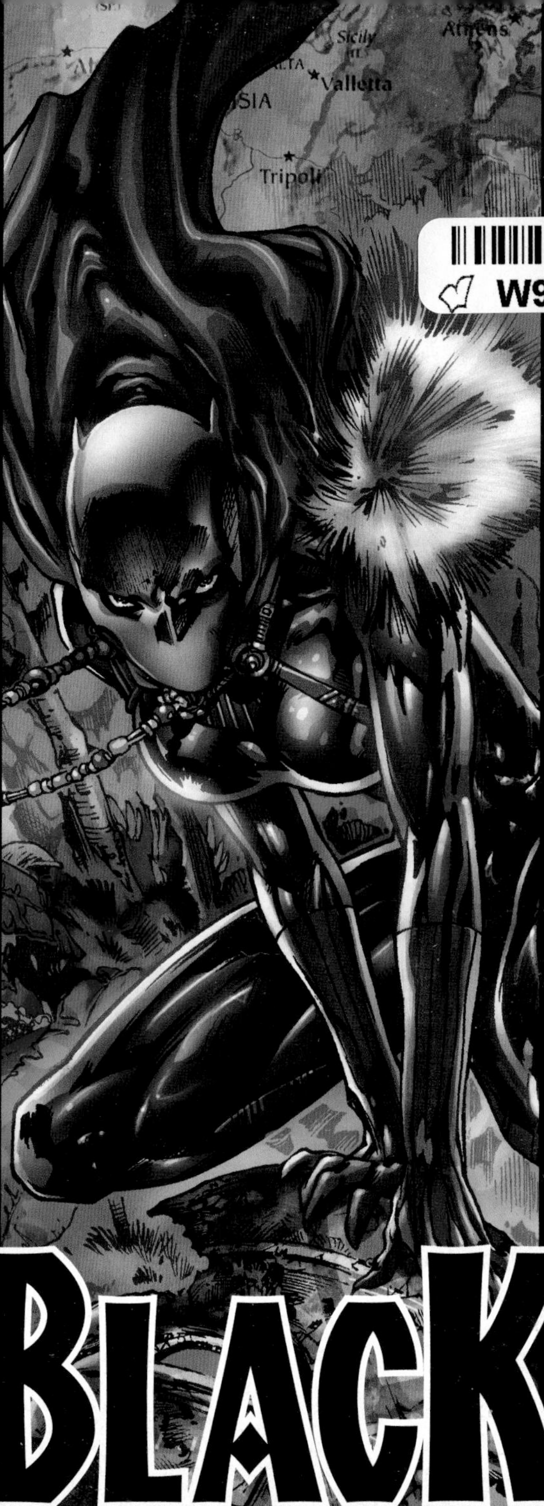
Sicily
Valletta
Tripoli

BLACK PANTHER

THE COMPLETE COLLECTION BY REGINALD HUDLIN

BLACK PANTHE

WRITTEN BY

REGINALD HUDLIN
& **JASON AARON** (BLACK PANTHER #39-41)

BLACK PANTHER (2005) #35-38

"BACK TO AFRICA"

PENCILS BY

CAFU (#35) & **FRANCIS PORTELA** (#36-38) WITH **CARLOS RODRIGUEZ** & **KEVIN SHARPE** (#38)

INKS BY

FRANCIS PORTELA WITH **BIT** & **ANDREW HENNESSY** (#38)

COLORS BY

VAL STAPLE

BLACK PANTHER (2005) #39-41

"SEE WAKANDA AND DIE"

ART BY

JEFTE PALO

COLORS BY

LEE LOUGHRIDGE

BLACK PANTHER (2009) #1-6

"THE DEADLIEST OF THE SPECIES"

PENCILS BY

KEN LASHLEY

INKS BY

PAUL NEARY

COLORS BY

PAUL MOUNTS

SPECIAL THANKS T

ENRICA JANG & **JONATH**

CAPTAIN AMERICA/BLACK PANTHER: FLAGS OF OUR FATHERS #1-4

PENCILS BY

DENYS COWAN

INKS BY

KLAUS JANSON (#1-2) & **TOM PALMER** (#3-4) WITH **SANDU FLOREA** (#4)

COLORS BY

PETE PANTAZIS

SPECIAL

CHRIS R

BLACK PANTHER SAGA

WRITTEN BY

JOHN RHETT THOMAS

DESIGNED BY

BRIAN O'DELL

MARVEL SPOTLIGHT: BLACK PANTHER

WRITTEN BY

JESS HARROLD & **GEORGE KHOURY**

DESIGNED BY

ROMMEL ALAMA & **BRIAN O'DELL**

EDIT

JOHN RHET

LETTERS BY

VC's CORY PETIT (BLACK PANTHER) & **JOE SABINO** (FLAGS OF OUR FATHERS)

ASSISTANT EDITORS

DANIEL KETCHUM, SEBASTIAN GIRNER & **JODY LEHEUP**

EDITOR

AXEL ALONSO

COVERS BY

DAVE WILKINS (BLACK PANTHER #35), **ALAN DAVIS, MARK**
PAUL MOUNTS (BLACK PANTHER #36-38), **JASON PEARSON** (BLAC
J. SCOTT CAMPBELL & **EDGAR DELGADO** (BLACK PANT
DENYS COWAN, KLAUS JANSON & **DEAN WHITE** (FLAGS O
DENYS COWAN, SANDU FLOREA & **PETE PANTAZIS** (FLAGS OF
JOHN ROMITA JR., KLAUS JANSON & **DEAN WHITE** (BLA

BLACK PANTHER CREATED BY **STAN LEE** & **JACK KIRBY**

COLLECTION EDITOR **MARK D. BEAZLEY**
ASSISTANT EDITOR **CAITLIN O'CONNELL**
ASSOCIATE MANAGING EDITOR **KATERI WOODY**
ASSOCIATE MANAGER, DIGITAL ASSETS **JOE HOCHSTEIN**
SENIOR EDITOR, SPECIAL PROJECTS **JENNIFER GRÜNWALD**
VP PRODUCTION & SPECIAL PROJECTS **JEFF YOUNGQUIST**
RESEARCH & LAYOUT **JEPH YORK**
BOOK DESIGNER **ADAM DEL RE**
SVP PRINT, SALES & MARKETING **DAVID GABRIEL**

EDITOR IN CHIEF **C.B. CEBULSKI**
CHIEF CREATIVE OFFICER **JOE QUESADA**
PRESIDENT **DAN BUCKLEY**
EXECUTIVE PRODUCER **ALAN FINE**

BLACK PANTHER BY REGINALD HUDLIN: THE COMPLETE COLLECTION VOL. 3. Contains material originally published in
PANTHER (2005) #35-41, BLACK PANTHER (2009) #1-6, BLACK PANTHER/CAPTAIN AMERICA: FLAGS OF OUR FATHERS #1-4
Second printing 2018. ISBN 978-1-302-91035-8. Published by MARVEL WORLDWIDE, INC., a subsidiary of MARVEL ENTEP
PUBLICATION: 135 West 50th Street, New York, NY 10020. Copyright © 2018 MARVEL No similarity between any of the names,
institutions in this magazine with those of any living or dead person or institution is intended, and any such similarity which may
Printed in the U.S.A. DAN BUCKLEY, President, Marvel Entertainment; JOHN NEE, Publisher; JOE QUESADA, Chief Creative O
of Publishing; DAVID BOGART, SVP of Business Affairs & Operations, Publishing & Partnership; DAVID GABRIEL, SVP of Sales &
YOUNGQUIST, VP of Production & Special Projects; DAN CARR, Executive Director of Publishing Technology; ALEX MORALES, Direc
SUSAN CRESPI, Production Manager; STAN LEE, Chairman Emeritus. For information regarding advertising in Marvel Comic
contact Vit DeBellis, Custom Solutions & Integrated Advertising Manager, at vdebellis@marvel.com. For Marvel subscription in
5480. **Manufactured between 3/21/2018 and 4/10/2018 by LSC COMMUNICATIONS INC., KENDALLVILLE, IN, USA.**

1 0 9 8 7 6 5 4 3 2

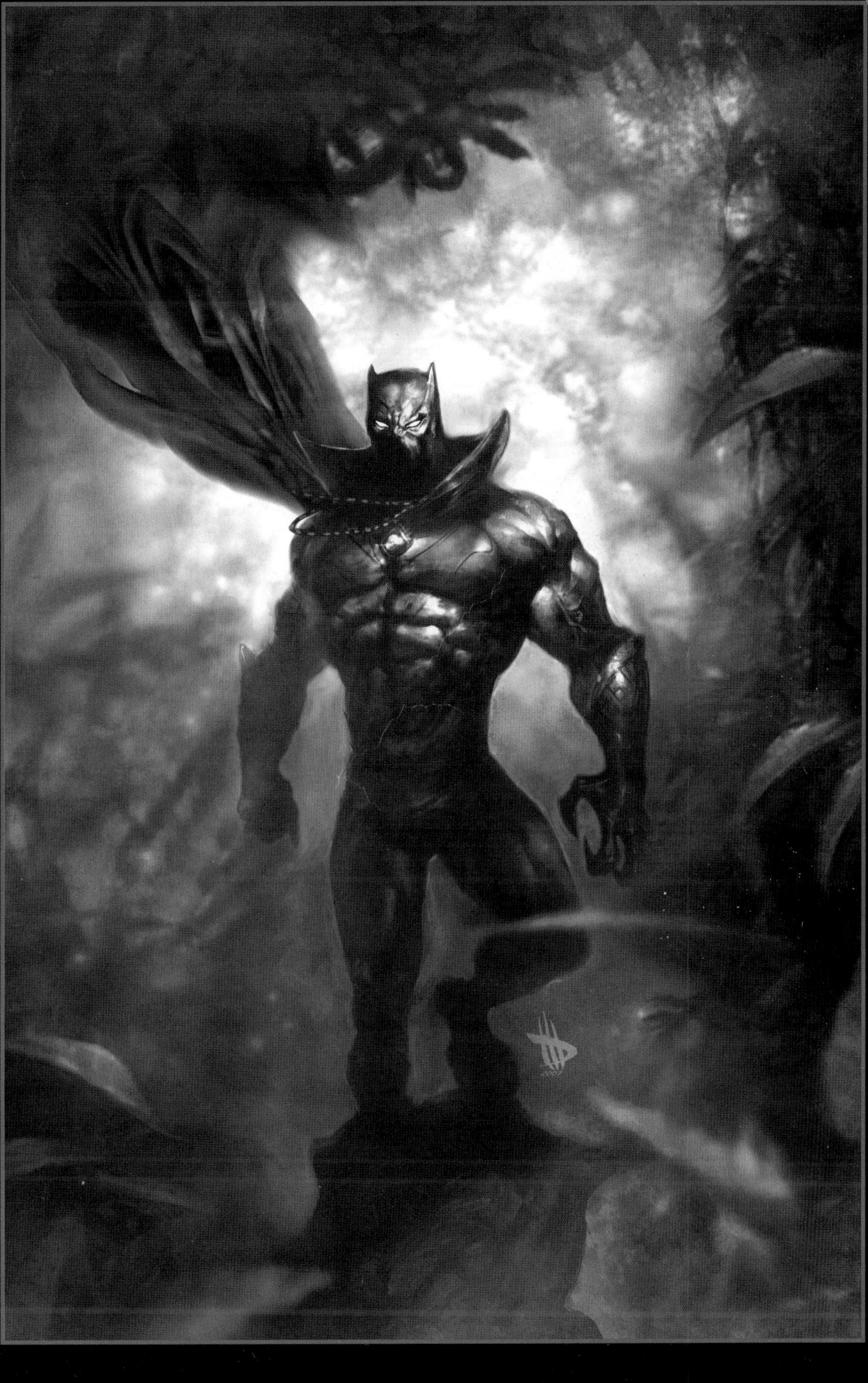

BLACK PANTHER (2005) 35

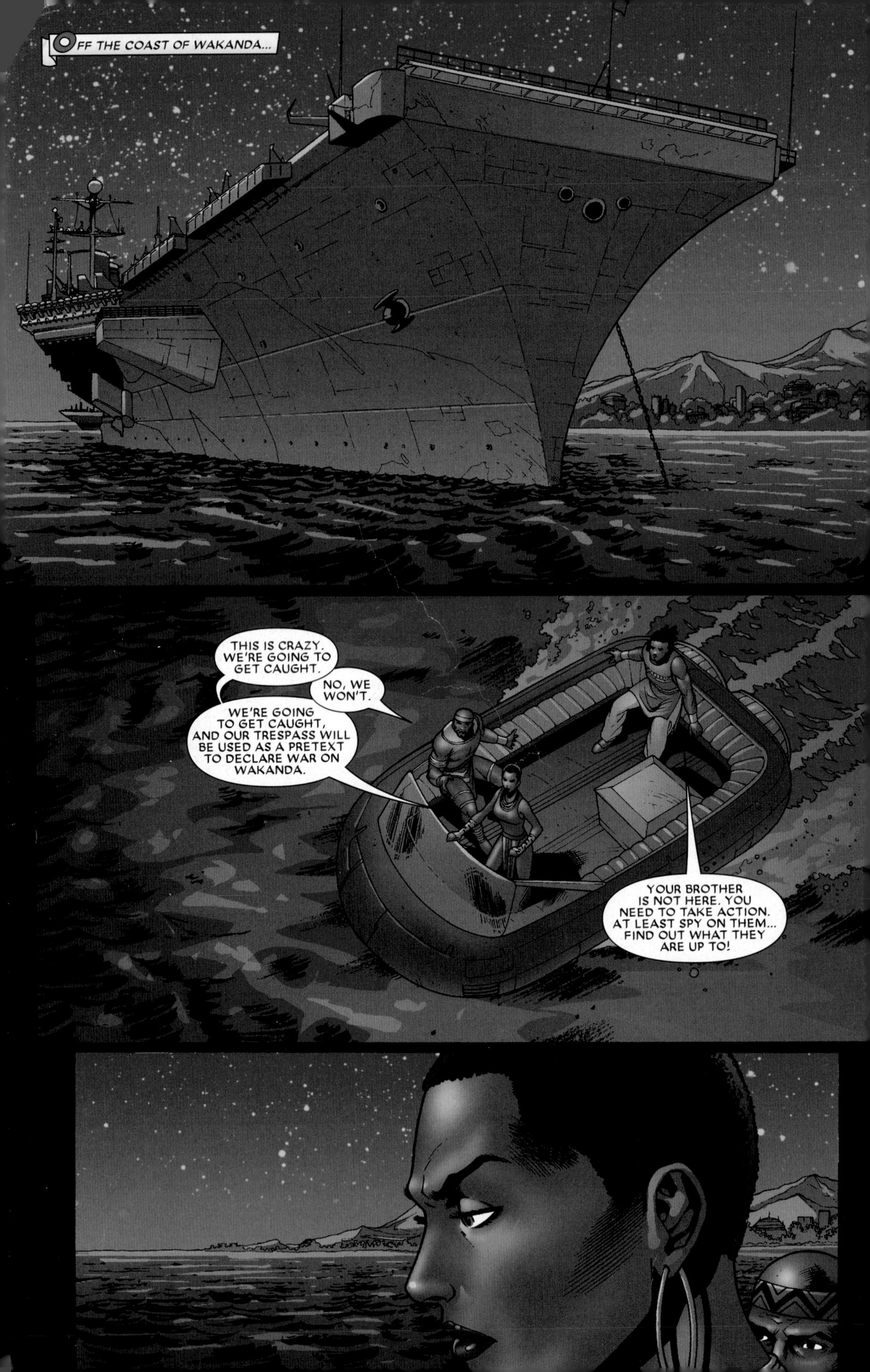
OFF THE COAST OF WAKANDA...
THIS IS CRAZY. WE'RE GOING TO GET CAUGHT.
NO, WE WON'T.
WE'RE GOING TO GET CAUGHT, AND OUR TRESPASS WILL BE USED AS A PRETEXT TO DECLARE WAR ON WAKANDA.
YOUR BROTHER IS NOT HERE. YOU NEED TO TAKE ACTION. AT LEAST SPY ON THEM... FIND OUT WHAT THEY ARE UP TO!

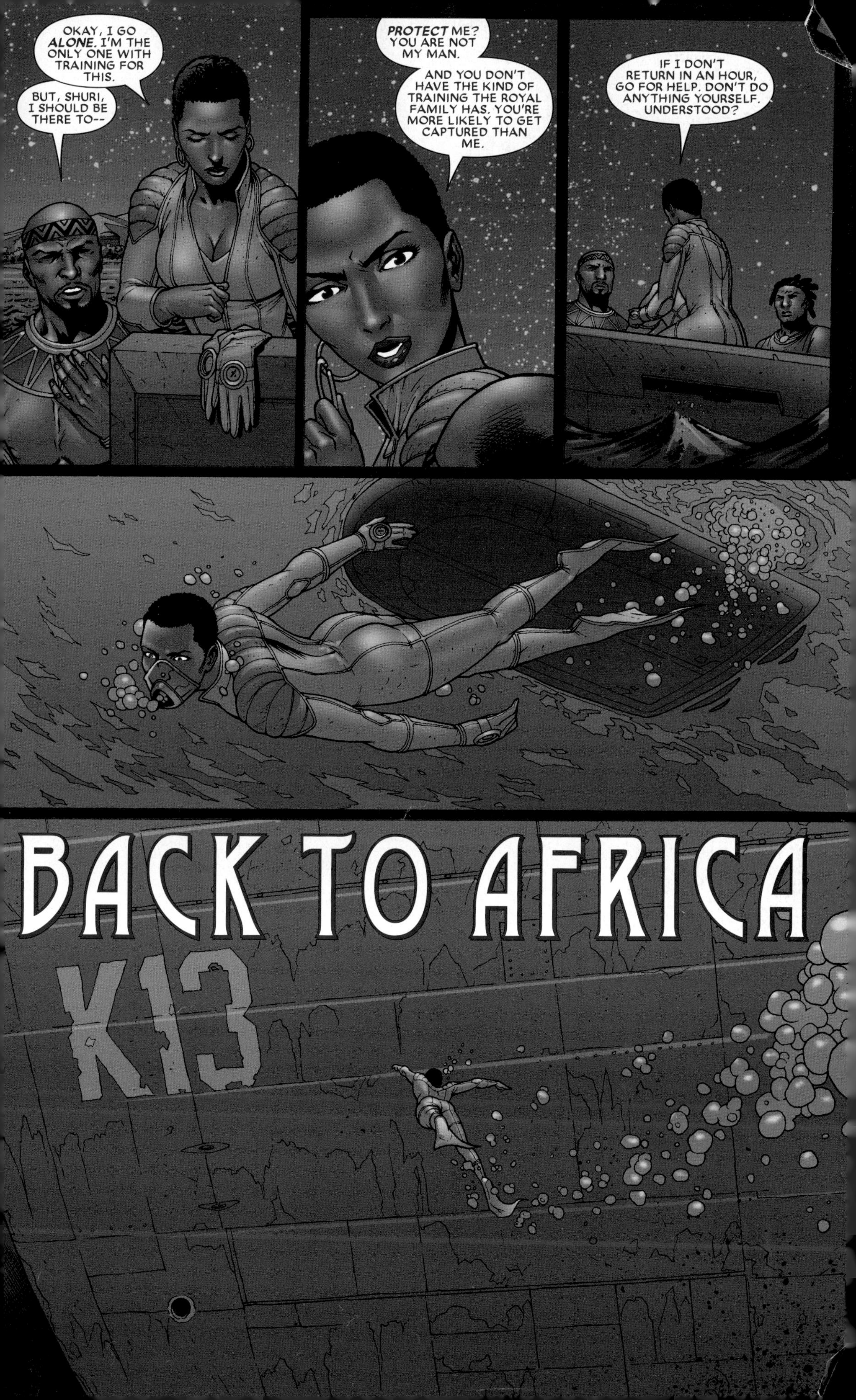
OKAY, I GO ALONE. I'M THE ONLY ONE WITH TRAINING FOR THIS.
BUT, SHURI, I SHOULD BE THERE TO--
PROTECT ME? YOU ARE NOT MY MAN.
AND YOU DON'T HAVE THE KIND OF TRAINING THE ROYAL FAMILY HAS. YOU'RE MORE LIKELY TO GET CAPTURED THAN ME.
IF I DON'T RETURN IN AN HOUR, GO FOR HELP. DON'T DO ANYTHING YOURSELF. UNDERSTOOD?
BACK TO AFRICA
K13

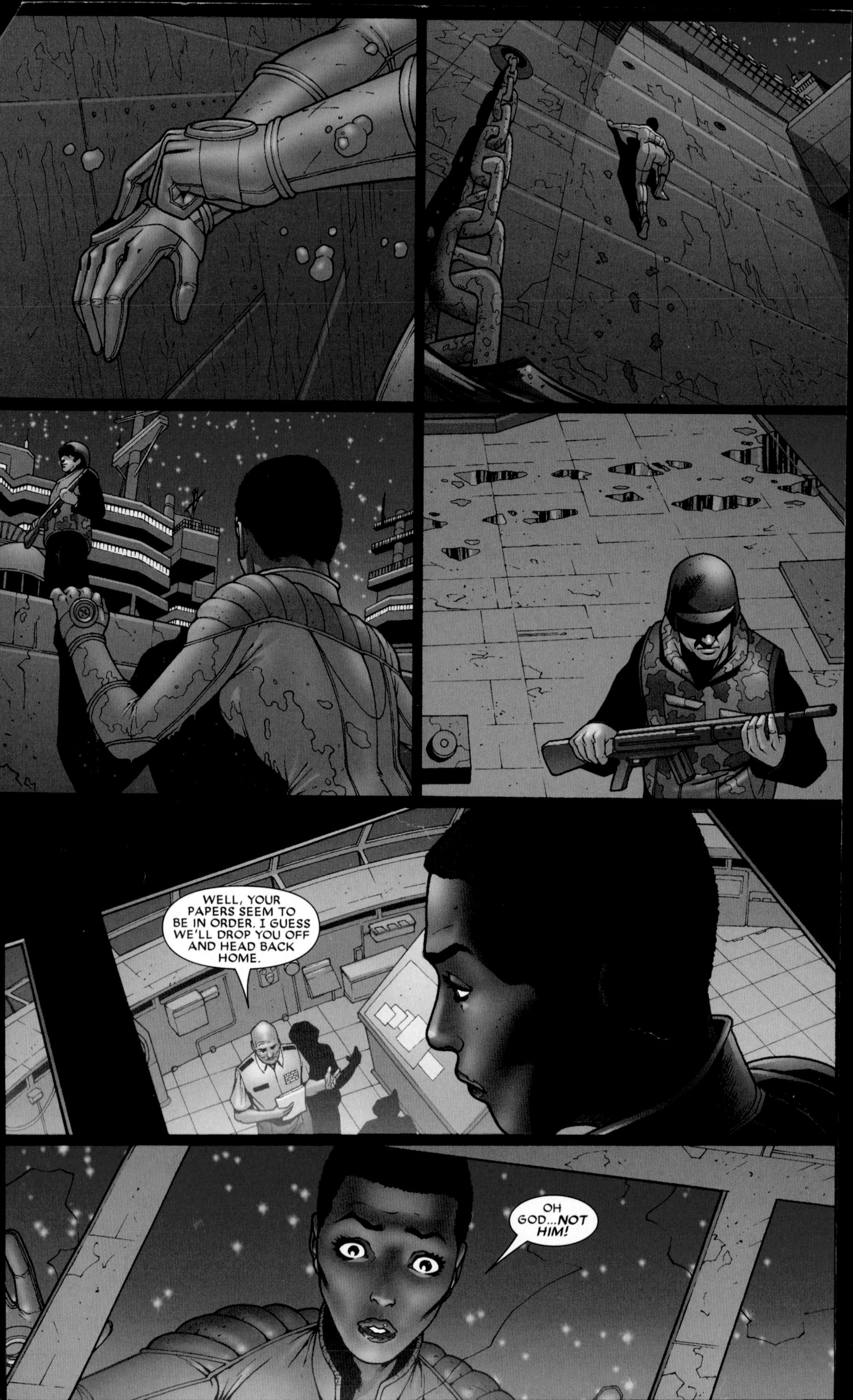
WELL, YOUR PAPERS SEEM TO BE IN ORDER. I GUESS WE'LL DROP YOU OFF AND HEAD BACK HOME.
OH GOD...NOT HIM!

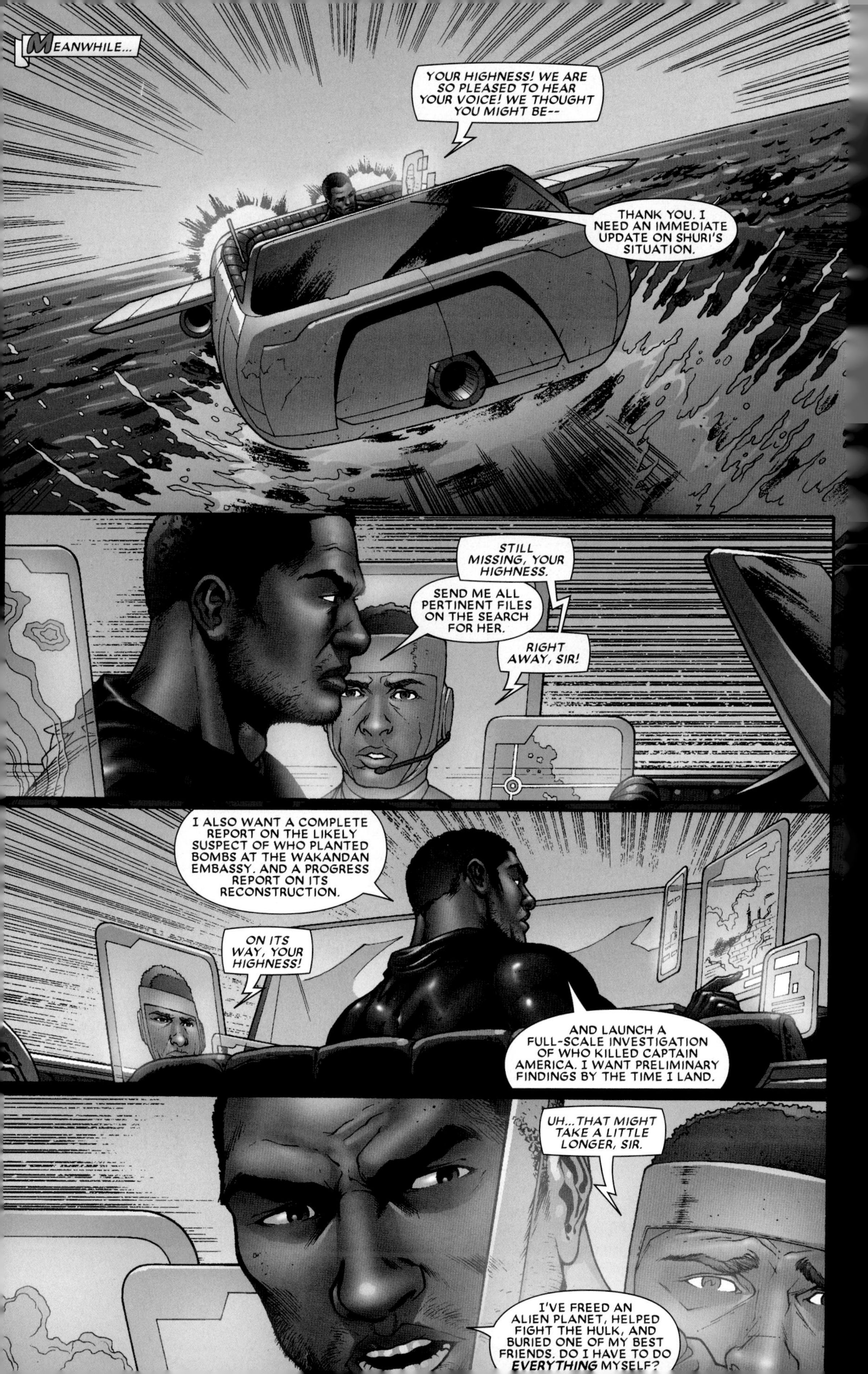
MEANWHILE...
YOUR HIGHNESS! WE ARE SO PLEASED TO HEAR YOUR VOICE! WE THOUGHT YOU MIGHT BE--
THANK YOU. I NEED AN IMMEDIATE UPDATE ON SHURI'S SITUATION.
STILL MISSING, YOUR HIGHNESS.
SEND ME ALL PERTINENT FILES ON THE SEARCH FOR HER.
RIGHT AWAY, SIR!
I ALSO WANT A COMPLETE REPORT ON THE LIKELY SUSPECT OF WHO PLANTED BOMBS AT THE WAKANDAN EMBASSY. AND A PROGRESS REPORT ON ITS RECONSTRUCTION.
ON ITS WAY, YOUR HIGHNESS!
AND LAUNCH A FULL-SCALE INVESTIGATION OF WHO KILLED CAPTAIN AMERICA. I WANT PRELIMINARY FINDINGS BY THE TIME I LAND.
UH...THAT MIGHT TAKE A LITTLE LONGER, SIR.
I'VE FREED AN ALIEN PLANET, HELPED FIGHT THE HULK, AND BURIED ONE OF MY BEST FRIENDS. DO I HAVE TO DO EVERYTHING MYSELF?

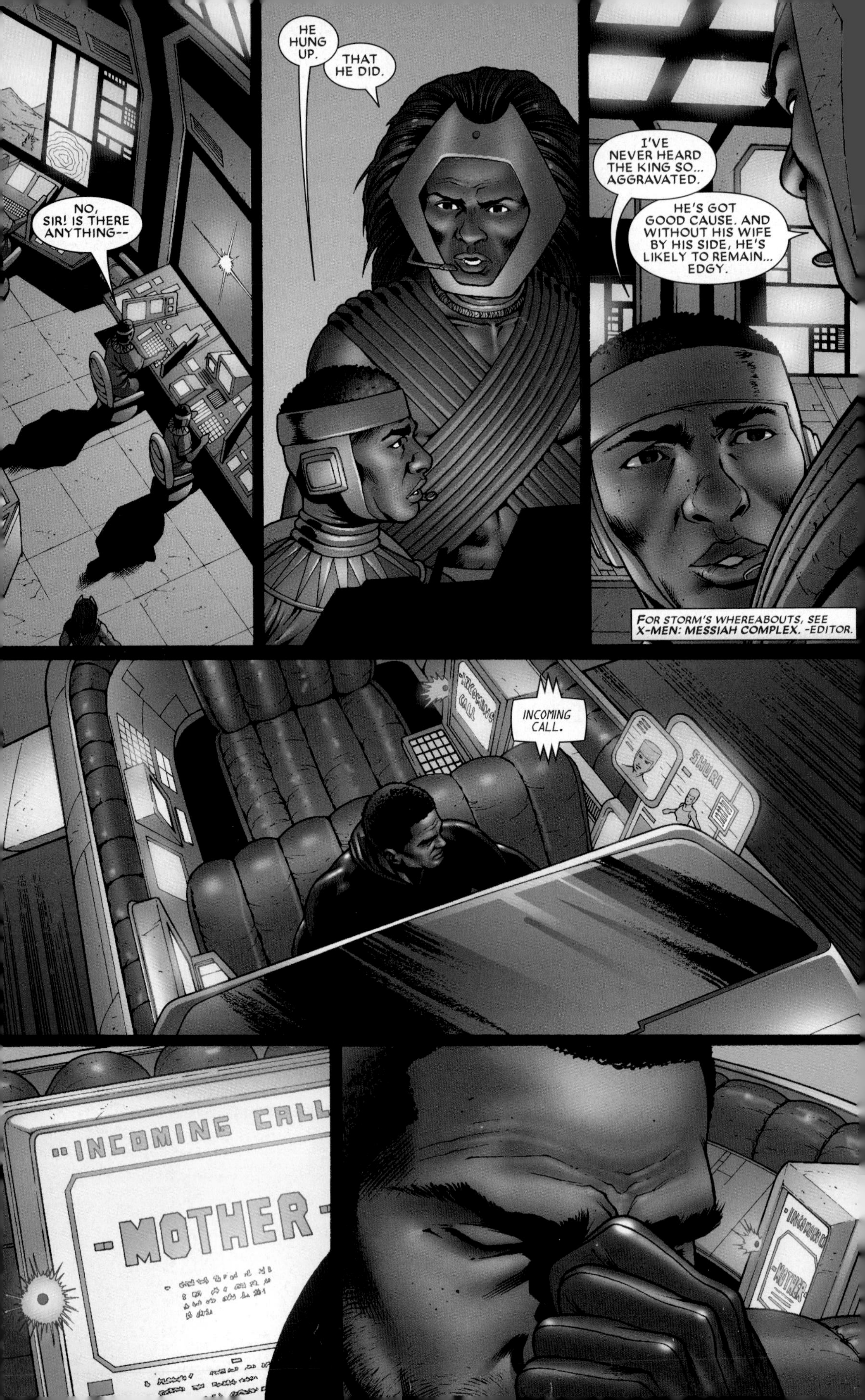

NO, SIR! IS THERE ANYTHING--
HE HUNG UP.
THAT HE DID.
I'VE NEVER HEARD THE KING SO... AGGRAVATED.
HE'S GOT GOOD CAUSE. AND WITHOUT HIS WIFE BY HIS SIDE, HE'S LIKELY TO REMAIN... EDGY.
FOR STORM'S WHEREABOUTS, SEE X-MEN: MESSIAH COMPLEX. -EDITOR.
INCOMING CALL
INCOMING CALL.
SHURI
INCOMING CALL
-MOTHER-

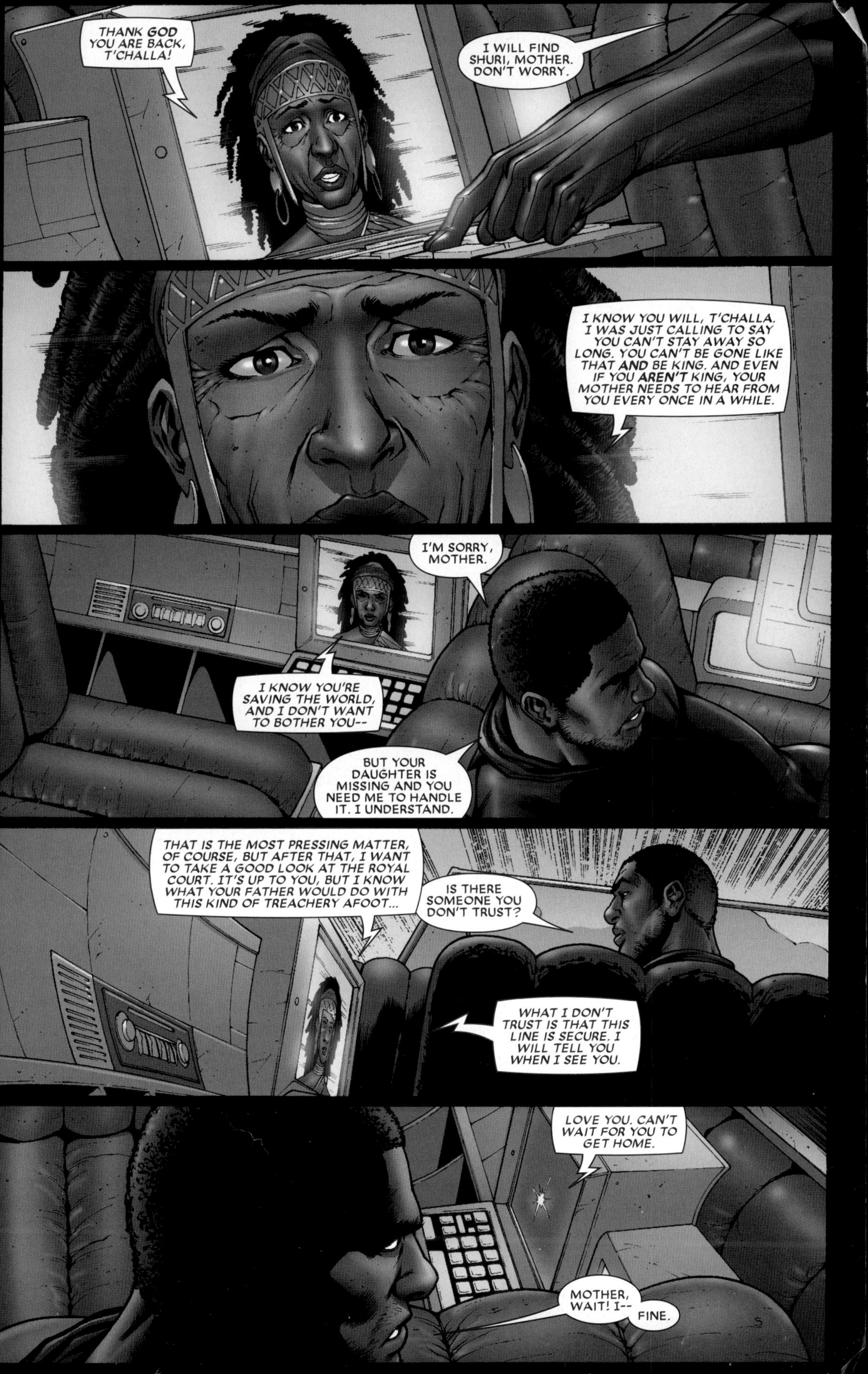
THANK GOD YOU ARE BACK, T'CHALLA!
I WILL FIND SHURI, MOTHER. DON'T WORRY.
I KNOW YOU WILL, T'CHALLA. I WAS JUST CALLING TO SAY YOU CAN'T STAY AWAY SO LONG. YOU CAN'T BE GONE LIKE THAT AND BE KING. AND EVEN IF YOU AREN'T KING, YOUR MOTHER NEEDS TO HEAR FROM YOU EVERY ONCE IN A WHILE.
I'M SORRY, MOTHER.
I KNOW YOU'RE SAVING THE WORLD, AND I DON'T WANT TO BOTHER YOU--
BUT YOUR DAUGHTER IS MISSING AND YOU NEED ME TO HANDLE IT. I UNDERSTAND.
THAT IS THE MOST PRESSING MATTER, OF COURSE, BUT AFTER THAT, I WANT TO TAKE A GOOD LOOK AT THE ROYAL COURT. IT'S UP TO YOU, BUT I KNOW WHAT YOUR FATHER WOULD DO WITH THIS KIND OF TREACHERY AFOOT...
IS THERE SOMEONE YOU DON'T TRUST?
WHAT I DON'T TRUST IS THAT THIS LINE IS SECURE. I WILL TELL YOU WHEN I SEE YOU.
LOVE YOU. CAN'T WAIT FOR YOU TO GET HOME.
MOTHER, WAIT! I--
FINE.

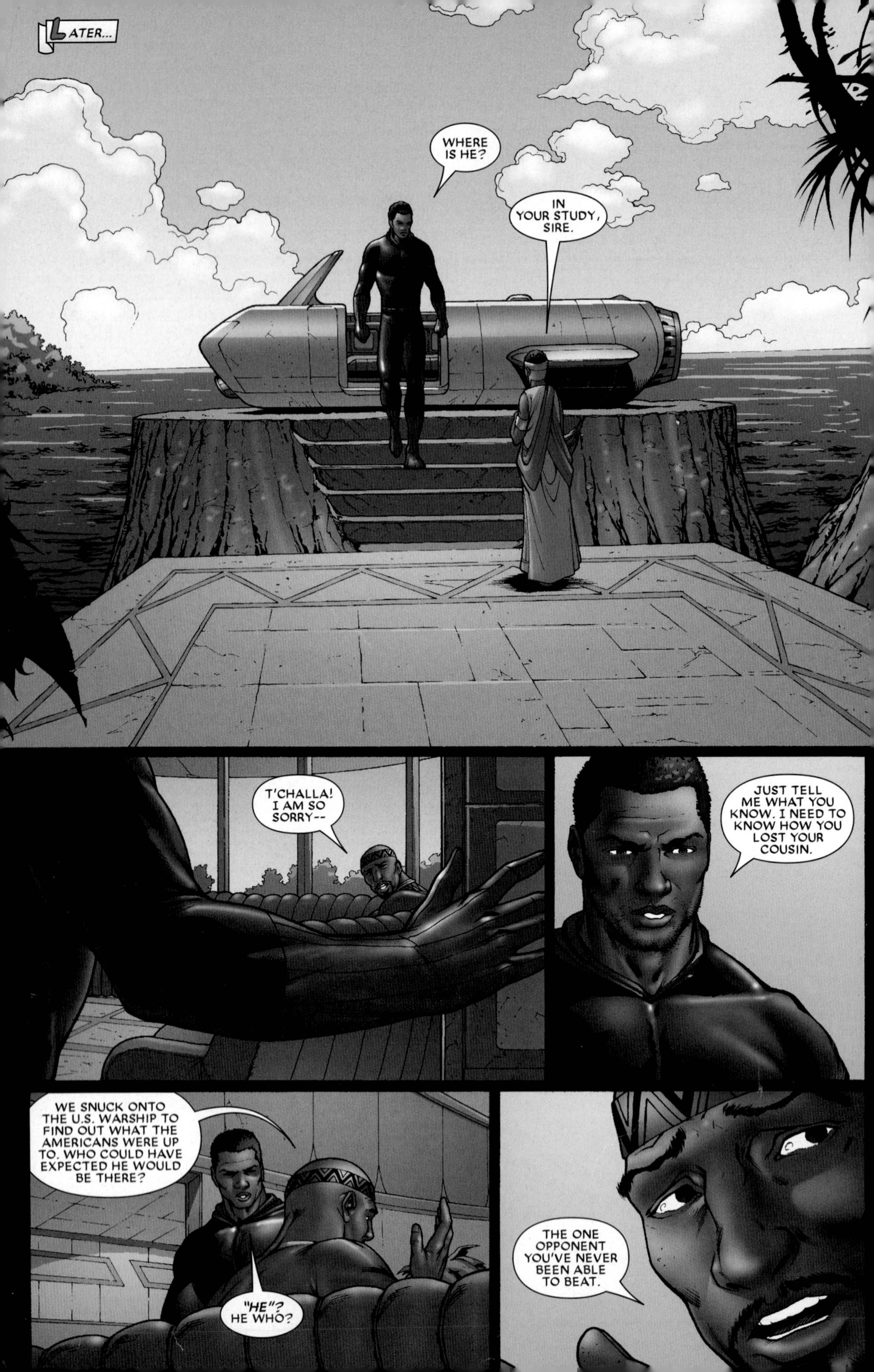
LATER...
WHERE IS HE?
IN YOUR STUDY, SIRE.
T'CHALLA! I AM SO SORRY--
JUST TELL ME WHAT YOU KNOW. I NEED TO KNOW HOW YOU LOST YOUR COUSIN.
WE SNUCK ONTO THE U.S. WARSHIP TO FIND OUT WHAT THE AMERICANS WERE UP TO. WHO COULD HAVE EXPECTED HE WOULD BE THERE?
"HE"? HE WHO?
THE ONE OPPONENT YOU'VE NEVER BEEN ABLE TO BEAT.

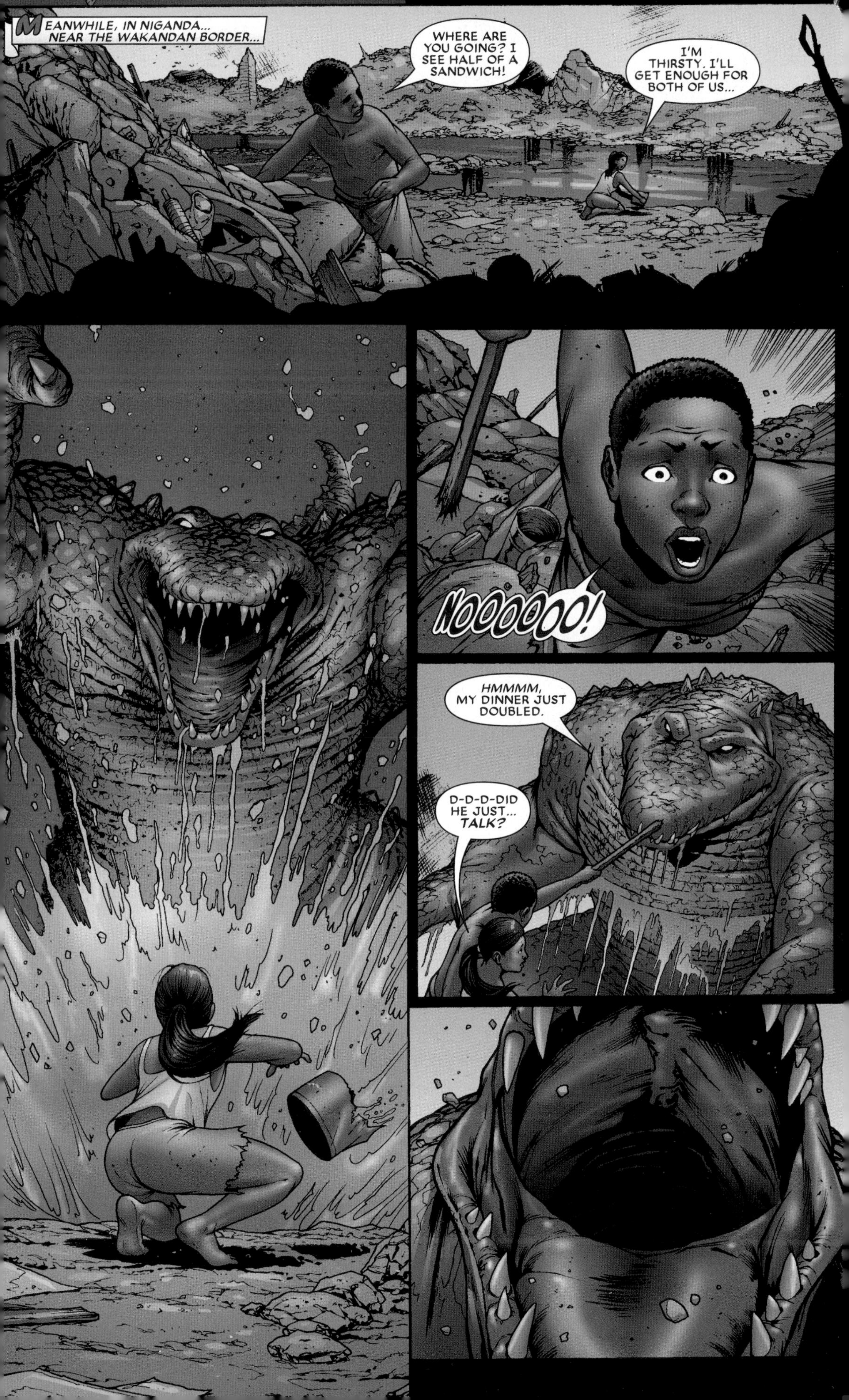
MEANWHILE, IN NIGANDA... NEAR THE WAKANDAN BORDER...
WHERE ARE YOU GOING? I SEE HALF OF A SANDWICH!
I'M THIRSTY. I'LL GET ENOUGH FOR BOTH OF US...
NOOOOOO!
HMMMM, MY DINNER JUST DOUBLED.
D-D-D-DID HE JUST... TALK?

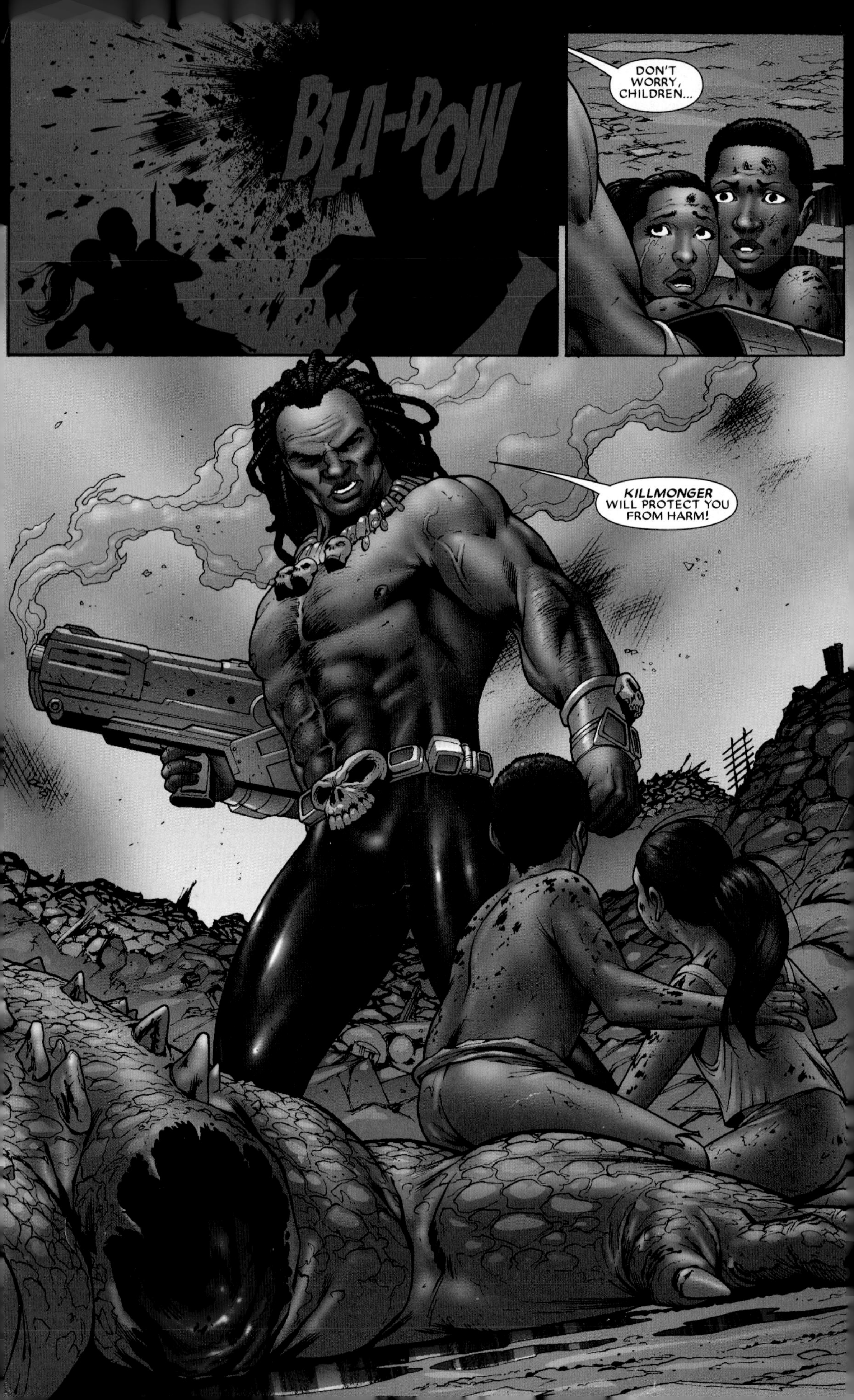
BLA-POW
DON'T WORRY, CHILDREN...
KILLMONGER WILL PROTECT YOU FROM HARM!

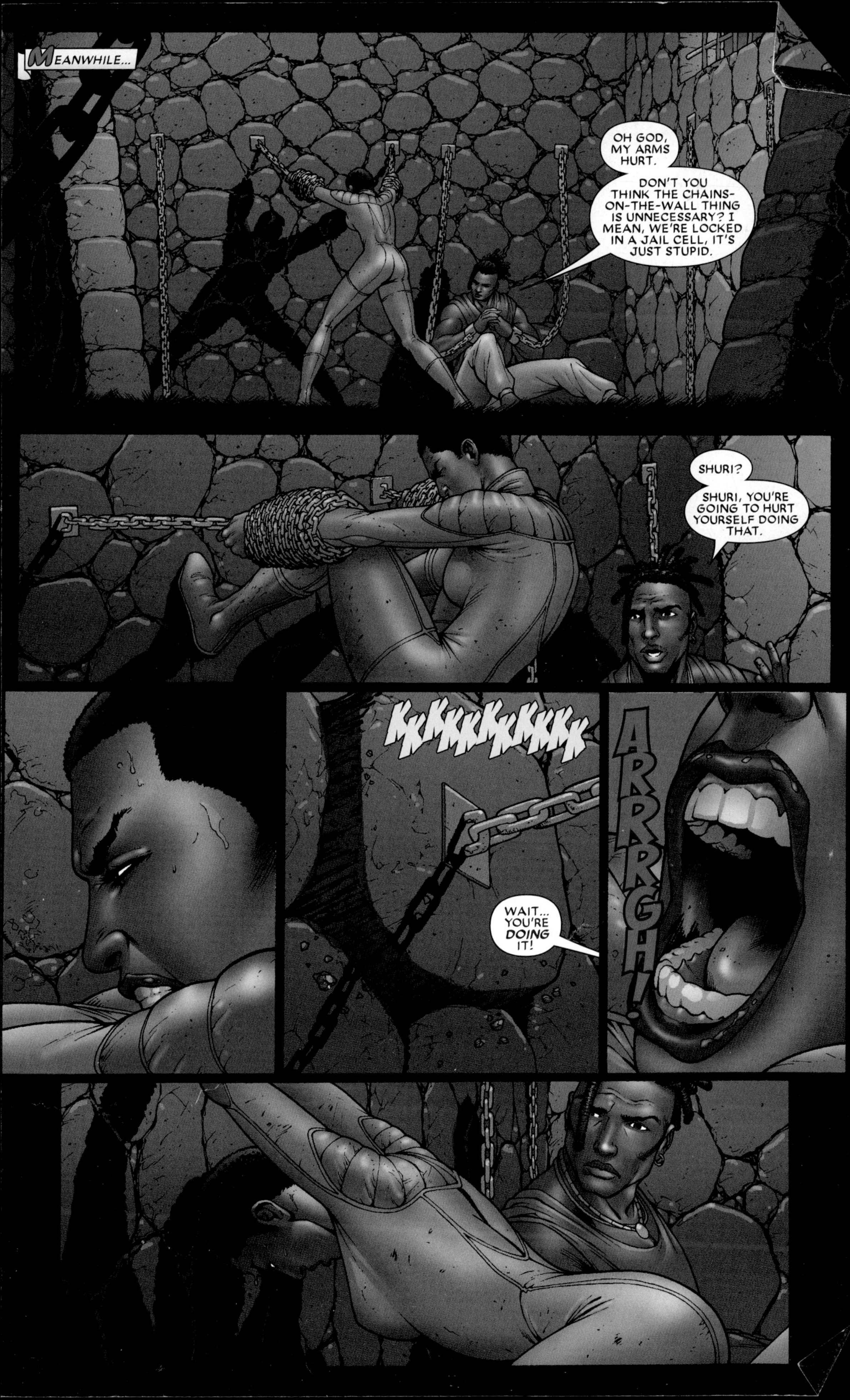
MEANWHILE...
OH GOD, MY ARMS HURT.
DON'T YOU THINK THE CHAINS-ON-THE-WALL THING IS UNNECESSARY? I MEAN, WE'RE LOCKED IN A JAIL CELL, IT'S JUST STUPID.
SHURI?
SHURI, YOU'RE GOING TO HURT YOURSELF DOING THAT.
KKKKKKKKKKKK
ARRRRGH!
WAIT... YOU'RE DOING IT!

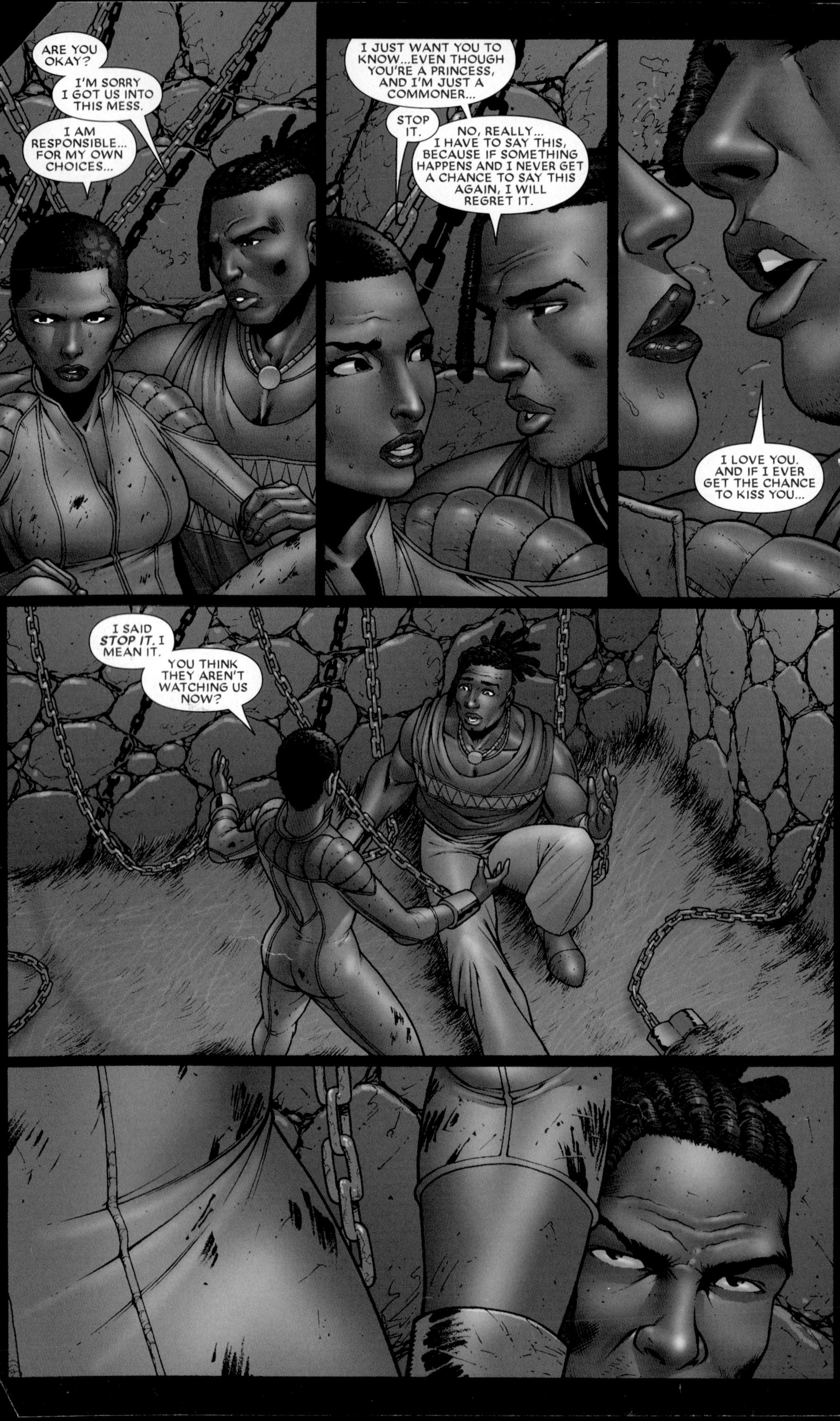
ARE YOU OKAY?
I'M SORRY I GOT US INTO THIS MESS.
I AM RESPONSIBLE... FOR MY OWN CHOICES...
I JUST WANT YOU TO KNOW...EVEN THOUGH YOU'RE A PRINCESS, AND I'M JUST A COMMONER...
STOP IT.
NO, REALLY... I HAVE TO SAY THIS, BECAUSE IF SOMETHING HAPPENS AND I NEVER GET A CHANCE TO SAY THIS AGAIN, I WILL REGRET IT.
I LOVE YOU. AND IF I EVER GET THE CHANCE TO KISS YOU...
I SAID *STOP IT.* I MEAN IT.
YOU THINK THEY AREN'T WATCHING US NOW?

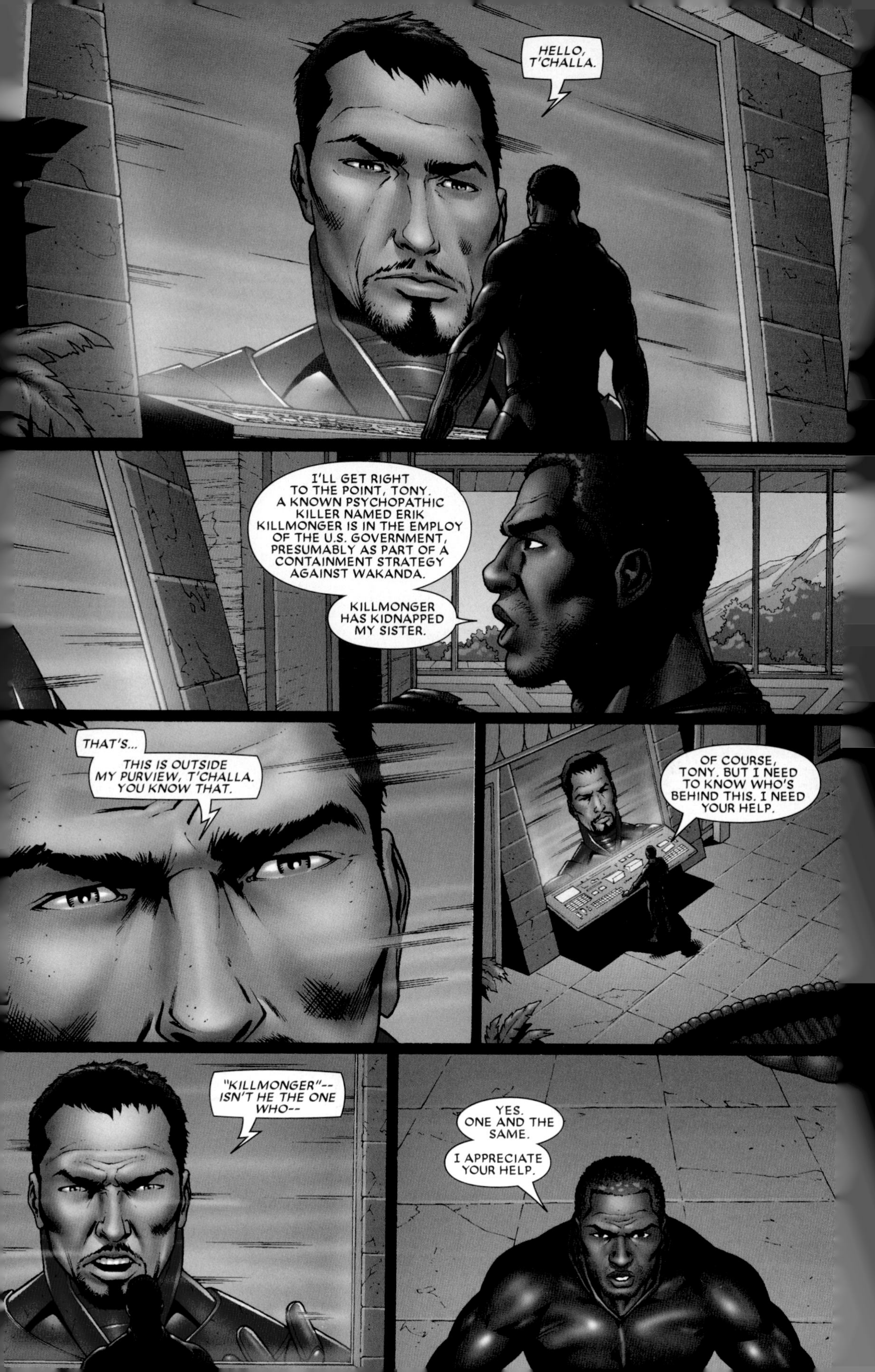
HELLO, T'CHALLA.
I'LL GET RIGHT TO THE POINT, TONY. A KNOWN PSYCHOPATHIC KILLER NAMED ERIK KILLMONGER IS IN THE EMPLOY OF THE U.S. GOVERNMENT, PRESUMABLY AS PART OF A CONTAINMENT STRATEGY AGAINST WAKANDA.
KILLMONGER HAS KIDNAPPED MY SISTER.
THAT'S...
THIS IS OUTSIDE MY PURVIEW, T'CHALLA. YOU KNOW THAT.
OF COURSE, TONY. BUT I NEED TO KNOW WHO'S BEHIND THIS. I NEED YOUR HELP.
"KILLMONGER"-- ISN'T HE THE ONE WHO--
YES. ONE AND THE SAME.
I APPRECIATE YOUR HELP.

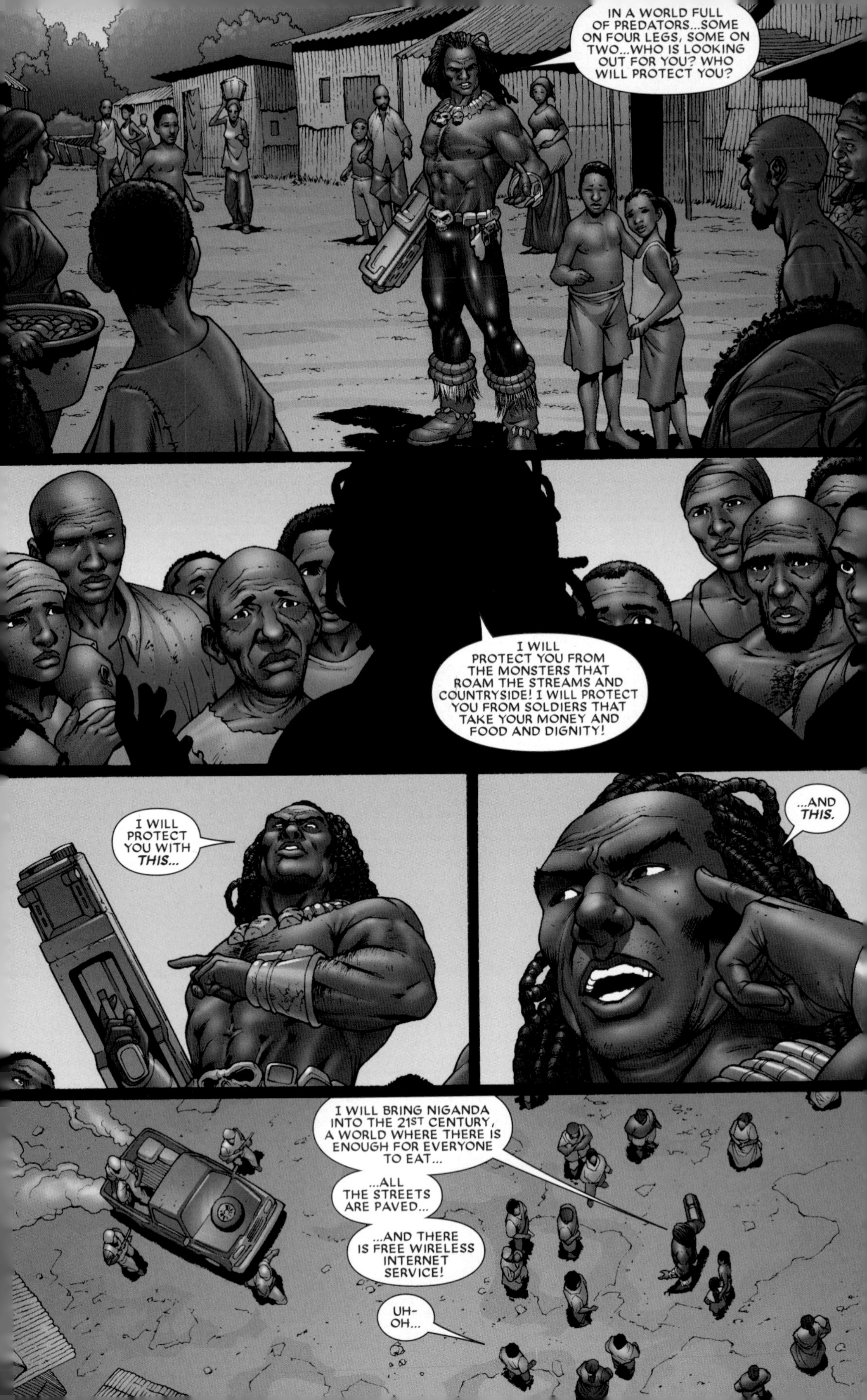
IN A WORLD FULL OF PREDATORS...SOME ON FOUR LEGS, SOME ON TWO...WHO IS LOOKING OUT FOR YOU? WHO WILL PROTECT YOU?
I WILL PROTECT YOU FROM THE MONSTERS THAT ROAM THE STREAMS AND COUNTRYSIDE! I WILL PROTECT YOU FROM SOLDIERS THAT TAKE YOUR MONEY AND FOOD AND DIGNITY!
I WILL PROTECT YOU WITH *THIS*...
...AND *THIS.*
I WILL BRING NIGANDA INTO THE 21ST CENTURY, A WORLD WHERE THERE IS ENOUGH FOR EVERYONE TO EAT...
...ALL THE STREETS ARE PAVED...
...AND THERE IS FREE WIRELESS INTERNET SERVICE!
UH-OH...

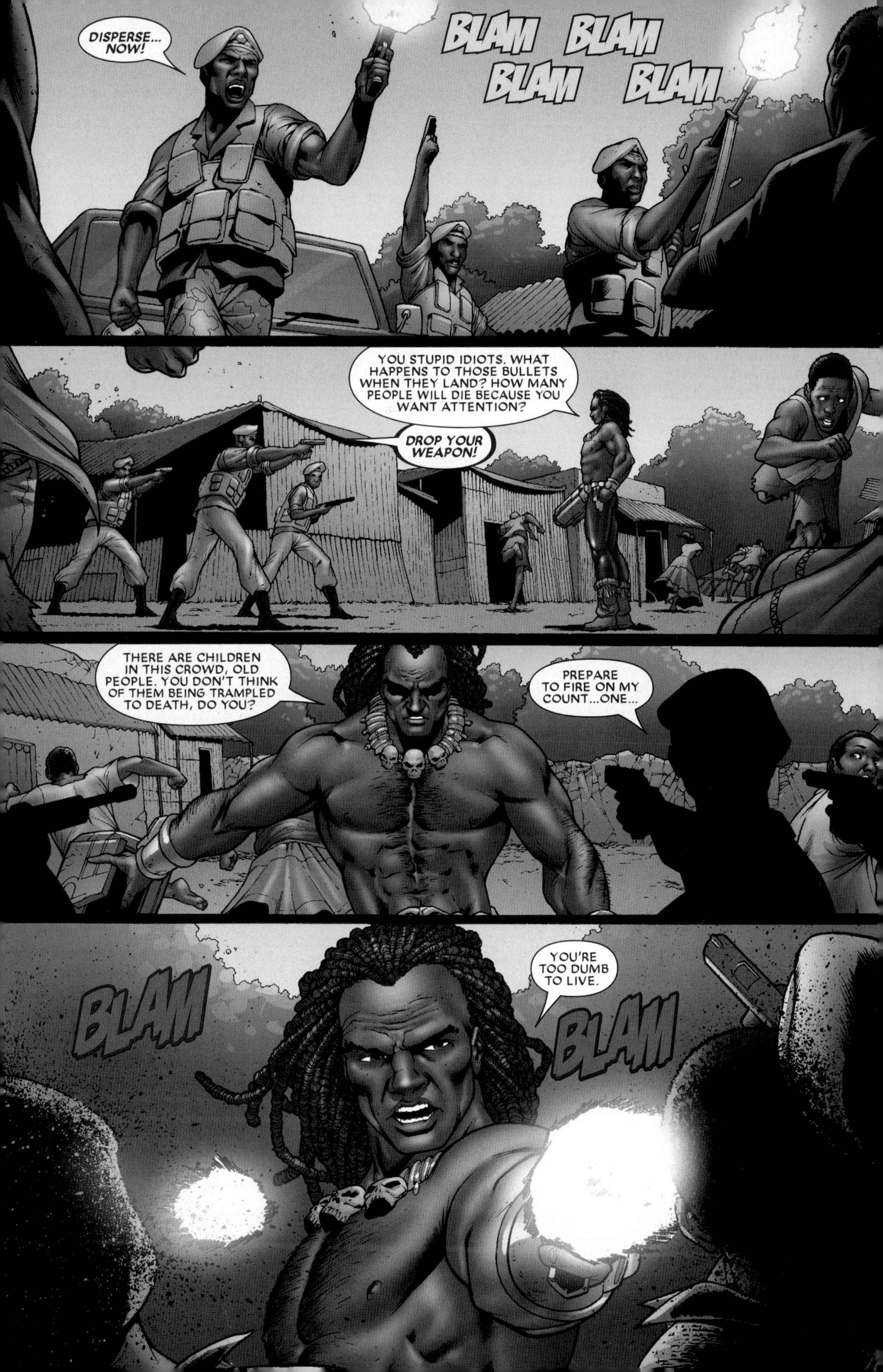
DISPERSE... NOW!
BLAM BLAM BLAM BLAM
YOU STUPID IDIOTS. WHAT HAPPENS TO THOSE BULLETS WHEN THEY LAND? HOW MANY PEOPLE WILL DIE BECAUSE YOU WANT ATTENTION?
DROP YOUR WEAPON!
THERE ARE CHILDREN IN THIS CROWD, OLD PEOPLE. YOU DON'T THINK OF THEM BEING TRAMPLED TO DEATH, DO YOU?
PREPARE TO FIRE ON MY COUNT...ONE...
BLAM
YOU'RE TOO DUMB TO LIVE.
BLAM

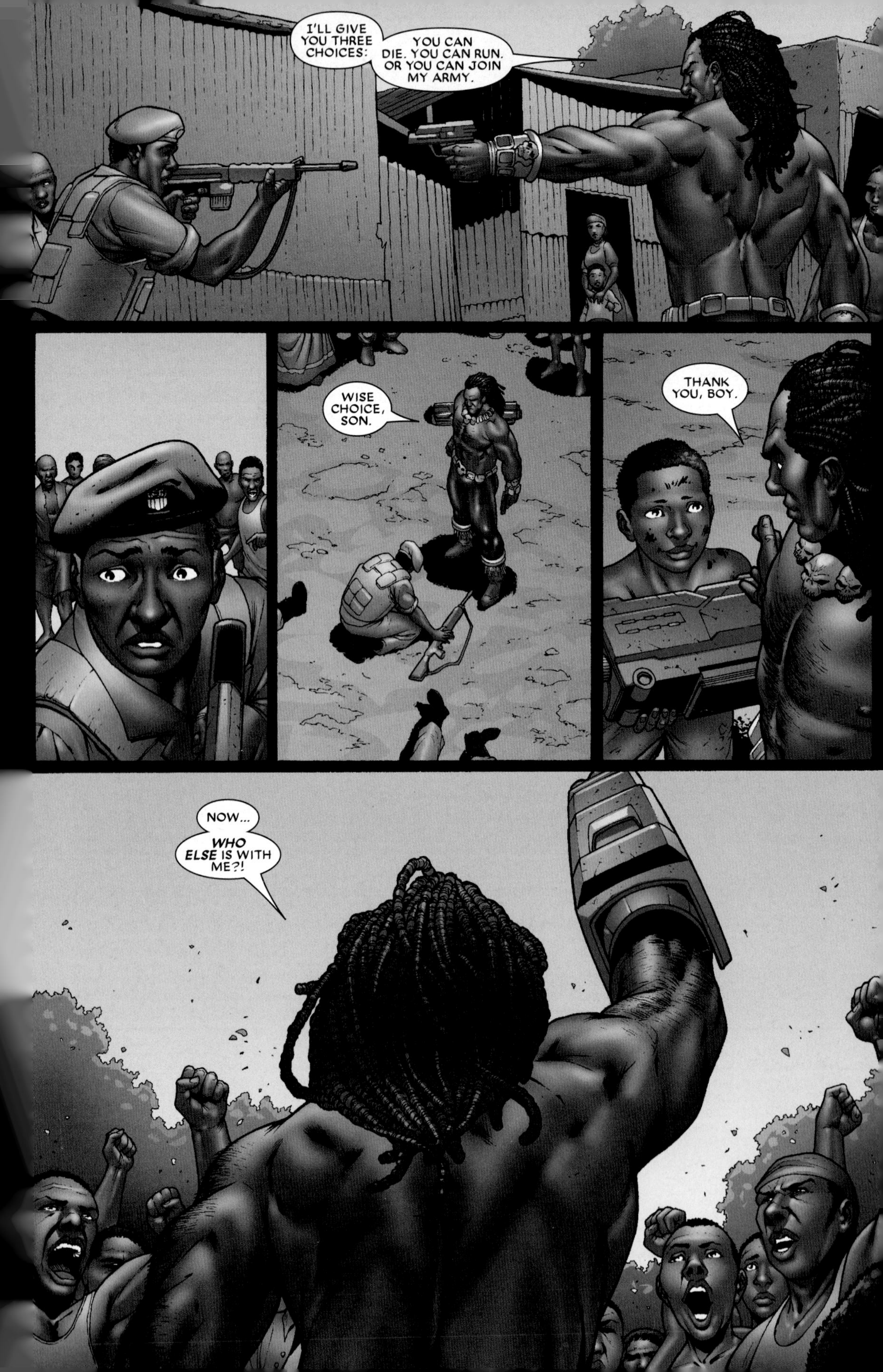

I'LL GIVE YOU THREE CHOICES:
YOU CAN DIE. YOU CAN RUN. OR YOU CAN JOIN MY ARMY.
WISE CHOICE, SON.
THANK YOU, BOY.
NOW...
WHO ELSE IS WITH ME?!

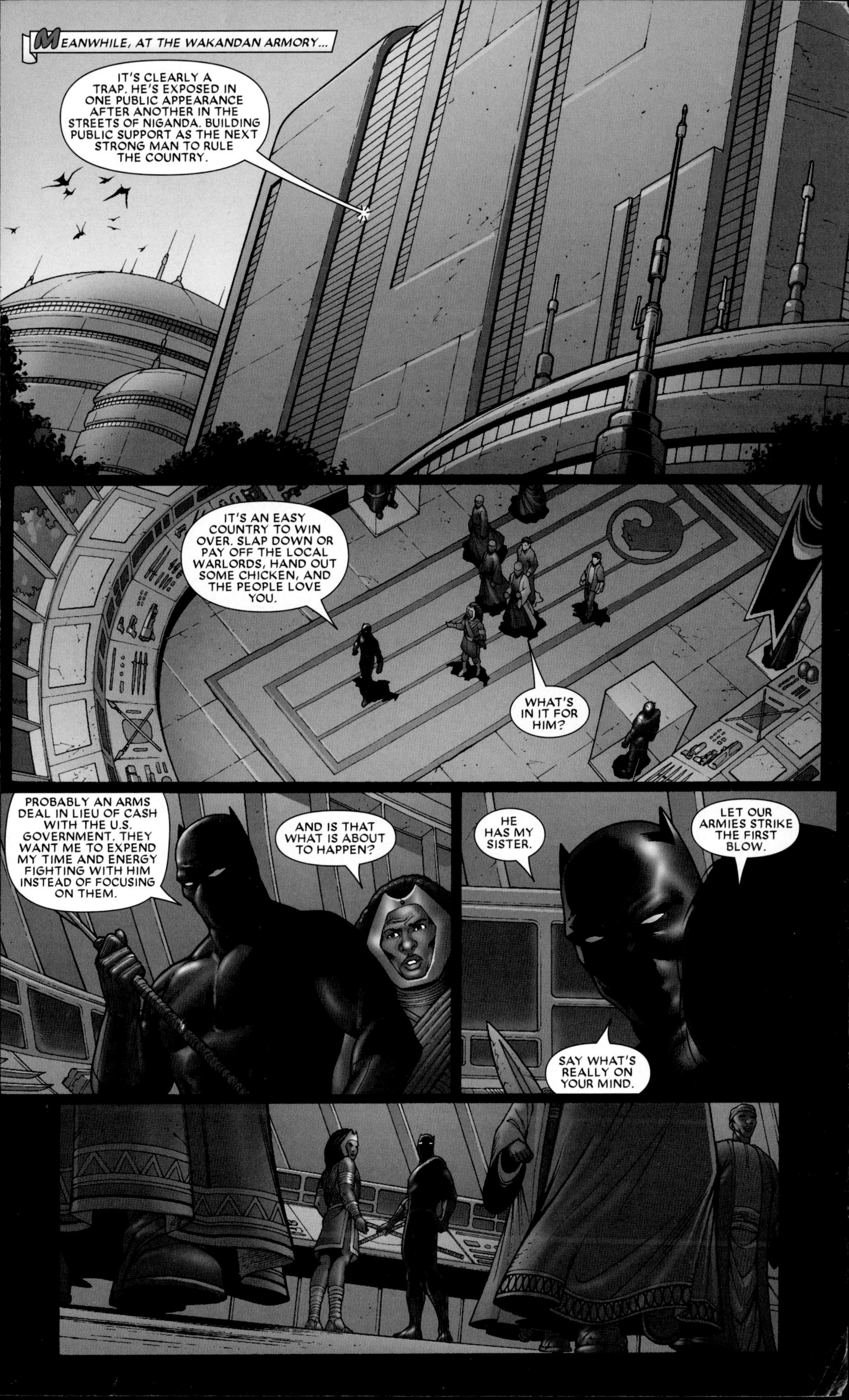
MEANWHILE, AT THE WAKANDAN ARMORY...
IT'S CLEARLY A TRAP. HE'S EXPOSED IN ONE PUBLIC APPEARANCE AFTER ANOTHER IN THE STREETS OF NIGANDA. BUILDING PUBLIC SUPPORT AS THE NEXT STRONG MAN TO RULE THE COUNTRY.
IT'S AN EASY COUNTRY TO WIN OVER. SLAP DOWN OR PAY OFF THE LOCAL WARLORDS, HAND OUT SOME CHICKEN, AND THE PEOPLE LOVE YOU.
WHAT'S IN IT FOR HIM?
PROBABLY AN ARMS DEAL IN LIEU OF CASH WITH THE U.S. GOVERNMENT. THEY WANT ME TO EXPEND MY TIME AND ENERGY FIGHTING WITH HIM INSTEAD OF FOCUSING ON THEM.
AND IS THAT WHAT IS ABOUT TO HAPPEN?
HE HAS MY SISTER.
LET OUR ARMIES STRIKE THE FIRST BLOW.
SAY WHAT'S REALLY ON YOUR MIND.

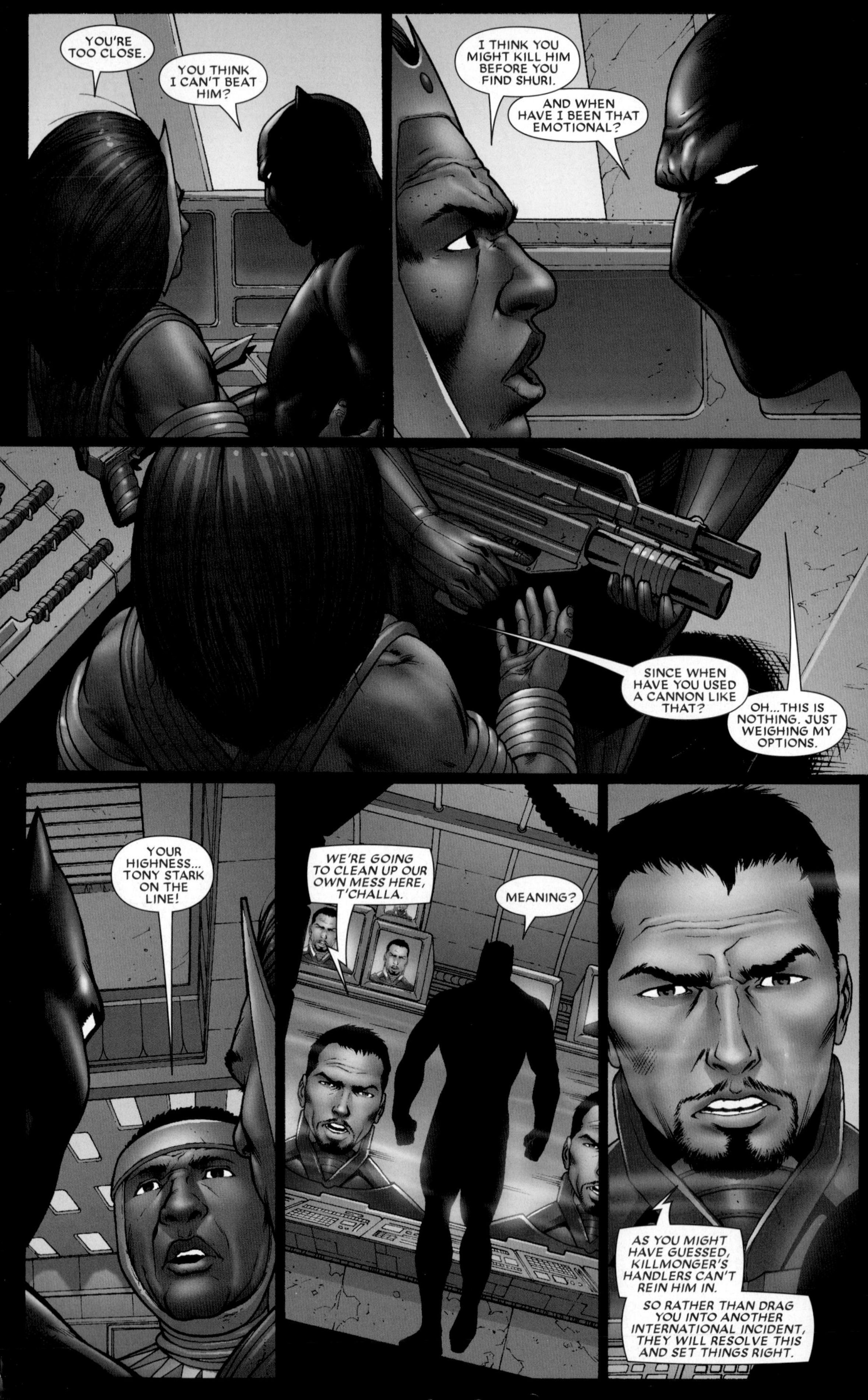
YOU'RE TOO CLOSE.
YOU THINK I CAN'T BEAT HIM?
I THINK YOU MIGHT KILL HIM BEFORE YOU FIND SHURI.
AND WHEN HAVE I BEEN THAT EMOTIONAL?
SINCE WHEN HAVE YOU USED A CANNON LIKE THAT?
OH...THIS IS NOTHING. JUST WEIGHING MY OPTIONS.
YOUR HIGHNESS... TONY STARK ON THE LINE!
WE'RE GOING TO CLEAN UP OUR OWN MESS HERE, T'CHALLA.
MEANING?
AS YOU MIGHT HAVE GUESSED, KILLMONGER'S HANDLERS CAN'T REIN HIM IN.
SO RATHER THAN DRAG YOU INTO ANOTHER INTERNATIONAL INCIDENT, THEY WILL RESOLVE THIS AND SET THINGS RIGHT.

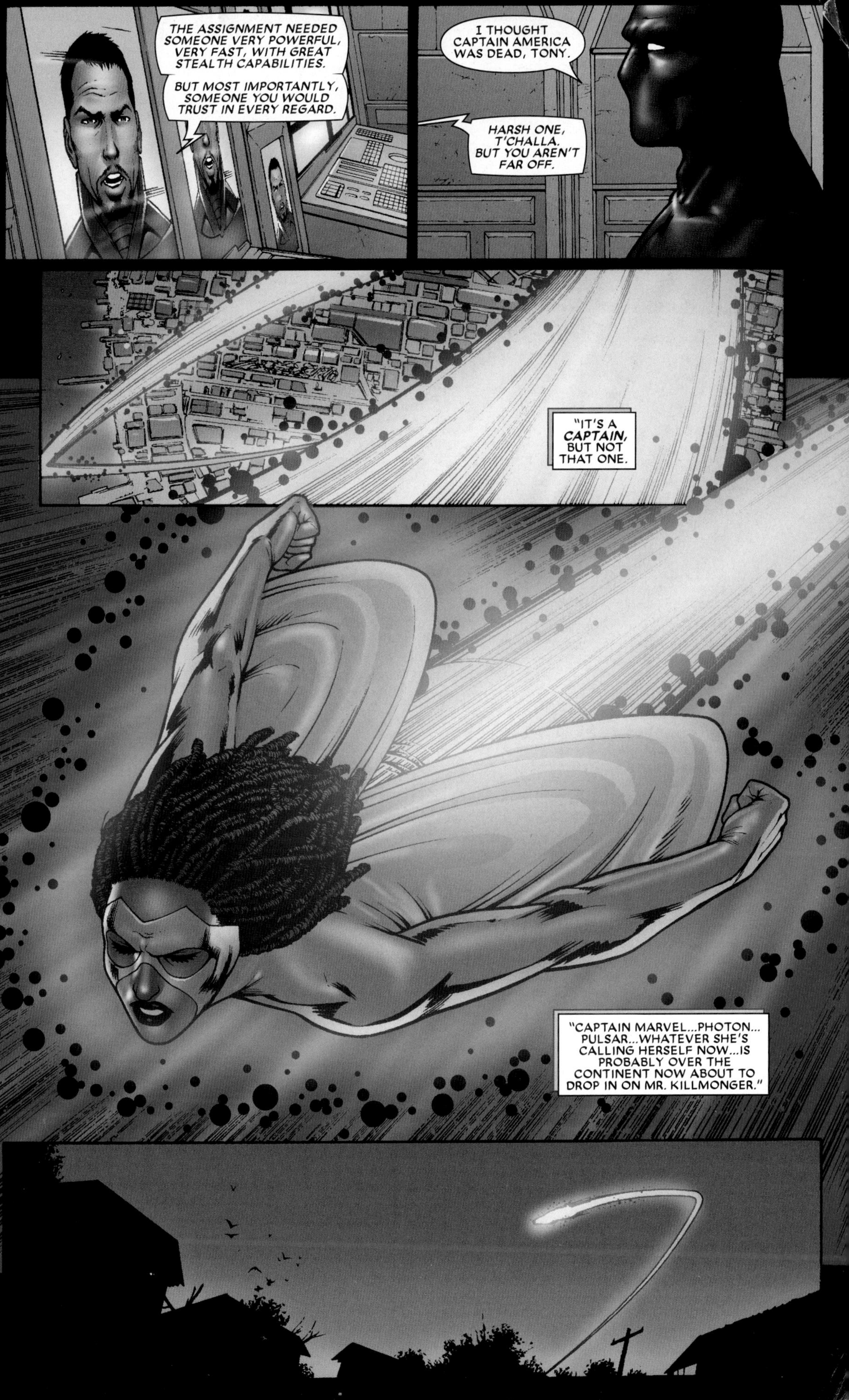
THE ASSIGNMENT NEEDED SOMEONE VERY POWERFUL, VERY FAST, WITH GREAT STEALTH CAPABILITIES.
BUT MOST IMPORTANTLY, SOMEONE YOU WOULD TRUST IN EVERY REGARD.
I THOUGHT CAPTAIN AMERICA WAS DEAD, TONY.
HARSH ONE, T'CHALLA. BUT YOU AREN'T FAR OFF.
"IT'S A CAPTAIN, BUT NOT THAT ONE.
"CAPTAIN MARVEL...PHOTON... PULSAR...WHATEVER SHE'S CALLING HERSELF NOW...IS PROBABLY OVER THE CONTINENT NOW ABOUT TO DROP IN ON MR. KILLMONGER."

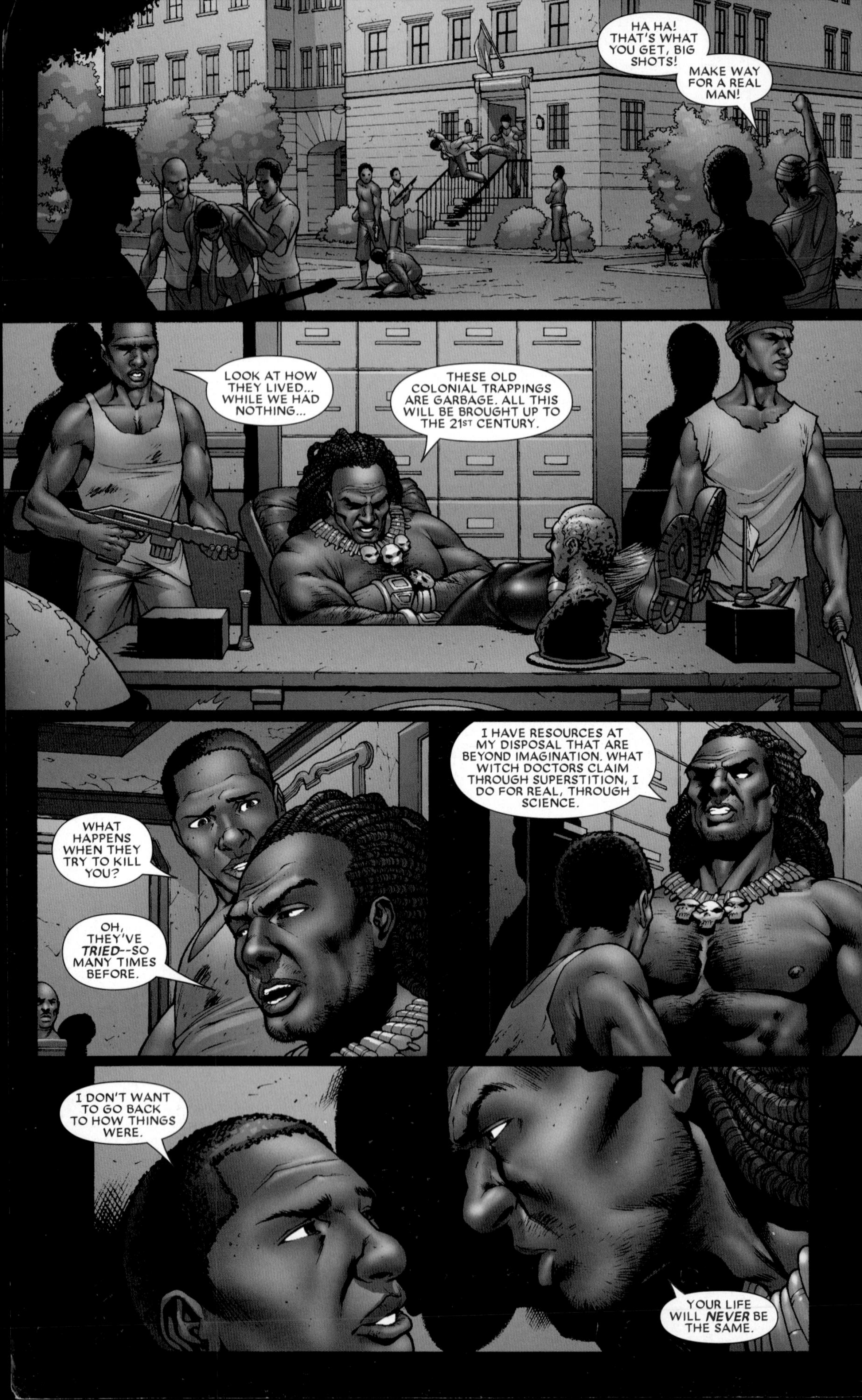
HA HA! THAT'S WHAT YOU GET, BIG SHOTS!
MAKE WAY FOR A REAL MAN!
LOOK AT HOW THEY LIVED... WHILE WE HAD NOTHING...
THESE OLD COLONIAL TRAPPINGS ARE GARBAGE. ALL THIS WILL BE BROUGHT UP TO THE 21ST CENTURY.
WHAT HAPPENS WHEN THEY TRY TO KILL YOU?
OH, THEY'VE *TRIED*--SO MANY TIMES BEFORE.
I HAVE RESOURCES AT MY DISPOSAL THAT ARE BEYOND IMAGINATION. WHAT WITCH DOCTORS CLAIM THROUGH SUPERSTITION, I DO FOR REAL, THROUGH SCIENCE.
I DON'T WANT TO GO BACK TO HOW THINGS WERE.
YOUR LIFE WILL ***NEVER*** BE THE SAME.

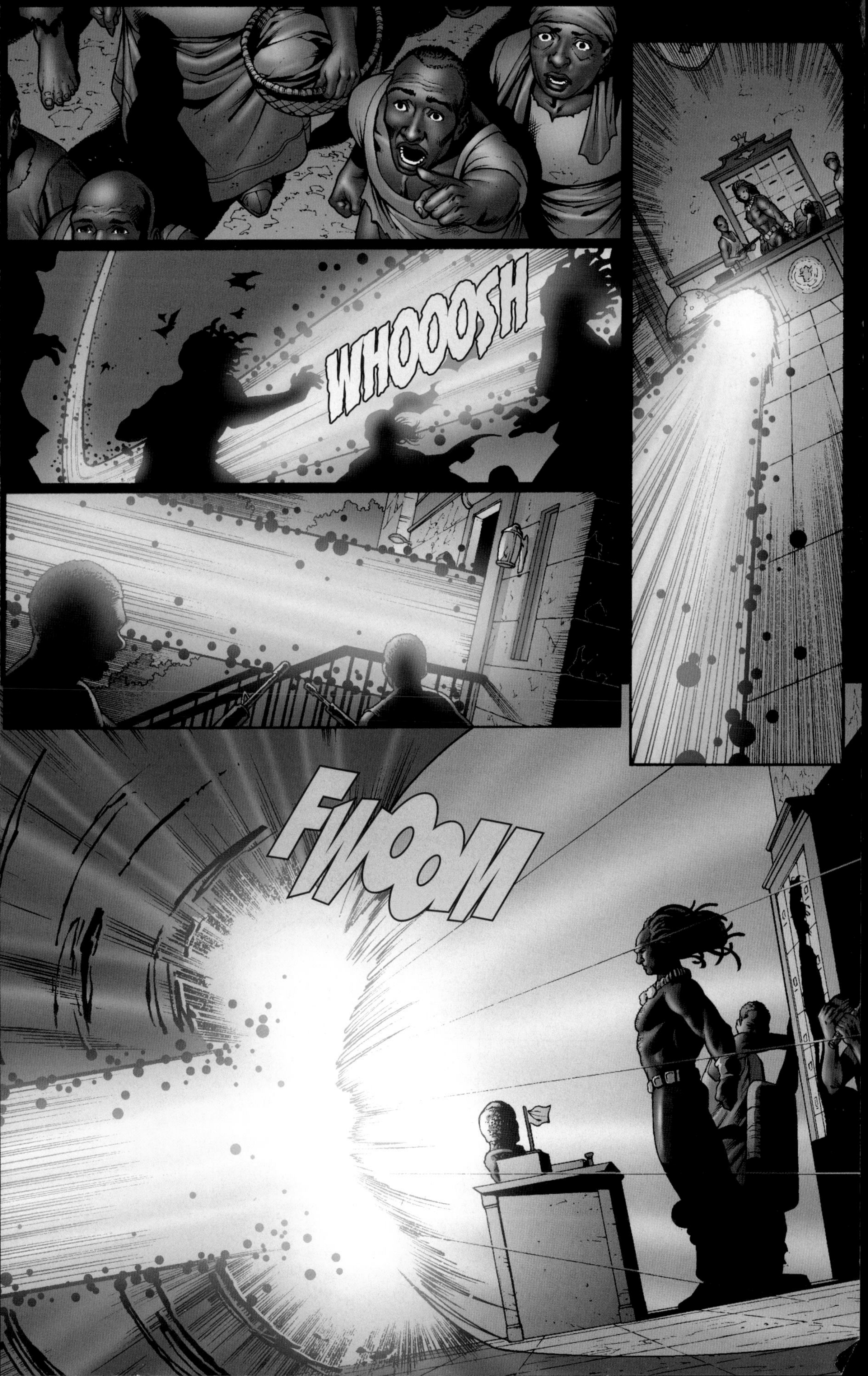
WHOOOSH
FWOOM

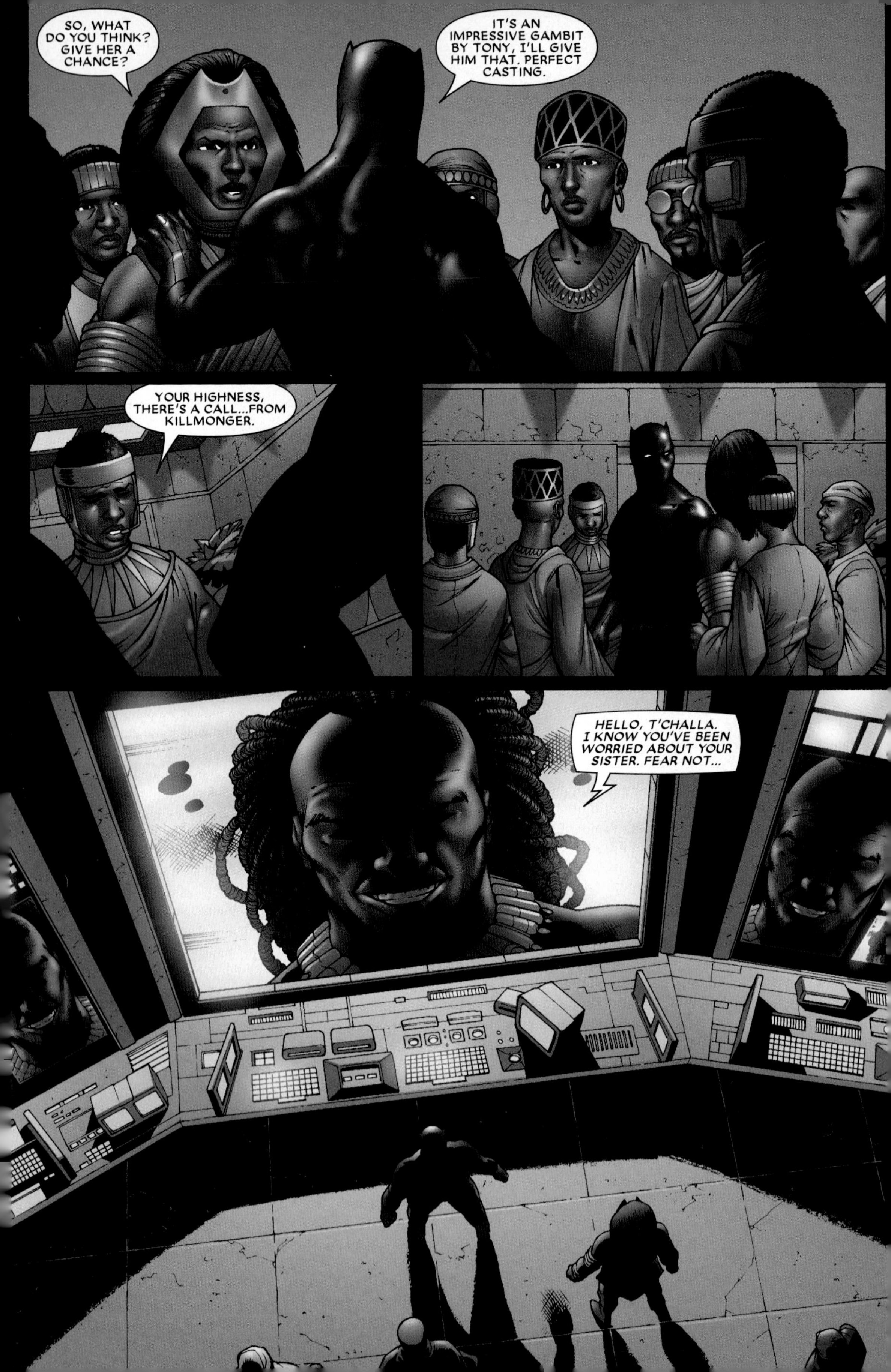

SO, WHAT DO YOU THINK? GIVE HER A CHANCE?
IT'S AN IMPRESSIVE GAMBIT BY TONY, I'LL GIVE HIM THAT. PERFECT CASTING.
YOUR HIGHNESS, THERE'S A CALL...FROM KILLMONGER.
HELLO, T'CHALLA. I KNOW YOU'VE BEEN WORRIED ABOUT YOUR SISTER. FEAR NOT...

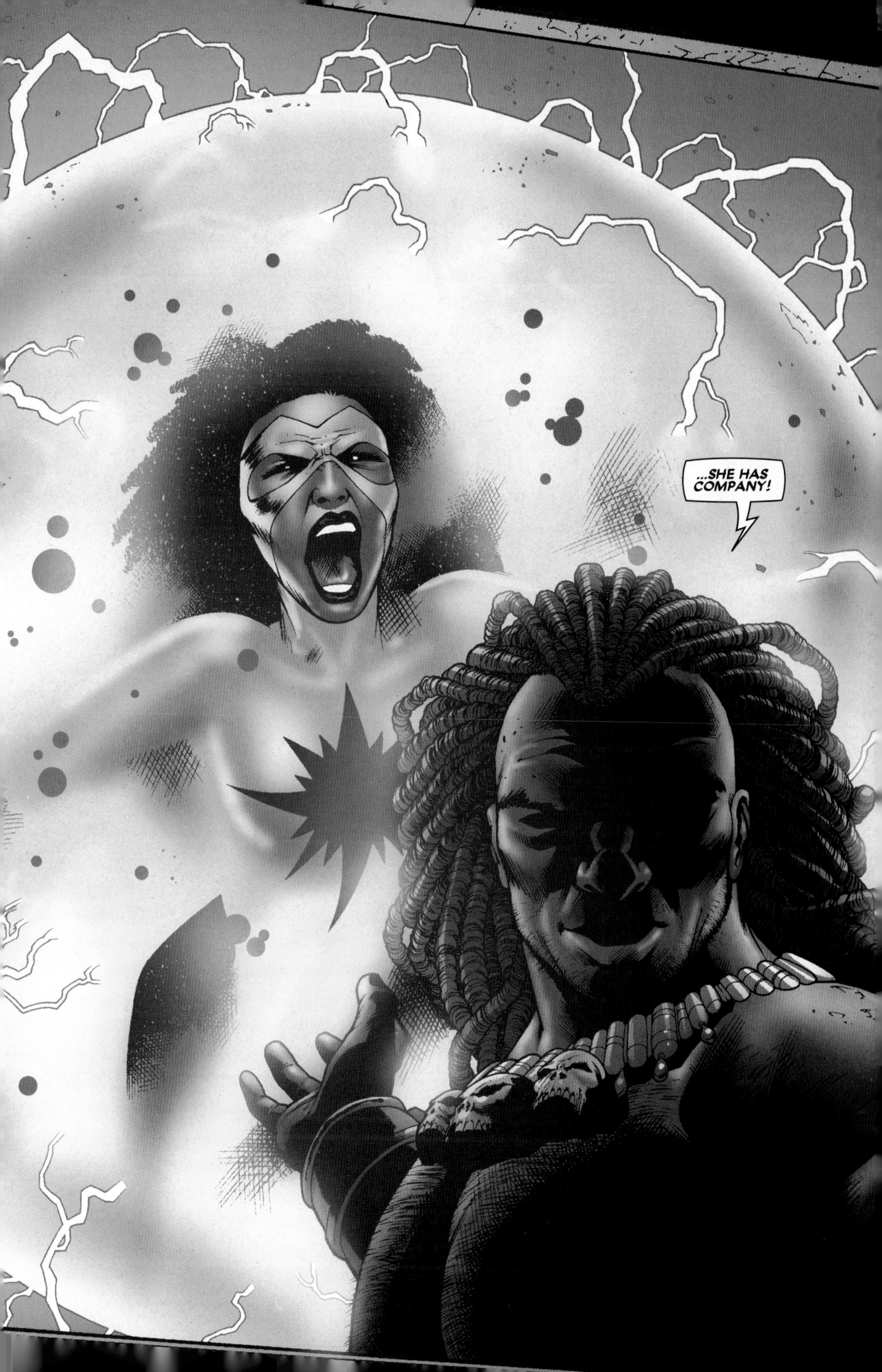
...SHE HAS COMPANY!

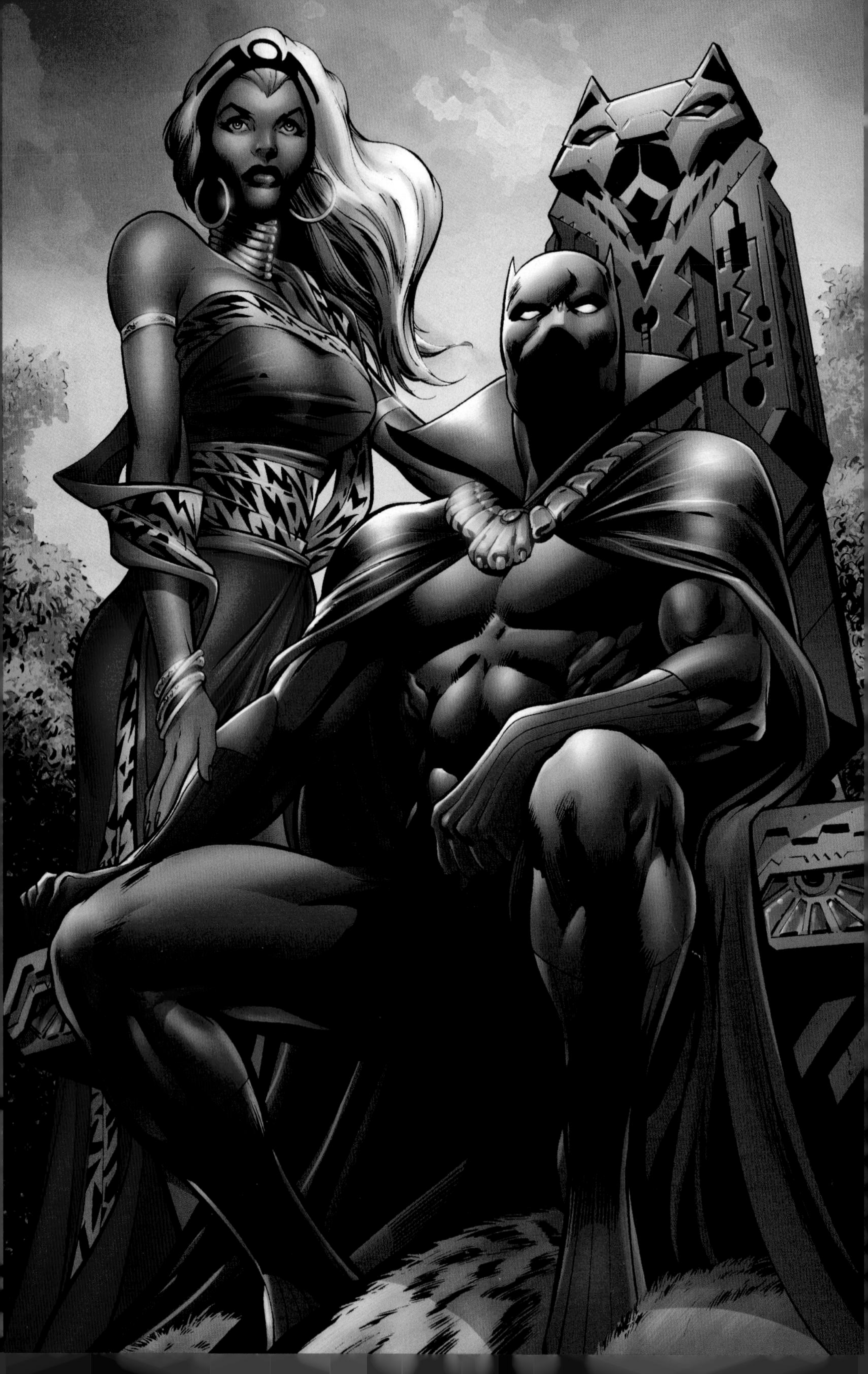

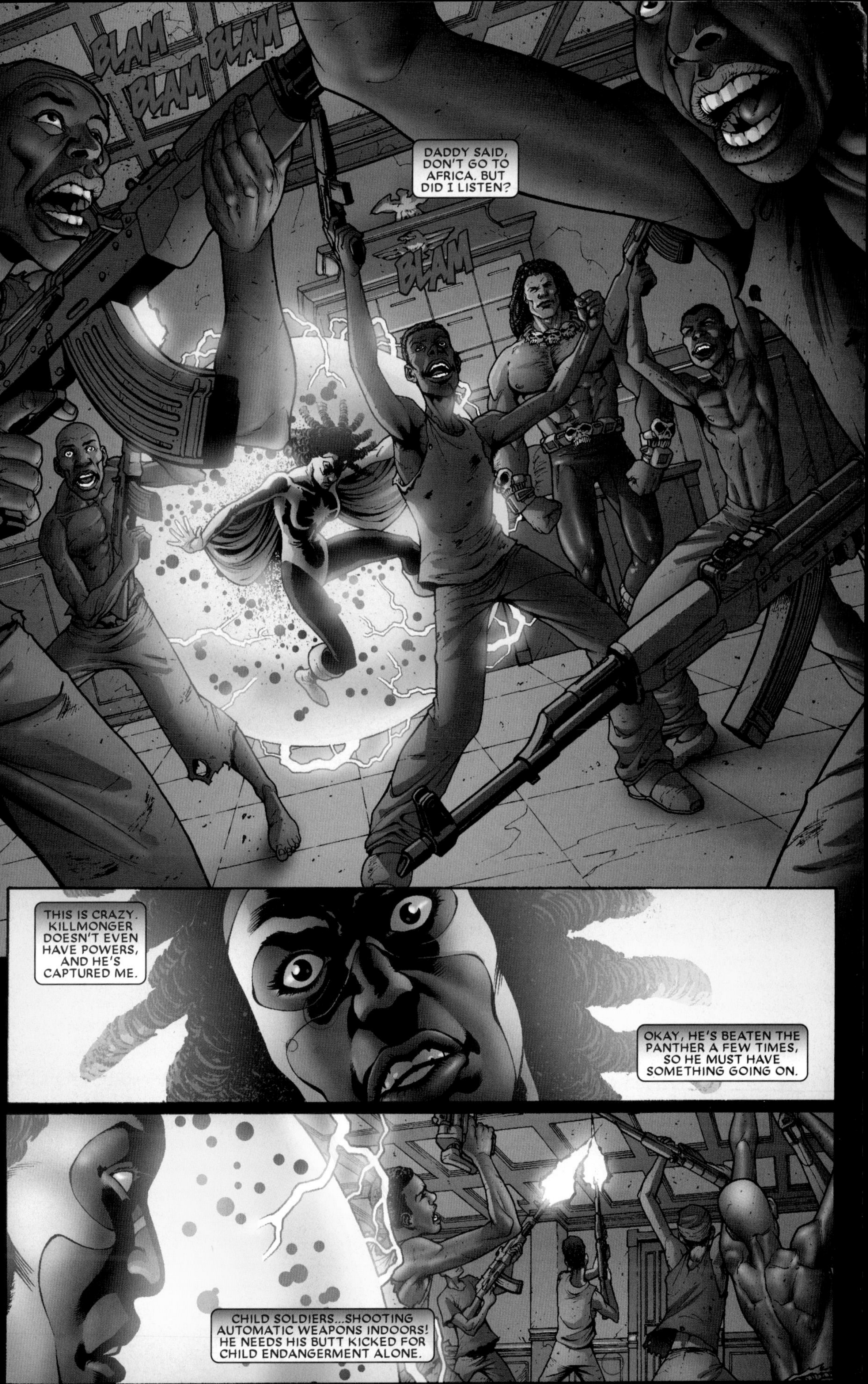
BLAM BLAM BLAM
DADDY SAID, DON'T GO TO AFRICA. BUT DID I LISTEN?
BLAM
THIS IS CRAZY. KILLMONGER DOESN'T EVEN HAVE POWERS, AND HE'S CAPTURED ME.
OKAY, HE'S BEATEN THE PANTHER A FEW TIMES, SO HE MUST HAVE SOMETHING GOING ON.
CHILD SOLDIERS...SHOOTING AUTOMATIC WEAPONS INDOORS! HE NEEDS HIS BUTT KICKED FOR CHILD ENDANGERMENT ALONE.

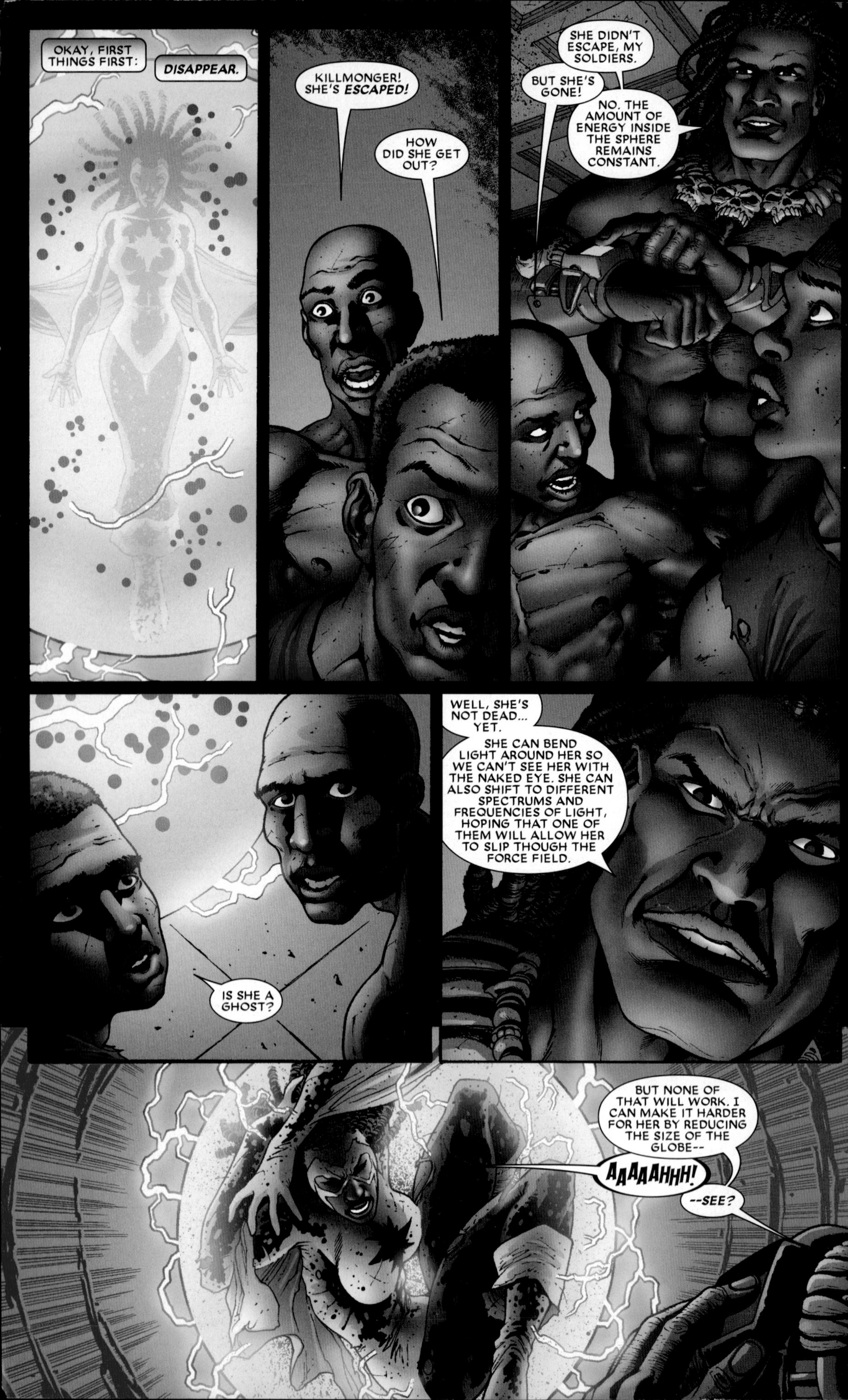
OKAY, FIRST THINGS FIRST:
DISAPPEAR.
KILLMONGER! SHE'S ESCAPED!
HOW DID SHE GET OUT?
SHE DIDN'T ESCAPE, MY SOLDIERS.
BUT SHE'S GONE!
NO. THE AMOUNT OF ENERGY INSIDE THE SPHERE REMAINS CONSTANT.
IS SHE A GHOST?
WELL, SHE'S NOT DEAD... YET.
SHE CAN BEND LIGHT AROUND HER SO WE CAN'T SEE HER WITH THE NAKED EYE. SHE CAN ALSO SHIFT TO DIFFERENT SPECTRUMS AND FREQUENCIES OF LIGHT, HOPING THAT ONE OF THEM WILL ALLOW HER TO SLIP THOUGH THE FORCE FIELD.
BUT NONE OF THAT WILL WORK. I CAN MAKE IT HARDER FOR HER BY REDUCING THE SIZE OF THE GLOBE--
AAAAAHHH!
--SEE?

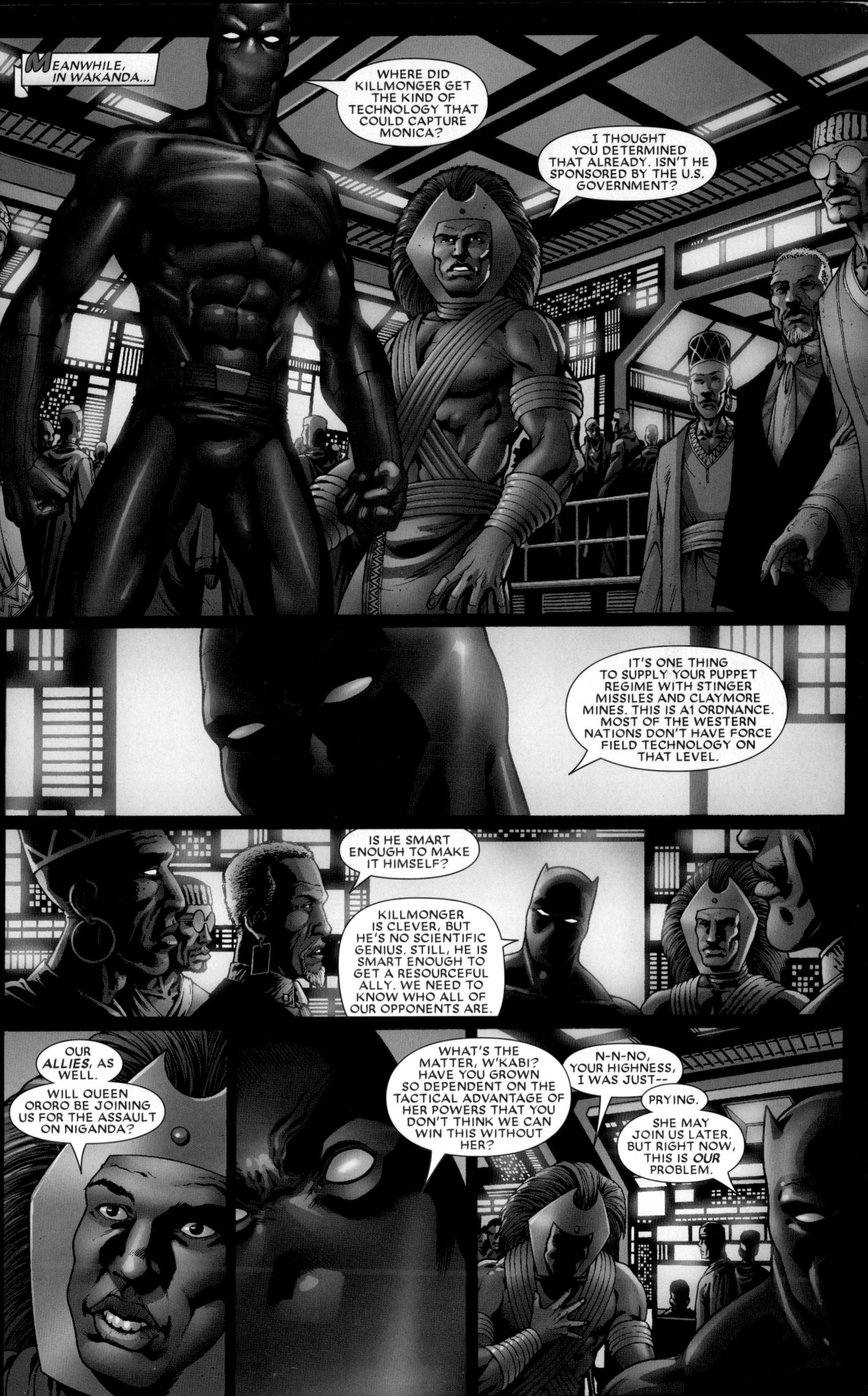
MEANWHILE, IN WAKANDA...
WHERE DID KILLMONGER GET THE KIND OF TECHNOLOGY THAT COULD CAPTURE MONICA?
I THOUGHT YOU DETERMINED THAT ALREADY. ISN'T HE SPONSORED BY THE U.S. GOVERNMENT?
IT'S ONE THING TO SUPPLY YOUR PUPPET REGIME WITH STINGER MISSILES AND CLAYMORE MINES. THIS IS A1 ORDNANCE. MOST OF THE WESTERN NATIONS DON'T HAVE FORCE FIELD TECHNOLOGY ON THAT LEVEL.
IS HE SMART ENOUGH TO MAKE IT HIMSELF?
KILLMONGER IS CLEVER, BUT HE'S NO SCIENTIFIC GENIUS. STILL, HE IS SMART ENOUGH TO GET A RESOURCEFUL ALLY. WE NEED TO KNOW WHO ALL OF OUR OPPONENTS ARE.
OUR *ALLIES*, AS WELL.
WILL QUEEN ORORO BE JOINING US FOR THE ASSAULT ON NIGANDA?
WHAT'S THE MATTER, W'KABI? HAVE YOU GROWN SO DEPENDENT ON THE TACTICAL ADVANTAGE OF HER POWERS THAT YOU DON'T THINK WE CAN WIN THIS WITHOUT HER?
N-N-NO, YOUR HIGHNESS, I WAS JUST--
PRYING.
SHE MAY JOIN US LATER. BUT RIGHT NOW, THIS IS *OUR* PROBLEM.

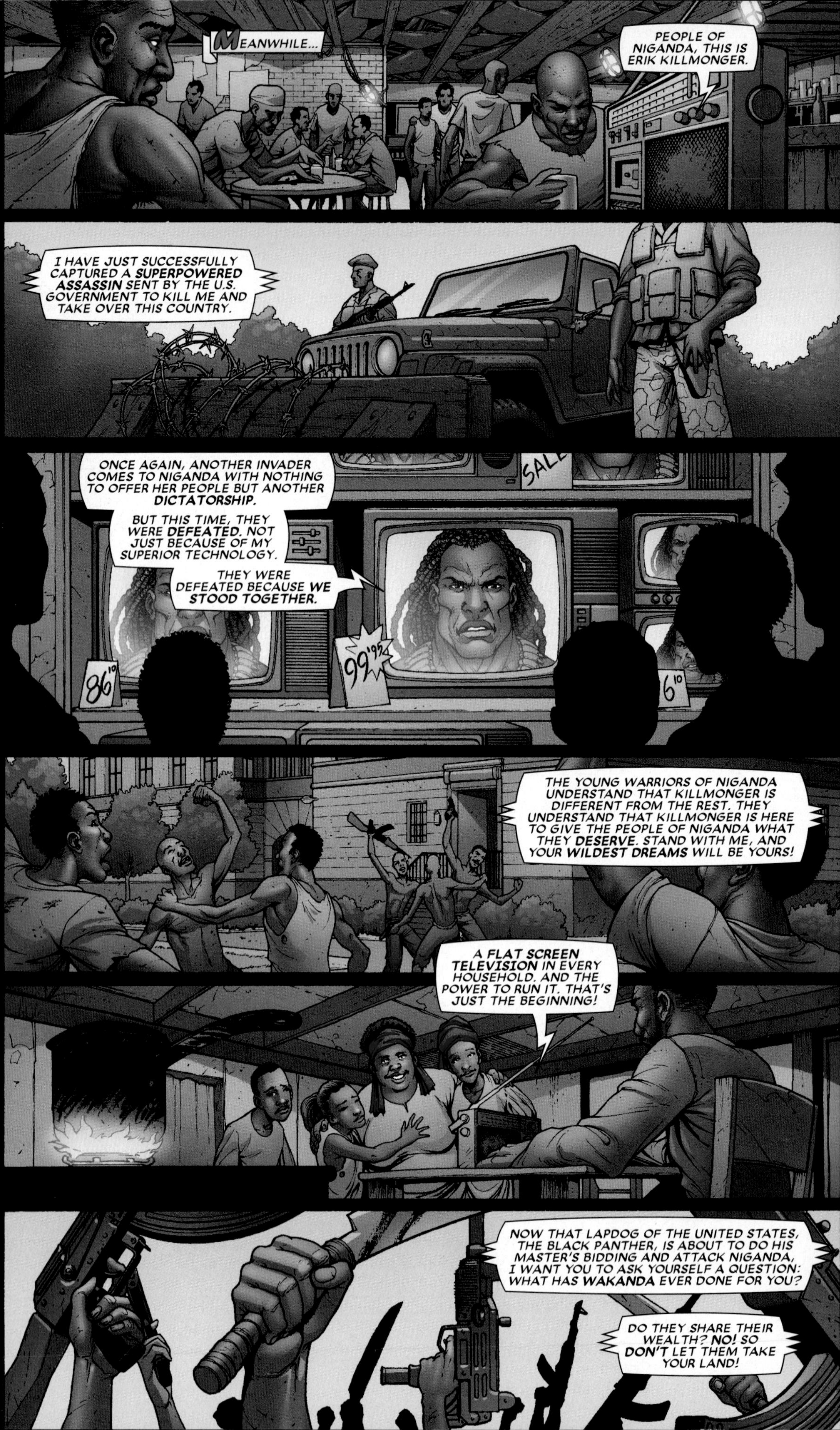
MEANWHILE...
PEOPLE OF NIGANDA, THIS IS ERIK KILLMONGER.
I HAVE JUST SUCCESSFULLY CAPTURED A SUPERPOWERED ASSASSIN SENT BY THE U.S. GOVERNMENT TO KILL ME AND TAKE OVER THIS COUNTRY.
ONCE AGAIN, ANOTHER INVADER COMES TO NIGANDA WITH NOTHING TO OFFER HER PEOPLE BUT ANOTHER DICTATORSHIP.
BUT THIS TIME, THEY WERE DEFEATED. NOT JUST BECAUSE OF MY SUPERIOR TECHNOLOGY.
THEY WERE DEFEATED BECAUSE WE STOOD TOGETHER.
SALE
86.10
99.95
6.10
THE YOUNG WARRIORS OF NIGANDA UNDERSTAND THAT KILLMONGER IS DIFFERENT FROM THE REST. THEY UNDERSTAND THAT KILLMONGER IS HERE TO GIVE THE PEOPLE OF NIGANDA WHAT THEY DESERVE. STAND WITH ME, AND YOUR WILDEST DREAMS WILL BE YOURS!
A FLAT SCREEN TELEVISION IN EVERY HOUSEHOLD. AND THE POWER TO RUN IT. THAT'S JUST THE BEGINNING!
NOW THAT LAPDOG OF THE UNITED STATES, THE BLACK PANTHER, IS ABOUT TO DO HIS MASTER'S BIDDING AND ATTACK NIGANDA, I WANT YOU TO ASK YOURSELF A QUESTION: WHAT HAS WAKANDA EVER DONE FOR YOU?
DO THEY SHARE THEIR WEALTH? NO! SO DON'T LET THEM TAKE YOUR LAND!

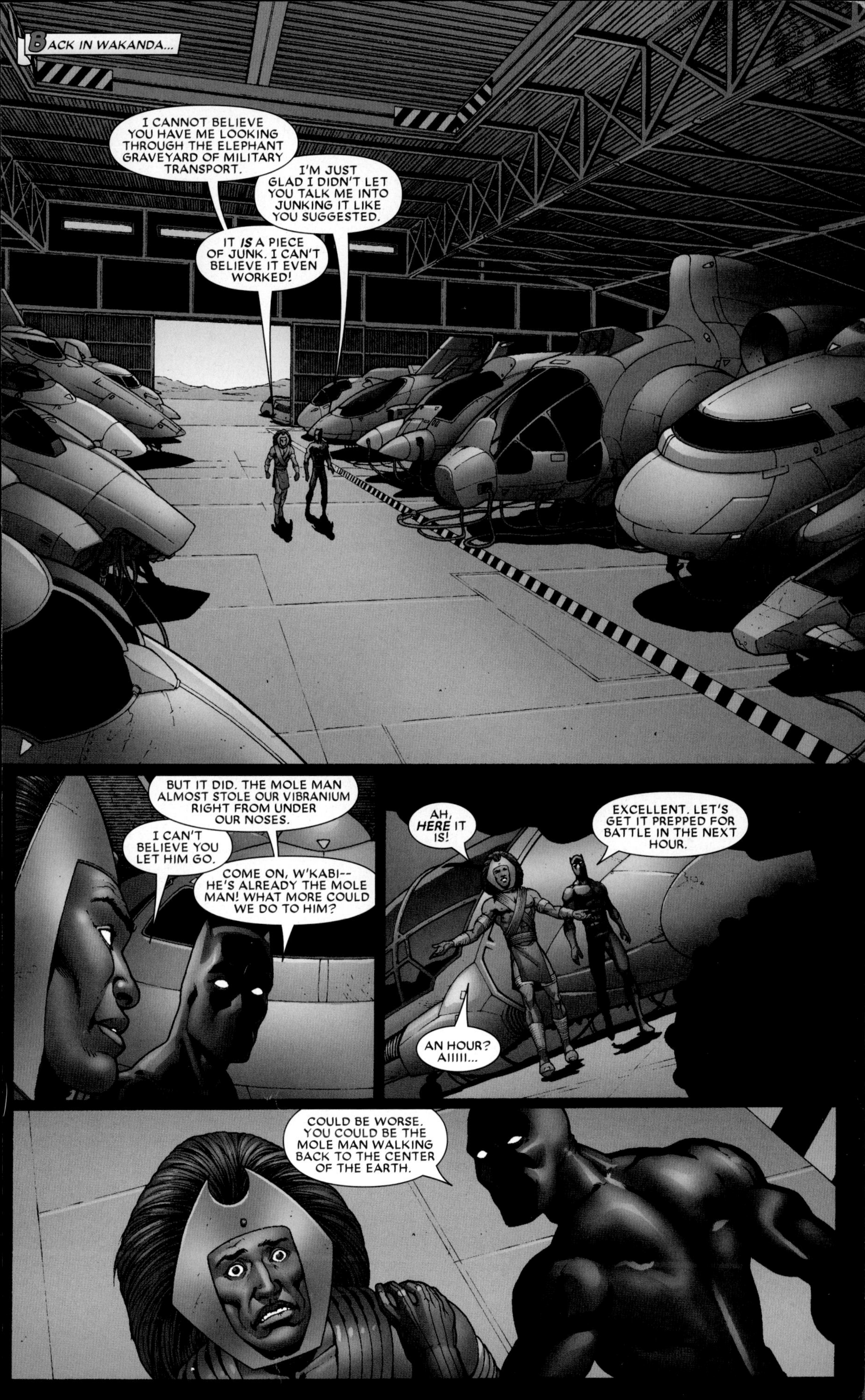
BACK IN WAKANDA...
I CANNOT BELIEVE YOU HAVE ME LOOKING THROUGH THE ELEPHANT GRAVEYARD OF MILITARY TRANSPORT.
I'M JUST GLAD I DIDN'T LET YOU TALK ME INTO JUNKING IT LIKE YOU SUGGESTED.
IT *IS* A PIECE OF JUNK. I CAN'T BELIEVE IT EVEN WORKED!
BUT IT DID. THE MOLE MAN ALMOST STOLE OUR VIBRANIUM RIGHT FROM UNDER OUR NOSES.
I CAN'T BELIEVE YOU LET HIM GO.
COME ON, W'KABI-- HE'S ALREADY THE MOLE MAN! WHAT MORE COULD WE DO TO HIM?
AH, *HERE* IT IS!
EXCELLENT. LET'S GET IT PREPPED FOR BATTLE IN THE NEXT HOUR.
AN HOUR? AIIIII...
COULD BE WORSE. YOU COULD BE THE MOLE MAN WALKING BACK TO THE CENTER OF THE EARTH.

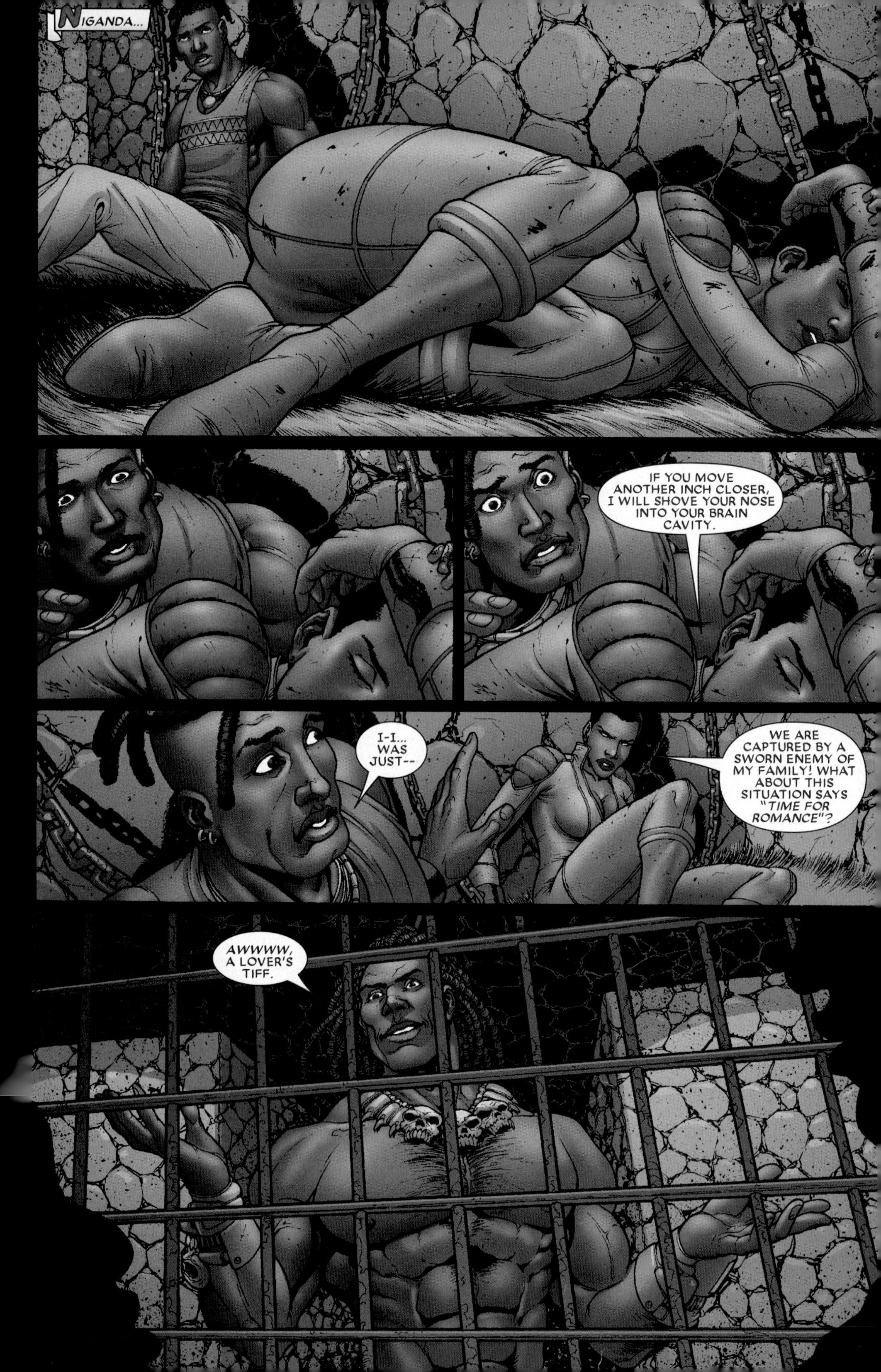
NIGANDA...
IF YOU MOVE ANOTHER INCH CLOSER, I WILL SHOVE YOUR NOSE INTO YOUR BRAIN CAVITY.
I-I... WAS JUST--
WE ARE CAPTURED BY A SWORN ENEMY OF MY FAMILY! WHAT ABOUT THIS SITUATION SAYS "TIME FOR ROMANCE"?
AWWWW, A LOVER'S TIFF.

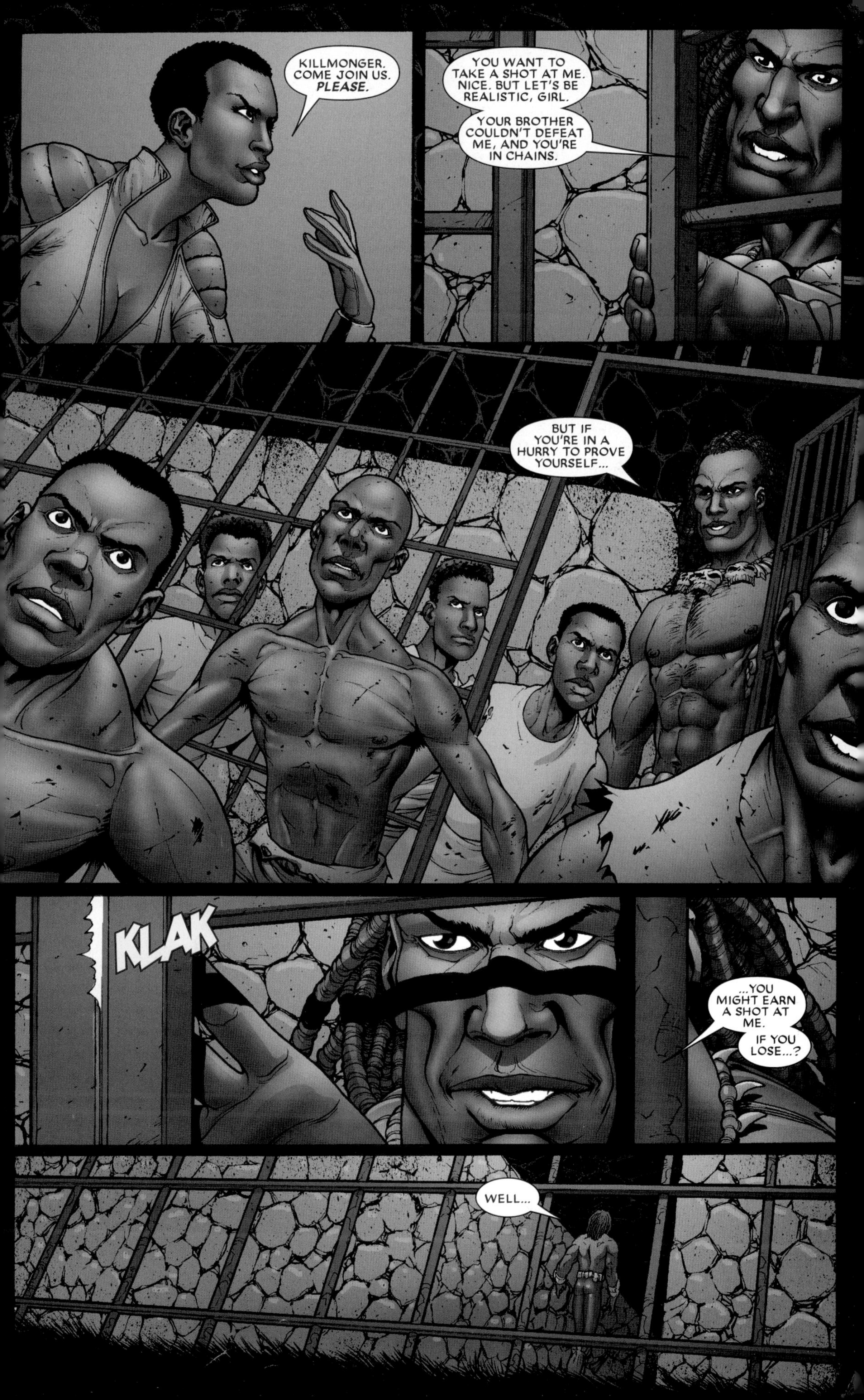
KILLMONGER. COME JOIN US. *PLEASE.*
YOU WANT TO TAKE A SHOT AT ME. NICE. BUT LET'S BE REALISTIC, GIRL.
YOUR BROTHER COULDN'T DEFEAT ME, AND YOU'RE IN CHAINS.
BUT IF YOU'RE IN A HURRY TO PROVE YOURSELF...
KLAK
...YOU MIGHT EARN A SHOT AT ME.
IF YOU LOSE...?
WELL...

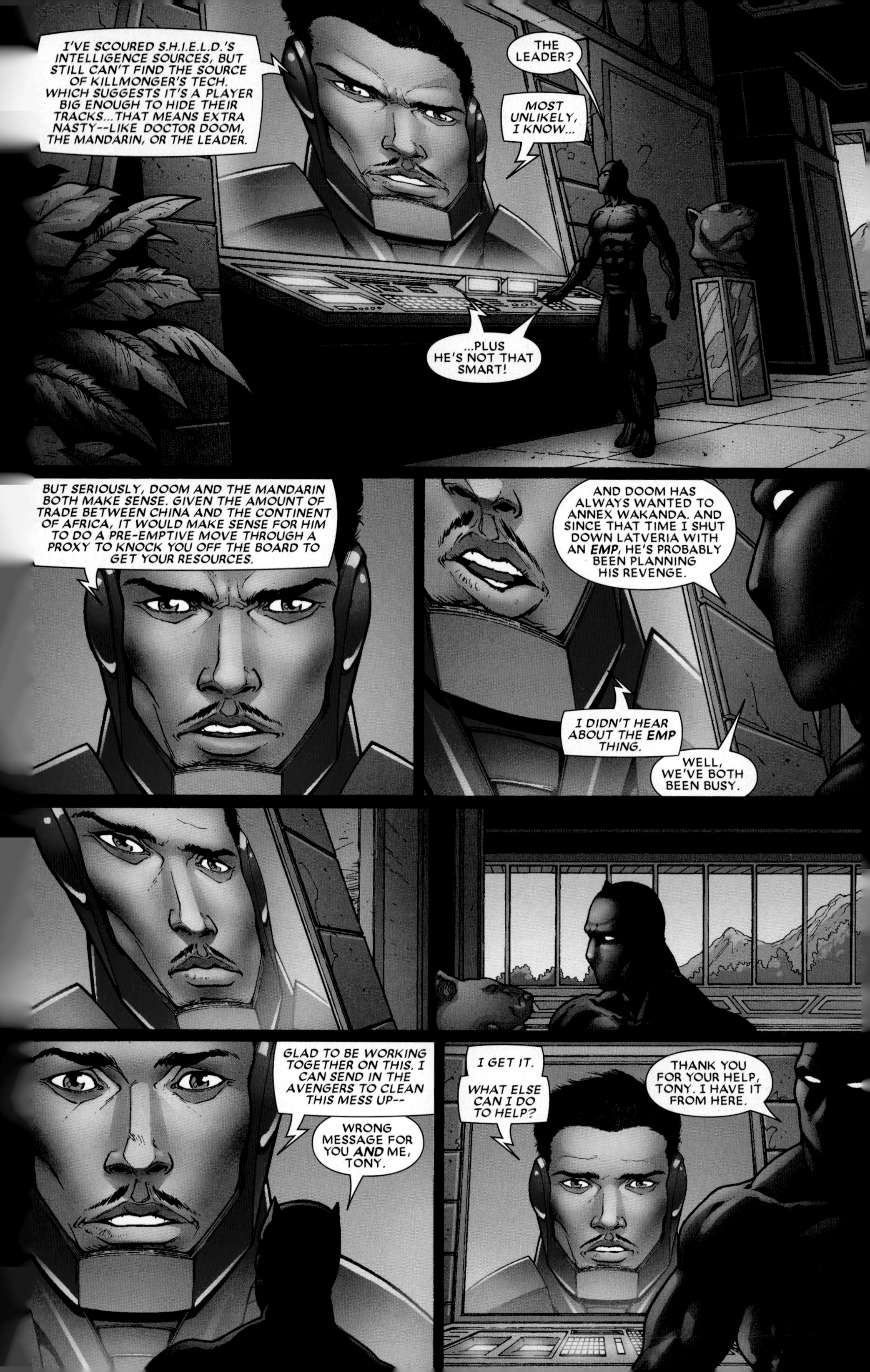
I'VE SCOURED S.H.I.E.L.D.'S INTELLIGENCE SOURCES, BUT STILL CAN'T FIND THE SOURCE OF KILLMONGER'S TECH. WHICH SUGGESTS IT'S A PLAYER BIG ENOUGH TO HIDE THEIR TRACKS...THAT MEANS EXTRA NASTY--LIKE DOCTOR DOOM, THE MANDARIN, OR THE LEADER.
THE LEADER?
MOST UNLIKELY, I KNOW...
...PLUS HE'S NOT THAT SMART!
BUT SERIOUSLY, DOOM AND THE MANDARIN BOTH MAKE SENSE. GIVEN THE AMOUNT OF TRADE BETWEEN CHINA AND THE CONTINENT OF AFRICA, IT WOULD MAKE SENSE FOR HIM TO DO A PRE-EMPTIVE MOVE THROUGH A PROXY TO KNOCK YOU OFF THE BOARD TO GET YOUR RESOURCES.
AND DOOM HAS ALWAYS WANTED TO ANNEX WAKANDA. AND SINCE THAT TIME I SHUT DOWN LATVERIA WITH AN EMP, HE'S PROBABLY BEEN PLANNING HIS REVENGE.
I DIDN'T HEAR ABOUT THE EMP THING.
WELL, WE'VE BOTH BEEN BUSY.
GLAD TO BE WORKING TOGETHER ON THIS. I CAN SEND IN THE AVENGERS TO CLEAN THIS MESS UP--
WRONG MESSAGE FOR YOU AND ME, TONY.
I GET IT.
WHAT ELSE CAN I DO TO HELP?
THANK YOU FOR YOUR HELP, TONY. I HAVE IT FROM HERE.

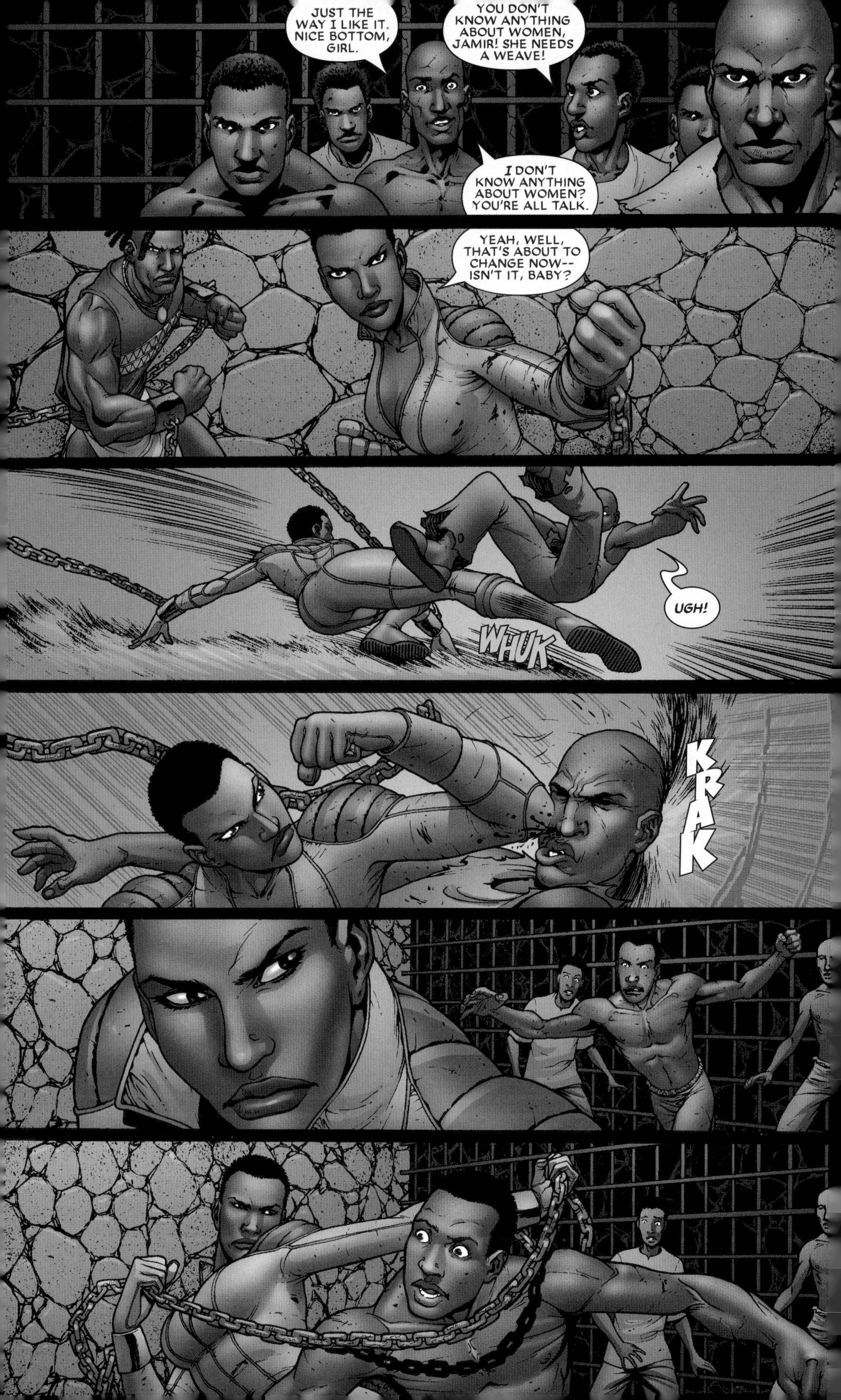
JUST THE WAY I LIKE IT. NICE BOTTOM, GIRL.
YOU DON'T KNOW ANYTHING ABOUT WOMEN, JAMIR! SHE NEEDS A WEAVE!
I DON'T KNOW ANYTHING ABOUT WOMEN? YOU'RE ALL TALK.
YEAH, WELL, THAT'S ABOUT TO CHANGE NOW-- ISN'T IT, BABY?
UGH!
WHUK
KRAK

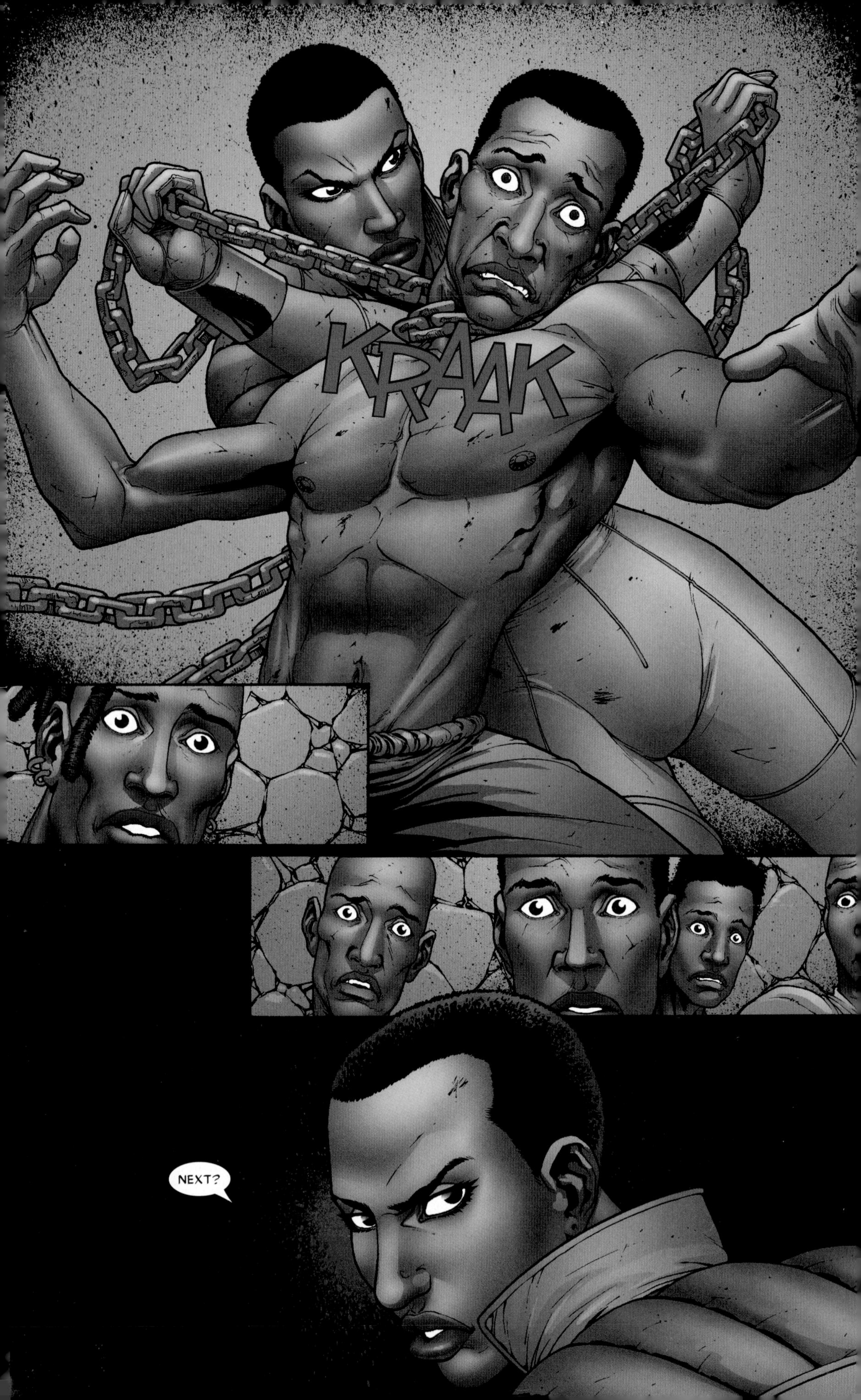
KRAAK
NEXT?

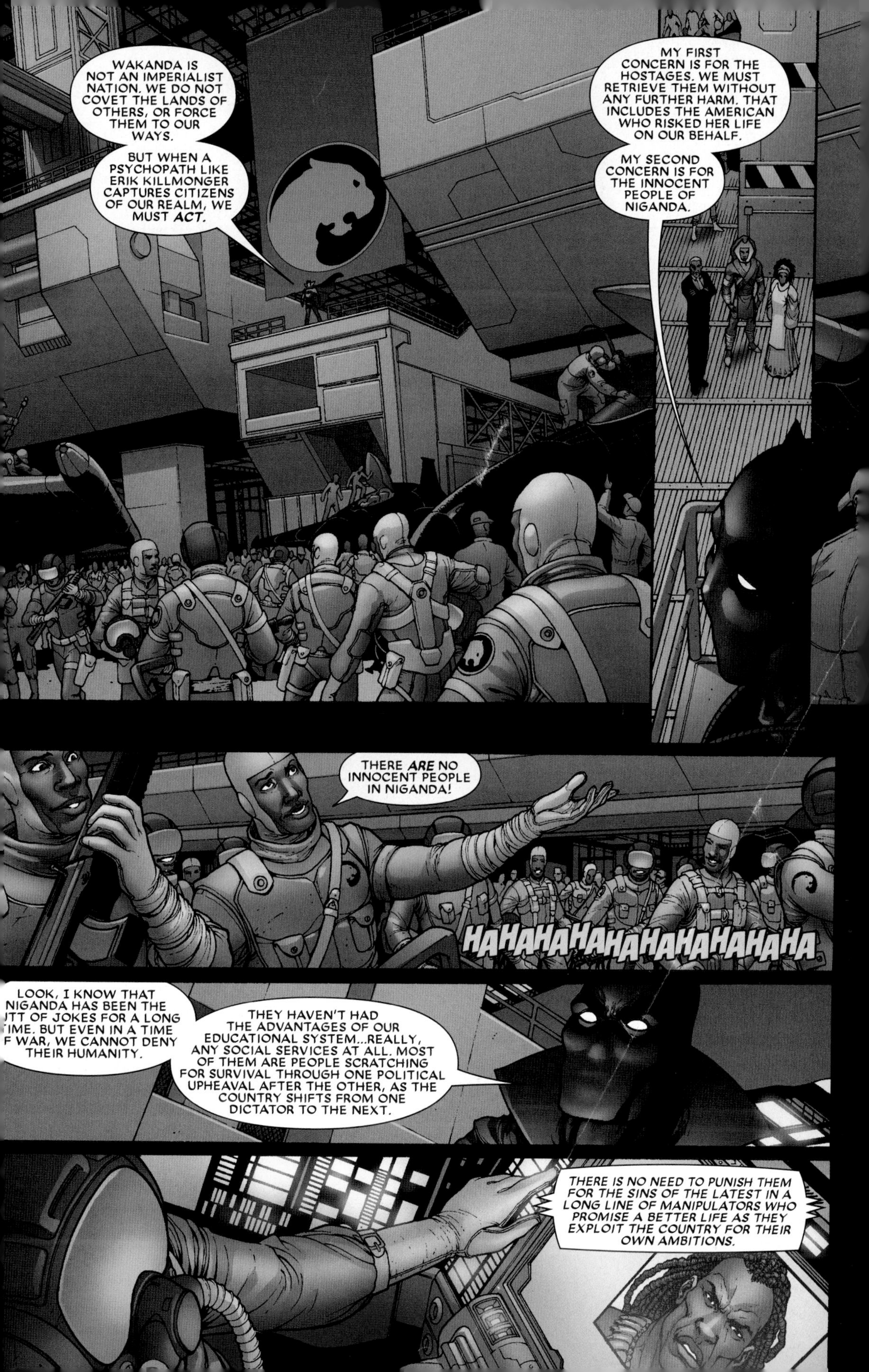

WAKANDA IS NOT AN IMPERIALIST NATION. WE DO NOT COVET THE LANDS OF OTHERS, OR FORCE THEM TO OUR WAYS.
BUT WHEN A PSYCHOPATH LIKE ERIK KILLMONGER CAPTURES CITIZENS OF OUR REALM, WE MUST ACT.
MY FIRST CONCERN IS FOR THE HOSTAGES. WE MUST RETRIEVE THEM WITHOUT ANY FURTHER HARM. THAT INCLUDES THE AMERICAN WHO RISKED HER LIFE ON OUR BEHALF.
MY SECOND CONCERN IS FOR THE INNOCENT PEOPLE OF NIGANDA.
THERE ARE NO INNOCENT PEOPLE IN NIGANDA!
HAHAHAHAHAHAHAHAHAHAHAHA
LOOK, I KNOW THAT NIGANDA HAS BEEN THE UTT OF JOKES FOR A LONG IME. BUT EVEN IN A TIME F WAR, WE CANNOT DENY THEIR HUMANITY.
THEY HAVEN'T HAD THE ADVANTAGES OF OUR EDUCATIONAL SYSTEM...REALLY, ANY SOCIAL SERVICES AT ALL. MOST OF THEM ARE PEOPLE SCRATCHING FOR SURVIVAL THROUGH ONE POLITICAL UPHEAVAL AFTER THE OTHER, AS THE COUNTRY SHIFTS FROM ONE DICTATOR TO THE NEXT.
THERE IS NO NEED TO PUNISH THEM FOR THE SINS OF THE LATEST IN A LONG LINE OF MANIPULATORS WHO PROMISE A BETTER LIFE AS THEY EXPLOIT THE COUNTRY FOR THEIR OWN AMBITIONS.

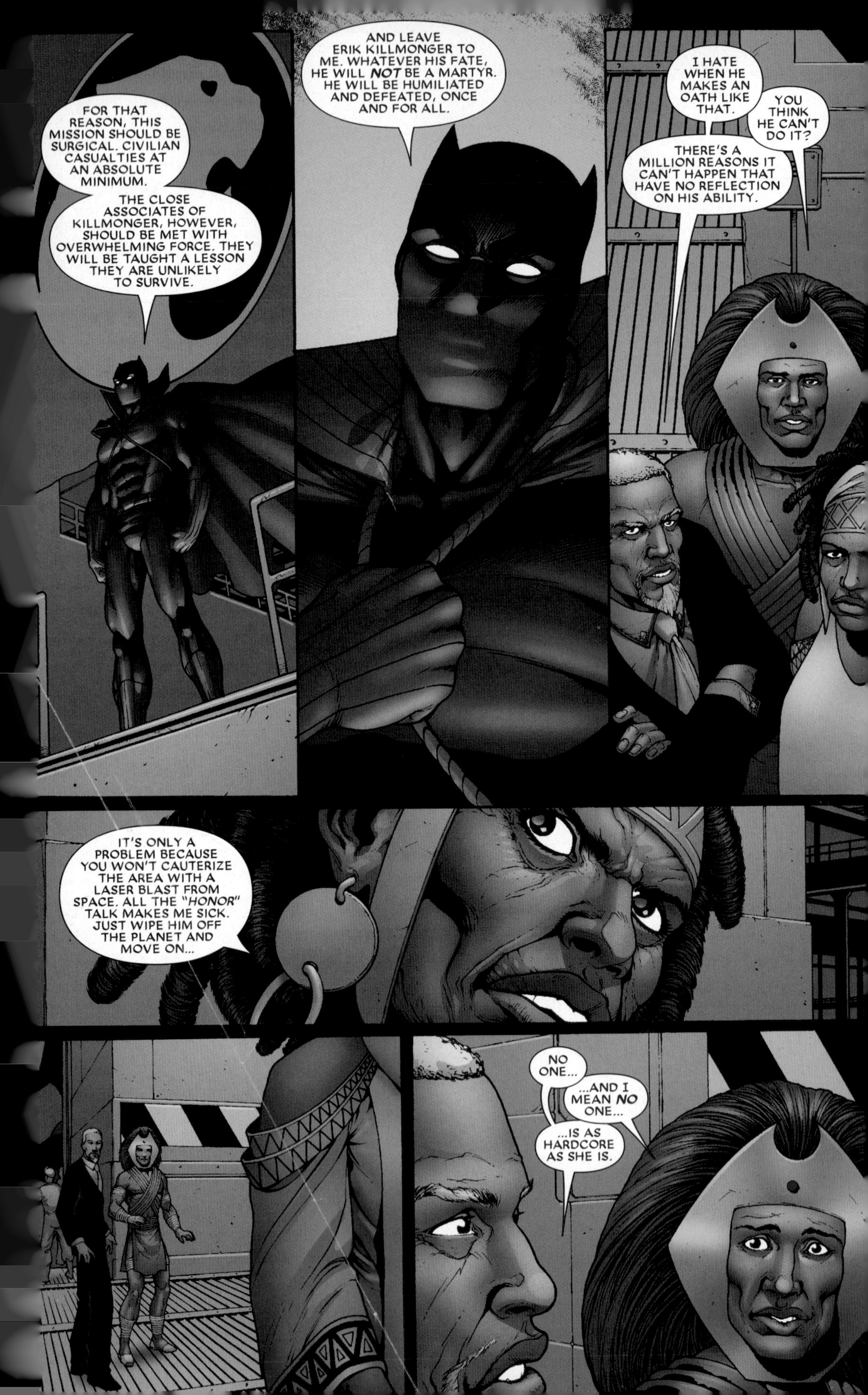
FOR THAT REASON, THIS MISSION SHOULD BE SURGICAL. CIVILIAN CASUALTIES AT AN ABSOLUTE MINIMUM.
THE CLOSE ASSOCIATES OF KILLMONGER, HOWEVER, SHOULD BE MET WITH OVERWHELMING FORCE. THEY WILL BE TAUGHT A LESSON THEY ARE UNLIKELY TO SURVIVE.
AND LEAVE ERIK KILLMONGER TO ME. WHATEVER HIS FATE, HE WILL *NOT* BE A MARTYR. HE WILL BE HUMILIATED AND DEFEATED, ONCE AND FOR ALL.
I HATE WHEN HE MAKES AN OATH LIKE THAT.
YOU THINK HE CAN'T DO IT?
THERE'S A MILLION REASONS IT CAN'T HAPPEN THAT HAVE NO REFLECTION ON HIS ABILITY.
IT'S ONLY A PROBLEM BECAUSE YOU WON'T CAUTERIZE THE AREA WITH A LASER BLAST FROM SPACE. ALL THE *"HONOR"* TALK MAKES ME SICK. JUST WIPE HIM OFF THE PLANET AND MOVE ON...
NO ONE...
...AND I MEAN *NO* ONE...
...IS AS HARDCORE AS SHE IS.

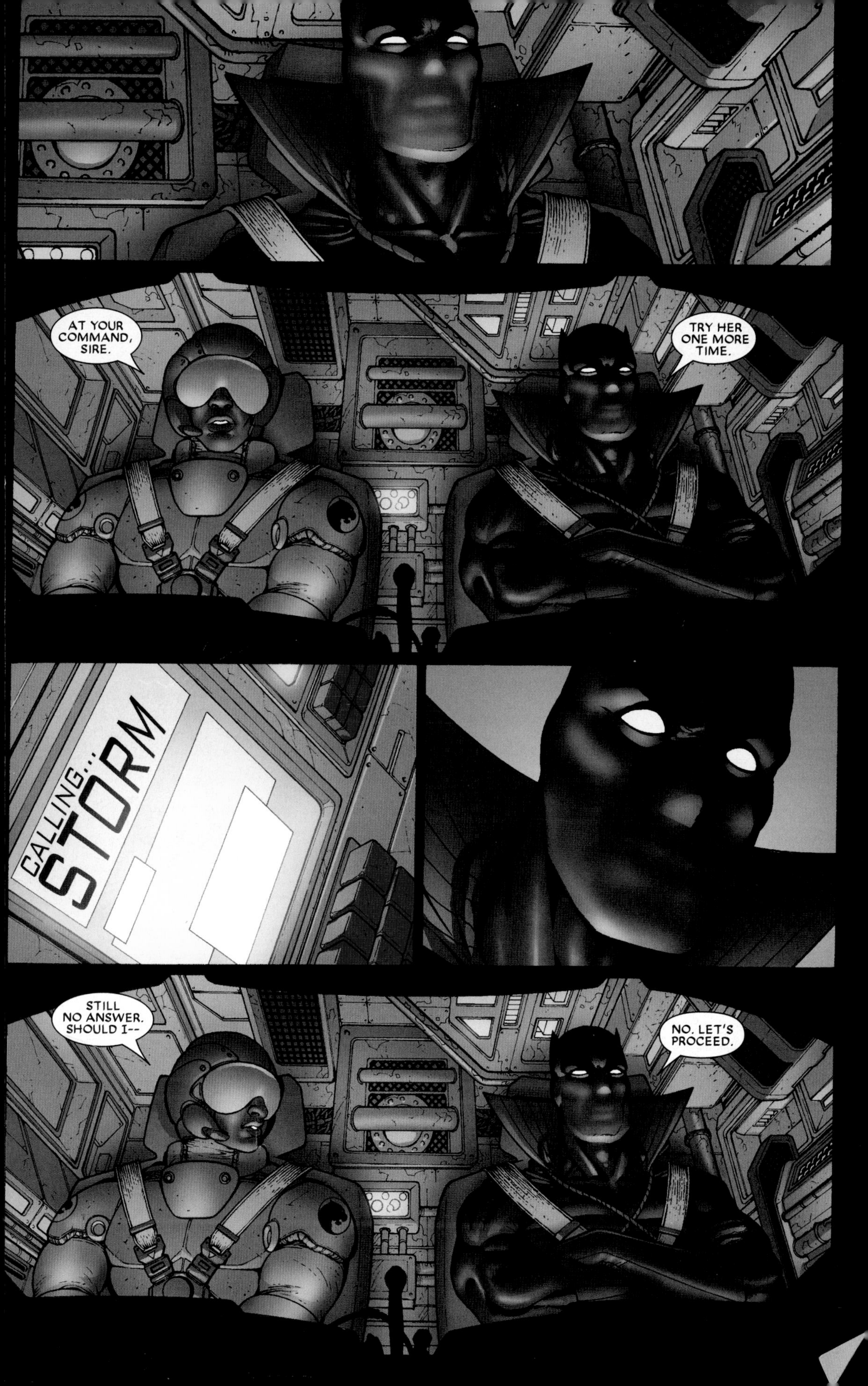

AT YOUR COMMAND, SIRE.
TRY HER ONE MORE TIME.
CALLING... STORM
STILL NO ANSWER. SHOULD I--
NO. LET'S PROCEED.

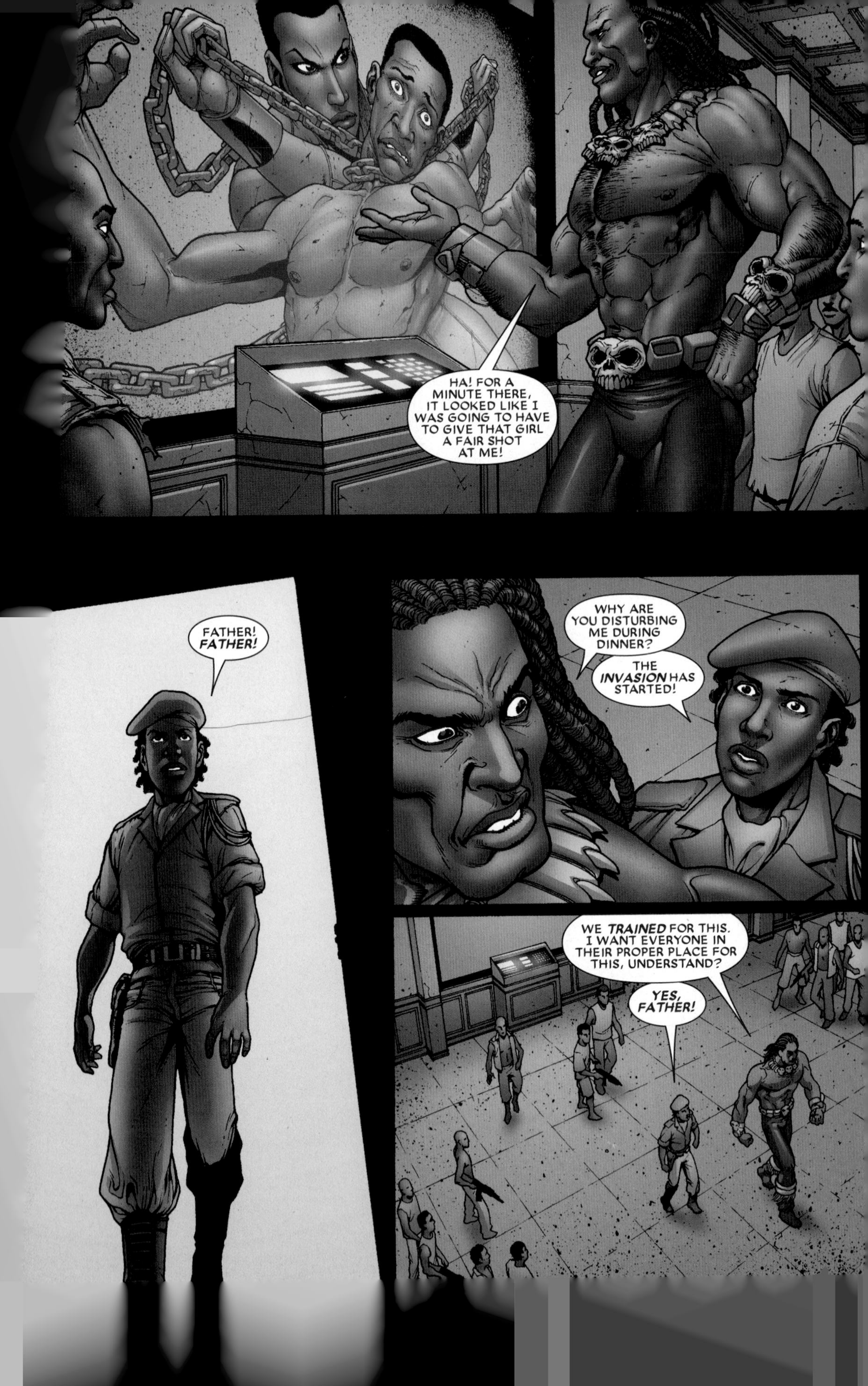
HA! FOR A MINUTE THERE, IT LOOKED LIKE I WAS GOING TO HAVE TO GIVE THAT GIRL A FAIR SHOT AT ME!
FATHER! FATHER!
WHY ARE YOU DISTURBING ME DURING DINNER?
THE INVASION HAS STARTED!
WE TRAINED FOR THIS. I WANT EVERYONE IN THEIR PROPER PLACE FOR THIS, UNDERSTAND?
YES, FATHER!

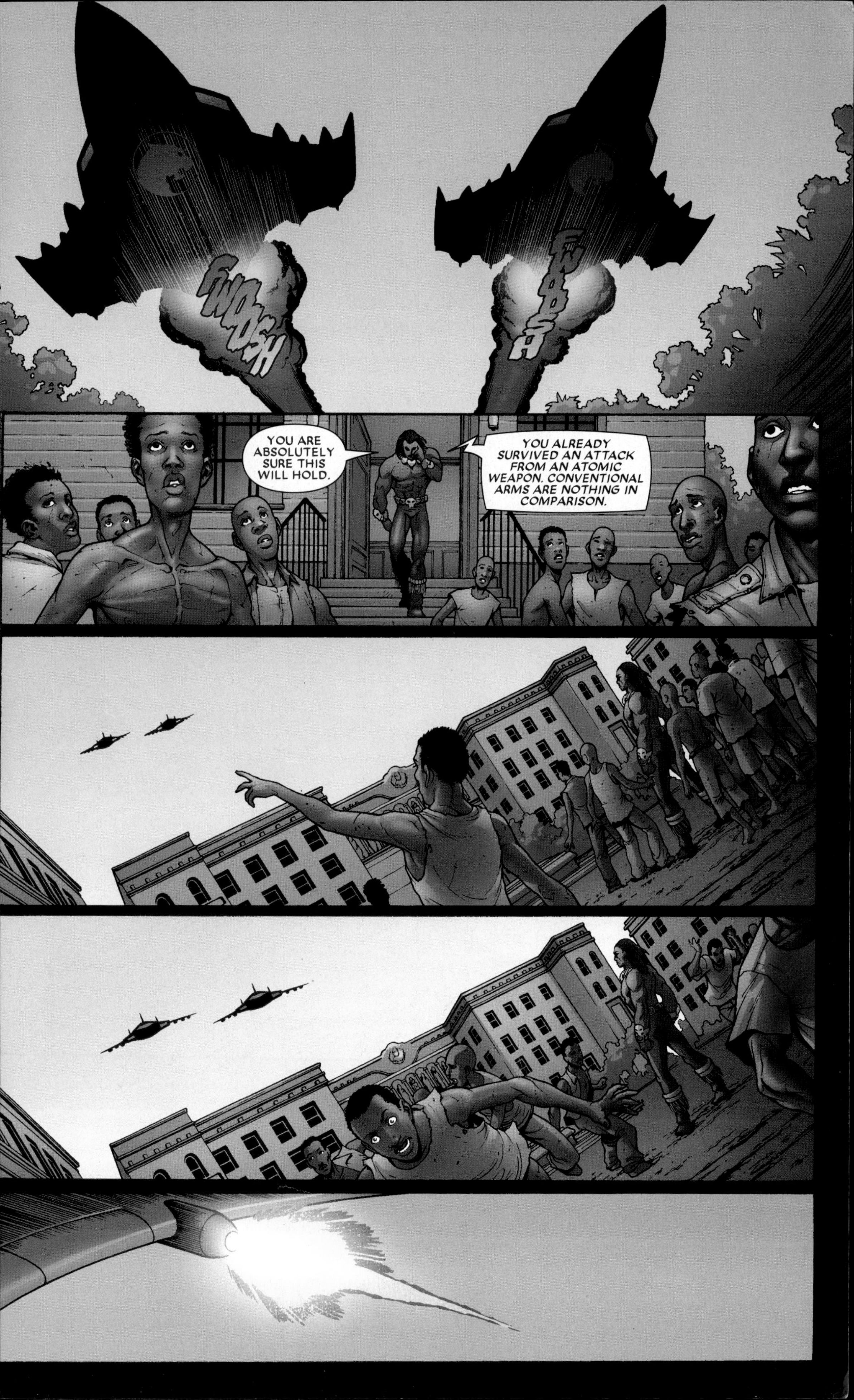
FWOOSH
FWOOSH
YOU ARE ABSOLUTELY SURE THIS WILL HOLD.
YOU ALREADY SURVIVED AN ATTACK FROM AN ATOMIC WEAPON. CONVENTIONAL ARMS ARE NOTHING IN COMPARISON.

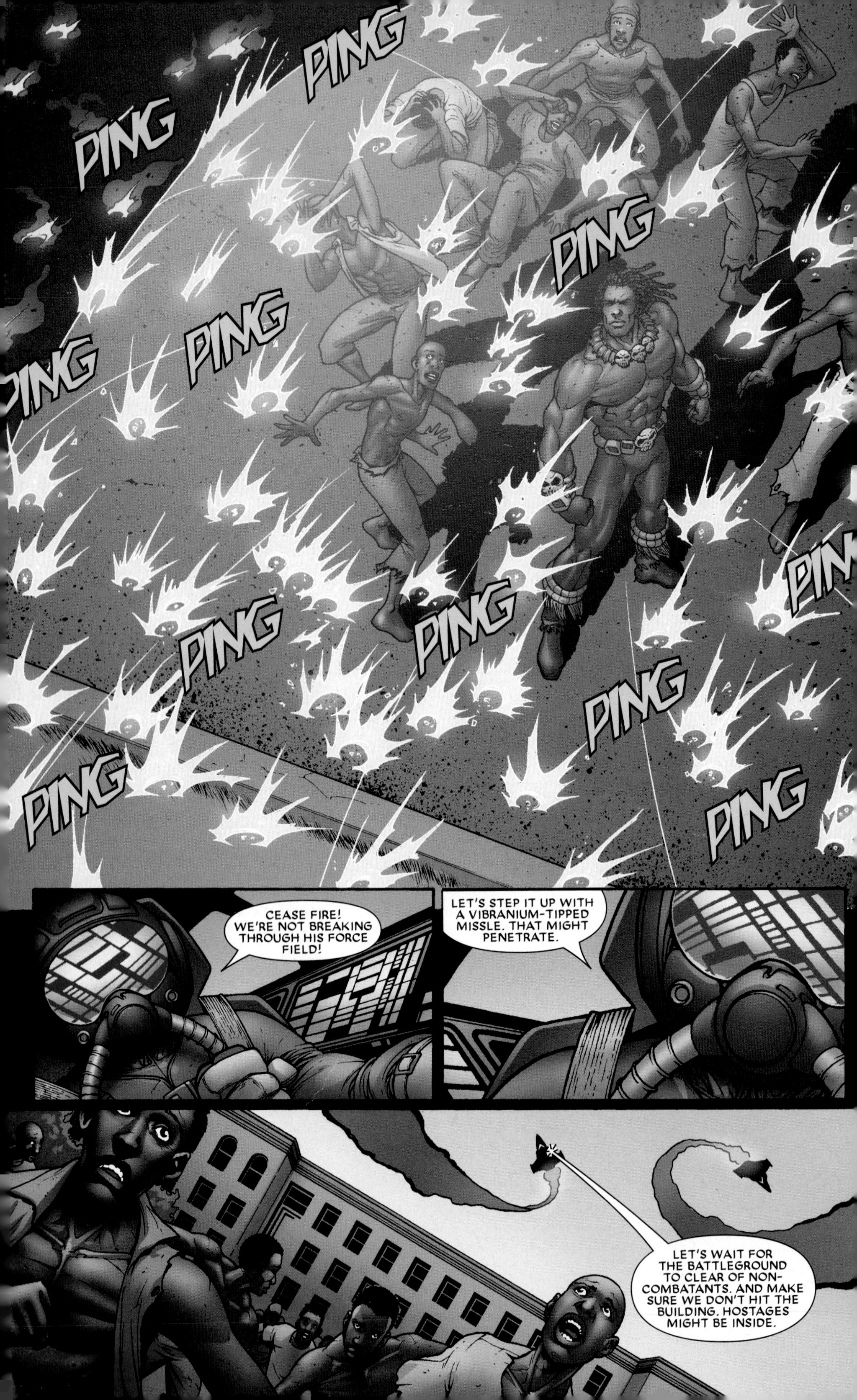
PING
PING
PING
PING
PING
PING
PING
PING
PING
PING
PING
PIN
CEASE FIRE! WE'RE NOT BREAKING THROUGH HIS FORCE FIELD!
LET'S STEP IT UP WITH A VIBRANIUM-TIPPED MISSLE. THAT MIGHT PENETRATE.
LET'S WAIT FOR THE BATTLEGROUND TO CLEAR OF NON-COMBATANTS. AND MAKE SURE WE DON'T HIT THE BUILDING. HOSTAGES MIGHT BE INSIDE.

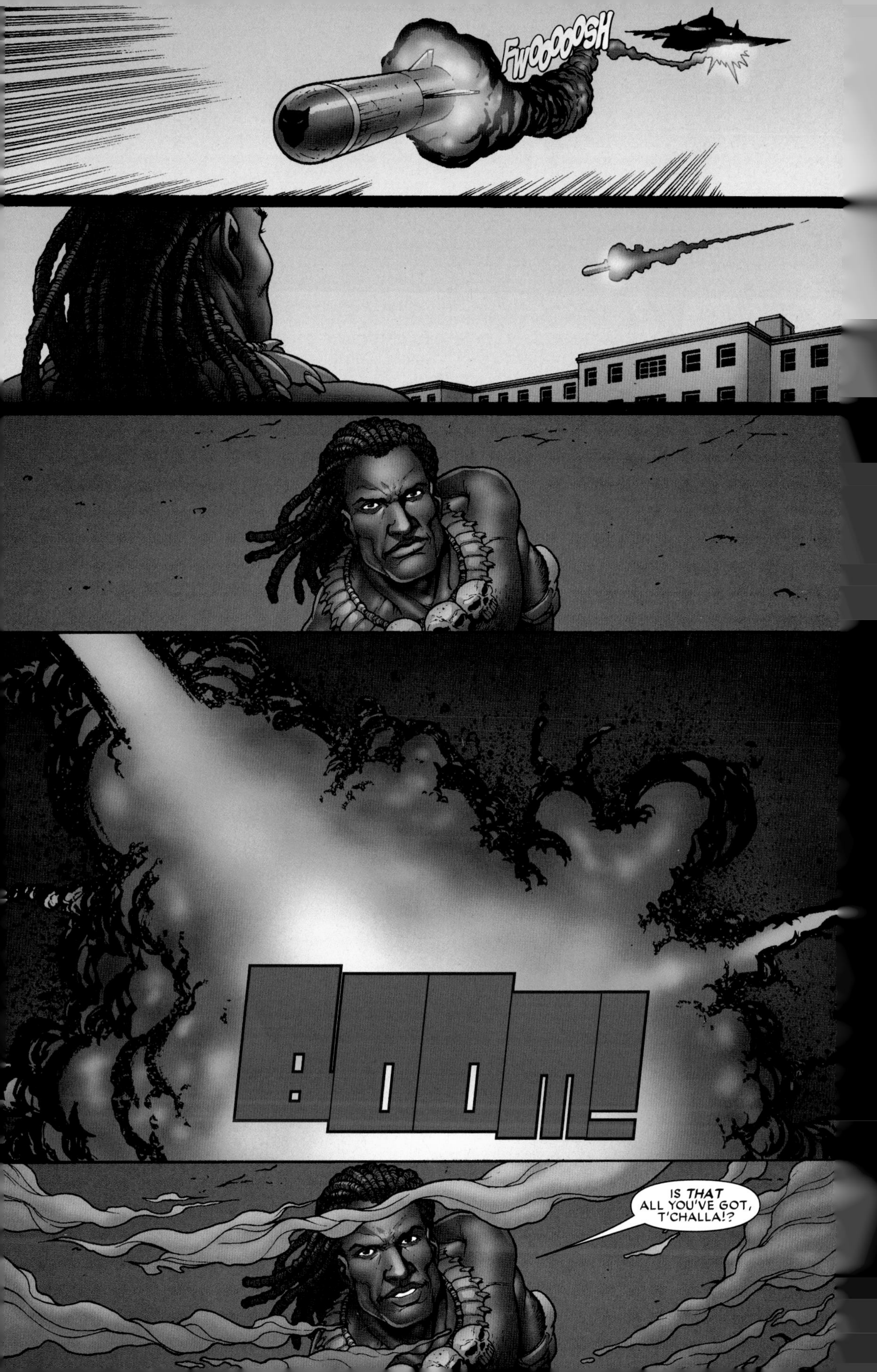
FWOOOOOSH
BOOOM!
IS THAT ALL YOU'VE GOT, T'CHALLA!?

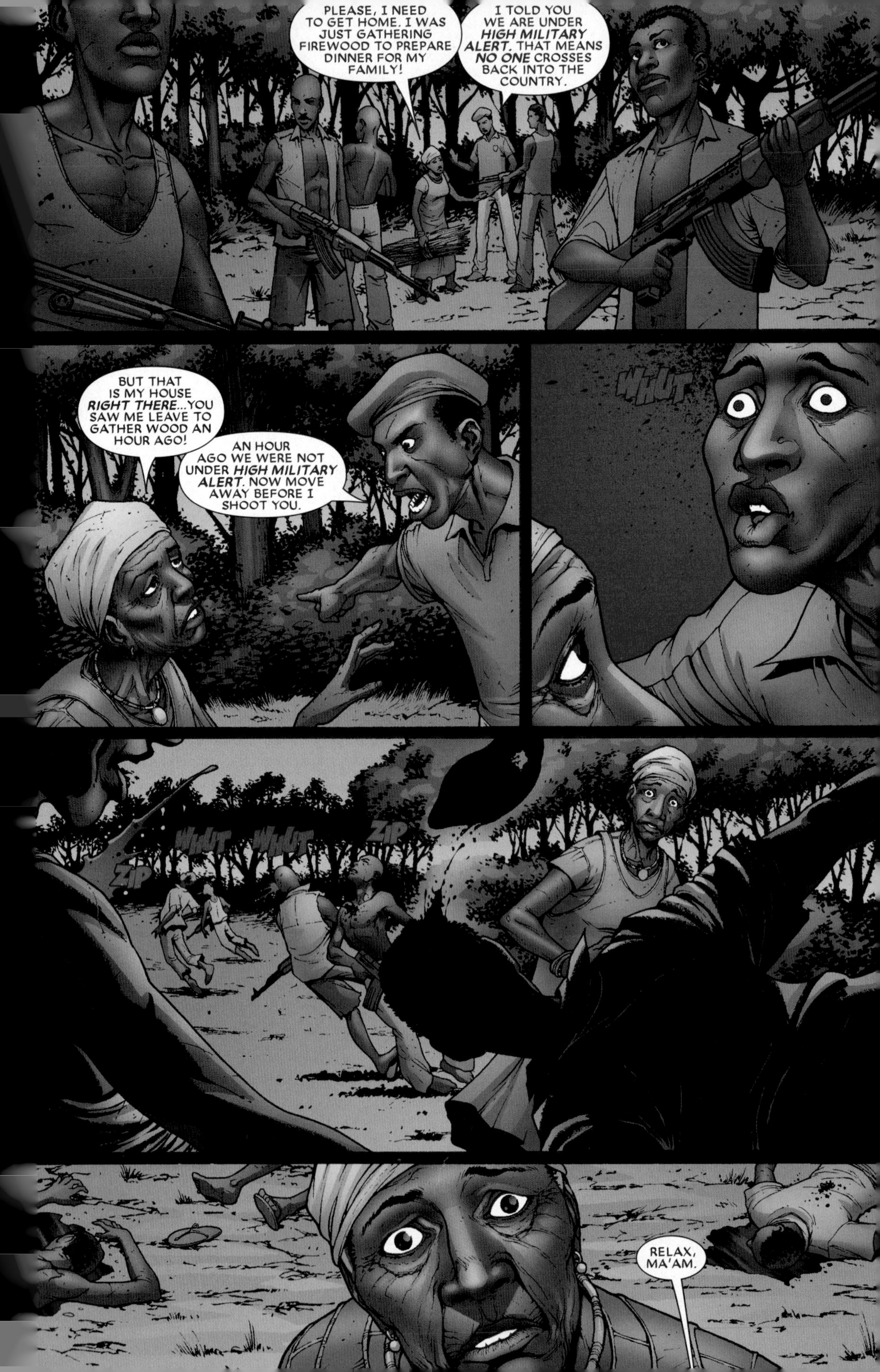

PLEASE, I NEED TO GET HOME. I WAS JUST GATHERING FIREWOOD TO PREPARE DINNER FOR MY FAMILY!
I TOLD YOU WE ARE UNDER *HIGH MILITARY ALERT.* THAT MEANS *NO ONE* CROSSES BACK INTO THE COUNTRY.
BUT THAT IS MY HOUSE *RIGHT THERE*...YOU SAW ME LEAVE TO GATHER WOOD AN HOUR AGO!
AN HOUR AGO WE WERE NOT UNDER *HIGH MILITARY ALERT*. NOW MOVE AWAY BEFORE I SHOOT YOU.
WHUT
ZIP
WHUT
WHUT
ZIP
RELAX, MA'AM.

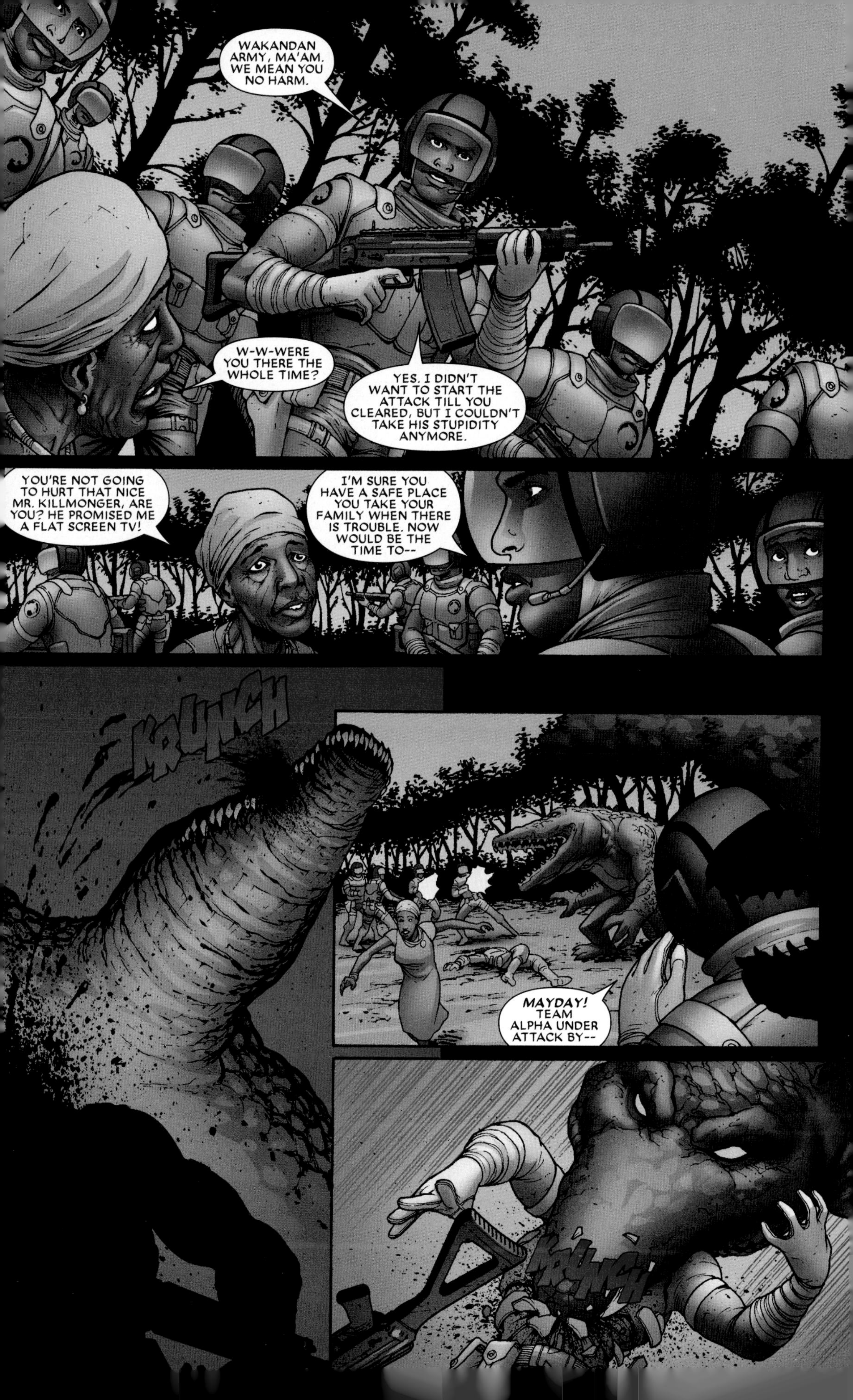
WAKANDAN ARMY, MA'AM. WE MEAN YOU NO HARM.
W-W-WERE YOU THERE THE WHOLE TIME?
YES. I DIDN'T WANT TO START THE ATTACK TILL YOU CLEARED, BUT I COULDN'T TAKE HIS STUPIDITY ANYMORE.
YOU'RE NOT GOING TO HURT THAT NICE MR. KILLMONGER, ARE YOU? HE PROMISED ME A FLAT SCREEN TV!
I'M SURE YOU HAVE A SAFE PLACE YOU TAKE YOUR FAMILY WHEN THERE IS TROUBLE. NOW WOULD BE THE TIME TO--
KRUNCH
MAYDAY! TEAM ALPHA UNDER ATTACK BY--
KRUNCH

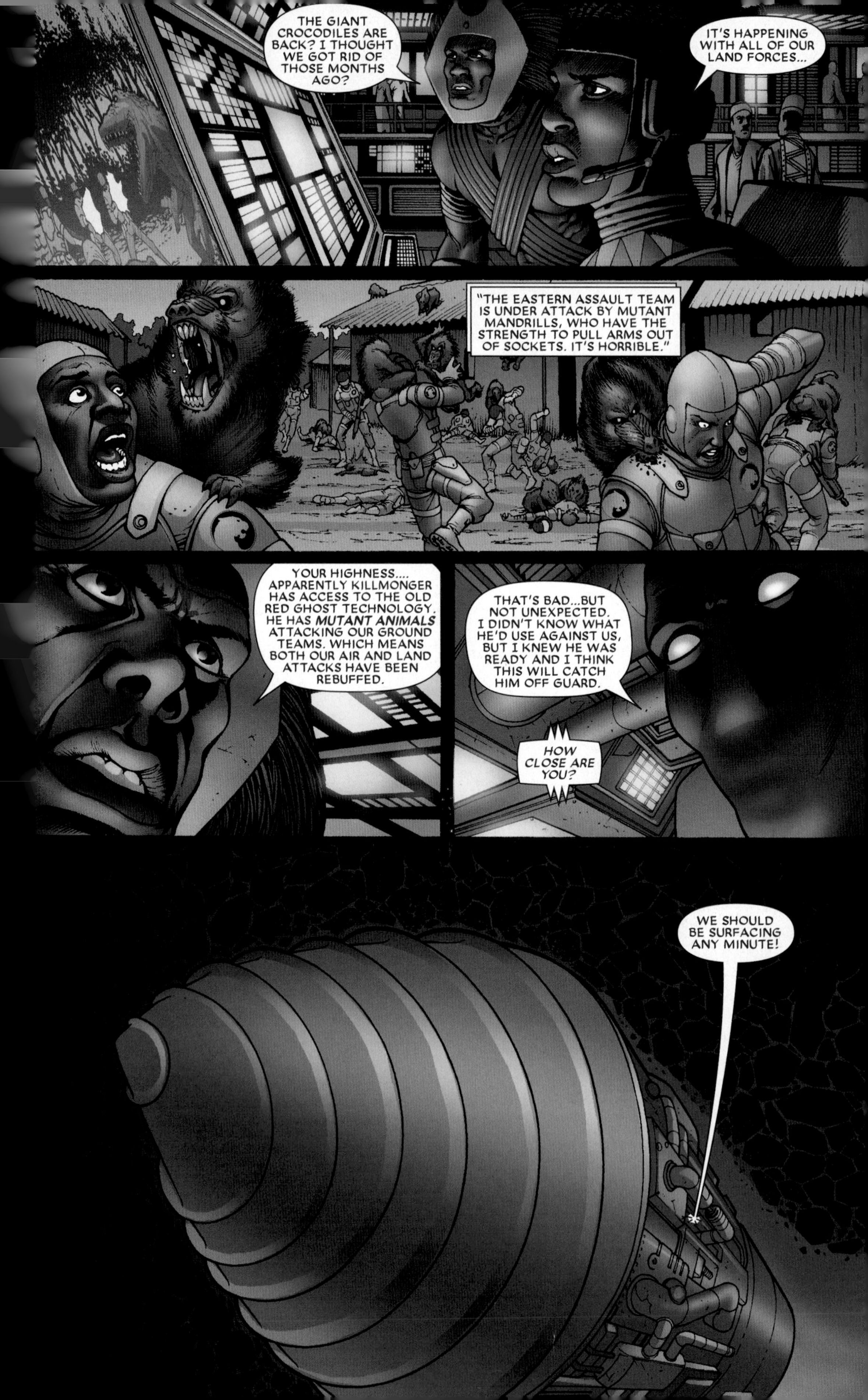
THE GIANT CROCODILES ARE BACK? I THOUGHT WE GOT RID OF THOSE MONTHS AGO?
IT'S HAPPENING WITH ALL OF OUR LAND FORCES...
"THE EASTERN ASSAULT TEAM IS UNDER ATTACK BY MUTANT MANDRILLS, WHO HAVE THE STRENGTH TO PULL ARMS OUT OF SOCKETS. IT'S HORRIBLE."
YOUR HIGHNESS.... APPARENTLY KILLMONGER HAS ACCESS TO THE OLD RED GHOST TECHNOLOGY. HE HAS MUTANT ANIMALS ATTACKING OUR GROUND TEAMS. WHICH MEANS BOTH OUR AIR AND LAND ATTACKS HAVE BEEN REBUFFED.
THAT'S BAD...BUT NOT UNEXPECTED. I DIDN'T KNOW WHAT HE'D USE AGAINST US, BUT I KNEW HE WAS READY AND I THINK THIS WILL CATCH HIM OFF GUARD.
HOW CLOSE ARE YOU?
WE SHOULD BE SURFACING ANY MINUTE!

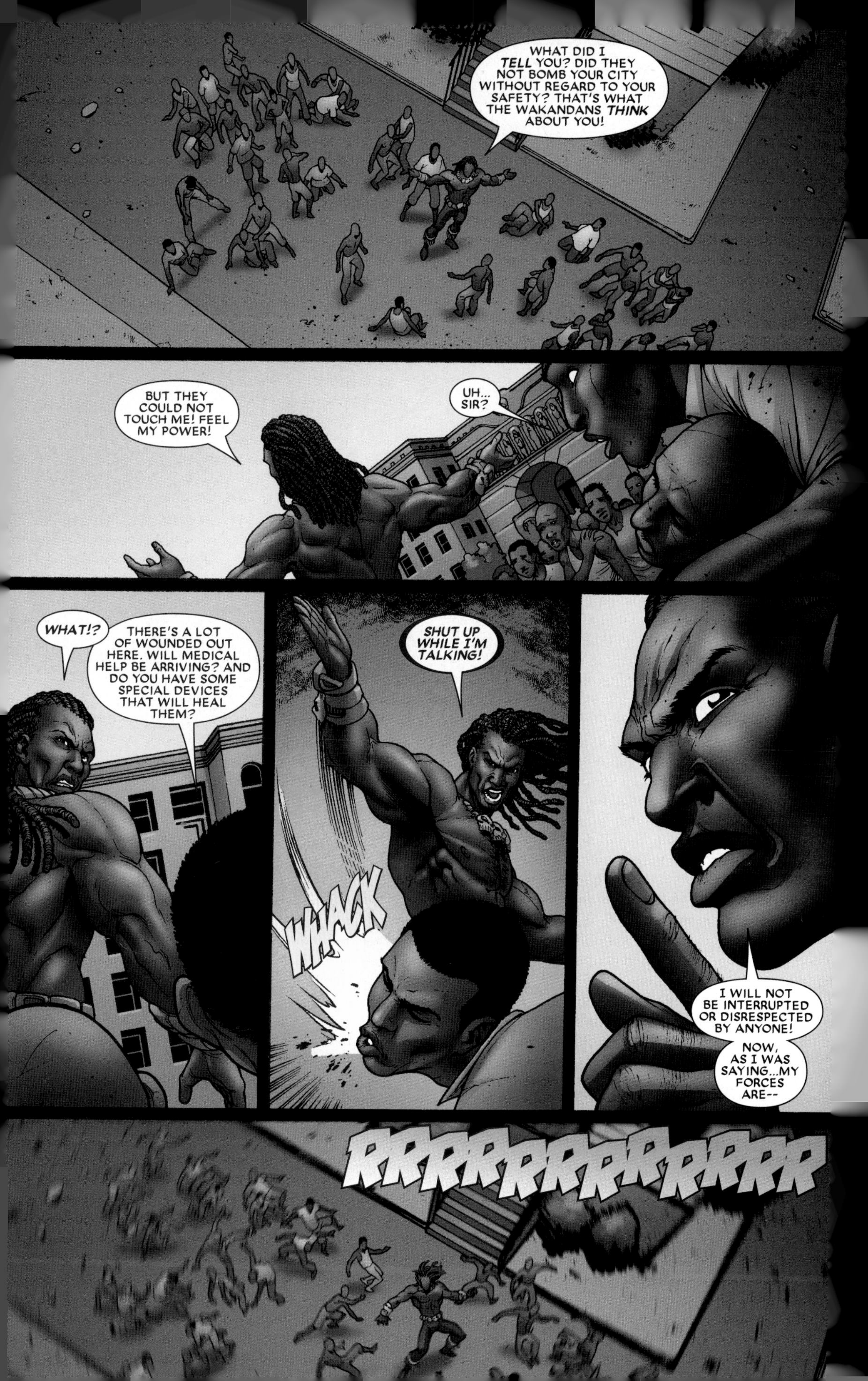
WHAT DID I TELL YOU? DID THEY NOT BOMB YOUR CITY WITHOUT REGARD TO YOUR SAFETY? THAT'S WHAT THE WAKANDANS THINK ABOUT YOU!
BUT THEY COULD NOT TOUCH ME! FEEL MY POWER!
UH... SIR?
WHAT!?
THERE'S A LOT OF WOUNDED OUT HERE. WILL MEDICAL HELP BE ARRIVING? AND DO YOU HAVE SOME SPECIAL DEVICES THAT WILL HEAL THEM?
SHUT UP WHILE I'M TALKING!
WHACK
I WILL NOT BE INTERRUPTED OR DISRESPECTED BY ANYONE!
NOW, AS I WAS SAYING...MY FORCES ARE--
RRRRRRRRRRRRRR

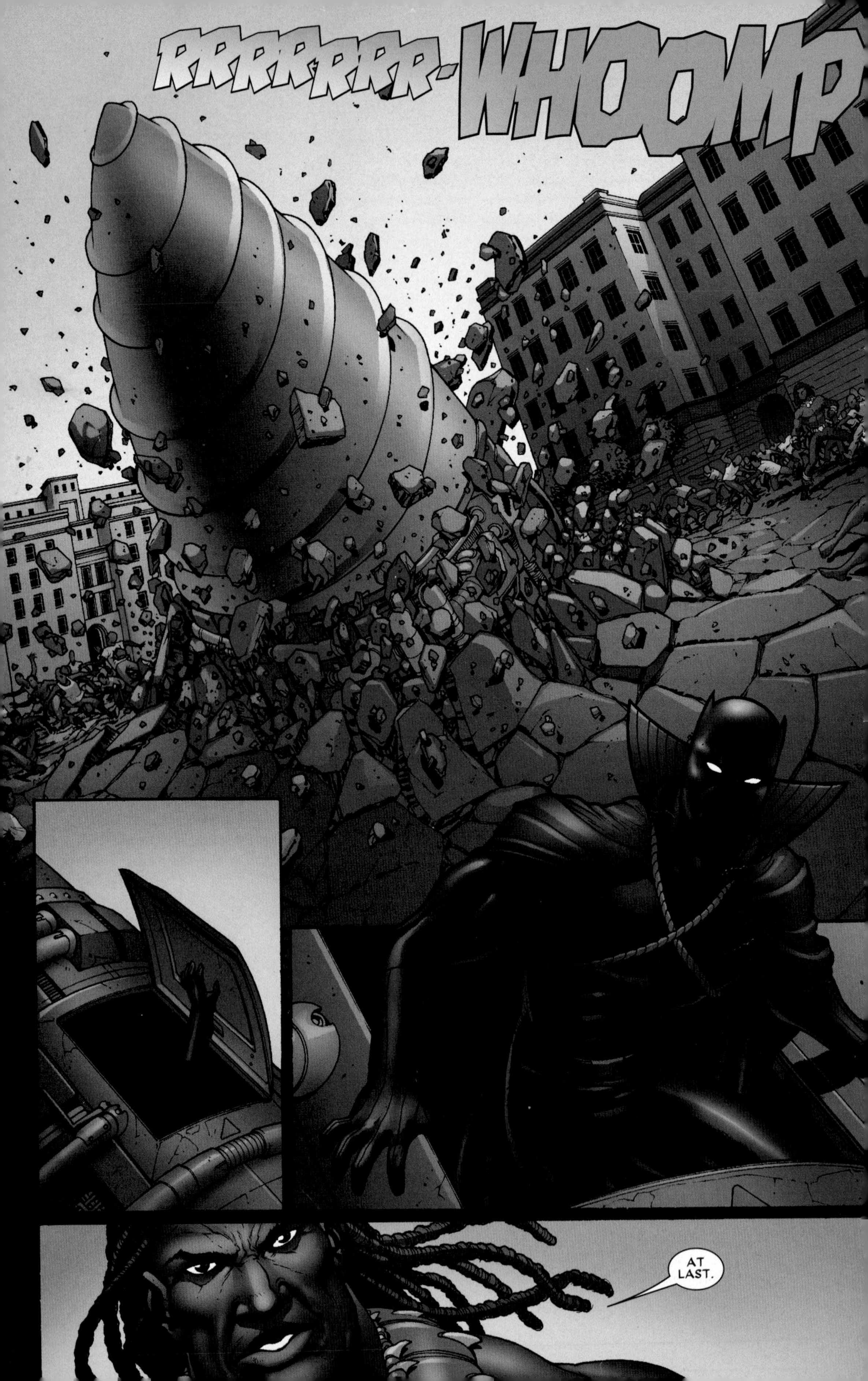
RRRRRRRR-WHOOMP!
AT LAST.

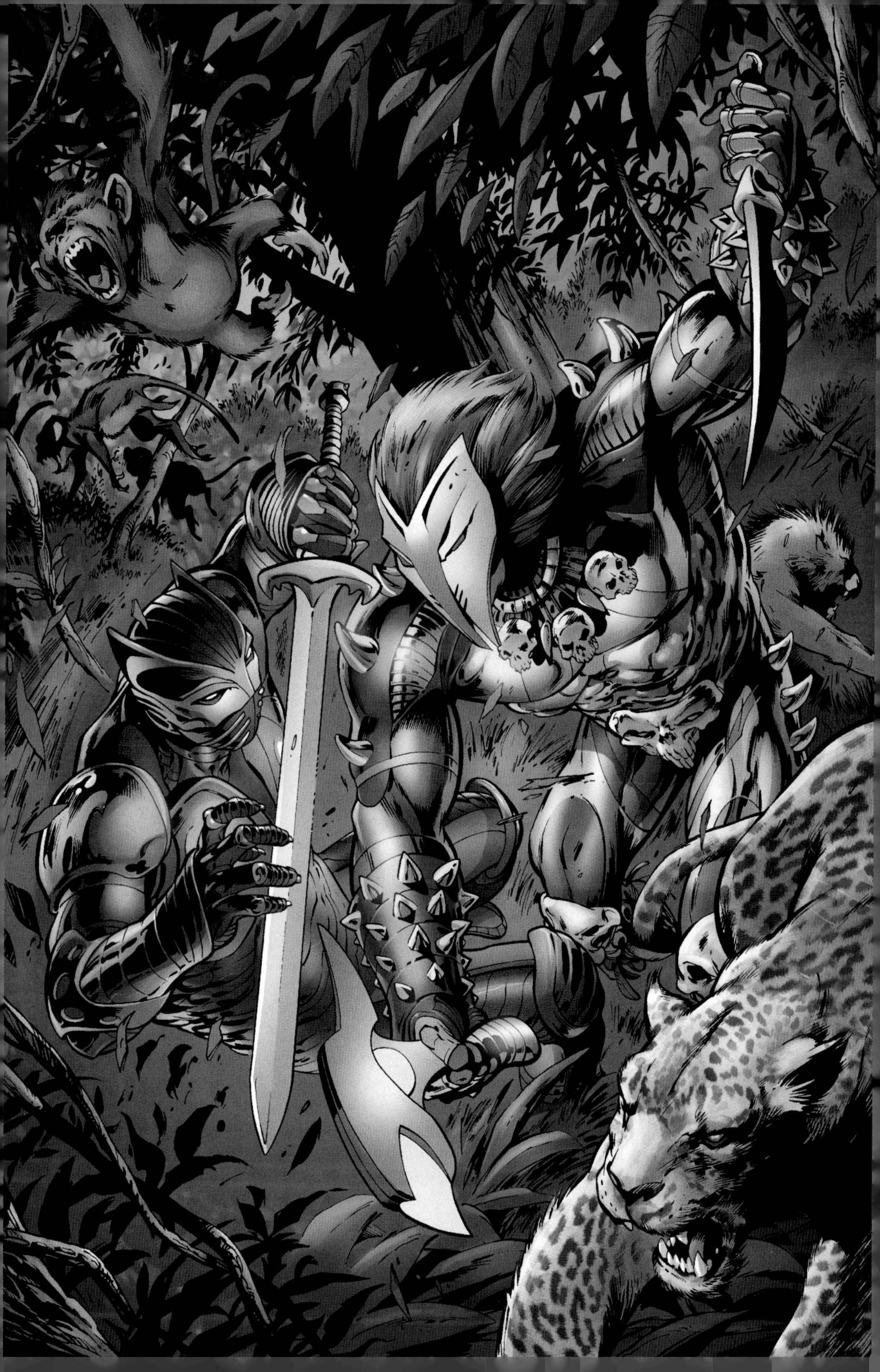

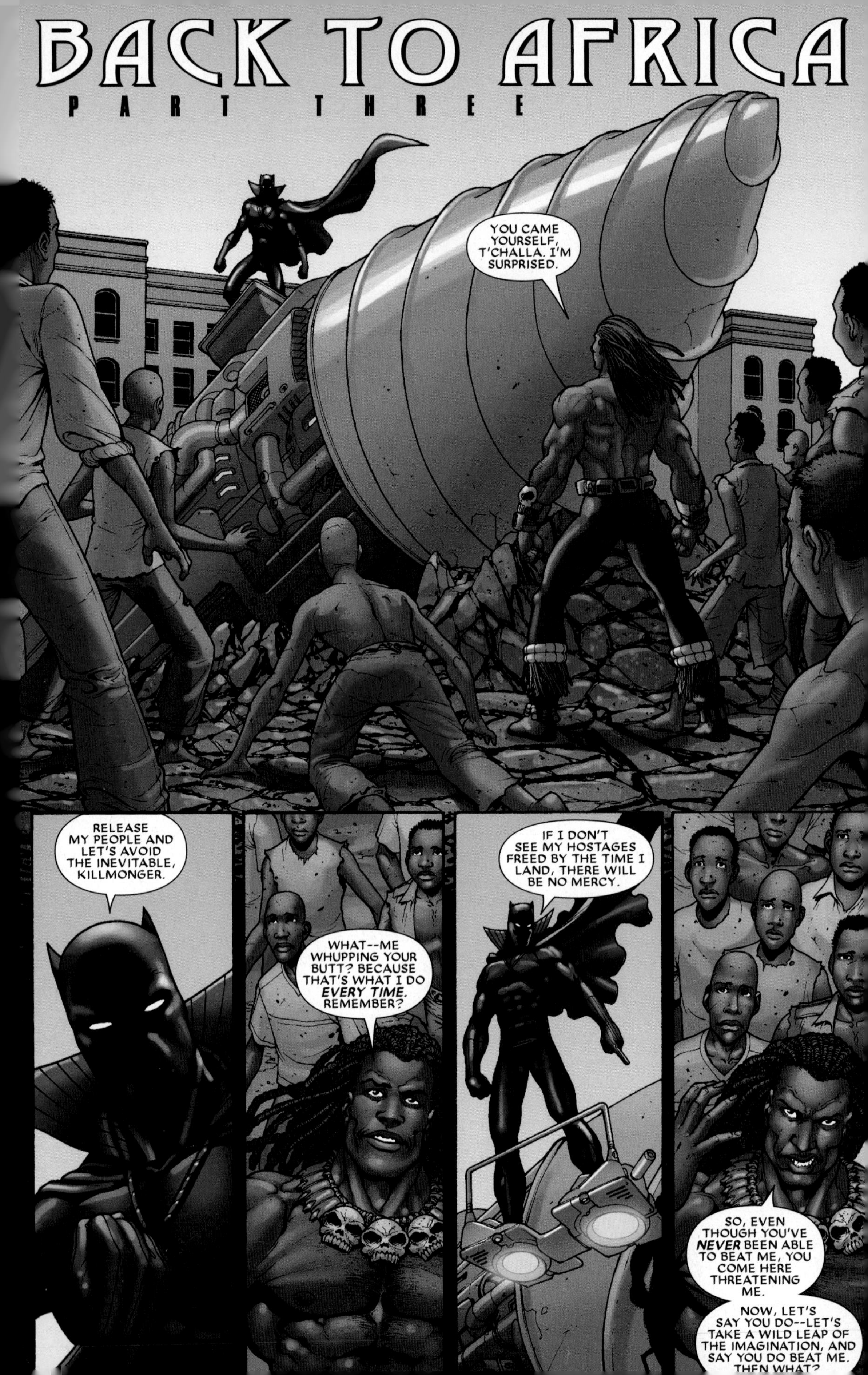
BACK TO AFRICA
PART THREE
YOU CAME YOURSELF, T'CHALLA. I'M SURPRISED.
RELEASE MY PEOPLE AND LET'S AVOID THE INEVITABLE, KILLMONGER.
WHAT--ME WHUPPING YOUR BUTT? BECAUSE THAT'S WHAT I DO *EVERY TIME.* REMEMBER?
IF I DON'T SEE MY HOSTAGES FREED BY THE TIME I LAND, THERE WILL BE NO MERCY.
SO, EVEN THOUGH YOU'VE ***NEVER*** BEEN ABLE TO BEAT ME, YOU COME HERE THREATENING ME.
NOW, LET'S SAY YOU DO--LET'S TAKE A WILD LEAP OF THE IMAGINATION, AND SAY YOU DO BEAT ME. THEN WHAT?

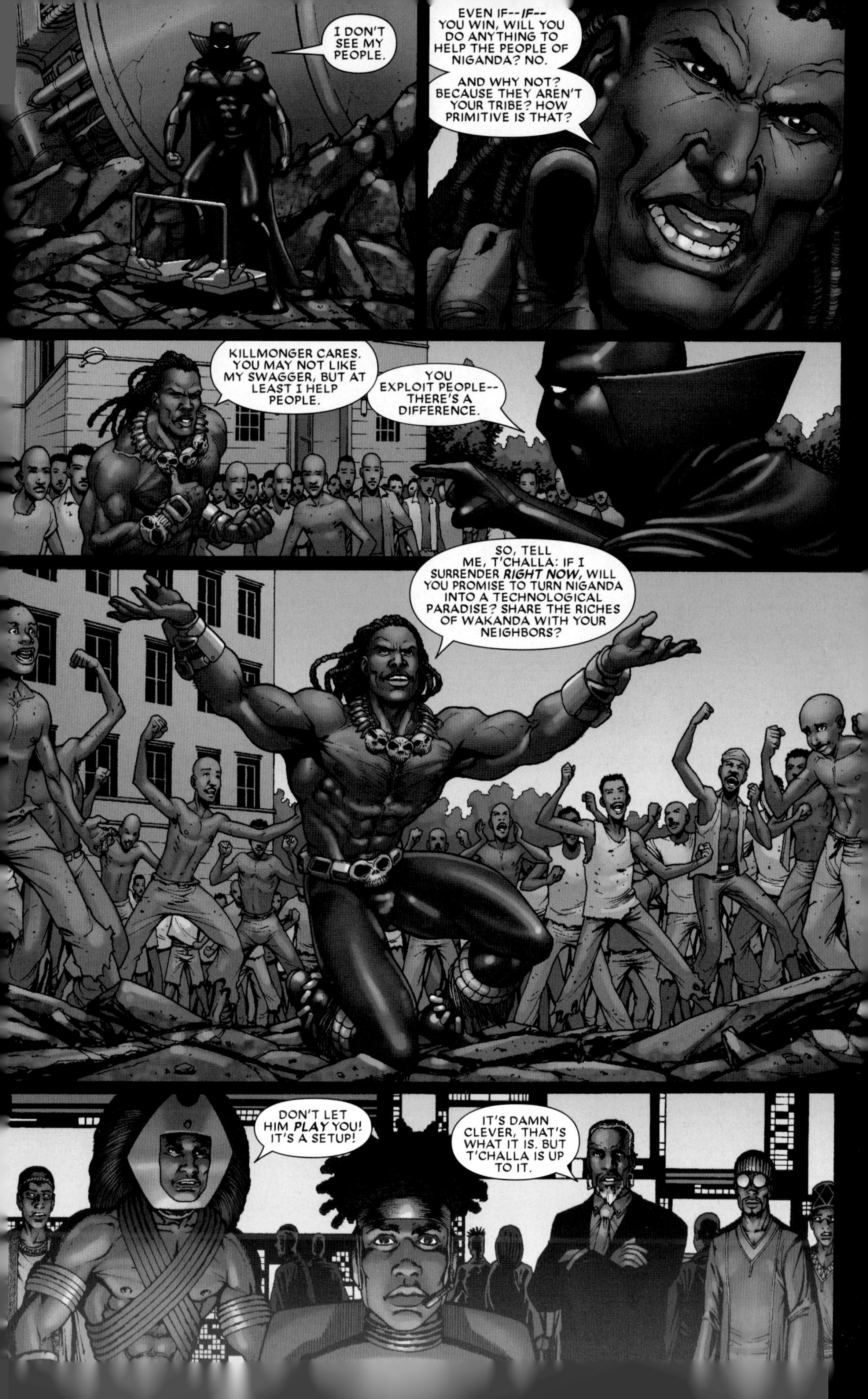
I DON'T SEE MY PEOPLE.
EVEN IF--IF--YOU WIN, WILL YOU DO ANYTHING TO HELP THE PEOPLE OF NIGANDA? NO.
AND WHY NOT? BECAUSE THEY AREN'T YOUR TRIBE? HOW PRIMITIVE IS THAT?
KILLMONGER CARES. YOU MAY NOT LIKE MY SWAGGER, BUT AT LEAST I HELP PEOPLE.
YOU EXPLOIT PEOPLE--THERE'S A DIFFERENCE.
SO, TELL ME, T'CHALLA: IF I SURRENDER RIGHT NOW, WILL YOU PROMISE TO TURN NIGANDA INTO A TECHNOLOGICAL PARADISE? SHARE THE RICHES OF WAKANDA WITH YOUR NEIGHBORS?
DON'T LET HIM PLAY YOU! IT'S A SETUP!
IT'S DAMN CLEVER, THAT'S WHAT IT IS. BUT T'CHALLA IS UP TO IT.

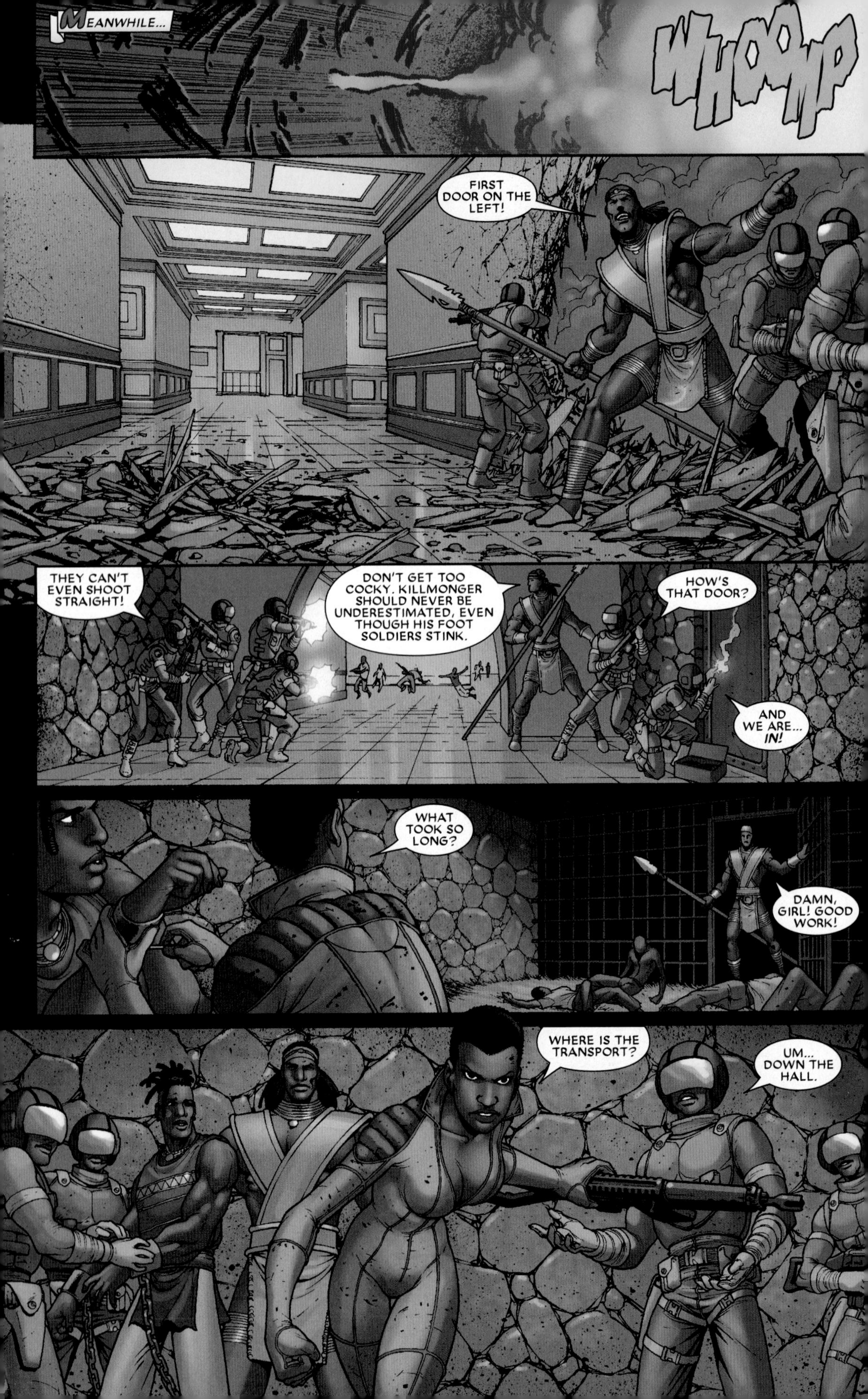
MEANWHILE...
WHOOMP
FIRST DOOR ON THE LEFT!
THEY CAN'T EVEN SHOOT STRAIGHT!
DON'T GET TOO COCKY. KILLMONGER SHOULD NEVER BE UNDERESTIMATED, EVEN THOUGH HIS FOOT SOLDIERS STINK.
HOW'S THAT DOOR?
AND WE ARE... IN!
WHAT TOOK SO LONG?
DAMN, GIRL! GOOD WORK!
WHERE IS THE TRANSPORT?
UM... DOWN THE HALL.

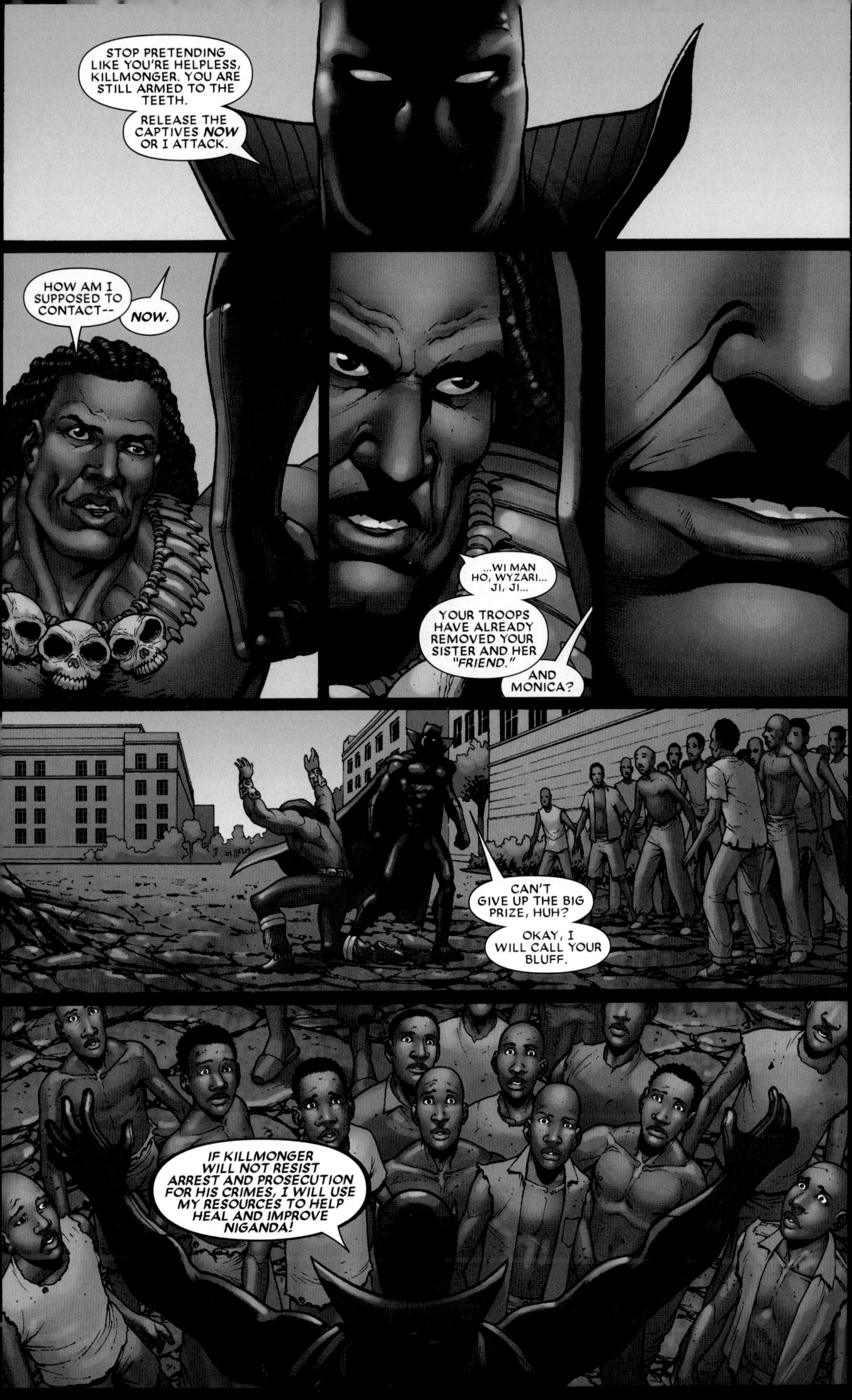
STOP PRETENDING LIKE YOU'RE HELPLESS, KILLMONGER. YOU ARE STILL ARMED TO THE TEETH.
RELEASE THE CAPTIVES NOW OR I ATTACK.
HOW AM I SUPPOSED TO CONTACT--
NOW.
...WI MAN HO, WYZARI... JI, JI...
YOUR TROOPS HAVE ALREADY REMOVED YOUR SISTER AND HER "FRIEND."
AND MONICA?
CAN'T GIVE UP THE BIG PRIZE, HUH?
OKAY, I WILL CALL YOUR BLUFF.
IF KILLMONGER WILL NOT RESIST ARREST AND PROSECUTION FOR HIS CRIMES, I WILL USE MY RESOURCES TO HELP HEAL AND IMPROVE NIGANDA!

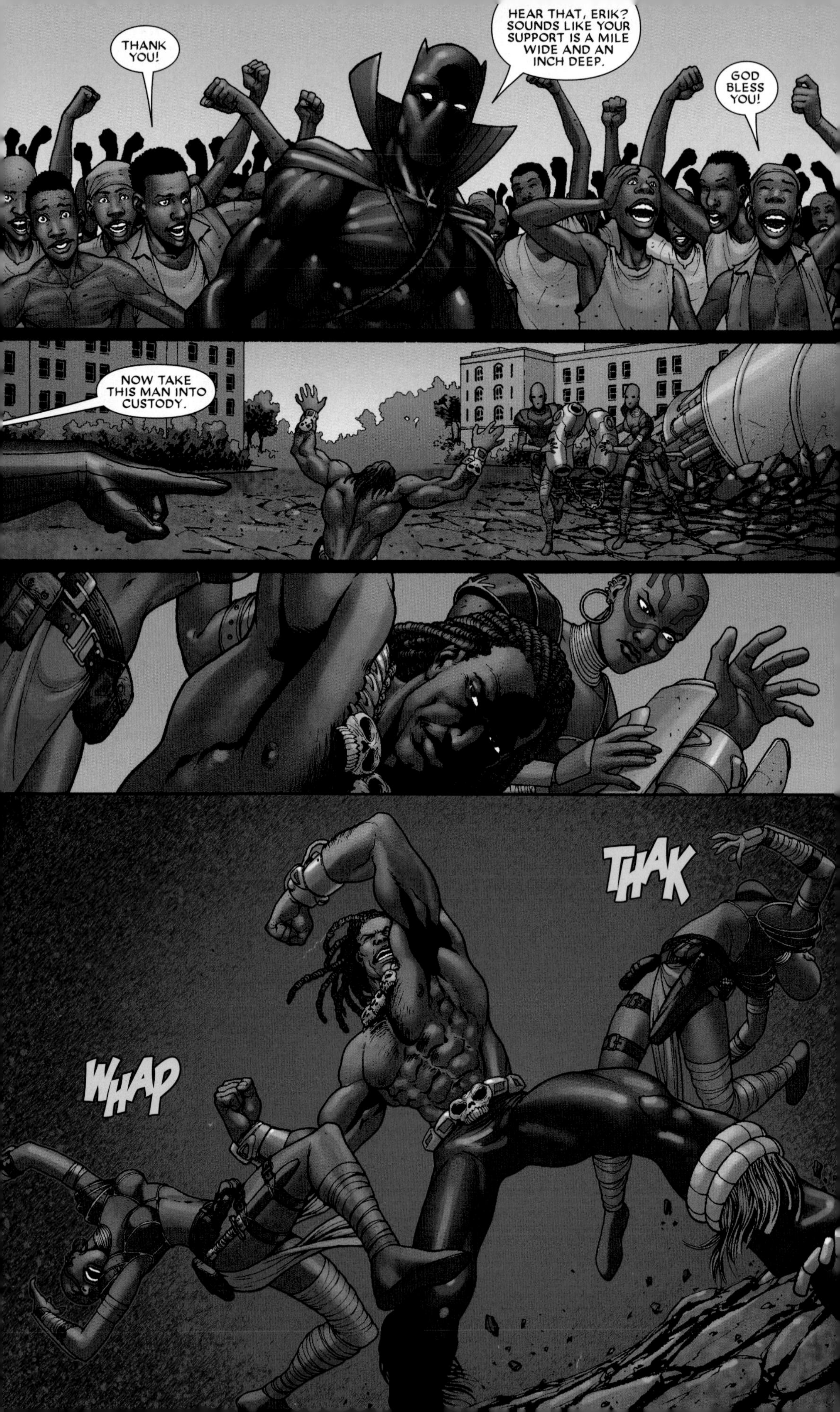
THANK YOU!
HEAR THAT, ERIK? SOUNDS LIKE YOUR SUPPORT IS A MILE WIDE AND AN INCH DEEP.
GOD BLESS YOU!
NOW TAKE THIS MAN INTO CUSTODY.
THAK
WHAP

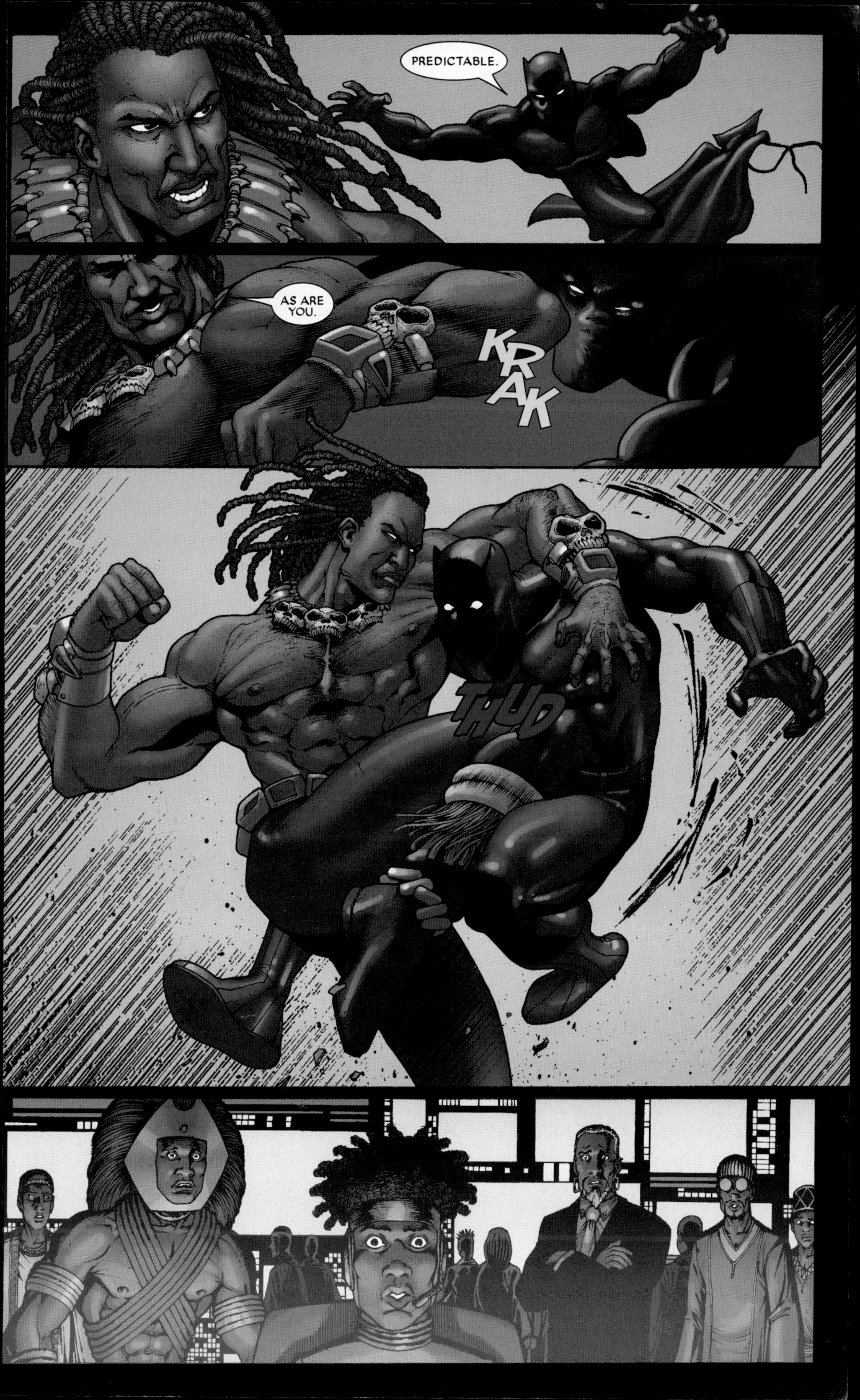
PREDICTABLE.
AS ARE YOU.
KRAK
THUD

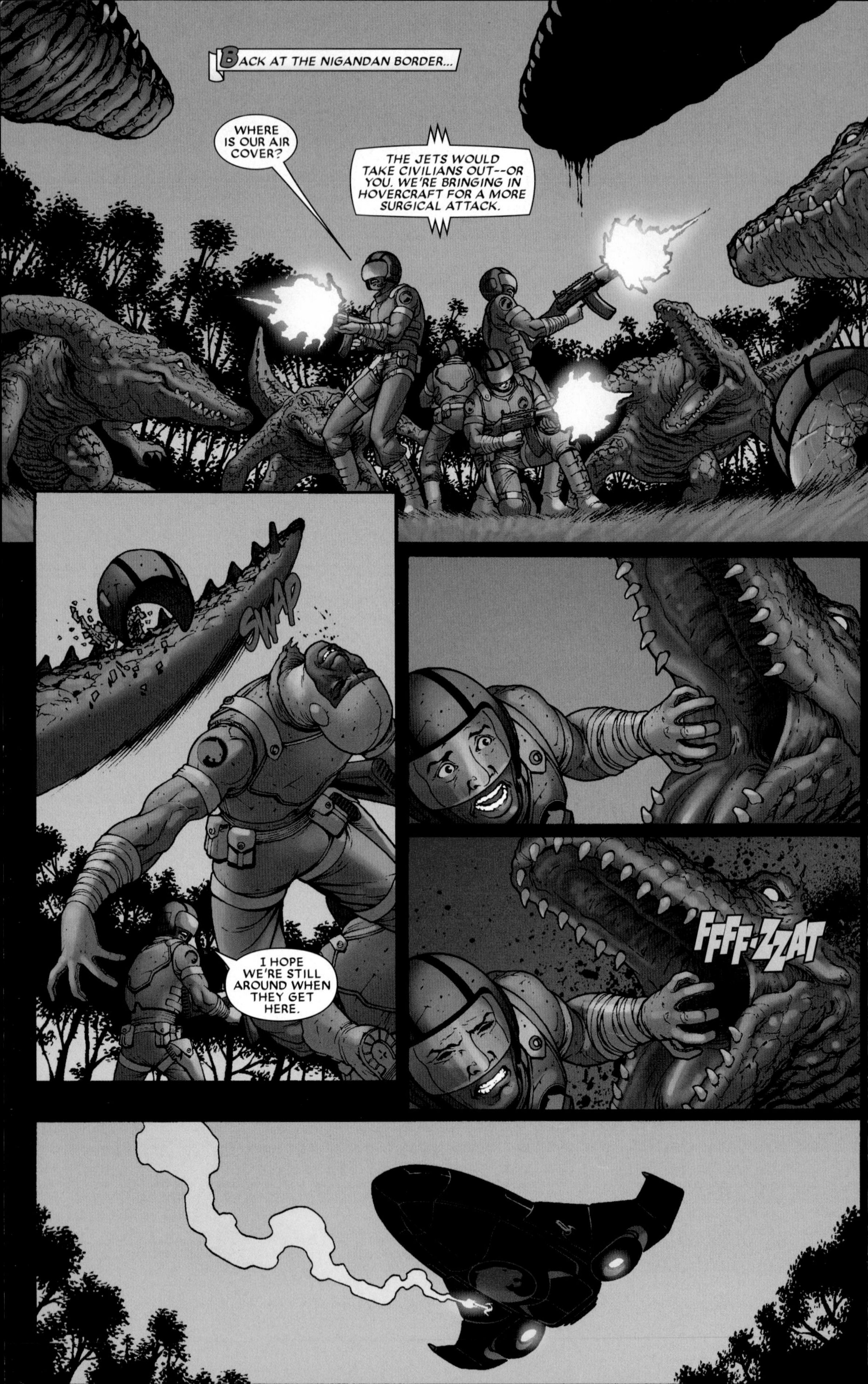
BACK AT THE NIGANDAN BORDER...
WHERE IS OUR AIR COVER?
THE JETS WOULD TAKE CIVILIANS OUT--OR YOU. WE'RE BRINGING IN HOVERCRAFT FOR A MORE SURGICAL ATTACK.
SWAP
I HOPE WE'RE STILL AROUND WHEN THEY GET HERE.
FFFF-ZZAT

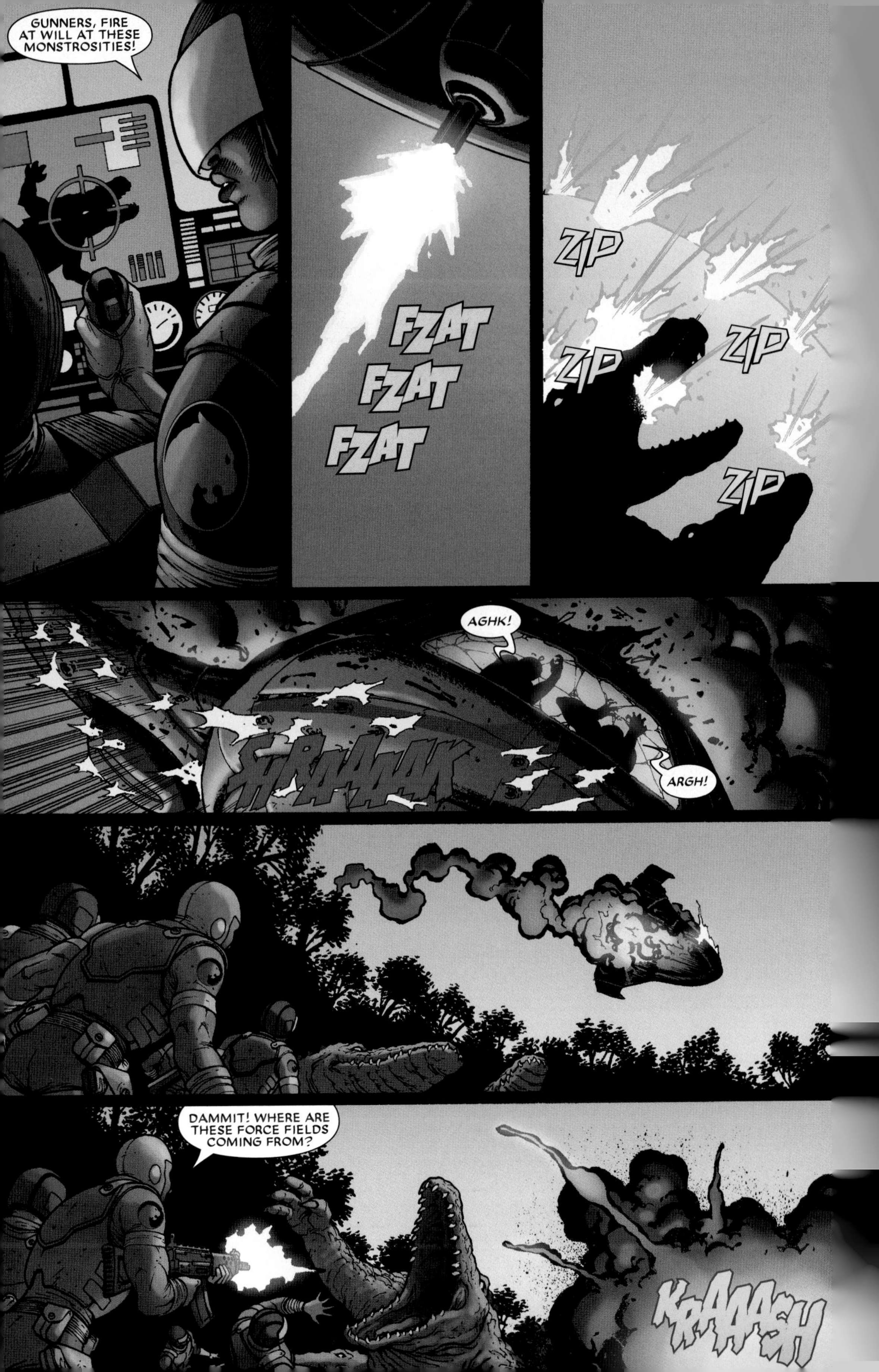
GUNNERS, FIRE AT WILL AT THESE MONSTROSITIES!
FZAT
FZAT
FZAT
ZIP
ZIP
ZIP
ZIP
AGHK!
SHRAAAAK
ARGH!
DAMMIT! WHERE ARE THESE FORCE FIELDS COMING FROM?
KRAAACH

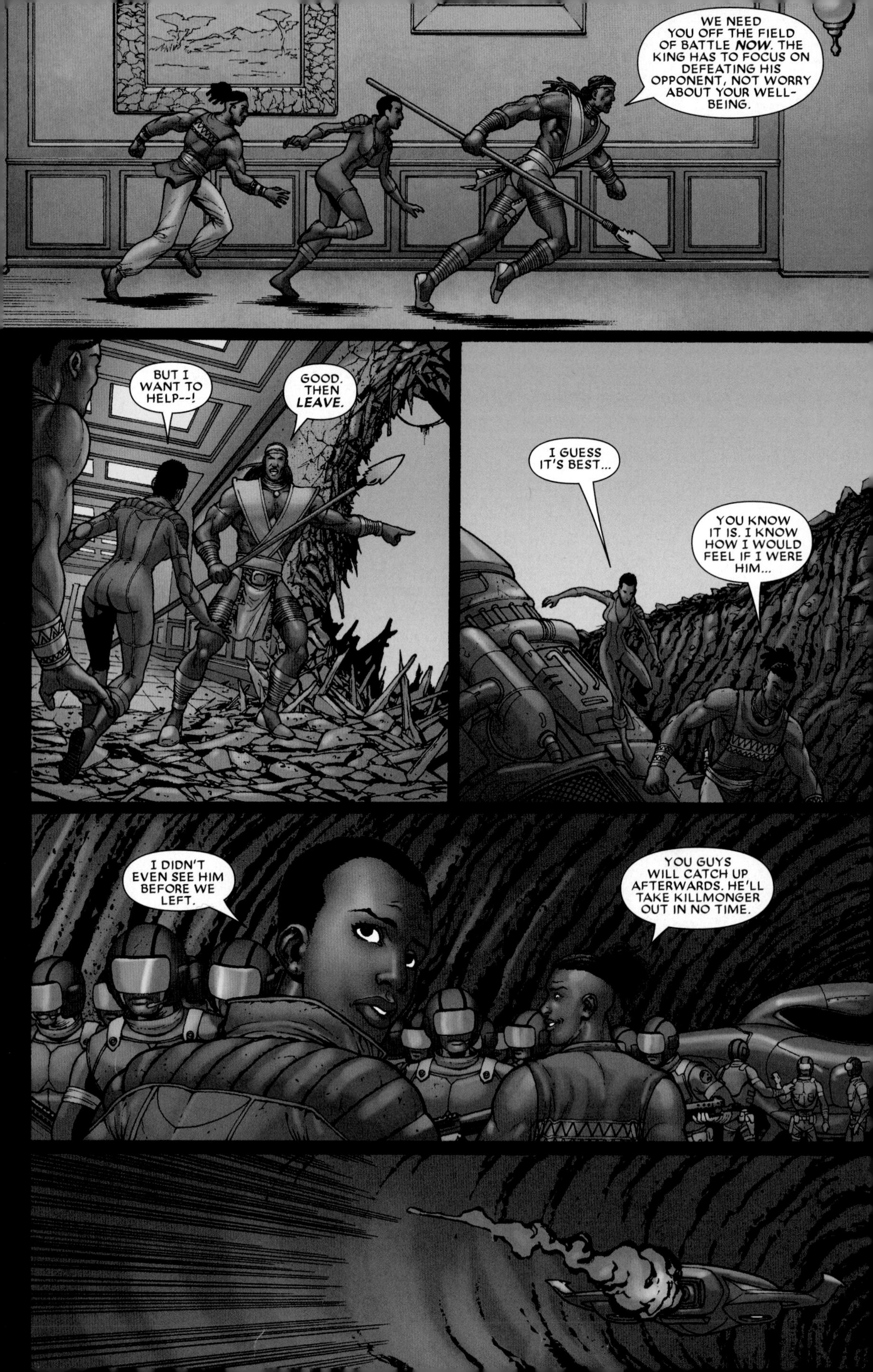
WE NEED YOU OFF THE FIELD OF BATTLE NOW. THE KING HAS TO FOCUS ON DEFEATING HIS OPPONENT, NOT WORRY ABOUT YOUR WELL-BEING.
BUT I WANT TO HELP--!
GOOD. THEN LEAVE.
I GUESS IT'S BEST...
YOU KNOW IT IS. I KNOW HOW I WOULD FEEL IF I WERE HIM...
I DIDN'T EVEN SEE HIM BEFORE WE LEFT.
YOU GUYS WILL CATCH UP AFTERWARDS. HE'LL TAKE KILLMONGER OUT IN NO TIME.

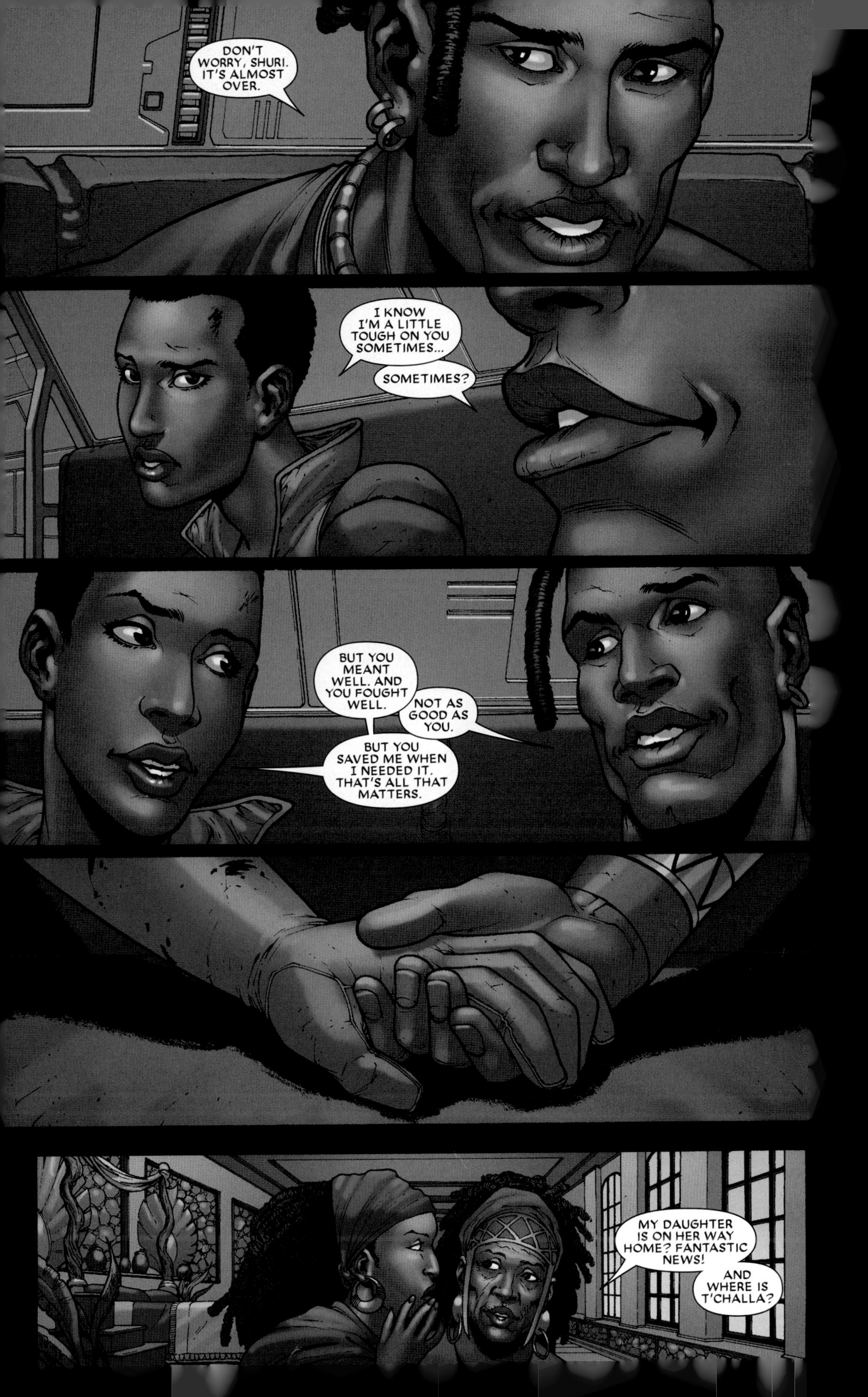
DON'T WORRY, SHURI. IT'S ALMOST OVER.
I KNOW I'M A LITTLE TOUGH ON YOU SOMETIMES...
SOMETIMES?
BUT YOU MEANT WELL. AND YOU FOUGHT WELL.
NOT AS GOOD AS YOU.
BUT YOU SAVED ME WHEN I NEEDED IT. THAT'S ALL THAT MATTERS.
MY DAUGHTER IS ON HER WAY HOME? FANTASTIC NEWS!
AND WHERE IS T'CHALLA?

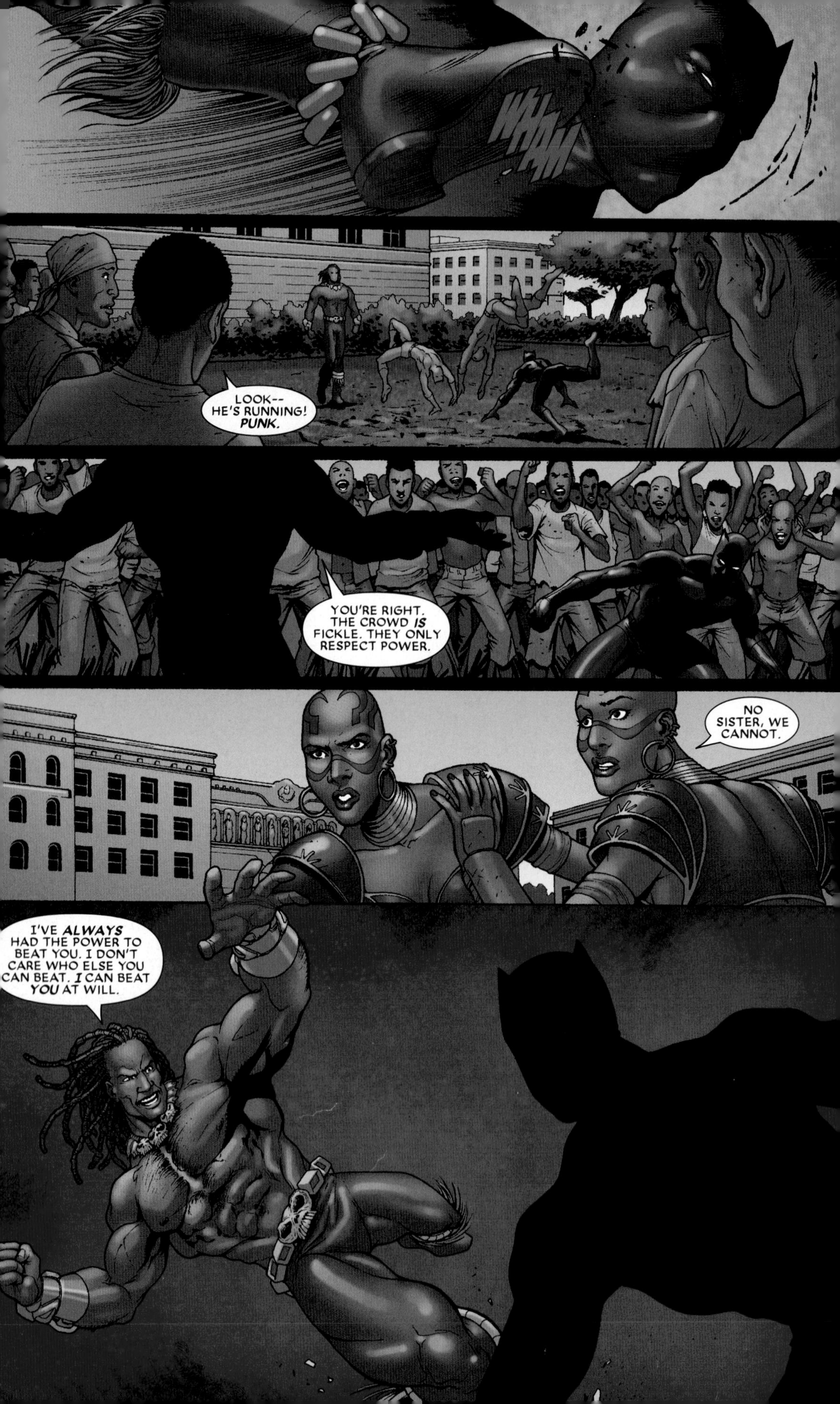
WHAM
LOOK-- HE'S RUNNING! PUNK.
YOU'RE RIGHT. THE CROWD IS FICKLE. THEY ONLY RESPECT POWER.
NO SISTER, WE CANNOT.
I'VE ALWAYS HAD THE POWER TO BEAT YOU. I DON'T CARE WHO ELSE YOU CAN BEAT. I CAN BEAT YOU AT WILL.

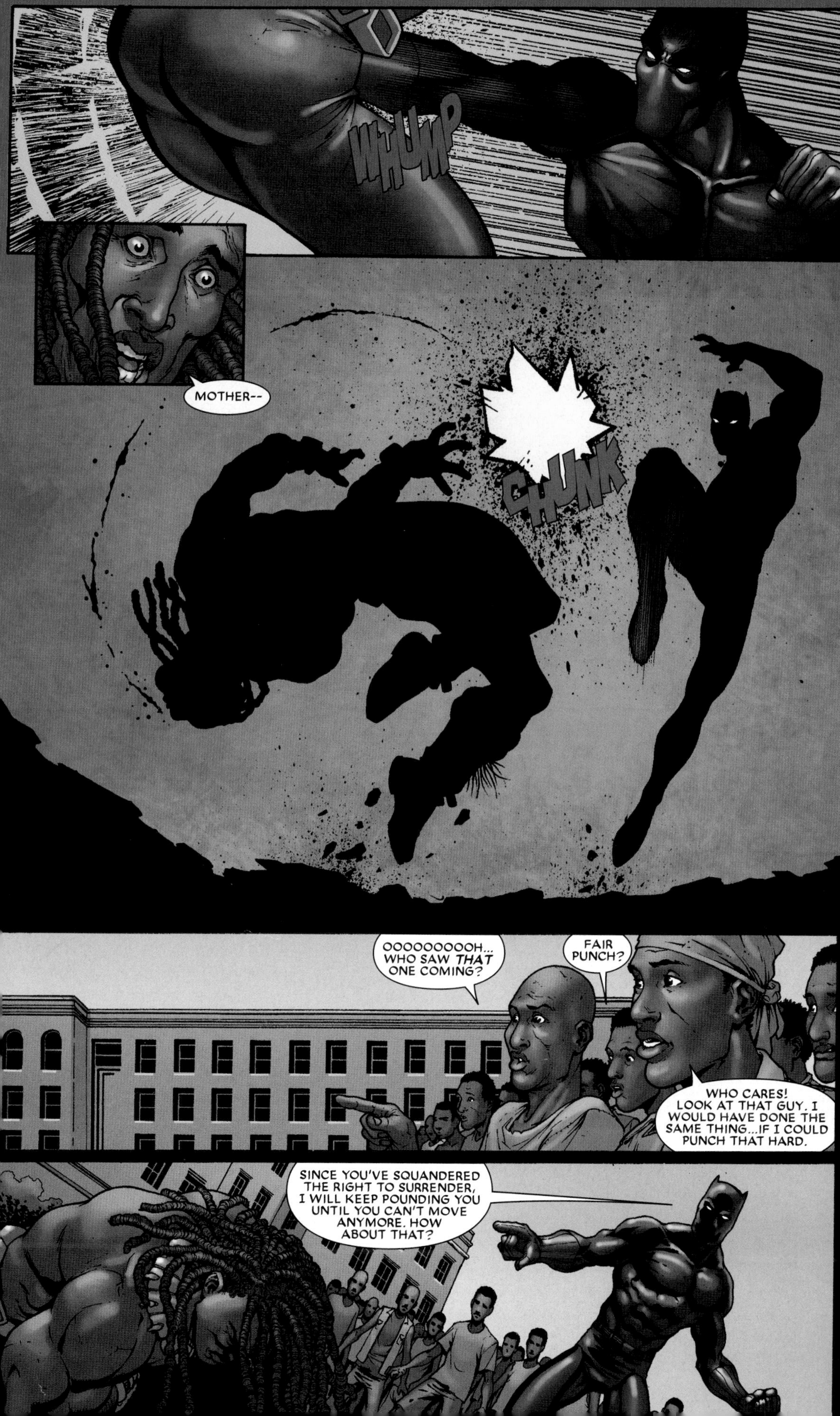
WHUMP
MOTHER--
CHUNK
OOOOOOOOOH... WHO SAW *THAT* ONE COMING?
FAIR PUNCH?
WHO CARES! LOOK AT THAT GUY. I WOULD HAVE DONE THE SAME THING...IF I COULD PUNCH THAT HARD.
SINCE YOU'VE SQUANDERED THE RIGHT TO SURRENDER, I WILL KEEP POUNDING YOU UNTIL YOU CAN'T MOVE ANYMORE. HOW ABOUT THAT?

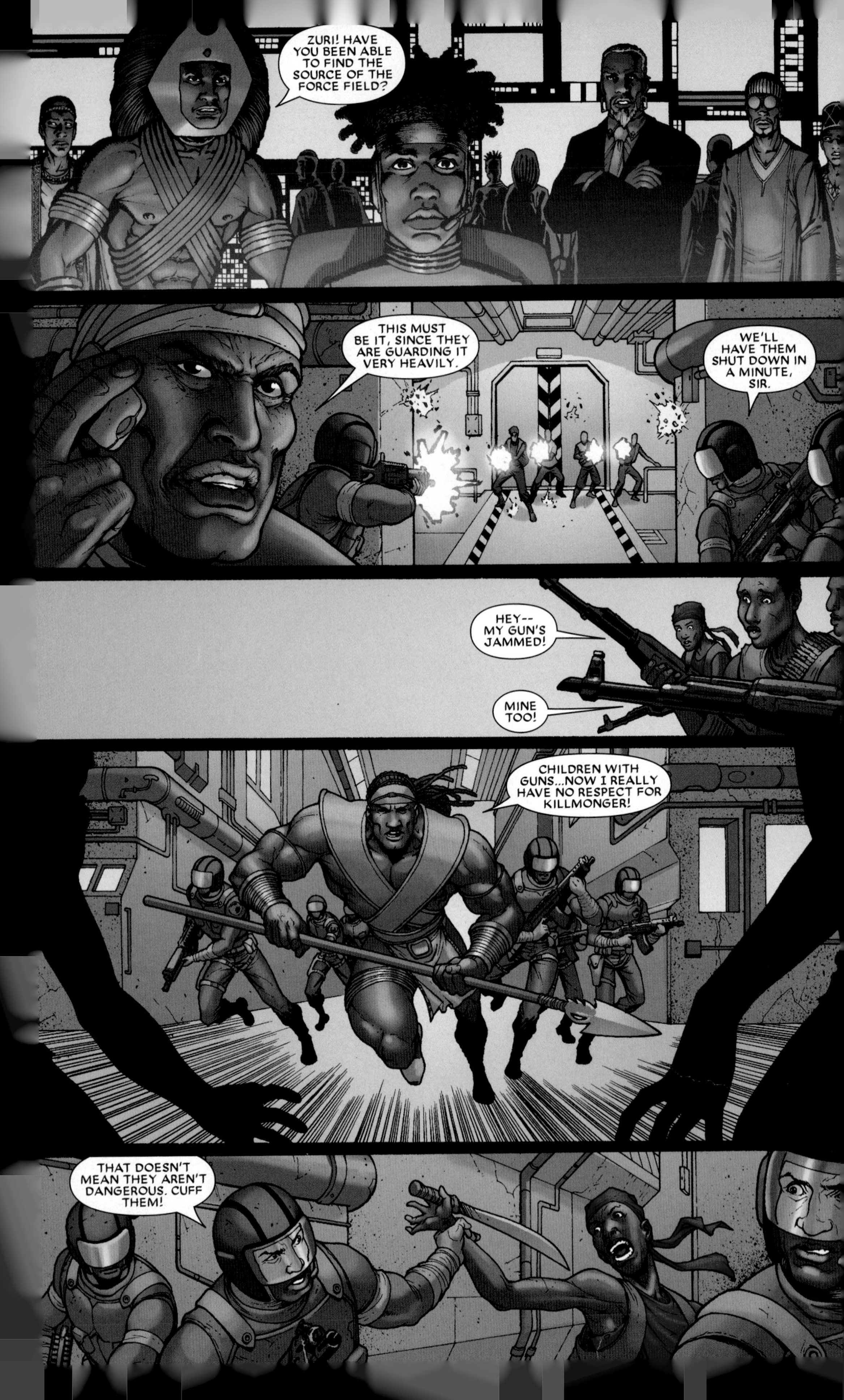
ZURI! HAVE YOU BEEN ABLE TO FIND THE SOURCE OF THE FORCE FIELD?
THIS MUST BE IT, SINCE THEY ARE GUARDING IT VERY HEAVILY.
WE'LL HAVE THEM SHUT DOWN IN A MINUTE, SIR.
HEY-- MY GUN'S JAMMED!
MINE TOO!
CHILDREN WITH GUNS...NOW I REALLY HAVE NO RESPECT FOR KILLMONGER!
THAT DOESN'T MEAN THEY AREN'T DANGEROUS. CUFF THEM!

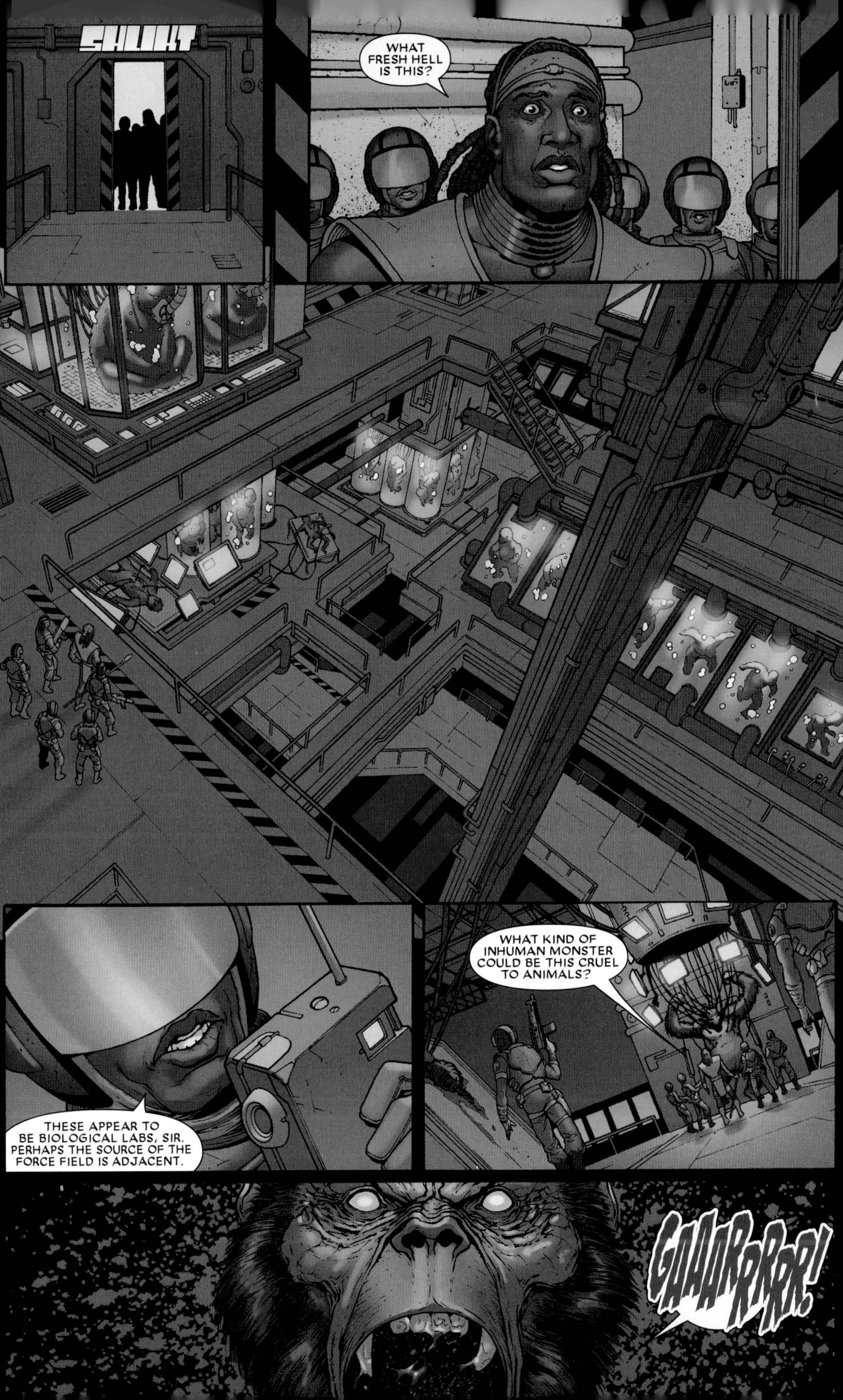
SHLIKT
WHAT FRESH HELL IS THIS?
THESE APPEAR TO BE BIOLOGICAL LABS, SIR. PERHAPS THE SOURCE OF THE FORCE FIELD IS ADJACENT.
WHAT KIND OF INHUMAN MONSTER COULD BE THIS CRUEL TO ANIMALS?
GOAARRRR!

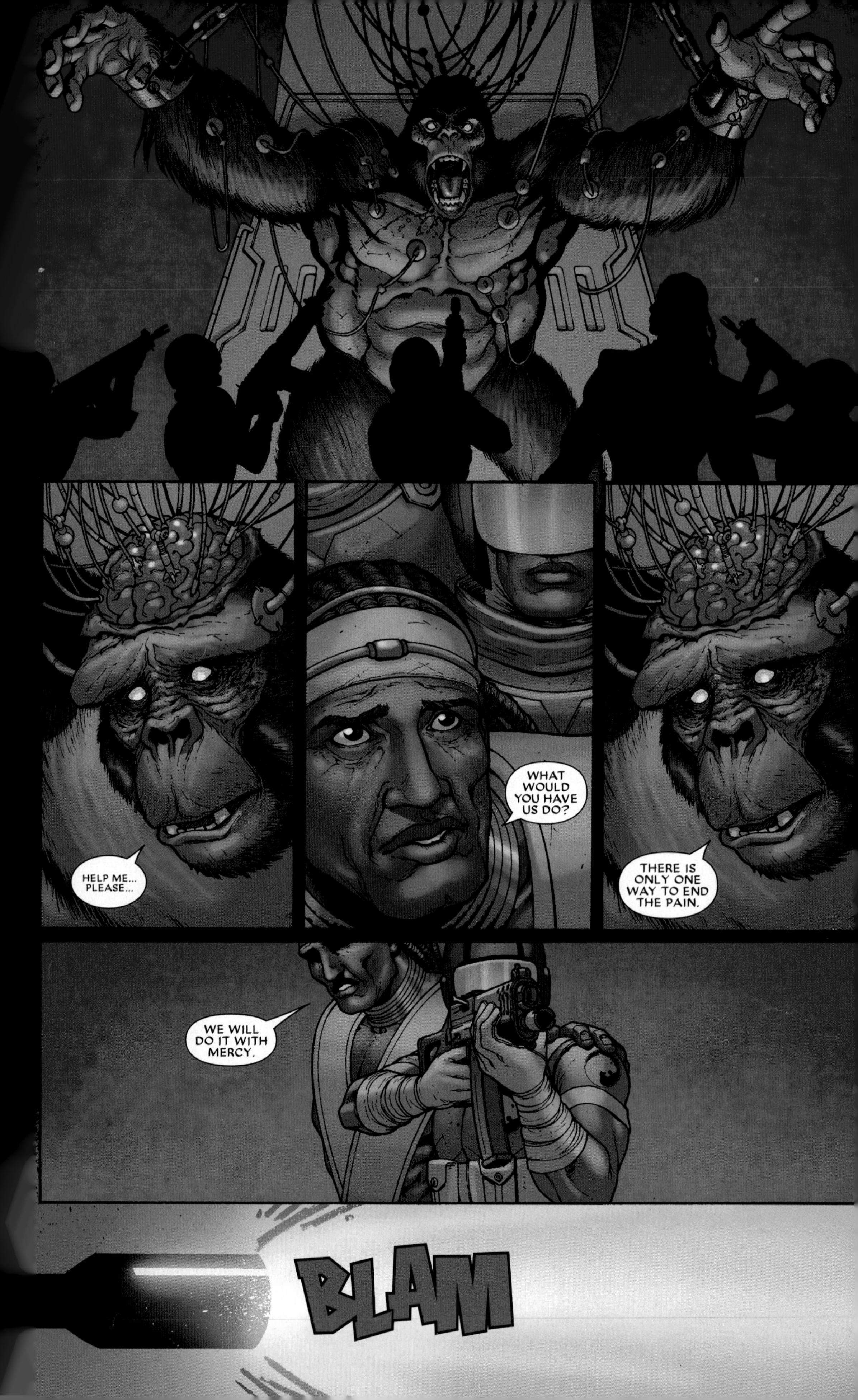
HELP ME... PLEASE...
WHAT WOULD YOU HAVE US DO?
THERE IS ONLY ONE WAY TO END THE PAIN.
WE WILL DO IT WITH MERCY.
BLAM

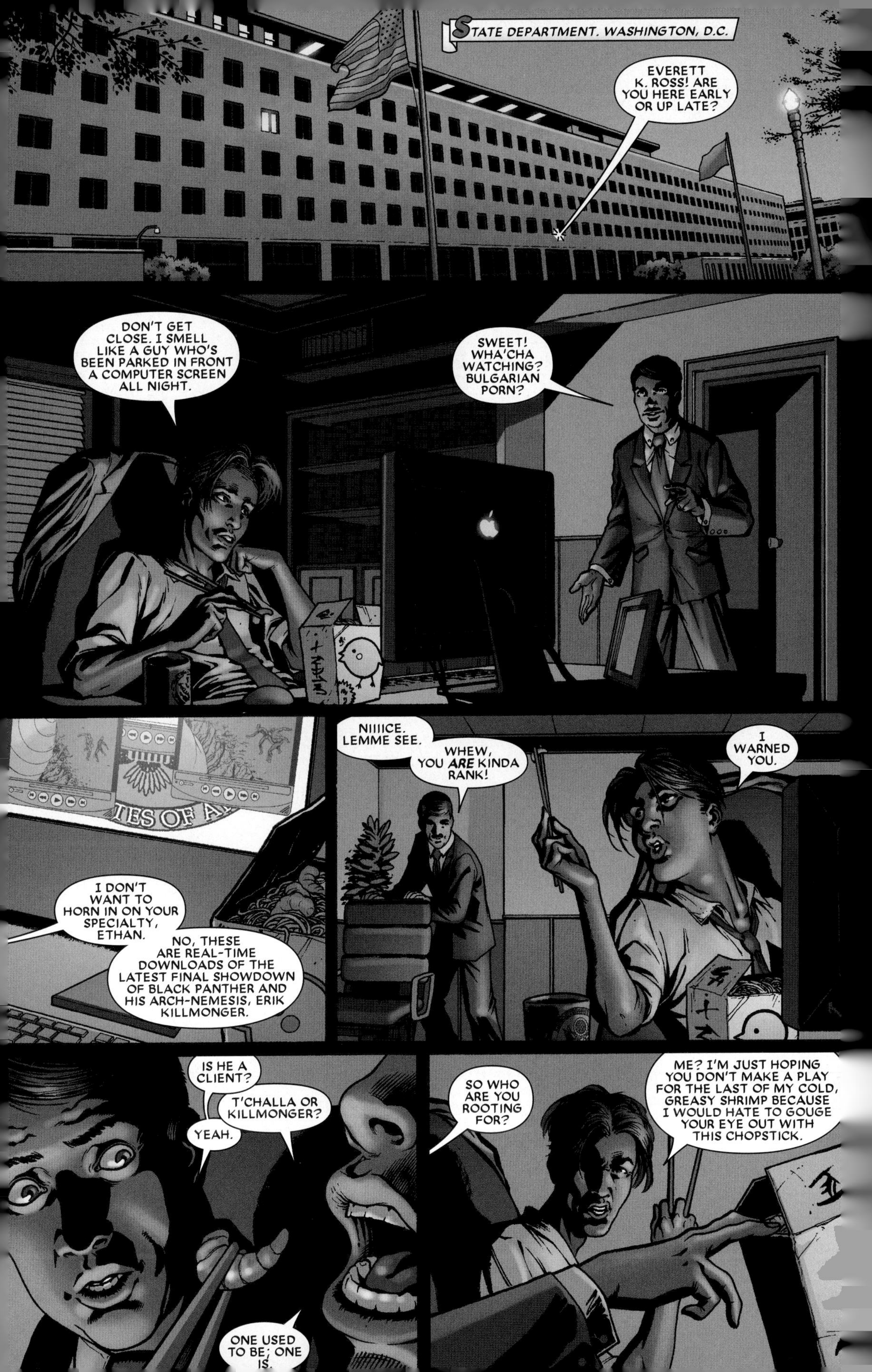
STATE DEPARTMENT. WASHINGTON, D.C.
EVERETT K. ROSS! ARE YOU HERE EARLY OR UP LATE?
DON'T GET CLOSE. I SMELL LIKE A GUY WHO'S BEEN PARKED IN FRONT A COMPUTER SCREEN ALL NIGHT.
SWEET! WHA'CHA WATCHING? BULGARIAN PORN?
I DON'T WANT TO HORN IN ON YOUR SPECIALTY, ETHAN.
NO, THESE ARE REAL-TIME DOWNLOADS OF THE LATEST FINAL SHOWDOWN OF BLACK PANTHER AND HIS ARCH-NEMESIS, ERIK KILLMONGER.
NIIIICE. LEMME SEE.
WHEW, YOU ARE KINDA RANK!
I WARNED YOU.
IS HE A CLIENT?
T'CHALLA OR KILLMONGER?
YEAH.
ONE USED TO BE; ONE IS.
SO WHO ARE YOU ROOTING FOR?
ME? I'M JUST HOPING YOU DON'T MAKE A PLAY FOR THE LAST OF MY COLD, GREASY SHRIMP BECAUSE I WOULD HATE TO GOUGE YOUR EYE OUT WITH THIS CHOPSTICK.

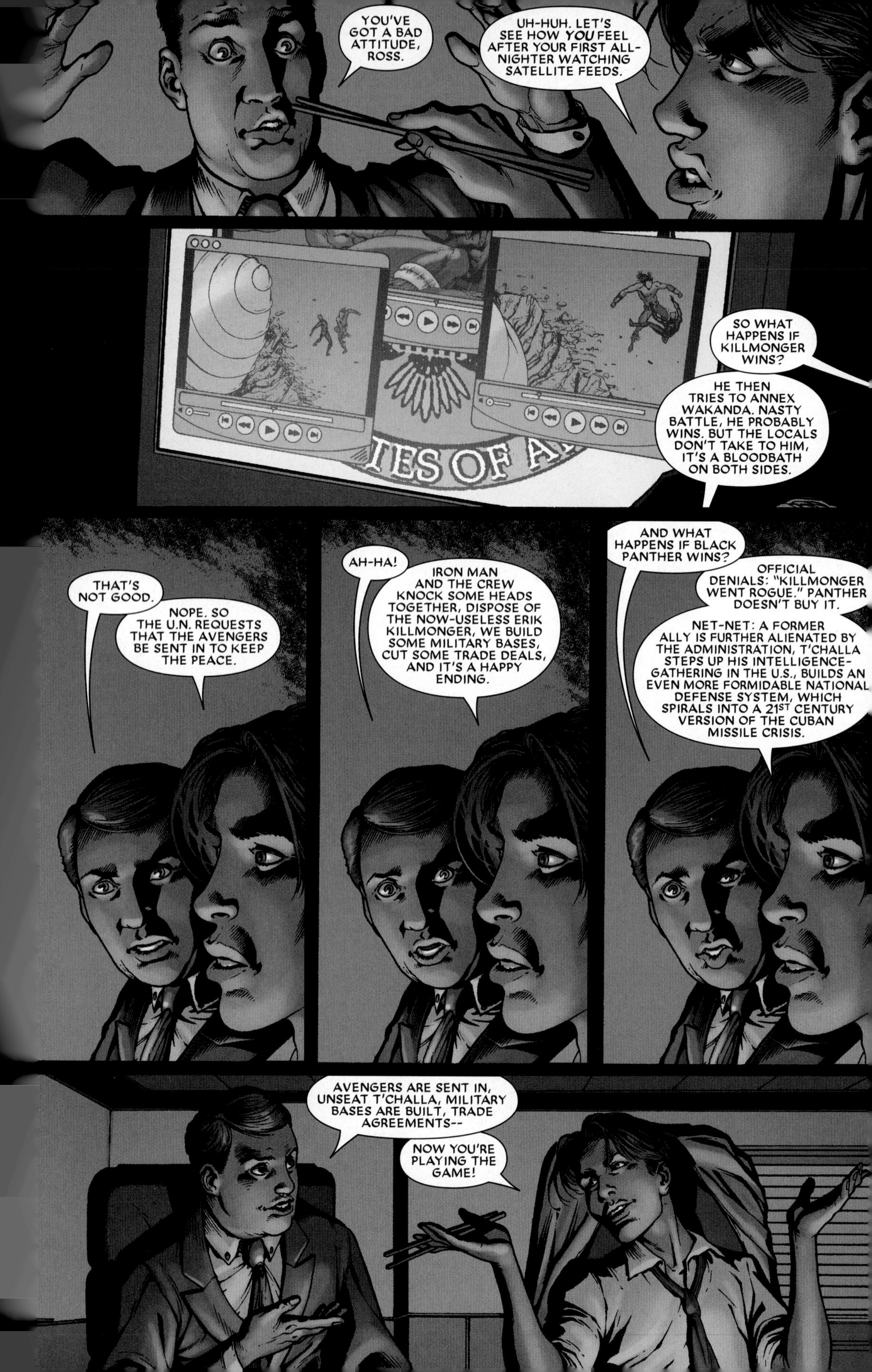

YOU'VE GOT A BAD ATTITUDE, ROSS.
UH-HUH. LET'S SEE HOW YOU FEEL AFTER YOUR FIRST ALL-NIGHTER WATCHING SATELLITE FEEDS.
SO WHAT HAPPENS IF KILLMONGER WINS?
HE THEN TRIES TO ANNEX WAKANDA. NASTY BATTLE, HE PROBABLY WINS. BUT THE LOCALS DON'T TAKE TO HIM, IT'S A BLOODBATH ON BOTH SIDES.
THAT'S NOT GOOD.
NOPE. SO THE U.N. REQUESTS THAT THE AVENGERS BE SENT IN TO KEEP THE PEACE.
AH-HA!
IRON MAN AND THE CREW KNOCK SOME HEADS TOGETHER, DISPOSE OF THE NOW-USELESS ERIK KILLMONGER, WE BUILD SOME MILITARY BASES, CUT SOME TRADE DEALS, AND IT'S A HAPPY ENDING.
AND WHAT HAPPENS IF BLACK PANTHER WINS?
OFFICIAL DENIALS: "KILLMONGER WENT ROGUE." PANTHER DOESN'T BUY IT.
NET-NET: A FORMER ALLY IS FURTHER ALIENATED BY THE ADMINISTRATION, T'CHALLA STEPS UP HIS INTELLIGENCE-GATHERING IN THE U.S., BUILDS AN EVEN MORE FORMIDABLE NATIONAL DEFENSE SYSTEM, WHICH SPIRALS INTO A 21ST CENTURY VERSION OF THE CUBAN MISSILE CRISIS.
AVENGERS ARE SENT IN, UNSEAT T'CHALLA, MILITARY BASES ARE BUILT, TRADE AGREEMENTS--
NOW YOU'RE PLAYING THE GAME!

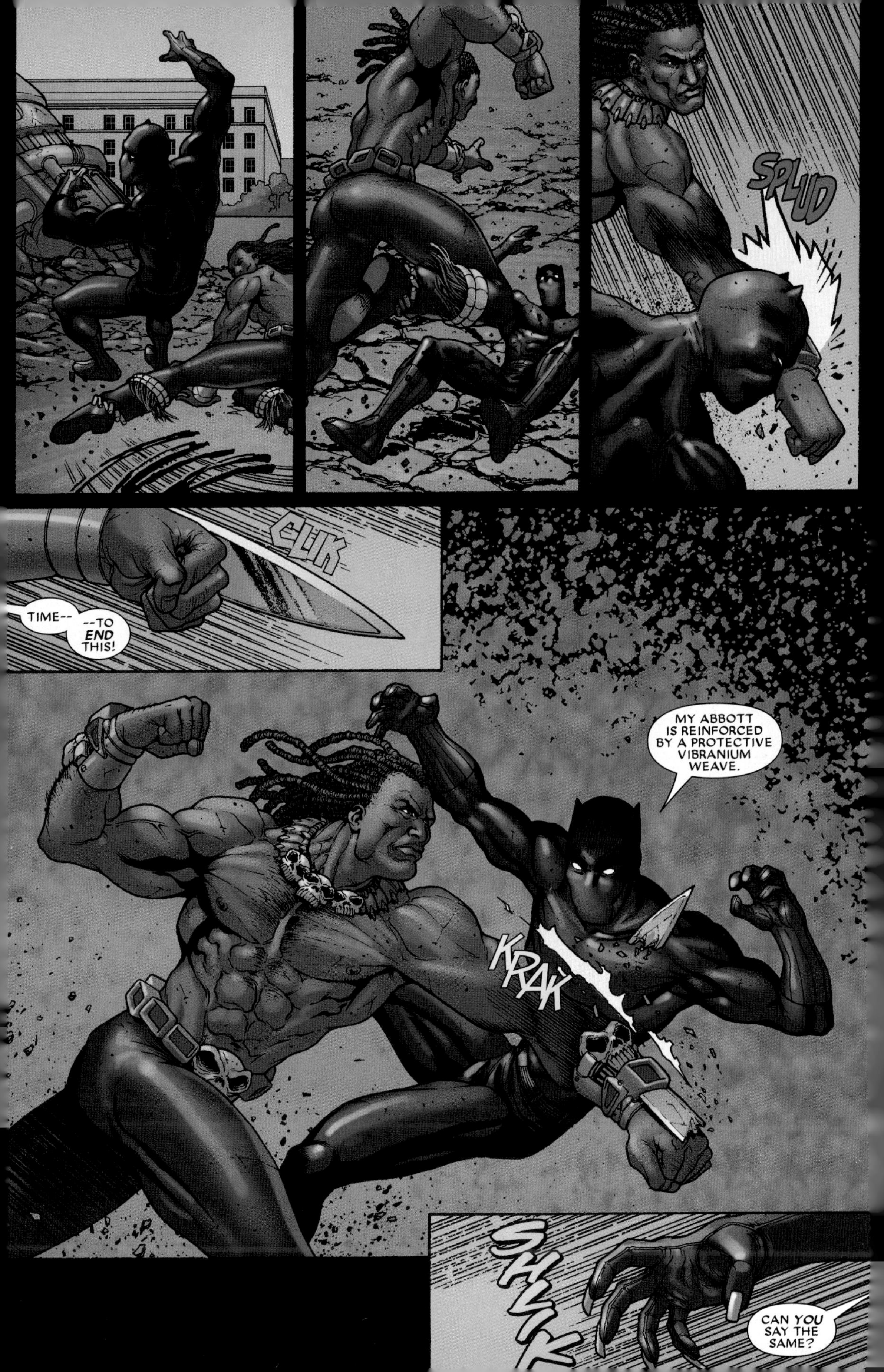
SPLUD
CLIK
TIME--
--TO END THIS!
MY ABBOTT IS REINFORCED BY A PROTECTIVE VIBRANIUM WEAVE.
KRAK
SHUK
CAN YOU SAY THE SAME?

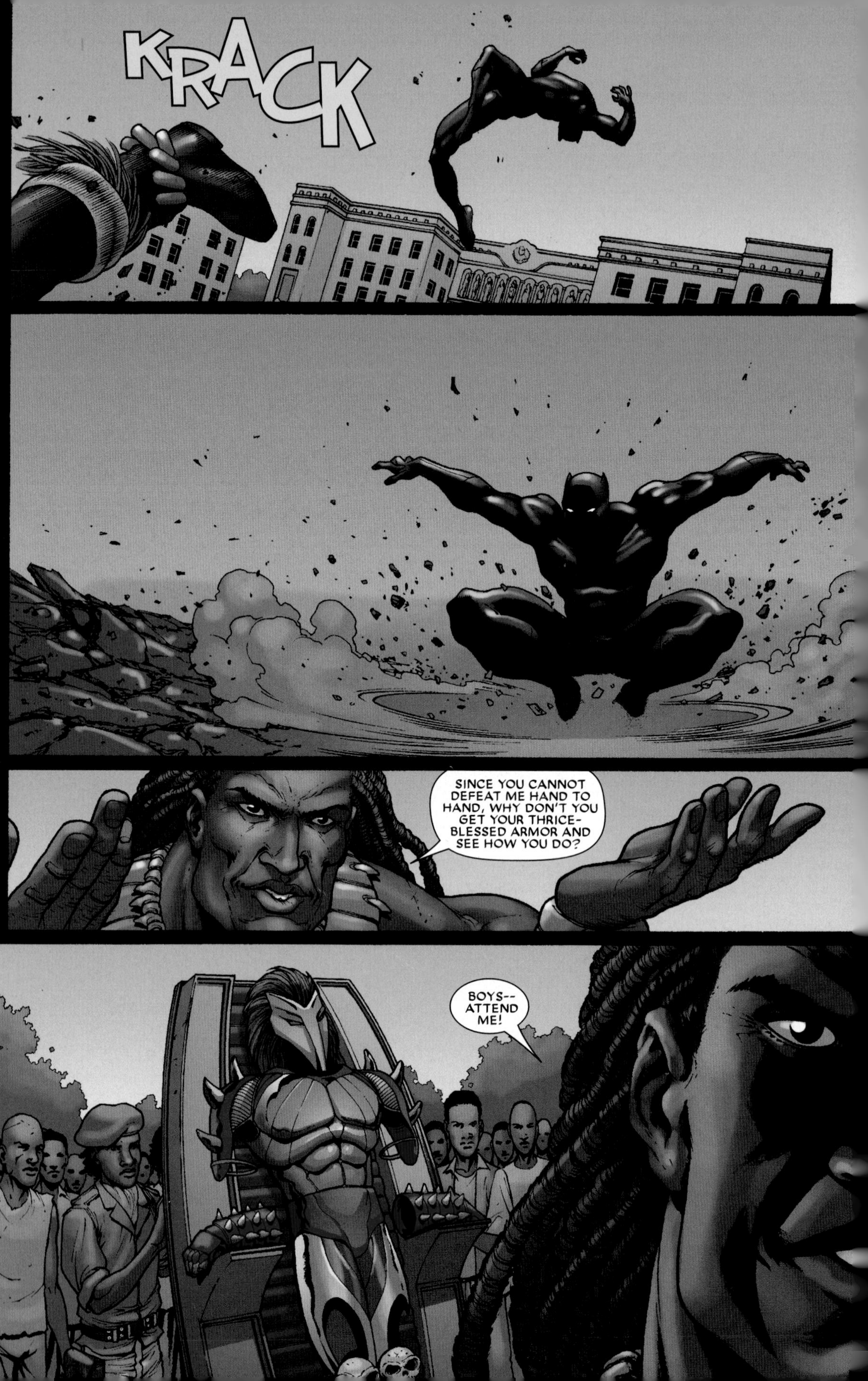
KRACK
SINCE YOU CANNOT DEFEAT ME HAND TO HAND, WHY DON'T YOU GET YOUR THRICE-BLESSED ARMOR AND SEE HOW YOU DO?
BOYS-- ATTEND ME!

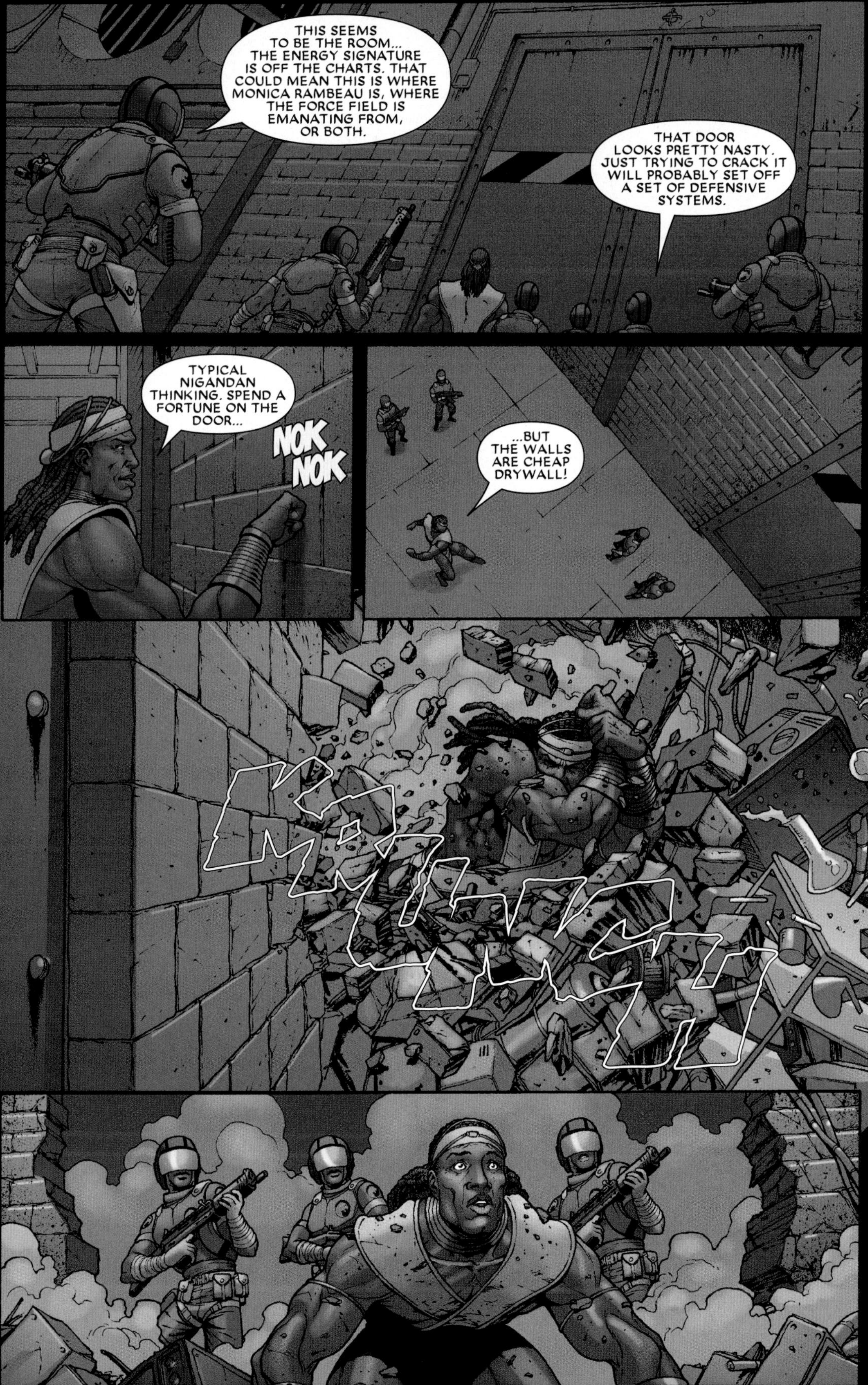
THIS SEEMS TO BE THE ROOM... THE ENERGY SIGNATURE IS OFF THE CHARTS. THAT COULD MEAN THIS IS WHERE MONICA RAMBEAU IS, WHERE THE FORCE FIELD IS EMANATING FROM, OR BOTH.
THAT DOOR LOOKS PRETTY NASTY. JUST TRYING TO CRACK IT WILL PROBABLY SET OFF A SET OF DEFENSIVE SYSTEMS.
TYPICAL NIGANDAN THINKING. SPEND A FORTUNE ON THE DOOR...
NOK NOK
...BUT THE WALLS ARE CHEAP DRYWALL!

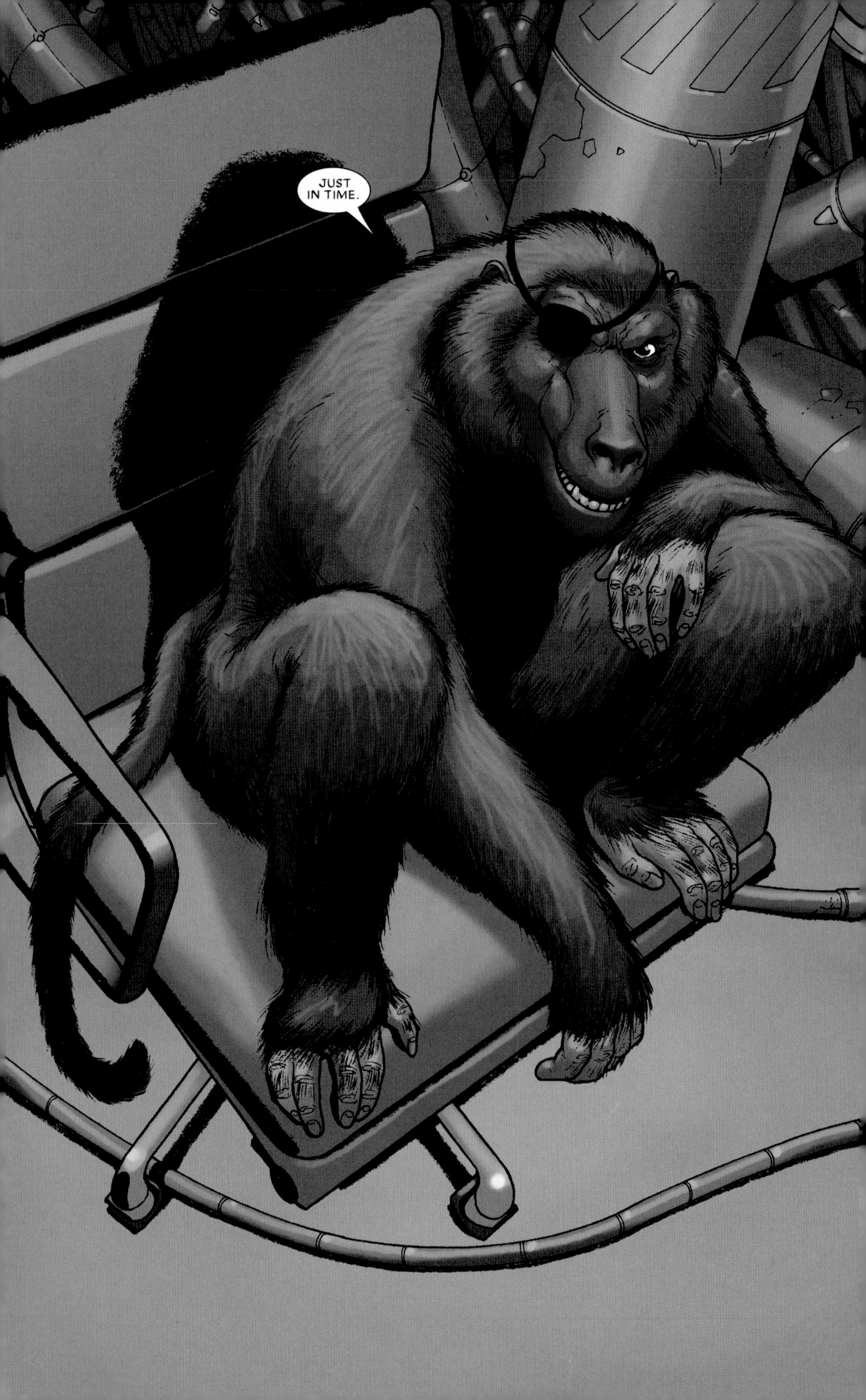
JUST IN TIME.

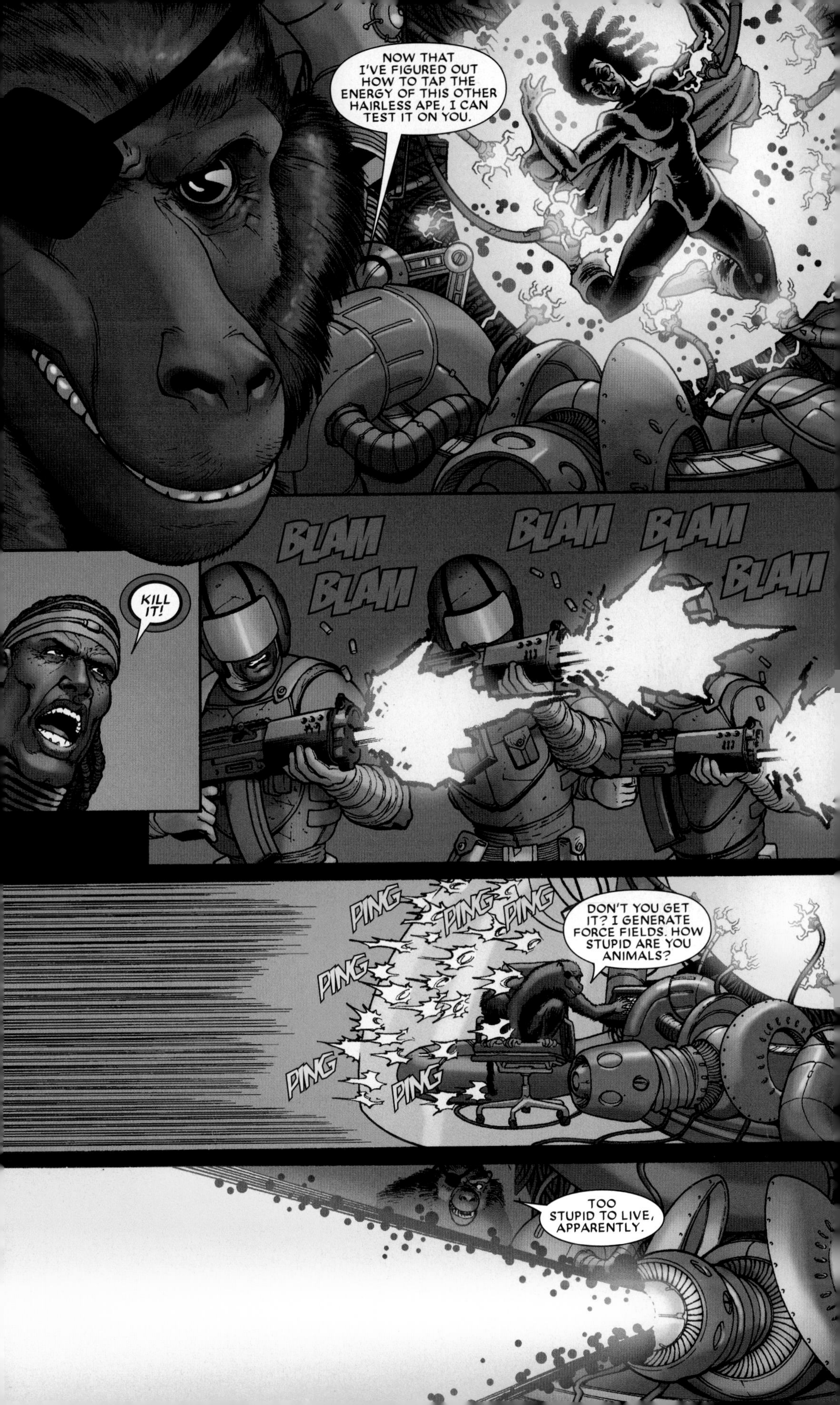
NOW THAT I'VE FIGURED OUT HOW TO TAP THE ENERGY OF THIS OTHER HAIRLESS APE, I CAN TEST IT ON YOU.
KILL IT!
BLAM
BLAM
BLAM
BLAM
BLAM
PING
PING
PING
PING
PING
PING
DON'T YOU GET IT? I GENERATE FORCE FIELDS. HOW STUPID ARE YOU ANIMALS?
TOO STUPID TO LIVE, APPARENTLY.

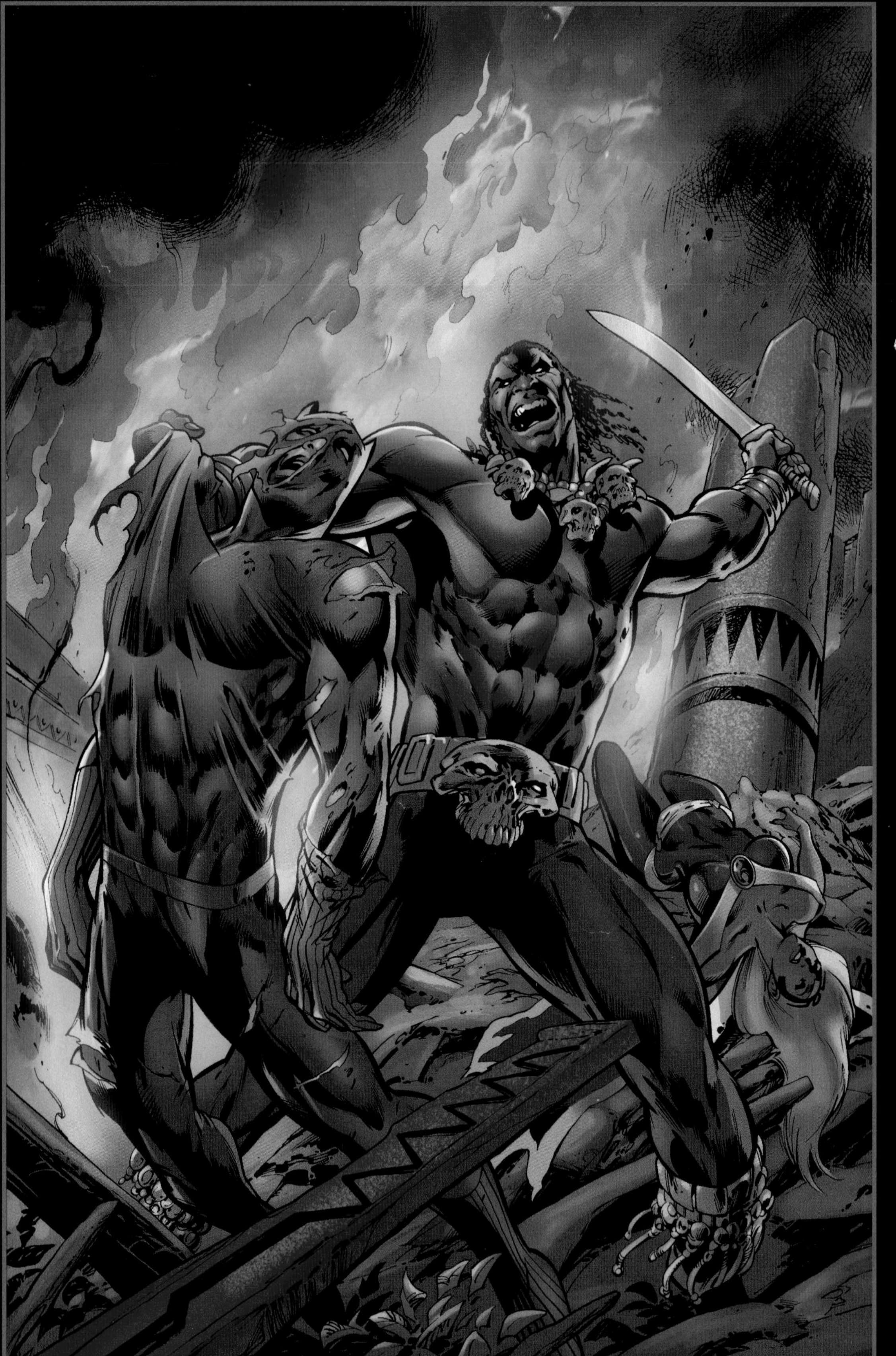

BLACK PANTHER (2005) **38**

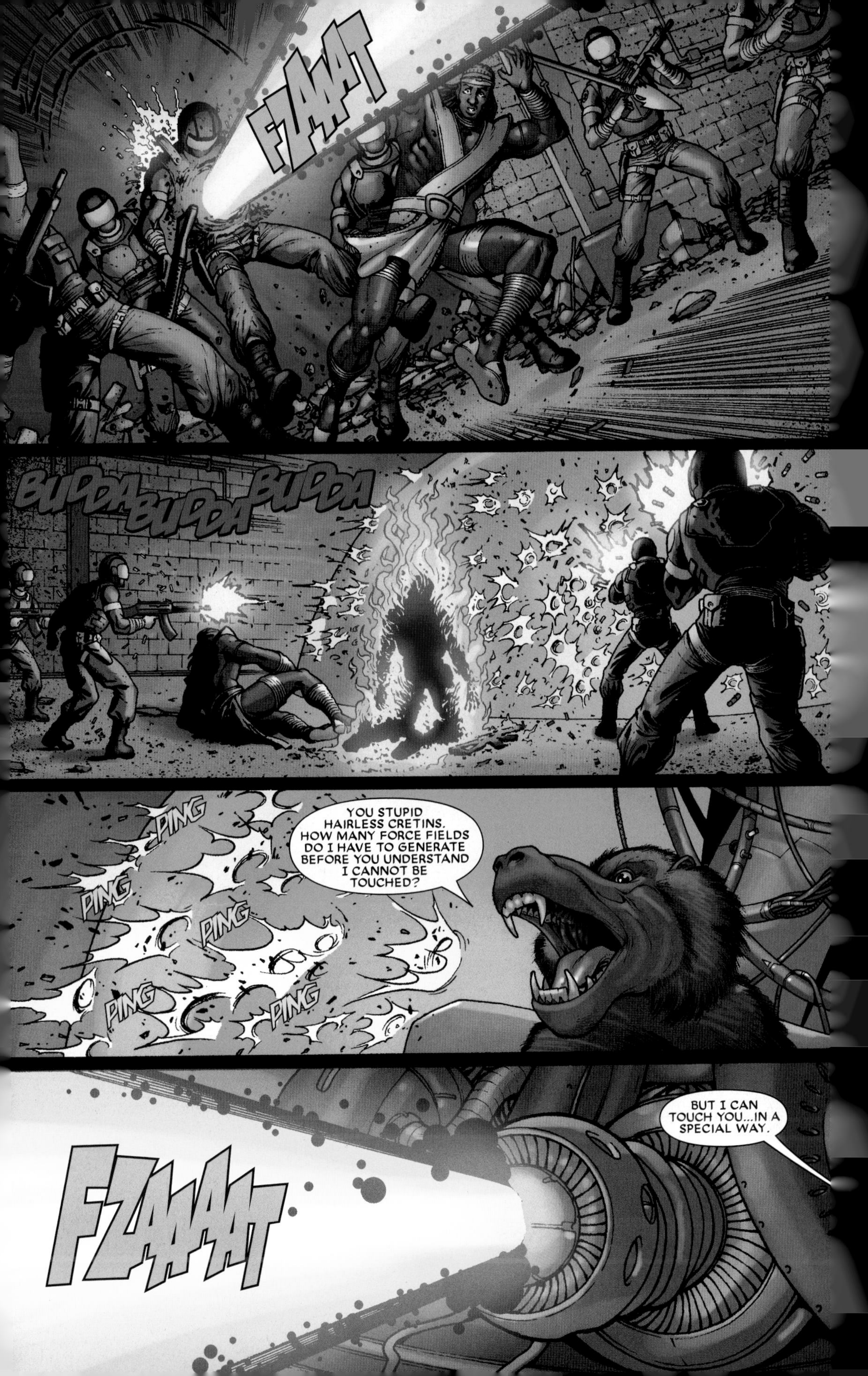
FZAAAT
BUDDA BUDDA BUDDA
PING
PING
PING
PING
PING
YOU STUPID HAIRLESS CRETINS. HOW MANY FORCE FIELDS DO I HAVE TO GENERATE BEFORE YOU UNDERSTAND I CANNOT BE TOUCHED?
BUT I CAN TOUCH YOU...IN A SPECIAL WAY.
FZAAAAT

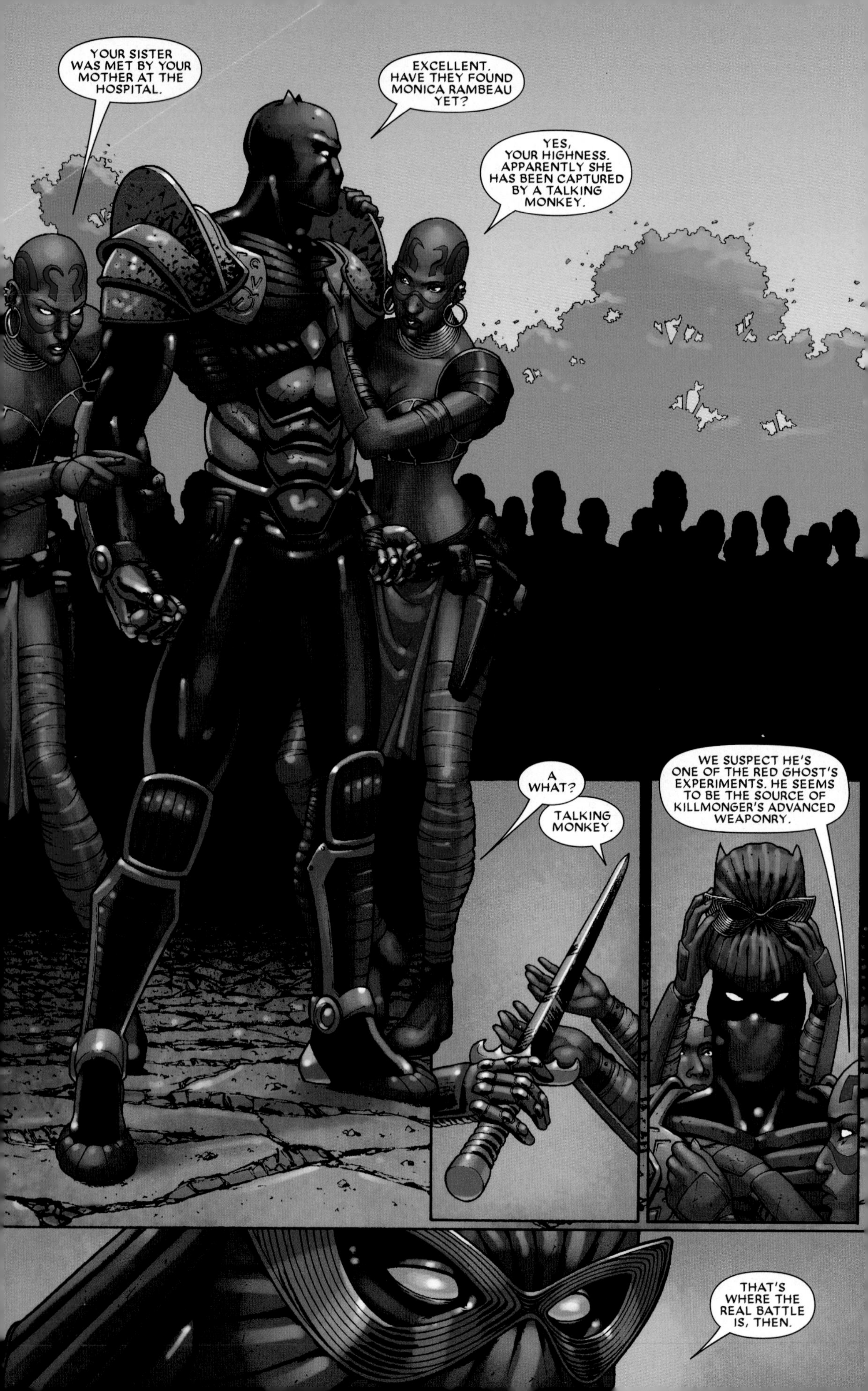
YOUR SISTER WAS MET BY YOUR MOTHER AT THE HOSPITAL.
EXCELLENT. HAVE THEY FOUND MONICA RAMBEAU YET?
YES, YOUR HIGHNESS. APPARENTLY SHE HAS BEEN CAPTURED BY A TALKING MONKEY.
A WHAT?
TALKING MONKEY.
WE SUSPECT HE'S ONE OF THE RED GHOST'S EXPERIMENTS. HE SEEMS TO BE THE SOURCE OF KILLMONGER'S ADVANCED WEAPONRY.
THAT'S WHERE THE REAL BATTLE IS, THEN.

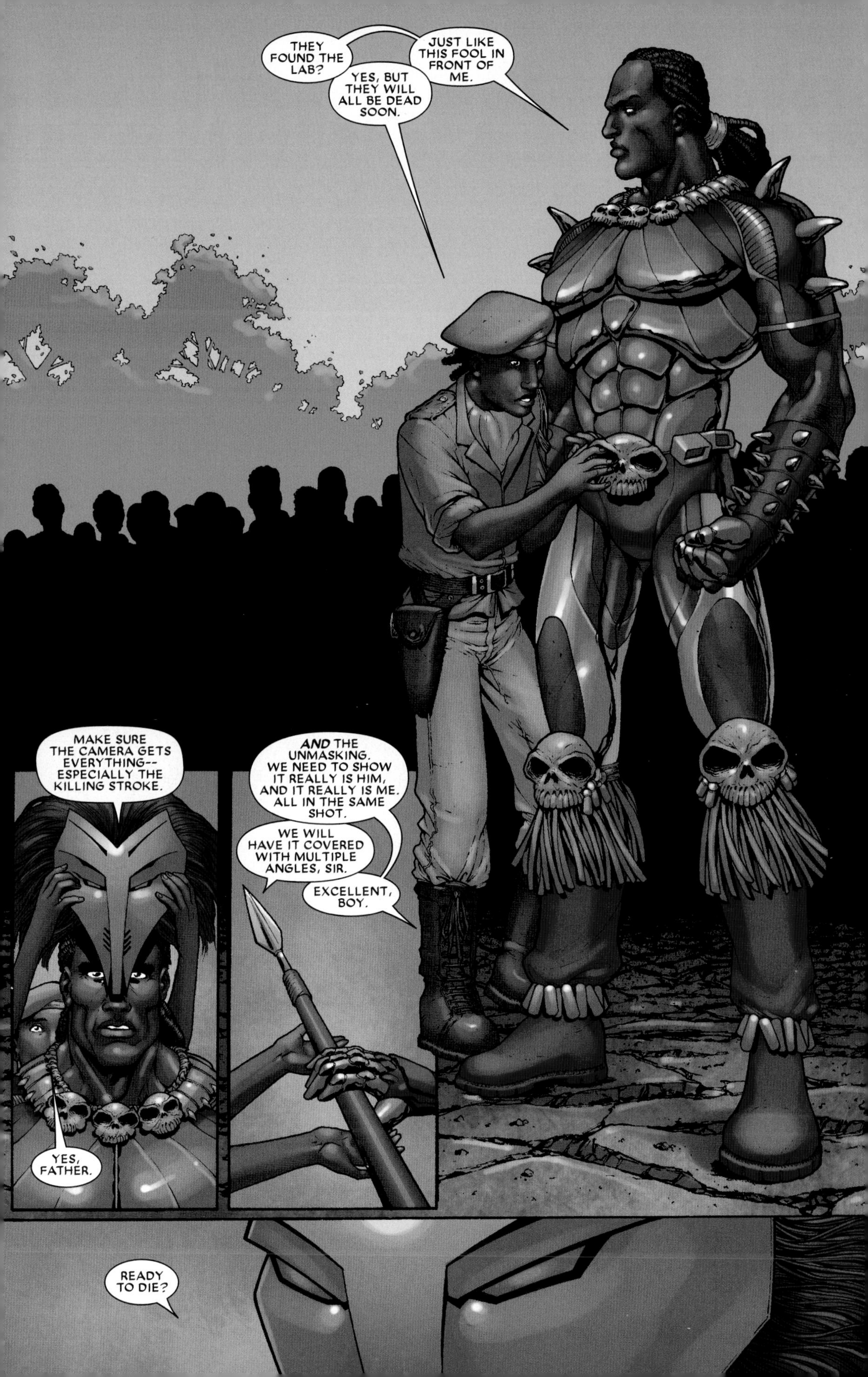
THEY FOUND THE LAB?
YES, BUT THEY WILL ALL BE DEAD SOON.
JUST LIKE THIS FOOL IN FRONT OF ME.
MAKE SURE THE CAMERA GETS EVERYTHING-- ESPECIALLY THE KILLING STROKE.
YES, FATHER.
AND THE UNMASKING. WE NEED TO SHOW IT REALLY IS HIM, AND IT REALLY IS ME. ALL IN THE SAME SHOT.
WE WILL HAVE IT COVERED WITH MULTIPLE ANGLES, SIR.
EXCELLENT, BOY.
READY TO DIE?

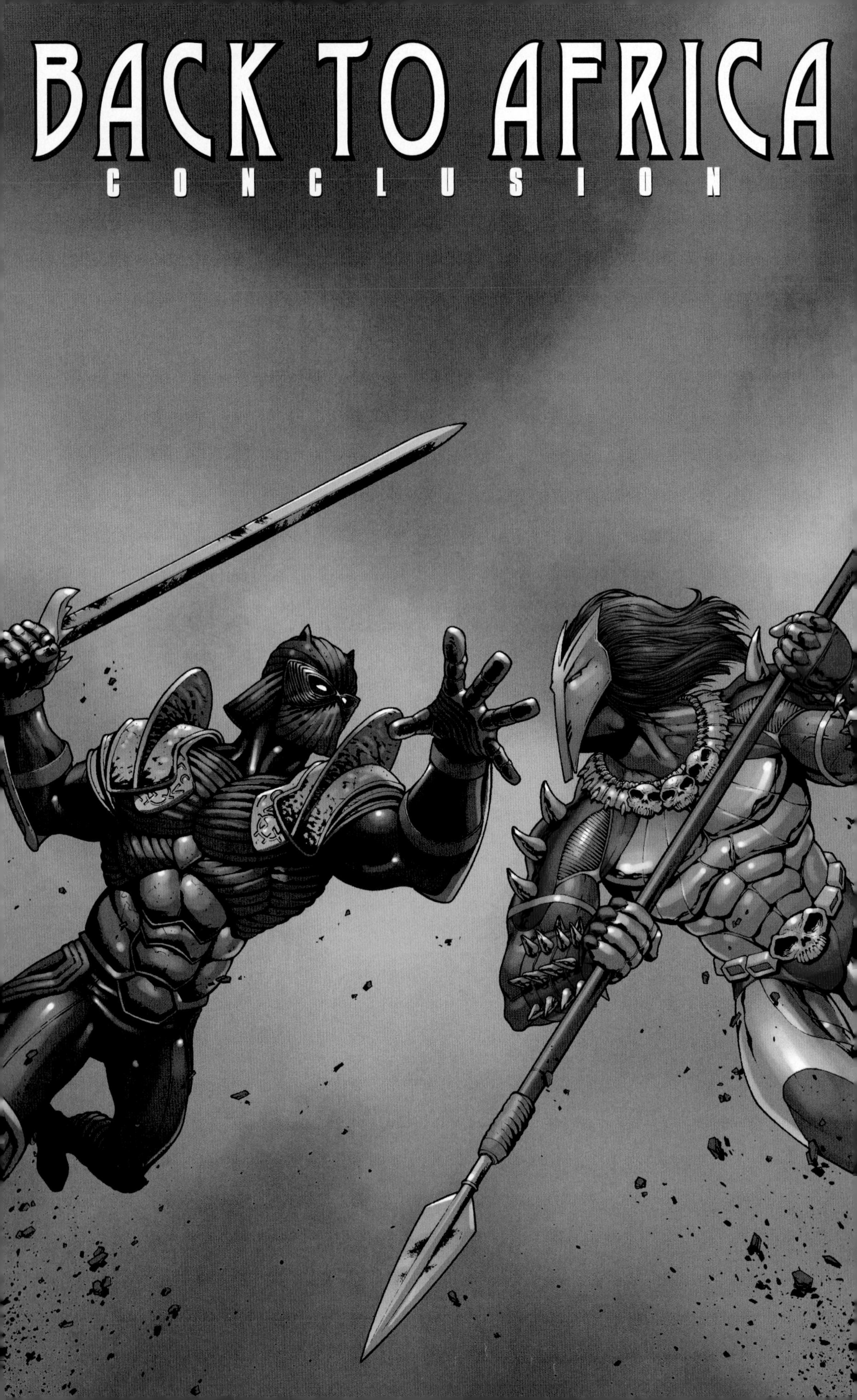
BACK TO AFRICA
CONCLUSION

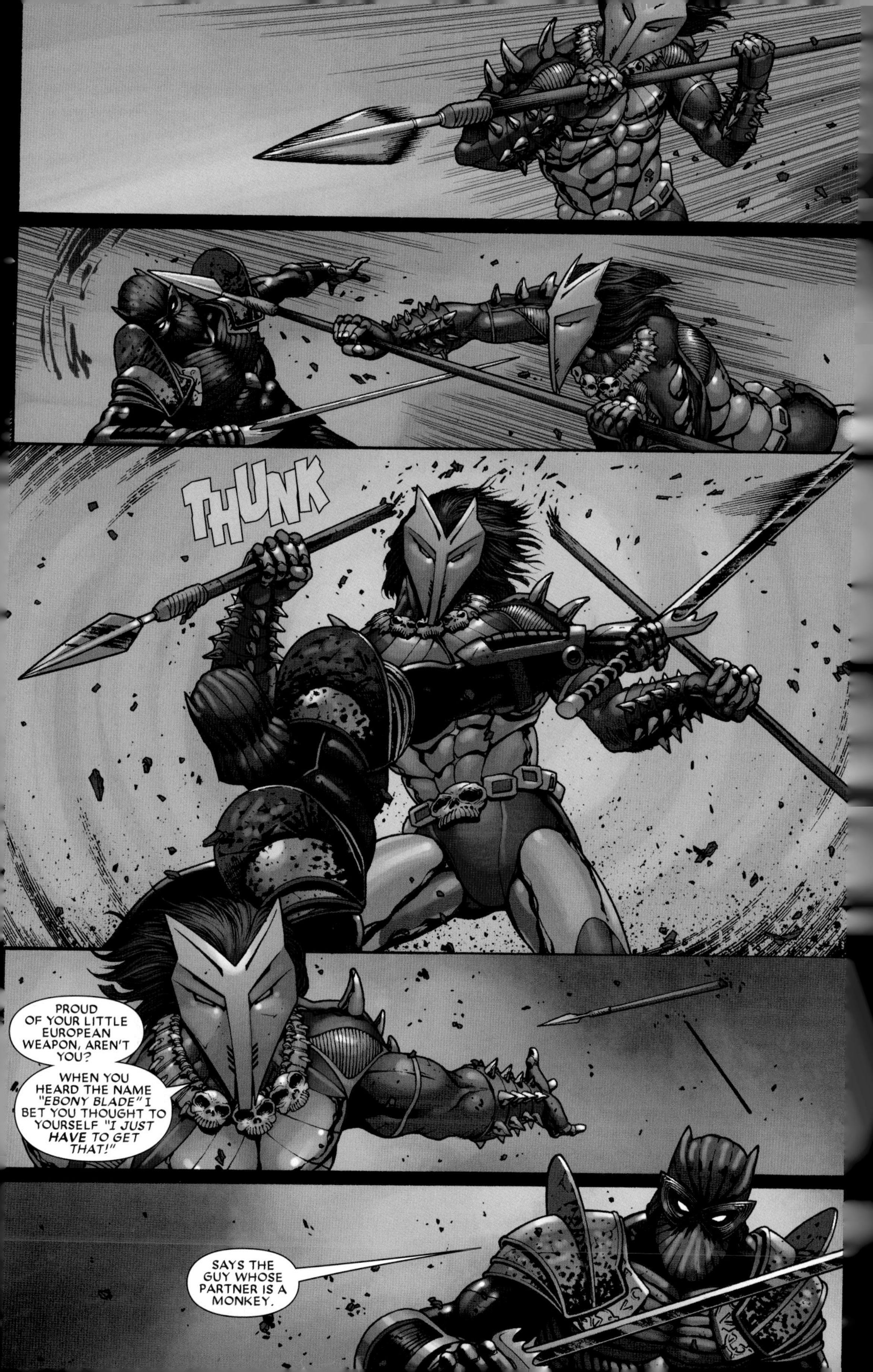
THUNK
PROUD OF YOUR LITTLE EUROPEAN WEAPON, AREN'T YOU?
WHEN YOU HEARD THE NAME "EBONY BLADE" I BET YOU THOUGHT TO YOURSELF "I JUST HAVE TO GET THAT!"
SAYS THE GUY WHOSE PARTNER IS A MONKEY.

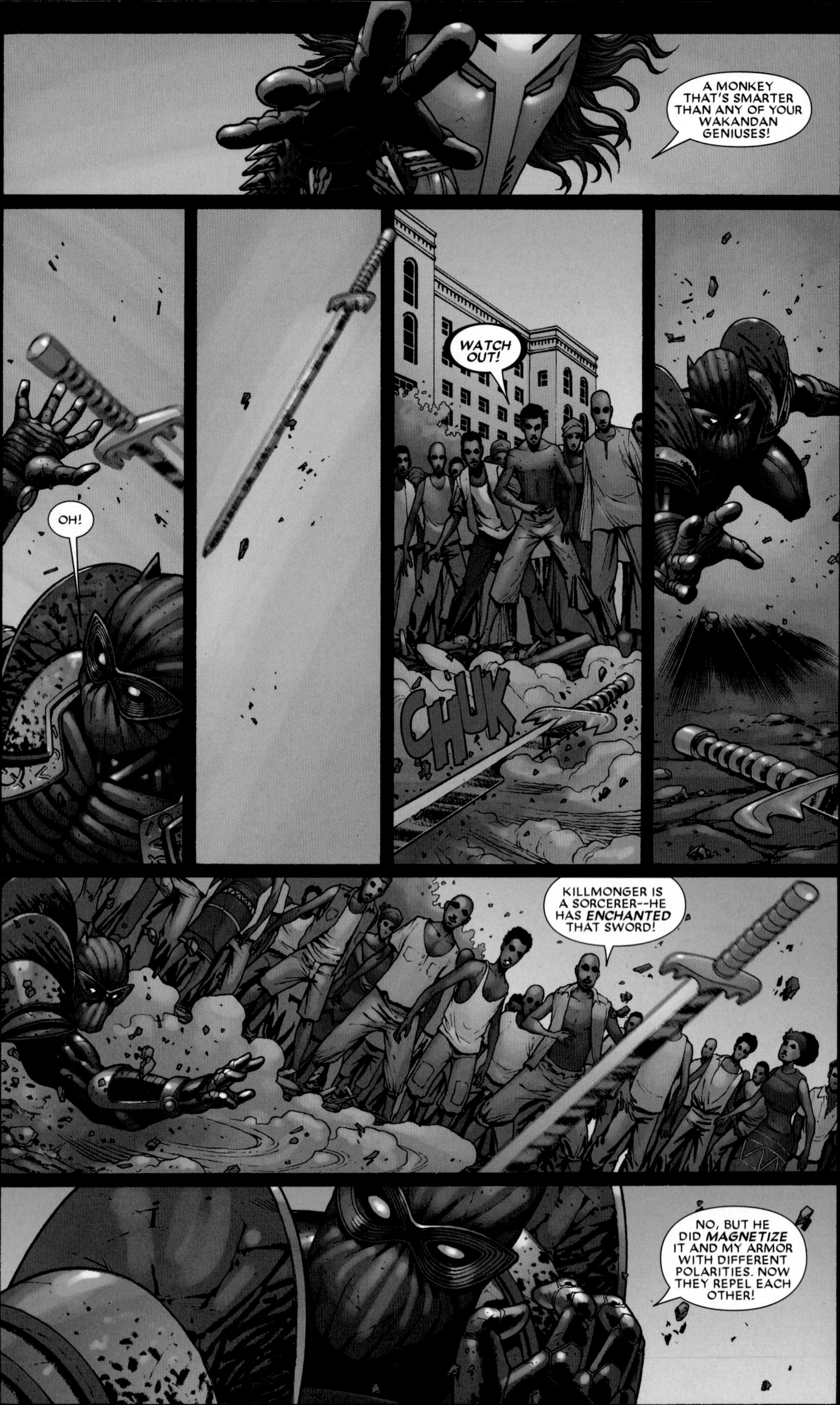
A MONKEY THAT'S SMARTER THAN ANY OF YOUR WAKANDAN GENIUSES!
OH!
WATCH OUT!
CHUK
KILLMONGER IS A SORCERER--HE HAS *ENCHANTED* THAT SWORD!
NO, BUT HE DID *MAGNETIZE* IT AND MY ARMOR WITH DIFFERENT POLARITIES. NOW THEY REPEL EACH OTHER!

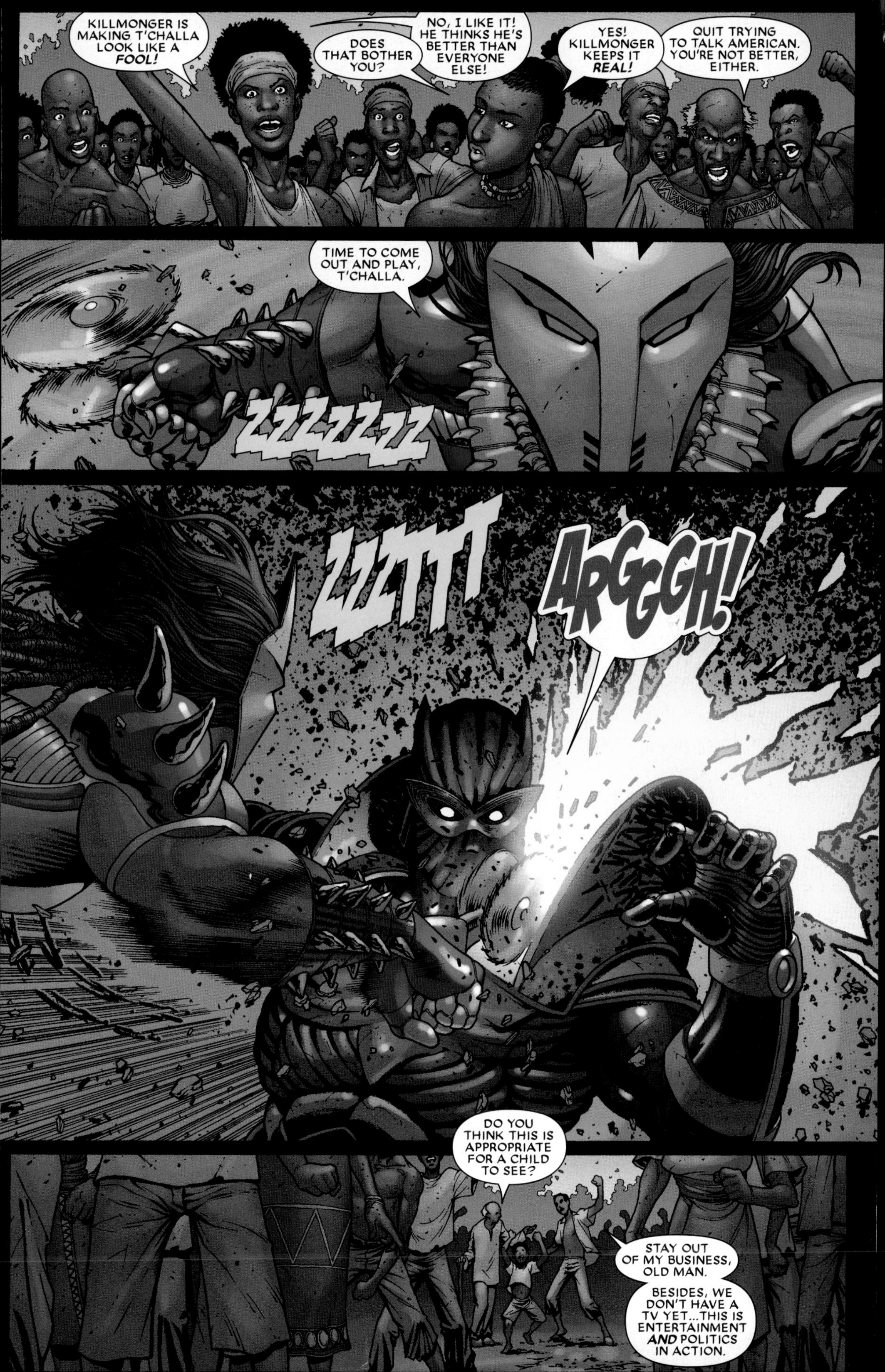
KILLMONGER IS MAKING T'CHALLA LOOK LIKE A FOOL!
DOES THAT BOTHER YOU?
NO, I LIKE IT! HE THINKS HE'S BETTER THAN EVERYONE ELSE!
YES! KILLMONGER KEEPS IT REAL!
QUIT TRYING TO TALK AMERICAN. YOU'RE NOT BETTER, EITHER.
TIME TO COME OUT AND PLAY, T'CHALLA.
ZZZZZZZZ
ZZZTTT
ARGGGH!
DO YOU THINK THIS IS APPROPRIATE FOR A CHILD TO SEE?
STAY OUT OF MY BUSINESS, OLD MAN.
BESIDES, WE DON'T HAVE A TV YET...THIS IS ENTERTAINMENT AND POLITICS IN ACTION.

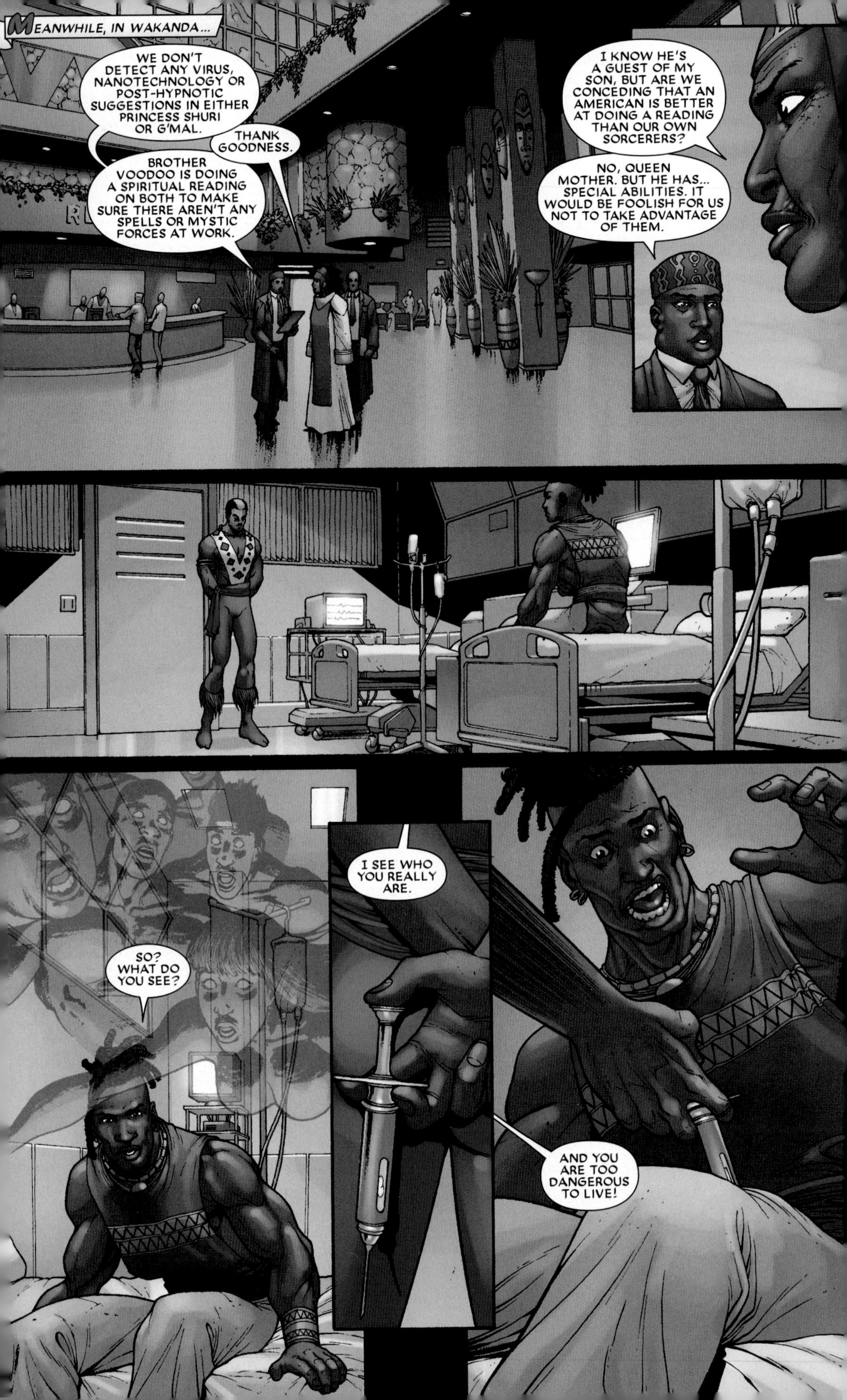
MEANWHILE, IN WAKANDA...
WE DON'T DETECT ANY VIRUS, NANOTECHNOLOGY OR POST-HYPNOTIC SUGGESTIONS IN EITHER PRINCESS SHURI OR G'MAL.
THANK GOODNESS.
BROTHER VOODOO IS DOING A SPIRITUAL READING ON BOTH TO MAKE SURE THERE AREN'T ANY SPELLS OR MYSTIC FORCES AT WORK.
I KNOW HE'S A GUEST OF MY SON, BUT ARE WE CONCEDING THAT AN AMERICAN IS BETTER AT DOING A READING THAN OUR OWN SORCERERS?
NO, QUEEN MOTHER. BUT HE HAS... SPECIAL ABILITIES. IT WOULD BE FOOLISH FOR US NOT TO TAKE ADVANTAGE OF THEM.
SO? WHAT DO YOU SEE?
I SEE WHO YOU REALLY ARE.
AND YOU ARE TOO DANGEROUS TO LIVE!

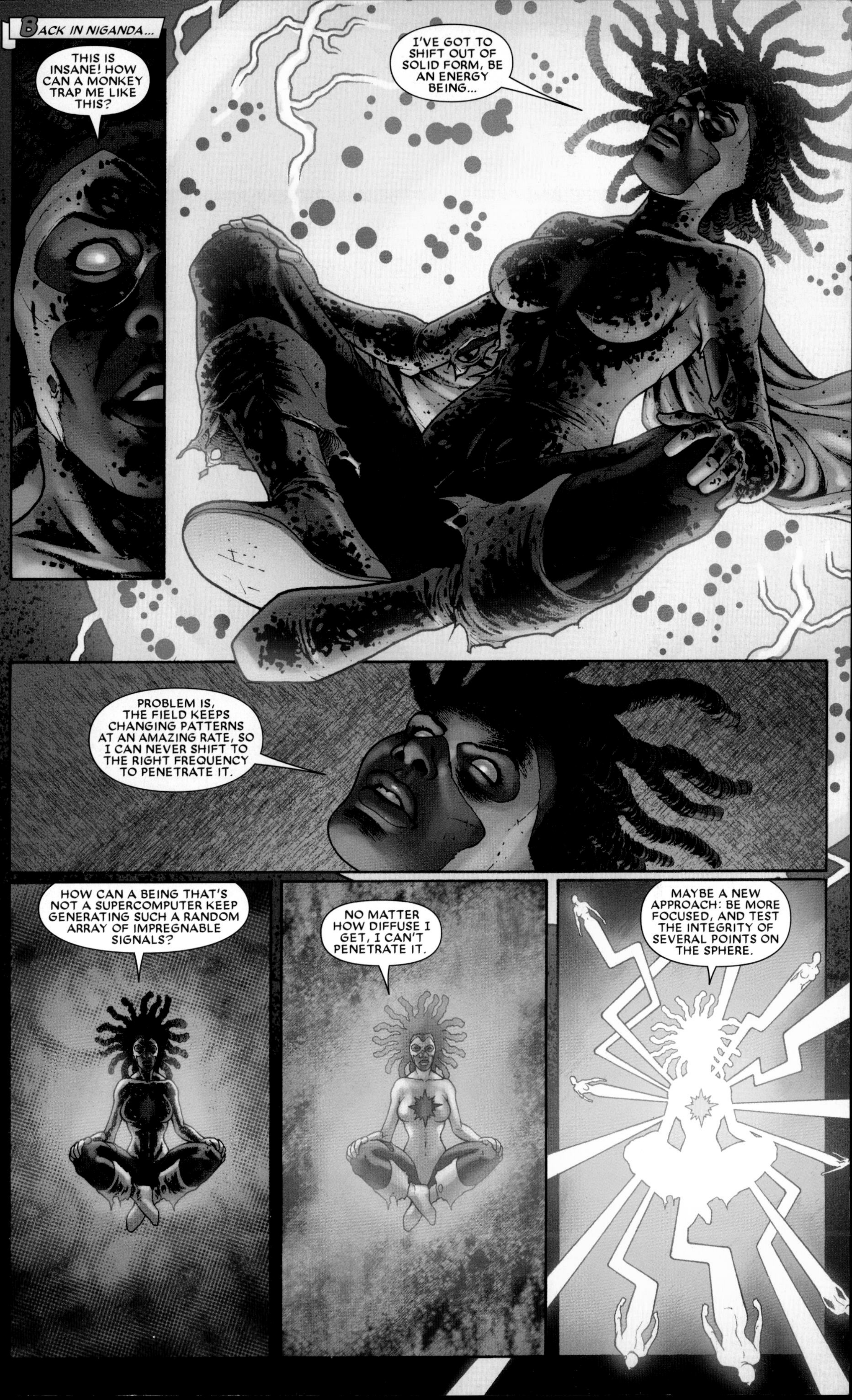
BACK IN NIGANDA...
THIS IS INSANE! HOW CAN A MONKEY TRAP ME LIKE THIS?
I'VE GOT TO SHIFT OUT OF SOLID FORM, BE AN ENERGY BEING...
PROBLEM IS, THE FIELD KEEPS CHANGING PATTERNS AT AN AMAZING RATE, SO I CAN NEVER SHIFT TO THE RIGHT FREQUENCY TO PENETRATE IT.
HOW CAN A BEING THAT'S NOT A SUPERCOMPUTER KEEP GENERATING SUCH A RANDOM ARRAY OF IMPREGNABLE SIGNALS?
NO MATTER HOW DIFFUSE I GET, I CAN'T PENETRATE IT.
MAYBE A NEW APPROACH: BE MORE FOCUSED, AND TEST THE INTEGRITY OF SEVERAL POINTS ON THE SPHERE.

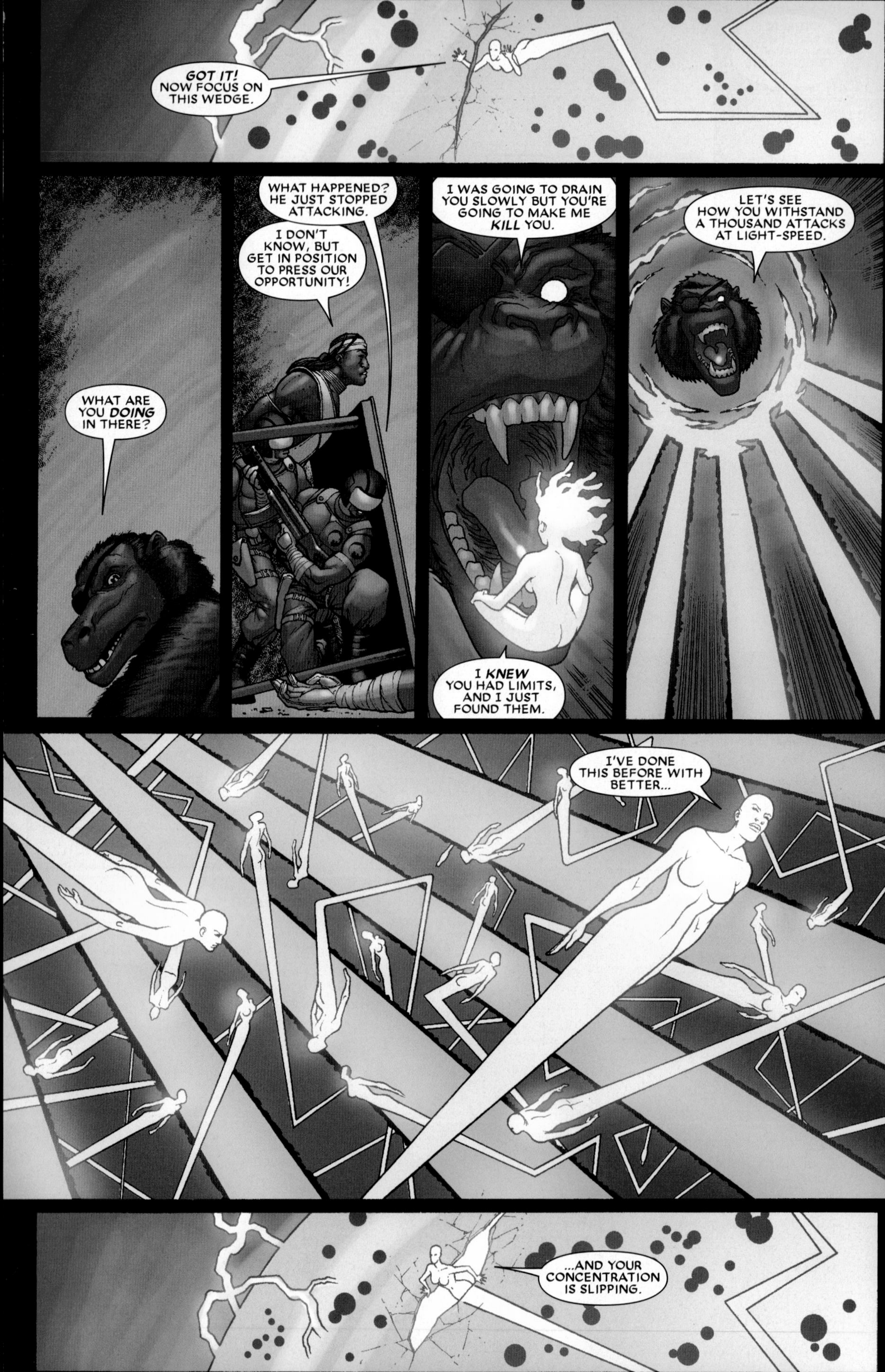
GOT IT! NOW FOCUS ON THIS WEDGE.
WHAT ARE YOU DOING IN THERE?
WHAT HAPPENED? HE JUST STOPPED ATTACKING.
I DON'T KNOW, BUT GET IN POSITION TO PRESS OUR OPPORTUNITY!
I WAS GOING TO DRAIN YOU SLOWLY BUT YOU'RE GOING TO MAKE ME KILL YOU.
I KNEW YOU HAD LIMITS, AND I JUST FOUND THEM.
LET'S SEE HOW YOU WITHSTAND A THOUSAND ATTACKS AT LIGHT-SPEED.
I'VE DONE THIS BEFORE WITH BETTER...
...AND YOUR CONCENTRATION IS SLIPPING.

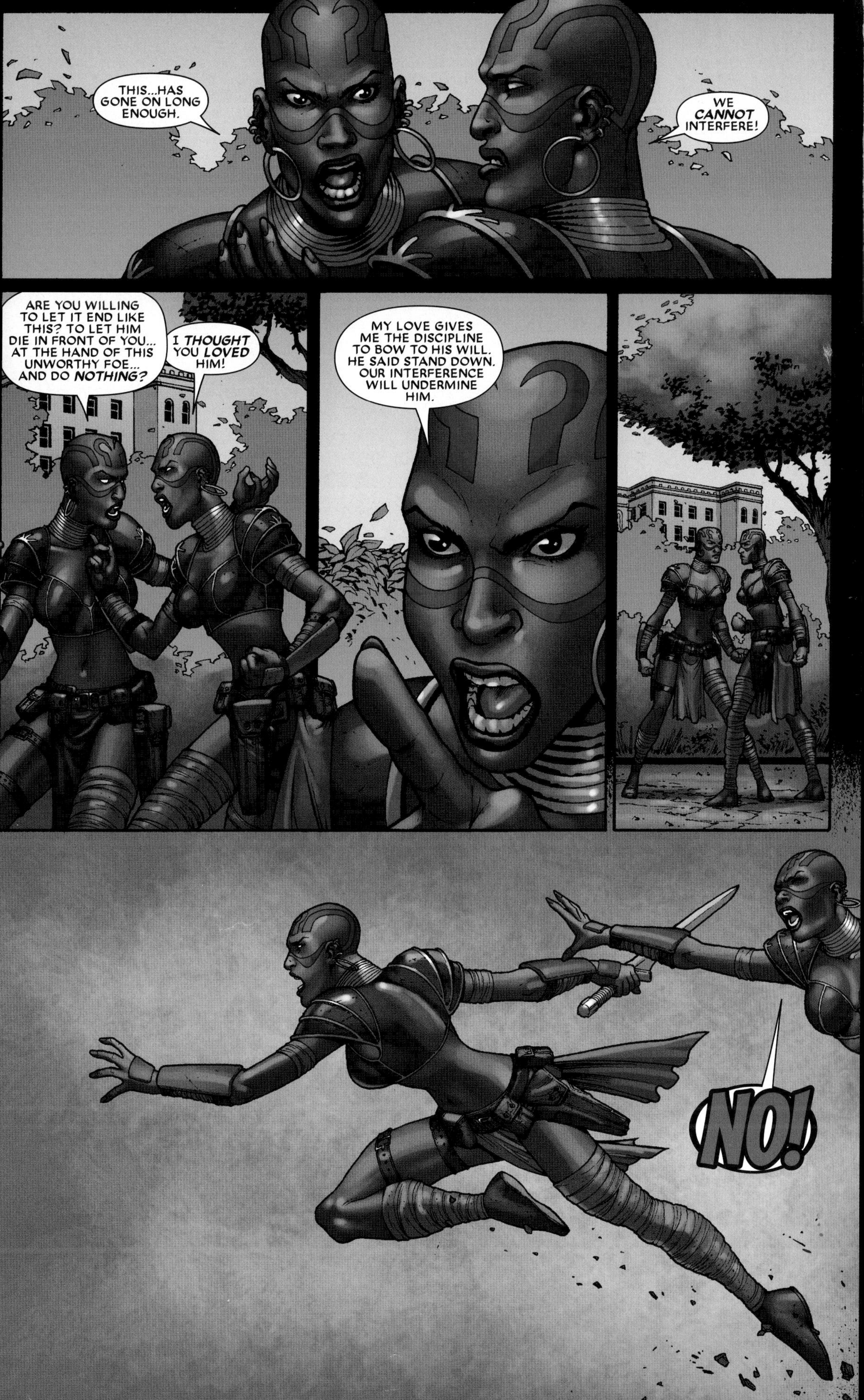
THIS...HAS GONE ON LONG ENOUGH.
WE CANNOT INTERFERE!
ARE YOU WILLING TO LET IT END LIKE THIS? TO LET HIM DIE IN FRONT OF YOU... AT THE HAND OF THIS UNWORTHY FOE... AND DO NOTHING?
I THOUGHT YOU LOVED HIM!
MY LOVE GIVES ME THE DISCIPLINE TO BOW TO HIS WILL. HE SAID STAND DOWN. OUR INTERFERENCE WILL UNDERMINE HIM.
NO!

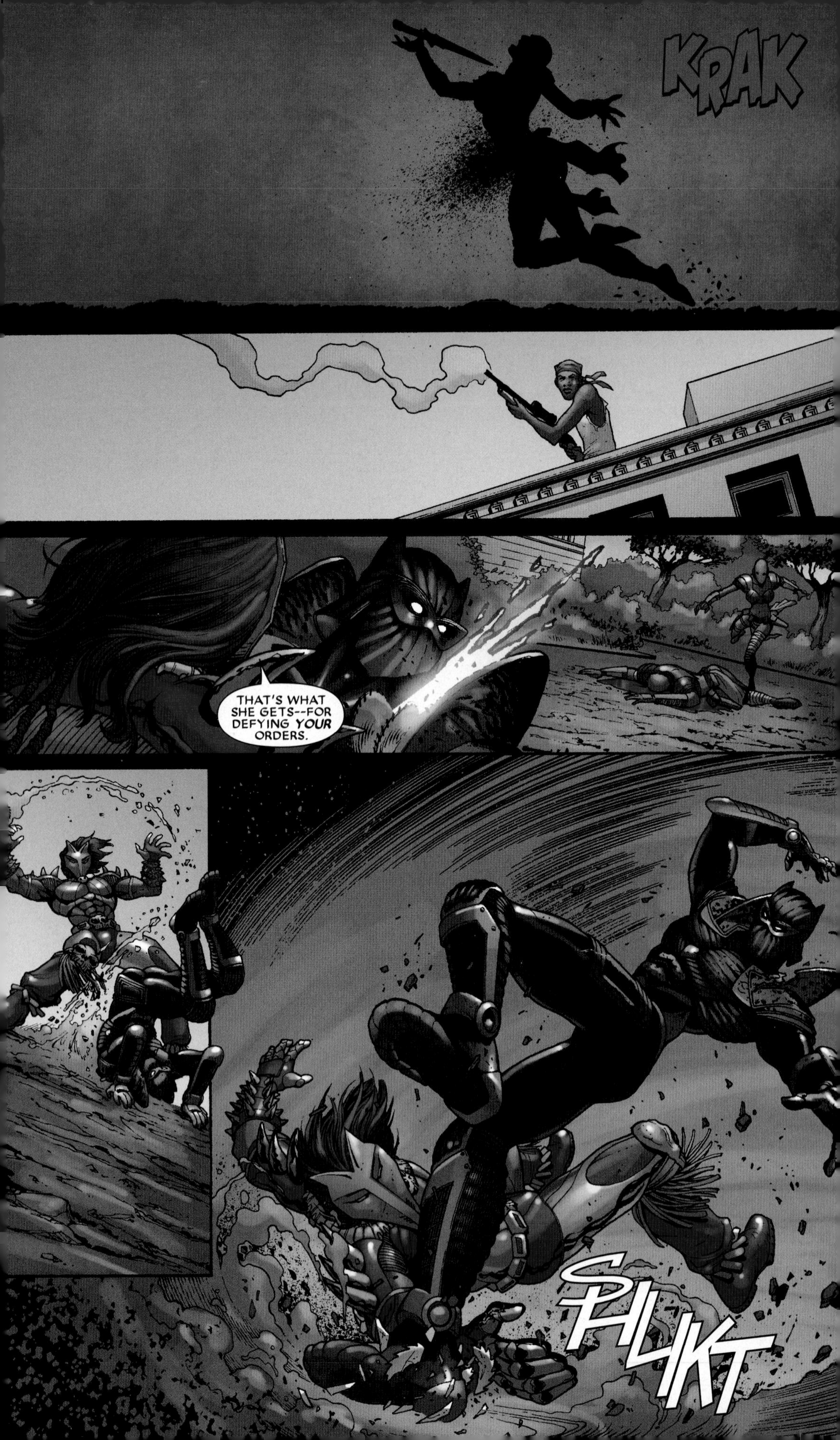
KRAK
THAT'S WHAT SHE GETS--FOR DEFYING YOUR ORDERS.
SHLIKT

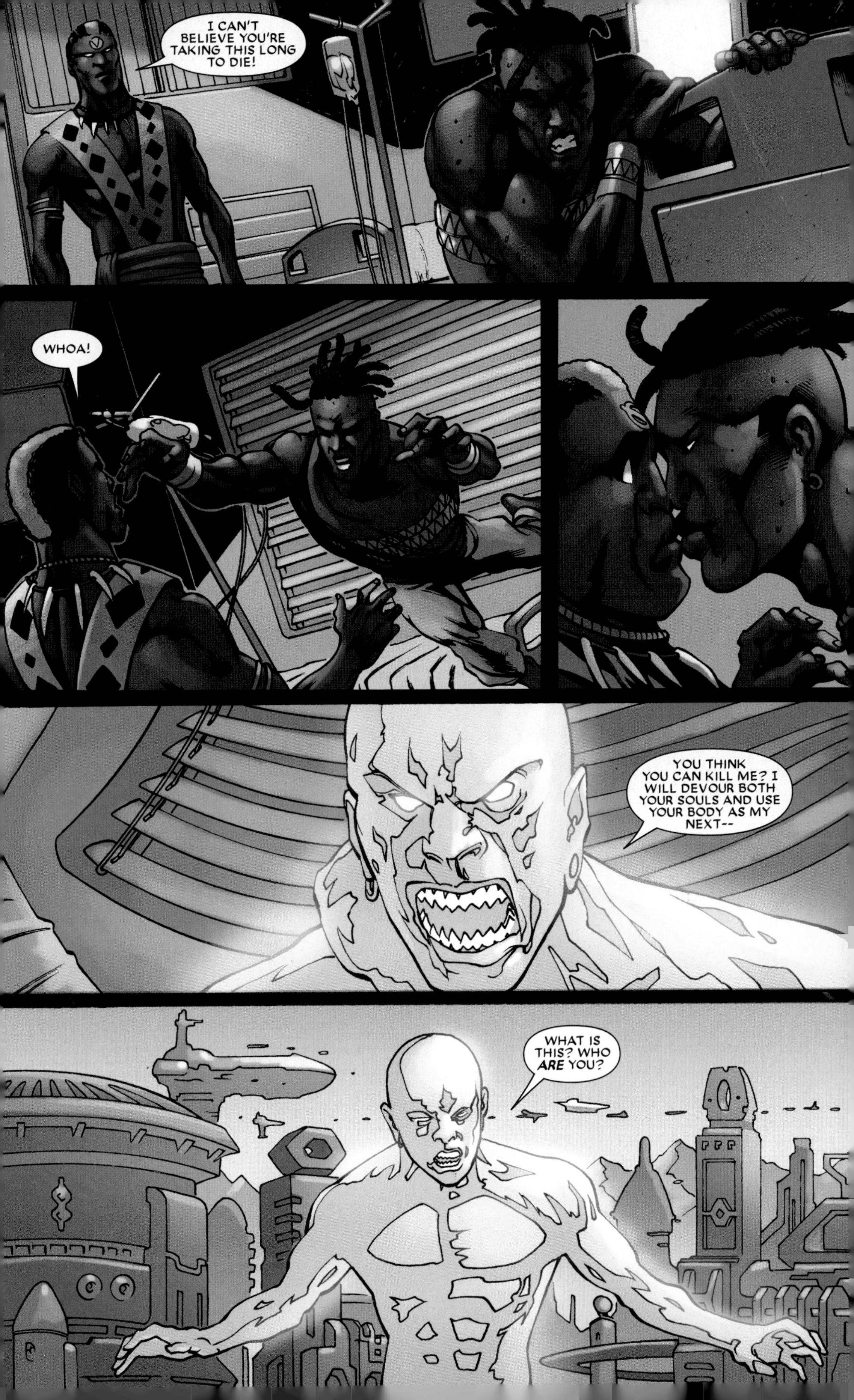
I CAN'T BELIEVE YOU'RE TAKING THIS LONG TO DIE!
WHOA!
YOU THINK YOU CAN KILL ME? I WILL DEVOUR BOTH YOUR SOULS AND USE YOUR BODY AS MY NEXT--
WHAT IS THIS? WHO *ARE* YOU?

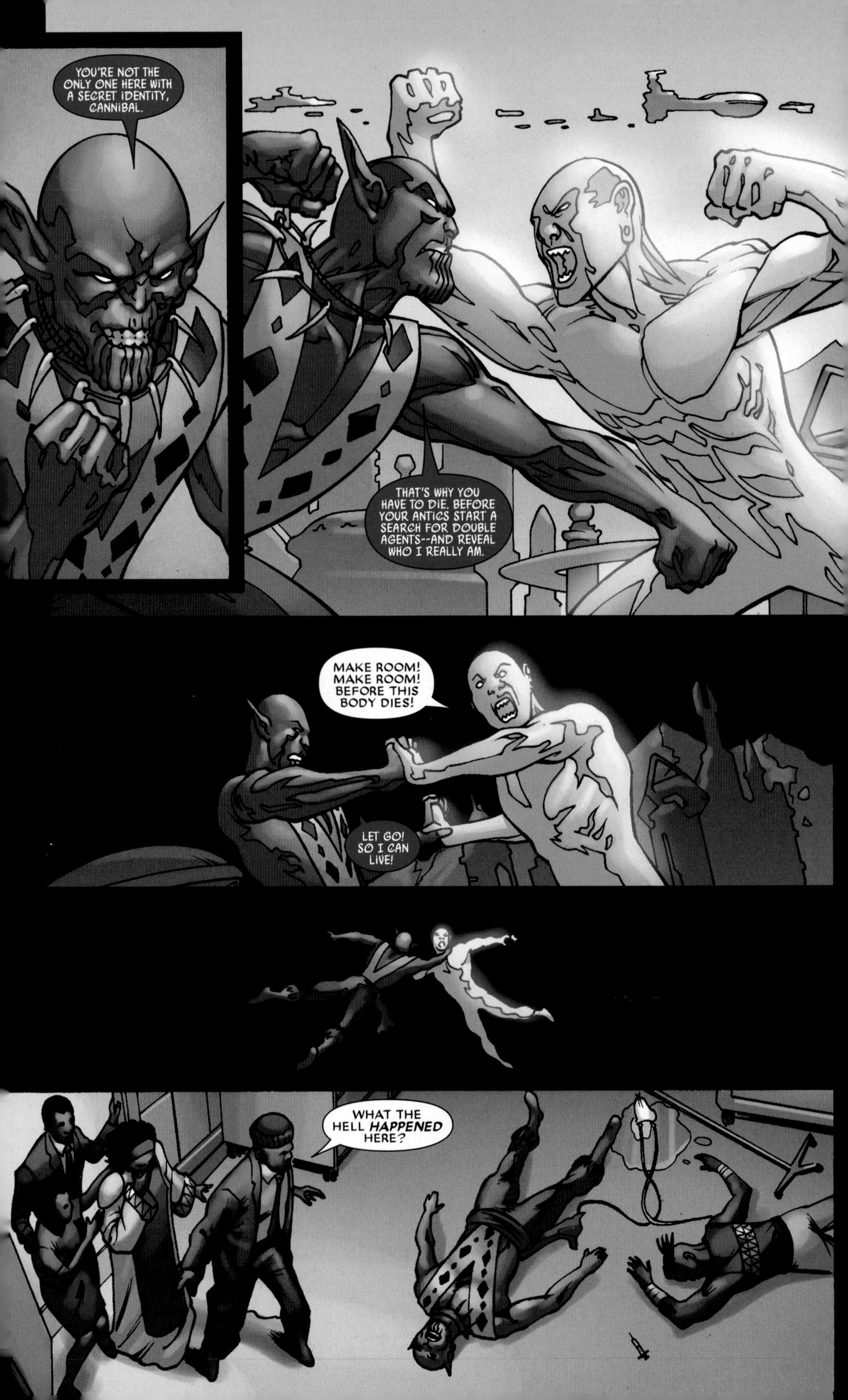
YOU'RE NOT THE ONLY ONE HERE WITH A SECRET IDENTITY, CANNIBAL.
THAT'S WHY YOU HAVE TO DIE. BEFORE YOUR ANTICS START A SEARCH FOR DOUBLE AGENTS--AND REVEAL WHO I REALLY AM.
MAKE ROOM! MAKE ROOM! BEFORE THIS BODY DIES!
LET GO! SO I CAN LIVE!
WHAT THE HELL HAPPENED HERE?

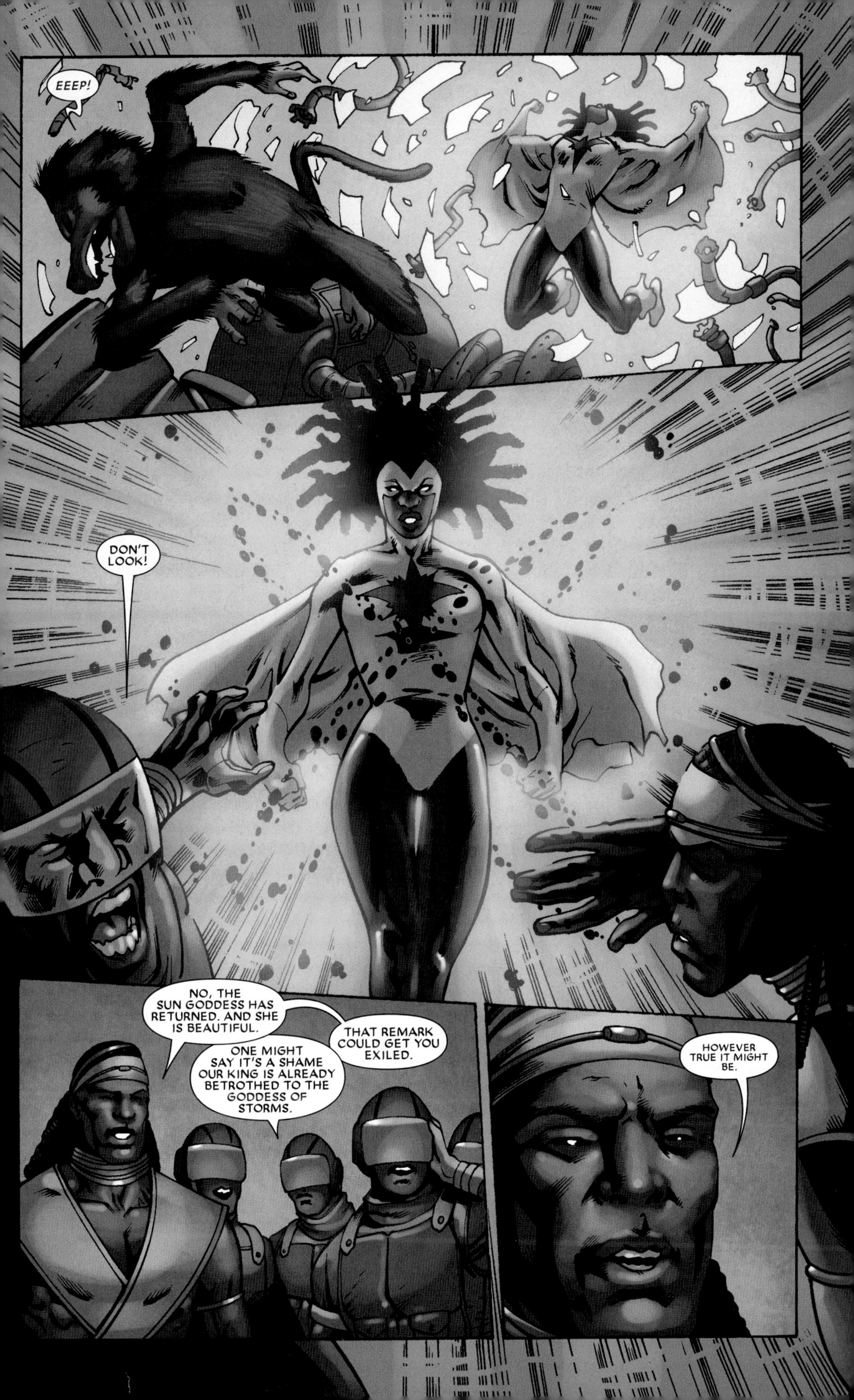

EEEP!
DON'T LOOK!
NO, THE SUN GODDESS HAS RETURNED. AND SHE IS BEAUTIFUL.
THAT REMARK COULD GET YOU EXILED.
ONE MIGHT SAY IT'S A SHAME OUR KING IS ALREADY BETROTHED TO THE GODDESS OF STORMS.
HOWEVER TRUE IT MIGHT BE.

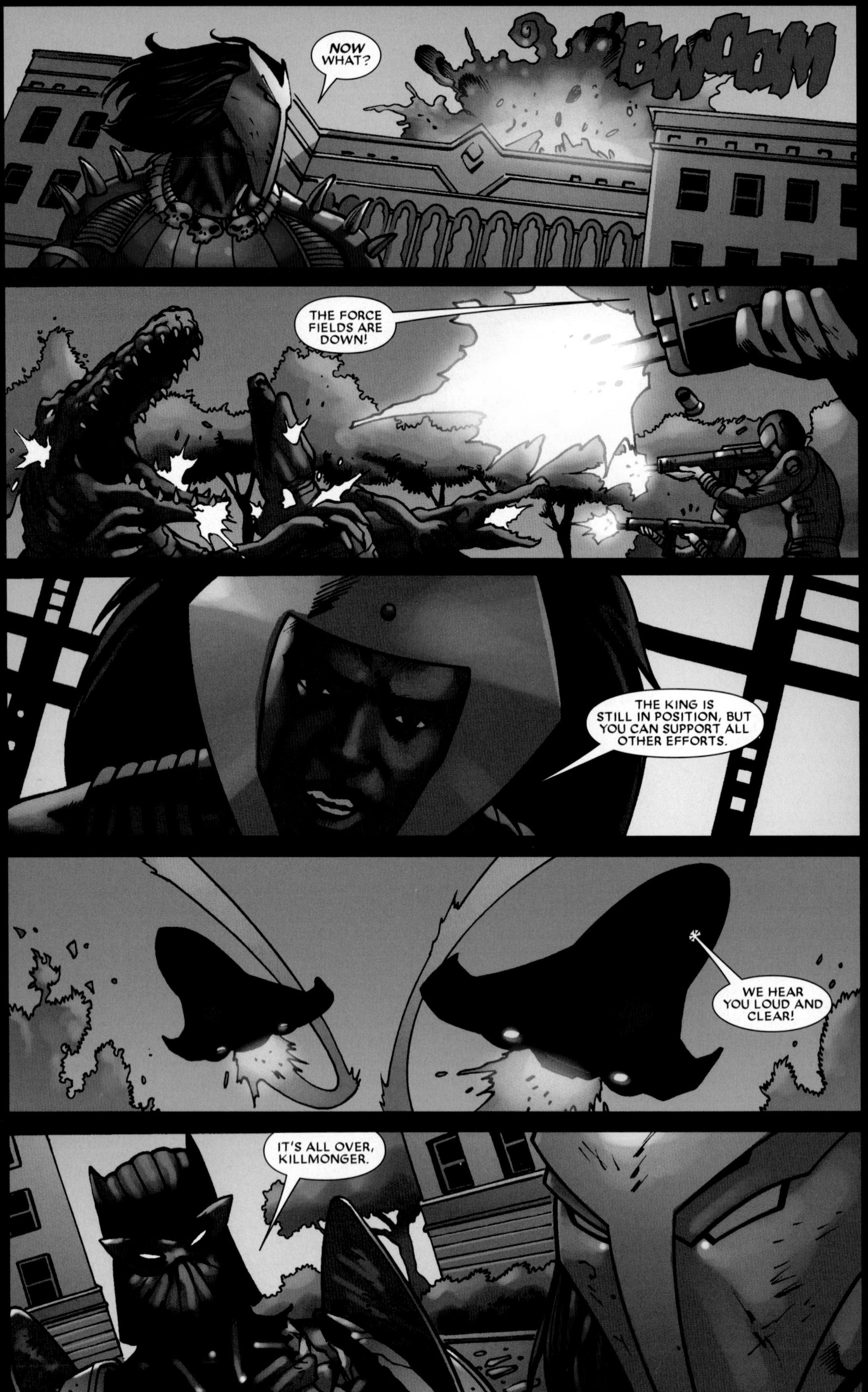
NOW WHAT?
BWOOM
THE FORCE FIELDS ARE DOWN!
THE KING IS STILL IN POSITION, BUT YOU CAN SUPPORT ALL OTHER EFFORTS.
WE HEAR YOU LOUD AND CLEAR!
IT'S ALL OVER, KILLMONGER.

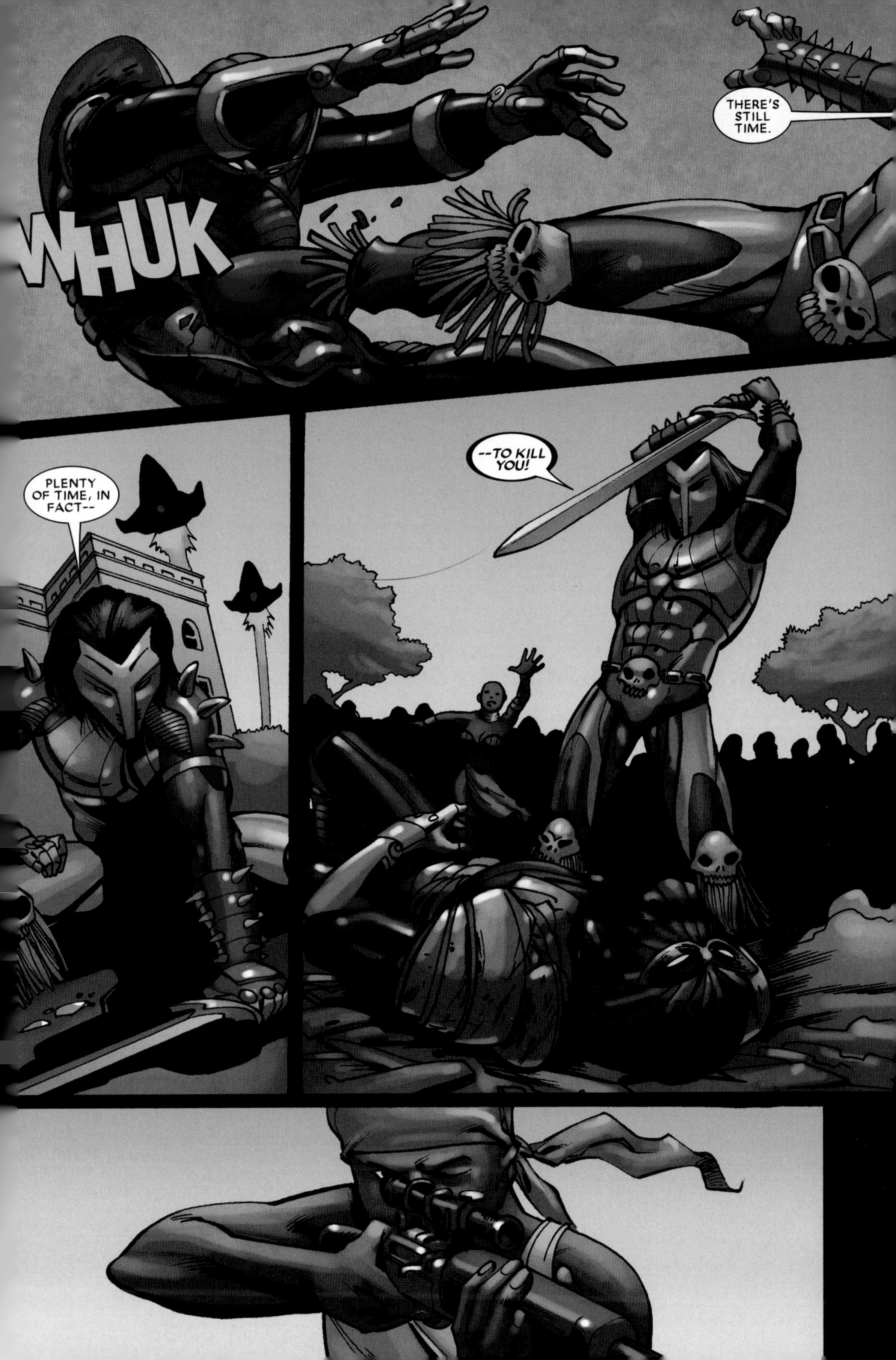
THERE'S STILL TIME.
WHUK
PLENTY OF TIME, IN FACT--
--TO KILL YOU!

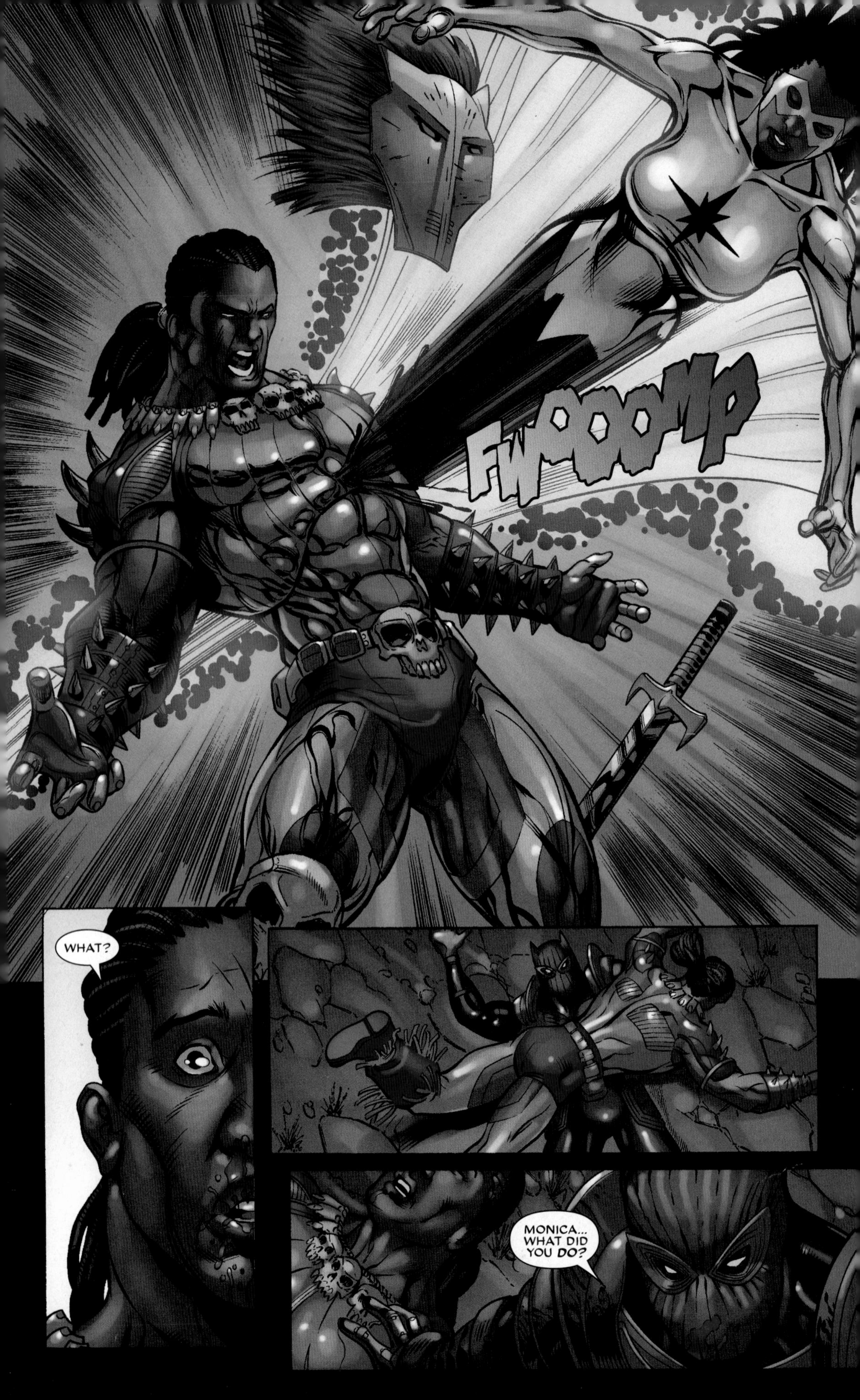
FWOOOMP
WHAT?
MONICA... WHAT DID YOU DO?

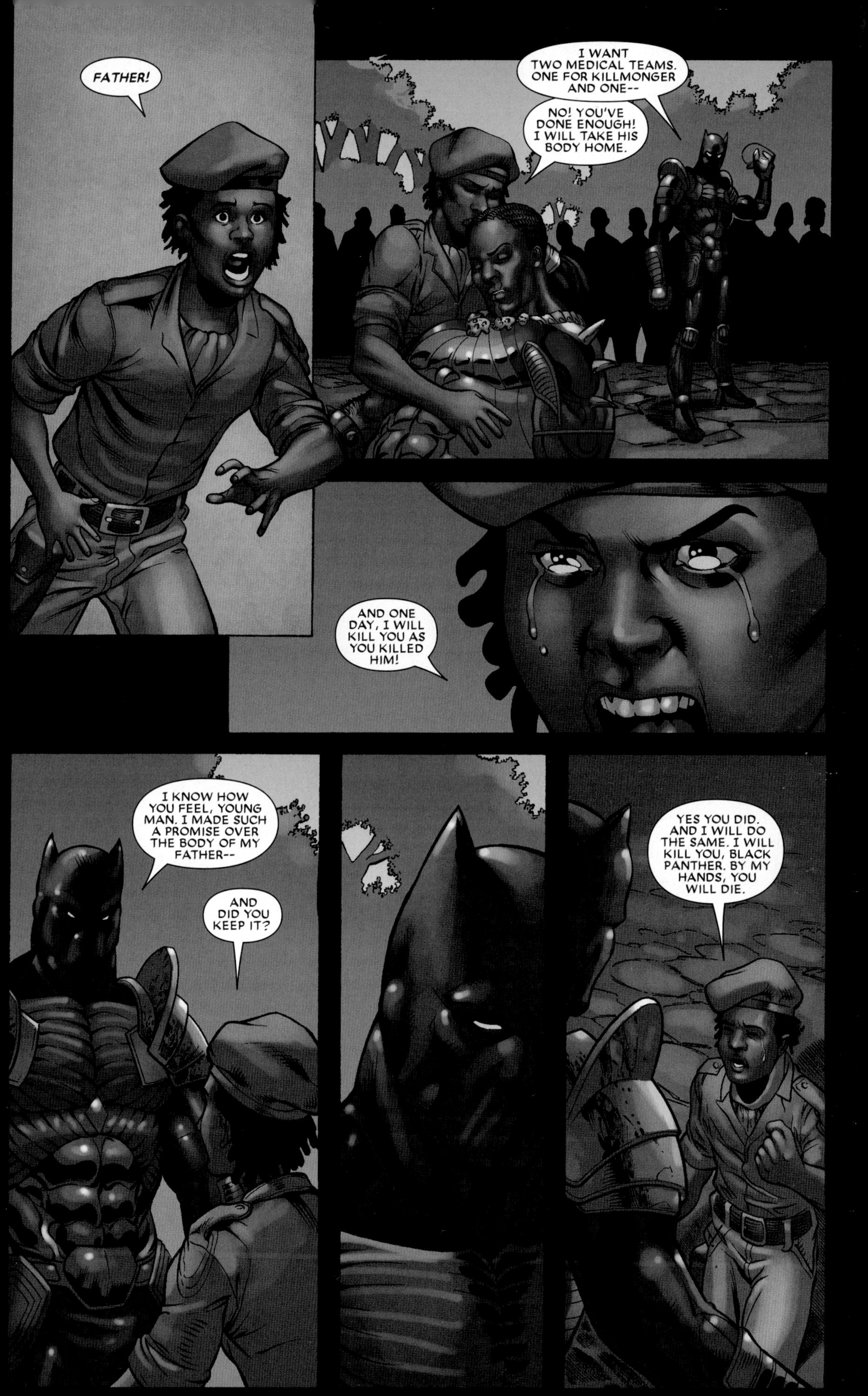
FATHER!
I WANT TWO MEDICAL TEAMS. ONE FOR KILLMONGER AND ONE--
NO! YOU'VE DONE ENOUGH! I WILL TAKE HIS BODY HOME.
AND ONE DAY, I WILL KILL YOU AS YOU KILLED HIM!
I KNOW HOW YOU FEEL, YOUNG MAN. I MADE SUCH A PROMISE OVER THE BODY OF MY FATHER--
AND DID YOU KEEP IT?
YES YOU DID. AND I WILL DO THE SAME. I WILL KILL YOU, BLACK PANTHER. BY MY HANDS, YOU WILL DIE.

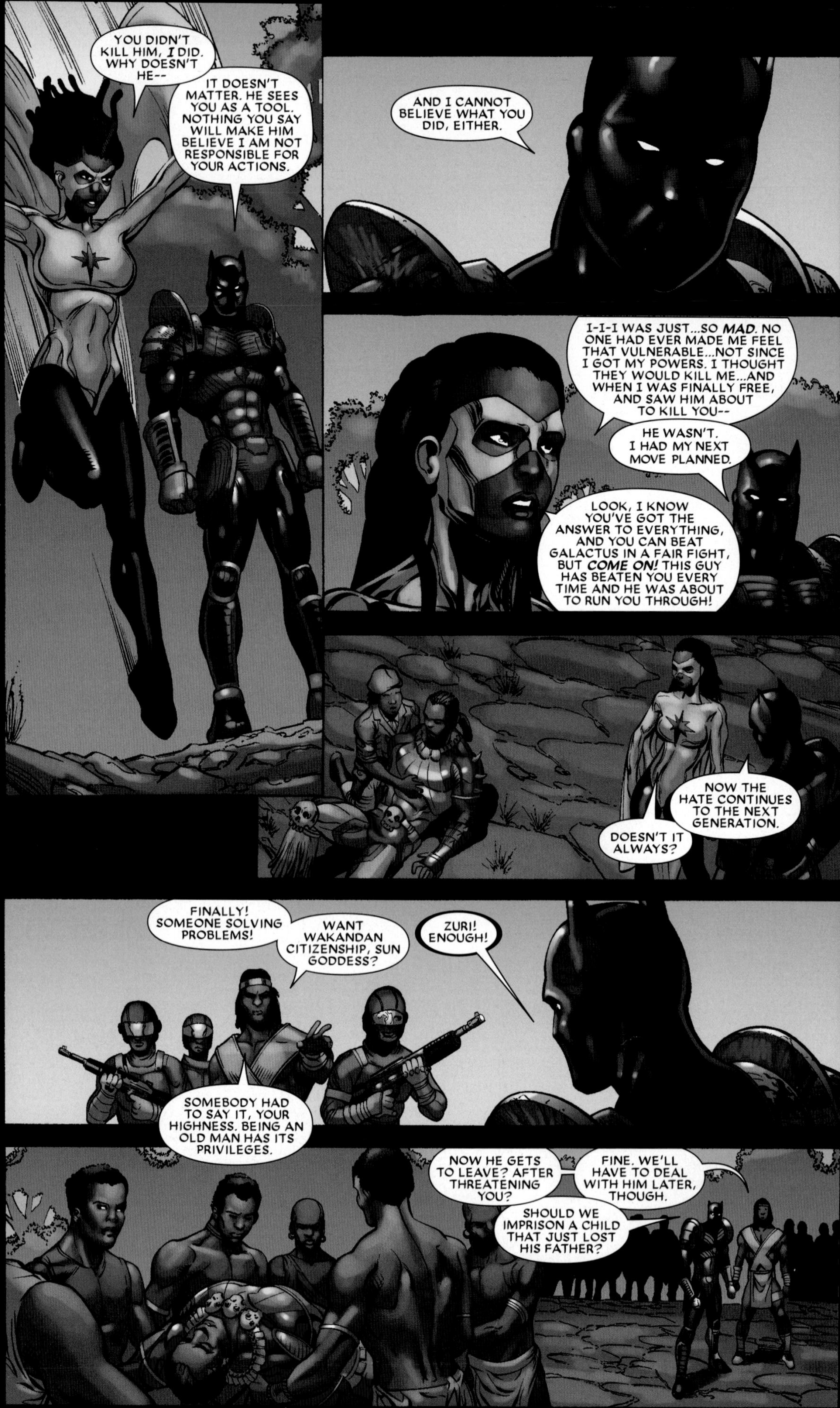
YOU DIDN'T KILL HIM, I DID. WHY DOESN'T HE--
IT DOESN'T MATTER. HE SEES YOU AS A TOOL. NOTHING YOU SAY WILL MAKE HIM BELIEVE I AM NOT RESPONSIBLE FOR YOUR ACTIONS.
AND I CANNOT BELIEVE WHAT YOU DID, EITHER.
I-I-I WAS JUST...SO MAD. NO ONE HAD EVER MADE ME FEEL THAT VULNERABLE...NOT SINCE I GOT MY POWERS. I THOUGHT THEY WOULD KILL ME...AND WHEN I WAS FINALLY FREE, AND SAW HIM ABOUT TO KILL YOU--
HE WASN'T. I HAD MY NEXT MOVE PLANNED.
LOOK, I KNOW YOU'VE GOT THE ANSWER TO EVERYTHING, AND YOU CAN BEAT GALACTUS IN A FAIR FIGHT, BUT COME ON! THIS GUY HAS BEATEN YOU EVERY TIME AND HE WAS ABOUT TO RUN YOU THROUGH!
NOW THE HATE CONTINUES TO THE NEXT GENERATION.
DOESN'T IT ALWAYS?
FINALLY! SOMEONE SOLVING PROBLEMS!
WANT WAKANDAN CITIZENSHIP, SUN GODDESS?
ZURI! ENOUGH!
SOMEBODY HAD TO SAY IT, YOUR HIGHNESS. BEING AN OLD MAN HAS ITS PRIVILEGES.
NOW HE GETS TO LEAVE? AFTER THREATENING YOU?
FINE. WE'LL HAVE TO DEAL WITH HIM LATER, THOUGH.
SHOULD WE IMPRISON A CHILD THAT JUST LOST HIS FATHER?

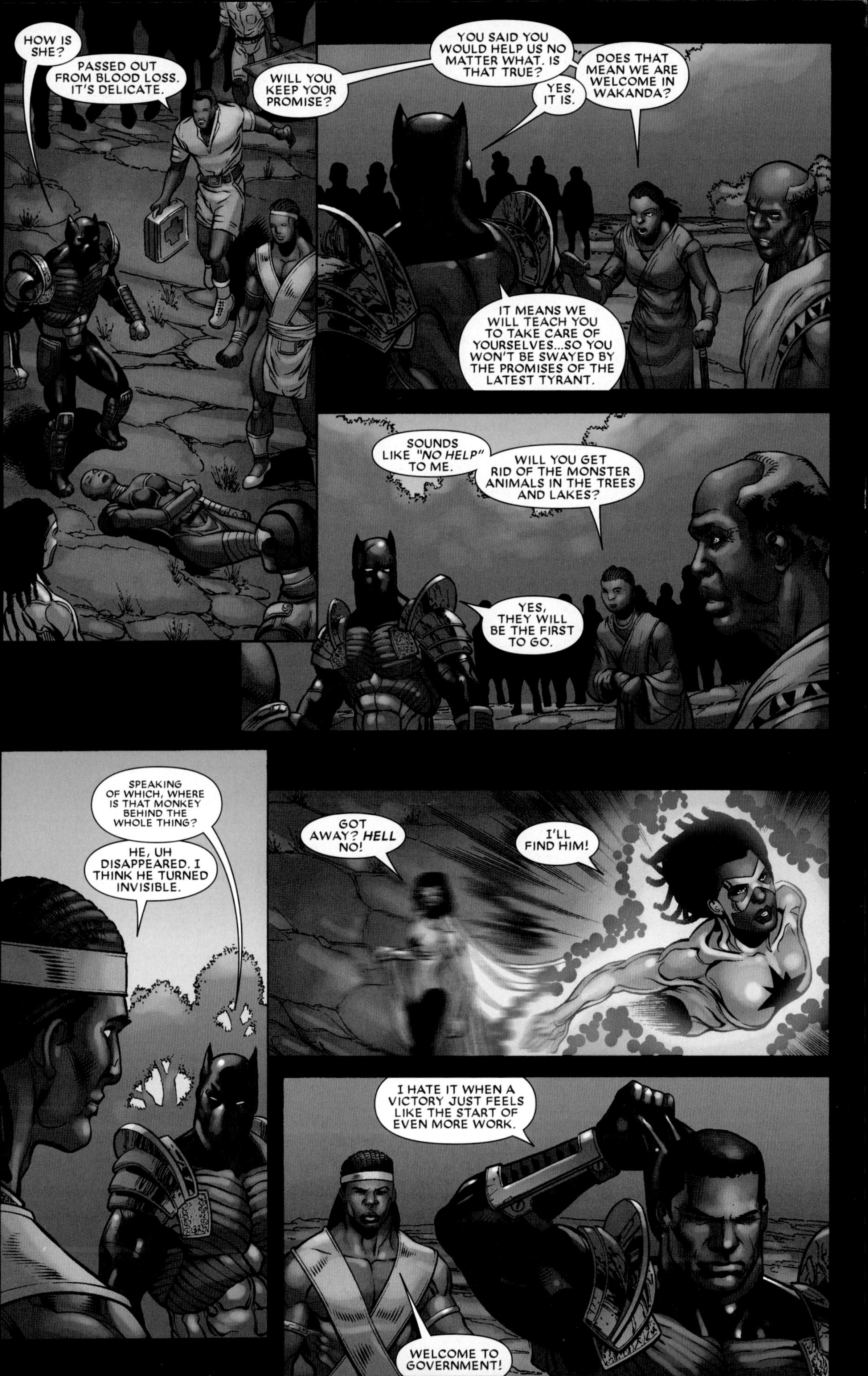
HOW IS SHE?
PASSED OUT FROM BLOOD LOSS. IT'S DELICATE.
WILL YOU KEEP YOUR PROMISE?
YOU SAID YOU WOULD HELP US NO MATTER WHAT. IS THAT TRUE?
YES, IT IS.
DOES THAT MEAN WE ARE WELCOME IN WAKANDA?
IT MEANS WE WILL TEACH YOU TO TAKE CARE OF YOURSELVES...SO YOU WON'T BE SWAYED BY THE PROMISES OF THE LATEST TYRANT.
SOUNDS LIKE *"NO HELP"* TO ME.
WILL YOU GET RID OF THE MONSTER ANIMALS IN THE TREES AND LAKES?
YES, THEY WILL BE THE FIRST TO GO.
SPEAKING OF WHICH, WHERE IS THAT MONKEY BEHIND THE WHOLE THING?
HE, UH DISAPPEARED. I THINK HE TURNED INVISIBLE.
GOT AWAY? ***HELL*** NO!
I'LL FIND HIM!
I HATE IT WHEN A VICTORY JUST FEELS LIKE THE START OF EVEN MORE WORK.
WELCOME TO GOVERNMENT!

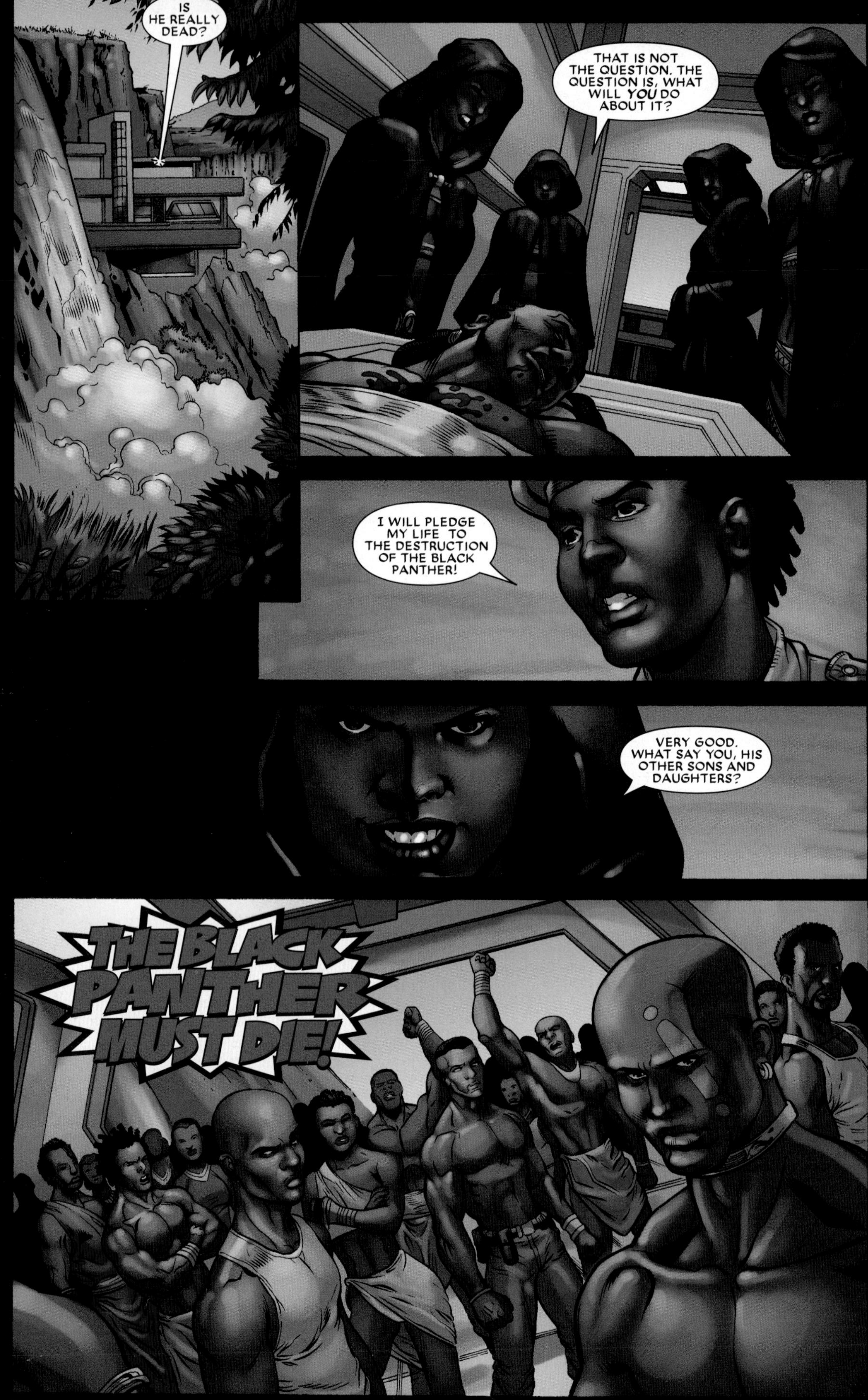
IS HE REALLY DEAD?
THAT IS NOT THE QUESTION. THE QUESTION IS, WHAT WILL YOU DO ABOUT IT?
I WILL PLEDGE MY LIFE TO THE DESTRUCTION OF THE BLACK PANTHER!
VERY GOOD. WHAT SAY YOU, HIS OTHER SONS AND DAUGHTERS?
THE BLACK PANTHER MUST DIE!

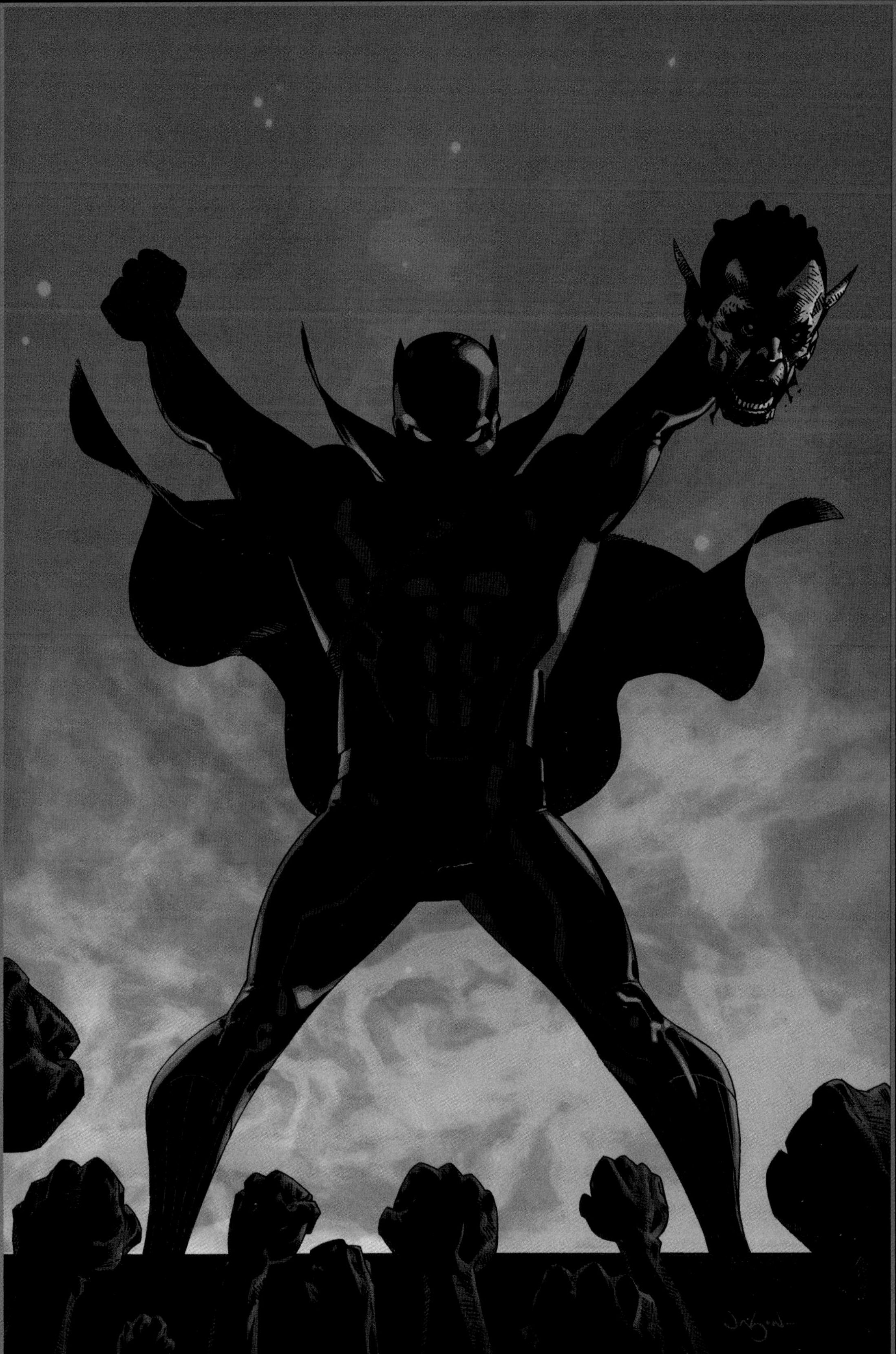

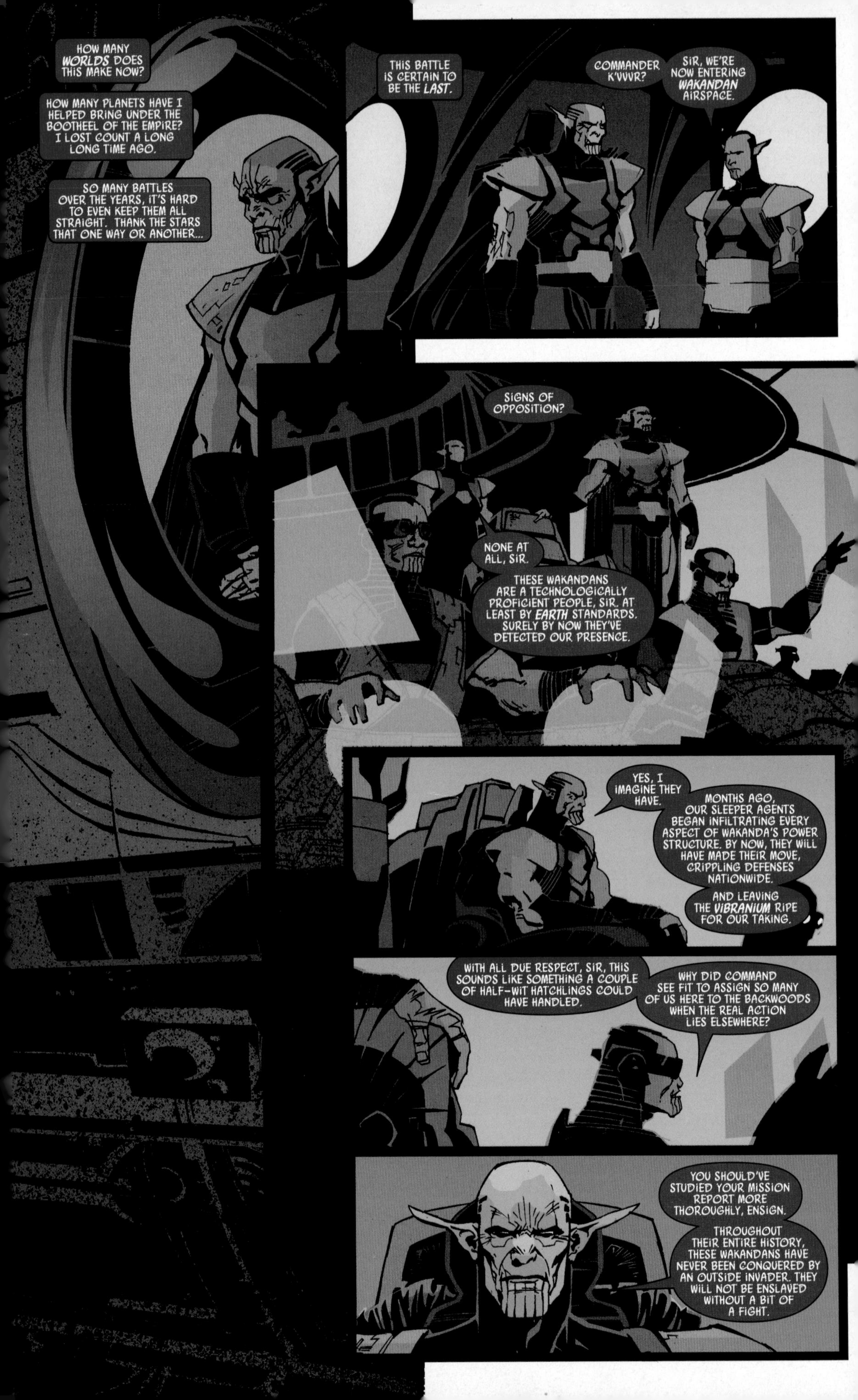
HOW MANY WORLDS DOES THIS MAKE NOW?
HOW MANY PLANETS HAVE I HELPED BRING UNDER THE BOOTHEEL OF THE EMPIRE? I LOST COUNT A LONG LONG TIME AGO.
SO MANY BATTLES OVER THE YEARS, IT'S HARD TO EVEN KEEP THEM ALL STRAIGHT. THANK THE STARS THAT ONE WAY OR ANOTHER...
THIS BATTLE IS CERTAIN TO BE THE LAST.
COMMANDER K'VVVR?
SIR, WE'RE NOW ENTERING WAKANDAN AIRSPACE.
SIGNS OF OPPOSITION?
NONE AT ALL, SIR.
THESE WAKANDANS ARE A TECHNOLOGICALLY PROFICIENT PEOPLE, SIR. AT LEAST BY EARTH STANDARDS. SURELY BY NOW THEY'VE DETECTED OUR PRESENCE.
YES, I IMAGINE THEY HAVE.
MONTHS AGO, OUR SLEEPER AGENTS BEGAN INFILTRATING EVERY ASPECT OF WAKANDA'S POWER STRUCTURE. BY NOW, THEY WILL HAVE MADE THEIR MOVE, CRIPPLING DEFENSES NATIONWIDE.
AND LEAVING THE VIBRANIUM RIPE FOR OUR TAKING.
WITH ALL DUE RESPECT, SIR, THIS SOUNDS LIKE SOMETHING A COUPLE OF HALF-WIT HATCHLINGS COULD HAVE HANDLED.
WHY DID COMMAND SEE FIT TO ASSIGN SO MANY OF US HERE TO THE BACKWOODS WHEN THE REAL ACTION LIES ELSEWHERE?
YOU SHOULD'VE STUDIED YOUR MISSION REPORT MORE THOROUGHLY, ENSIGN.
THROUGHOUT THEIR ENTIRE HISTORY, THESE WAKANDANS HAVE NEVER BEEN CONQUERED BY AN OUTSIDE INVADER. THEY WILL NOT BE ENSLAVED WITHOUT A BIT OF A FIGHT.

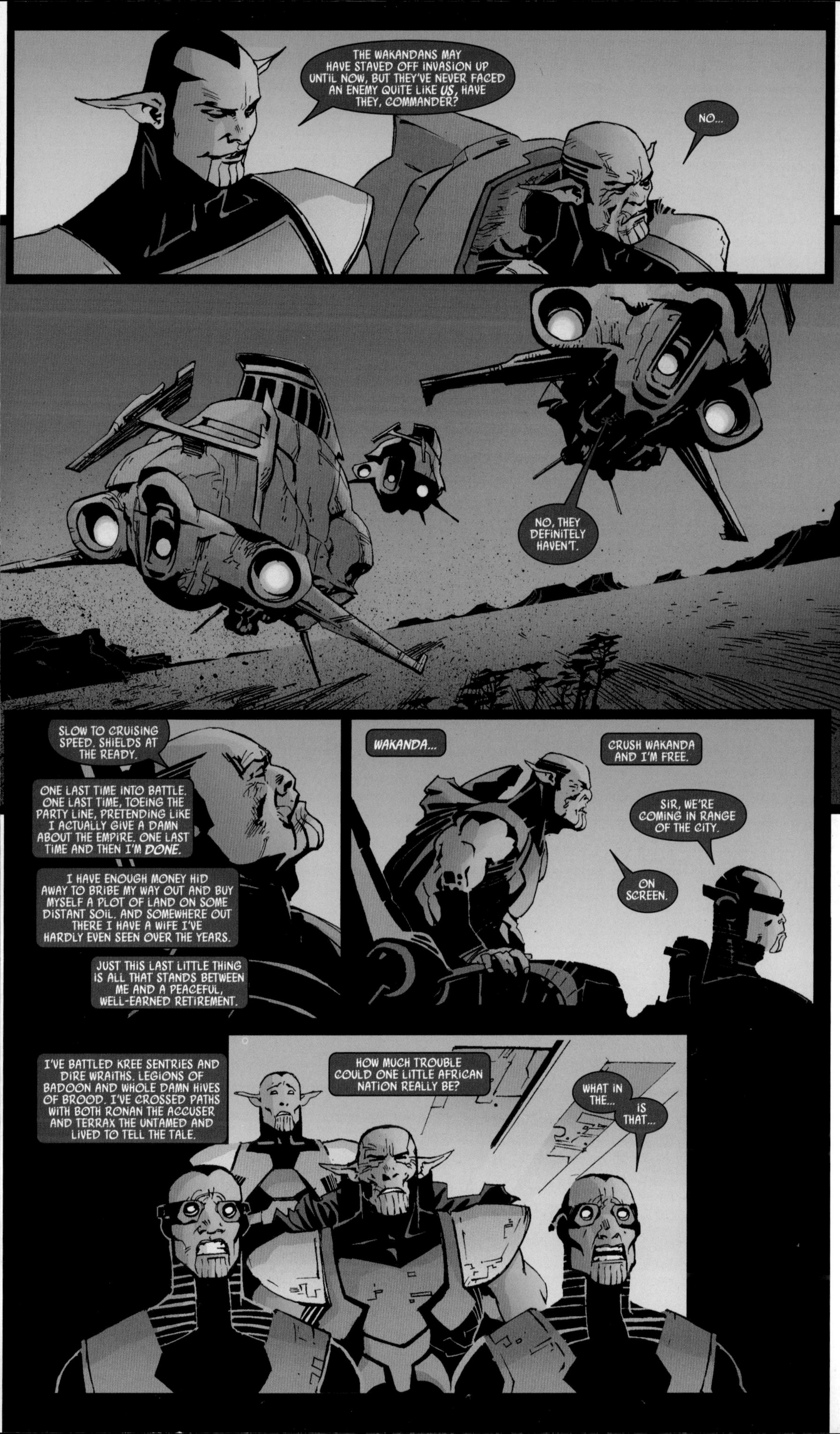
THE WAKANDANS MAY HAVE STAVED OFF INVASION UP UNTIL NOW, BUT THEY'VE NEVER FACED AN ENEMY QUITE LIKE US, HAVE THEY, COMMANDER?
NO...
NO, THEY DEFINITELY HAVEN'T.
SLOW TO CRUISING SPEED. SHIELDS AT THE READY.
ONE LAST TIME INTO BATTLE. ONE LAST TIME, TOEING THE PARTY LINE, PRETENDING LIKE I ACTUALLY GIVE A DAMN ABOUT THE EMPIRE. ONE LAST TIME AND THEN I'M DONE.
I HAVE ENOUGH MONEY HID AWAY TO BRIBE MY WAY OUT AND BUY MYSELF A PLOT OF LAND ON SOME DISTANT SOIL. AND SOMEWHERE OUT THERE I HAVE A WIFE I'VE HARDLY EVEN SEEN OVER THE YEARS.
JUST THIS LAST LITTLE THING IS ALL THAT STANDS BETWEEN ME AND A PEACEFUL, WELL-EARNED RETIREMENT.
WAKANDA...
CRUSH WAKANDA AND I'M FREE.
SIR, WE'RE COMING IN RANGE OF THE CITY.
ON SCREEN.
I'VE BATTLED KREE SENTRIES AND DIRE WRAITHS. LEGIONS OF BADOON AND WHOLE DAMN HIVES OF BROOD. I'VE CROSSED PATHS WITH BOTH RONAN THE ACCUSER AND TERRAX THE UNTAMED AND LIVED TO TELL THE TALE.
HOW MUCH TROUBLE COULD ONE LITTLE AFRICAN NATION REALLY BE?
WHAT IN THE... IS THAT...

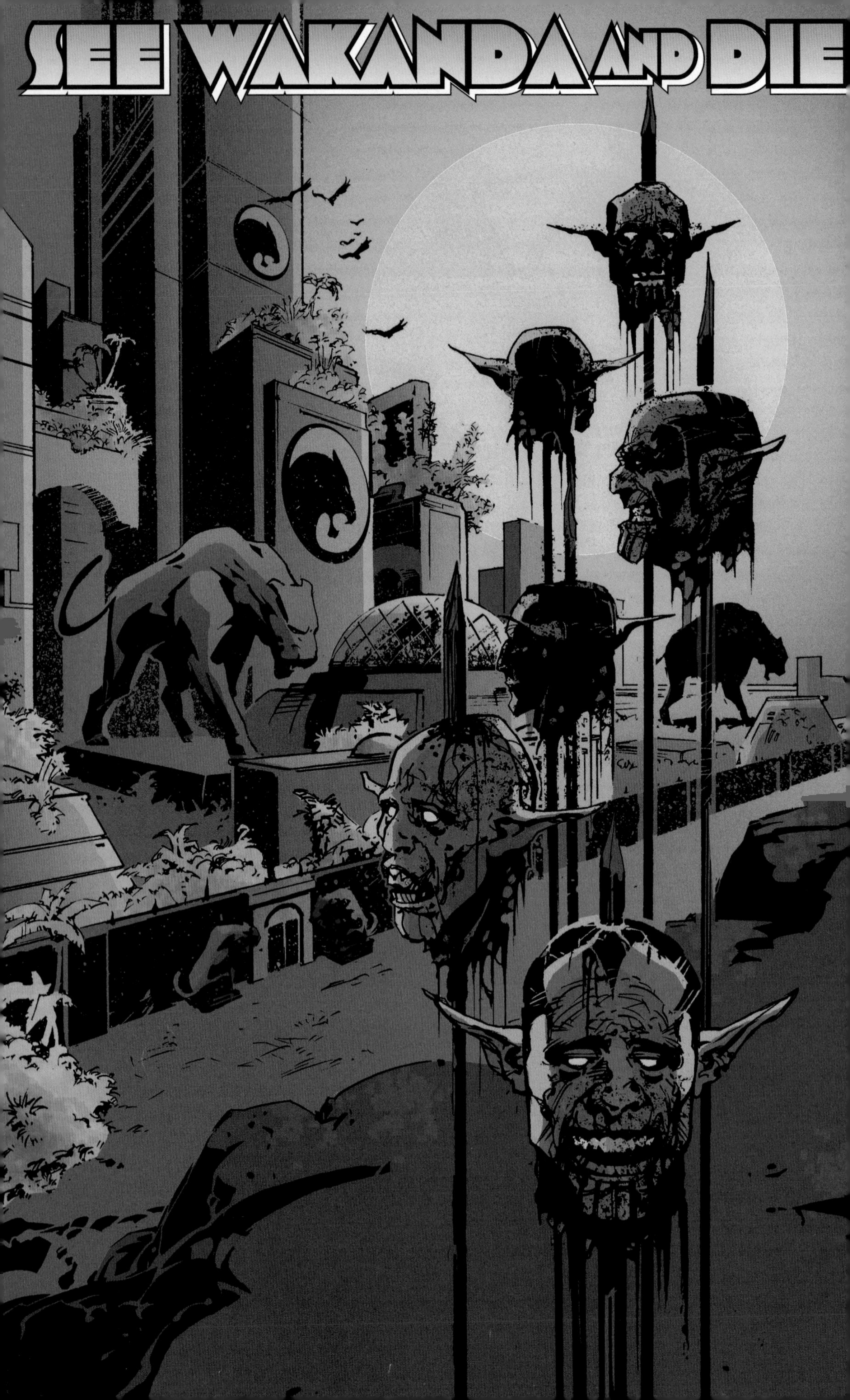
SEE WAKANDA AND DIE

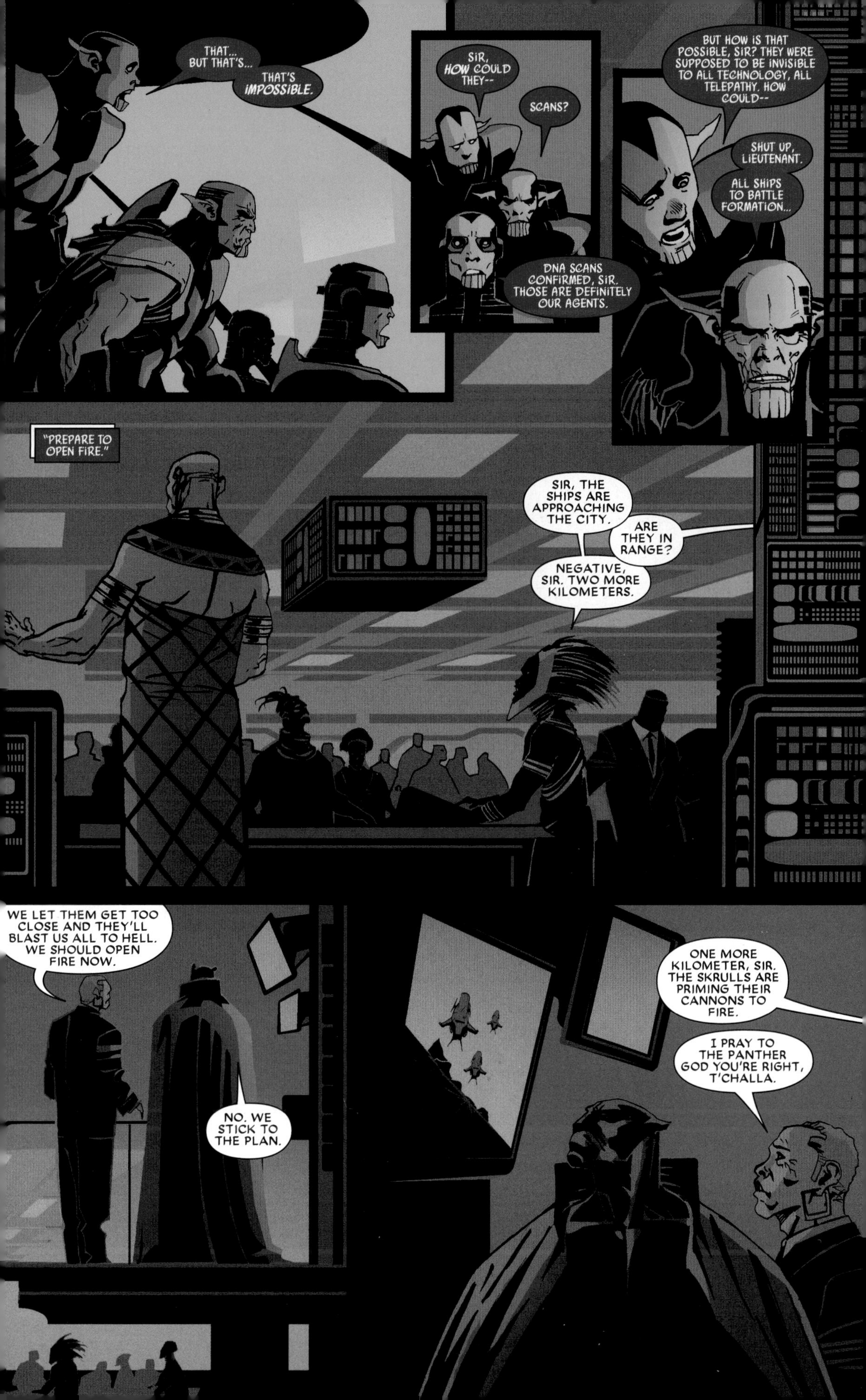
THAT... BUT THAT'S...
THAT'S IMPOSSIBLE.
SIR, HOW COULD THEY--
SCANS?
DNA SCANS CONFIRMED, SIR. THOSE ARE DEFINITELY OUR AGENTS.
BUT HOW IS THAT POSSIBLE, SIR? THEY WERE SUPPOSED TO BE INVISIBLE TO ALL TECHNOLOGY, ALL TELEPATHY. HOW COULD--
SHUT UP, LIEUTENANT.
ALL SHIPS TO BATTLE FORMATION...
"PREPARE TO OPEN FIRE."
SIR, THE SHIPS ARE APPROACHING THE CITY.
ARE THEY IN RANGE?
NEGATIVE, SIR. TWO MORE KILOMETERS.
WE LET THEM GET TOO CLOSE AND THEY'LL BLAST US ALL TO HELL. WE SHOULD OPEN FIRE NOW.
NO. WE STICK TO THE PLAN.
ONE MORE KILOMETER, SIR. THE SKRULLS ARE PRIMING THEIR CANNONS TO FIRE.
I PRAY TO THE PANTHER GOD YOU'RE RIGHT, T'CHALLA.

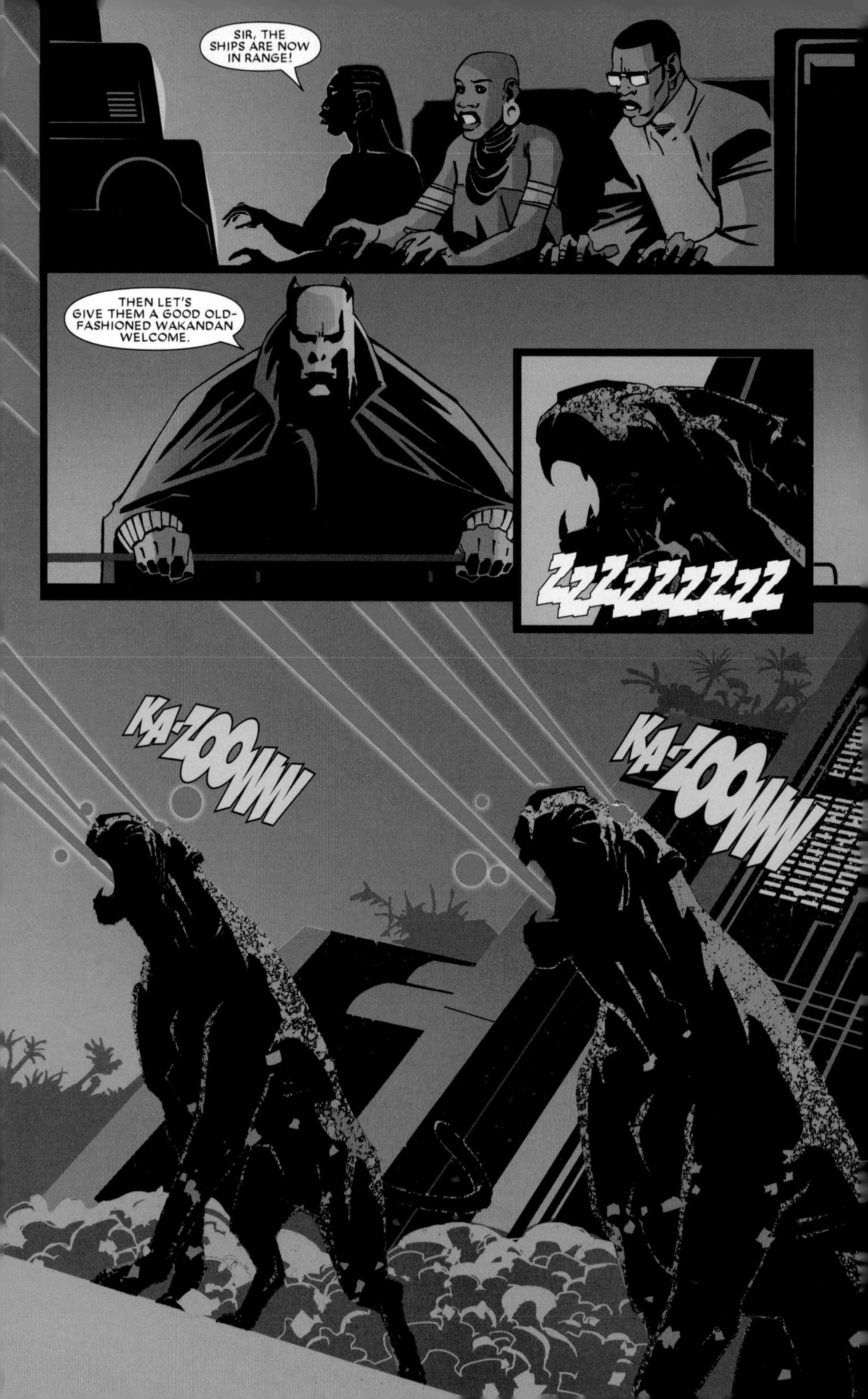
SIR, THE SHIPS ARE NOW IN RANGE!
THEN LET'S GIVE THEM A GOOD OLD-FASHIONED WAKANDAN WELCOME.
ZZZZZZZZZZ
KA-ZOOMM
KA-ZOOMM

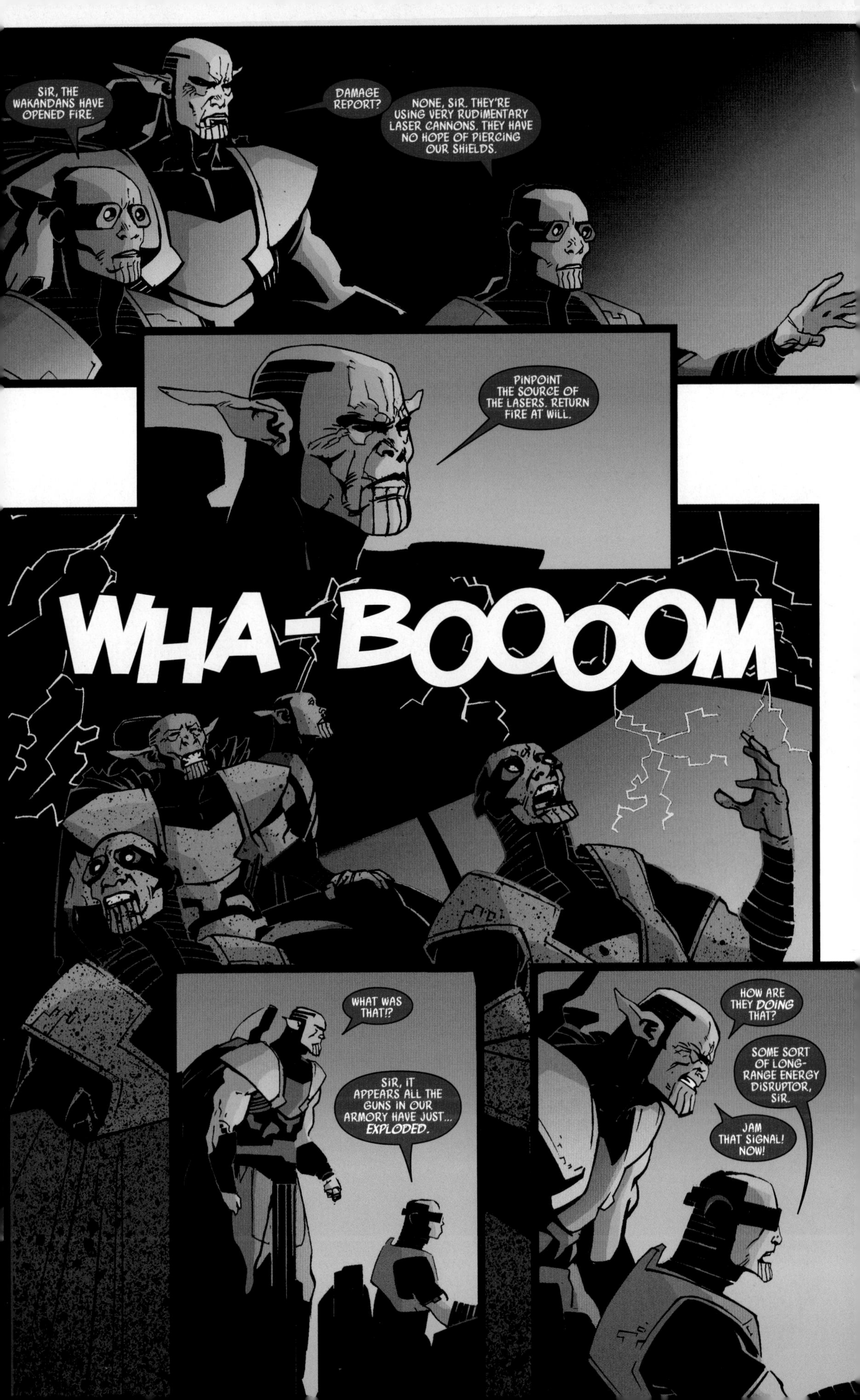
SiR, THE WAKANDANS HAVE OPENED FiRE.
DAMAGE REPORT?
NONE, SiR. THEY'RE USiNG VERY RUDiMENTARY LASER CANNONS. THEY HAVE NO HOPE OF PiERCiNG OUR SHiELDS.
PiNPOiNT THE SOURCE OF THE LASERS. RETURN FiRE AT WiLL.
WHA-BOOOOOM
WHAT WAS THAT!?
SiR, iT APPEARS ALL THE GUNS iN OUR ARMORY HAVE JUST... *EXPLODED*.
HOW ARE THEY *DOING* THAT?
SOME SORT OF LONG-RANGE ENERGY DiSRUPTOR, SiR.
JAM THAT SIGNAL! NOW!

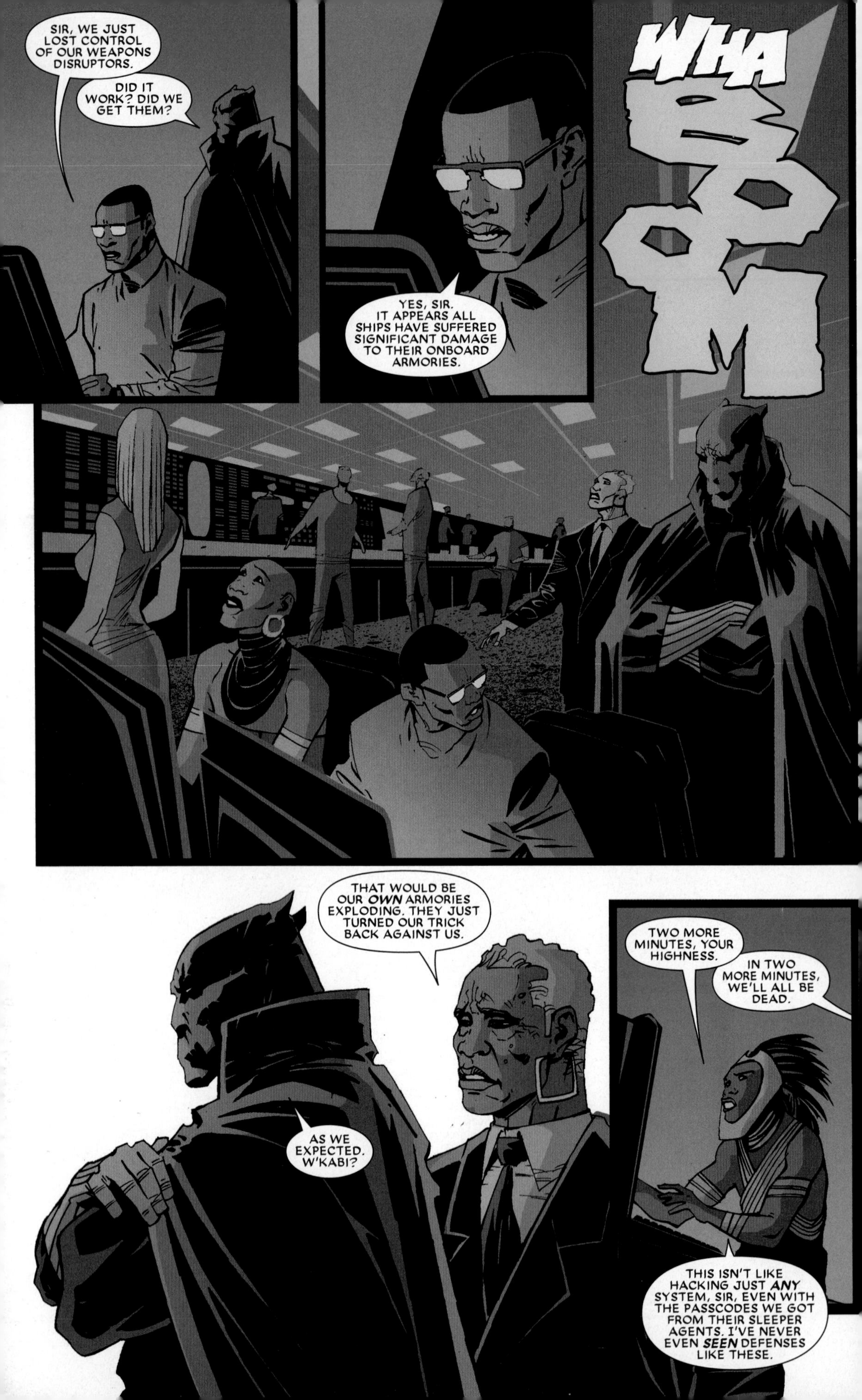
SIR, WE JUST LOST CONTROL OF OUR WEAPONS DISRUPTORS.
DID IT WORK? DID WE GET THEM?
YES, SIR. IT APPEARS ALL SHIPS HAVE SUFFERED SIGNIFICANT DAMAGE TO THEIR ONBOARD ARMORIES.
WHA BOOM
THAT WOULD BE OUR OWN ARMORIES EXPLODING. THEY JUST TURNED OUR TRICK BACK AGAINST US.
AS WE EXPECTED. W'KABI?
TWO MORE MINUTES, YOUR HIGHNESS.
IN TWO MORE MINUTES, WE'LL ALL BE DEAD.
THIS ISN'T LIKE HACKING JUST ANY SYSTEM, SIR, EVEN WITH THE PASSCODES WE GOT FROM THEIR SLEEPER AGENTS. I'VE NEVER EVEN SEEN DEFENSES LIKE THESE.

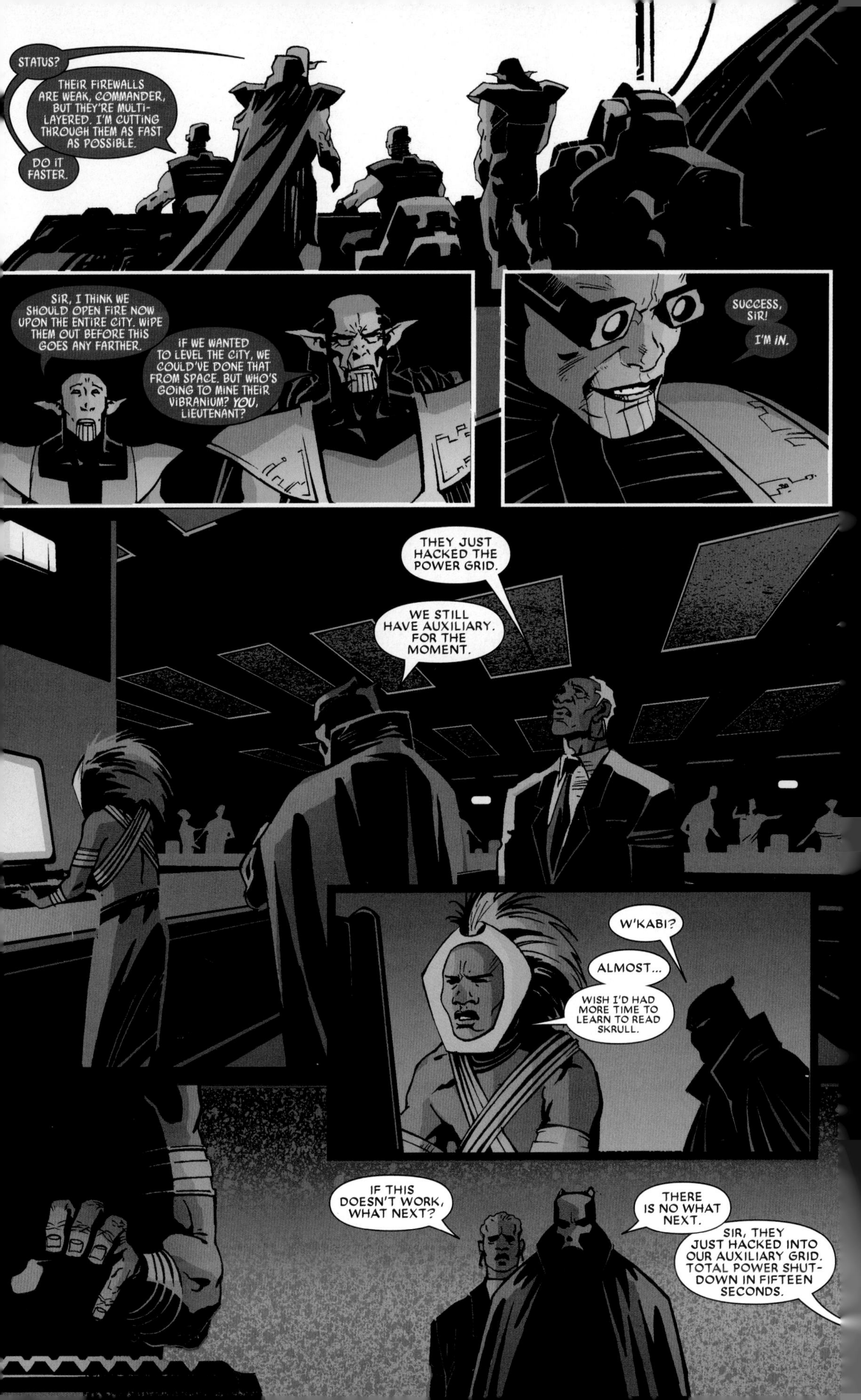
STATUS?
THEIR FIREWALLS ARE WEAK, COMMANDER, BUT THEY'RE MULTI-LAYERED. I'M CUTTING THROUGH THEM AS FAST AS POSSIBLE.
DO IT FASTER.
SIR, I THINK WE SHOULD OPEN FIRE NOW UPON THE ENTIRE CITY. WIPE THEM OUT BEFORE THIS GOES ANY FARTHER.
IF WE WANTED TO LEVEL THE CITY, WE COULD'VE DONE THAT FROM SPACE. BUT WHO'S GOING TO MINE THEIR VIBRANIUM? YOU, LIEUTENANT?
SUCCESS, SIR!
I'M IN.
THEY JUST HACKED THE POWER GRID.
WE STILL HAVE AUXILIARY. FOR THE MOMENT.
W'KABI?
ALMOST...
WISH I'D HAD MORE TIME TO LEARN TO READ SKRULL.
IF THIS DOESN'T WORK, WHAT NEXT?
THERE IS NO WHAT NEXT.
SIR, THEY JUST HACKED INTO OUR AUXILIARY GRID. TOTAL POWER SHUT-DOWN IN FIFTEEN SECONDS.

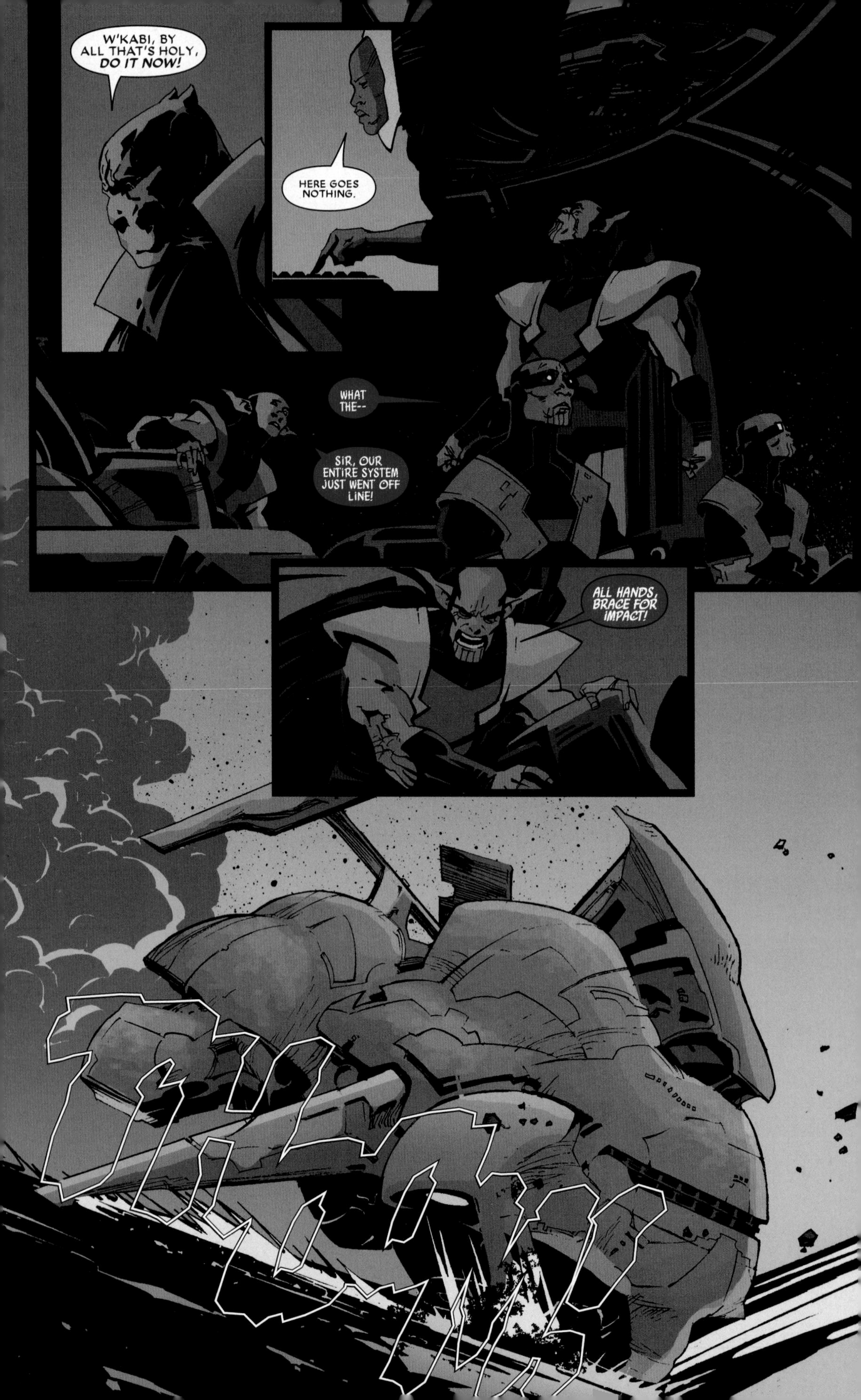
W'KABI, BY ALL THAT'S HOLY, *DO IT NOW!*
HERE GOES NOTHING.
WHAT THE--
SIR, OUR ENTIRE SYSTEM JUST WENT OFF LINE!
ALL HANDS, BRACE FOR IMPACT!

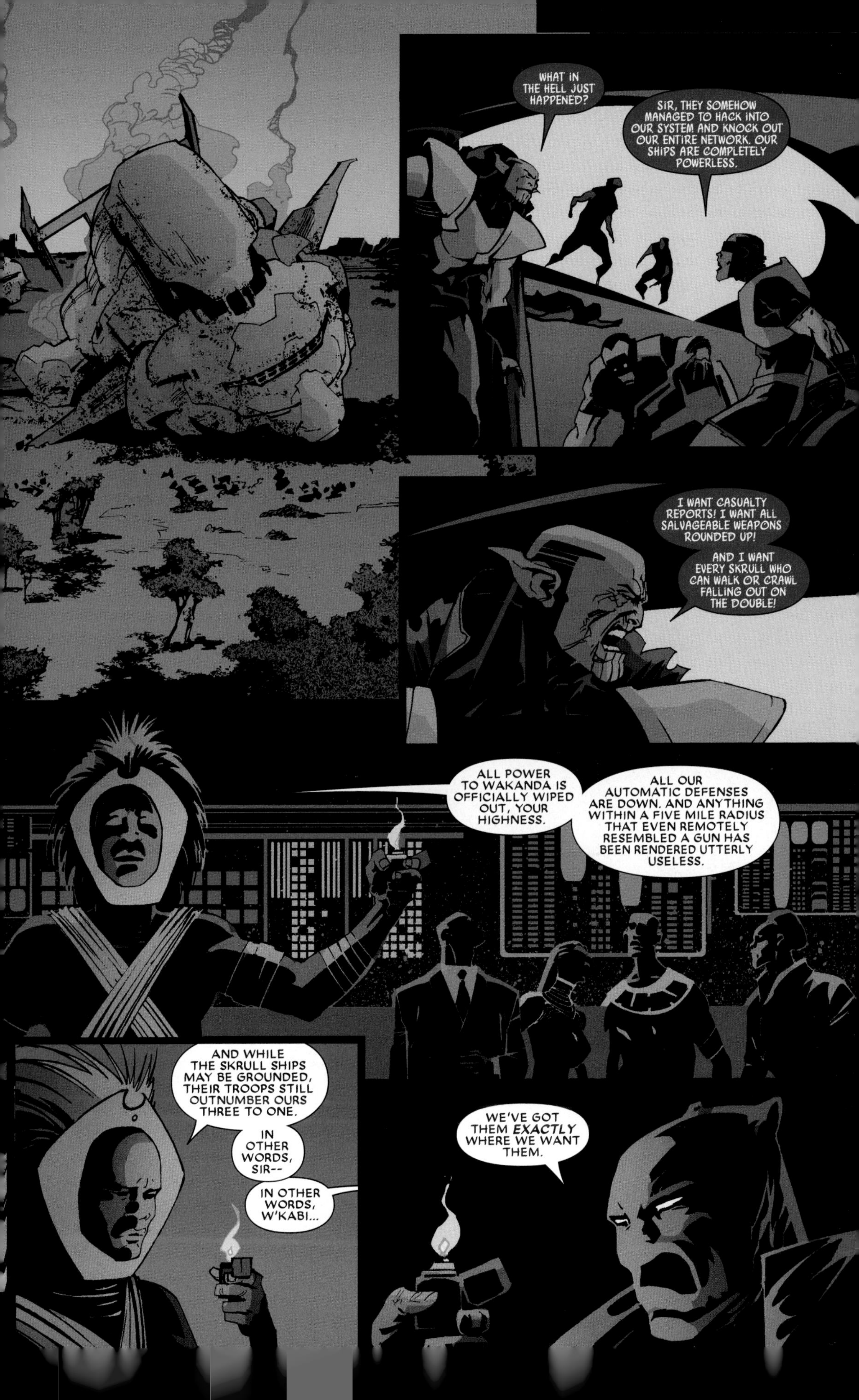
WHAT IN THE HELL JUST HAPPENED?
SIR, THEY SOMEHOW MANAGED TO HACK INTO OUR SYSTEM AND KNOCK OUT OUR ENTIRE NETWORK. OUR SHIPS ARE COMPLETELY POWERLESS.
I WANT CASUALTY REPORTS! I WANT ALL SALVAGEABLE WEAPONS ROUNDED UP!
AND I WANT EVERY SKRULL WHO CAN WALK OR CRAWL FALLING OUT ON THE DOUBLE!
ALL POWER TO WAKANDA IS OFFICIALLY WIPED OUT, YOUR HIGHNESS.
ALL OUR AUTOMATIC DEFENSES ARE DOWN. AND ANYTHING WITHIN A FIVE MILE RADIUS THAT EVEN REMOTELY RESEMBLED A GUN HAS BEEN RENDERED UTTERLY USELESS.
AND WHILE THE SKRULL SHIPS MAY BE GROUNDED, THEIR TROOPS STILL OUTNUMBER OURS THREE TO ONE.
IN OTHER WORDS, SIR--
IN OTHER WORDS, W'KABI...
WE'VE GOT THEM *EXACTLY* WHERE WE WANT THEM.

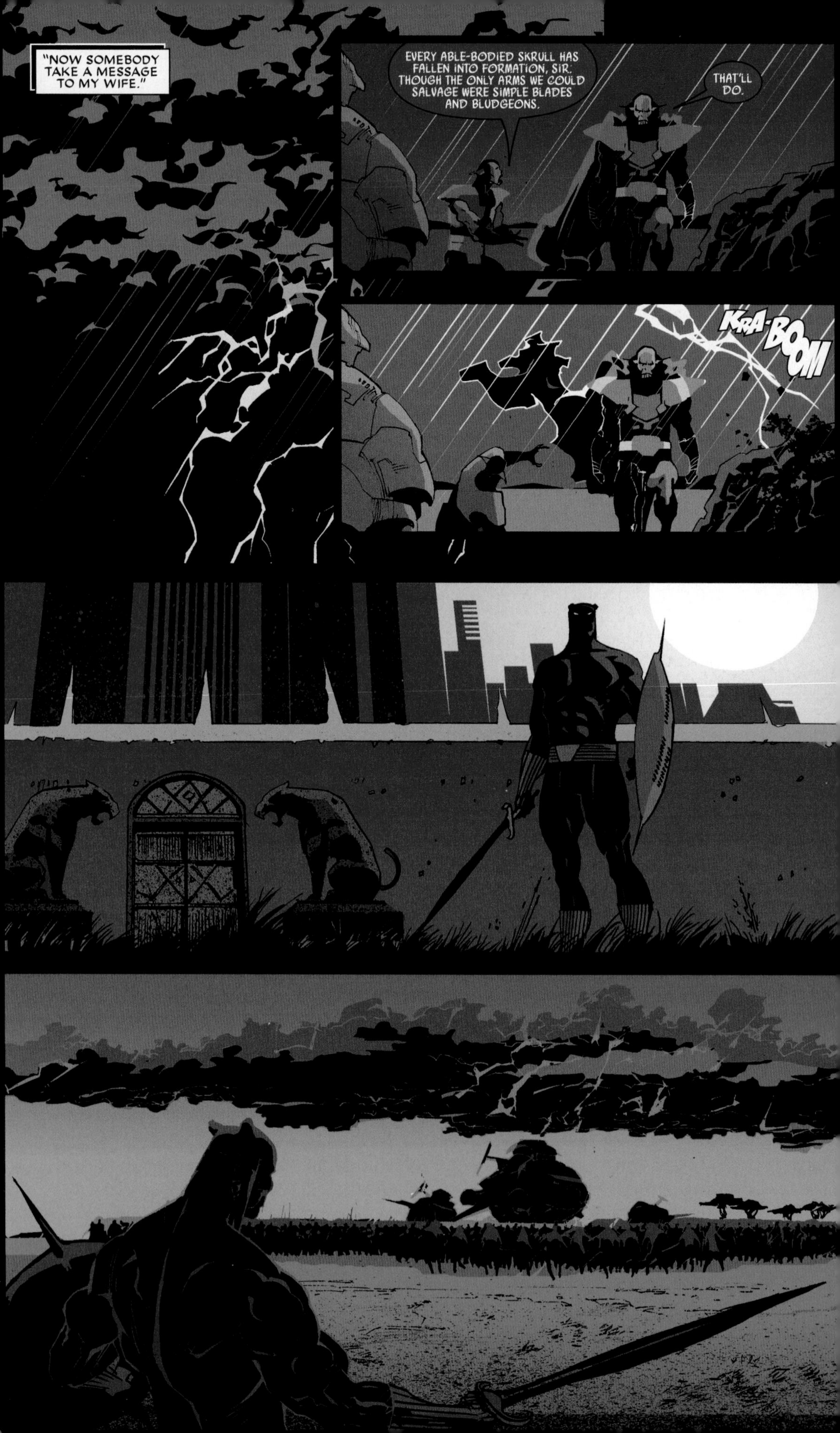
"NOW SOMEBODY TAKE A MESSAGE TO MY WIFE."
EVERY ABLE-BODIED SKRULL HAS FALLEN INTO FORMATION, SIR. THOUGH THE ONLY ARMS WE COULD SALVAGE WERE SIMPLE BLADES AND BLUDGEONS.
THAT'LL DO.
KRA-BOOM

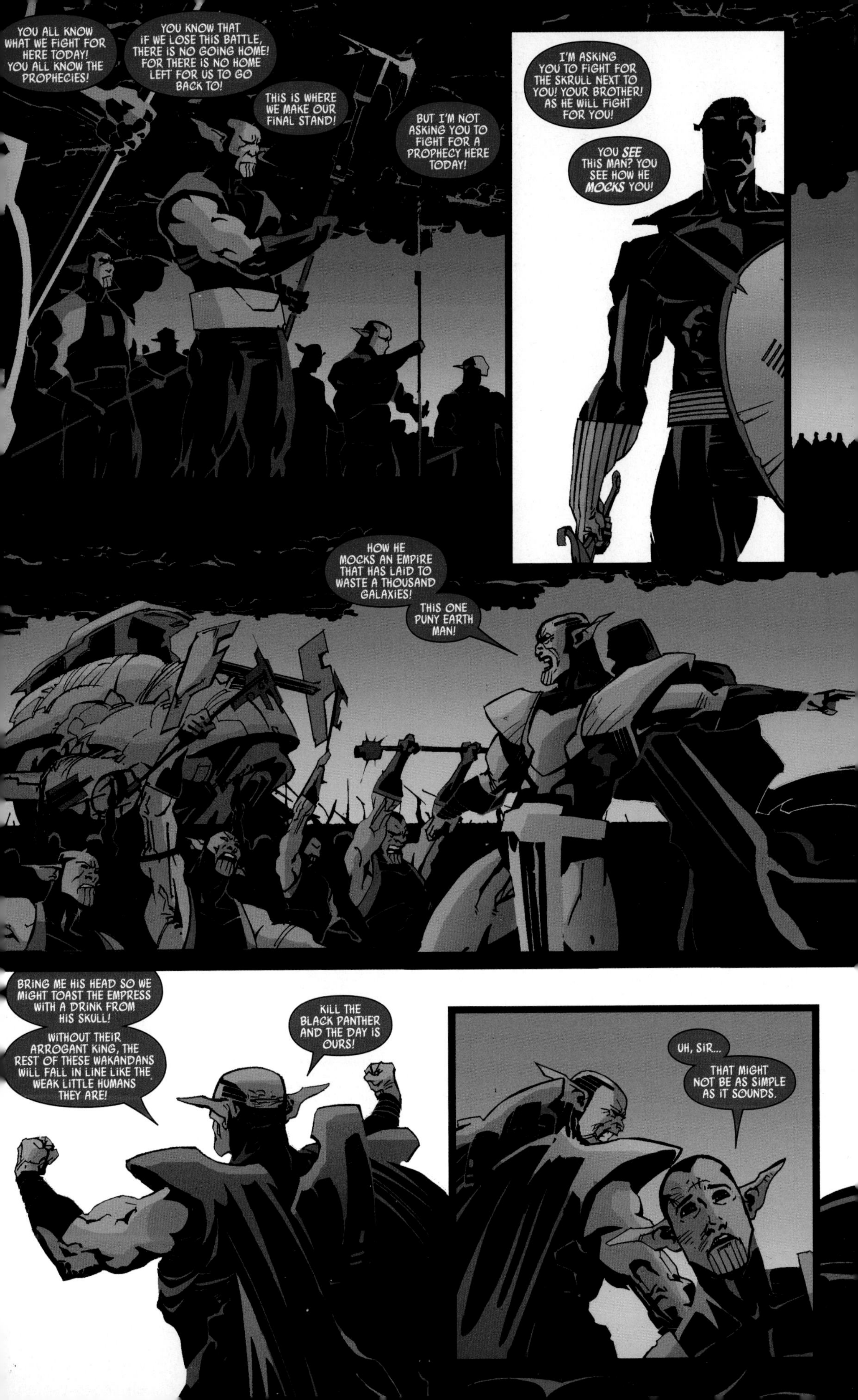
YOU ALL KNOW WHAT WE FIGHT FOR HERE TODAY! YOU ALL KNOW THE PROPHECIES!
YOU KNOW THAT IF WE LOSE THIS BATTLE, THERE IS NO GOING HOME! FOR THERE IS NO HOME LEFT FOR US TO GO BACK TO!
THIS IS WHERE WE MAKE OUR FINAL STAND!
BUT I'M NOT ASKING YOU TO FIGHT FOR A PROPHECY HERE TODAY!
I'M ASKING YOU TO FIGHT FOR THE SKRULL NEXT TO YOU! YOUR BROTHER! AS HE WILL FIGHT FOR YOU!
YOU SEE THIS MAN? YOU SEE HOW HE MOCKS YOU!
HOW HE MOCKS AN EMPIRE THAT HAS LAID TO WASTE A THOUSAND GALAXIES!
THIS ONE PUNY EARTH MAN!
BRING ME HIS HEAD SO WE MIGHT TOAST THE EMPRESS WITH A DRINK FROM HIS SKULL!
WITHOUT THEIR ARROGANT KING, THE REST OF THESE WAKANDANS WILL FALL IN LINE LIKE THE WEAK LITTLE HUMANS THEY ARE!
KILL THE BLACK PANTHER AND THE DAY IS OURS!
UH, SIR...
THAT MIGHT NOT BE AS SIMPLE AS IT SOUNDS.

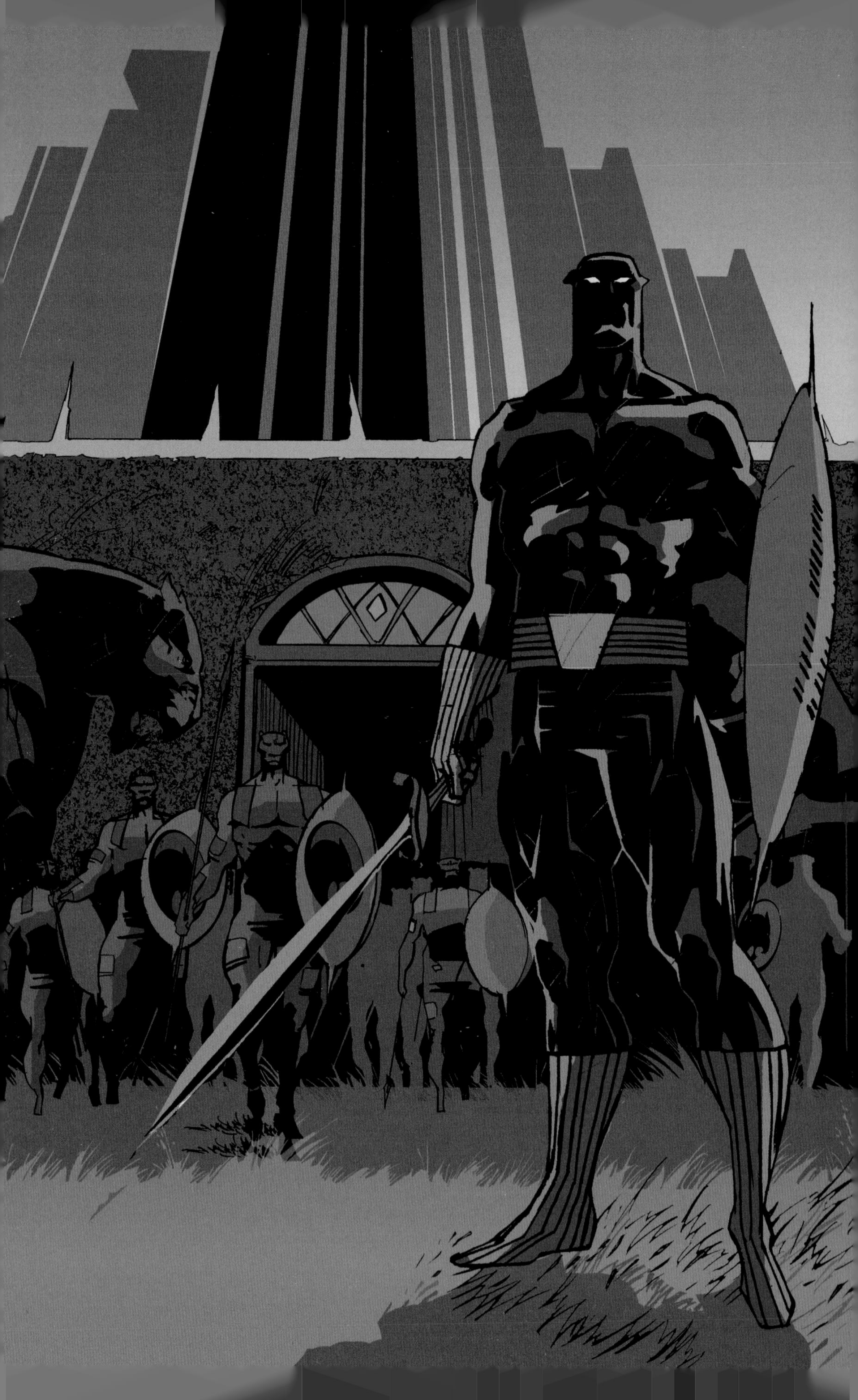

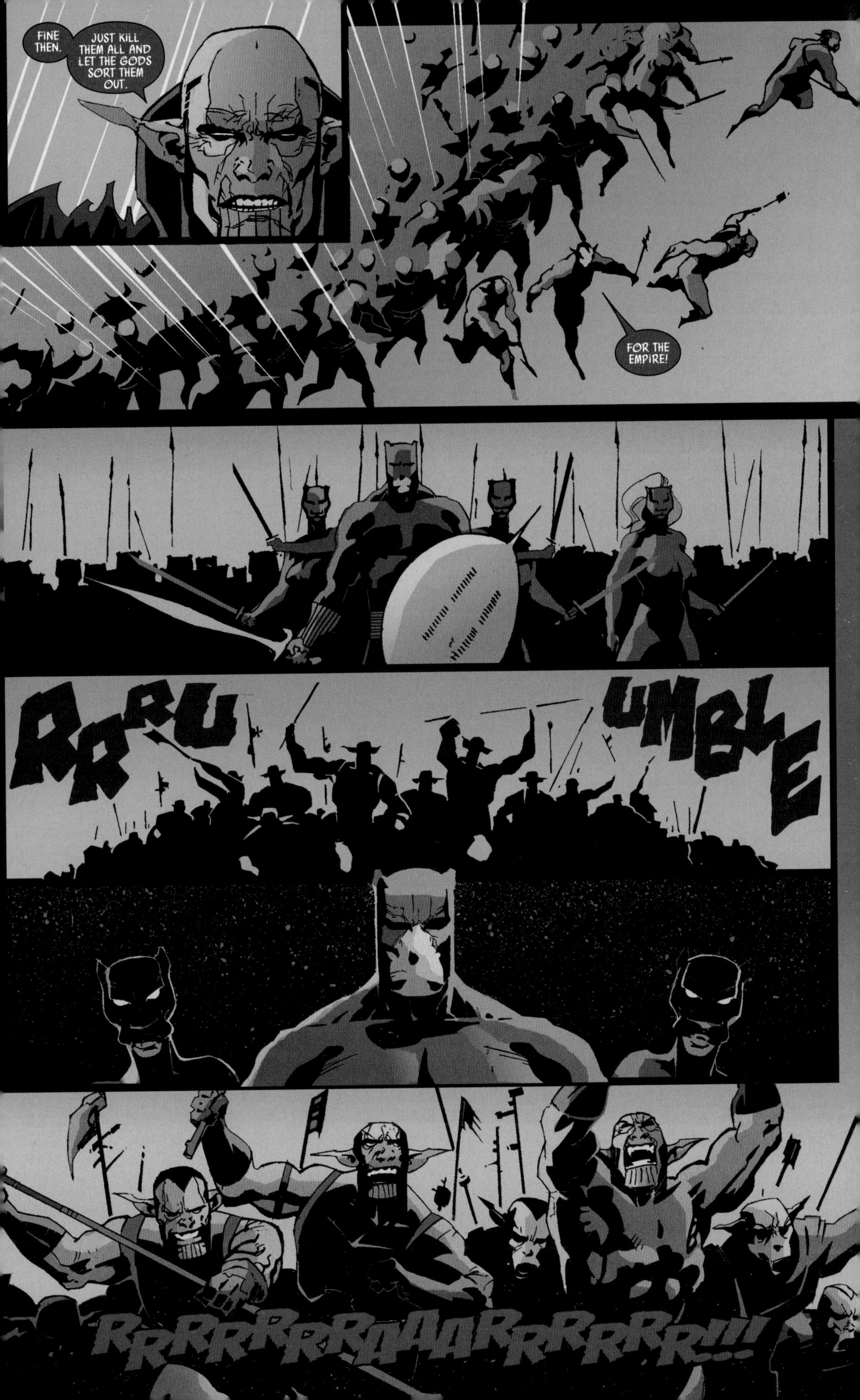
FINE THEN.
JUST KILL THEM ALL AND LET THE GODS SORT THEM OUT.
FOR THE EMPIRE!
RRRRUUMBLE
RRRRRRRRAAARRRRRRR!!!

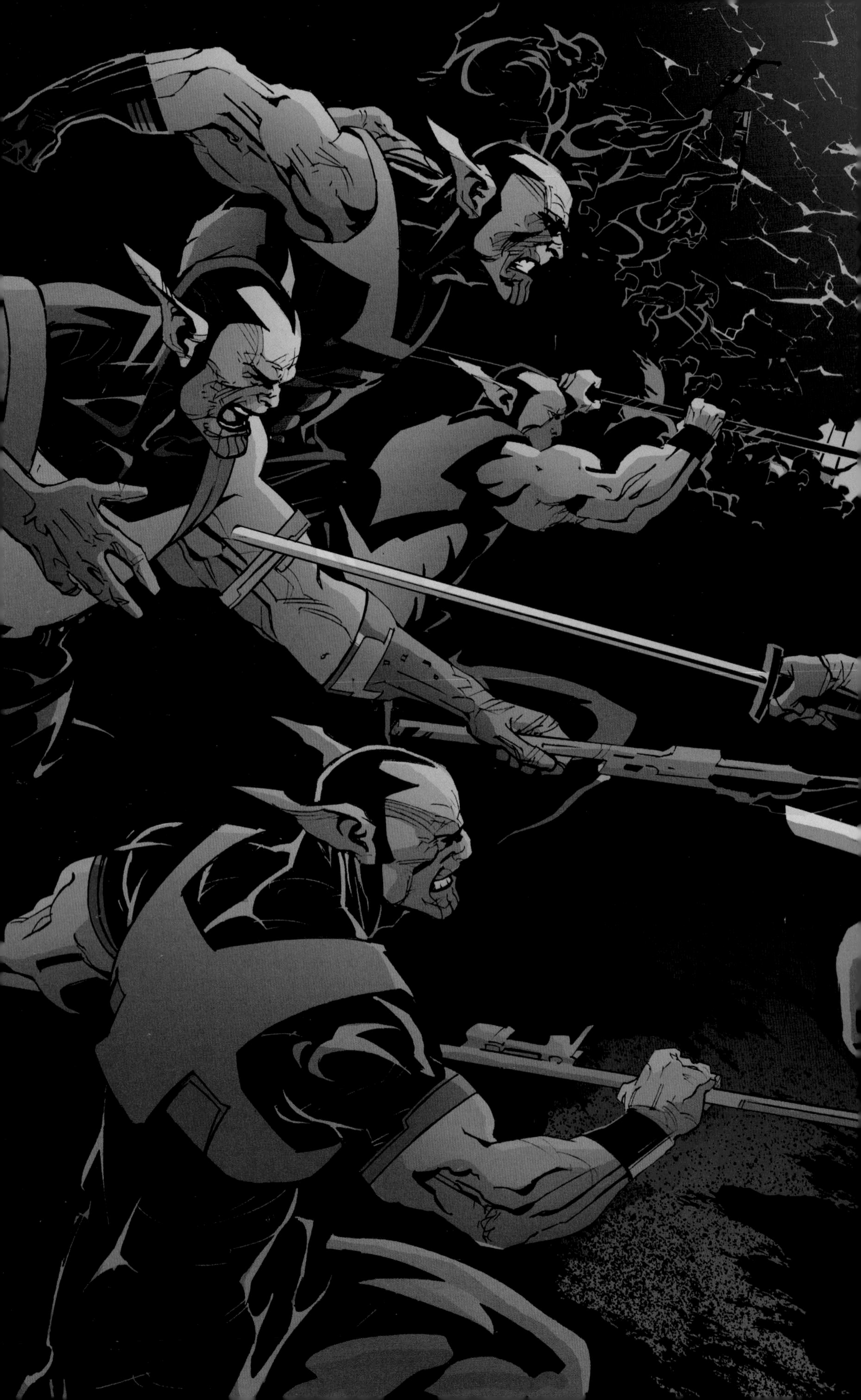

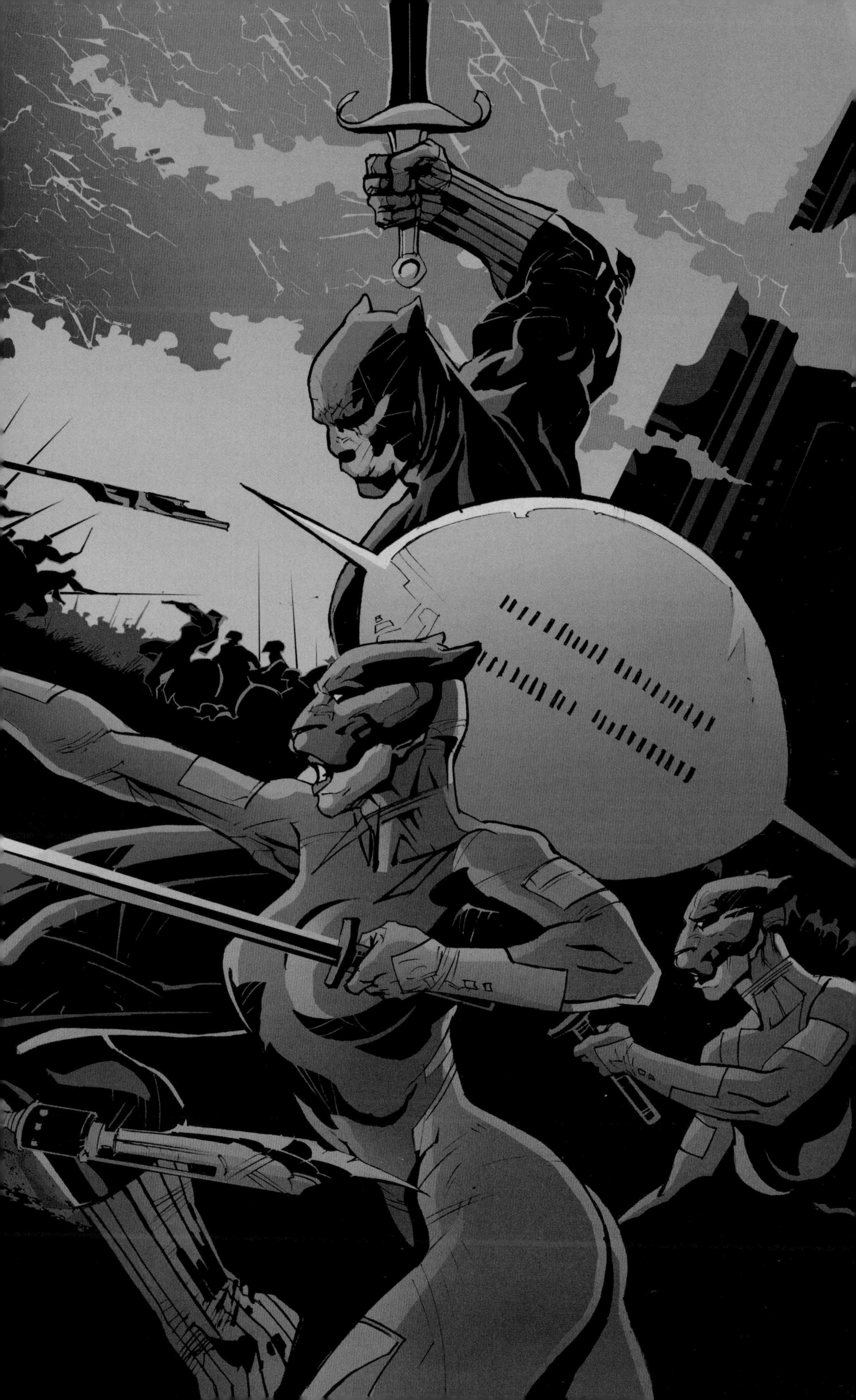

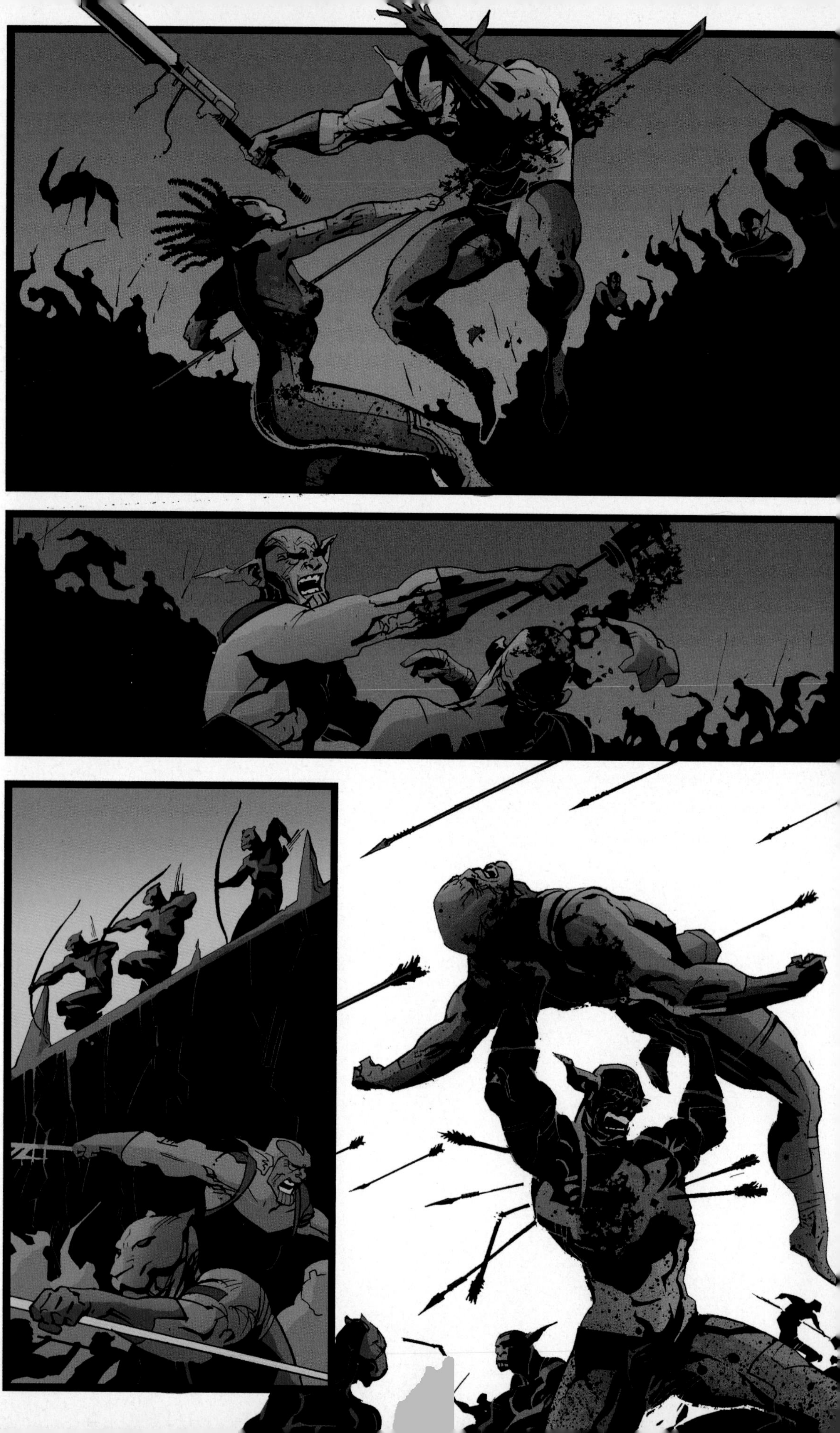

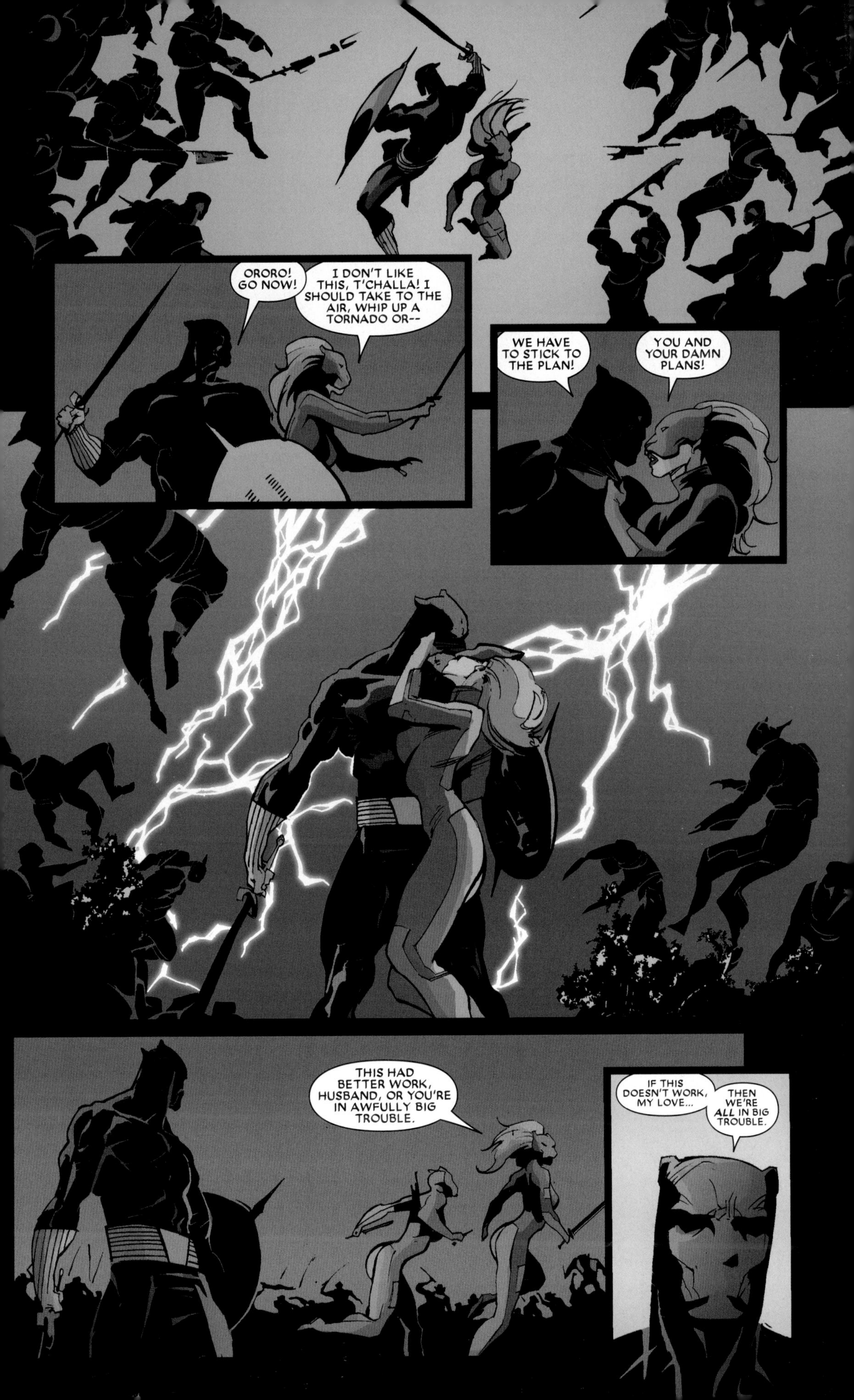
ORORO! GO NOW!
I DON'T LIKE THIS, T'CHALLA! I SHOULD TAKE TO THE AIR, WHIP UP A TORNADO OR--
WE HAVE TO STICK TO THE PLAN!
YOU AND YOUR DAMN PLANS!
THIS HAD BETTER WORK, HUSBAND, OR YOU'RE IN AWFULLY BIG TROUBLE.
IF THIS DOESN'T WORK, MY LOVE...
THEN WE'RE *ALL* IN BIG TROUBLE.

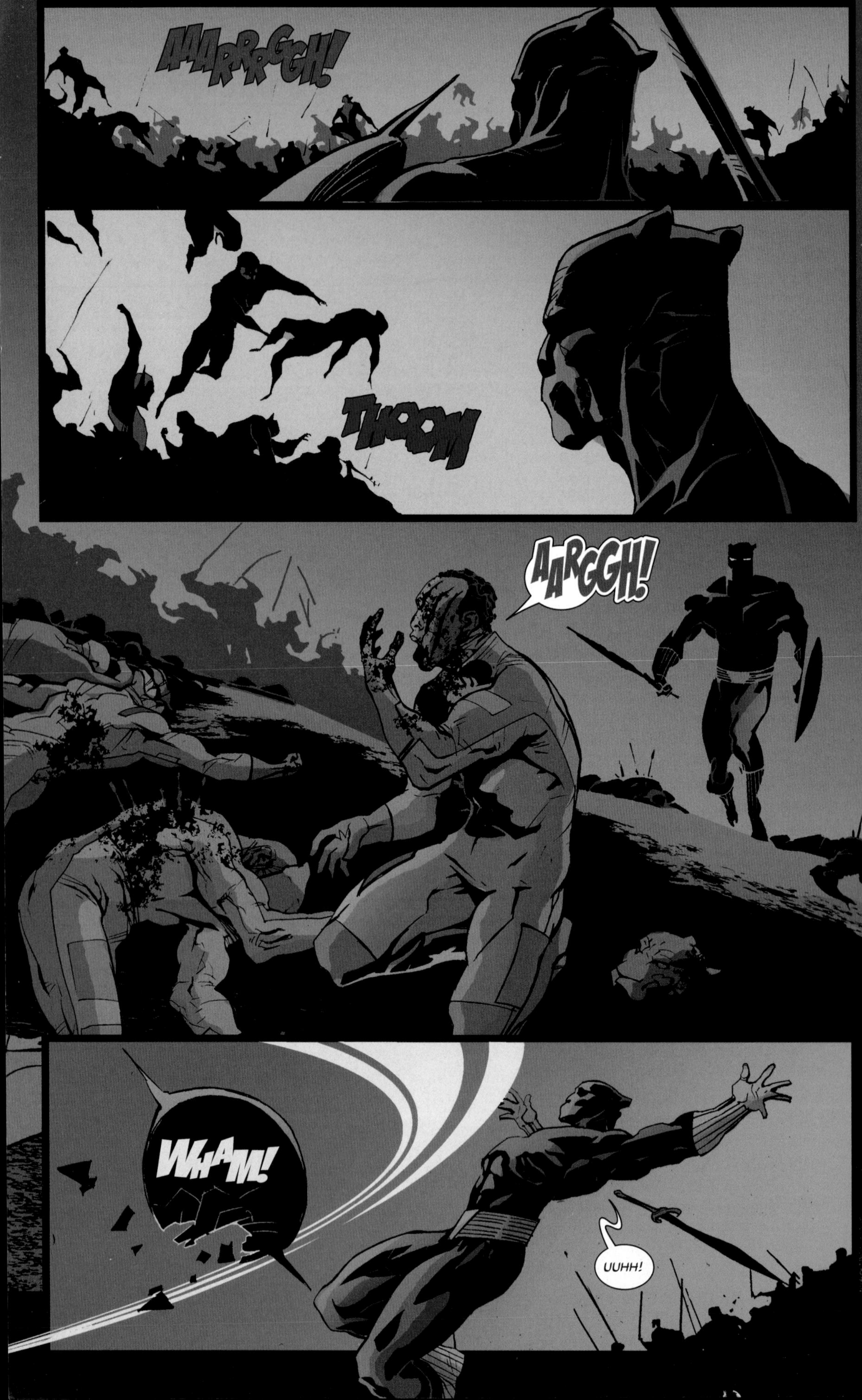
AAARRRGGH!
THOOM
AARGGH!
WHAM!
UUHH!

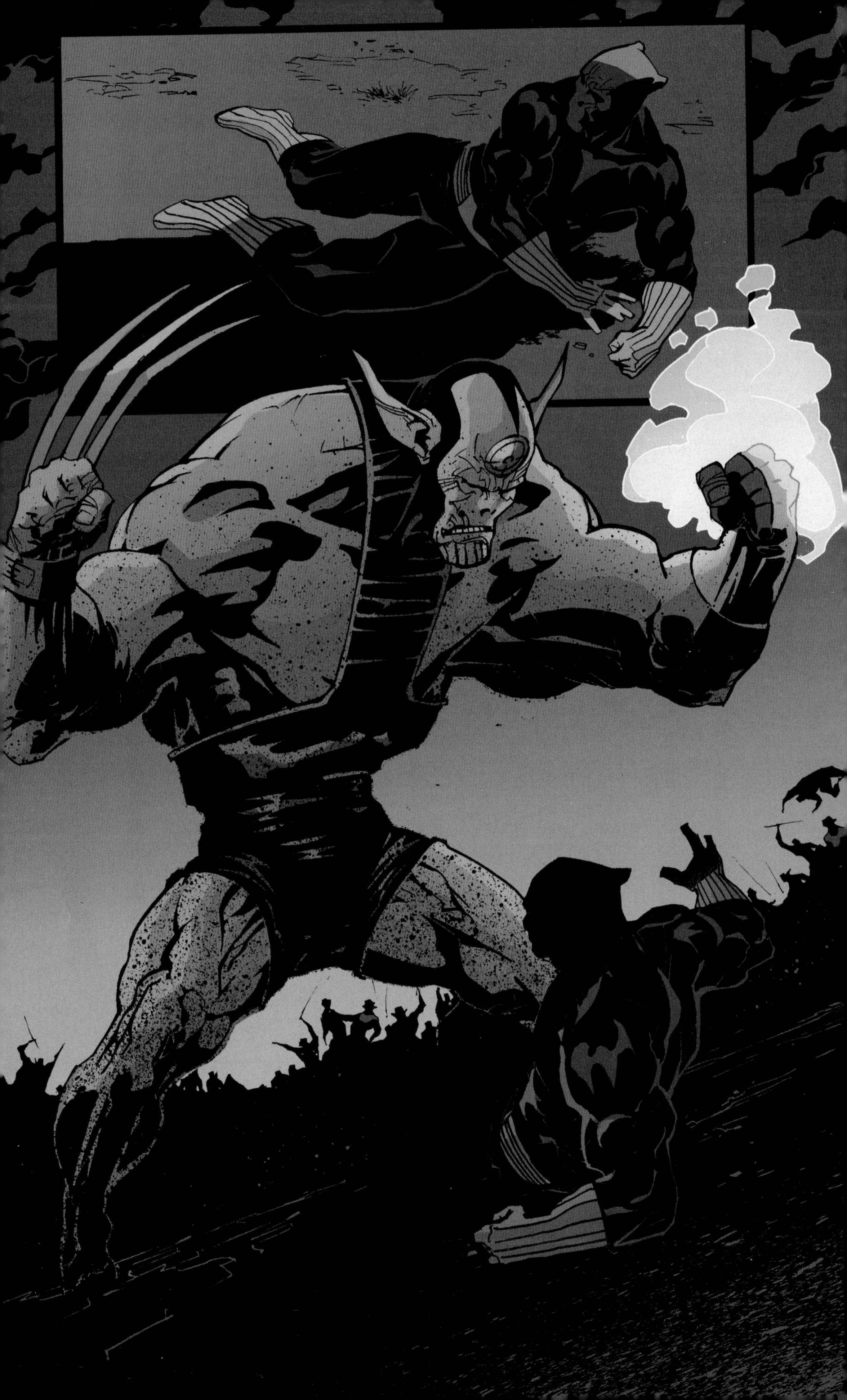

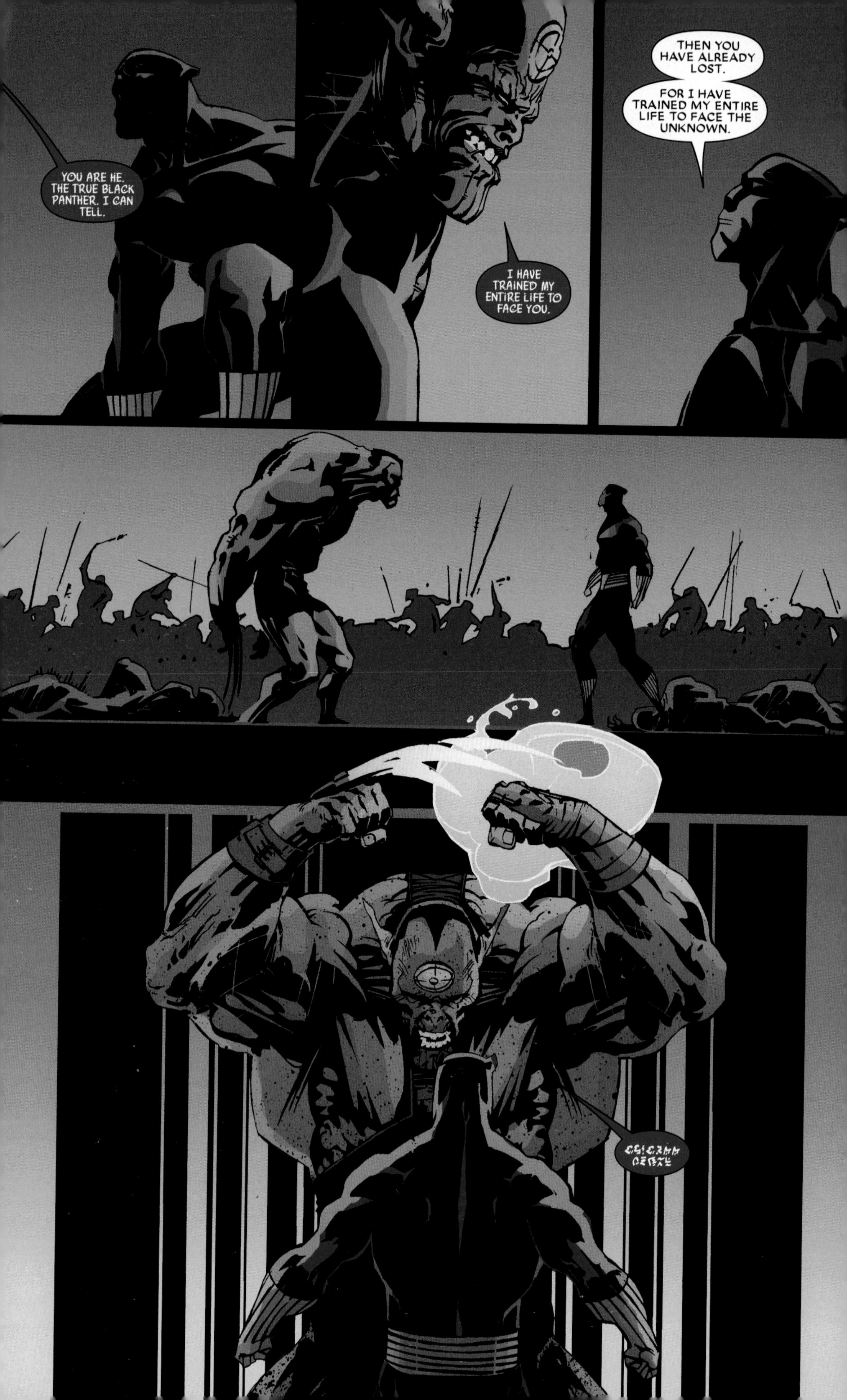
YOU ARE HE. THE TRUE BLACK PANTHER. I CAN TELL.
I HAVE TRAINED MY ENTIRE LIFE TO FACE YOU.
THEN YOU HAVE ALREADY LOST.
FOR I HAVE TRAINED MY ENTIRE LIFE TO FACE THE UNKNOWN.

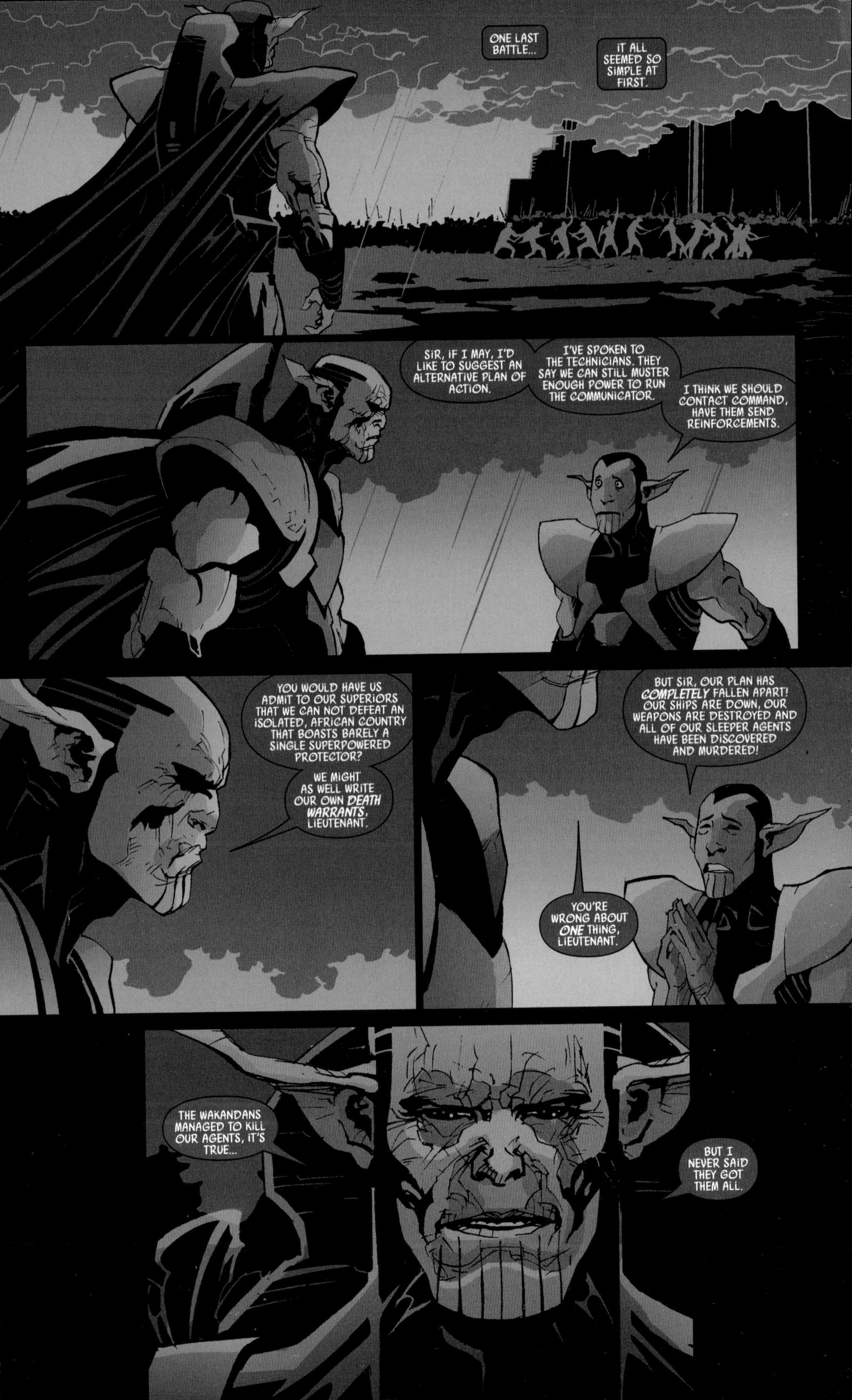
ONE LAST BATTLE...
IT ALL SEEMED SO SIMPLE AT FIRST.
SIR, IF I MAY, I'D LIKE TO SUGGEST AN ALTERNATIVE PLAN OF ACTION.
I'VE SPOKEN TO THE TECHNICIANS. THEY SAY WE CAN STILL MUSTER ENOUGH POWER TO RUN THE COMMUNICATOR.
I THINK WE SHOULD CONTACT COMMAND, HAVE THEM SEND REINFORCEMENTS.
YOU WOULD HAVE US ADMIT TO OUR SUPERIORS THAT WE CAN NOT DEFEAT AN ISOLATED, AFRICAN COUNTRY THAT BOASTS BARELY A SINGLE SUPERPOWERED PROTECTOR?
WE MIGHT AS WELL WRITE OUR OWN DEATH WARRANTS, LIEUTENANT.
BUT SIR, OUR PLAN HAS COMPLETELY FALLEN APART! OUR SHIPS ARE DOWN, OUR WEAPONS ARE DESTROYED AND ALL OF OUR SLEEPER AGENTS HAVE BEEN DISCOVERED AND MURDERED!
YOU'RE WRONG ABOUT ONE THING, LIEUTENANT.
THE WAKANDANS MANAGED TO KILL OUR AGENTS, IT'S TRUE...
BUT I NEVER SAID THEY GOT THEM ALL.

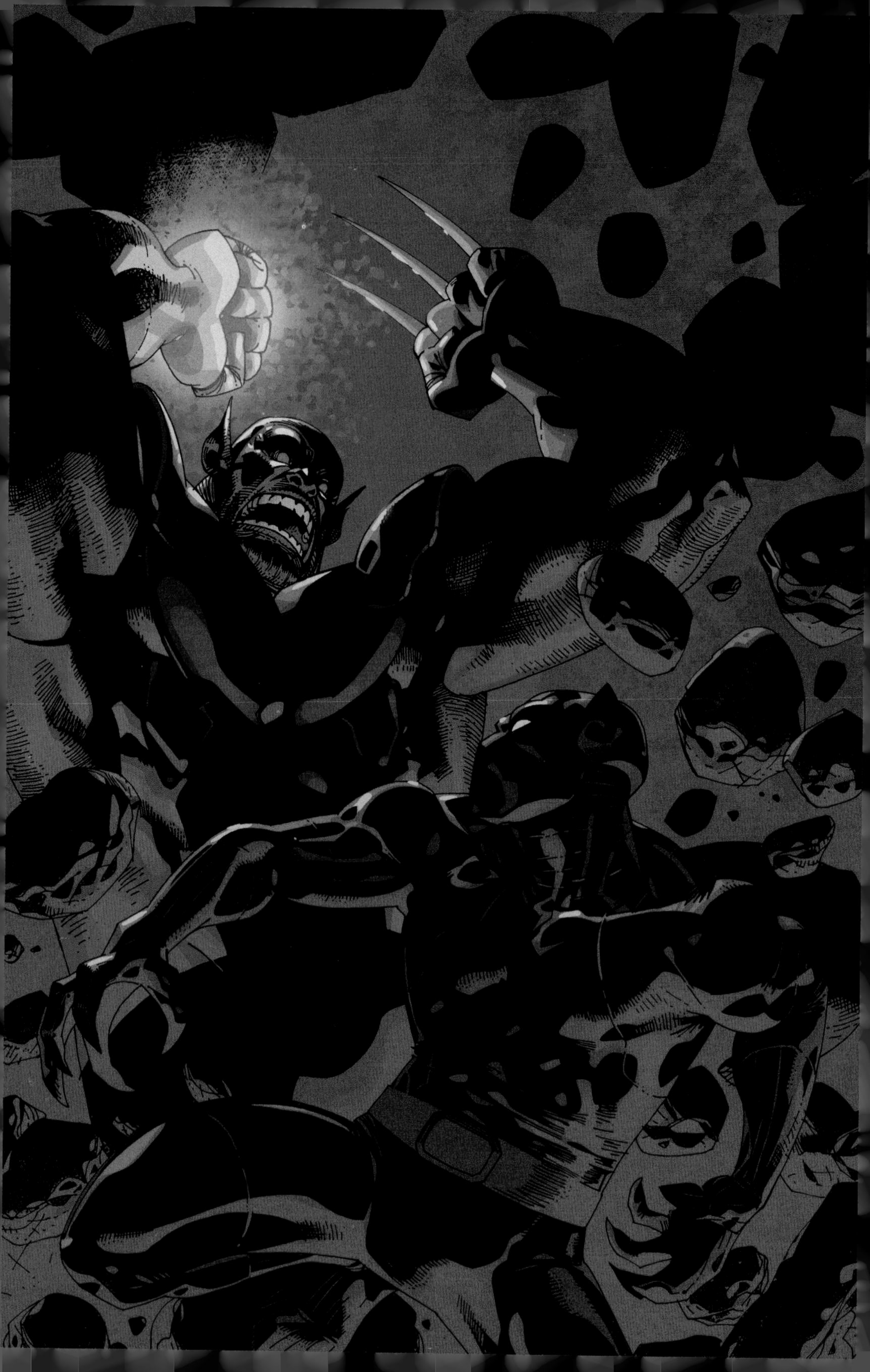

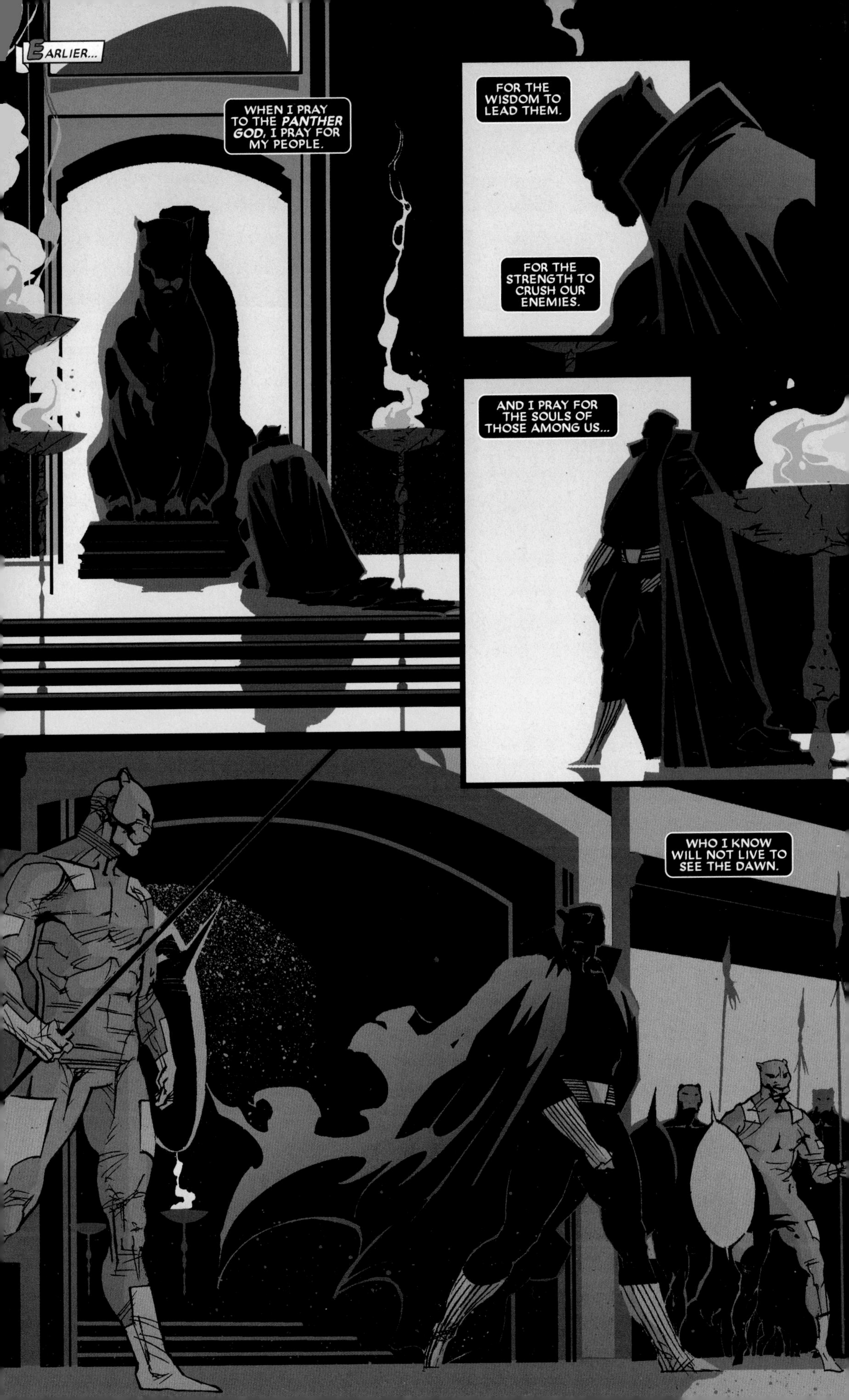
EARLIER...
WHEN I PRAY TO THE PANTHER GOD, I PRAY FOR MY PEOPLE.
FOR THE WISDOM TO LEAD THEM.
FOR THE STRENGTH TO CRUSH OUR ENEMIES.
AND I PRAY FOR THE SOULS OF THOSE AMONG US...
WHO I KNOW WILL NOT LIVE TO SEE THE DAWN.

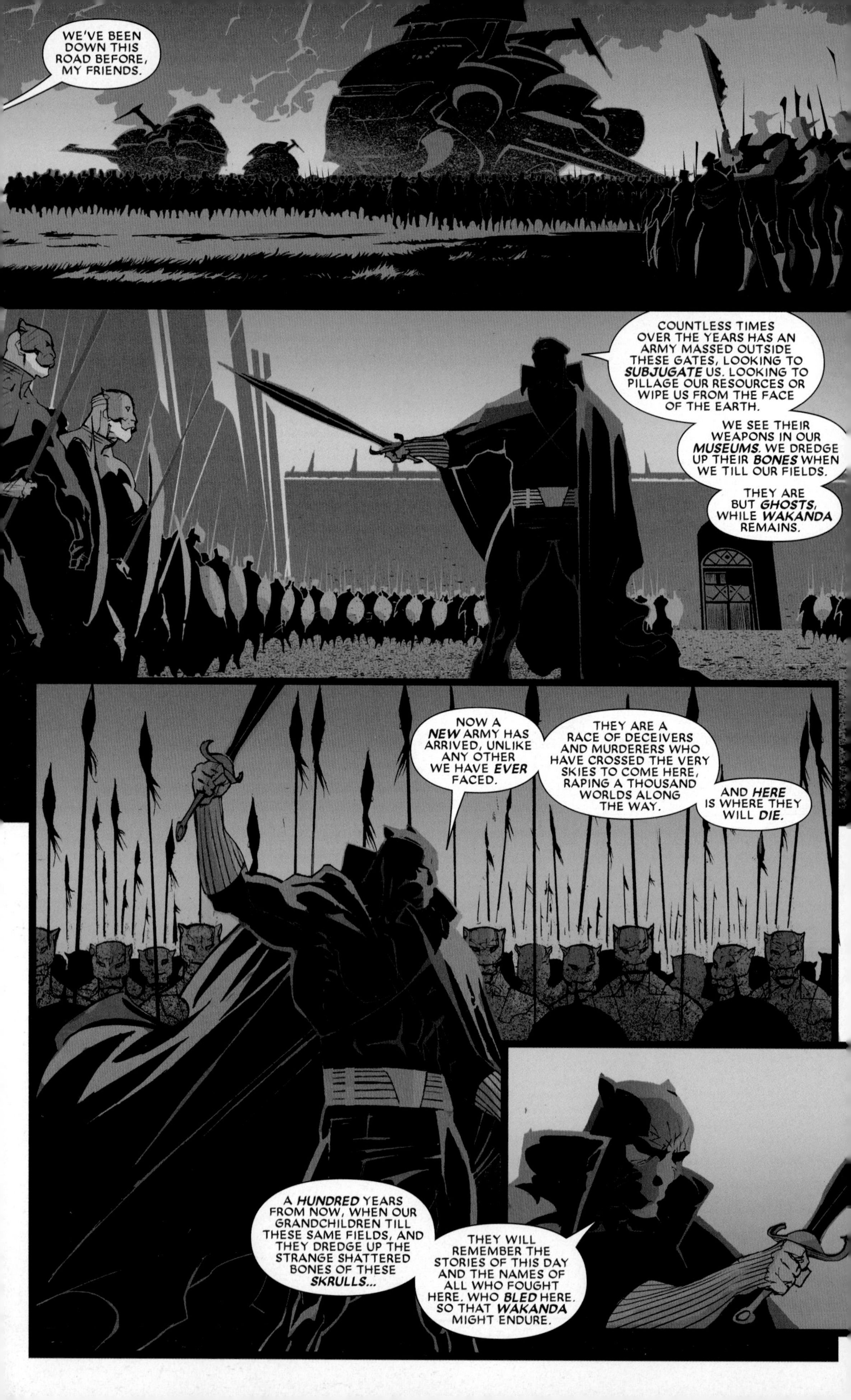
WE'VE BEEN DOWN THIS ROAD BEFORE, MY FRIENDS.
COUNTLESS TIMES OVER THE YEARS HAS AN ARMY MASSED OUTSIDE THESE GATES, LOOKING TO SUBJUGATE US. LOOKING TO PILLAGE OUR RESOURCES OR WIPE US FROM THE FACE OF THE EARTH.
WE SEE THEIR WEAPONS IN OUR MUSEUMS. WE DREDGE UP THEIR BONES WHEN WE TILL OUR FIELDS.
THEY ARE BUT GHOSTS, WHILE WAKANDA REMAINS.
NOW A NEW ARMY HAS ARRIVED, UNLIKE ANY OTHER WE HAVE EVER FACED.
THEY ARE A RACE OF DECEIVERS AND MURDERERS WHO HAVE CROSSED THE VERY SKIES TO COME HERE, RAPING A THOUSAND WORLDS ALONG THE WAY.
AND HERE IS WHERE THEY WILL DIE.
A HUNDRED YEARS FROM NOW, WHEN OUR GRANDCHILDREN TILL THESE SAME FIELDS, AND THEY DREDGE UP THE STRANGE SHATTERED BONES OF THESE SKRULLS...
THEY WILL REMEMBER THE STORIES OF THIS DAY AND THE NAMES OF ALL WHO FOUGHT HERE. WHO BLED HERE. SO THAT WAKANDA MIGHT ENDURE.

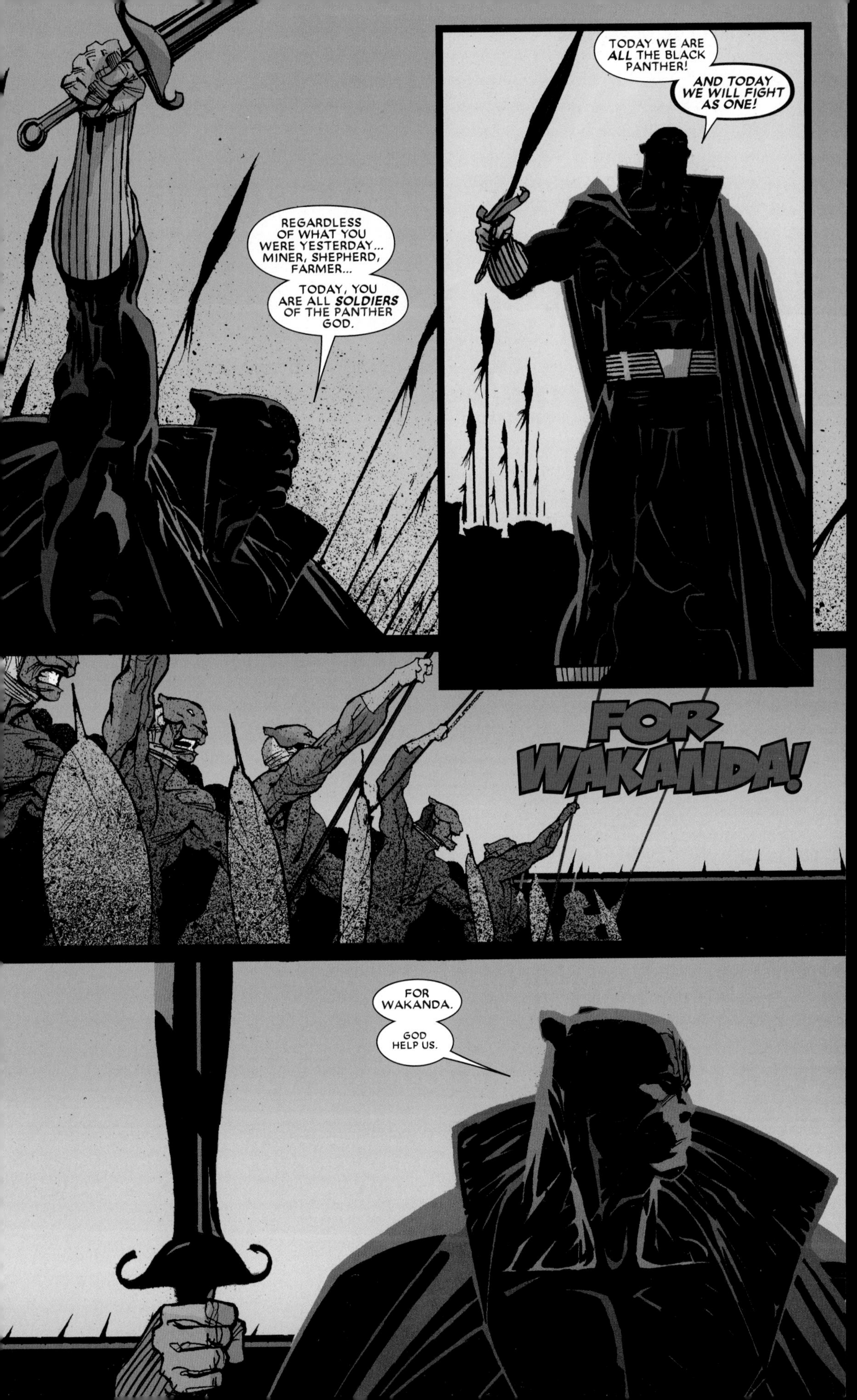
REGARDLESS OF WHAT YOU WERE YESTERDAY... MINER, SHEPHERD, FARMER...
TODAY, YOU ARE ALL *SOLDIERS* OF THE PANTHER GOD.
TODAY WE ARE *ALL* THE BLACK PANTHER!
AND TODAY WE WILL FIGHT AS ONE!
FOR WAKANDA!
FOR WAKANDA.
GOD HELP US.

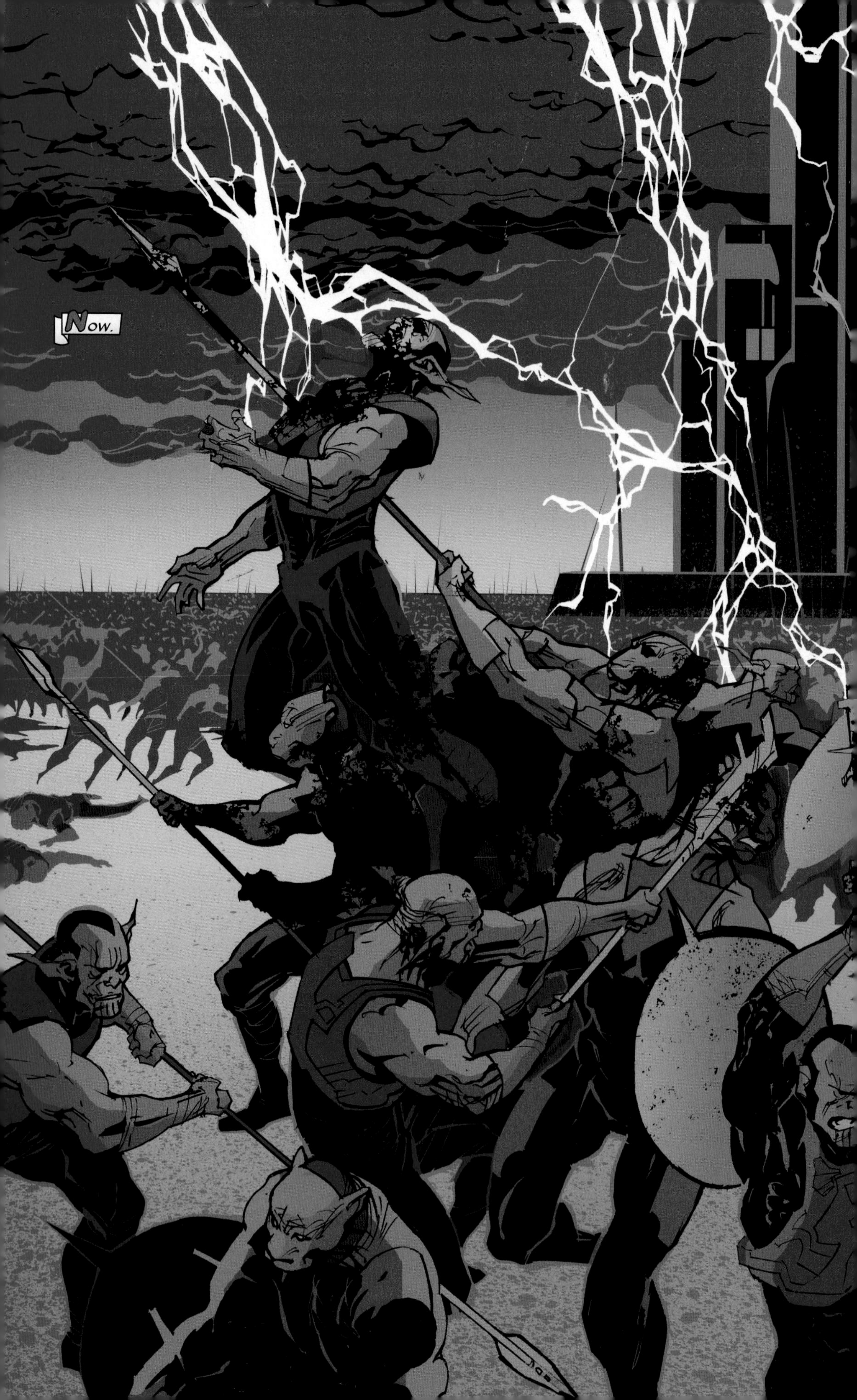
Now.

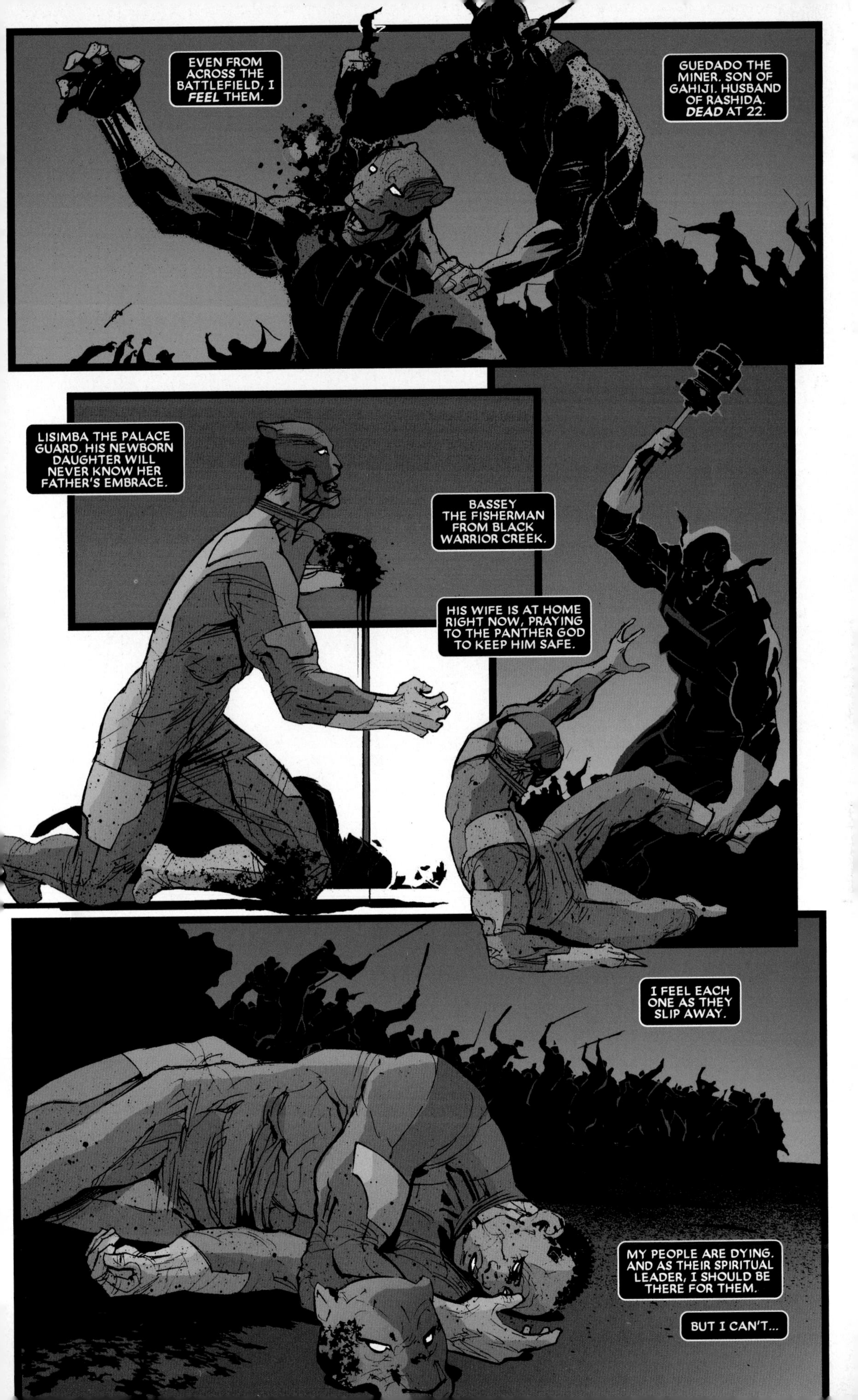
EVEN FROM ACROSS THE BATTLEFIELD, I *FEEL* THEM.
GUEDADO THE MINER. SON OF GAHIJI. HUSBAND OF RASHIDA. *DEAD* AT 22.
LISIMBA THE PALACE GUARD. HIS NEWBORN DAUGHTER WILL NEVER KNOW HER FATHER'S EMBRACE.
BASSEY THE FISHERMAN FROM BLACK WARRIOR CREEK.
HIS WIFE IS AT HOME RIGHT NOW, PRAYING TO THE PANTHER GOD TO KEEP HIM SAFE.
I FEEL EACH ONE AS THEY SLIP AWAY.
MY PEOPLE ARE DYING. AND AS THEIR SPIRITUAL LEADER, I SHOULD BE THERE FOR THEM.
BUT I CAN'T...

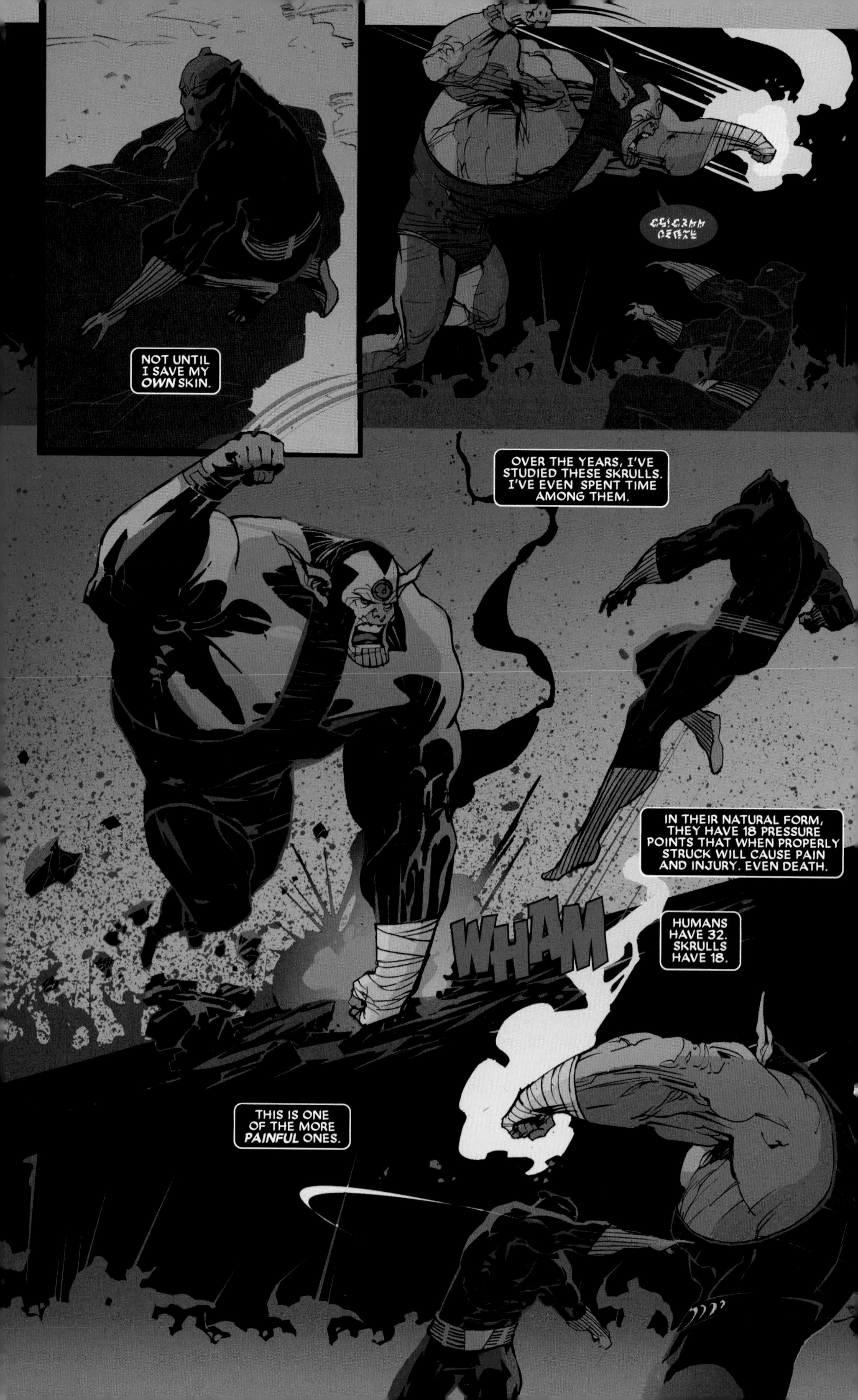
NOT UNTIL I SAVE MY *OWN* SKIN.
OVER THE YEARS, I'VE STUDIED THESE SKRULLS. I'VE EVEN SPENT TIME AMONG THEM.
IN THEIR NATURAL FORM, THEY HAVE 18 PRESSURE POINTS THAT WHEN PROPERLY STRUCK WILL CAUSE PAIN AND INJURY. EVEN DEATH.
WHAM
HUMANS HAVE 32. SKRULLS HAVE 18.
THIS IS ONE OF THE MORE *PAINFUL* ONES.

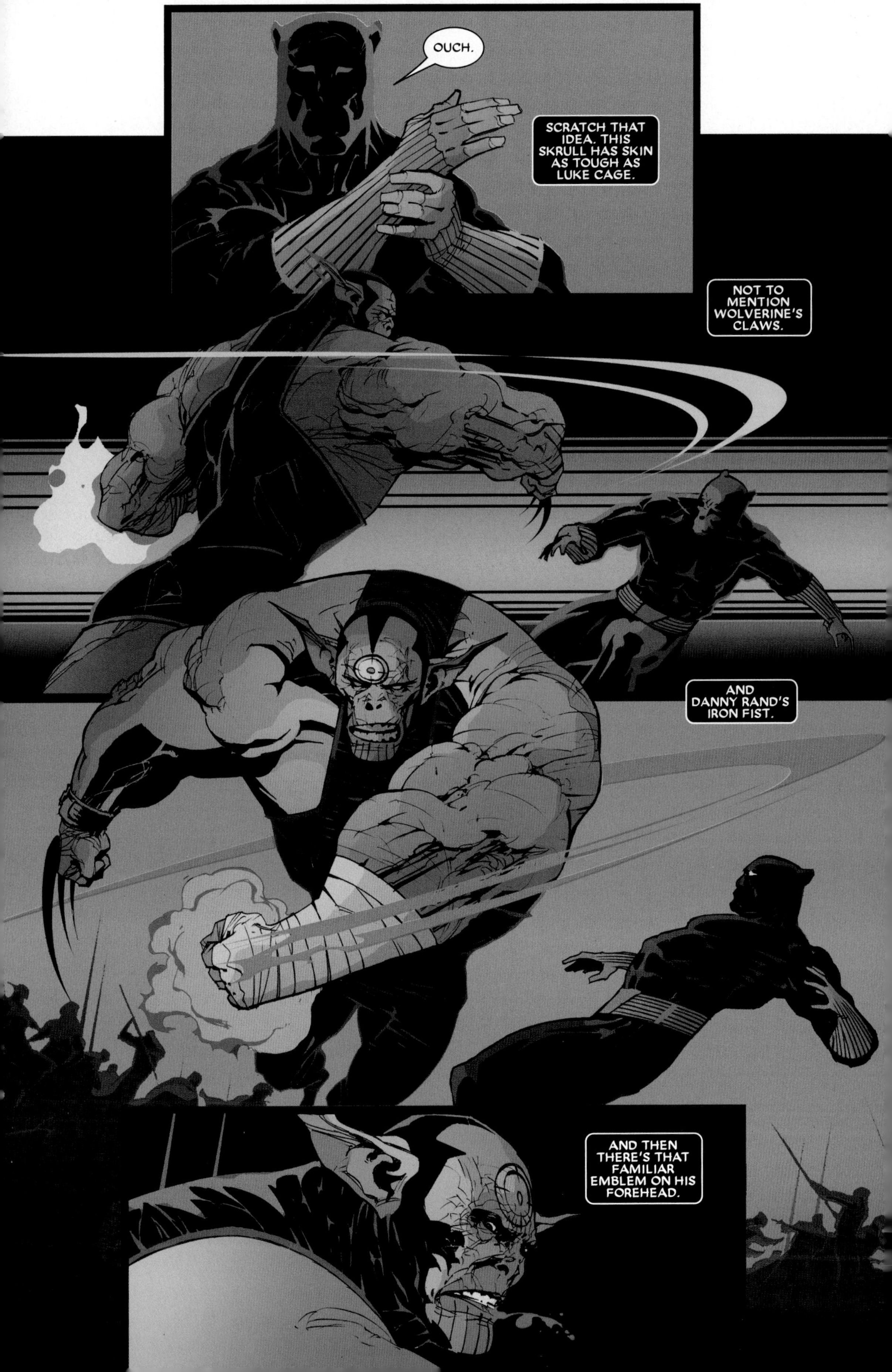
OUCH.
SCRATCH THAT IDEA. THIS SKRULL HAS SKIN AS TOUGH AS LUKE CAGE.
NOT TO MENTION WOLVERINE'S CLAWS.
AND DANNY RAND'S IRON FIST.
AND THEN THERE'S THAT FAMILIAR EMBLEM ON HIS FOREHEAD.

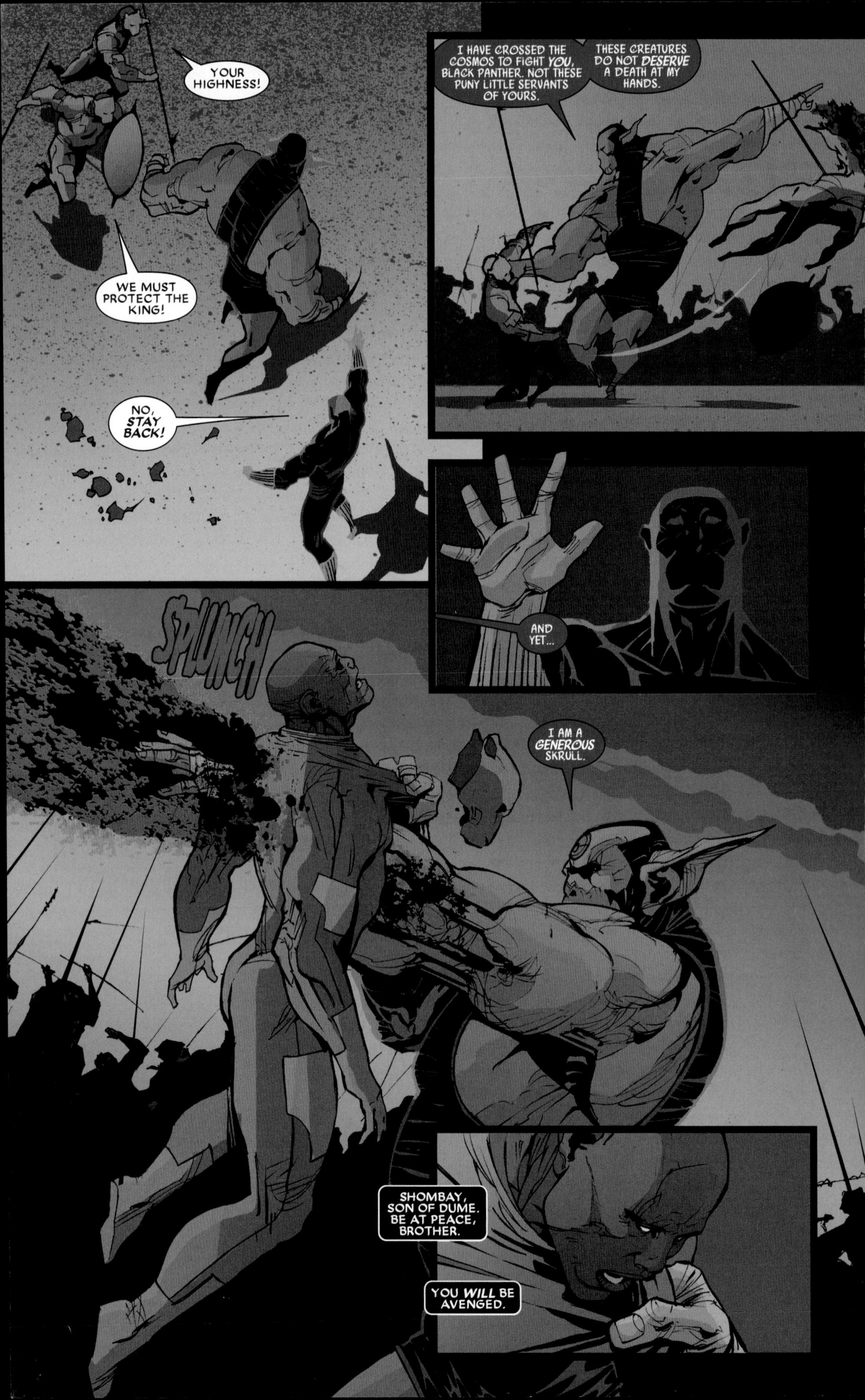
YOUR HIGHNESS!
WE MUST PROTECT THE KING!
NO, STAY BACK!
I HAVE CROSSED THE COSMOS TO FIGHT YOU, BLACK PANTHER. NOT THESE PUNY LITTLE SERVANTS OF YOURS.
THESE CREATURES DO NOT DESERVE A DEATH AT MY HANDS.
AND YET...
SPLUNCH
I AM A GENEROUS SKRULL.
SHOMBAY, SON OF DUME. BE AT PEACE, BROTHER.
YOU WILL BE AVENGED.

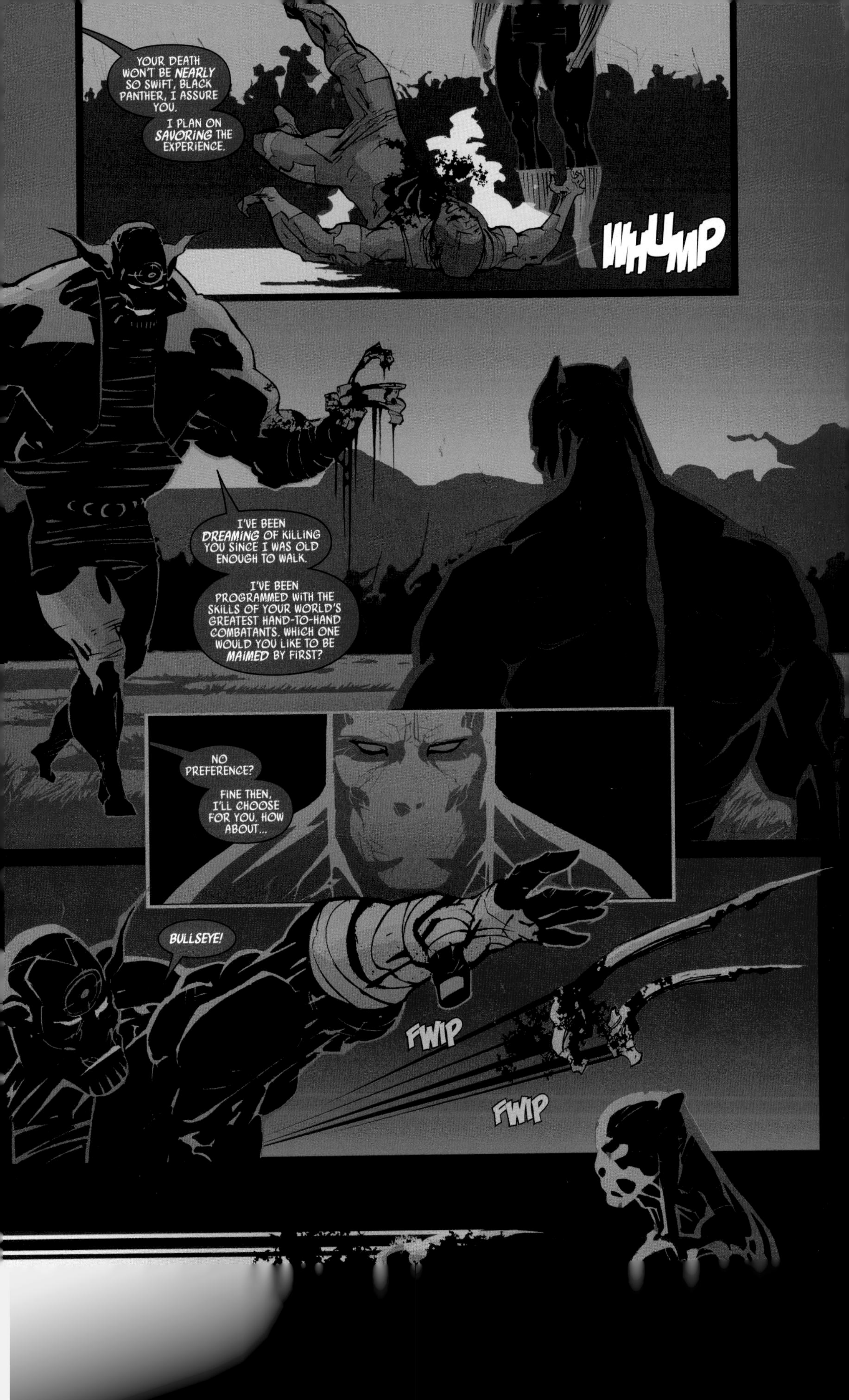
YOUR DEATH WON'T BE NEARLY SO SWIFT, BLACK PANTHER, I ASSURE YOU.
I PLAN ON SAVORING THE EXPERIENCE.
WHUMP
I'VE BEEN DREAMING OF KILLING YOU SINCE I WAS OLD ENOUGH TO WALK.
I'VE BEEN PROGRAMMED WITH THE SKILLS OF YOUR WORLD'S GREATEST HAND-TO-HAND COMBATANTS. WHICH ONE WOULD YOU LIKE TO BE MAIMED BY FIRST?
NO PREFERENCE?
FINE THEN, I'LL CHOOSE FOR YOU. HOW ABOUT...
BULLSEYE!
FWIP
FWIP

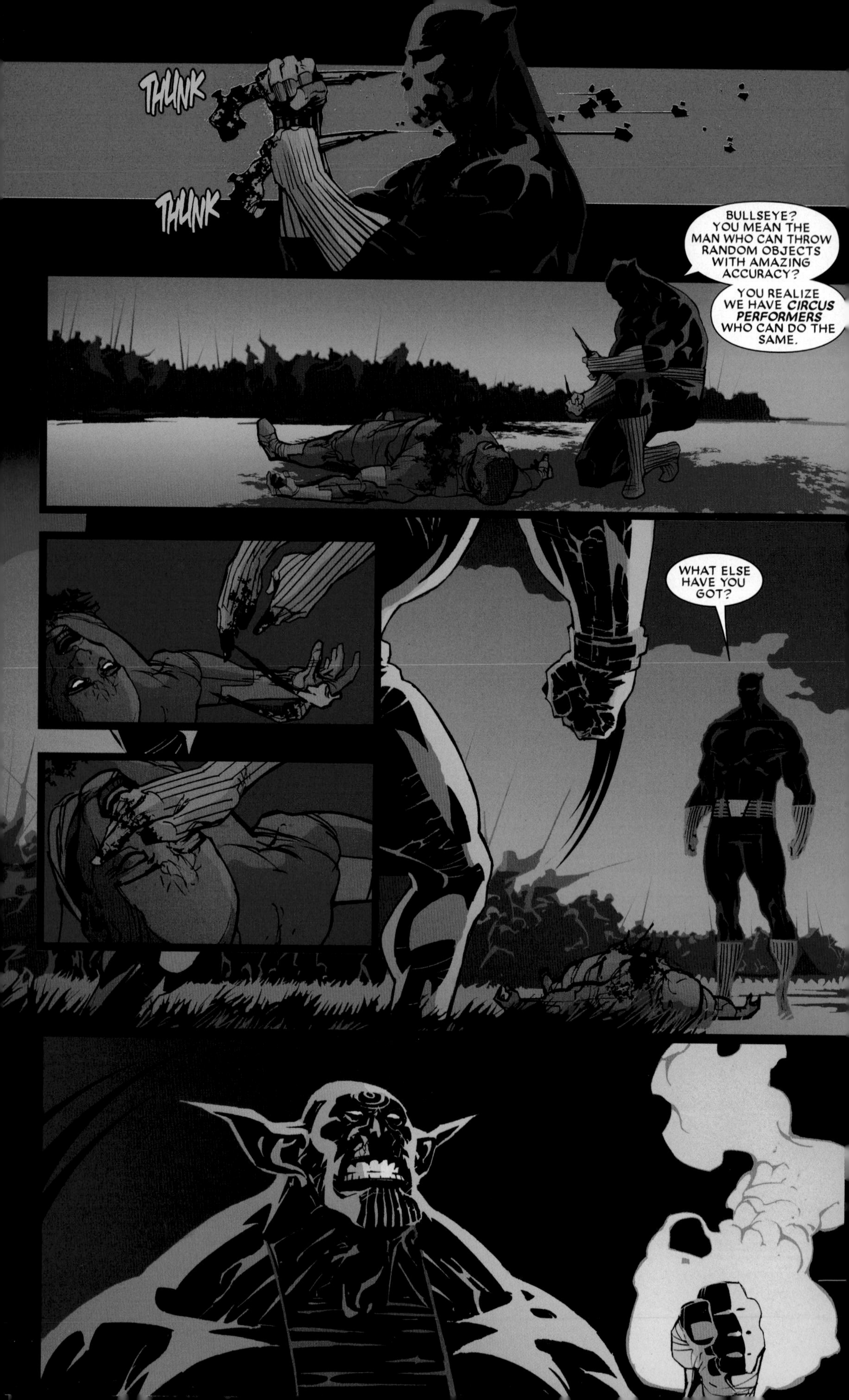
THUNK
THUNK
BULLSEYE? YOU MEAN THE MAN WHO CAN THROW RANDOM OBJECTS WITH AMAZING ACCURACY?
YOU REALIZE WE HAVE CIRCUS PERFORMERS WHO CAN DO THE SAME.
WHAT ELSE HAVE YOU GOT?

MOON KNIGHT. SHANG CHI. CAPTAIN AMERICA. DAREDEVIL. ELEKTRA. EVEN ME.

HE HAS THE STYLES OF THEM ALL DOWN PAT.

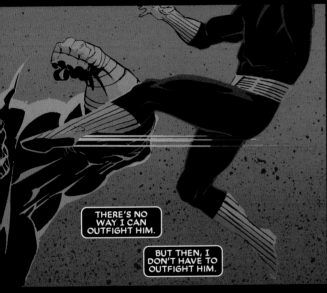

THERE'S NO WAY I CAN OUTFIGHT HIM.

BUT THEN, I DON'T HAVE TO OUTFIGHT HIM.

ALL I HAVE TO DO IS JUST SURVIVE LONG ENOUGH...

...TO FIGURE OUT HIS WEAKNESS.

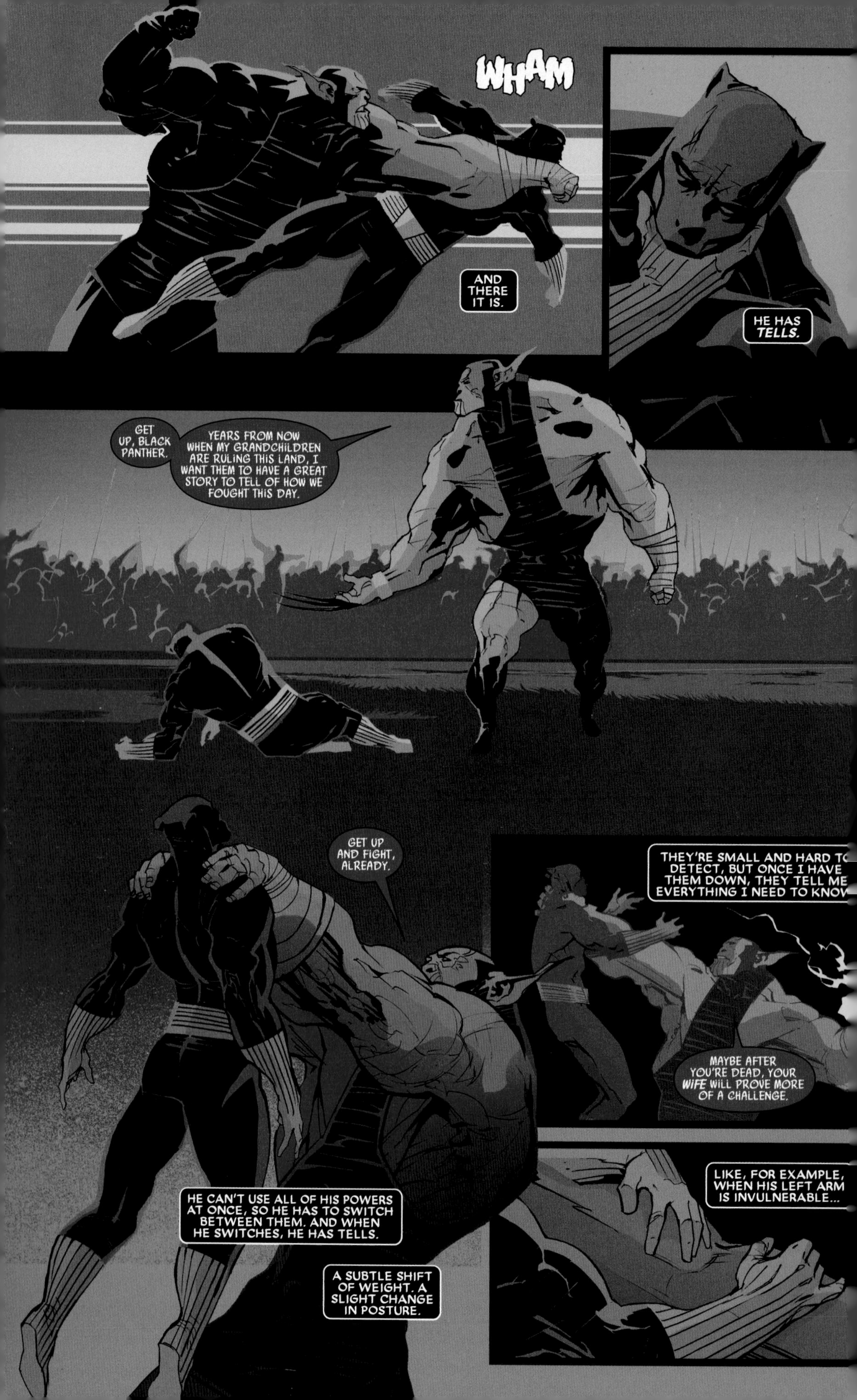
WHAM
AND THERE IT IS.
HE HAS TELLS.
GET UP, BLACK PANTHER.
YEARS FROM NOW WHEN MY GRANDCHILDREN ARE RULING THIS LAND, I WANT THEM TO HAVE A GREAT STORY TO TELL OF HOW WE FOUGHT THIS DAY.
GET UP AND FIGHT, ALREADY.
HE CAN'T USE ALL OF HIS POWERS AT ONCE, SO HE HAS TO SWITCH BETWEEN THEM. AND WHEN HE SWITCHES, HE HAS TELLS.
A SUBTLE SHIFT OF WEIGHT. A SLIGHT CHANGE IN POSTURE.
THEY'RE SMALL AND HARD TO DETECT, BUT ONCE I HAVE THEM DOWN, THEY TELL ME EVERYTHING I NEED TO KNOW
MAYBE AFTER YOU'RE DEAD, YOUR WIFE WILL PROVE MORE OF A CHALLENGE.
LIKE, FOR EXAMPLE, WHEN HIS LEFT ARM IS INVULNERABLE...

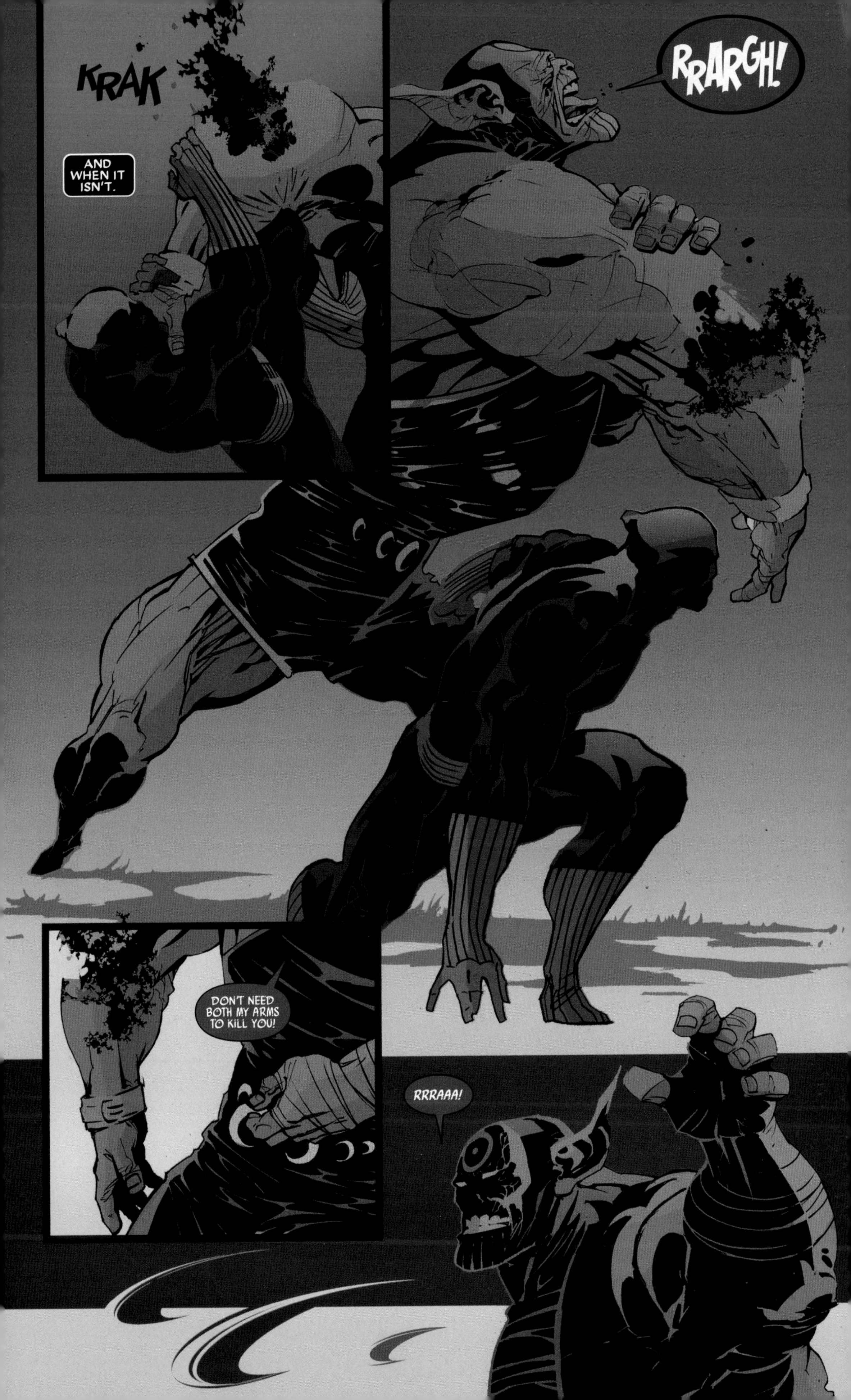
KRAK
AND WHEN IT ISN'T.
RRARGH!
DON'T NEED BOTH MY ARMS TO KILL YOU!
RRRAAA!

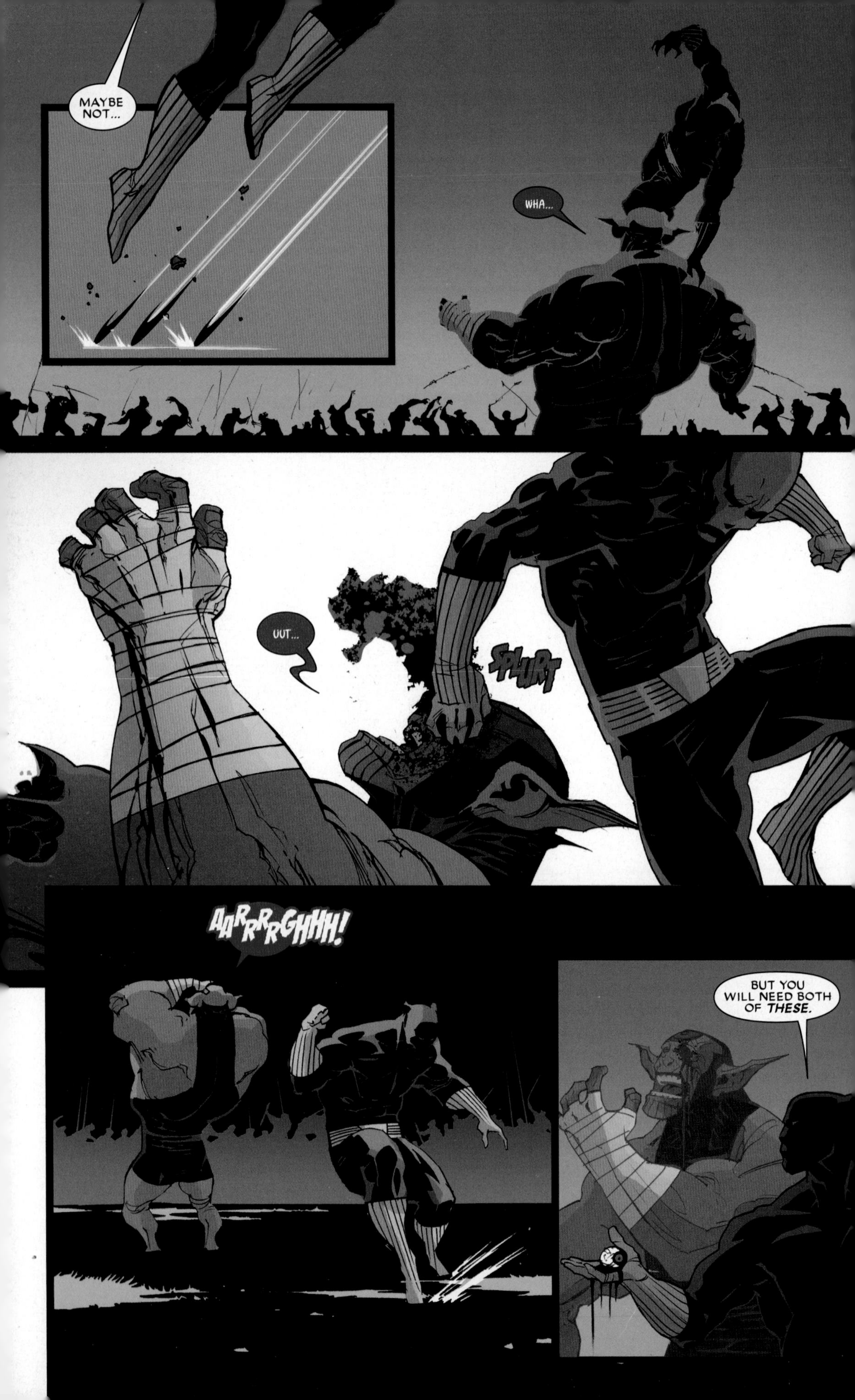
MAYBE NOT...
WHA...
UUT...
SPLURT
AARRRRGHHH!
BUT YOU WILL NEED BOTH OF *THESE.*

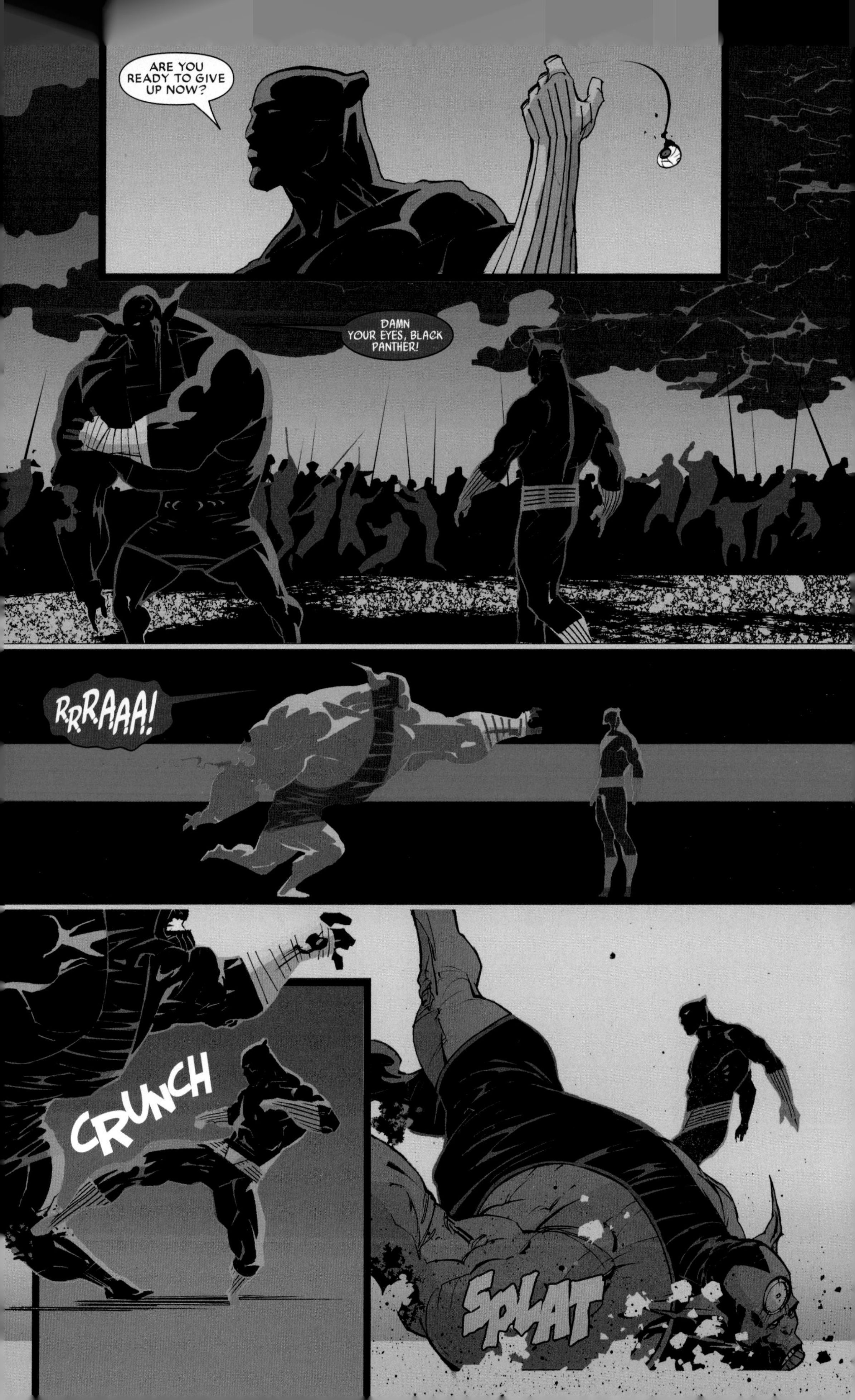
ARE YOU READY TO GIVE UP NOW?
DAMN YOUR EYES, BLACK PANTHER!
RRRAAA!
CRUNCH
SPLAT

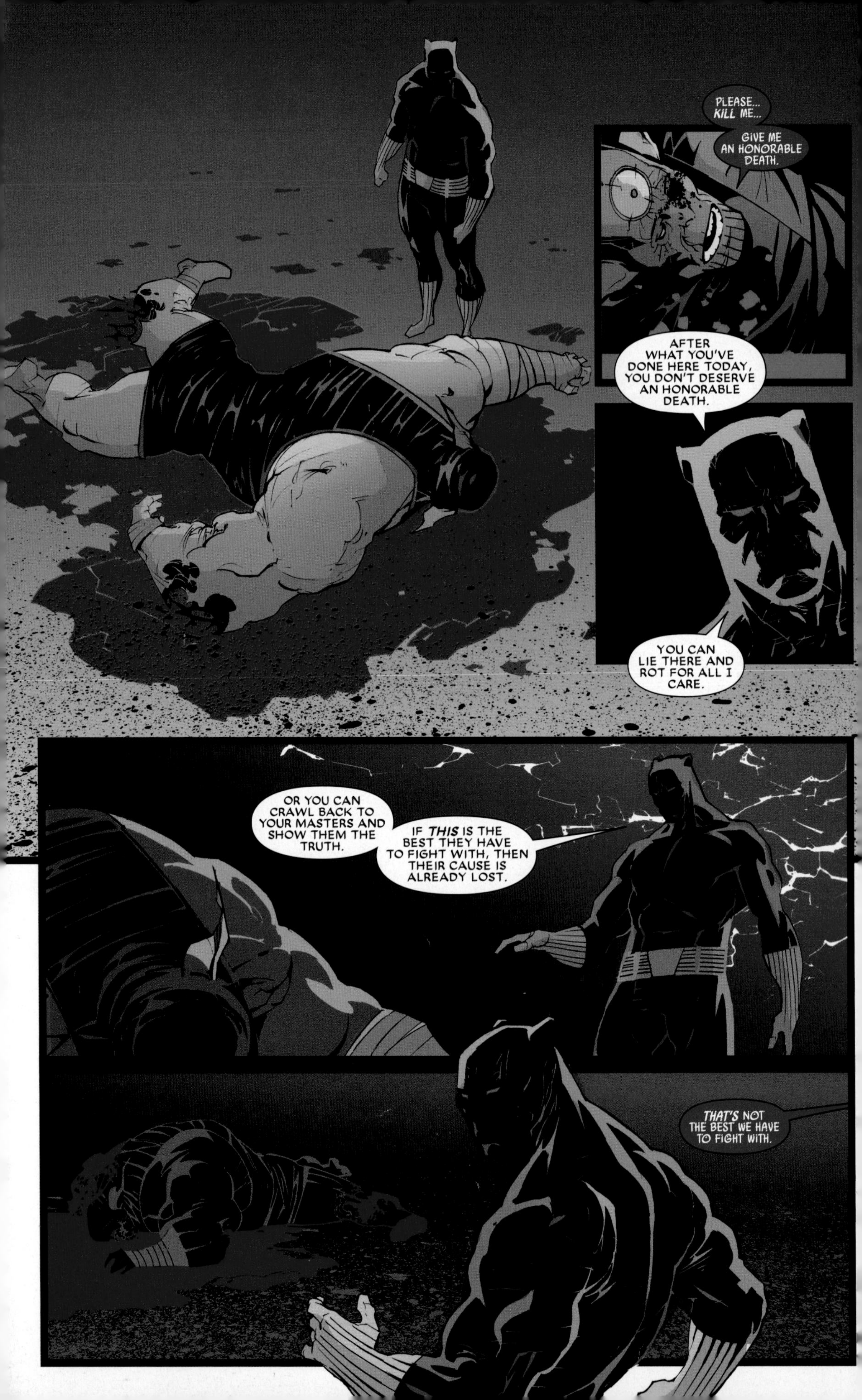
PLEASE... KILL ME...
GIVE ME AN HONORABLE DEATH.
AFTER WHAT YOU'VE DONE HERE TODAY, YOU DON'T DESERVE AN HONORABLE DEATH.
YOU CAN LIE THERE AND ROT FOR ALL I CARE.
OR YOU CAN CRAWL BACK TO YOUR MASTERS AND SHOW THEM THE TRUTH.
IF THIS IS THE BEST THEY HAVE TO FIGHT WITH, THEN THEIR CAUSE IS ALREADY LOST.
THAT'S NOT THE BEST WE HAVE TO FIGHT WITH.

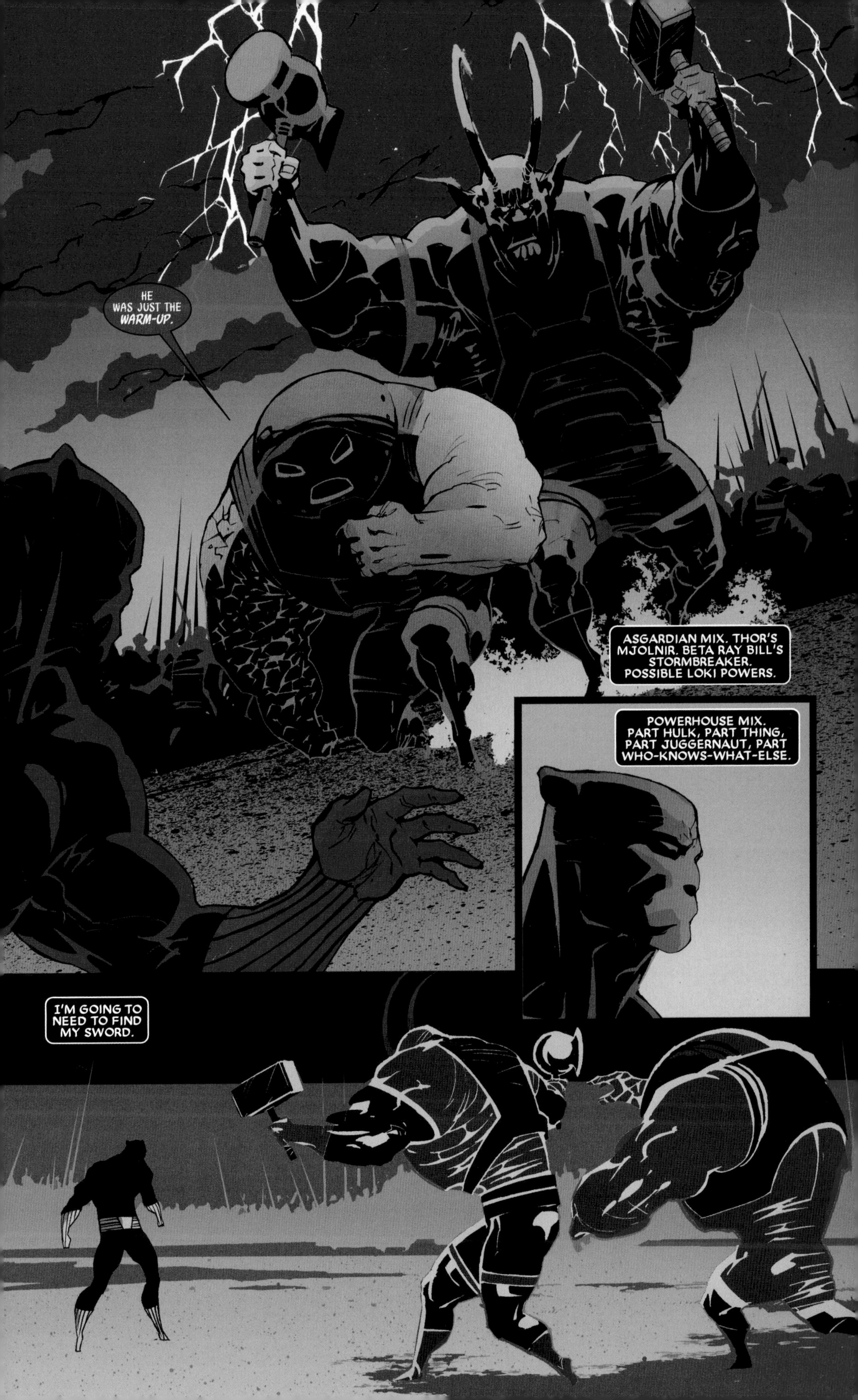
HE WAS JUST THE WARM-UP.
ASGARDIAN MIX. THOR'S MJOLNIR. BETA RAY BILL'S STORMBREAKER. POSSIBLE LOKI POWERS.
POWERHOUSE MIX. PART HULK, PART THING, PART JUGGERNAUT, PART WHO-KNOWS-WHAT-ELSE.
I'M GOING TO NEED TO FIND MY SWORD.

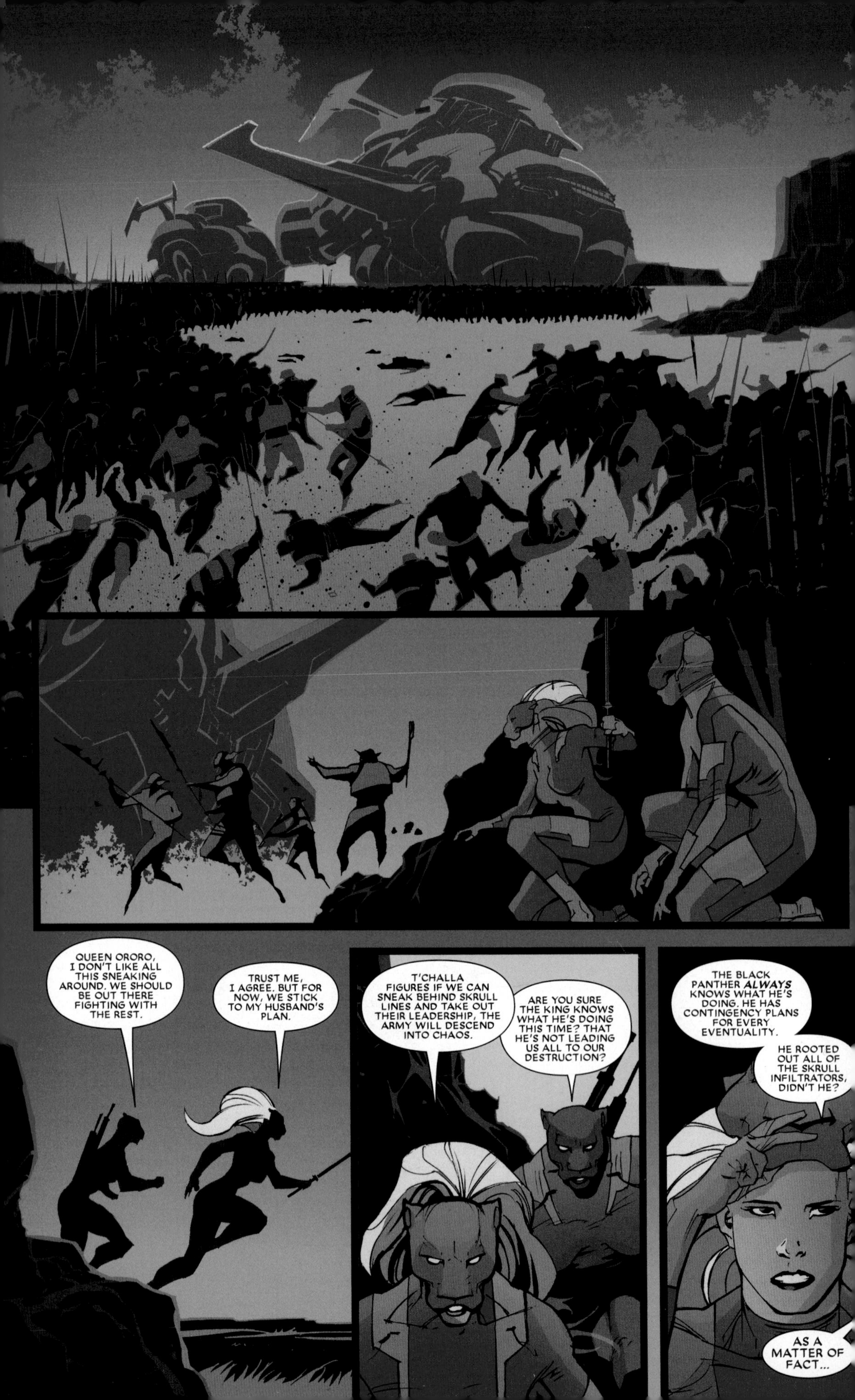
QUEEN ORORO, I DON'T LIKE ALL THIS SNEAKING AROUND. WE SHOULD BE OUT THERE FIGHTING WITH THE REST.
TRUST ME, I AGREE. BUT FOR NOW, WE STICK TO MY HUSBAND'S PLAN.
T'CHALLA FIGURES IF WE CAN SNEAK BEHIND SKRULL LINES AND TAKE OUT THEIR LEADERSHIP, THE ARMY WILL DESCEND INTO CHAOS.
ARE YOU SURE THE KING KNOWS WHAT HE'S DOING THIS TIME? THAT HE'S NOT LEADING US ALL TO OUR DESTRUCTION?
THE BLACK PANTHER *ALWAYS* KNOWS WHAT HE'S DOING. HE HAS CONTINGENCY PLANS FOR EVERY EVENTUALITY.
HE ROOTED OUT ALL OF THE SKRULL INFILTRATORS, DIDN'T HE?
AS A MATTER OF FACT...

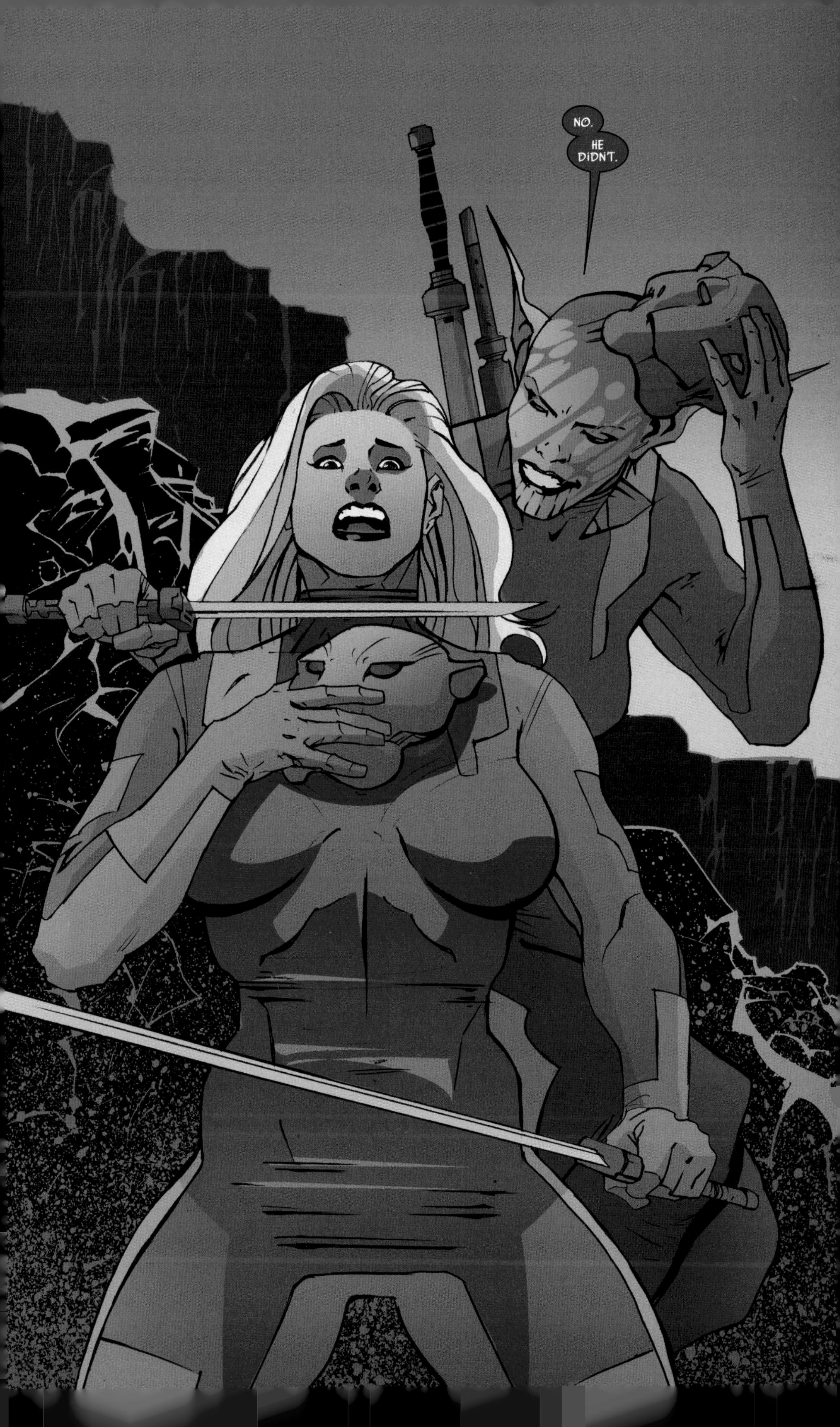
NO.
HE DIDN'T.

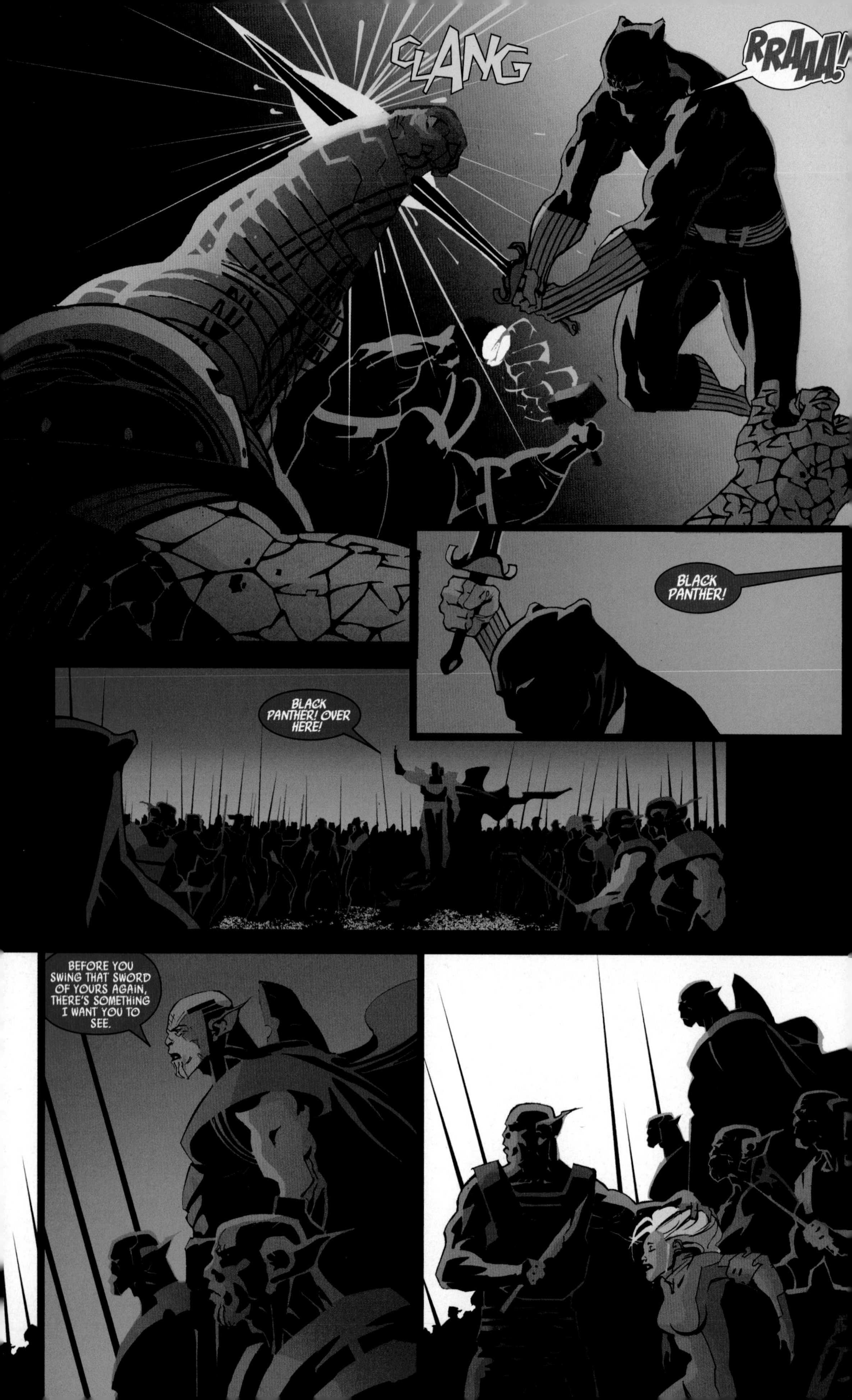
CLANG
RRAAA!
BLACK PANTHER!
BLACK PANTHER! OVER HERE!
BEFORE YOU SWING THAT SWORD OF YOURS AGAIN, THERE'S SOMETHING I WANT YOU TO SEE.

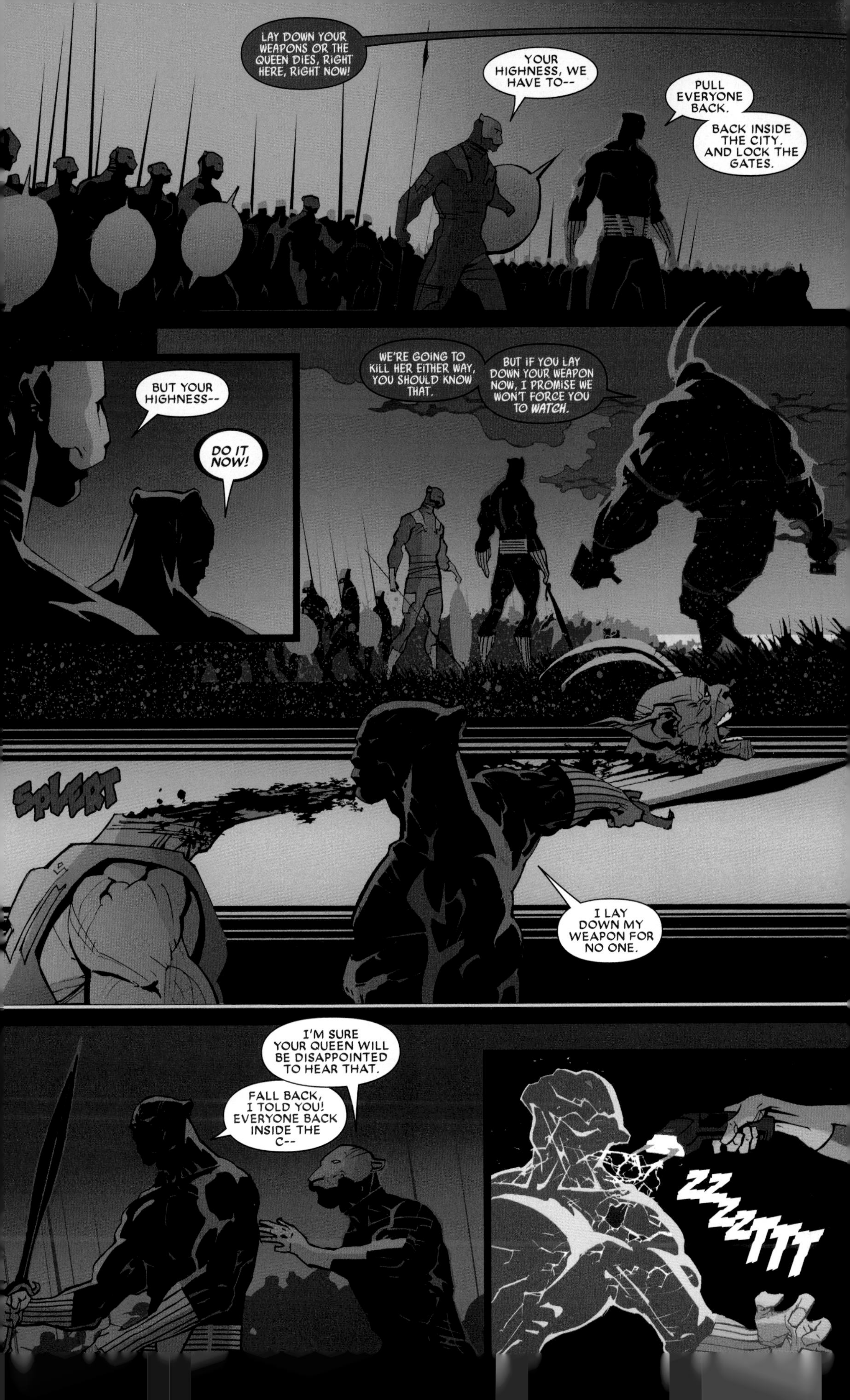
LAY DOWN YOUR WEAPONS OR THE QUEEN DIES, RIGHT HERE, RIGHT NOW!
YOUR HIGHNESS, WE HAVE TO--
PULL EVERYONE BACK.
BACK INSIDE THE CITY. AND LOCK THE GATES.
BUT YOUR HIGHNESS--
DO IT NOW!
WE'RE GOING TO KILL HER EITHER WAY, YOU SHOULD KNOW THAT.
BUT IF YOU LAY DOWN YOUR WEAPON NOW, I PROMISE WE WON'T FORCE YOU TO WATCH.
SPLERT
I LAY DOWN MY WEAPON FOR NO ONE.
I'M SURE YOUR QUEEN WILL BE DISAPPOINTED TO HEAR THAT.
FALL BACK, I TOLD YOU! EVERYONE BACK INSIDE THE C--
ZZZZTTTT

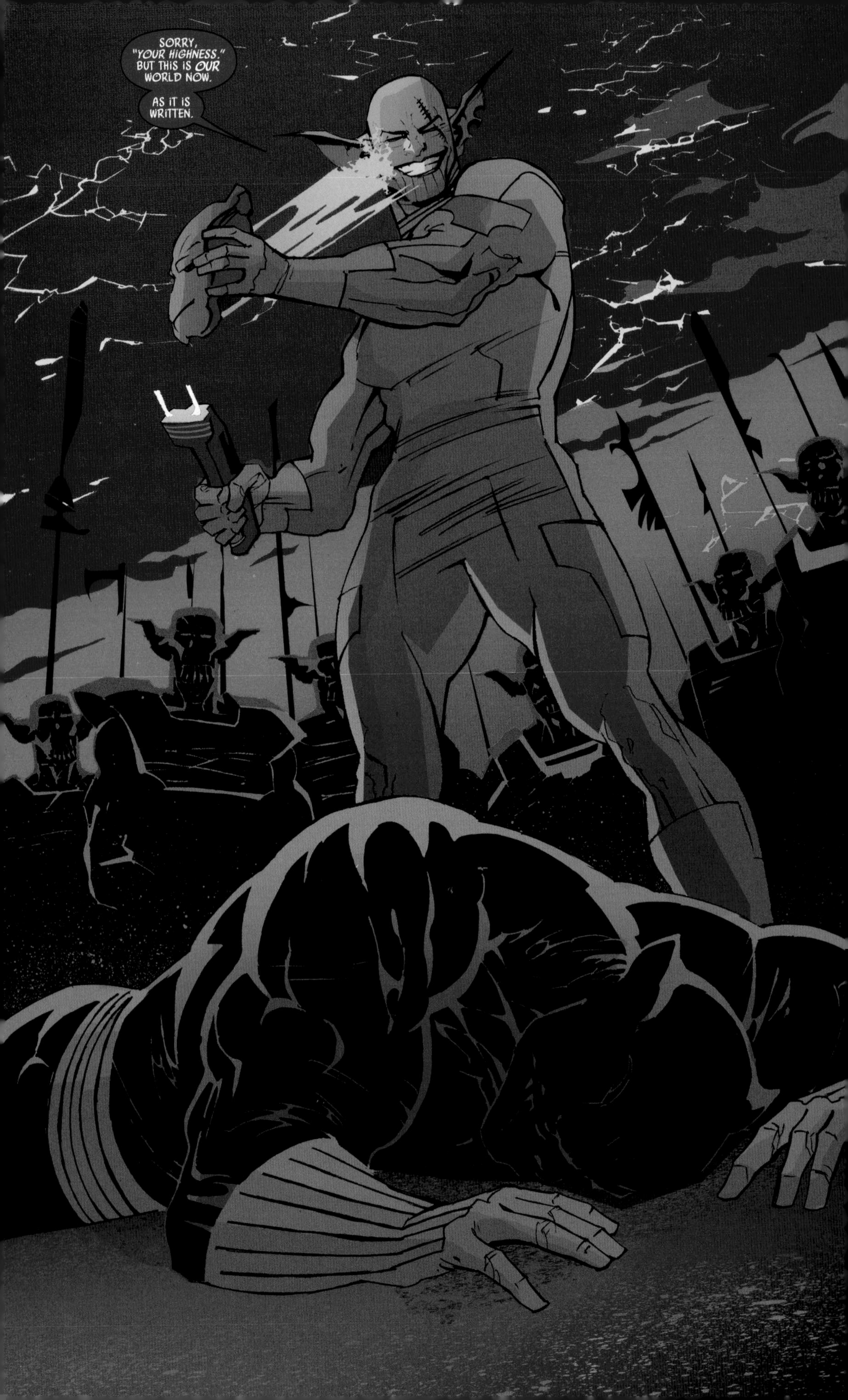
SORRY, "YOUR HIGHNESS." BUT THIS IS OUR WORLD NOW.
AS IT IS WRITTEN.

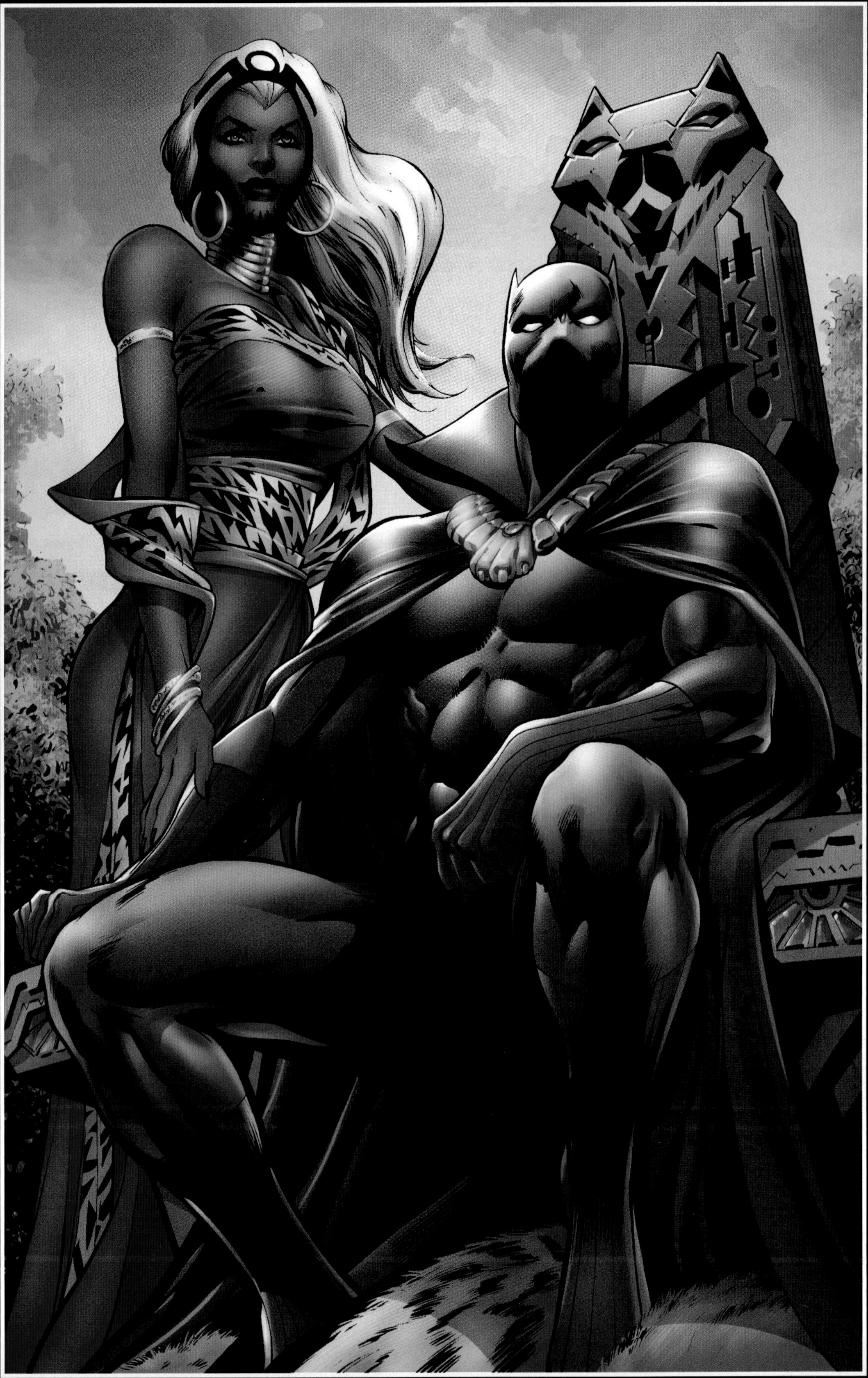

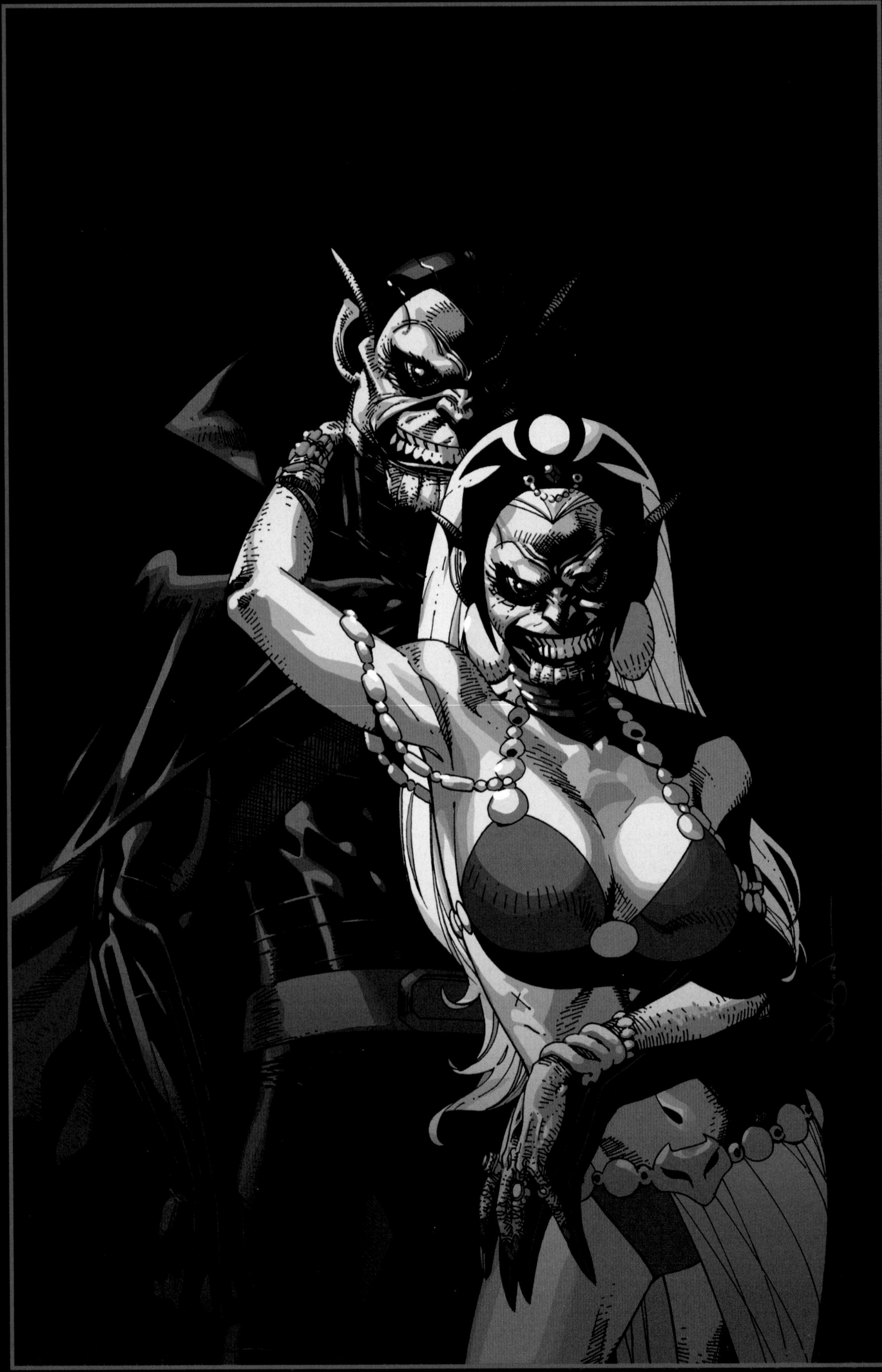

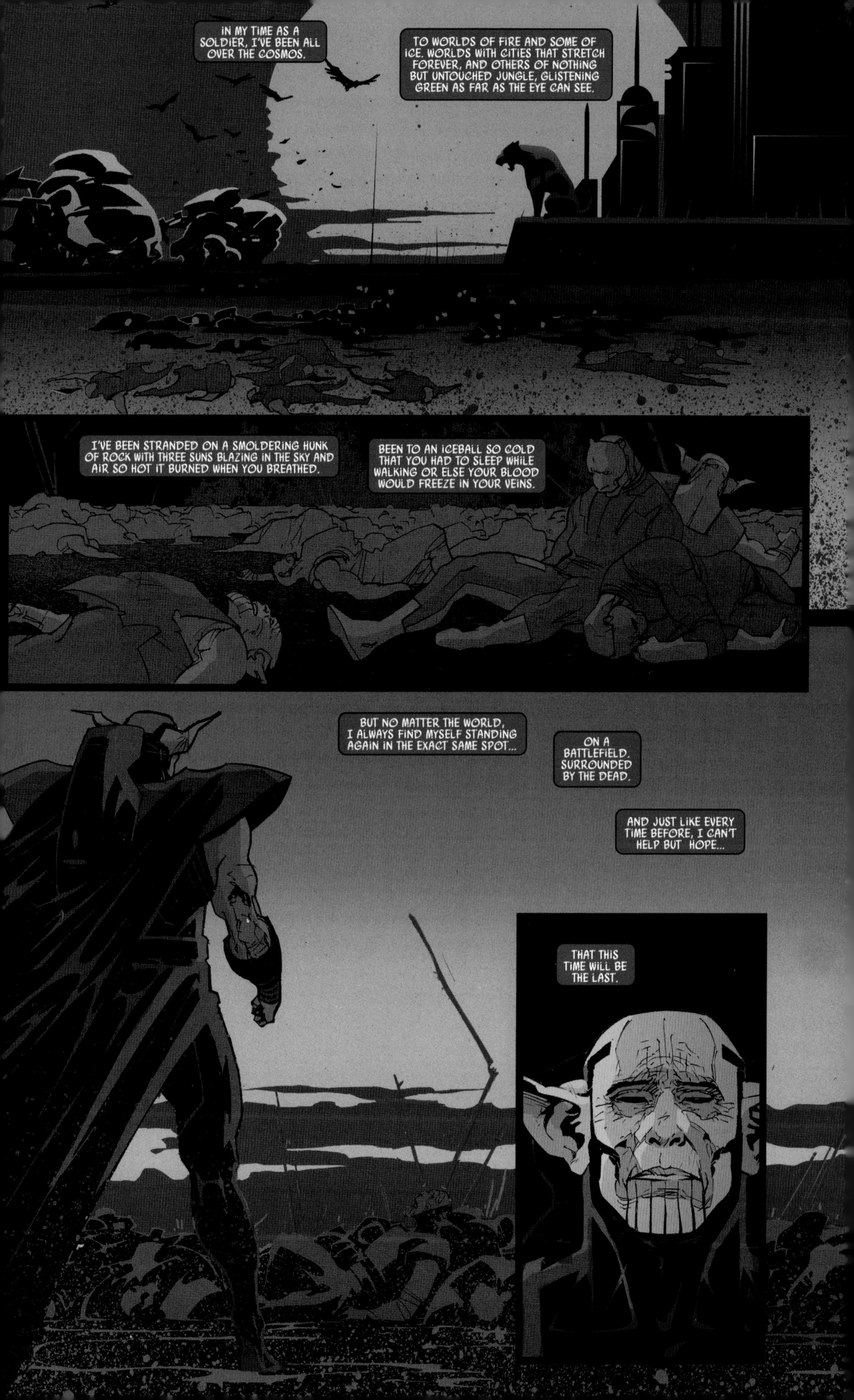
IN MY TIME AS A SOLDIER, I'VE BEEN ALL OVER THE COSMOS.
TO WORLDS OF FIRE AND SOME OF ICE. WORLDS WITH CITIES THAT STRETCH FOREVER, AND OTHERS OF NOTHING BUT UNTOUCHED JUNGLE, GLISTENING GREEN AS FAR AS THE EYE CAN SEE.
I'VE BEEN STRANDED ON A SMOLDERING HUNK OF ROCK WITH THREE SUNS BLAZING IN THE SKY AND AIR SO HOT IT BURNED WHEN YOU BREATHED.
BEEN TO AN ICEBALL SO COLD THAT YOU HAD TO SLEEP WHILE WALKING OR ELSE YOUR BLOOD WOULD FREEZE IN YOUR VEINS.
BUT NO MATTER THE WORLD, I ALWAYS FIND MYSELF STANDING AGAIN IN THE EXACT SAME SPOT...
ON A BATTLEFIELD, SURROUNDED BY THE DEAD.
AND JUST LIKE EVERY TIME BEFORE, I CAN'T HELP BUT HOPE...
THAT THIS TIME WILL BE THE LAST.

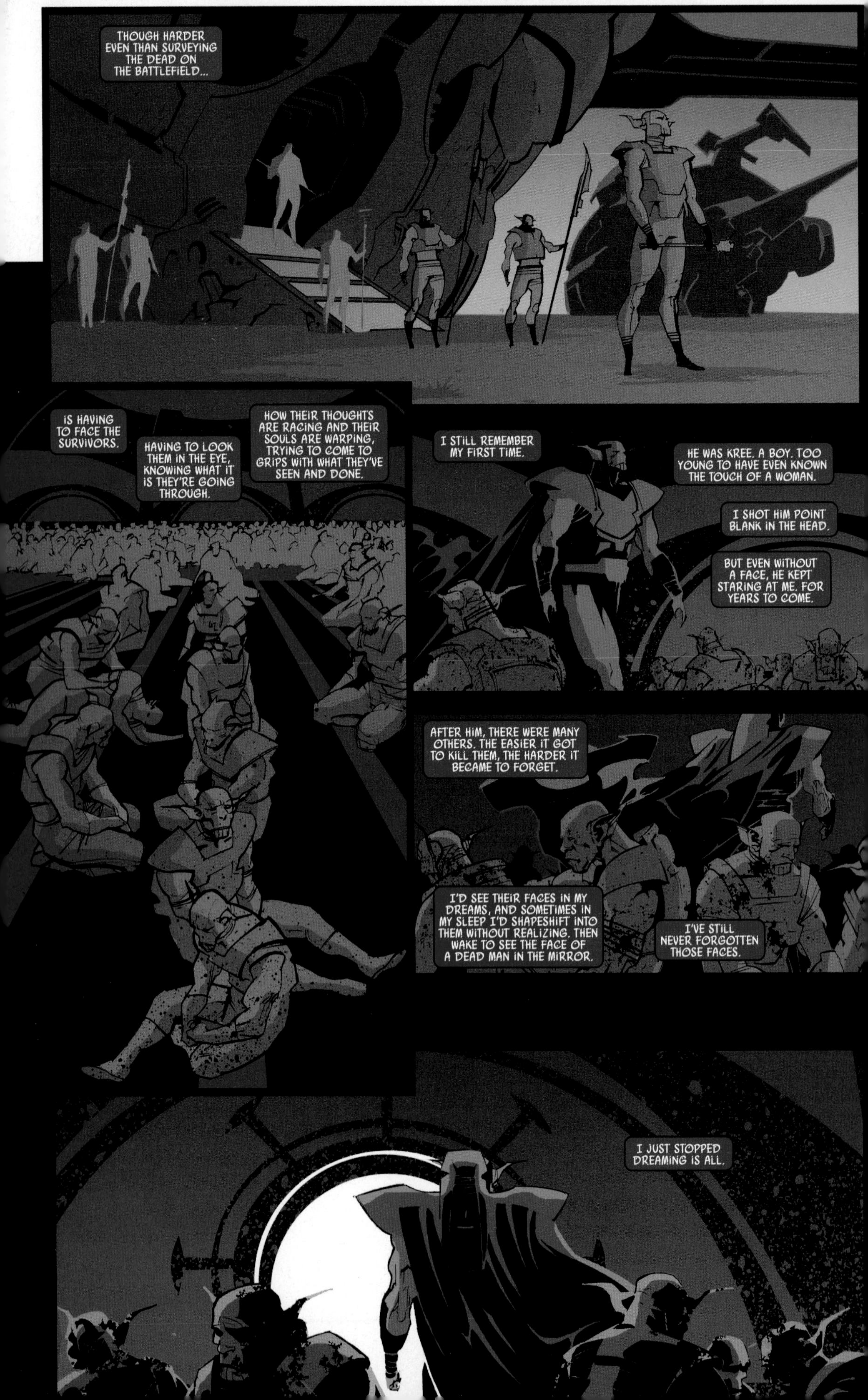
THOUGH HARDER EVEN THAN SURVEYING THE DEAD ON THE BATTLEFIELD...
IS HAVING TO FACE THE SURVIVORS.
HAVING TO LOOK THEM IN THE EYE, KNOWING WHAT IT IS THEY'RE GOING THROUGH.
HOW THEIR THOUGHTS ARE RACING AND THEIR SOULS ARE WARPING, TRYING TO COME TO GRIPS WITH WHAT THEY'VE SEEN AND DONE.
I STILL REMEMBER MY FIRST TIME.
HE WAS KREE. A BOY. TOO YOUNG TO HAVE EVEN KNOWN THE TOUCH OF A WOMAN.
I SHOT HIM POINT BLANK IN THE HEAD.
BUT EVEN WITHOUT A FACE, HE KEPT STARING AT ME. FOR YEARS TO COME.
AFTER HIM, THERE WERE MANY OTHERS. THE EASIER IT GOT TO KILL THEM, THE HARDER IT BECAME TO FORGET.
I'D SEE THEIR FACES IN MY DREAMS, AND SOMETIMES IN MY SLEEP I'D SHAPESHIFT INTO THEM WITHOUT REALIZING. THEN WAKE TO SEE THE FACE OF A DEAD MAN IN THE MIRROR.
I'VE STILL NEVER FORGOTTEN THOSE FACES.
I JUST STOPPED DREAMING IS ALL.

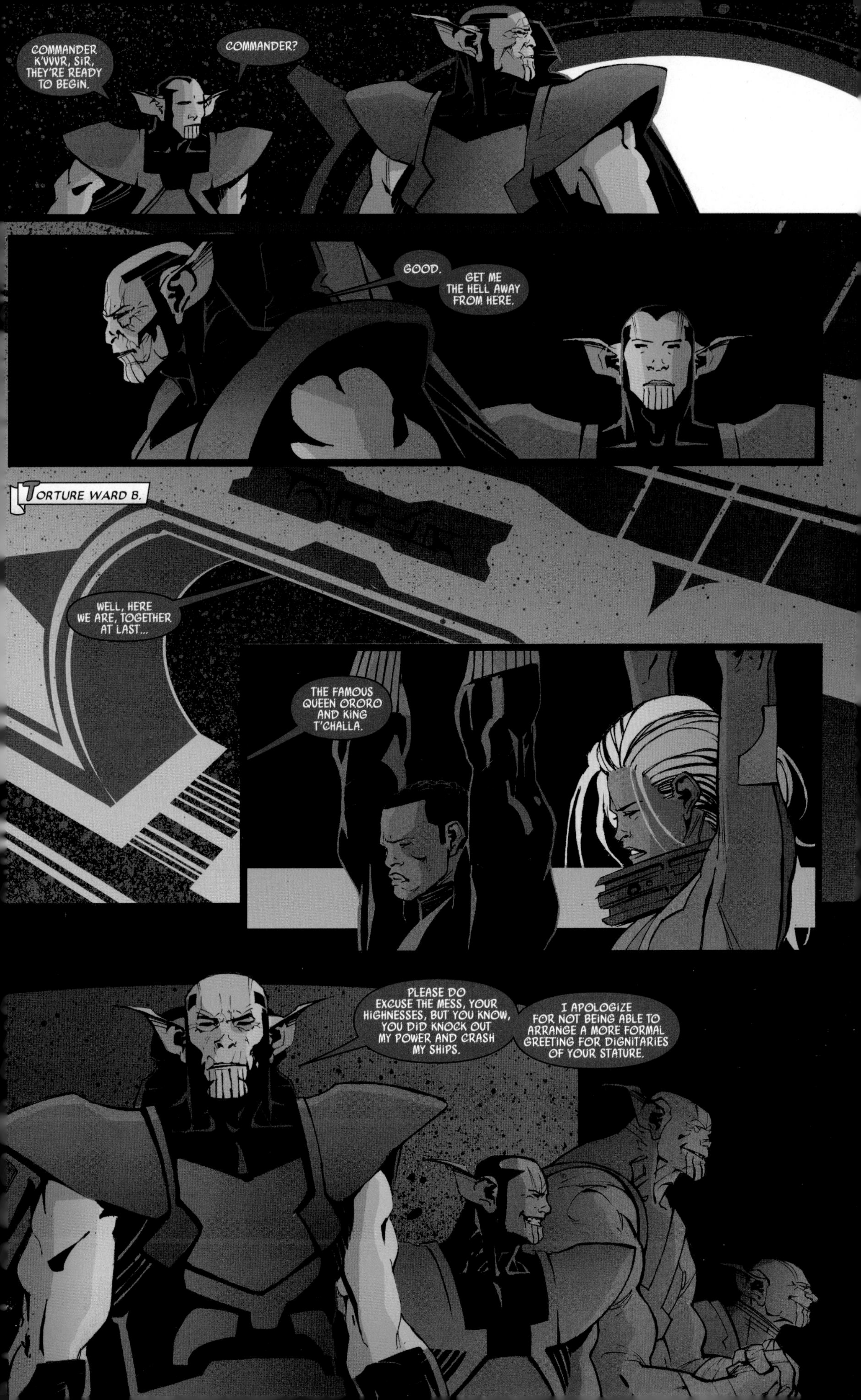
COMMANDER K'VVVR, SIR, THEY'RE READY TO BEGIN.
COMMANDER?
GOOD.
GET ME THE HELL AWAY FROM HERE.
TORTURE WARD B.
WELL, HERE WE ARE, TOGETHER AT LAST...
THE FAMOUS QUEEN ORORO AND KING T'CHALLA.
PLEASE DO EXCUSE THE MESS, YOUR HIGHNESSES, BUT YOU KNOW, YOU DID KNOCK OUT MY POWER AND CRASH MY SHIPS.
I APOLOGIZE FOR NOT BEING ABLE TO ARRANGE A MORE FORMAL GREETING FOR DIGNITARIES OF YOUR STATURE.

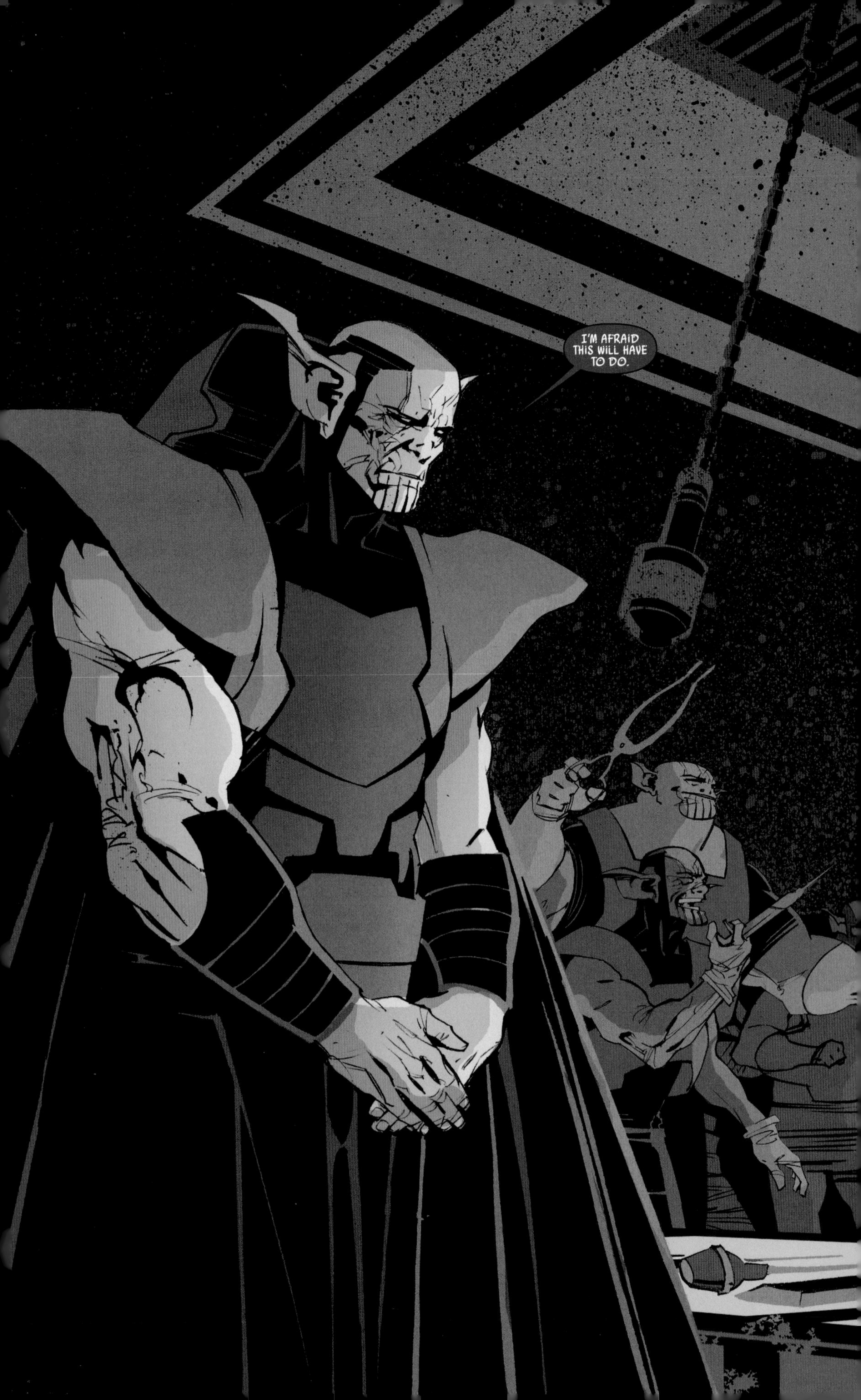
I'M AFRAID THIS WILL HAVE TO DO.

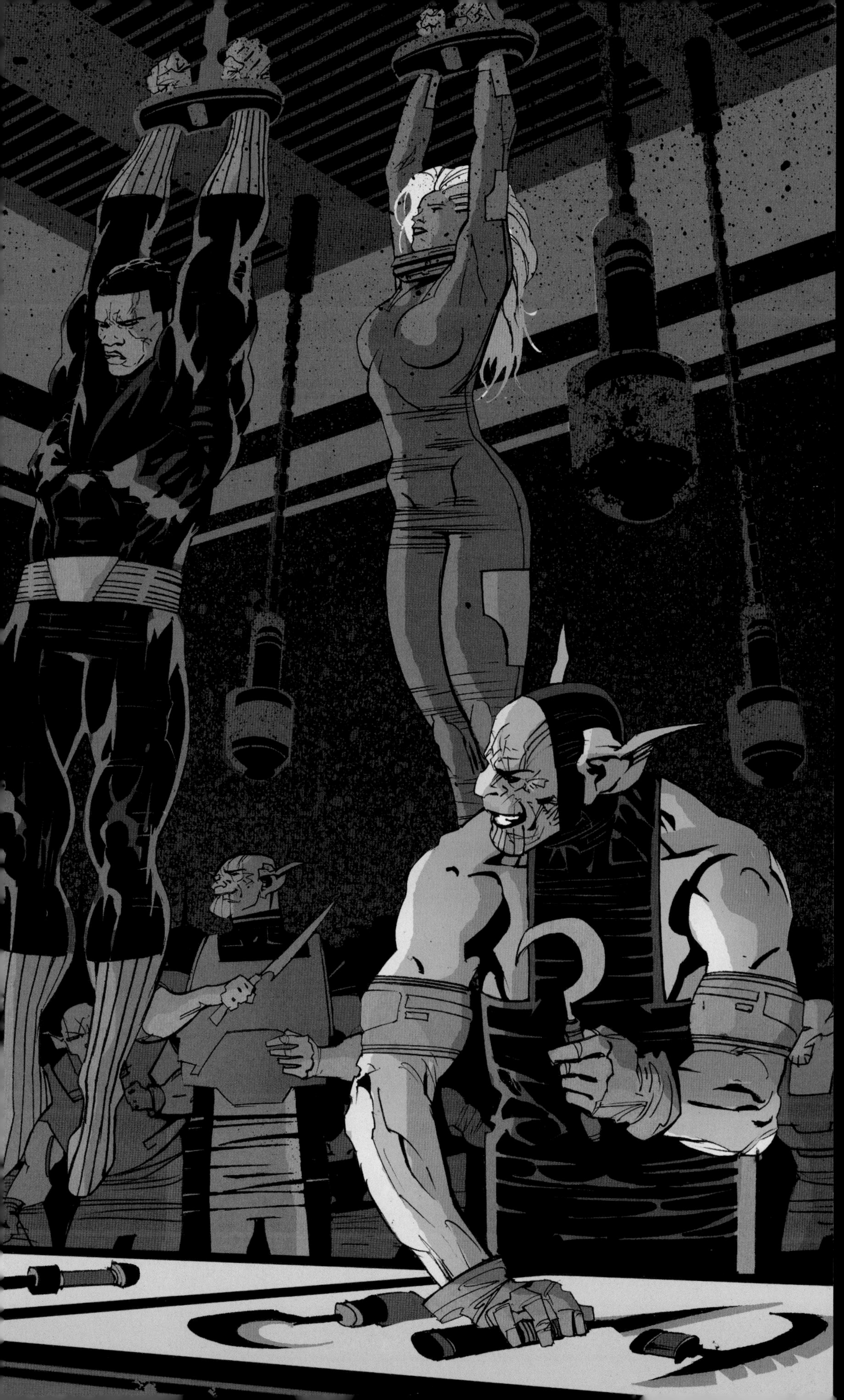

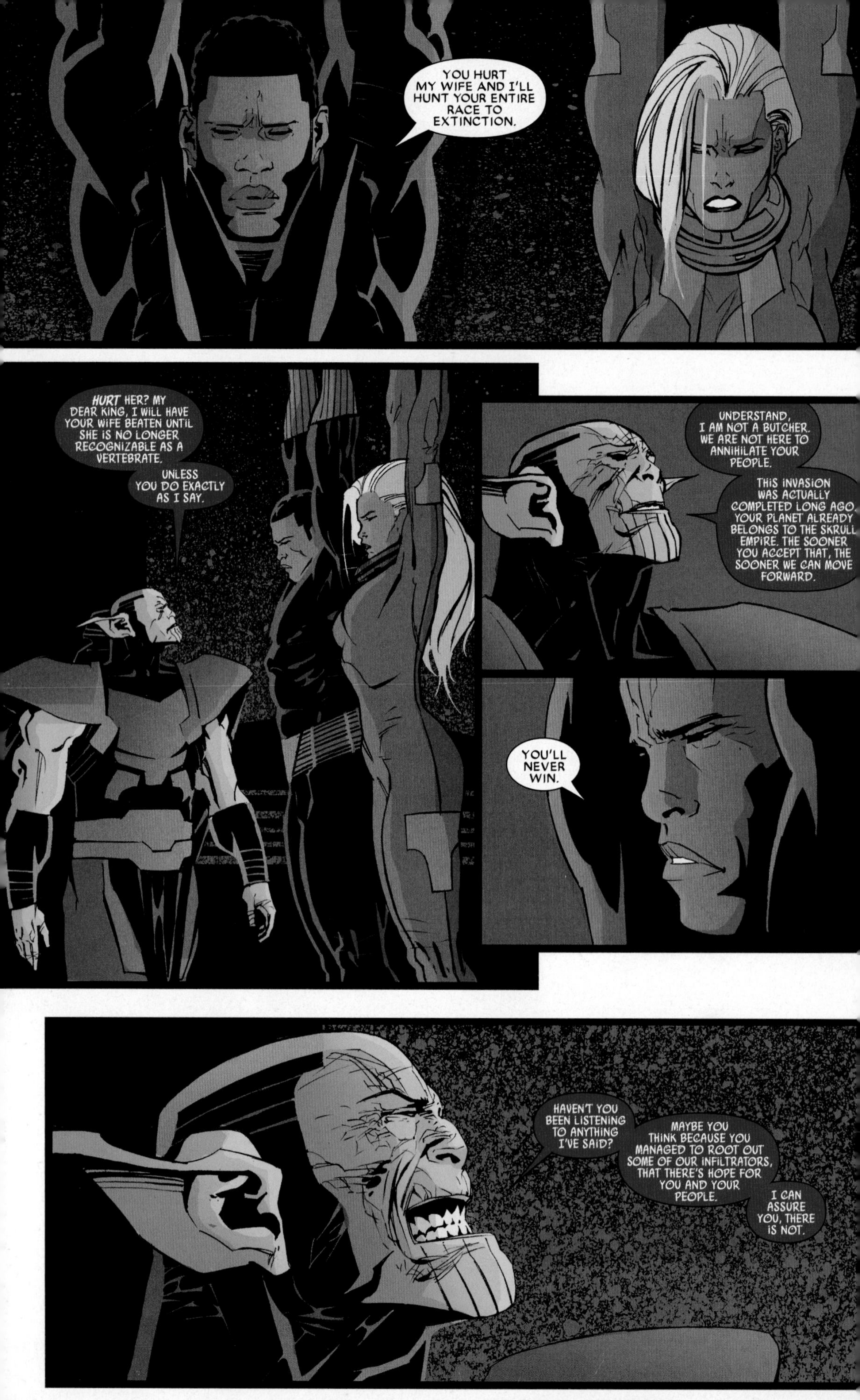
YOU HURT MY WIFE AND I'LL HUNT YOUR ENTIRE RACE TO EXTINCTION.
HURT HER? MY DEAR KING, I WILL HAVE YOUR WIFE BEATEN UNTIL SHE IS NO LONGER RECOGNIZABLE AS A VERTEBRATE.
UNLESS YOU DO EXACTLY AS I SAY.
UNDERSTAND, I AM NOT A BUTCHER. WE ARE NOT HERE TO ANNIHILATE YOUR PEOPLE.
THIS INVASION WAS ACTUALLY COMPLETED LONG AGO. YOUR PLANET ALREADY BELONGS TO THE SKRULL EMPIRE. THE SOONER YOU ACCEPT THAT, THE SOONER WE CAN MOVE FORWARD.
YOU'LL NEVER WIN.
HAVEN'T YOU BEEN LISTENING TO ANYTHING I'VE SAID?
MAYBE YOU THINK BECAUSE YOU MANAGED TO ROOT OUT SOME OF OUR INFILTRATORS, THAT THERE'S HOPE FOR YOU AND YOUR PEOPLE.
I CAN ASSURE YOU, THERE IS NOT.

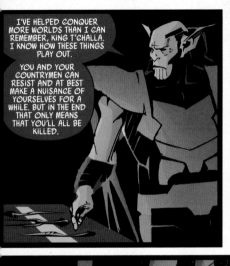

I'VE HELPED CONQUER MORE WORLDS THAN I CAN REMEMBER, KING T'CHALLA. I KNOW HOW THESE THINGS PLAY OUT.

YOU AND YOUR COUNTRYMEN CAN RESIST AND AT BEST MAKE A NUISANCE OF YOURSELVES FOR A WHILE. BUT IN THE END THAT ONLY MEANS THAT YOU'LL ALL BE KILLED.

LOOK AT YOUR WIFE. THAT COLLAR NEUTRALIZES HER POWERS, MAKING THEM AS USEFUL AS A BOSOM ON A BROOD QUEEN.

YOU HAVE NO MORE OPTIONS. ACCEPT THAT YOU'VE LOST. TELL YOUR PEOPLE TO STAND DOWN.

TELL THEM TO GO TO HELL, HONEY.

GO TO HELL, YOU BASTARDS.

I UNDERSTAND. YOU ARE OF ROYAL BLOOD. YOU COME FROM A LONG LINE OF KINGS. YOUR PRIDE WILL NOT LET YOU GIVE IN, DESPITE THE HOPELESSNESS OF YOUR SITUATION.

DO NOT WORRY THOUGH...

WE HAVE BEATEN THE PRIDE OUT OF GREATER KINGS THAN YOU.

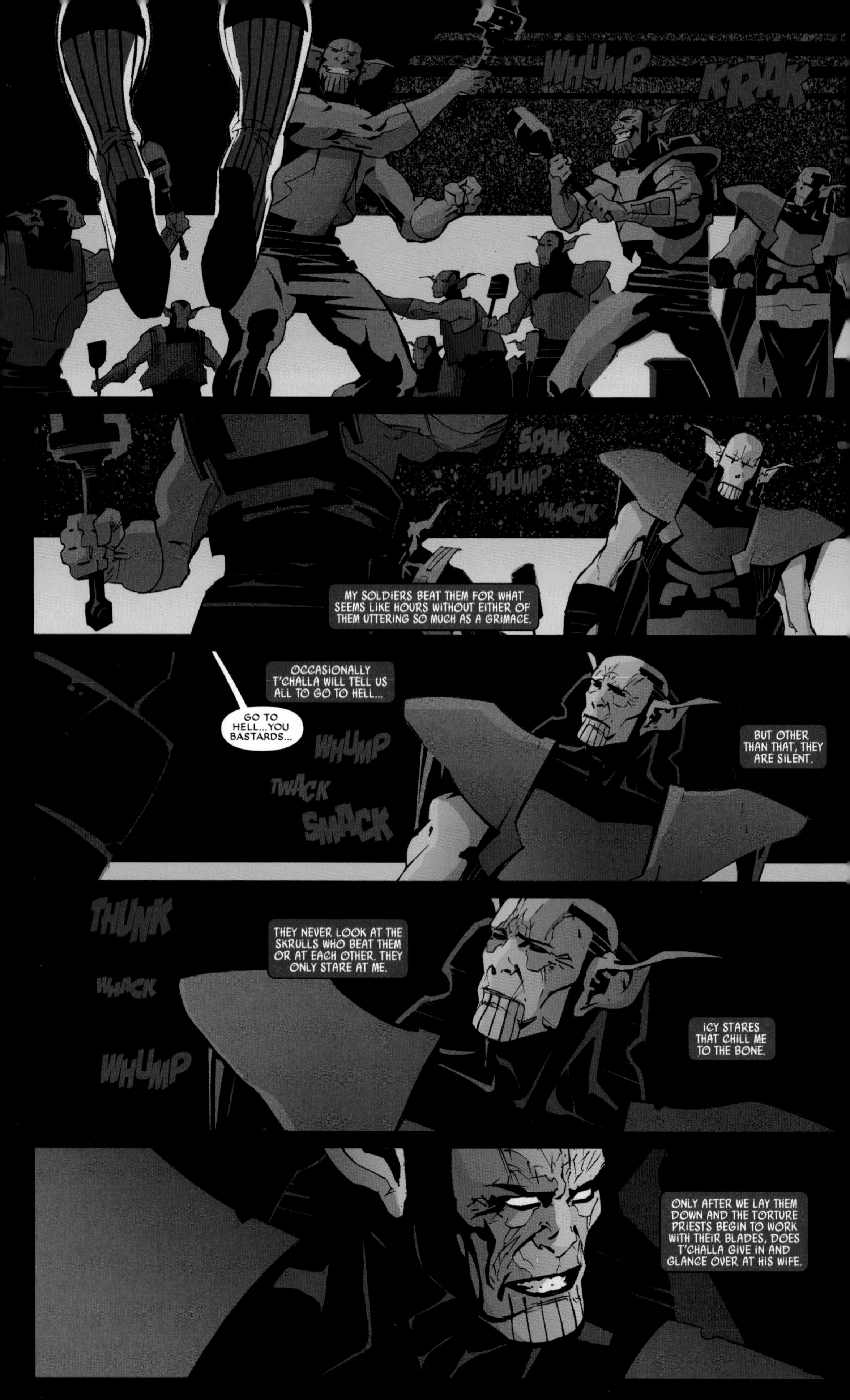
WHUMP
KRAK
SPAK
THUMP
WHACK
MY SOLDIERS BEAT THEM FOR WHAT SEEMS LIKE HOURS WITHOUT EITHER OF THEM UTTERING SO MUCH AS A GRIMACE.
OCCASIONALLY T'CHALLA WILL TELL US ALL TO GO TO HELL...
GO TO HELL...YOU BASTARDS...
WHUMP
TWACK
SMACK
BUT OTHER THAN THAT, THEY ARE SILENT.
THUNK
WHACK
WHUMP
THEY NEVER LOOK AT THE SKRULLS WHO BEAT THEM OR AT EACH OTHER. THEY ONLY STARE AT ME.
ICY STARES THAT CHILL ME TO THE BONE.
ONLY AFTER WE LAY THEM DOWN AND THE TORTURE PRIESTS BEGIN TO WORK WITH THEIR BLADES, DOES T'CHALLA GIVE IN AND GLANCE OVER AT HIS WIFE.

AAAAARRRGGGHHHH!!

AND THEN HE SCREAMS.

RRRAARRGGHH!!

THEY BOTH DO.

AAAARRGGHHH!! GGGAAAGGHH!!

I DON'T LIKE IT. WE SHOULD MOVE OUT NOW.

NO, SHURI. WE *WAIT.* WE STICK TO T'CHALLA'S PLAN.

AND PRAY HE KNOWS WHAT HE'S DOING.

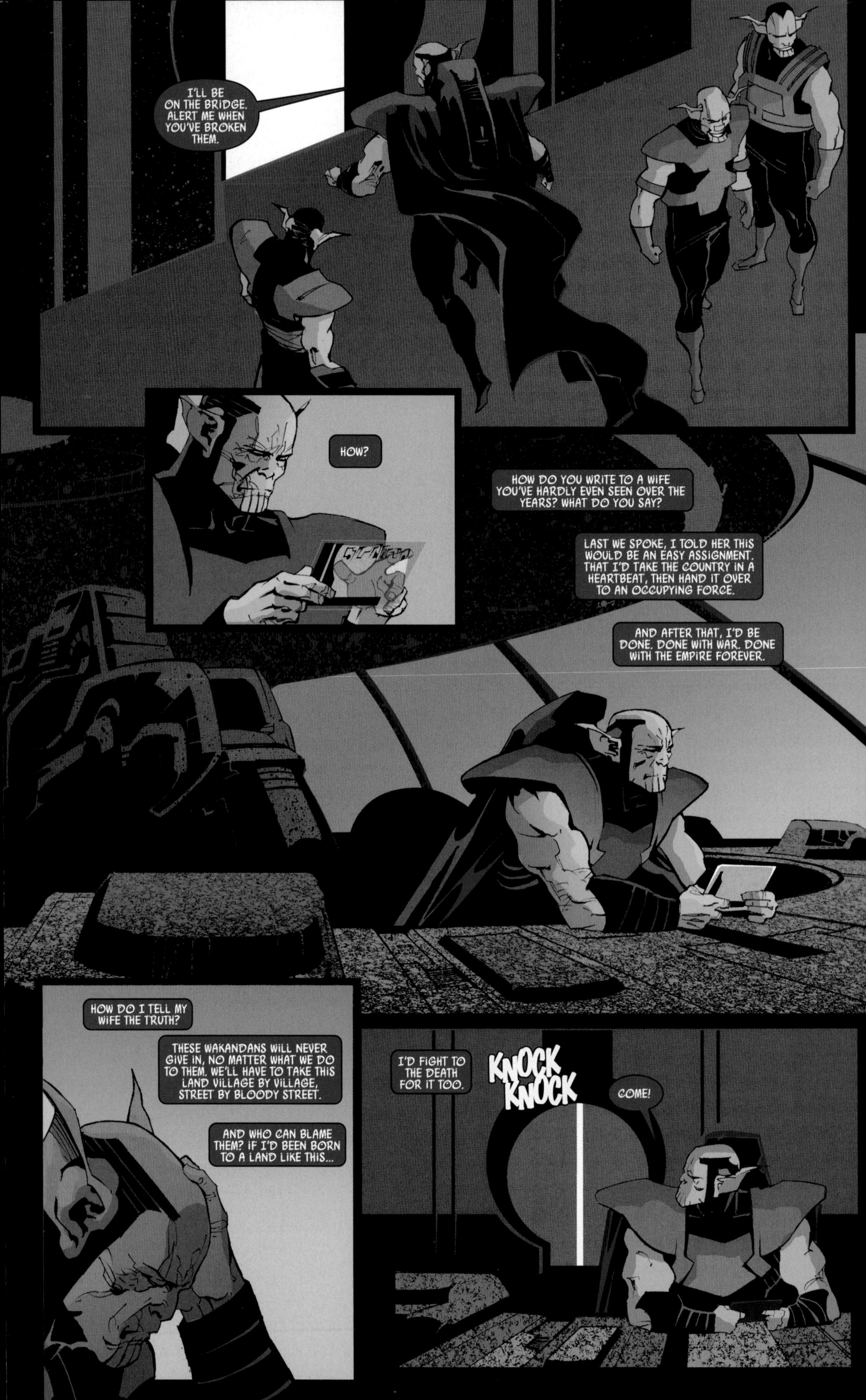
I'LL BE ON THE BRIDGE. ALERT ME WHEN YOU'VE BROKEN THEM.
HOW?
HOW DO YOU WRITE TO A WIFE YOU'VE HARDLY EVEN SEEN OVER THE YEARS? WHAT DO YOU SAY?
LAST WE SPOKE, I TOLD HER THIS WOULD BE AN EASY ASSIGNMENT. THAT I'D TAKE THE COUNTRY IN A HEARTBEAT, THEN HAND IT OVER TO AN OCCUPYING FORCE.
AND AFTER THAT, I'D BE DONE. DONE WITH WAR. DONE WITH THE EMPIRE FOREVER.
HOW DO I TELL MY WIFE THE TRUTH?
THESE WAKANDANS WILL NEVER GIVE IN, NO MATTER WHAT WE DO TO THEM. WE'LL HAVE TO TAKE THIS LAND VILLAGE BY VILLAGE, STREET BY BLOODY STREET.
AND WHO CAN BLAME THEM? IF I'D BEEN BORN TO A LAND LIKE THIS...
I'D FIGHT TO THE DEATH FOR IT TOO.
KNOCK KNOCK
COME!

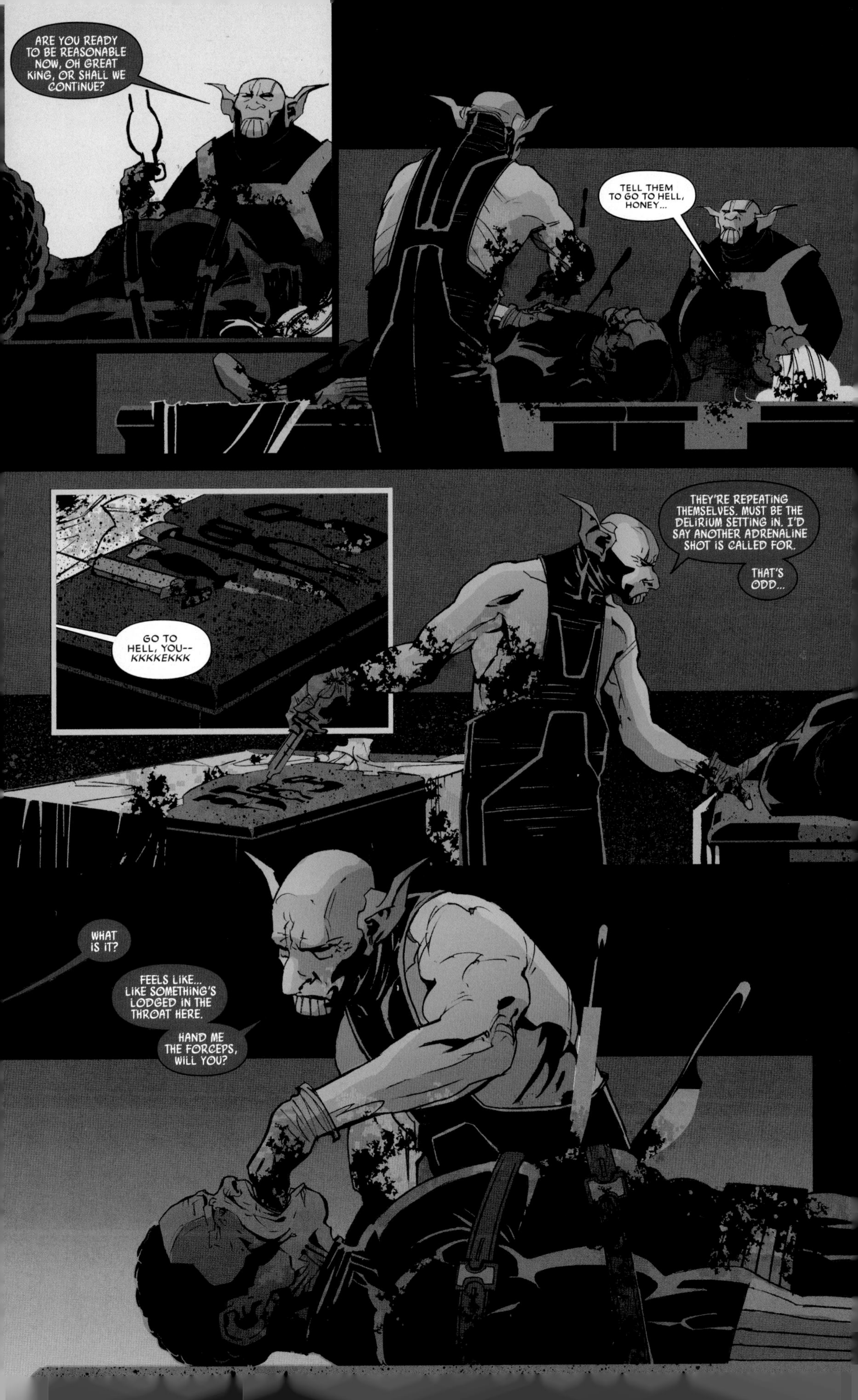
ARE YOU READY TO BE REASONABLE NOW, OH GREAT KING, OR SHALL WE CONTINUE?
TELL THEM TO GO TO HELL, HONEY...
GO TO HELL, YOU-- KKKKEKKK
THEY'RE REPEATING THEMSELVES. MUST BE THE DELIRIUM SETTING IN. I'D SAY ANOTHER ADRENALINE SHOT IS CALLED FOR.
THAT'S ODD...
WHAT IS IT?
FEELS LIKE... LIKE SOMETHING'S LODGED IN THE THROAT HERE.
HAND ME THE FORCEPS, WILL YOU?

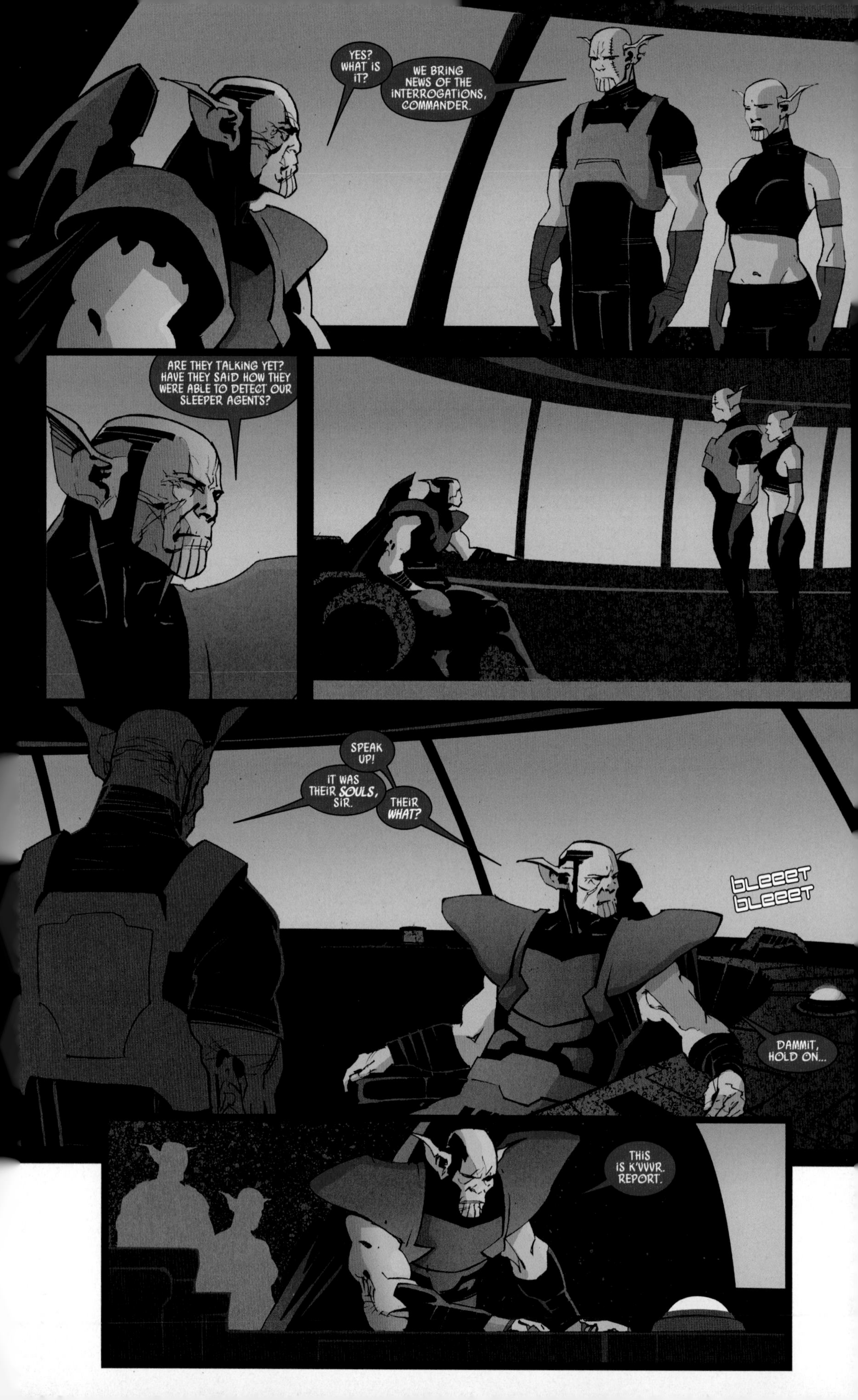
YES? WHAT iS iT?
WE BRING NEWS OF THE iNTERROGATiONS, COMMANDER.
ARE THEY TALKiNG YET? HAVE THEY SAiD HOW THEY WERE ABLE TO DETECT OUR SLEEPER AGENTS?
SPEAK UP!
iT WAS THEiR SOULS, SiR.
THEiR WHAT?
BLEEET BLEEET
DAMMiT, HOLD ON...
THiS iS K'VVVR. REPORT.

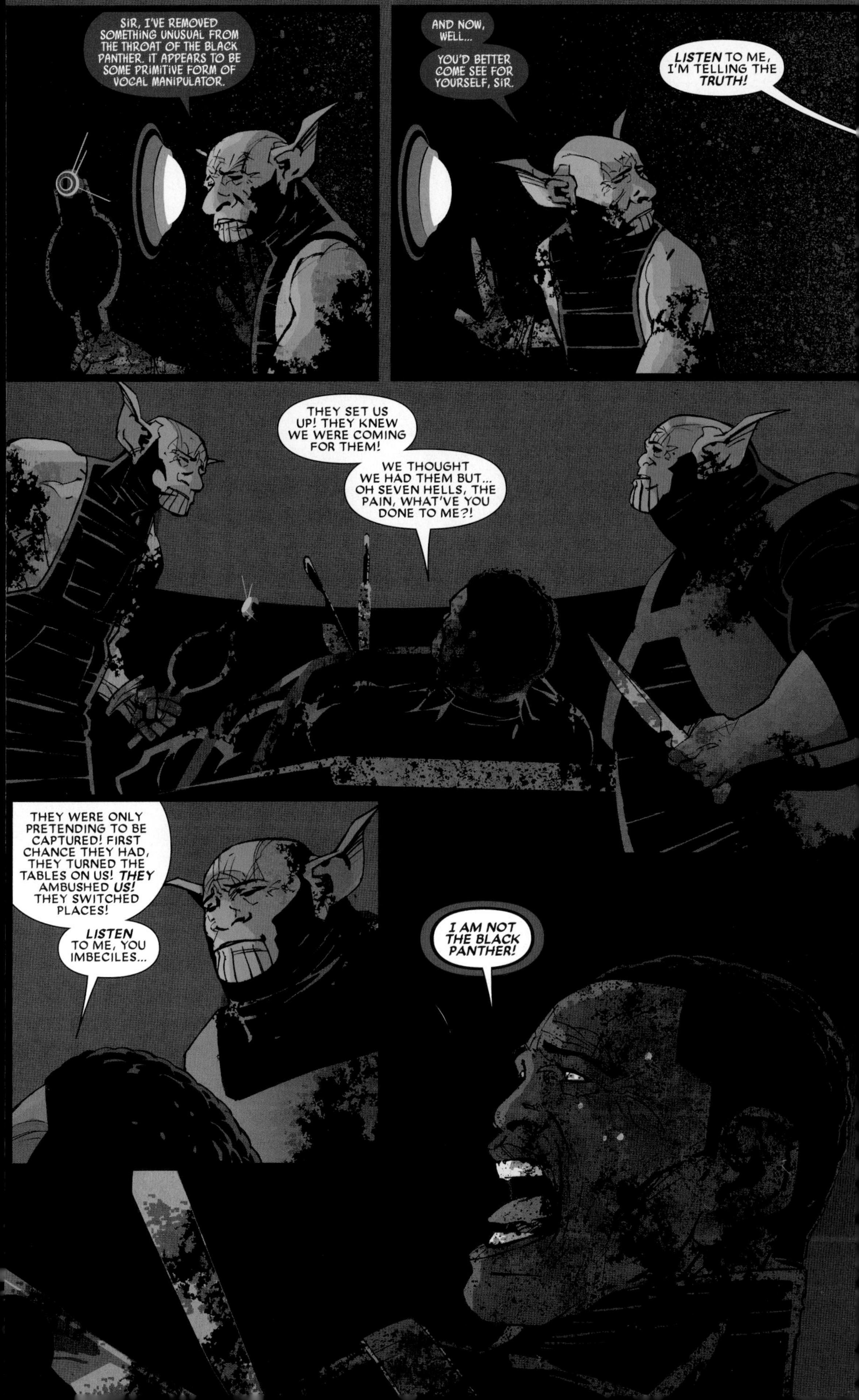
SIR, I'VE REMOVED SOMETHING UNUSUAL FROM THE THROAT OF THE BLACK PANTHER. IT APPEARS TO BE SOME PRIMITIVE FORM OF VOCAL MANIPULATOR.
AND NOW, WELL...
YOU'D BETTER COME SEE FOR YOURSELF, SIR.
LISTEN TO ME, I'M TELLING THE TRUTH!
THEY SET US UP! THEY KNEW WE WERE COMING FOR THEM!
WE THOUGHT WE HAD THEM BUT... OH SEVEN HELLS, THE PAIN, WHAT'VE YOU DONE TO ME?!
THEY WERE ONLY PRETENDING TO BE CAPTURED! FIRST CHANCE THEY HAD, THEY TURNED THE TABLES ON US! THEY AMBUSHED US! THEY SWITCHED PLACES!
LISTEN TO ME, YOU IMBECILES...
I AM NOT THE BLACK PANTHER!

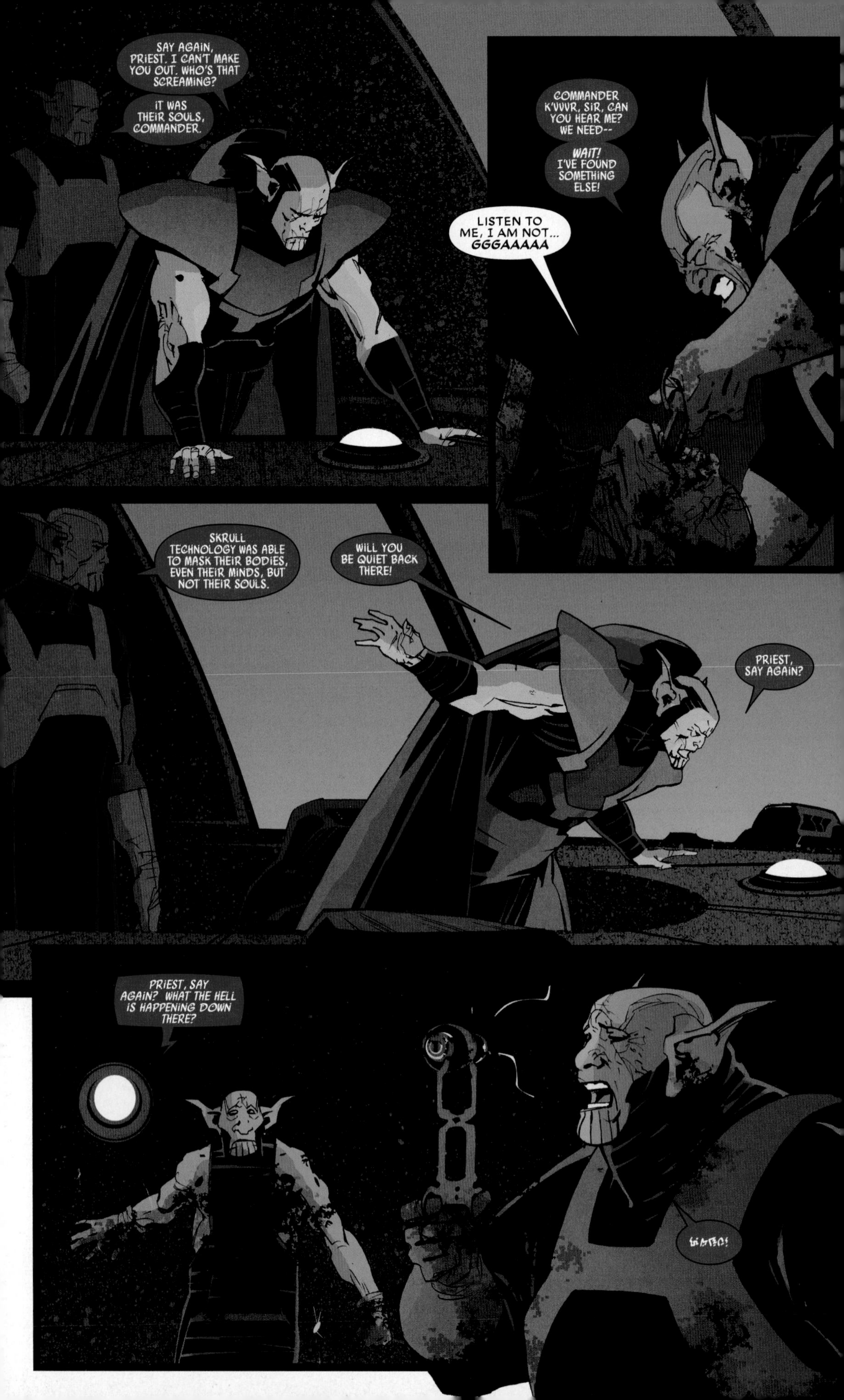
SAY AGAIN, PRIEST. I CAN'T MAKE YOU OUT. WHO'S THAT SCREAMING?
IT WAS THEIR SOULS, COMMANDER.
COMMANDER K'VVVR, SIR, CAN YOU HEAR ME? WE NEED--
WAIT! I'VE FOUND SOMETHING ELSE!
LISTEN TO ME, I AM NOT... GGGAAAAAA
SKRULL TECHNOLOGY WAS ABLE TO MASK THEIR BODIES, EVEN THEIR MINDS, BUT NOT THEIR SOULS.
WILL YOU BE QUIET BACK THERE!
PRIEST, SAY AGAIN?
PRIEST, SAY AGAIN? WHAT THE HELL IS HAPPENING DOWN THERE?

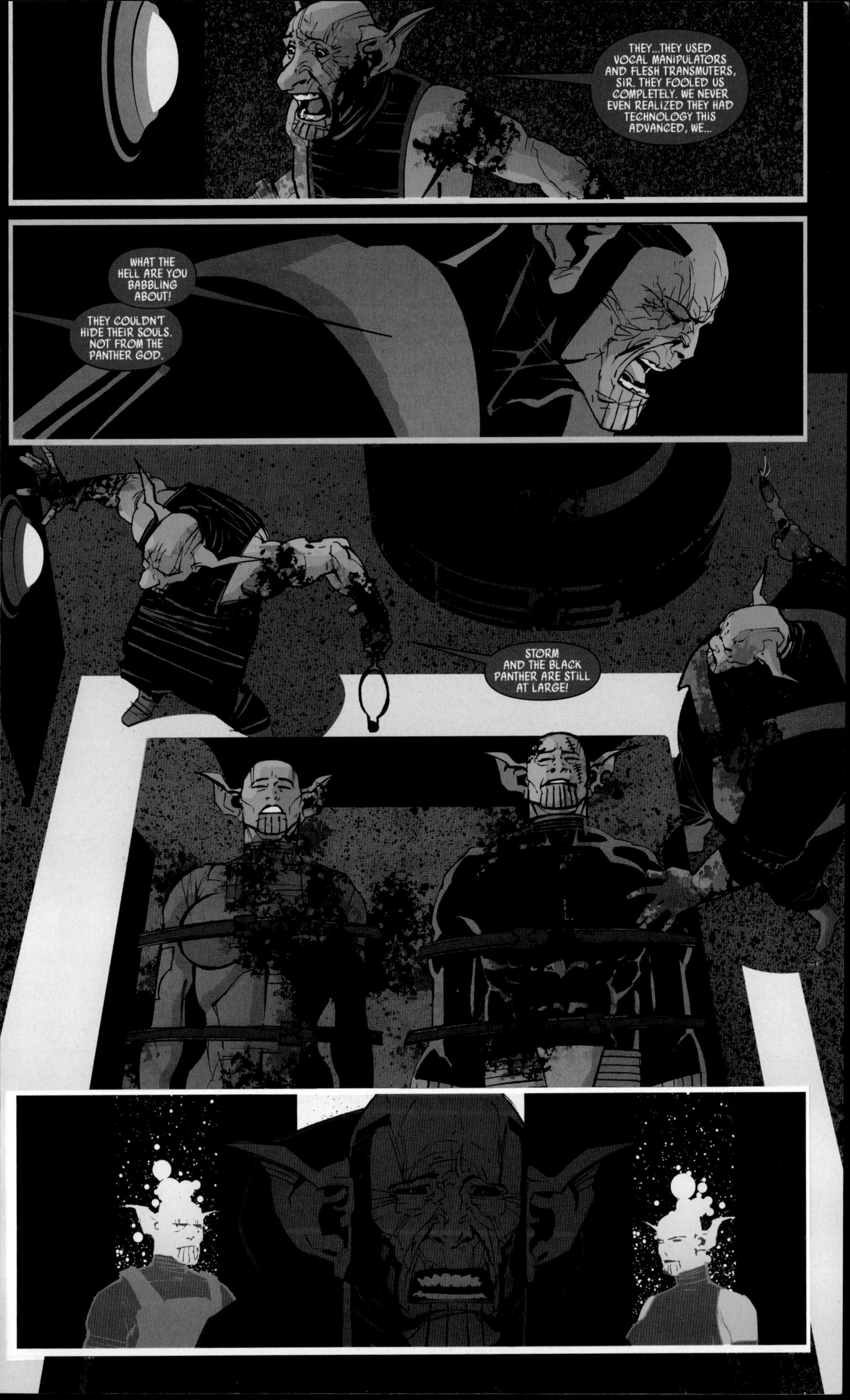
THEY...THEY USED VOCAL MANIPULATORS AND FLESH TRANSMUTERS, SIR. THEY FOOLED US COMPLETELY. WE NEVER EVEN REALIZED THEY HAD TECHNOLOGY THIS ADVANCED, WE...
WHAT THE HELL ARE YOU BABBLING ABOUT!
THEY COULDN'T HIDE THEIR SOULS. NOT FROM THE PANTHER GOD.
STORM AND THE BLACK PANTHER ARE STILL AT LARGE!

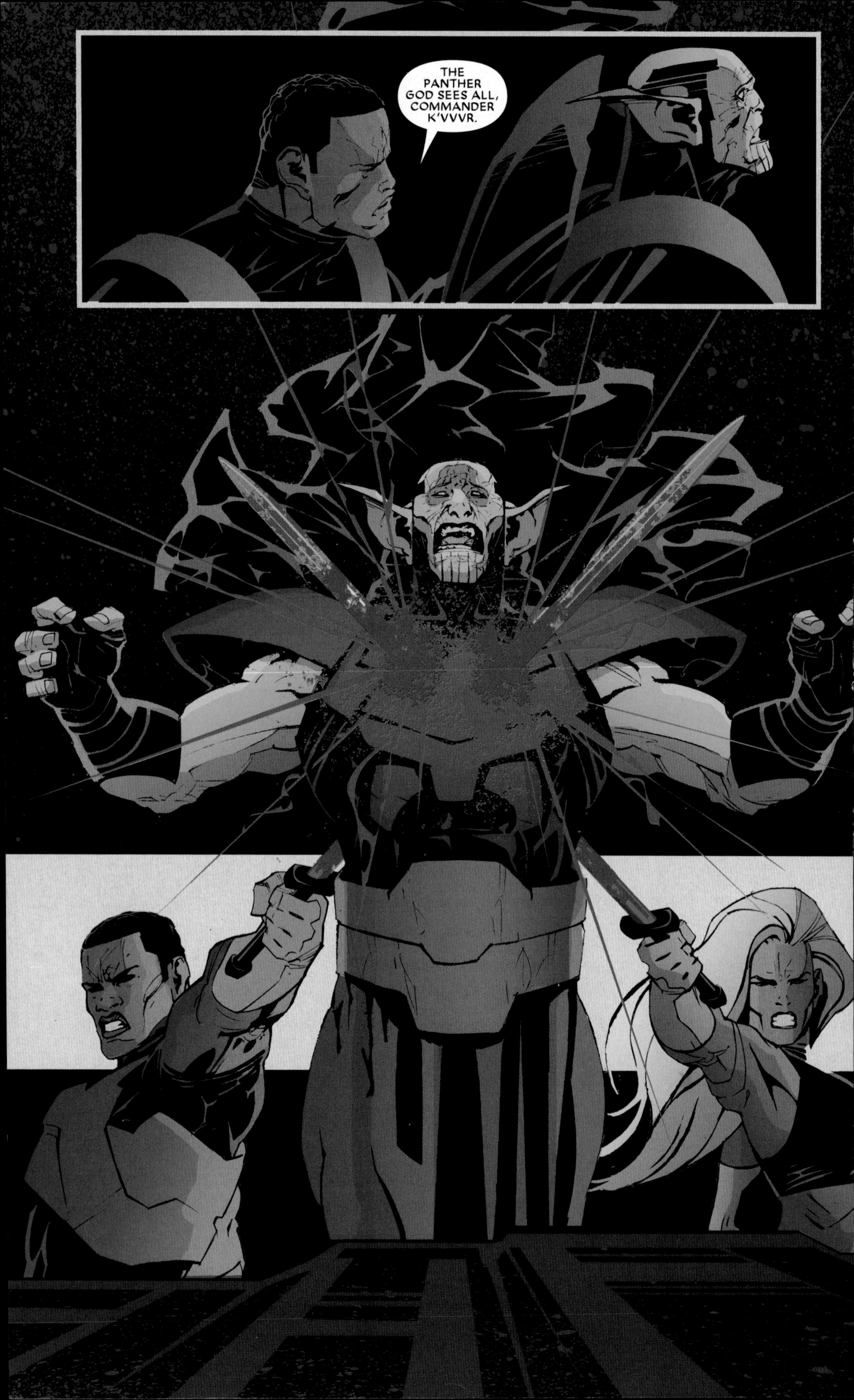
THE PANTHER GOD SEES ALL, COMMANDER K'VVVR.

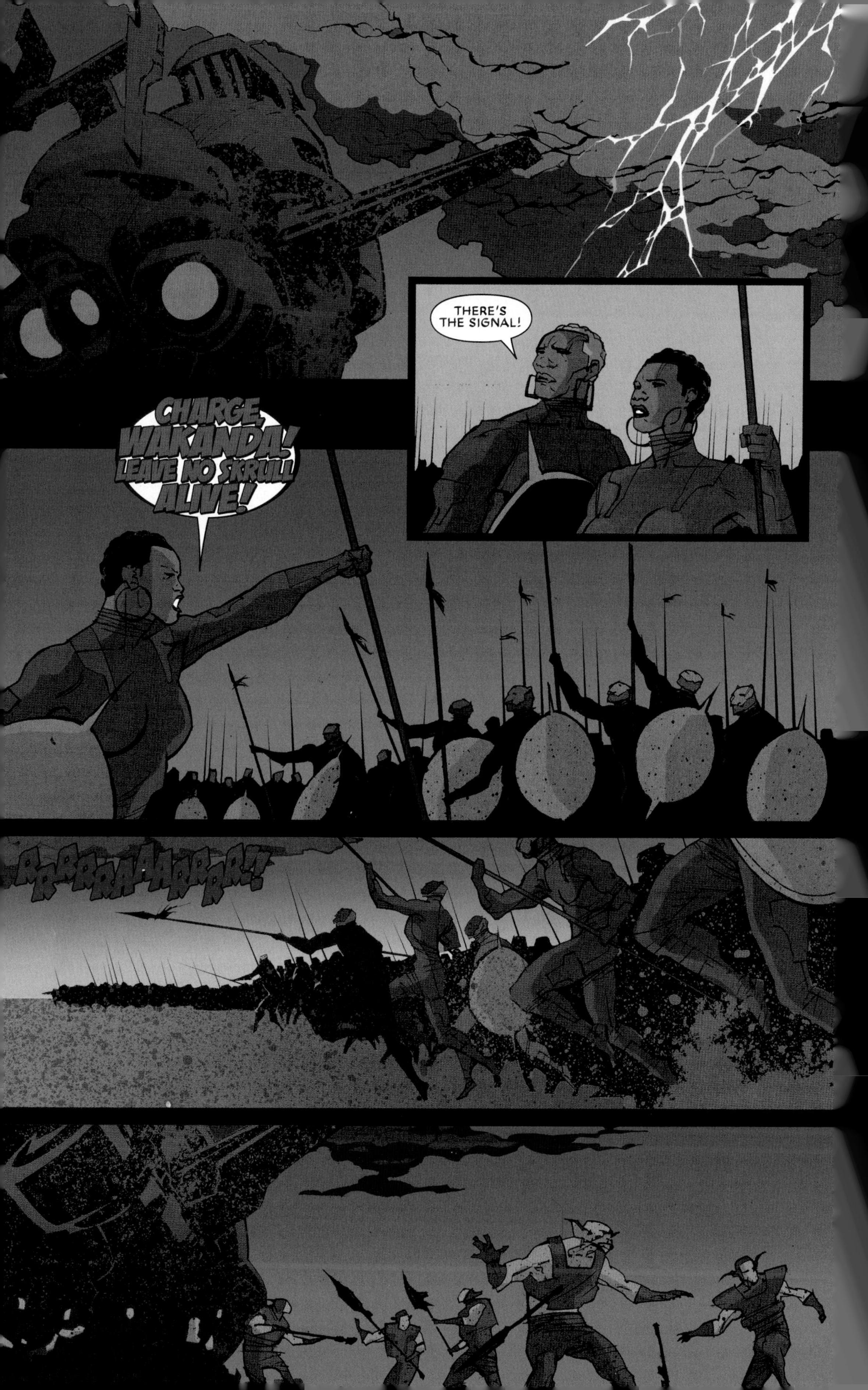
THERE'S THE SIGNAL!
CHARGE, WAKANDA! LEAVE NO SKRULL ALIVE!
RRRRRAAARRRR!!

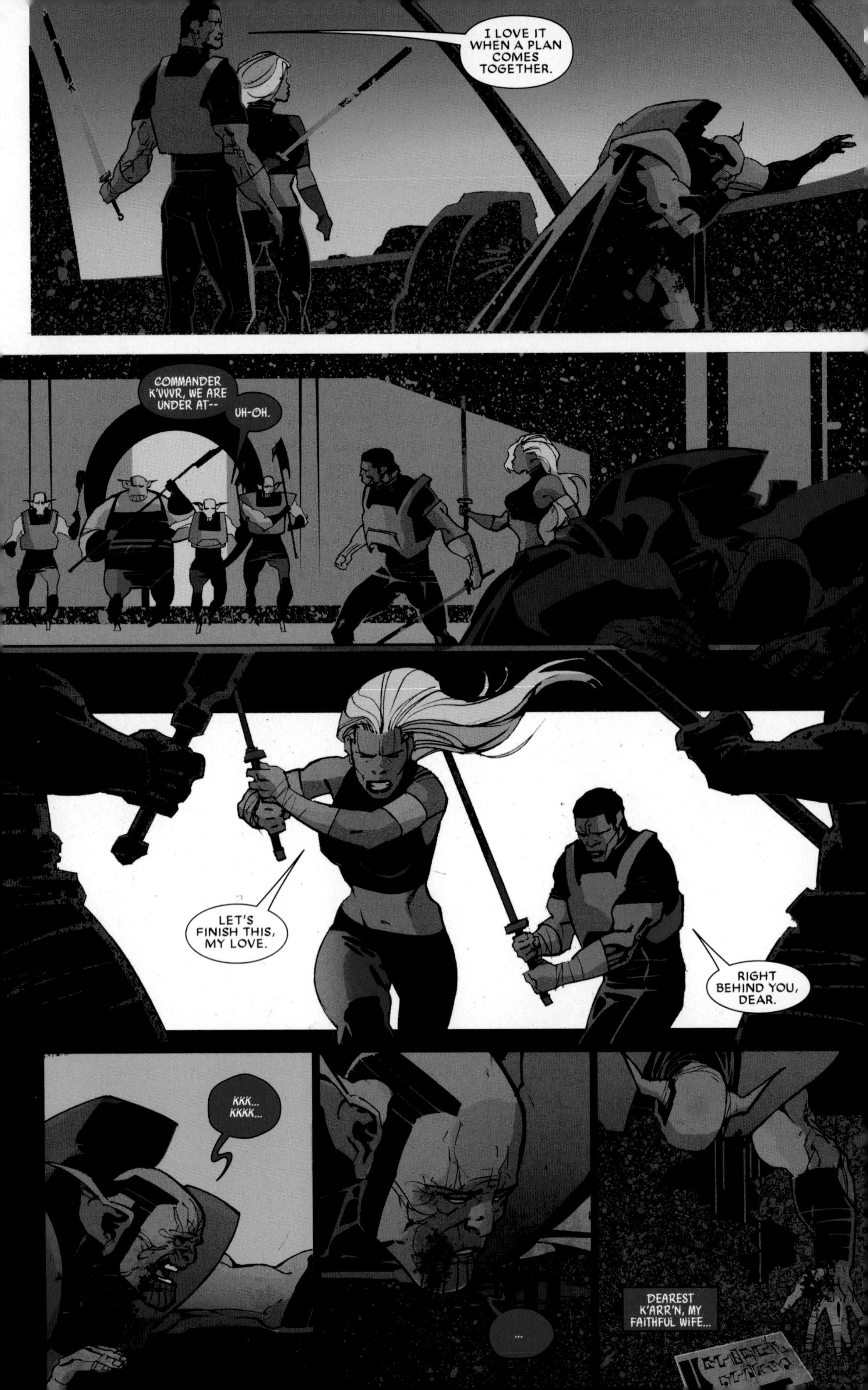
I LOVE IT WHEN A PLAN COMES TOGETHER.
COMMANDER K'VVVR, WE ARE UNDER AT--
UH-OH.
LET'S FINISH THIS, MY LOVE.
RIGHT BEHIND YOU, DEAR.
KKK... KKKK...
...
DEAREST K'ARR'N, MY FAITHFUL WIFE...

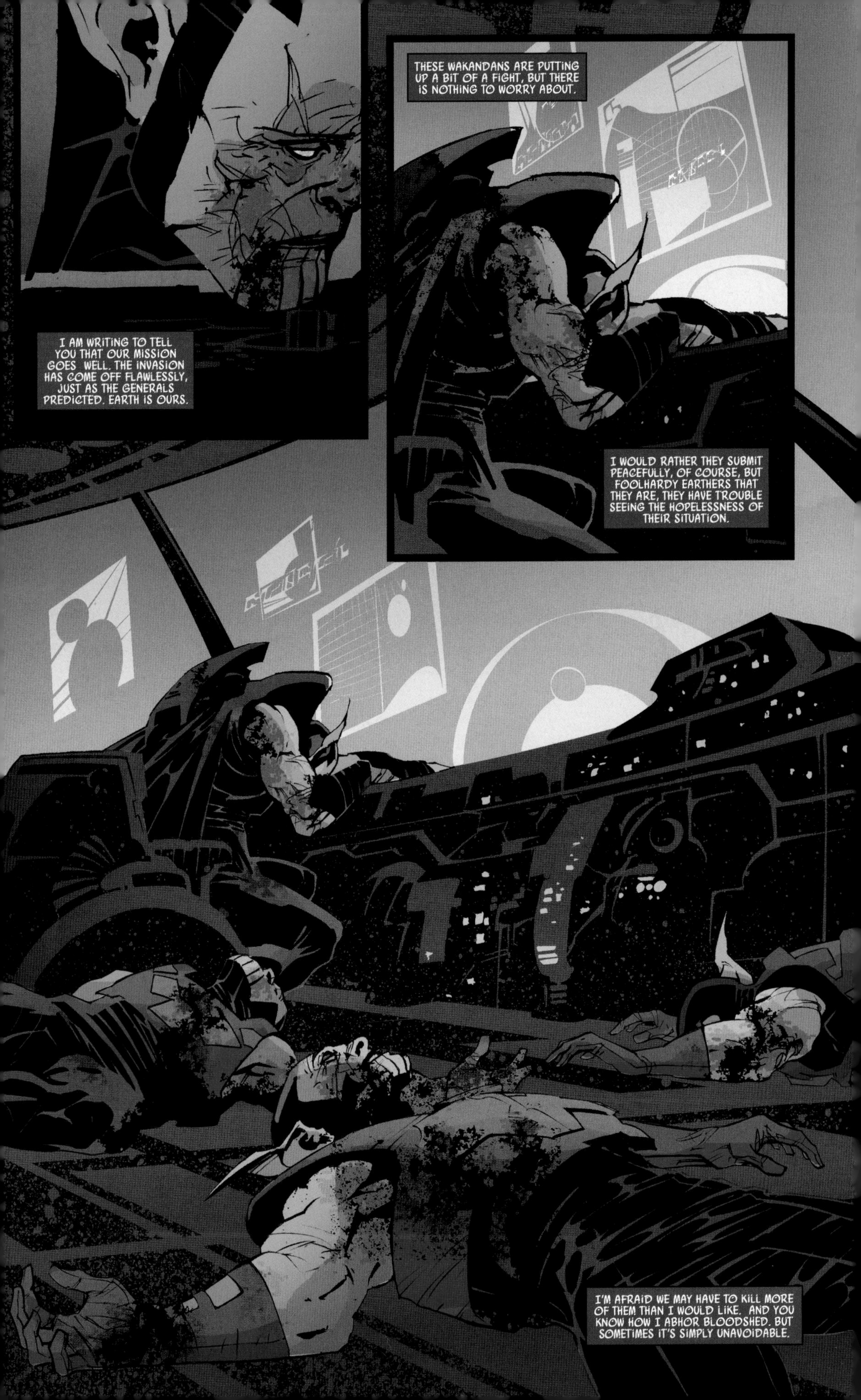
I AM WRITING TO TELL YOU THAT OUR MISSION GOES WELL. THE INVASION HAS COME OFF FLAWLESSLY, JUST AS THE GENERALS PREDICTED. EARTH IS OURS.
THESE WAKANDANS ARE PUTTING UP A BIT OF A FIGHT, BUT THERE IS NOTHING TO WORRY ABOUT.
I WOULD RATHER THEY SUBMIT PEACEFULLY, OF COURSE, BUT FOOLHARDY EARTHERS THAT THEY ARE, THEY HAVE TROUBLE SEEING THE HOPELESSNESS OF THEIR SITUATION.
I'M AFRAID WE MAY HAVE TO KILL MORE OF THEM THAN I WOULD LIKE. AND YOU KNOW HOW I ABHOR BLOODSHED. BUT SOMETIMES IT'S SIMPLY UNAVOIDABLE.

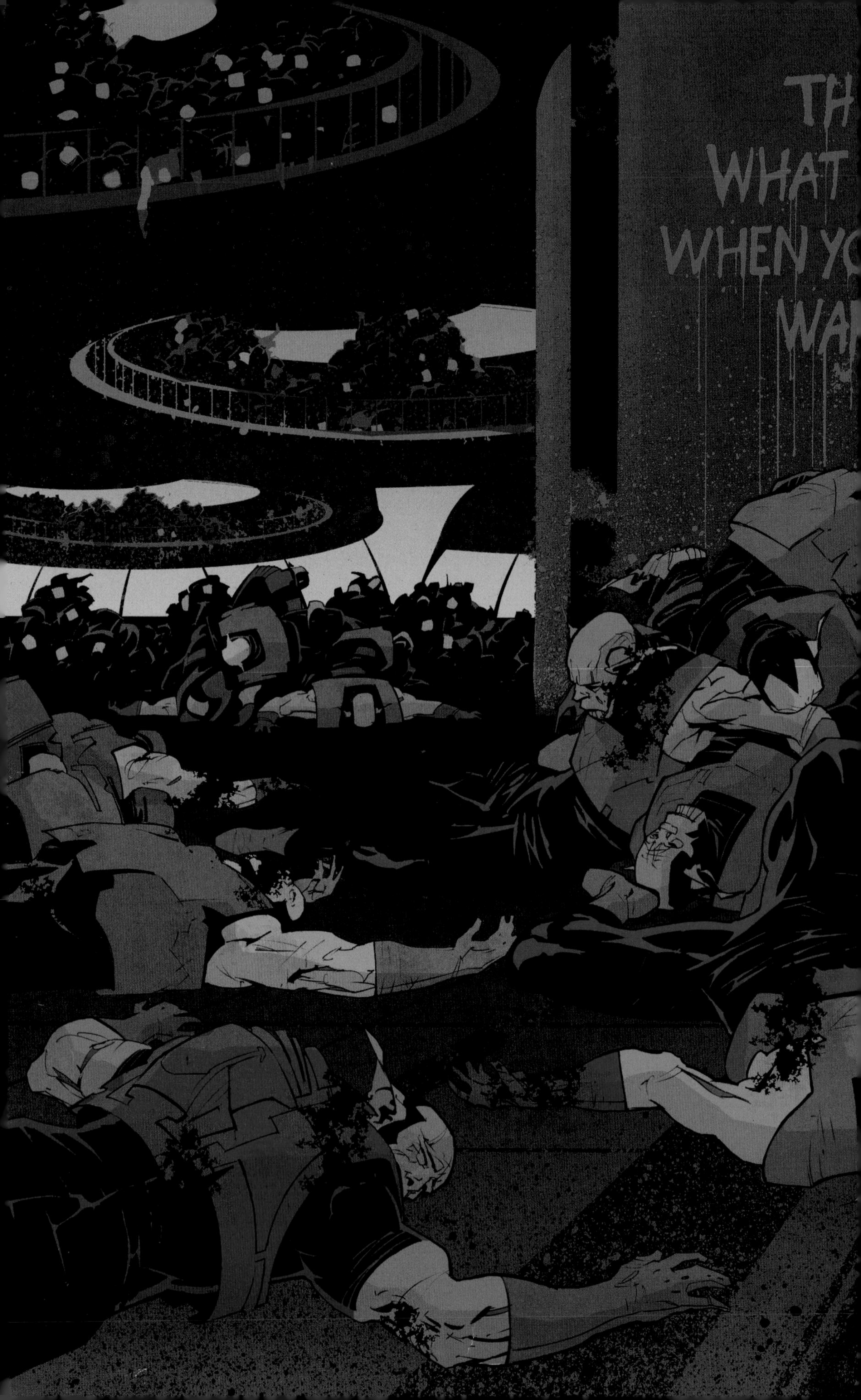
TH
WHAT
WHEN YO
WA

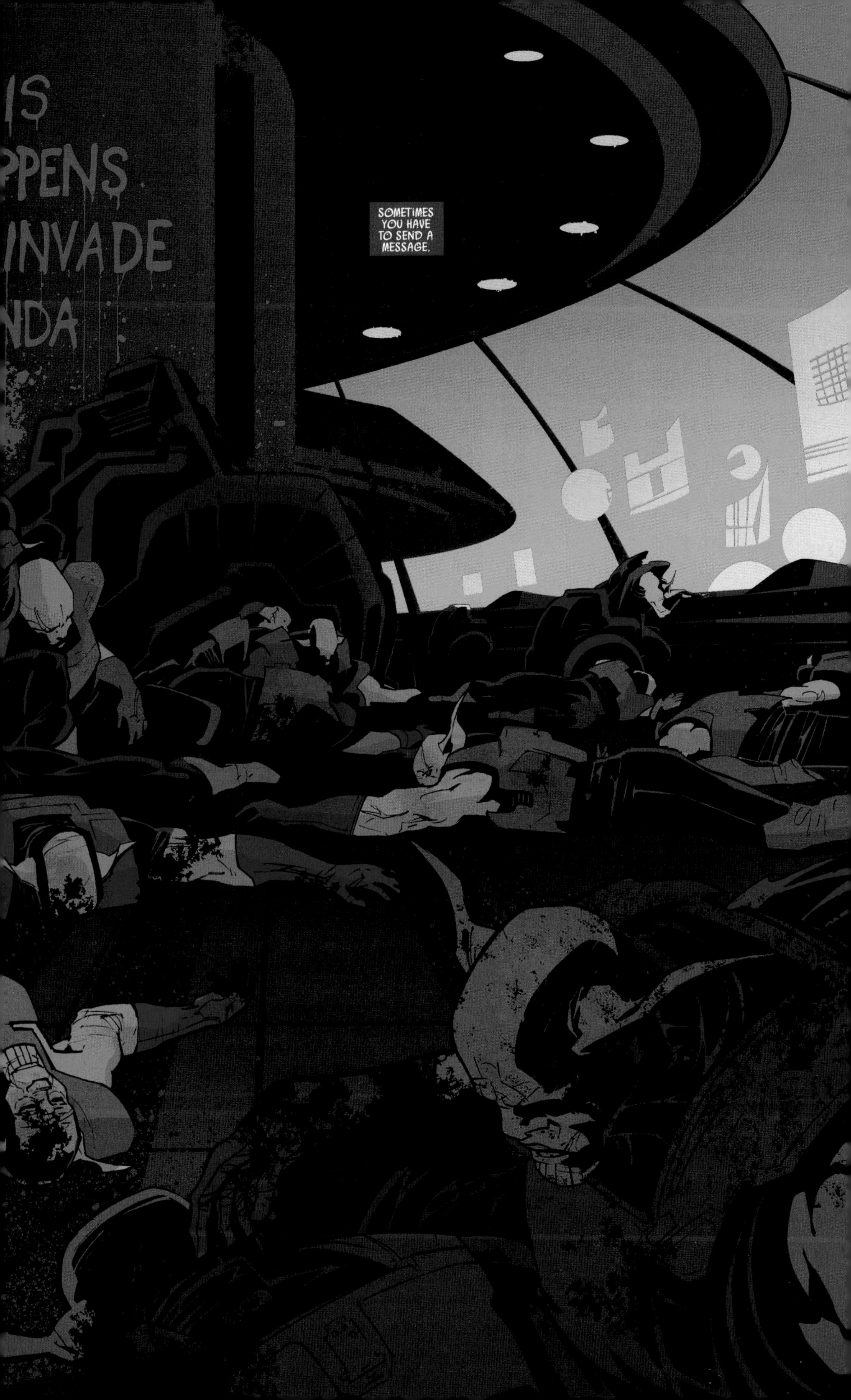
IS
PPENS
INVADE
NDA
SOMETIMES YOU HAVE TO SEND A MESSAGE.

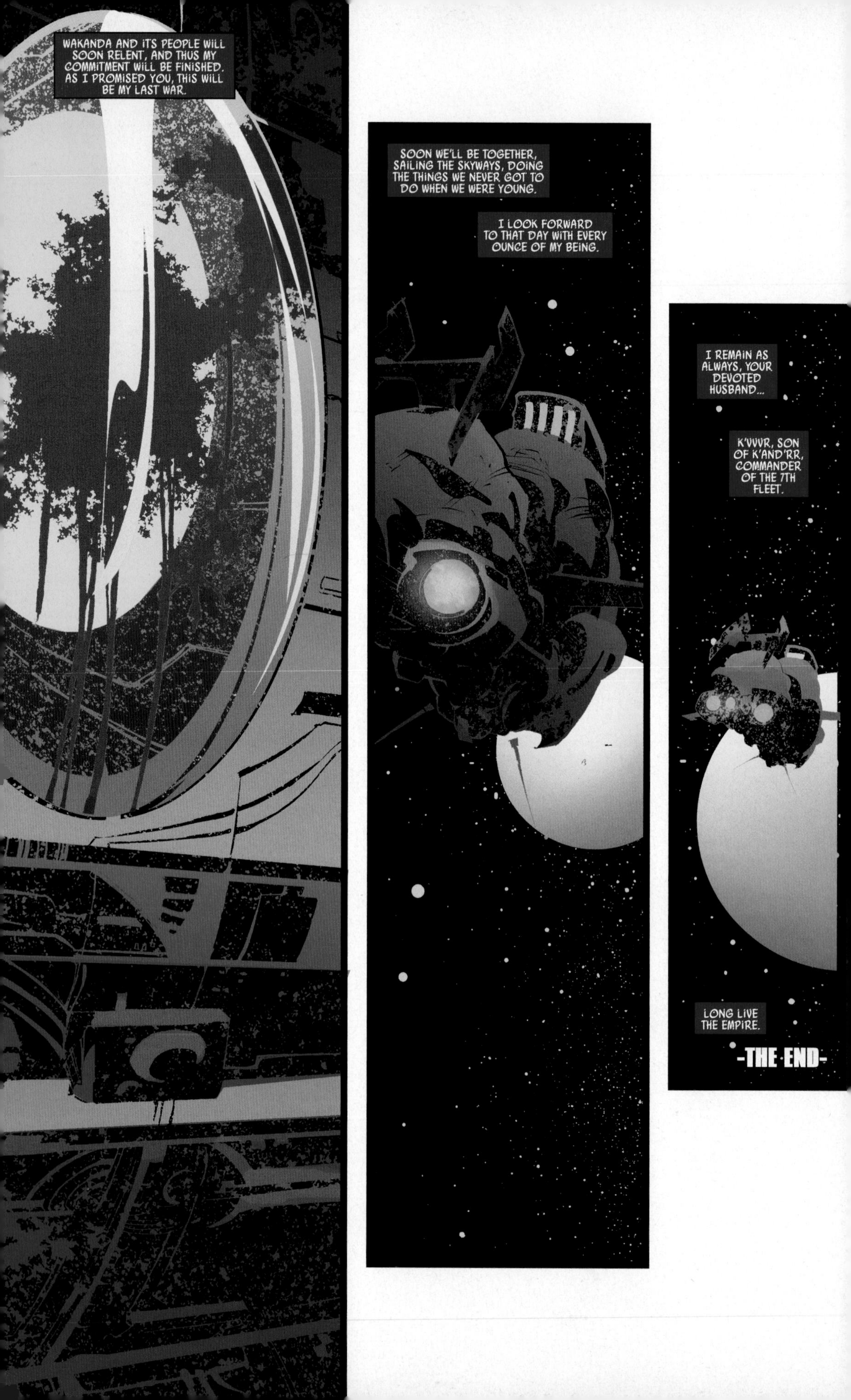

WAKANDA AND ITS PEOPLE WILL SOON RELENT, AND THUS MY COMMITMENT WILL BE FINISHED. AS I PROMISED YOU, THIS WILL BE MY LAST WAR.
SOON WE'LL BE TOGETHER, SAILING THE SKYWAYS, DOING THE THINGS WE NEVER GOT TO DO WHEN WE WERE YOUNG.
I LOOK FORWARD TO THAT DAY WITH EVERY OUNCE OF MY BEING.
I REMAIN AS ALWAYS, YOUR DEVOTED HUSBAND...
K'VVVR, SON OF K'AND'RR, COMMANDER OF THE 7TH FLEET.
LONG LIVE THE EMPIRE.
-THE END-

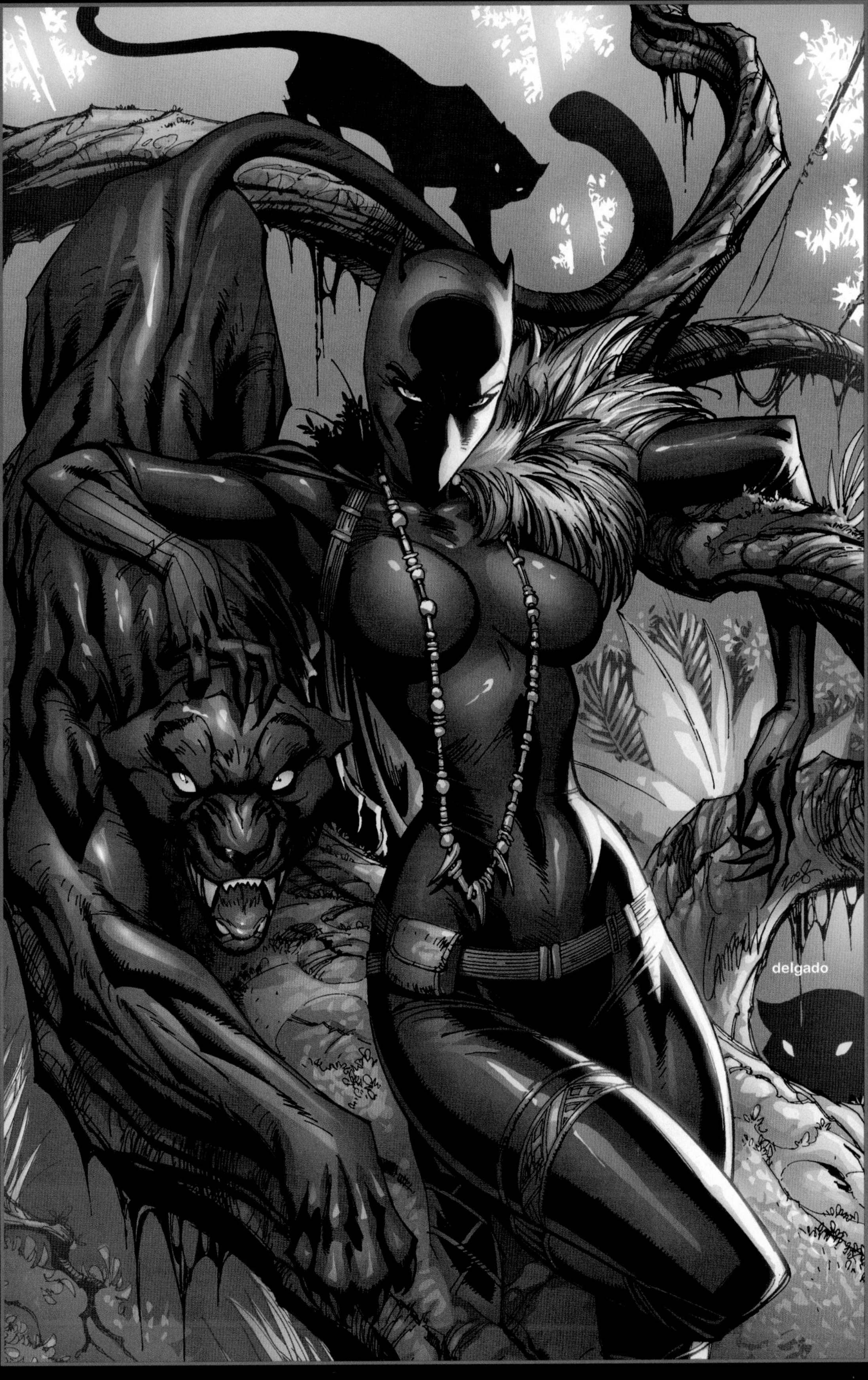
delgado

BLACK PANTHER (2009) **1:** THE DEADLIEST OF THE SPECIES, PART 1

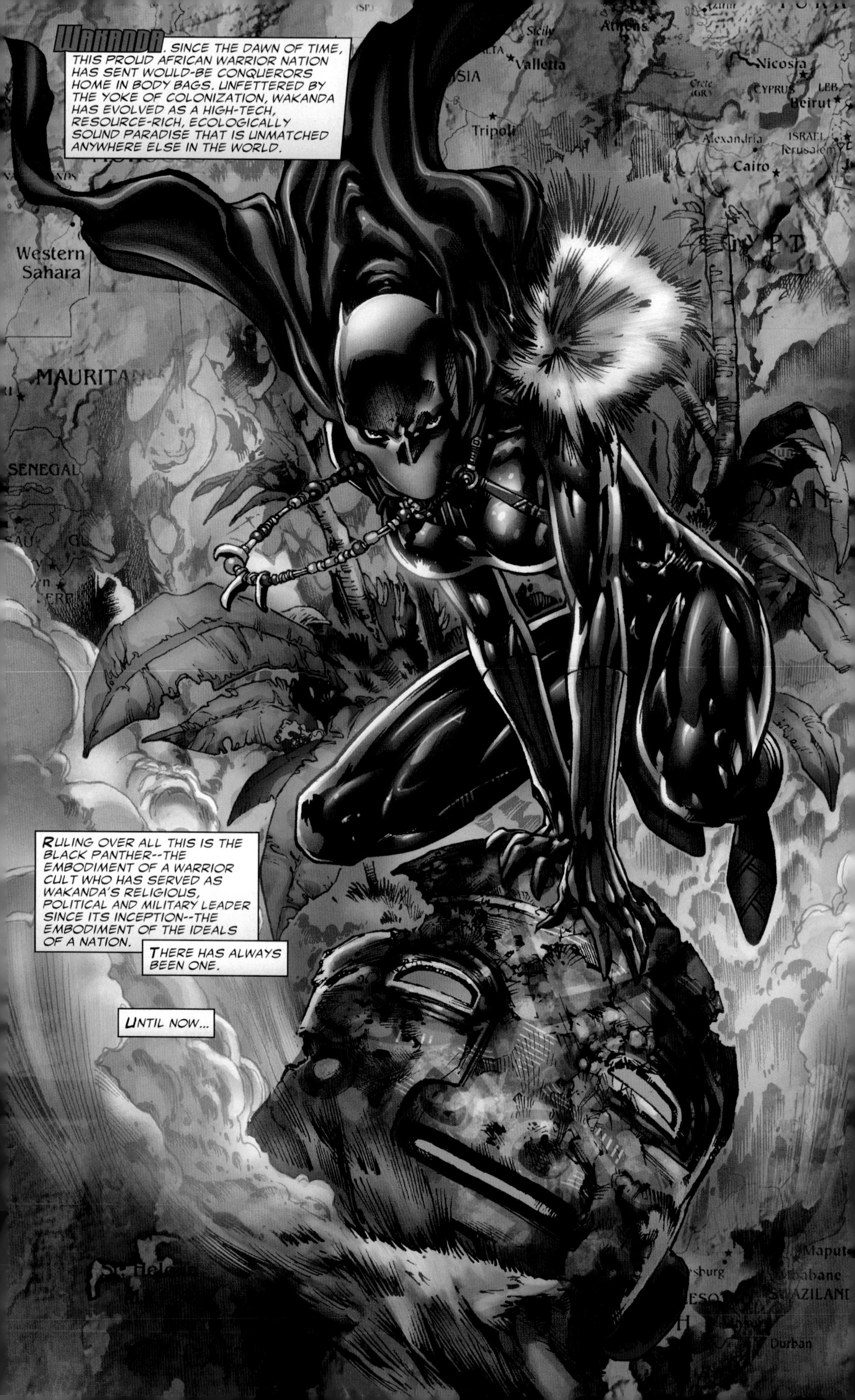
WAKANDA. SINCE THE DAWN OF TIME, THIS PROUD AFRICAN WARRIOR NATION HAS SENT WOULD-BE CONQUERORS HOME IN BODY BAGS. UNFETTERED BY THE YOKE OF COLONIZATION, WAKANDA HAS EVOLVED AS A HIGH-TECH, RESOURCE-RICH, ECOLOGICALLY SOUND PARADISE THAT IS UNMATCHED ANYWHERE ELSE IN THE WORLD.
RULING OVER ALL THIS IS THE BLACK PANTHER--THE EMBODIMENT OF A WARRIOR CULT WHO HAS SERVED AS WAKANDA'S RELIGIOUS, POLITICAL AND MILITARY LEADER SINCE ITS INCEPTION--THE EMBODIMENT OF THE IDEALS OF A NATION.
THERE HAS ALWAYS BEEN ONE.
UNTIL NOW...

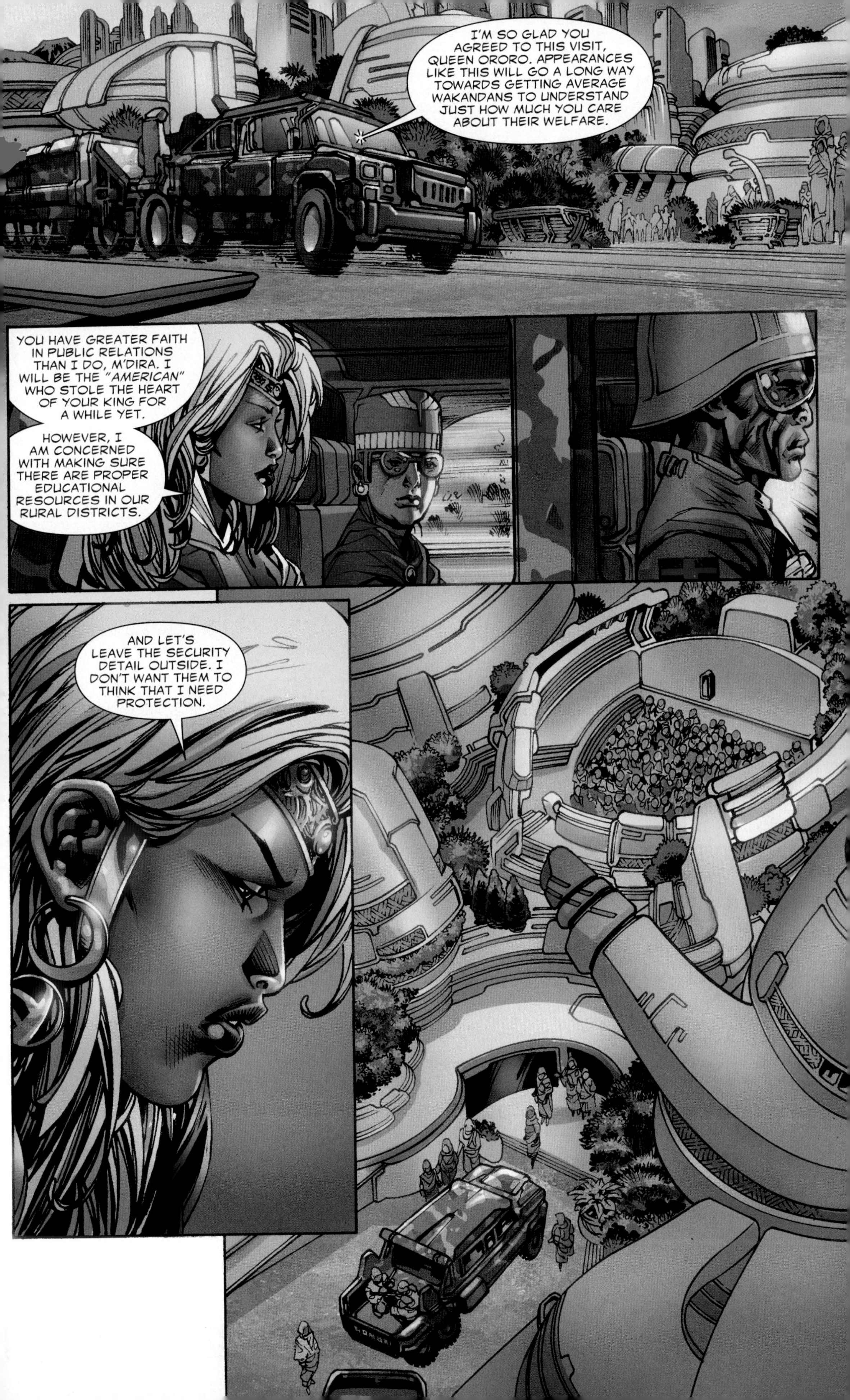
I'M SO GLAD YOU AGREED TO THIS VISIT, QUEEN ORORO. APPEARANCES LIKE THIS WILL GO A LONG WAY TOWARDS GETTING AVERAGE WAKANDANS TO UNDERSTAND JUST HOW MUCH YOU CARE ABOUT THEIR WELFARE.
YOU HAVE GREATER FAITH IN PUBLIC RELATIONS THAN I DO, M'DIRA. I WILL BE THE "AMERICAN" WHO STOLE THE HEART OF YOUR KING FOR A WHILE YET.
HOWEVER, I AM CONCERNED WITH MAKING SURE THERE ARE PROPER EDUCATIONAL RESOURCES IN OUR RURAL DISTRICTS.
AND LET'S LEAVE THE SECURITY DETAIL OUTSIDE. I DON'T WANT THEM TO THINK THAT I NEED PROTECTION.

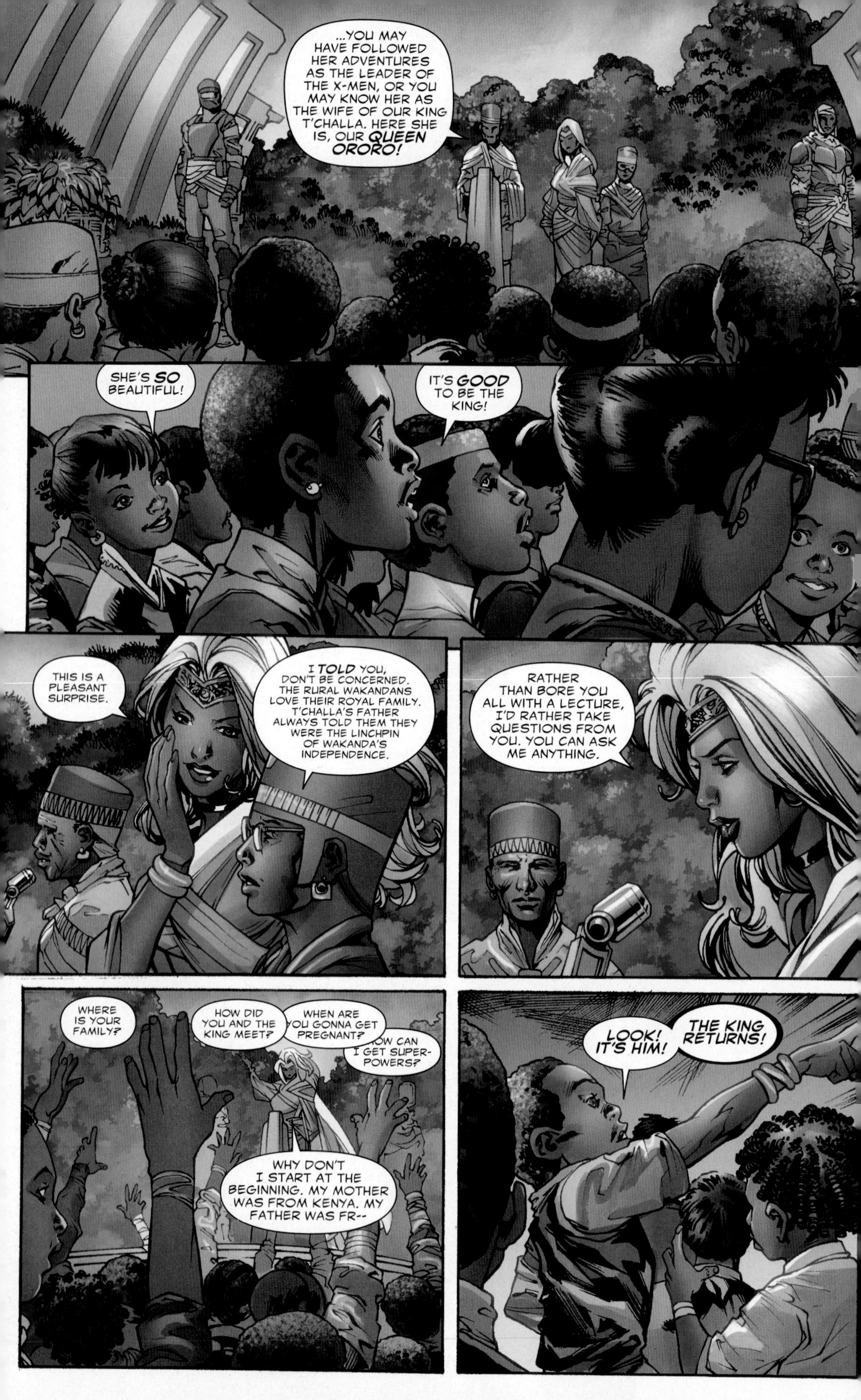
...YOU MAY HAVE FOLLOWED HER ADVENTURES AS THE LEADER OF THE X-MEN, OR YOU MAY KNOW HER AS THE WIFE OF OUR KING T'CHALLA. HERE SHE IS, OUR QUEEN ORORO!
SHE'S SO BEAUTIFUL!
IT'S GOOD TO BE THE KING!
THIS IS A PLEASANT SURPRISE.
I TOLD YOU, DON'T BE CONCERNED. THE RURAL WAKANDANS LOVE THEIR ROYAL FAMILY. T'CHALLA'S FATHER ALWAYS TOLD THEM THEY WERE THE LINCHPIN OF WAKANDA'S INDEPENDENCE.
RATHER THAN BORE YOU ALL WITH A LECTURE, I'D RATHER TAKE QUESTIONS FROM YOU. YOU CAN ASK ME ANYTHING.
WHERE IS YOUR FAMILY?
HOW DID YOU AND THE KING MEET?
WHEN ARE YOU GONNA GET PREGNANT?
HOW CAN I GET SUPER-POWERS?
WHY DON'T I START AT THE BEGINNING. MY MOTHER WAS FROM KENYA. MY FATHER WAS FR--
LOOK! IT'S HIM!
THE KING RETURNS!

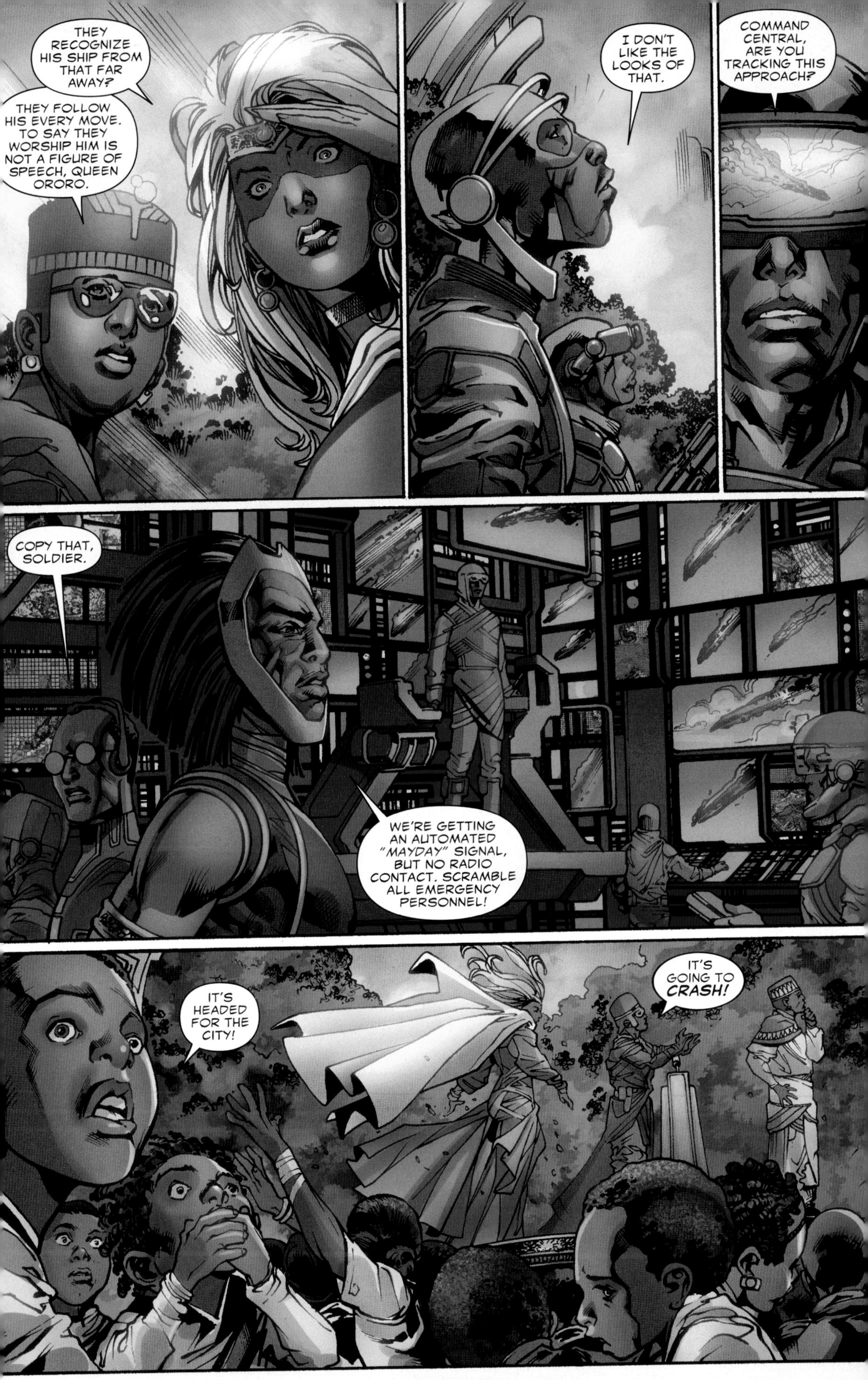
THEY RECOGNIZE HIS SHIP FROM THAT FAR AWAY?
THEY FOLLOW HIS EVERY MOVE. TO SAY THEY WORSHIP HIM IS NOT A FIGURE OF SPEECH, QUEEN ORORO.
I DON'T LIKE THE LOOKS OF THAT.
COMMAND CENTRAL, ARE YOU TRACKING THIS APPROACH?
COPY THAT, SOLDIER.
WE'RE GETTING AN AUTOMATED "MAYDAY" SIGNAL, BUT NO RADIO CONTACT. SCRAMBLE ALL EMERGENCY PERSONNEL!
IT'S HEADED FOR THE CITY!
IT'S GOING TO CRASH!

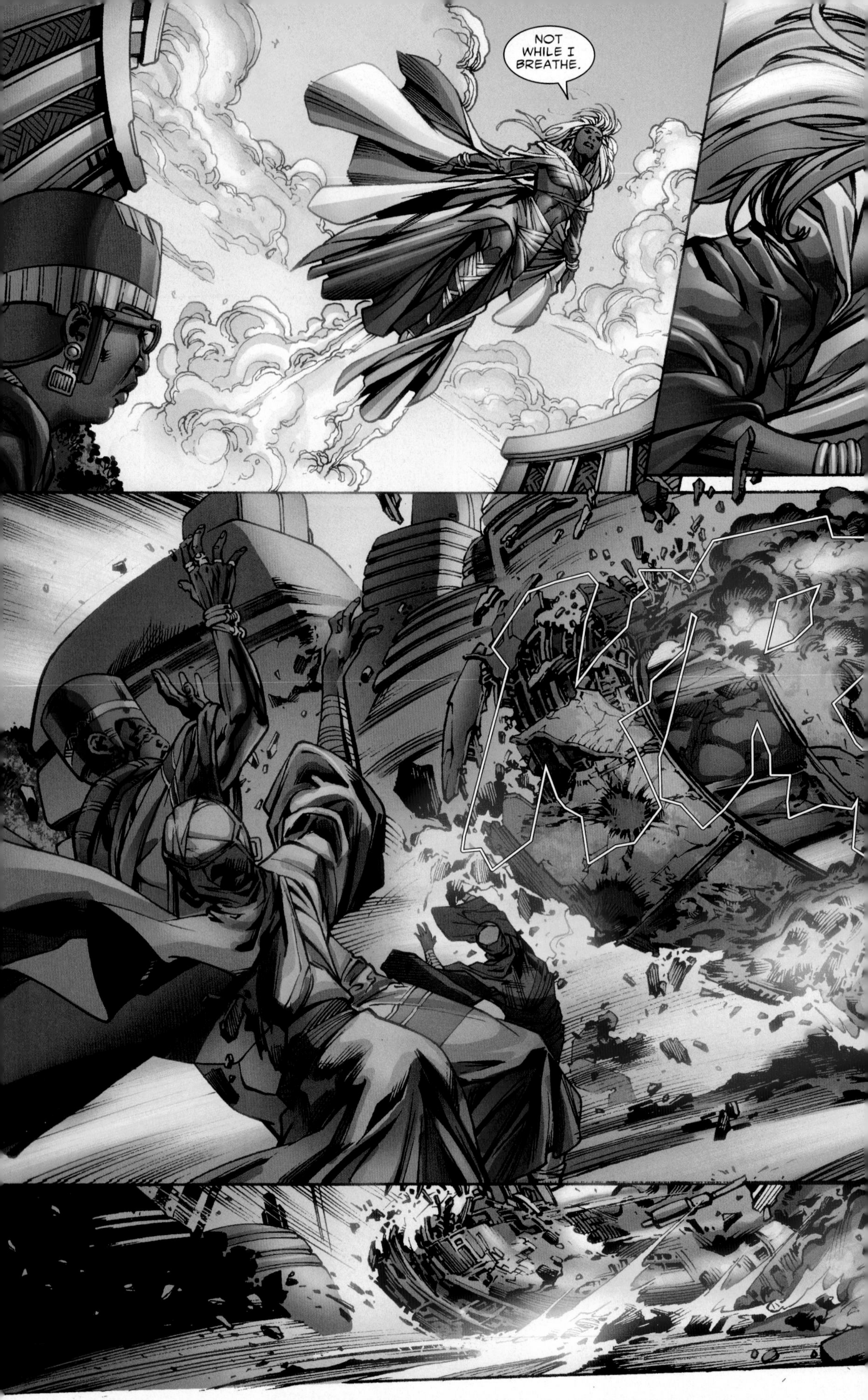
NOT WHILE I BREATHE.

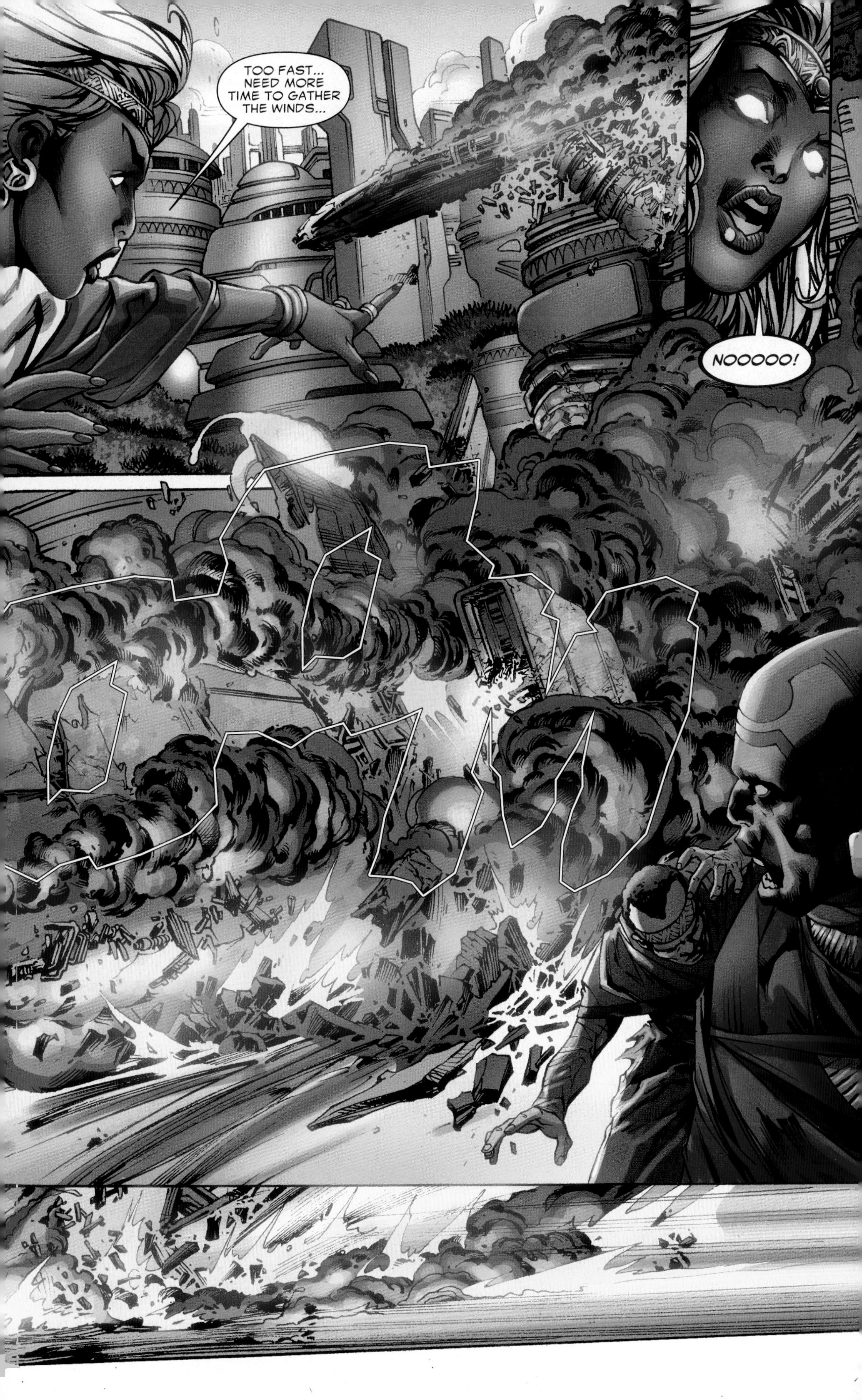
TOO FAST... NEED MORE TIME TO GATHER THE WINDS...
NOOOOO!

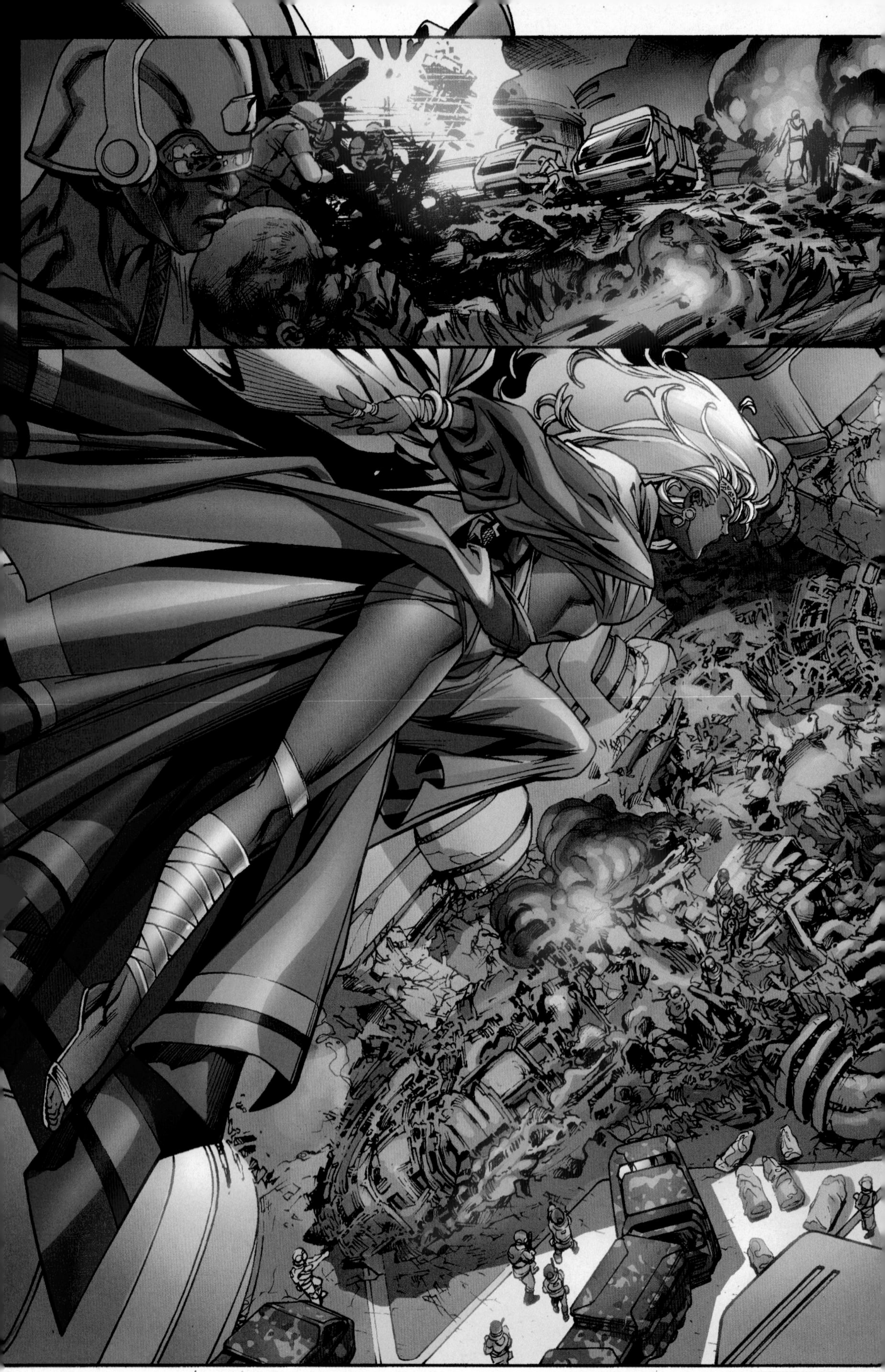

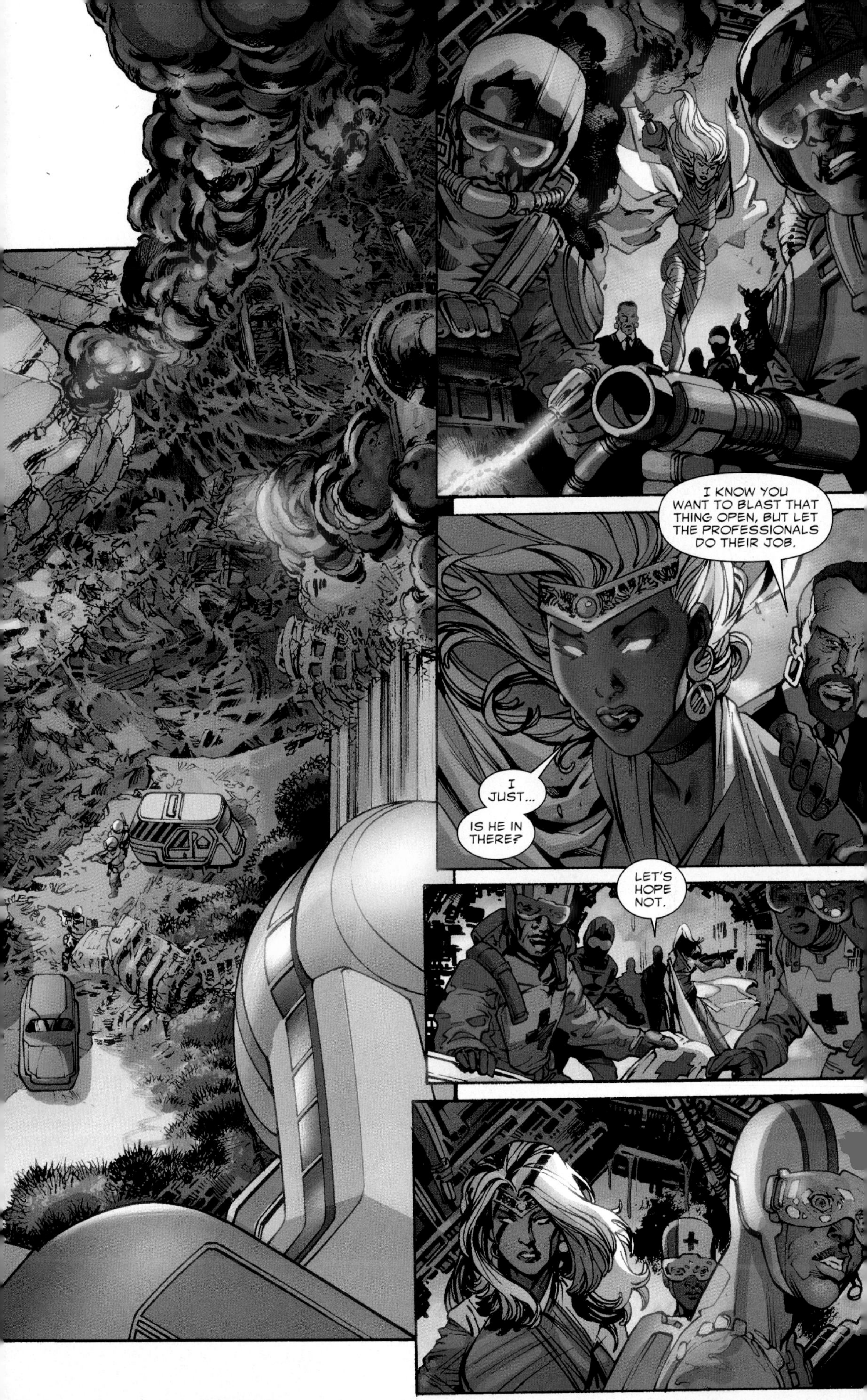

I KNOW YOU WANT TO BLAST THAT THING OPEN, BUT LET THE PROFESSIONALS DO THEIR JOB.
I JUST...
IS HE IN THERE?
LET'S HOPE NOT.

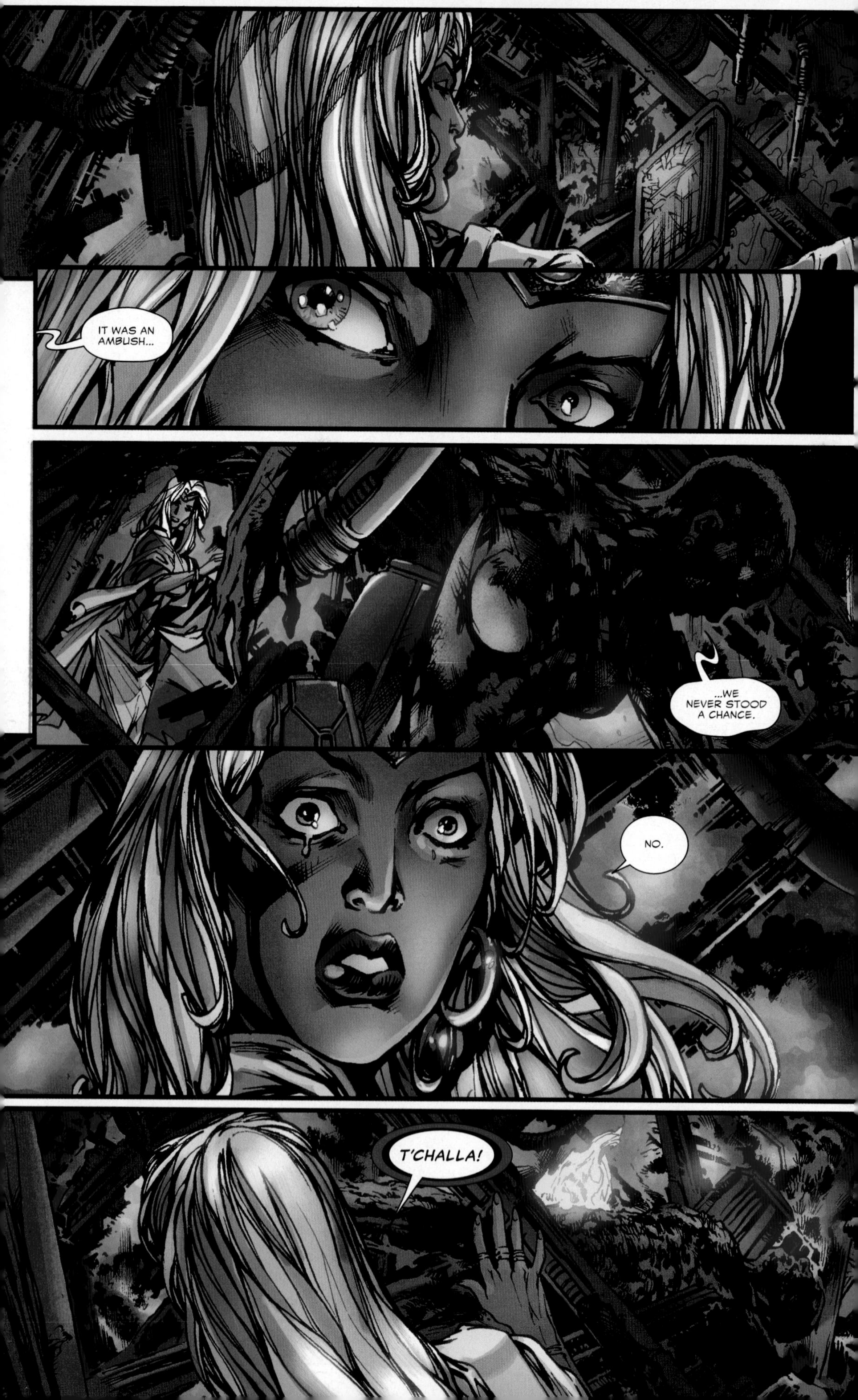
IT WAS AN AMBUSH...
...WE NEVER STOOD A CHANCE.
NO.
T'CHALLA!

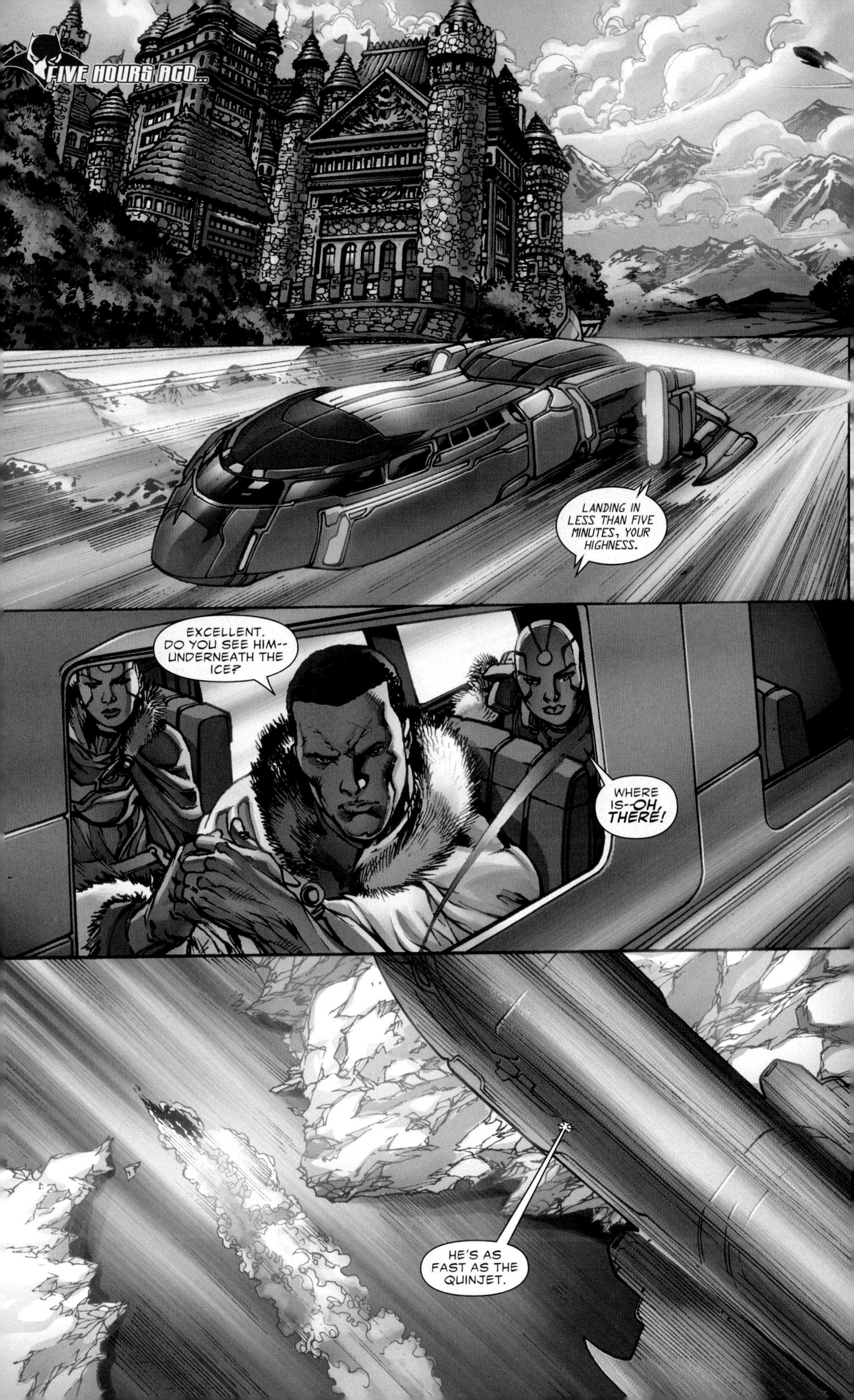
FIVE HOURS AGO...
LANDING IN LESS THAN FIVE MINUTES, YOUR HIGHNESS.
EXCELLENT. DO YOU SEE HIM-- UNDERNEATH THE ICE?
WHERE IS--OH, THERE!
HE'S AS FAST AS THE QUINJET.

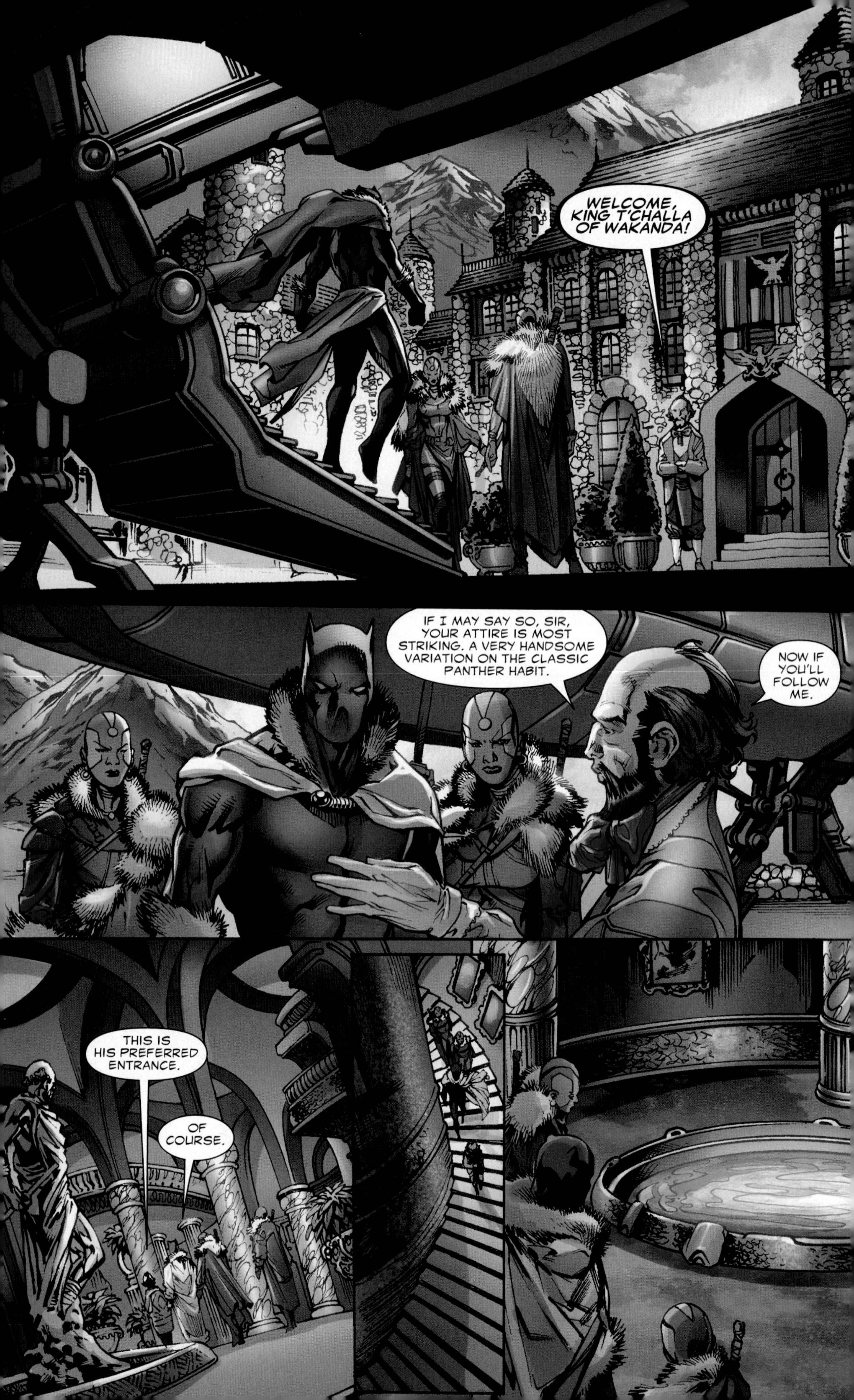
WELCOME, KING T'CHALLA OF WAKANDA!
IF I MAY SAY SO, SIR, YOUR ATTIRE IS MOST STRIKING. A VERY HANDSOME VARIATION ON THE CLASSIC PANTHER HABIT.
NOW IF YOU'LL FOLLOW ME.
THIS IS HIS PREFERRED ENTRANCE.
OF COURSE.

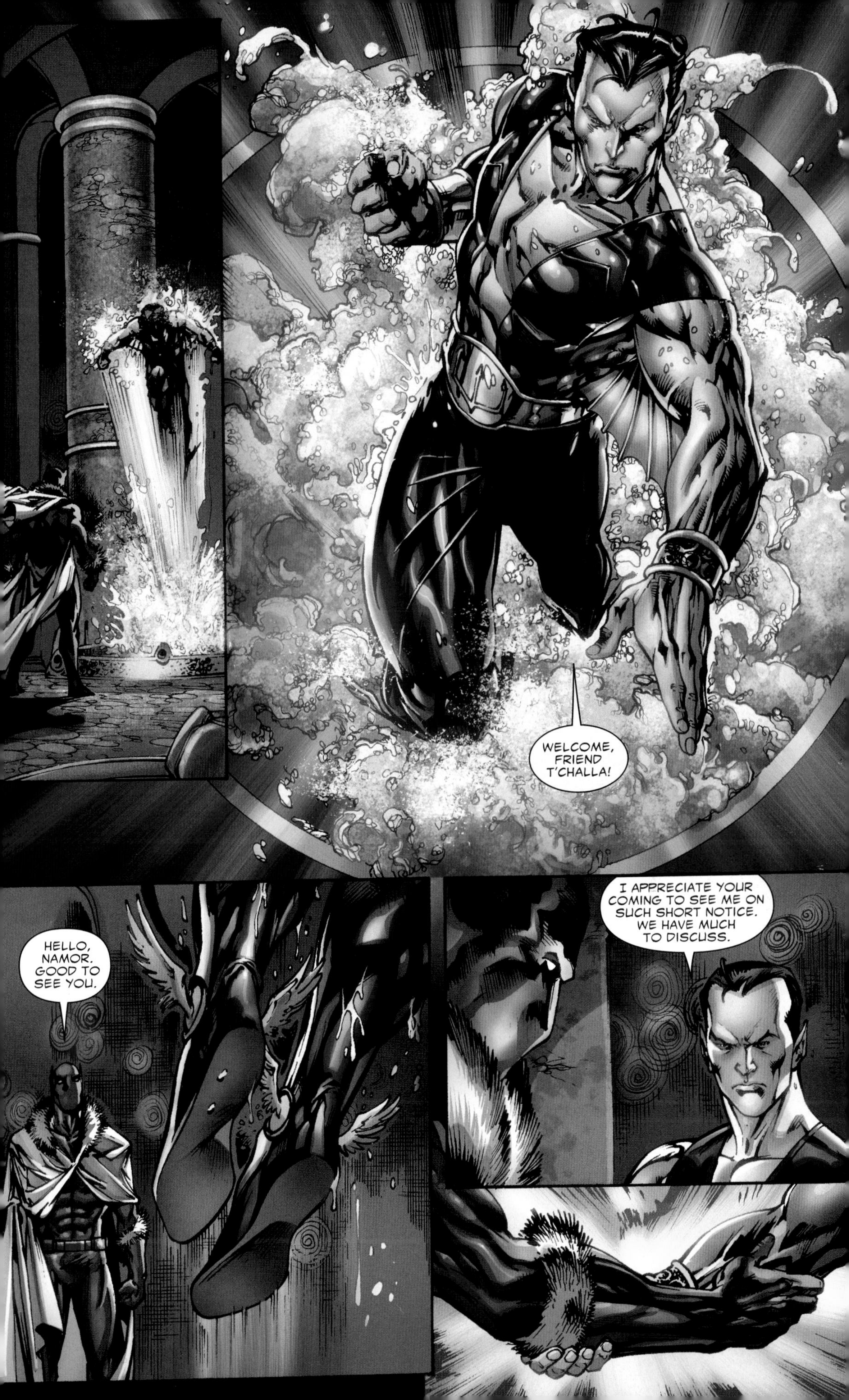
WELCOME, FRIEND T'CHALLA!
HELLO, NAMOR. GOOD TO SEE YOU.
I APPRECIATE YOUR COMING TO SEE ME ON SUCH SHORT NOTICE. WE HAVE MUCH TO DISCUSS.

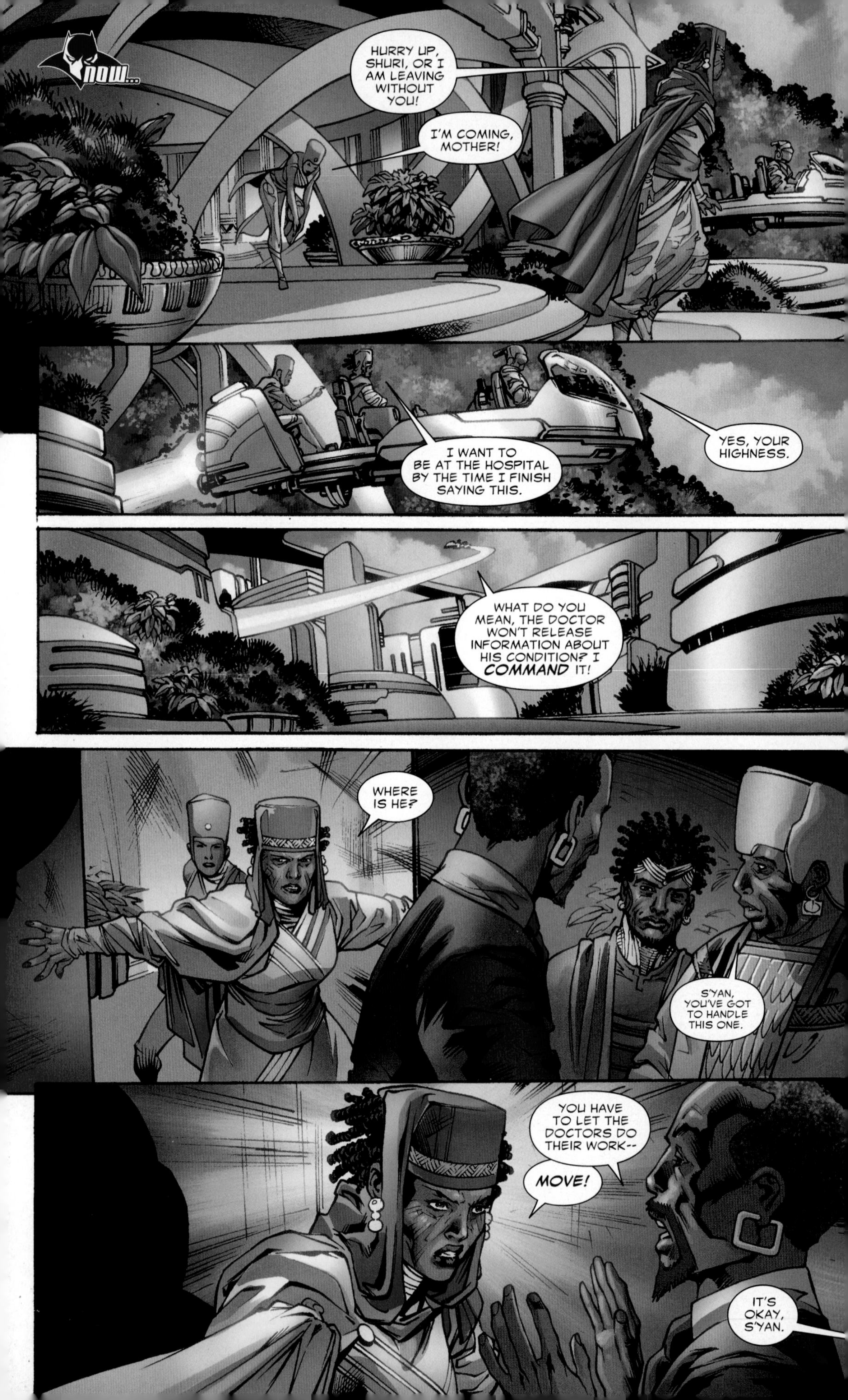
NOW...
HURRY UP, SHURI, OR I AM LEAVING WITHOUT YOU!
I'M COMING, MOTHER!
I WANT TO BE AT THE HOSPITAL BY THE TIME I FINISH SAYING THIS.
YES, YOUR HIGHNESS.
WHAT DO YOU MEAN, THE DOCTOR WON'T RELEASE INFORMATION ABOUT HIS CONDITION? I COMMAND IT!
WHERE IS HE?
S'YAN, YOU'VE GOT TO HANDLE THIS ONE.
YOU HAVE TO LET THE DOCTORS DO THEIR WORK--
MOVE!
IT'S OKAY, S'YAN.

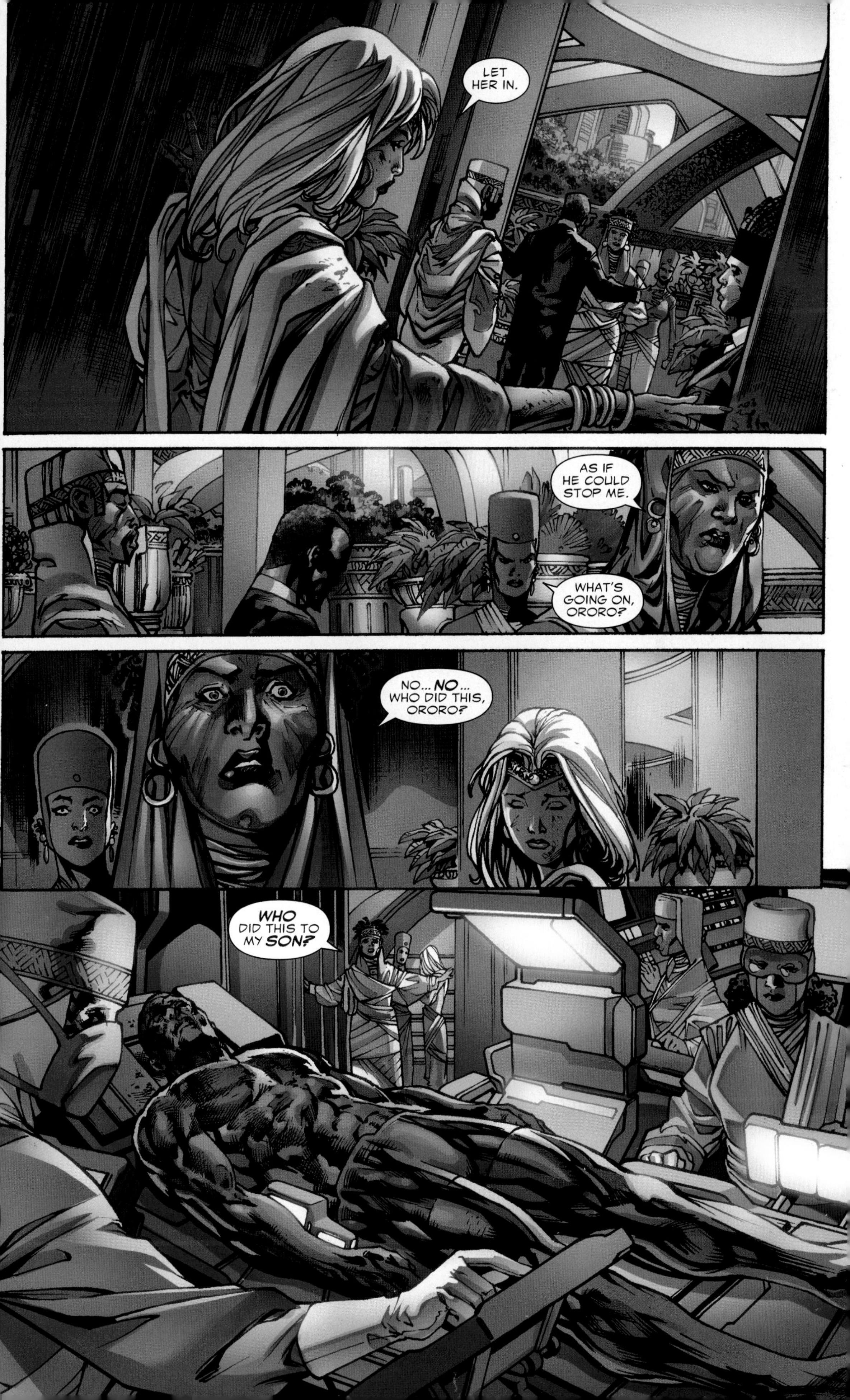
LET HER IN.
AS IF HE COULD STOP ME.
WHAT'S GOING ON, ORORO?
NO... **NO**... WHO DID THIS, ORORO?
WHO DID THIS TO MY **SON?**

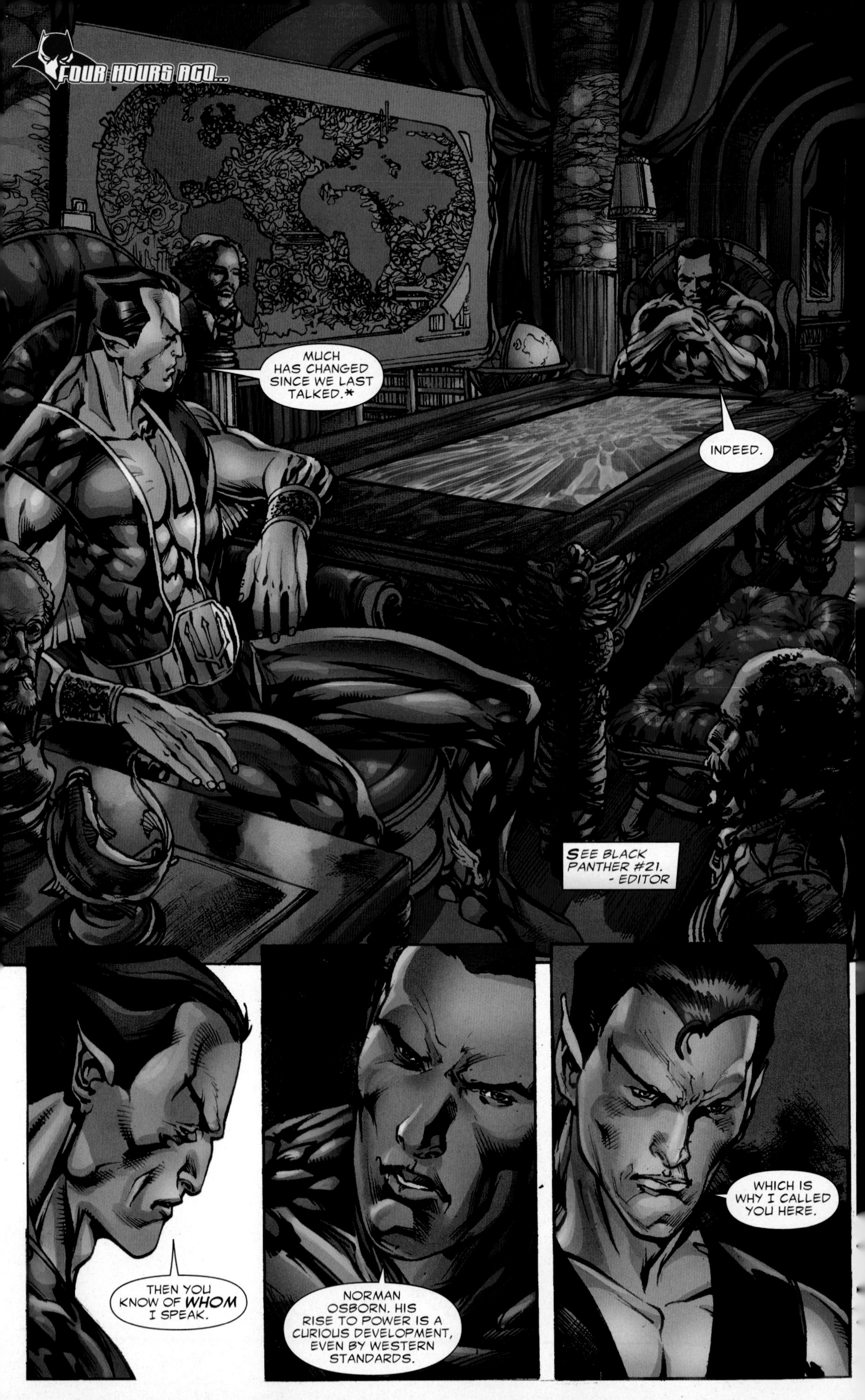
FOUR HOURS AGO...
MUCH HAS CHANGED SINCE WE LAST TALKED.*
INDEED.
SEE BLACK PANTHER #21. - EDITOR
THEN YOU KNOW OF WHOM I SPEAK.
NORMAN OSBORN. HIS RISE TO POWER IS A CURIOUS DEVELOPMENT, EVEN BY WESTERN STANDARDS.
WHICH IS WHY I CALLED YOU HERE.

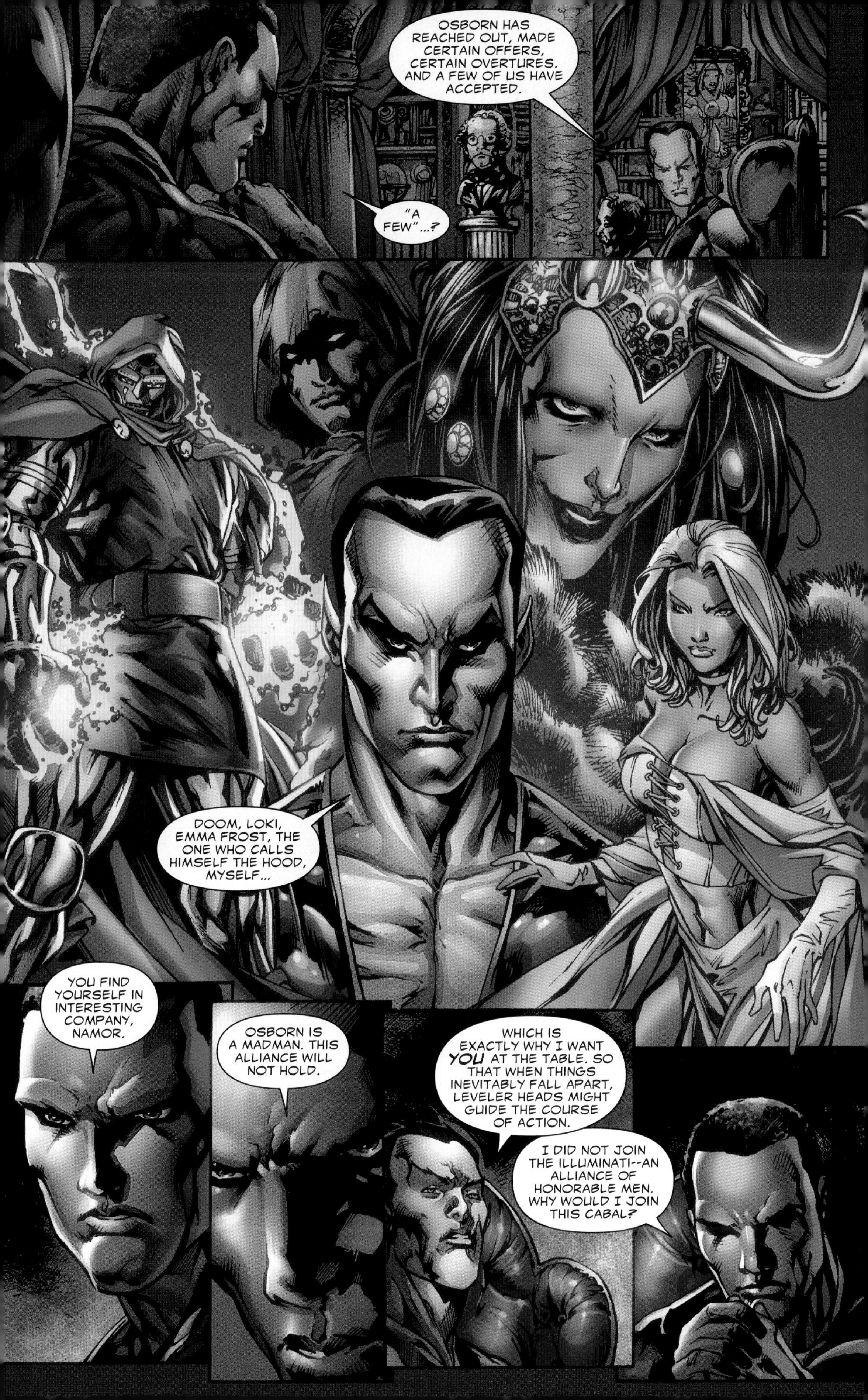
OSBORN HAS REACHED OUT, MADE CERTAIN OFFERS, CERTAIN OVERTURES. AND A FEW OF US HAVE ACCEPTED.
"A FEW"...?
DOOM, LOKI, EMMA FROST, THE ONE WHO CALLS HIMSELF THE HOOD, MYSELF...
YOU FIND YOURSELF IN INTERESTING COMPANY, NAMOR.
OSBORN IS A MADMAN. THIS ALLIANCE WILL NOT HOLD.
WHICH IS EXACTLY WHY I WANT YOU AT THE TABLE. SO THAT WHEN THINGS INEVITABLY FALL APART, LEVELER HEADS MIGHT GUIDE THE COURSE OF ACTION.
I DID NOT JOIN THE ILLUMINATI--AN ALLIANCE OF HONORABLE MEN. WHY WOULD I JOIN THIS CABAL?

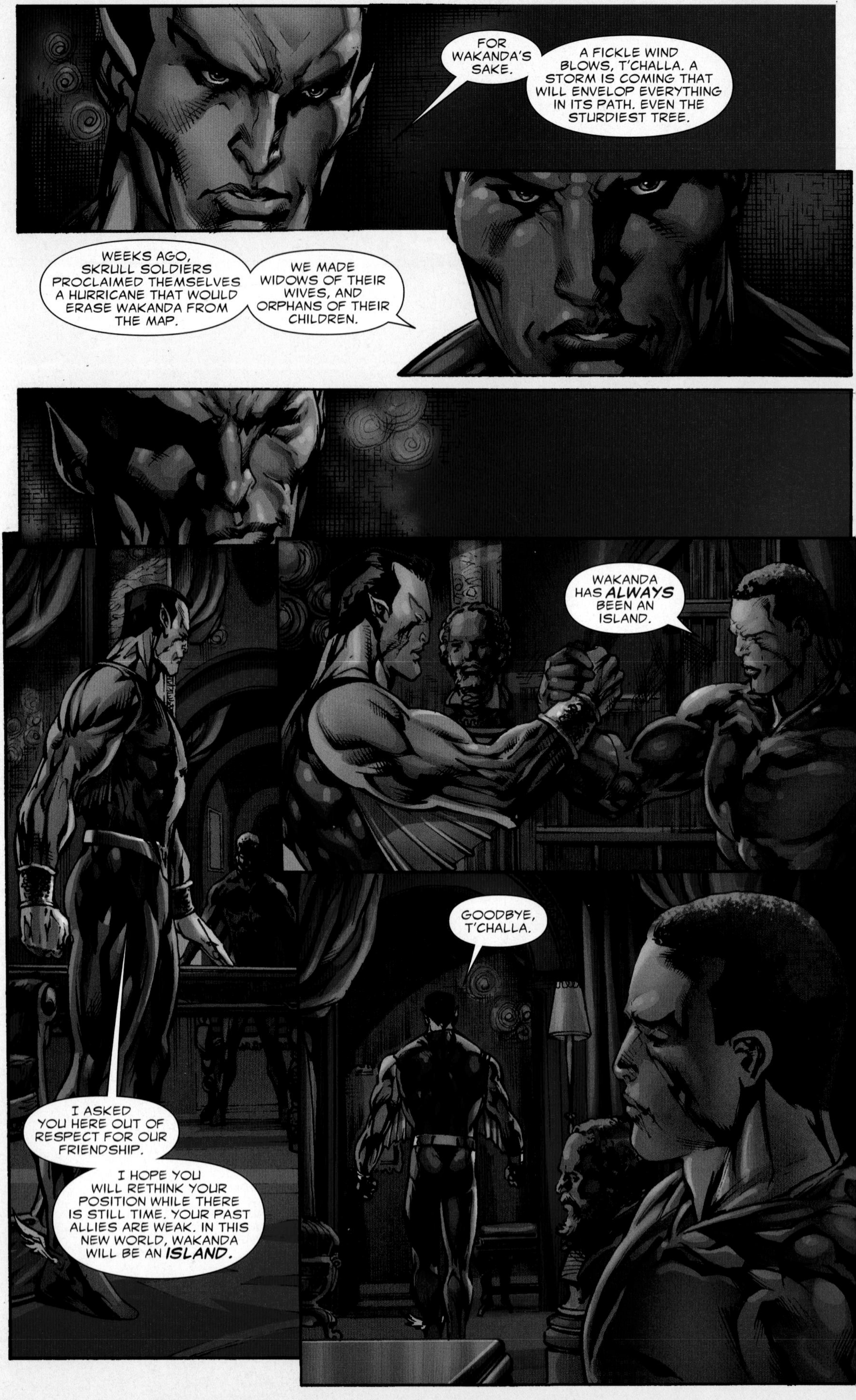
FOR WAKANDA'S SAKE.
A FICKLE WIND BLOWS, T'CHALLA. A STORM IS COMING THAT WILL ENVELOP EVERYTHING IN ITS PATH. EVEN THE STURDIEST TREE.
WEEKS AGO, SKRULL SOLDIERS PROCLAIMED THEMSELVES A HURRICANE THAT WOULD ERASE WAKANDA FROM THE MAP.
WE MADE WIDOWS OF THEIR WIVES, AND ORPHANS OF THEIR CHILDREN.
I ASKED YOU HERE OUT OF RESPECT FOR OUR FRIENDSHIP.
I HOPE YOU WILL RETHINK YOUR POSITION WHILE THERE IS STILL TIME. YOUR PAST ALLIES ARE WEAK. IN THIS NEW WORLD, WAKANDA WILL BE AN ***ISLAND.***
WAKANDA HAS ***ALWAYS*** BEEN AN ISLAND.
GOODBYE, T'CHALLA.

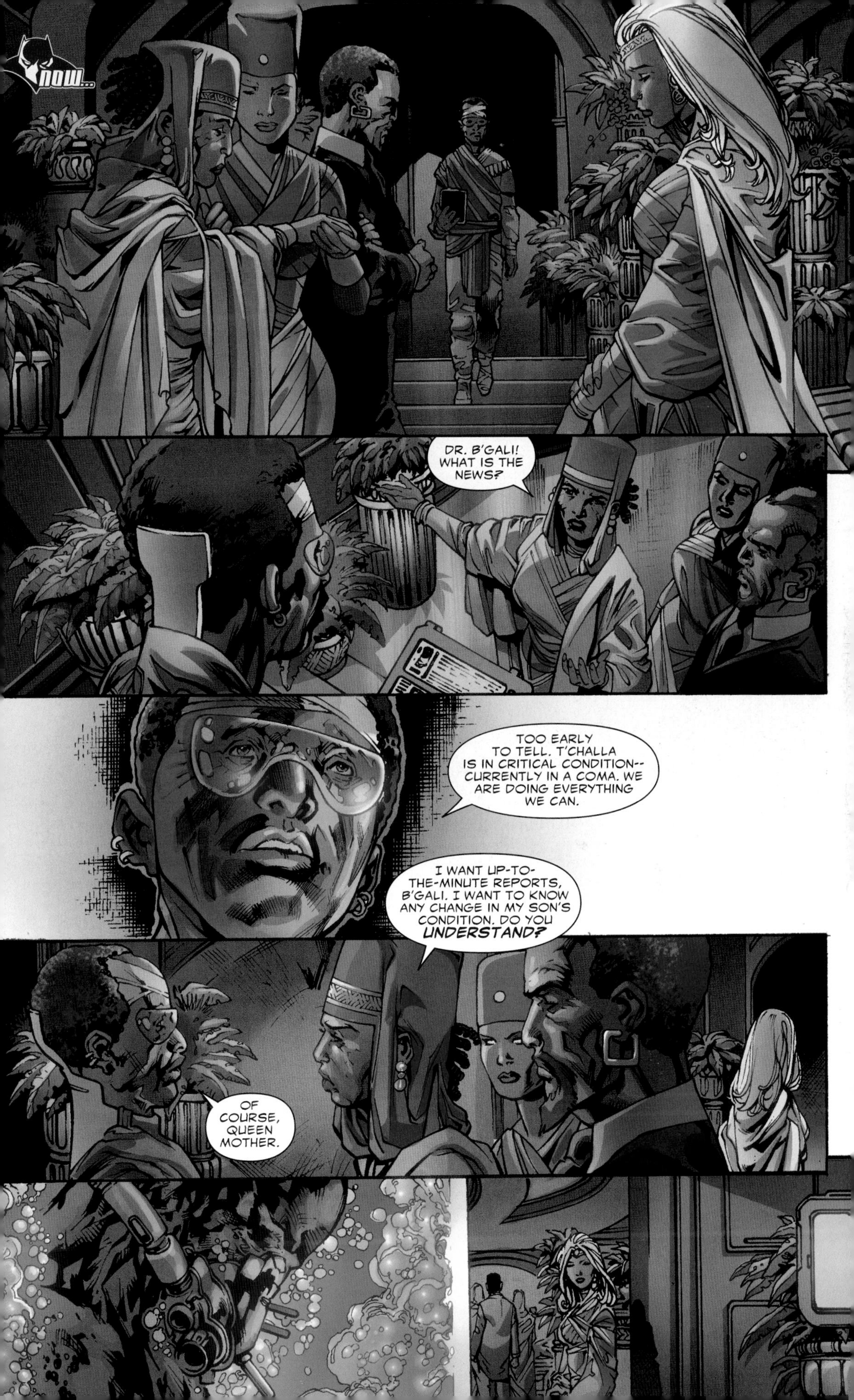
NOW...
DR. B'GALI! WHAT IS THE NEWS?
TOO EARLY TO TELL. T'CHALLA IS IN CRITICAL CONDITION-- CURRENTLY IN A COMA. WE ARE DOING EVERYTHING WE CAN.
I WANT UP-TO-THE-MINUTE REPORTS, B'GALI. I WANT TO KNOW ANY CHANGE IN MY SON'S CONDITION. DO YOU **UNDERSTAND?**
OF COURSE, QUEEN MOTHER.

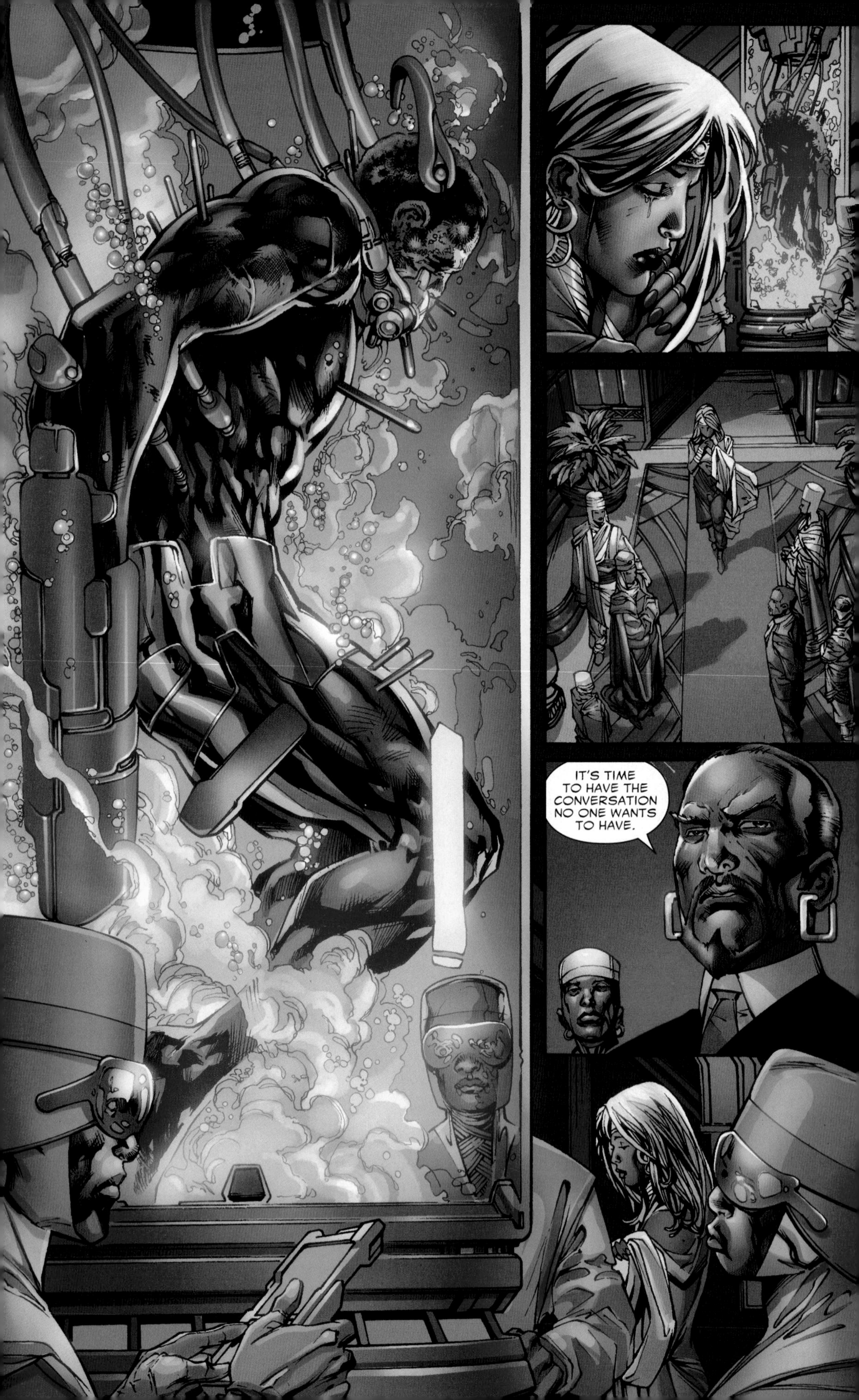
IT'S TIME TO HAVE THE CONVERSATION NO ONE WANTS TO HAVE.

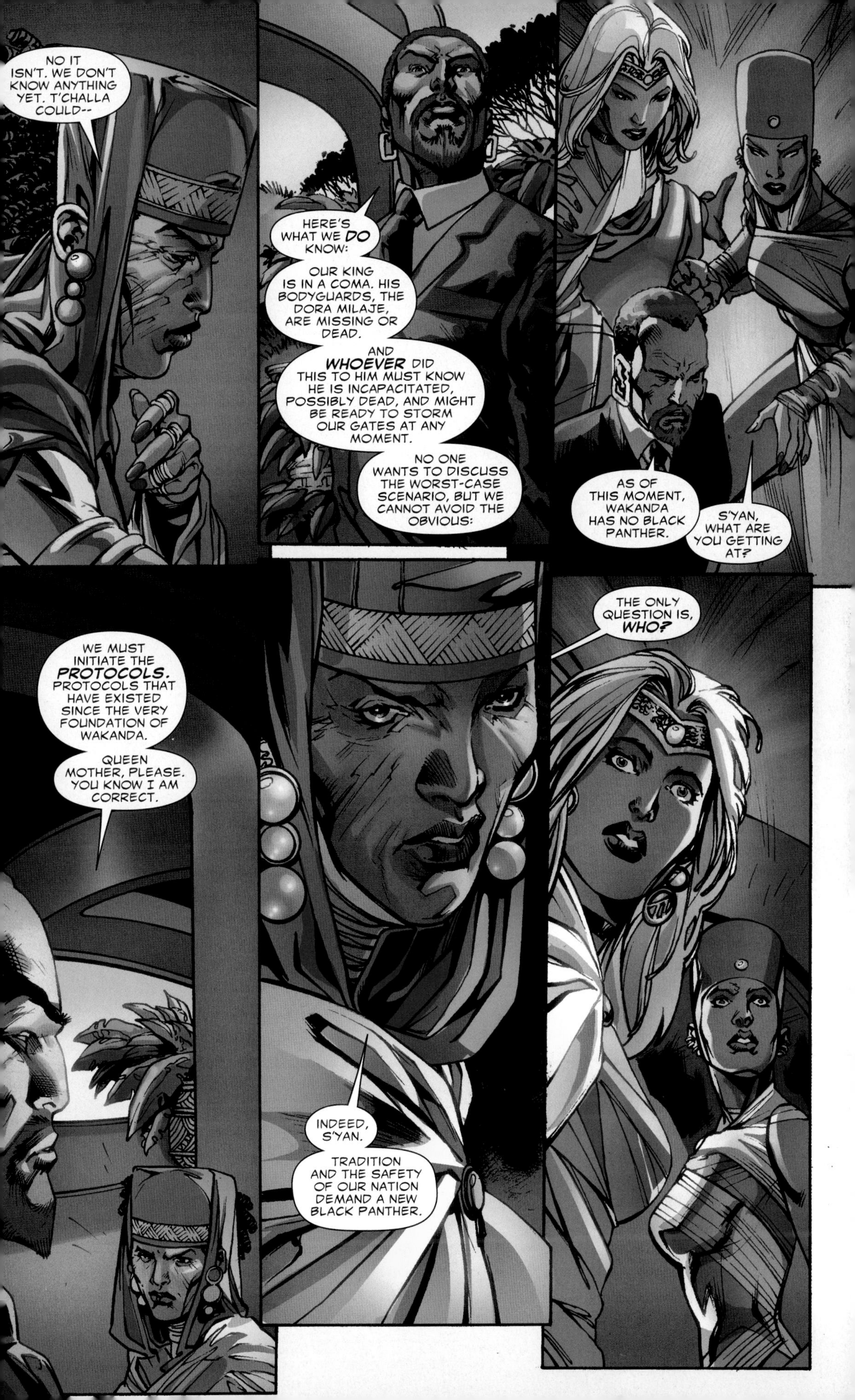
NO IT ISN'T. WE DON'T KNOW ANYTHING YET. T'CHALLA COULD--
HERE'S WHAT WE DO KNOW:
OUR KING IS IN A COMA. HIS BODYGUARDS, THE DORA MILAJE, ARE MISSING OR DEAD.
AND WHOEVER DID THIS TO HIM MUST KNOW HE IS INCAPACITATED, POSSIBLY DEAD, AND MIGHT BE READY TO STORM OUR GATES AT ANY MOMENT.
NO ONE WANTS TO DISCUSS THE WORST-CASE SCENARIO, BUT WE CANNOT AVOID THE OBVIOUS:
AS OF THIS MOMENT, WAKANDA HAS NO BLACK PANTHER.
S'YAN, WHAT ARE YOU GETTING AT?
WE MUST INITIATE THE PROTOCOLS. PROTOCOLS THAT HAVE EXISTED SINCE THE VERY FOUNDATION OF WAKANDA.
QUEEN MOTHER, PLEASE. YOU KNOW I AM CORRECT.
INDEED, S'YAN.
TRADITION AND THE SAFETY OF OUR NATION DEMAND A NEW BLACK PANTHER.
THE ONLY QUESTION IS, WHO?

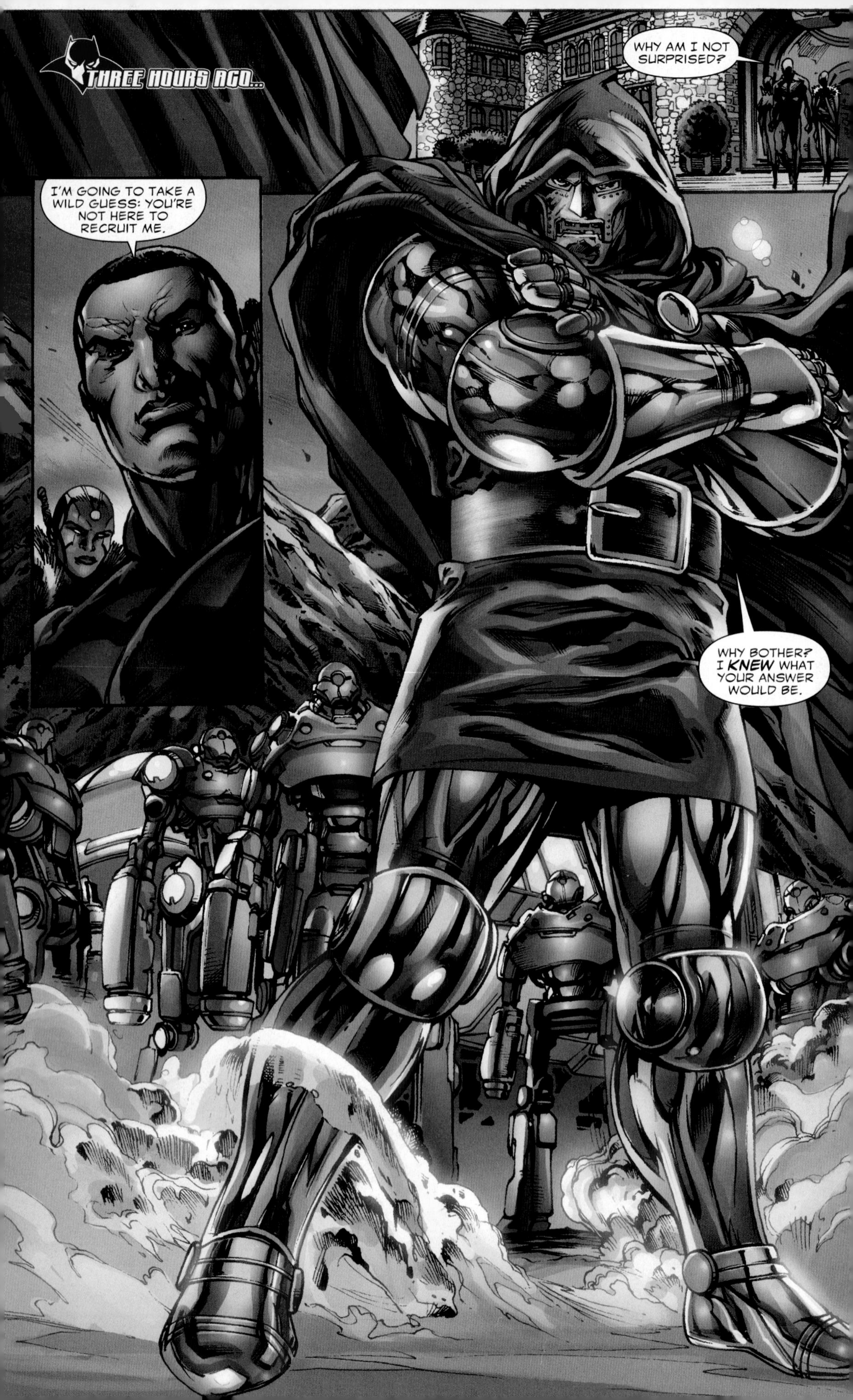
THREE HOURS AGO...
I'M GOING TO TAKE A WILD GUESS: YOU'RE NOT HERE TO RECRUIT ME.
WHY AM I NOT SURPRISED?
WHY BOTHER? I KNEW WHAT YOUR ANSWER WOULD BE.

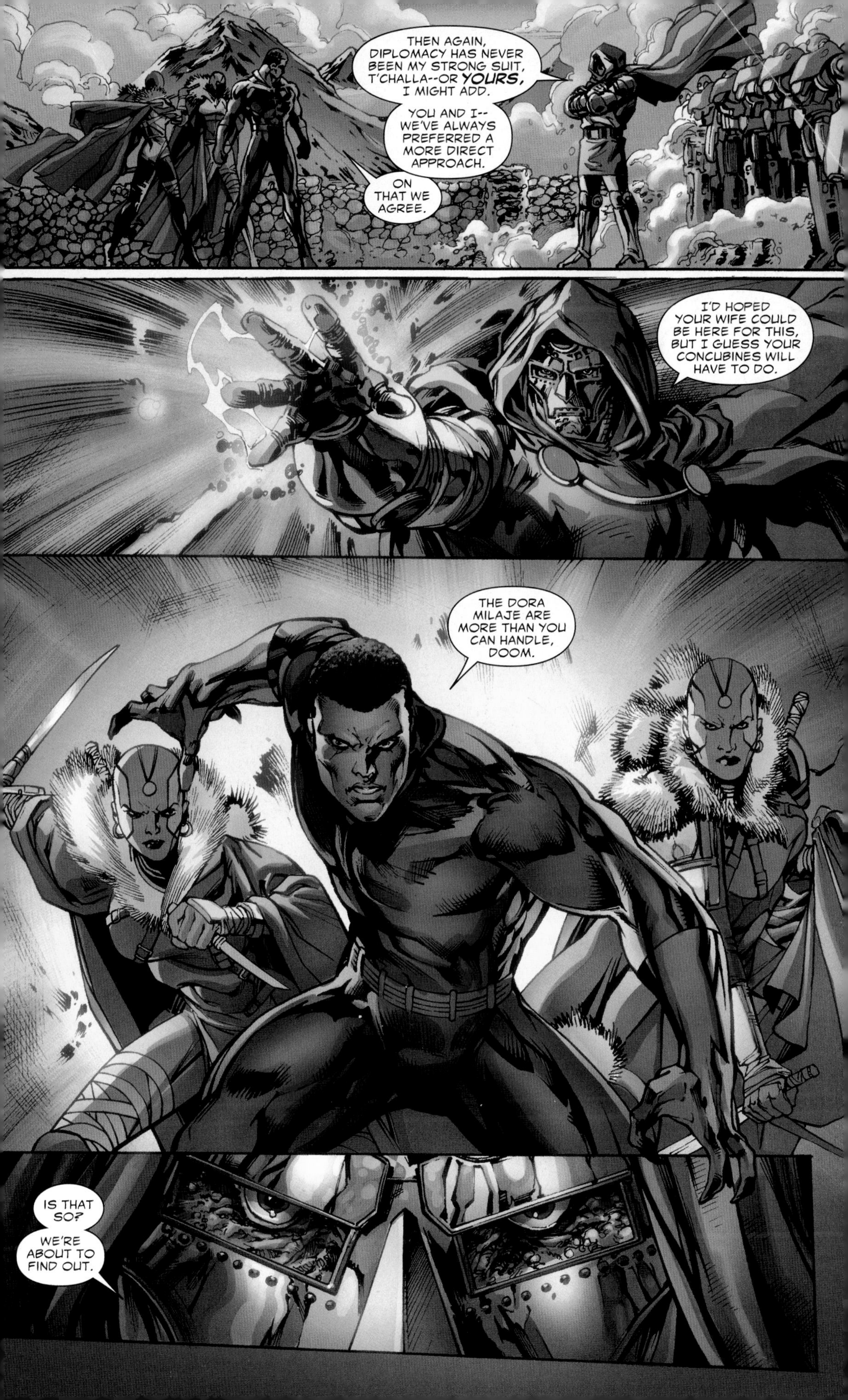
THEN AGAIN, DIPLOMACY HAS NEVER BEEN MY STRONG SUIT, T'CHALLA--OR YOURS, I MIGHT ADD.
YOU AND I-- WE'VE ALWAYS PREFERRED A MORE DIRECT APPROACH.
ON THAT WE AGREE.
I'D HOPED YOUR WIFE COULD BE HERE FOR THIS, BUT I GUESS YOUR CONCUBINES WILL HAVE TO DO.
THE DORA MILAJE ARE MORE THAN YOU CAN HANDLE, DOOM.
IS THAT SO?
WE'RE ABOUT TO FIND OUT.

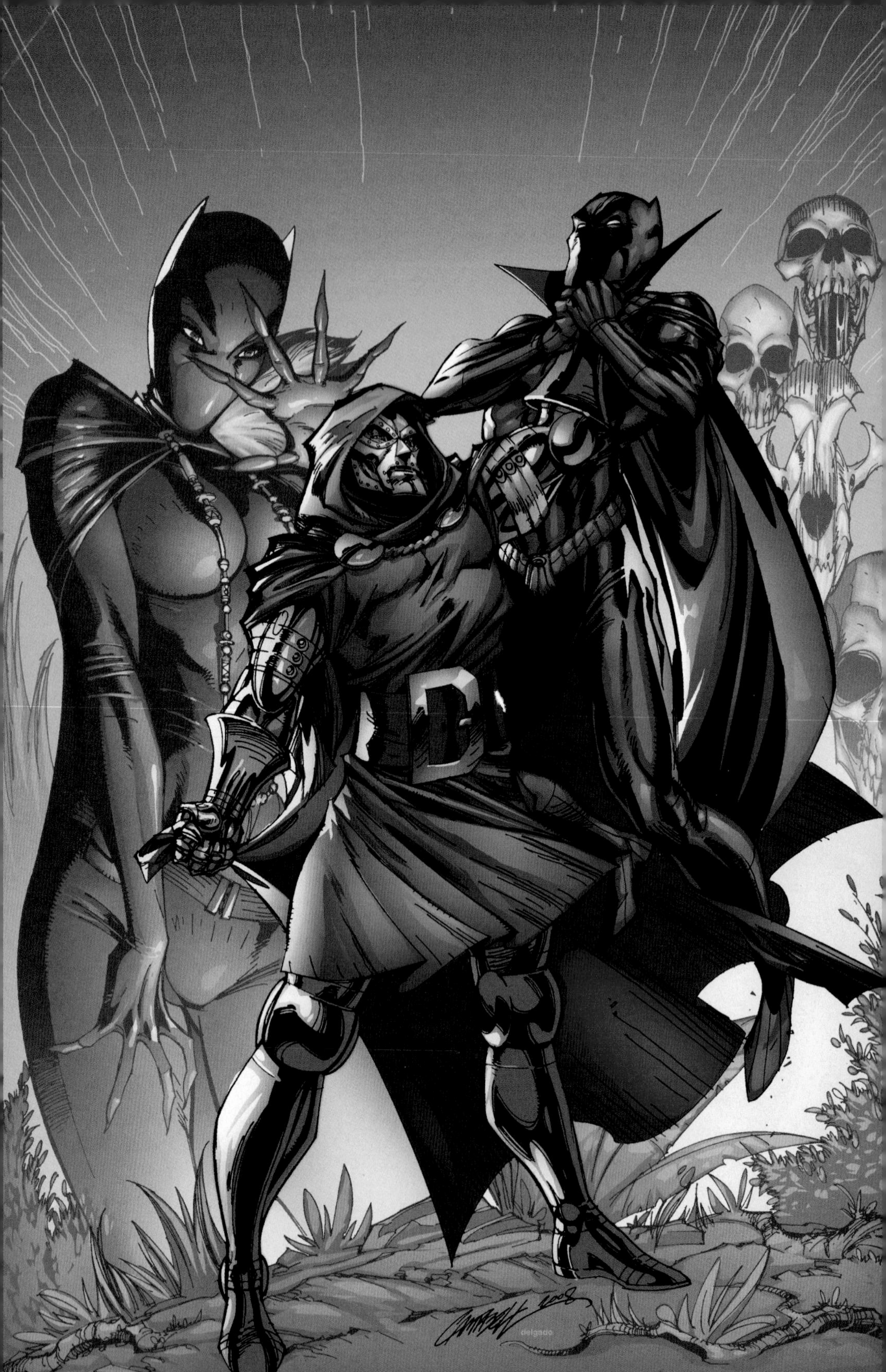

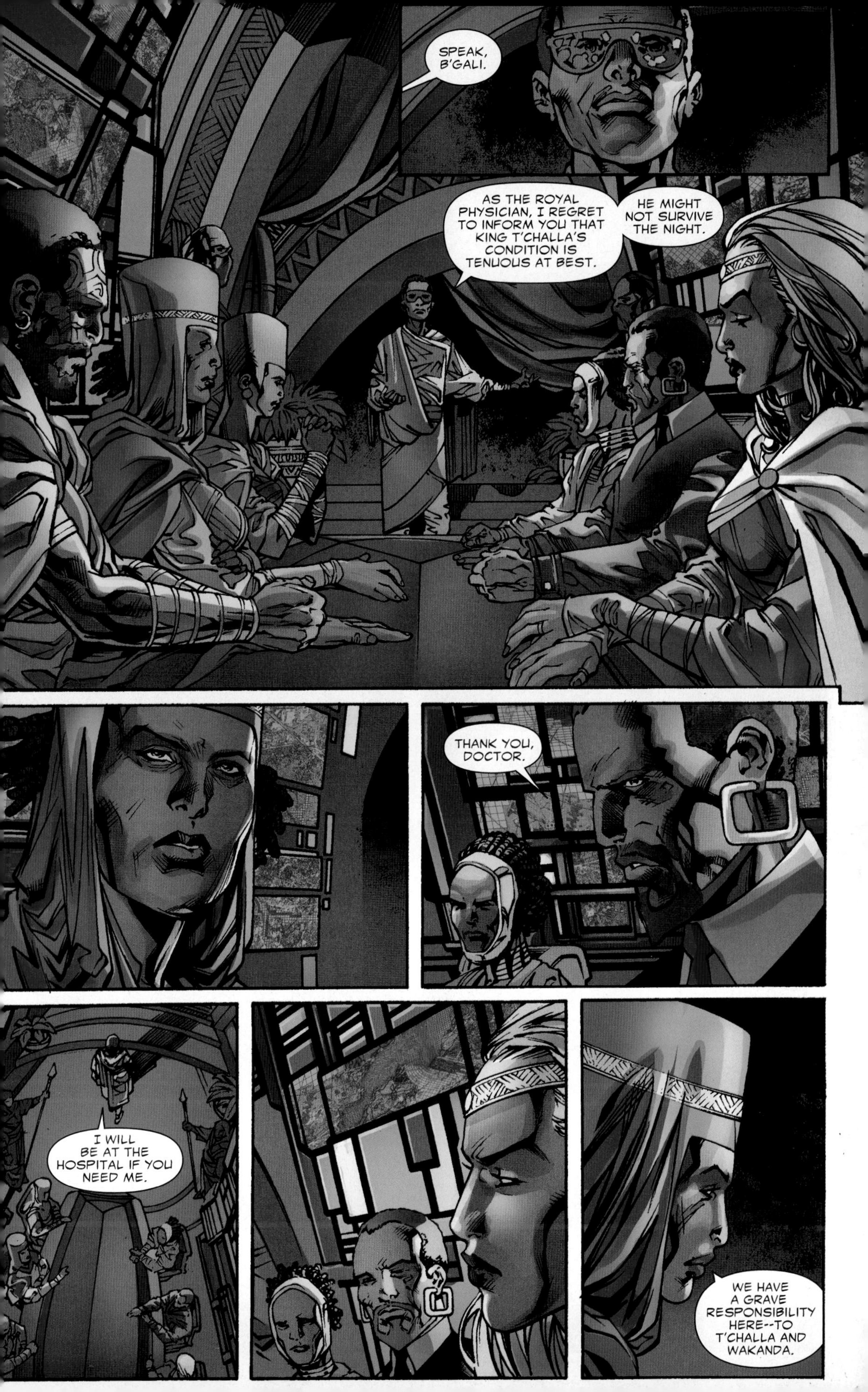
SPEAK, B'GALI.
AS THE ROYAL PHYSICIAN, I REGRET TO INFORM YOU THAT KING T'CHALLA'S CONDITION IS TENUOUS AT BEST.
HE MIGHT NOT SURVIVE THE NIGHT.
THANK YOU, DOCTOR.
I WILL BE AT THE HOSPITAL IF YOU NEED ME.
WE HAVE A GRAVE RESPONSIBILITY HERE--TO T'CHALLA AND WAKANDA.

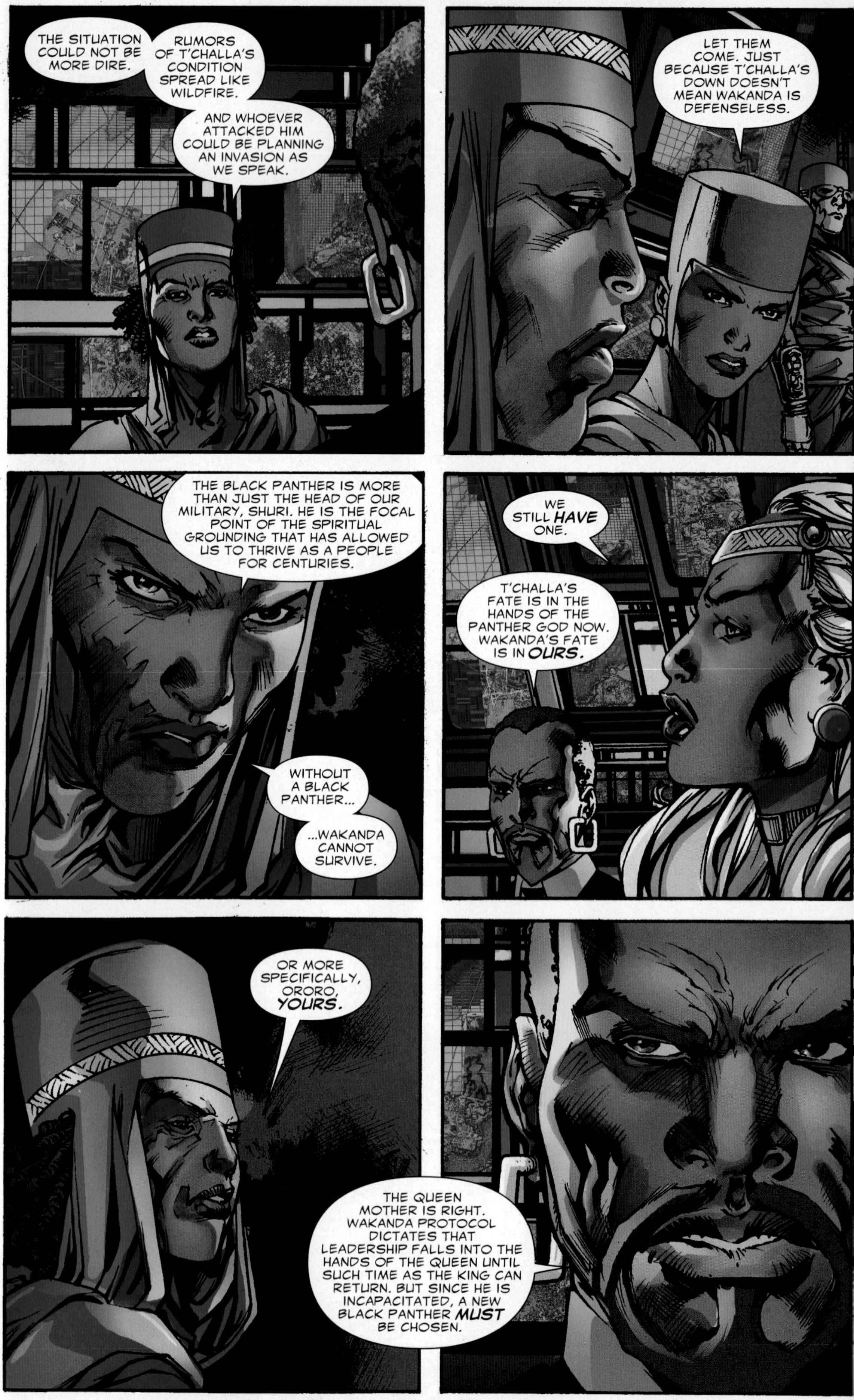
THE SITUATION COULD NOT BE MORE DIRE.
RUMORS OF T'CHALLA'S CONDITION SPREAD LIKE WILDFIRE.
AND WHOEVER ATTACKED HIM COULD BE PLANNING AN INVASION AS WE SPEAK.
LET THEM COME. JUST BECAUSE T'CHALLA'S DOWN DOESN'T MEAN WAKANDA IS DEFENSELESS.
THE BLACK PANTHER IS MORE THAN JUST THE HEAD OF OUR MILITARY, SHURI. HE IS THE FOCAL POINT OF THE SPIRITUAL GROUNDING THAT HAS ALLOWED US TO THRIVE AS A PEOPLE FOR CENTURIES.
WITHOUT A BLACK PANTHER...
...WAKANDA CANNOT SURVIVE.
WE STILL HAVE ONE.
T'CHALLA'S FATE IS IN THE HANDS OF THE PANTHER GOD NOW. WAKANDA'S FATE IS IN OURS.
OR MORE SPECIFICALLY, ORORO, YOURS.
THE QUEEN MOTHER IS RIGHT. WAKANDA PROTOCOL DICTATES THAT LEADERSHIP FALLS INTO THE HANDS OF THE QUEEN UNTIL SUCH TIME AS THE KING CAN RETURN. BUT SINCE HE IS INCAPACITATED, A NEW BLACK PANTHER MUST BE CHOSEN.

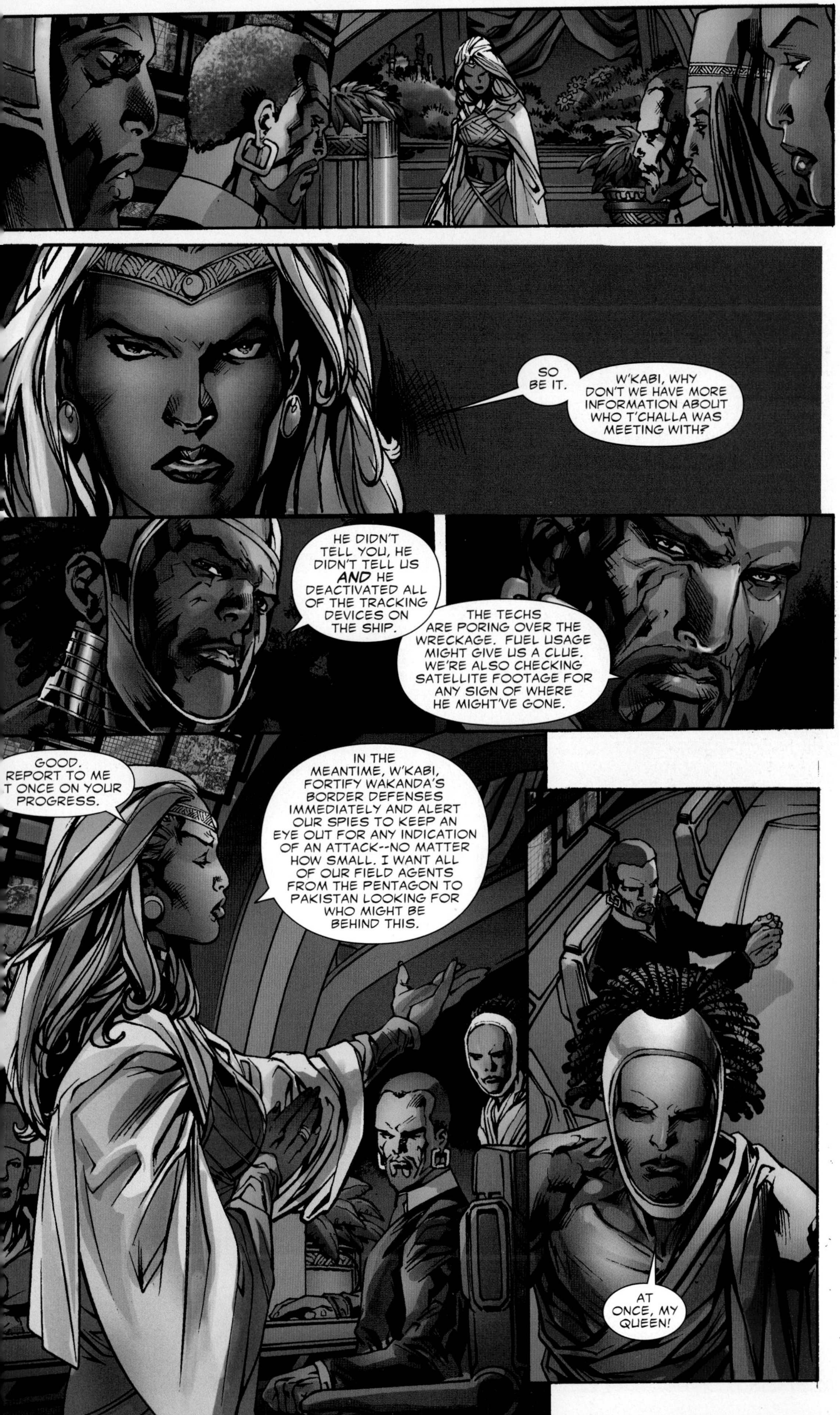
SO BE IT.
W'KABI, WHY DON'T WE HAVE MORE INFORMATION ABOUT WHO T'CHALLA WAS MEETING WITH?
HE DIDN'T TELL YOU, HE DIDN'T TELL US AND HE DEACTIVATED ALL OF THE TRACKING DEVICES ON THE SHIP.
THE TECHS ARE PORING OVER THE WRECKAGE. FUEL USAGE MIGHT GIVE US A CLUE. WE'RE ALSO CHECKING SATELLITE FOOTAGE FOR ANY SIGN OF WHERE HE MIGHT'VE GONE.
GOOD. REPORT TO ME T ONCE ON YOUR PROGRESS.
IN THE MEANTIME, W'KABI, FORTIFY WAKANDA'S BORDER DEFENSES IMMEDIATELY AND ALERT OUR SPIES TO KEEP AN EYE OUT FOR ANY INDICATION OF AN ATTACK--NO MATTER HOW SMALL. I WANT ALL OF OUR FIELD AGENTS FROM THE PENTAGON TO PAKISTAN LOOKING FOR WHO MIGHT BE BEHIND THIS.
AT ONCE, MY QUEEN!

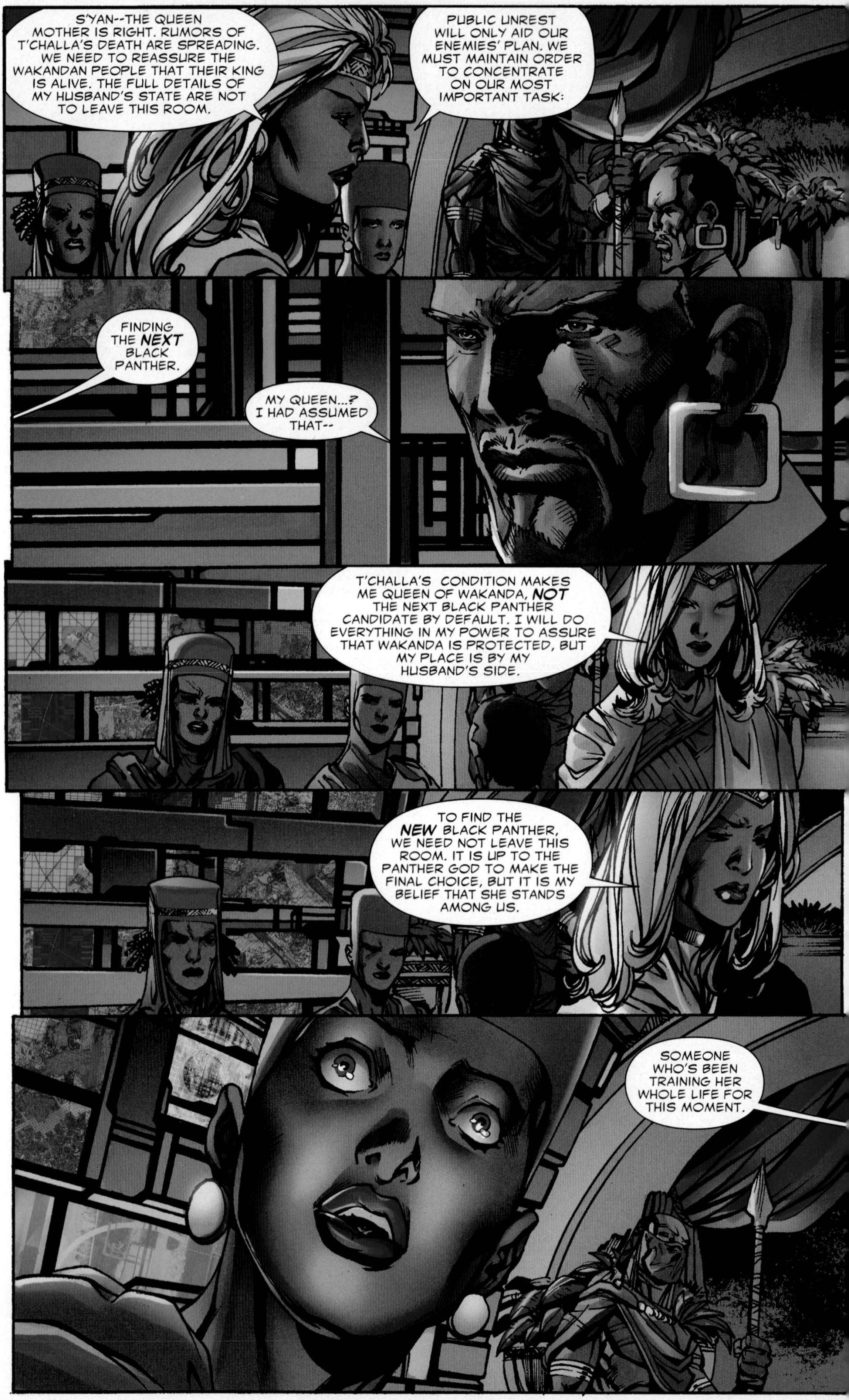
S'YAN--THE QUEEN MOTHER IS RIGHT. RUMORS OF T'CHALLA'S DEATH ARE SPREADING. WE NEED TO REASSURE THE WAKANDAN PEOPLE THAT THEIR KING IS ALIVE. THE FULL DETAILS OF MY HUSBAND'S STATE ARE NOT TO LEAVE THIS ROOM.
PUBLIC UNREST WILL ONLY AID OUR ENEMIES' PLAN. WE MUST MAINTAIN ORDER TO CONCENTRATE ON OUR MOST IMPORTANT TASK:
FINDING THE **NEXT** BLACK PANTHER.
MY QUEEN...? I HAD ASSUMED THAT--
T'CHALLA'S CONDITION MAKES ME QUEEN OF WAKANDA, **NOT** THE NEXT BLACK PANTHER CANDIDATE BY DEFAULT. I WILL DO EVERYTHING IN MY POWER TO ASSURE THAT WAKANDA IS PROTECTED, BUT MY PLACE IS BY MY HUSBAND'S SIDE.
TO FIND THE **NEW** BLACK PANTHER, WE NEED NOT LEAVE THIS ROOM. IT IS UP TO THE PANTHER GOD TO MAKE THE FINAL CHOICE, BUT IT IS MY BELIEF THAT SHE STANDS AMONG US.
SOMEONE WHO'S BEEN TRAINING HER WHOLE LIFE FOR THIS MOMENT.

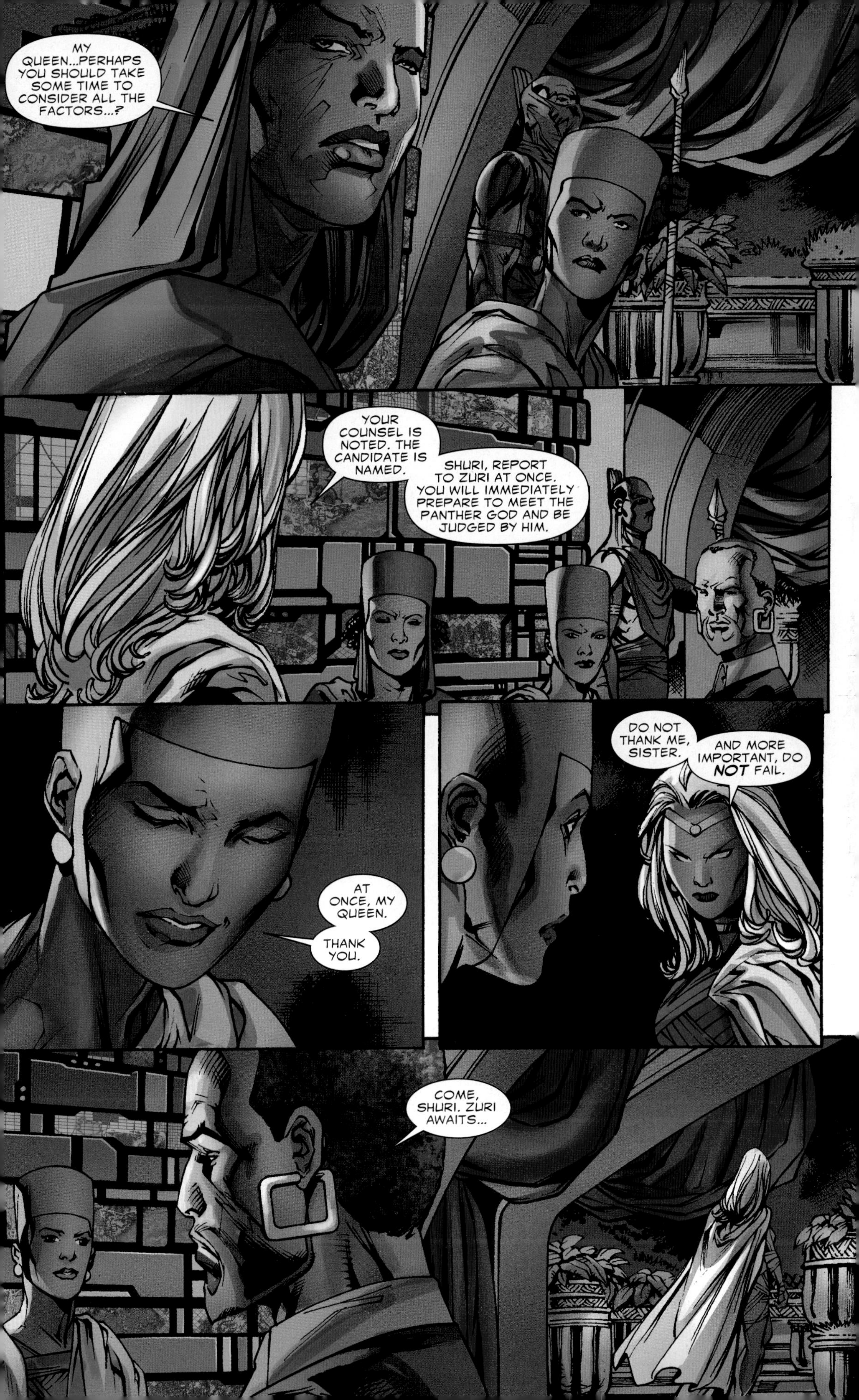
MY QUEEN...PERHAPS YOU SHOULD TAKE SOME TIME TO CONSIDER ALL THE FACTORS...?
YOUR COUNSEL IS NOTED. THE CANDIDATE IS NAMED.
SHURI, REPORT TO ZURI AT ONCE. YOU WILL IMMEDIATELY PREPARE TO MEET THE PANTHER GOD AND BE JUDGED BY HIM.
AT ONCE, MY QUEEN.
THANK YOU.
DO NOT THANK ME, SISTER.
AND MORE IMPORTANT, DO NOT FAIL.
COME, SHURI. ZURI AWAITS...

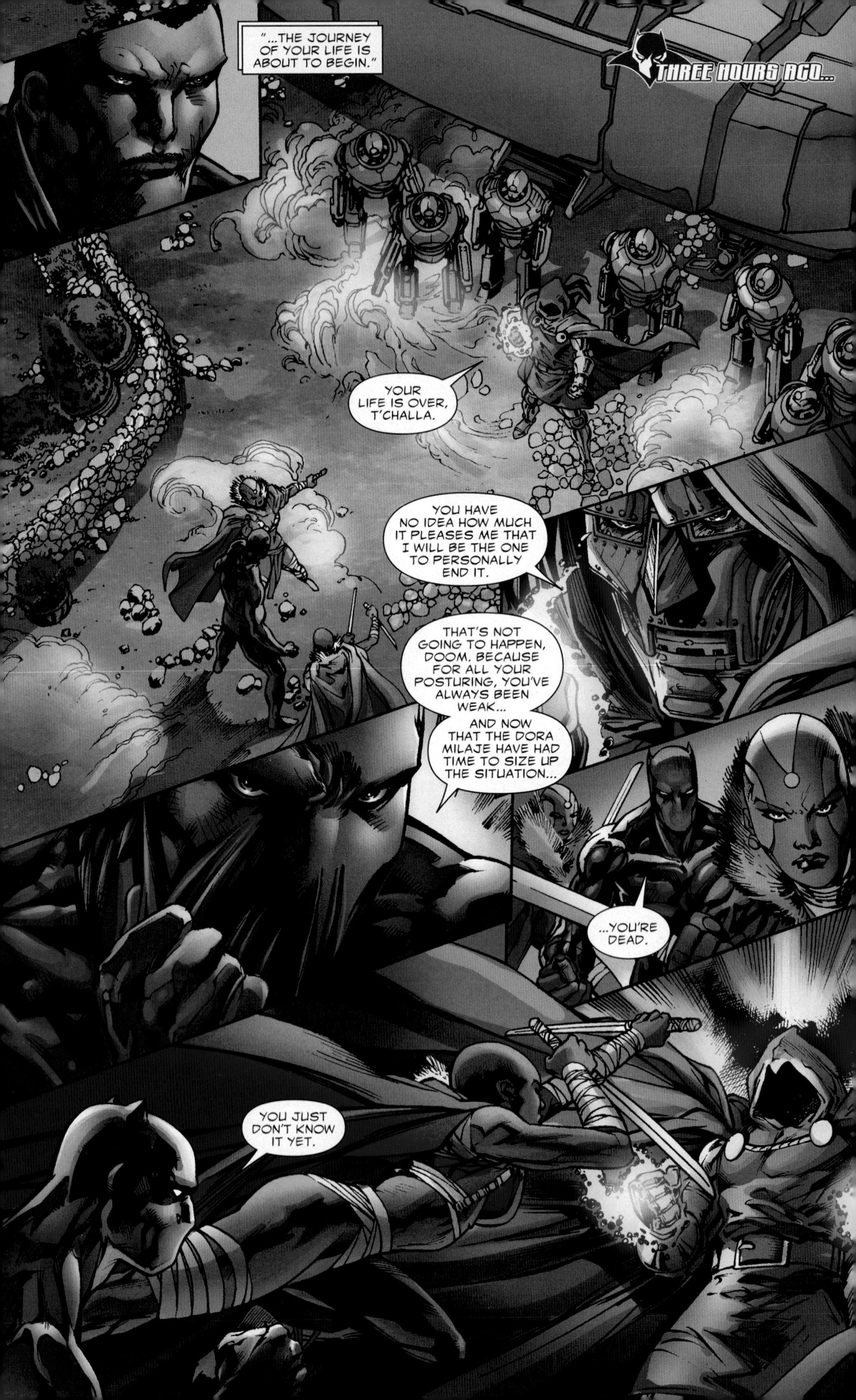
"...THE JOURNEY OF YOUR LIFE IS ABOUT TO BEGIN."
THREE HOURS AGO...
YOUR LIFE IS OVER, T'CHALLA.
YOU HAVE NO IDEA HOW MUCH IT PLEASES ME THAT I WILL BE THE ONE TO PERSONALLY END IT.
THAT'S NOT GOING TO HAPPEN, DOOM. BECAUSE FOR ALL YOUR POSTURING, YOU'VE ALWAYS BEEN WEAK...
AND NOW THAT THE DORA MILAJE HAVE HAD TIME TO SIZE UP THE SITUATION...
...YOU'RE DEAD.
YOU JUST DON'T KNOW IT YET.

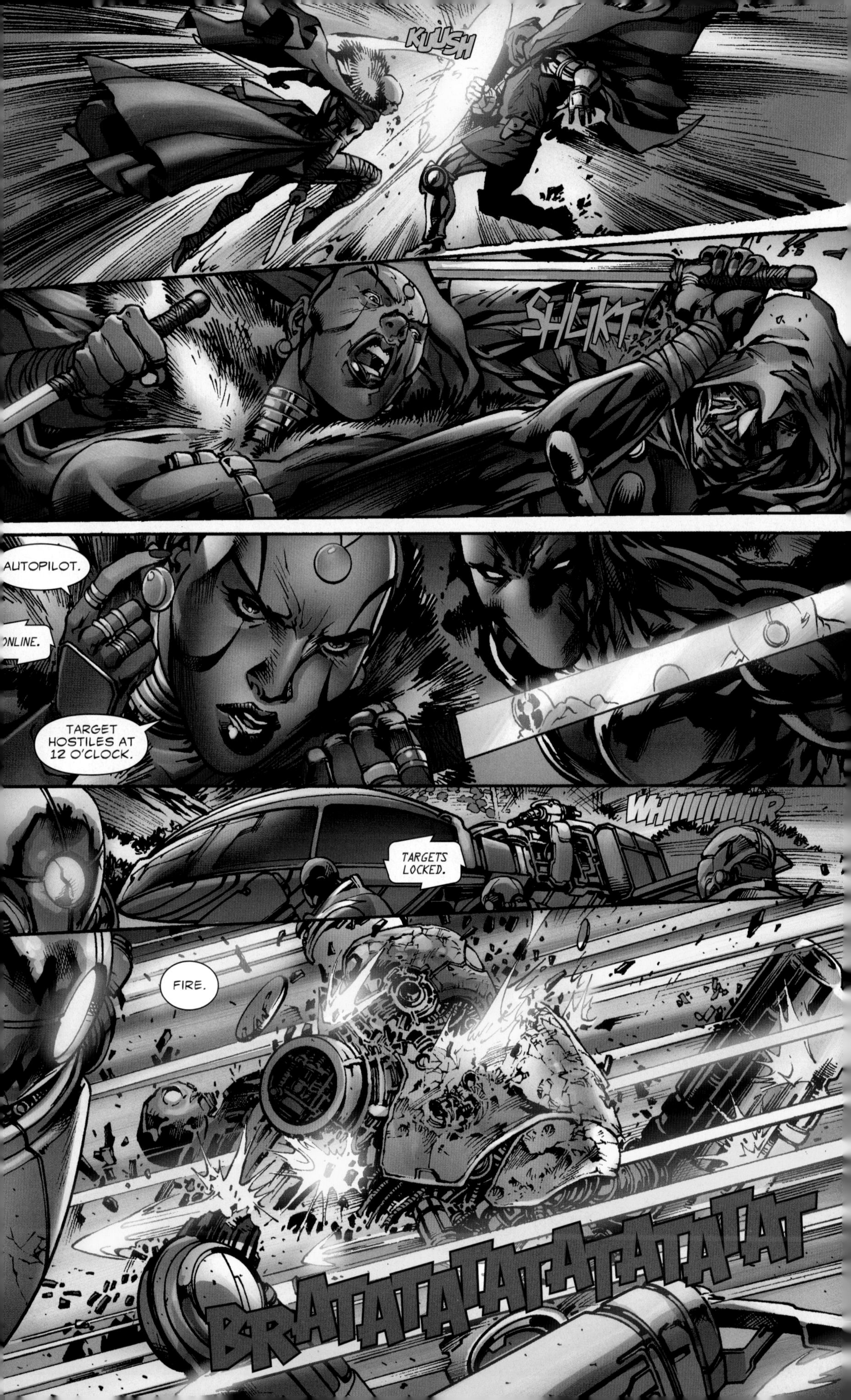
KUUSH
SHLIKT
AUTOPILOT.
ONLINE.
TARGET HOSTILES AT 12 O'CLOCK.
WHIIIIIIIIIIR
TARGETS LOCKED.
FIRE.
BRATATATATATATATATAT

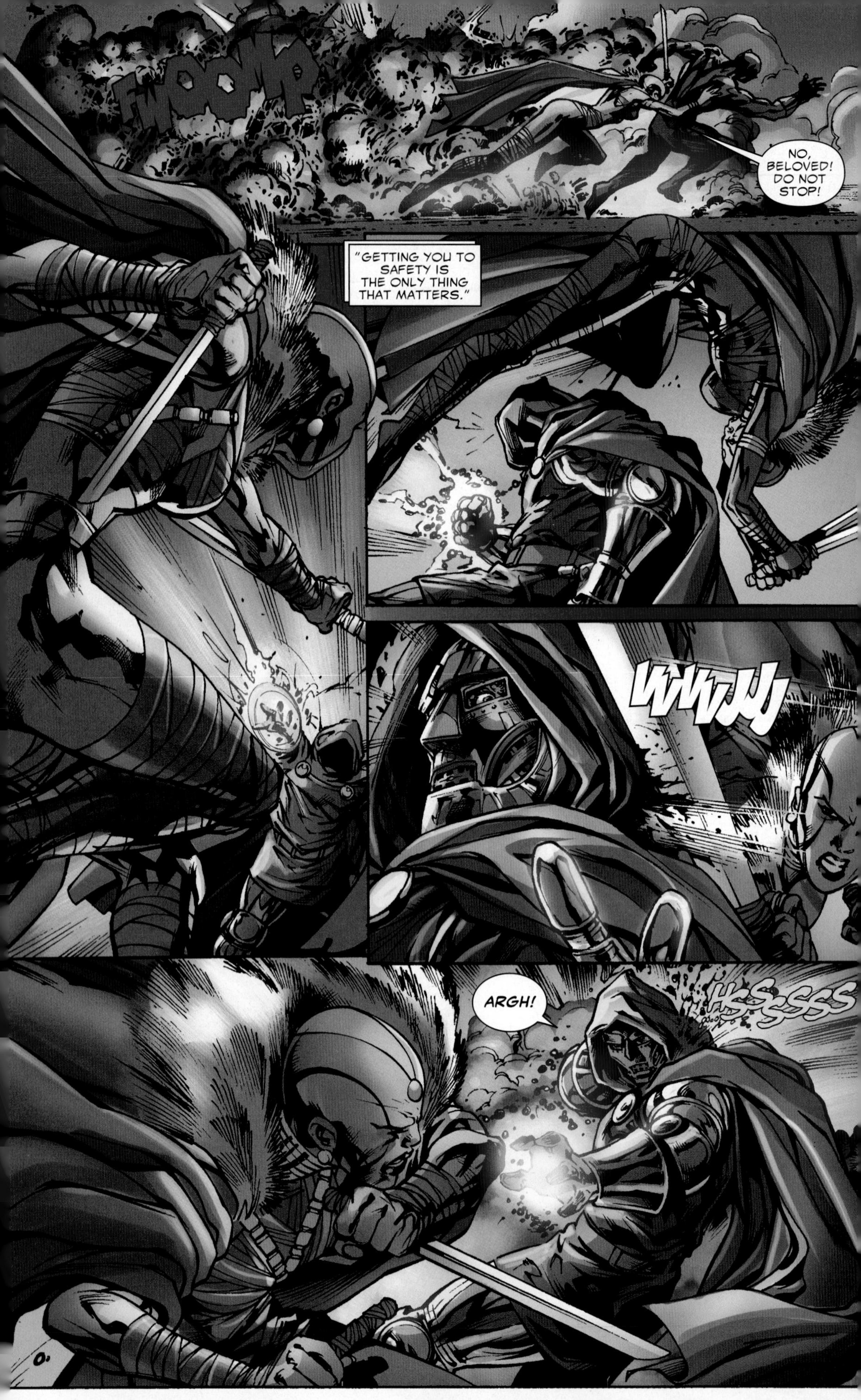
FWOOMP
NO, BELOVED! DO NOT STOP!
"GETTING YOU TO SAFETY IS THE ONLY THING THAT MATTERS."
WWWJJ
ARGH!
HSSSSSS

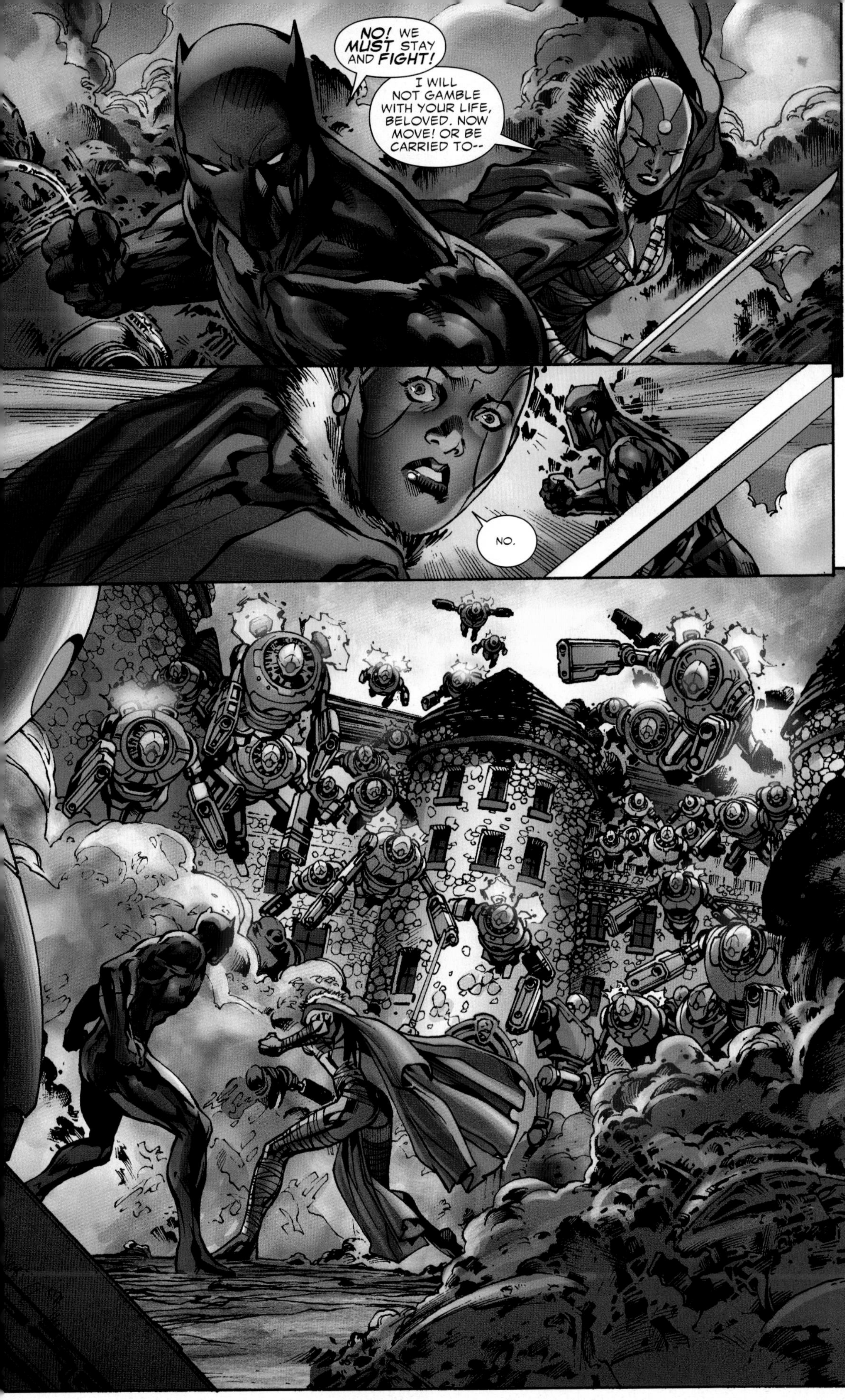
NO! WE MUST STAY AND FIGHT!
I WILL NOT GAMBLE WITH YOUR LIFE, BELOVED. NOW MOVE! OR BE CARRIED TO--
NO.

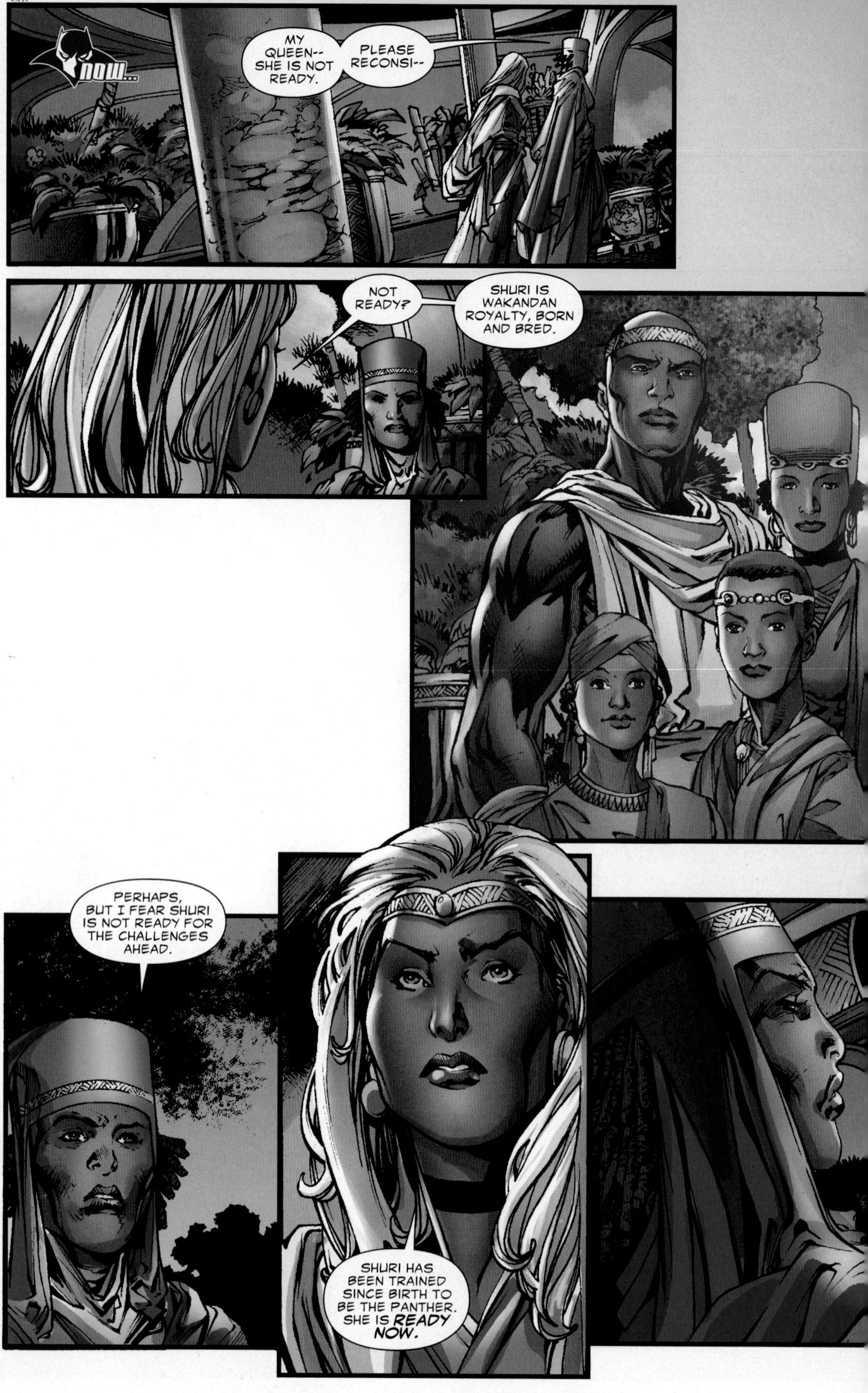
NOW...
MY QUEEN-- SHE IS NOT READY.
PLEASE RECONSI--
NOT READY?
SHURI IS WAKANDAN ROYALTY, BORN AND BRED.
PERHAPS, BUT I FEAR SHURI IS NOT READY FOR THE CHALLENGES AHEAD.
SHURI HAS BEEN TRAINED SINCE BIRTH TO BE THE PANTHER. SHE IS READY NOW.

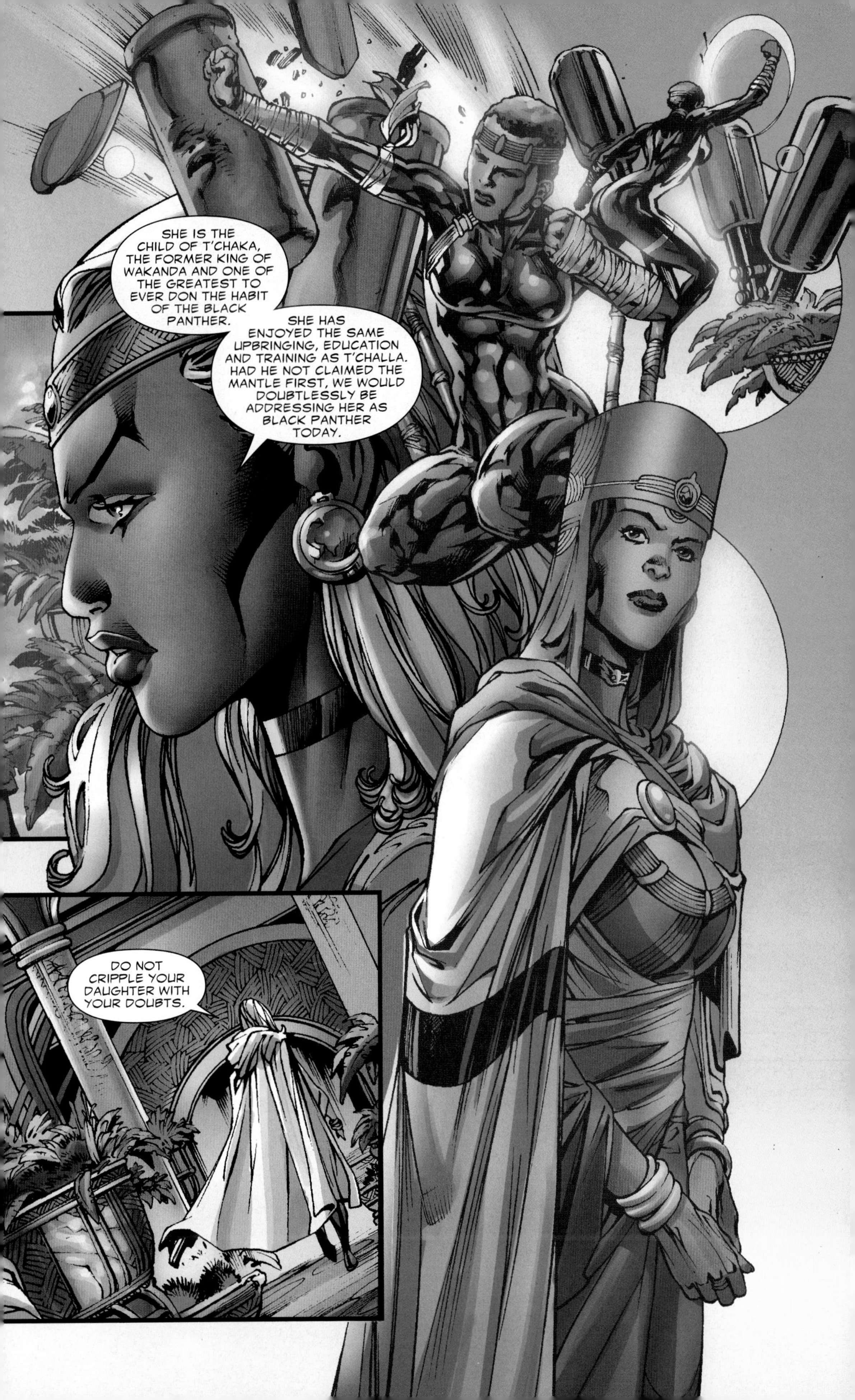
SHE IS THE CHILD OF T'CHAKA, THE FORMER KING OF WAKANDA AND ONE OF THE GREATEST TO EVER DON THE HABIT OF THE BLACK PANTHER.
SHE HAS ENJOYED THE SAME UPBRINGING, EDUCATION AND TRAINING AS T'CHALLA. HAD HE NOT CLAIMED THE MANTLE FIRST, WE WOULD DOUBTLESSLY BE ADDRESSING HER AS BLACK PANTHER TODAY.
DO NOT CRIPPLE YOUR DAUGHTER WITH YOUR DOUBTS.

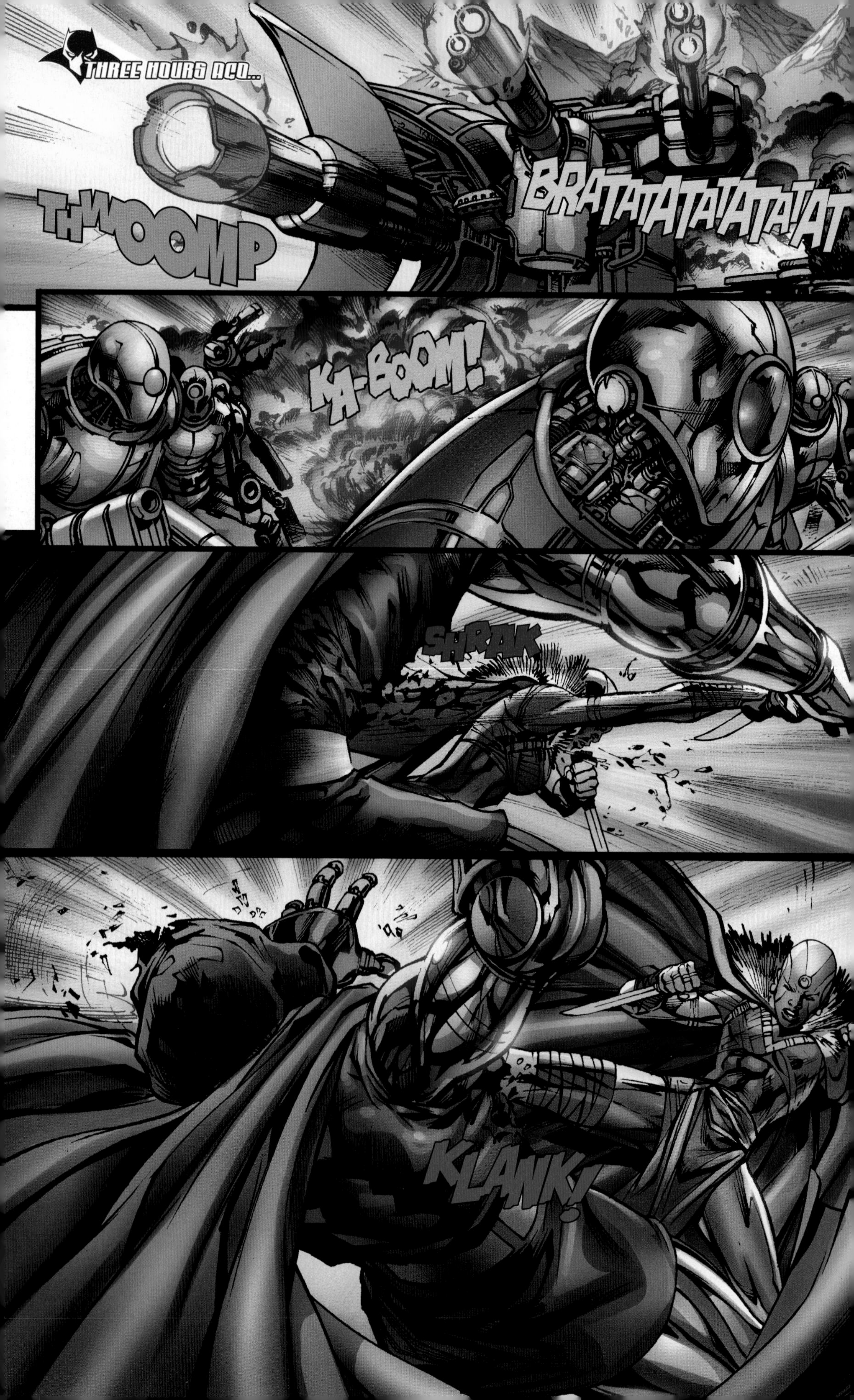
THREE HOURS AGO...
THWOOMP
BRATATATATATATAT
KA-BOOM!
SHRAK
KLANK!

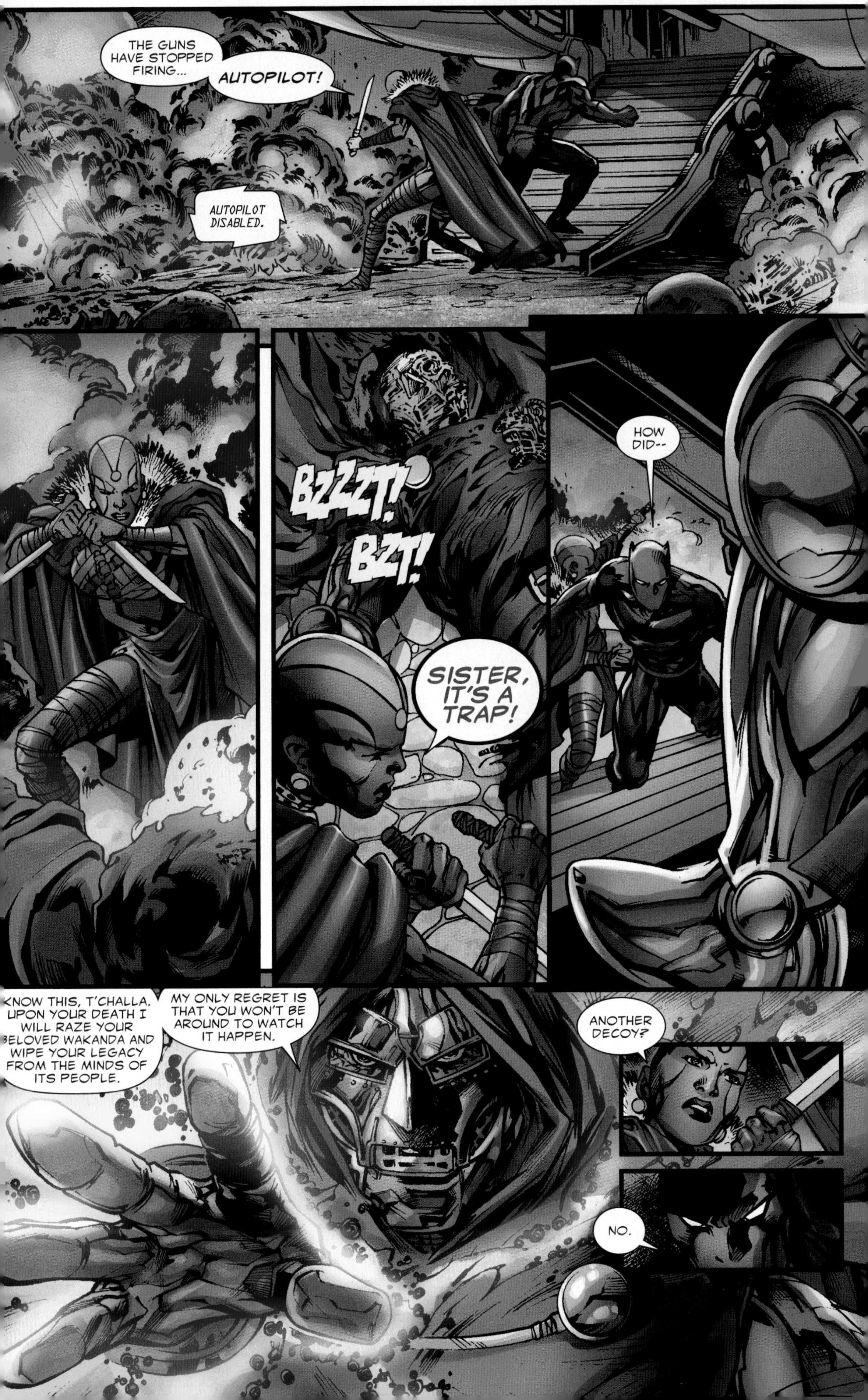
THE GUNS HAVE STOPPED FIRING...
AUTOPILOT!
AUTOPILOT DISABLED.
BZZZT!
BZZT!
SISTER, IT'S A TRAP!
HOW DID--
KNOW THIS, T'CHALLA. UPON YOUR DEATH I WILL RAZE YOUR BELOVED WAKANDA AND WIPE YOUR LEGACY FROM THE MINDS OF ITS PEOPLE.
MY ONLY REGRET IS THAT YOU WON'T BE AROUND TO WATCH IT HAPPEN.
ANOTHER DECOY?
NO.

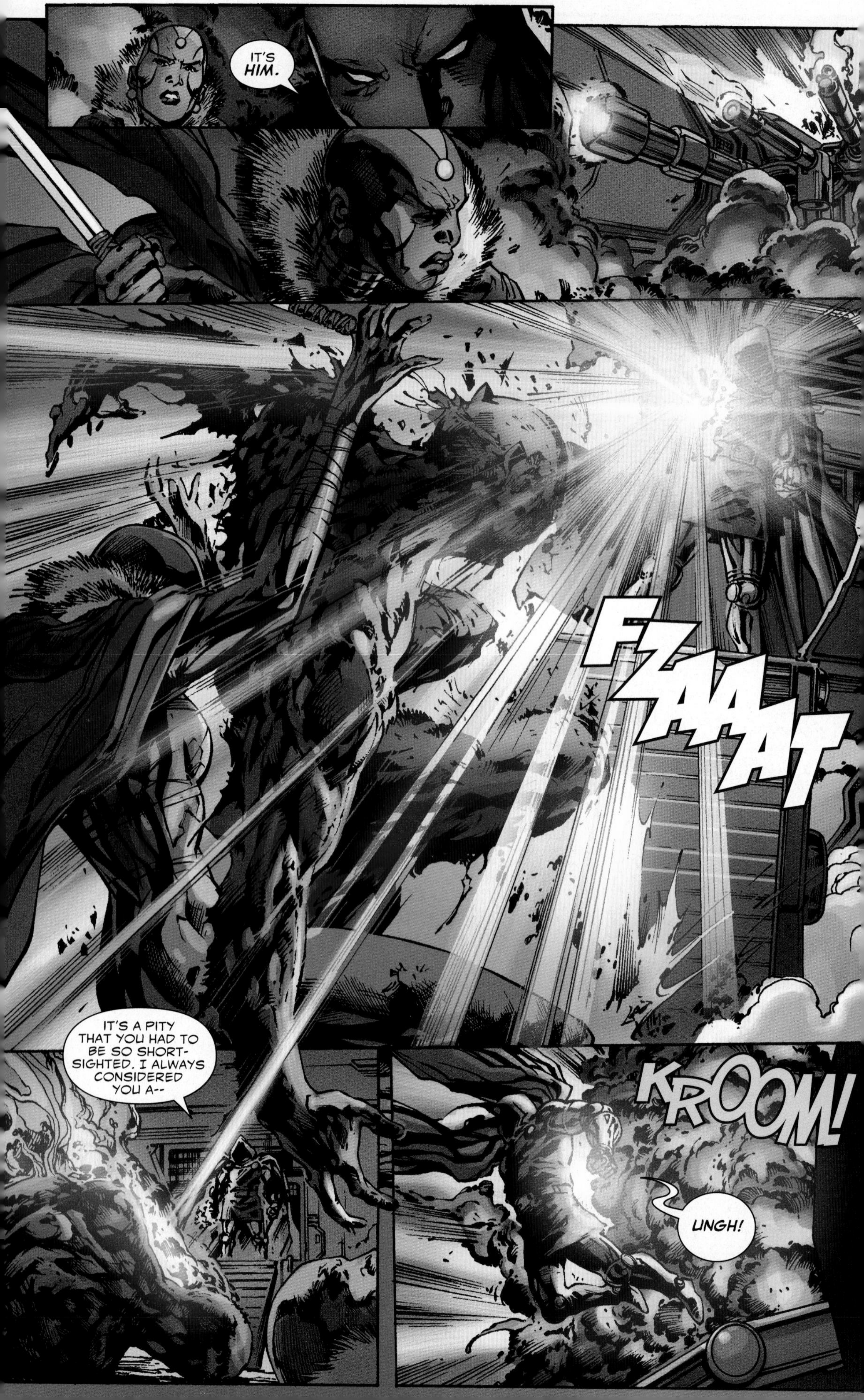
IT'S HIM.
FZAAAT
IT'S A PITY THAT YOU HAD TO BE SO SHORT-SIGHTED. I ALWAYS CONSIDERED YOU A--
KROOM!
UNGH!

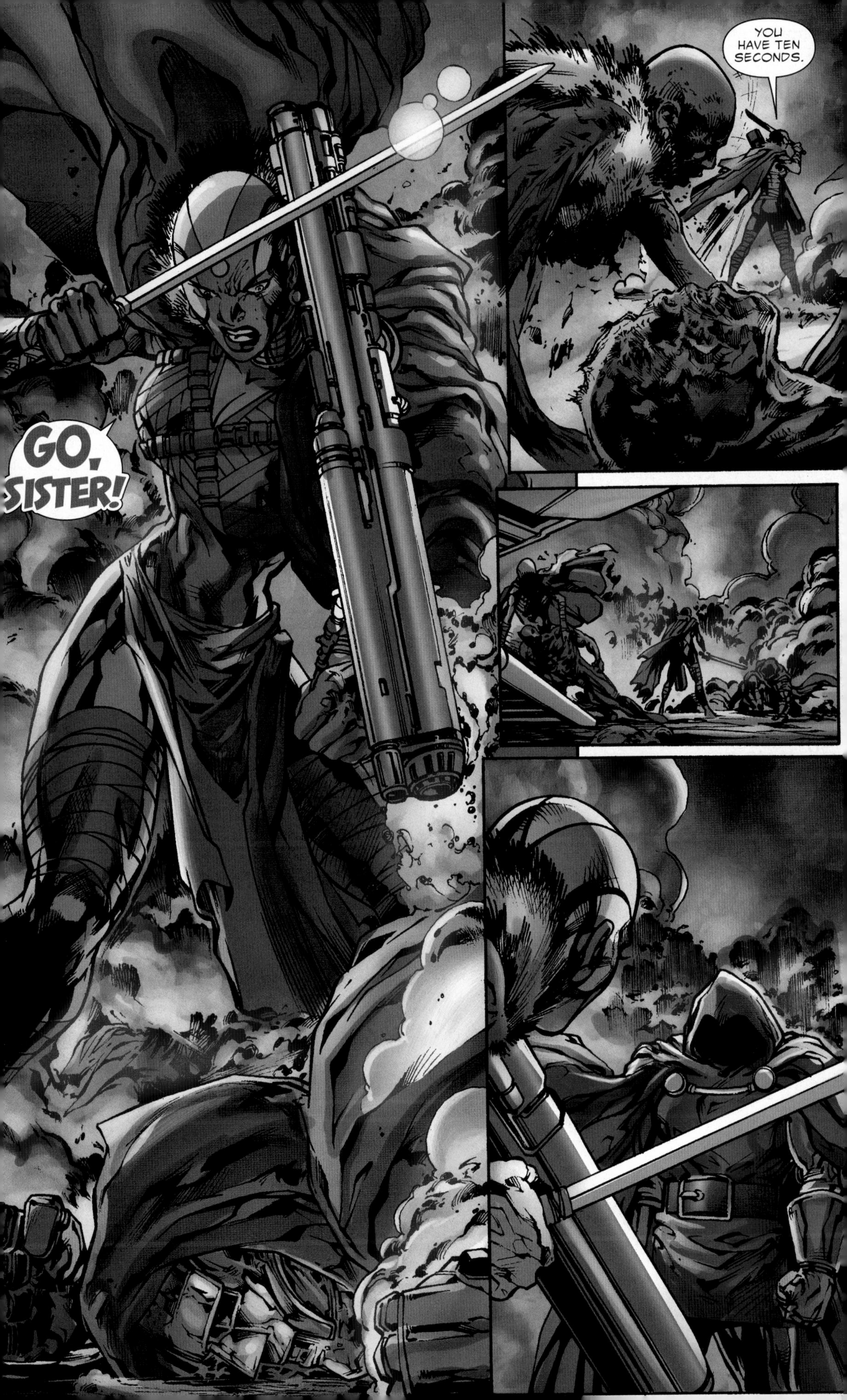
GO, SISTER!
YOU HAVE TEN SECONDS.

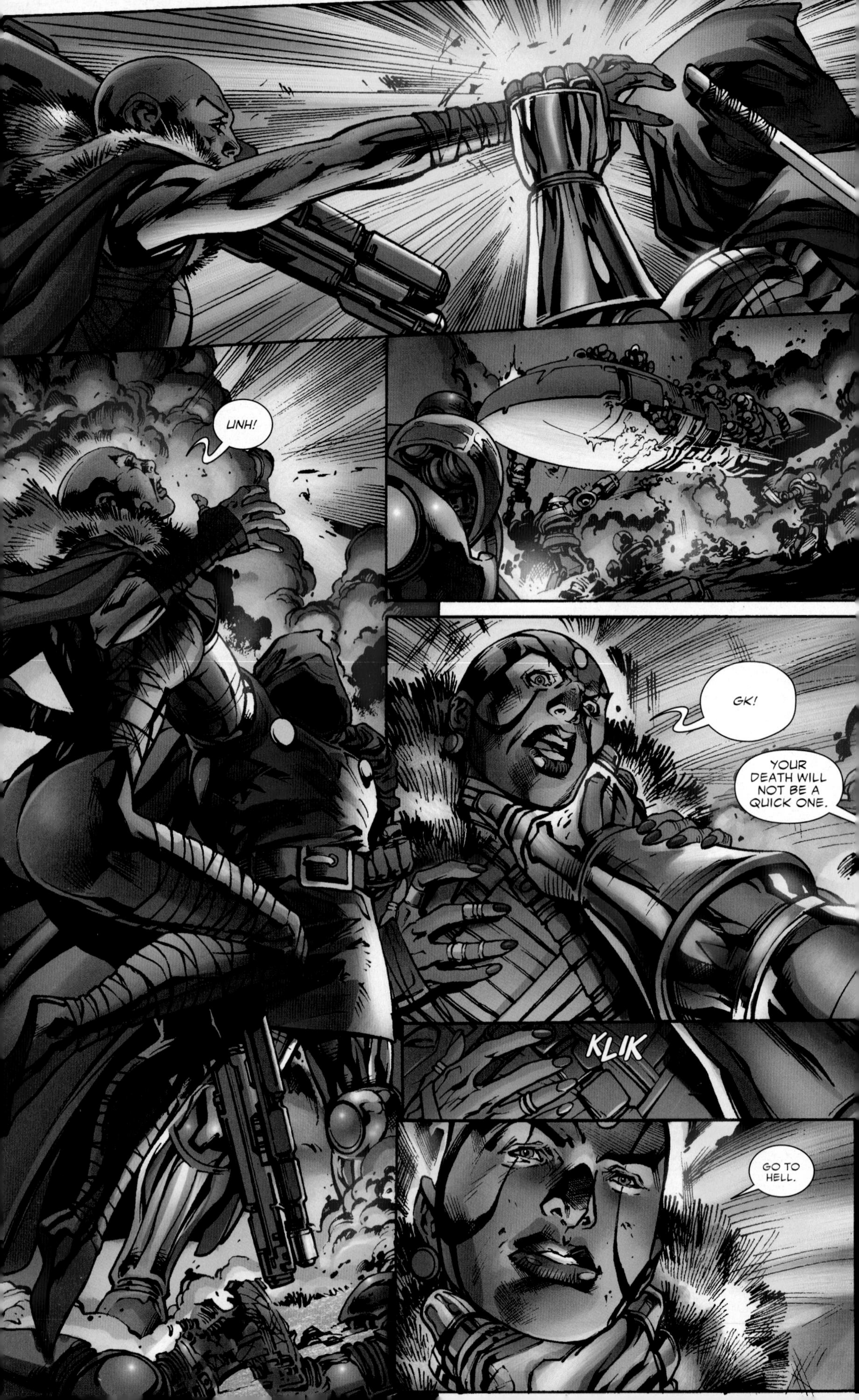
UNH!
GK!
YOUR DEATH WILL NOT BE A QUICK ONE.
KLIK
GO TO HELL.

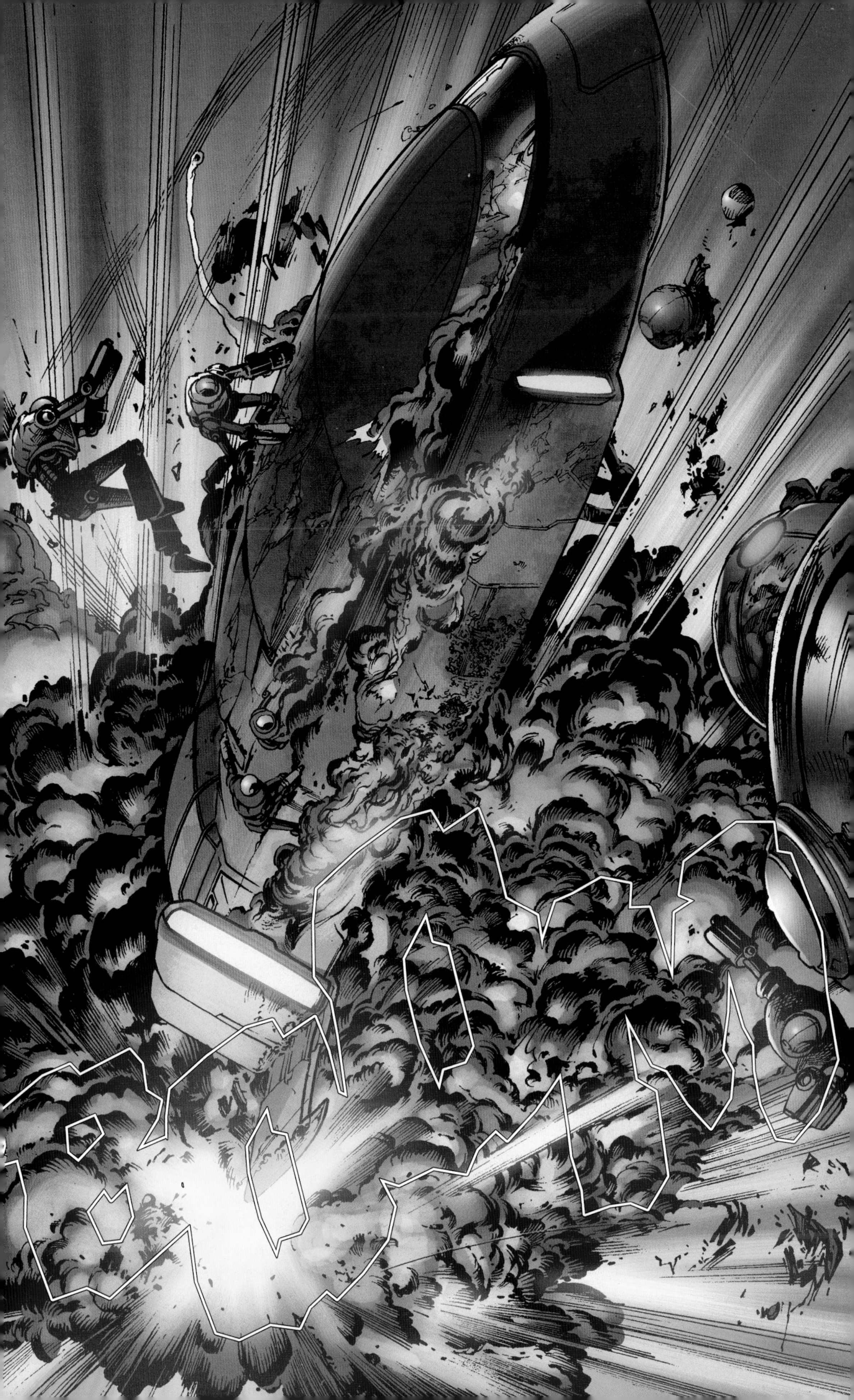
BOOM

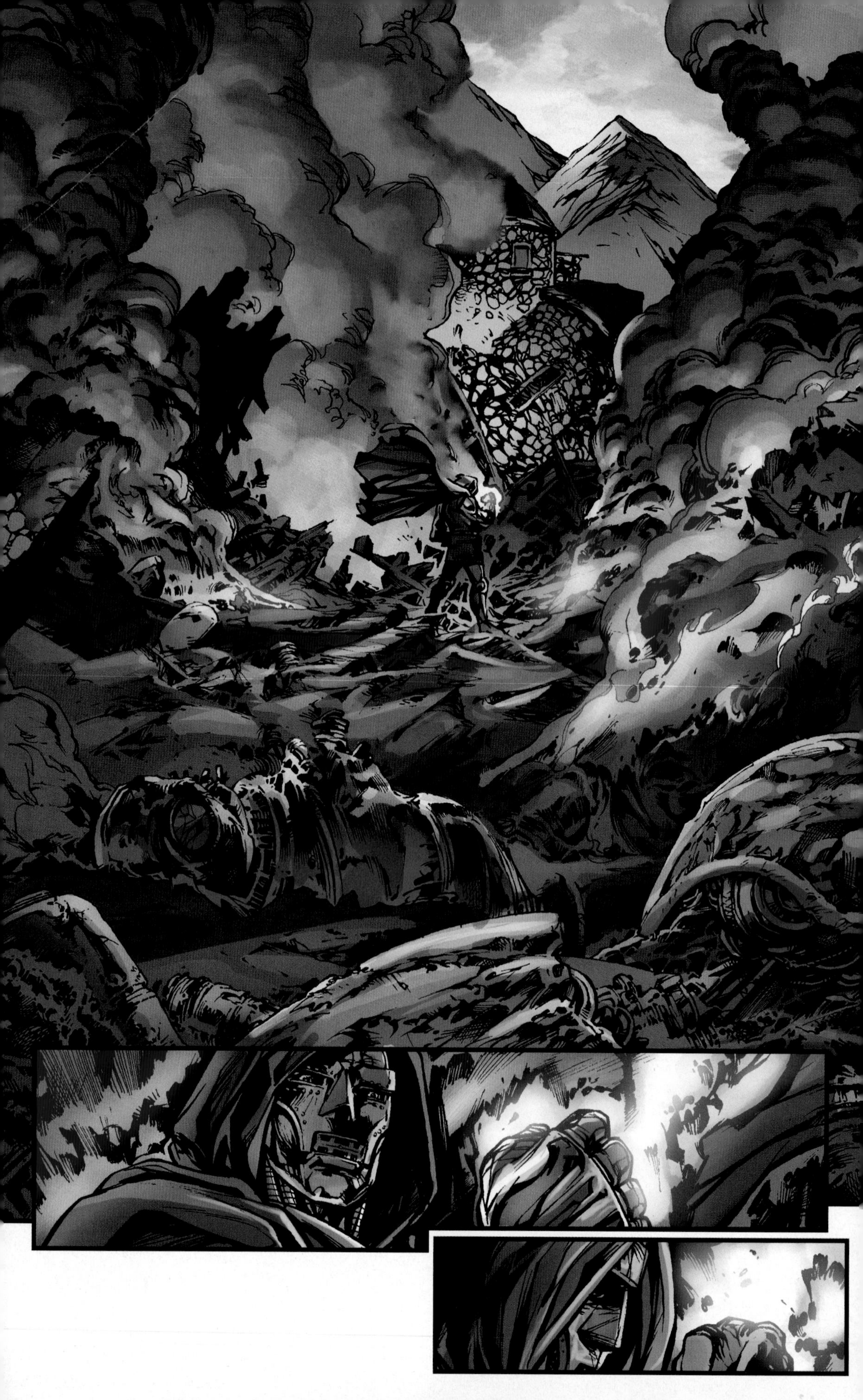

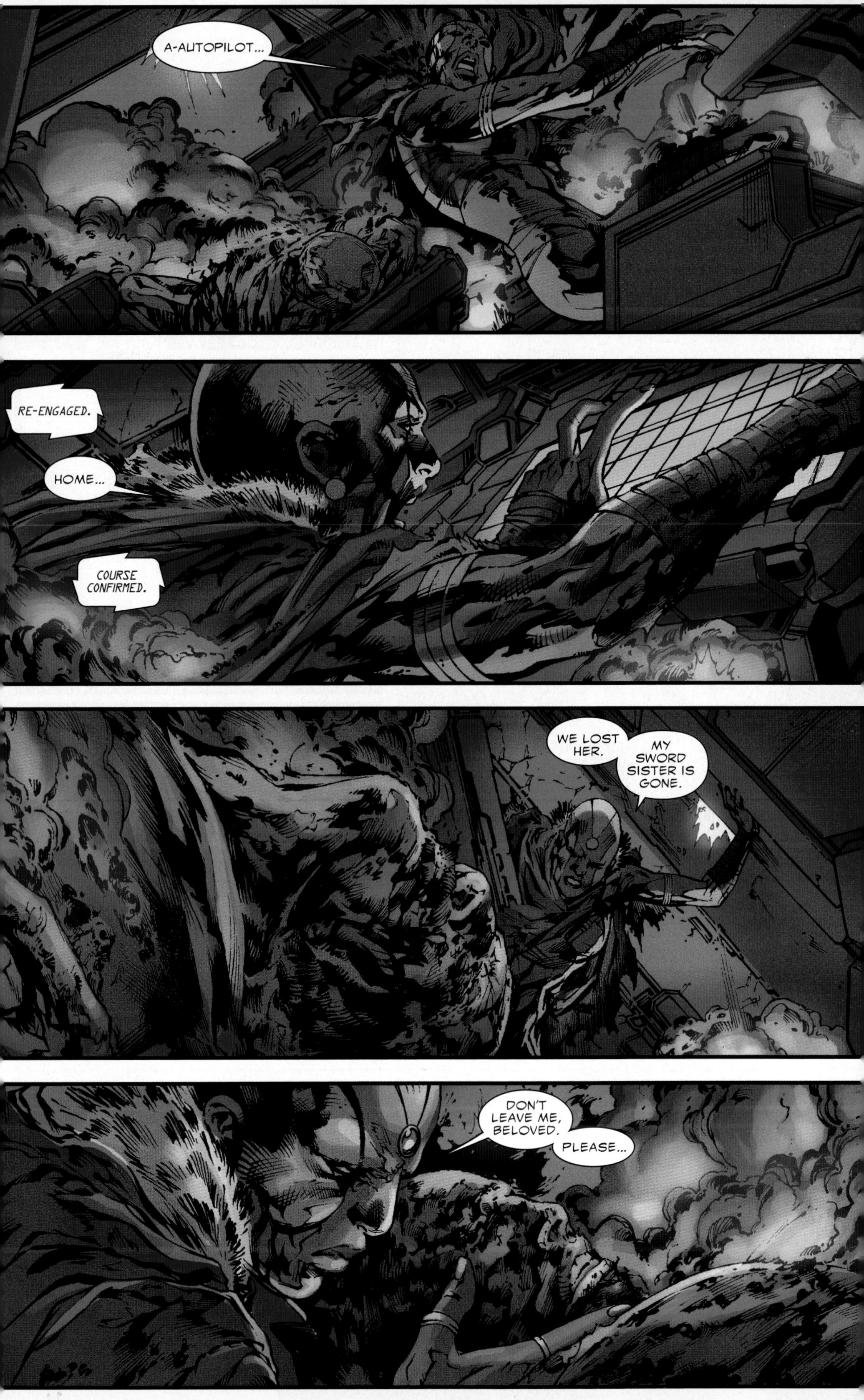
A-AUTOPILOT...
RE-ENGAGED.
HOME...
COURSE CONFIRMED.
WE LOST HER.
MY SWORD SISTER IS GONE.
DON'T LEAVE ME, BELOVED.
PLEASE...

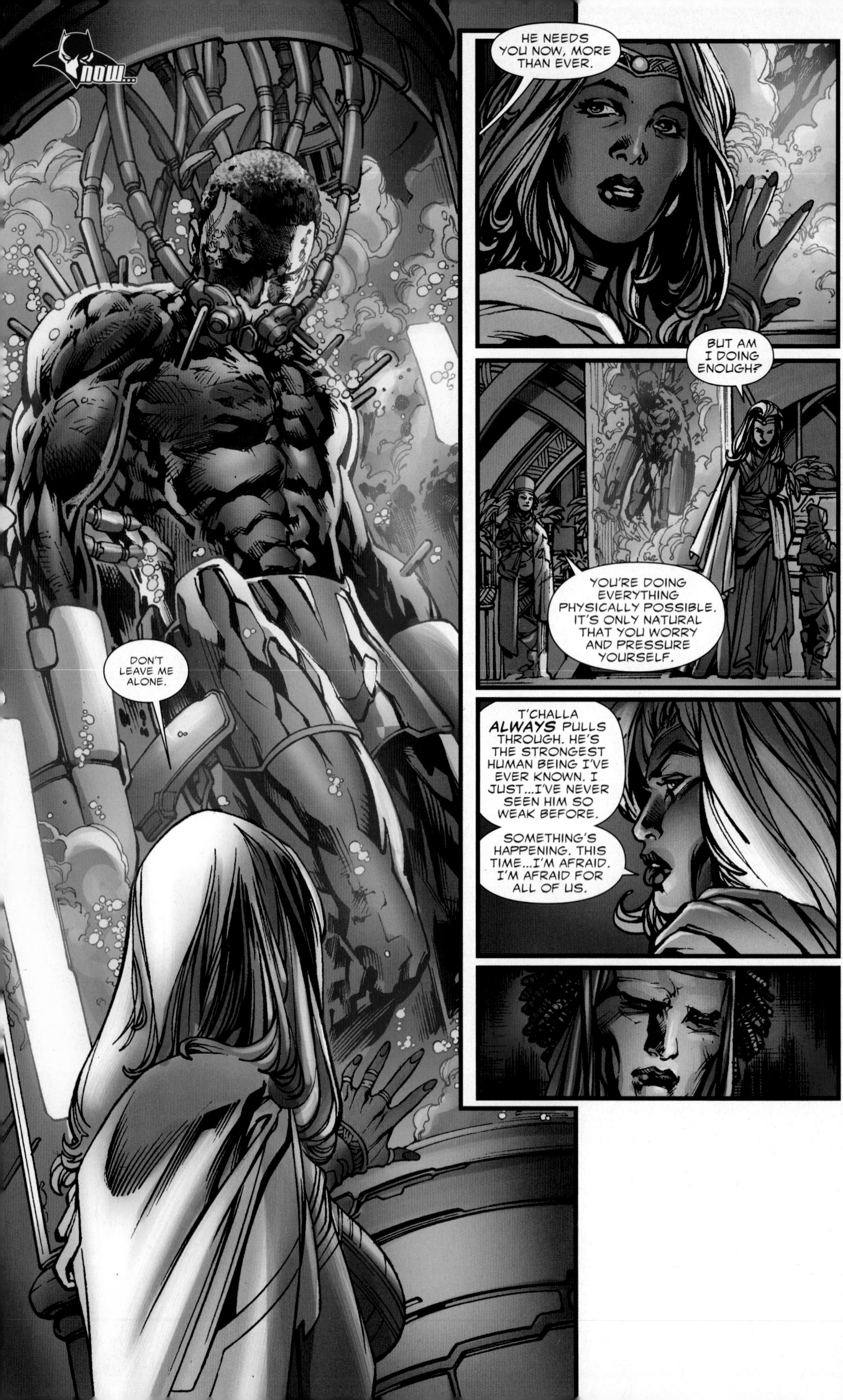
NOW...
DON'T LEAVE ME ALONE.
HE NEEDS YOU NOW, MORE THAN EVER.
BUT AM I DOING ENOUGH?
YOU'RE DOING EVERYTHING PHYSICALLY POSSIBLE. IT'S ONLY NATURAL THAT YOU WORRY AND PRESSURE YOURSELF.
T'CHALLA ALWAYS PULLS THROUGH. HE'S THE STRONGEST HUMAN BEING I'VE EVER KNOWN. I JUST...I'VE NEVER SEEN HIM SO WEAK BEFORE.
SOMETHING'S HAPPENING. THIS TIME...I'M AFRAID. I'M AFRAID FOR ALL OF US.

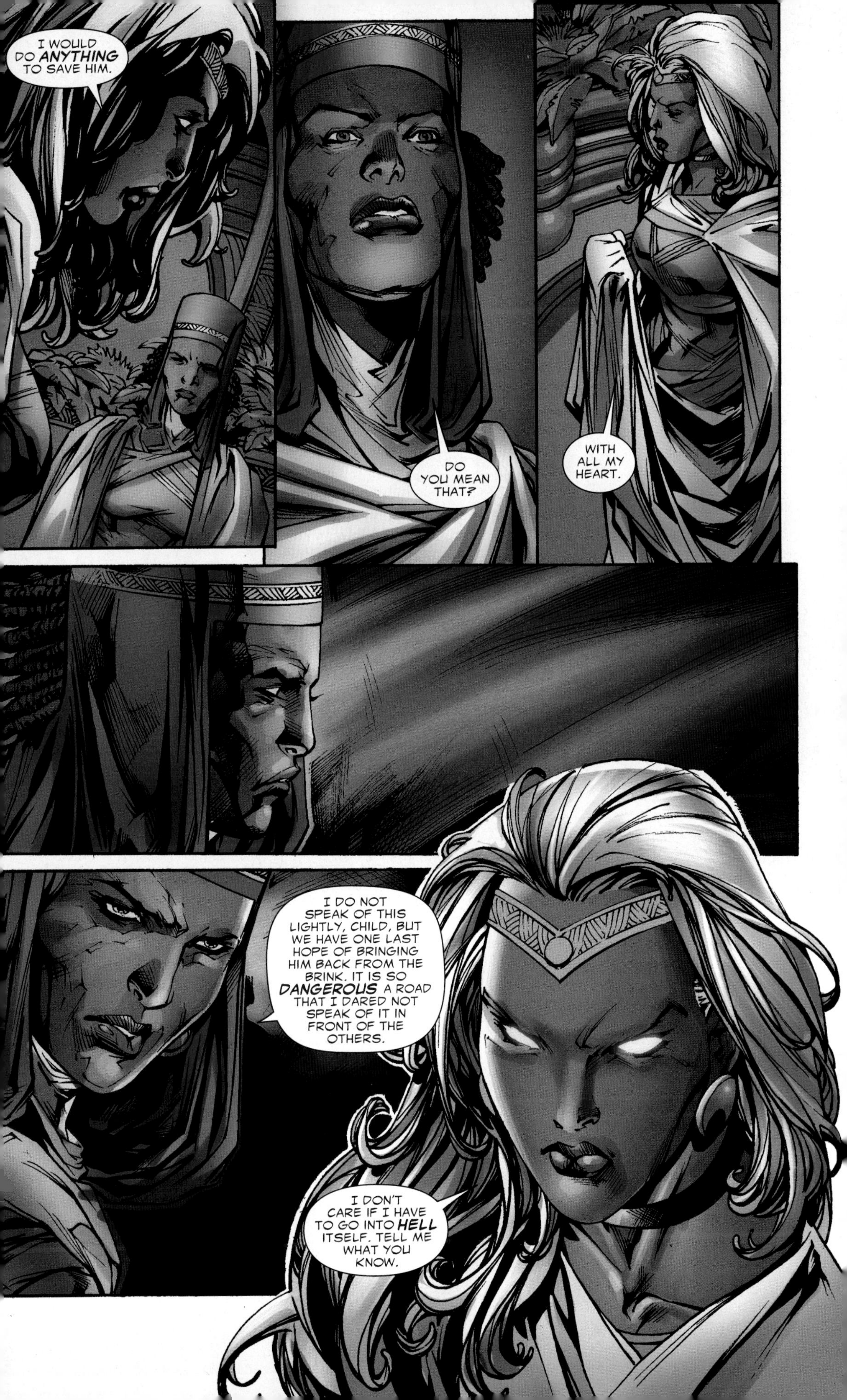
I WOULD DO ANYTHING TO SAVE HIM.
DO YOU MEAN THAT?
WITH ALL MY HEART.
I DO NOT SPEAK OF THIS LIGHTLY, CHILD, BUT WE HAVE ONE LAST HOPE OF BRINGING HIM BACK FROM THE BRINK. IT IS SO DANGEROUS A ROAD THAT I DARED NOT SPEAK OF IT IN FRONT OF THE OTHERS.
I DON'T CARE IF I HAVE TO GO INTO HELL ITSELF. TELL ME WHAT YOU KNOW.

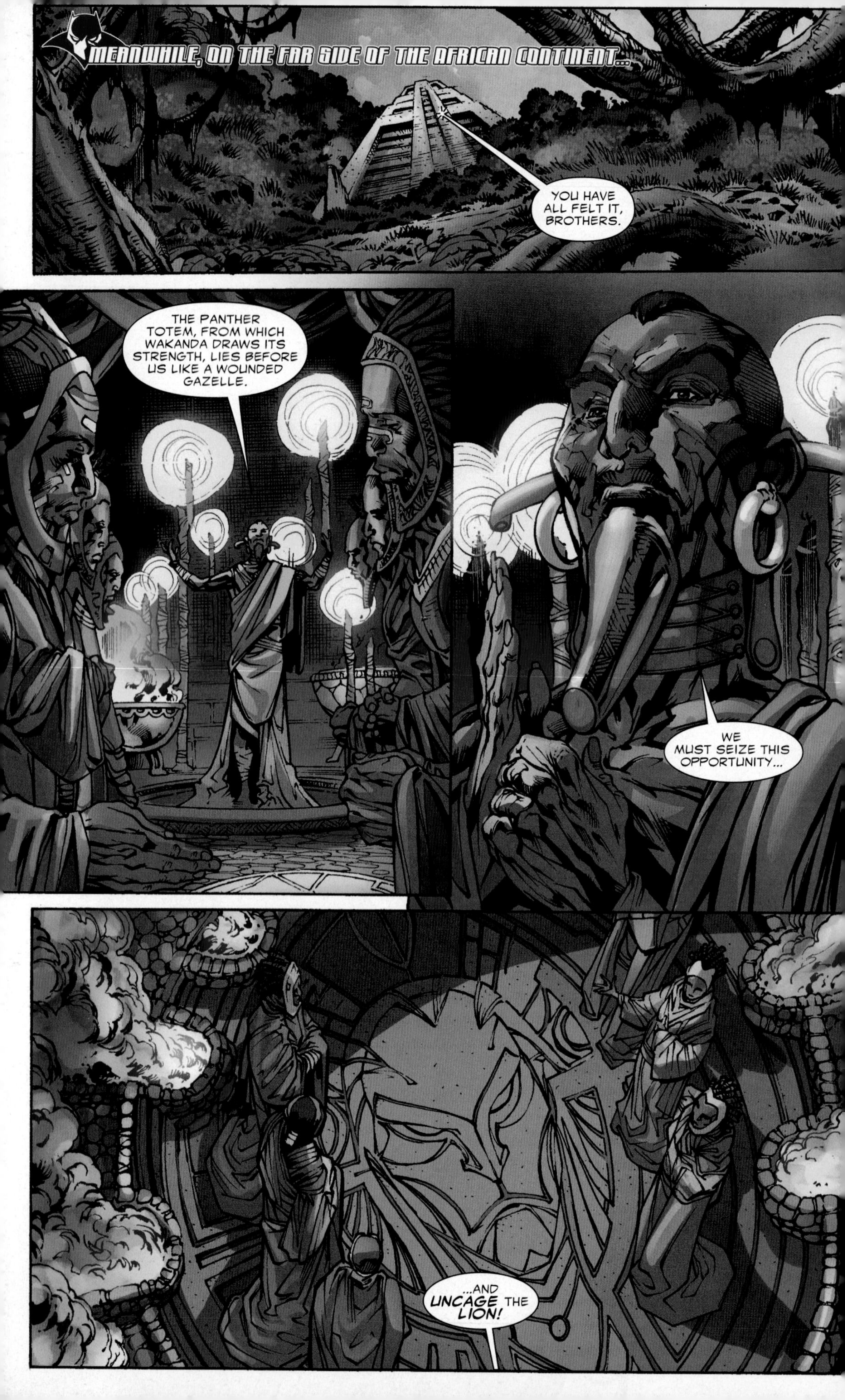
MEANWHILE, ON THE FAR SIDE OF THE AFRICAN CONTINENT...
YOU HAVE ALL FELT IT, BROTHERS.
THE PANTHER TOTEM, FROM WHICH WAKANDA DRAWS ITS STRENGTH, LIES BEFORE US LIKE A WOUNDED GAZELLE.
WE MUST SEIZE THIS OPPORTUNITY...
...AND UNCAGE THE LION!

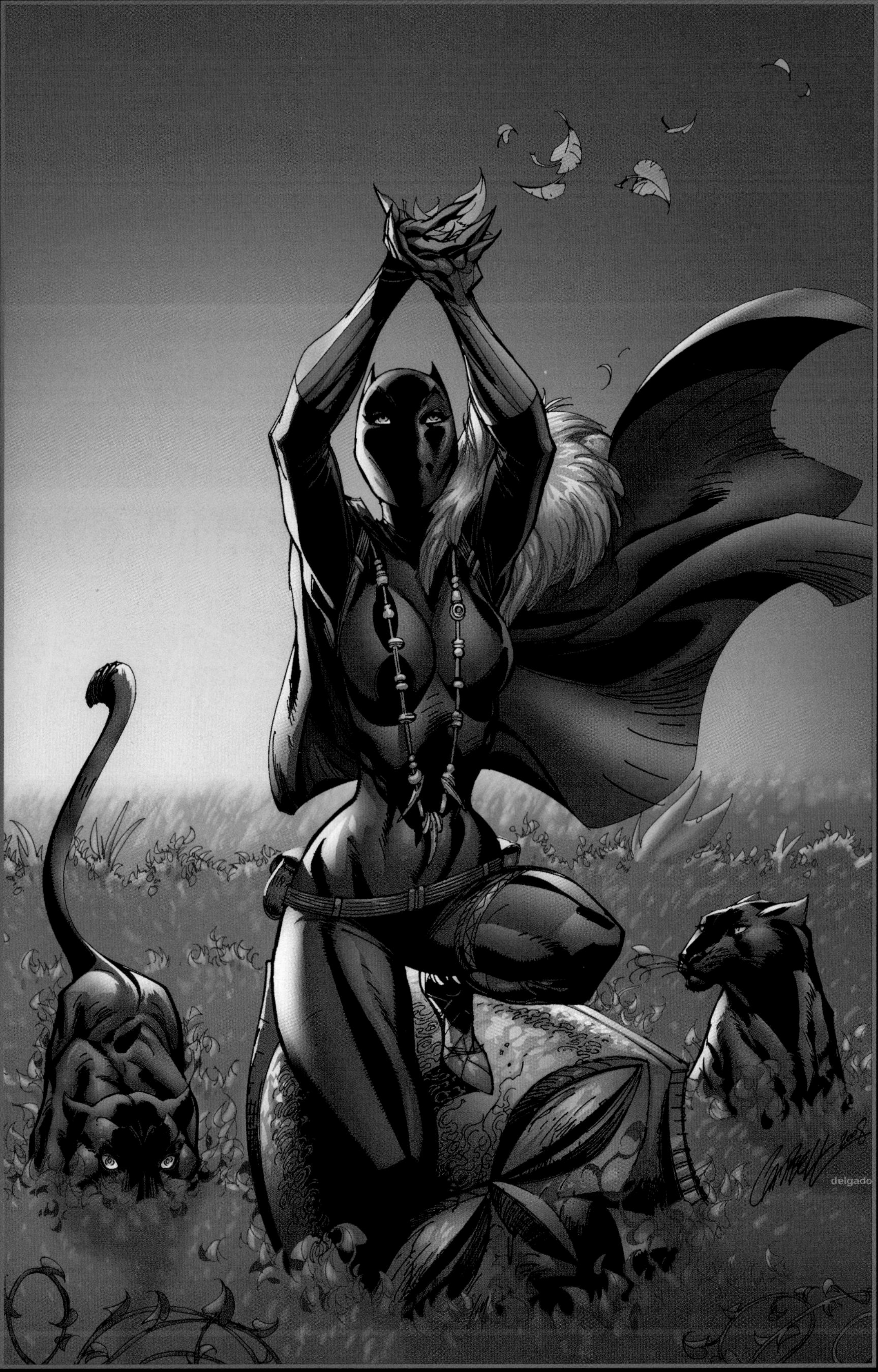
delgado

BLACK PANTHER (2009) **3:** THE DEADLIEST OF THE SPECIES, PART 3

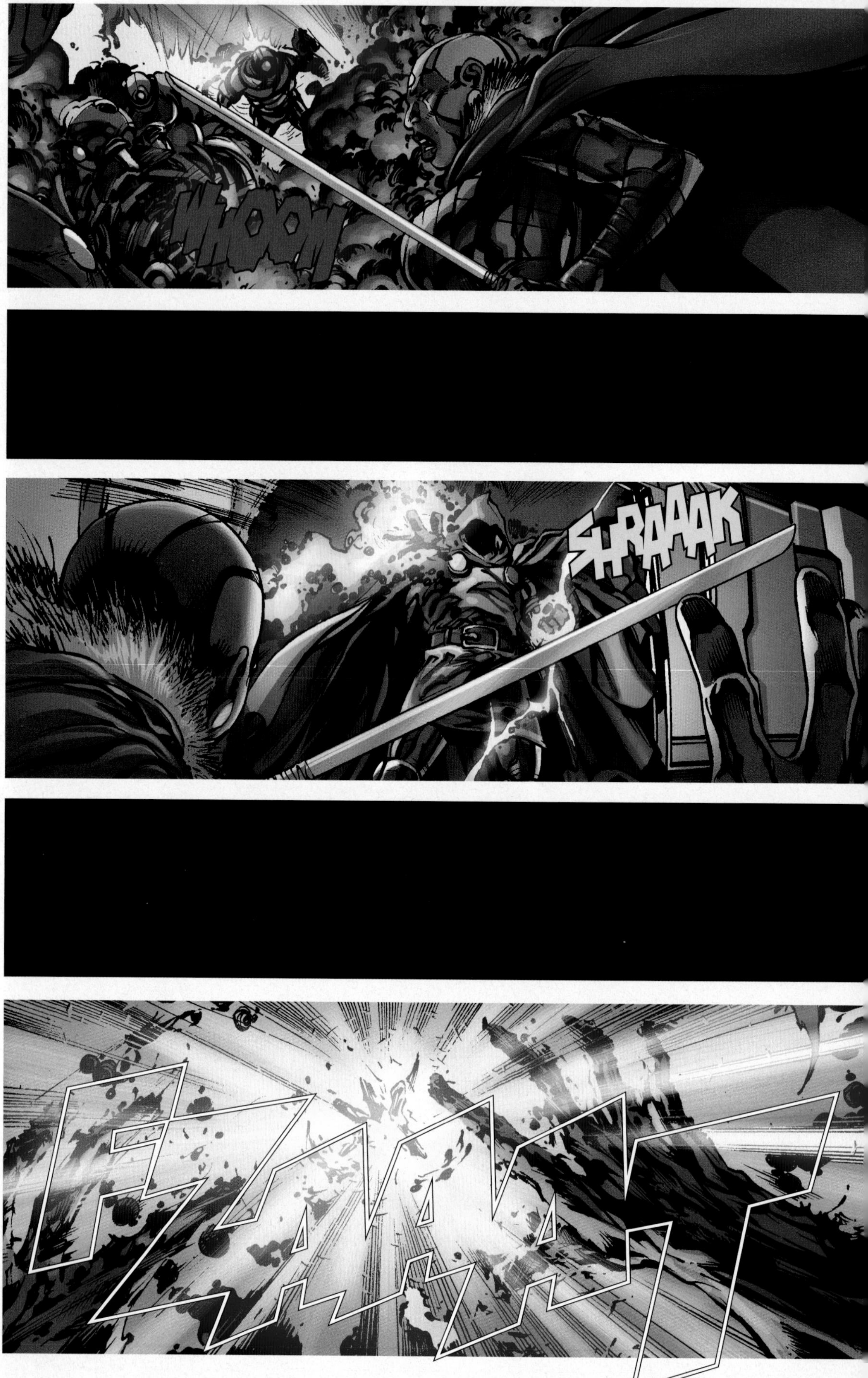
WHOOM
SHRAAAK

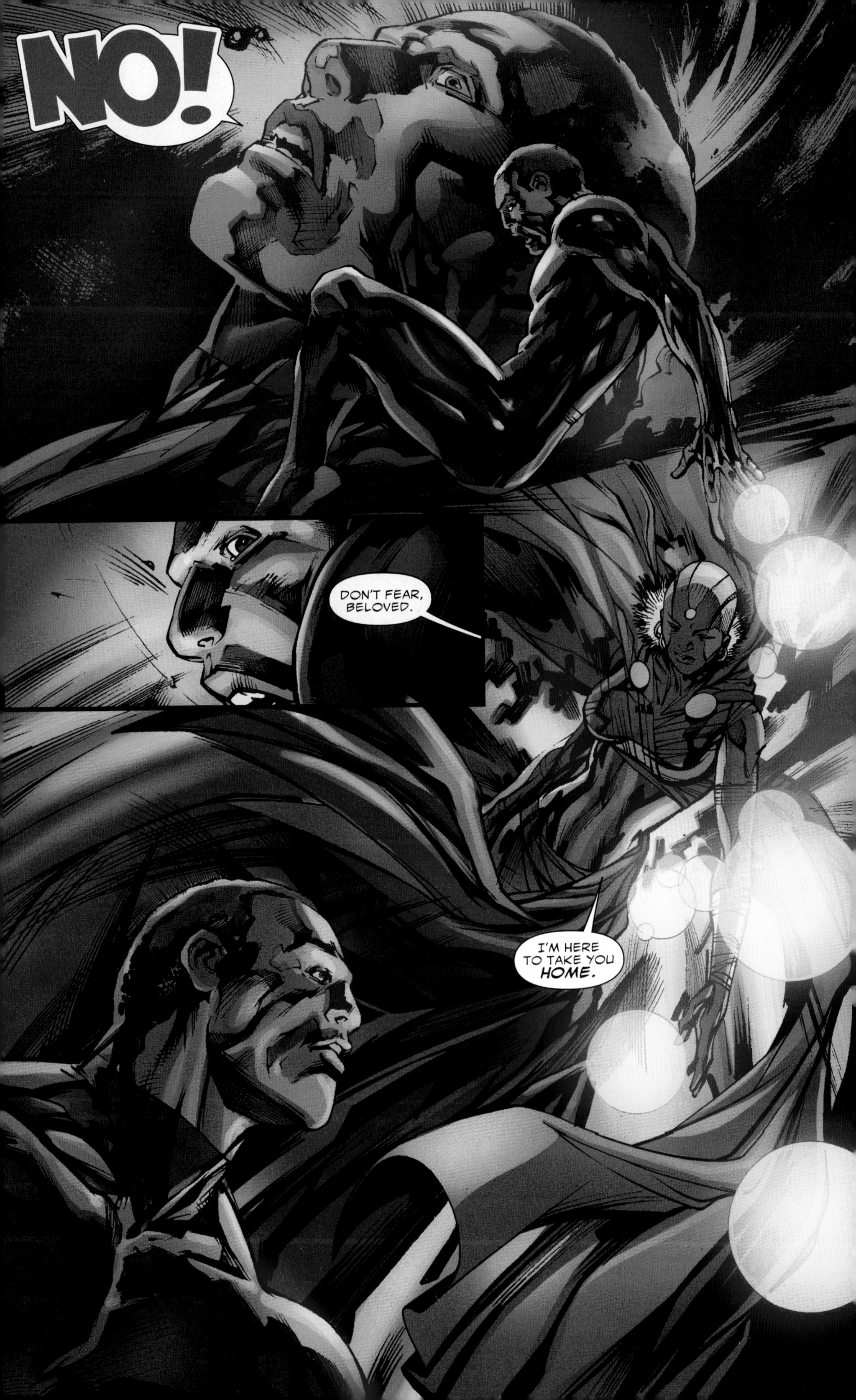
NO!
DON'T FEAR, BELOVED.
I'M HERE TO TAKE YOU HOME.

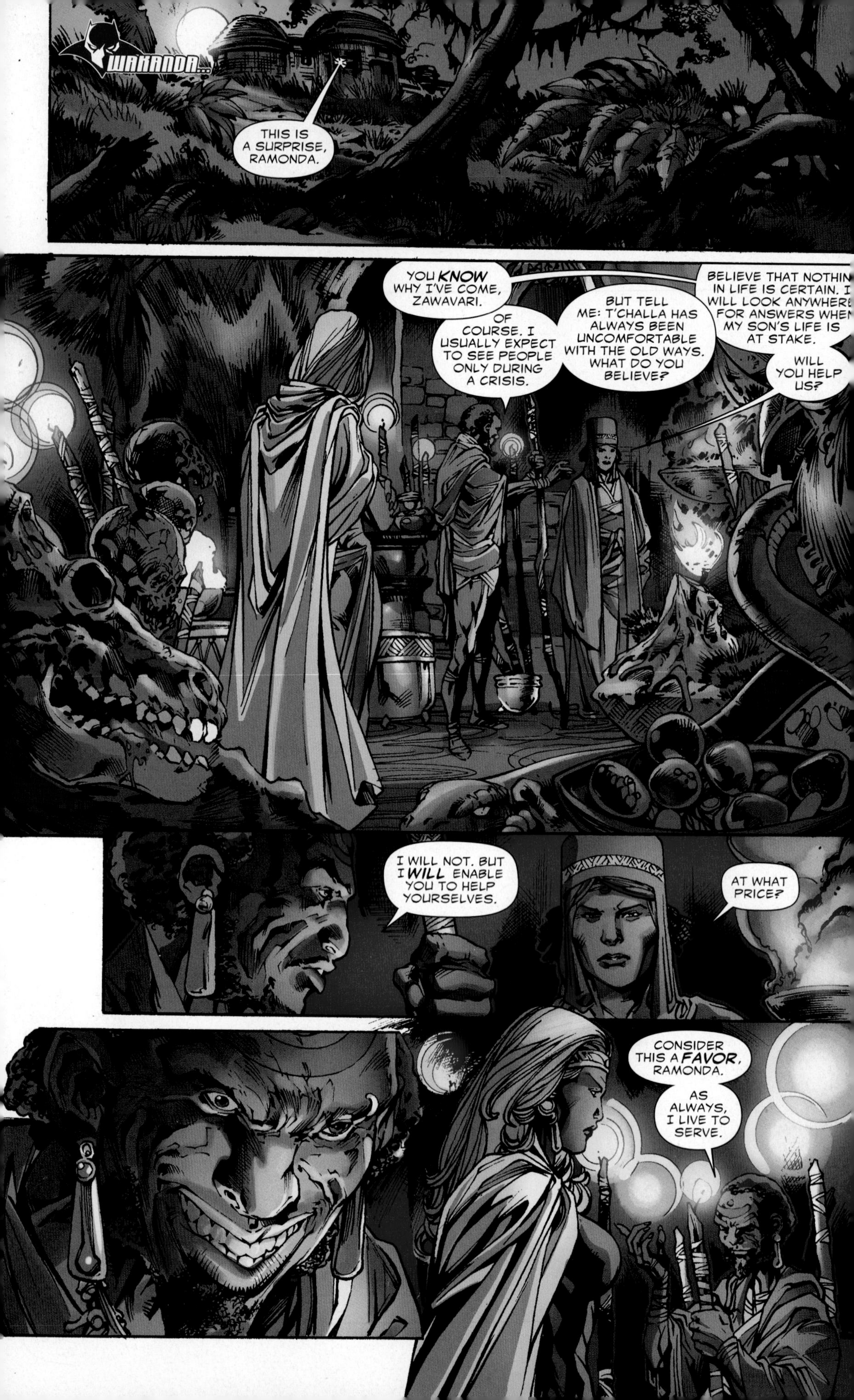
WAKANDA...
THIS IS A SURPRISE, RAMONDA.
YOU KNOW WHY I'VE COME, ZAWAVARI.
OF COURSE. I USUALLY EXPECT TO SEE PEOPLE ONLY DURING A CRISIS.
BUT TELL ME: T'CHALLA HAS ALWAYS BEEN UNCOMFORTABLE WITH THE OLD WAYS. WHAT DO YOU BELIEVE?
BELIEVE THAT NOTHIN IN LIFE IS CERTAIN. I WILL LOOK ANYWHERE FOR ANSWERS WHEN MY SON'S LIFE IS AT STAKE.
WILL YOU HELP US?
I WILL NOT. BUT I WILL ENABLE YOU TO HELP YOURSELVES.
AT WHAT PRICE?
CONSIDER THIS A FAVOR, RAMONDA.
AS ALWAYS, I LIVE TO SERVE.

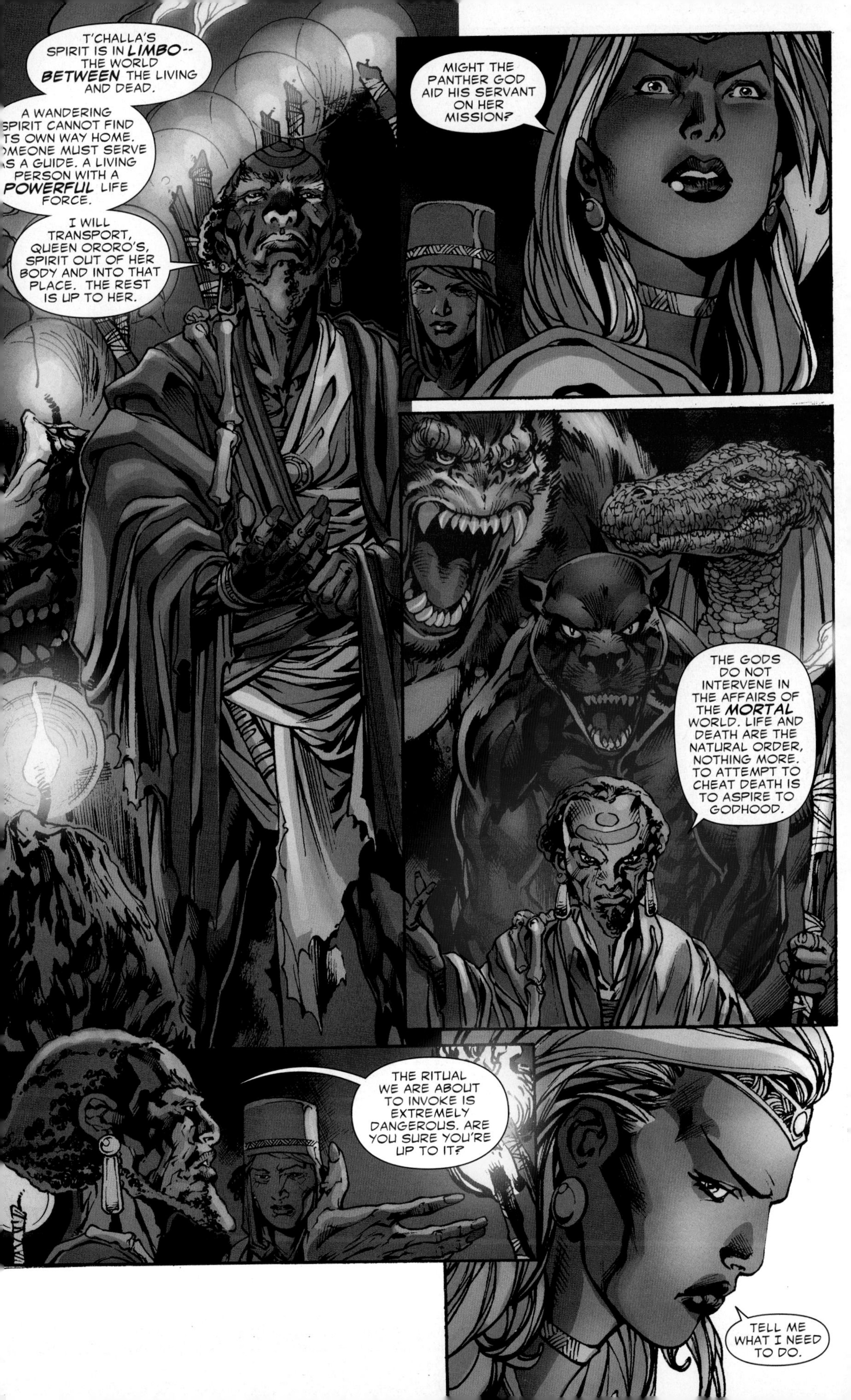
T'CHALLA'S SPIRIT IS IN LIMBO-- THE WORLD BETWEEN THE LIVING AND DEAD.
A WANDERING SPIRIT CANNOT FIND ITS OWN WAY HOME. SOMEONE MUST SERVE AS A GUIDE. A LIVING PERSON WITH A POWERFUL LIFE FORCE.
I WILL TRANSPORT, QUEEN ORORO'S, SPIRIT OUT OF HER BODY AND INTO THAT PLACE. THE REST IS UP TO HER.
MIGHT THE PANTHER GOD AID HIS SERVANT ON HER MISSION?
THE GODS DO NOT INTERVENE IN THE AFFAIRS OF THE MORTAL WORLD. LIFE AND DEATH ARE THE NATURAL ORDER, NOTHING MORE. TO ATTEMPT TO CHEAT DEATH IS TO ASPIRE TO GODHOOD.
THE RITUAL WE ARE ABOUT TO INVOKE IS EXTREMELY DANGEROUS. ARE YOU SURE YOU'RE UP TO IT?
TELL ME WHAT I NEED TO DO.

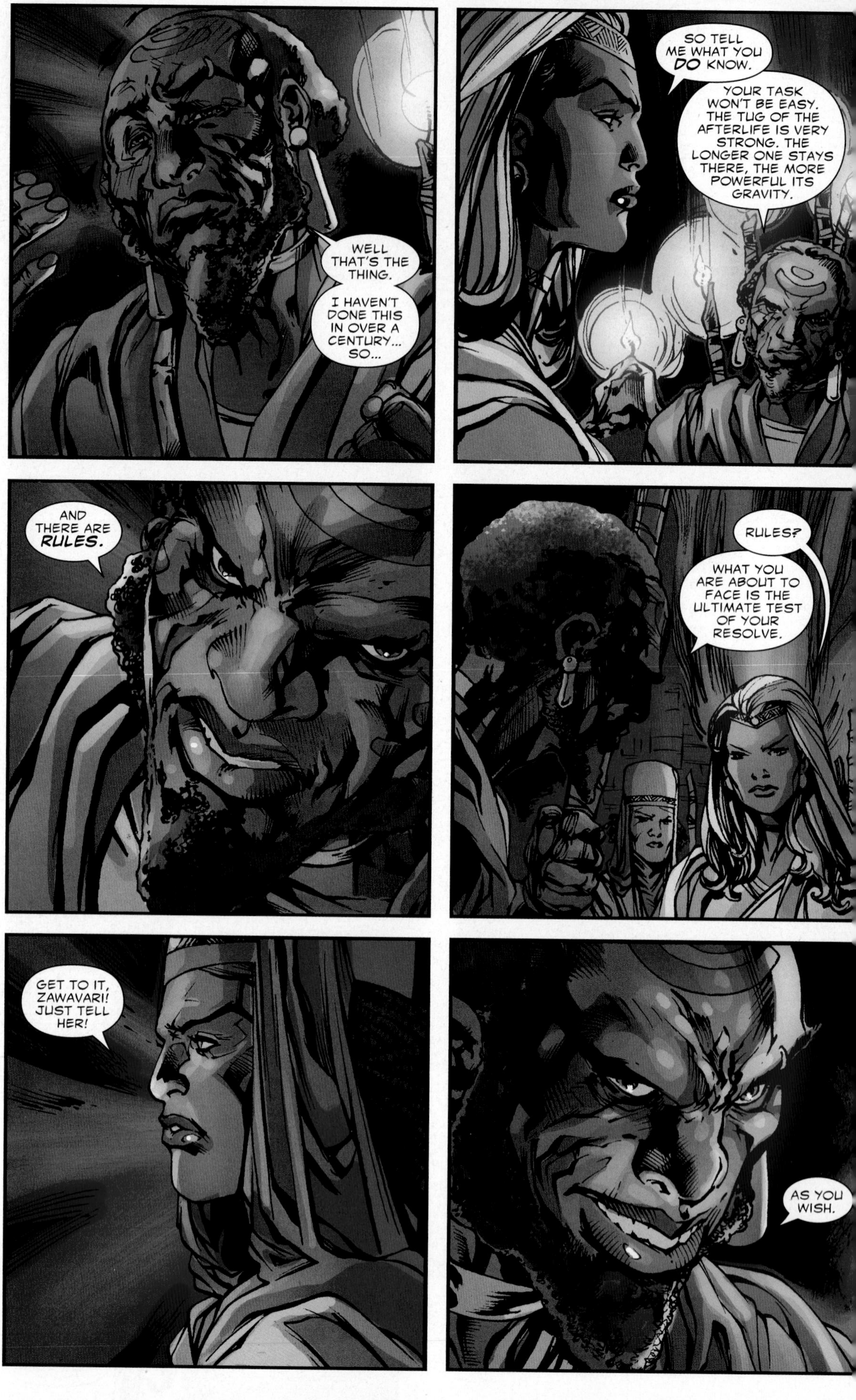
WELL THAT'S THE THING.
I HAVEN'T DONE THIS IN OVER A CENTURY... SO...
SO TELL ME WHAT YOU DO KNOW.
YOUR TASK WON'T BE EASY. THE TUG OF THE AFTERLIFE IS VERY STRONG. THE LONGER ONE STAYS THERE, THE MORE POWERFUL ITS GRAVITY.
AND THERE ARE RULES.
RULES?
WHAT YOU ARE ABOUT TO FACE IS THE ULTIMATE TEST OF YOUR RESOLVE.
GET TO IT, ZAWAVARI! JUST TELL HER!
AS YOU WISH.

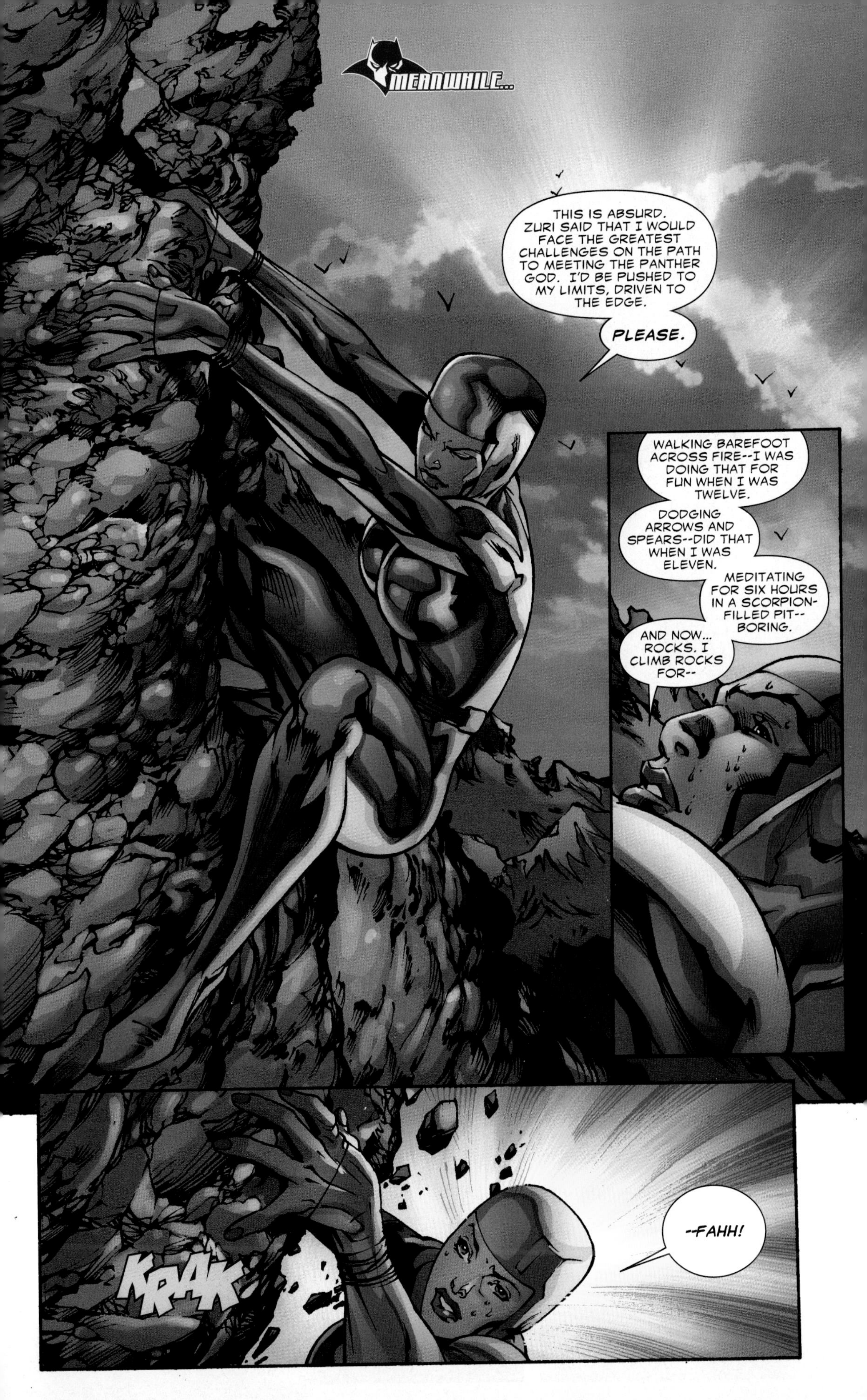
MEANWHILE...
THIS IS ABSURD. ZURI SAID THAT I WOULD FACE THE GREATEST CHALLENGES ON THE PATH TO MEETING THE PANTHER GOD. I'D BE PUSHED TO MY LIMITS, DRIVEN TO THE EDGE.
PLEASE.
WALKING BAREFOOT ACROSS FIRE--I WAS DOING THAT FOR FUN WHEN I WAS TWELVE.
DODGING ARROWS AND SPEARS--DID THAT WHEN I WAS ELEVEN.
MEDITATING FOR SIX HOURS IN A SCORPION-FILLED PIT--BORING.
AND NOW... ROCKS. I CLIMB ROCKS FOR--
KRAK
--FAHH!

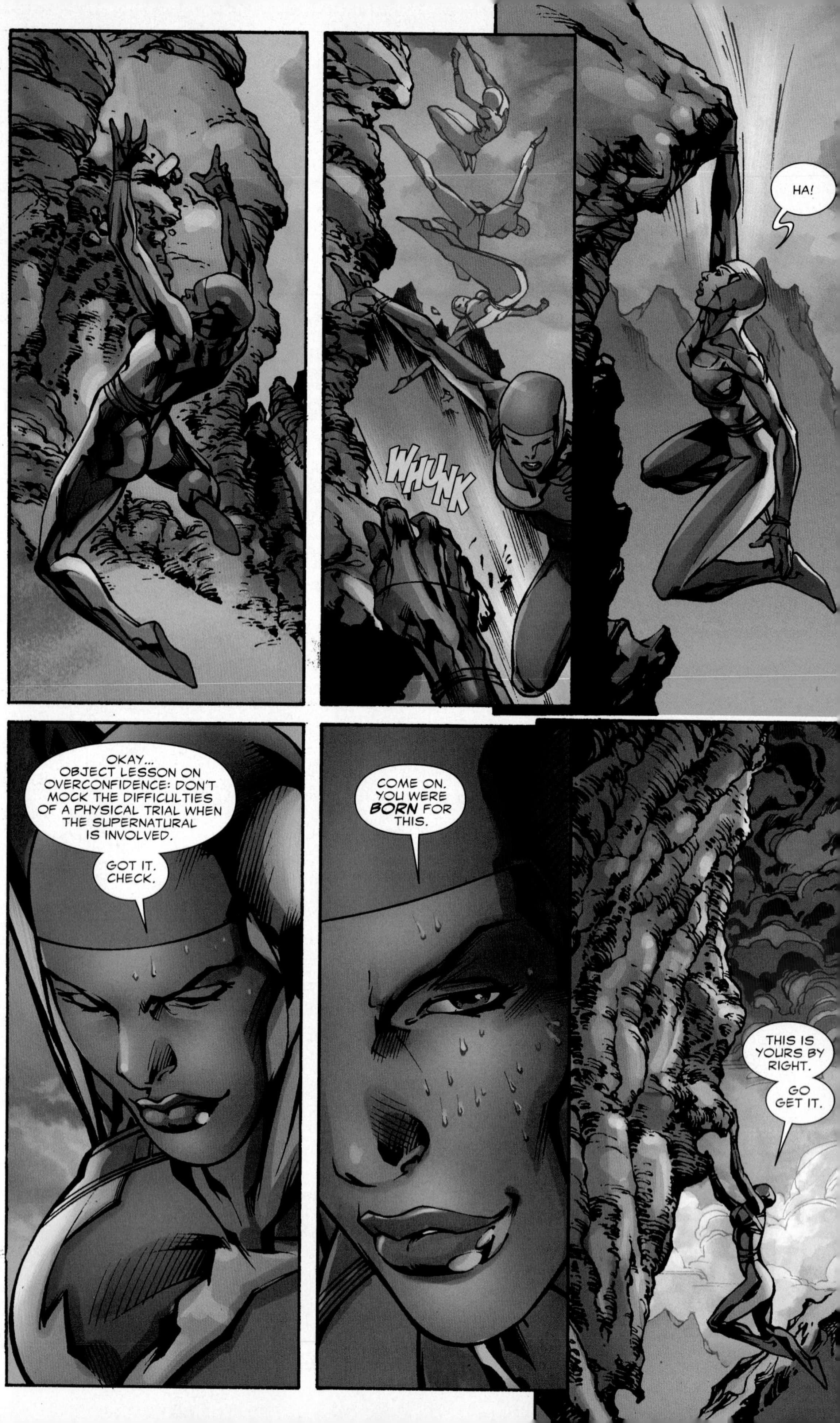
WHUNK
HA!
OKAY... OBJECT LESSON ON OVERCONFIDENCE: DON'T MOCK THE DIFFICULTIES OF A PHYSICAL TRIAL WHEN THE SUPERNATURAL IS INVOLVED.
GOT IT. CHECK.
COME ON. YOU WERE *BORN* FOR THIS.
THIS IS YOURS BY RIGHT.
GO GET IT.

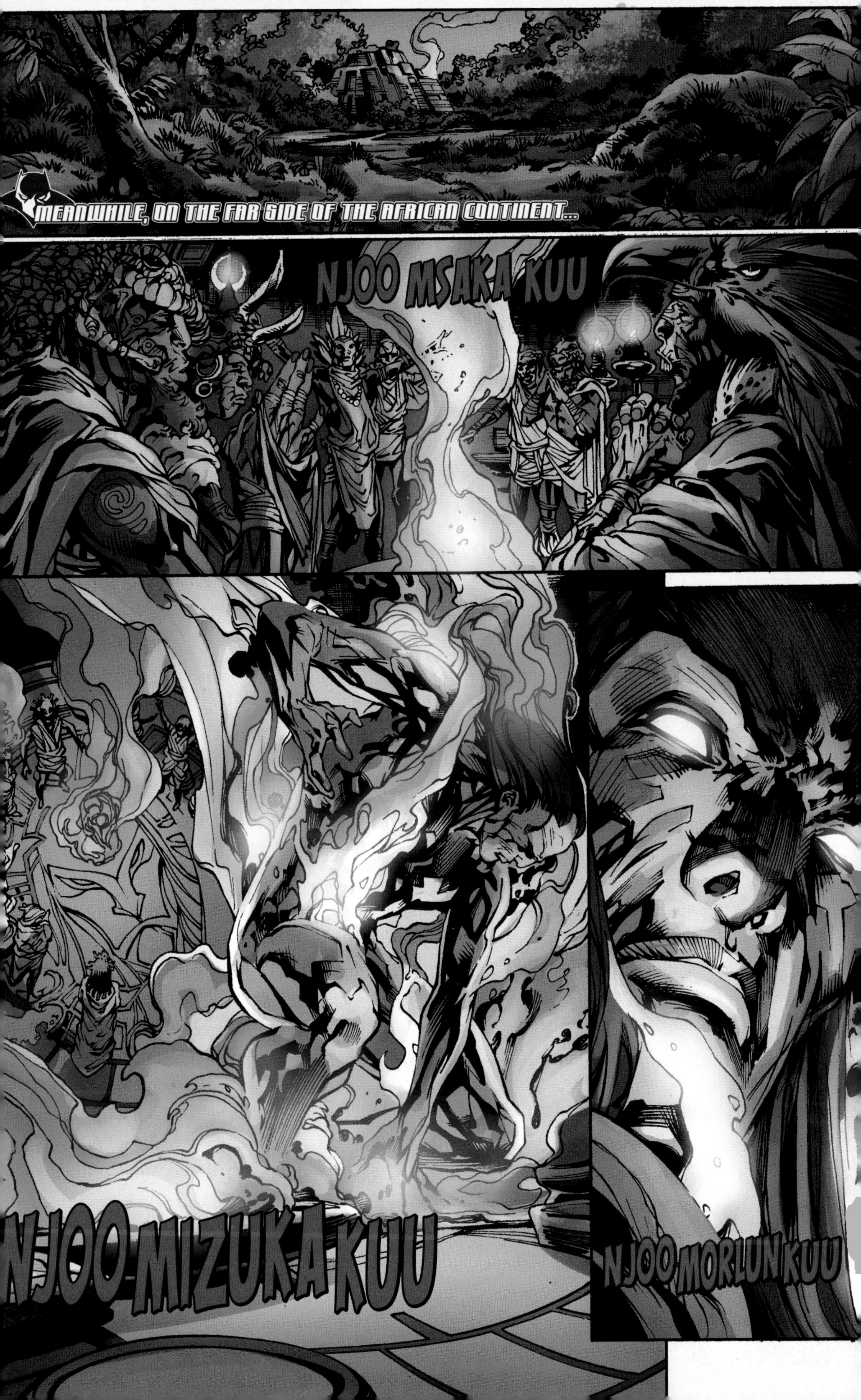
MEANWHILE, ON THE FAR SIDE OF THE AFRICAN CONTINENT...
NJOO MSAKA KUU
NJOO MIZUKA KUU
NJOO MORLUN KUU

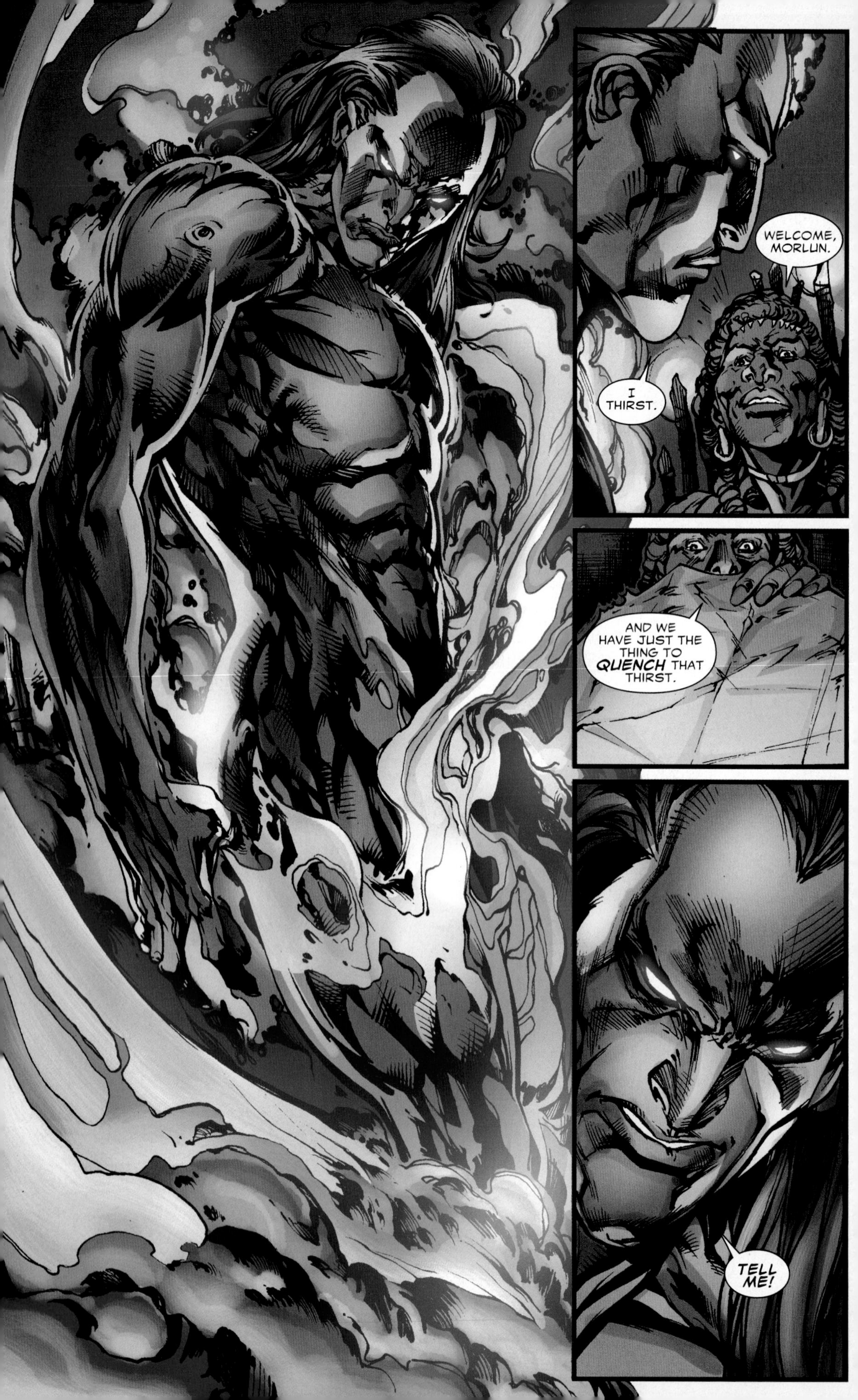
WELCOME, MORLUN.
I THIRST.
AND WE HAVE JUST THE THING TO QUENCH THAT THIRST.
TELL ME!

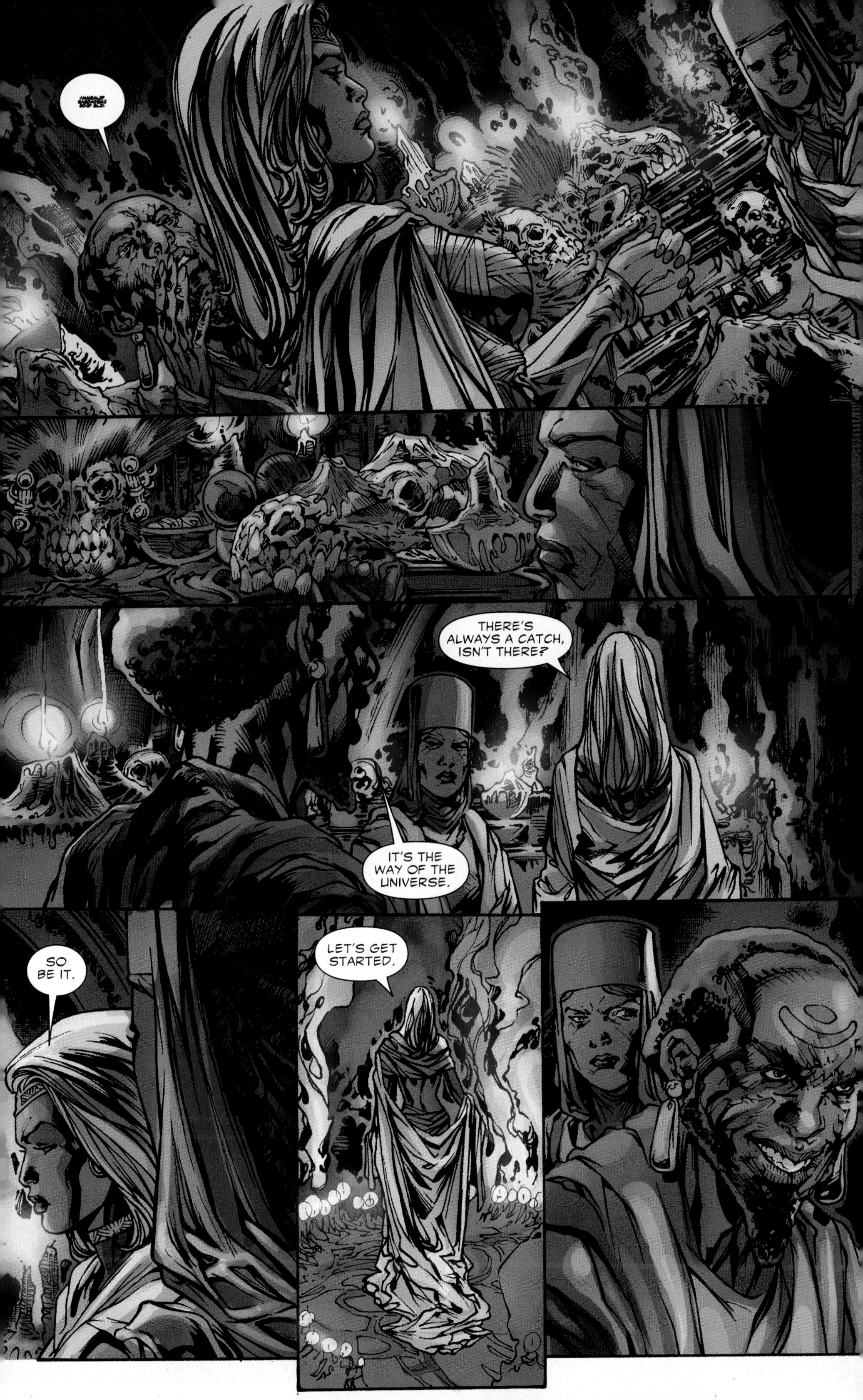
THERE'S ALWAYS A CATCH, ISN'T THERE?
IT'S THE WAY OF THE UNIVERSE.
SO BE IT.
LET'S GET STARTED.

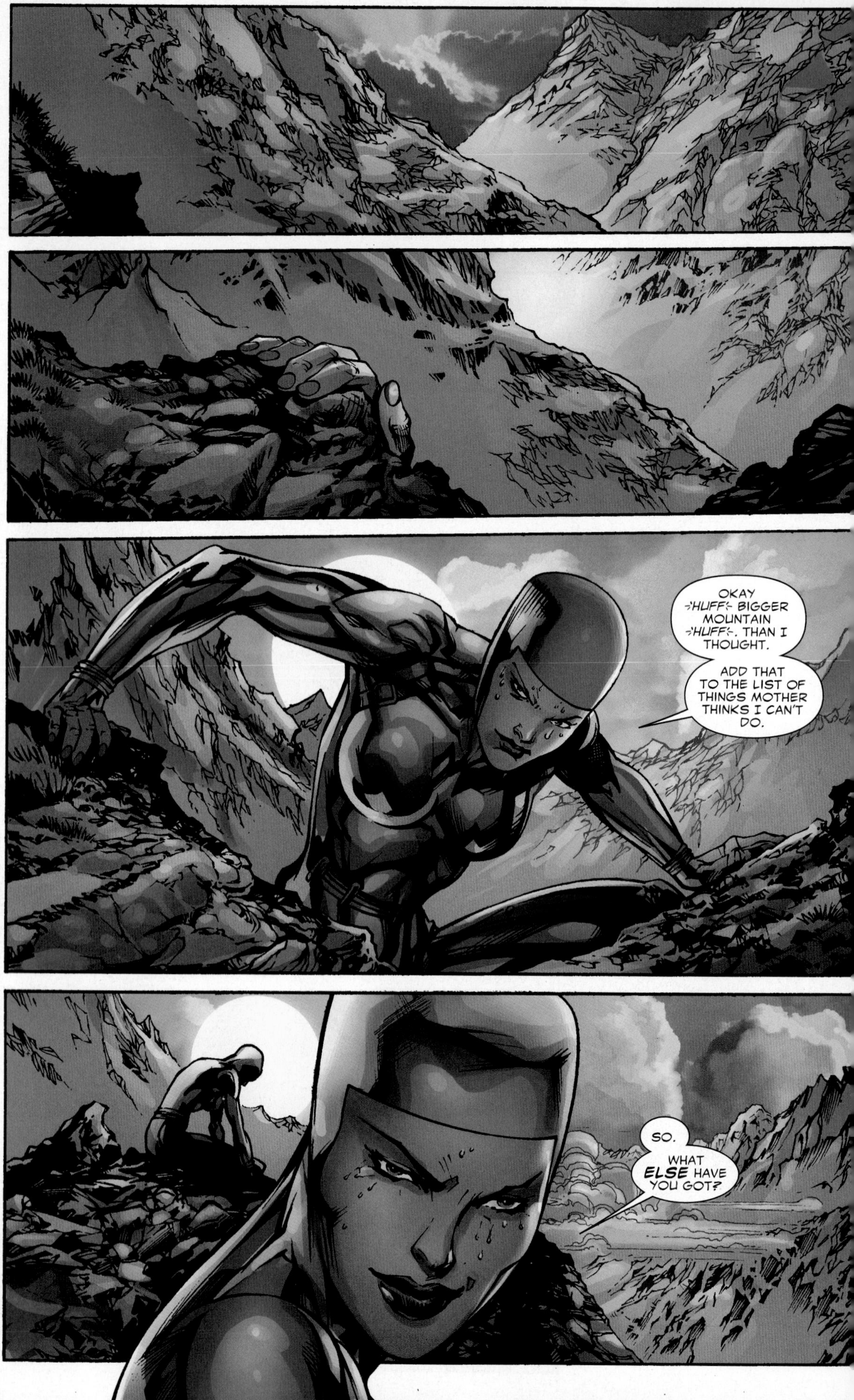
OKAY -HUFF- BIGGER MOUNTAIN -HUFF-. THAN I THOUGHT.
ADD THAT TO THE LIST OF THINGS MOTHER THINKS I CAN'T DO.
SO.
WHAT ELSE HAVE YOU GOT?

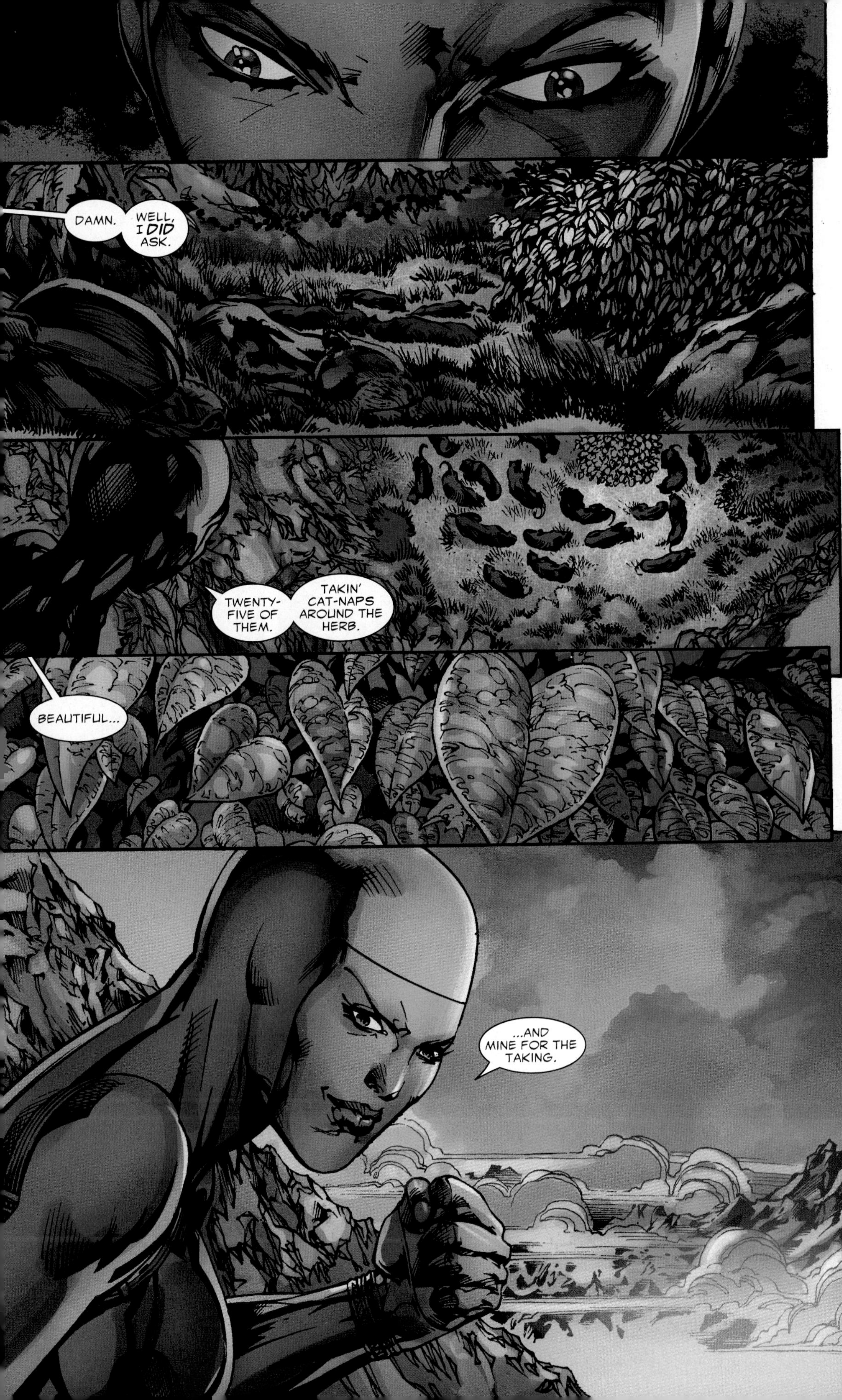
DAMN.
WELL, I DID ASK.
TWENTY-FIVE OF THEM.
TAKIN' CAT-NAPS AROUND THE HERB.
BEAUTIFUL...
...AND MINE FOR THE TAKING.

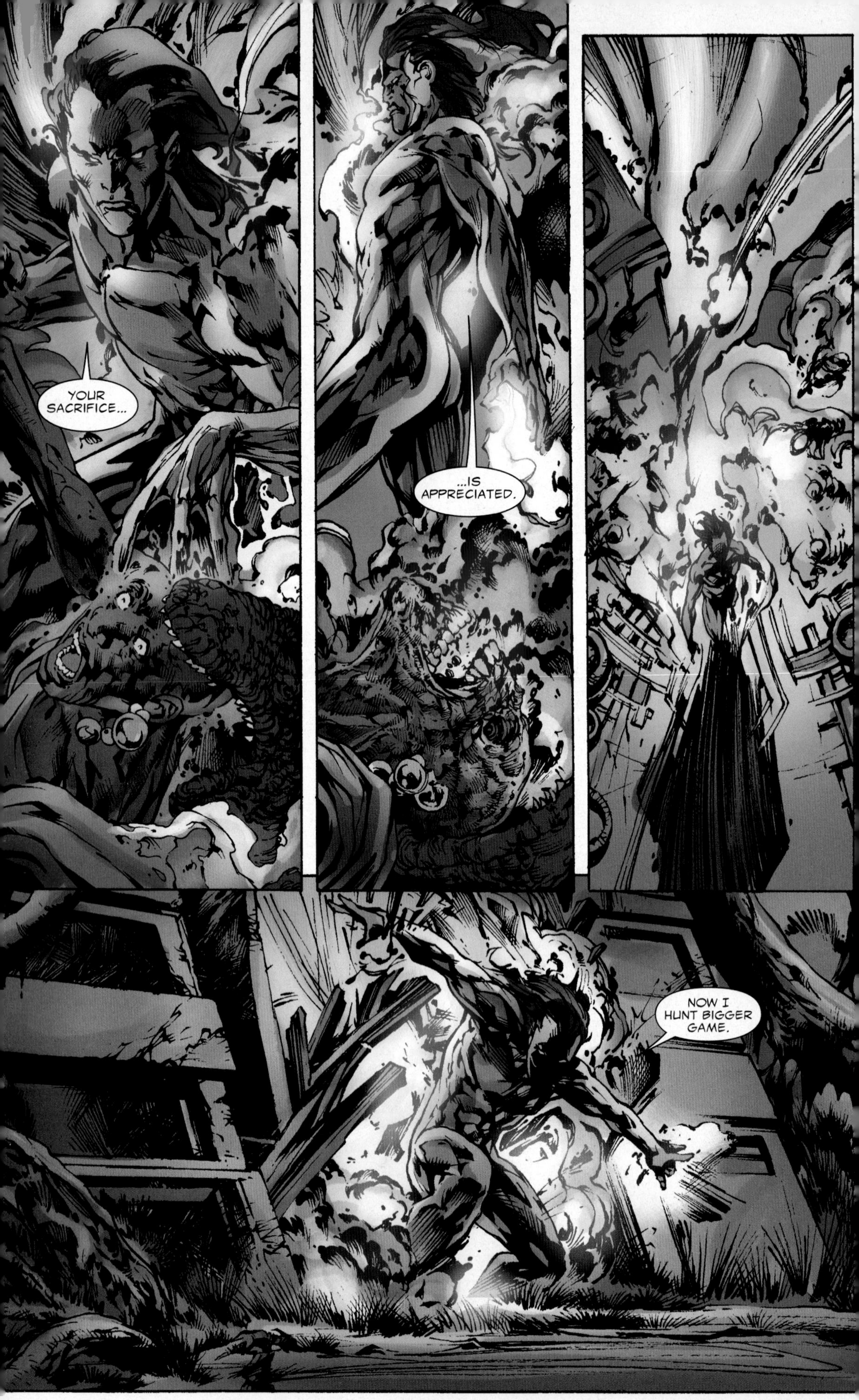
YOUR SACRIFICE...
...IS APPRECIATED.
NOW I HUNT BIGGER GAME.

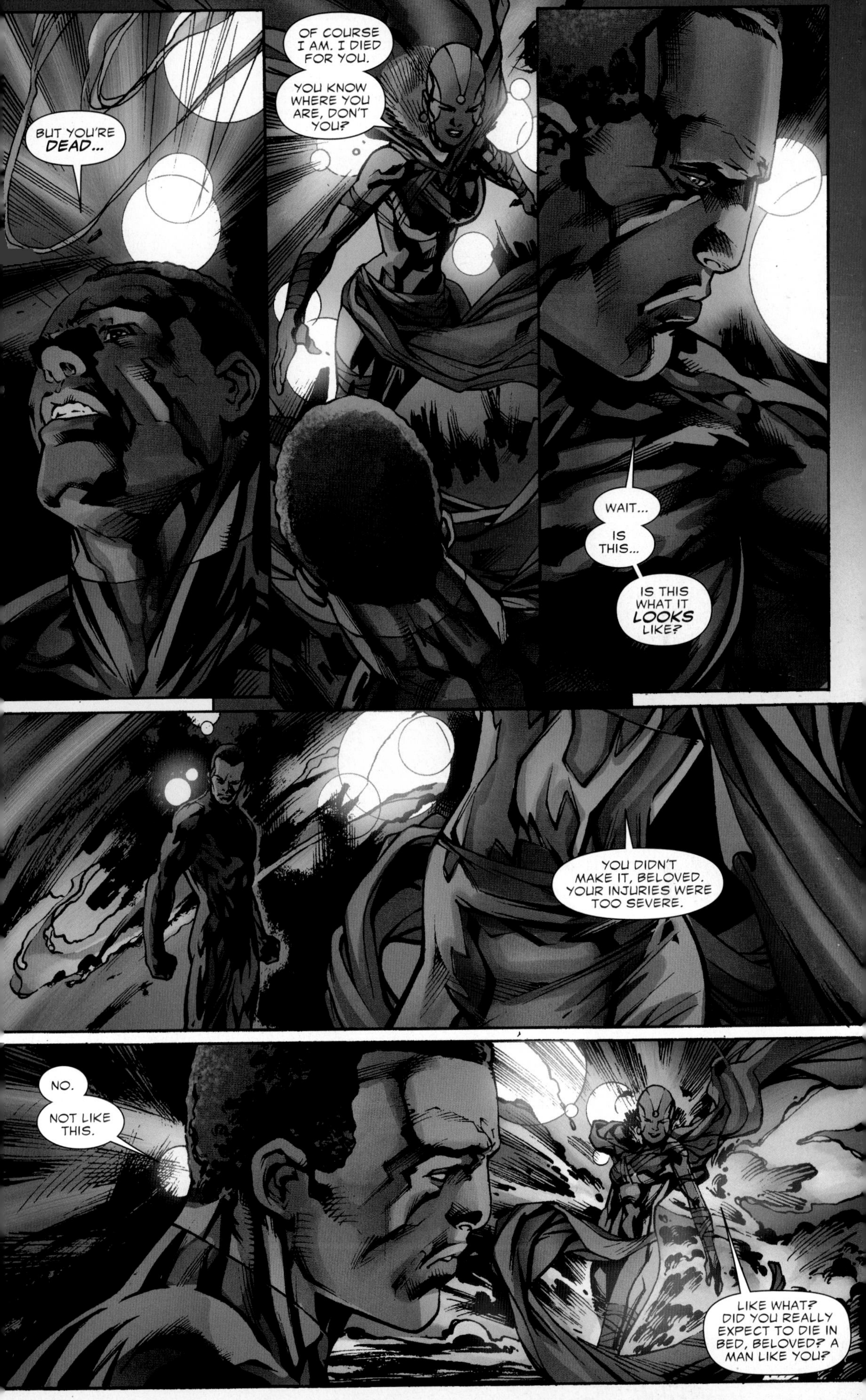

BUT YOU'RE DEAD...
OF COURSE I AM. I DIED FOR YOU.
YOU KNOW WHERE YOU ARE, DON'T YOU?
WAIT...
IS THIS...
IS THIS WHAT IT LOOKS LIKE?
YOU DIDN'T MAKE IT, BELOVED. YOUR INJURIES WERE TOO SEVERE.
NO.
NOT LIKE THIS.
LIKE WHAT? DID YOU REALLY EXPECT TO DIE IN BED, BELOVED? A MAN LIKE YOU?

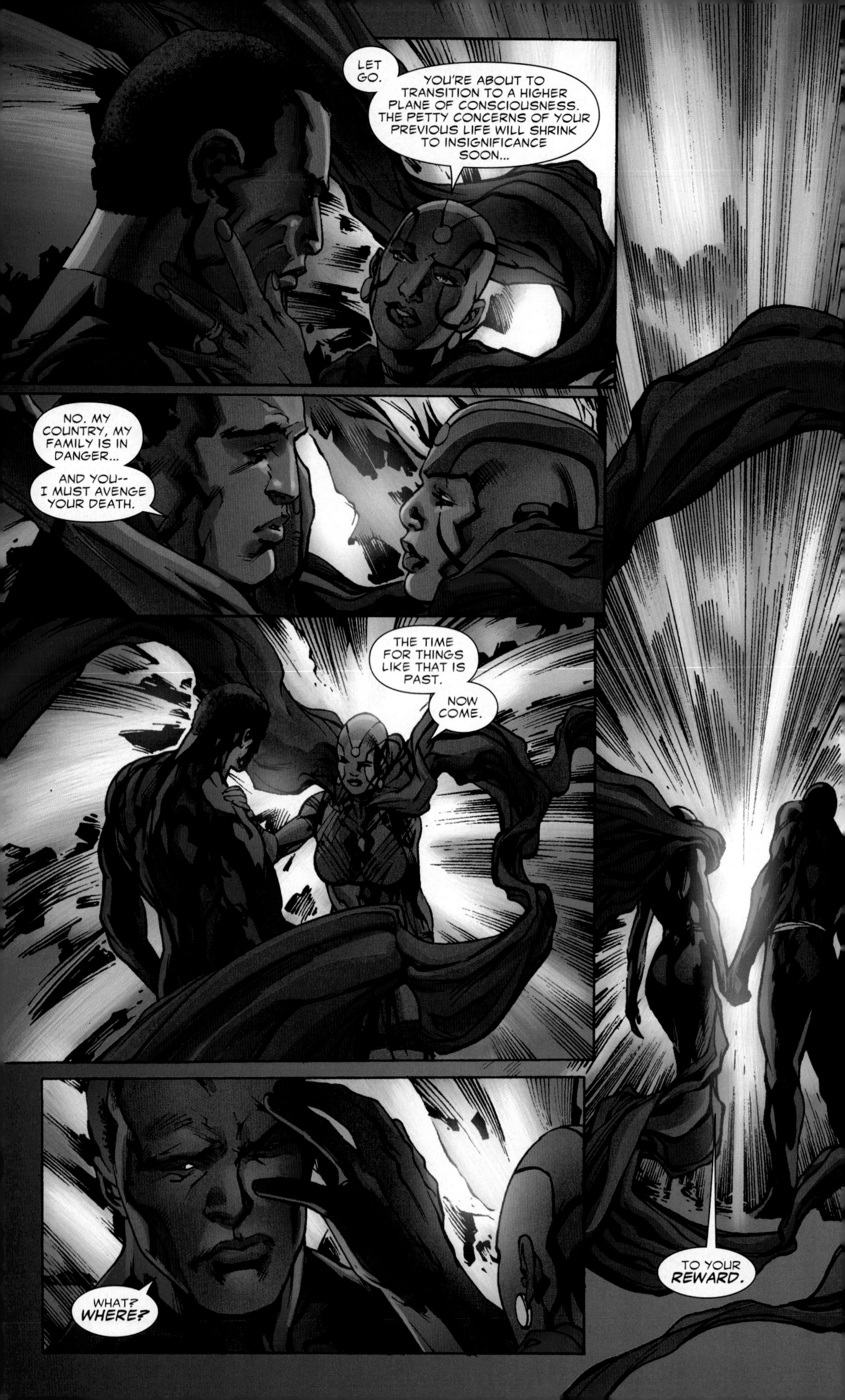
LET GO.
YOU'RE ABOUT TO TRANSITION TO A HIGHER PLANE OF CONSCIOUSNESS. THE PETTY CONCERNS OF YOUR PREVIOUS LIFE WILL SHRINK TO INSIGNIFICANCE SOON...
NO. MY COUNTRY, MY FAMILY IS IN DANGER...
AND YOU-- I MUST AVENGE YOUR DEATH.
THE TIME FOR THINGS LIKE THAT IS PAST.
NOW COME.
WHAT? **WHERE?**
TO YOUR **REWARD.**

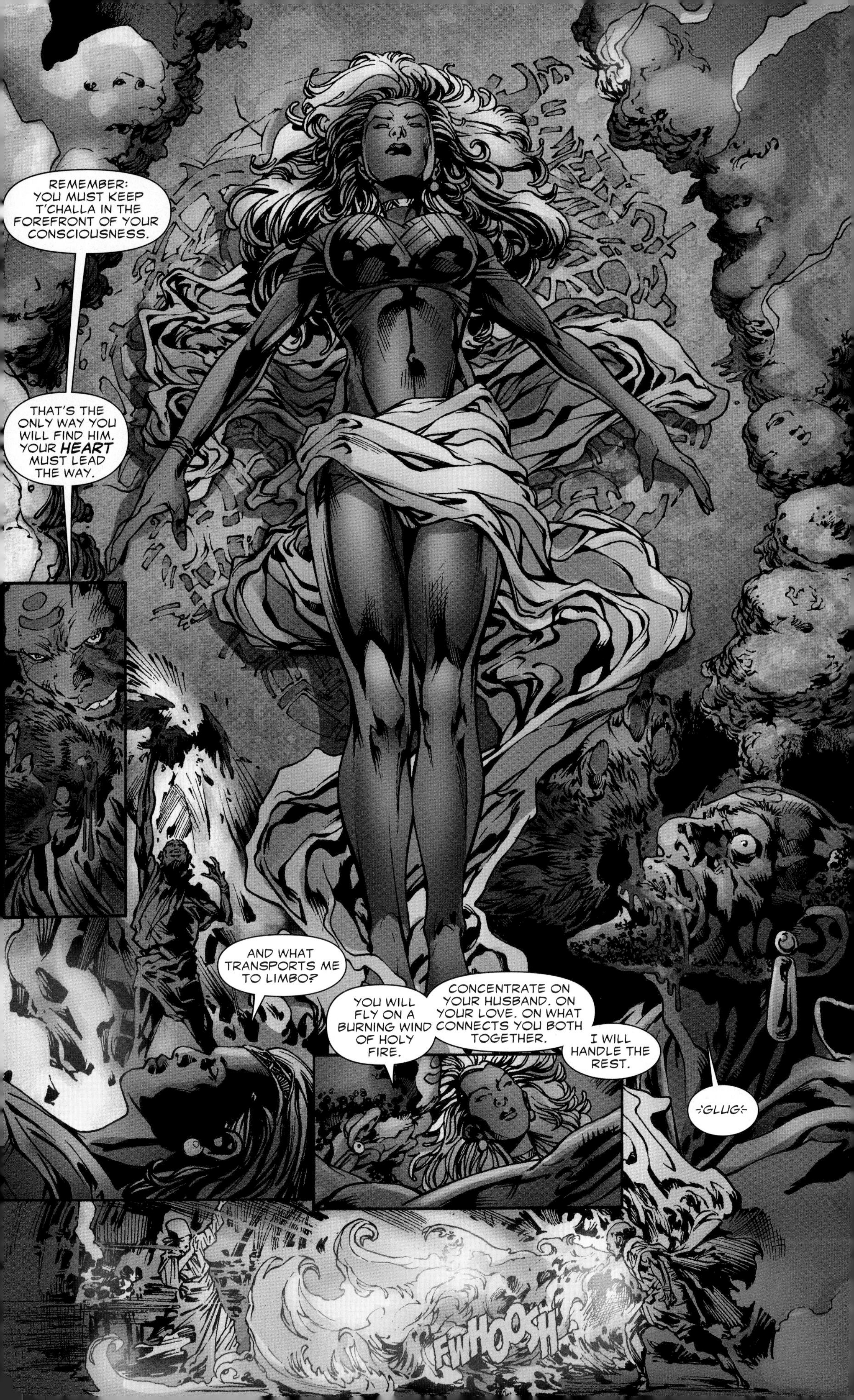
REMEMBER: YOU MUST KEEP T'CHALLA IN THE FOREFRONT OF YOUR CONSCIOUSNESS.
THAT'S THE ONLY WAY YOU WILL FIND HIM. YOUR **HEART** MUST LEAD THE WAY.
AND WHAT TRANSPORTS ME TO LIMBO?
YOU WILL FLY ON A BURNING WIND OF HOLY FIRE.
CONCENTRATE ON YOUR HUSBAND. ON YOUR LOVE. ON WHAT CONNECTS YOU BOTH TOGETHER.
I WILL HANDLE THE REST.
-GLUG-
FWHOOSH!

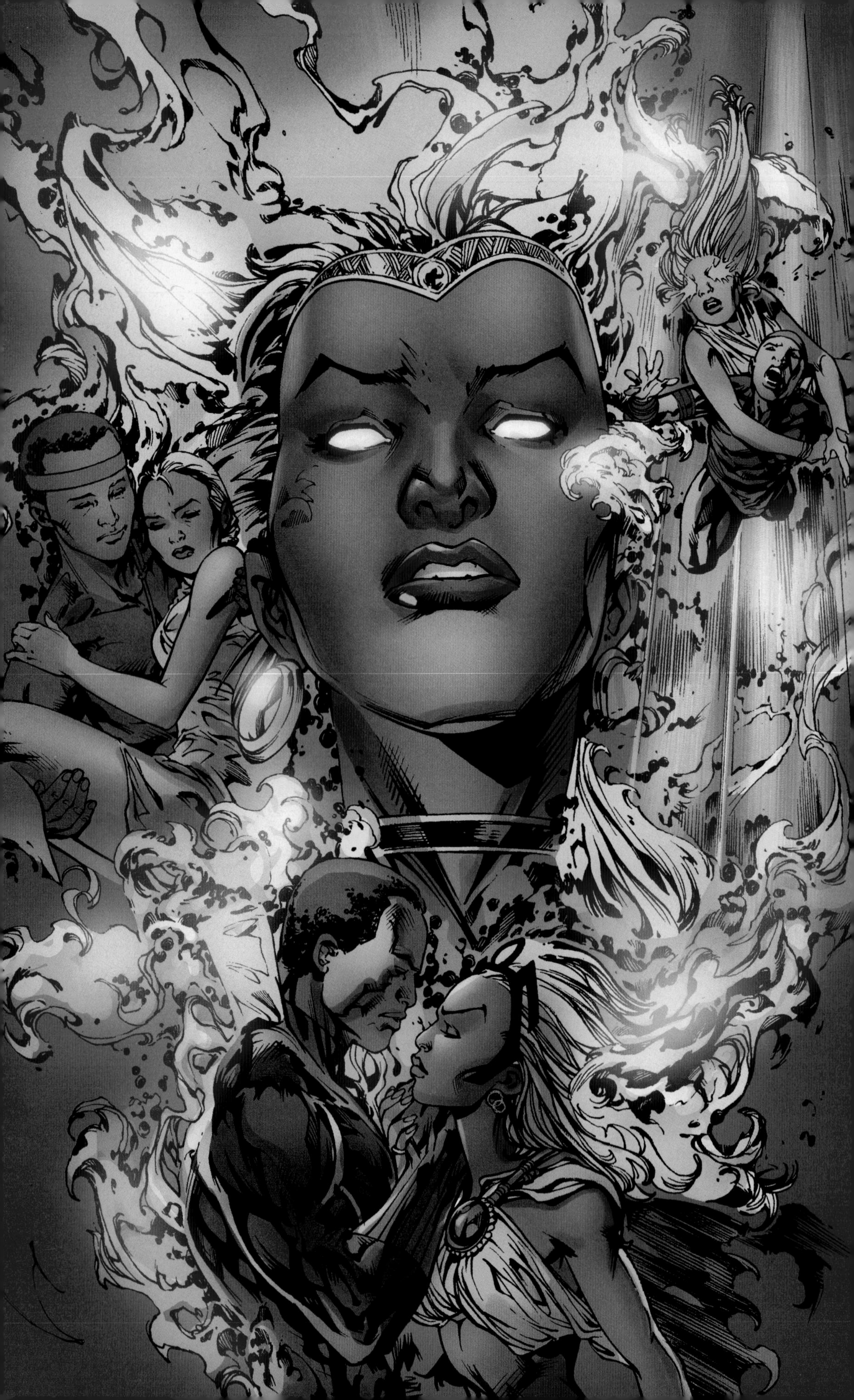

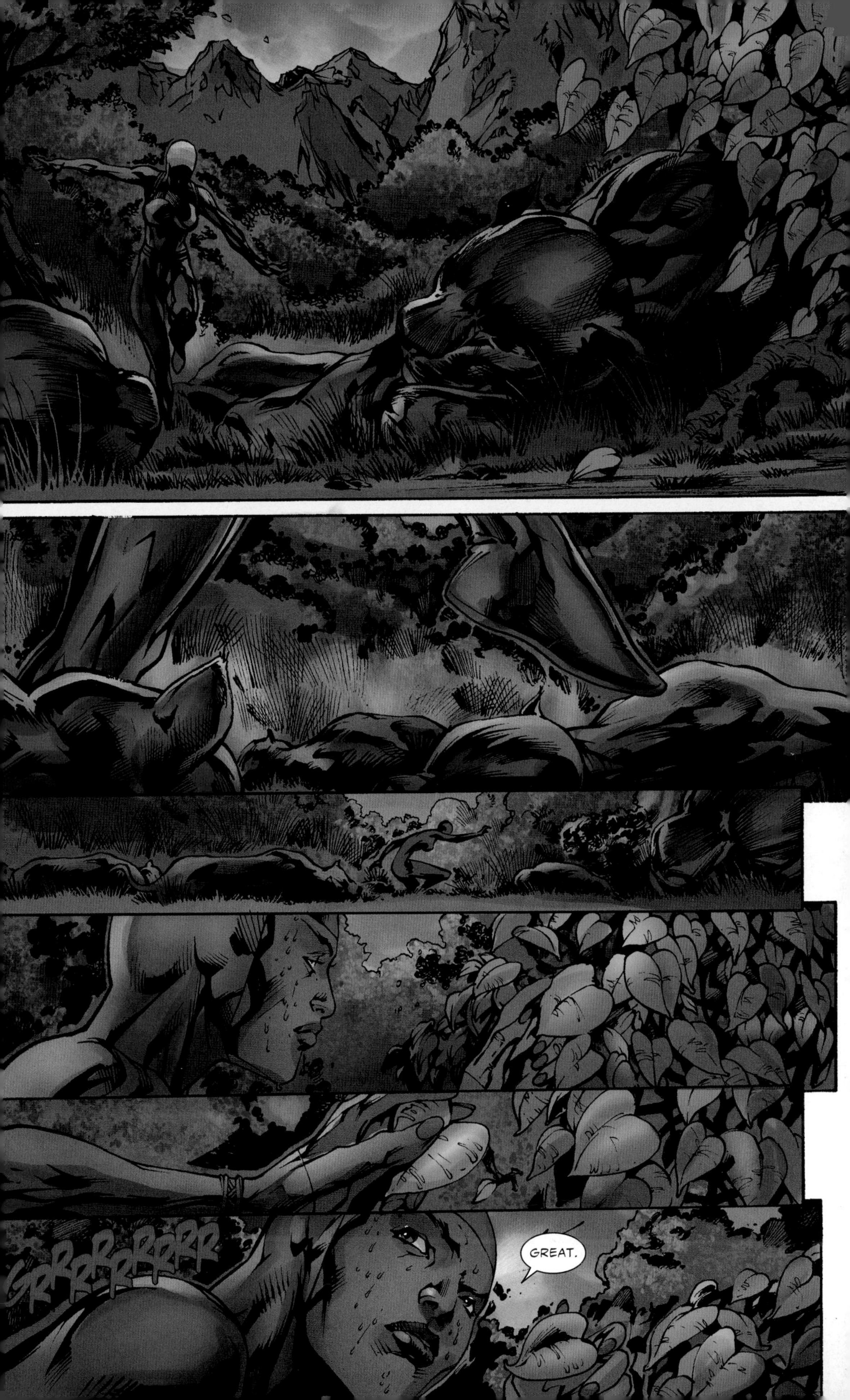
GRRRRRRRR
GREAT.

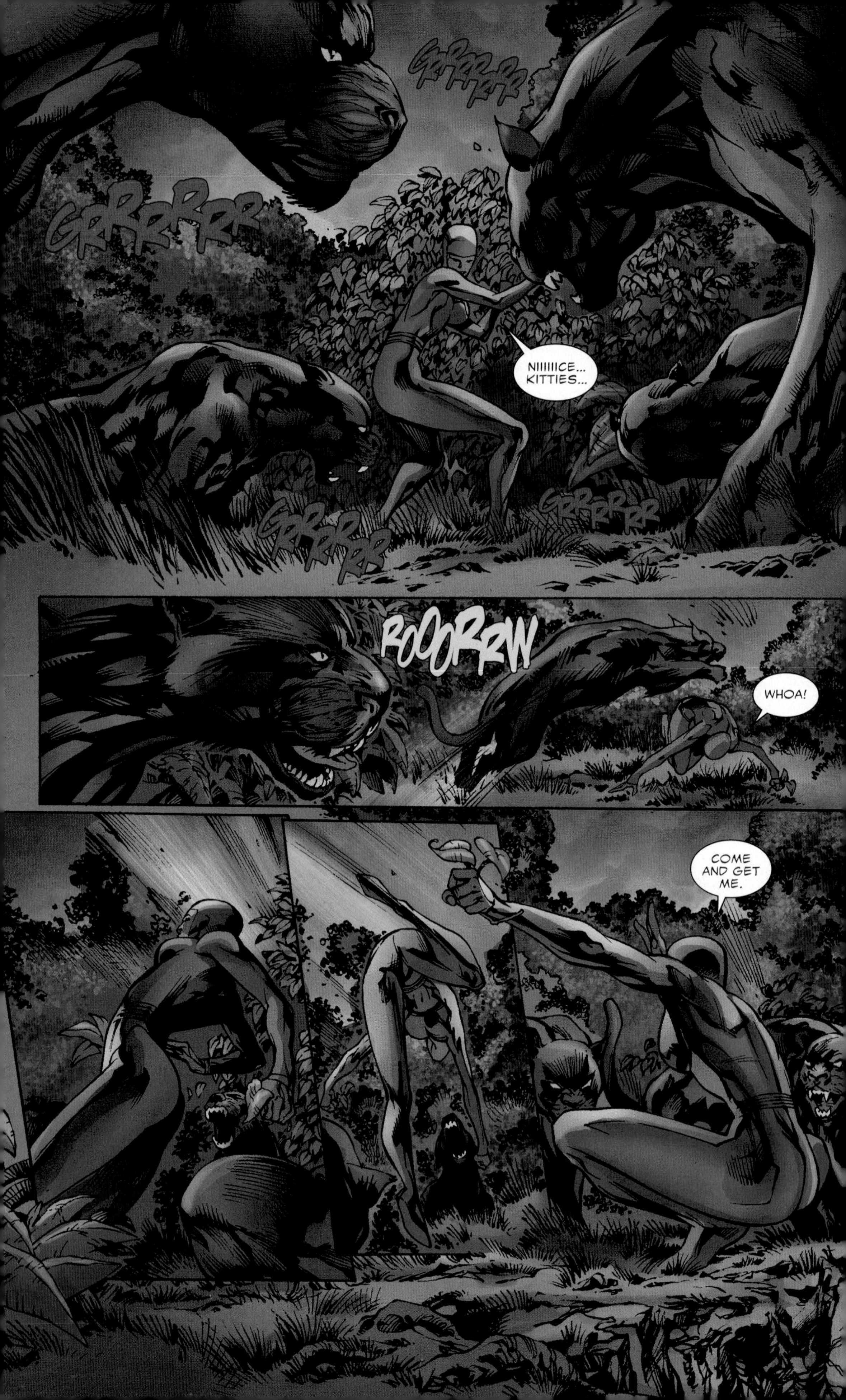
GRRRRRR
GRRRRRR
NIIIIIICE... KITTIES...
GRRRRRR
GRRRRRR
ROOORRW
WHOA!
COME AND GET ME.

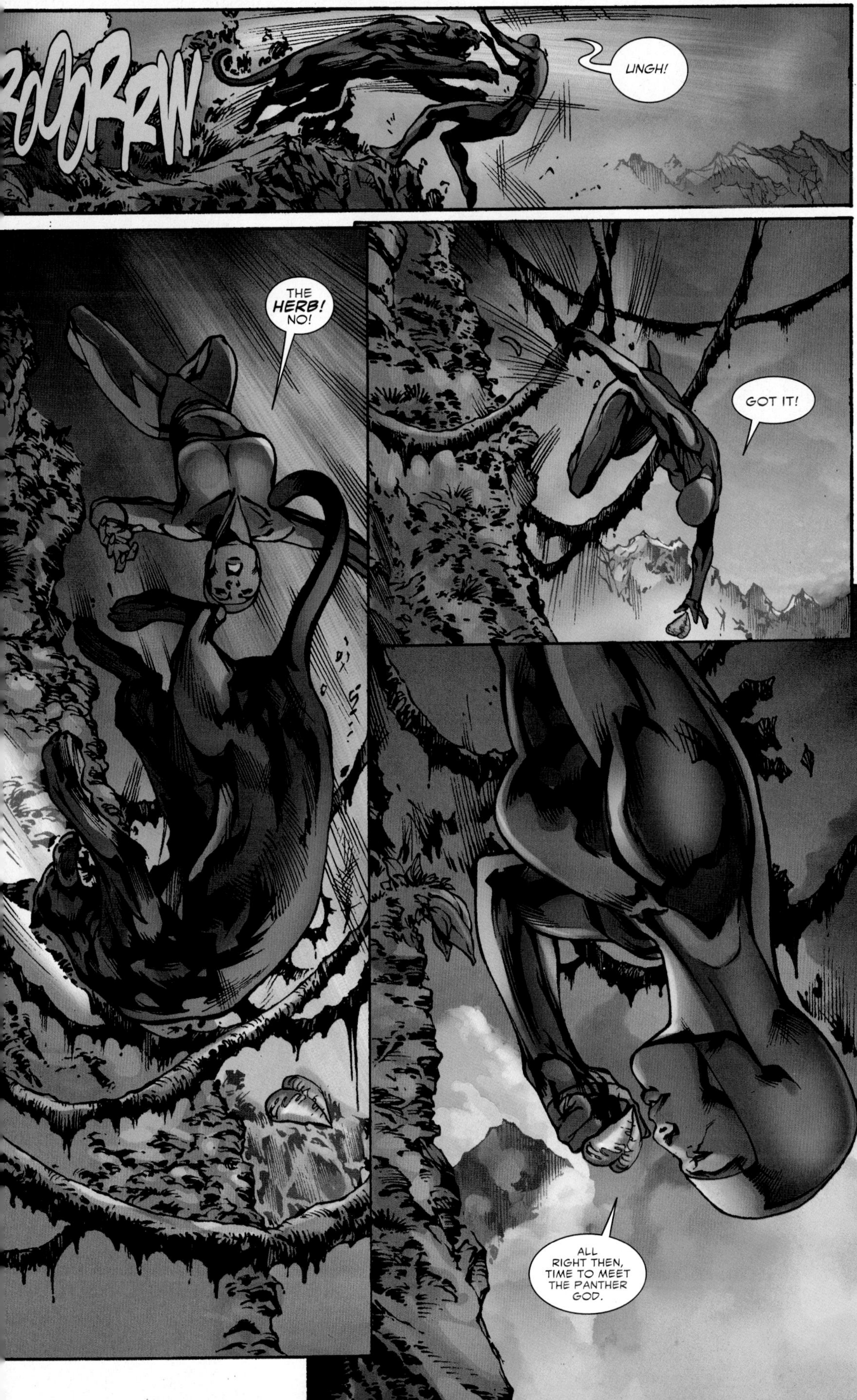
ROOORRW
UNGH!
THE HERB! NO!
GOT IT!
ALL RIGHT THEN, TIME TO MEET THE PANTHER GOD.

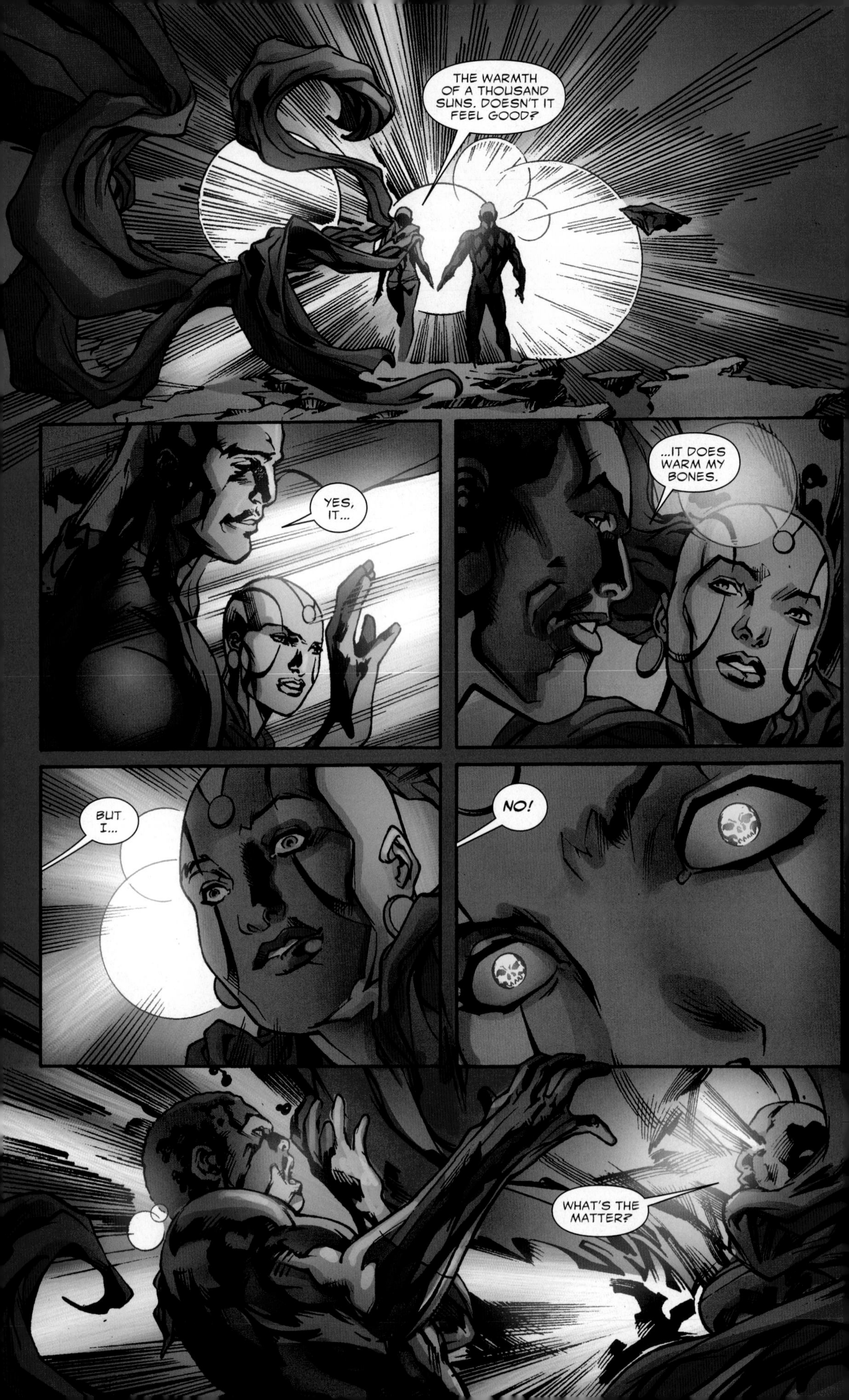
THE WARMTH OF A THOUSAND SUNS. DOESN'T IT FEEL GOOD?
YES, IT...
...IT DOES WARM MY BONES.
BUT I...
NO!
WHAT'S THE MATTER?

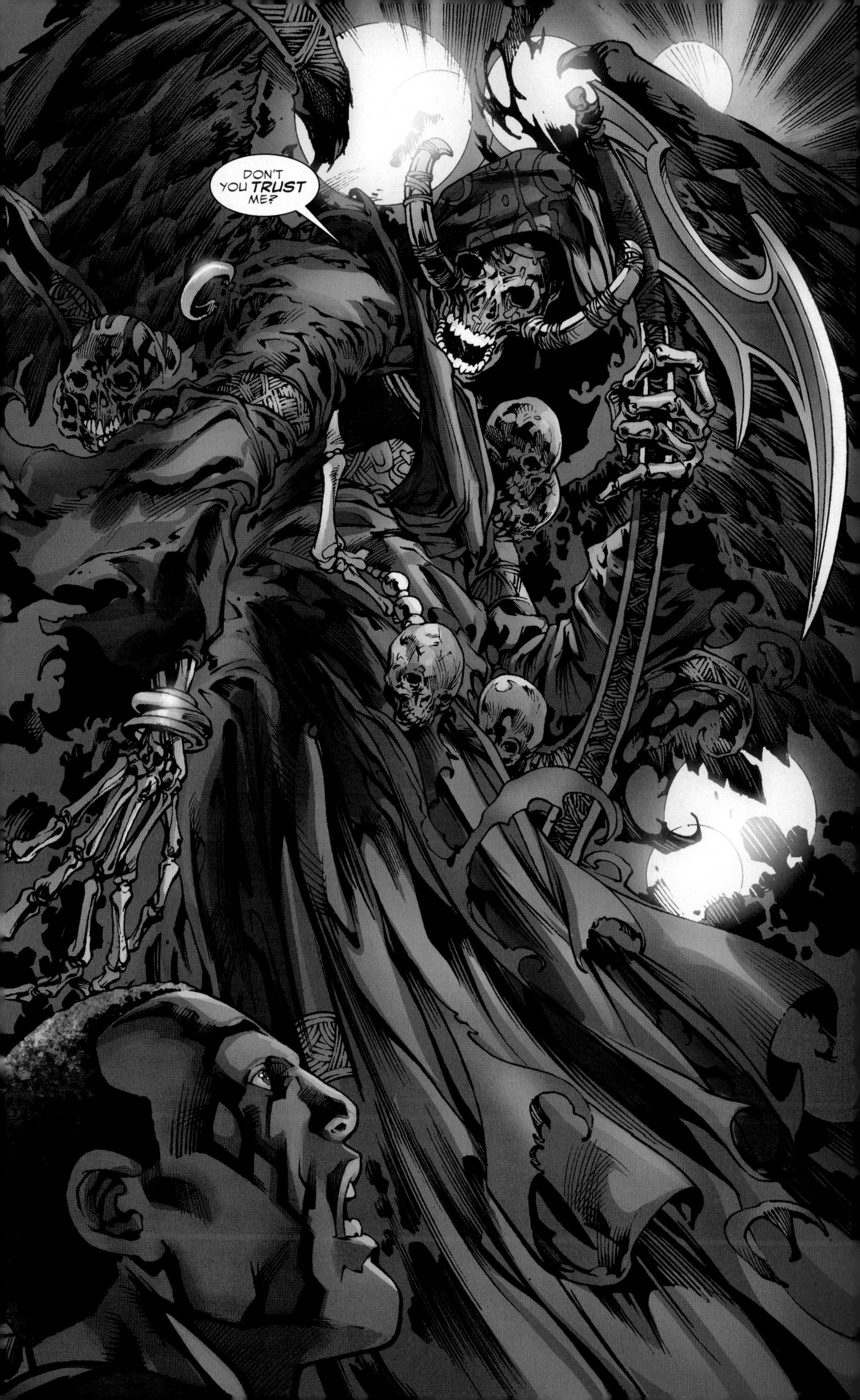
DON'T YOU TRUST ME?

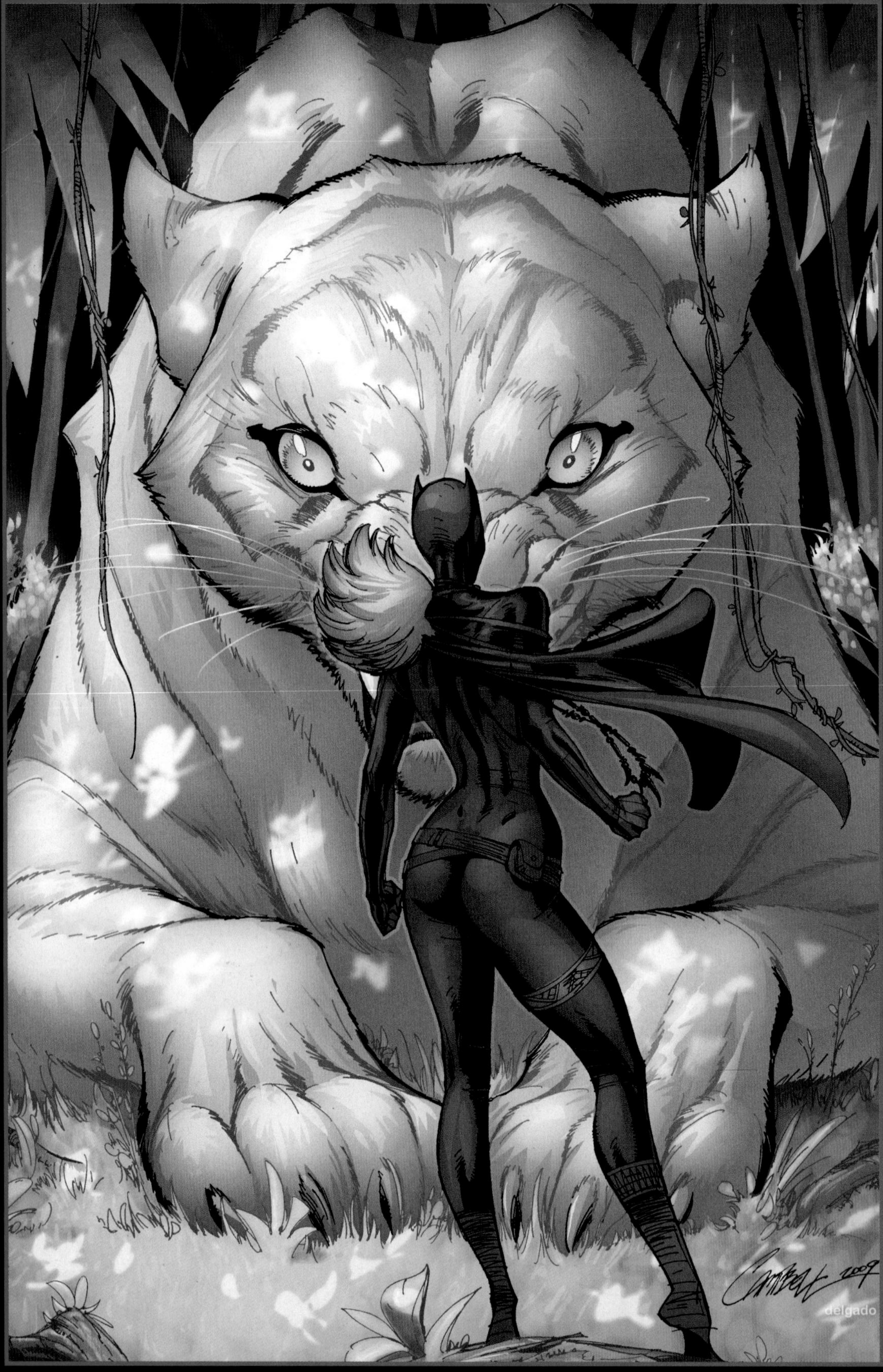
delgado

BLACK PANTHER (2009) **4:** THE DEADLIEST OF THE SPECIES, PART 4

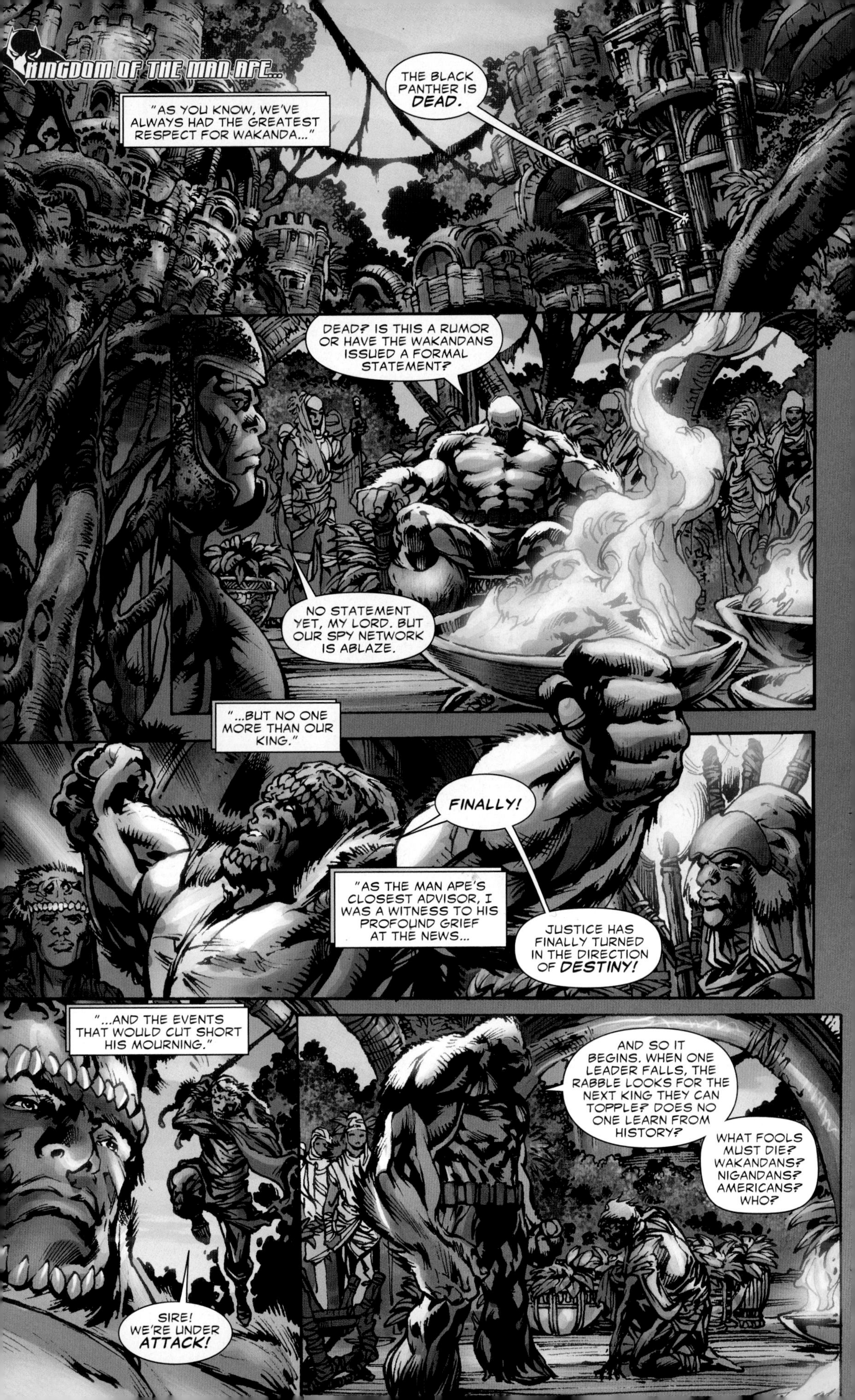
KINGDOM OF THE MAN APE...
"AS YOU KNOW, WE'VE ALWAYS HAD THE GREATEST RESPECT FOR WAKANDA..."
THE BLACK PANTHER IS DEAD.
DEAD? IS THIS A RUMOR OR HAVE THE WAKANDANS ISSUED A FORMAL STATEMENT?
NO STATEMENT YET, MY LORD. BUT OUR SPY NETWORK IS ABLAZE.
"...BUT NO ONE MORE THAN OUR KING."
FINALLY!
"AS THE MAN APE'S CLOSEST ADVISOR, I WAS A WITNESS TO HIS PROFOUND GRIEF AT THE NEWS...
JUSTICE HAS FINALLY TURNED IN THE DIRECTION OF DESTINY!
"...AND THE EVENTS THAT WOULD CUT SHORT HIS MOURNING."
SIRE! WE'RE UNDER ATTACK!
AND SO IT BEGINS. WHEN ONE LEADER FALLS, THE RABBLE LOOKS FOR THE NEXT KING THEY CAN TOPPLE? DOES NO ONE LEARN FROM HISTORY?
WHAT FOOLS MUST DIE? WAKANDANS? NIGANDANS? AMERICANS? WHO?

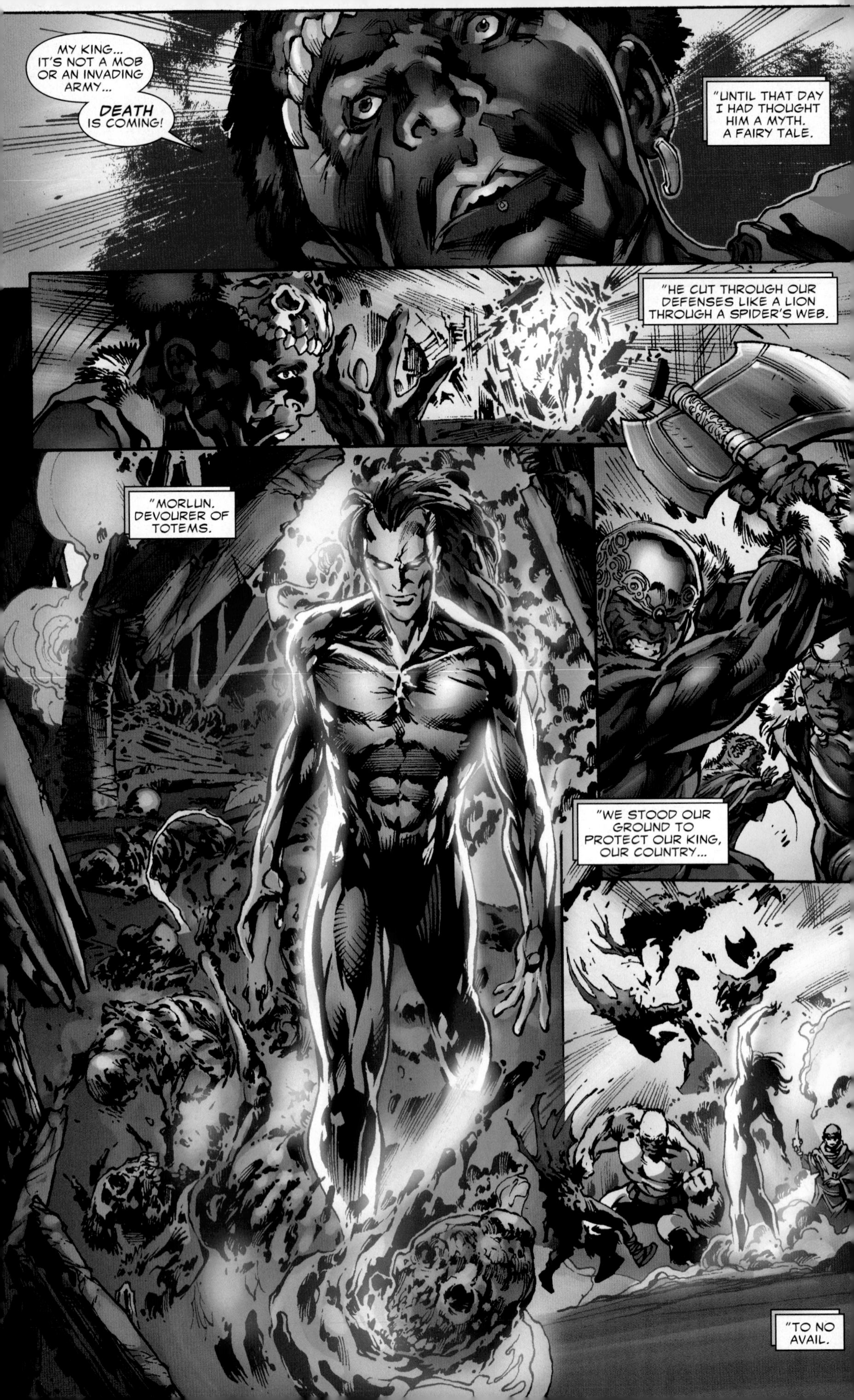

MY KING... IT'S NOT A MOB OR AN INVADING ARMY...
DEATH IS COMING!
"UNTIL THAT DAY I HAD THOUGHT HIM A MYTH. A FAIRY TALE.
"HE CUT THROUGH OUR DEFENSES LIKE A LION THROUGH A SPIDER'S WEB.
"MORLUN. DEVOURER OF TOTEMS.
"WE STOOD OUR GROUND TO PROTECT OUR KING, OUR COUNTRY...
"TO NO AVAIL.

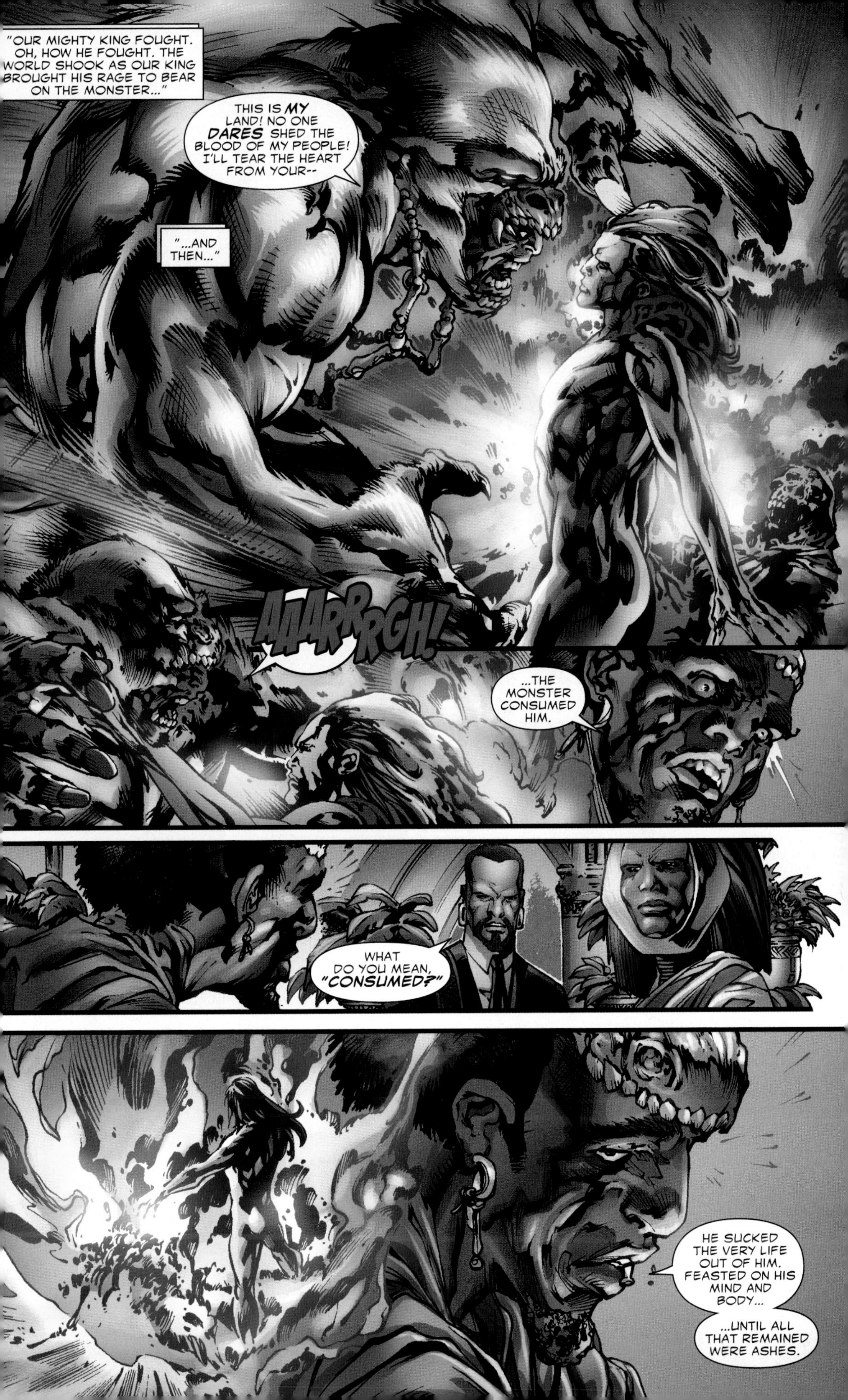
"OUR MIGHTY KING FOUGHT. OH, HOW HE FOUGHT. THE WORLD SHOOK AS OUR KING BROUGHT HIS RAGE TO BEAR ON THE MONSTER..."
THIS IS MY LAND! NO ONE DARES SHED THE BLOOD OF MY PEOPLE! I'LL TEAR THE HEART FROM YOUR--
"...AND THEN..."
AAARRRGH!
...THE MONSTER CONSUMED HIM.
WHAT DO YOU MEAN, "CONSUMED?"
HE SUCKED THE VERY LIFE OUT OF HIM. FEASTED ON HIS MIND AND BODY...
...UNTIL ALL THAT REMAINED WERE ASHES.

SO HOW DID *YOU* SURVIVE?

WITH HIS DYING BREATH, MY KING BID ME LEAVE...

...TO SPREAD THE WORD THAT HE HAD DIED BRAVELY IN BATTLE...

...AND TO FIND SOME WAY TO AVENGE HIS DEATH.

WHY COME *HERE?* YOUR MASTER WAS NOT FOND OF THE BLACK PANTHER.

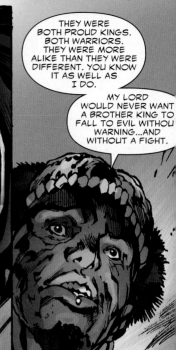

THEY WERE BOTH PROUD KINGS. BOTH WARRIORS. THEY WERE MORE ALIKE THAN THEY WERE DIFFERENT. YOU KNOW IT AS WELL AS I DO.

MY LORD WOULD NEVER WANT A BROTHER KING TO FALL TO EVIL WITHOUT WARNING...AND WITHOUT A FIGHT.

BESIDES, I KNEW THAT WITH PROPER WARNING, YOU WOULD ERECT ADEQUATE DEFENSES TO STOP MORLUN. AND THAT THE GENEROUS NATION OF WAKANDA WOULD PROTECT AND REWARD SOMEONE WHO PROVIDED THE INFORMATION THAT MIGHT SAVE ITS PEOPLE.

W'KABI, PUT OUR FORCES ON DEFENSE ALERT ALPHA. AND HAVE YOUR NETWORK VERIFY THIS MAN'S STORY.

AT ONCE.

IF THIS IS TRUE, THEN WE COULD BE FACING A TIDAL WAVE OF REFUGEES AT THE VERY TIME WE SHOULD BE CLOSING OUR BORDERS.

DO YOU THINK IT'S ALL RELATED?

BETTER TO ASSUME THE WORST, AND PREPARE FOR IT.

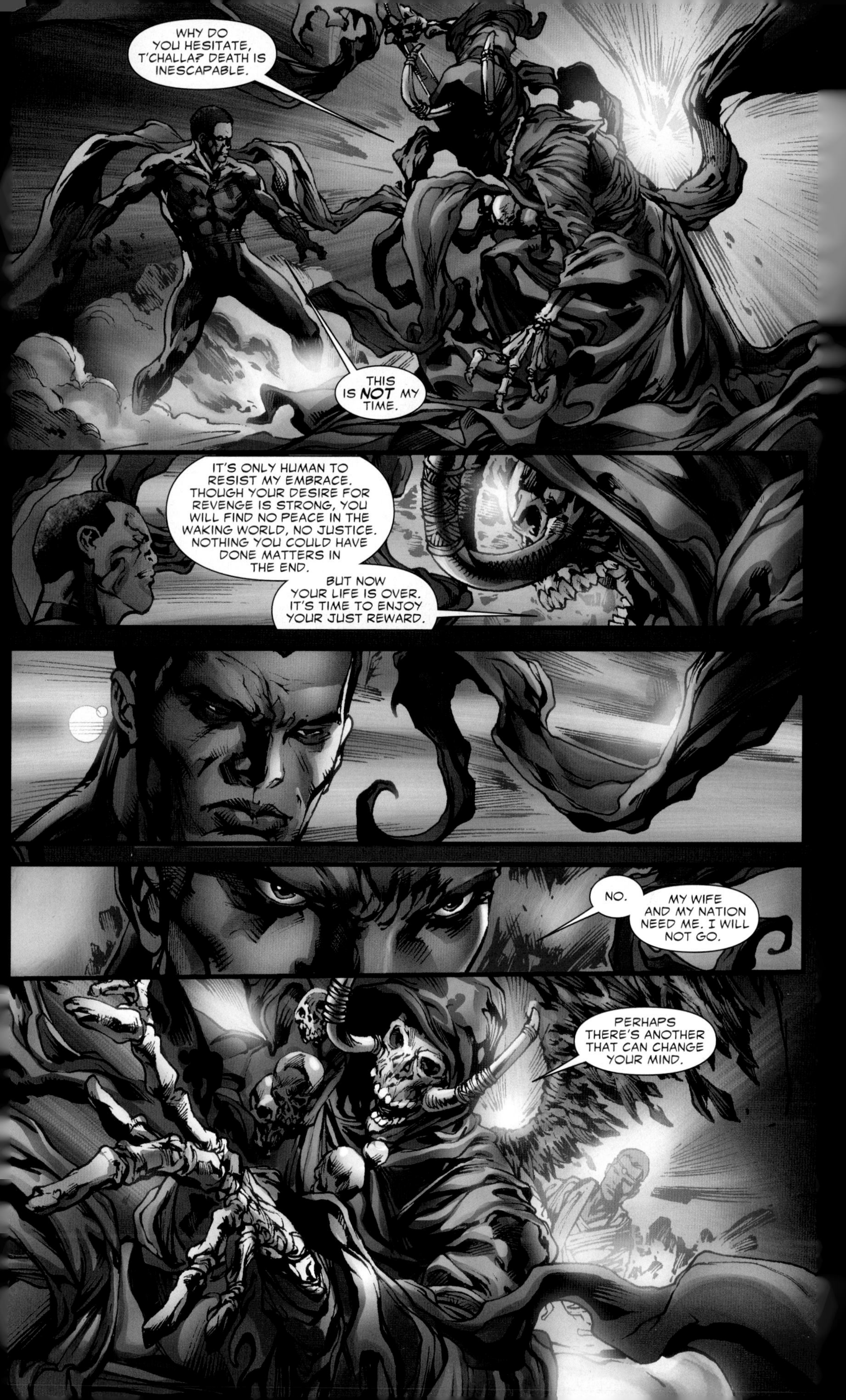
WHY DO YOU HESITATE, T'CHALLA? DEATH IS INESCAPABLE.
THIS IS NOT MY TIME.
IT'S ONLY HUMAN TO RESIST MY EMBRACE. THOUGH YOUR DESIRE FOR REVENGE IS STRONG, YOU WILL FIND NO PEACE IN THE WAKING WORLD, NO JUSTICE. NOTHING YOU COULD HAVE DONE MATTERS IN THE END.
BUT NOW YOUR LIFE IS OVER. IT'S TIME TO ENJOY YOUR JUST REWARD.
NO.
MY WIFE AND MY NATION NEED ME. I WILL NOT GO.
PERHAPS THERE'S ANOTHER THAT CAN CHANGE YOUR MIND.

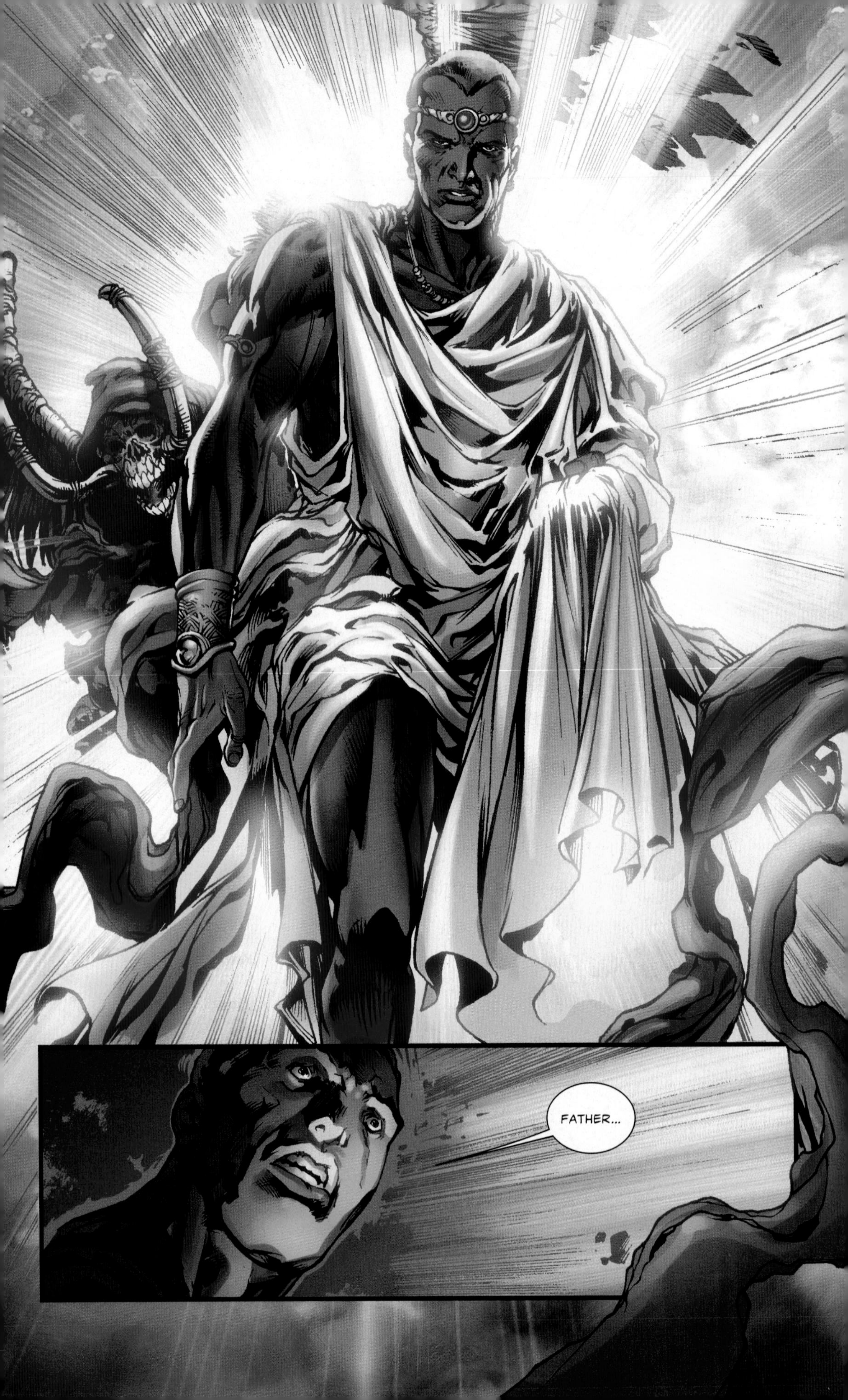
FATHER...

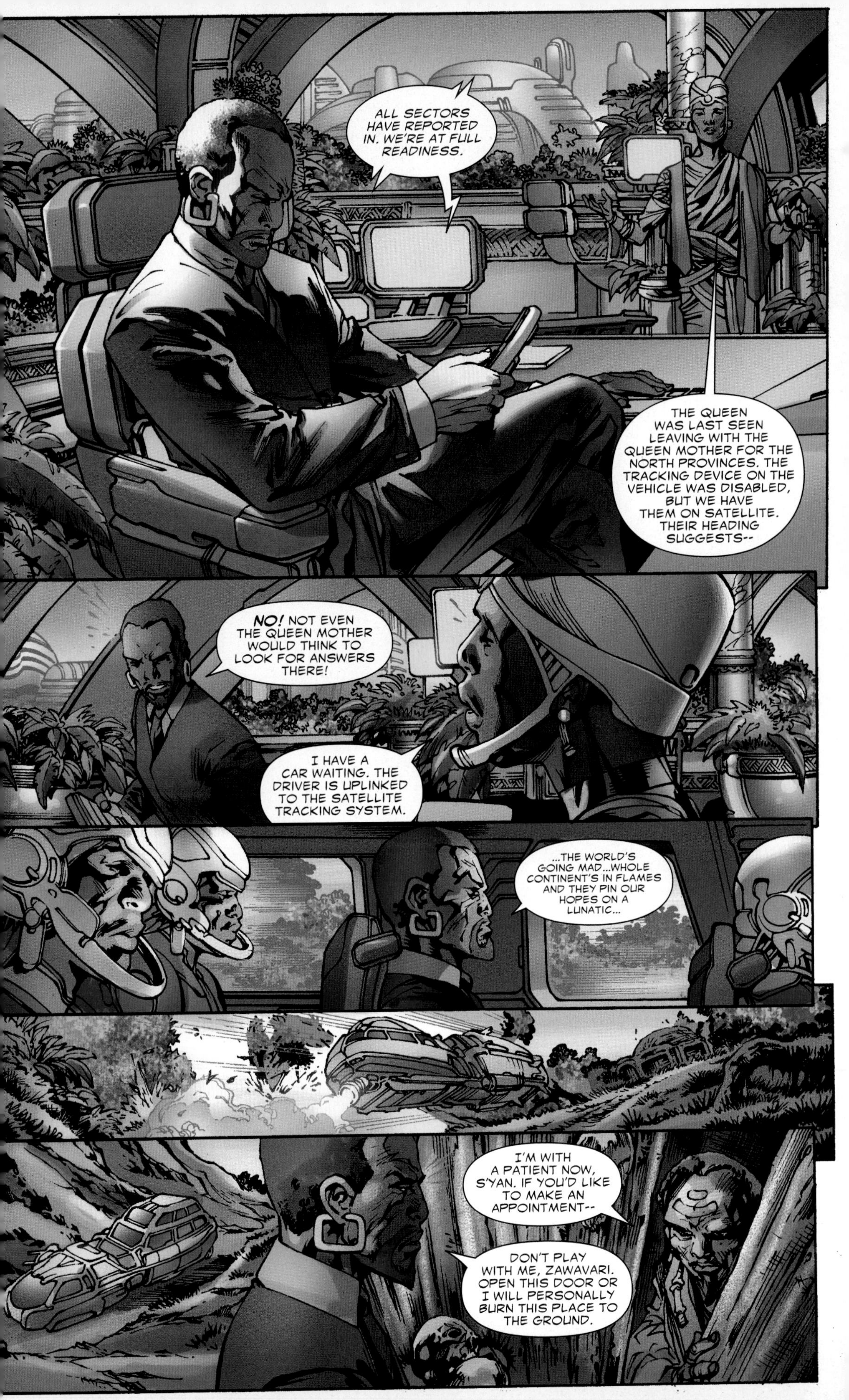
ALL SECTORS HAVE REPORTED IN. WE'RE AT FULL READINESS.
THE QUEEN WAS LAST SEEN LEAVING WITH THE QUEEN MOTHER FOR THE NORTH PROVINCES. THE TRACKING DEVICE ON THE VEHICLE WAS DISABLED, BUT WE HAVE THEM ON SATELLITE. THEIR HEADING SUGGESTS--
NO! NOT EVEN THE QUEEN MOTHER WOULD THINK TO LOOK FOR ANSWERS THERE!
I HAVE A CAR WAITING. THE DRIVER IS UPLINKED TO THE SATELLITE TRACKING SYSTEM.
...THE WORLD'S GOING MAD...WHOLE CONTINENT'S IN FLAMES AND THEY PIN OUR HOPES ON A LUNATIC...
I'M WITH A PATIENT NOW, S'YAN. IF YOU'D LIKE TO MAKE AN APPOINTMENT--
DON'T PLAY WITH ME, ZAWAVARI. OPEN THIS DOOR OR I WILL PERSONALLY BURN THIS PLACE TO THE GROUND.

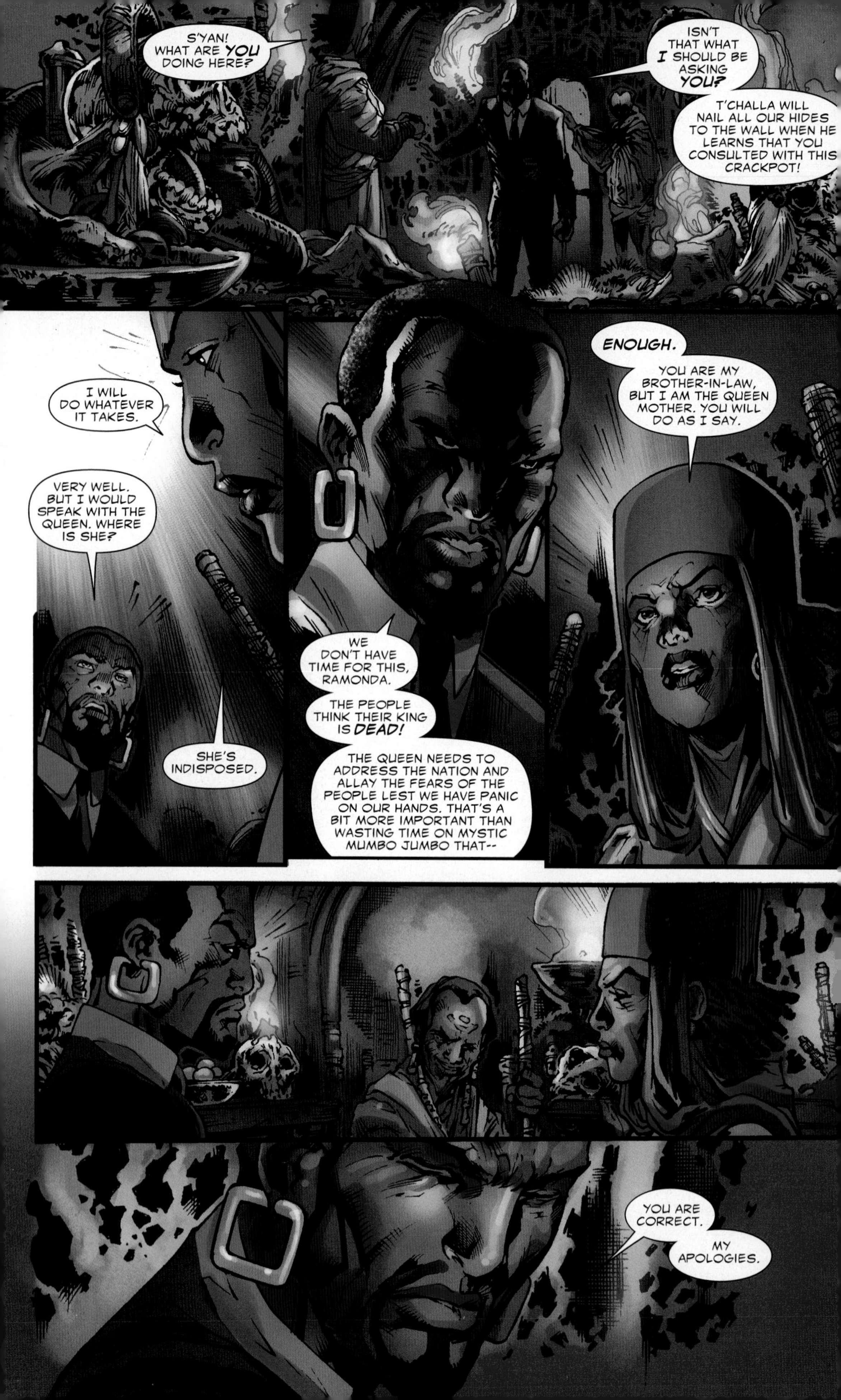
S'YAN! WHAT ARE YOU DOING HERE?
ISN'T THAT WHAT I SHOULD BE ASKING YOU?
T'CHALLA WILL NAIL ALL OUR HIDES TO THE WALL WHEN HE LEARNS THAT YOU CONSULTED WITH THIS CRACKPOT!
I WILL DO WHATEVER IT TAKES.
VERY WELL. BUT I WOULD SPEAK WITH THE QUEEN. WHERE IS SHE?
SHE'S INDISPOSED.
WE DON'T HAVE TIME FOR THIS, RAMONDA.
THE PEOPLE THINK THEIR KING IS DEAD!
THE QUEEN NEEDS TO ADDRESS THE NATION AND ALLAY THE FEARS OF THE PEOPLE LEST WE HAVE PANIC ON OUR HANDS. THAT'S A BIT MORE IMPORTANT THAN WASTING TIME ON MYSTIC MUMBO JUMBO THAT--
ENOUGH.
YOU ARE MY BROTHER-IN-LAW, BUT I AM THE QUEEN MOTHER. YOU WILL DO AS I SAY.
YOU ARE CORRECT.
MY APOLOGIES.

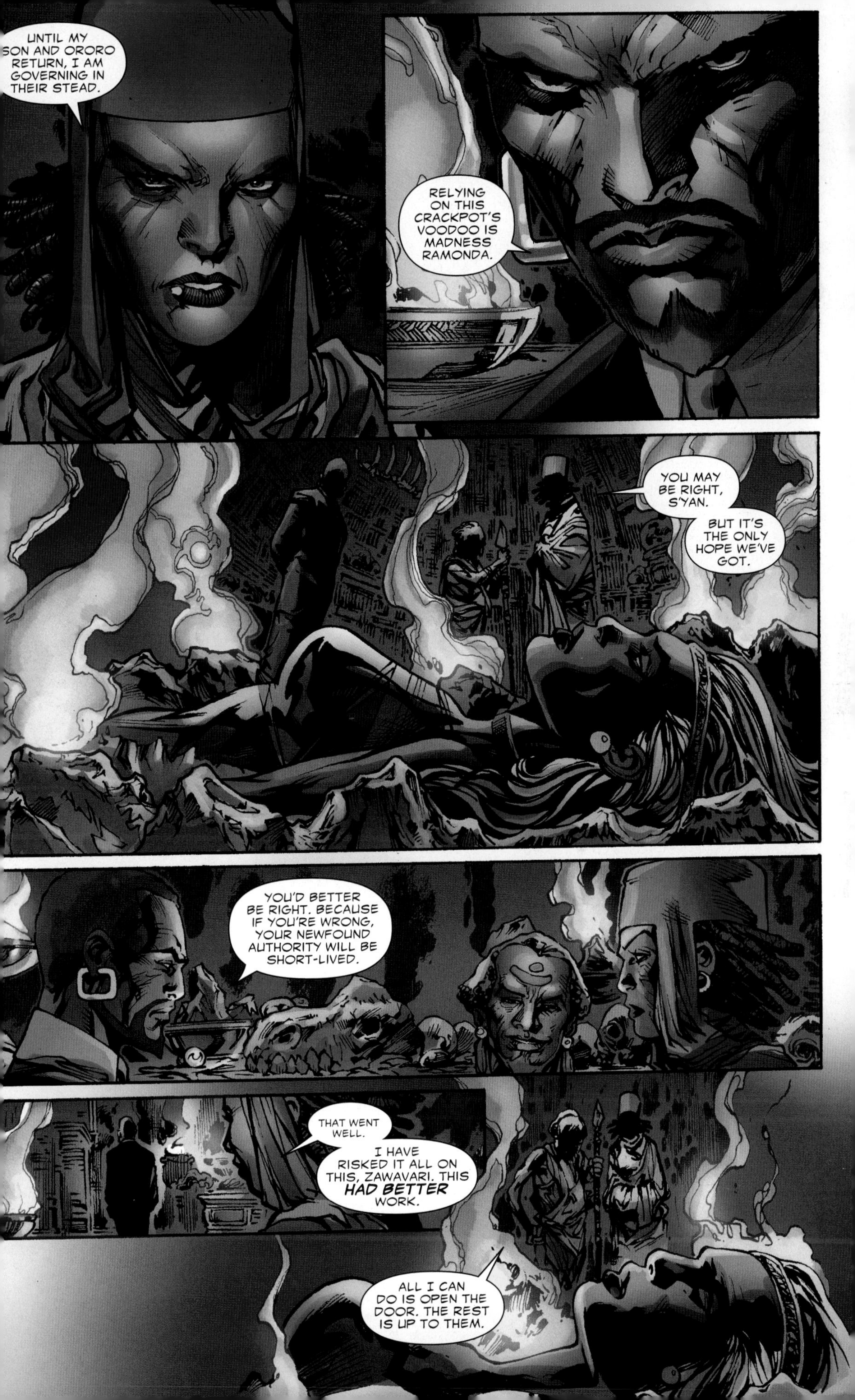
UNTIL MY SON AND ORORO RETURN, I AM GOVERNING IN THEIR STEAD.
RELYING ON THIS CRACKPOT'S VOODOO IS MADNESS RAMONDA.
YOU MAY BE RIGHT, S'YAN.
BUT IT'S THE ONLY HOPE WE'VE GOT.
YOU'D BETTER BE RIGHT. BECAUSE IF YOU'RE WRONG, YOUR NEWFOUND AUTHORITY WILL BE SHORT-LIVED.
THAT WENT WELL.
I HAVE RISKED IT ALL ON THIS, ZAWAVARI. THIS **HAD BETTER** WORK.
ALL I CAN DO IS OPEN THE DOOR. THE REST IS UP TO THEM.

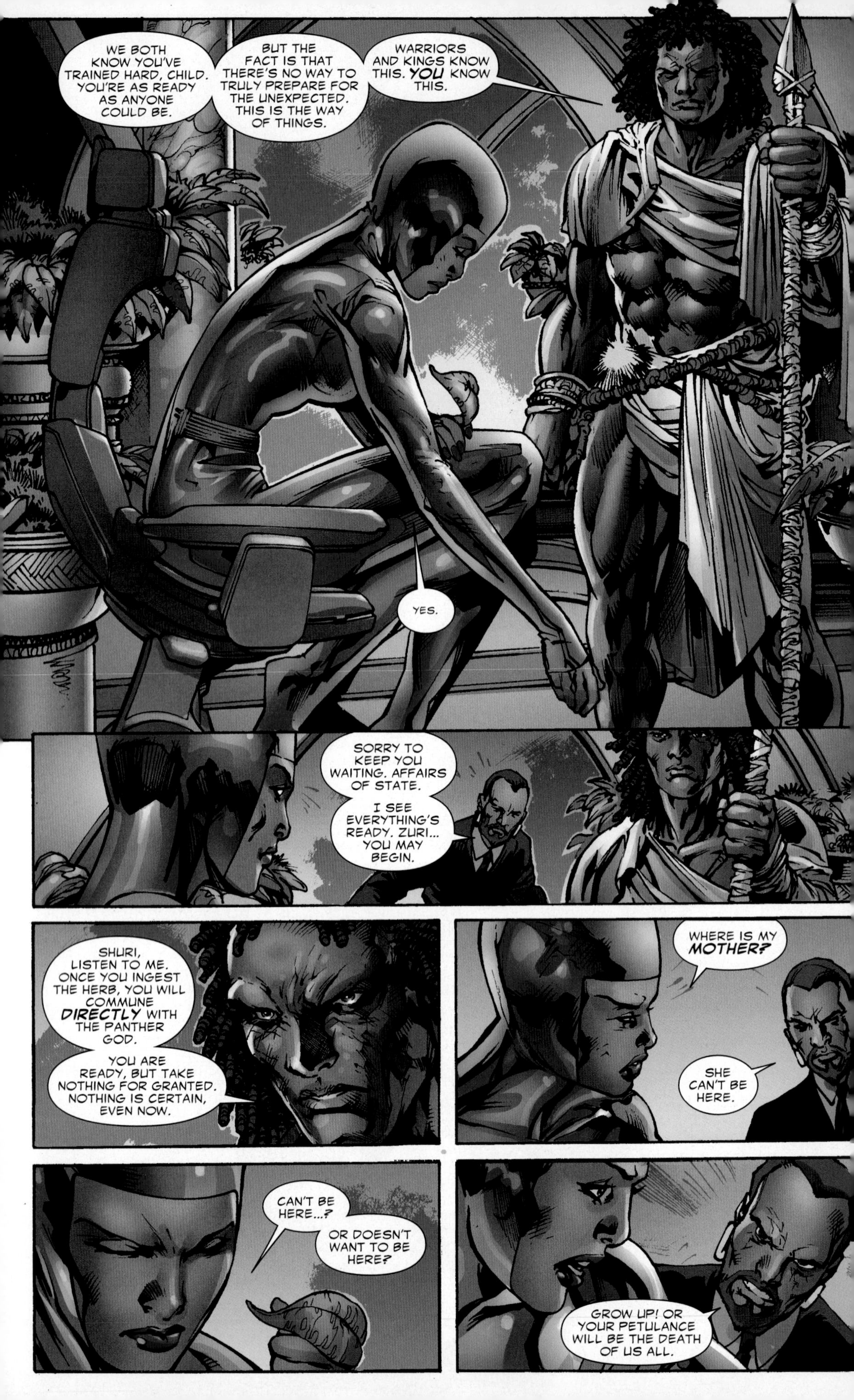
WE BOTH KNOW YOU'VE TRAINED HARD, CHILD. YOU'RE AS READY AS ANYONE COULD BE.
BUT THE FACT IS THAT THERE'S NO WAY TO TRULY PREPARE FOR THE UNEXPECTED. THIS IS THE WAY OF THINGS.
WARRIORS AND KINGS KNOW THIS. YOU KNOW THIS.
YES.
SORRY TO KEEP YOU WAITING. AFFAIRS OF STATE.
I SEE EVERYTHING'S READY. ZURI... YOU MAY BEGIN.
SHURI, LISTEN TO ME. ONCE YOU INGEST THE HERB, YOU WILL COMMUNE DIRECTLY WITH THE PANTHER GOD.
YOU ARE READY, BUT TAKE NOTHING FOR GRANTED. NOTHING IS CERTAIN, EVEN NOW.
WHERE IS MY MOTHER?
SHE CAN'T BE HERE.
CAN'T BE HERE...?
OR DOESN'T WANT TO BE HERE?
GROW UP! OR YOUR PETULANCE WILL BE THE DEATH OF US ALL.

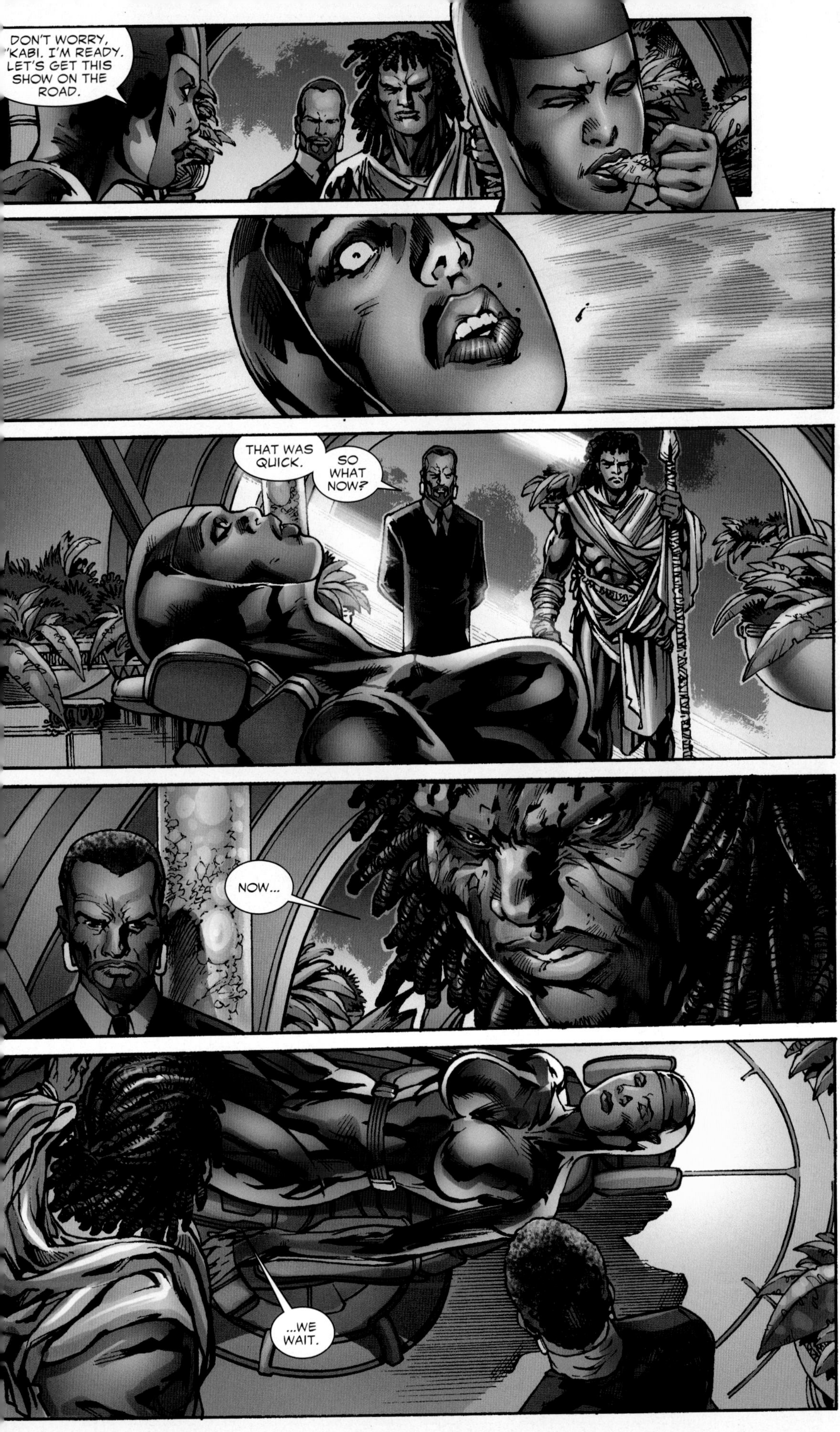
DON'T WORRY, 'KABI. I'M READY. LET'S GET THIS SHOW ON THE ROAD.
THAT WAS QUICK.
SO WHAT NOW?
NOW...
...WE WAIT.

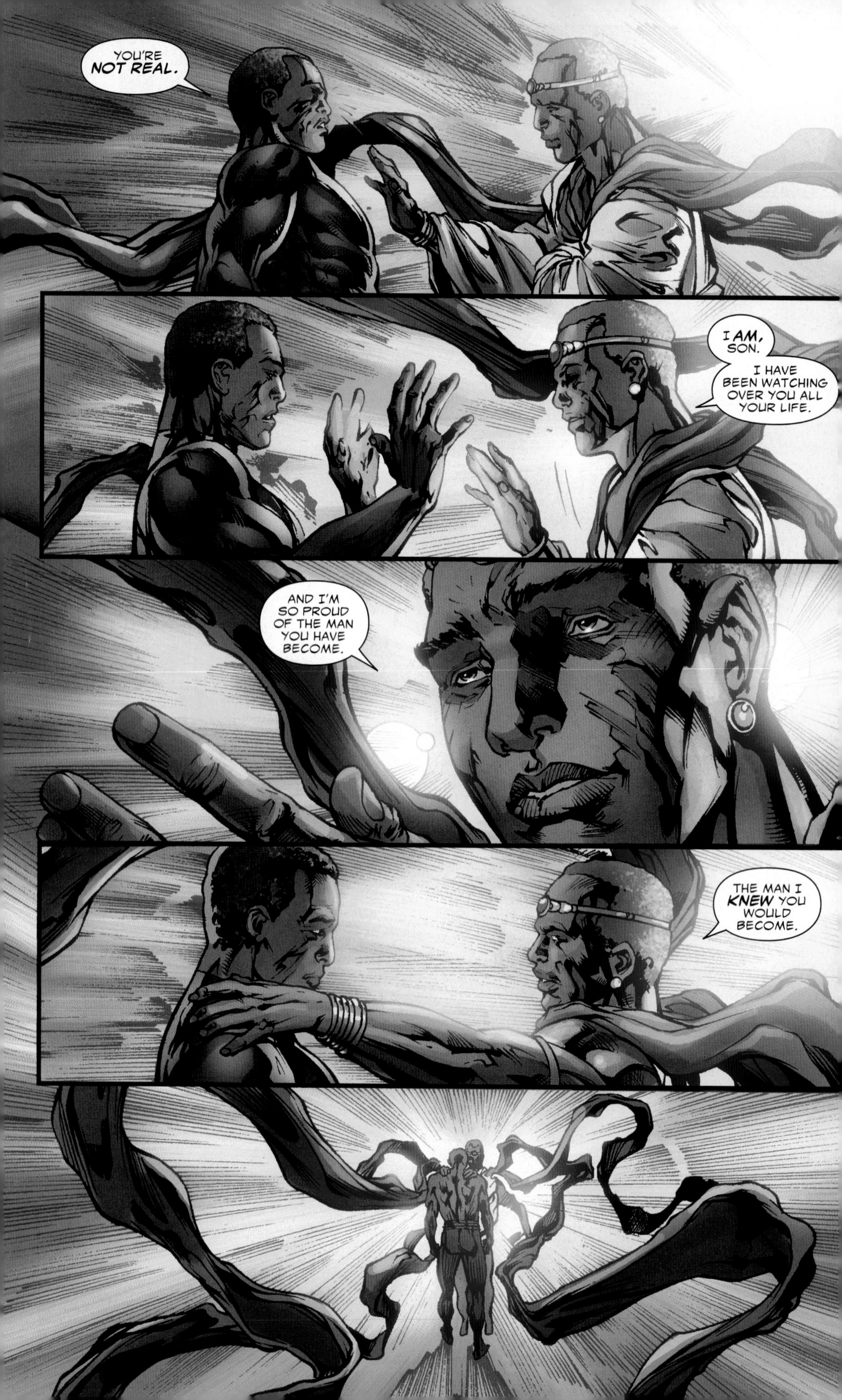

YOU'RE NOT REAL.
I AM, SON.
I HAVE BEEN WATCHING OVER YOU ALL YOUR LIFE.
AND I'M SO PROUD OF THE MAN YOU HAVE BECOME.
THE MAN I KNEW YOU WOULD BECOME.

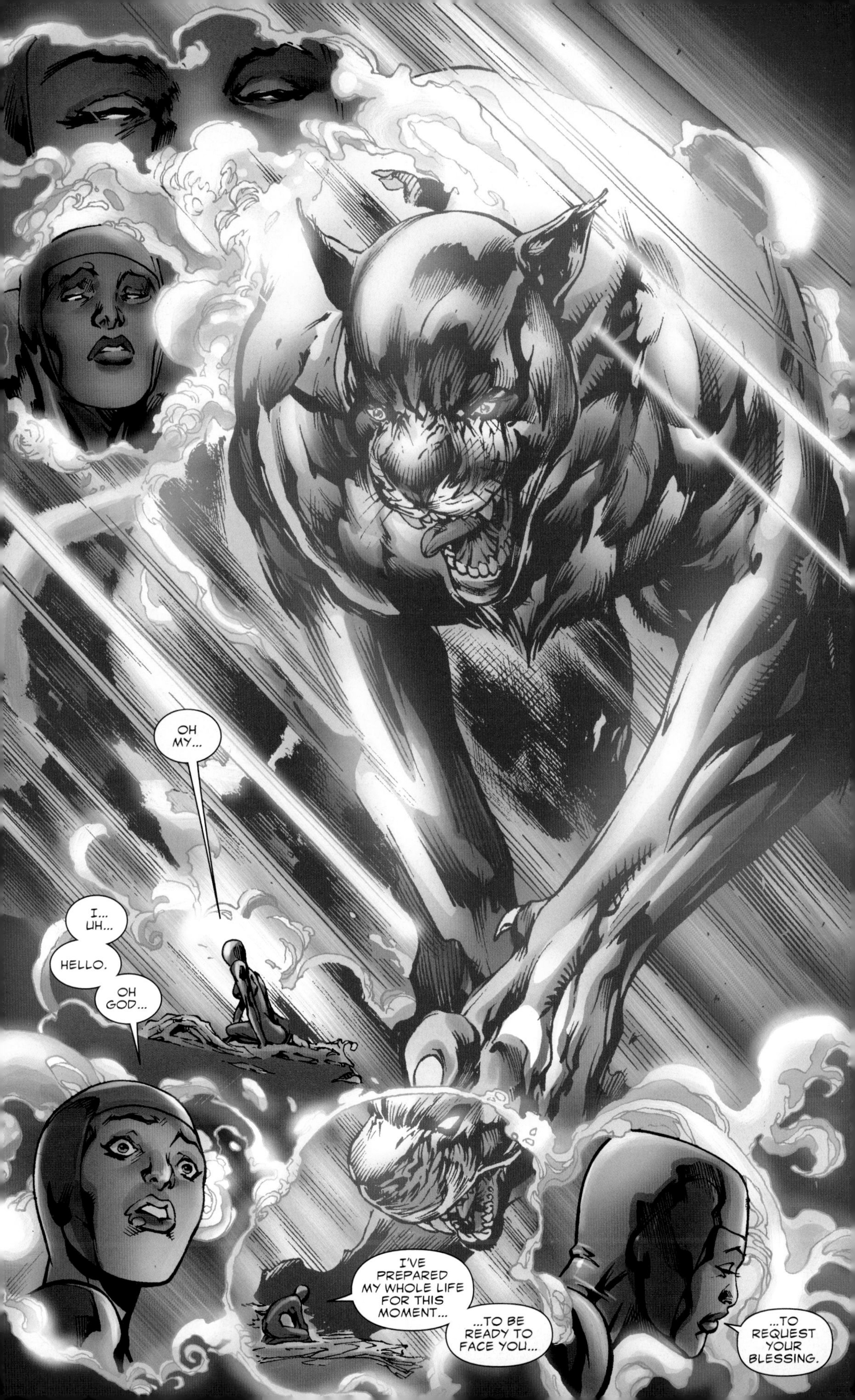
OH MY...
I... UH...
HELLO.
OH GOD...
I'VE PREPARED MY WHOLE LIFE FOR THIS MOMENT...
...TO BE READY TO FACE YOU...
...TO REQUEST YOUR BLESSING.

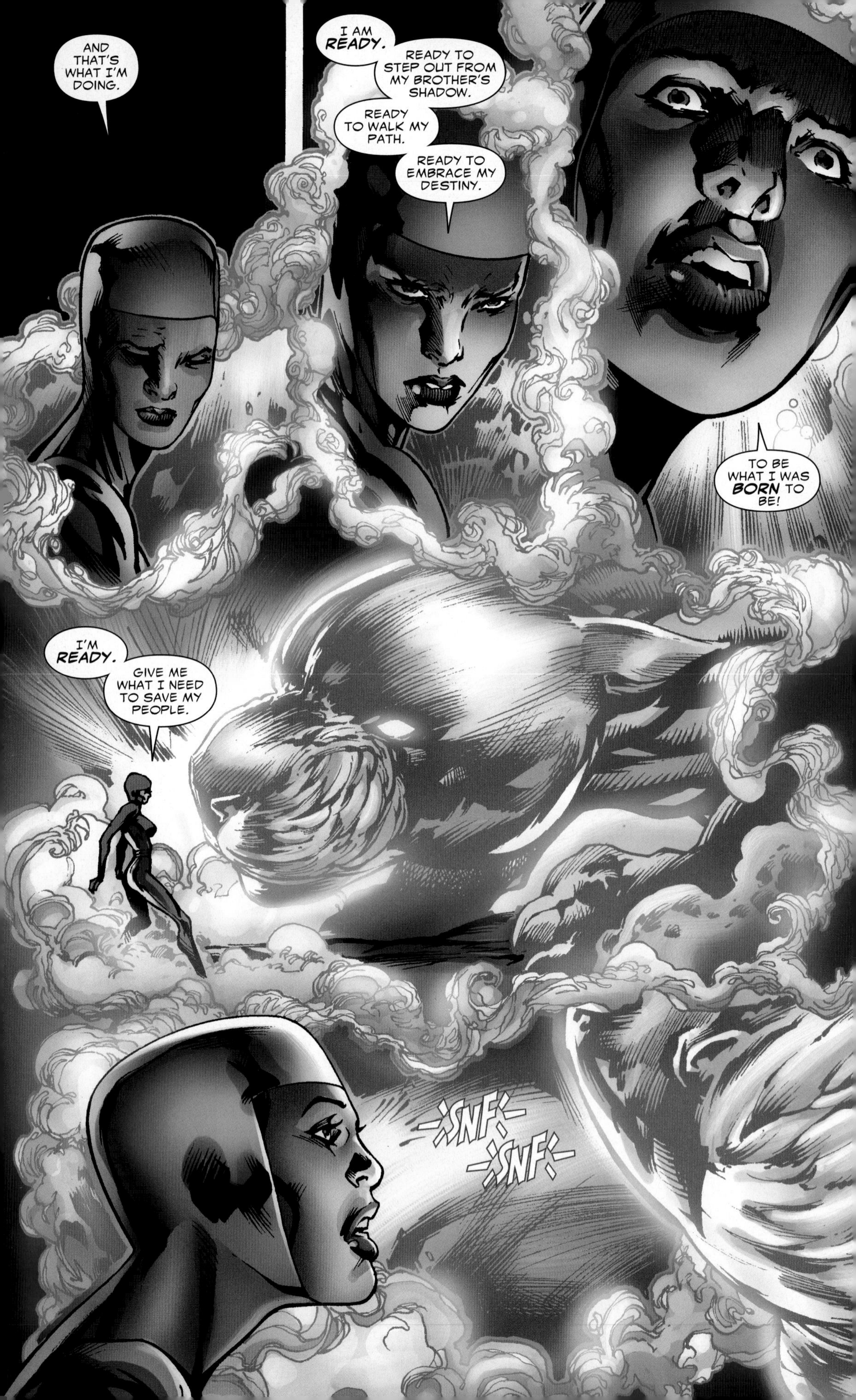
AND THAT'S WHAT I'M DOING.
I AM **READY.**
READY TO STEP OUT FROM MY BROTHER'S SHADOW.
READY TO WALK MY PATH.
READY TO EMBRACE MY DESTINY.
TO BE WHAT I WAS **BORN** TO BE!
I'M **READY.**
GIVE ME WHAT I NEED TO SAVE MY PEOPLE.
SNF
SNF

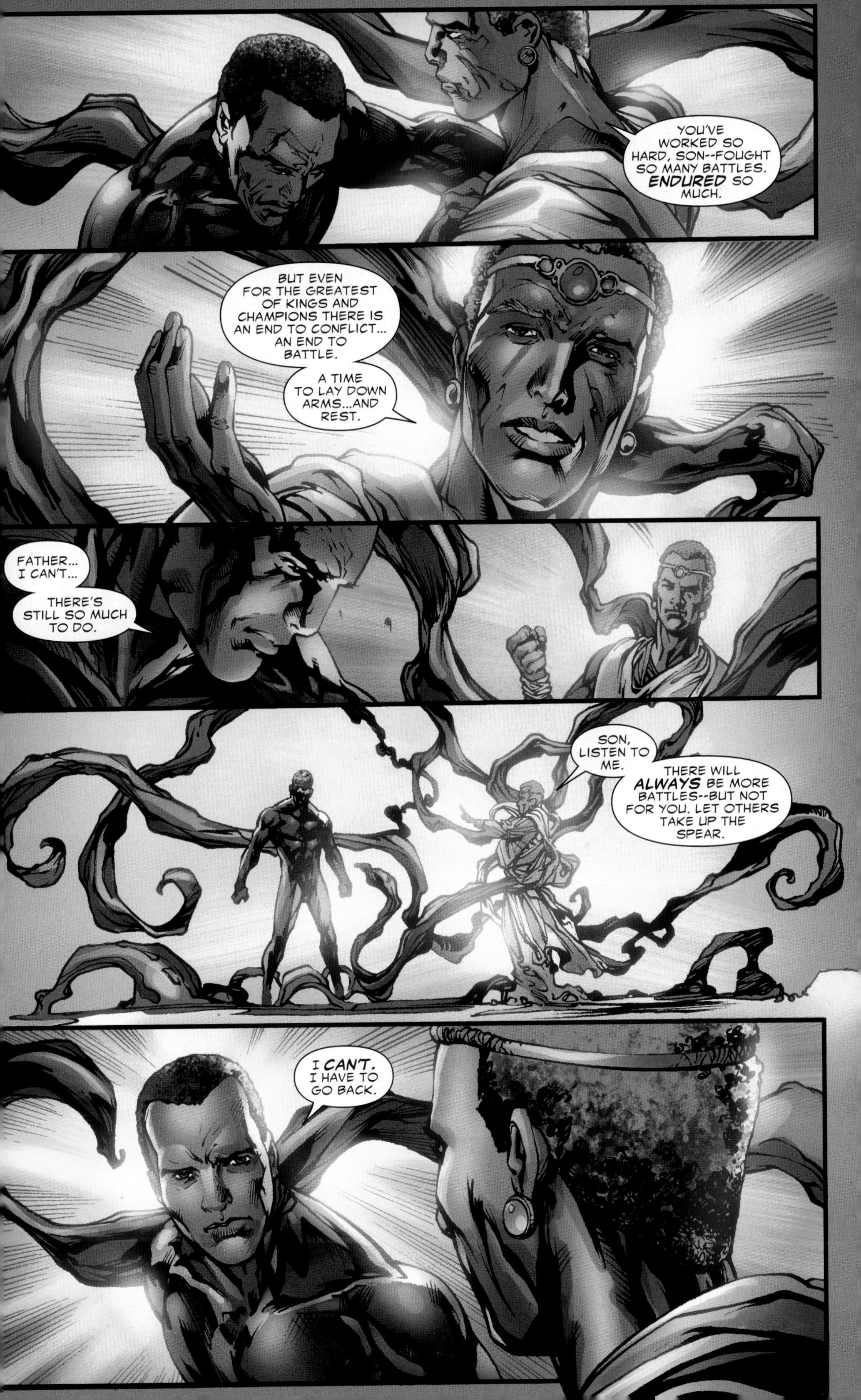
YOU'VE WORKED SO HARD, SON--FOUGHT SO MANY BATTLES. ENDURED SO MUCH.
BUT EVEN FOR THE GREATEST OF KINGS AND CHAMPIONS THERE IS AN END TO CONFLICT... AN END TO BATTLE.
A TIME TO LAY DOWN ARMS...AND REST.
FATHER... I CAN'T...
THERE'S STILL SO MUCH TO DO.
SON, LISTEN TO ME.
THERE WILL ALWAYS BE MORE BATTLES--BUT NOT FOR YOU. LET OTHERS TAKE UP THE SPEAR.
I CAN'T. I HAVE TO GO BACK.

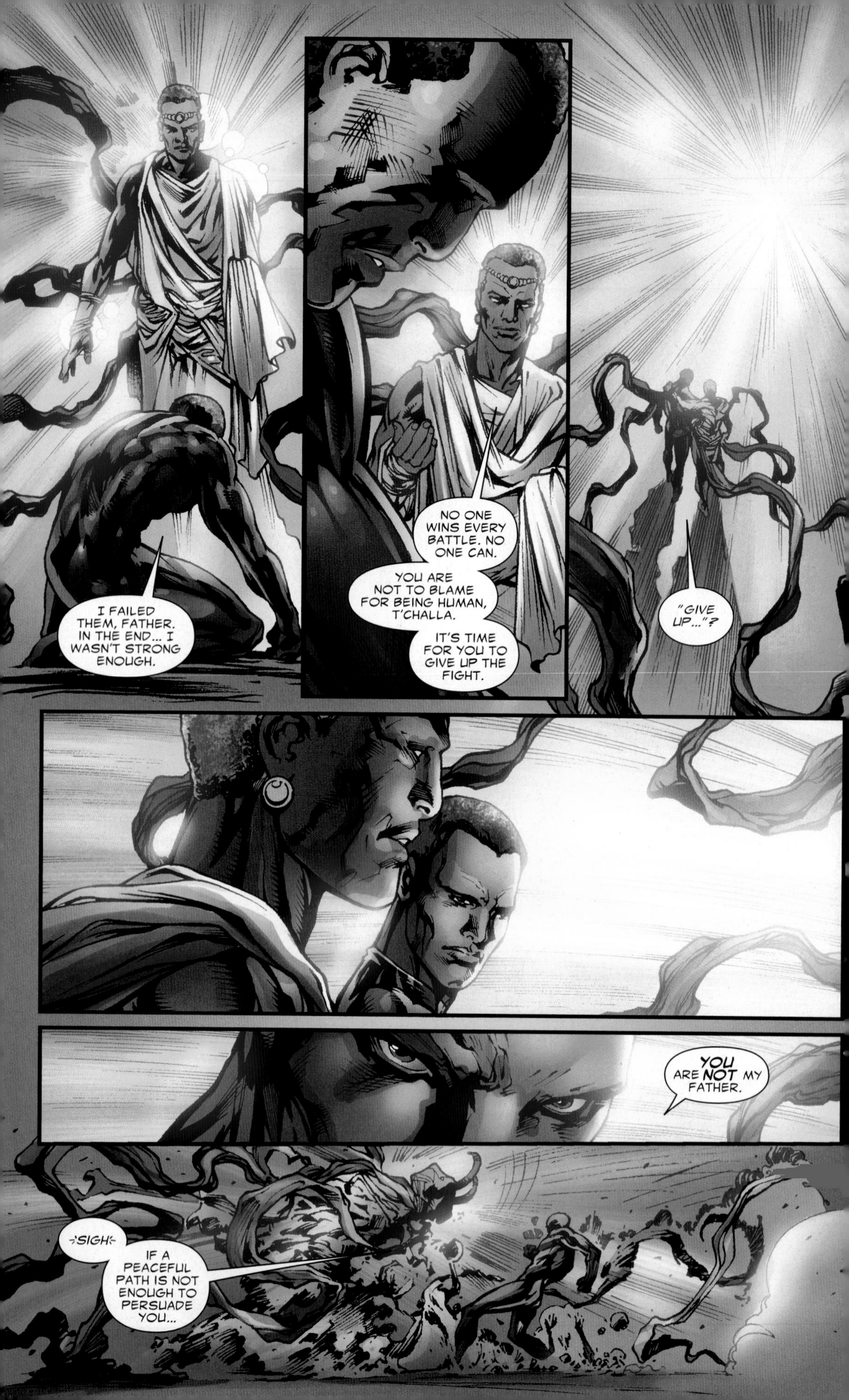
I FAILED THEM, FATHER. IN THE END... I WASN'T STRONG ENOUGH.
NO ONE WINS EVERY BATTLE. NO ONE CAN.
YOU ARE NOT TO BLAME FOR BEING HUMAN, T'CHALLA.
IT'S TIME FOR YOU TO GIVE UP THE FIGHT.
"GIVE UP..."?
YOU ARE NOT MY FATHER.
-SIGH-
IF A PEACEFUL PATH IS NOT ENOUGH TO PERSUADE YOU...

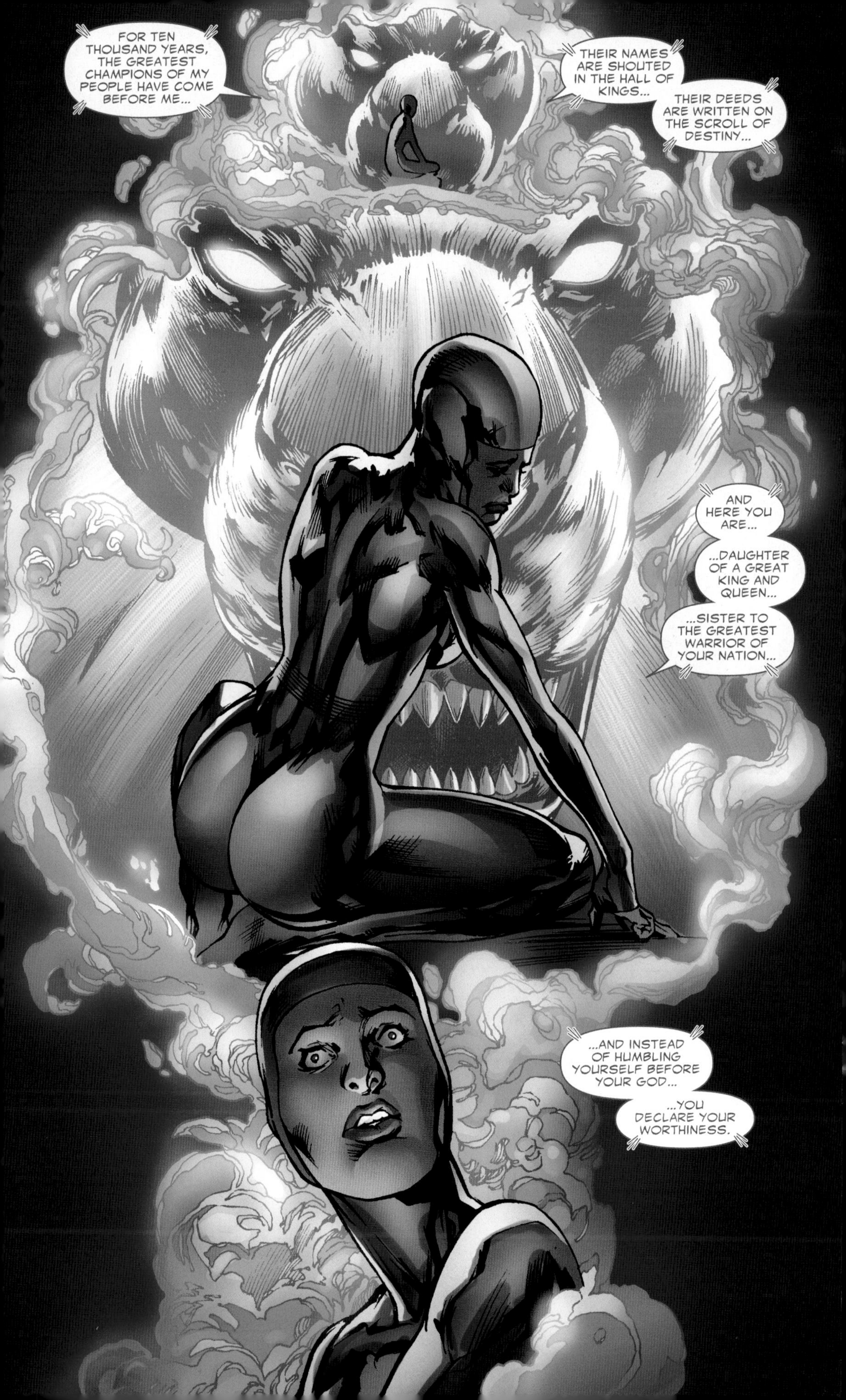
FOR TEN THOUSAND YEARS, THE GREATEST CHAMPIONS OF MY PEOPLE HAVE COME BEFORE ME...
THEIR NAMES ARE SHOUTED IN THE HALL OF KINGS...
THEIR DEEDS ARE WRITTEN ON THE SCROLL OF DESTINY...
AND HERE YOU ARE...
...DAUGHTER OF A GREAT KING AND QUEEN...
...SISTER TO THE GREATEST WARRIOR OF YOUR NATION...
...AND INSTEAD OF HUMBLING YOURSELF BEFORE YOUR GOD...
...YOU DECLARE YOUR WORTHINESS.

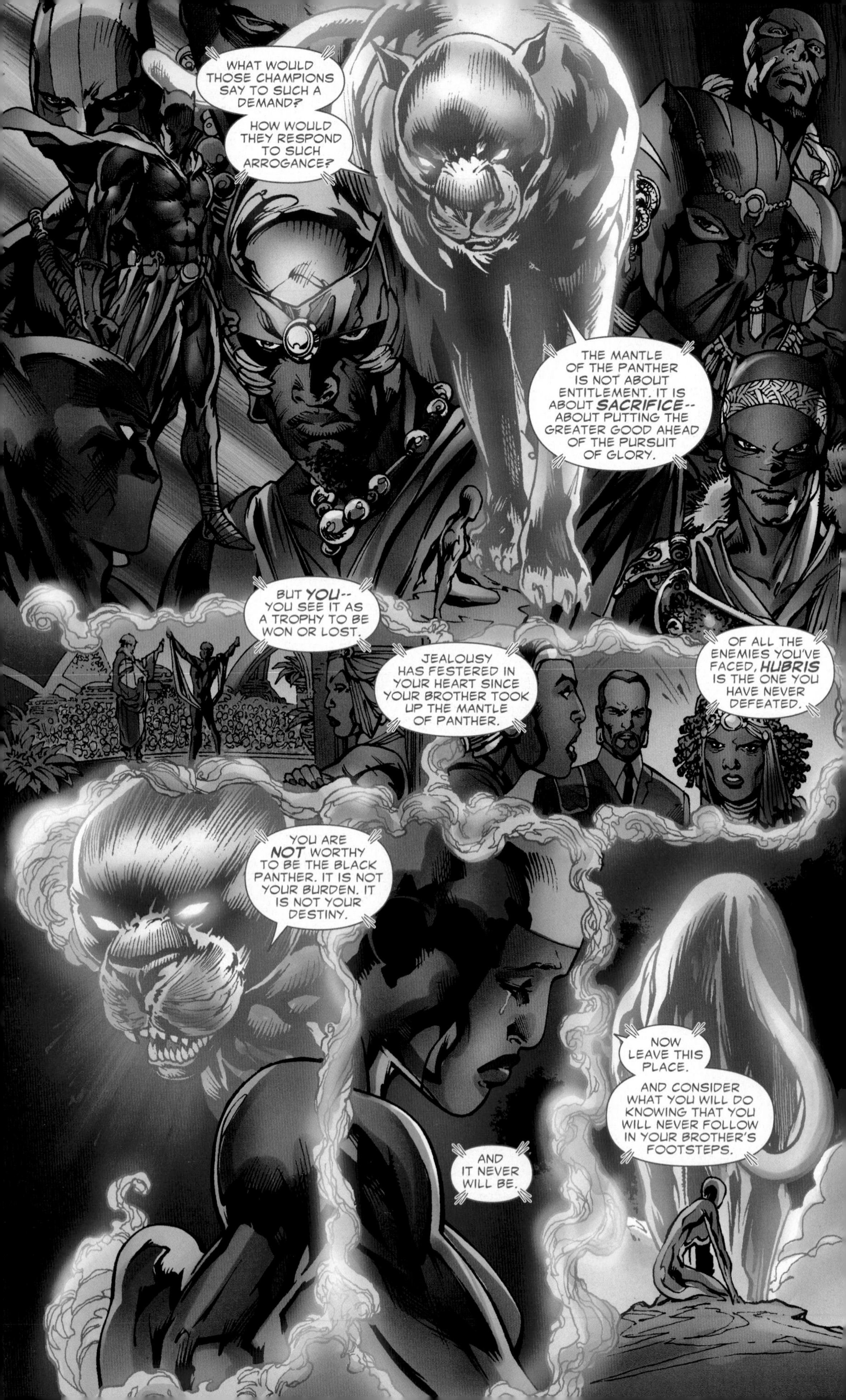
WHAT WOULD THOSE CHAMPIONS SAY TO SUCH A DEMAND?
HOW WOULD THEY RESPOND TO SUCH ARROGANCE?
THE MANTLE OF THE PANTHER IS NOT ABOUT ENTITLEMENT. IT IS ABOUT SACRIFICE-- ABOUT PUTTING THE GREATER GOOD AHEAD OF THE PURSUIT OF GLORY.
BUT YOU-- YOU SEE IT AS A TROPHY TO BE WON OR LOST.
JEALOUSY HAS FESTERED IN YOUR HEART SINCE YOUR BROTHER TOOK UP THE MANTLE OF PANTHER.
OF ALL THE ENEMIES YOU'VE FACED, HUBRIS IS THE ONE YOU HAVE NEVER DEFEATED.
YOU ARE NOT WORTHY TO BE THE BLACK PANTHER. IT IS NOT YOUR BURDEN. IT IS NOT YOUR DESTINY.
AND IT NEVER WILL BE.
NOW LEAVE THIS PLACE.
AND CONSIDER WHAT YOU WILL DO KNOWING THAT YOU WILL NEVER FOLLOW IN YOUR BROTHER'S FOOTSTEPS.

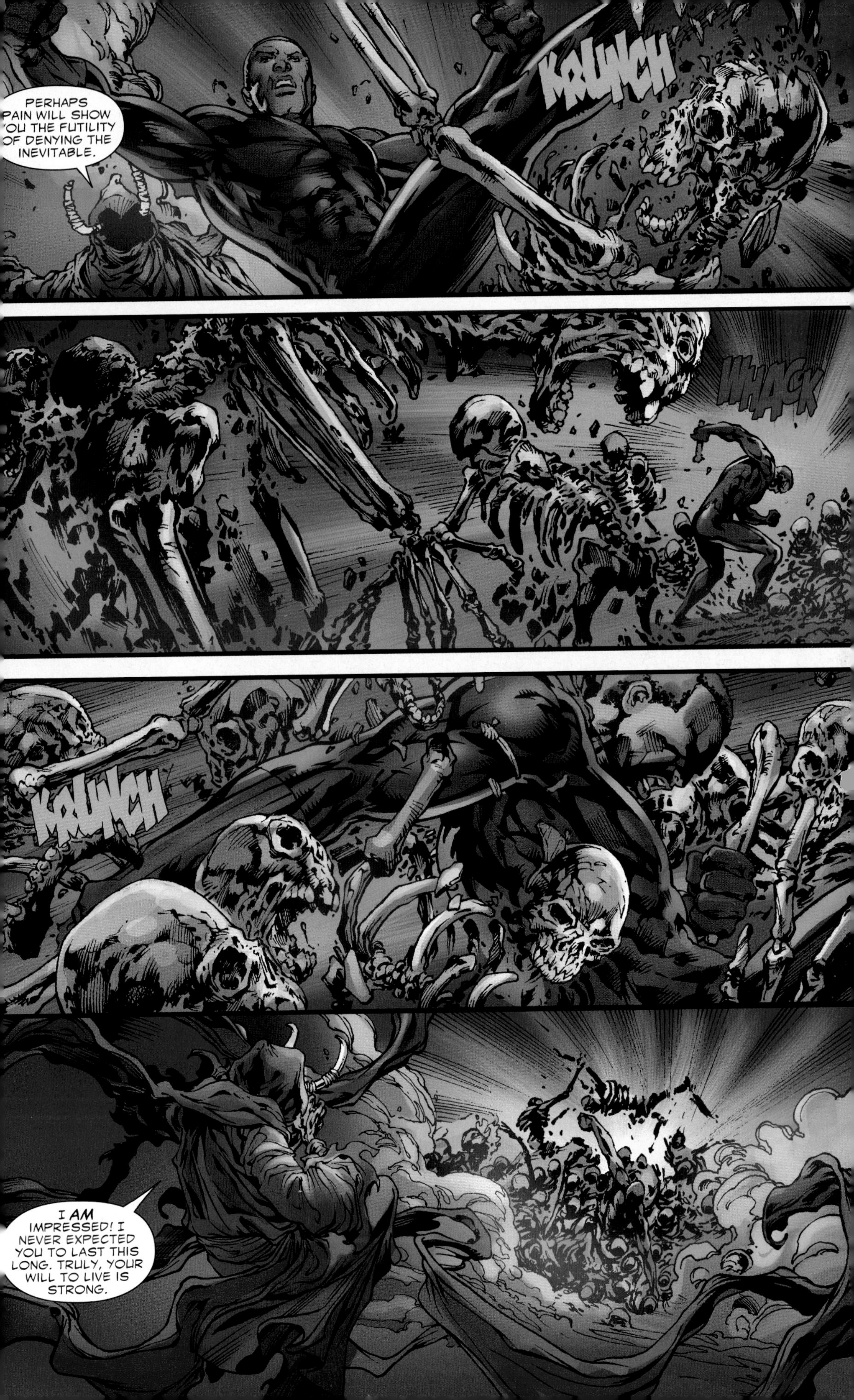
PERHAPS PAIN WILL SHOW YOU THE FUTILITY OF DENYING THE INEVITABLE.
KRUNCH
WHACK
KRUNCH
I AM IMPRESSED! I NEVER EXPECTED YOU TO LAST THIS LONG. TRULY, YOUR WILL TO LIVE IS STRONG.

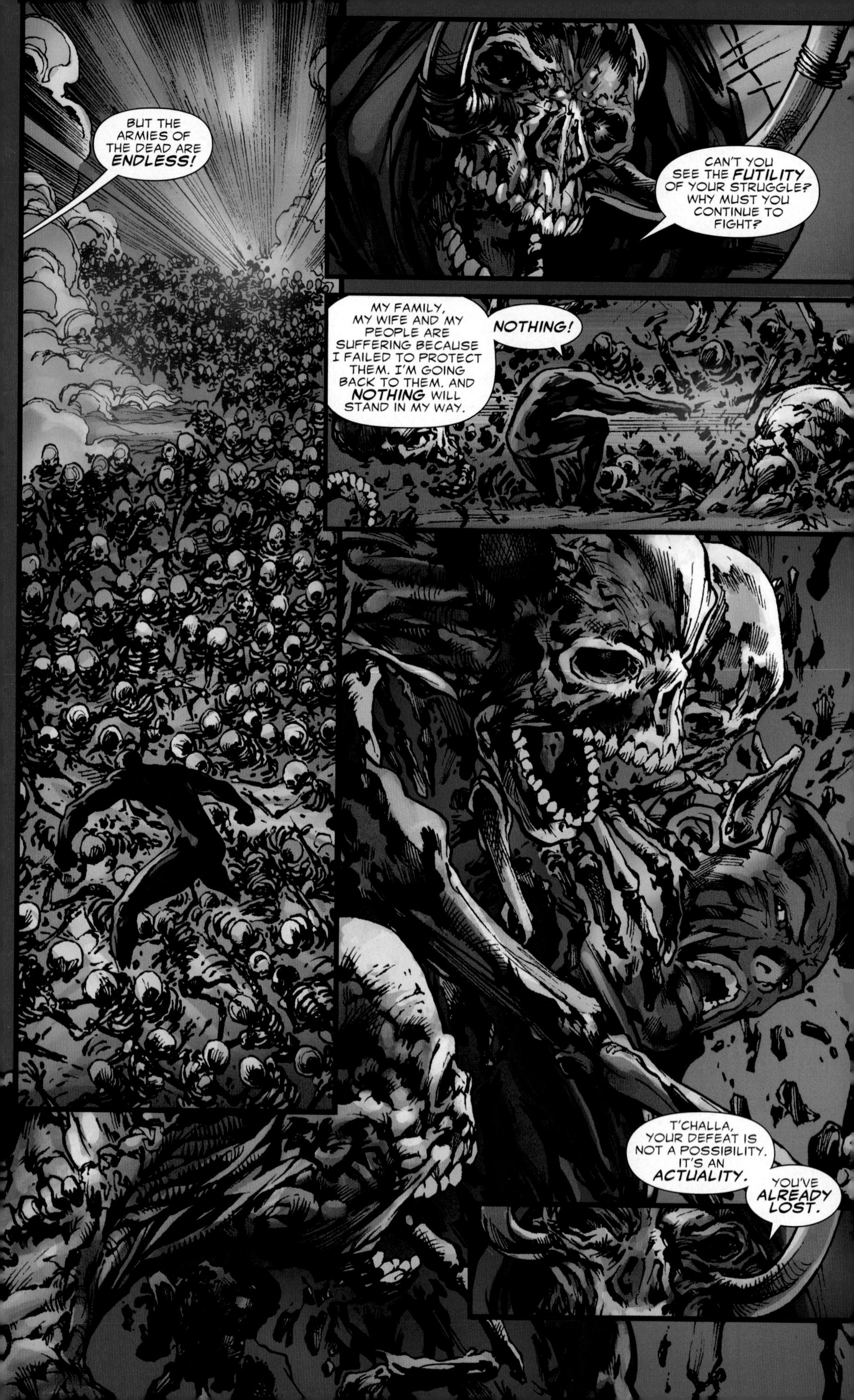
BUT THE ARMIES OF THE DEAD ARE ENDLESS!
CAN'T YOU SEE THE FUTILITY OF YOUR STRUGGLE? WHY MUST YOU CONTINUE TO FIGHT?
MY FAMILY, MY WIFE AND MY PEOPLE ARE SUFFERING BECAUSE I FAILED TO PROTECT THEM. I'M GOING BACK TO THEM. AND NOTHING WILL STAND IN MY WAY.
NOTHING!
T'CHALLA, YOUR DEFEAT IS NOT A POSSIBILITY. IT'S AN ACTUALITY.
YOU'VE ALREADY LOST.

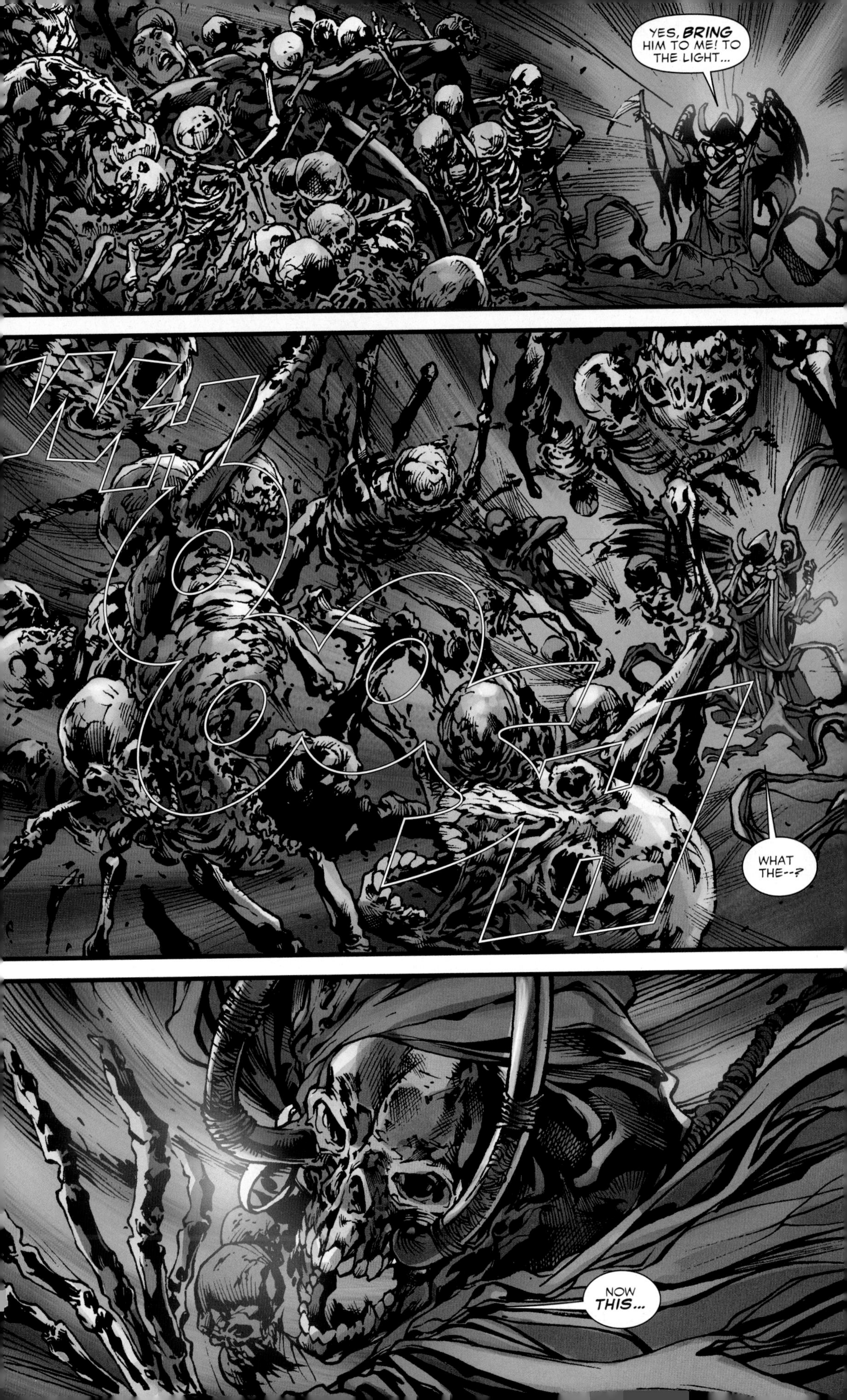
YES, BRING HIM TO ME! TO THE LIGHT...
WHAT THE--?
NOW THIS...

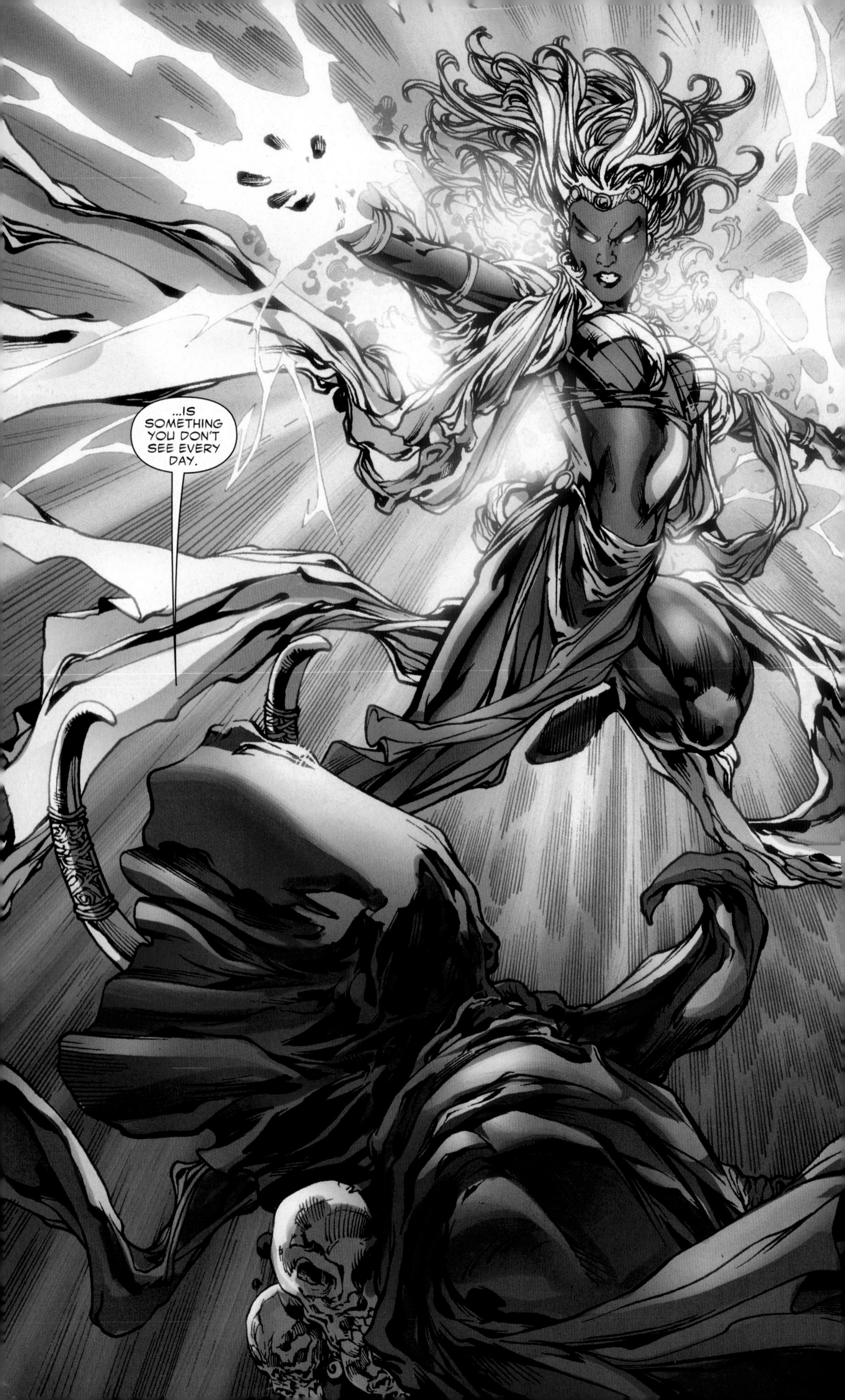
...IS SOMETHING YOU DON'T SEE EVERY DAY.

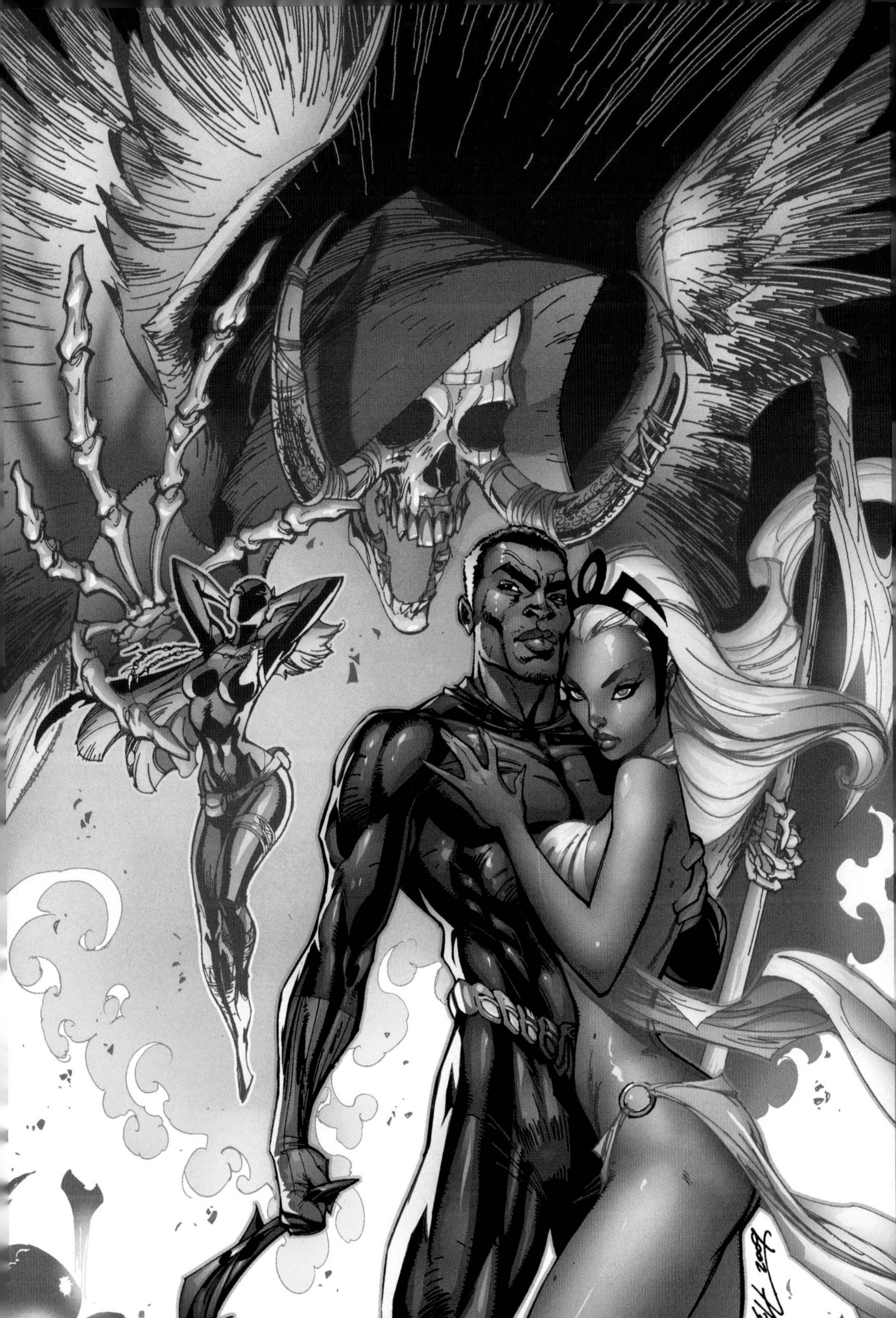
delgado

CK PANTH

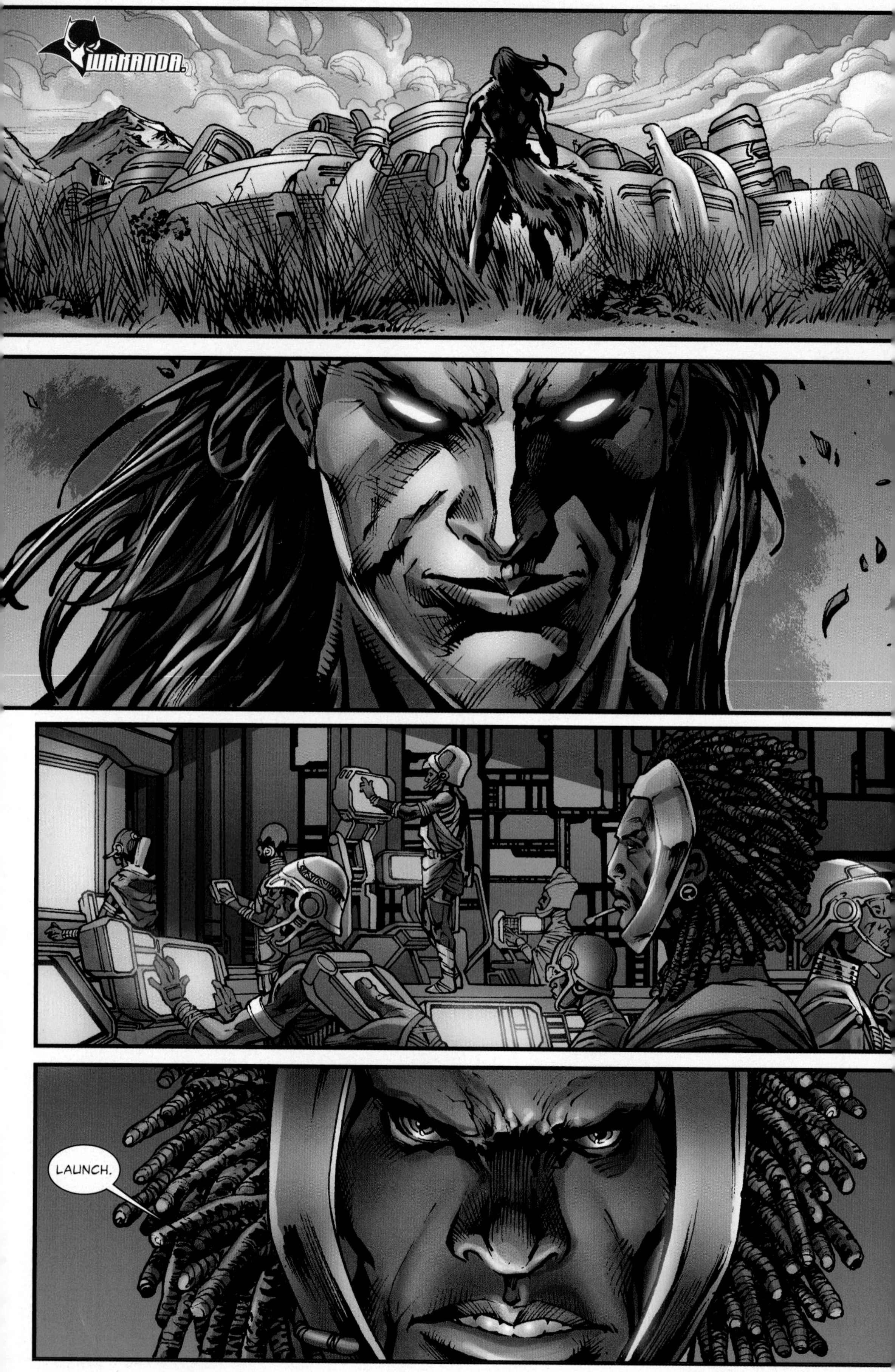
WAKANDA.
LAUNCH.

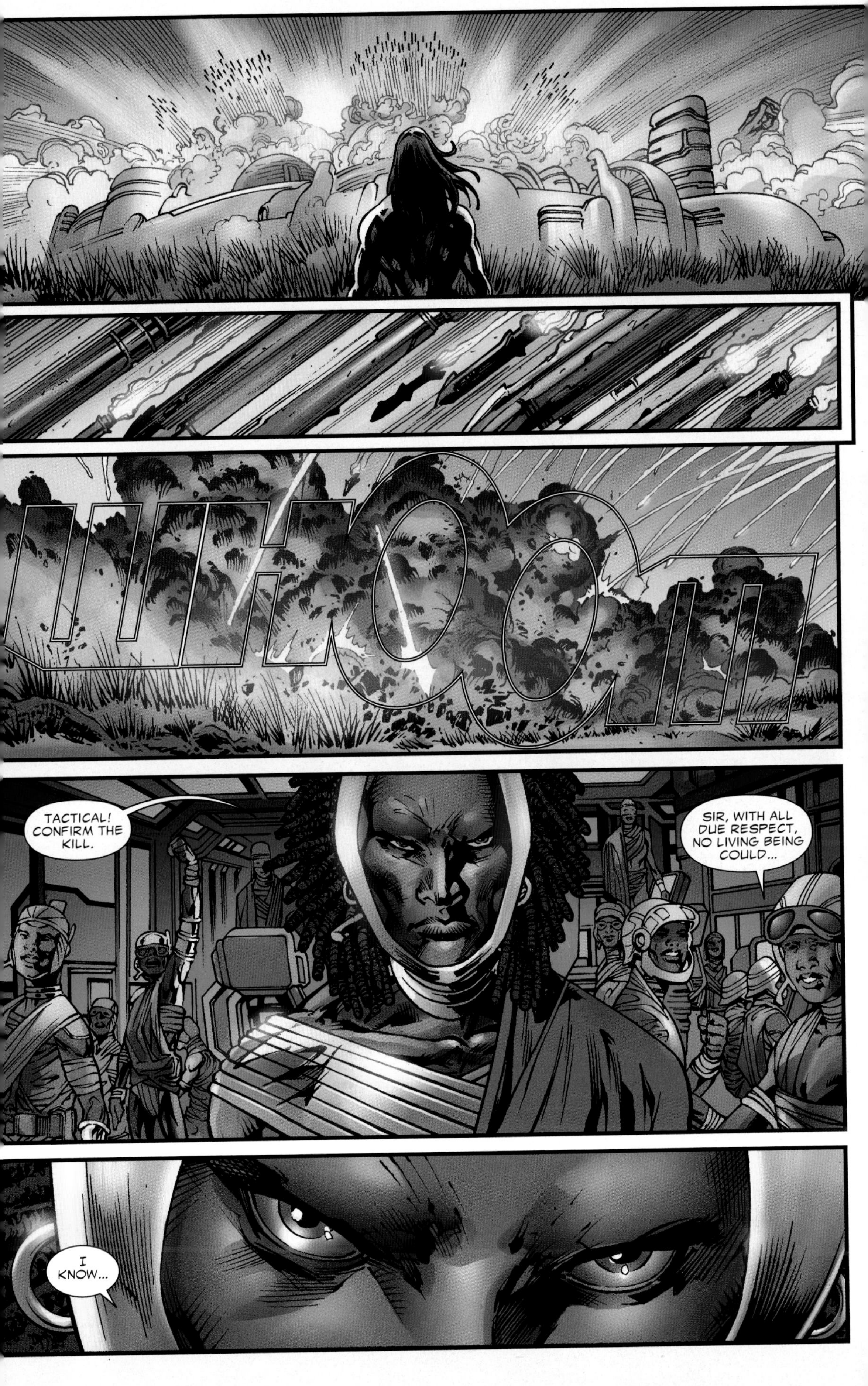
WHOOM
TACTICAL! CONFIRM THE KILL.
SIR, WITH ALL DUE RESPECT, NO LIVING BEING COULD...
I KNOW...

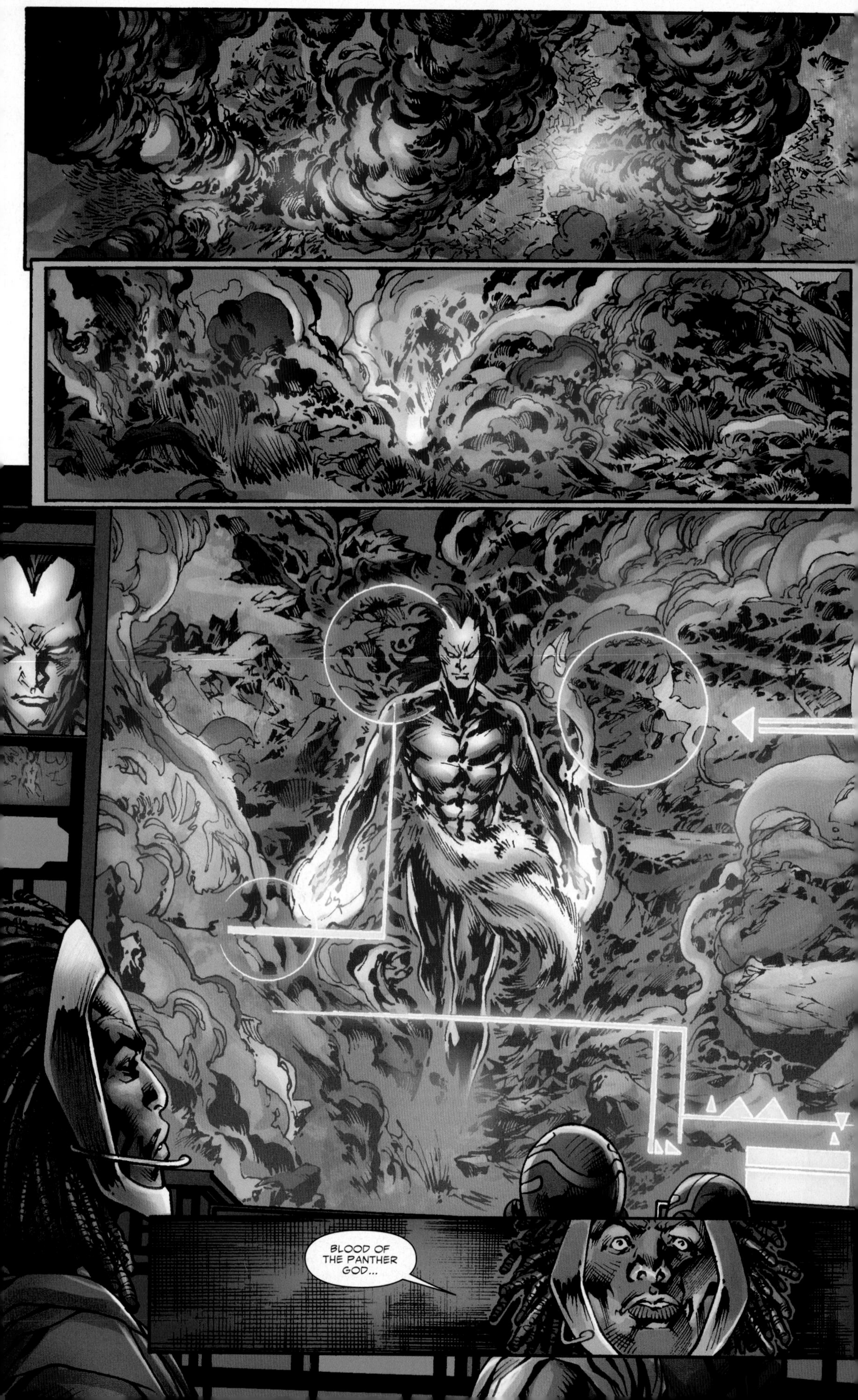
BLOOD OF THE PANTHER GOD...

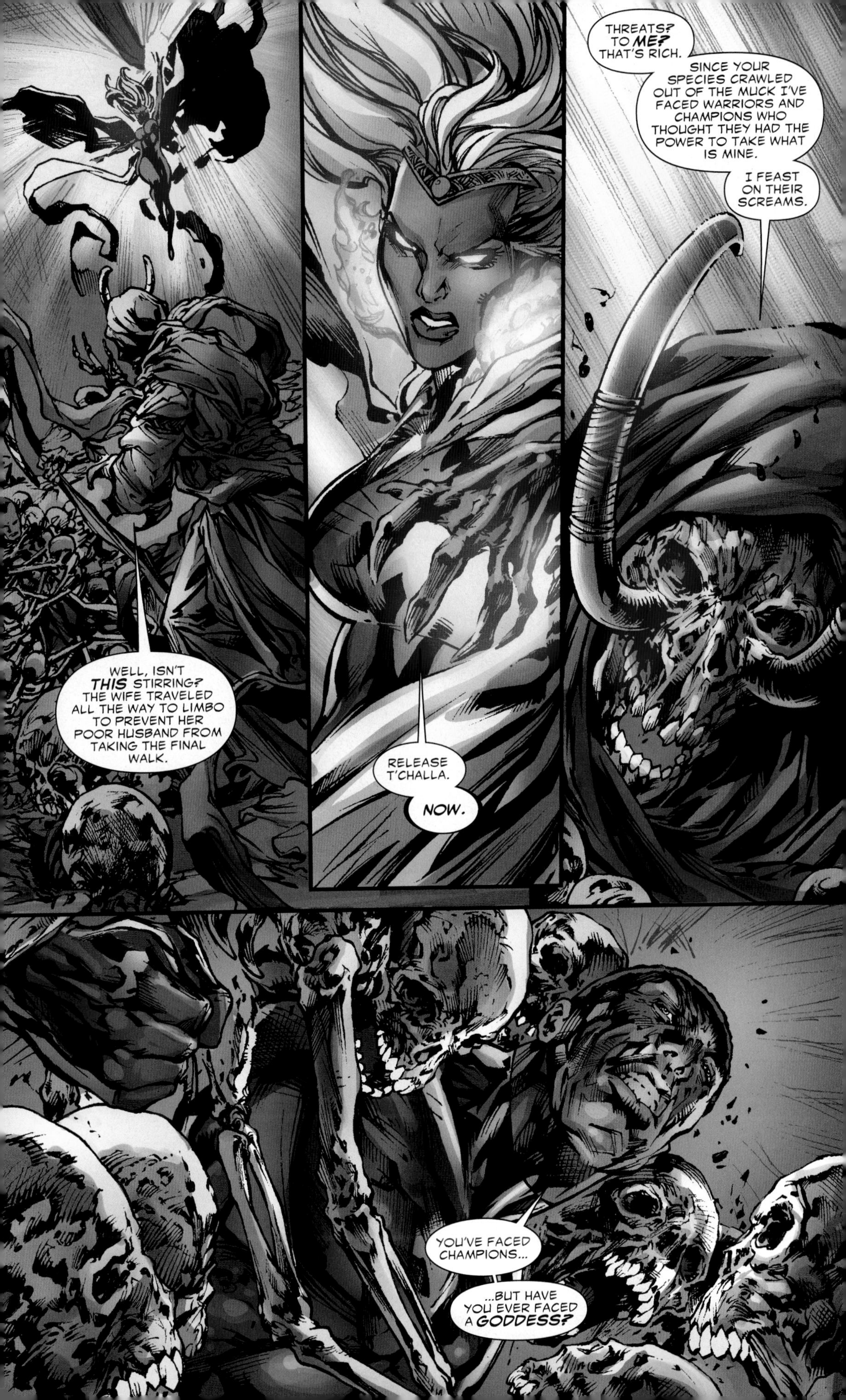
WELL, ISN'T THIS STIRRING? THE WIFE TRAVELED ALL THE WAY TO LIMBO TO PREVENT HER POOR HUSBAND FROM TAKING THE FINAL WALK.
RELEASE T'CHALLA.
NOW.
THREATS? TO ME? THAT'S RICH.
SINCE YOUR SPECIES CRAWLED OUT OF THE MUCK I'VE FACED WARRIORS AND CHAMPIONS WHO THOUGHT THEY HAD THE POWER TO TAKE WHAT IS MINE.
I FEAST ON THEIR SCREAMS.
YOU'VE FACED CHAMPIONS...
...BUT HAVE YOU EVER FACED A GODDESS?

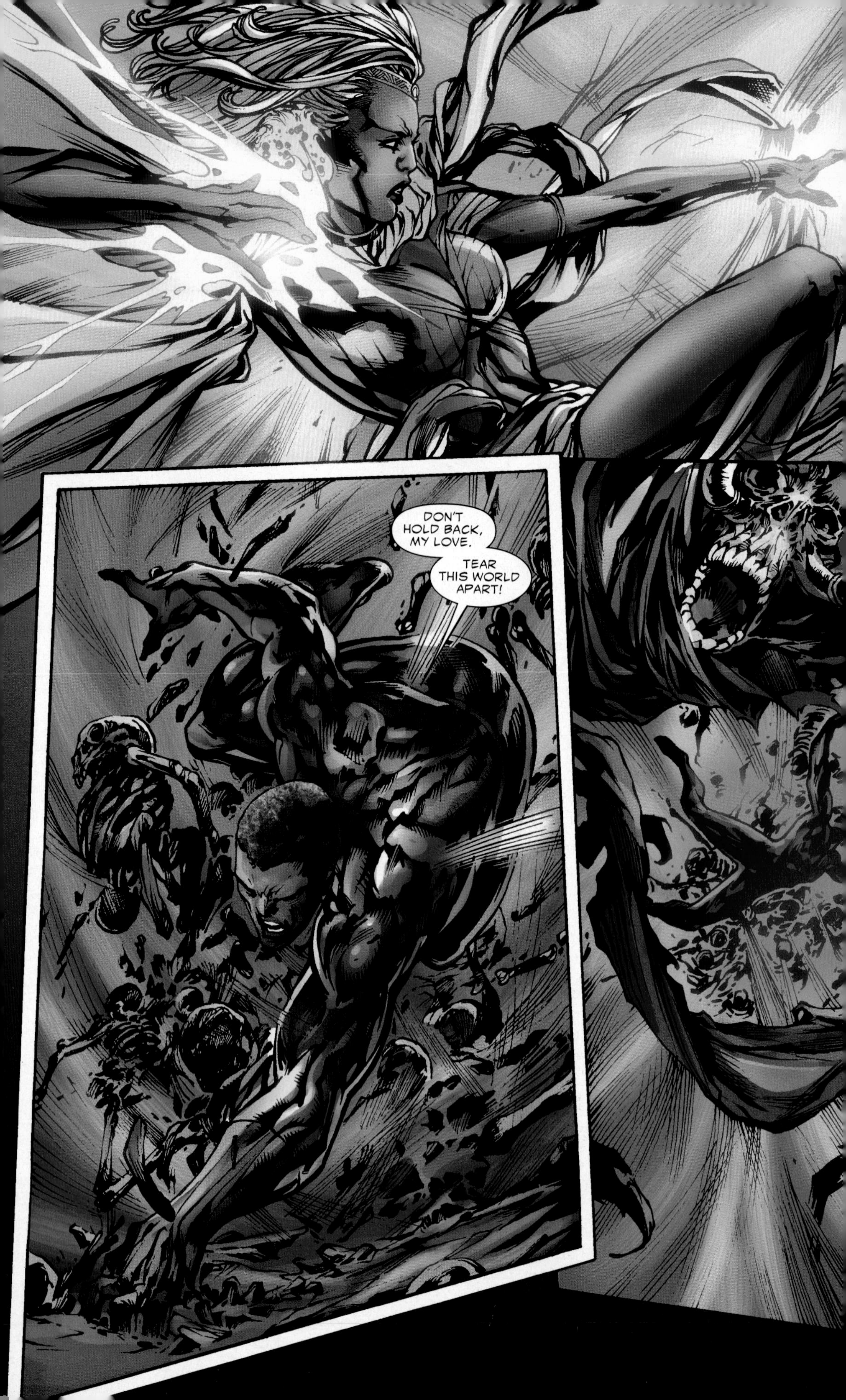
DON'T HOLD BACK, MY LOVE.
TEAR THIS WORLD APART!

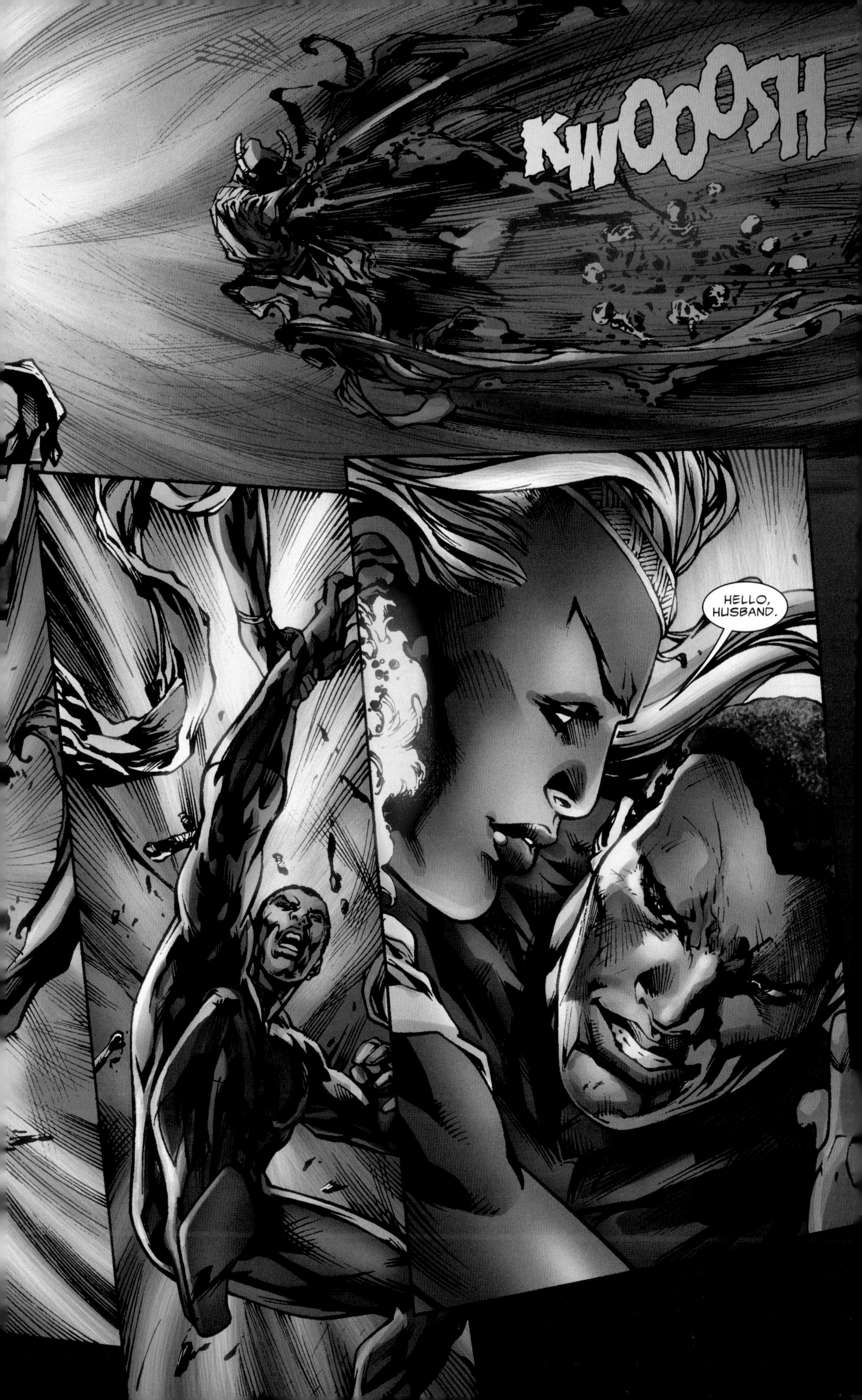
KWOOOSH
HELLO, HUSBAND.

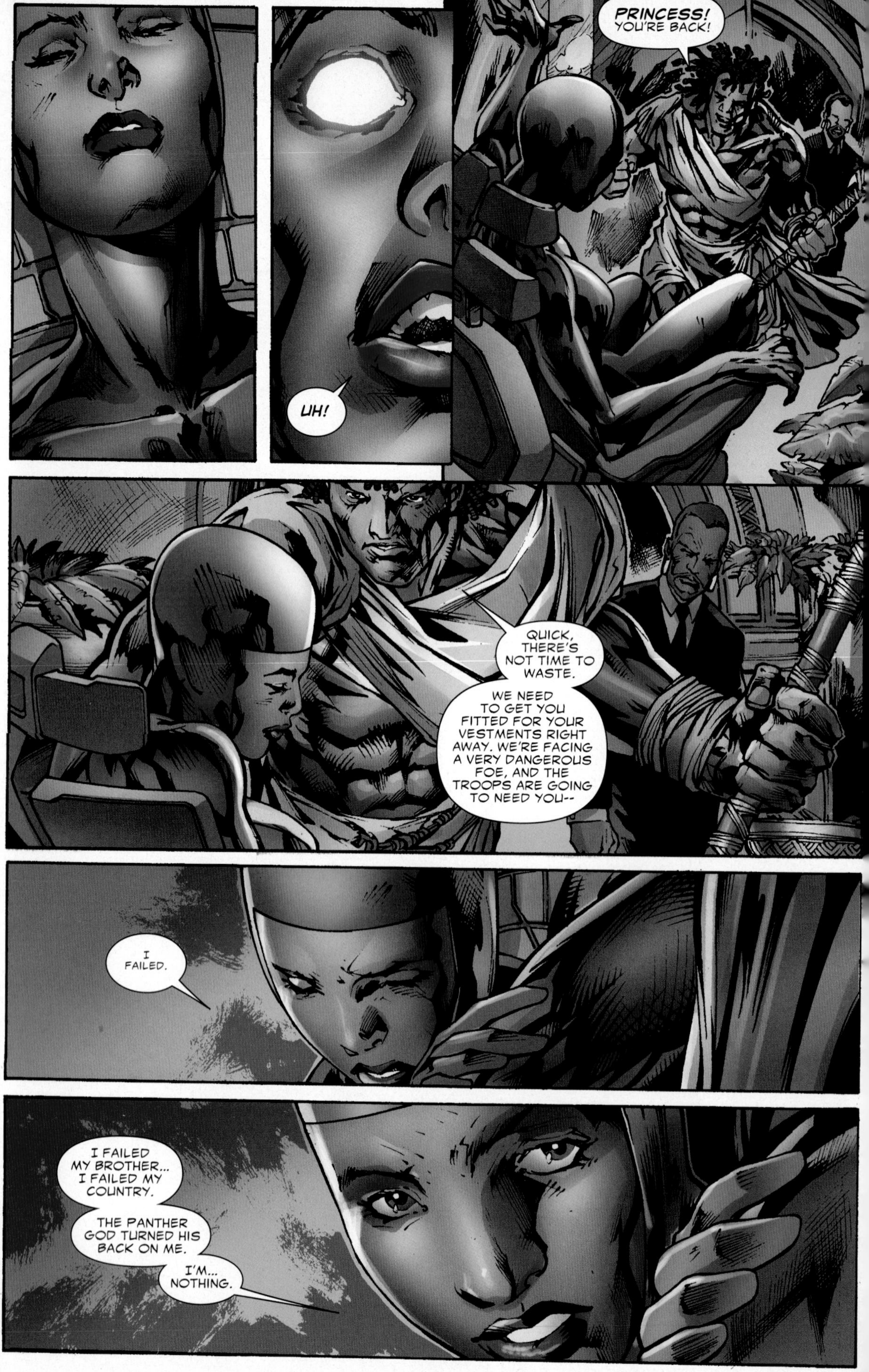
UH!
PRINCESS! YOU'RE BACK!
QUICK, THERE'S NOT TIME TO WASTE.
WE NEED TO GET YOU FITTED FOR YOUR VESTMENTS RIGHT AWAY. WE'RE FACING A VERY DANGEROUS FOE, AND THE TROOPS ARE GOING TO NEED YOU--
I FAILED.
I FAILED MY BROTHER... I FAILED MY COUNTRY.
THE PANTHER GOD TURNED HIS BACK ON ME.
I'M... NOTHING.

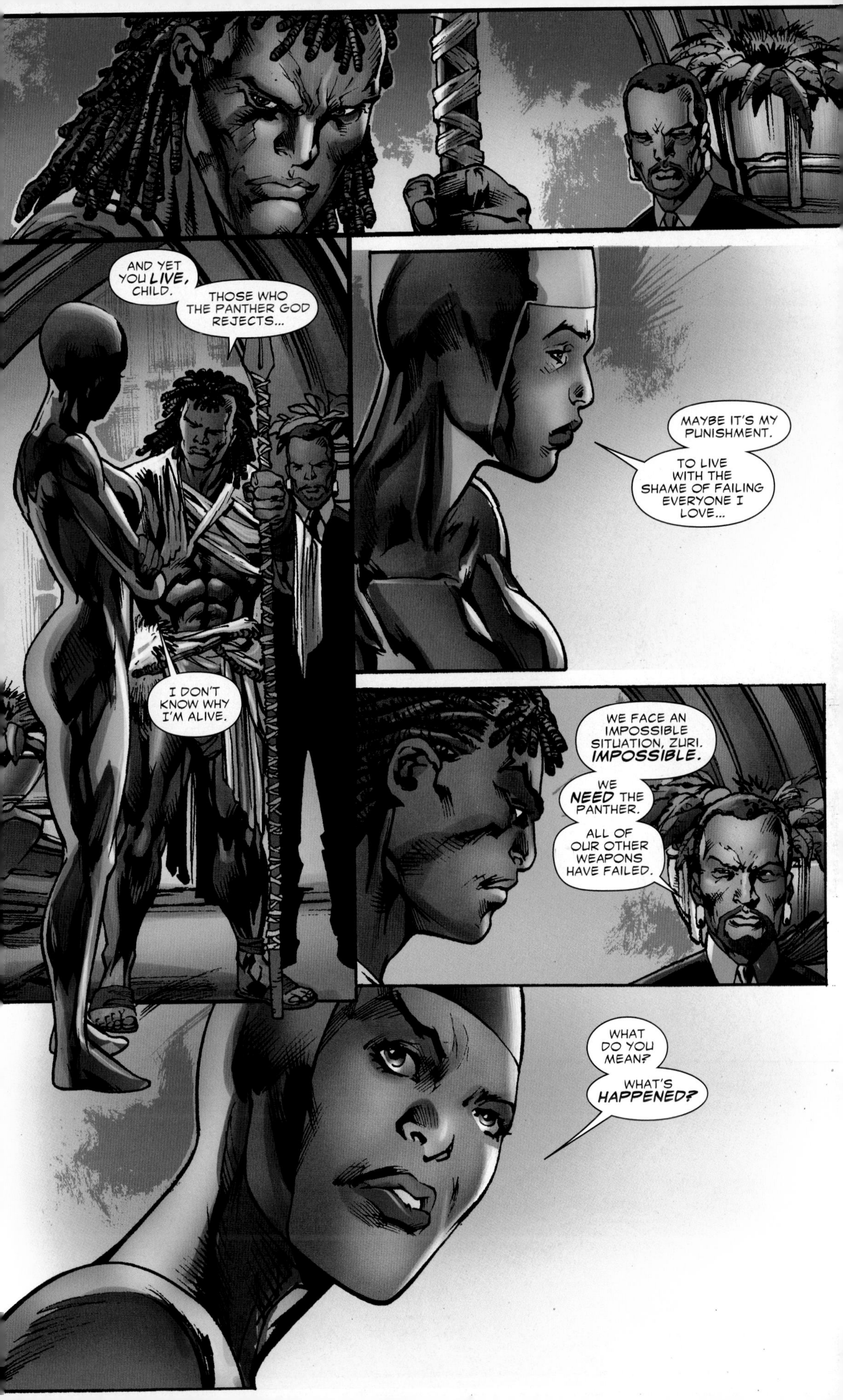
AND YET YOU LIVE, CHILD.
THOSE WHO THE PANTHER GOD REJECTS...
I DON'T KNOW WHY I'M ALIVE.
MAYBE IT'S MY PUNISHMENT.
TO LIVE WITH THE SHAME OF FAILING EVERYONE I LOVE...
WE FACE AN IMPOSSIBLE SITUATION, ZURI. IMPOSSIBLE.
WE NEED THE PANTHER.
ALL OF OUR OTHER WEAPONS HAVE FAILED.
WHAT DO YOU MEAN?
WHAT'S HAPPENED?

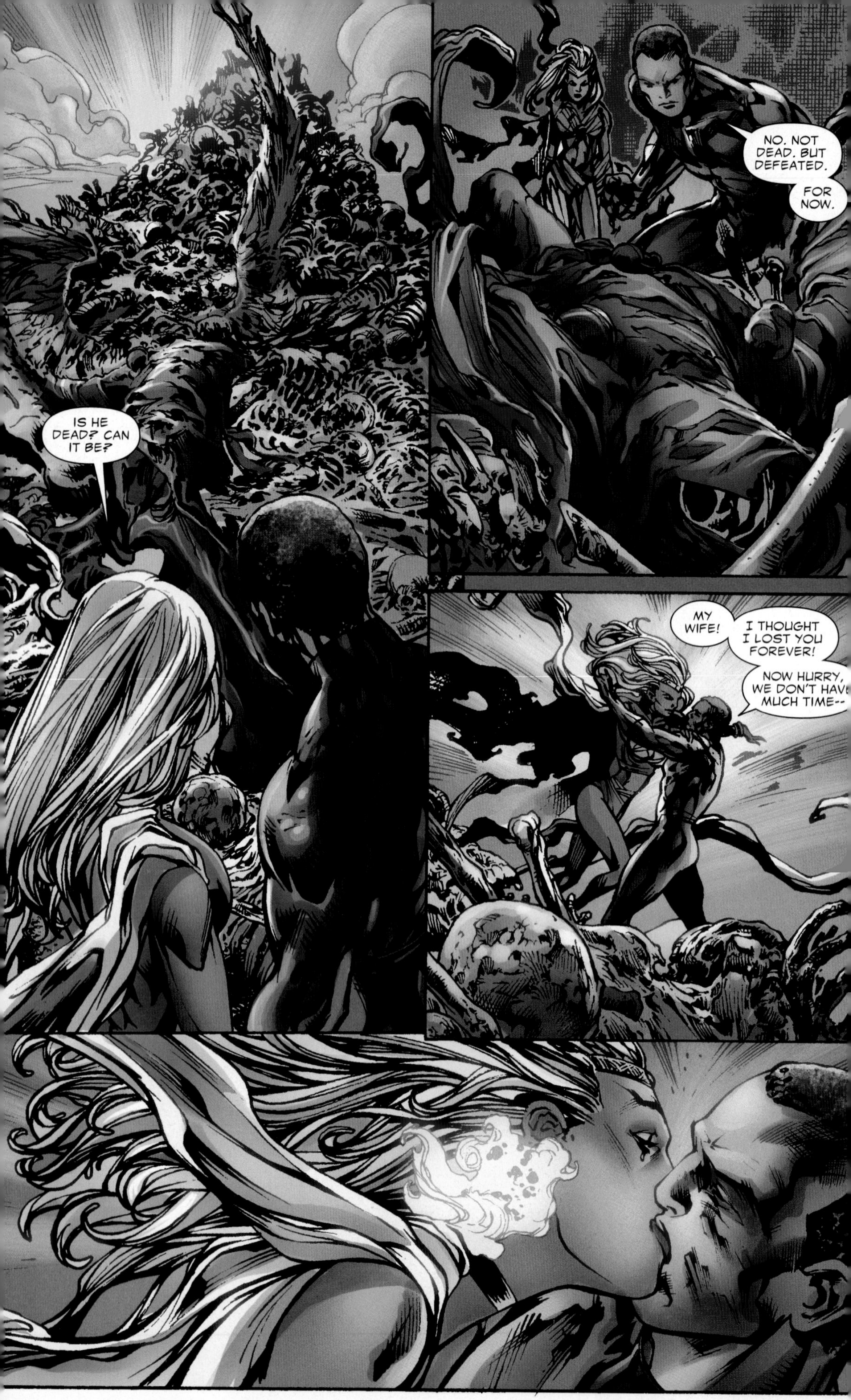
IS HE DEAD? CAN IT BE?
NO. NOT DEAD. BUT DEFEATED.
FOR NOW.
MY WIFE!
I THOUGHT I LOST YOU FOREVER!
NOW HURRY, WE DON'T HAV MUCH TIME--

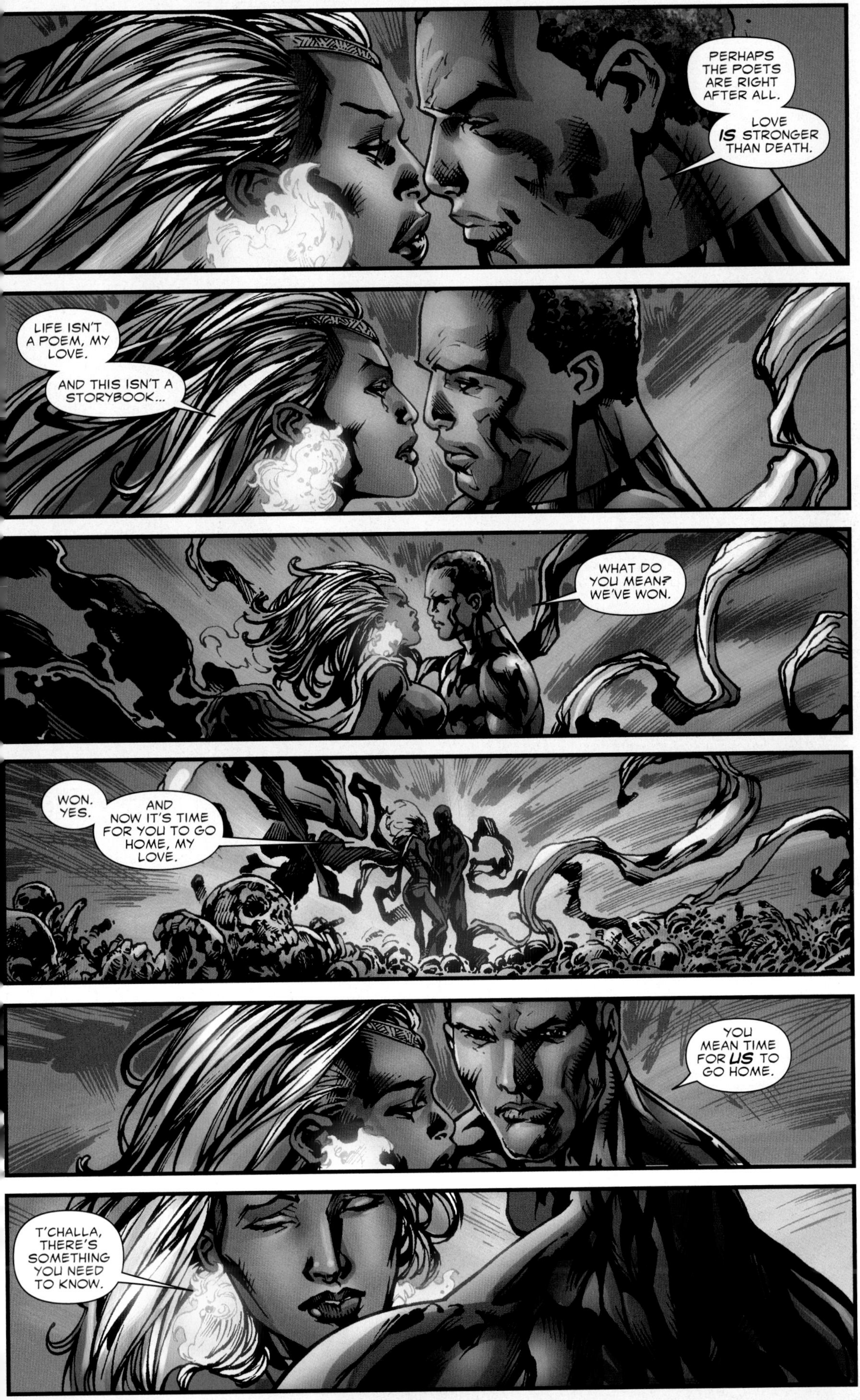
PERHAPS THE POETS ARE RIGHT AFTER ALL.
LOVE IS STRONGER THAN DEATH.
LIFE ISN'T A POEM, MY LOVE.
AND THIS ISN'T A STORYBOOK...
WHAT DO YOU MEAN? WE'VE WON.
WON. YES.
AND NOW IT'S TIME FOR YOU TO GO HOME, MY LOVE.
YOU MEAN TIME FOR US TO GO HOME.
T'CHALLA, THERE'S SOMETHING YOU NEED TO KNOW.

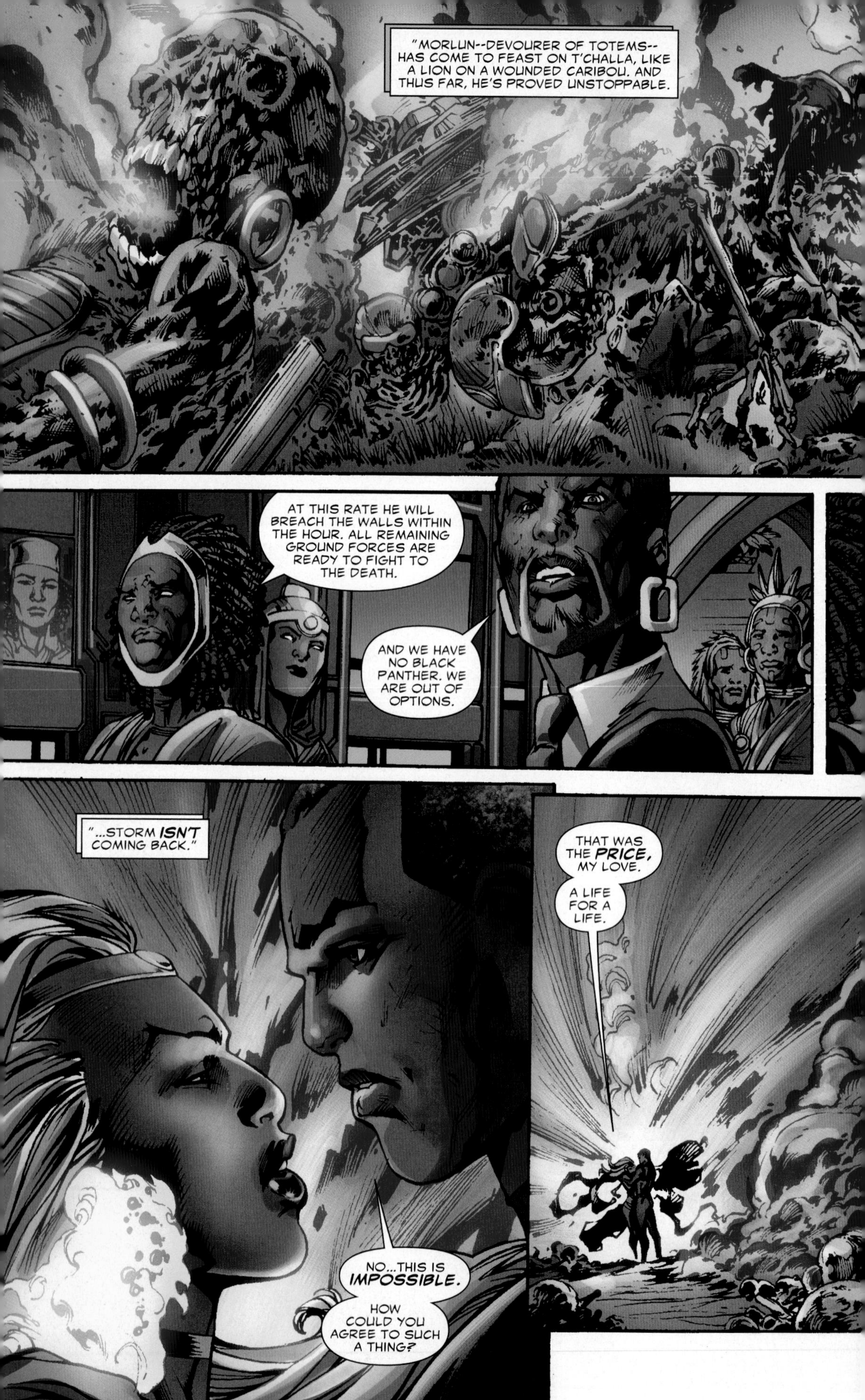
"MORLUN--DEVOURER OF TOTEMS--
HAS COME TO FEAST ON T'CHALLA, LIKE
A LION ON A WOUNDED CARIBOU. AND
THUS FAR, HE'S PROVED UNSTOPPABLE.
AT THIS RATE HE WILL BREACH THE WALLS WITHIN THE HOUR. ALL REMAINING GROUND FORCES ARE READY TO FIGHT TO THE DEATH.
AND WE HAVE NO BLACK PANTHER. WE ARE OUT OF OPTIONS.
"...STORM ISN'T COMING BACK."
NO...THIS IS IMPOSSIBLE.
HOW COULD YOU AGREE TO SUCH A THING?
THAT WAS THE PRICE, MY LOVE.
A LIFE FOR A LIFE.

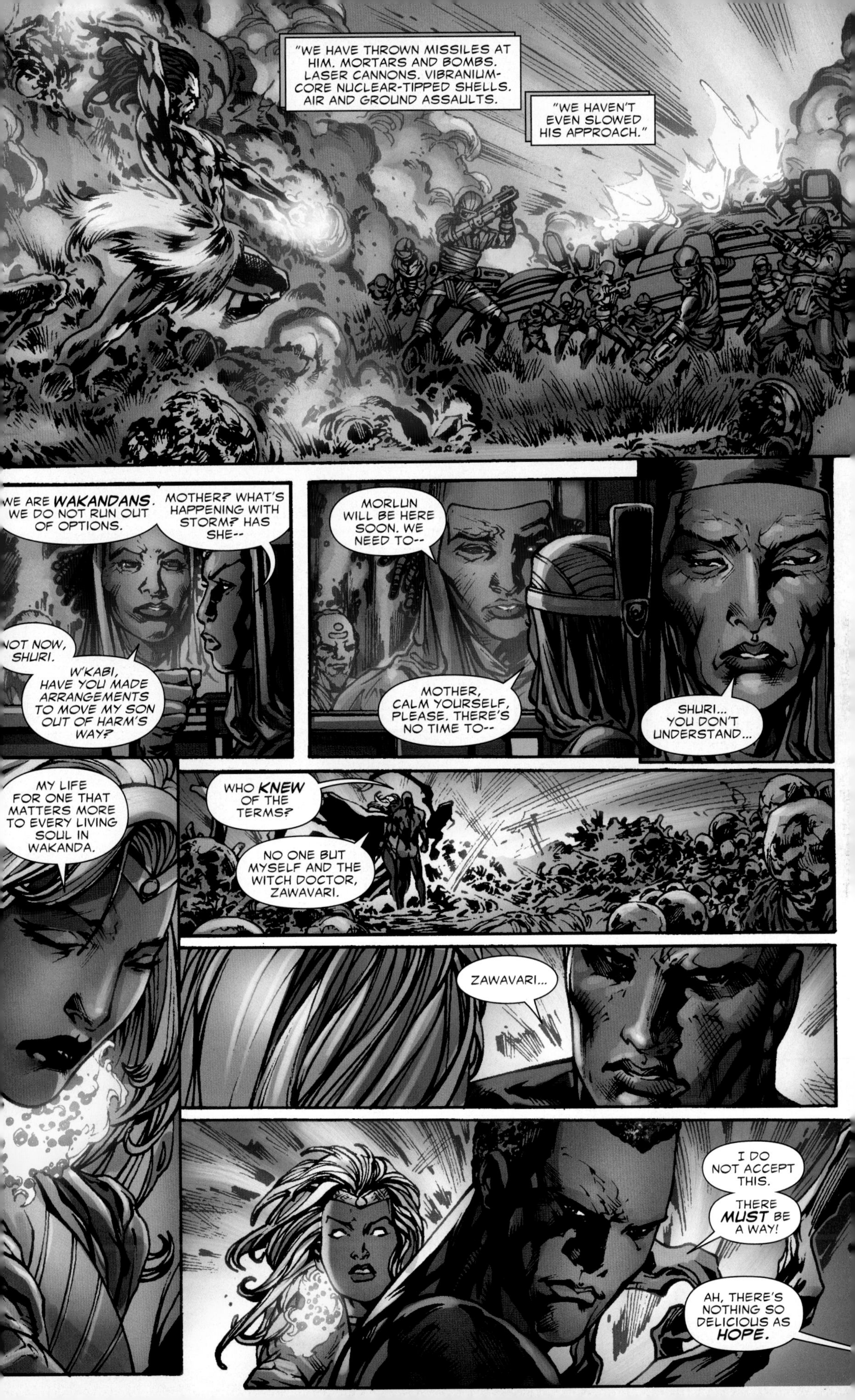

"WE HAVE THROWN MISSILES AT HIM. MORTARS AND BOMBS. LASER CANNONS. VIBRANIUM-CORE NUCLEAR-TIPPED SHELLS. AIR AND GROUND ASSAULTS.
"WE HAVEN'T EVEN SLOWED HIS APPROACH."
WE ARE WAKANDANS. WE DO NOT RUN OUT OF OPTIONS.
MOTHER? WHAT'S HAPPENING WITH STORM? HAS SHE--
NOT NOW, SHURI.
W'KABI, HAVE YOU MADE ARRANGEMENTS TO MOVE MY SON OUT OF HARM'S WAY?
MORLUN WILL BE HERE SOON. WE NEED TO--
MOTHER, CALM YOURSELF, PLEASE. THERE'S NO TIME TO--
SHURI... YOU DON'T UNDERSTAND...
MY LIFE FOR ONE THAT MATTERS MORE TO EVERY LIVING SOUL IN WAKANDA.
WHO KNEW OF THE TERMS?
NO ONE BUT MYSELF AND THE WITCH DOCTOR, ZAWAVARI.
ZAWAVARI...
I DO NOT ACCEPT THIS.
THERE MUST BE A WAY!
AH, THERE'S NOTHING SO DELICIOUS AS HOPE.

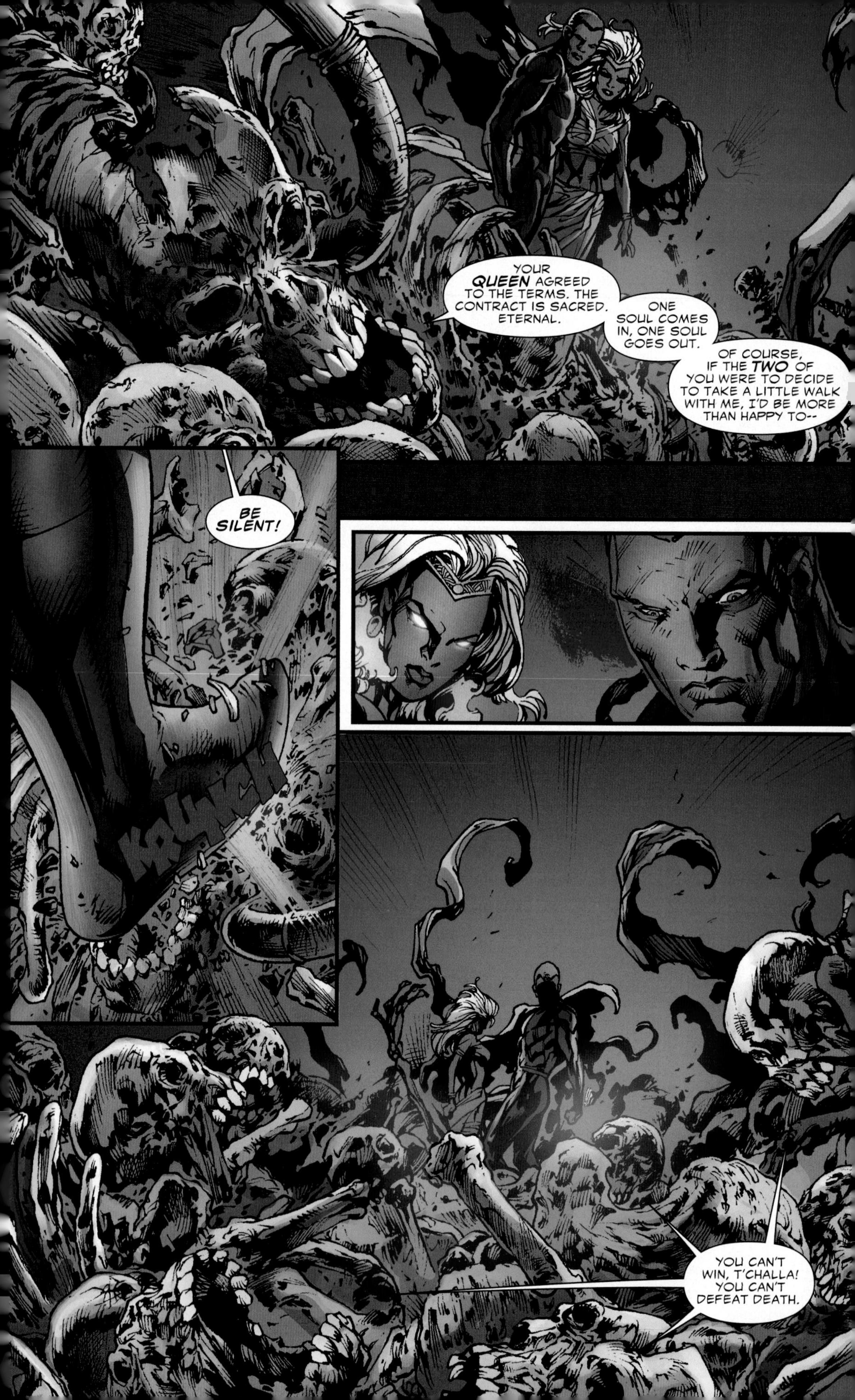
YOUR QUEEN AGREED TO THE TERMS. THE CONTRACT IS SACRED. ETERNAL.
ONE SOUL COMES IN, ONE SOUL GOES OUT.
OF COURSE, IF THE TWO OF YOU WERE TO DECIDE TO TAKE A LITTLE WALK WITH ME, I'D BE MORE THAN HAPPY TO--
BE SILENT!
YOU CAN'T WIN, T'CHALLA! YOU CAN'T DEFEAT DEATH.

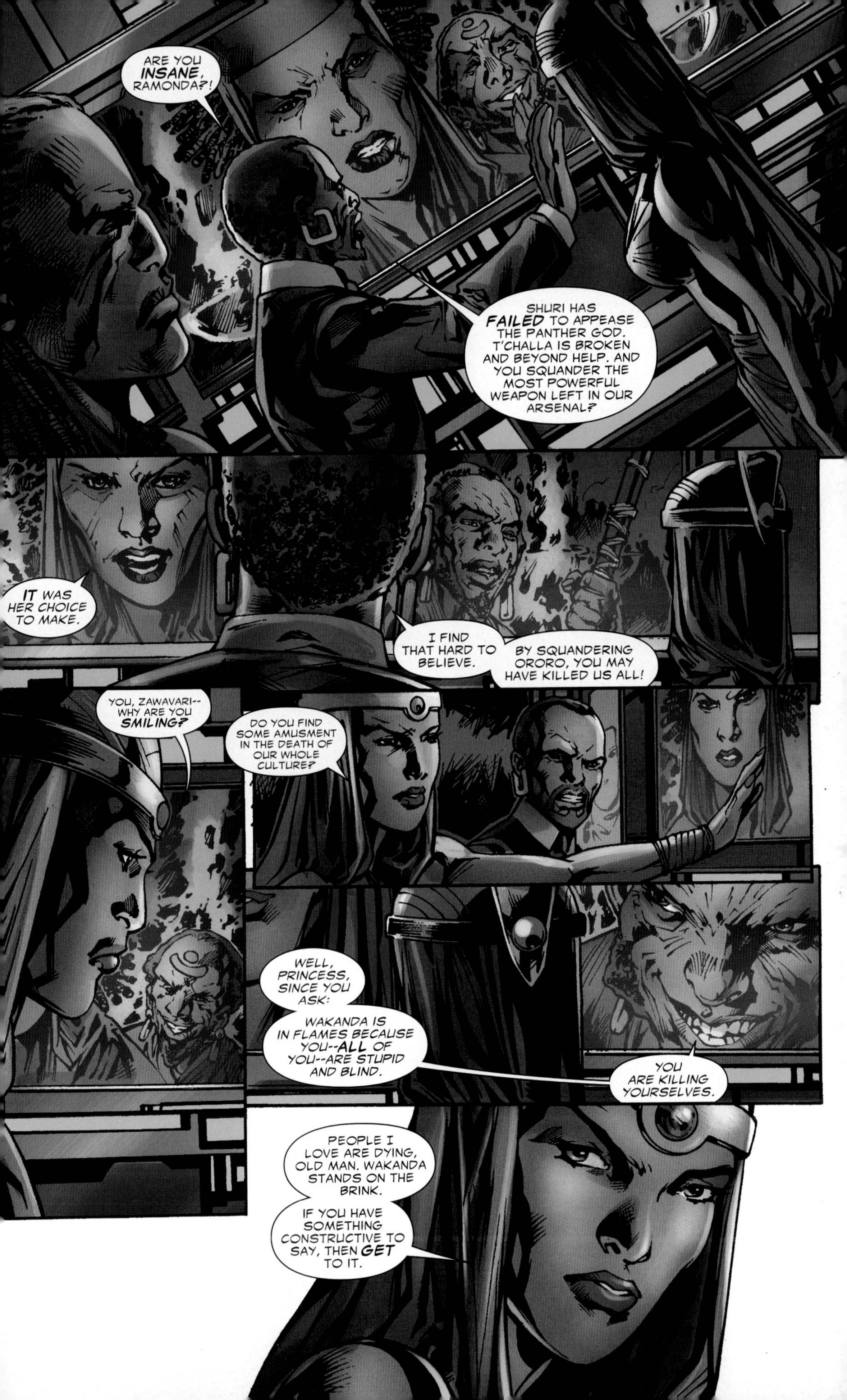
ARE YOU INSANE, RAMONDA?!
SHURI HAS FAILED TO APPEASE THE PANTHER GOD. T'CHALLA IS BROKEN AND BEYOND HELP. AND YOU SQUANDER THE MOST POWERFUL WEAPON LEFT IN OUR ARSENAL?
IT WAS HER CHOICE TO MAKE.
I FIND THAT HARD TO BELIEVE.
BY SQUANDERING ORORO, YOU MAY HAVE KILLED US ALL!
YOU, ZAWAVARI-- WHY ARE YOU SMILING?
DO YOU FIND SOME AMUSMENT IN THE DEATH OF OUR WHOLE CULTURE?
WELL, PRINCESS, SINCE YOU ASK:
WAKANDA IS IN FLAMES BECAUSE YOU--ALL OF YOU--ARE STUPID AND BLIND.
YOU ARE KILLING YOURSELVES.
PEOPLE I LOVE ARE DYING, OLD MAN. WAKANDA STANDS ON THE BRINK.
IF YOU HAVE SOMETHING CONSTRUCTIVE TO SAY, THEN GET TO IT.

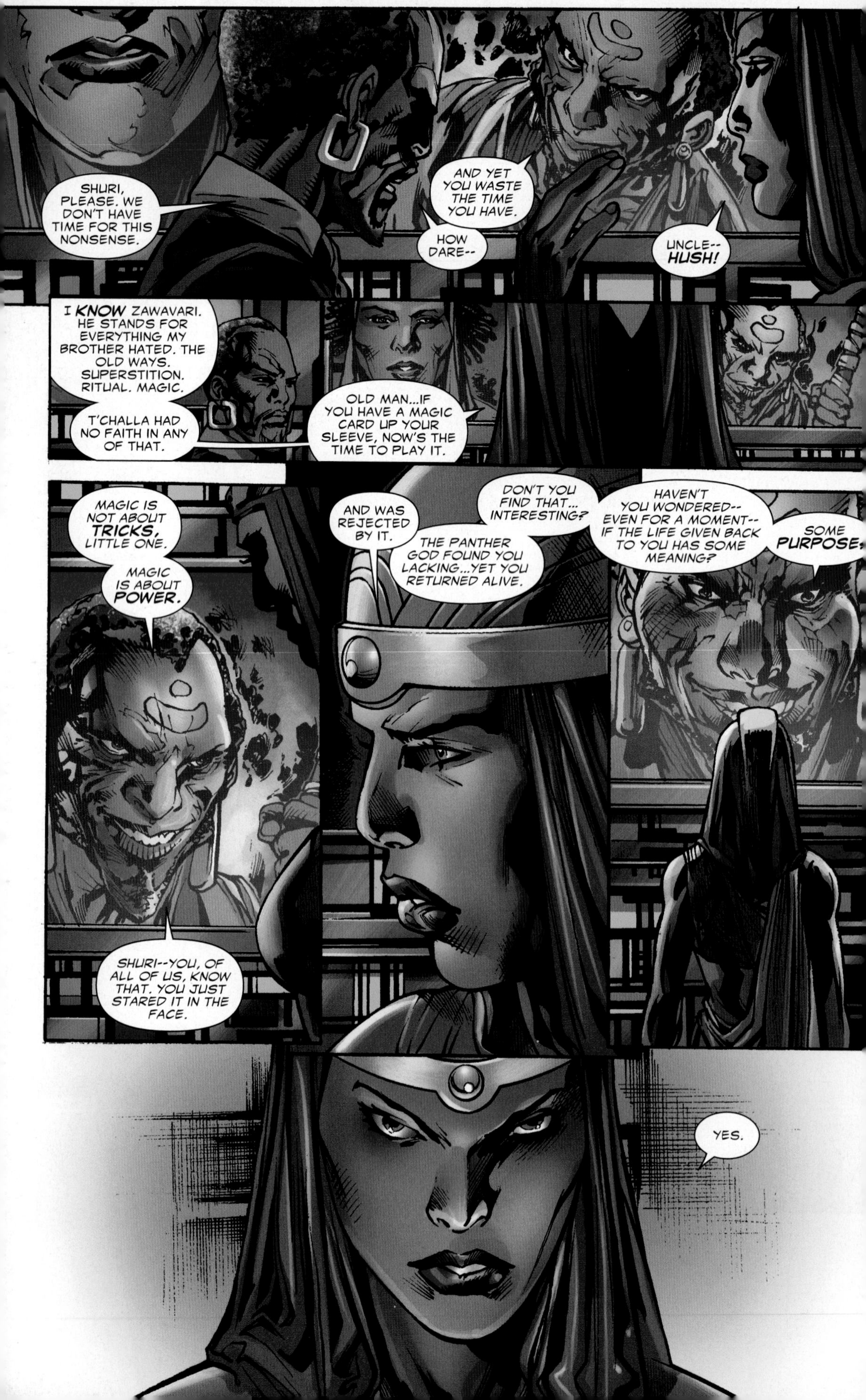
SHURI, PLEASE. WE DON'T HAVE TIME FOR THIS NONSENSE.
AND YET YOU WASTE THE TIME YOU HAVE.
HOW DARE--
UNCLE-- HUSH!
I KNOW ZAWAVARI. HE STANDS FOR EVERYTHING MY BROTHER HATED. THE OLD WAYS. SUPERSTITION. RITUAL. MAGIC.
T'CHALLA HAD NO FAITH IN ANY OF THAT.
OLD MAN...IF YOU HAVE A MAGIC CARD UP YOUR SLEEVE, NOW'S THE TIME TO PLAY IT.
MAGIC IS NOT ABOUT TRICKS, LITTLE ONE.
MAGIC IS ABOUT POWER.
SHURI--YOU, OF ALL OF US, KNOW THAT. YOU JUST STARED IT IN THE FACE.
AND WAS REJECTED BY IT.
THE PANTHER GOD FOUND YOU LACKING...YET YOU RETURNED ALIVE.
DON'T YOU FIND THAT... INTERESTING?
HAVEN'T YOU WONDERED-- EVEN FOR A MOMENT-- IF THE LIFE GIVEN BACK TO YOU HAS SOME MEANING?
SOME PURPOSE?
YES.

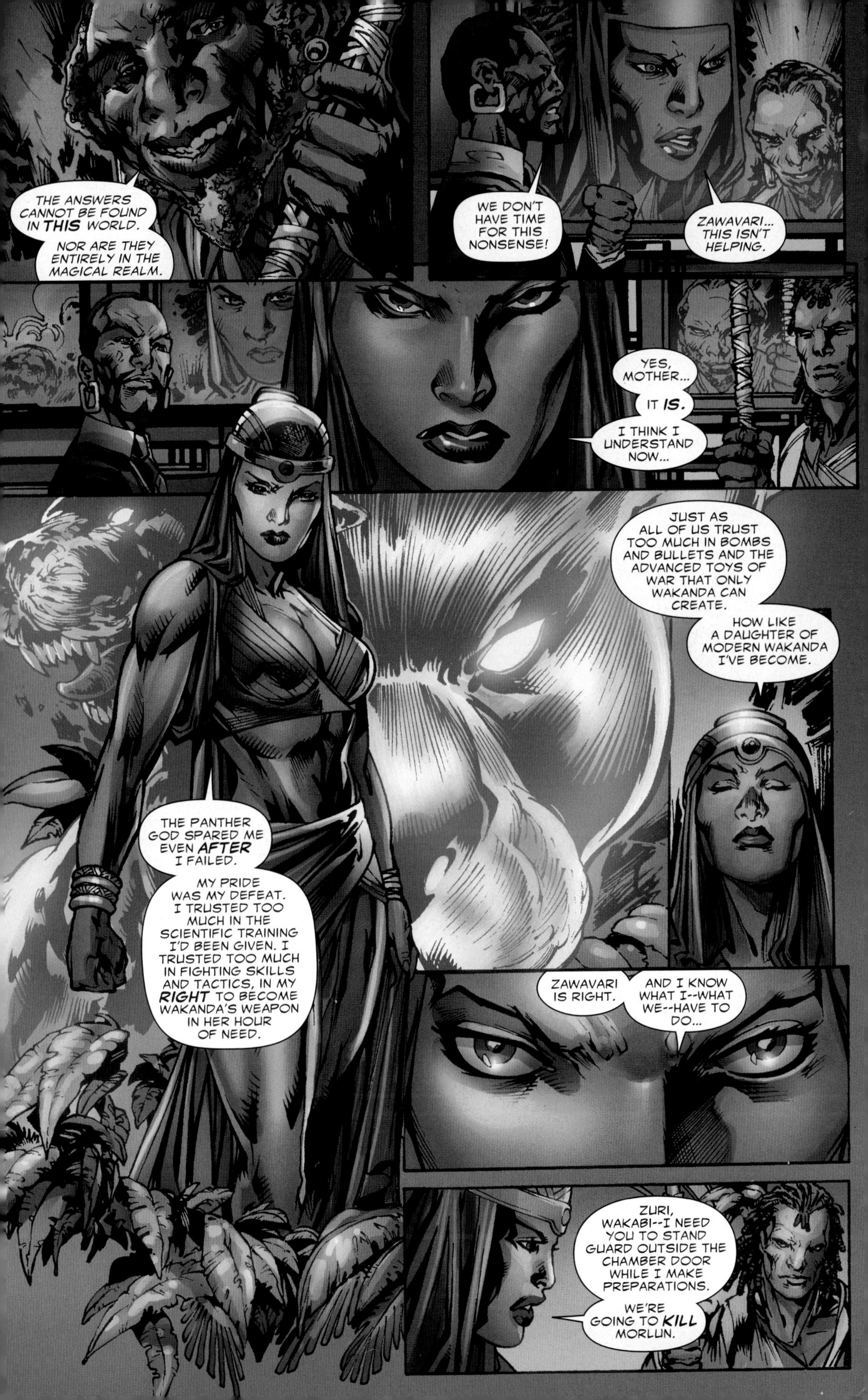
THE ANSWERS CANNOT BE FOUND IN THIS WORLD.
NOR ARE THEY ENTIRELY IN THE MAGICAL REALM.
WE DON'T HAVE TIME FOR THIS NONSENSE!
ZAWAVARI... THIS ISN'T HELPING.
YES, MOTHER...
IT IS.
I THINK I UNDERSTAND NOW...
THE PANTHER GOD SPARED ME EVEN AFTER I FAILED.
MY PRIDE WAS MY DEFEAT. I TRUSTED TOO MUCH IN THE SCIENTIFIC TRAINING I'D BEEN GIVEN. I TRUSTED TOO MUCH IN FIGHTING SKILLS AND TACTICS, IN MY RIGHT TO BECOME WAKANDA'S WEAPON IN HER HOUR OF NEED.
JUST AS ALL OF US TRUST TOO MUCH IN BOMBS AND BULLETS AND THE ADVANCED TOYS OF WAR THAT ONLY WAKANDA CAN CREATE.
HOW LIKE A DAUGHTER OF MODERN WAKANDA I'VE BECOME.
ZAWAVARI IS RIGHT.
AND I KNOW WHAT I--WHAT WE--HAVE TO DO...
ZURI, WAKABI--I NEED YOU TO STAND GUARD OUTSIDE THE CHAMBER DOOR WHILE I MAKE PREPARATIONS.
WE'RE GOING TO KILL MORLUN.

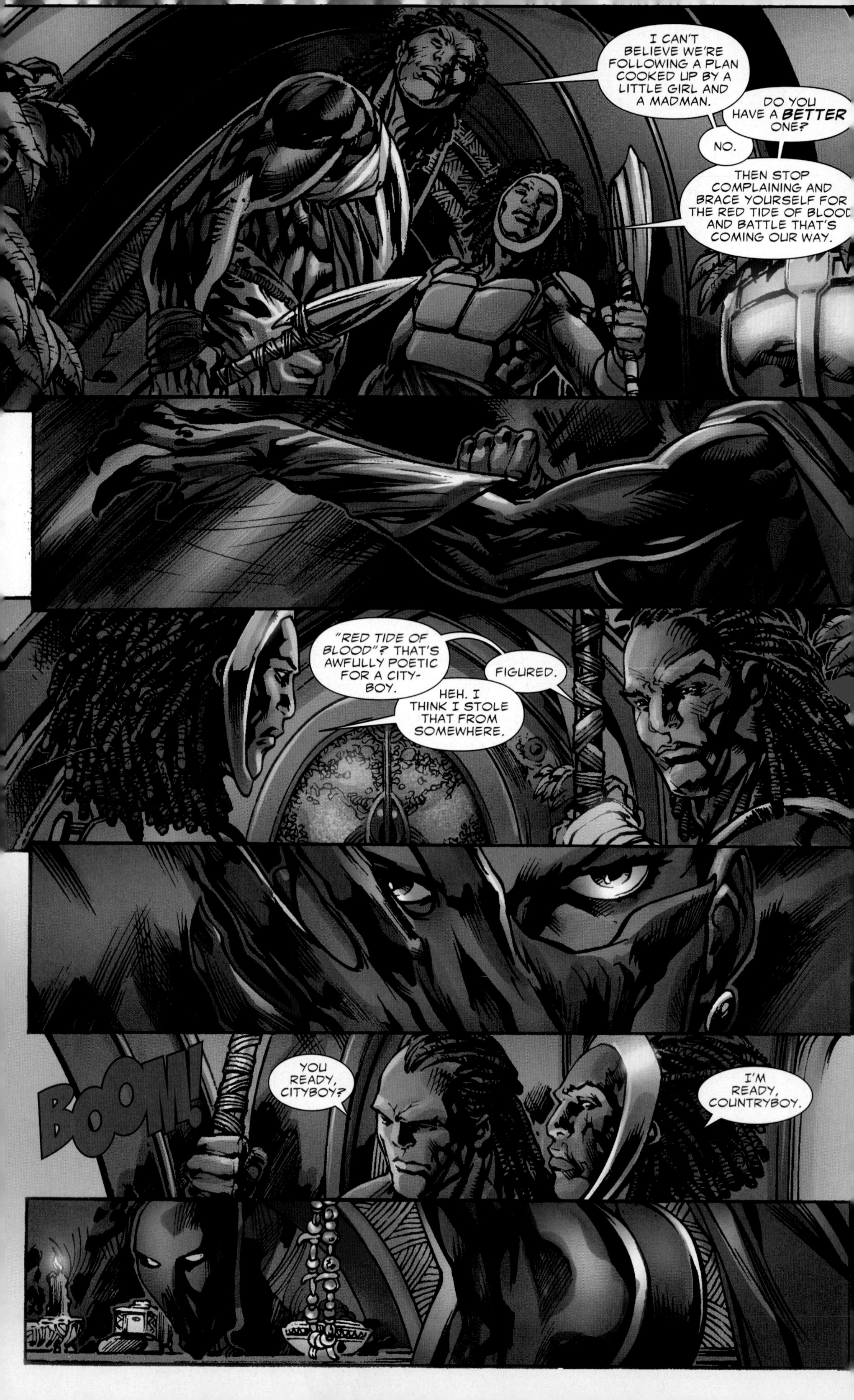
I CAN'T BELIEVE WE'RE FOLLOWING A PLAN COOKED UP BY A LITTLE GIRL AND A MADMAN.
DO YOU HAVE A **BETTER** ONE?
NO.
THEN STOP COMPLAINING AND BRACE YOURSELF FOR THE RED TIDE OF BLOOD AND BATTLE THAT'S COMING OUR WAY.
"RED TIDE OF BLOOD"? THAT'S AWFULLY POETIC FOR A CITY-BOY.
FIGURED.
HEH. I THINK I STOLE THAT FROM SOMEWHERE.
BOOM!
YOU READY, CITYBOY?
I'M READY, COUNTRYBOY.

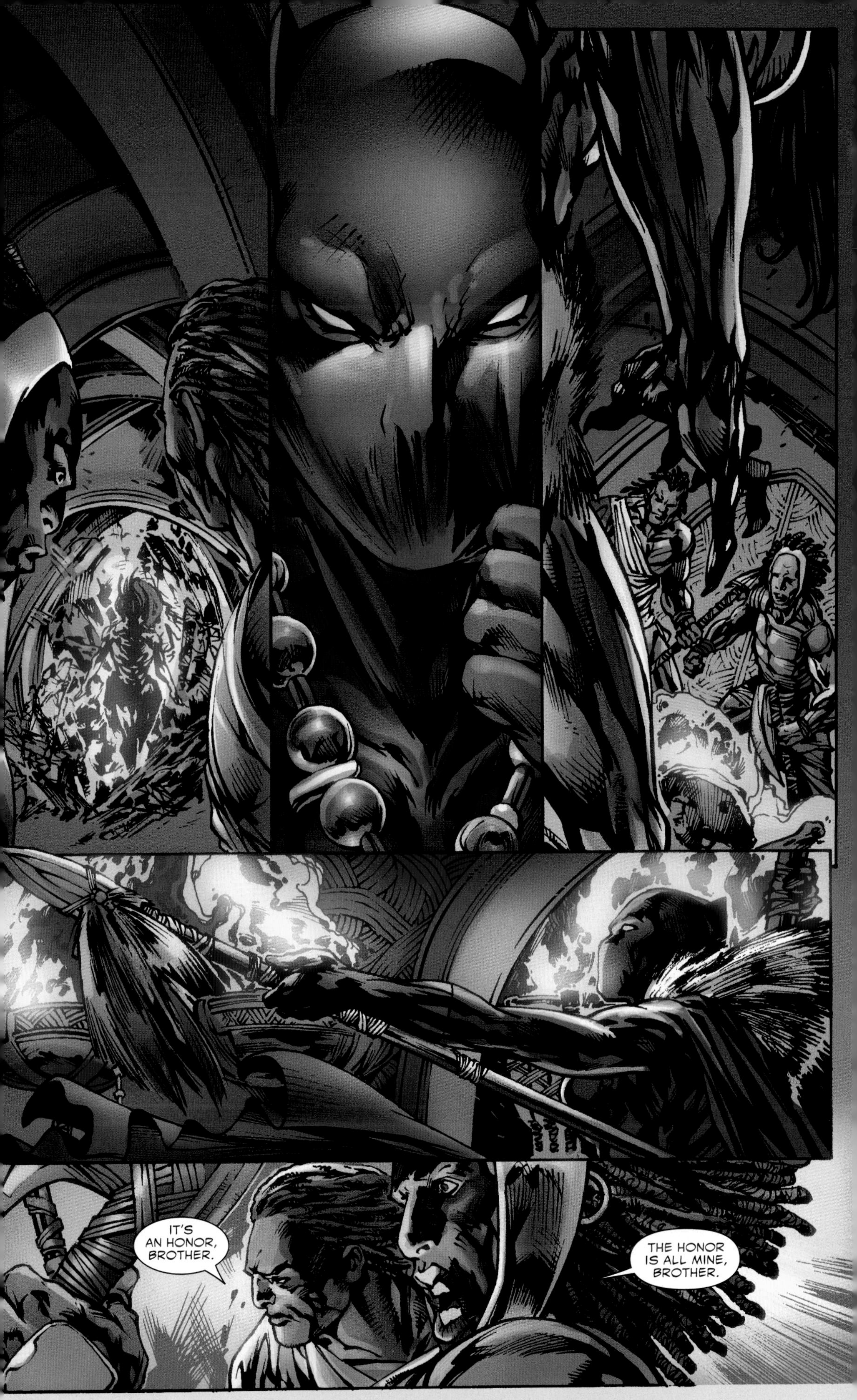
IT'S AN HONOR, BROTHER.
THE HONOR IS ALL MINE, BROTHER.

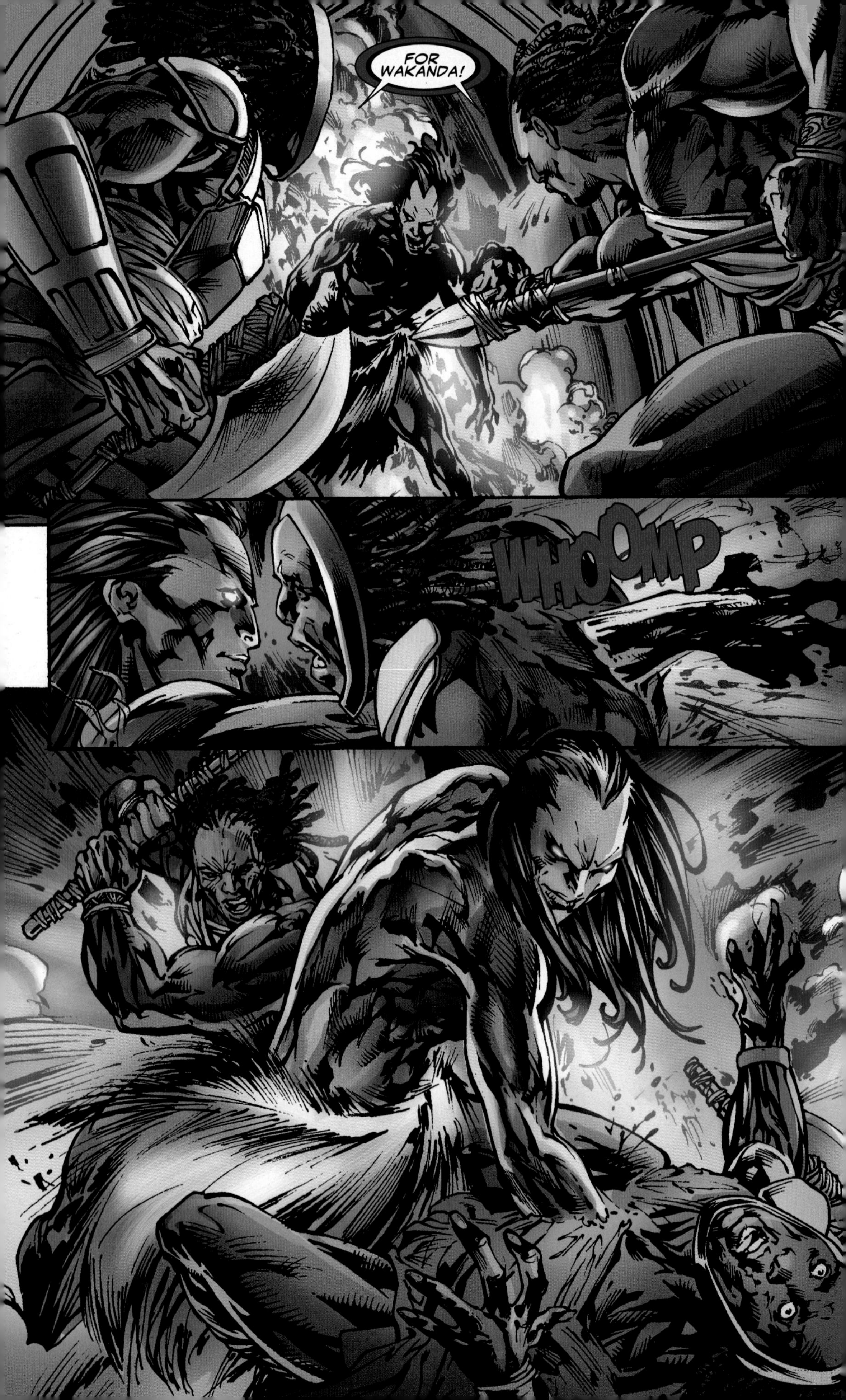
FOR WAKANDA!
WHOOMP

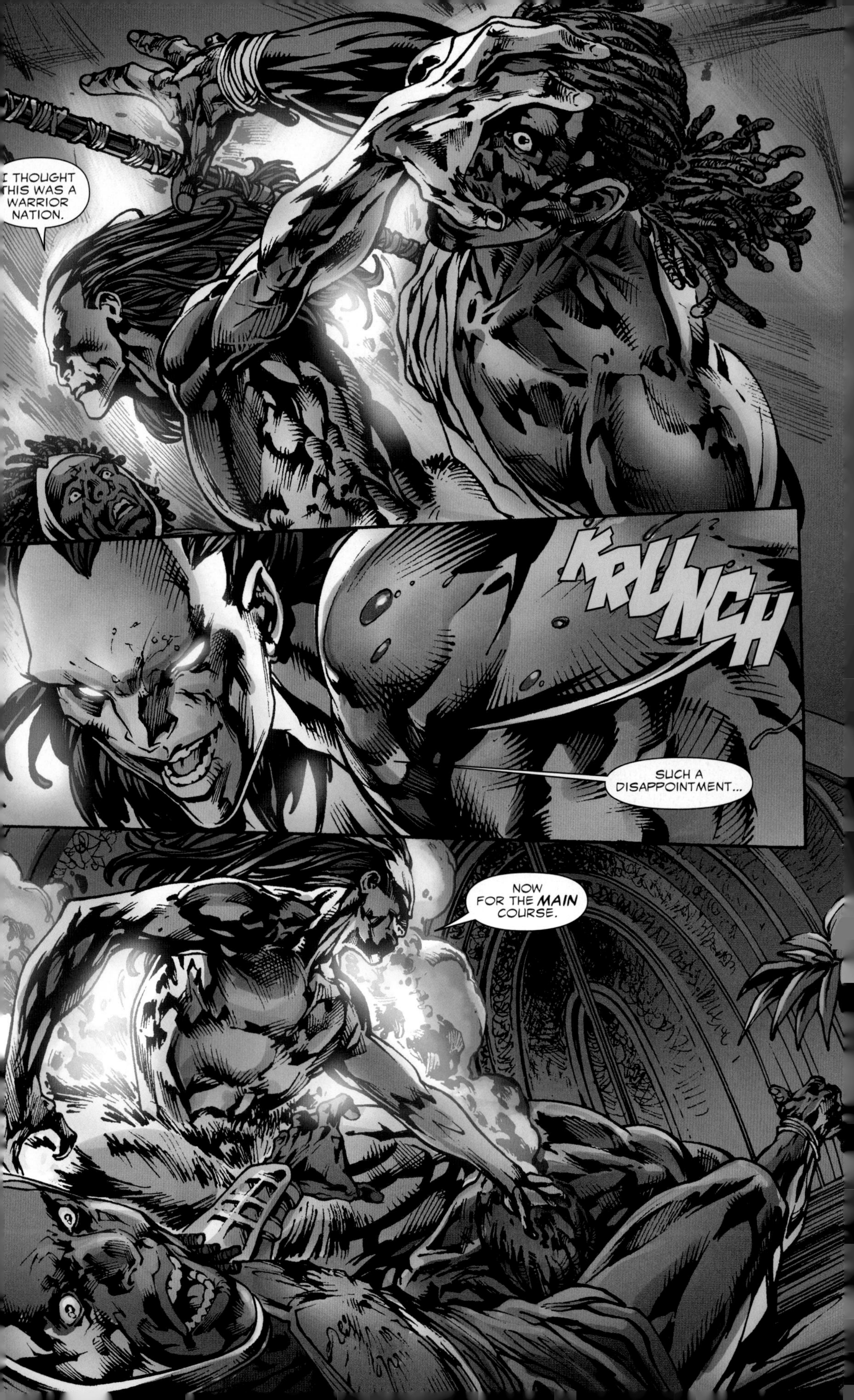
I THOUGHT THIS WAS A WARRIOR NATION.
KRUNCH
SUCH A DISAPPOINTMENT...
NOW FOR THE MAIN COURSE.

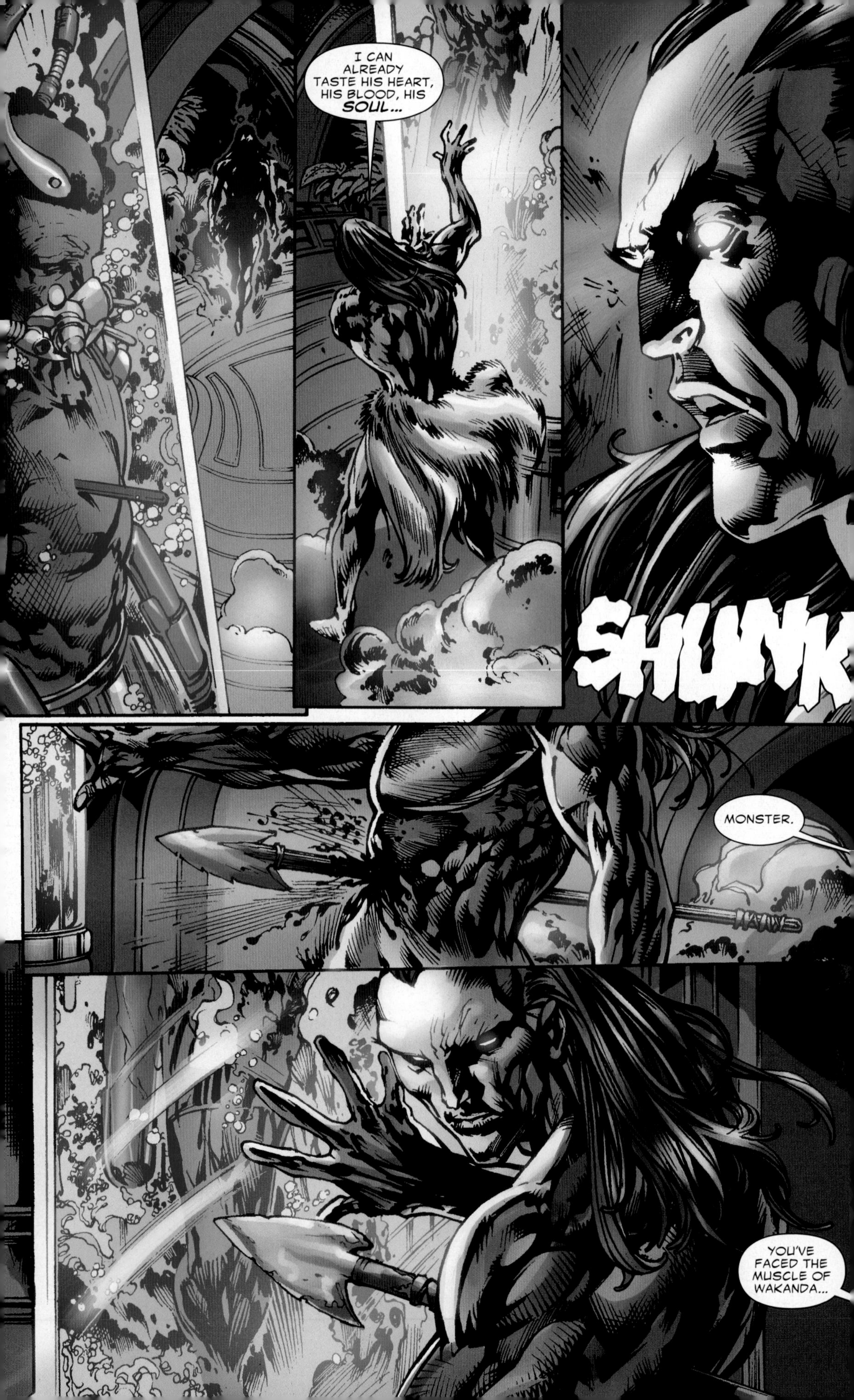
I CAN ALREADY TASTE HIS HEART, HIS BLOOD, HIS SOUL...
SHUNK
MONSTER.
YOU'VE FACED THE MUSCLE OF WAKANDA...

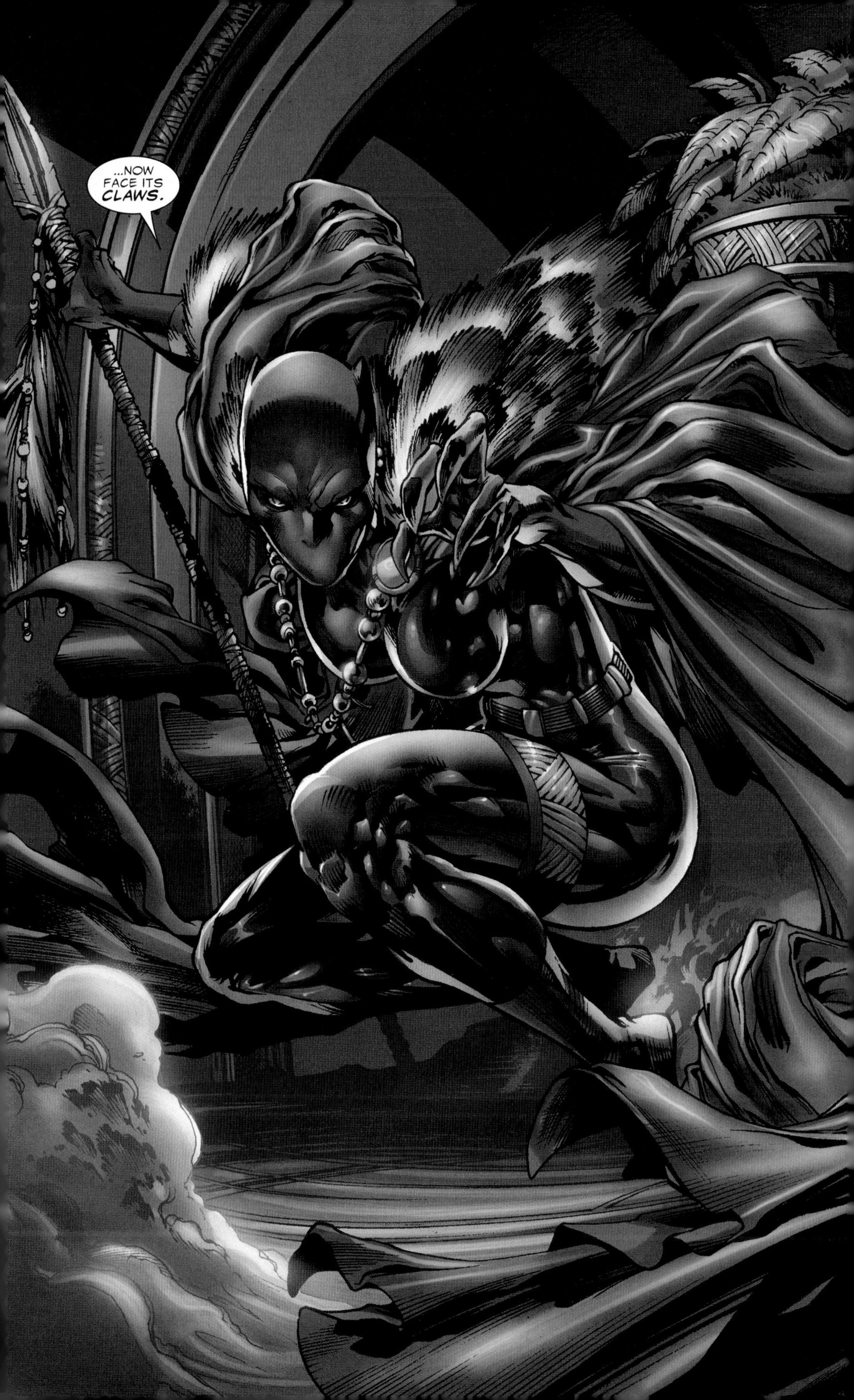
...NOW FACE ITS CLAWS.

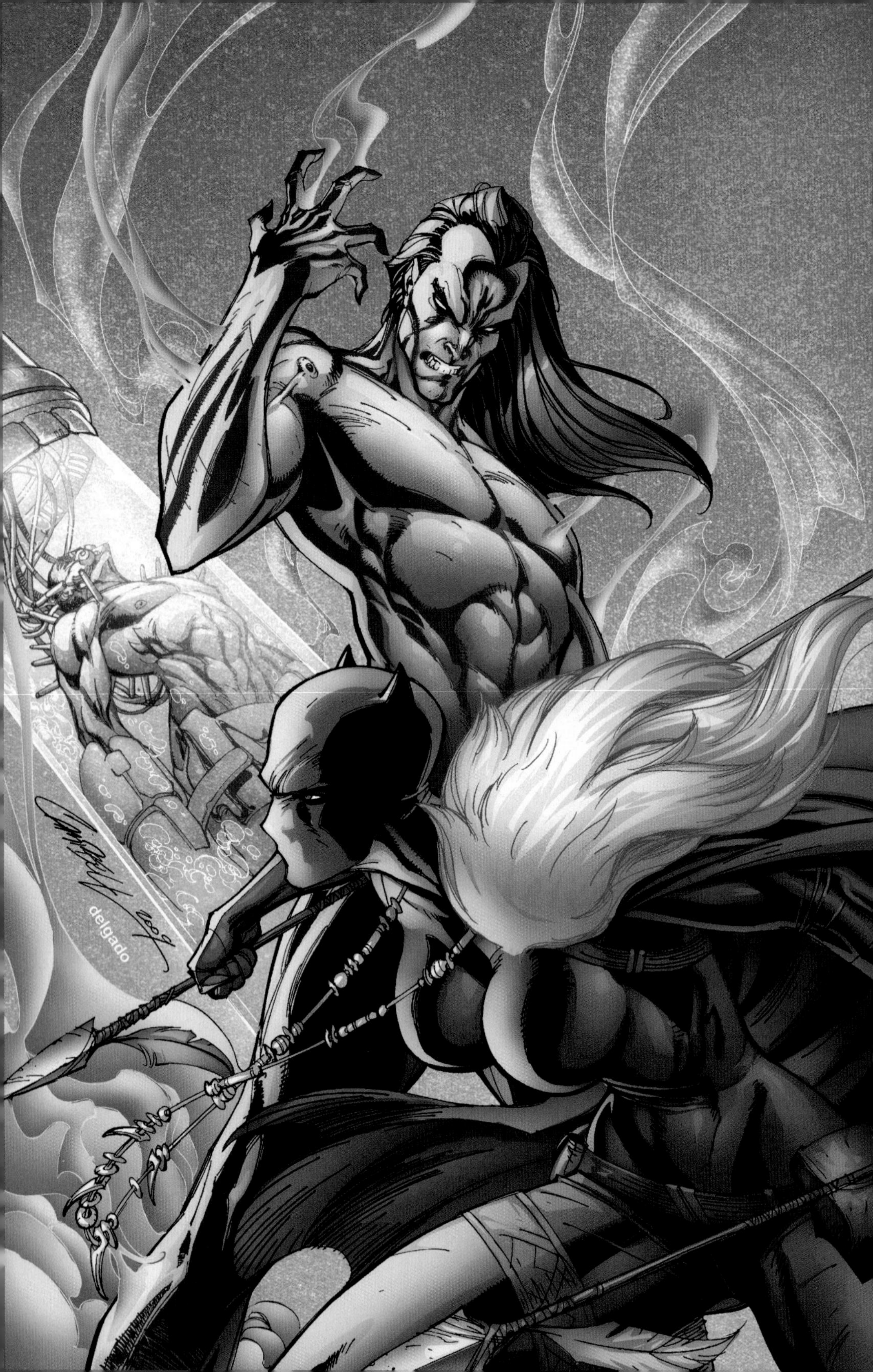
delgado

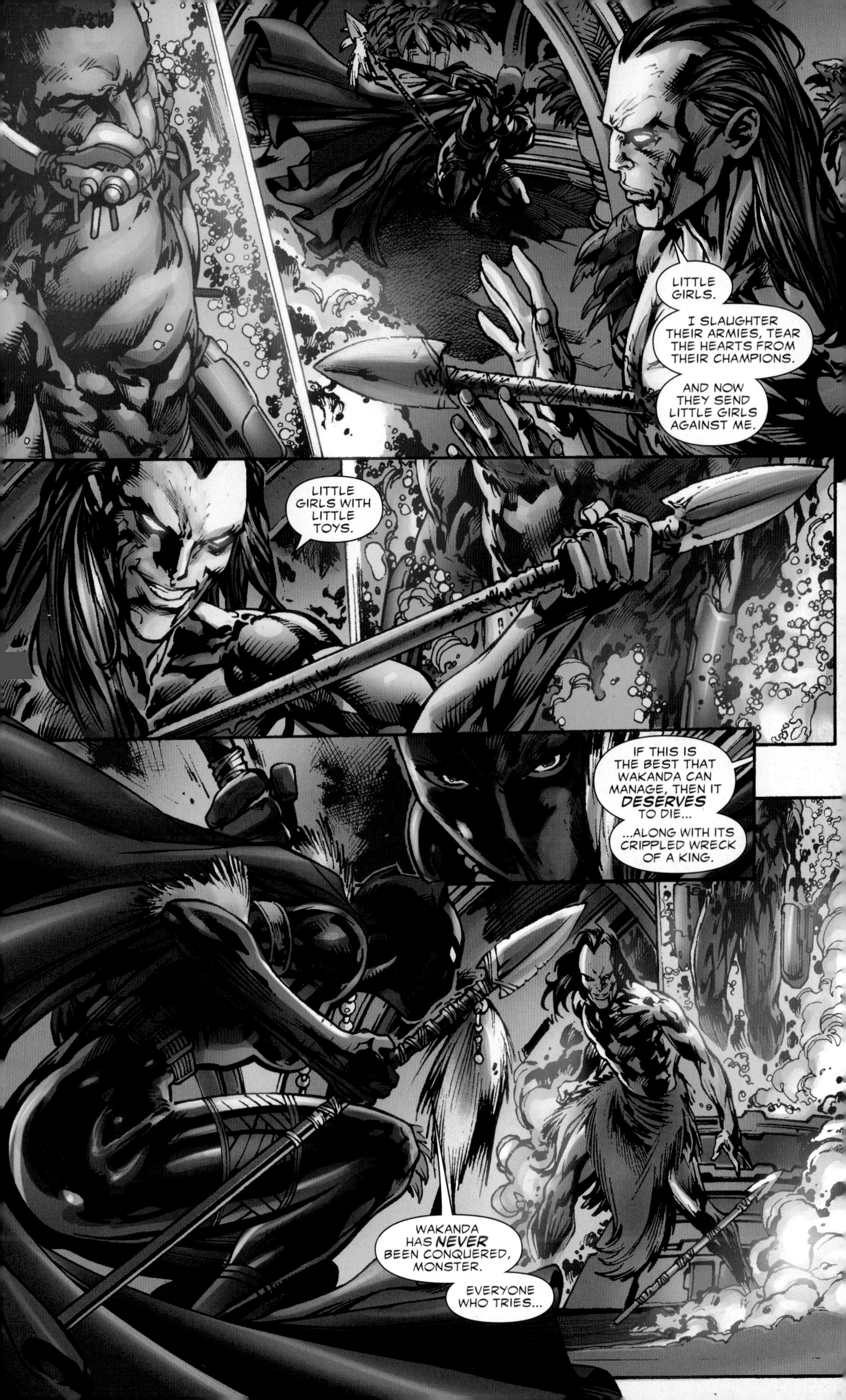
LITTLE GIRLS.
I SLAUGHTER THEIR ARMIES, TEAR THE HEARTS FROM THEIR CHAMPIONS.
AND NOW THEY SEND LITTLE GIRLS AGAINST ME.
LITTLE GIRLS WITH LITTLE TOYS.
IF THIS IS THE BEST THAT WAKANDA CAN MANAGE, THEN IT **DESERVES** TO DIE...
...ALONG WITH ITS CRIPPLED WRECK OF A KING.
WAKANDA HAS **NEVER** BEEN CONQUERED, MONSTER.
EVERYONE WHO TRIES...

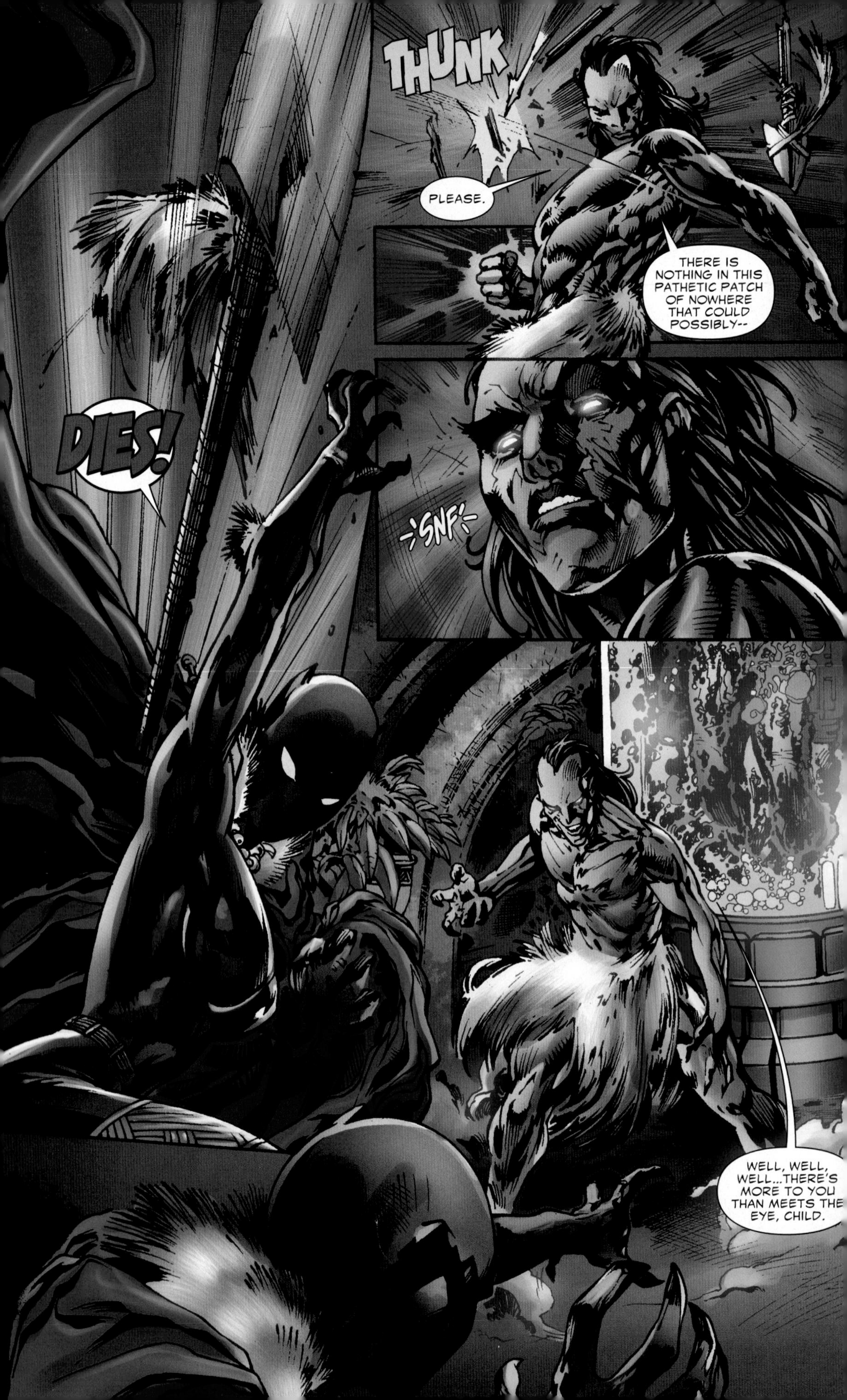
THUNK
PLEASE.
THERE IS NOTHING IN THIS PATHETIC PATCH OF NOWHERE THAT COULD POSSIBLY--
DIES!
SNF
WELL, WELL, WELL...THERE'S MORE TO YOU THAN MEETS THE EYE, CHILD.

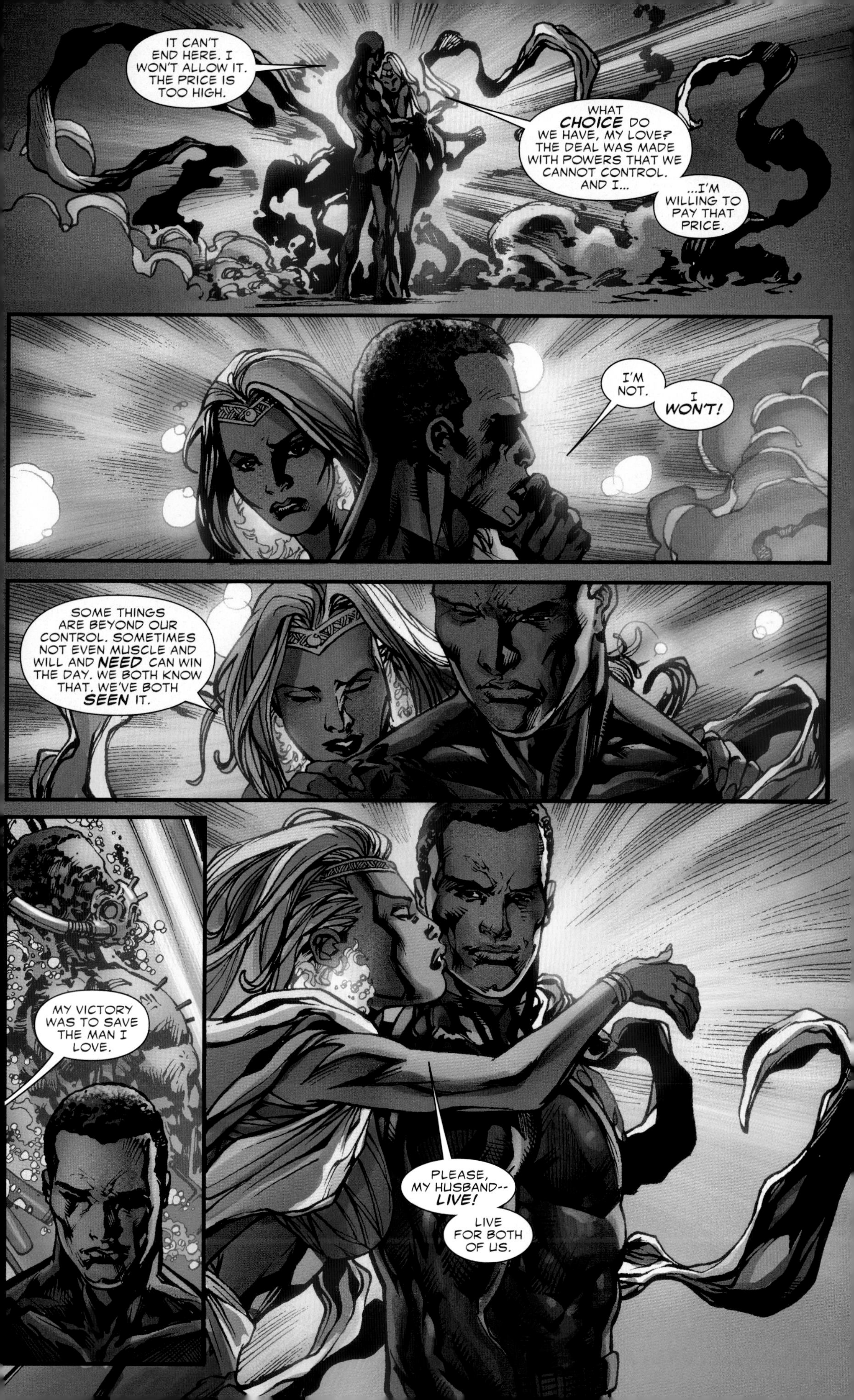
IT CAN'T END HERE. I WON'T ALLOW IT. THE PRICE IS TOO HIGH.
WHAT CHOICE DO WE HAVE, MY LOVE? THE DEAL WAS MADE WITH POWERS THAT WE CANNOT CONTROL. AND I...
...I'M WILLING TO PAY THAT PRICE.
I'M NOT.
I WON'T!
SOME THINGS ARE BEYOND OUR CONTROL. SOMETIMES NOT EVEN MUSCLE AND WILL AND NEED CAN WIN THE DAY. WE BOTH KNOW THAT. WE'VE BOTH SEEN IT.
MY VICTORY WAS TO SAVE THE MAN I LOVE.
PLEASE, MY HUSBAND-- LIVE!
LIVE FOR BOTH OF US.

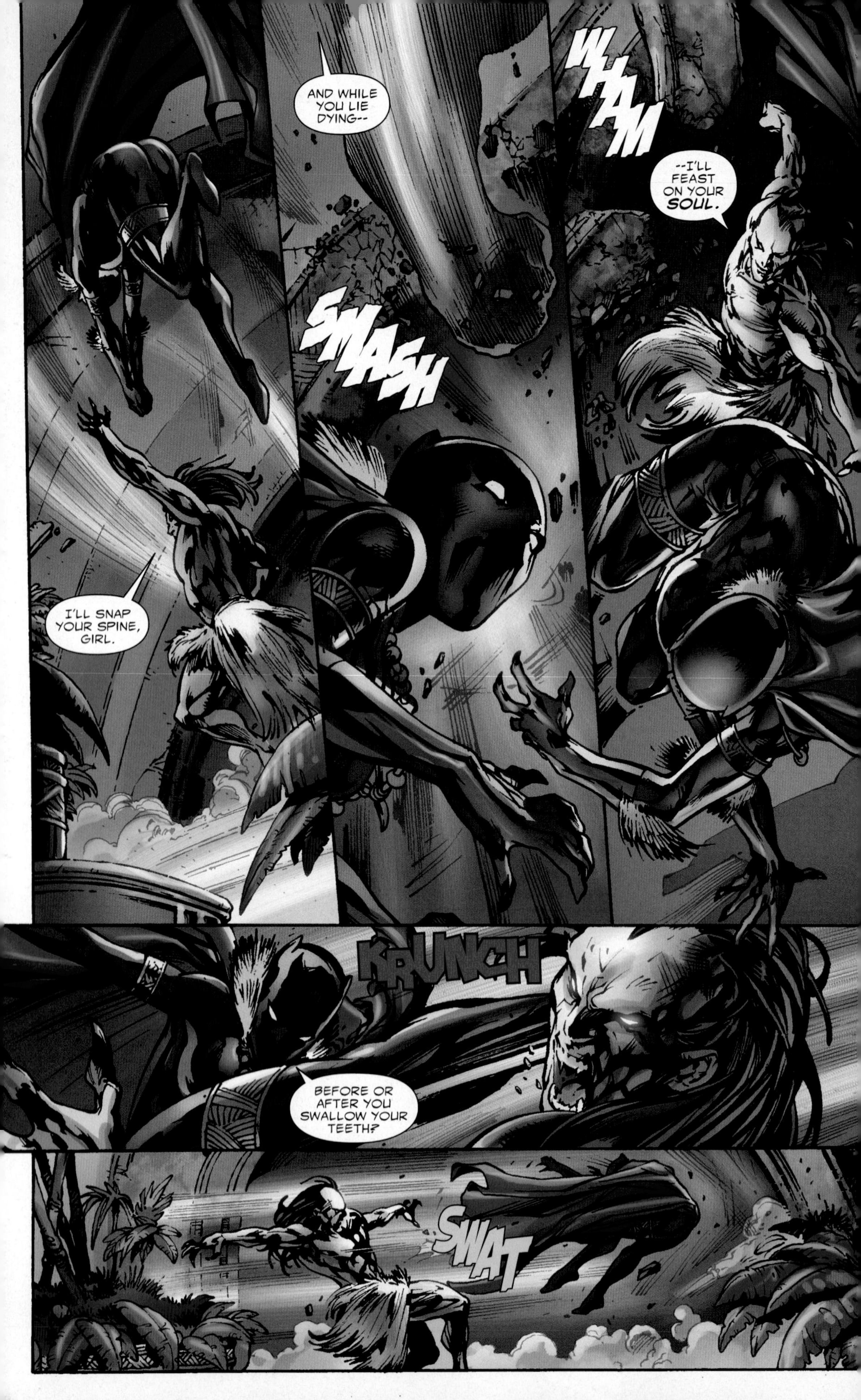
AND WHILE YOU LIE DYING--
I'LL SNAP YOUR SPINE, GIRL.
SMASH
WHAM
--I'LL FEAST ON YOUR SOUL.
KRUNCH
BEFORE OR AFTER YOU SWALLOW YOUR TEETH?
SWAT

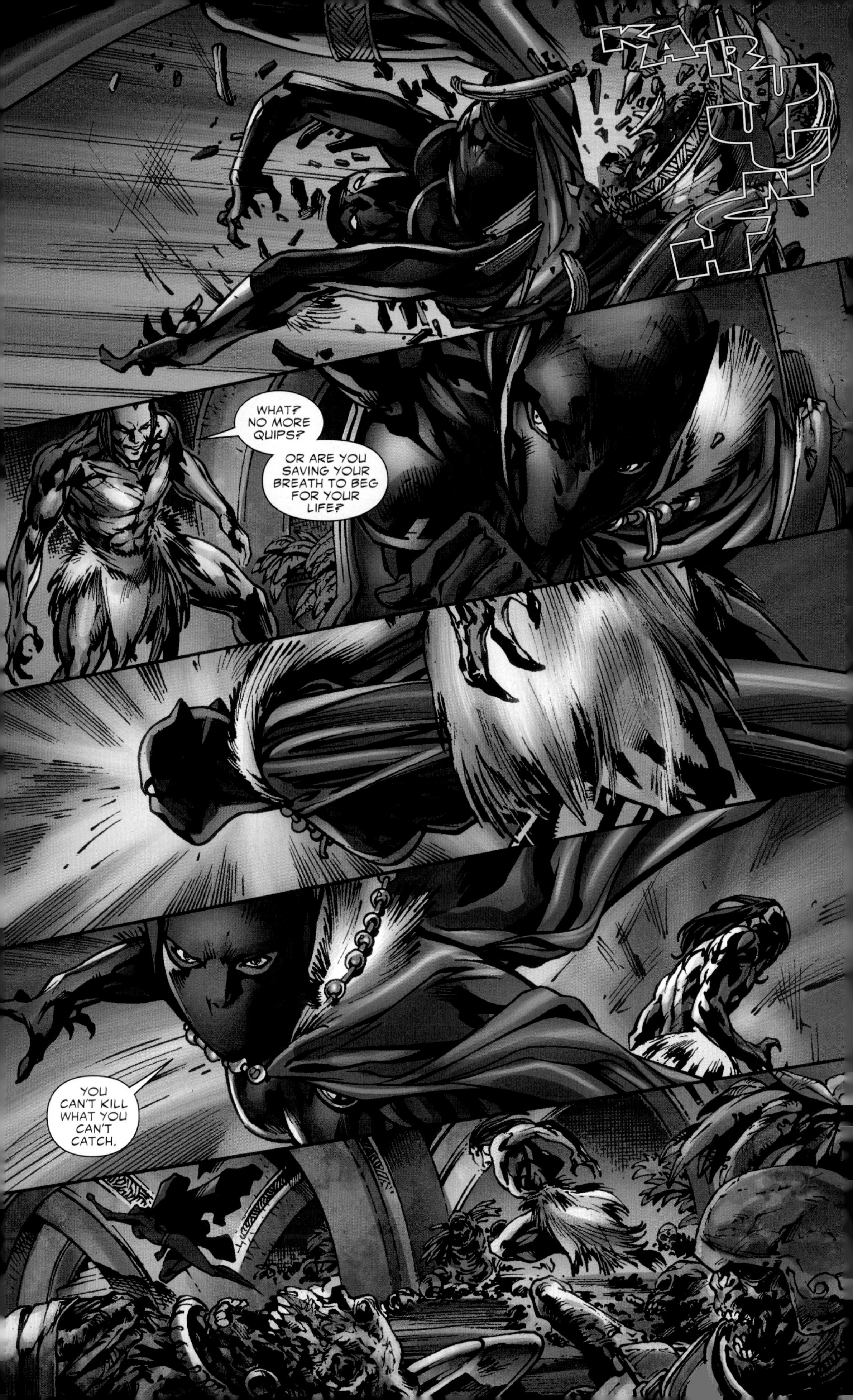
KA-RUNCH
WHAT? NO MORE QUIPS?
OR ARE YOU SAVING YOUR BREATH TO BEG FOR YOUR LIFE?
YOU CAN'T KILL WHAT YOU CAN'T CATCH.

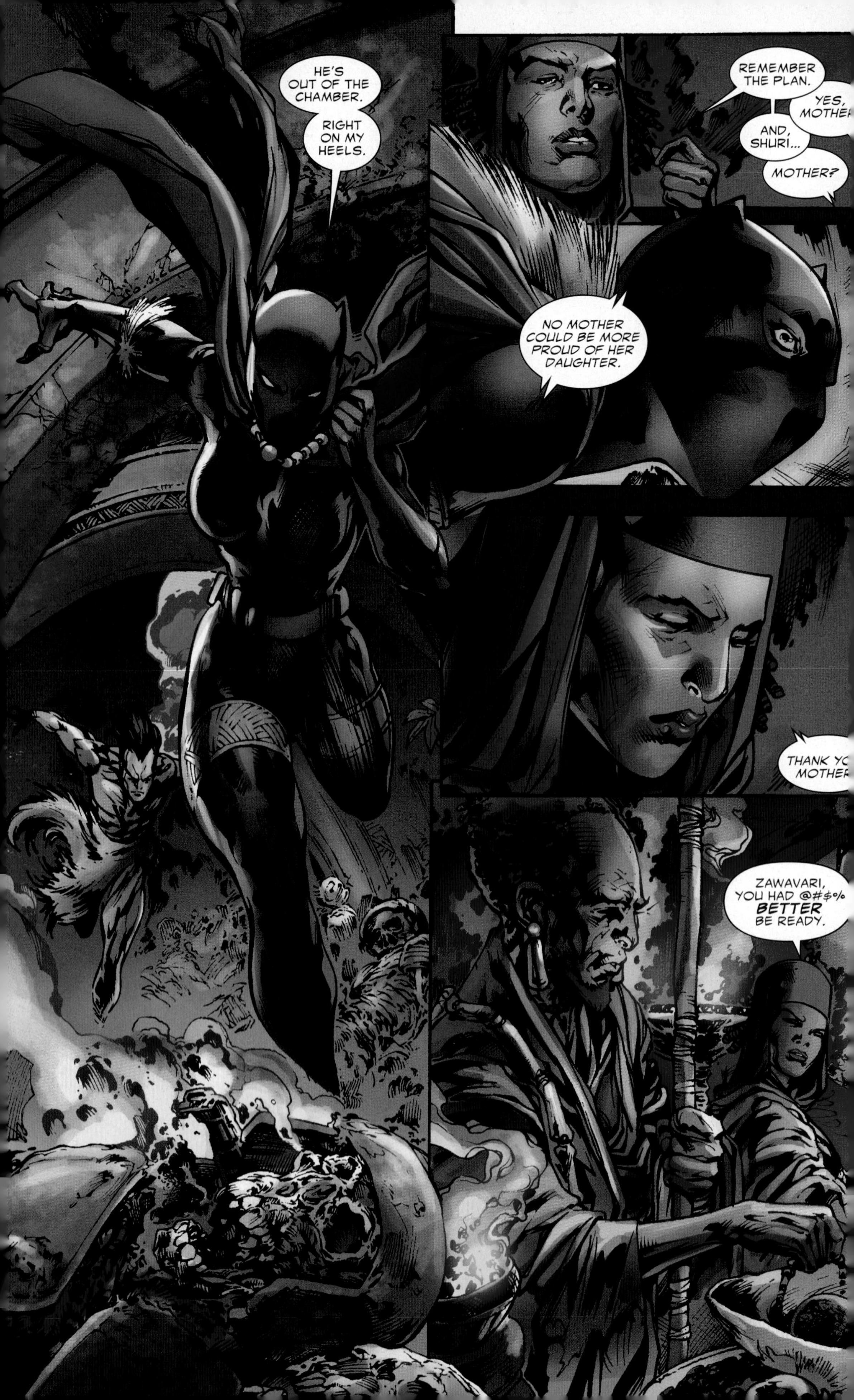

HE'S OUT OF THE CHAMBER.
RIGHT ON MY HEELS.
REMEMBER THE PLAN.
YES, MOTHER
AND, SHURI...
MOTHER?
NO MOTHER COULD BE MORE PROUD OF HER DAUGHTER.
THANK YO MOTHER
ZAWAVARI, YOU HAD @#$% BETTER BE READY.

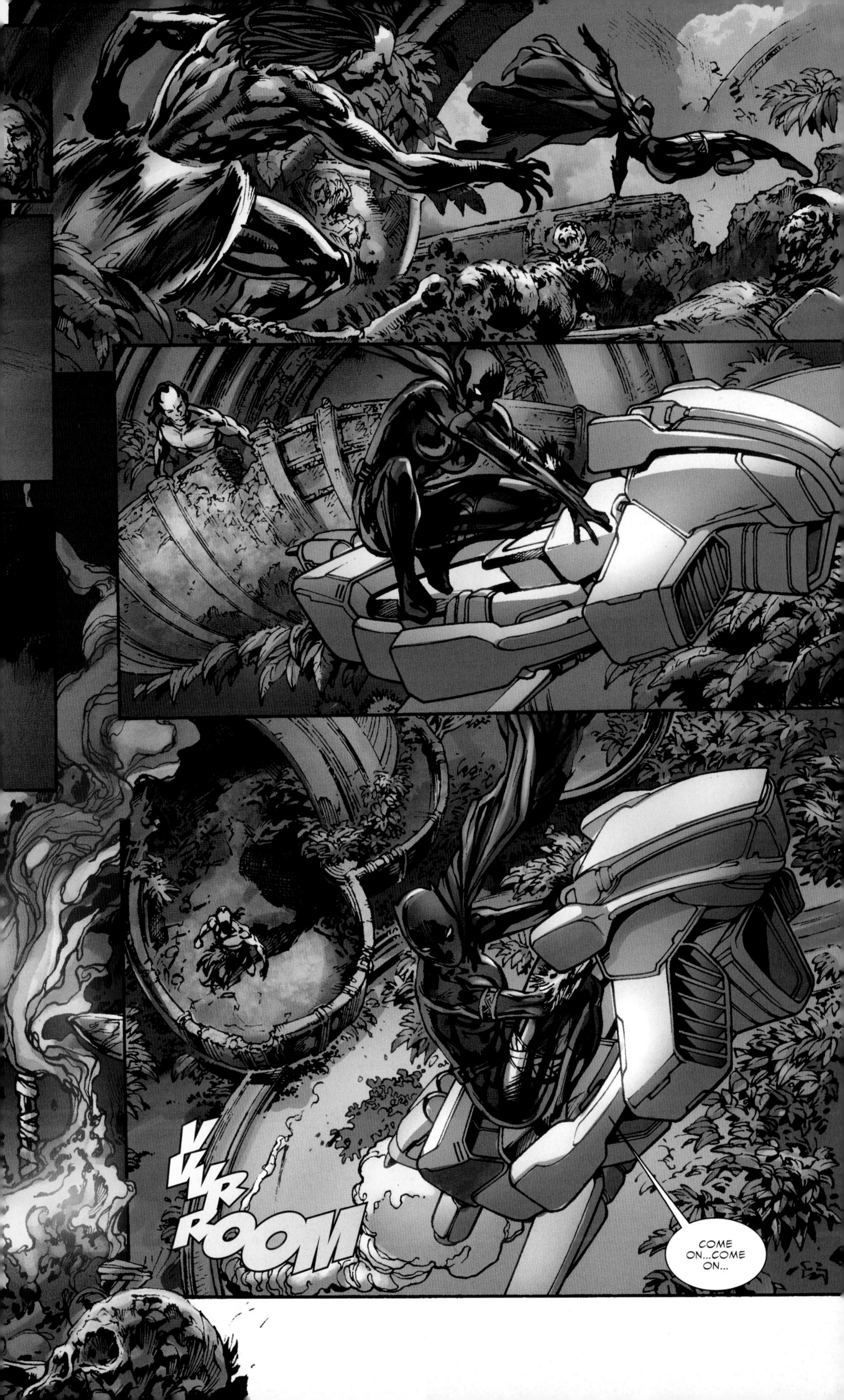
VVVRROOM
COME ON...COME ON...

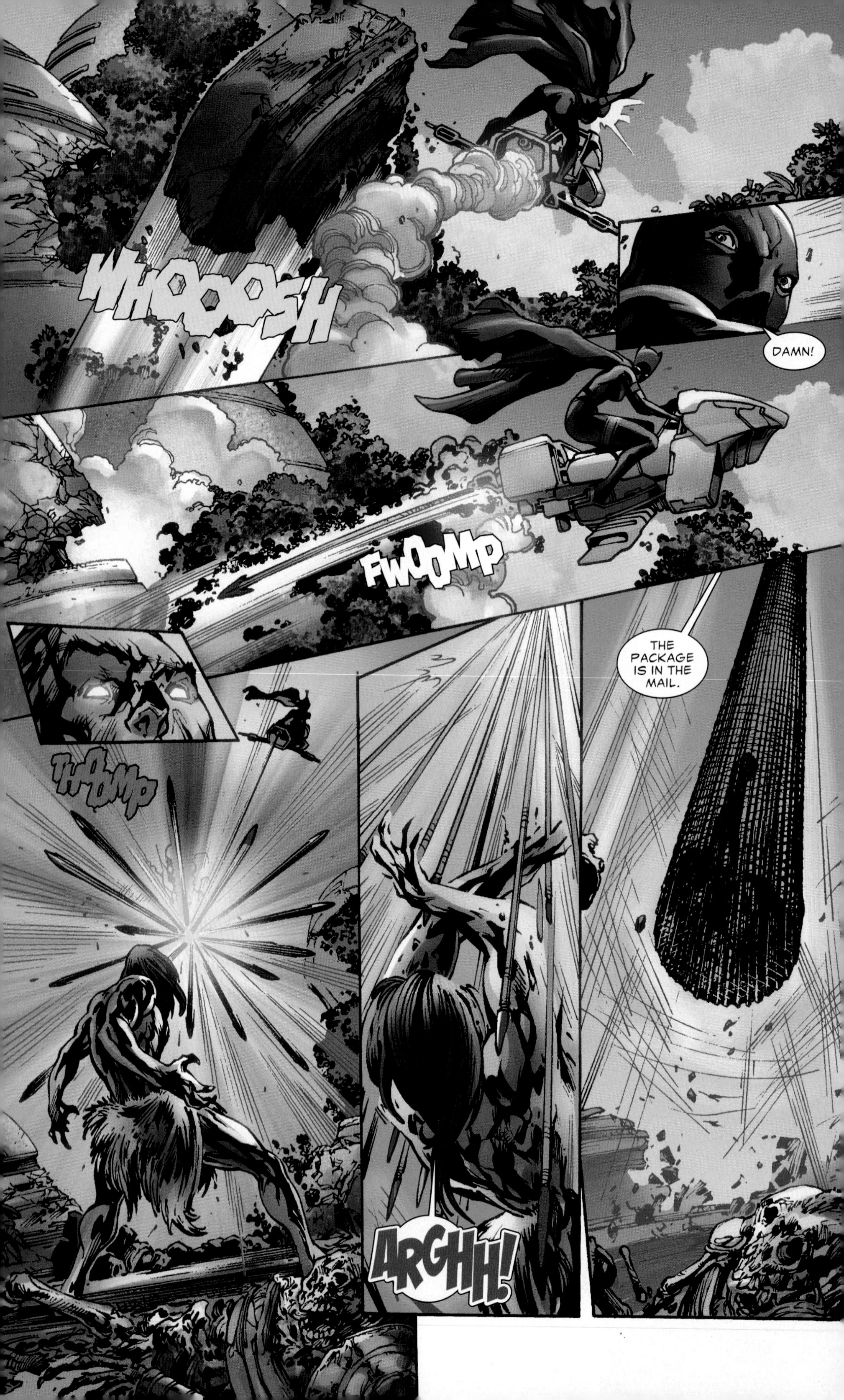
WHOOOSH
DAMN!
FWOOMP
THE PACKAGE IS IN THE MAIL.
THOOMP
ARGHH!

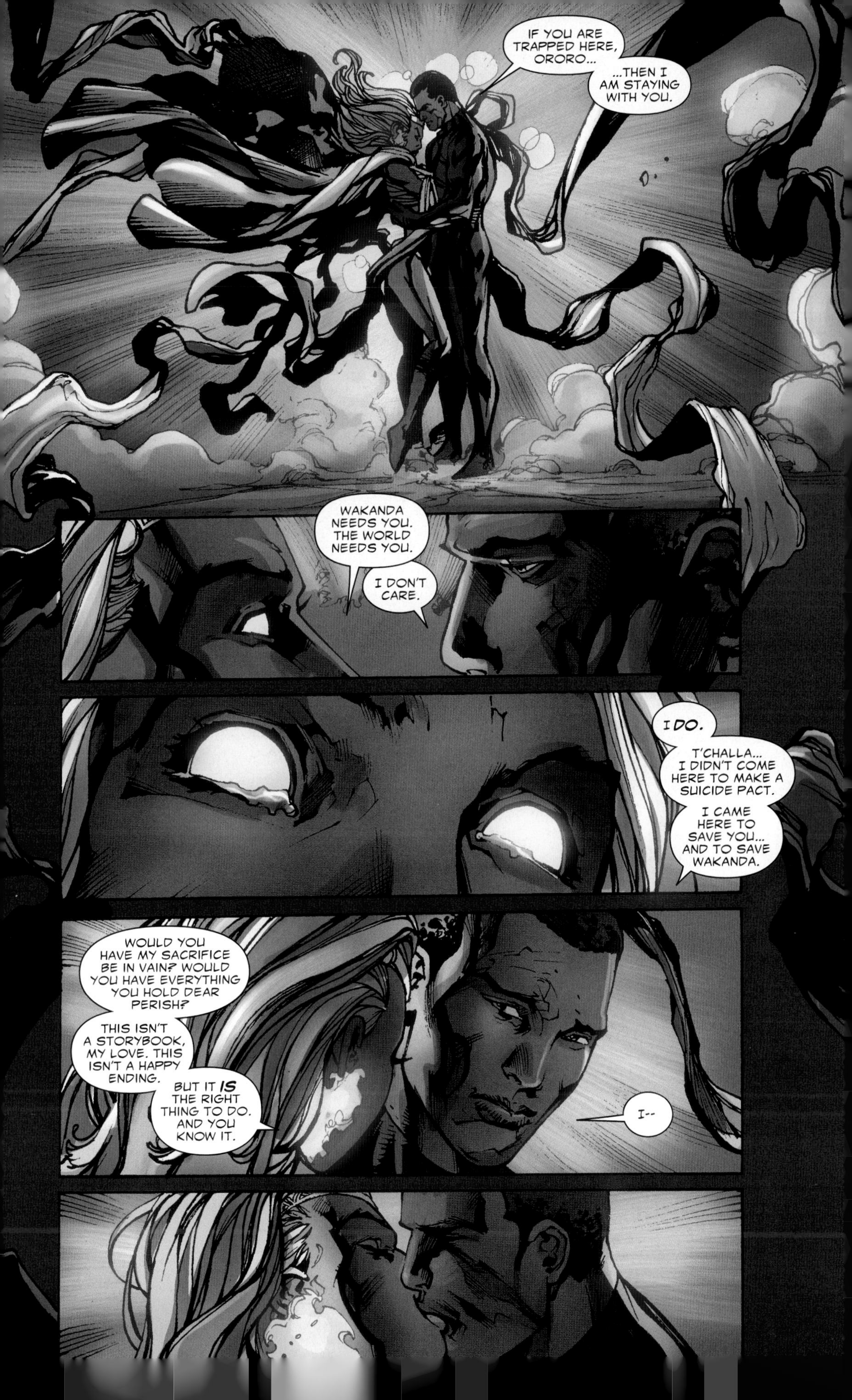
IF YOU ARE TRAPPED HERE, ORORO...
...THEN I AM STAYING WITH YOU.
WAKANDA NEEDS YOU. THE WORLD NEEDS YOU.
I DON'T CARE.
I DO.
T'CHALLA... I DIDN'T COME HERE TO MAKE A SUICIDE PACT.
I CAME HERE TO SAVE YOU... AND TO SAVE WAKANDA.
WOULD YOU HAVE MY SACRIFICE BE IN VAIN? WOULD YOU HAVE EVERYTHING YOU HOLD DEAR PERISH?
THIS ISN'T A STORYBOOK, MY LOVE. THIS ISN'T A HAPPY ENDING.
BUT IT IS THE RIGHT THING TO DO. AND YOU KNOW IT.
I--

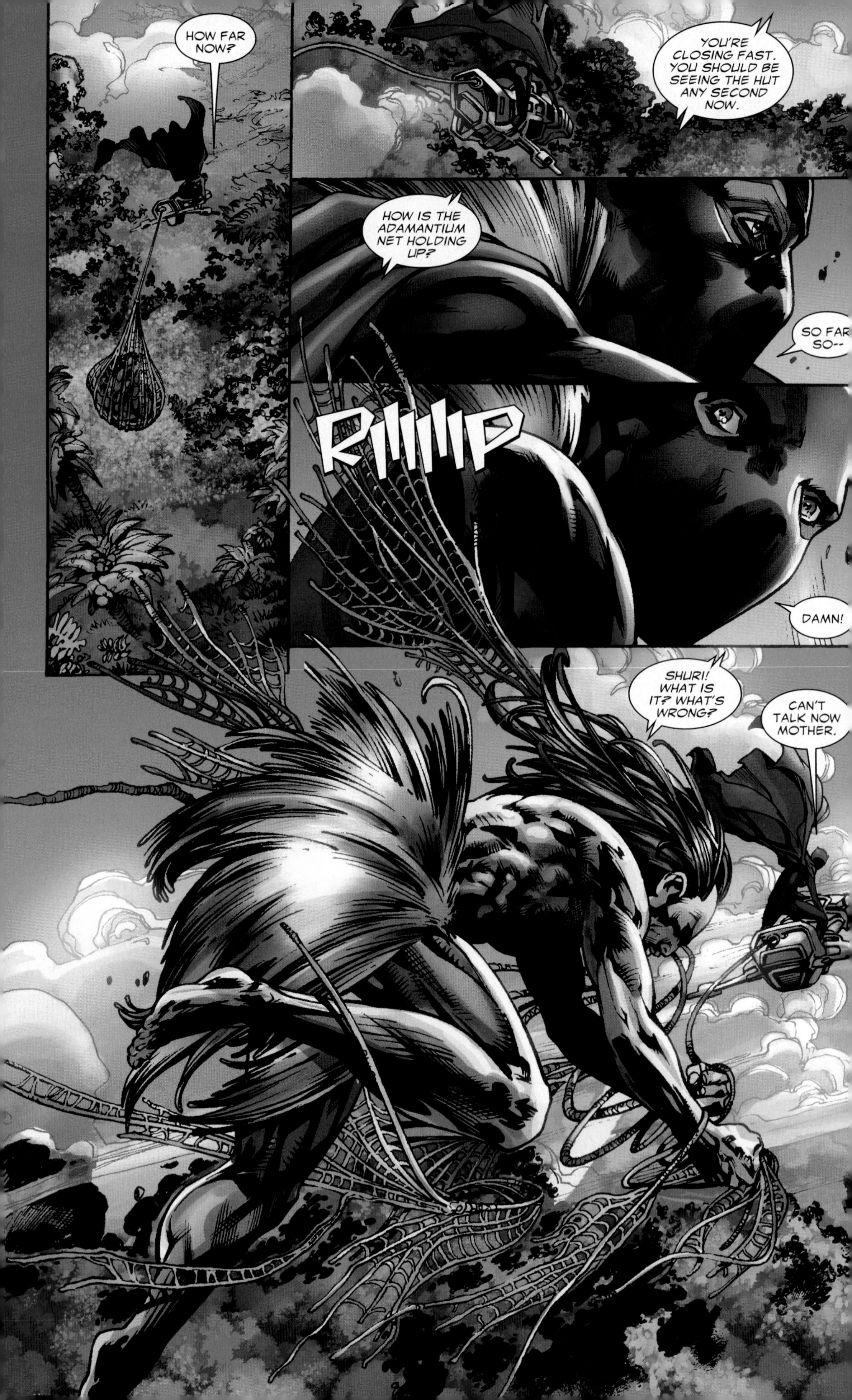
HOW FAR NOW?
YOU'RE CLOSING FAST. YOU SHOULD BE SEEING THE HUT ANY SECOND NOW.
HOW IS THE ADAMANTIUM NET HOLDING UP?
SO FAR SO--
RIIIIIP
DAMN!
SHURI! WHAT IS IT? WHAT'S WRONG?
CAN'T TALK NOW MOTHER.

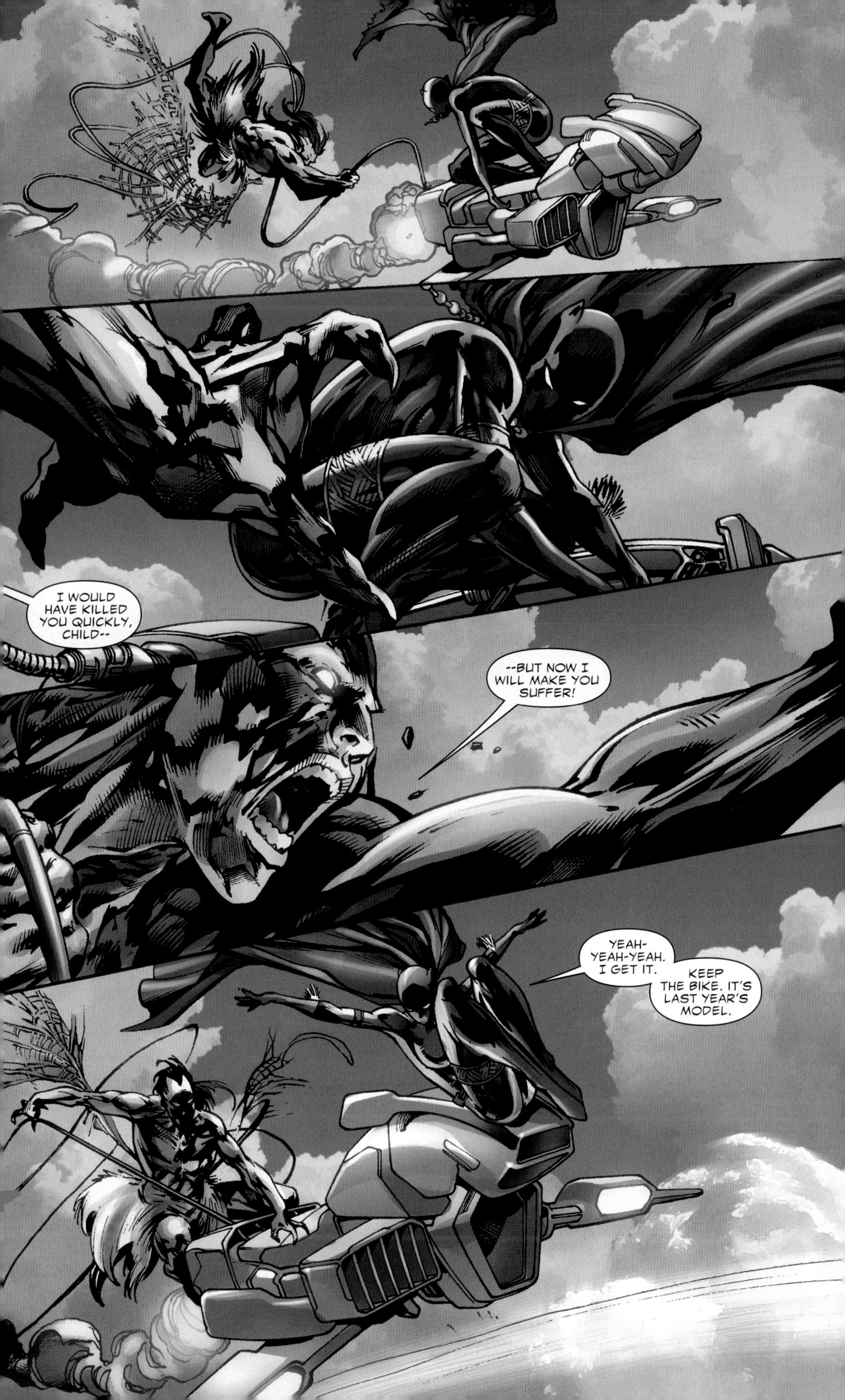
I WOULD HAVE KILLED YOU QUICKLY, CHILD--
--BUT NOW I WILL MAKE YOU SUFFER!
YEAH-YEAH-YEAH. I GET IT.
KEEP THE BIKE. IT'S LAST YEAR'S MODEL.

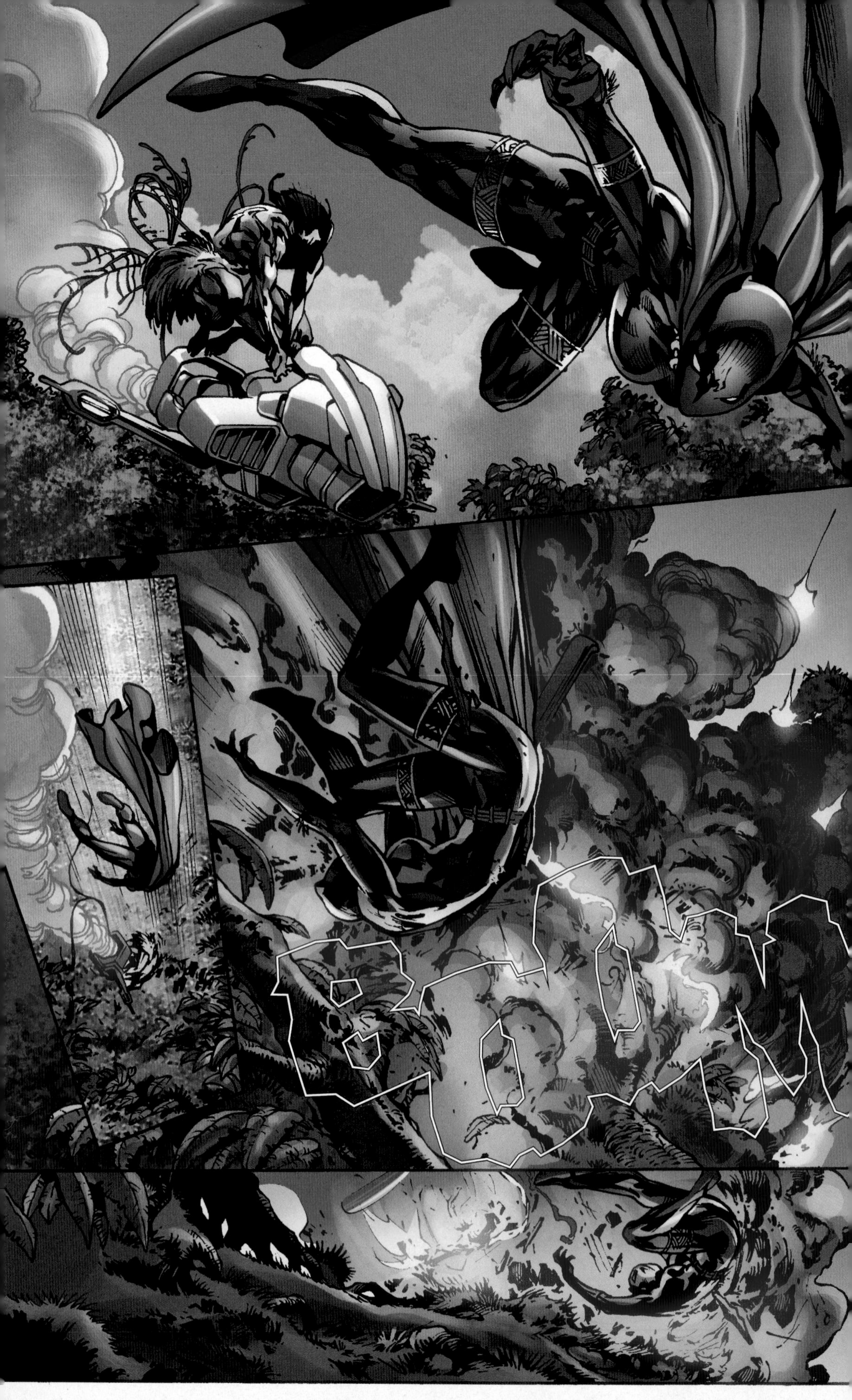
BOOM

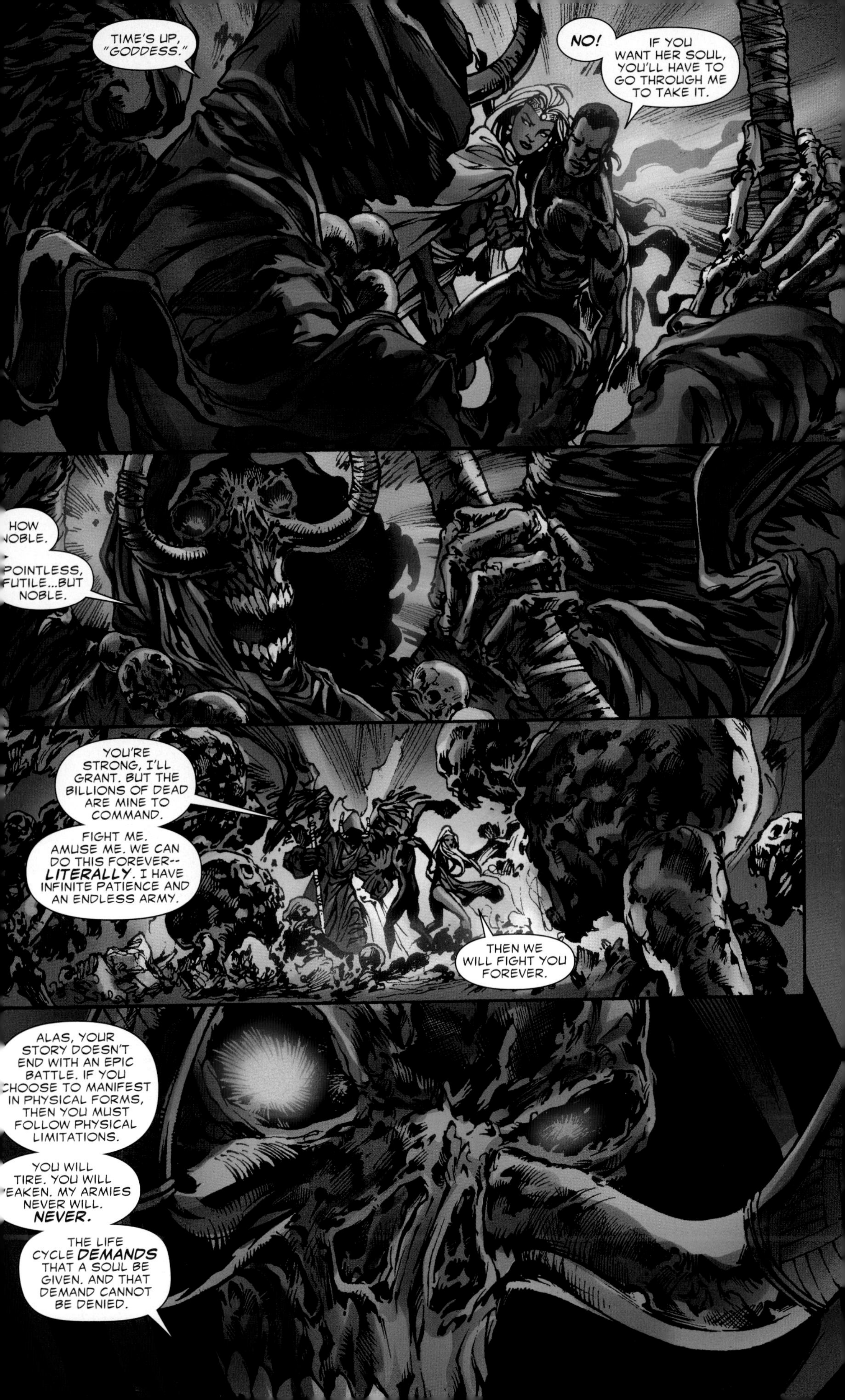
TIME'S UP, "GODDESS."
NO!
IF YOU WANT HER SOUL, YOU'LL HAVE TO GO THROUGH ME TO TAKE IT.
HOW NOBLE.
POINTLESS, FUTILE...BUT NOBLE.
YOU'RE STRONG, I'LL GRANT. BUT THE BILLIONS OF DEAD ARE MINE TO COMMAND.
FIGHT ME. AMUSE ME. WE CAN DO THIS FOREVER-- LITERALLY. I HAVE INFINITE PATIENCE AND AN ENDLESS ARMY.
THEN WE WILL FIGHT YOU FOREVER.
ALAS, YOUR STORY DOESN'T END WITH AN EPIC BATTLE. IF YOU CHOOSE TO MANIFEST IN PHYSICAL FORMS, THEN YOU MUST FOLLOW PHYSICAL LIMITATIONS.
YOU WILL TIRE. YOU WILL WEAKEN. MY ARMIES NEVER WILL. NEVER.
THE LIFE CYCLE DEMANDS THAT A SOUL BE GIVEN. AND THAT DEMAND CANNOT BE DENIED.

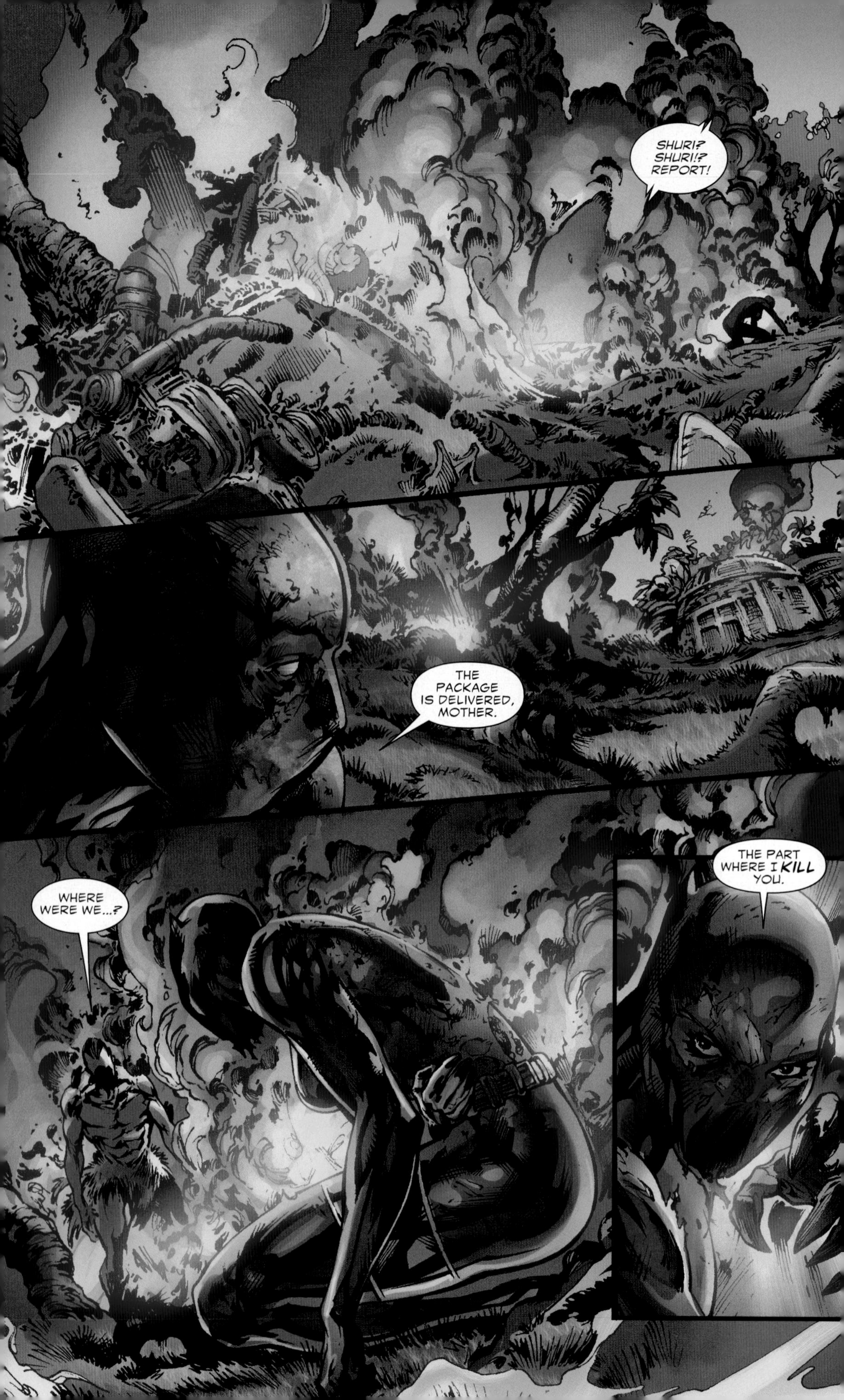
SHURI? SHURI!? REPORT!
THE PACKAGE IS DELIVERED, MOTHER.
WHERE WERE WE...?
THE PART WHERE I KILL YOU.

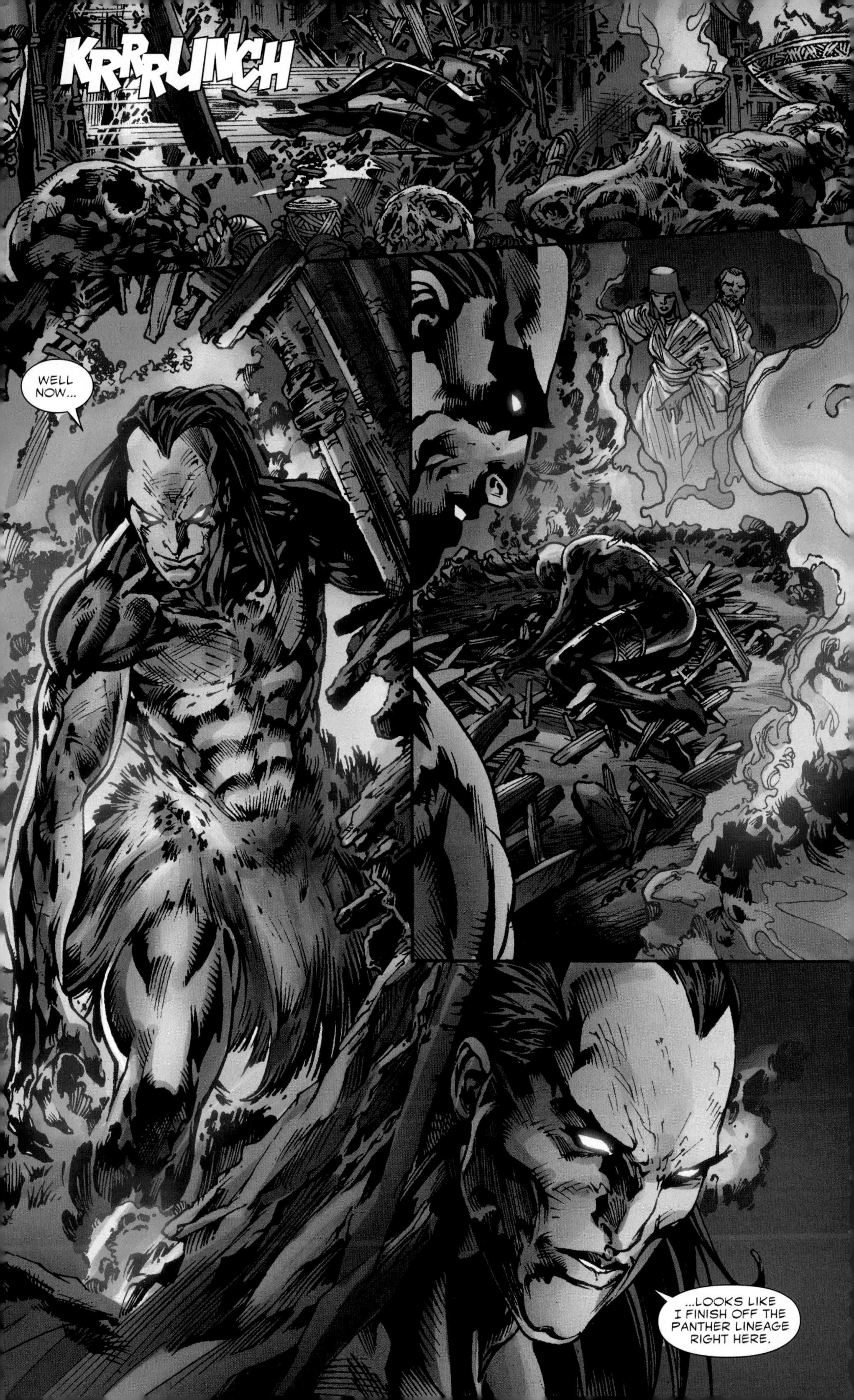
KRRRUNCH
WELL NOW...
...LOOKS LIKE I FINISH OFF THE PANTHER LINEAGE RIGHT HERE.

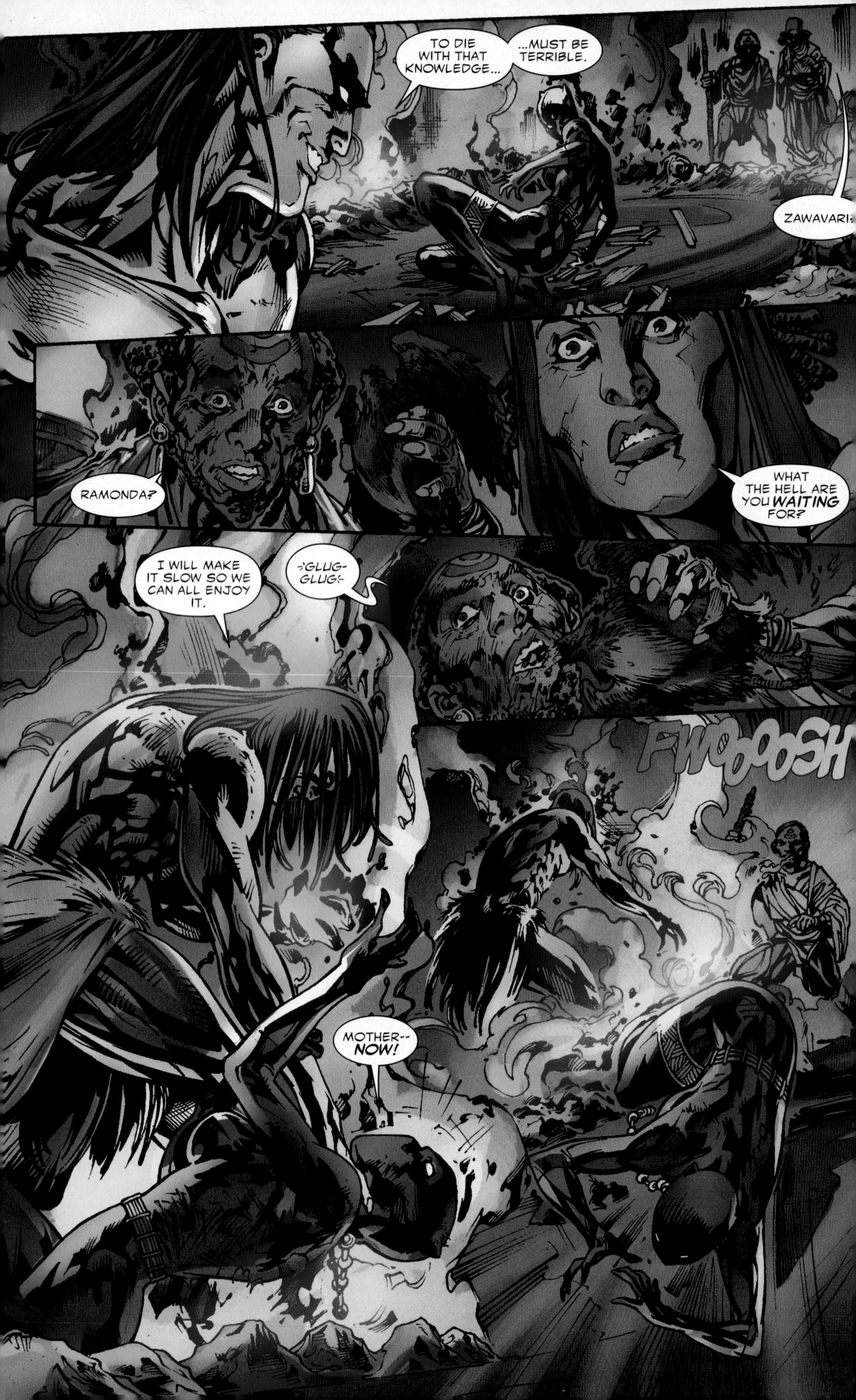

TO DIE WITH THAT KNOWLEDGE...
...MUST BE TERRIBLE.
ZAWAVARI:
RAMONDA?
WHAT THE HELL ARE YOU WAITING FOR?
I WILL MAKE IT SLOW SO WE CAN ALL ENJOY IT.
-GLUG-GLUG-
FWOOOOSH
MOTHER--NOW!

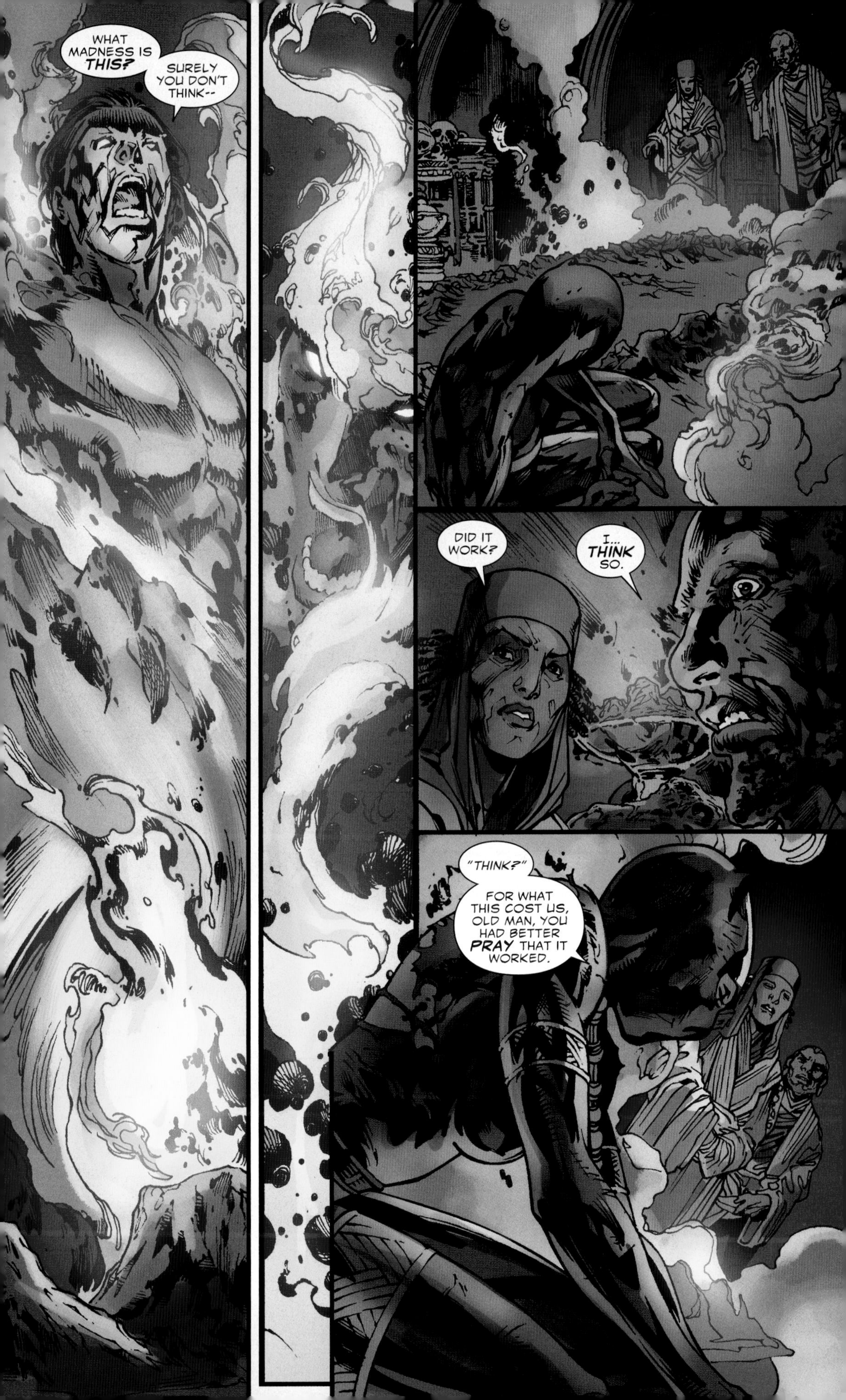

WHAT MADNESS IS THIS?
SURELY YOU DON'T THINK--
DID IT WORK?
I... THINK SO.
"THINK?"
FOR WHAT THIS COST US, OLD MAN, YOU HAD BETTER PRAY THAT IT WORKED.

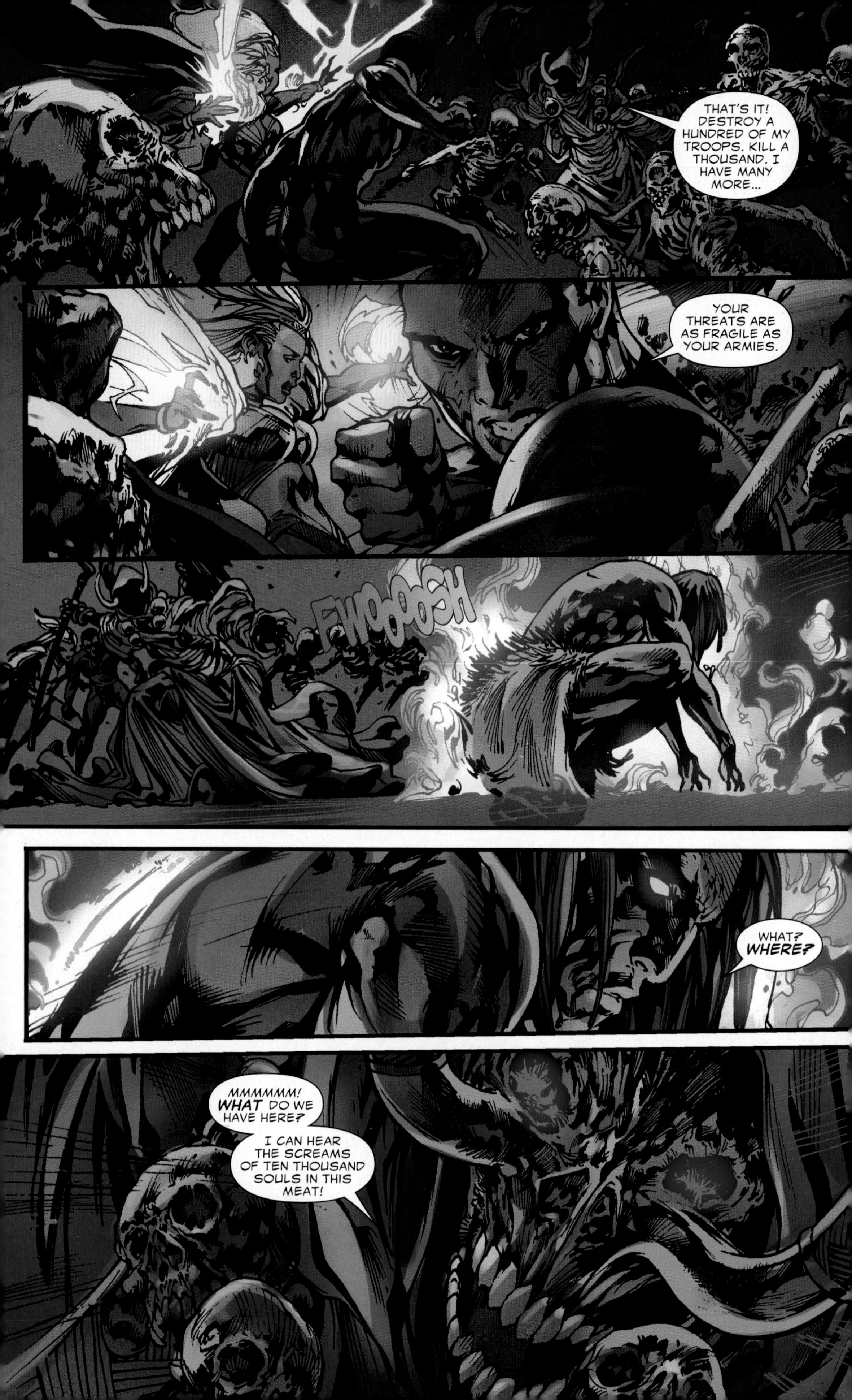

THAT'S IT! DESTROY A HUNDRED OF MY TROOPS. KILL A THOUSAND. I HAVE MANY MORE...
YOUR THREATS ARE AS FRAGILE AS YOUR ARMIES.
FWOOOOSH
WHAT? WHERE?
MMMMMM! WHAT DO WE HAVE HERE?
I CAN HEAR THE SCREAMS OF TEN THOUSAND SOULS IN THIS MEAT!

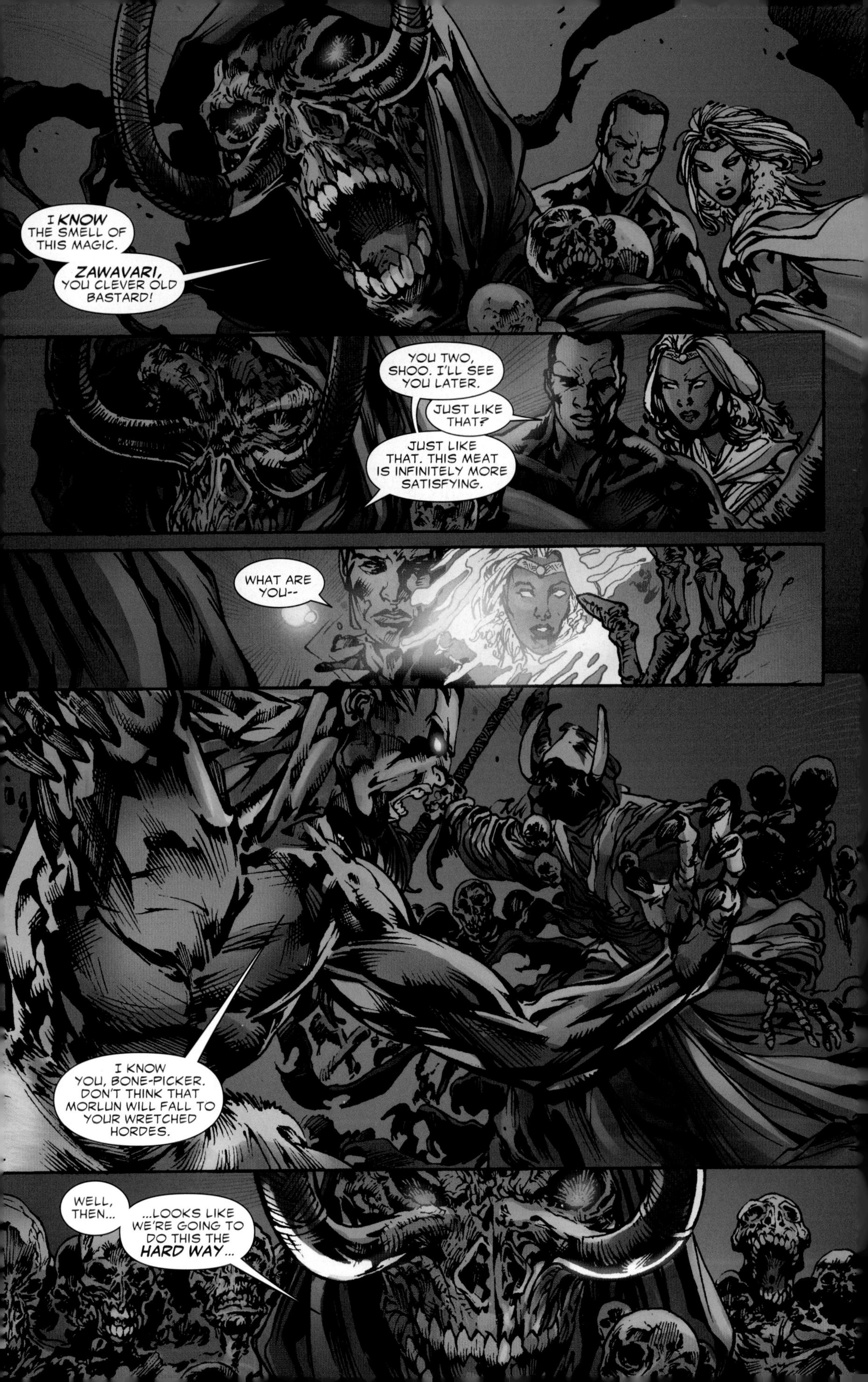
I KNOW THE SMELL OF THIS MAGIC.
ZAWAVARI, YOU CLEVER OLD BASTARD!
YOU TWO, SHOO. I'LL SEE YOU LATER.
JUST LIKE THAT?
JUST LIKE THAT. THIS MEAT IS INFINITELY MORE SATISFYING.
WHAT ARE YOU--
I KNOW YOU, BONE-PICKER. DON'T THINK THAT MORLUN WILL FALL TO YOUR WRETCHED HORDES.
WELL, THEN...
...LOOKS LIKE WE'RE GOING TO DO THIS THE HARD WAY...

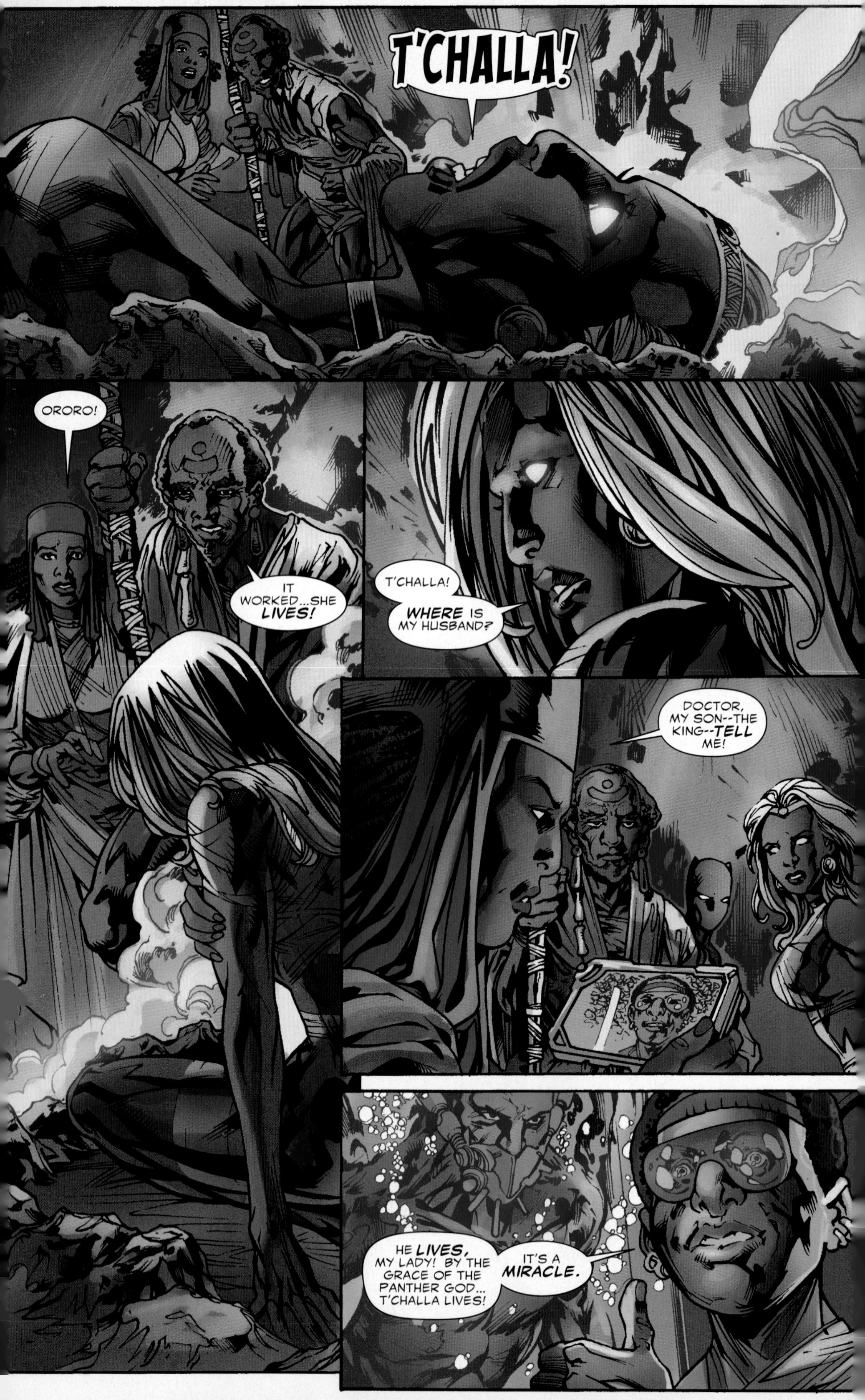
T'CHALLA!
ORORO!
IT WORKED...SHE LIVES!
T'CHALLA!
WHERE IS MY HUSBAND?
DOCTOR, MY SON--THE KING--TELL ME!
HE LIVES, MY LADY! BY THE GRACE OF THE PANTHER GOD... T'CHALLA LIVES!
IT'S A MIRACLE.

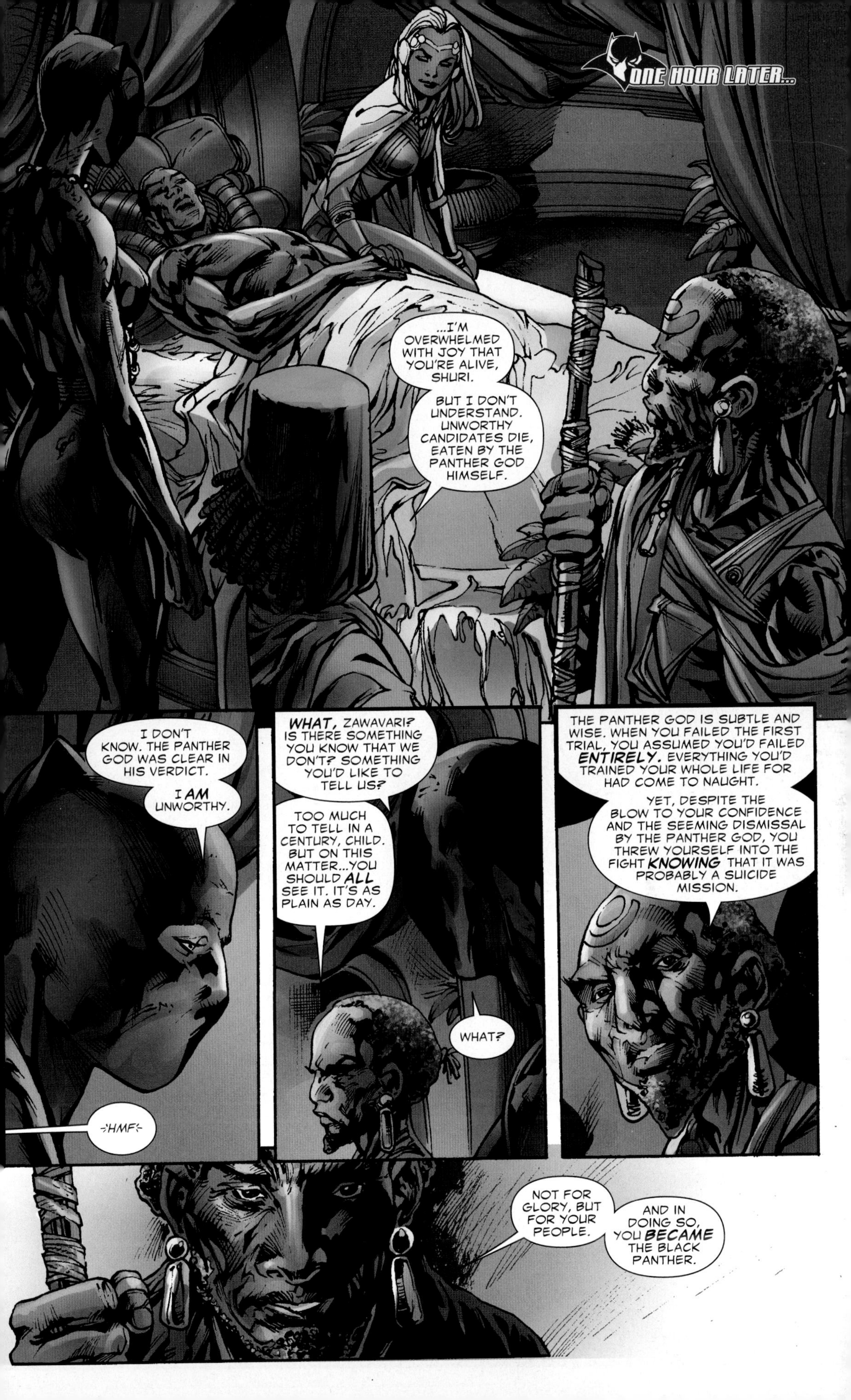
ONE HOUR LATER...
...I'M OVERWHELMED WITH JOY THAT YOU'RE ALIVE, SHURI.
BUT I DON'T UNDERSTAND. UNWORTHY CANDIDATES DIE, EATEN BY THE PANTHER GOD HIMSELF.
I DON'T KNOW. THE PANTHER GOD WAS CLEAR IN HIS VERDICT.
I AM UNWORTHY.
-HMF-
WHAT, ZAWAVARI? IS THERE SOMETHING YOU KNOW THAT WE DON'T? SOMETHING YOU'D LIKE TO TELL US?
TOO MUCH TO TELL IN A CENTURY, CHILD. BUT ON THIS MATTER...YOU SHOULD ALL SEE IT. IT'S AS PLAIN AS DAY.
WHAT?
THE PANTHER GOD IS SUBTLE AND WISE. WHEN YOU FAILED THE FIRST TRIAL, YOU ASSUMED YOU'D FAILED ENTIRELY. EVERYTHING YOU'D TRAINED YOUR WHOLE LIFE FOR HAD COME TO NAUGHT.
YET, DESPITE THE BLOW TO YOUR CONFIDENCE AND THE SEEMING DISMISSAL BY THE PANTHER GOD, YOU THREW YOURSELF INTO THE FIGHT KNOWING THAT IT WAS PROBABLY A SUICIDE MISSION.
NOT FOR GLORY, BUT FOR YOUR PEOPLE.
AND IN DOING SO, YOU BECAME THE BLACK PANTHER.

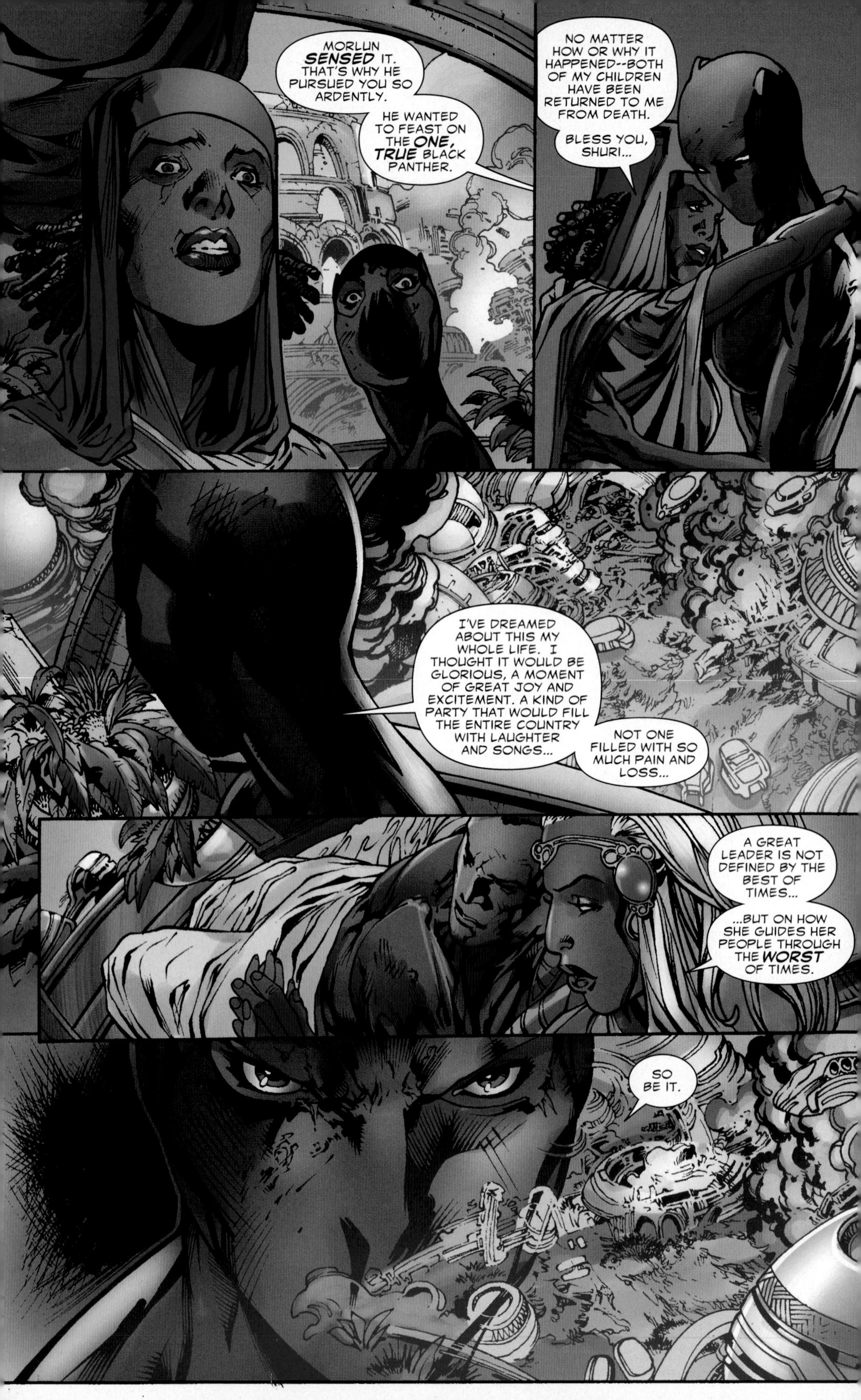

MORLUN SENSED IT. THAT'S WHY HE PURSUED YOU SO ARDENTLY.
HE WANTED TO FEAST ON THE ONE, TRUE BLACK PANTHER.
NO MATTER HOW OR WHY IT HAPPENED--BOTH OF MY CHILDREN HAVE BEEN RETURNED TO ME FROM DEATH.
BLESS YOU, SHURI...
I'VE DREAMED ABOUT THIS MY WHOLE LIFE. I THOUGHT IT WOULD BE GLORIOUS, A MOMENT OF GREAT JOY AND EXCITEMENT. A KIND OF PARTY THAT WOULD FILL THE ENTIRE COUNTRY WITH LAUGHTER AND SONGS...
NOT ONE FILLED WITH SO MUCH PAIN AND LOSS...
A GREAT LEADER IS NOT DEFINED BY THE BEST OF TIMES...
...BUT ON HOW SHE GUIDES HER PEOPLE THROUGH THE WORST OF TIMES.
SO BE IT.

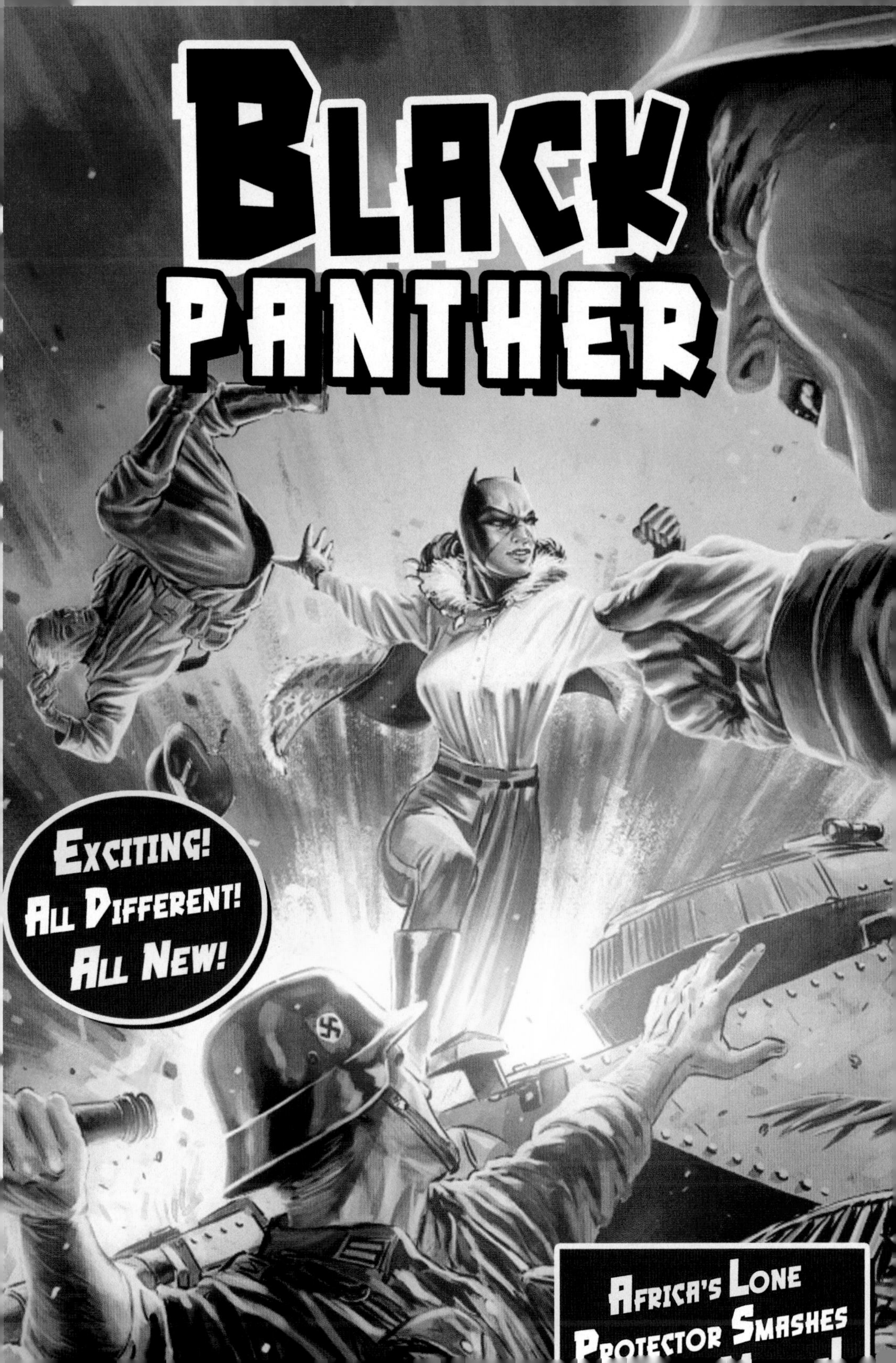
BLACK
PANTHER
EXCITING!
ALL DIFFERENT!
ALL NEW!
AFRICA'S LONE
PROTECTOR SMASHES

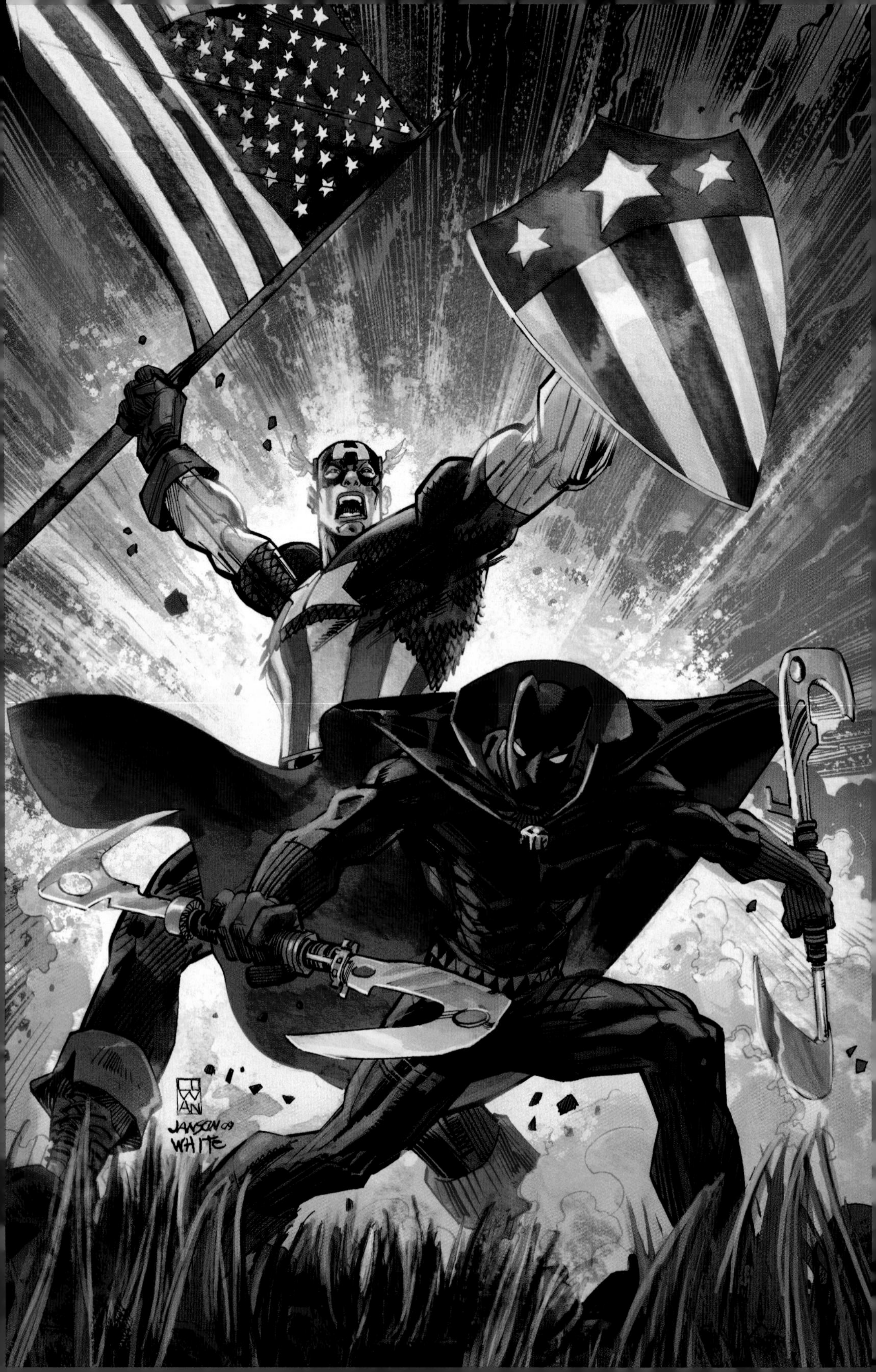
JANSON 09
WHITE

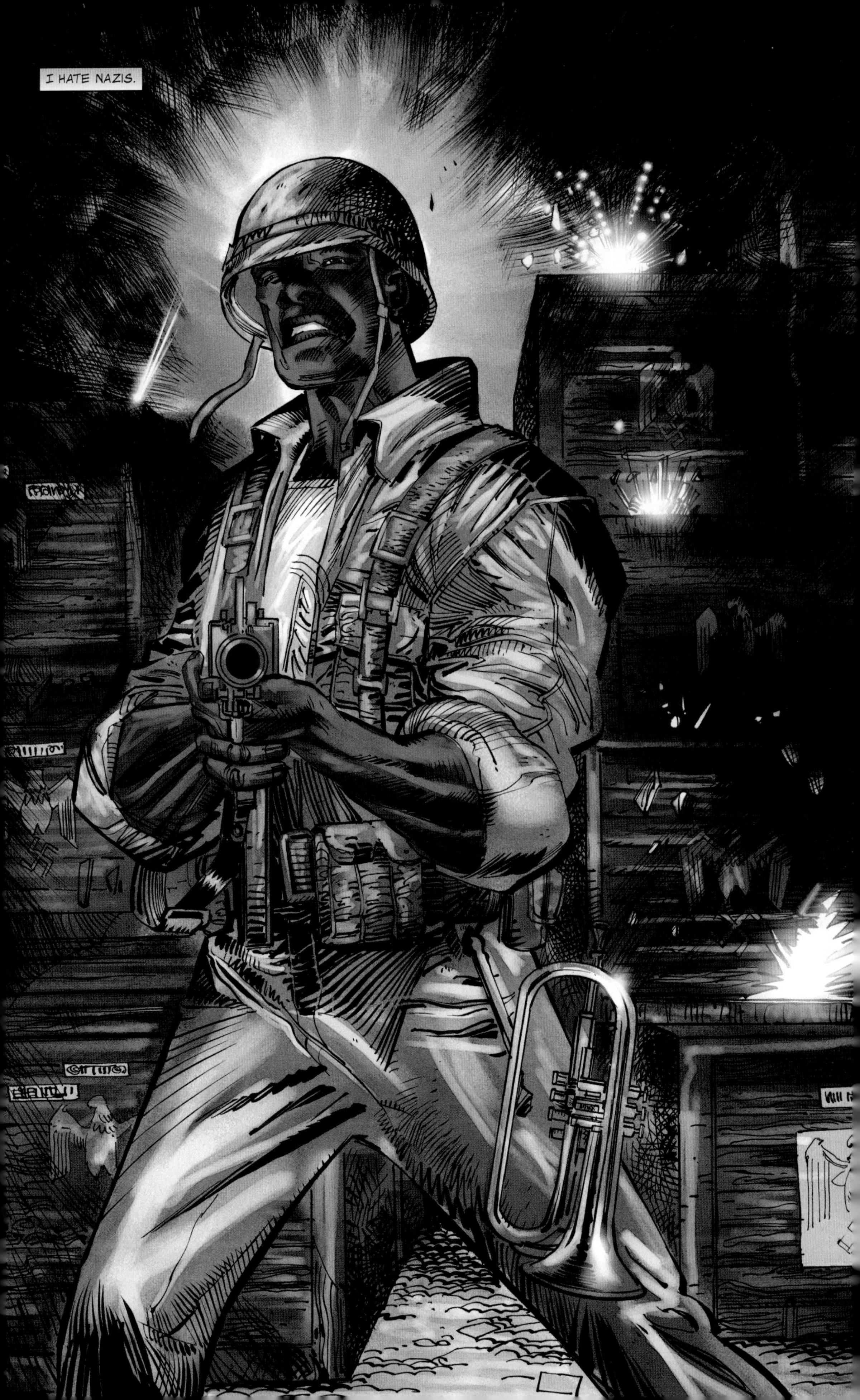
I HATE NAZIS.

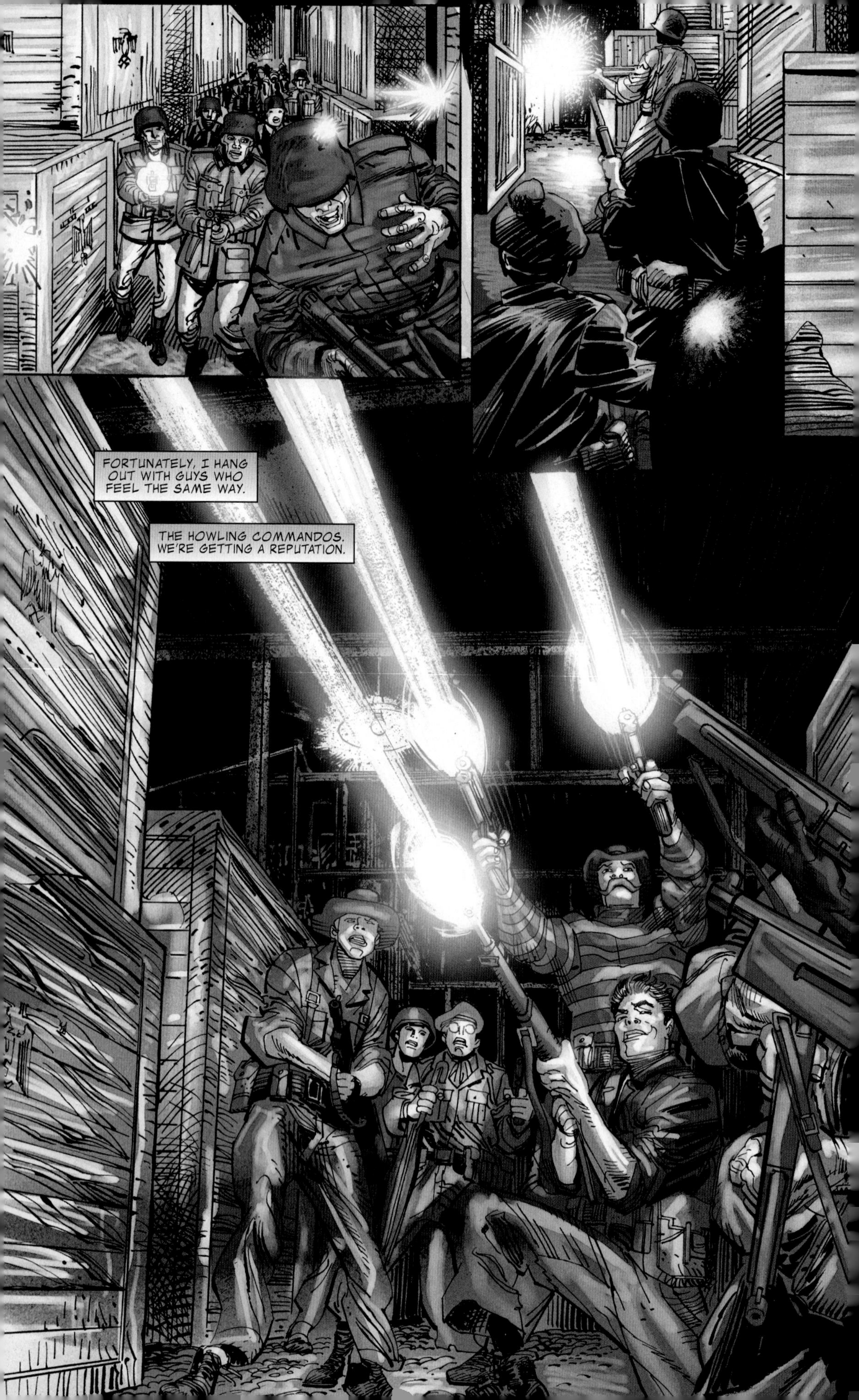
FORTUNATELY, I HANG OUT WITH GUYS WHO FEEL THE SAME WAY.
THE HOWLING COMMANDOS. WE'RE GETTING A REPUTATION.

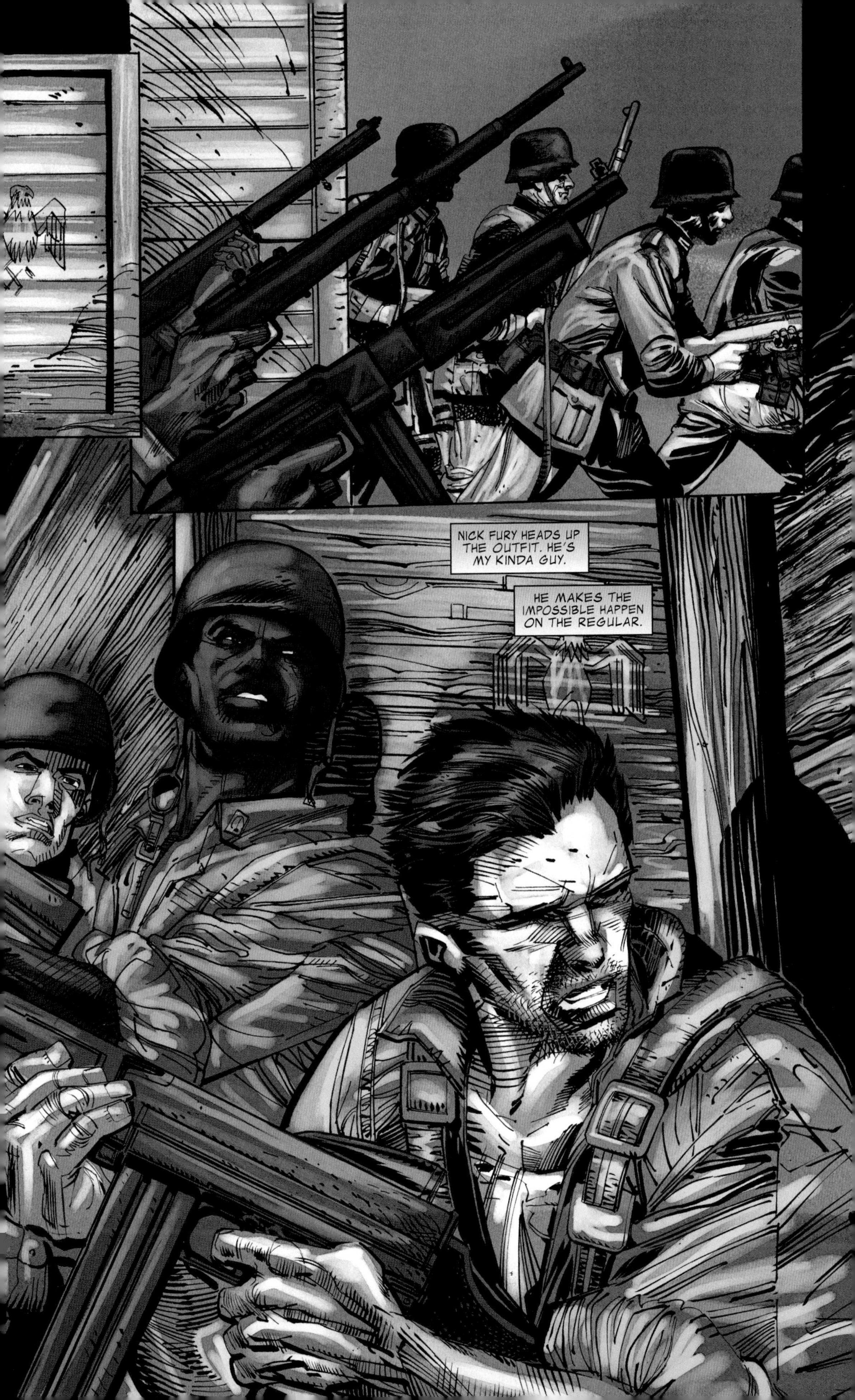
NICK FURY HEADS UP THE OUTFIT. HE'S MY KINDA GUY.
HE MAKES THE IMPOSSIBLE HAPPEN ON THE REGULAR.

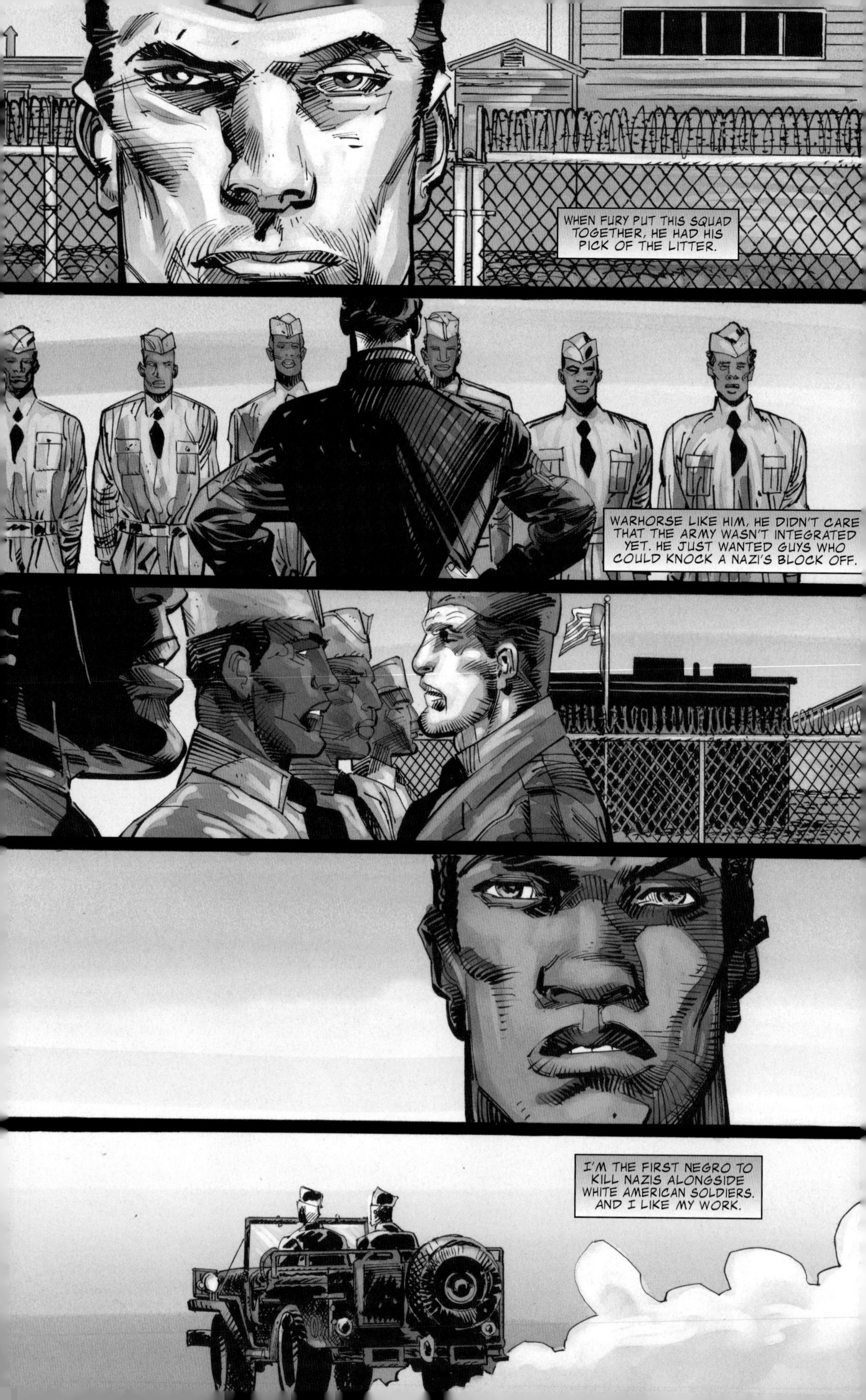
WHEN FURY PUT THIS SQUAD TOGETHER, HE HAD HIS PICK OF THE LITTER.
WARHORSE LIKE HIM, HE DIDN'T CARE THAT THE ARMY WASN'T INTEGRATED YET. HE JUST WANTED GUYS WHO COULD KNOCK A NAZI'S BLOCK OFF.
I'M THE FIRST NEGRO TO KILL NAZIS ALONGSIDE WHITE AMERICAN SOLDIERS. AND I LIKE MY WORK.

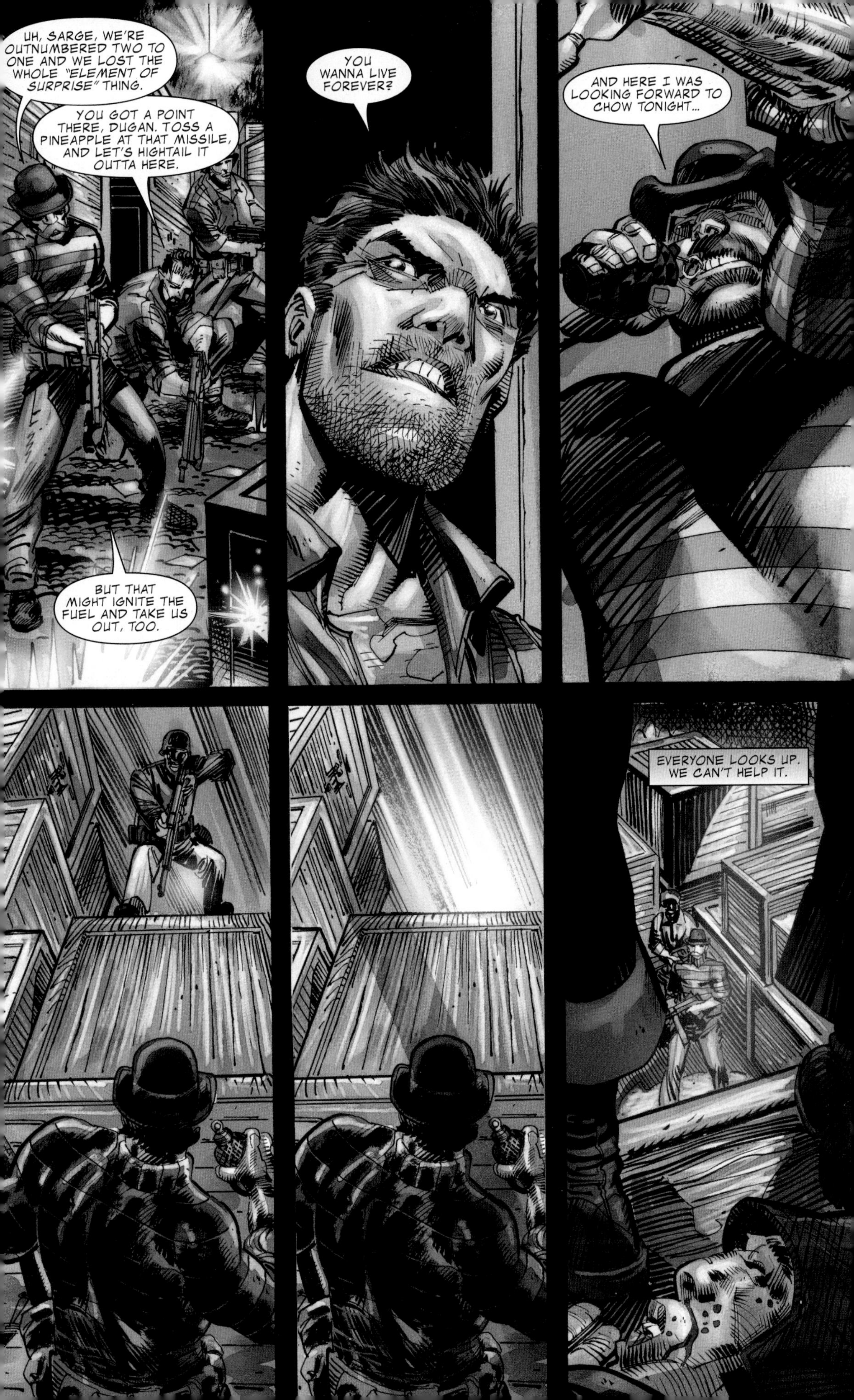
UH, SARGE, WE'RE OUTNUMBERED TWO TO ONE AND WE LOST THE WHOLE "ELEMENT OF SURPRISE" THING.
YOU GOT A POINT THERE, DUGAN. TOSS A PINEAPPLE AT THAT MISSILE, AND LET'S HIGHTAIL IT OUTTA HERE.
BUT THAT MIGHT IGNITE THE FUEL AND TAKE US OUT, TOO.
YOU WANNA LIVE FOREVER?
AND HERE I WAS LOOKING FORWARD TO CHOW TONIGHT...
EVERYONE LOOKS UP. WE CAN'T HELP IT.

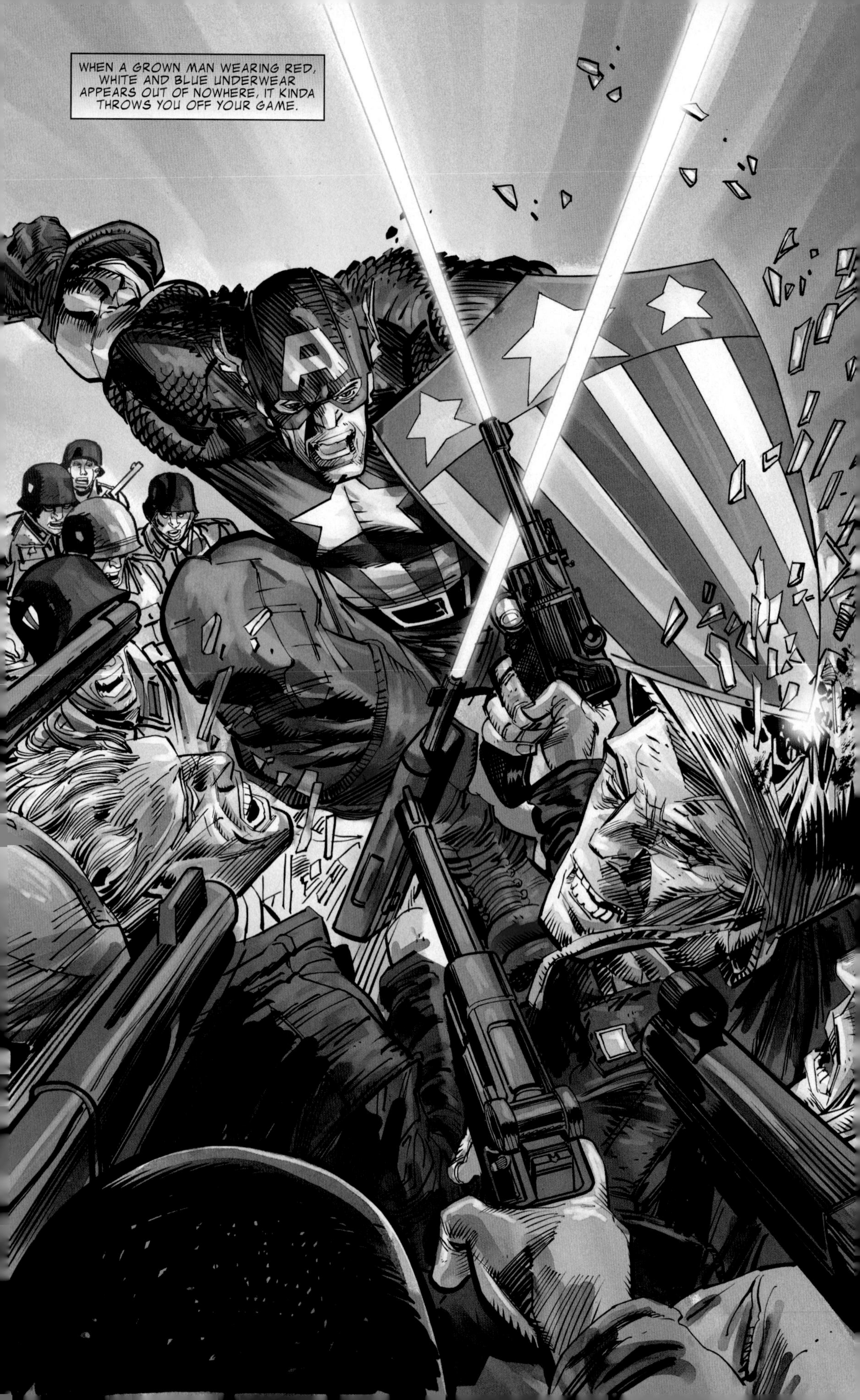
WHEN A GROWN MAN WEARING RED, WHITE AND BLUE UNDERWEAR APPEARS OUT OF NOWHERE, IT KINDA THROWS YOU OFF YOUR GAME.

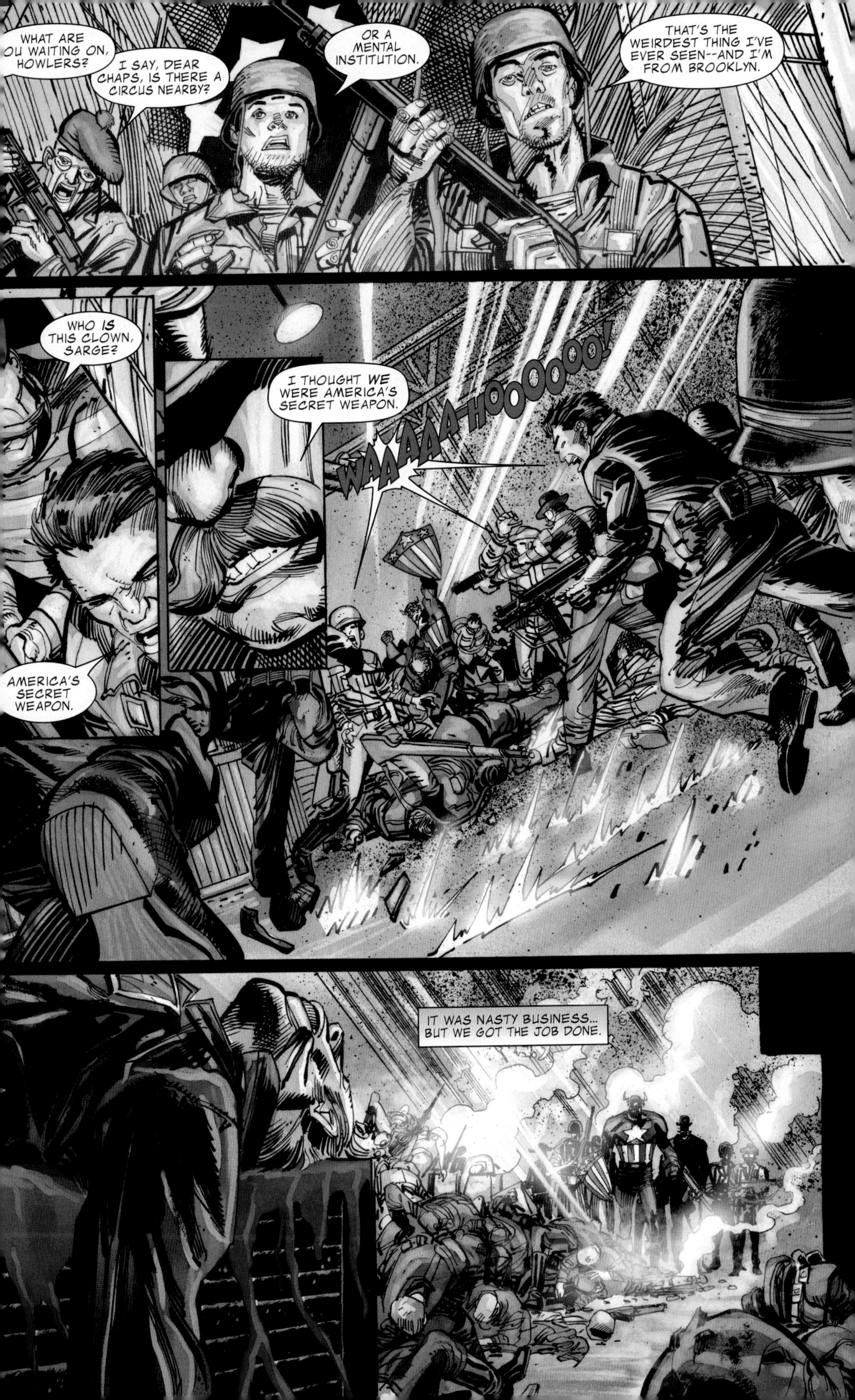
WHAT ARE OU WAITING ON, HOWLERS?
I SAY, DEAR CHAPS, IS THERE A CIRCUS NEARBY?
OR A MENTAL INSTITUTION.
THAT'S THE WEIRDEST THING I'VE EVER SEEN--AND I'M FROM BROOKLYN.
WHO IS THIS CLOWN, SARGE?
AMERICA'S SECRET WEAPON.
I THOUGHT WE WERE AMERICA'S SECRET WEAPON.
WAAAAA-HOOOOOOO!
IT WAS NASTY BUSINESS... BUT WE GOT THE JOB DONE.

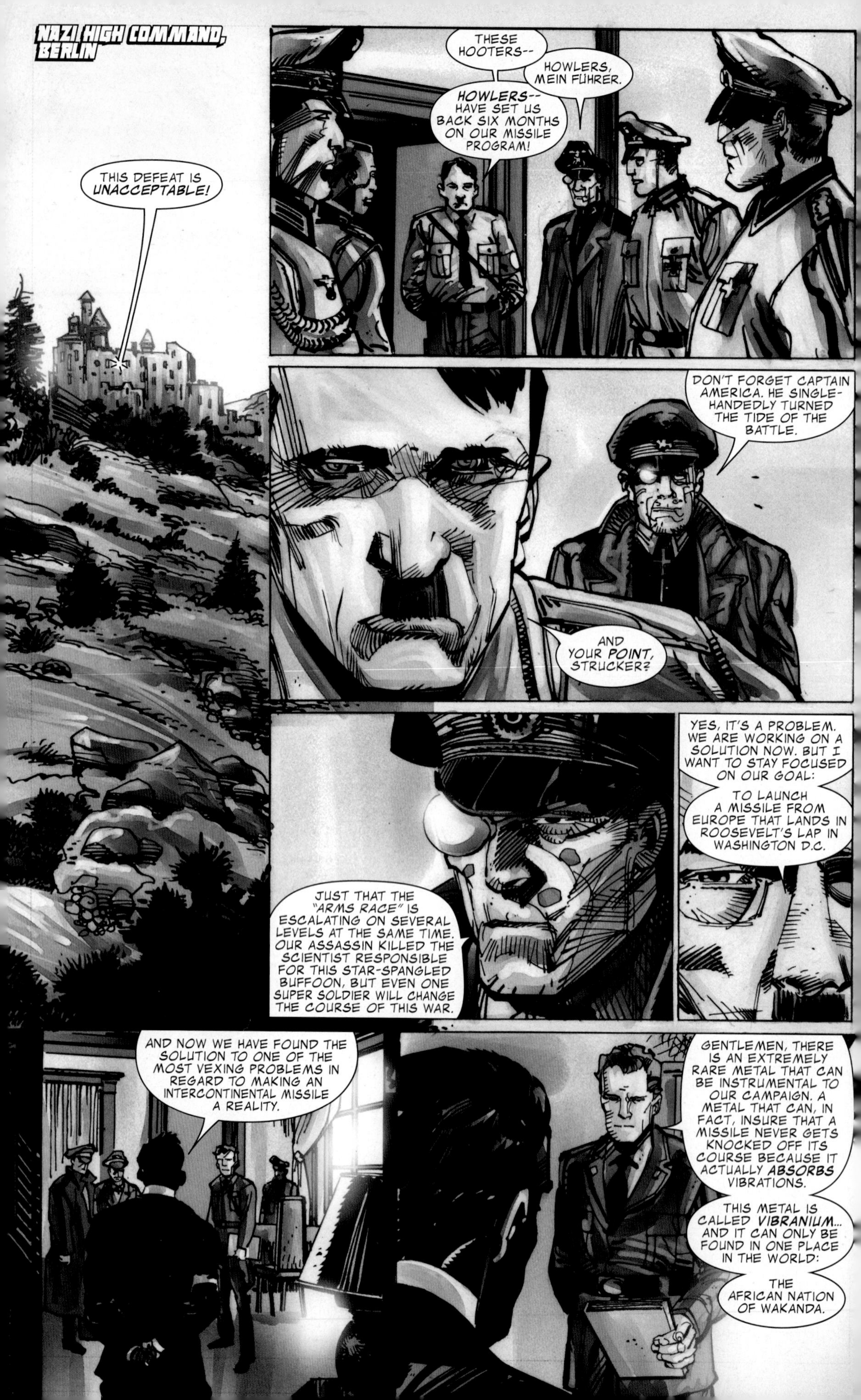
NAZI HIGH COMMAND, BERLIN
THIS DEFEAT IS UNACCEPTABLE!
THESE HOOTERS--
HOWLERS, MEIN FÜHRER.
HOWLERS-- HAVE SET US BACK SIX MONTHS ON OUR MISSILE PROGRAM!
DON'T FORGET CAPTAIN AMERICA. HE SINGLE-HANDEDLY TURNED THE TIDE OF THE BATTLE.
AND YOUR POINT, STRUCKER?
JUST THAT THE "ARMS RACE" IS ESCALATING ON SEVERAL LEVELS AT THE SAME TIME. OUR ASSASSIN KILLED THE SCIENTIST RESPONSIBLE FOR THIS STAR-SPANGLED BUFFOON, BUT EVEN ONE SUPER SOLDIER WILL CHANGE THE COURSE OF THIS WAR.
YES, IT'S A PROBLEM. WE ARE WORKING ON A SOLUTION NOW. BUT I WANT TO STAY FOCUSED ON OUR GOAL:
TO LAUNCH A MISSILE FROM EUROPE THAT LANDS IN ROOSEVELT'S LAP IN WASHINGTON D.C.
AND NOW WE HAVE FOUND THE SOLUTION TO ONE OF THE MOST VEXING PROBLEMS IN REGARD TO MAKING AN INTERCONTINENTAL MISSILE A REALITY.
GENTLEMEN, THERE IS AN EXTREMELY RARE METAL THAT CAN BE INSTRUMENTAL TO OUR CAMPAIGN. A METAL THAT CAN, IN FACT, INSURE THAT A MISSILE NEVER GETS KNOCKED OFF ITS COURSE BECAUSE IT ACTUALLY ABSORBS VIBRATIONS.
THIS METAL IS CALLED VIBRANIUM... AND IT CAN ONLY BE FOUND IN ONE PLACE IN THE WORLD:
THE AFRICAN NATION OF WAKANDA.

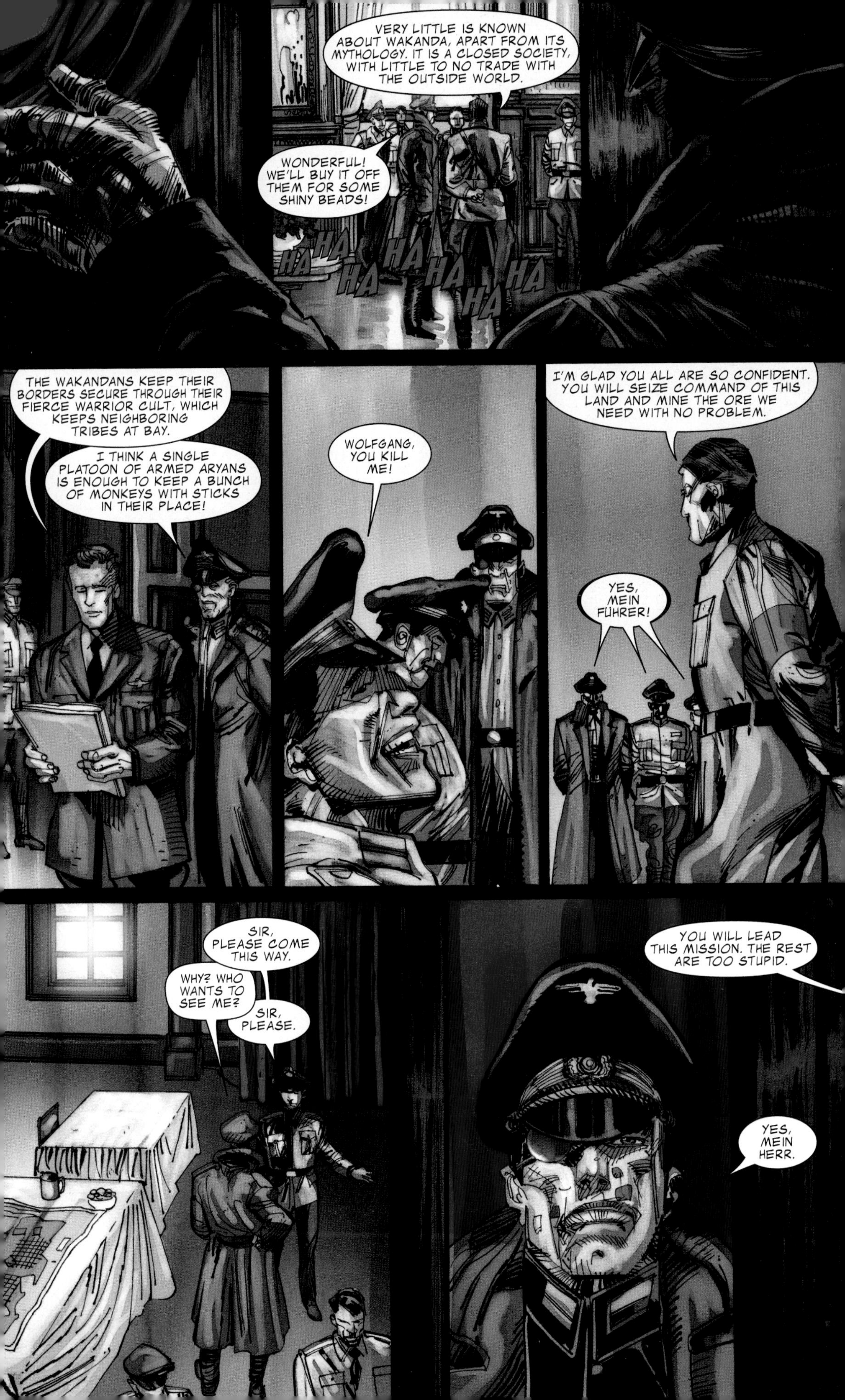
VERY LITTLE IS KNOWN ABOUT WAKANDA, APART FROM ITS MYTHOLOGY. IT IS A CLOSED SOCIETY, WITH LITTLE TO NO TRADE WITH THE OUTSIDE WORLD.
WONDERFUL! WE'LL BUY IT OFF THEM FOR SOME SHINY BEADS!
HA HA HA HA HA HA HA HA HA
THE WAKANDANS KEEP THEIR BORDERS SECURE THROUGH THEIR FIERCE WARRIOR CULT, WHICH KEEPS NEIGHBORING TRIBES AT BAY.
I THINK A SINGLE PLATOON OF ARMED ARYANS IS ENOUGH TO KEEP A BUNCH OF MONKEYS WITH STICKS IN THEIR PLACE!
WOLFGANG, YOU KILL ME!
I'M GLAD YOU ALL ARE SO CONFIDENT. YOU WILL SEIZE COMMAND OF THIS LAND AND MINE THE ORE WE NEED WITH NO PROBLEM.
YES, MEIN FÜHRER!
SIR, PLEASE COME THIS WAY.
WHY? WHO WANTS TO SEE ME?
SIR, PLEASE.
YOU WILL LEAD THIS MISSION. THE REST ARE TOO STUPID.
YES, MEIN HERR.

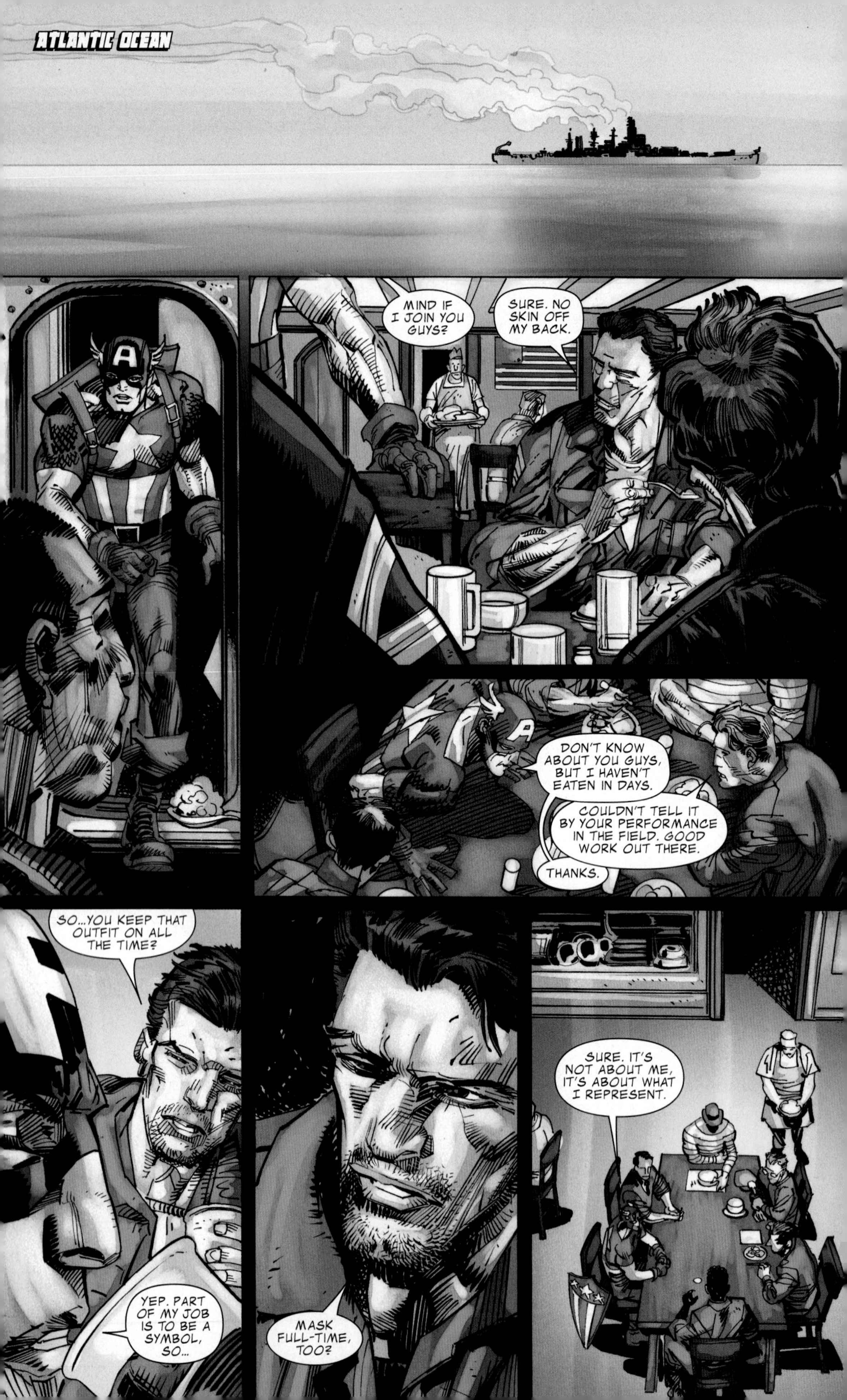
ATLANTIC OCEAN
MIND IF I JOIN YOU GUYS?
SURE. NO SKIN OFF MY BACK.
DON'T KNOW ABOUT YOU GUYS, BUT I HAVEN'T EATEN IN DAYS.
COULDN'T TELL IT BY YOUR PERFORMANCE IN THE FIELD. GOOD WORK OUT THERE.
THANKS.
SO...YOU KEEP THAT OUTFIT ON ALL THE TIME?
YEP. PART OF MY JOB IS TO BE A SYMBOL, SO...
MASK FULL-TIME, TOO?
SURE. IT'S NOT ABOUT ME, IT'S ABOUT WHAT I REPRESENT.

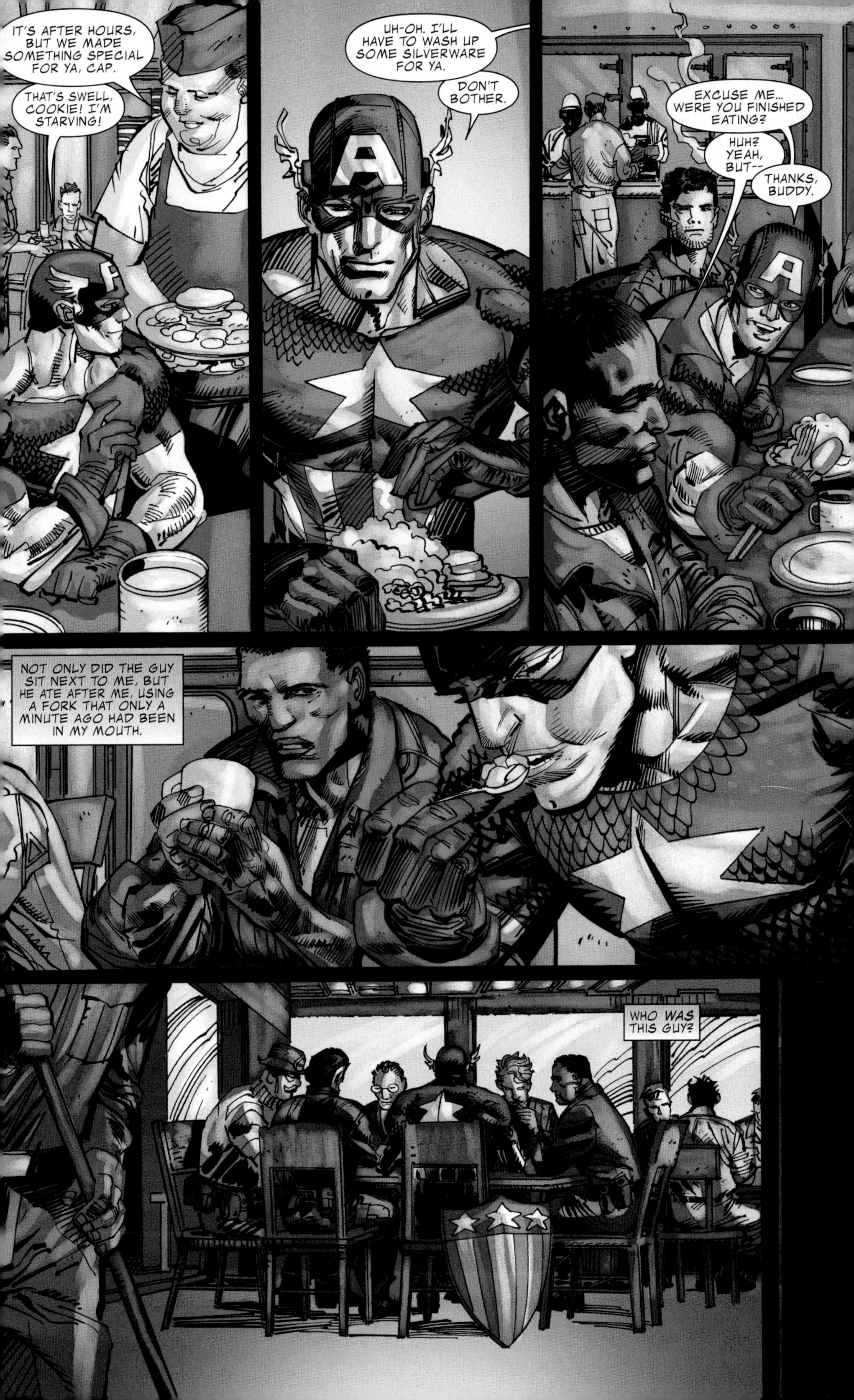
IT'S AFTER HOURS, BUT WE MADE SOMETHING SPECIAL FOR YA, CAP.
THAT'S SWELL, COOKIE! I'M STARVING!
UH-OH. I'LL HAVE TO WASH UP SOME SILVERWARE FOR YA.
DON'T BOTHER.
EXCUSE ME... WERE YOU FINISHED EATING?
HUH? YEAH, BUT--
THANKS, BUDDY.
NOT ONLY DID THE GUY SIT NEXT TO ME, BUT HE ATE AFTER ME, USING A FORK THAT ONLY A MINUTE AGO HAD BEEN IN MY MOUTH.
WHO WAS THIS GUY?

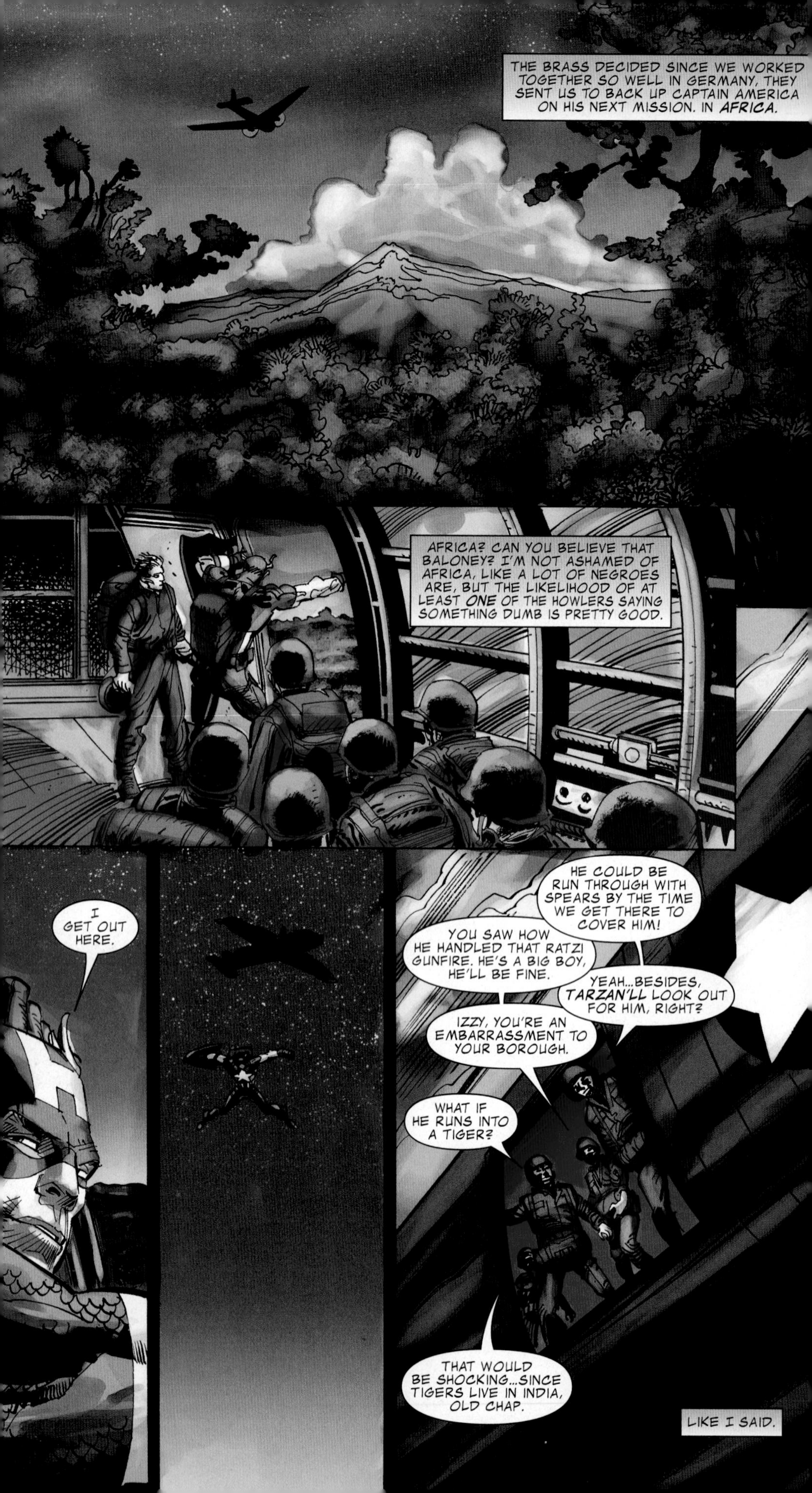
THE BRASS DECIDED SINCE WE WORKED TOGETHER SO WELL IN GERMANY, THEY SENT US TO BACK UP CAPTAIN AMERICA ON HIS NEXT MISSION. IN AFRICA.
AFRICA? CAN YOU BELIEVE THAT BALONEY? I'M NOT ASHAMED OF AFRICA, LIKE A LOT OF NEGROES ARE, BUT THE LIKELIHOOD OF AT LEAST ONE OF THE HOWLERS SAYING SOMETHING DUMB IS PRETTY GOOD.
I GET OUT HERE.
HE COULD BE RUN THROUGH WITH SPEARS BY THE TIME WE GET THERE TO COVER HIM!
YOU SAW HOW HE HANDLED THAT RATZI GUNFIRE. HE'S A BIG BOY, HE'LL BE FINE.
YEAH...BESIDES, TARZAN'LL LOOK OUT FOR HIM, RIGHT?
IZZY, YOU'RE AN EMBARRASSMENT TO YOUR BOROUGH.
WHAT IF HE RUNS INTO A TIGER?
THAT WOULD BE SHOCKING...SINCE TIGERS LIVE IN INDIA, OLD CHAP.
LIKE I SAID.

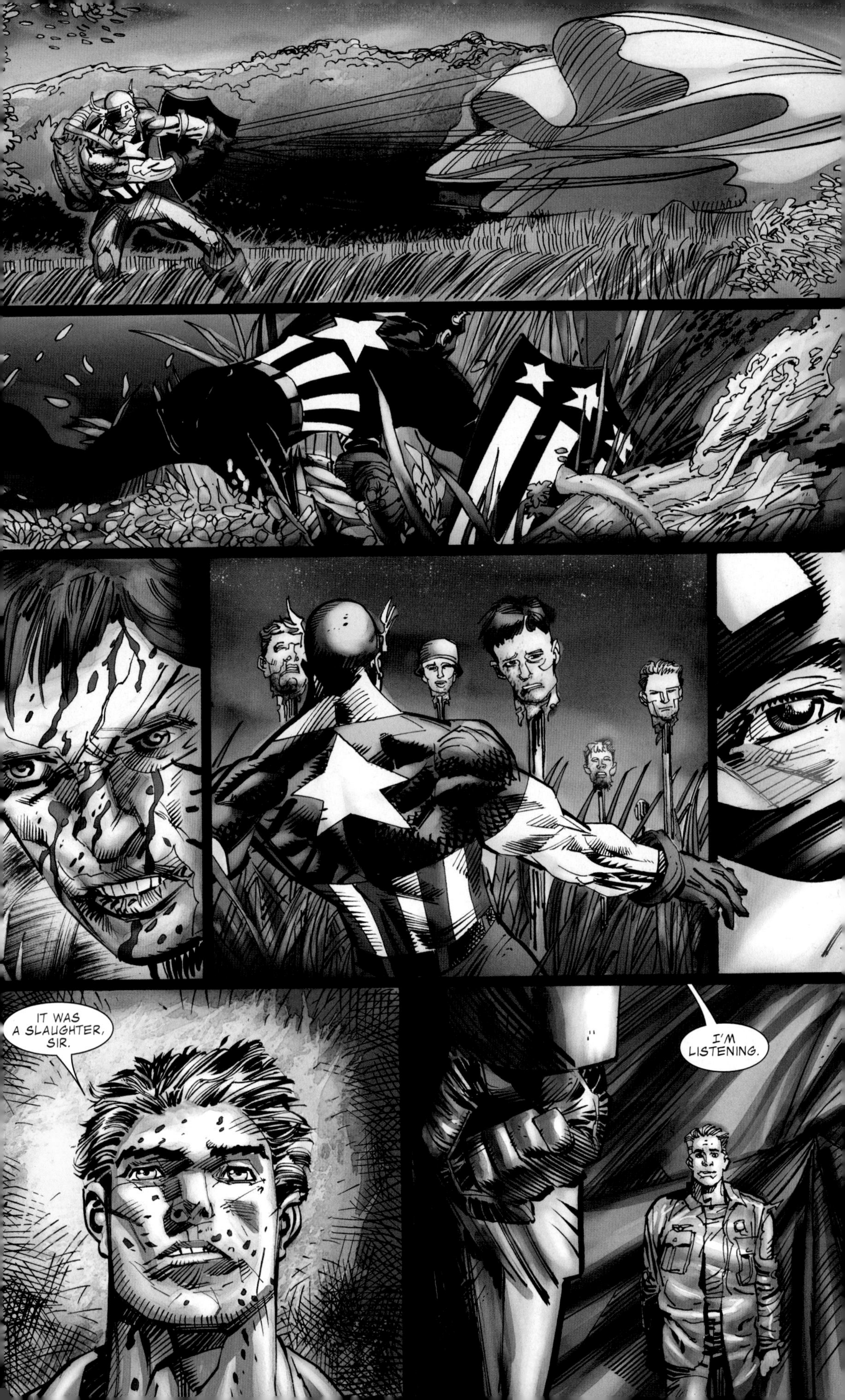
IT WAS A SLAUGHTER, SIR.
I'M LISTENING.

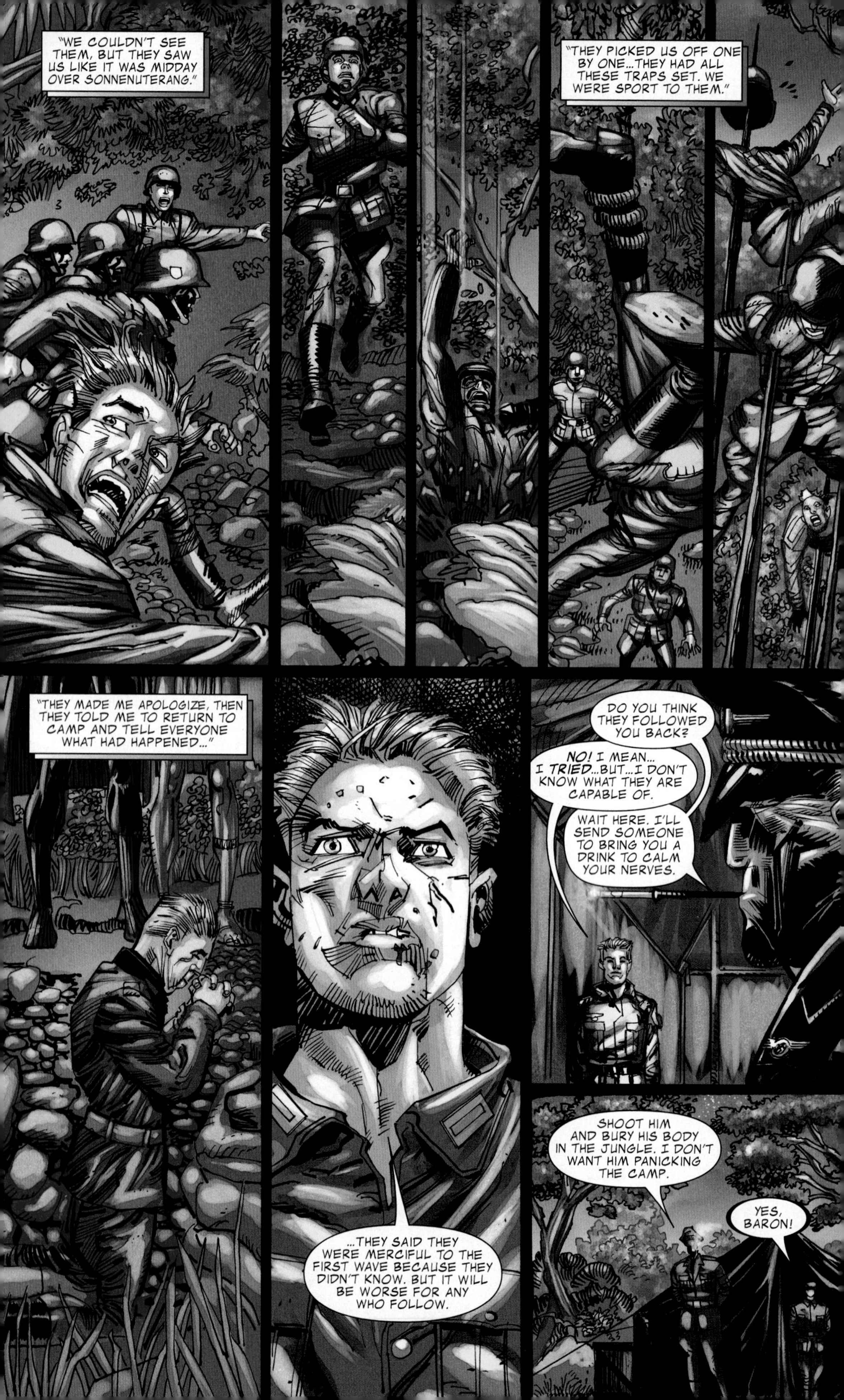
"WE COULDN'T SEE THEM, BUT THEY SAW US LIKE IT WAS MIDDAY OVER SONNENUTERANG."
"THEY PICKED US OFF ONE BY ONE...THEY HAD ALL THESE TRAPS SET. WE WERE SPORT TO THEM."
"THEY MADE ME APOLOGIZE, THEN THEY TOLD ME TO RETURN TO CAMP AND TELL EVERYONE WHAT HAD HAPPENED..."
...THEY SAID THEY WERE MERCIFUL TO THE FIRST WAVE BECAUSE THEY DIDN'T KNOW. BUT IT WILL BE WORSE FOR ANY WHO FOLLOW.
DO YOU THINK THEY FOLLOWED YOU BACK?
NO! I MEAN... I TRIED...BUT...I DON'T KNOW WHAT THEY ARE CAPABLE OF.
WAIT HERE. I'LL SEND SOMEONE TO BRING YOU A DRINK TO CALM YOUR NERVES.
SHOOT HIM AND BURY HIS BODY IN THE JUNGLE. I DON'T WANT HIM PANICKING THE CAMP.
YES, BARON!

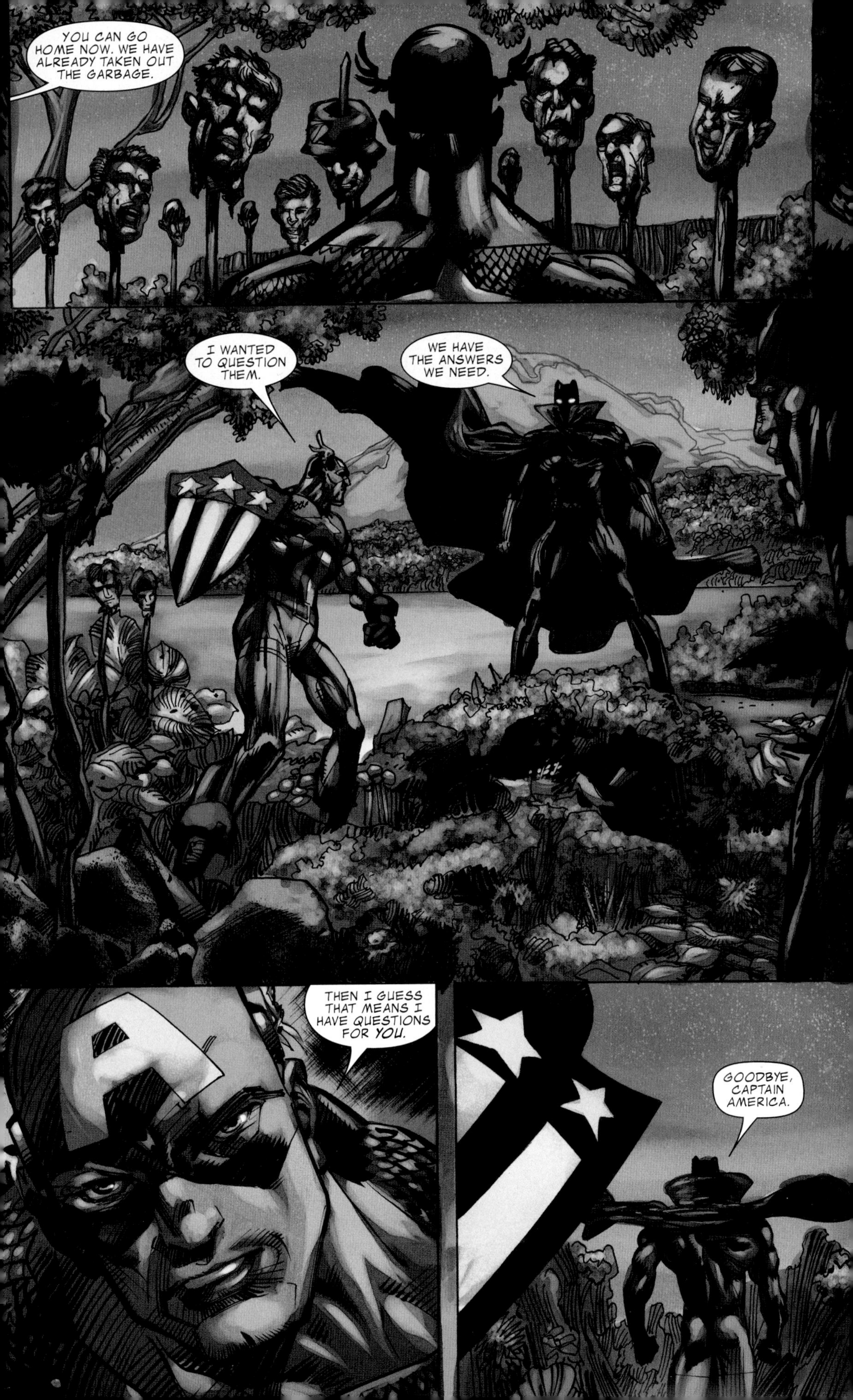
YOU CAN GO HOME NOW. WE HAVE ALREADY TAKEN OUT THE GARBAGE.
I WANTED TO QUESTION THEM.
WE HAVE THE ANSWERS WE NEED.
THEN I GUESS THAT MEANS I HAVE QUESTIONS FOR YOU.
GOODBYE, CAPTAIN AMERICA.

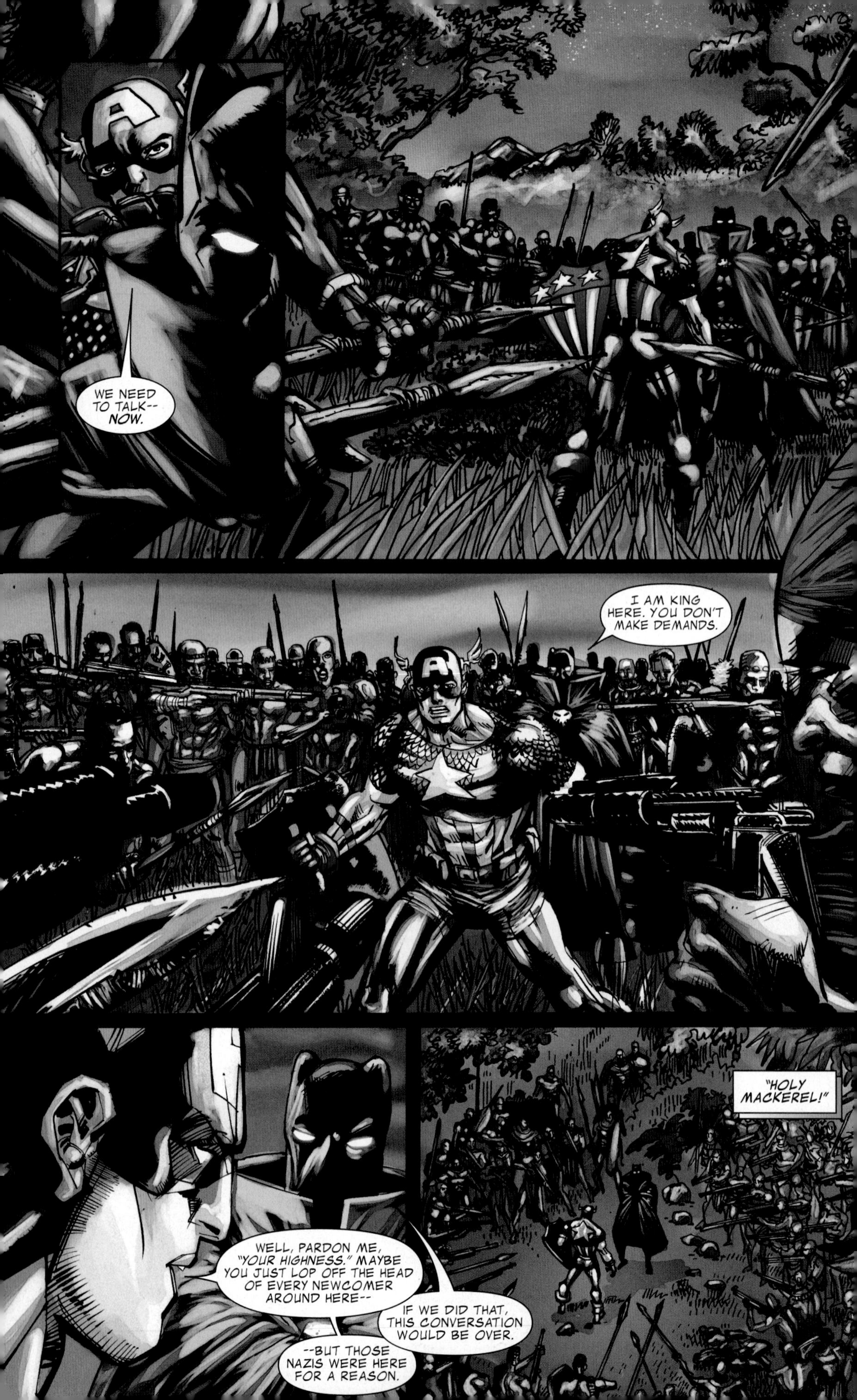
WE NEED TO TALK-- NOW.
I AM KING HERE. YOU DON'T MAKE DEMANDS.
WELL, PARDON ME, "YOUR HIGHNESS." MAYBE YOU JUST LOP OFF THE HEAD OF EVERY NEWCOMER AROUND HERE--
IF WE DID THAT, THIS CONVERSATION WOULD BE OVER.
--BUT THOSE NAZIS WERE HERE FOR A REASON.
"HOLY MACKEREL!"

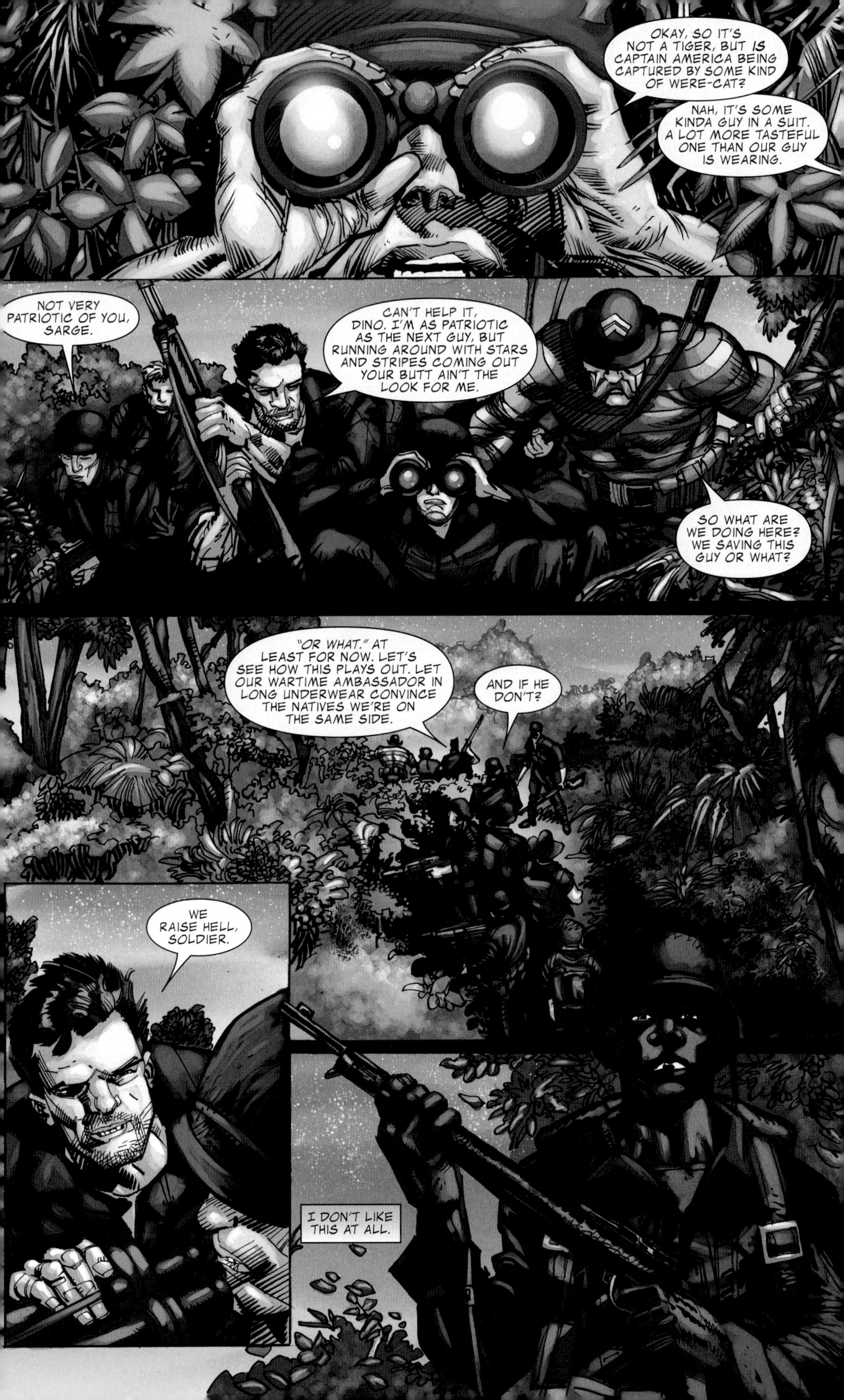
OKAY, SO IT'S NOT A TIGER, BUT IS CAPTAIN AMERICA BEING CAPTURED BY SOME KIND OF WERE-CAT?
NAH, IT'S SOME KINDA GUY IN A SUIT. A LOT MORE TASTEFUL ONE THAN OUR GUY IS WEARING.
NOT VERY PATRIOTIC OF YOU, SARGE.
CAN'T HELP IT, DINO. I'M AS PATRIOTIC AS THE NEXT GUY, BUT RUNNING AROUND WITH STARS AND STRIPES COMING OUT YOUR BUTT AIN'T THE LOOK FOR ME.
SO WHAT ARE WE DOING HERE? WE SAVING THIS GUY OR WHAT?
"OR WHAT." AT LEAST FOR NOW. LET'S SEE HOW THIS PLAYS OUT. LET OUR WARTIME AMBASSADOR IN LONG UNDERWEAR CONVINCE THE NATIVES WE'RE ON THE SAME SIDE.
AND IF HE DON'T?
WE RAISE HELL, SOLDIER.
I DON'T LIKE THIS AT ALL.

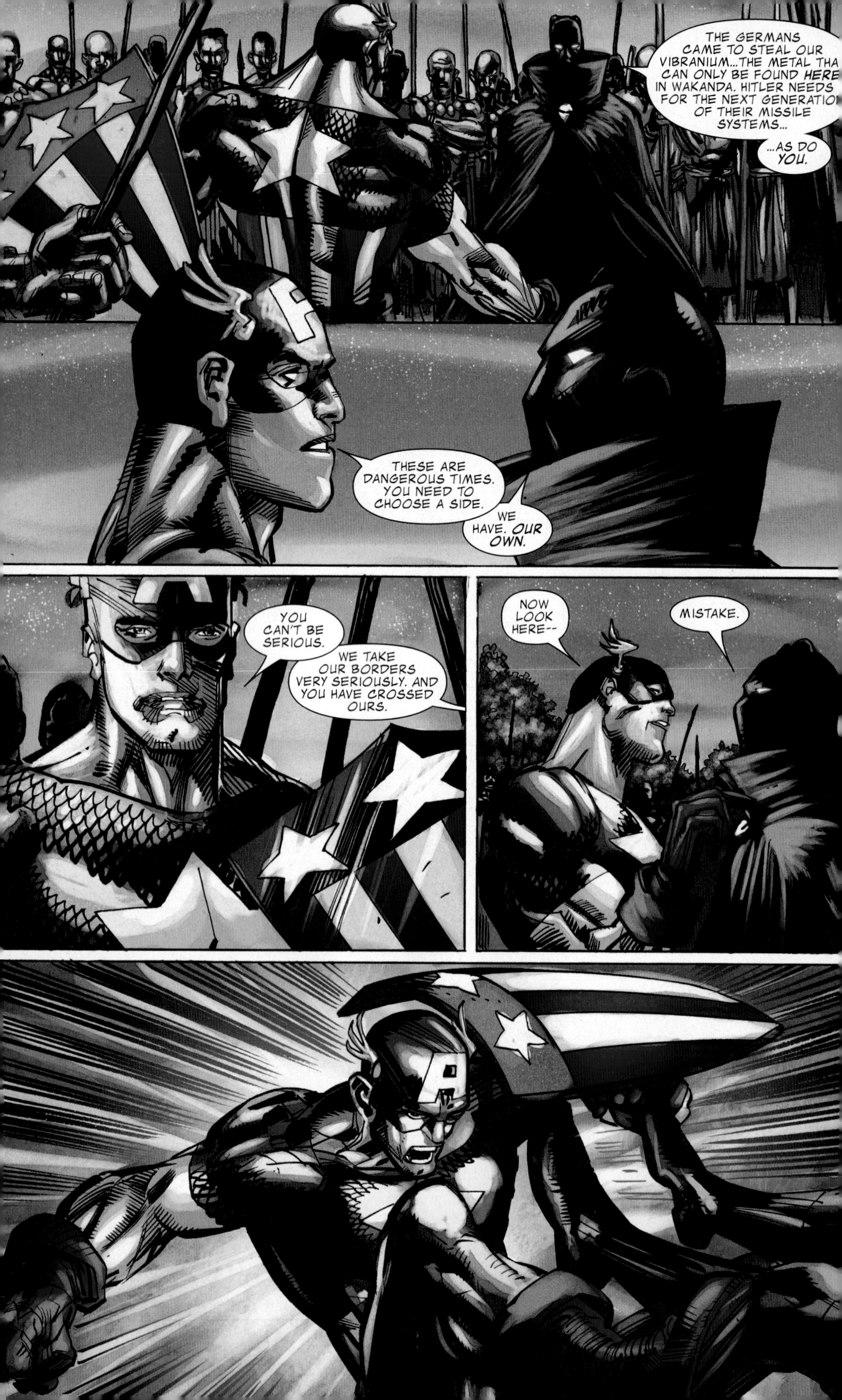
THE GERMANS CAME TO STEAL OUR VIBRANIUM...THE METAL THA CAN ONLY BE FOUND HERE IN WAKANDA. HITLER NEEDS FOR THE NEXT GENERATIO OF THEIR MISSILE SYSTEMS...
...AS DO YOU.
THESE ARE DANGEROUS TIMES. YOU NEED TO CHOOSE A SIDE.
WE HAVE. OUR OWN.
YOU CAN'T BE SERIOUS.
WE TAKE OUR BORDERS VERY SERIOUSLY. AND YOU HAVE CROSSED OURS.
NOW LOOK HERE--
MISTAKE.

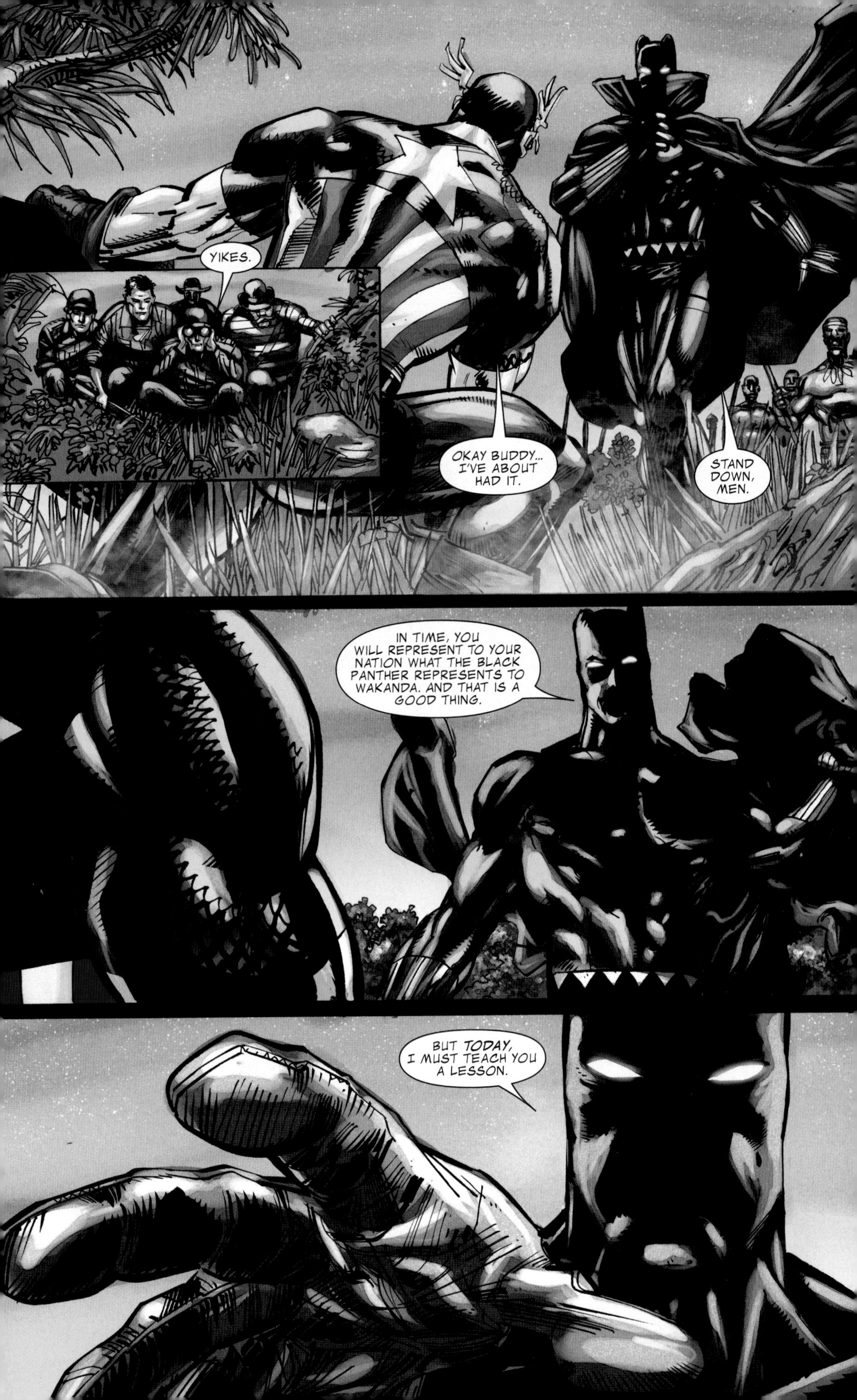
YIKES.
OKAY BUDDY... I'VE ABOUT HAD IT.
STAND DOWN, MEN.
IN TIME, YOU WILL REPRESENT TO YOUR NATION WHAT THE BLACK PANTHER REPRESENTS TO WAKANDA. AND THAT IS A GOOD THING.
BUT TODAY, I MUST TEACH YOU A LESSON.

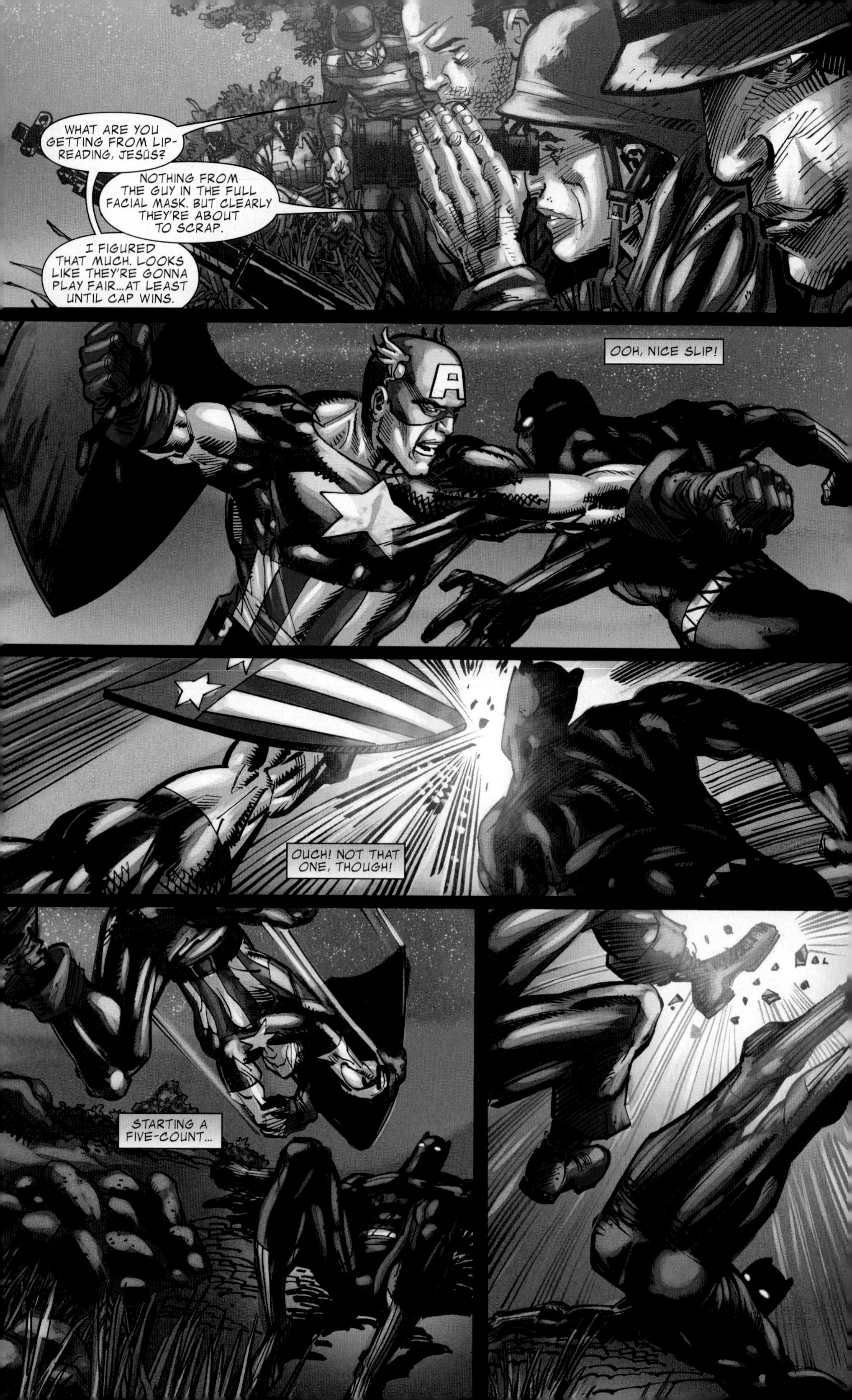
WHAT ARE YOU GETTING FROM LIP-READING, JESÚS?
NOTHING FROM THE GUY IN THE FULL FACIAL MASK. BUT CLEARLY THEY'RE ABOUT TO SCRAP.
I FIGURED THAT MUCH. LOOKS LIKE THEY'RE GONNA PLAY FAIR...AT LEAST UNTIL CAP WINS.
OOH, NICE SLIP!
OUCH! NOT THAT ONE, THOUGH!
STARTING A FIVE-COUNT...

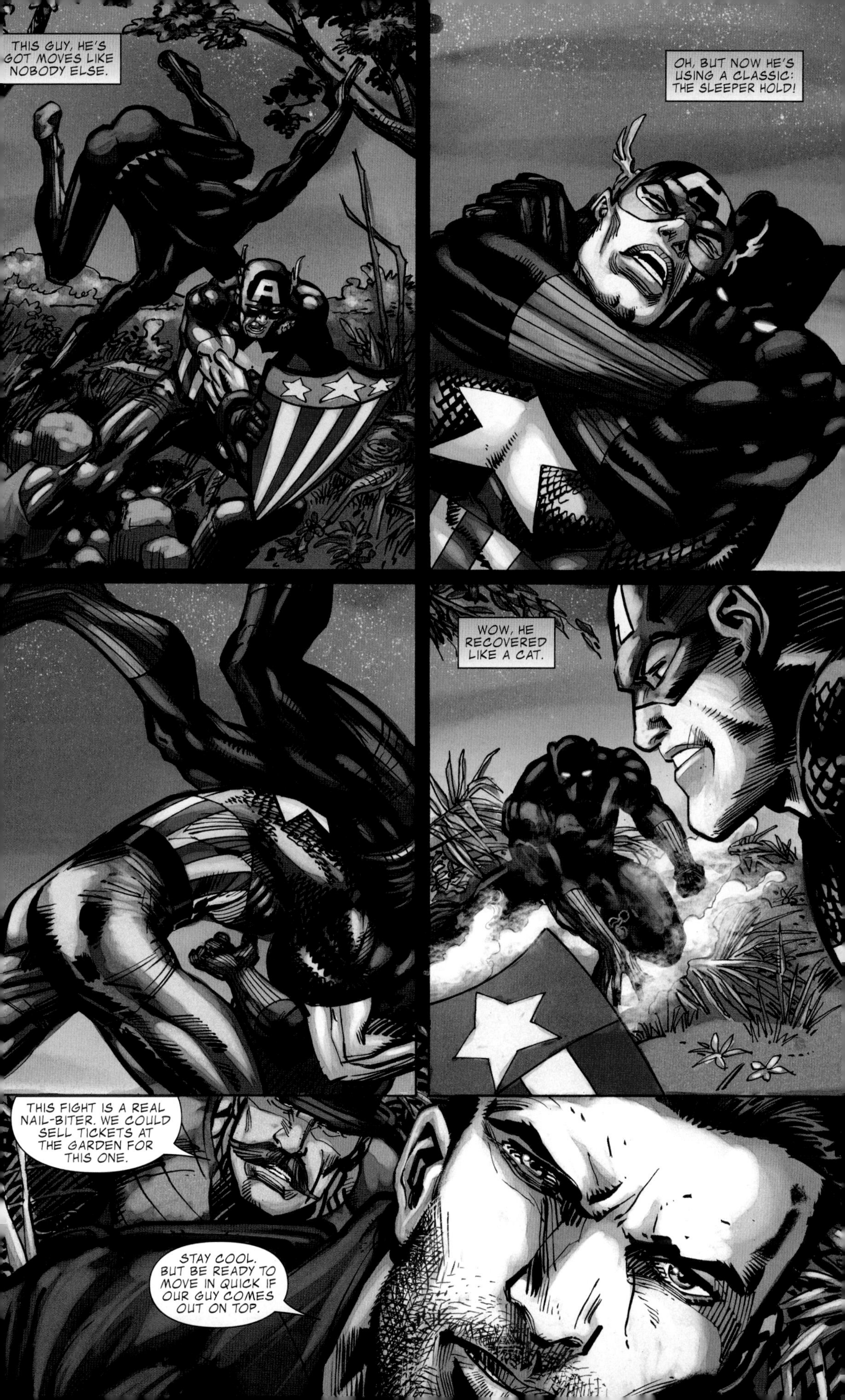
THIS GUY, HE'S GOT MOVES LIKE NOBODY ELSE.
OH, BUT NOW HE'S USING A CLASSIC: THE SLEEPER HOLD!
WOW, HE RECOVERED LIKE A CAT.
THIS FIGHT IS A REAL NAIL-BITER. WE COULD SELL TICKETS AT THE GARDEN FOR THIS ONE.
STAY COOL. BUT BE READY TO MOVE IN QUICK IF OUR GUY COMES OUT ON TOP.

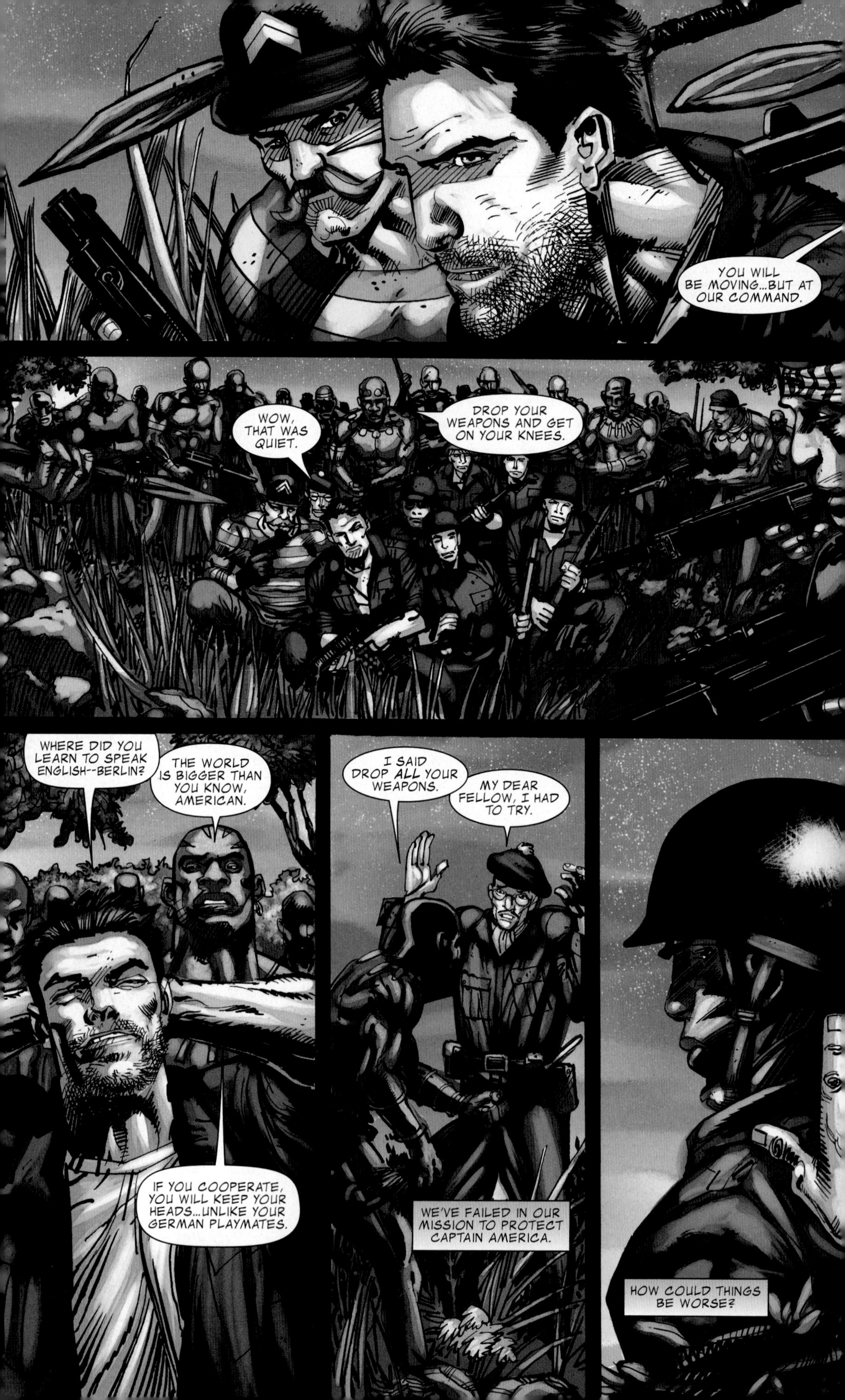
YOU WILL BE MOVING...BUT AT OUR COMMAND.
WOW, THAT WAS QUIET.
DROP YOUR WEAPONS AND GET ON YOUR KNEES.
WHERE DID YOU LEARN TO SPEAK ENGLISH--BERLIN?
THE WORLD IS BIGGER THAN YOU KNOW, AMERICAN.
IF YOU COOPERATE, YOU WILL KEEP YOUR HEADS...UNLIKE YOUR GERMAN PLAYMATES.
I SAID DROP ALL YOUR WEAPONS.
MY DEAR FELLOW, I HAD TO TRY.
WE'VE FAILED IN OUR MISSION TO PROTECT CAPTAIN AMERICA.
HOW COULD THINGS BE WORSE?

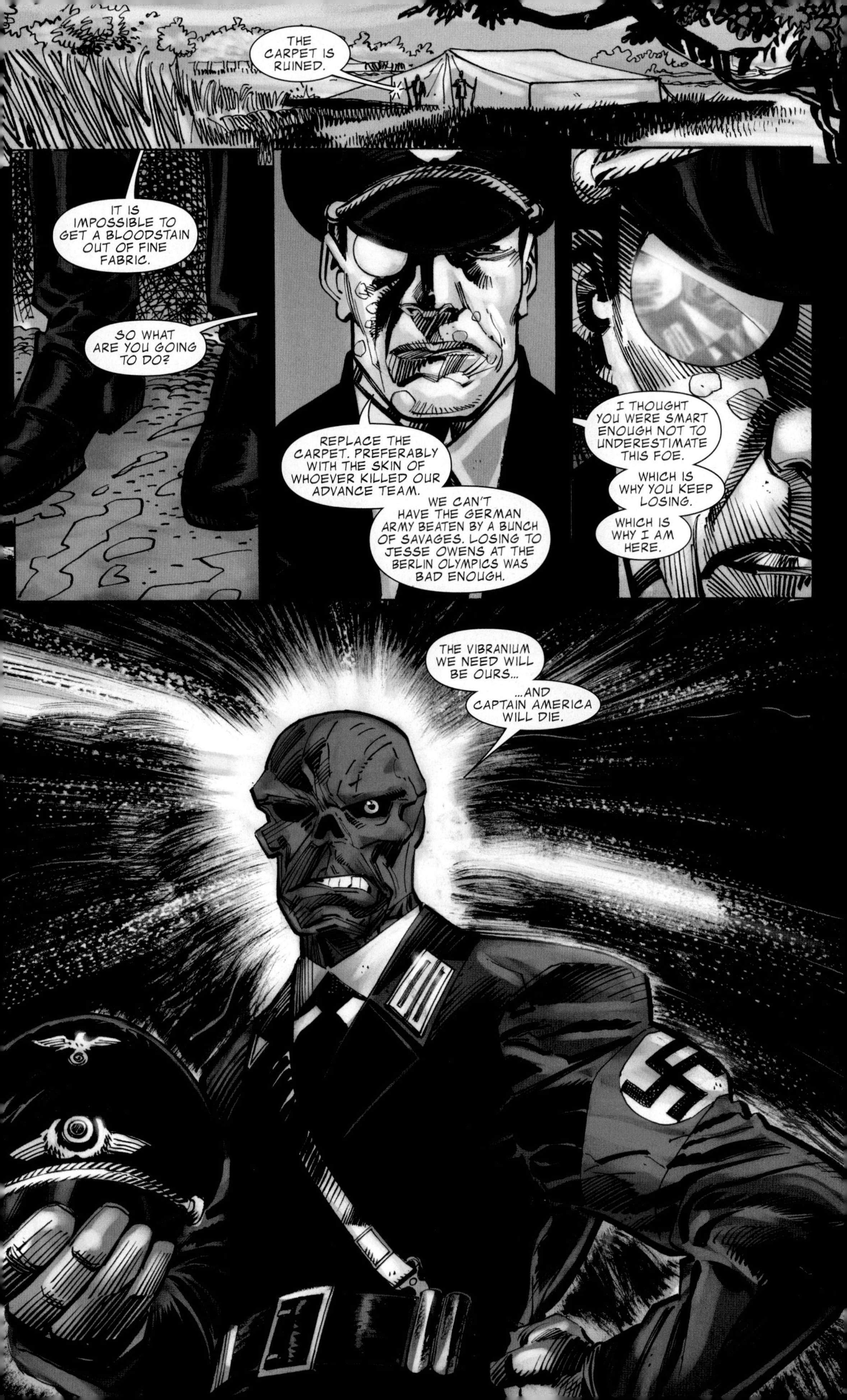
THE CARPET IS RUINED.
IT IS IMPOSSIBLE TO GET A BLOODSTAIN OUT OF FINE FABRIC.
SO WHAT ARE YOU GOING TO DO?
REPLACE THE CARPET. PREFERABLY WITH THE SKIN OF WHOEVER KILLED OUR ADVANCE TEAM.
WE CAN'T HAVE THE GERMAN ARMY BEATEN BY A BUNCH OF SAVAGES. LOSING TO JESSE OWENS AT THE BERLIN OLYMPICS WAS BAD ENOUGH.
I THOUGHT YOU WERE SMART ENOUGH NOT TO UNDERESTIMATE THIS FOE.
WHICH IS WHY YOU KEEP LOSING.
WHICH IS WHY I AM HERE.
THE VIBRANIUM WE NEED WILL BE OURS...
...AND CAPTAIN AMERICA WILL DIE.

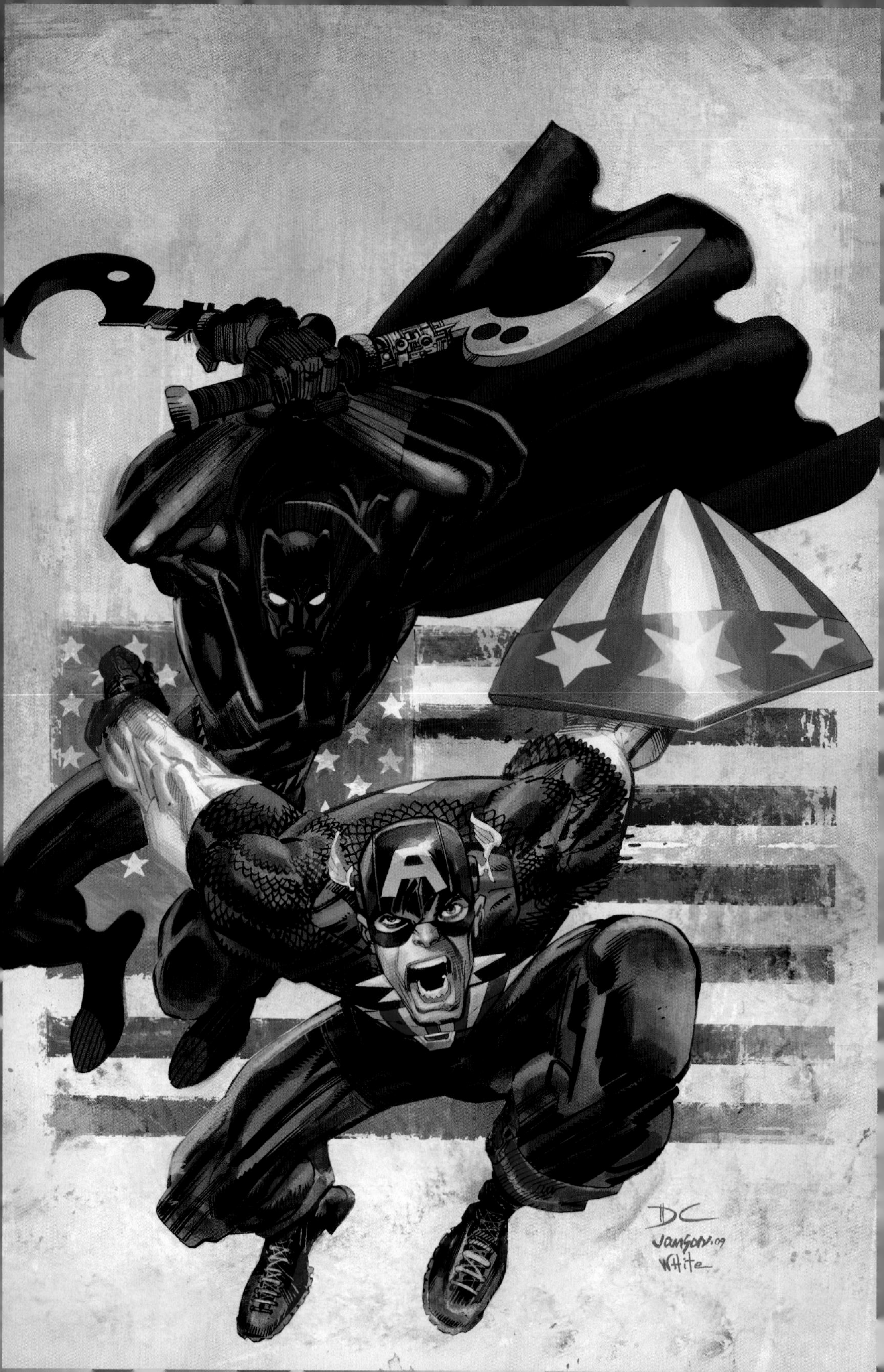

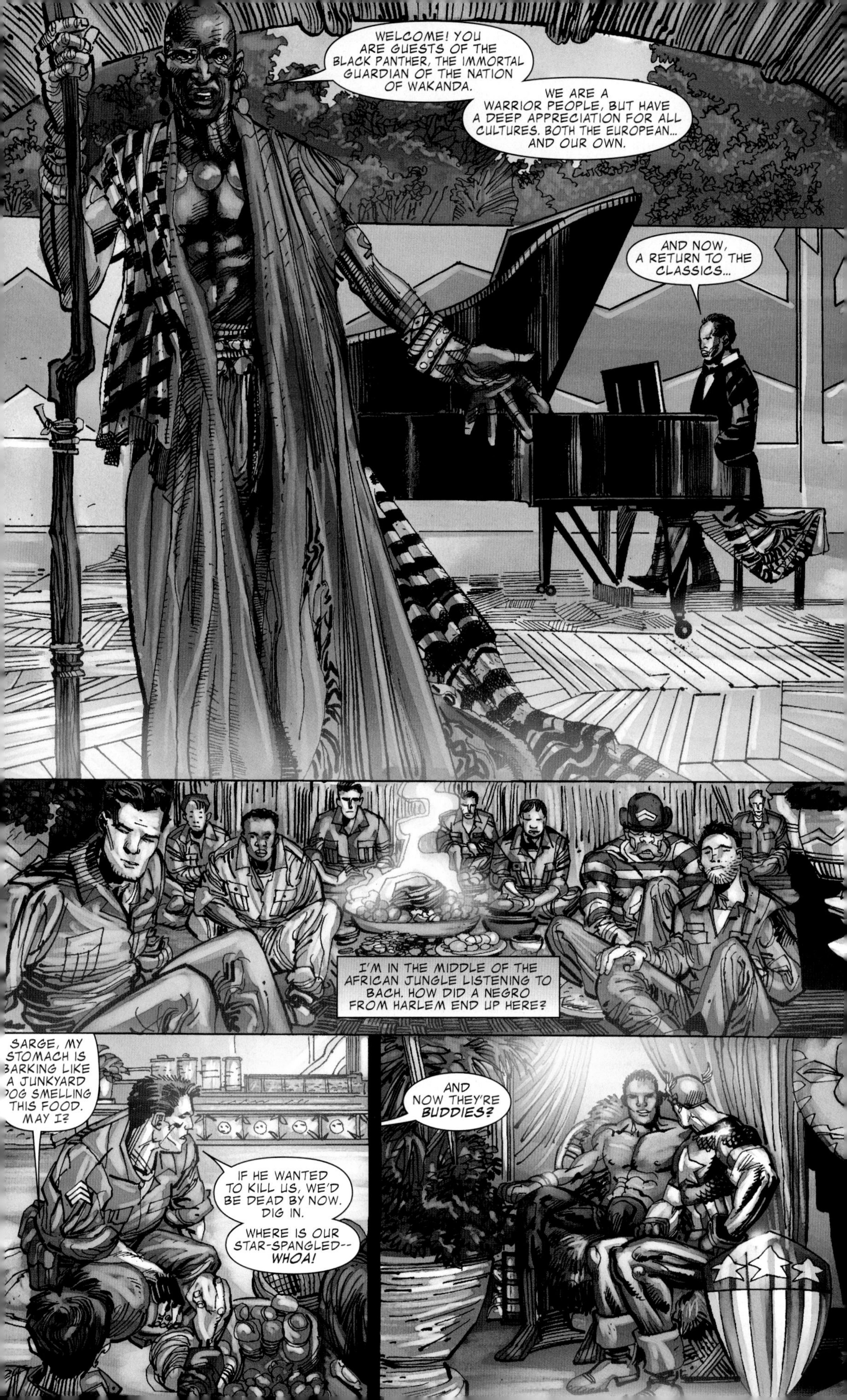

WELCOME! YOU ARE GUESTS OF THE BLACK PANTHER, THE IMMORTAL GUARDIAN OF THE NATION OF WAKANDA.
WE ARE A WARRIOR PEOPLE, BUT HAVE A DEEP APPRECIATION FOR ALL CULTURES. BOTH THE EUROPEAN... AND OUR OWN.
AND NOW, A RETURN TO THE CLASSICS...
I'M IN THE MIDDLE OF THE AFRICAN JUNGLE LISTENING TO BACH. HOW DID A NEGRO FROM HARLEM END UP HERE?
SARGE, MY STOMACH IS BARKING LIKE A JUNKYARD DOG SMELLING THIS FOOD. MAY I?
IF HE WANTED TO KILL US, WE'D BE DEAD BY NOW. DIG IN.
WHERE IS OUR STAR-SPANGLED-- WHOA!
AND NOW THEY'RE BUDDIES?

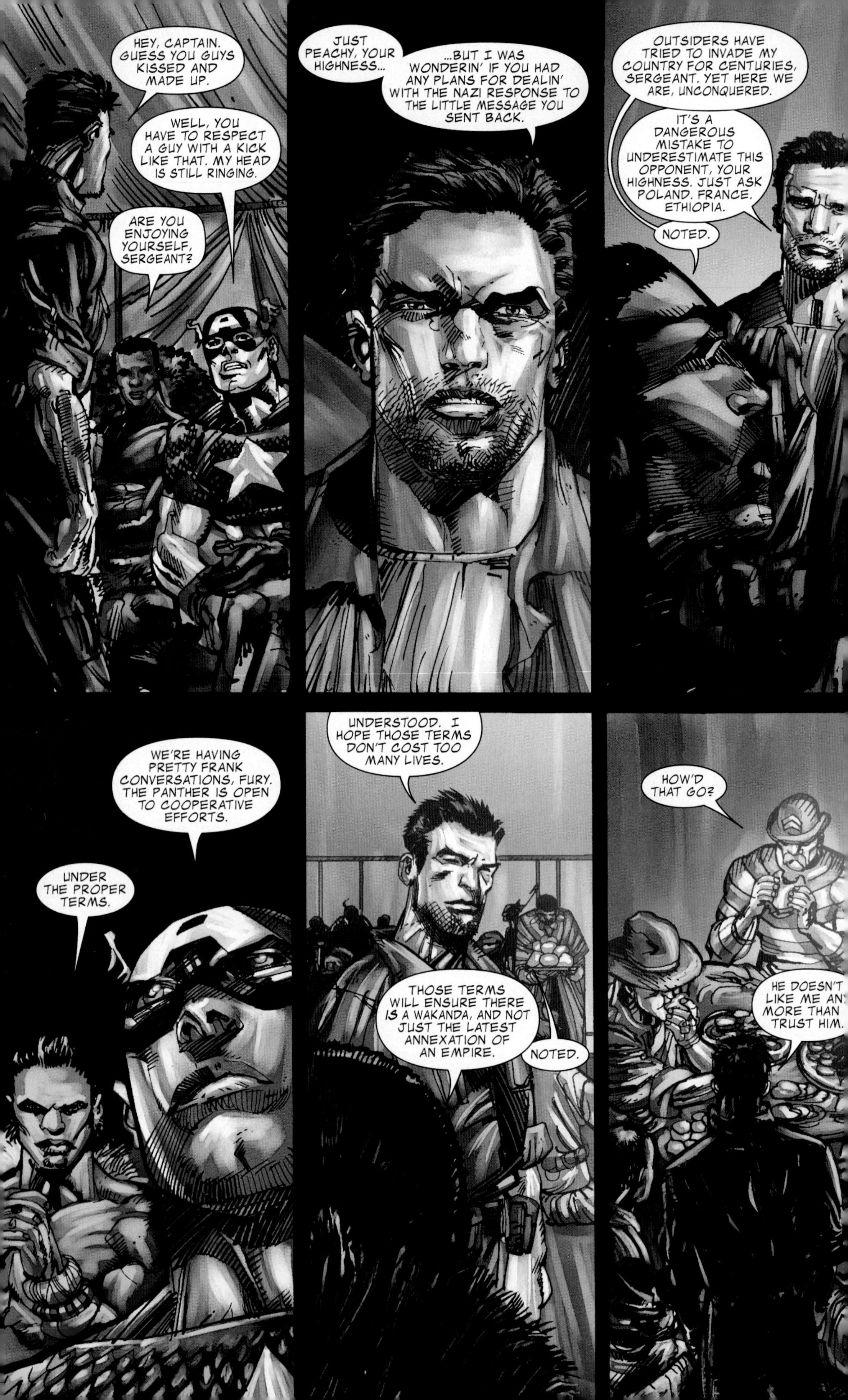
HEY, CAPTAIN. GUESS YOU GUYS KISSED AND MADE UP.
WELL, YOU HAVE TO RESPECT A GUY WITH A KICK LIKE THAT. MY HEAD IS STILL RINGING.
ARE YOU ENJOYING YOURSELF, SERGEANT?
JUST PEACHY, YOUR HIGHNESS...
...BUT I WAS WONDERIN' IF YOU HAD ANY PLANS FOR DEALIN' WITH THE NAZI RESPONSE TO THE LITTLE MESSAGE YOU SENT BACK.
OUTSIDERS HAVE TRIED TO INVADE MY COUNTRY FOR CENTURIES, SERGEANT. YET HERE WE ARE, UNCONQUERED.
IT'S A DANGEROUS MISTAKE TO UNDERESTIMATE THIS OPPONENT, YOUR HIGHNESS. JUST ASK POLAND. FRANCE. ETHIOPIA.
NOTED.
WE'RE HAVING PRETTY FRANK CONVERSATIONS, FURY. THE PANTHER IS OPEN TO COOPERATIVE EFFORTS.
UNDER THE PROPER TERMS.
UNDERSTOOD. I HOPE THOSE TERMS DON'T COST TOO MANY LIVES.
THOSE TERMS WILL ENSURE THERE IS A WAKANDA, AND NOT JUST THE LATEST ANNEXATION OF AN EMPIRE.
NOTED.
HOW'D THAT GO?
HE DOESN'T LIKE ME AN MORE THAN TRUST HIM.

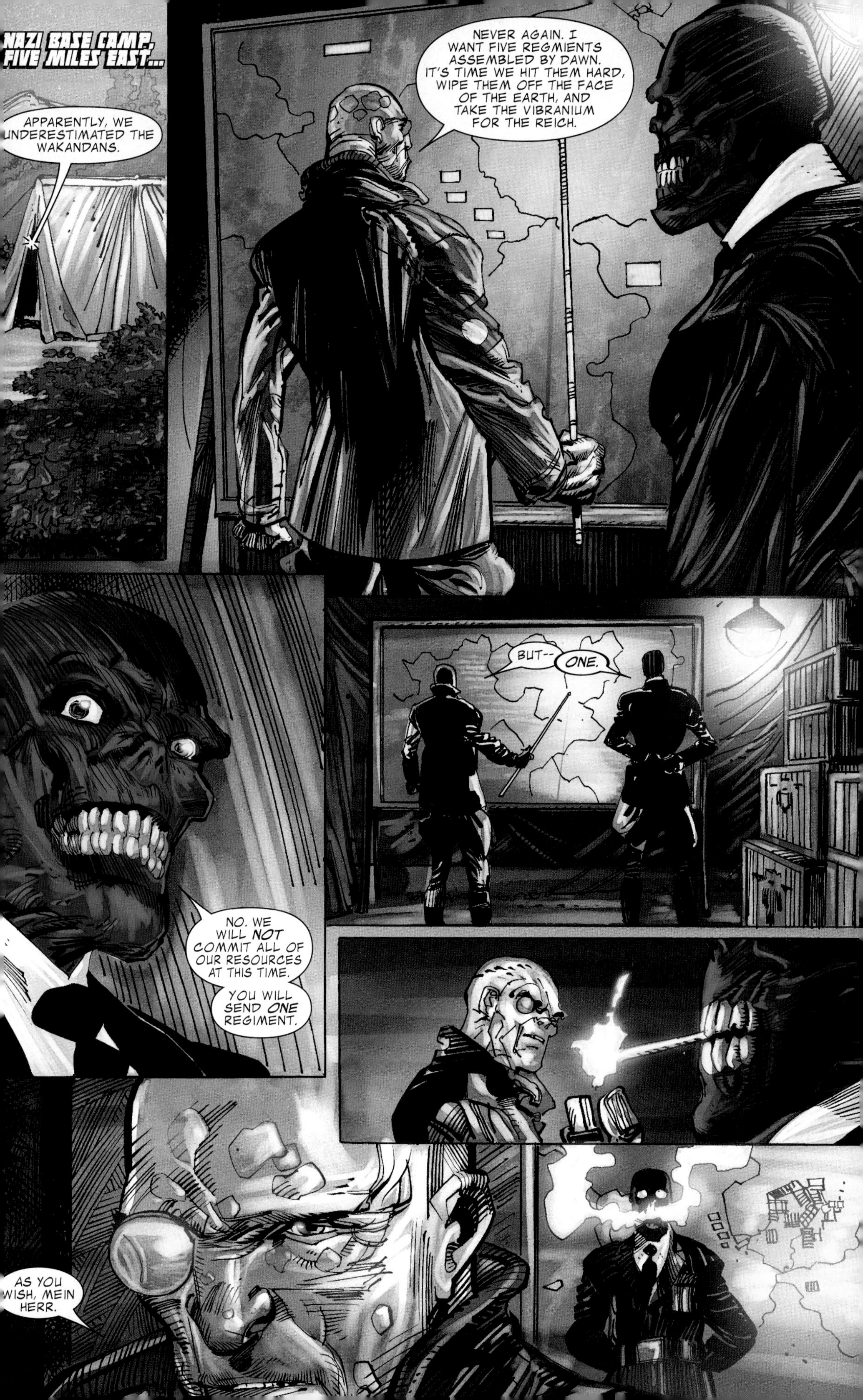
NAZI BASE CAMP, FIVE MILES EAST...
APPARENTLY, WE UNDERESTIMATED THE WAKANDANS.
NEVER AGAIN. I WANT FIVE REGMIENTS ASSEMBLED BY DAWN. IT'S TIME WE HIT THEM HARD, WIPE THEM OFF THE FACE OF THE EARTH, AND TAKE THE VIBRANIUM FOR THE REICH.
NO. WE WILL NOT COMMIT ALL OF OUR RESOURCES AT THIS TIME.
YOU WILL SEND ONE REGIMENT.
BUT--
ONE.
AS YOU WISH, MEIN HERR.

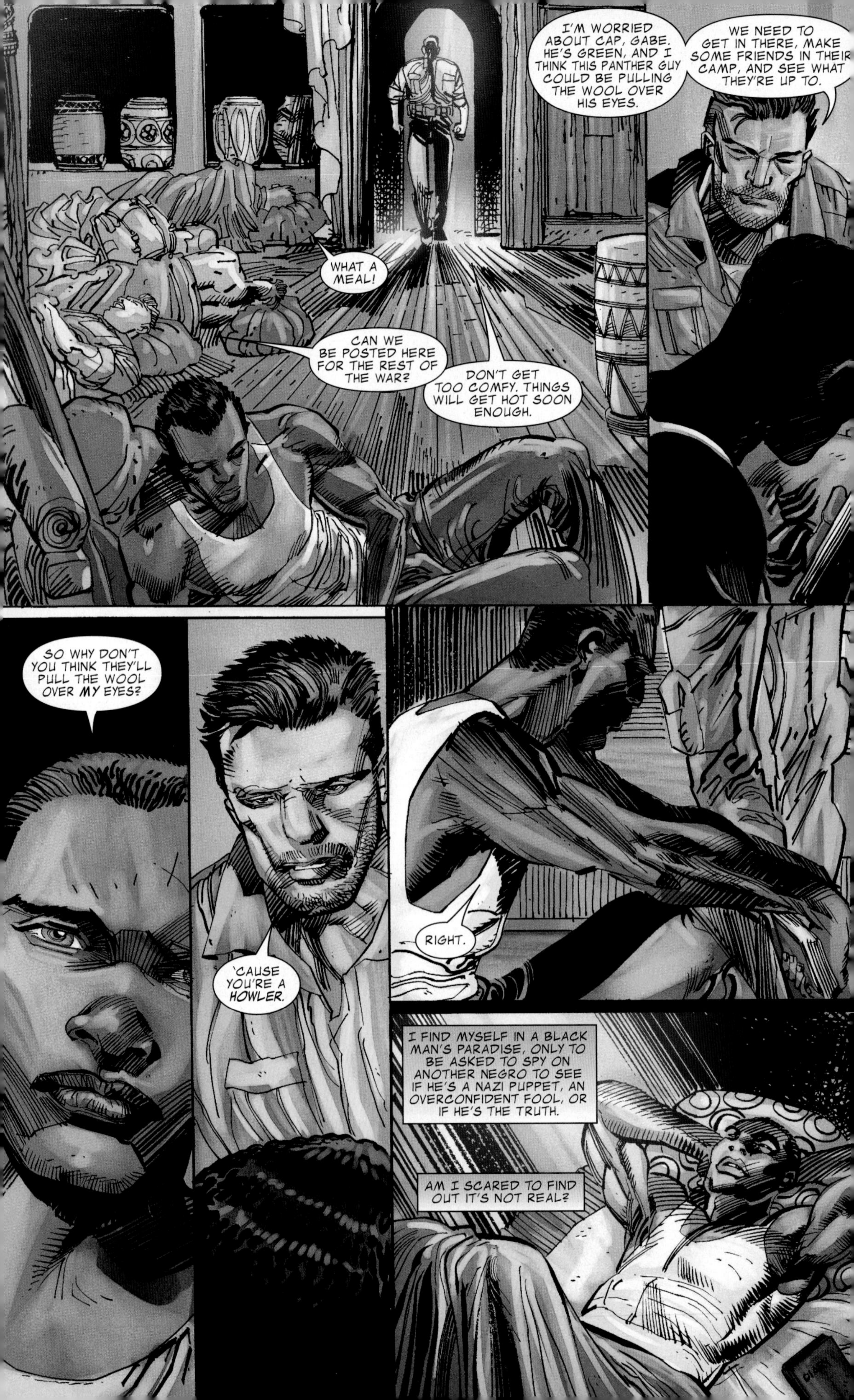
WHAT A MEAL!
CAN WE BE POSTED HERE FOR THE REST OF THE WAR?
DON'T GET TOO COMFY. THINGS WILL GET HOT SOON ENOUGH.
I'M WORRIED ABOUT CAP, GABE. HE'S GREEN, AND I THINK THIS PANTHER GUY COULD BE PULLING THE WOOL OVER HIS EYES.
WE NEED TO GET IN THERE, MAKE SOME FRIENDS IN THEIR CAMP, AND SEE WHAT THEY'RE UP TO.
SO WHY DON'T YOU THINK THEY'LL PULL THE WOOL OVER MY EYES?
'CAUSE YOU'RE A HOWLER.
RIGHT.
I FIND MYSELF IN A BLACK MAN'S PARADISE, ONLY TO BE ASKED TO SPY ON ANOTHER NEGRO TO SEE IF HE'S A NAZI PUPPET, AN OVERCONFIDENT FOOL, OR IF HE'S THE TRUTH.
AM I SCARED TO FIND OUT IT'S NOT REAL?

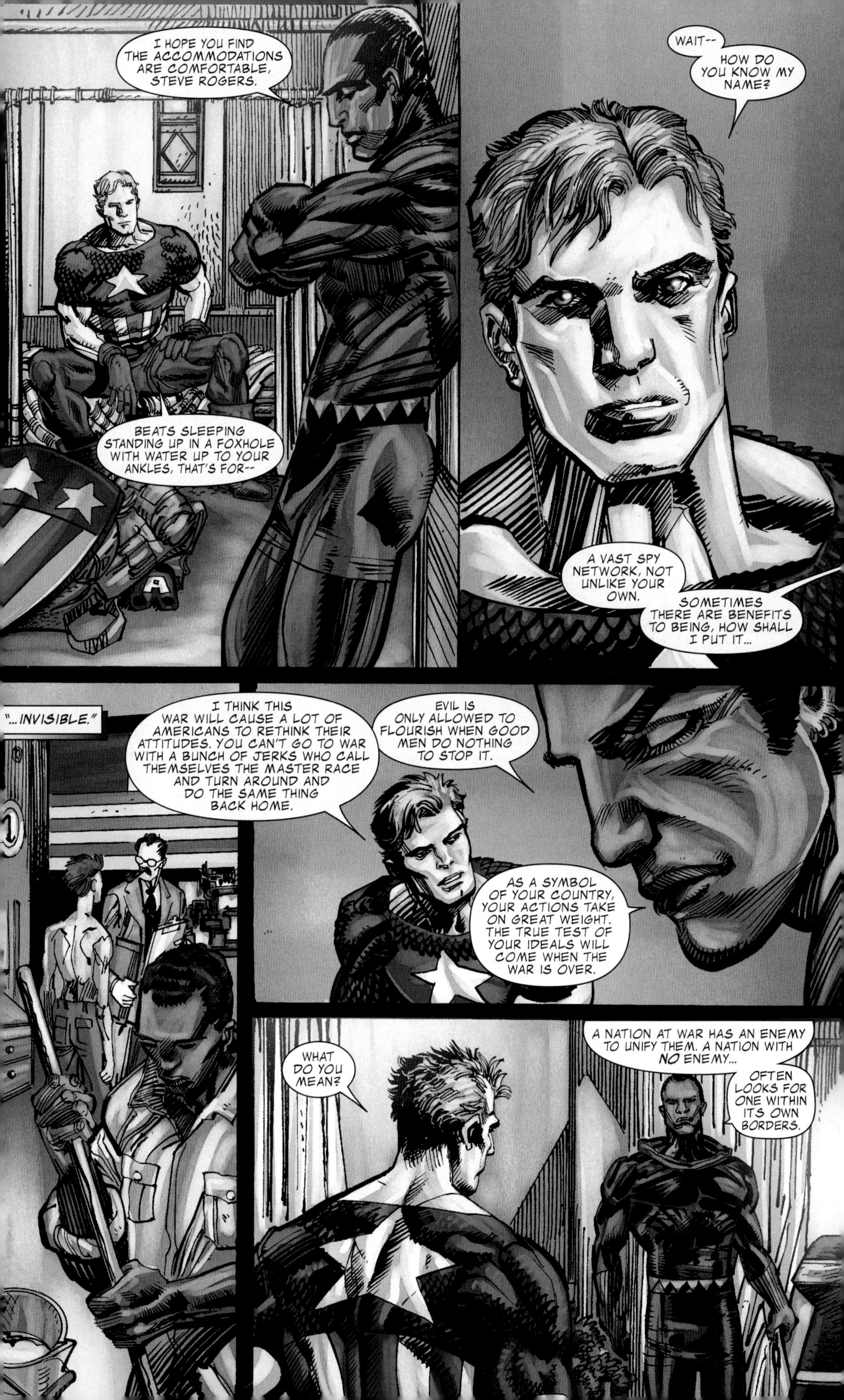
I HOPE YOU FIND THE ACCOMMODATIONS ARE COMFORTABLE, STEVE ROGERS.
BEATS SLEEPING STANDING UP IN A FOXHOLE WITH WATER UP TO YOUR ANKLES, THAT'S FOR--
WAIT--
HOW DO YOU KNOW MY NAME?
A VAST SPY NETWORK, NOT UNLIKE YOUR OWN.
SOMETIMES THERE ARE BENEFITS TO BEING, HOW SHALL I PUT IT...
"...INVISIBLE."
I THINK THIS WAR WILL CAUSE A LOT OF AMERICANS TO RETHINK THEIR ATTITUDES. YOU CAN'T GO TO WAR WITH A BUNCH OF JERKS WHO CALL THEMSELVES THE MASTER RACE AND TURN AROUND AND DO THE SAME THING BACK HOME.
EVIL IS ONLY ALLOWED TO FLOURISH WHEN GOOD MEN DO NOTHING TO STOP IT.
AS A SYMBOL OF YOUR COUNTRY, YOUR ACTIONS TAKE ON GREAT WEIGHT. THE TRUE TEST OF YOUR IDEALS WILL COME WHEN THE WAR IS OVER.
WHAT DO YOU MEAN?
A NATION AT WAR HAS AN ENEMY TO UNIFY THEM. A NATION WITH NO ENEMY...
OFTEN LOOKS FOR ONE WITHIN ITS OWN BORDERS.

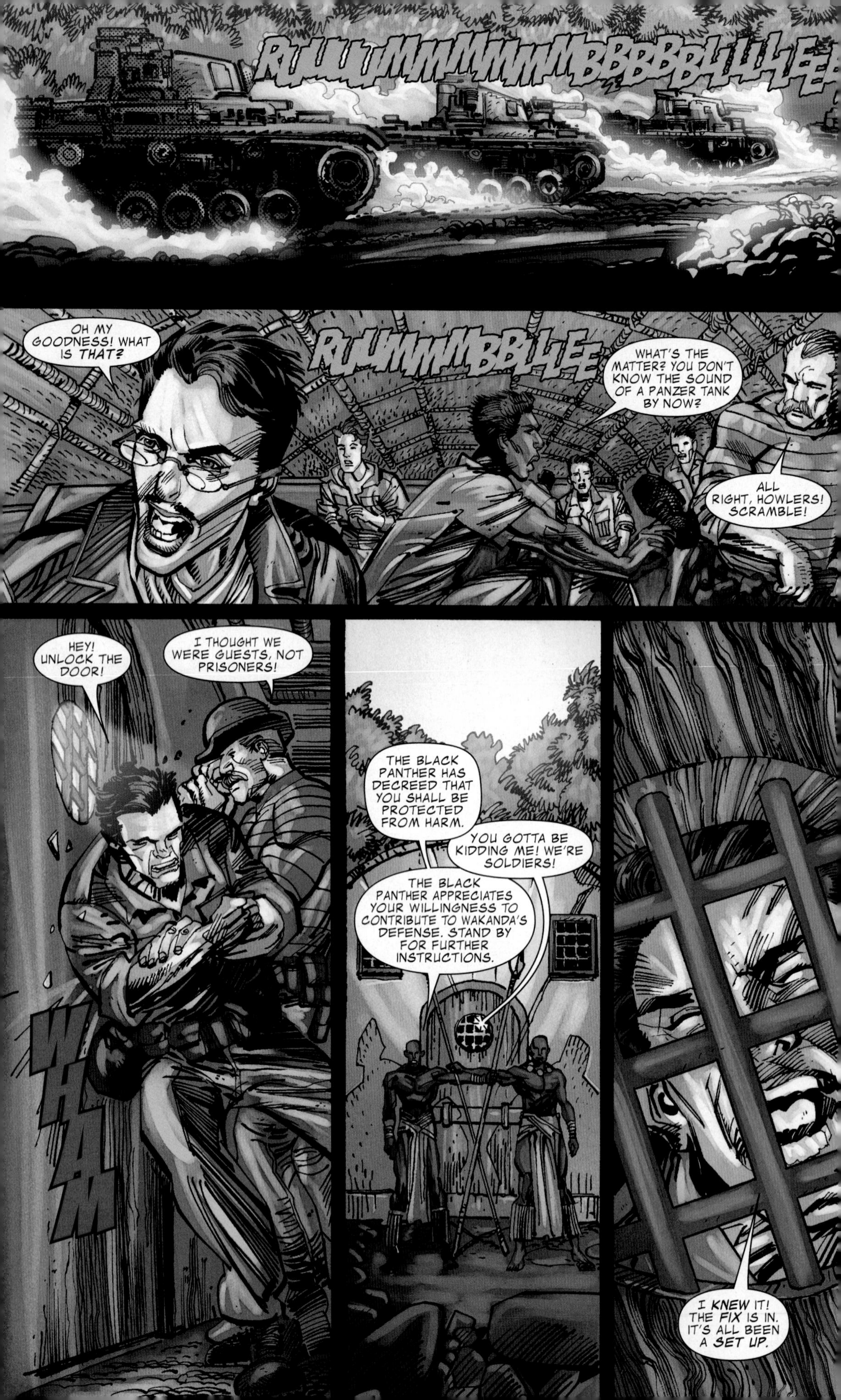
RUUUUMMMMMMMBBBBBLLLEE!
OH MY GOODNESS! WHAT IS THAT?
RUUMMMBBLLEE
WHAT'S THE MATTER? YOU DON'T KNOW THE SOUND OF A PANZER TANK BY NOW?
ALL RIGHT, HOWLERS! SCRAMBLE!
HEY! UNLOCK THE DOOR!
I THOUGHT WE WERE GUESTS, NOT PRISONERS!
WHAM
THE BLACK PANTHER HAS DECREED THAT YOU SHALL BE PROTECTED FROM HARM.
YOU GOTTA BE KIDDING ME! WE'RE SOLDIERS!
THE BLACK PANTHER APPRECIATES YOUR WILLINGNESS TO CONTRIBUTE TO WAKANDA'S DEFENSE. STAND BY FOR FURTHER INSTRUCTIONS.
I KNEW IT! THE FIX IS IN. IT'S ALL BEEN A SET UP.

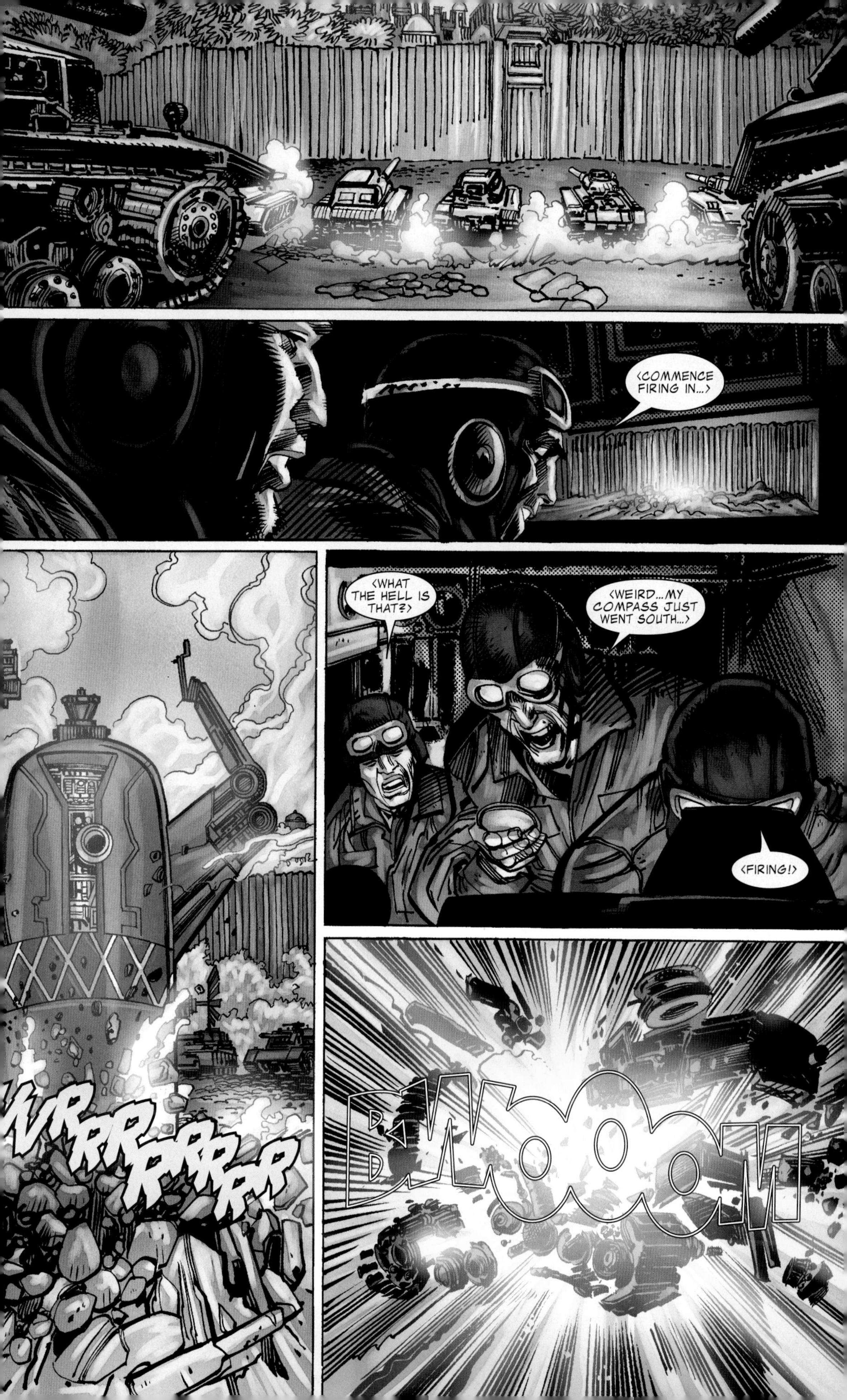
<COMMENCE FIRING IN...>
<WHAT THE HELL IS THAT?>
<WEIRD...MY COMPASS JUST WENT SOUTH...>
<FIRING!>
VRRRRRRRR
BWOOOOM

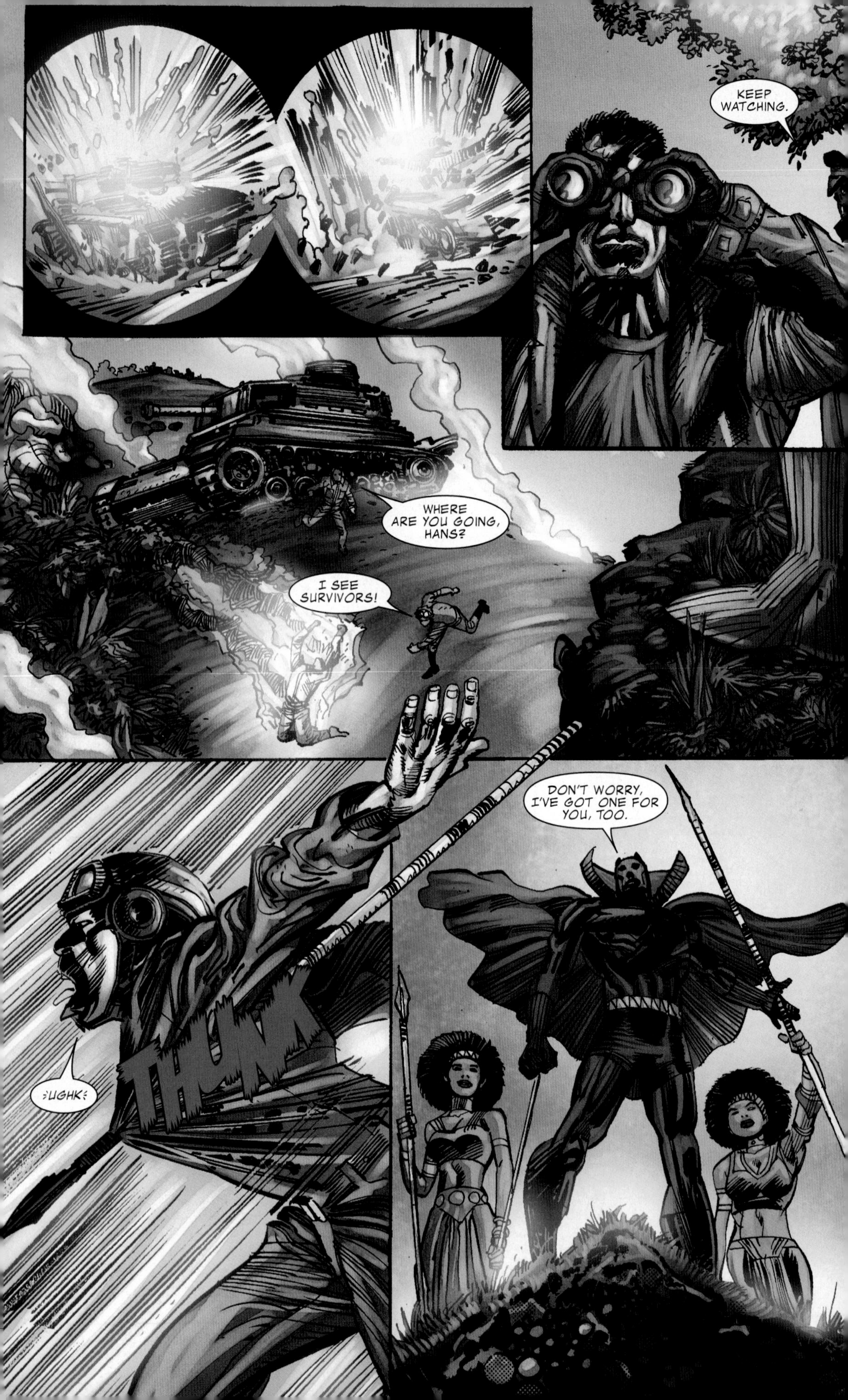
KEEP WATCHING.
WHERE ARE YOU GOING, HANS?
I SEE SURVIVORS!
THUNK
UGHK
DON'T WORRY, I'VE GOT ONE FOR YOU, TOO.

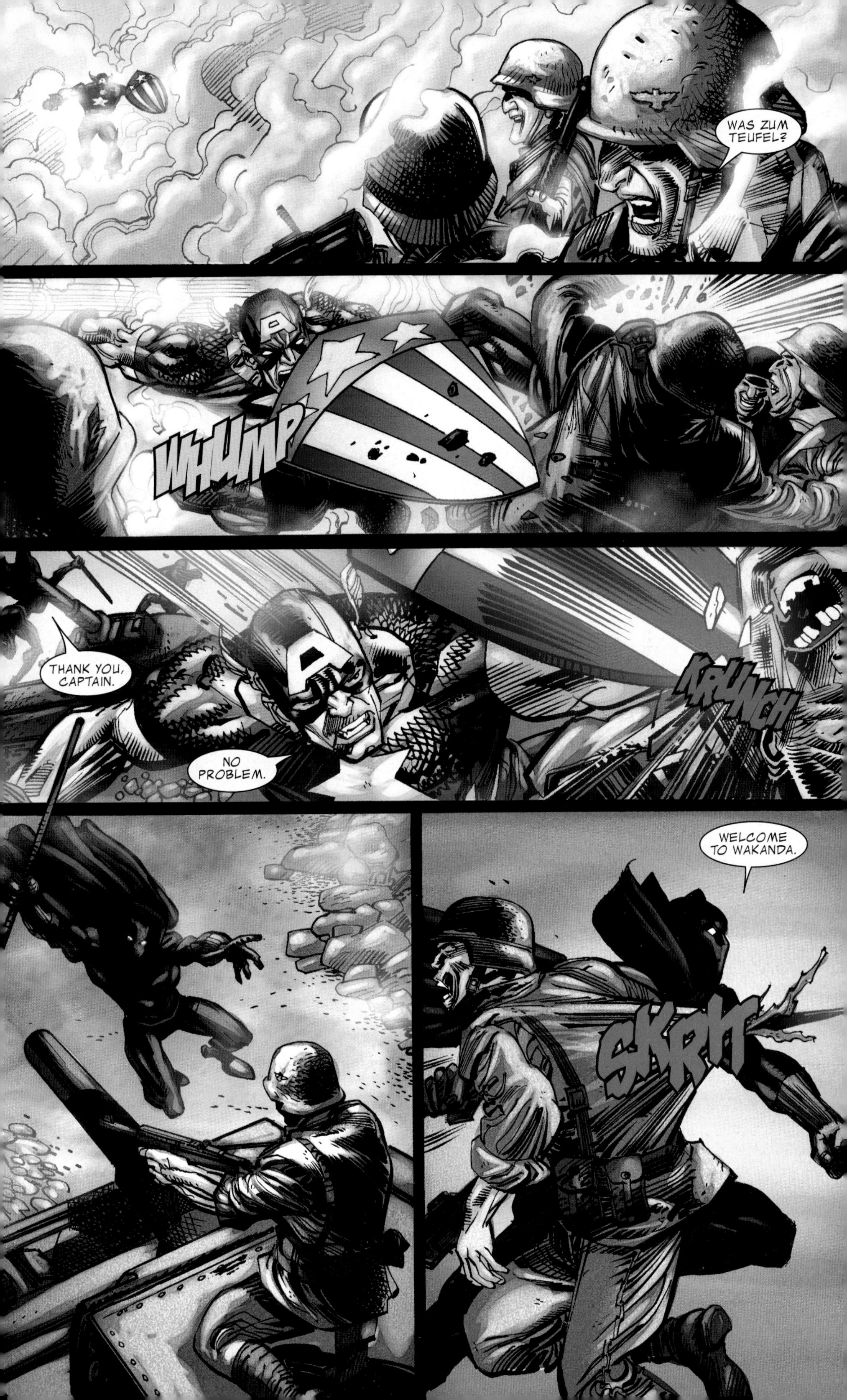
WAS ZUM TEUFEL?
WHUMP
THANK YOU, CAPTAIN.
KRUNCH
NO PROBLEM.
WELCOME TO WAKANDA.
SKRIT

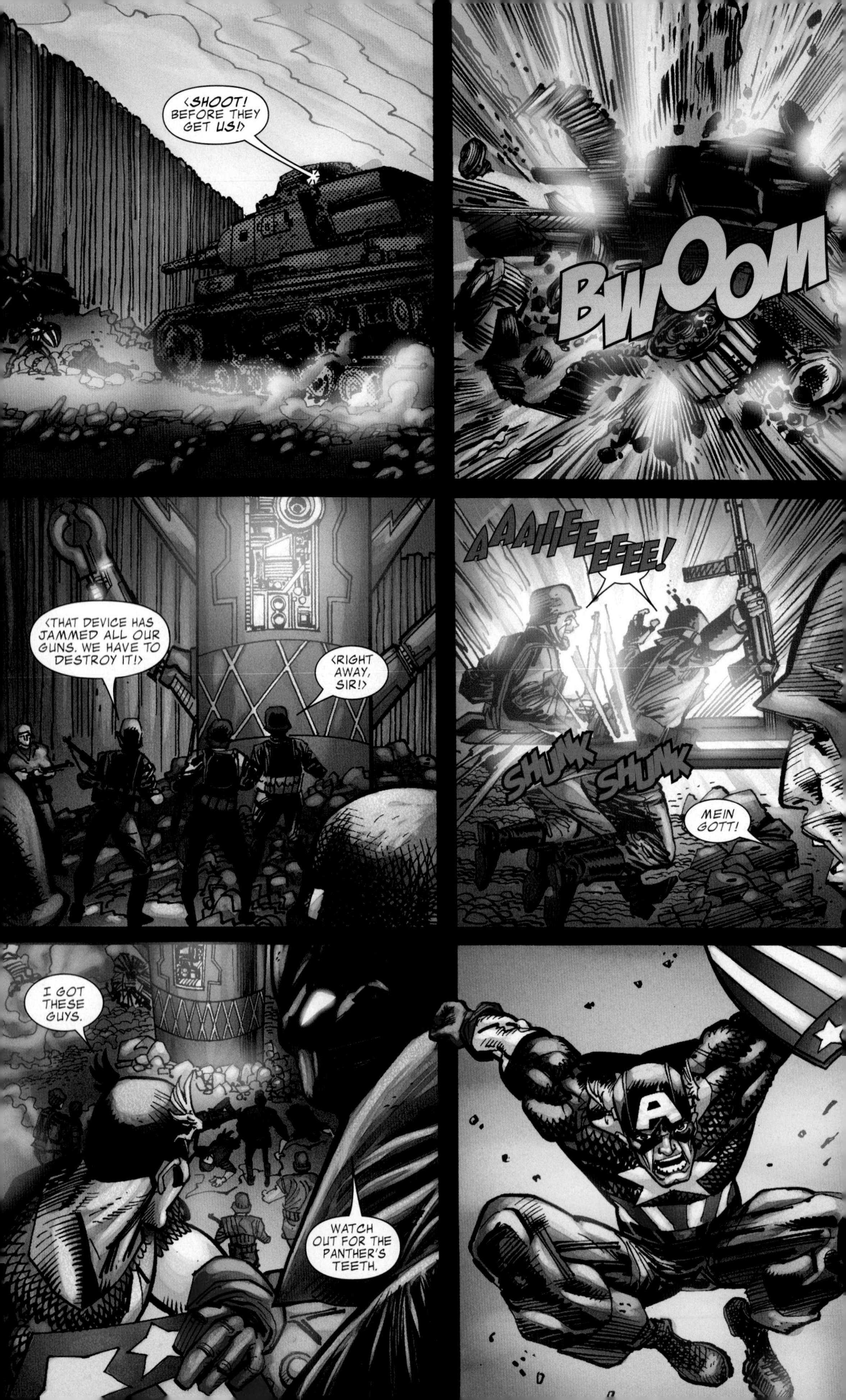

<SHOOT! BEFORE THEY GET US!>
BWOOOM
<THAT DEVICE HAS JAMMED ALL OUR GUNS. WE HAVE TO DESTROY IT!>
<RIGHT AWAY, SIR!>
AAAIIEEEEEEE!
SHUNK
SHUNK
MEIN GOTT!
I GOT THESE GUYS.
WATCH OUT FOR THE PANTHER'S TEETH.

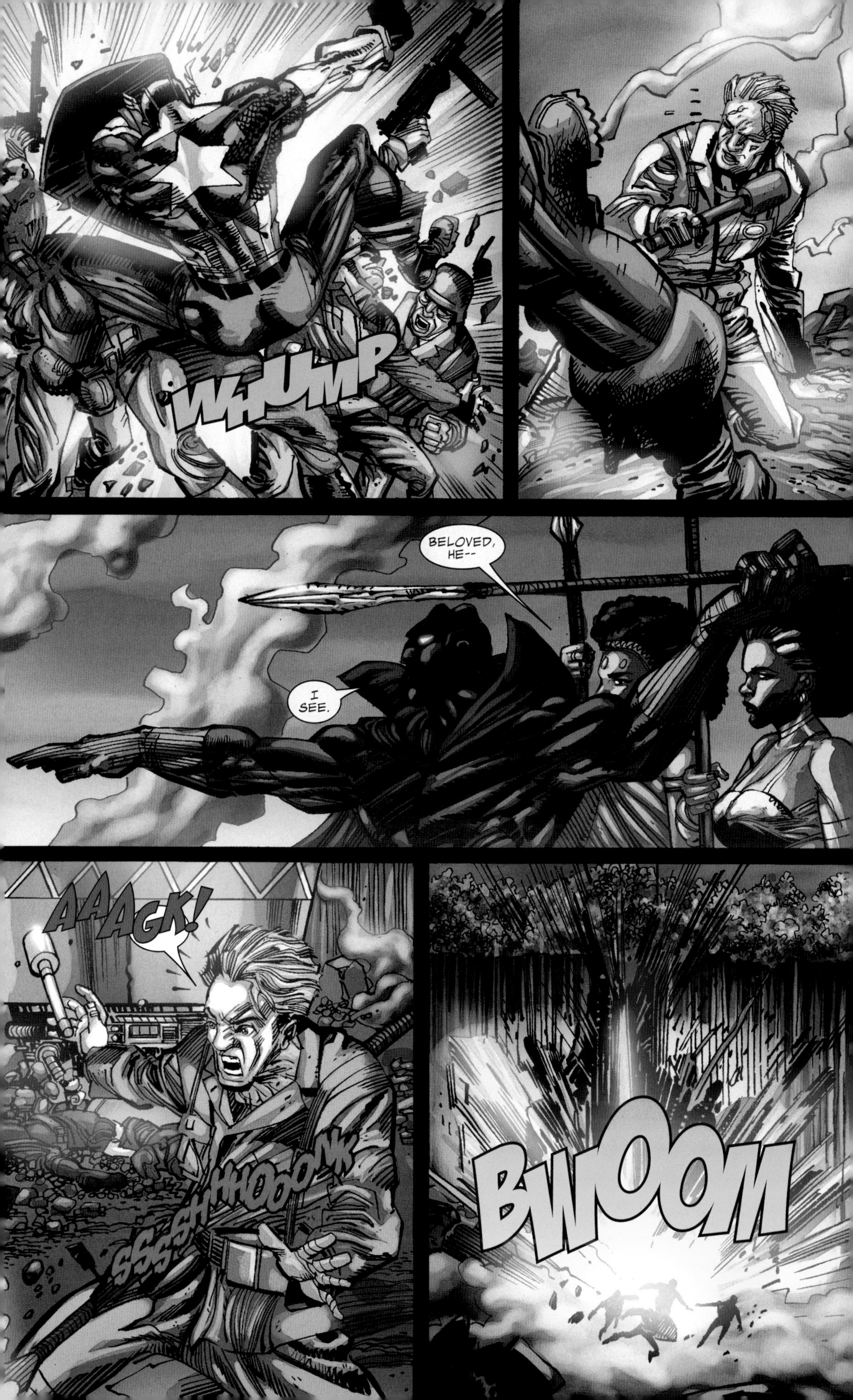
WHUMP
BELOVED, HE--
I SEE.
AAAGK!
SSSSHHHOOONK
BWOOOM

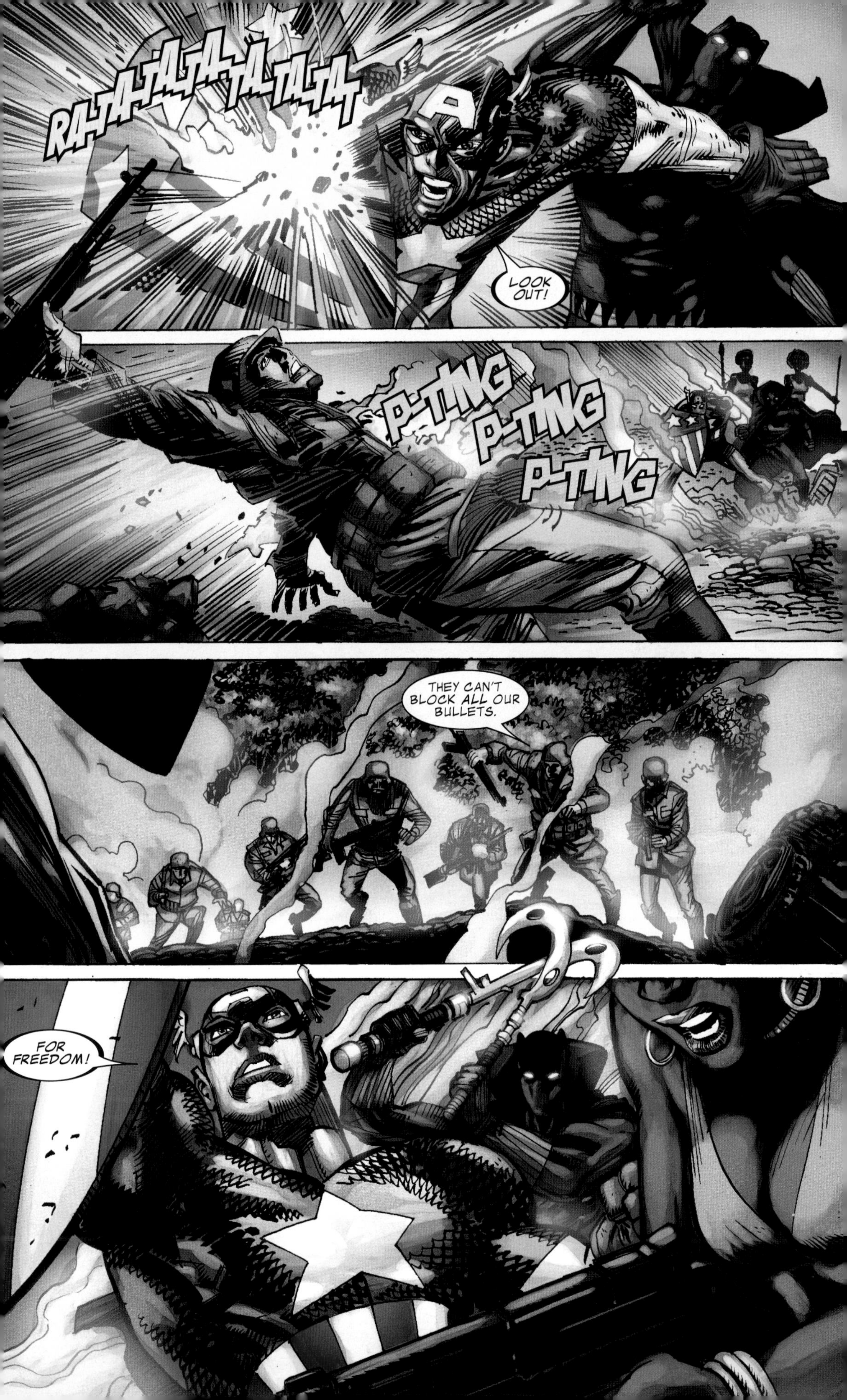
RA-TA-TA-TA-TA-TA-TA
LOOK OUT!
P-TING
P-TING
P-TING
THEY CAN'T BLOCK ALL OUR BULLETS.
FOR FREEDOM!

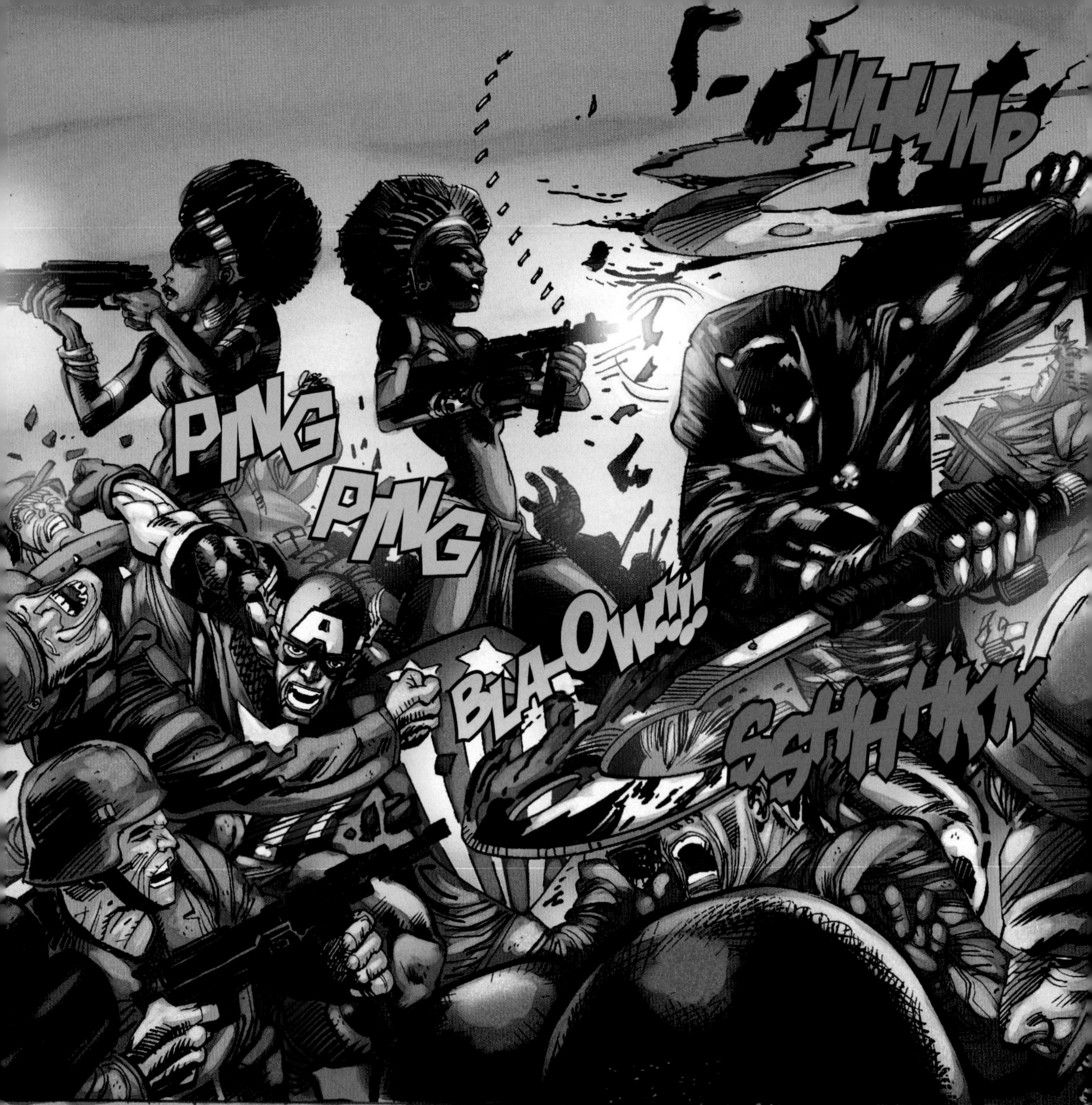
WHUMP
PING
PING
BLA-OW!!!
SSHHHKK

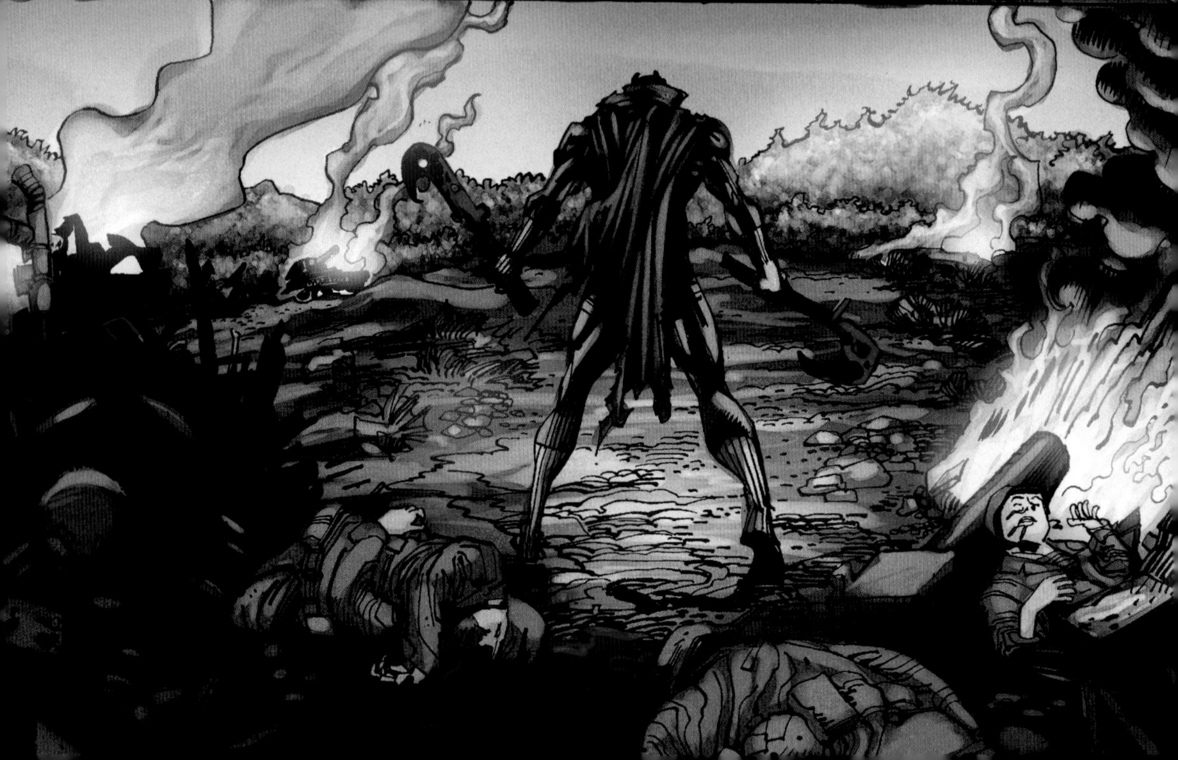

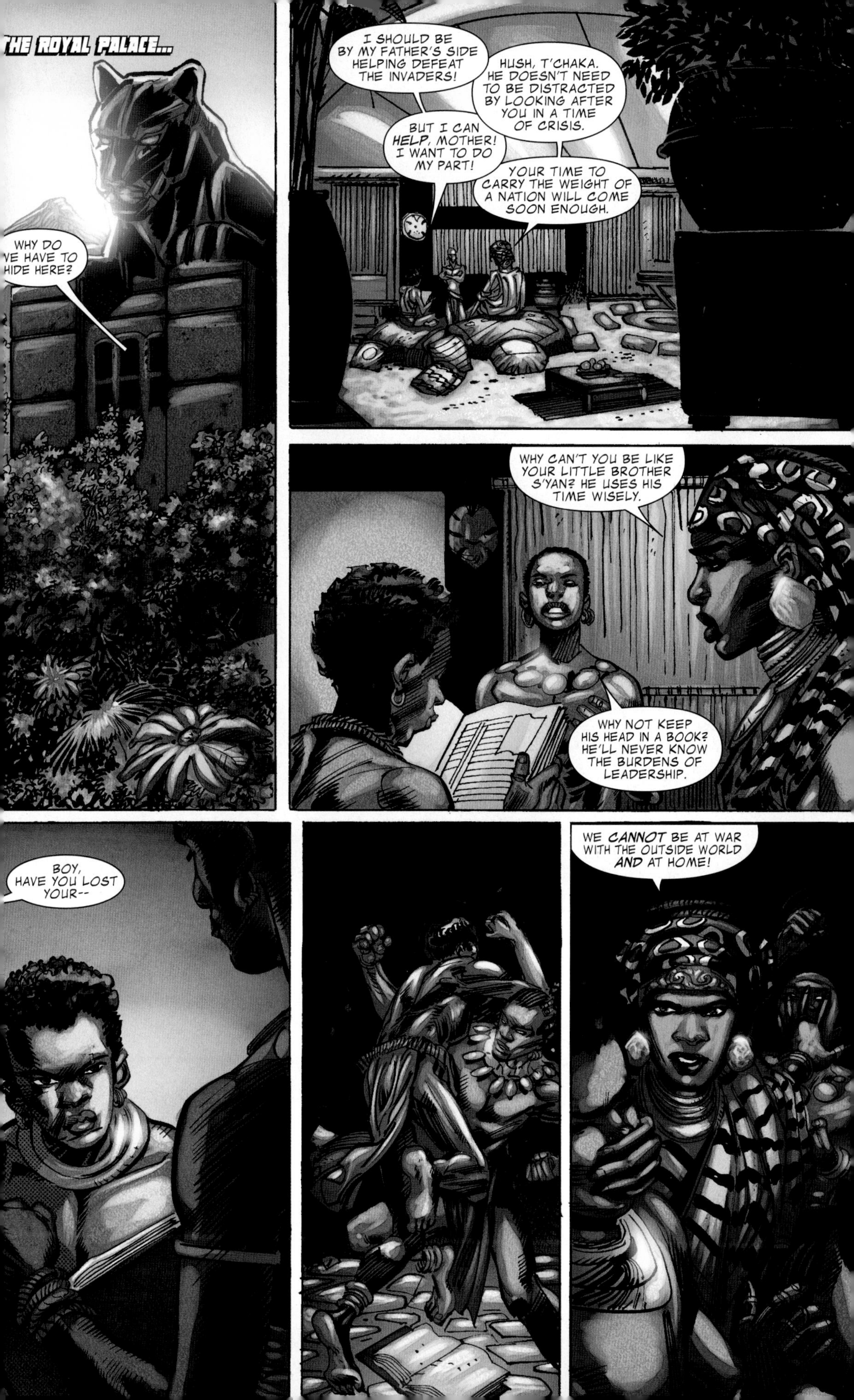
THE ROYAL PALACE...
WHY DO WE HAVE TO HIDE HERE?
I SHOULD BE BY MY FATHER'S SIDE HELPING DEFEAT THE INVADERS!
HUSH, T'CHAKA. HE DOESN'T NEED TO BE DISTRACTED BY LOOKING AFTER YOU IN A TIME OF CRISIS.
BUT I CAN HELP, MOTHER! I WANT TO DO MY PART!
YOUR TIME TO CARRY THE WEIGHT OF A NATION WILL COME SOON ENOUGH.
WHY CAN'T YOU BE LIKE YOUR LITTLE BROTHER S'YAN? HE USES HIS TIME WISELY.
WHY NOT KEEP HIS HEAD IN A BOOK? HE'LL NEVER KNOW THE BURDENS OF LEADERSHIP.
BOY, HAVE YOU LOST YOUR--
WE CANNOT BE AT WAR WITH THE OUTSIDE WORLD AND AT HOME!

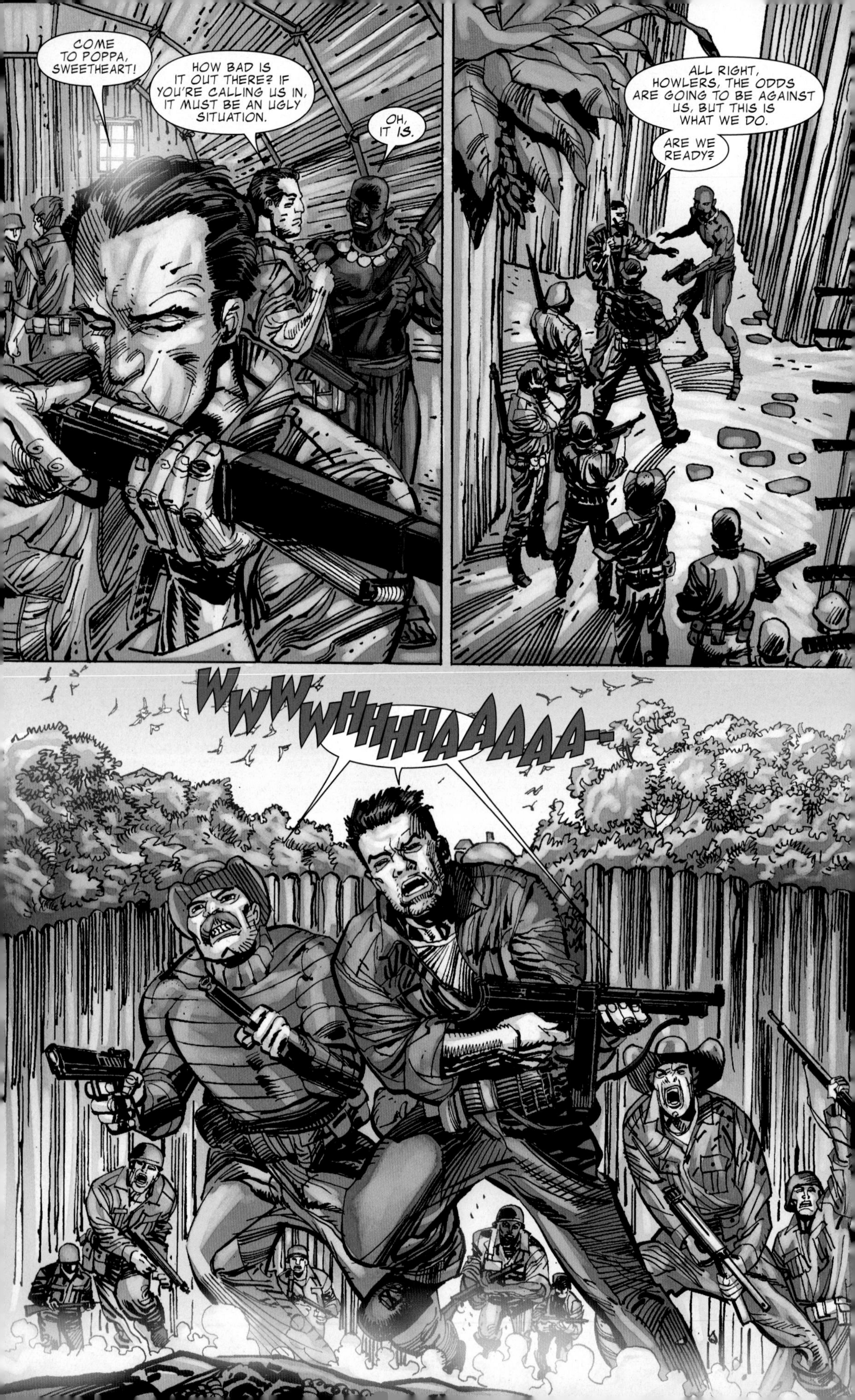
COME TO POPPA, SWEETHEART!
HOW BAD IS IT OUT THERE? IF YOU'RE CALLING US IN, IT MUST BE AN UGLY SITUATION.
OH, IT IS.
ALL RIGHT, HOWLERS, THE ODDS ARE GOING TO BE AGAINST US, BUT THIS IS WHAT WE DO.
ARE WE READY?
WWWWHHHHAAAAA-

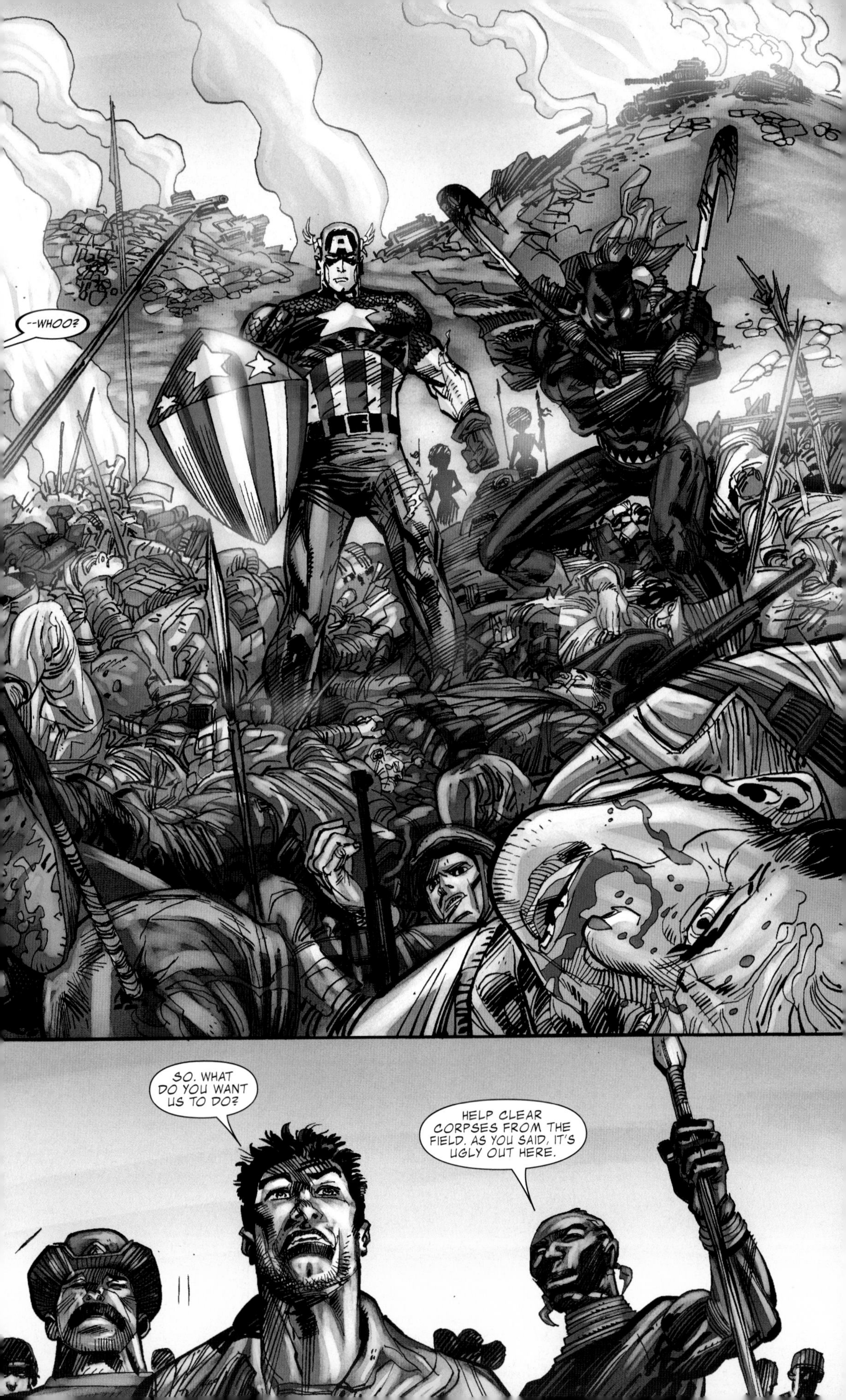
--WHOO?
SO. WHAT DO YOU WANT US TO DO?
HELP CLEAR CORPSES FROM THE FIELD. AS YOU SAID, IT'S UGLY OUT HERE.

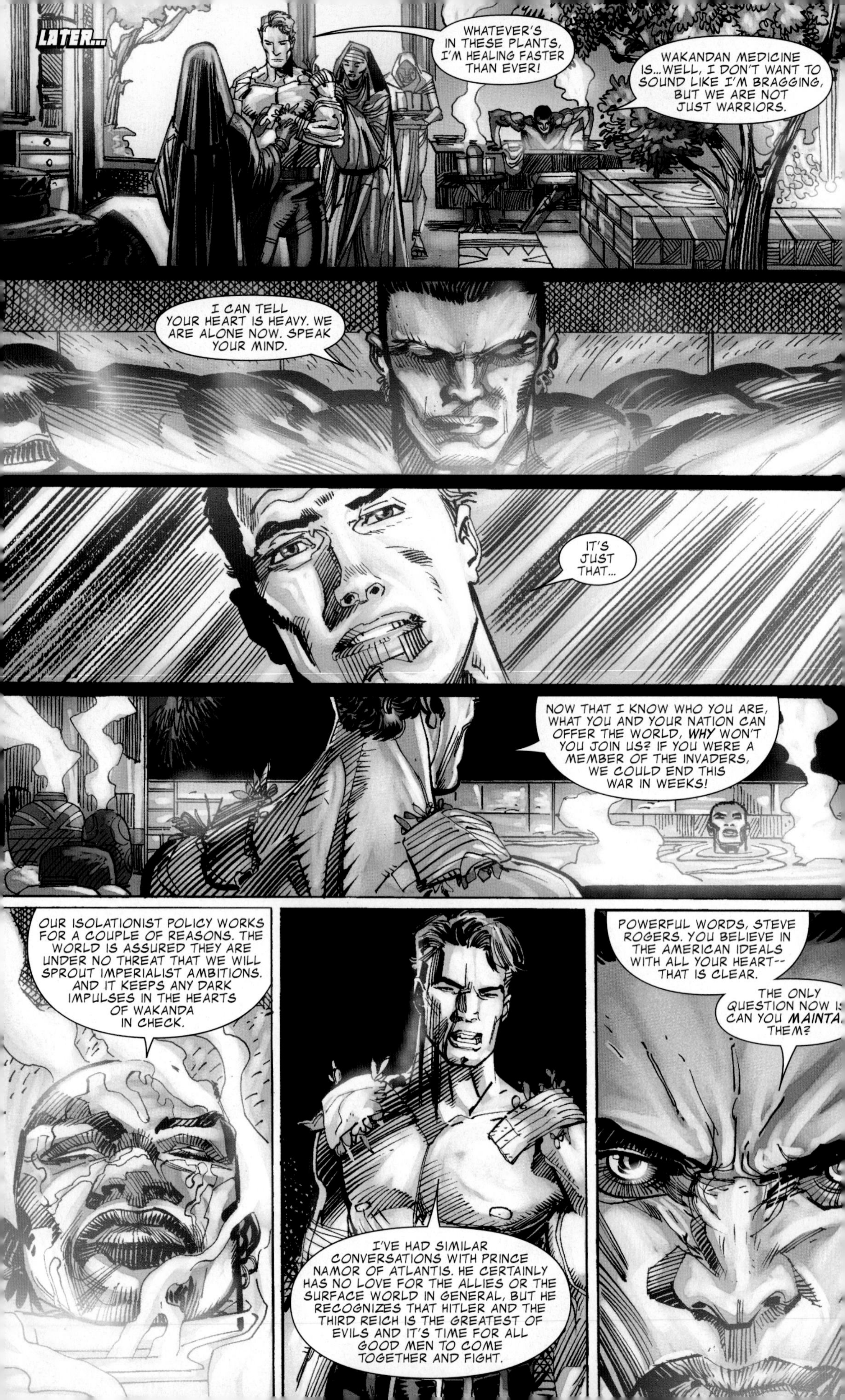
LATER...
WHATEVER'S IN THESE PLANTS, I'M HEALING FASTER THAN EVER!
WAKANDAN MEDICINE IS...WELL, I DON'T WANT TO SOUND LIKE I'M BRAGGING, BUT WE ARE NOT JUST WARRIORS.
I CAN TELL YOUR HEART IS HEAVY. WE ARE ALONE NOW. SPEAK YOUR MIND.
IT'S JUST THAT...
NOW THAT I KNOW WHO YOU ARE, WHAT YOU AND YOUR NATION CAN OFFER THE WORLD, WHY WON'T YOU JOIN US? IF YOU WERE A MEMBER OF THE INVADERS, WE COULD END THIS WAR IN WEEKS!
OUR ISOLATIONIST POLICY WORKS FOR A COUPLE OF REASONS. THE WORLD IS ASSURED THEY ARE UNDER NO THREAT THAT WE WILL SPROUT IMPERIALIST AMBITIONS. AND IT KEEPS ANY DARK IMPULSES IN THE HEARTS OF WAKANDA IN CHECK.
I'VE HAD SIMILAR CONVERSATIONS WITH PRINCE NAMOR OF ATLANTIS. HE CERTAINLY HAS NO LOVE FOR THE ALLIES OR THE SURFACE WORLD IN GENERAL, BUT HE RECOGNIZES THAT HITLER AND THE THIRD REICH IS THE GREATEST OF EVILS AND IT'S TIME FOR ALL GOOD MEN TO COME TOGETHER AND FIGHT.
POWERFUL WORDS, STEVE ROGERS. YOU BELIEVE IN THE AMERICAN IDEALS WITH ALL YOUR HEART-- THAT IS CLEAR.
THE ONLY QUESTION NOW IS CAN YOU MAINTA THEM?

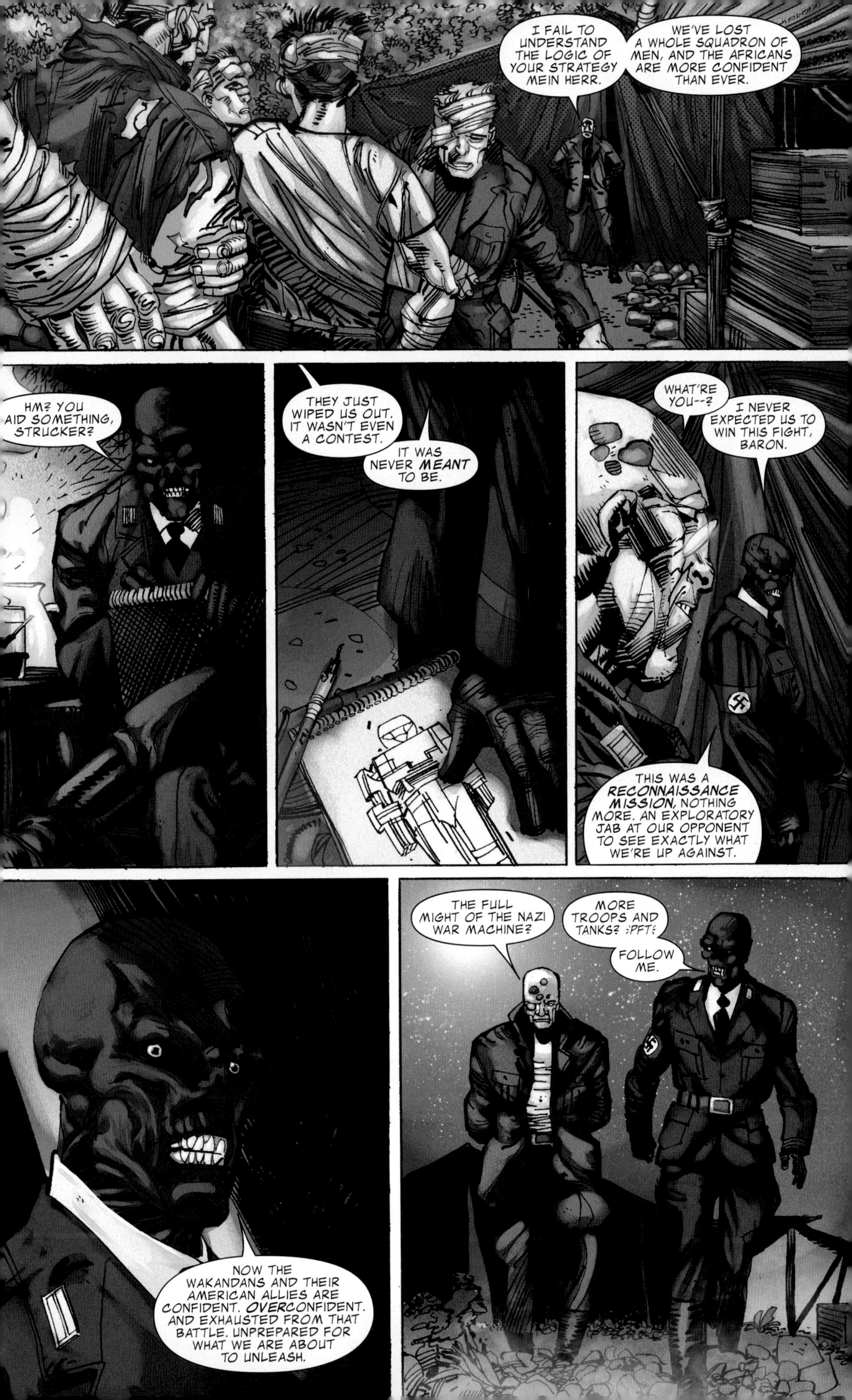
I FAIL TO UNDERSTAND THE LOGIC OF YOUR STRATEGY MEIN HERR.
WE'VE LOST A WHOLE SQUADRON OF MEN, AND THE AFRICANS ARE MORE CONFIDENT THAN EVER.
HM? YOU AID SOMETHING, STRUCKER?
THEY JUST WIPED US OUT. IT WASN'T EVEN A CONTEST.
IT WAS NEVER **MEANT** TO BE.
WHAT'RE YOU--?
I NEVER EXPECTED US TO WIN THIS FIGHT, BARON.
THIS WAS A ***RECONNAISSANCE MISSION***, NOTHING MORE. AN EXPLORATORY JAB AT OUR OPPONENT TO SEE EXACTLY WHAT WE'RE UP AGAINST.
NOW THE WAKANDANS AND THEIR AMERICAN ALLIES ARE CONFIDENT. ***OVER***CONFIDENT. AND EXHAUSTED FROM THAT BATTLE. UNPREPARED FOR WHAT WE ARE ABOUT TO UNLEASH.
THE FULL MIGHT OF THE NAZI WAR MACHINE?
MORE TROOPS AND TANKS? :PFT:
FOLLOW ME.

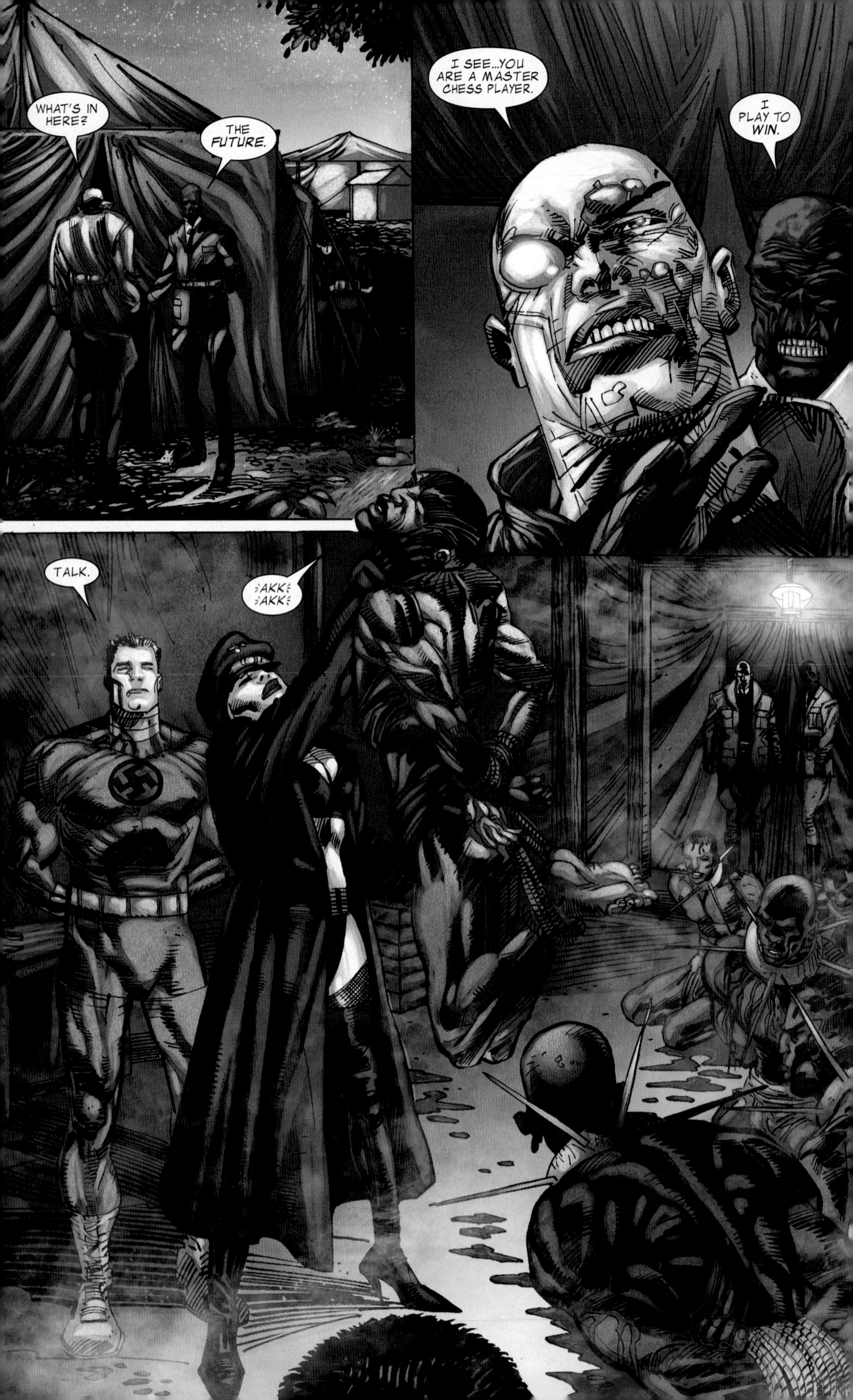
WHAT'S IN HERE?
THE FUTURE.
I SEE...YOU ARE A MASTER CHESS PLAYER.
I PLAY TO WIN.
TALK.
AKK AKK

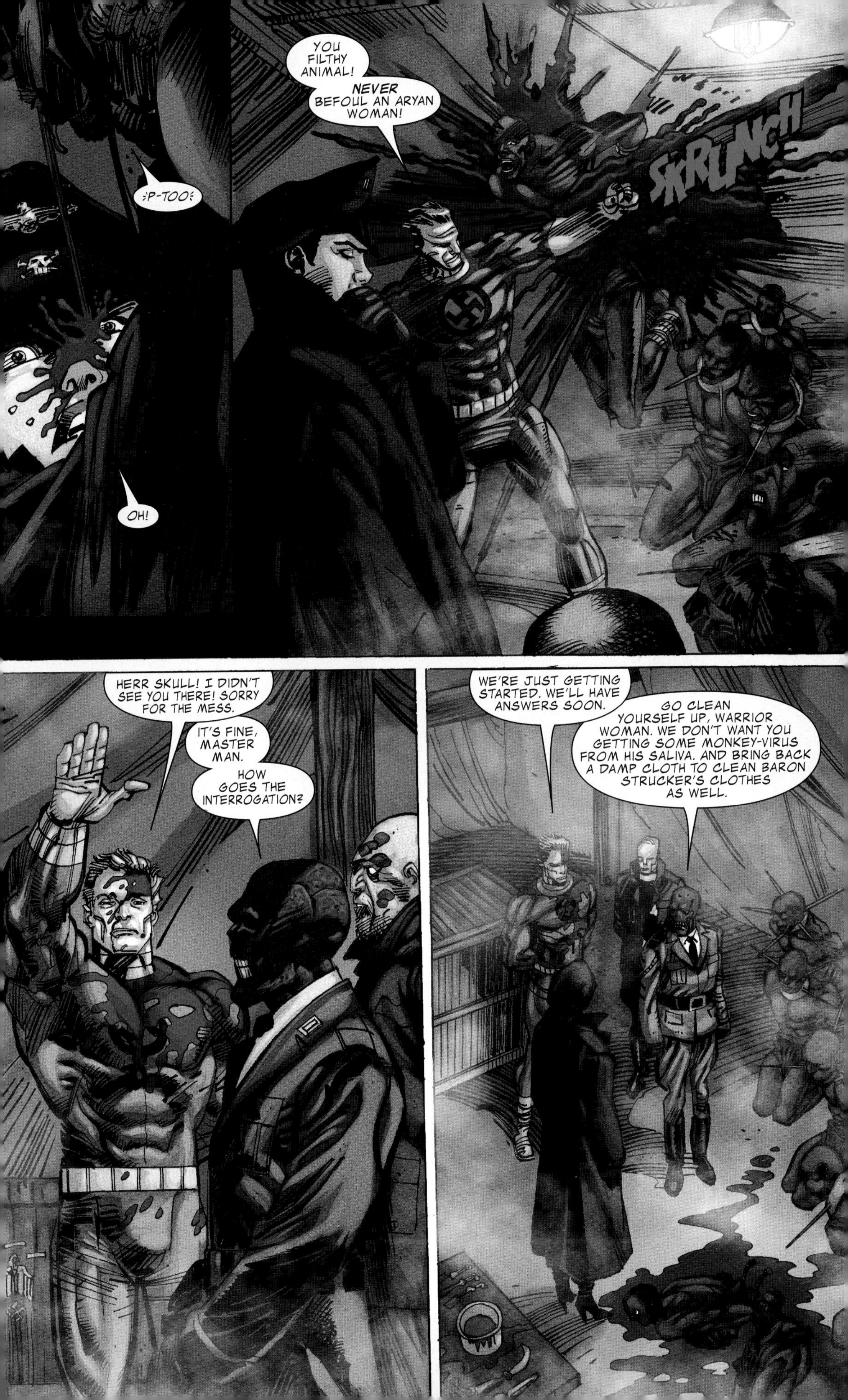

:P-TOO:
OH!
YOU FILTHY ANIMAL! NEVER BEFOUL AN ARYAN WOMAN!
SKRUNCH
HERR SKULL! I DIDN'T SEE YOU THERE! SORRY FOR THE MESS.
IT'S FINE, MASTER MAN.
HOW GOES THE INTERROGATION?
WE'RE JUST GETTING STARTED. WE'LL HAVE ANSWERS SOON.
GO CLEAN YOURSELF UP, WARRIOR WOMAN. WE DON'T WANT YOU GETTING SOME MONKEY-VIRUS FROM HIS SALIVA. AND BRING BACK A DAMP CLOTH TO CLEAN BARON STRUCKER'S CLOTHES AS WELL.

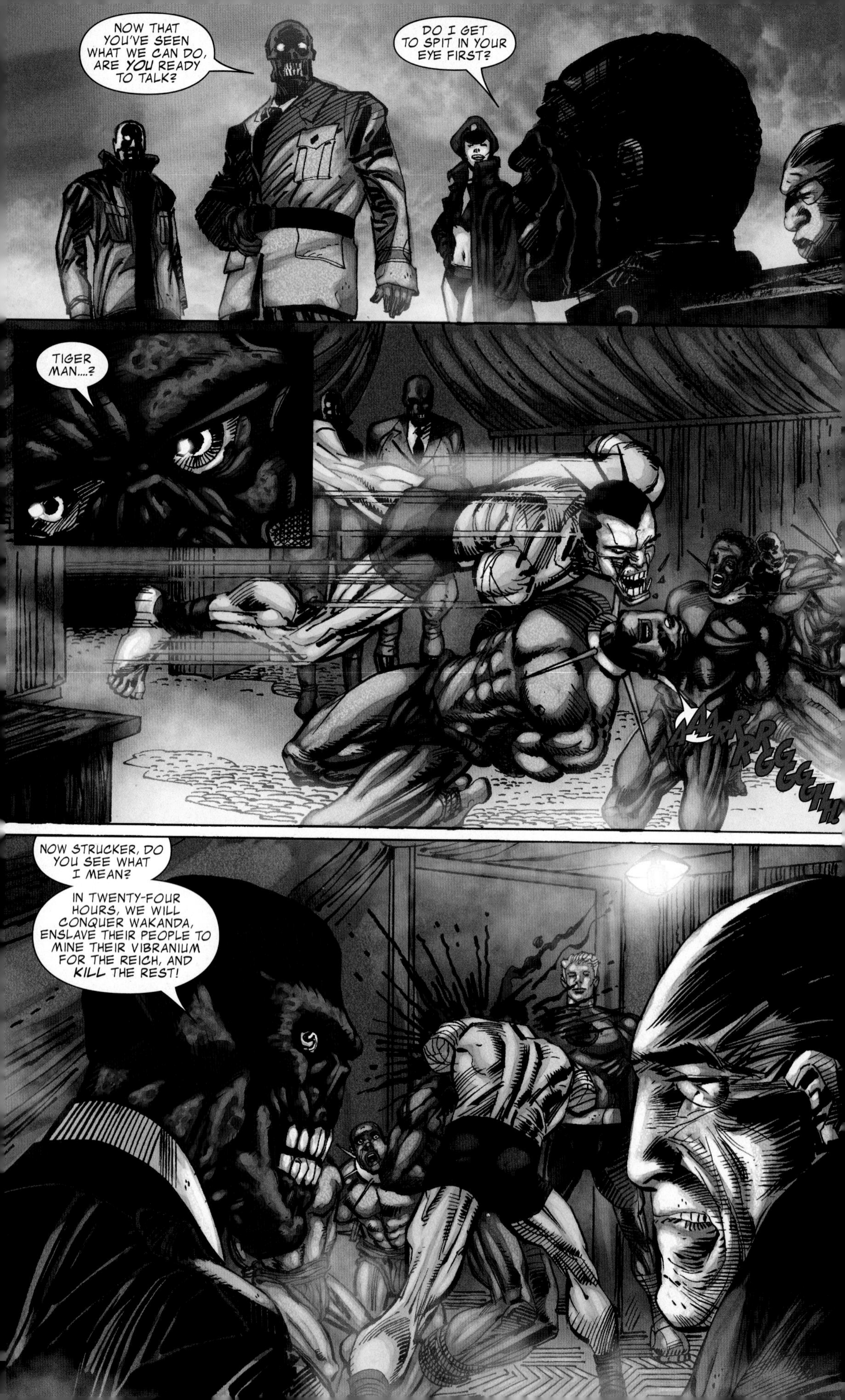
NOW THAT YOU'VE SEEN WHAT WE CAN DO, ARE YOU READY TO TALK?
DO I GET TO SPIT IN YOUR EYE FIRST?
TIGER MAN...?
AAARRRRGGGGHH!
NOW STRUCKER, DO YOU SEE WHAT I MEAN?
IN TWENTY-FOUR HOURS, WE WILL CONQUER WAKANDA, ENSLAVE THEIR PEOPLE TO MINE THEIR VIBRANIUM FOR THE REICH, AND KILL THE REST!

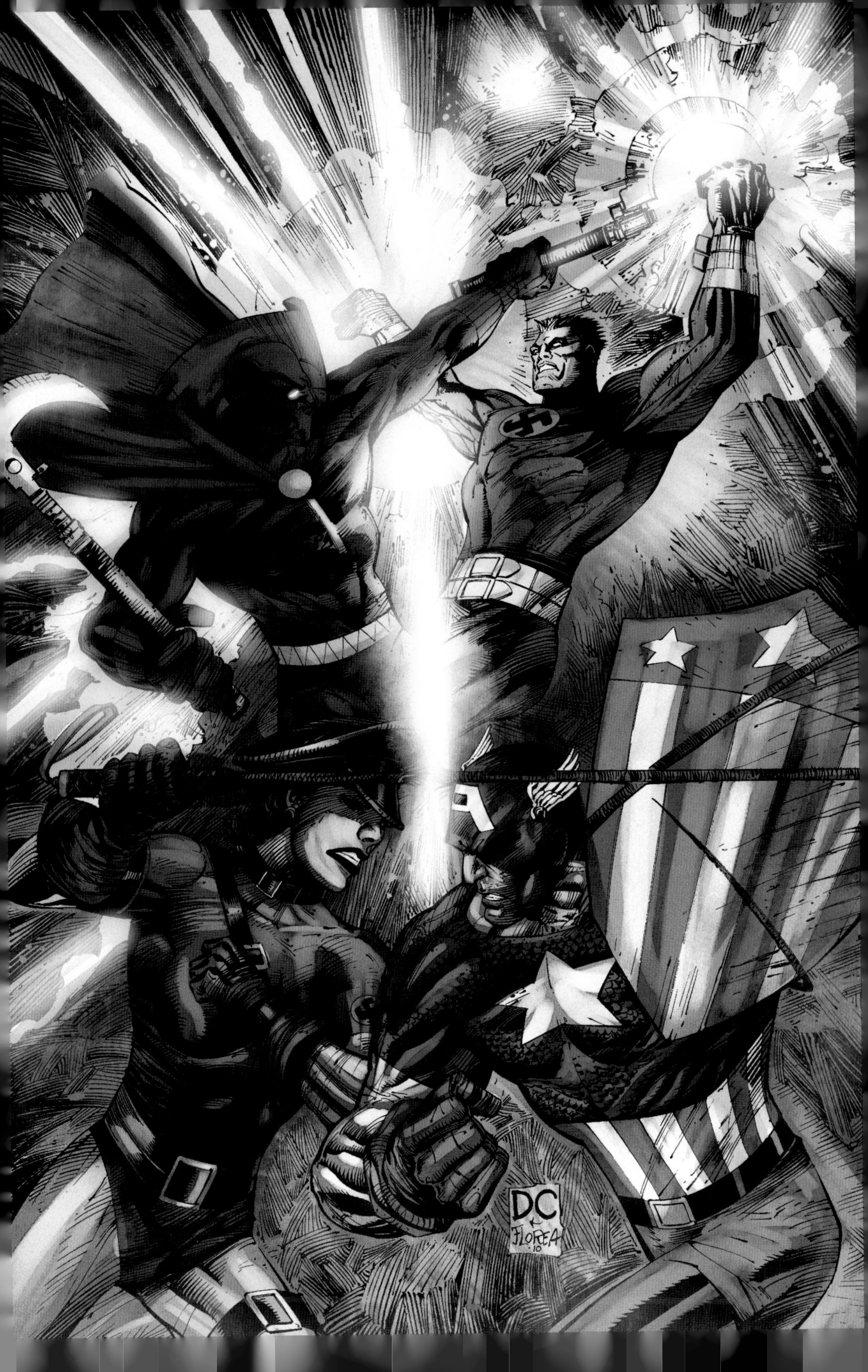
DC
FLOREA
10

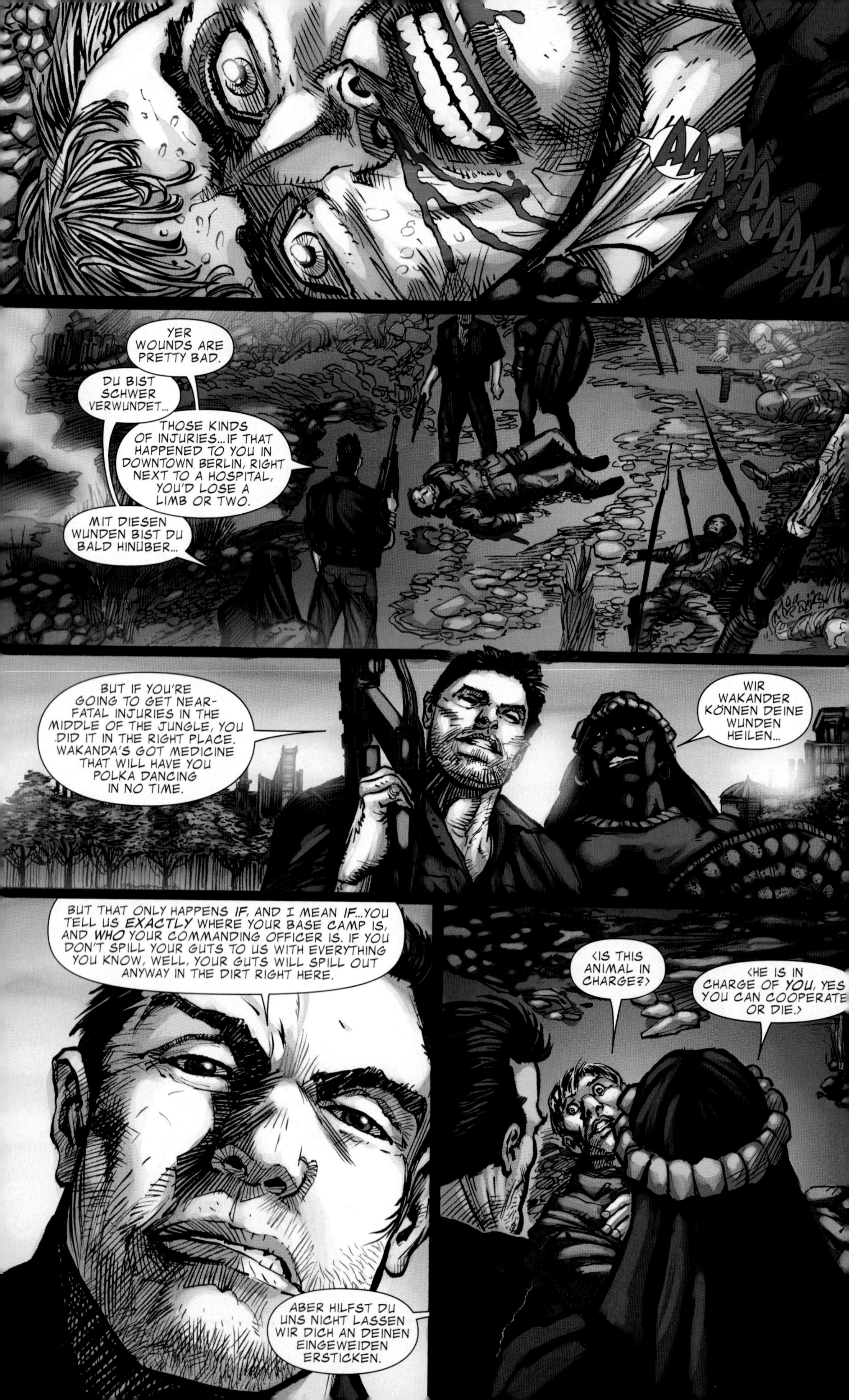
AAAAAAAAAAAA!
YER WOUNDS ARE PRETTY BAD.
DU BIST SCHWER VERWUNDET...
THOSE KINDS OF INJURIES...IF THAT HAPPENED TO YOU IN DOWNTOWN BERLIN, RIGHT NEXT TO A HOSPITAL, YOU'D LOSE A LIMB OR TWO.
MIT DIESEN WUNDEN BIST DU BALD HINÜBER...
BUT IF YOU'RE GOING TO GET NEAR-FATAL INJURIES IN THE MIDDLE OF THE JUNGLE, YOU DID IT IN THE RIGHT PLACE. WAKANDA'S GOT MEDICINE THAT WILL HAVE YOU POLKA DANCING IN NO TIME.
WIR WAKANDER KÖNNEN DEINE WUNDEN HEILEN...
BUT THAT ONLY HAPPENS *IF*, AND I MEAN *IF*...YOU TELL US ***EXACTLY*** WHERE YOUR BASE CAMP IS, AND ***WHO*** YOUR COMMANDING OFFICER IS. IF YOU DON'T SPILL YOUR GUTS TO US WITH EVERYTHING YOU KNOW, WELL, YOUR GUTS WILL SPILL OUT ANYWAY IN THE DIRT RIGHT HERE.
ABER HILFST DU UNS NICHT LASSEN WIR DICH AN DEINEN EINGEWEIDEN ERSTICKEN.
<IS THIS ANIMAL IN CHARGE?>
<HE IS IN CHARGE OF ***YOU***, YES. YOU CAN COOPERATE OR DIE.>

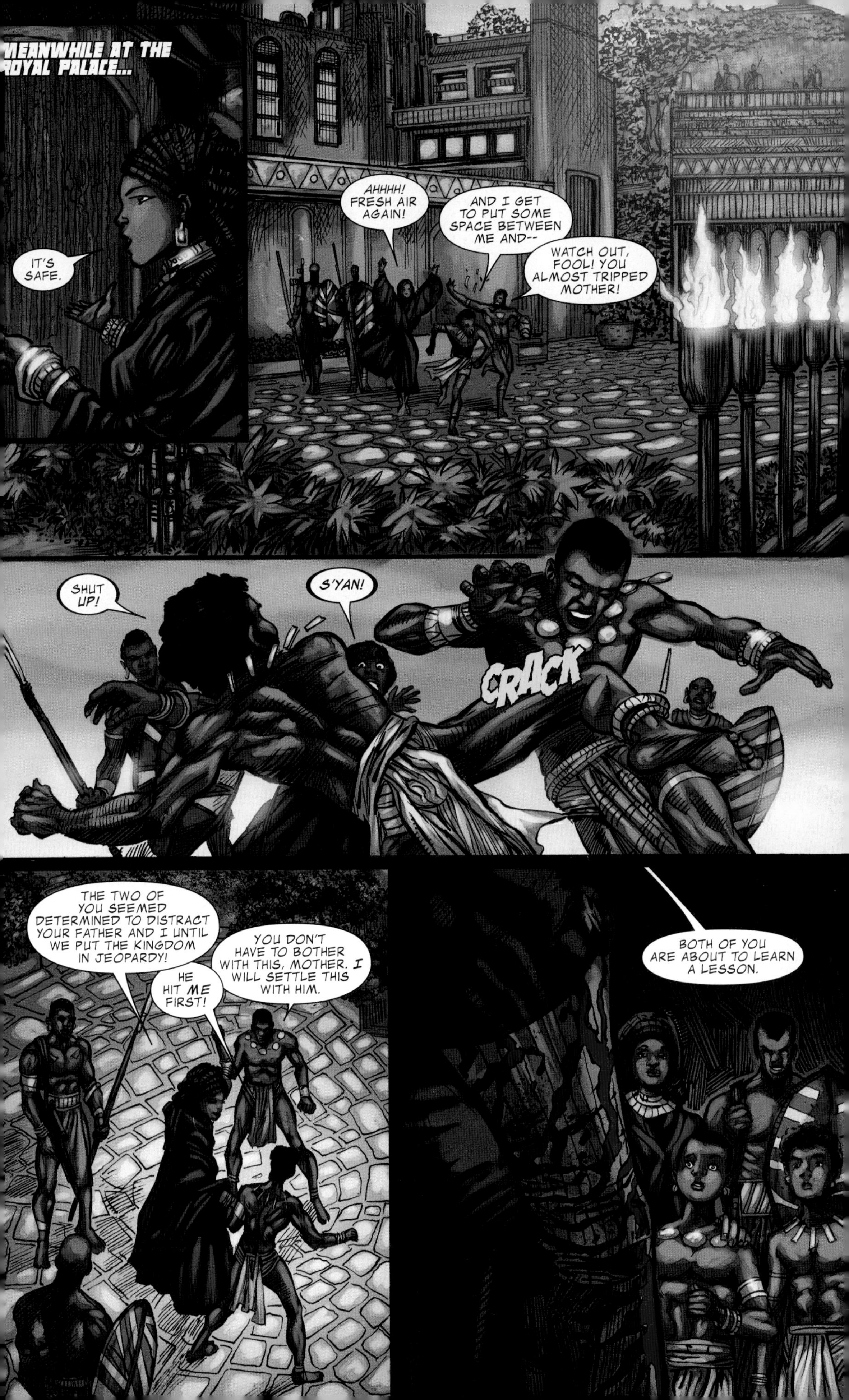
MEANWHILE AT THE ROYAL PALACE...
IT'S SAFE.
AHHHH! FRESH AIR AGAIN!
AND I GET TO PUT SOME SPACE BETWEEN ME AND--
WATCH OUT, FOOL! YOU ALMOST TRIPPED MOTHER!
SHUT UP!
S'YAN!
CRACK
THE TWO OF YOU SEEMED DETERMINED TO DISTRACT YOUR FATHER AND I UNTIL WE PUT THE KINGDOM IN JEOPARDY!
HE HIT ME FIRST!
YOU DON'T HAVE TO BOTHER WITH THIS, MOTHER. I WILL SETTLE THIS WITH HIM.
BOTH OF YOU ARE ABOUT TO LEARN A LESSON.

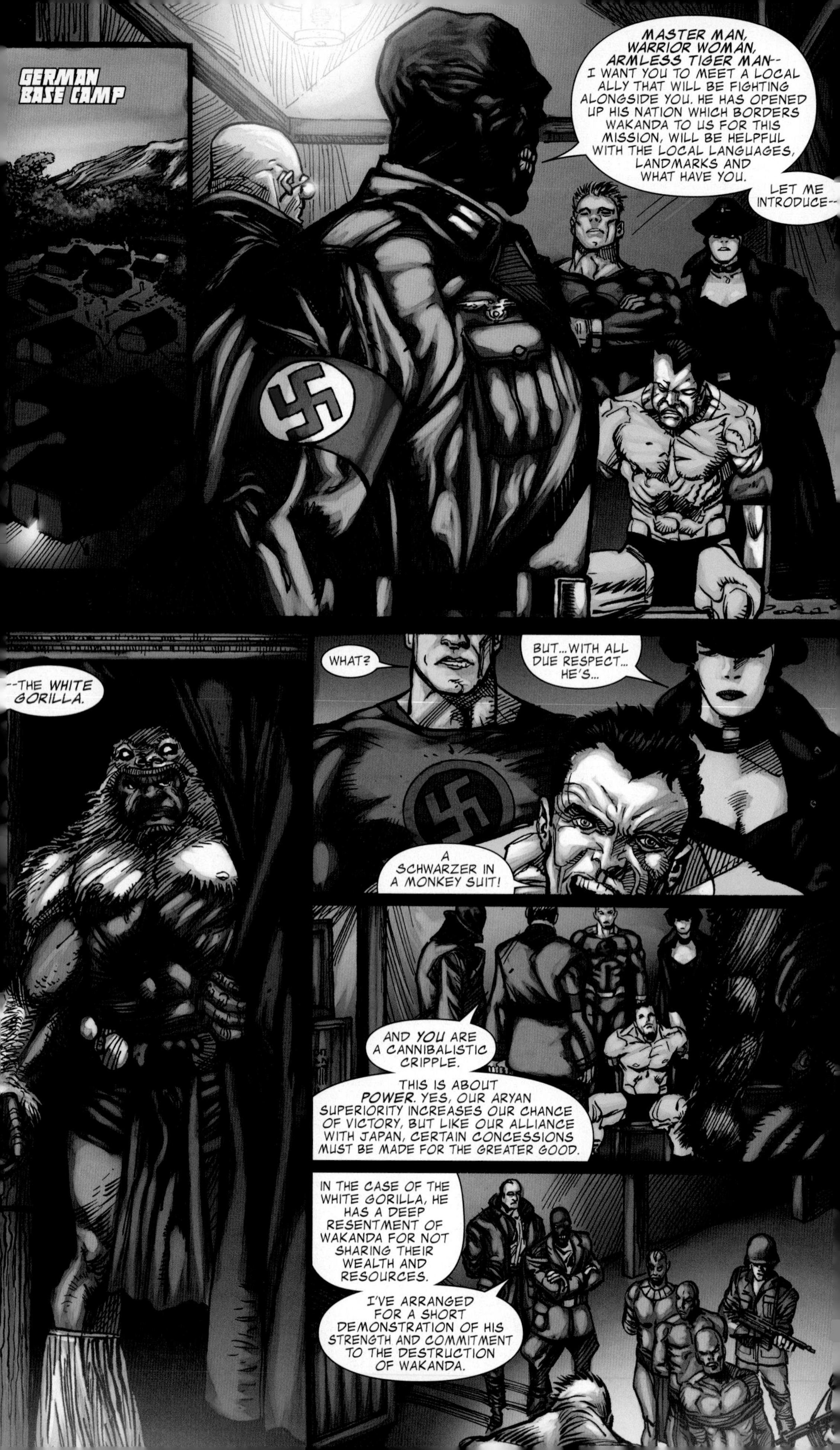
GERMAN BASE CAMP
MASTER MAN, WARRIOR WOMAN, ARMLESS TIGER MAN-- I WANT YOU TO MEET A LOCAL ALLY THAT WILL BE FIGHTING ALONGSIDE YOU. HE HAS OPENED UP HIS NATION WHICH BORDERS WAKANDA TO US FOR THIS MISSION, WILL BE HELPFUL WITH THE LOCAL LANGUAGES, LANDMARKS AND WHAT HAVE YOU.
LET ME INTRODUCE--
--THE WHITE GORILLA.
WHAT?
BUT...WITH ALL DUE RESPECT... HE'S...
A SCHWARZER IN A MONKEY SUIT!
AND YOU ARE A CANNIBALISTIC CRIPPLE.
THIS IS ABOUT POWER. YES, OUR ARYAN SUPERIORITY INCREASES OUR CHANCE OF VICTORY, BUT LIKE OUR ALLIANCE WITH JAPAN, CERTAIN CONCESSIONS MUST BE MADE FOR THE GREATER GOOD.
IN THE CASE OF THE WHITE GORILLA, HE HAS A DEEP RESENTMENT OF WAKANDA FOR NOT SHARING THEIR WEALTH AND RESOURCES.
I'VE ARRANGED FOR A SHORT DEMONSTRATION OF HIS STRENGTH AND COMMITMENT TO THE DESTRUCTION OF WAKANDA.

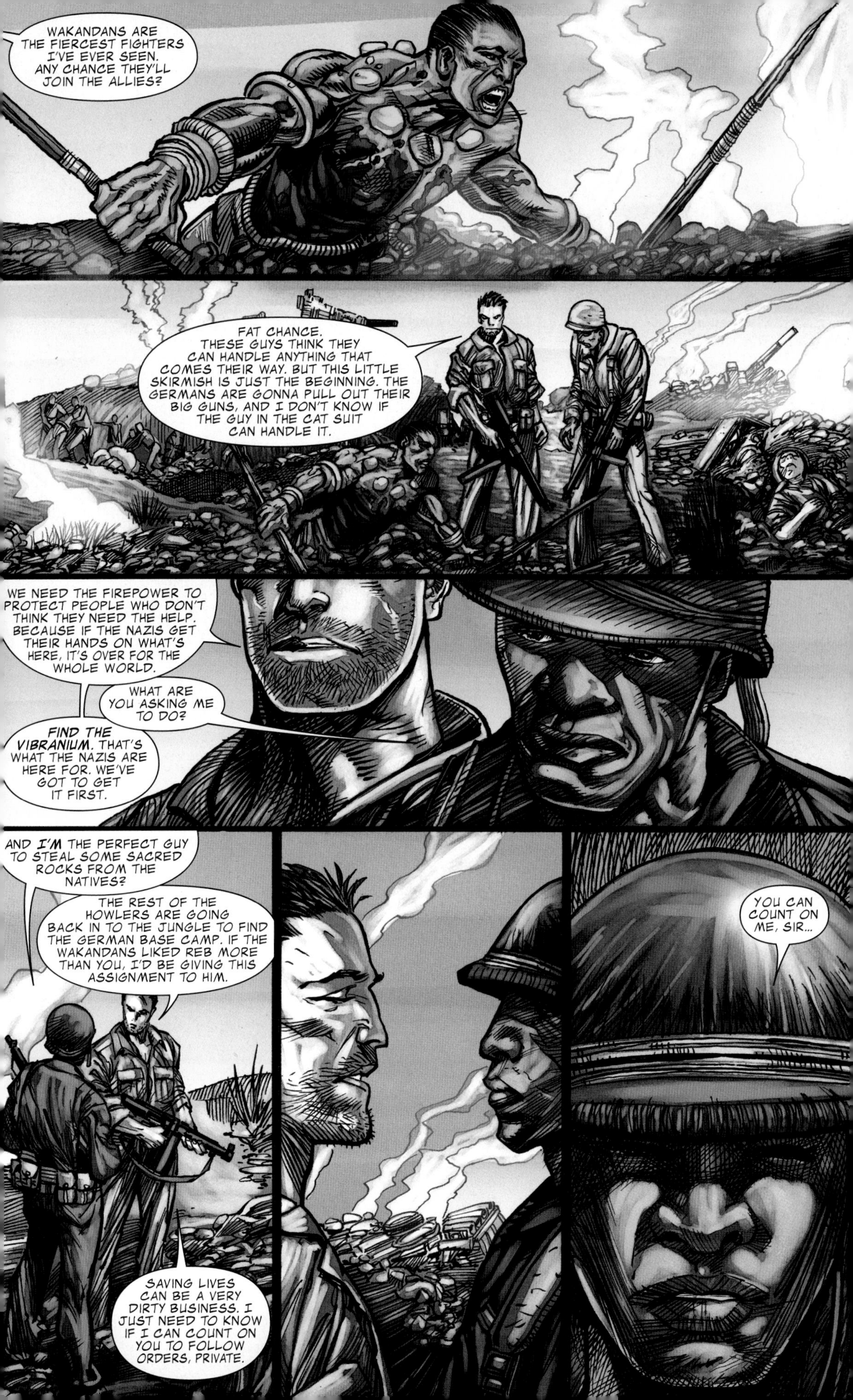
WAKANDANS ARE THE FIERCEST FIGHTERS I'VE EVER SEEN. ANY CHANCE THEY'LL JOIN THE ALLIES?
FAT CHANCE. THESE GUYS THINK THEY CAN HANDLE ANYTHING THAT COMES THEIR WAY. BUT THIS LITTLE SKIRMISH IS JUST THE BEGINNING. THE GERMANS ARE GONNA PULL OUT THEIR BIG GUNS, AND I DON'T KNOW IF THE GUY IN THE CAT SUIT CAN HANDLE IT.
WE NEED THE FIREPOWER TO PROTECT PEOPLE WHO DON'T THINK THEY NEED THE HELP. BECAUSE IF THE NAZIS GET THEIR HANDS ON WHAT'S HERE, IT'S OVER FOR THE WHOLE WORLD.
WHAT ARE YOU ASKING ME TO DO?
FIND THE VIBRANIUM. THAT'S WHAT THE NAZIS ARE HERE FOR. WE'VE GOT TO GET IT FIRST.
AND *I'M* THE PERFECT GUY TO STEAL SOME SACRED ROCKS FROM THE NATIVES?
THE REST OF THE HOWLERS ARE GOING BACK IN TO THE JUNGLE TO FIND THE GERMAN BASE CAMP. IF THE WAKANDANS LIKED REB MORE THAN YOU, I'D BE GIVING THIS ASSIGNMENT TO HIM.
SAVING LIVES CAN BE A VERY DIRTY BUSINESS. I JUST NEED TO KNOW IF I CAN COUNT ON YOU TO FOLLOW ORDERS, PRIVATE.
YOU CAN COUNT ON ME, SIR...

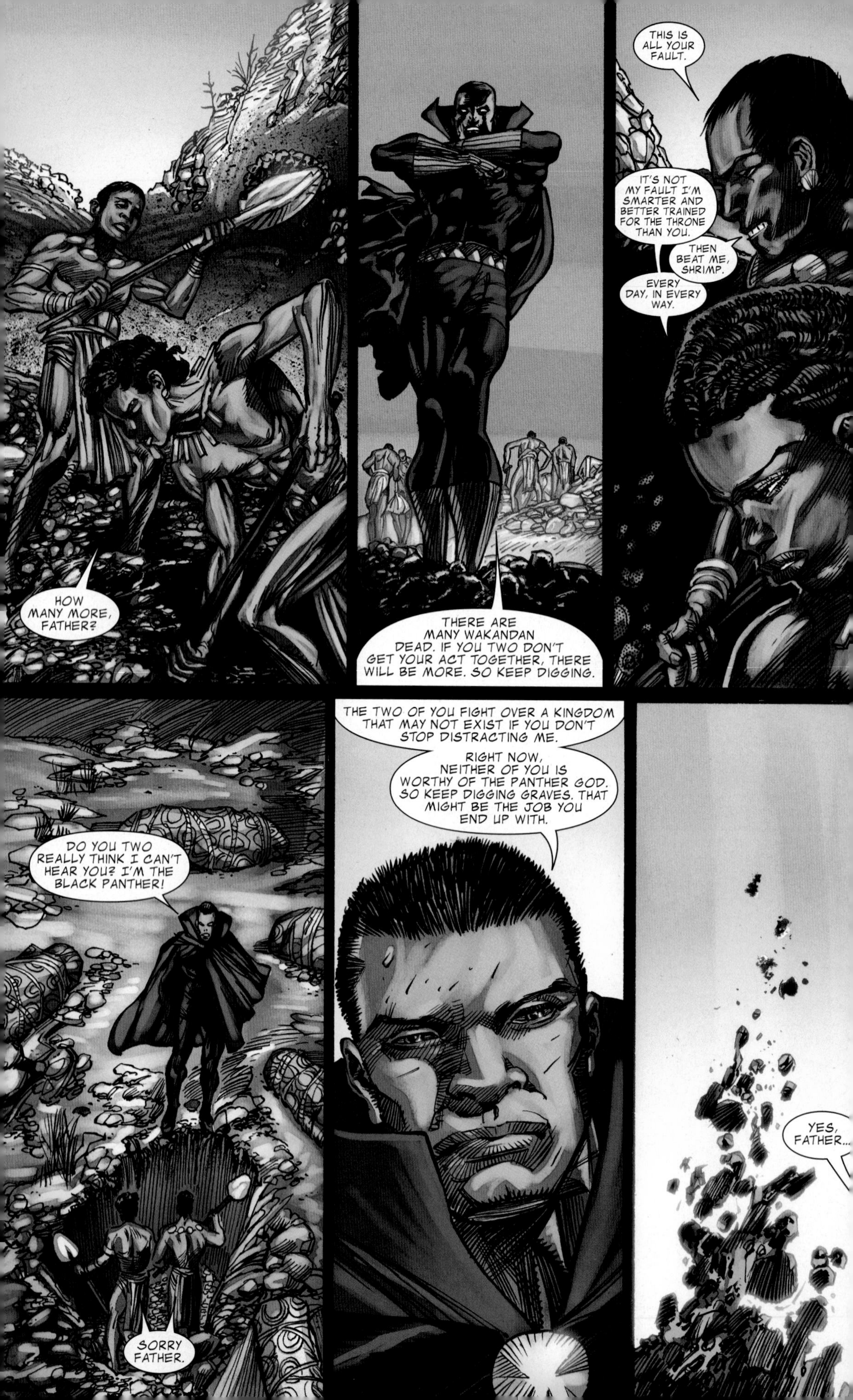
HOW MANY MORE, FATHER?
THERE ARE MANY WAKANDAN DEAD. IF YOU TWO DON'T GET YOUR ACT TOGETHER, THERE WILL BE MORE. SO KEEP DIGGING.
THIS IS ALL YOUR FAULT.
IT'S NOT MY FAULT I'M SMARTER AND BETTER TRAINED FOR THE THRONE THAN YOU.
THEN BEAT ME, SHRIMP.
EVERY DAY, IN EVERY WAY.
DO YOU TWO REALLY THINK I CAN'T HEAR YOU? I'M THE BLACK PANTHER!
SORRY FATHER.
THE TWO OF YOU FIGHT OVER A KINGDOM THAT MAY NOT EXIST IF YOU DON'T STOP DISTRACTING ME.
RIGHT NOW, NEITHER OF YOU IS WORTHY OF THE PANTHER GOD. SO KEEP DIGGING GRAVES. THAT MIGHT BE THE JOB YOU END UP WITH.
YES, FATHER...

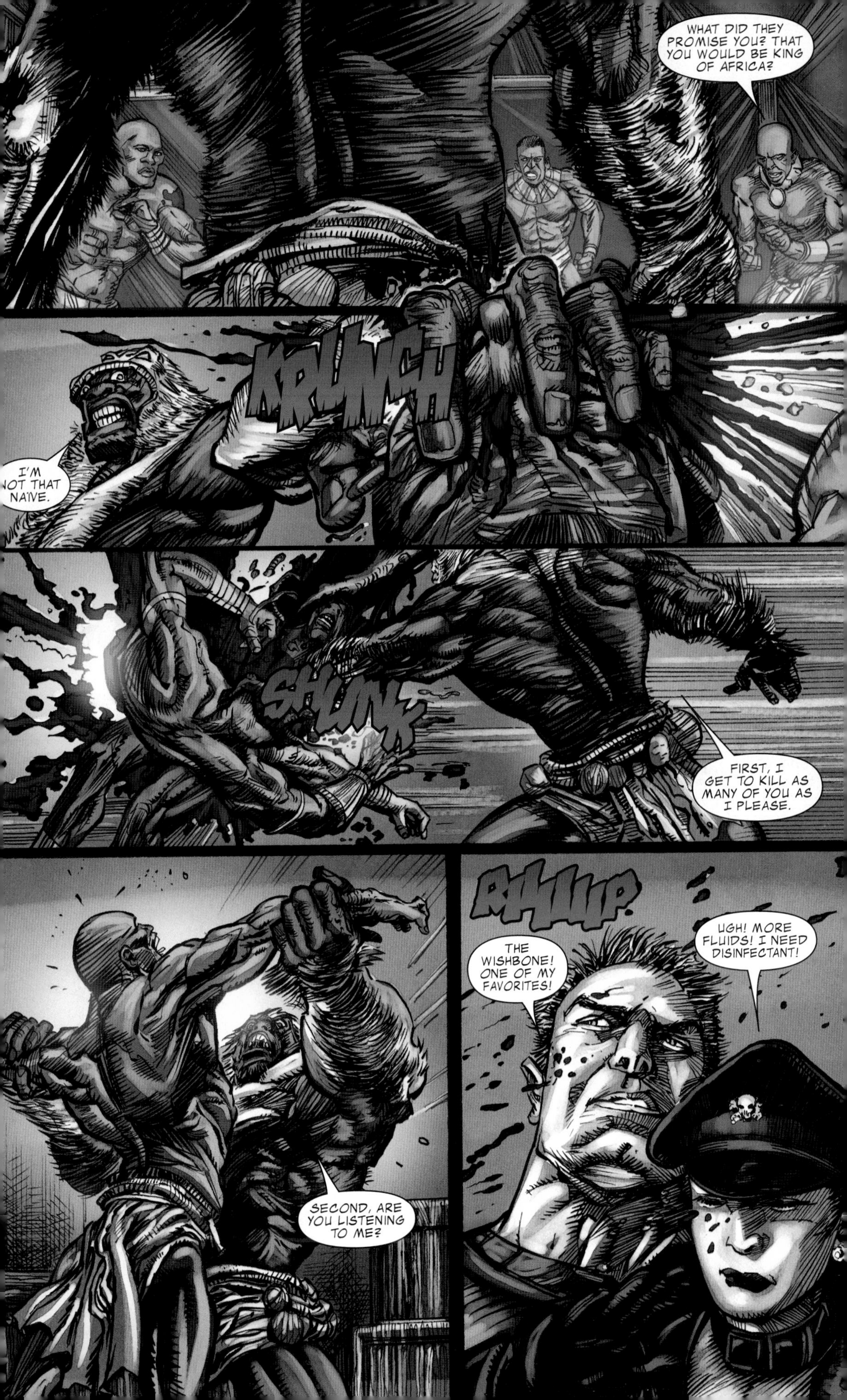
WHAT DID THEY PROMISE YOU? THAT YOU WOULD BE KING OF AFRICA?
KRUNCH
I'M NOT THAT NAÏVE.
SHUNK
FIRST, I GET TO KILL AS MANY OF YOU AS I PLEASE.
SECOND, ARE YOU LISTENING TO ME?
RAAAP
THE WISHBONE! ONE OF MY FAVORITES!
UGH! MORE FLUIDS! I NEED DISINFECTANT!

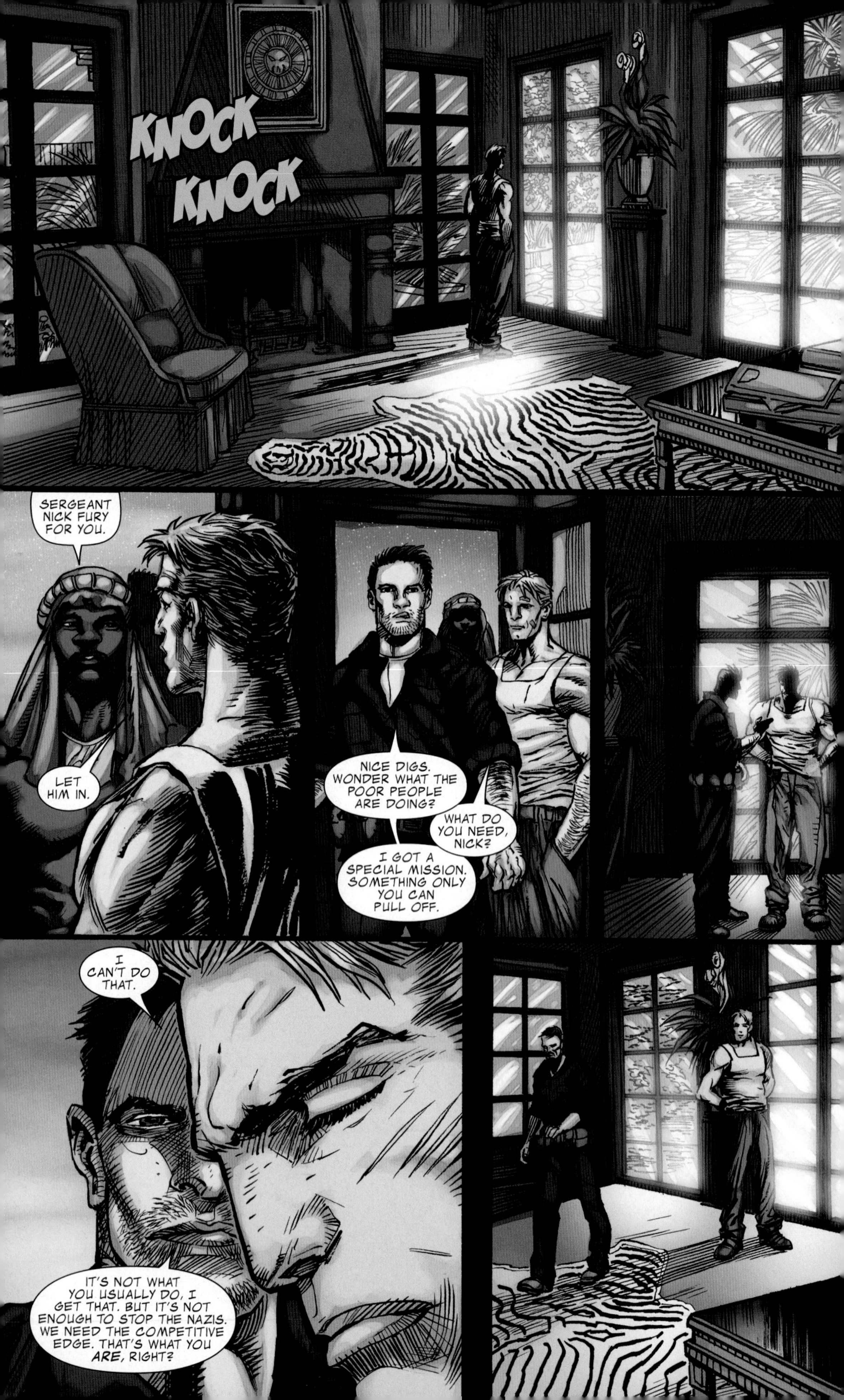
KNOCK
KNOCK
SERGEANT NICK FURY FOR YOU.
LET HIM IN.
NICE DIGS. WONDER WHAT THE POOR PEOPLE ARE DOING?
WHAT DO YOU NEED, NICK?
I GOT A SPECIAL MISSION. SOMETHING ONLY YOU CAN PULL OFF.
I CAN'T DO THAT.
IT'S NOT WHAT YOU USUALLY DO, I GET THAT. BUT IT'S NOT ENOUGH TO STOP THE NAZIS. WE NEED THE COMPETITIVE EDGE. THAT'S WHAT YOU ARE, RIGHT?

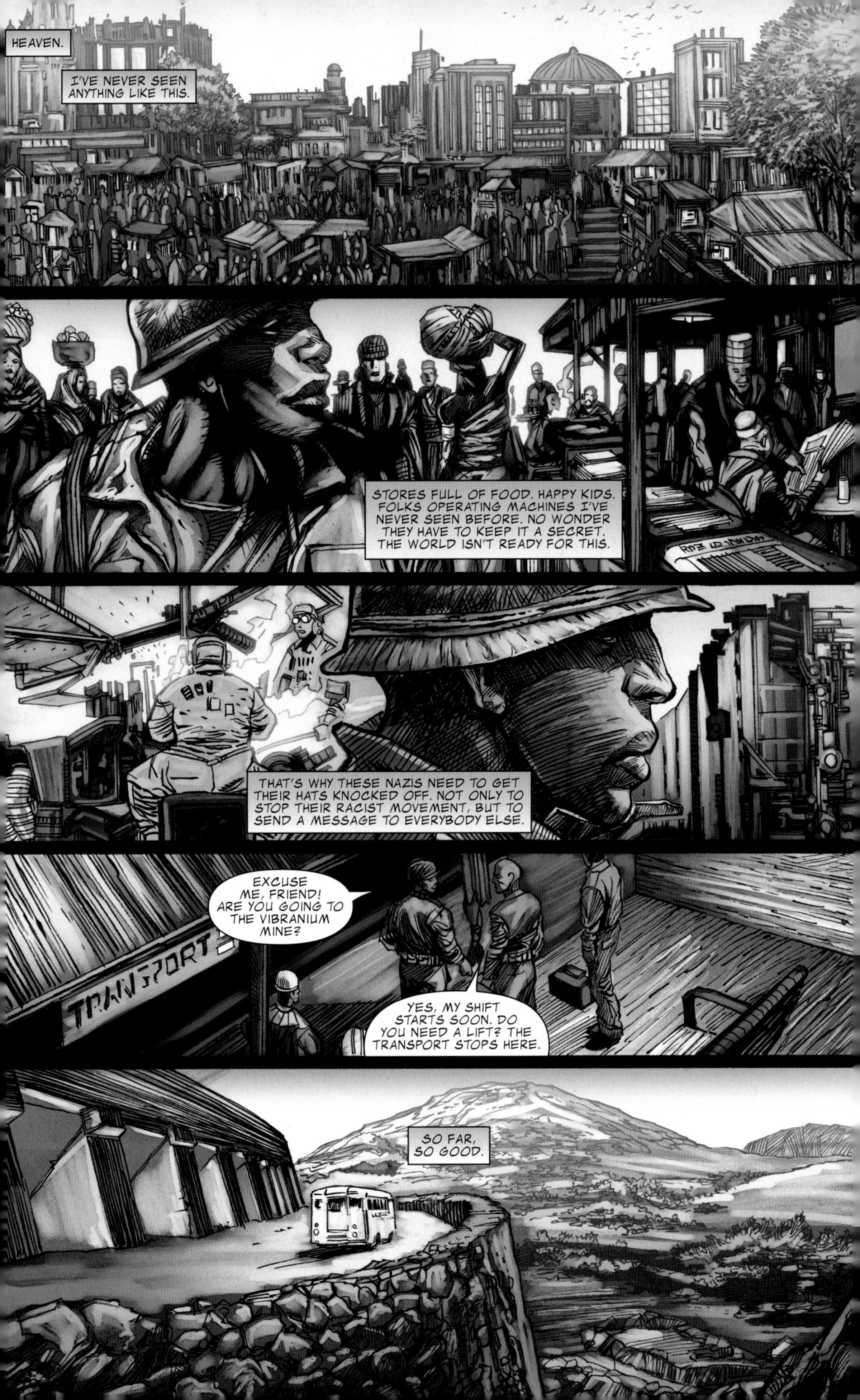
HEAVEN.
I'VE NEVER SEEN ANYTHING LIKE THIS.
STORES FULL OF FOOD. HAPPY KIDS. FOLKS OPERATING MACHINES I'VE NEVER SEEN BEFORE. NO WONDER THEY HAVE TO KEEP IT A SECRET. THE WORLD ISN'T READY FOR THIS.
THAT'S WHY THESE NAZIS NEED TO GET THEIR HATS KNOCKED OFF. NOT ONLY TO STOP THEIR RACIST MOVEMENT, BUT TO SEND A MESSAGE TO EVERYBODY ELSE.
TRANSPORT
EXCUSE ME, FRIEND! ARE YOU GOING TO THE VIBRANIUM MINE?
YES, MY SHIFT STARTS SOON. DO YOU NEED A LIFT? THE TRANSPORT STOPS HERE.
SO FAR, SO GOOD.

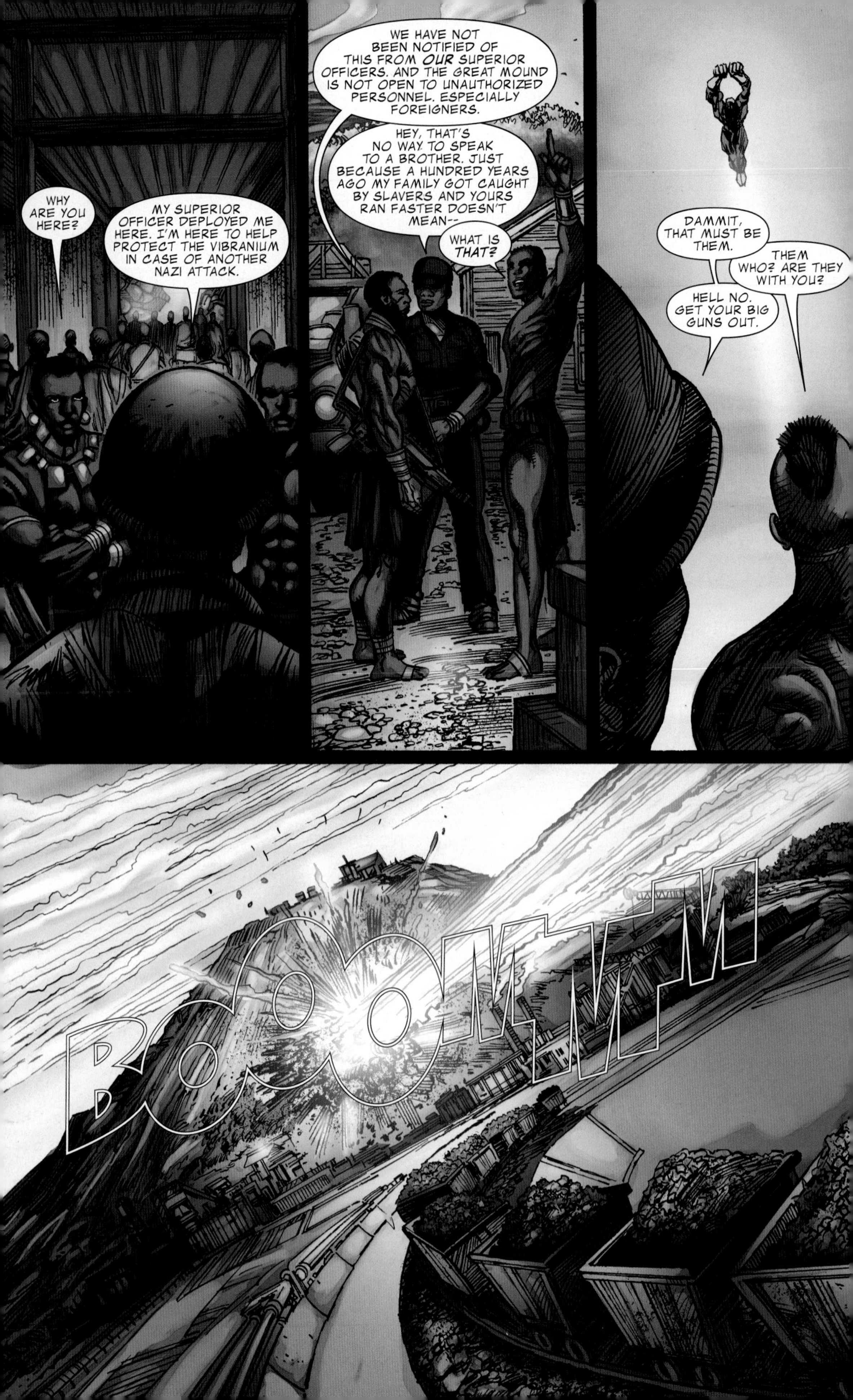
WHY ARE YOU HERE?
MY SUPERIOR OFFICER DEPLOYED ME HERE. I'M HERE TO HELP PROTECT THE VIBRANIUM IN CASE OF ANOTHER NAZI ATTACK.
WE HAVE NOT BEEN NOTIFIED OF THIS FROM OUR SUPERIOR OFFICERS. AND THE GREAT MOUND IS NOT OPEN TO UNAUTHORIZED PERSONNEL. ESPECIALLY FOREIGNERS.
HEY, THAT'S NO WAY TO SPEAK TO A BROTHER. JUST BECAUSE A HUNDRED YEARS AGO MY FAMILY GOT CAUGHT BY SLAVERS AND YOURS RAN FASTER DOESN'T MEAN--
WHAT IS THAT?
DAMMIT, THAT MUST BE THEM.
THEM WHO? ARE THEY WITH YOU?
HELL NO. GET YOUR BIG GUNS OUT.
BOOOMMM

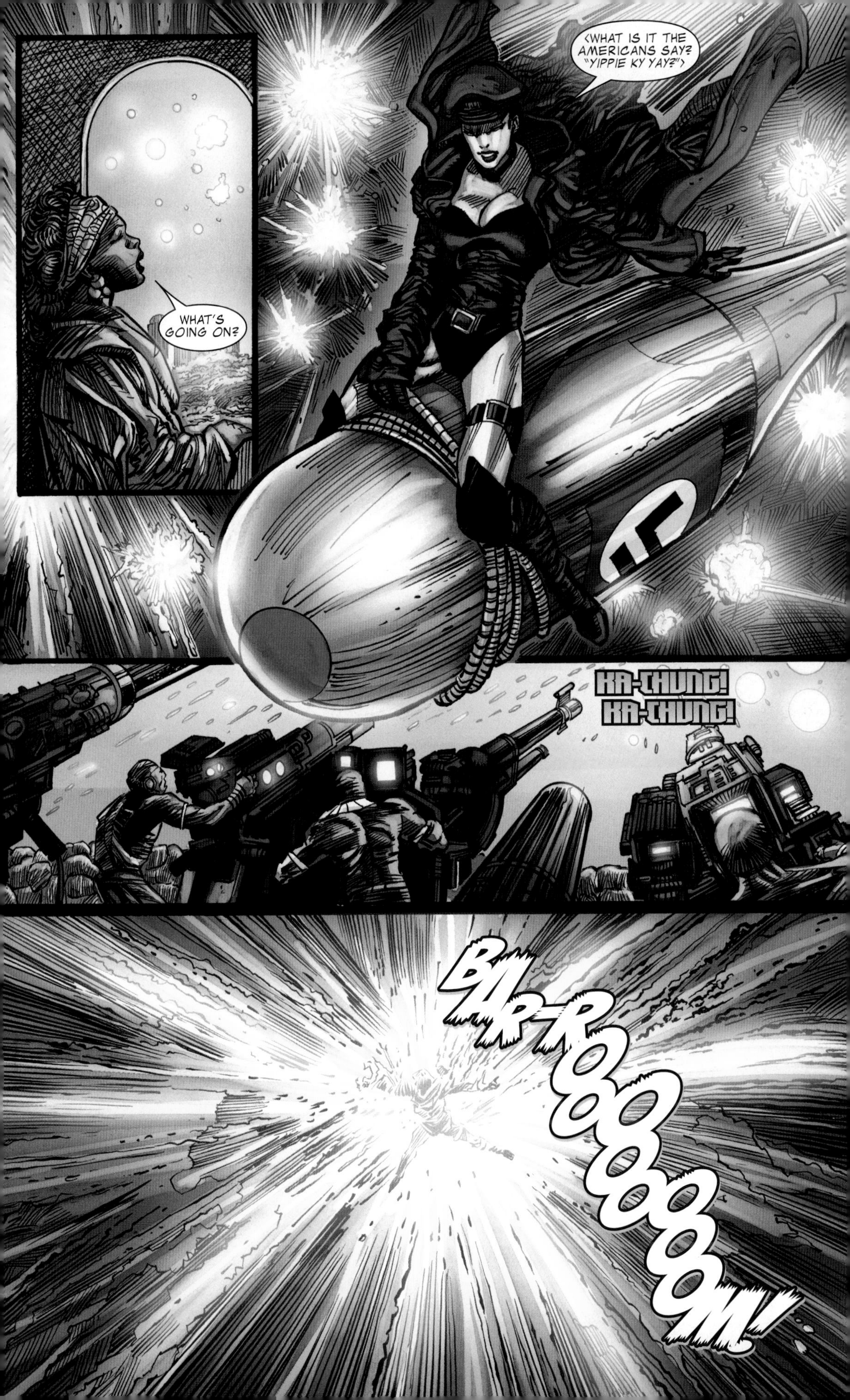

WHAT'S GOING ON?
<WHAT IS IT THE AMERICANS SAY? "YIPPIE KY YAY?">
KA-CHUNG! KA-CHUNG!
BAR-ROOOOOOOOM!

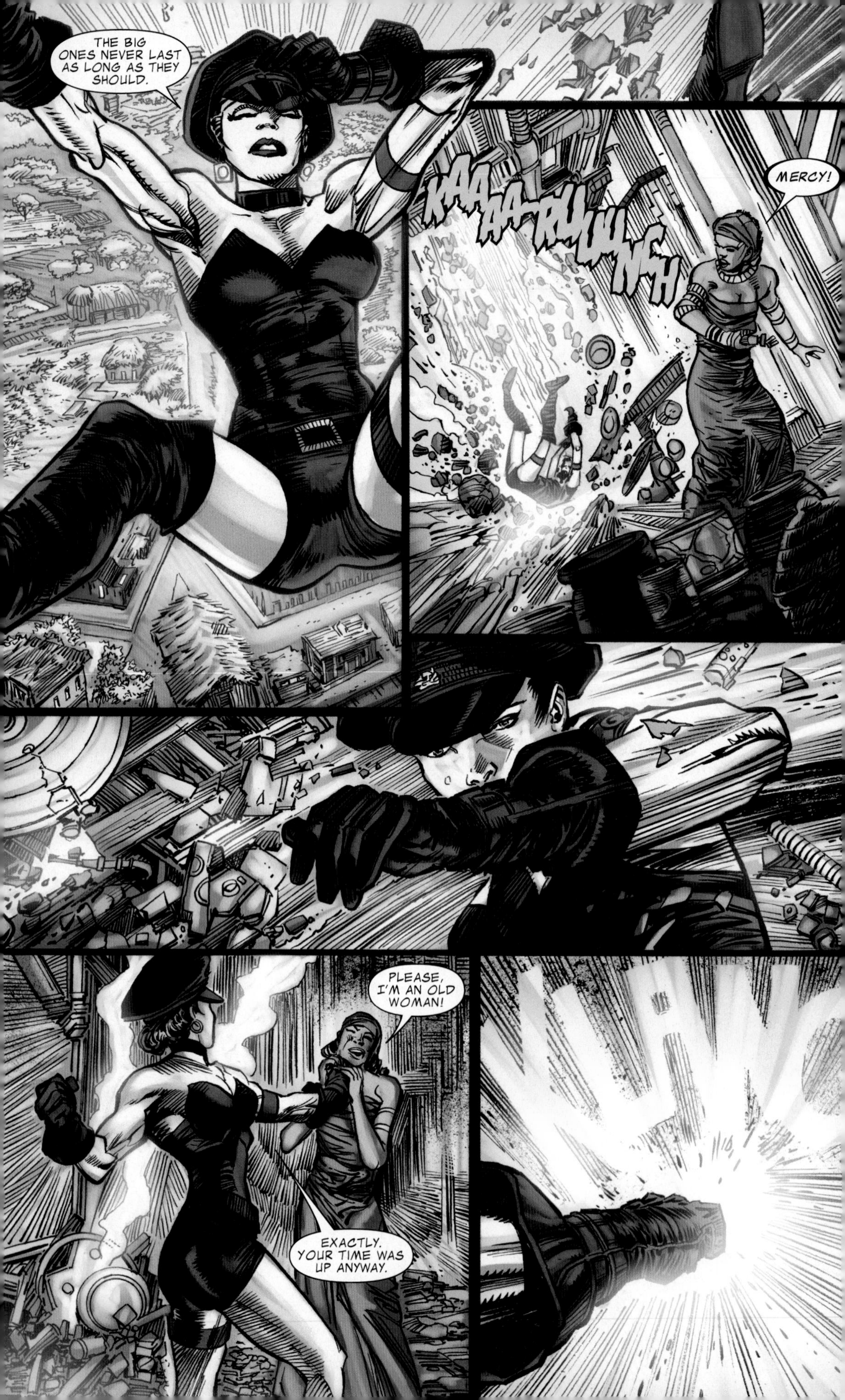
THE BIG ONES NEVER LAST AS LONG AS THEY SHOULD.
KAAAAA-RUUUNGH
MERCY!
PLEASE, I'M AN OLD WOMAN!
EXACTLY. YOUR TIME WAS UP ANYWAY.

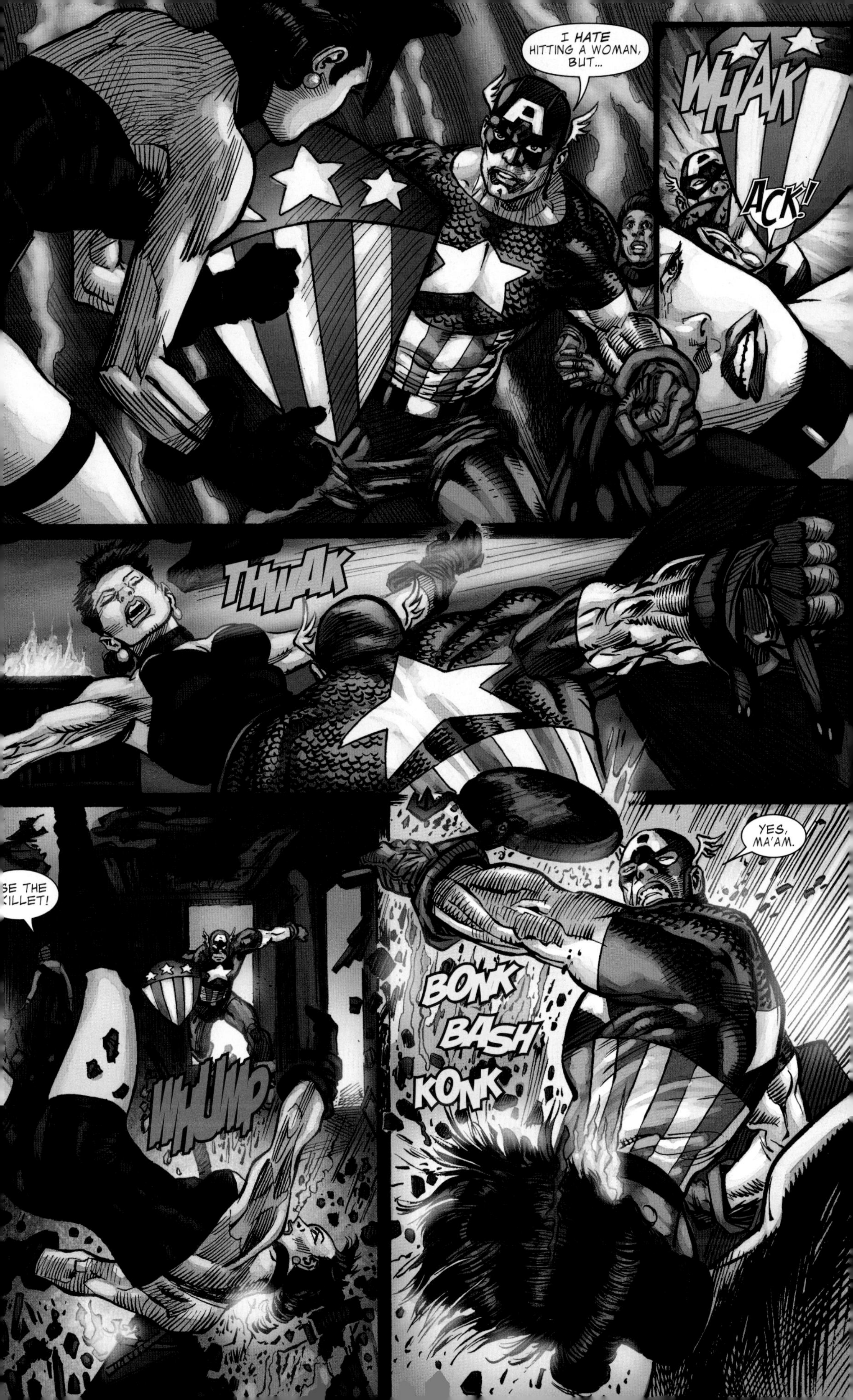
I HATE HITTING A WOMAN, BUT...
WHAK
ACK!
THWAK
SE THE KILLET!
WHUMP
YES, MA'AM.
BONK
BASH
KONK

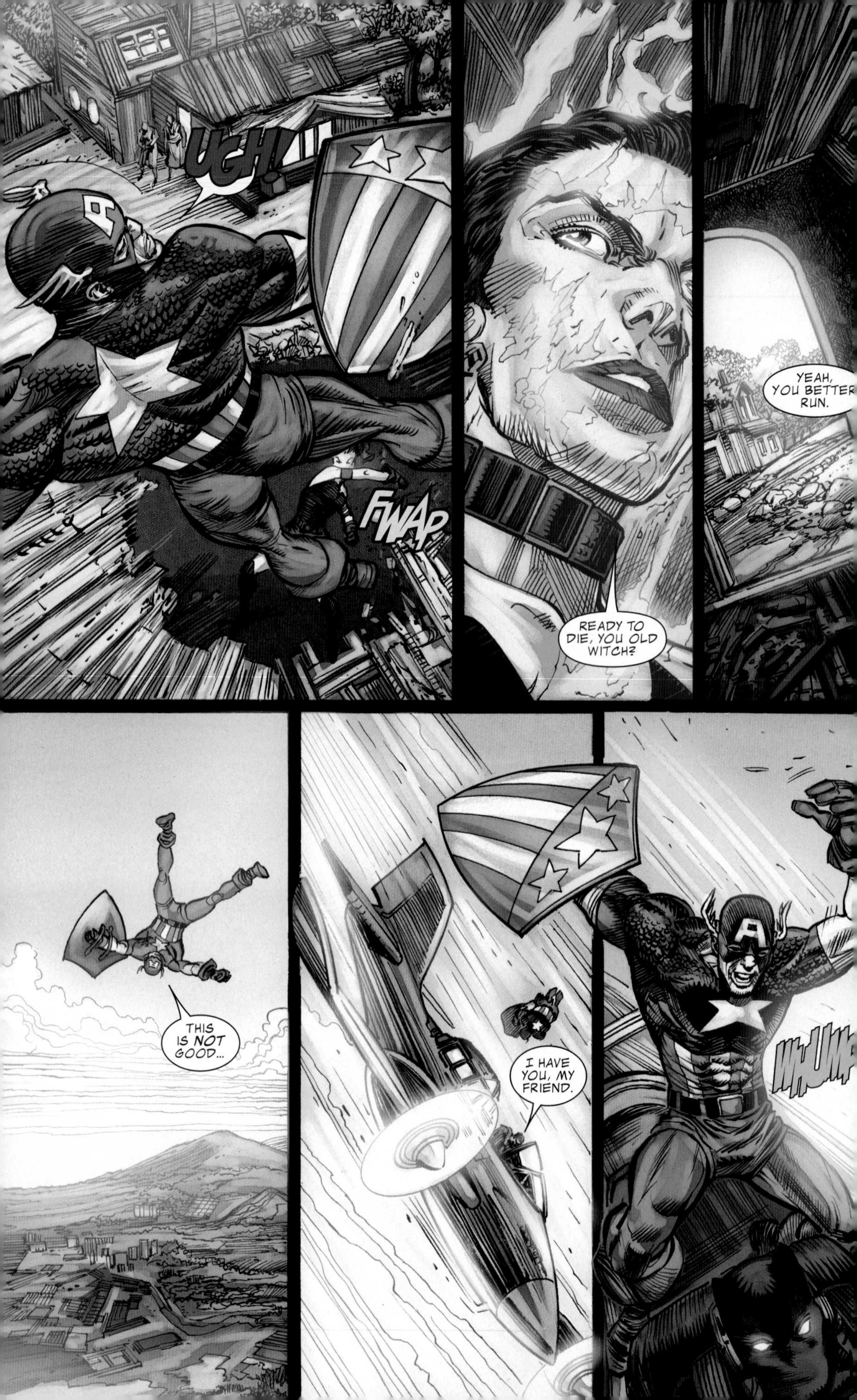
UGH!
FWAP
READY TO DIE, YOU OLD WITCH?
YEAH, YOU BETTER RUN.
THIS IS NOT GOOD...
I HAVE YOU, MY FRIEND.
WHUMP

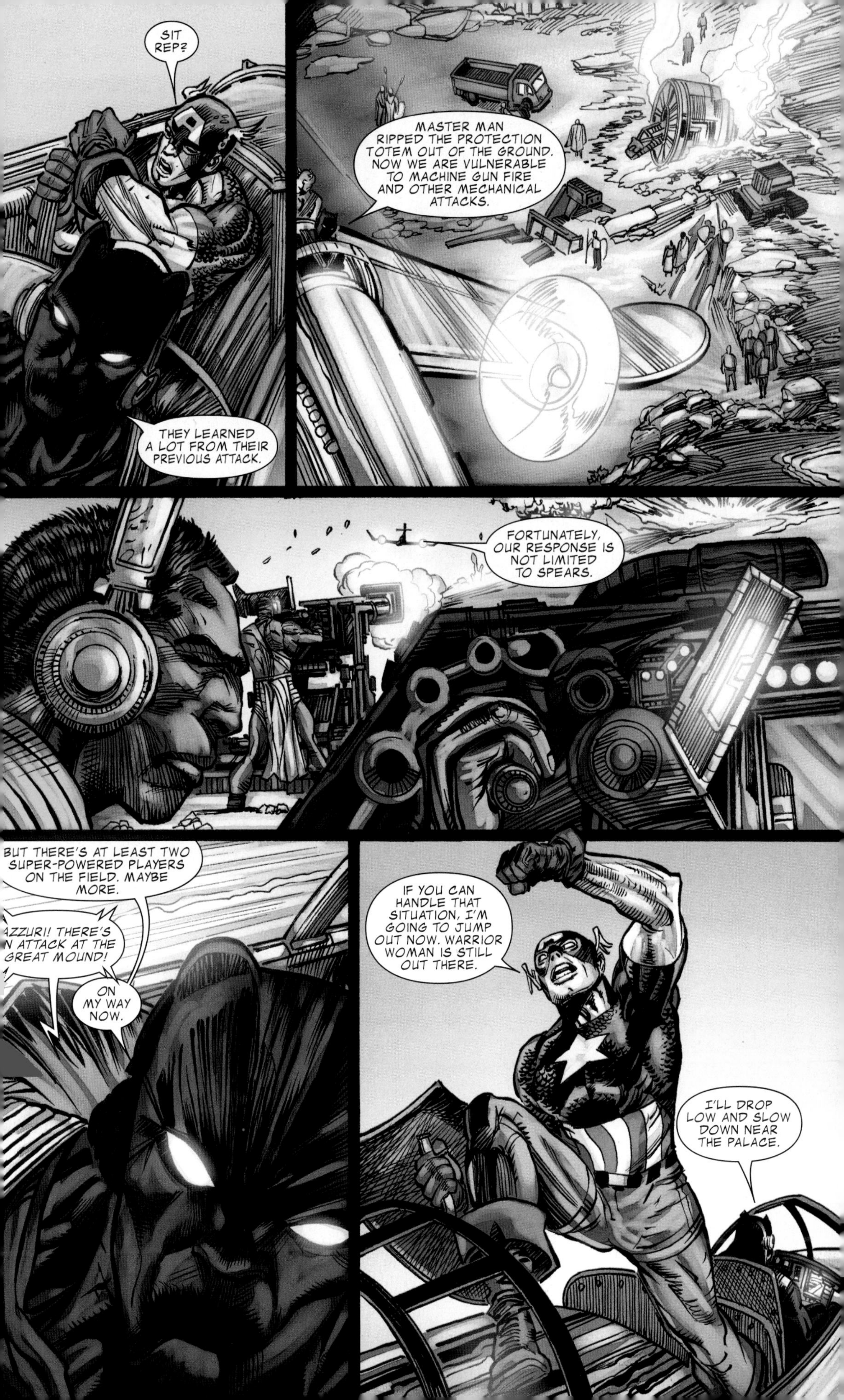
SIT REP?
MASTER MAN RIPPED THE PROTECTION TOTEM OUT OF THE GROUND. NOW WE ARE VULNERABLE TO MACHINE GUN FIRE AND OTHER MECHANICAL ATTACKS.
THEY LEARNED A LOT FROM THEIR PREVIOUS ATTACK.
FORTUNATELY, OUR RESPONSE IS NOT LIMITED TO SPEARS.
BUT THERE'S AT LEAST TWO SUPER-POWERED PLAYERS ON THE FIELD. MAYBE MORE.
AZZURI! THERE'S N ATTACK AT THE GREAT MOUND!
ON MY WAY NOW.
IF YOU CAN HANDLE THAT SITUATION, I'M GOING TO JUMP OUT NOW. WARRIOR WOMAN IS STILL OUT THERE.
I'LL DROP LOW AND SLOW DOWN NEAR THE PALACE.

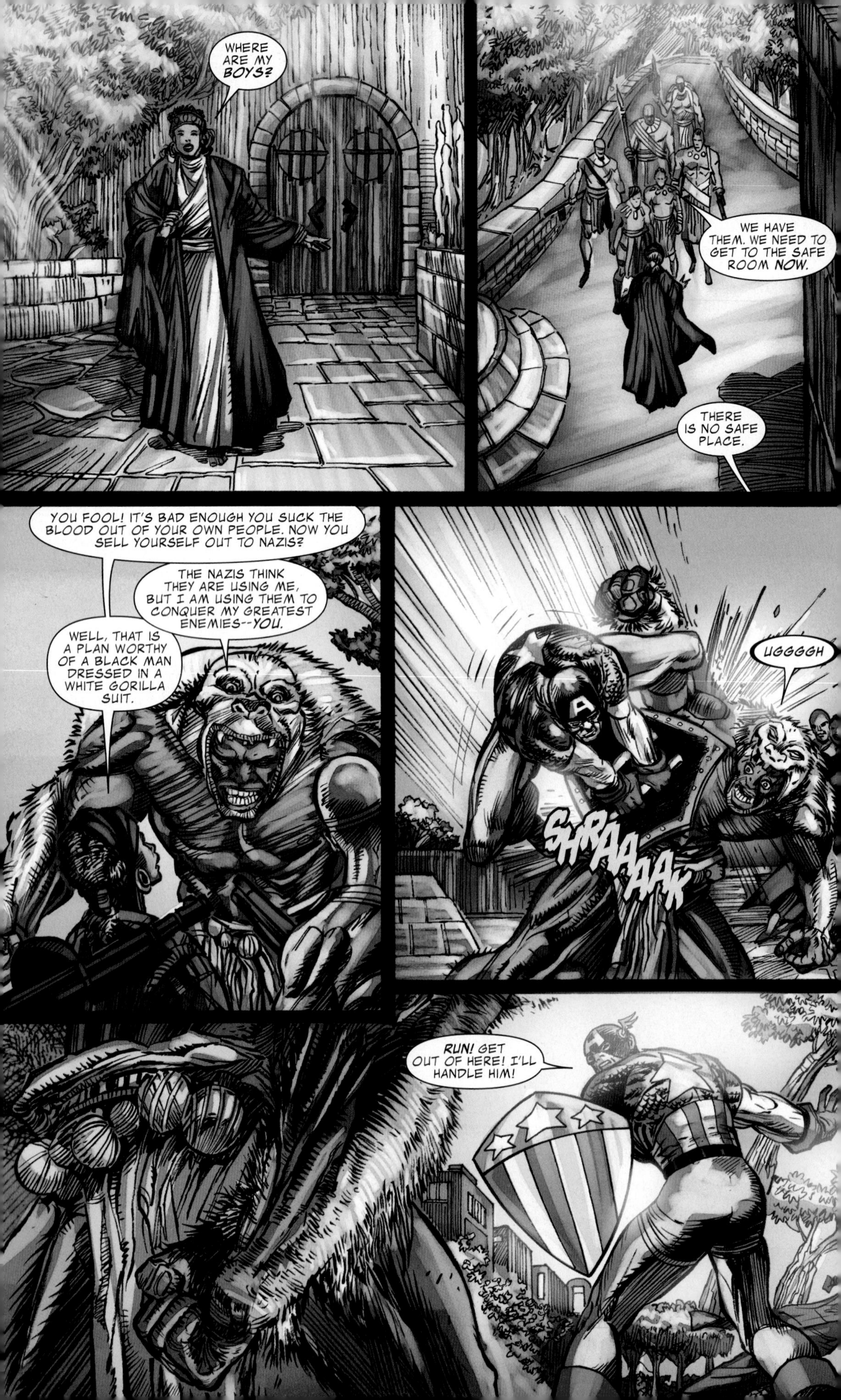
WHERE ARE MY BOYS?
WE HAVE THEM. WE NEED TO GET TO THE SAFE ROOM NOW.
THERE IS NO SAFE PLACE.
YOU FOOL! IT'S BAD ENOUGH YOU SUCK THE BLOOD OUT OF YOUR OWN PEOPLE. NOW YOU SELL YOURSELF OUT TO NAZIS?
THE NAZIS THINK THEY ARE USING ME, BUT I AM USING THEM TO CONQUER MY GREATEST ENEMIES--YOU.
WELL, THAT IS A PLAN WORTHY OF A BLACK MAN DRESSED IN A WHITE GORILLA SUIT.
UGGGGH
SHRAAAAAK
RUN! GET OUT OF HERE! I'LL HANDLE HIM!

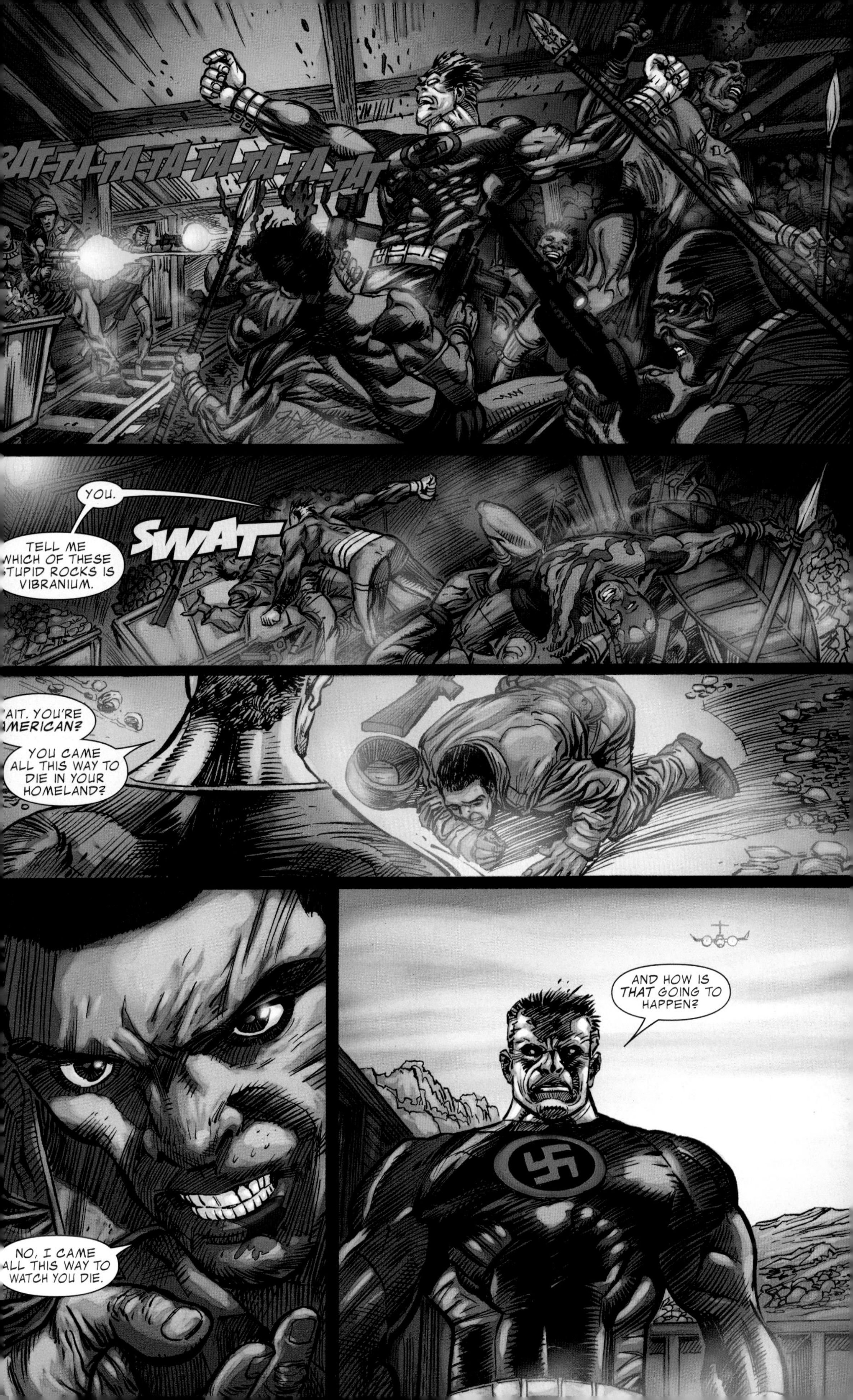
RAT-TA-TA-TA-TA-TA-TA-TAT
YOU.
SWAT
TELL ME WHICH OF THESE STUPID ROCKS IS VIBRANIUM.
AIT. YOU'RE AMERICAN?
YOU CAME ALL THIS WAY TO DIE IN YOUR HOMELAND?
NO, I CAME ALL THIS WAY TO WATCH YOU DIE.
AND HOW IS THAT GOING TO HAPPEN?

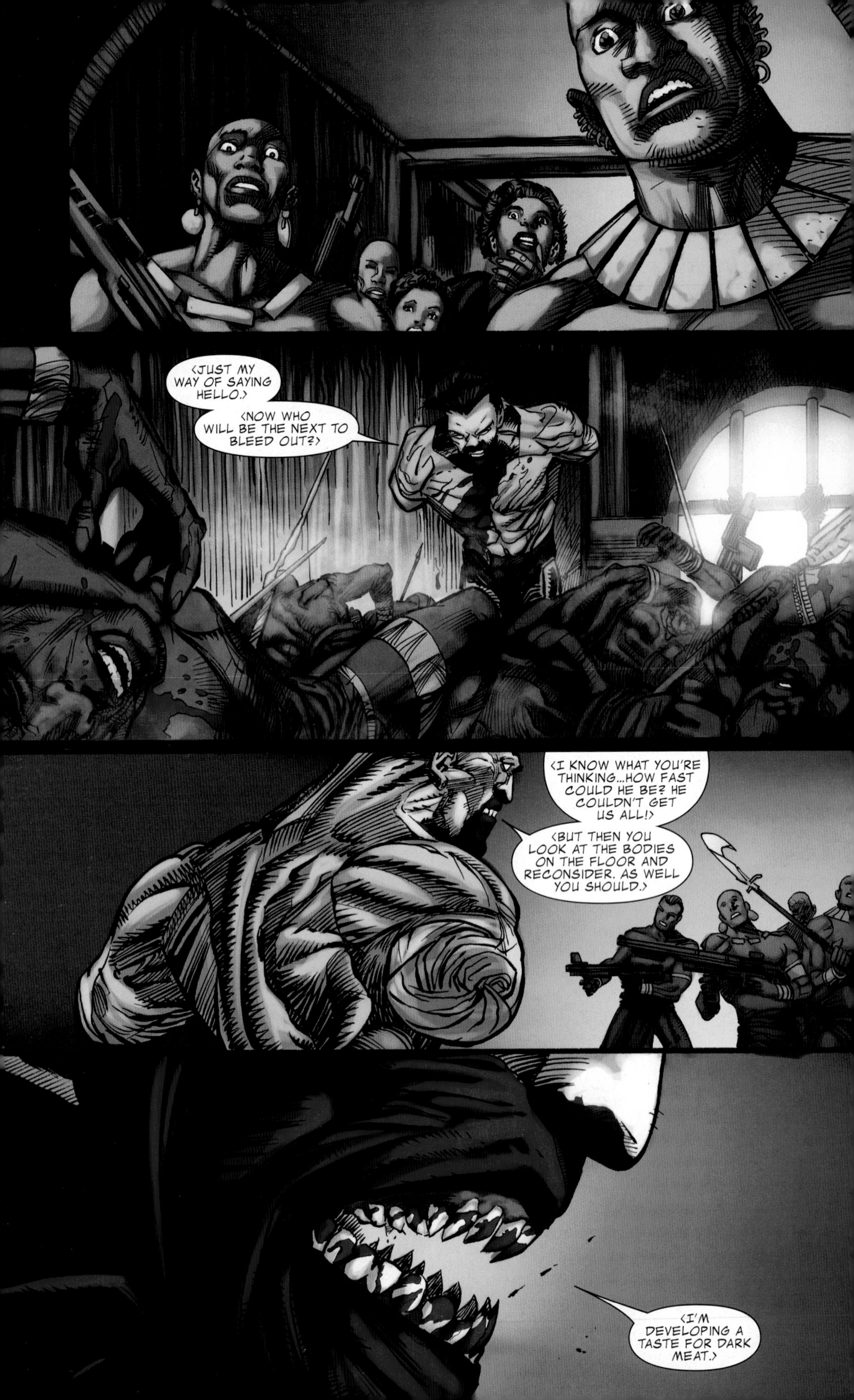

<JUST MY WAY OF SAYING HELLO.>
<NOW WHO WILL BE THE NEXT TO BLEED OUT?>
<I KNOW WHAT YOU'RE THINKING...HOW FAST COULD HE BE? HE COULDN'T GET US ALL!>
<BUT THEN YOU LOOK AT THE BODIES ON THE FLOOR AND RECONSIDER. AS WELL YOU SHOULD.>
<I'M DEVELOPING A TASTE FOR DARK MEAT.>

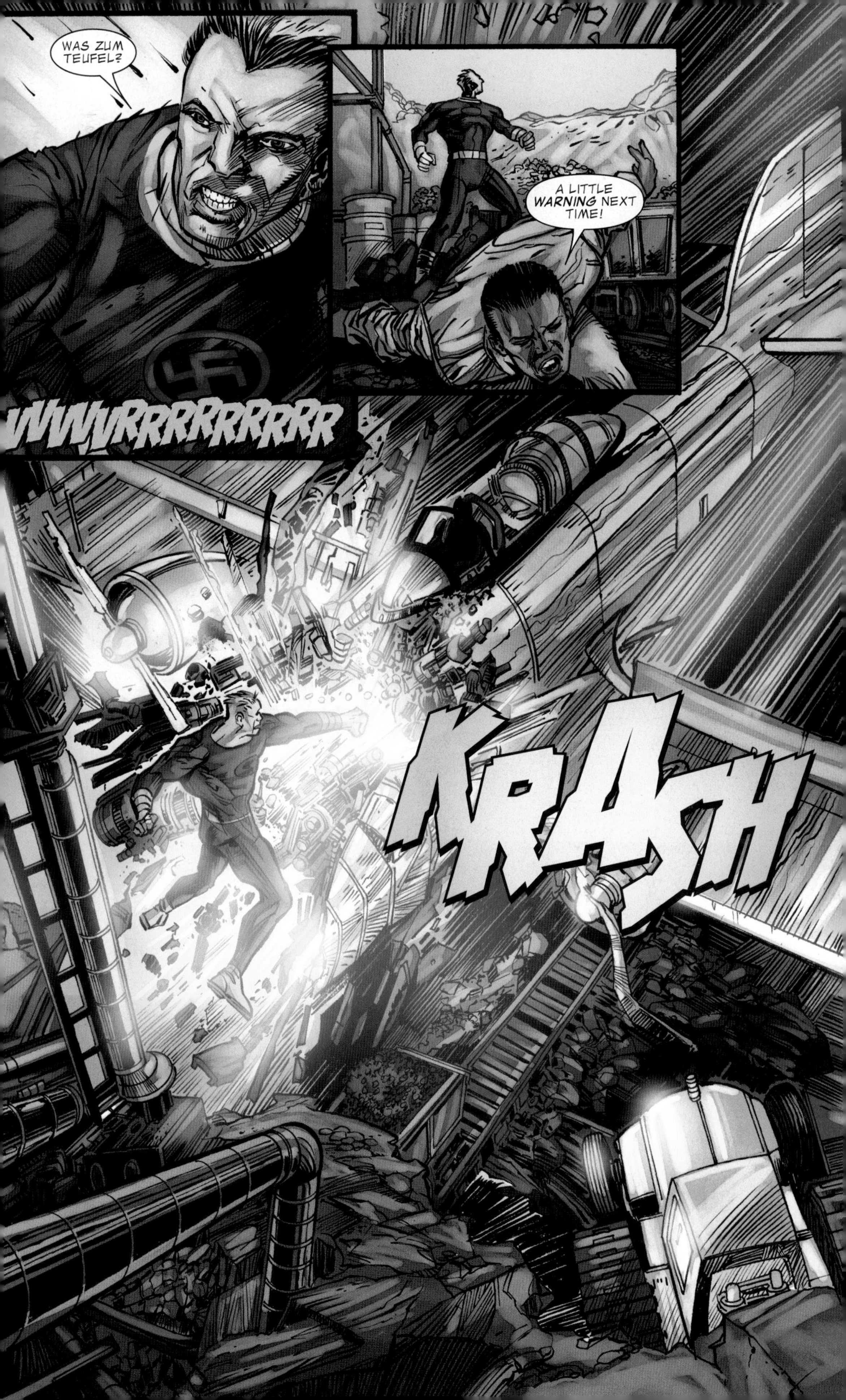
WAS ZUM TEUFEL?
A LITTLE WARNING NEXT TIME!
VVVVVRRRRRRRRRR
KRASH

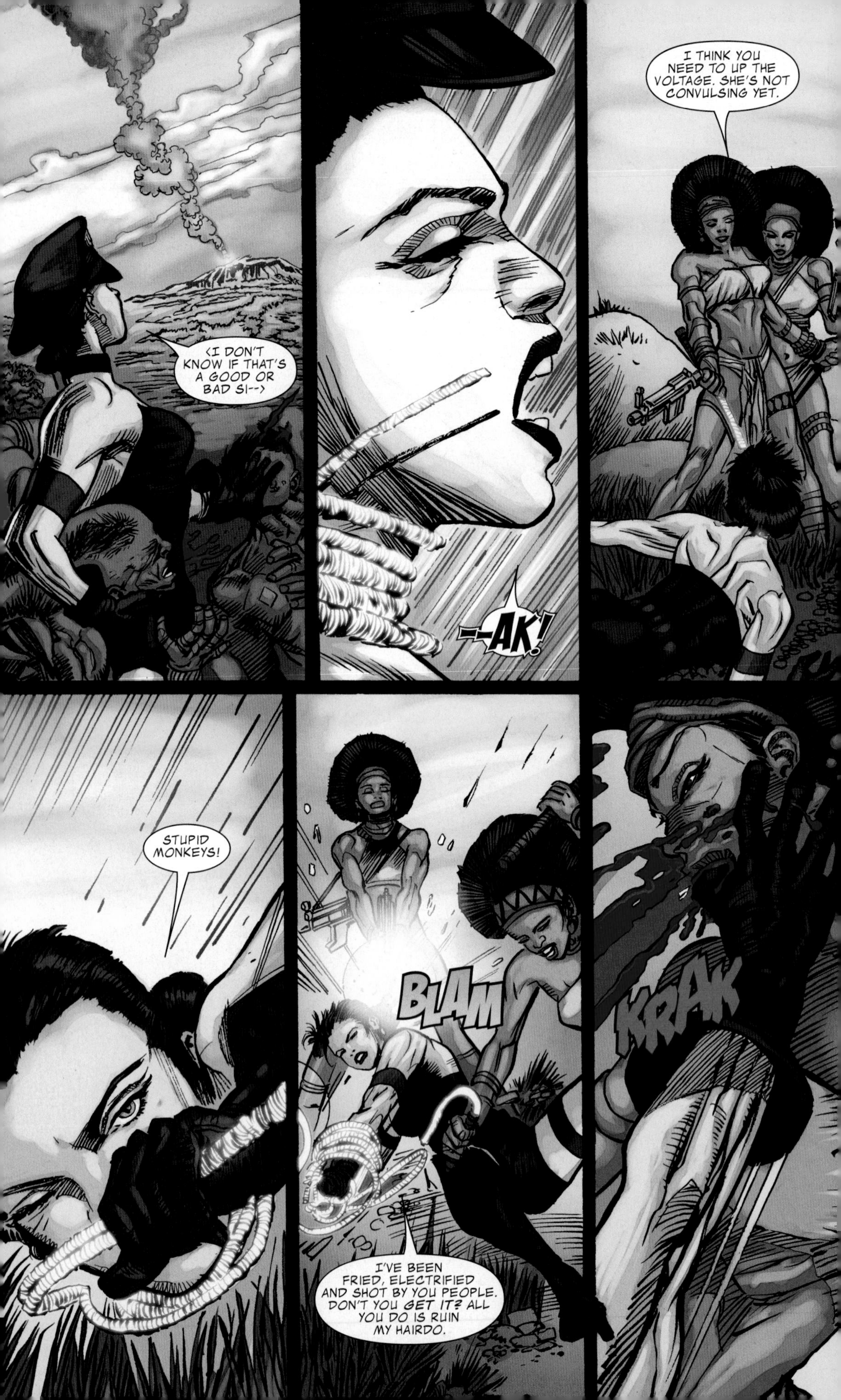
<I DON'T KNOW IF THAT'S A GOOD OR BAD SI-->
--AK!
I THINK YOU NEED TO UP THE VOLTAGE. SHE'S NOT CONVULSING YET.
STUPID MONKEYS!
BLAM
I'VE BEEN FRIED, ELECTRIFIED AND SHOT BY YOU PEOPLE. DON'T YOU GET IT? ALL YOU DO IS RUIN MY HAIRDO.
KRAK

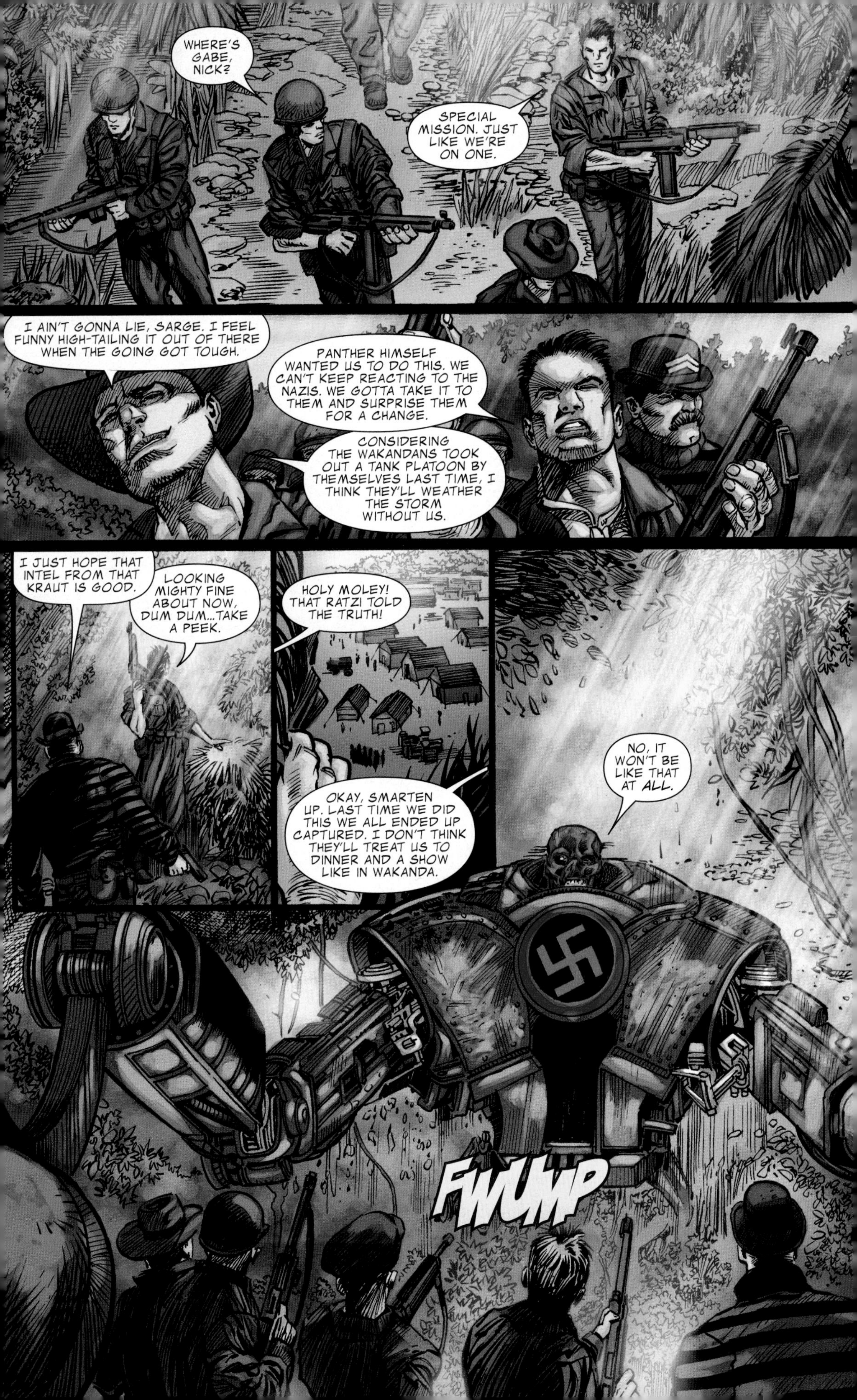
WHERE'S GABE, NICK?
SPECIAL MISSION. JUST LIKE WE'RE ON ONE.
I AIN'T GONNA LIE, SARGE. I FEEL FUNNY HIGH-TAILING IT OUT OF THERE WHEN THE GOING GOT TOUGH.
PANTHER HIMSELF WANTED US TO DO THIS. WE CAN'T KEEP REACTING TO THE NAZIS. WE GOTTA TAKE IT TO THEM AND SURPRISE THEM FOR A CHANGE.
CONSIDERING THE WAKANDANS TOOK OUT A TANK PLATOON BY THEMSELVES LAST TIME, I THINK THEY'LL WEATHER THE STORM WITHOUT US.
I JUST HOPE THAT INTEL FROM THAT KRAUT IS GOOD.
LOOKING MIGHTY FINE ABOUT NOW, DUM DUM...TAKE A PEEK.
HOLY MOLEY! THAT RATZI TOLD THE TRUTH!
OKAY, SMARTEN UP. LAST TIME WE DID THIS WE ALL ENDED UP CAPTURED. I DON'T THINK THEY'LL TREAT US TO DINNER AND A SHOW LIKE IN WAKANDA.
NO, IT WON'T BE LIKE THAT AT ALL.
FWUMP

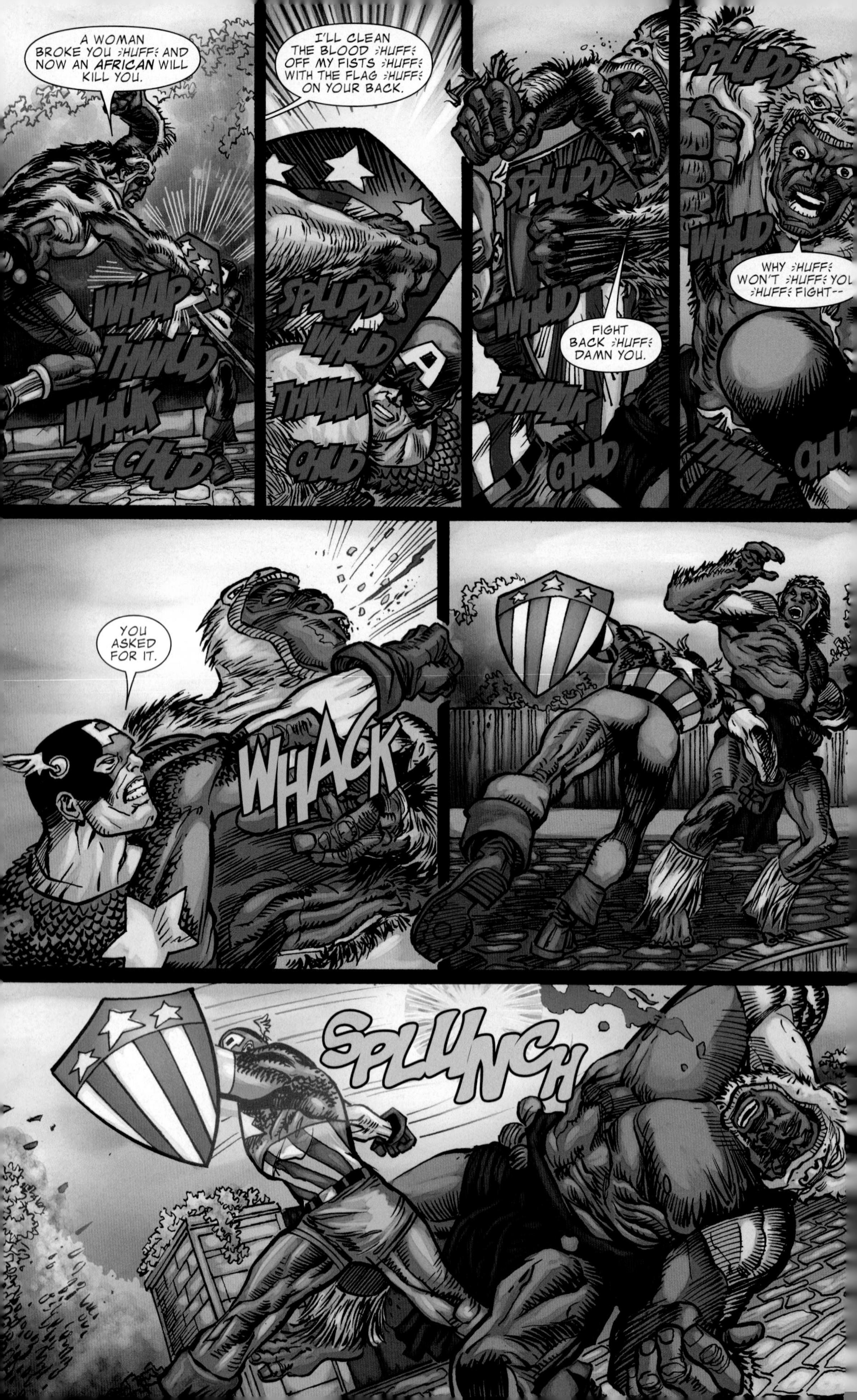

A WOMAN BROKE YOU >HUFF< AND NOW AN AFRICAN WILL KILL YOU.
WHAP
THWUD
WHUK
CHUD
I'LL CLEAN THE BLOOD >HUFF< OFF MY FISTS >HUFF< WITH THE FLAG >HUFF< ON YOUR BACK.
SPLUDD
WHUD
THWAK
CHUD
SPLUDD
WHUD
FIGHT BACK >HUFF< DAMN YOU.
THWAK
CHUD
SPLUDD
WHUD
WHY >HUFF< WON'T >HUFF< YOU >HUFF< FIGHT--
THWAK
CHUD
YOU ASKED FOR IT.
WHACK
SPLUNCH

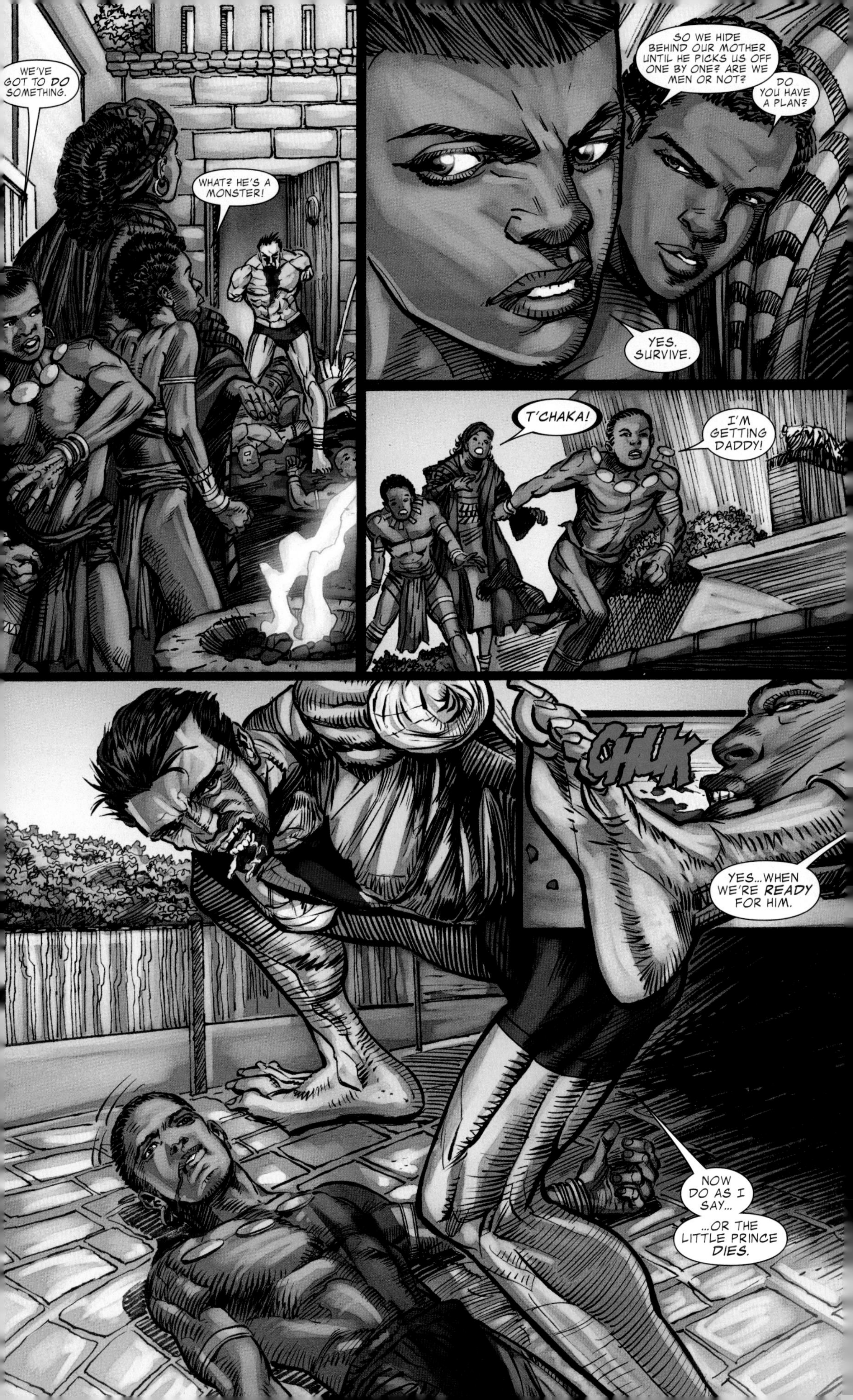
WE'VE GOT TO DO SOMETHING.
WHAT? HE'S A MONSTER!
SO WE HIDE BEHIND OUR MOTHER UNTIL HE PICKS US OFF ONE BY ONE? ARE WE MEN OR NOT?
DO YOU HAVE A PLAN?
YES. SURVIVE.
T'CHAKA!
I'M GETTING DADDY!
CHUK
YES...WHEN WE'RE READY FOR HIM.
NOW DO AS I SAY...
...OR THE LITTLE PRINCE DIES.

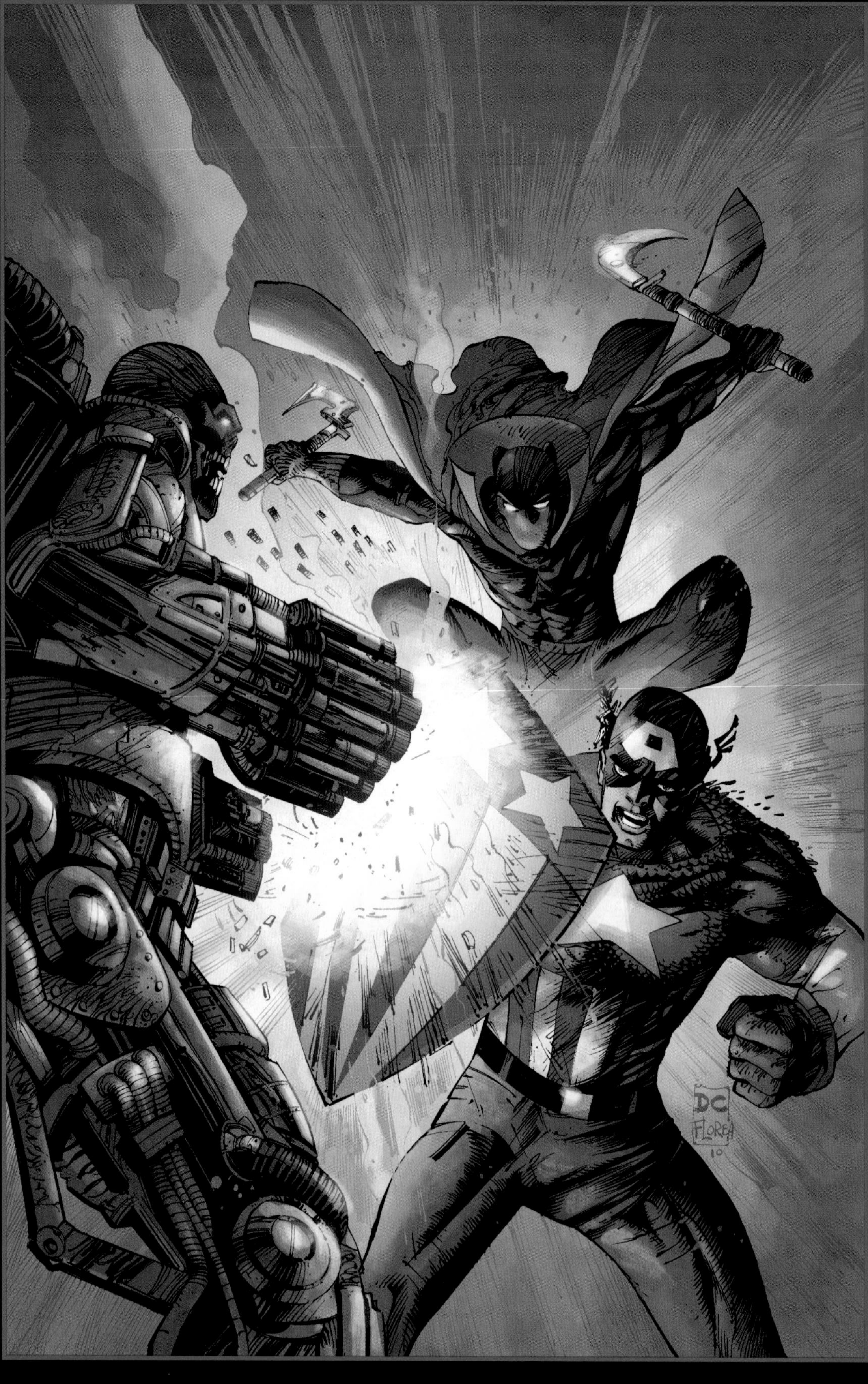
DC
FLOREA
10

CAPTAIN AMERICA / BLACK PANTHER: FLAGS OF OUR FATHERS 4

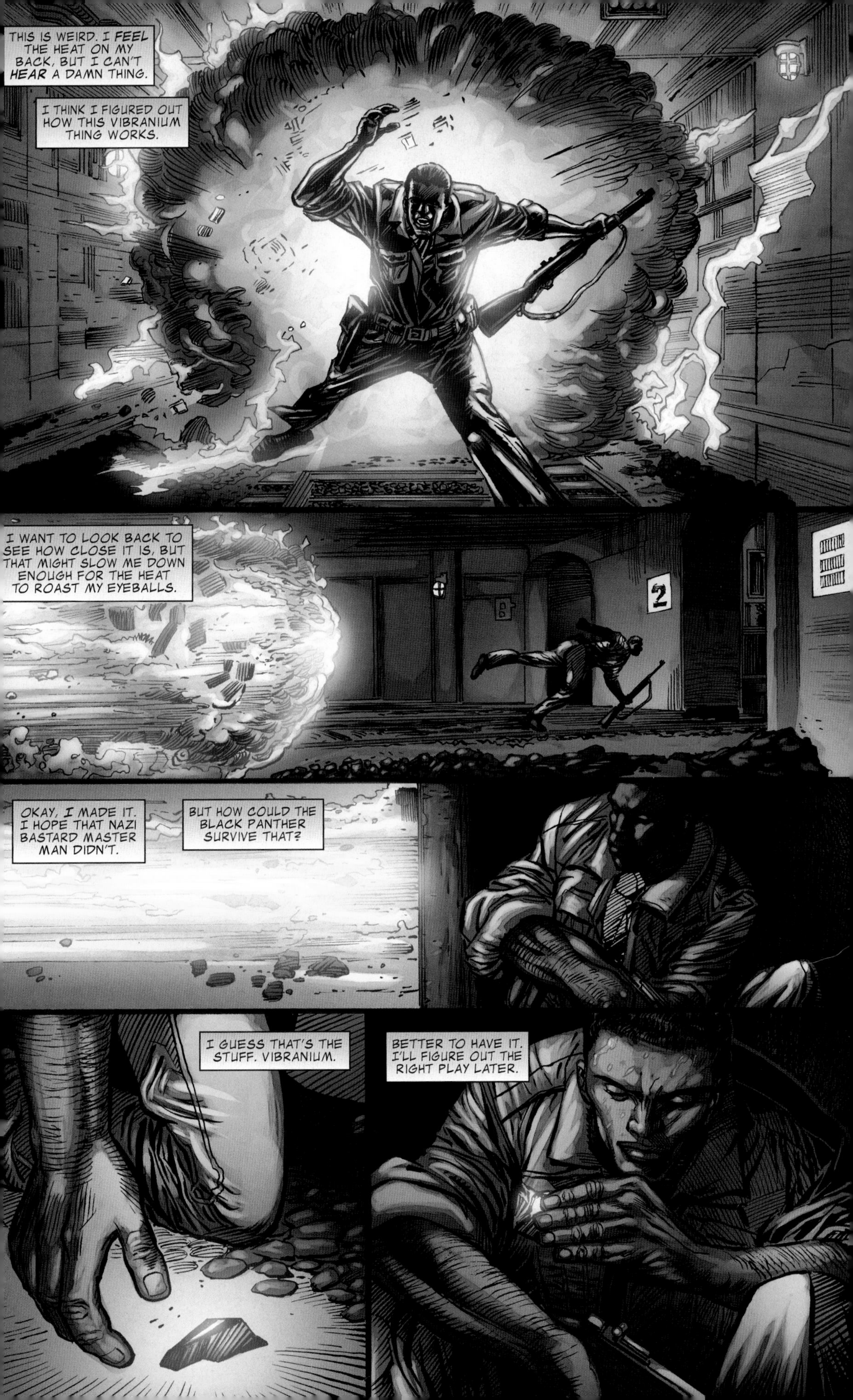
THIS IS WEIRD. I FEEL THE HEAT ON MY BACK, BUT I CAN'T HEAR A DAMN THING.
I THINK I FIGURED OUT HOW THIS VIBRANIUM THING WORKS.
I WANT TO LOOK BACK TO SEE HOW CLOSE IT IS, BUT THAT MIGHT SLOW ME DOWN ENOUGH FOR THE HEAT TO ROAST MY EYEBALLS.
2
OKAY, I MADE IT. I HOPE THAT NAZI BASTARD MASTER MAN DIDN'T.
BUT HOW COULD THE BLACK PANTHER SURVIVE THAT?
I GUESS THAT'S THE STUFF. VIBRANIUM.
BETTER TO HAVE IT. I'LL FIGURE OUT THE RIGHT PLAY LATER.

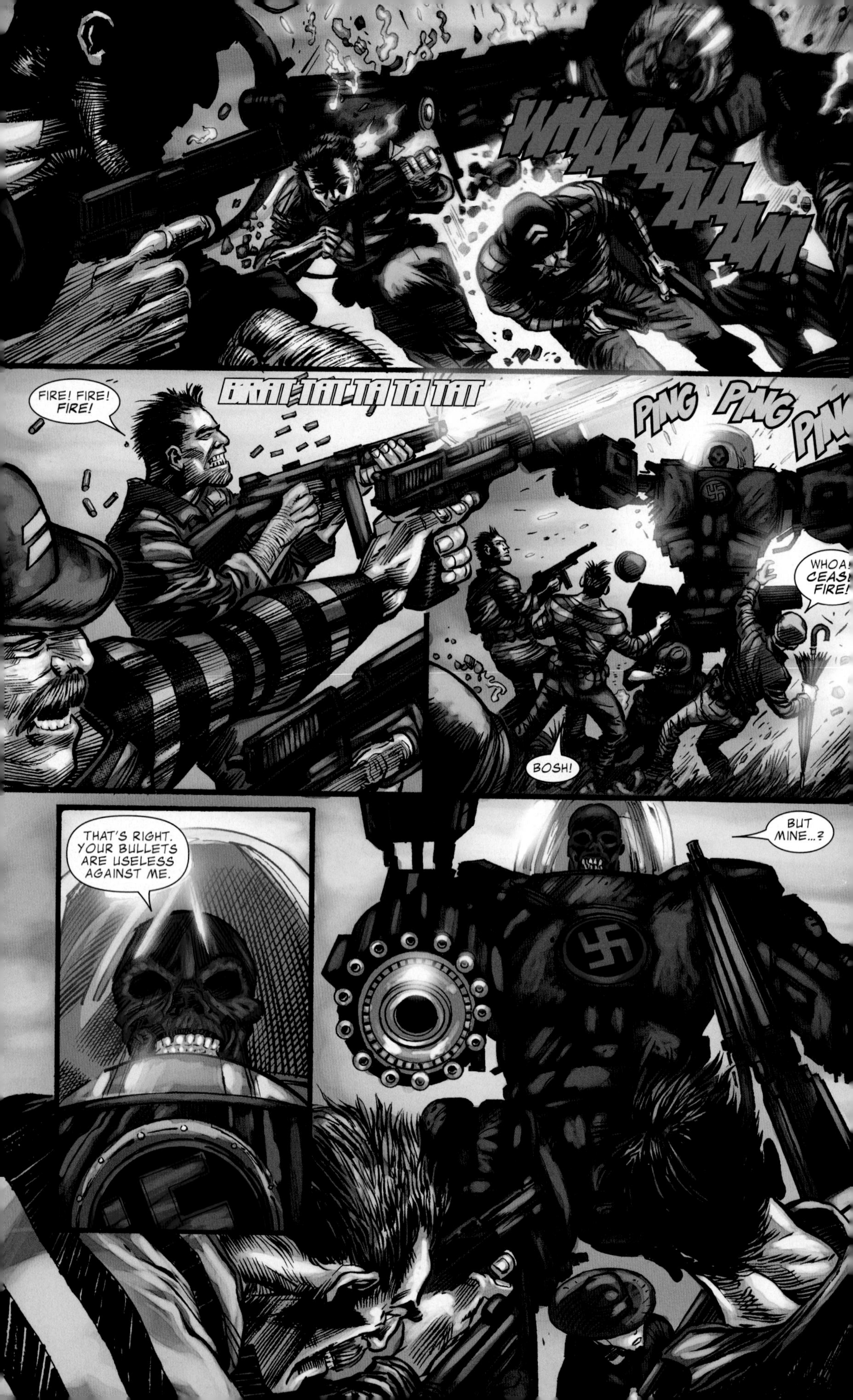
WHAAAAAAAM
FIRE! FIRE! FIRE!
BRAT TAT TA TA TAT
PING PING PIN
WHOA! CEAS FIRE!
BOSH!
THAT'S RIGHT. YOUR BULLETS ARE USELESS AGAINST ME.
BUT MINE...?

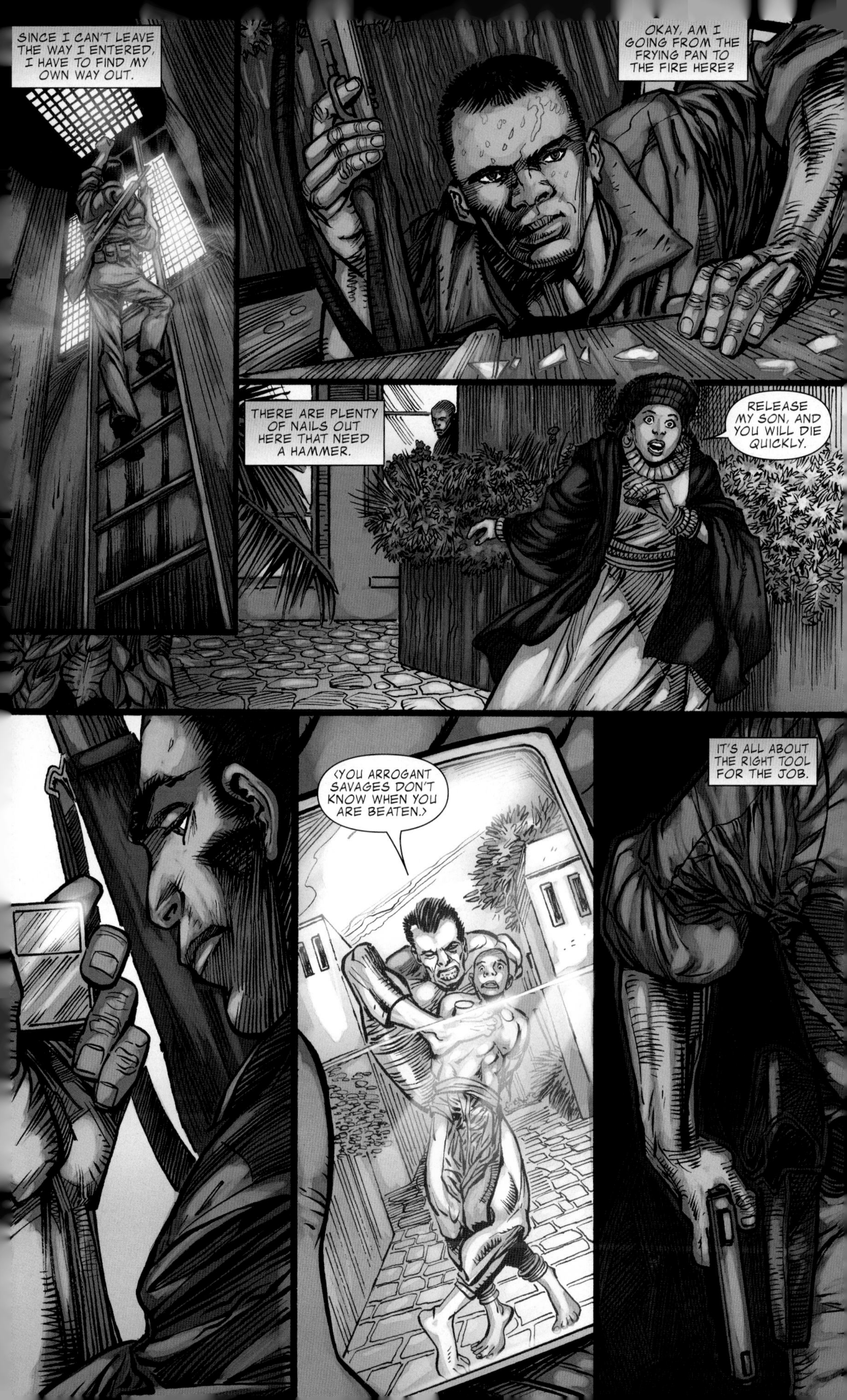
SINCE I CAN'T LEAVE THE WAY I ENTERED, I HAVE TO FIND MY OWN WAY OUT.
OKAY, AM I GOING FROM THE FRYING PAN TO THE FIRE HERE?
THERE ARE PLENTY OF NAILS OUT HERE THAT NEED A HAMMER.
RELEASE MY SON, AND YOU WILL DIE QUICKLY.
<YOU ARROGANT SAVAGES DON'T KNOW WHEN YOU ARE BEATEN.>
IT'S ALL ABOUT THE RIGHT TOOL FOR THE JOB.

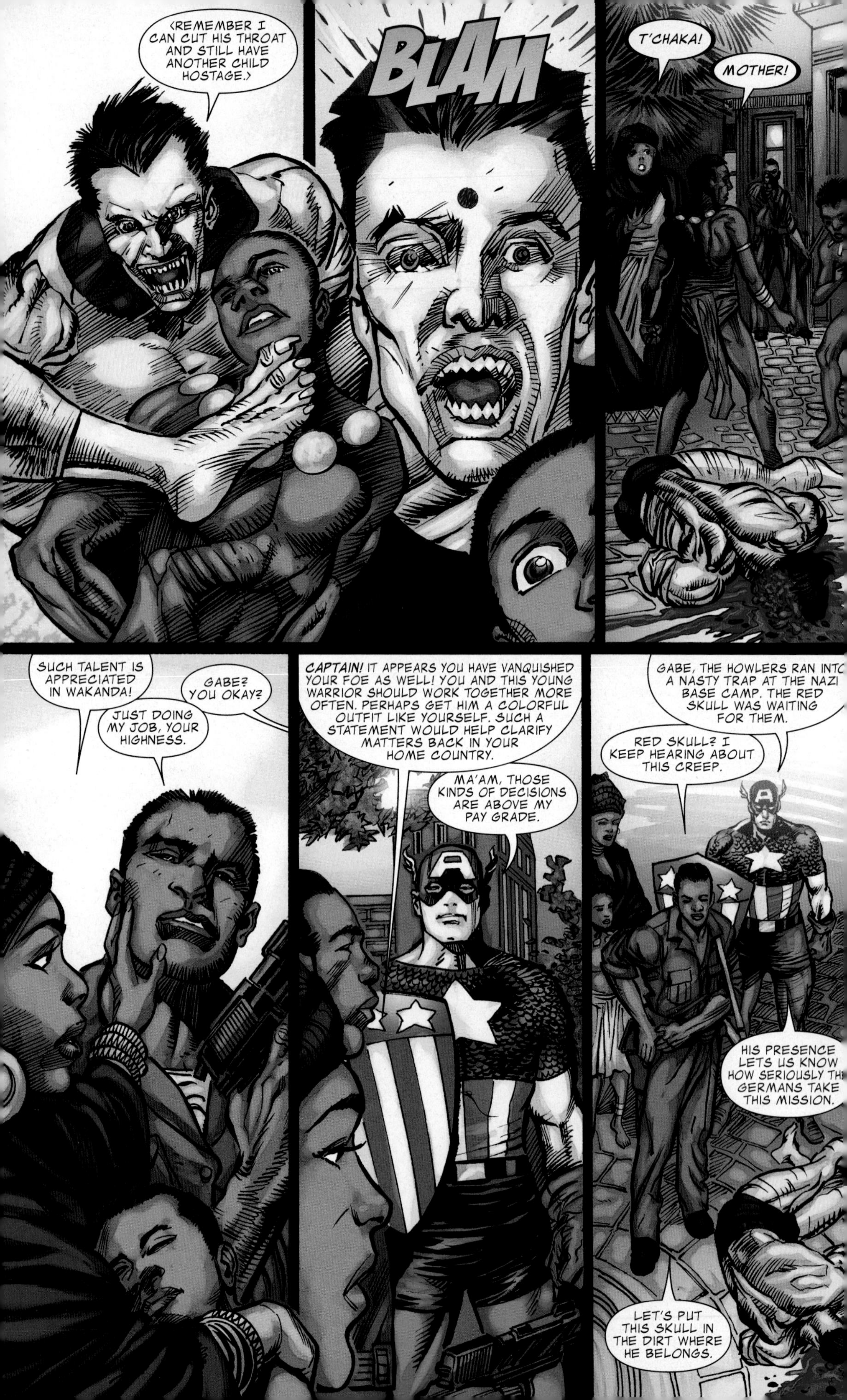
‹REMEMBER I CAN CUT HIS THROAT AND STILL HAVE ANOTHER CHILD HOSTAGE.›
BLAM
T'CHAKA!
MOTHER!
SUCH TALENT IS APPRECIATED IN WAKANDA!
JUST DOING MY JOB, YOUR HIGHNESS.
GABE? YOU OKAY?
CAPTAIN! IT APPEARS YOU HAVE VANQUISHED YOUR FOE AS WELL! YOU AND THIS YOUNG WARRIOR SHOULD WORK TOGETHER MORE OFTEN. PERHAPS GET HIM A COLORFUL OUTFIT LIKE YOURSELF. SUCH A STATEMENT WOULD HELP CLARIFY MATTERS BACK IN YOUR HOME COUNTRY.
MA'AM, THOSE KINDS OF DECISIONS ARE ABOVE MY PAY GRADE.
GABE, THE HOWLERS RAN INTO A NASTY TRAP AT THE NAZI BASE CAMP. THE RED SKULL WAS WAITING FOR THEM.
RED SKULL? I KEEP HEARING ABOUT THIS CREEP.
HIS PRESENCE LETS US KNOW HOW SERIOUSLY THE GERMANS TAKE THIS MISSION.
LET'S PUT THIS SKULL IN THE DIRT WHERE HE BELONGS.

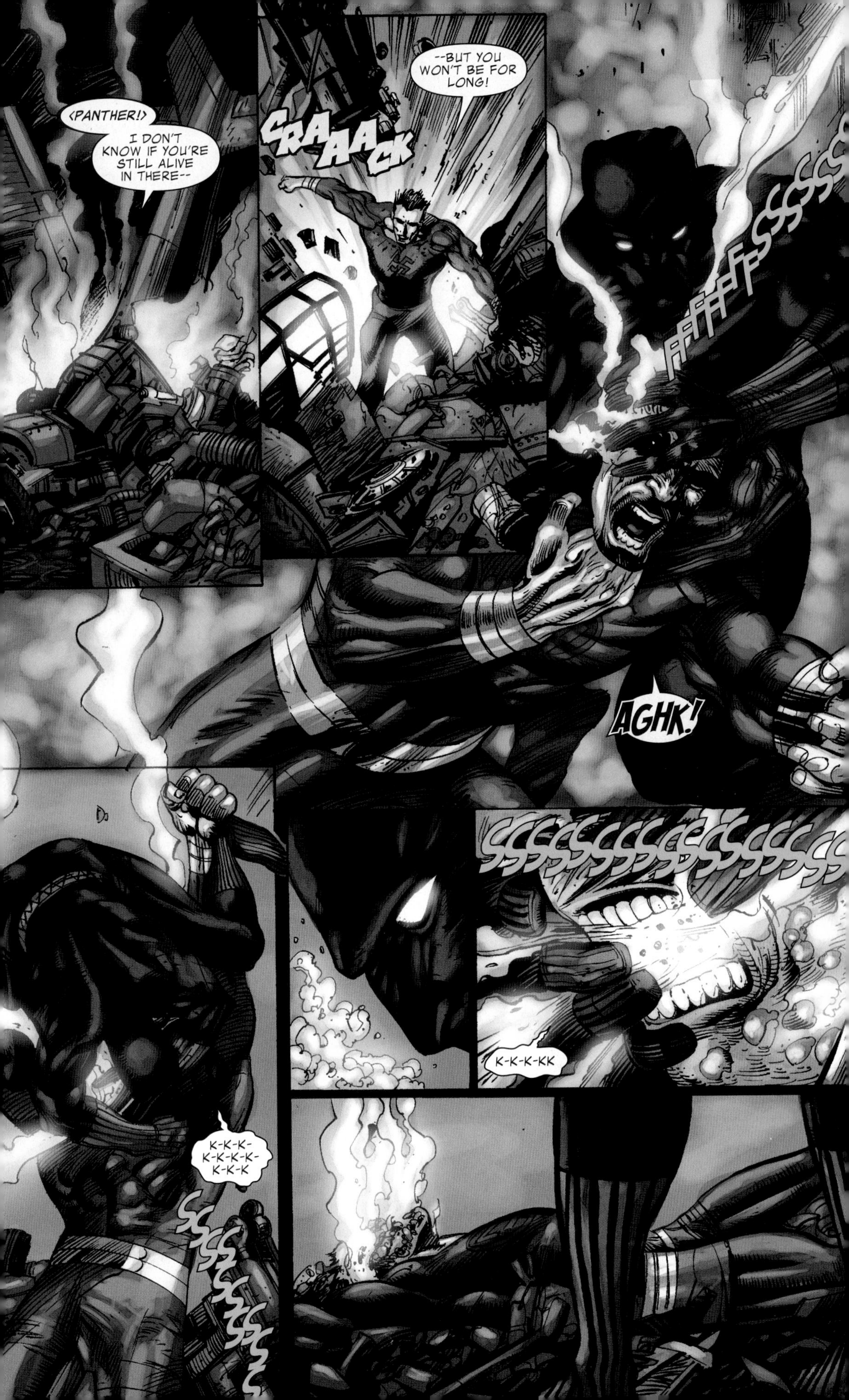

<PANTHER!>
I DON'T KNOW IF YOU'RE STILL ALIVE IN THERE--
CRAAACK
--BUT YOU WON'T BE FOR LONG!
AGHK!
K-K-K-KK
K-K-K- K-K-K-K- K-K-K

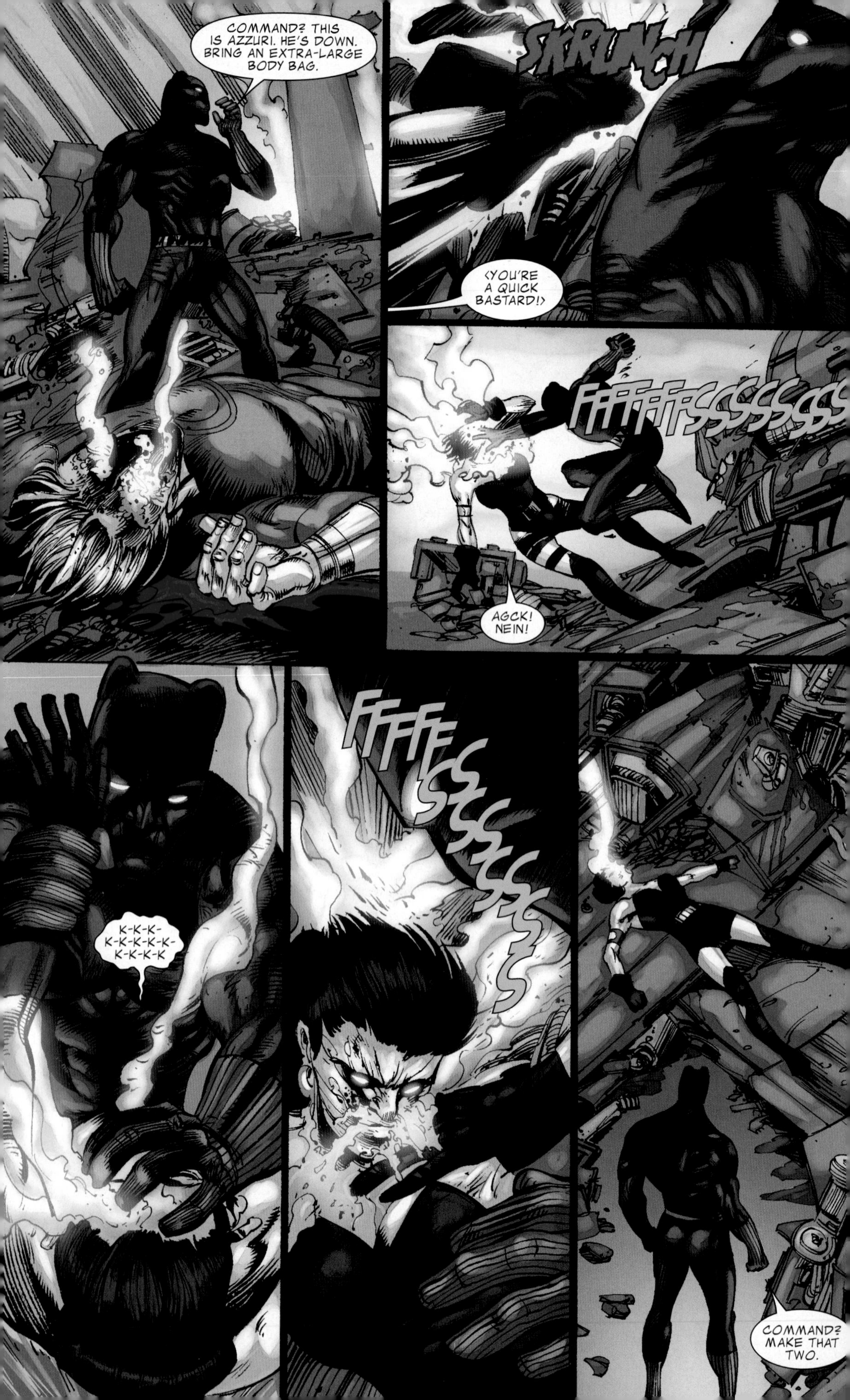
COMMAND? THIS IS AZZURI. HE'S DOWN. BRING AN EXTRA-LARGE BODY BAG.
SKRUNCH
‹YOU'RE A QUICK BASTARD!›
FFFFFFSSSSSSSSS
AGCK! NEIN!
K-K-K-
K-K-K-K-K-
K-K-K-K
FFFFSSSSSS
COMMAND? MAKE THAT TWO.

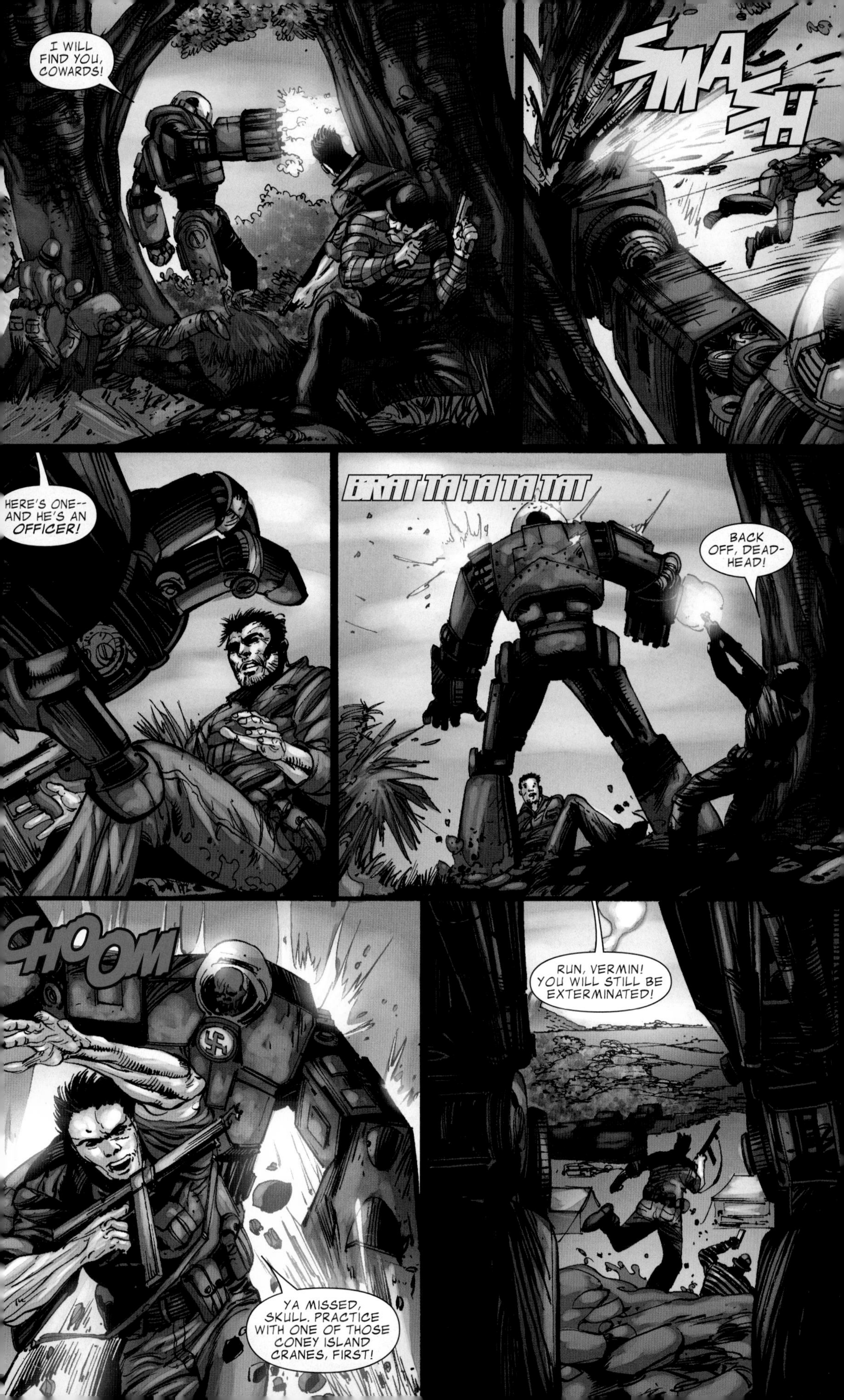
I WILL FIND YOU, COWARDS!
SMASH
HERE'S ONE-- AND HE'S AN OFFICER!
BRAT TA TA TA TAT
BACK OFF, DEAD-HEAD!
CHOOM
YA MISSED, SKULL. PRACTICE WITH ONE OF THOSE CONEY ISLAND CRANES, FIRST!
RUN, VERMIN! YOU WILL STILL BE EXTERMINATED!

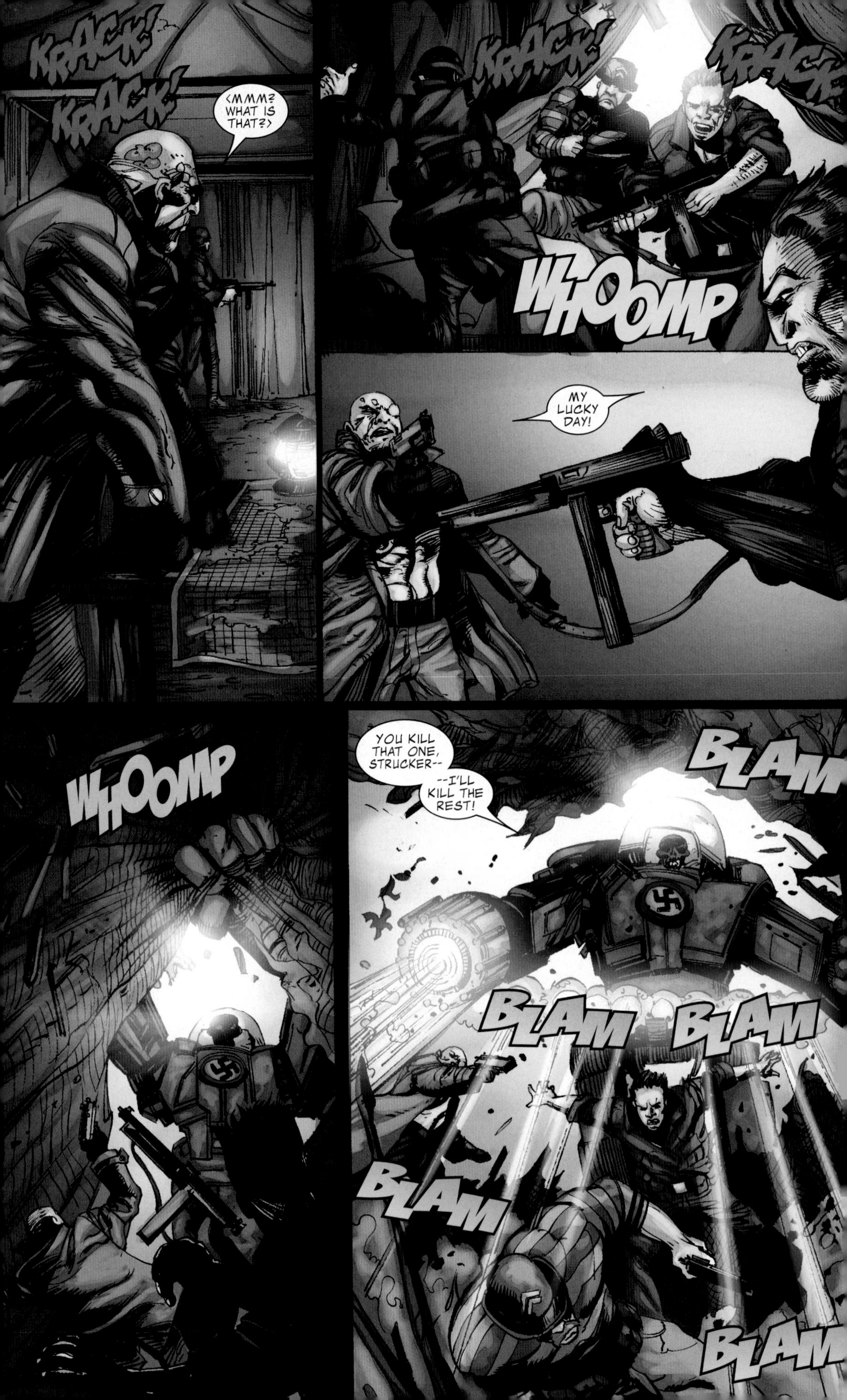
KRACK!
KRACK!
<MMM? WHAT IS THAT?>
KRACK!
KRACK!
WHOOMP
MY LUCKY DAY!
WHOOMP
YOU KILL THAT ONE, STRUCKER--
--I'LL KILL THE REST!
BLAM
BLAM
BLAM
BLAM
BLAM

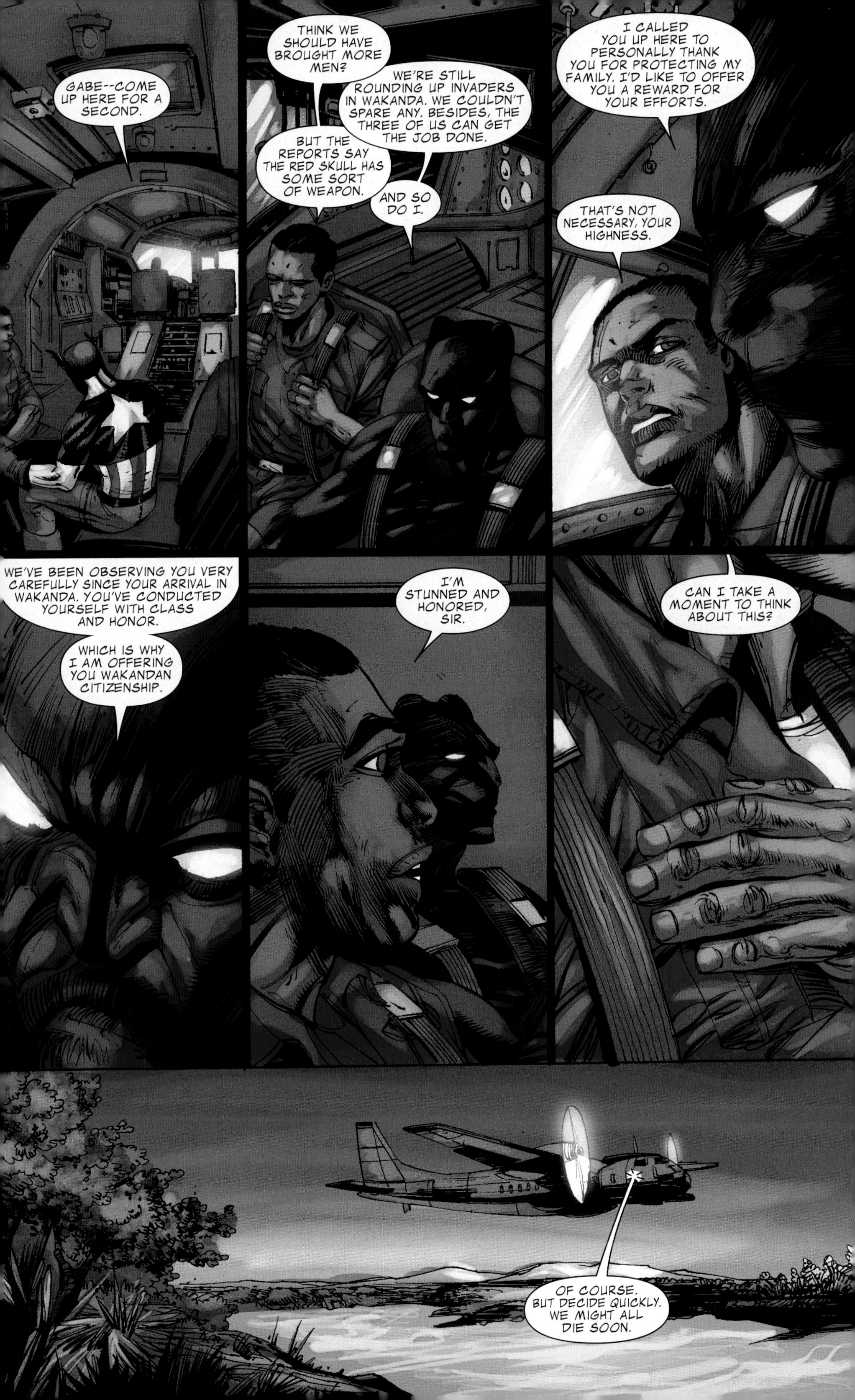
GABE--COME UP HERE FOR A SECOND.
THINK WE SHOULD HAVE BROUGHT MORE MEN?
WE'RE STILL ROUNDING UP INVADERS IN WAKANDA. WE COULDN'T SPARE ANY. BESIDES, THE THREE OF US CAN GET THE JOB DONE.
BUT THE REPORTS SAY THE RED SKULL HAS SOME SORT OF WEAPON.
AND SO DO I.
I CALLED YOU UP HERE TO PERSONALLY THANK YOU FOR PROTECTING MY FAMILY. I'D LIKE TO OFFER YOU A REWARD FOR YOUR EFFORTS.
THAT'S NOT NECESSARY, YOUR HIGHNESS.
WE'VE BEEN OBSERVING YOU VERY CAREFULLY SINCE YOUR ARRIVAL IN WAKANDA. YOU'VE CONDUCTED YOURSELF WITH CLASS AND HONOR.
WHICH IS WHY I AM OFFERING YOU WAKANDAN CITIZENSHIP.
I'M STUNNED AND HONORED, SIR.
CAN I TAKE A MOMENT TO THINK ABOUT THIS?
OF COURSE. BUT DECIDE QUICKLY. WE MIGHT ALL DIE SOON.

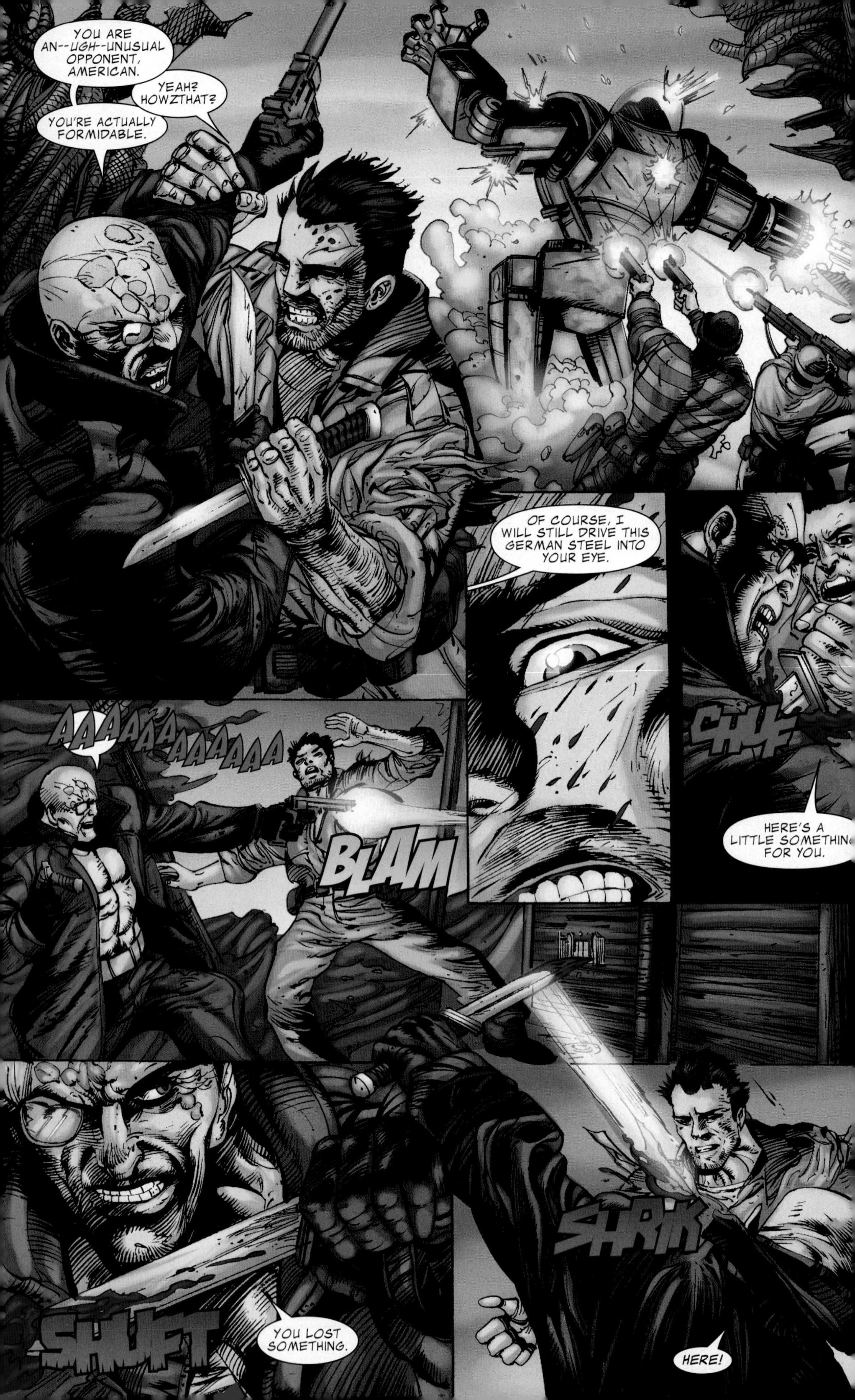

YOU ARE AN--UGH--UNUSUAL OPPONENT, AMERICAN.
YEAH? HOWZTHAT?
YOU'RE ACTUALLY FORMIDABLE.
OF COURSE, I WILL STILL DRIVE THIS GERMAN STEEL INTO YOUR EYE.
CHUF
HERE'S A LITTLE SOMETHING FOR YOU.
AAAAAAAAAAAAA
BLAM
SHUFT
YOU LOST SOMETHING.
SHRIK
HERE!

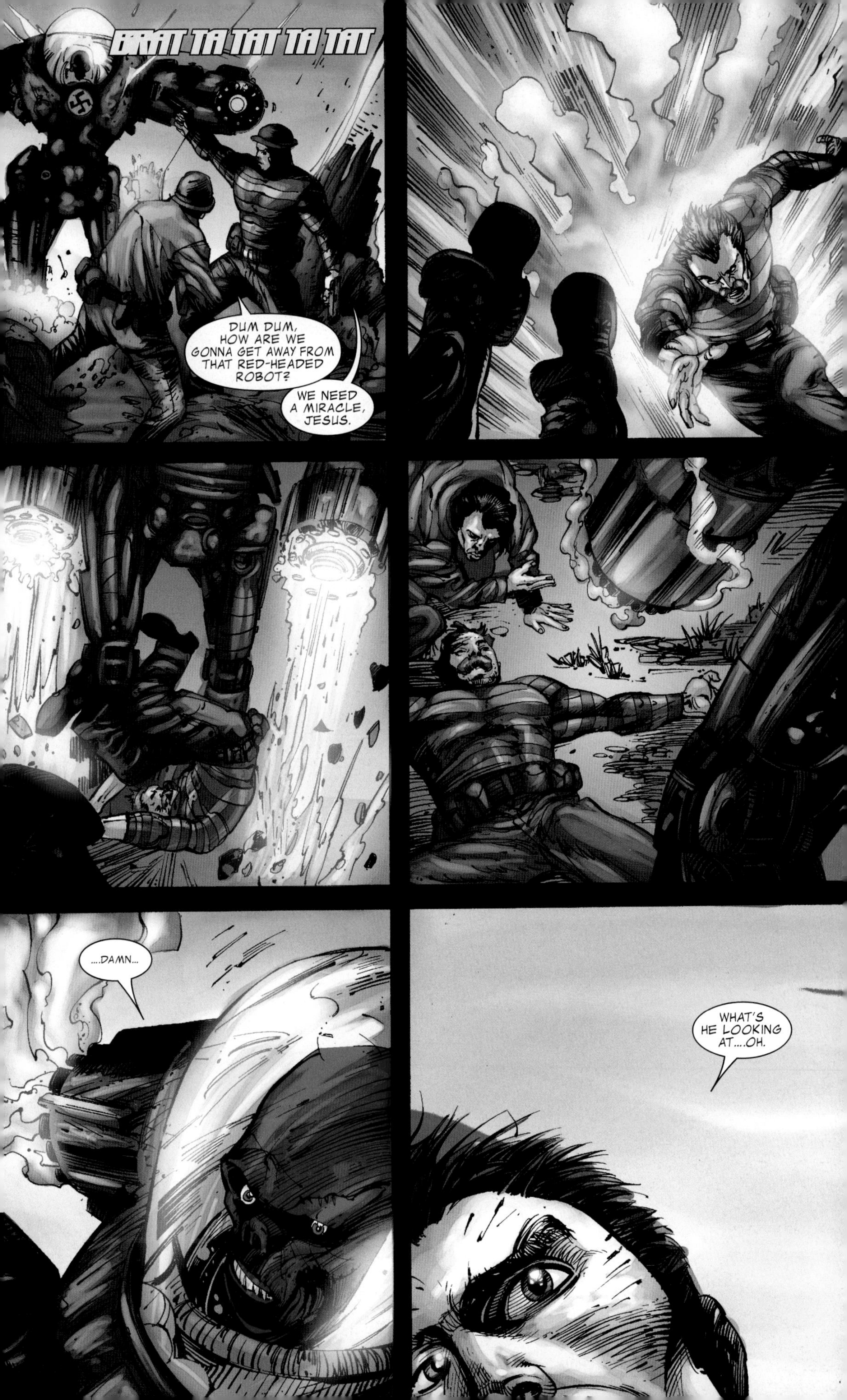
BRAT TA TAT TA TAT
DUM DUM, HOW ARE WE GONNA GET AWAY FROM THAT RED-HEADED ROBOT?
WE NEED A MIRACLE, JESUS.
....DAMN...
WHAT'S HE LOOKING AT....OH.

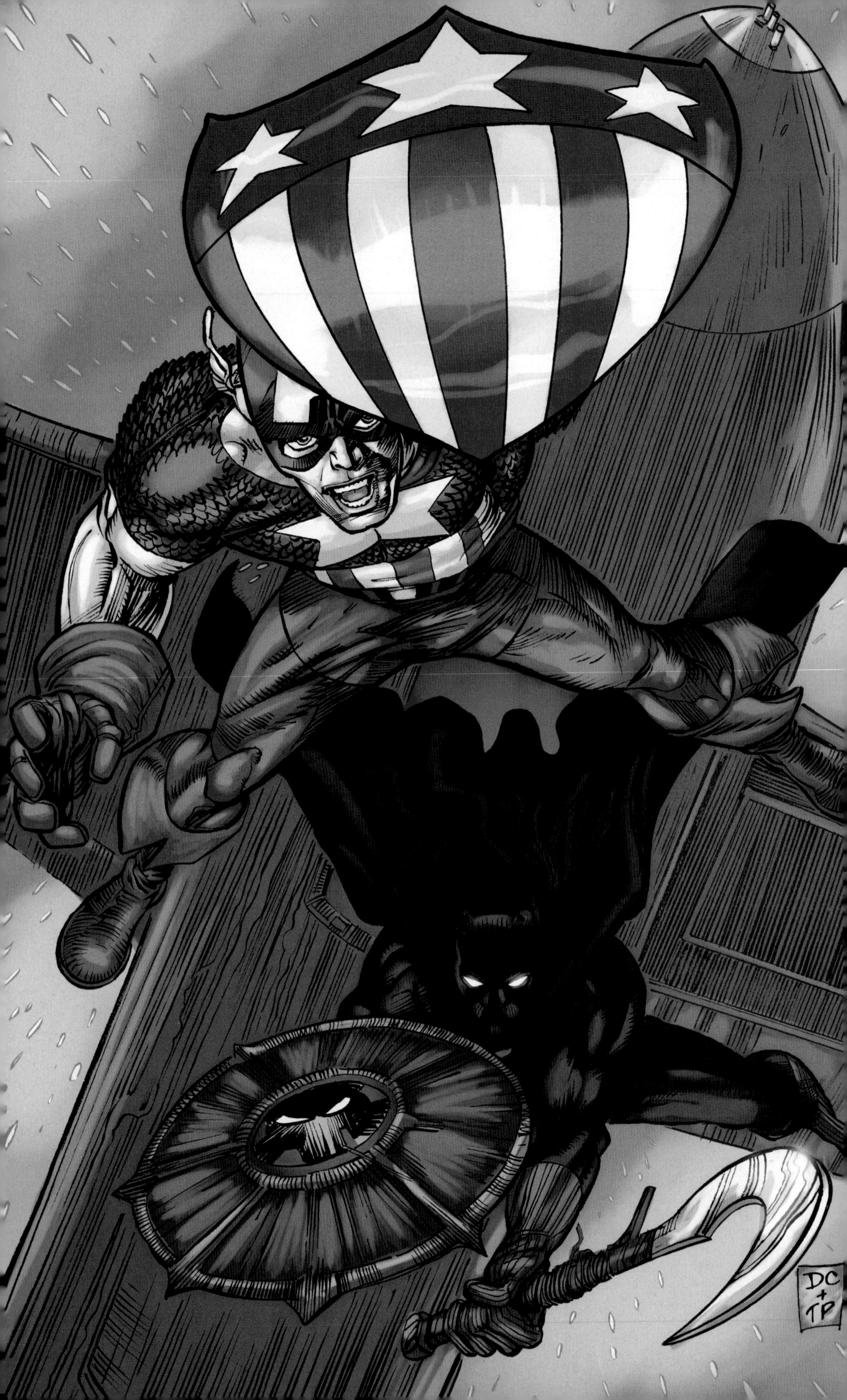
DC
+
TP

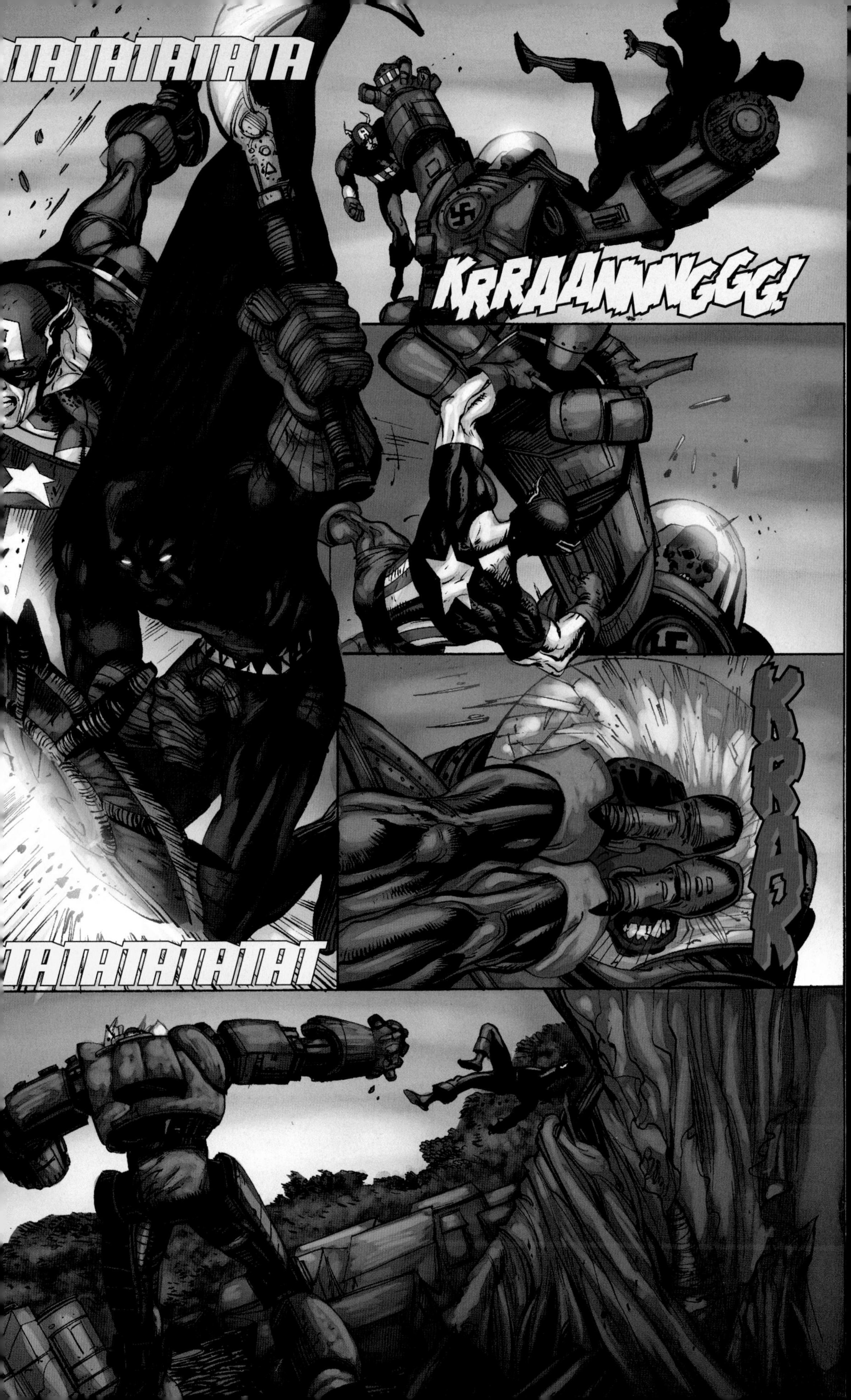
TATATATATATA
KRRAANNNGGG!
KRAK
TATATATATAT

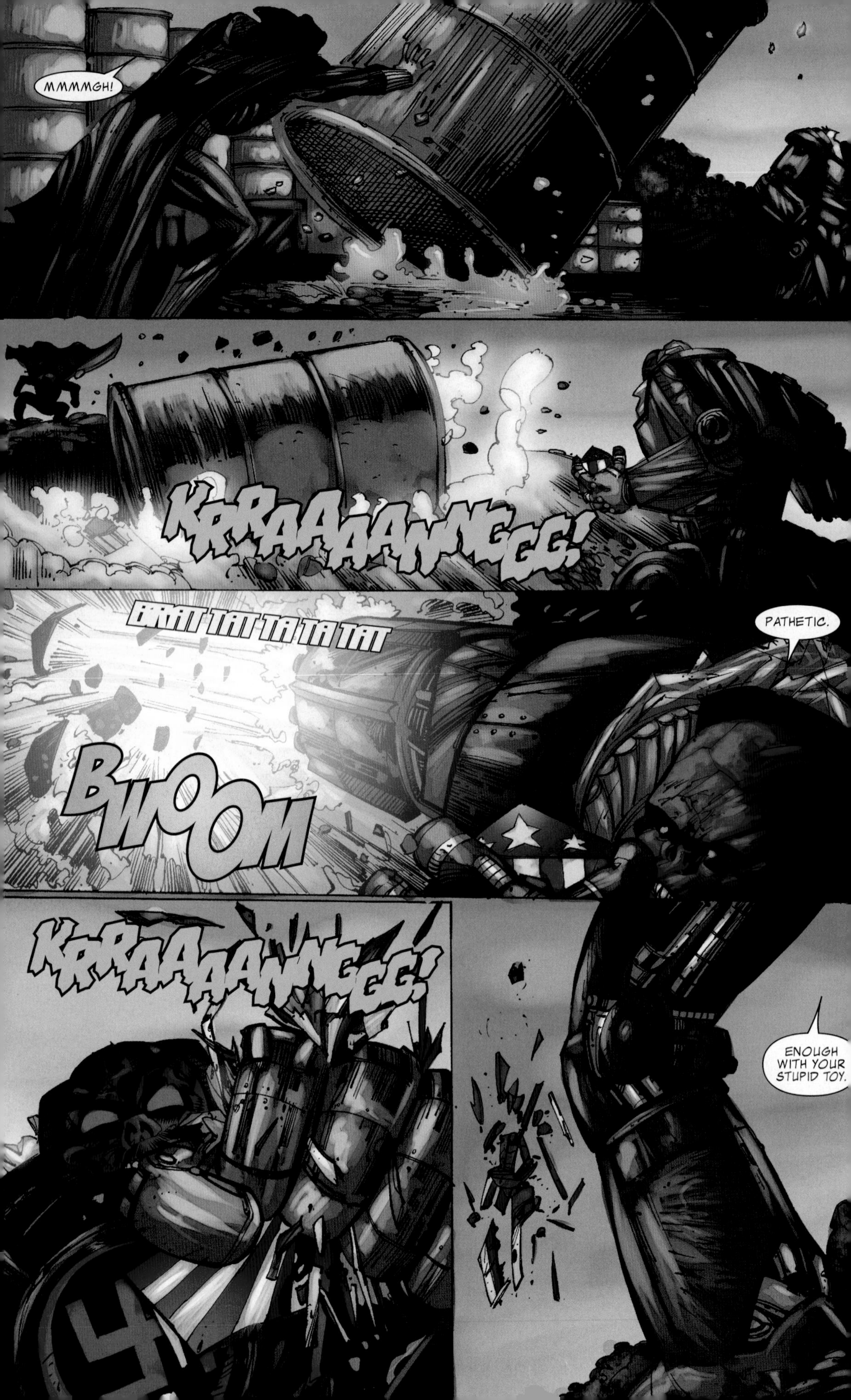
MMMMGH!
KRRAAAAANNGGG!
BRRAT TAT TA TA TAT
PATHETIC.
BWOOM
KRRAAAAANNGGG!
ENOUGH WITH YOUR STUPID TOY.

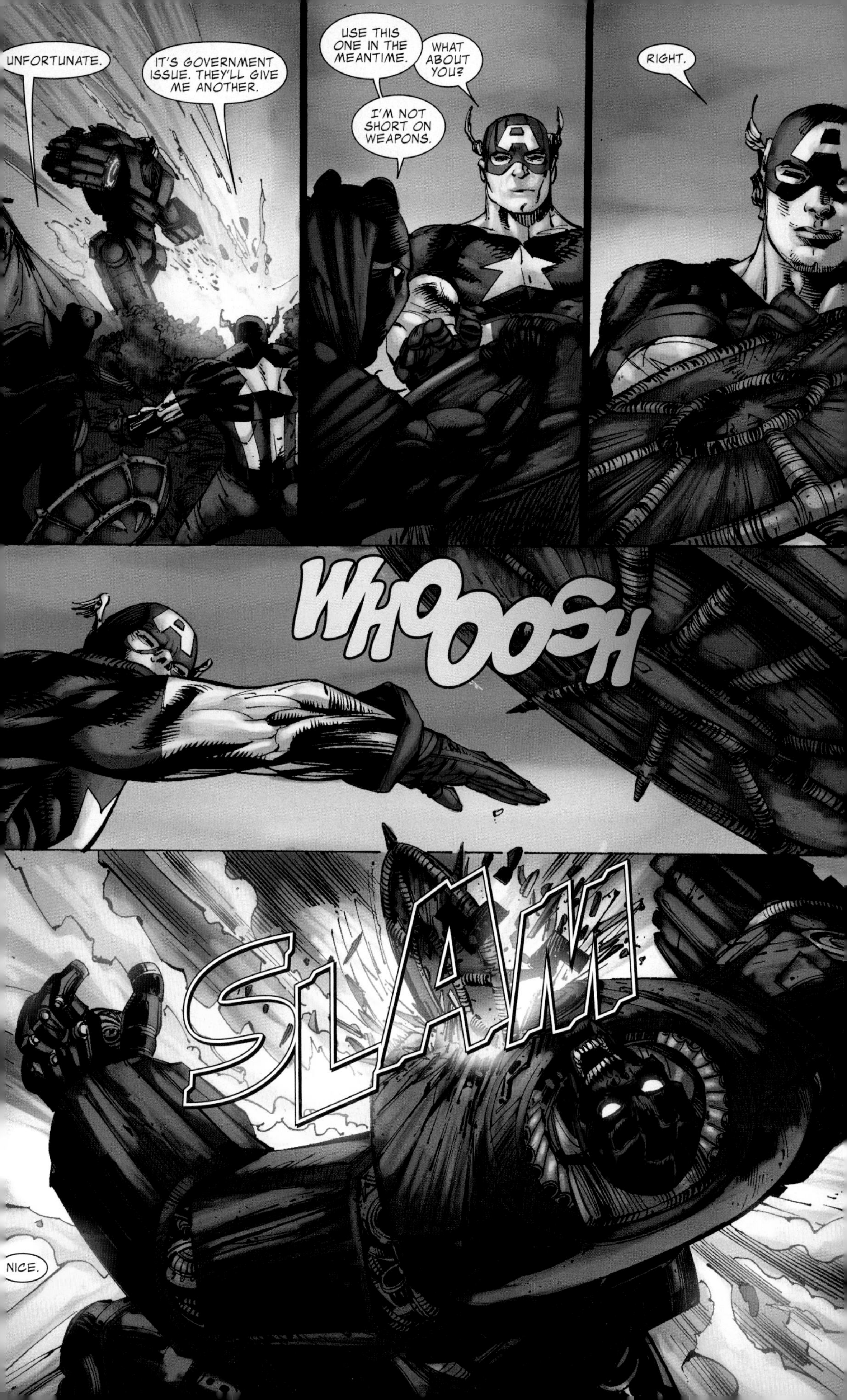
UNFORTUNATE.
IT'S GOVERNMENT ISSUE. THEY'LL GIVE ME ANOTHER.
USE THIS ONE IN THE MEANTIME.
WHAT ABOUT YOU?
I'M NOT SHORT ON WEAPONS.
RIGHT.
WHOOOOSH
SLAM
NICE.

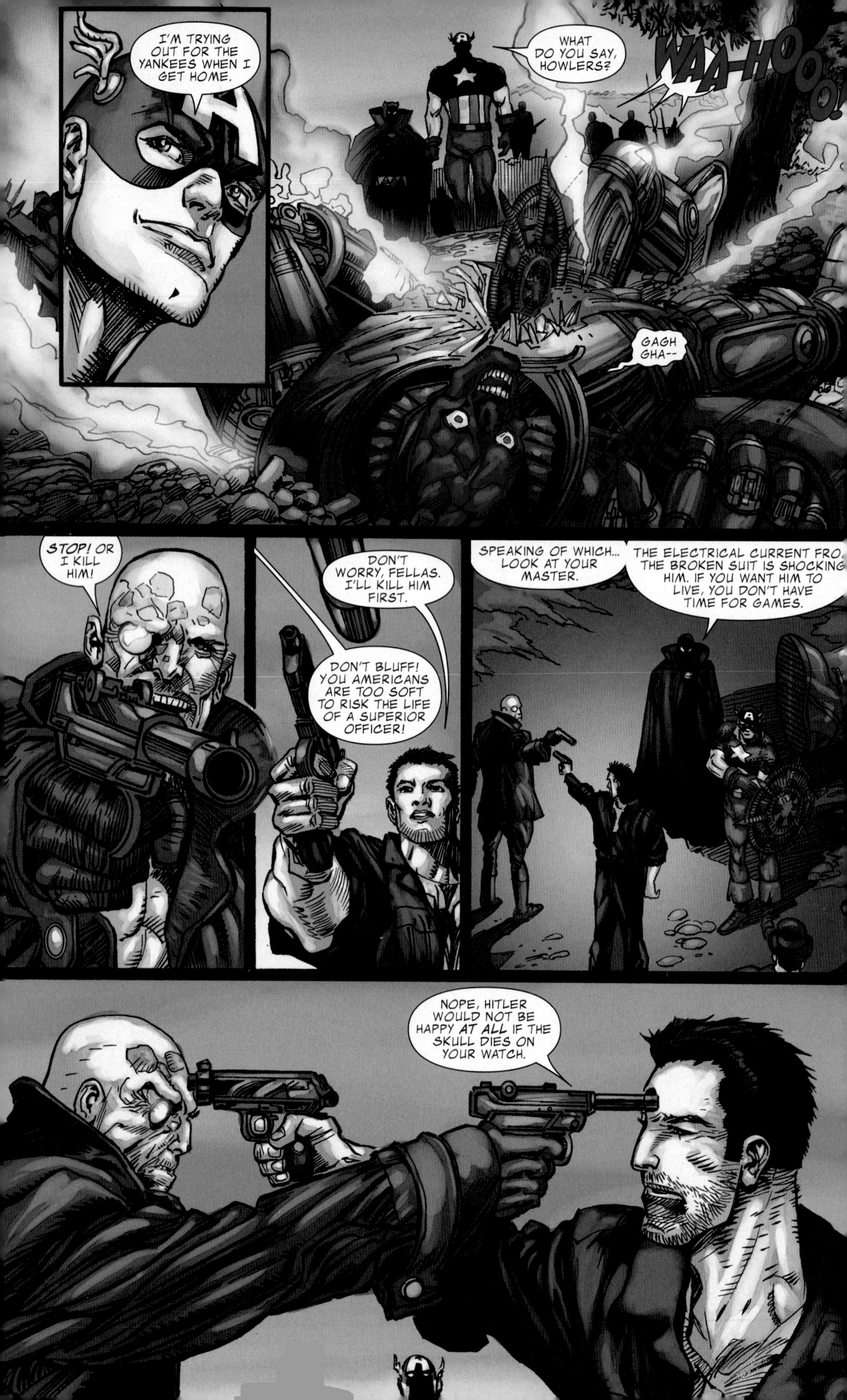

I'M TRYING OUT FOR THE YANKEES WHEN I GET HOME.
WHAT DO YOU SAY, HOWLERS?
WAA-HOOO!
KRAK
GAGH GHA--
STOP! OR I KILL HIM!
DON'T WORRY, FELLAS. I'LL KILL HIM FIRST.
DON'T BLUFF! YOU AMERICANS ARE TOO SOFT TO RISK THE LIFE OF A SUPERIOR OFFICER!
SPEAKING OF WHICH... LOOK AT YOUR MASTER.
THE ELECTRICAL CURRENT FRO THE BROKEN SUIT IS SHOCKING HIM. IF YOU WANT HIM TO LIVE, YOU DON'T HAVE TIME FOR GAMES.
NOPE, HITLER WOULD NOT BE HAPPY AT ALL IF THE SKULL DIES ON YOUR WATCH.

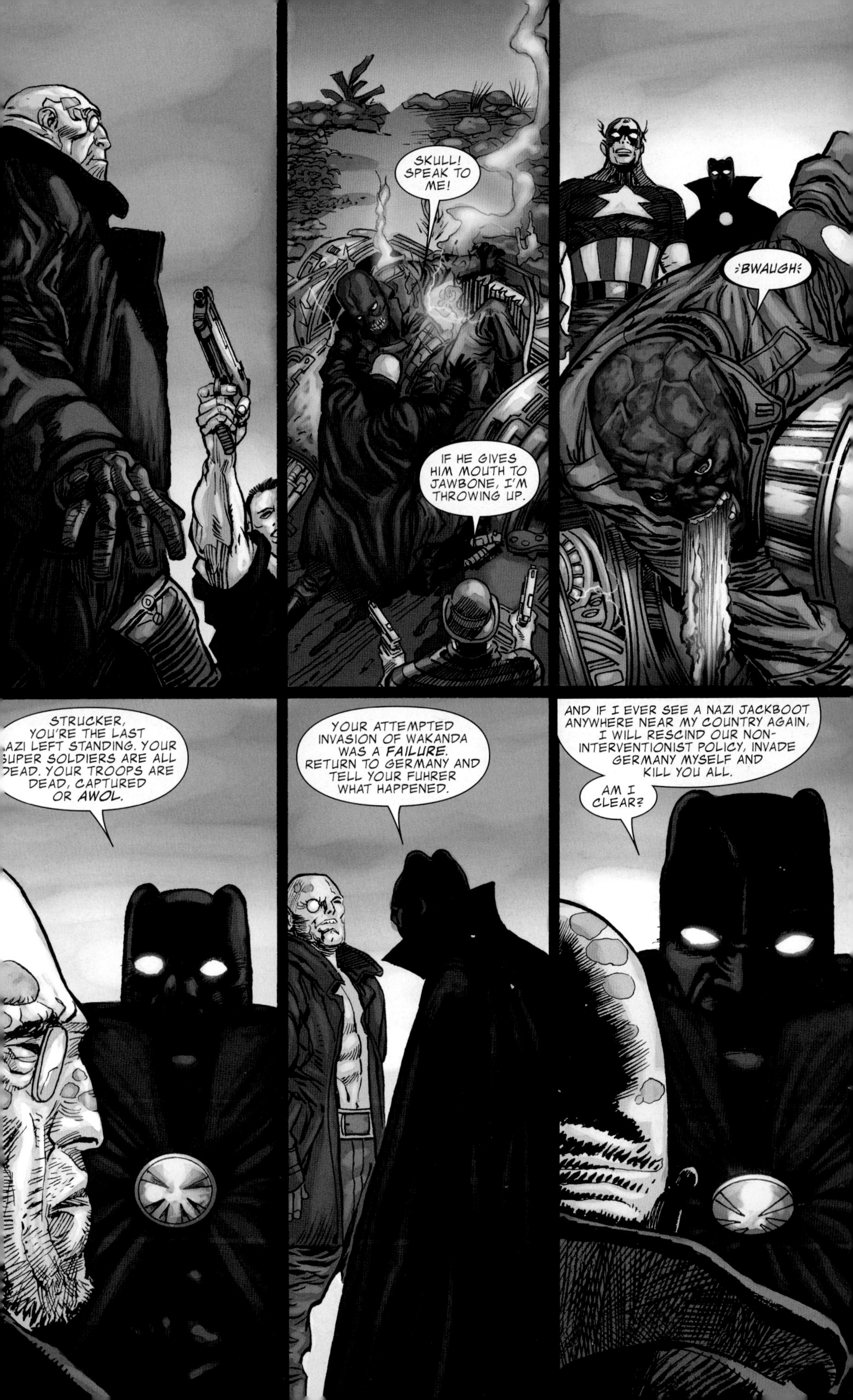
SKULL! SPEAK TO ME!
IF HE GIVES HIM MOUTH TO JAWBONE, I'M THROWING UP.
BWAUGH
STRUCKER, YOU'RE THE LAST NAZI LEFT STANDING. YOUR SUPER SOLDIERS ARE ALL DEAD. YOUR TROOPS ARE DEAD, CAPTURED OR AWOL.
YOUR ATTEMPTED INVASION OF WAKANDA WAS A FAILURE. RETURN TO GERMANY AND TELL YOUR FUHRER WHAT HAPPENED.
AND IF I EVER SEE A NAZI JACKBOOT ANYWHERE NEAR MY COUNTRY AGAIN, I WILL RESCIND OUR NON-INTERVENTIONIST POLICY, INVADE GERMANY MYSELF AND KILL YOU ALL.
AM I CLEAR?

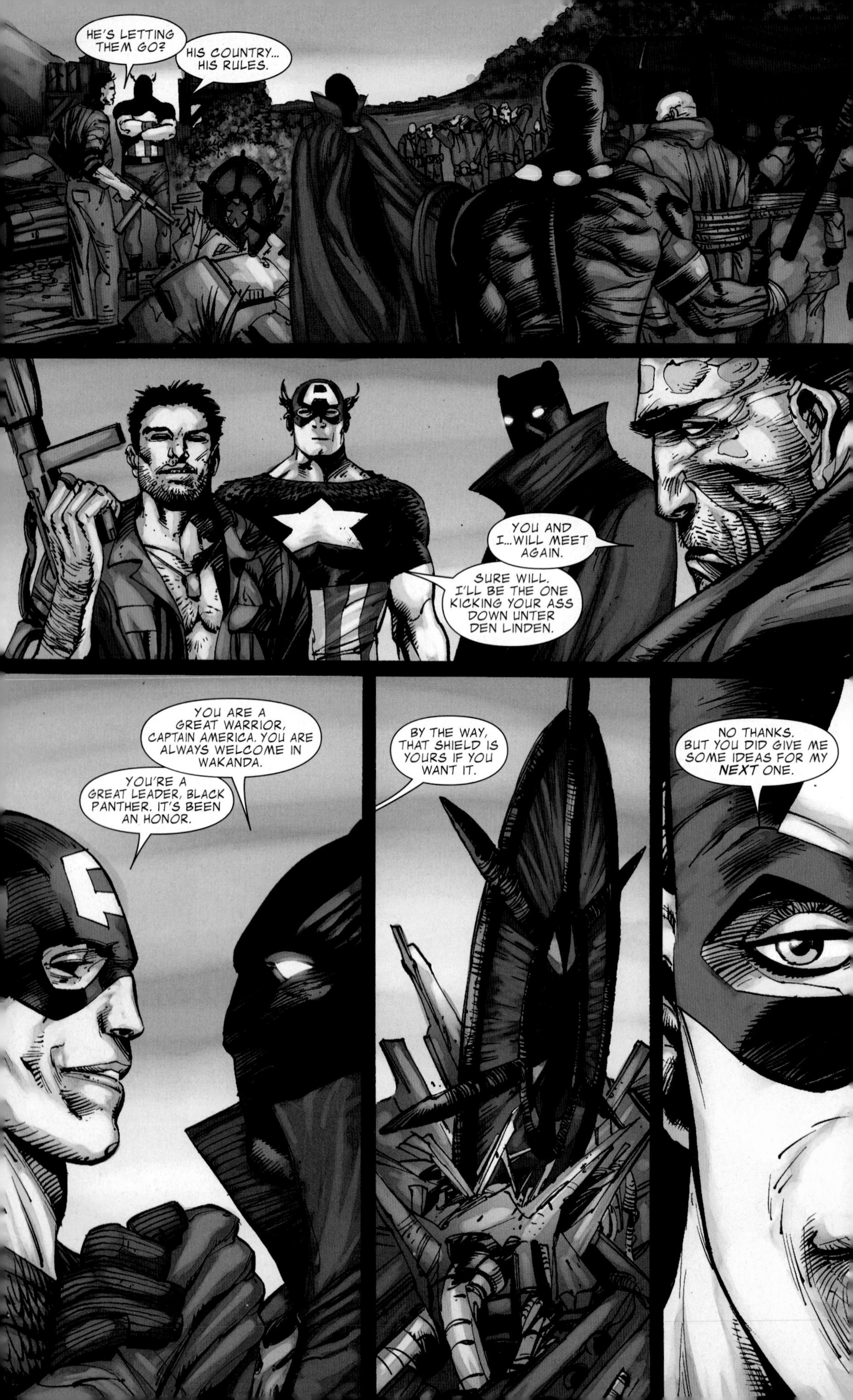
HE'S LETTING THEM GO?
HIS COUNTRY... HIS RULES.
YOU AND I...WILL MEET AGAIN.
SURE WILL. I'LL BE THE ONE KICKING YOUR ASS DOWN UNTER DEN LINDEN.
YOU ARE A GREAT WARRIOR, CAPTAIN AMERICA. YOU ARE ALWAYS WELCOME IN WAKANDA.
YOU'RE A GREAT LEADER, BLACK PANTHER. IT'S BEEN AN HONOR.
BY THE WAY, THAT SHIELD IS YOURS IF YOU WANT IT.
NO THANKS. BUT YOU DID GIVE ME SOME IDEAS FOR MY NEXT ONE.

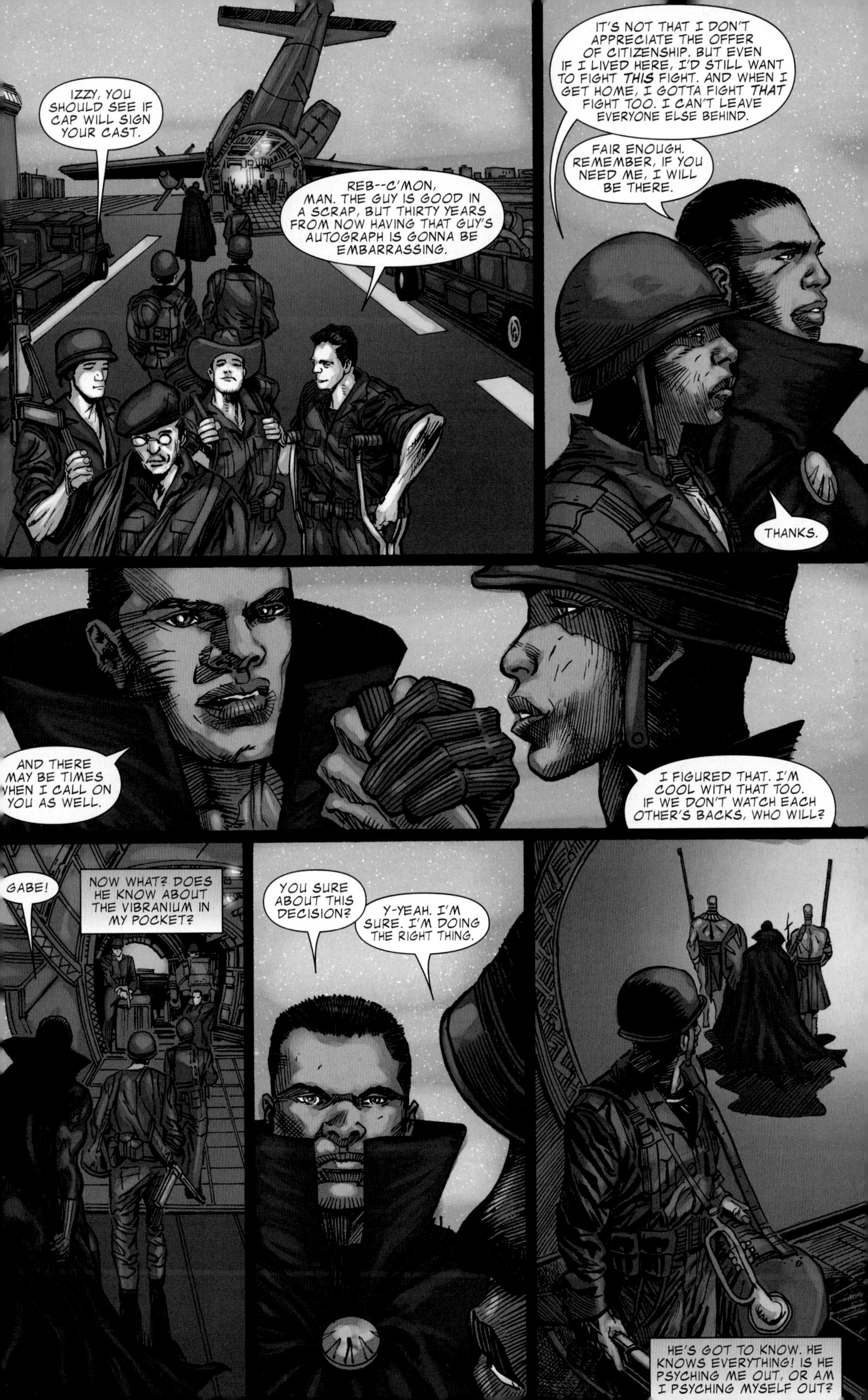
IZZY, YOU SHOULD SEE IF CAP WILL SIGN YOUR CAST.
REB--C'MON, MAN. THE GUY IS GOOD IN A SCRAP, BUT THIRTY YEARS FROM NOW HAVING THAT GUY'S AUTOGRAPH IS GONNA BE EMBARRASSING.
IT'S NOT THAT I DON'T APPRECIATE THE OFFER OF CITIZENSHIP. BUT EVEN IF I LIVED HERE, I'D STILL WANT TO FIGHT THIS FIGHT. AND WHEN I GET HOME, I GOTTA FIGHT THAT FIGHT TOO. I CAN'T LEAVE EVERYONE ELSE BEHIND.
FAIR ENOUGH. REMEMBER, IF YOU NEED ME, I WILL BE THERE.
THANKS.
AND THERE MAY BE TIMES WHEN I CALL ON YOU AS WELL.
I FIGURED THAT. I'M COOL WITH THAT TOO. IF WE DON'T WATCH EACH OTHER'S BACKS, WHO WILL?
GABE!
NOW WHAT? DOES HE KNOW ABOUT THE VIBRANIUM IN MY POCKET?
YOU SURE ABOUT THIS DECISION?
Y-YEAH. I'M SURE. I'M DOING THE RIGHT THING.
HE'S GOT TO KNOW. HE KNOWS EVERYTHING! IS HE PSYCHING ME OUT, OR AM I PSYCHING MYSELF OUT?

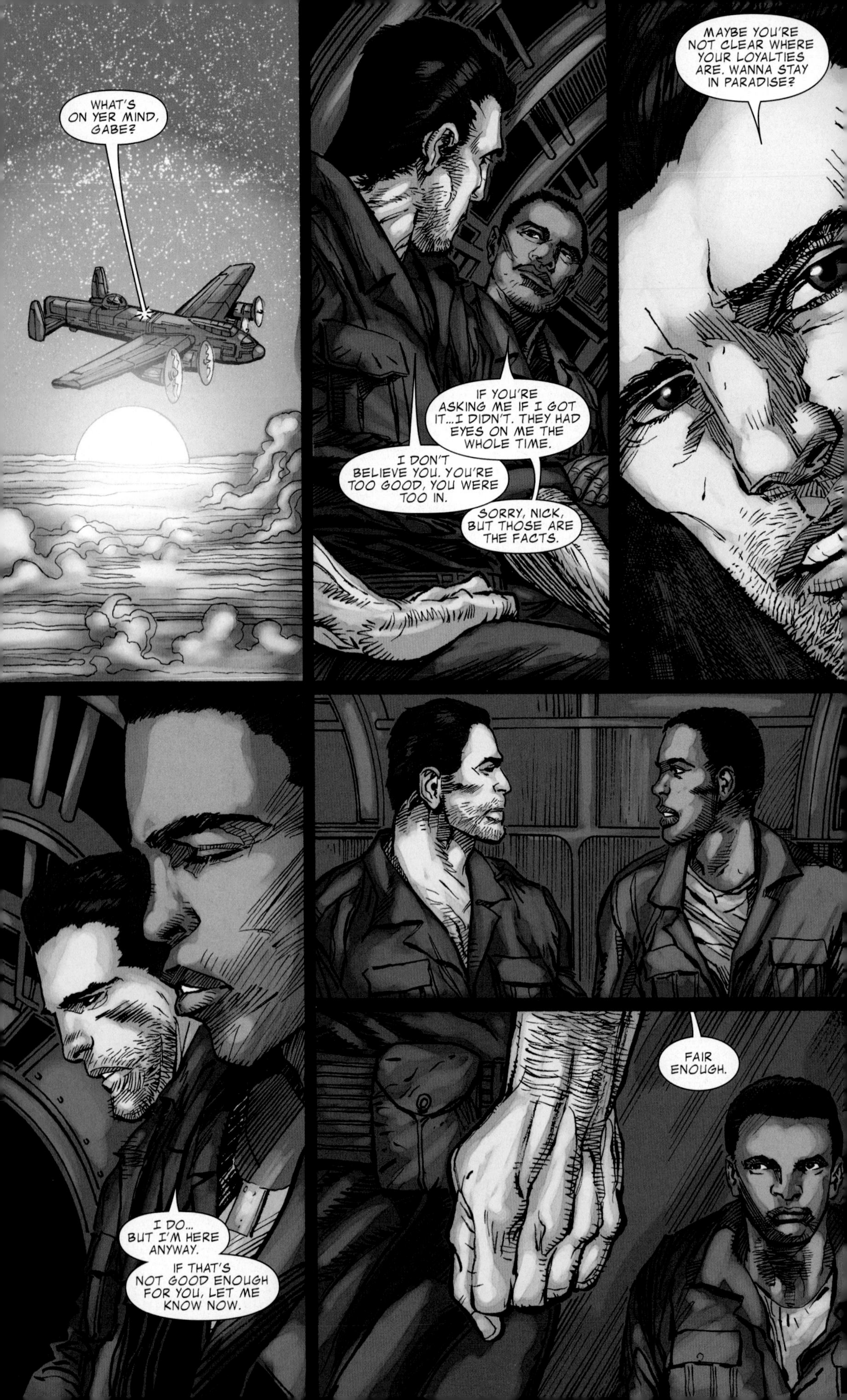
WHAT'S ON YER MIND, GABE?
IF YOU'RE ASKING ME IF I GOT IT...I DIDN'T. THEY HAD EYES ON ME THE WHOLE TIME.
I DON'T BELIEVE YOU. YOU'RE TOO GOOD, YOU WERE TOO IN.
SORRY, NICK, BUT THOSE ARE THE FACTS.
MAYBE YOU'RE NOT CLEAR WHERE YOUR LOYALTIES ARE. WANNA STAY IN PARADISE?
I DO... BUT I'M HERE ANYWAY.
IF THAT'S NOT GOOD ENOUGH FOR YOU, LET ME KNOW NOW.
FAIR ENOUGH.

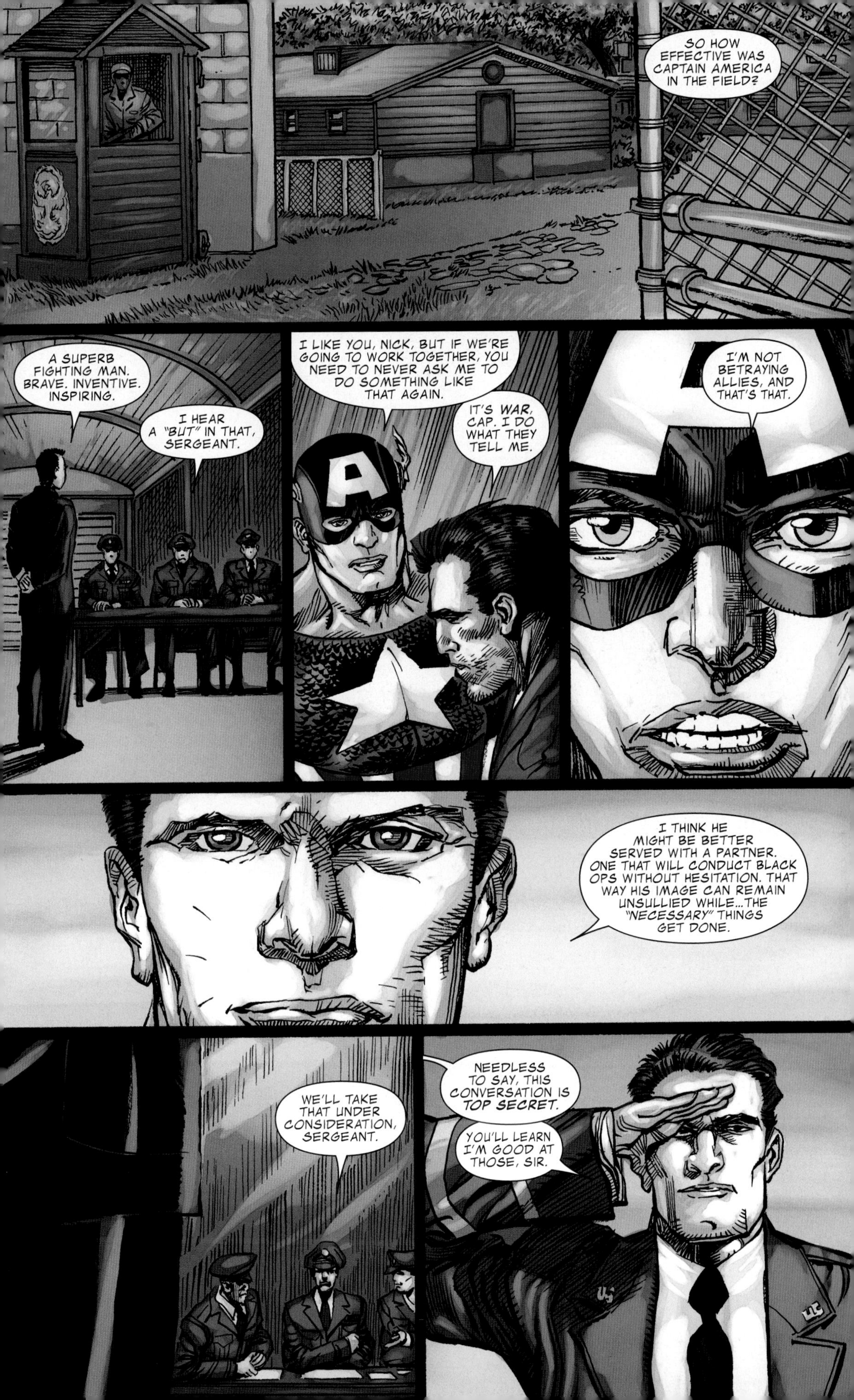
SO HOW EFFECTIVE WAS CAPTAIN AMERICA IN THE FIELD?
A SUPERB FIGHTING MAN. BRAVE. INVENTIVE. INSPIRING.
I HEAR A "BUT" IN THAT, SERGEANT.
I LIKE YOU, NICK, BUT IF WE'RE GOING TO WORK TOGETHER, YOU NEED TO NEVER ASK ME TO DO SOMETHING LIKE THAT AGAIN.
IT'S WAR, CAP. I DO WHAT THEY TELL ME.
I'M NOT BETRAYING ALLIES, AND THAT'S THAT.
I THINK HE MIGHT BE BETTER SERVED WITH A PARTNER. ONE THAT WILL CONDUCT BLACK OPS WITHOUT HESITATION. THAT WAY HIS IMAGE CAN REMAIN UNSULLIED WHILE...THE "NECESSARY" THINGS GET DONE.
WE'LL TAKE THAT UNDER CONSIDERATION, SERGEANT.
NEEDLESS TO SAY, THIS CONVERSATION IS TOP SECRET.
YOU'LL LEARN I'M GOOD AT THOSE, SIR.

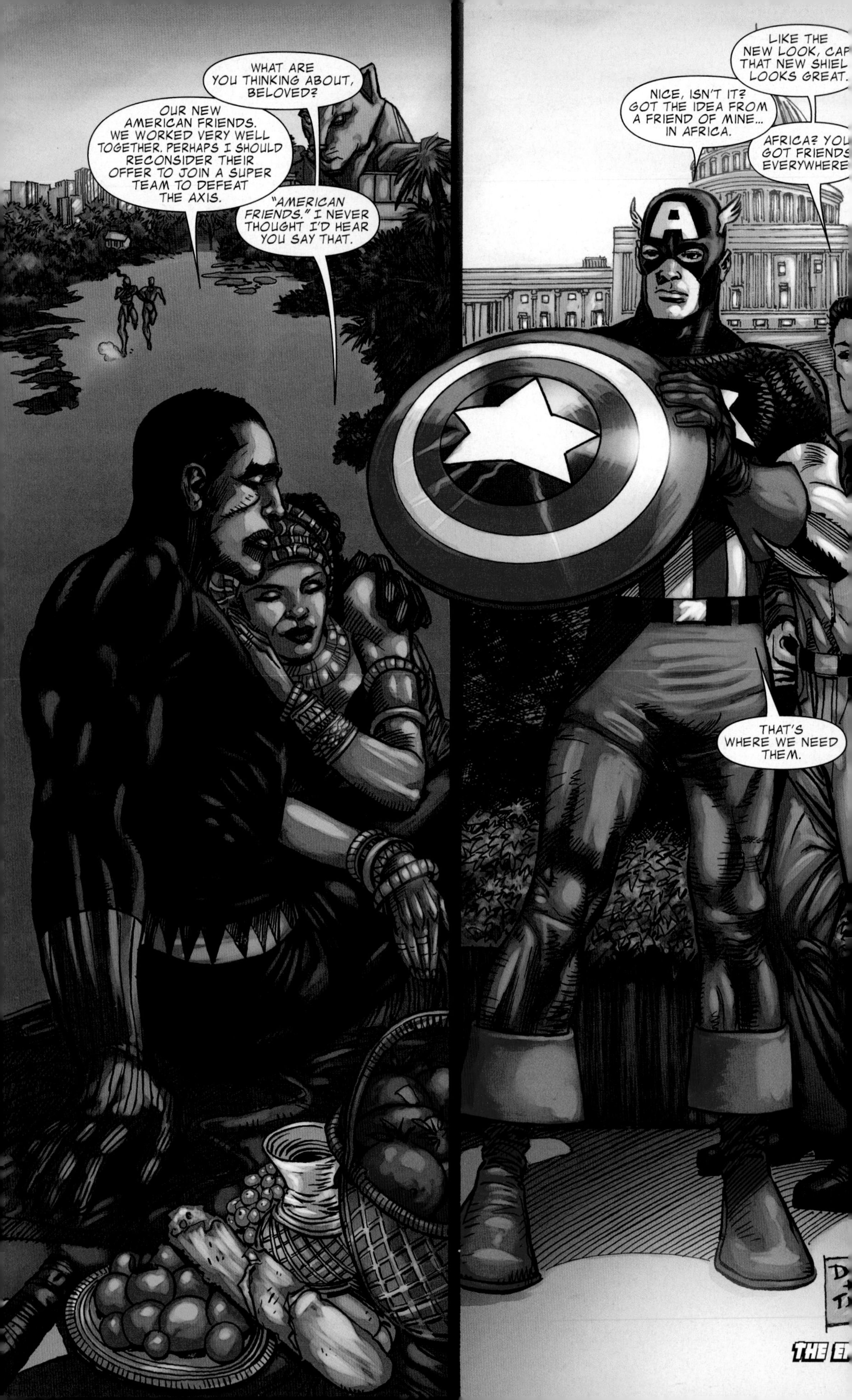
WHAT ARE YOU THINKING ABOUT, BELOVED?
OUR NEW AMERICAN FRIENDS. WE WORKED VERY WELL TOGETHER. PERHAPS I SHOULD RECONSIDER THEIR OFFER TO JOIN A SUPER TEAM TO DEFEAT THE AXIS.
"AMERICAN FRIENDS." I NEVER THOUGHT I'D HEAR YOU SAY THAT.
LIKE THE NEW LOOK, CAP THAT NEW SHIEL LOOKS GREAT.
NICE, ISN'T IT? GOT THE IDEA FROM A FRIEND OF MINE... IN AFRICA.
AFRICA? YOU GOT FRIENDS EVERYWHERE
THAT'S WHERE WE NEED THEM.

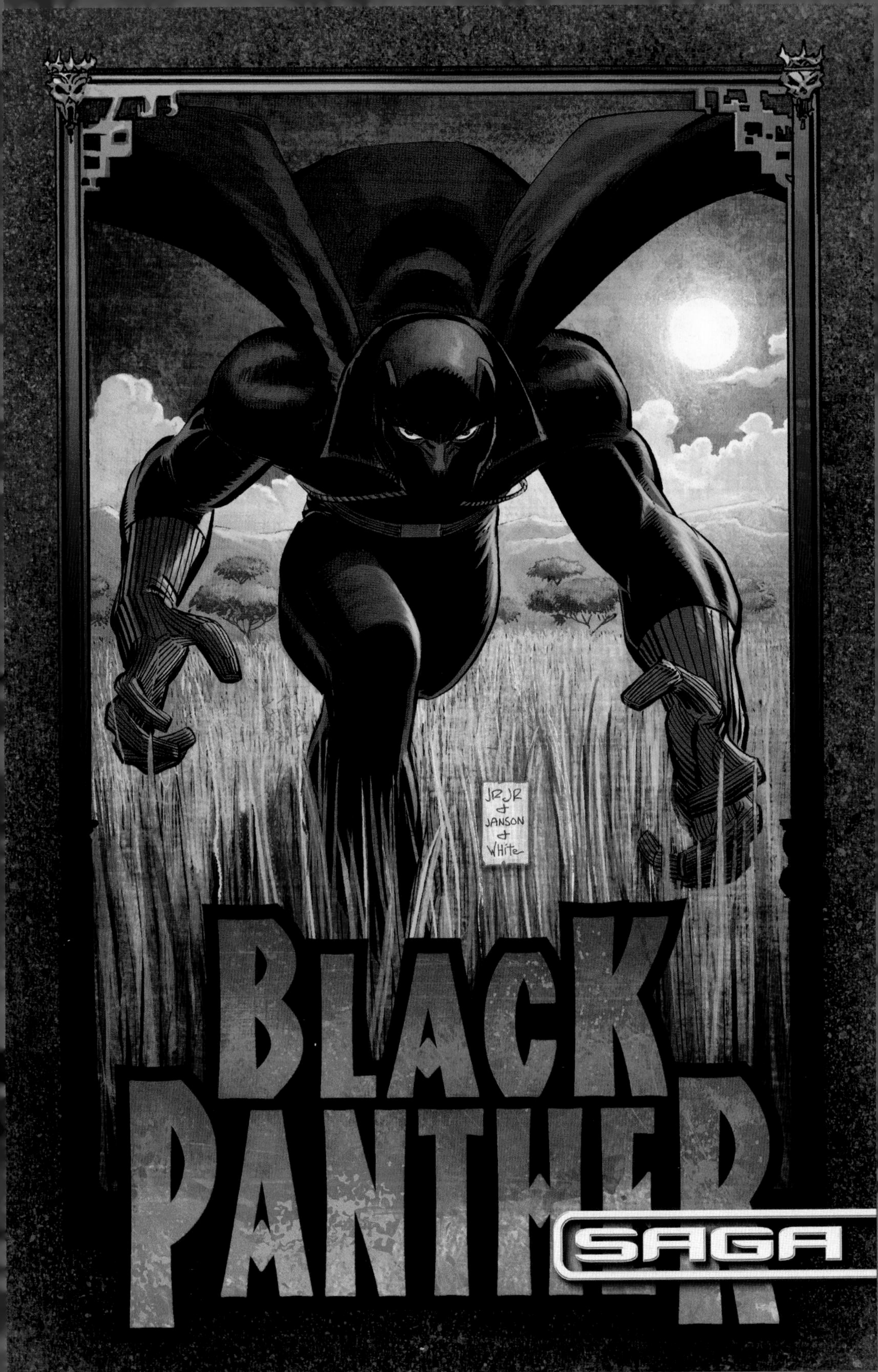
JRJR
&
JANSON
&
White
BLACK
PANTHER
SAGA

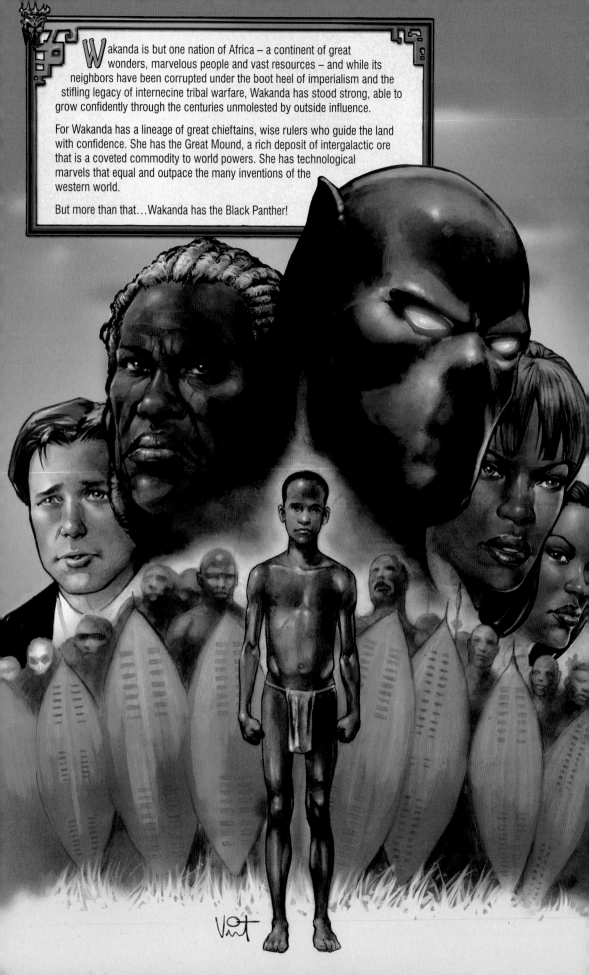

Wakanda is but one nation of Africa – a continent of great wonders, marvelous people and vast resources – and while its neighbors have been corrupted under the boot heel of imperialism and the stifling legacy of internecine tribal warfare, Wakanda has stood strong, able to grow confidently through the centuries unmolested by outside influence.

For Wakanda has a lineage of great chieftains, wise rulers who guide the land with confidence. She has the Great Mound, a rich deposit of intergalactic ore that is a coveted commodity to world powers. She has technological marvels that equal and outpace the many inventions of the western world.

But more than that…Wakanda has the Black Panther!

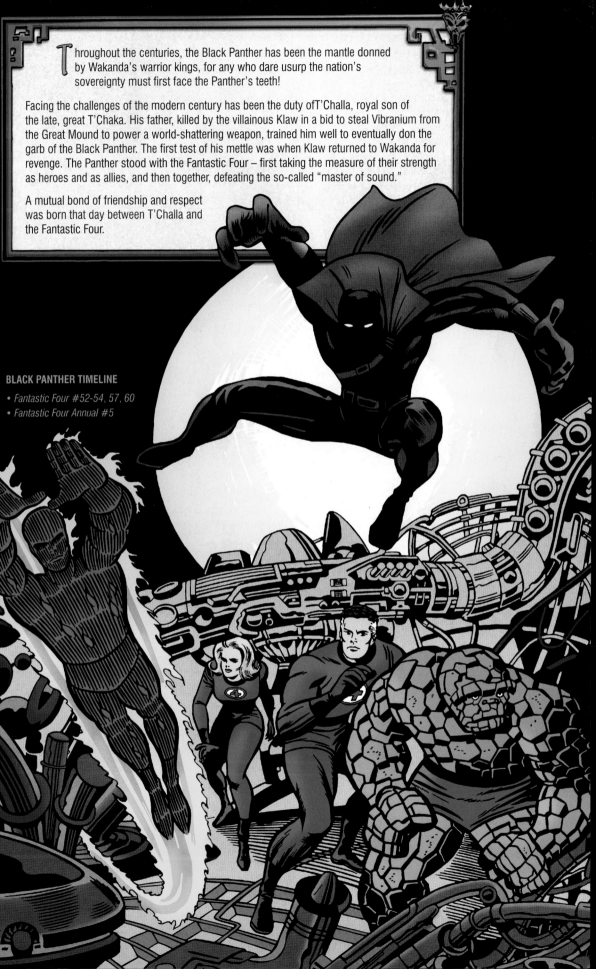

Throughout the centuries, the Black Panther has been the mantle donned by Wakanda's warrior kings, for any who dare usurp the nation's sovereignty must first face the Panther's teeth!

Facing the challenges of the modern century has been the duty of T'Challa, royal son of the late, great T'Chaka. His father, killed by the villainous Klaw in a bid to steal Vibranium from the Great Mound to power a world-shattering weapon, trained him well to eventually don the garb of the Black Panther. The first test of his mettle was when Klaw returned to Wakanda for revenge. The Panther stood with the Fantastic Four – first taking the measure of their strength as heroes and as allies, and then together, defeating the so-called "master of sound."

A mutual bond of friendship and respect was born that day between T'Challa and the Fantastic Four.

BLACK PANTHER TIMELINE

- *Fantastic Four #52-54, 57, 60*
- *Fantastic Four Annual #5*

T'Challa continued his interest in learning more about America, the great nation of the western hemisphere. He traveled across the ocean and took residence in its greatest city, joining the ranks of Earth's Mightiest Heroes, with whom he would avenge injustice against foes across the country, the world and throughout the cosmos. But the Panther also kept a watchful eye on his fellow heroes, for the wise king's ultimate loyalty was to the people of his homeland and he knew full well that there was destined to be a day when these friends may turn terrible foes — when the heroes of the West may turn against themselves, or even Wakanda. And on that day, the Black Panther would need to be armed with intelligence and insight.

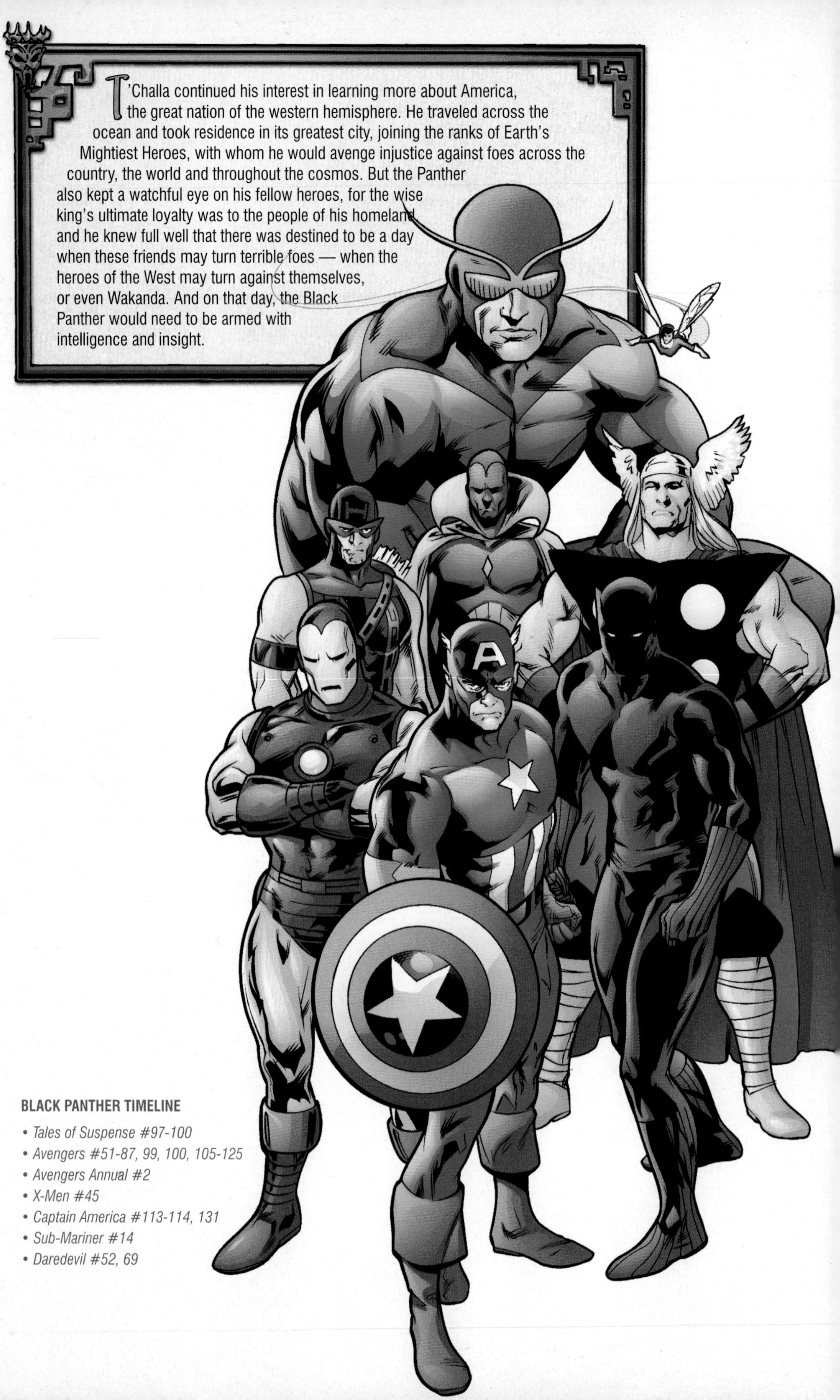

BLACK PANTHER TIMELINE

- *Tales of Suspense #97-100*
- *Avengers #51-87, 99, 100, 105-125*
- *Avengers Annual #2*
- *X-Men #45*
- *Captain America #113-114, 131*
- *Sub-Mariner #14*
- *Daredevil #52, 69*

His reputation with the heroes of the West now firmly established, the intervening years would continue to test the heroism of T'Challa and enhance the legacy of the Black Panther. In America, he would feel the Panther's rage as he stood against racism and intolerance, while in Wakanda, he would face down Erik Killmonger, a rebel leader and serious challenger to his leadership.

The Panther would also become embroiled in fantastic adventures with "The Collectors," who would lead him on wild goose chases throughout space and time at the whims of the ancient artifacts known as King Solomon's Frogs.

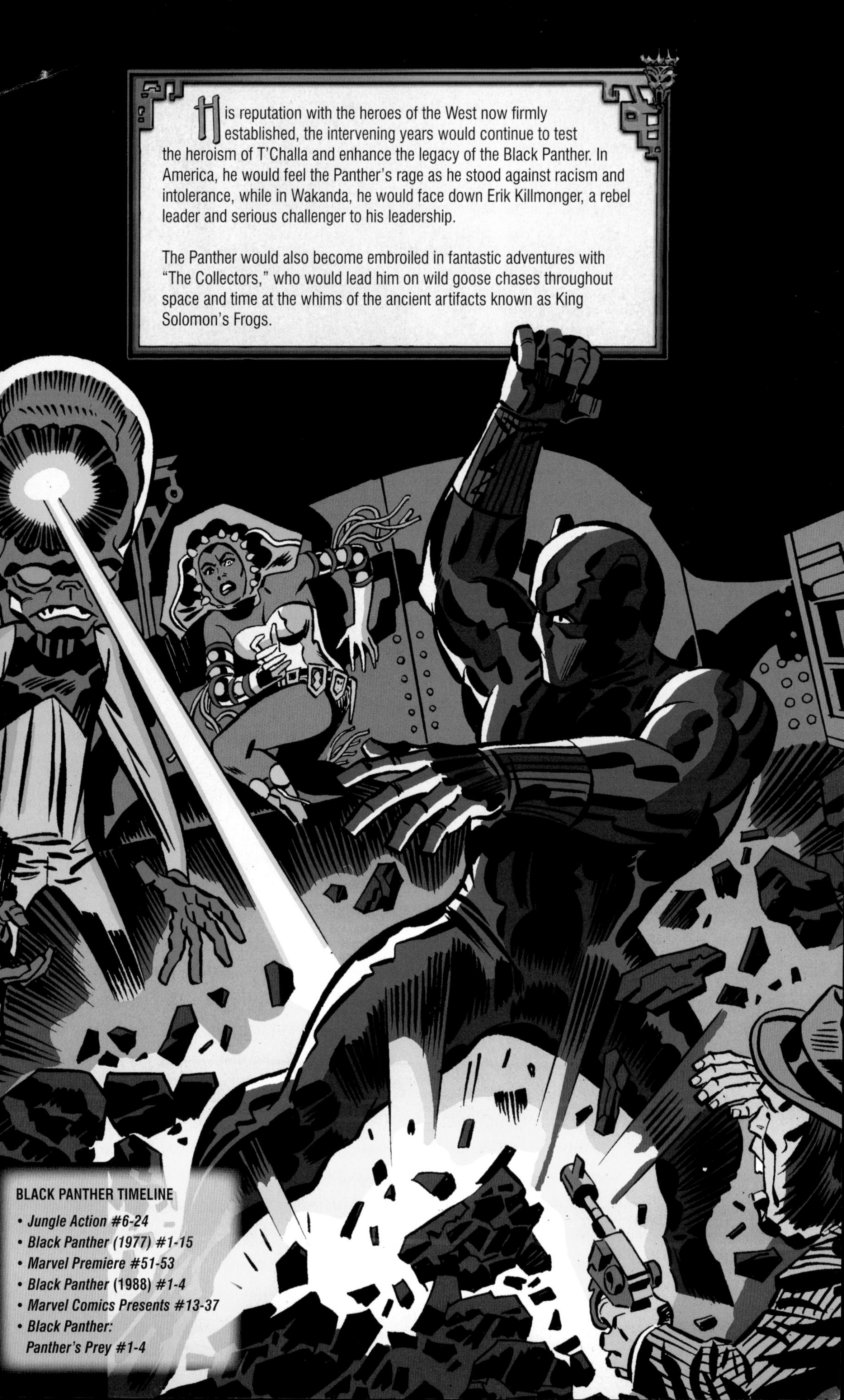

BLACK PANTHER TIMELINE

- *Jungle Action #6-24*
- *Black Panther (1977) #1-15*
- *Marvel Premiere #51-53*
- *Black Panther (1988) #1-4*
- *Marvel Comics Presents #13-37*
- *Black Panther: Panther's Prey #1-4*

After a period of relative calm in the Panther's life, mundane matters of statecraft would explode in his face. T'Challa's life was once more torn between royal duties in Wakanda and flashpoints of conflict in America: A Wakandan charity led by T'Challa was connected to an insidious murder plot fomented by the insane Achebe, a rebel challenger to the Panther's throne, and his half-brother, the White Wolf, a rogue element of the Wakandan secret police.

But the Panther, assisted by loyal aide Zuri and his Dora Milaje ("Adored Ones"), unraveled the plot and remained two steps ahead of his enemies. It would not be the last time forces inside the Panther's circle would subvert his authority. More such challenges would lie ahead…

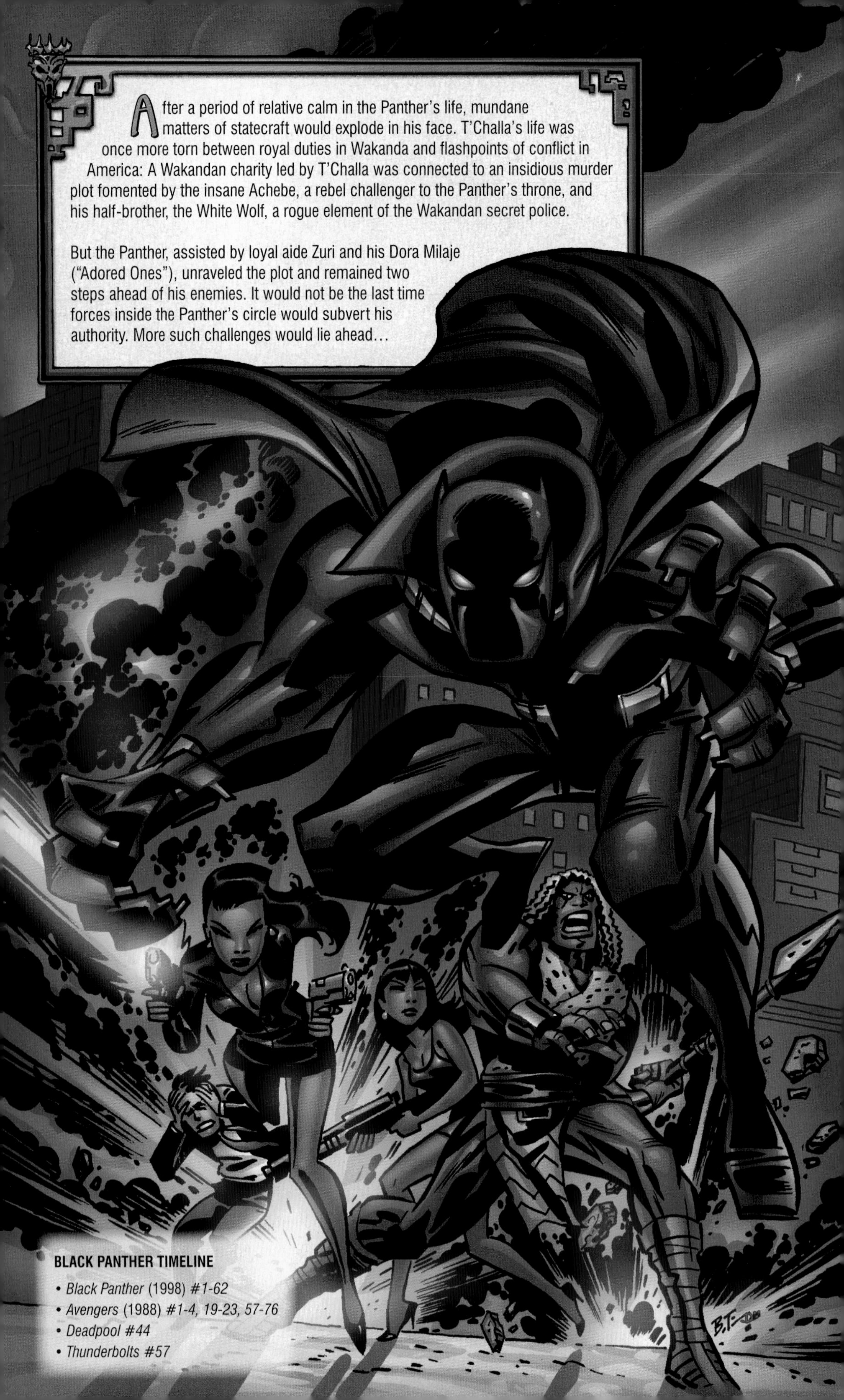

BLACK PANTHER TIMELINE

- *Black Panther* (1998) *#1-62*
- *Avengers* (1988) *#1-4, 19-23, 57-76*
- *Deadpool #44*
- *Thunderbolts #57*

ACK PANTHER TIMELINE

arvel Team-Up #100

torm #1-6

lack Panther (1998) *#26*

lack Panther (2005) *#8-41*

-Men #175-176

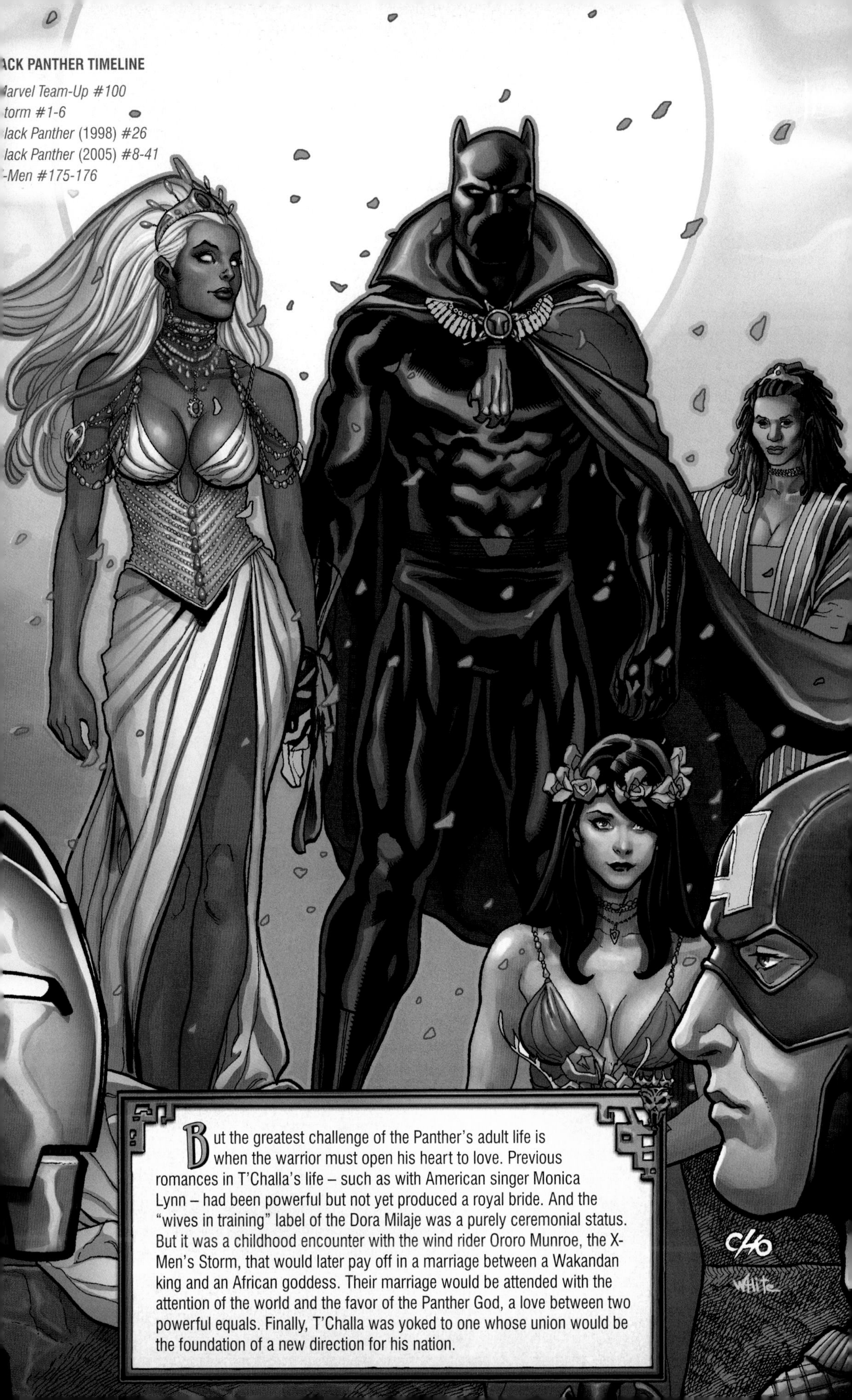

But the greatest challenge of the Panther's adult life is when the warrior must open his heart to love. Previous romances in T'Challa's life – such as with American singer Monica Lynn – had been powerful but not yet produced a royal bride. And the "wives in training" label of the Dora Milaje was a purely ceremonial status. But it was a childhood encounter with the wind rider Ororo Munroe, the X-Men's Storm, that would later pay off in a marriage between a Wakandan king and an African goddess. Their marriage would be attended with the attention of the world and the favor of the Panther God, a love between two powerful equals. Finally, T'Challa was yoked to one whose union would be the foundation of a new direction for his nation.

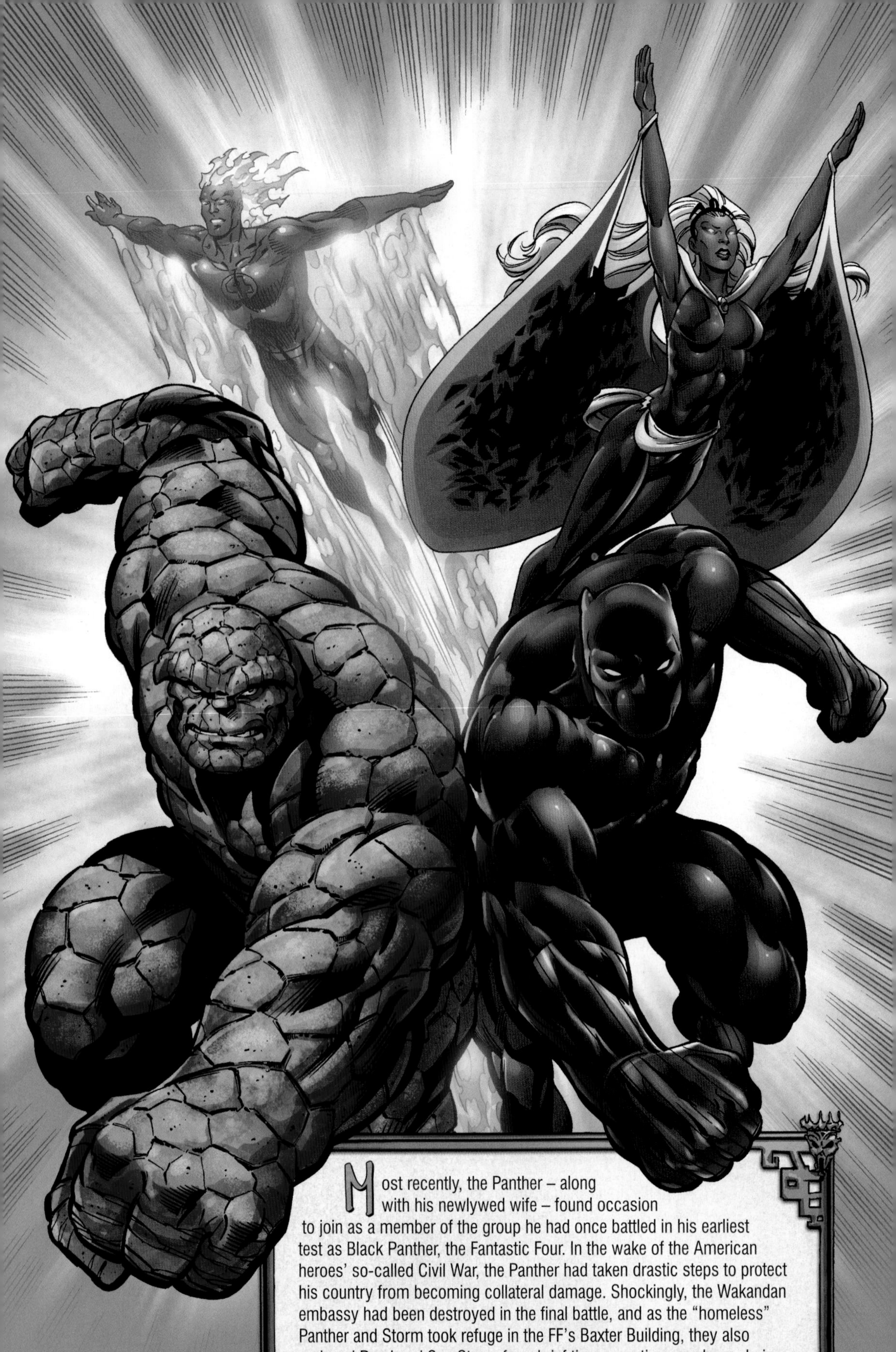

Most recently, the Panther – along with his newlywed wife – found occasion to join as a member of the group he had once battled in his earliest test as Black Panther, the Fantastic Four. In the wake of the American heroes' so-called Civil War, the Panther had taken drastic steps to protect his country from becoming collateral damage. Shockingly, the Wakandan embassy had been destroyed in the final battle, and as the "homeless" Panther and Storm took refuge in the FF's Baxter Building, they also replaced Reed and Sue Storm for a brief time as active members, during which they traveled the galaxy facing Galactus, the Silver Surfer and flesh-eating zombie creatures from another dimension.

BLACK PANTHER TIMELINE

- *Fantastic Four #544-550*
- *Black Panther* (2005) *#26-34*

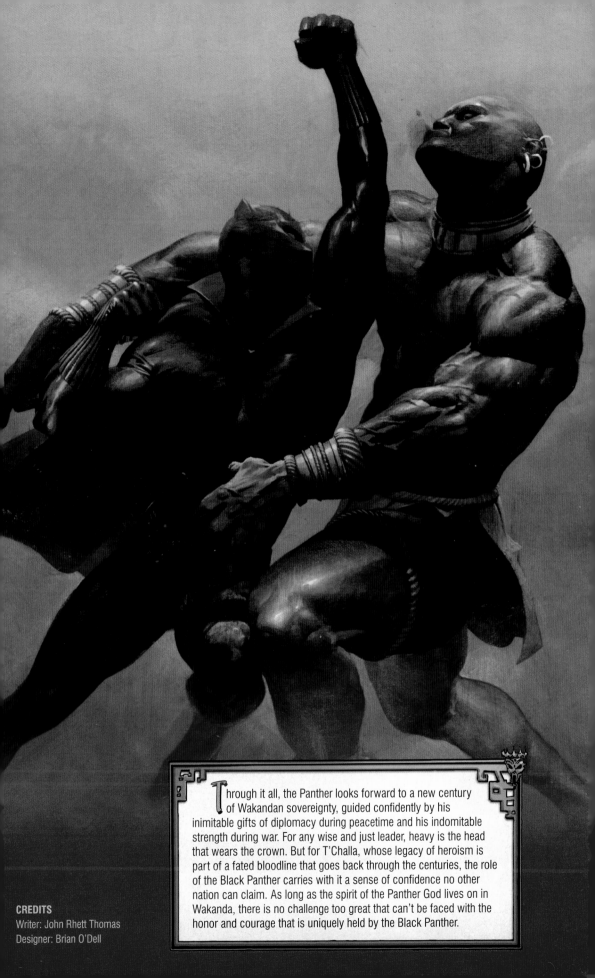

Through it all, the Panther looks forward to a new century of Wakandan sovereignty, guided confidently by his inimitable gifts of diplomacy during peacetime and his indomitable strength during war. For any wise and just leader, heavy is the head that wears the crown. But for T'Challa, whose legacy of heroism is part of a fated bloodline that goes back through the centuries, the role of the Black Panther carries with it a sense of confidence no other nation can claim. As long as the spirit of the Panther God lives on in Wakanda, there is no challenge too great that can't be faced with the honor and courage that is uniquely held by the Black Panther.

CREDITS
Writer: John Rhett Thomas
Designer: Brian O'Dell

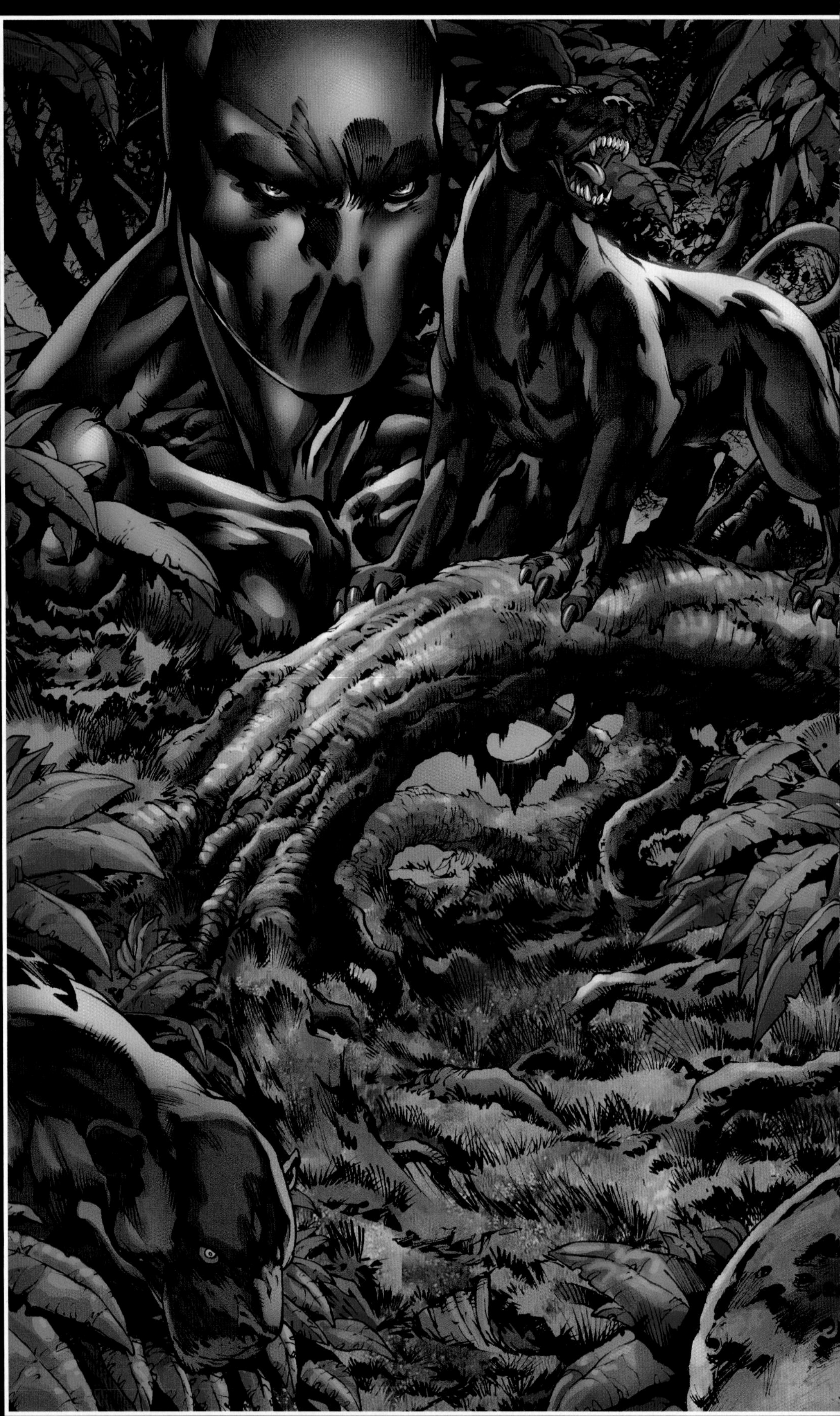

BY **KEN LASHLEY, PAUL NEARY** & **PAUL MOUNTS**

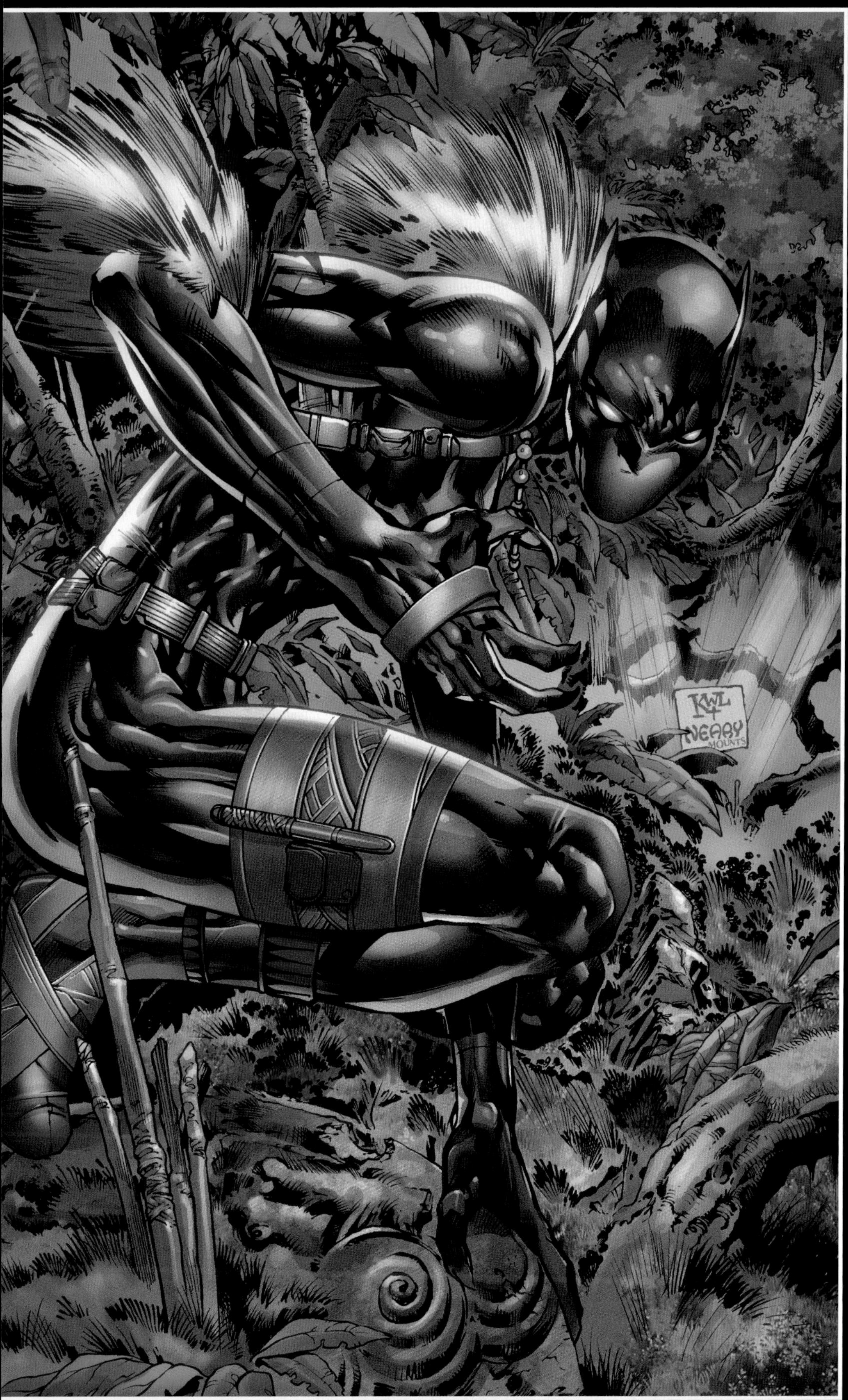
KWL
NEARY
MOUNTS

BLACK PANTHER (2009) #1 70TH ANNIVERSARY VARIANT BY **MARKO DJURDJEVIĆ**

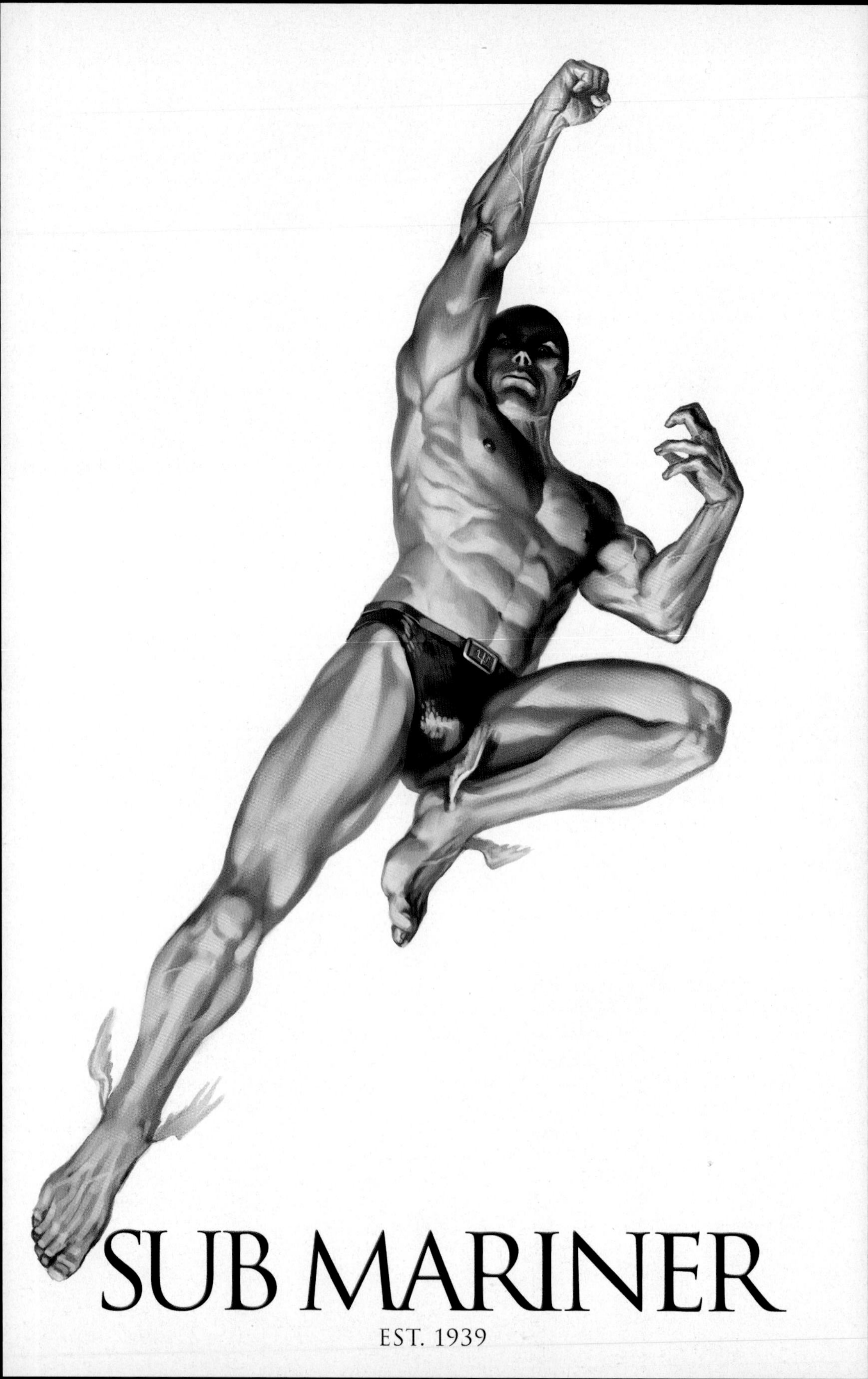
SUB MARINER
EST. 1939

BLACK PANTHER PAST, PRESENT, FUTURE

T'Challa, the warrior king of Wakanda, made his first appearance in the classic Stan Lee/Jack Kirby tale *"The Black Panther!"* way back in *Fantastic Four #52*, cover dated July 1966. In the nearly 43 years since that time, Black Panther has been at the center of dozens of timeless tales, including membership in the Avengers and a recent turn leading the legendary FF, not to mention the various solo titles he's earned throughout the decades.

After culling the last three-action packed issues of the series launched in 2005 by Reginald Hudlin and John Romita Jr., *Secret Invasion: Black Panther TPB* now takes a few looks back at some of the distinctive eras in Panther history. In addition, we'll serve up some scintillating sketch work by this book's penciling auteur, Jefte Palo. And finally, we'll preview the art of Ken Lashley, an artist whom will be taking over the new 2009 *Black Panther* series, and whose work will surely stand in the pantheon of great Panther art.

Black Panther #40, pg. 11, uncolored Jefte Palo pencil art.

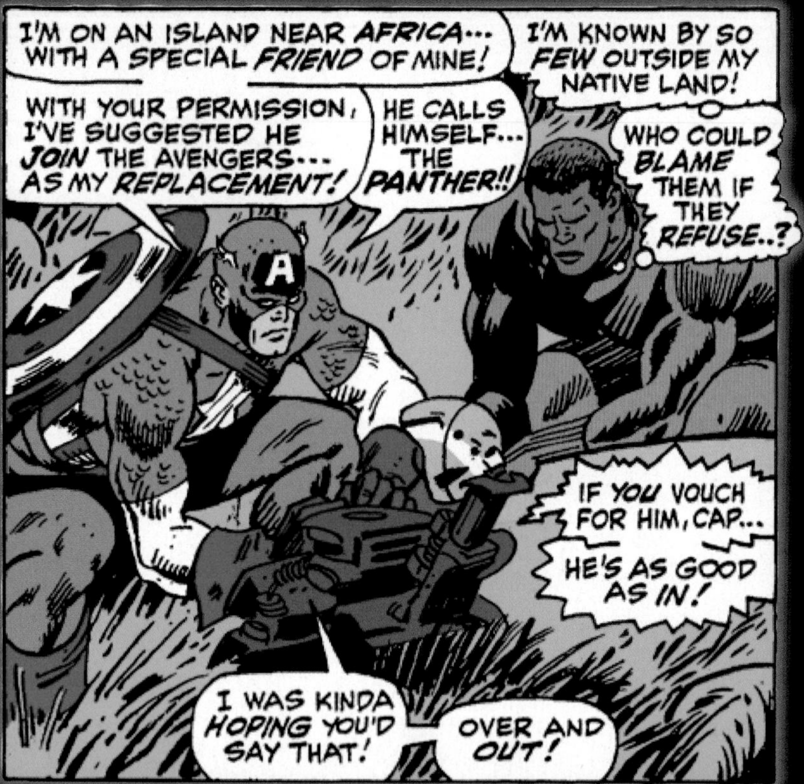
I'M ON AN ISLAND NEAR AFRICA... WITH A SPECIAL FRIEND OF MINE!
I'M KNOWN BY SO FEW OUTSIDE MY NATIVE LAND!
WITH YOUR PERMISSION, I'VE SUGGESTED HE JOIN THE AVENGERS... AS MY REPLACEMENT!
HE CALLS HIMSELF... THE PANTHER!!
WHO COULD BLAME THEM IF THEY REFUSE..?
IF YOU VOUCH FOR HIM, CAP...
HE'S AS GOOD AS IN!
I WAS KINDA HOPING YOU'D SAY THAT!
OVER AND OUT!

ONCE AN AVENGER...

ROY THOMAS TELLS ALL ABOUT T'CHALLA'S MEMBERSHIP WITH EARTH'S MIGHTIEST HEROES

BY JESS HARROLD

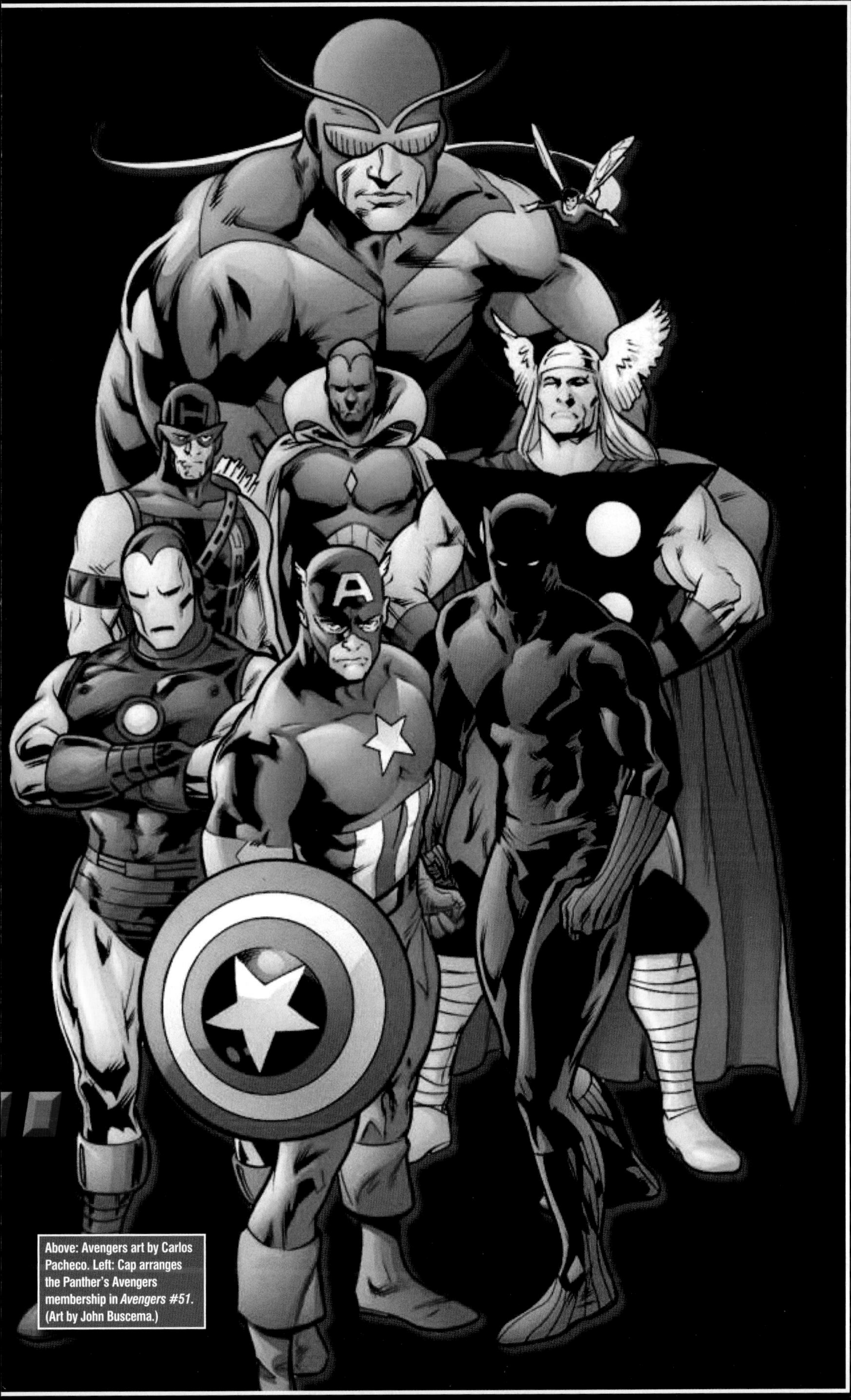

Above: Avengers art by Carlos Pacheco. Left: Cap arranges the Panther's Avengers membership in *Avengers #51*. (Art by John Buscema.)

WHEN BLACK PANTHER FIRST PROWLED INTO AVENGERS MANSION at Captain America's invitation in May 1968, he found Earth's Mightiest Heroes apparently slain at the hand – or, literally, the scythe – of the Grim Reaper. Proving his mettle by single-handedly defeating the Reaper and reviving the team, T'Challa cemented his place on the Avengers roster for years to come. While the Panther's initial stint on the team saw many changes in line-up, and several of the biggest names in comics history on art duties, one thing was constant – the stewardship of legendary Marvel writer 'Rascally' Roy Thomas. Roy, who had earlier found success on *X-Men*, would go on to test the Avengers to the limit with the classic Kree/Skrull War storyline, introduce *Conan the Barbarian* to Marvel Comics, and, in 1972, take over from Stan Lee as the company's editor-in-chief. During Roy's time with the Panther, T'Challa would behold the coming of the Vision, attend the wedding of Yellowjacket and the Wasp, and witness Hawkeye's transformation into Goliath. Yet somehow the Panther also found time to take on the civilian teacher guise Luke Charles and find love with the singer Monica Lynne. All the while, writing the character fed Roy's desire to one day see the continent of T'Challa's birth. Now Roy casts his mind back across the decades to the pioneering character he made a key part of *Avengers* history.

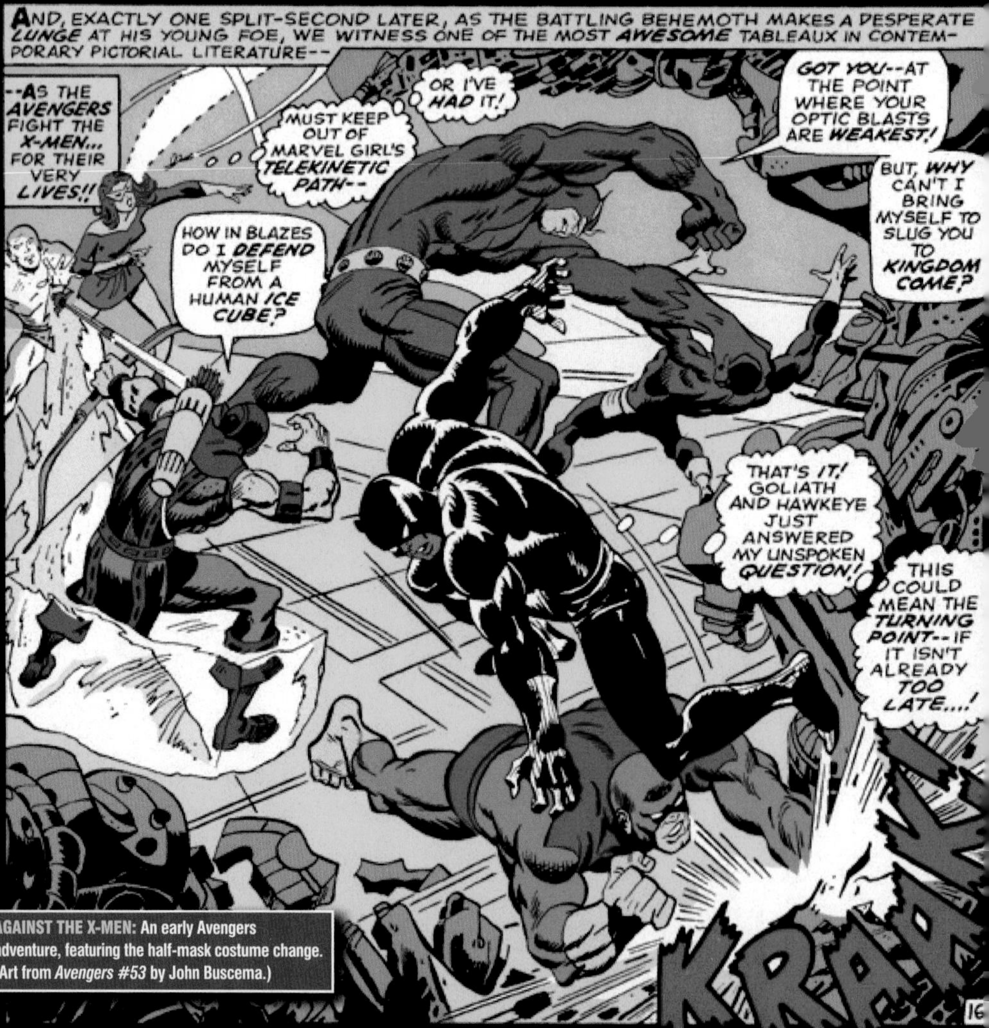
AND, EXACTLY ONE SPLIT-SECOND LATER, AS THE BATTLING BEHEMOTH MAKES A DESPERATE LUNGE AT HIS YOUNG FOE, WE WITNESS ONE OF THE MOST AWESOME TABLEAUX IN CONTEMPORARY PICTORIAL LITERATURE--
--AS THE AVENGERS FIGHT THE X-MEN... FOR THEIR VERY LIVES!!
MUST KEEP OUT OF MARVEL GIRL'S TELEKINETIC PATH--
OR I'VE HAD IT!
GOT YOU!--AT THE POINT WHERE YOUR OPTIC BLASTS ARE WEAKEST!
BUT, WHY CAN'T I BRING MYSELF TO SLUG YOU TO KINGDOM COME?
HOW IN BLAZES DO I DEFEND MYSELF FROM A HUMAN ICE CUBE?
THAT'S IT! GOLIATH AND HAWKEYE JUST ANSWERED MY UNSPOKEN QUESTION!
THIS COULD MEAN THE TURNING POINT-- IF IT ISN'T ALREADY TOO LATE...!
16
AGAINST THE X-MEN: An early Avengers adventure, featuring the half-mask costume change. (Art from *Avengers #53* by John Buscema.)

SPOTLIGHT: Whose idea was it for Black Panther to join the team in *Avengers #52*?

ROY: Stan wanted T'Challa to join the Avengers, probably agreeing with me at least to the extent that the mag needed one or two more popular heroes than a steady dose of second stringers like Goliath, Wasp and Hawkeye. The Panther was, of course, the first black super hero at Marvel, indeed in all of American comics. I was there when the character was created and brought in. I guess it was based on that Coal Tiger idea Jack had, of which I'd seen the drawing. It would have been a little weird because, of course, there aren't any tigers in Africa.

SPOTLIGHT: How important did you think it was to introduce racial diversity into the line-up of Earth's Mightiest Heroes at that time?

ROY: I didn't think it was important, exactly, but a good idea, since the character existed. Stan had been integrating in crowd scenes since the very beginning. At a time when everybody was 'white bread' at DC and other companies, Stan made sure that the crowds at Marvel Comics were integrated. They shouldn't all only be white faces. Then of course we had Bill Foster who was a lab assistant to Hank Pym. I think that was basically a good thing, and later on, when I wrote *Fantastic Four*, I put Luke Cage on the team's roster, just as I came up with the initial ideas for Banshee from Ireland, Sunfire from Japan, Wolverine from Canada, and later the Living Lightning in *Avengers West Coast*.

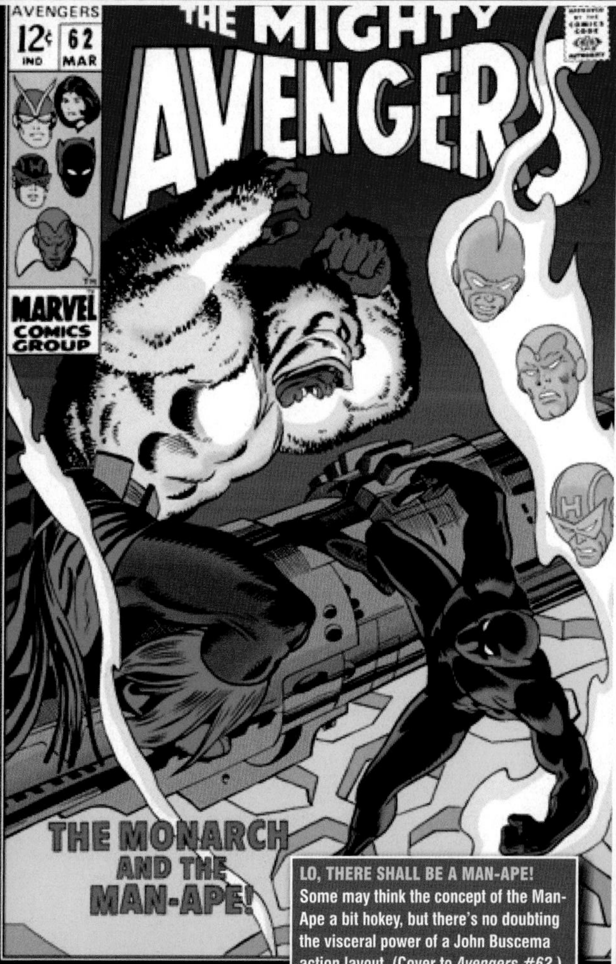
AVENGERS
12¢
62
IND
MAR
THE MIGHTY AVENGERS
MARVEL COMICS GROUP
THE MONARCH AND THE MAN-APE!

LO, THERE SHALL BE A MAN-APE! Some may think the concept of the Man-Ape a bit hokey, but there's no doubting the visceral power of a John Buscema action layout. (Cover to *Avengers #62*.)

"He was a foreigner, and would have a different outlook...a good action character, who also had lots of gimmicks that could augment those provided by Tony Stark."

– ROY THOMAS ON WHAT BLACK PANTHER BROUGHT TO THE TABLE IN AVENGERS

SPOTLIGHT: How was the Panther's arrival greeted by fans? Do you think it brought in new readers?

ROY: With enthusiasm, I believe. I think a couple of people, maybe more, wrote in saying it was good to see, not an African-American, but an African in the comic. I'm sure it did bring in readers, in the sense that I know we got some letters about it, but how many of them were already reading Marvel I don't know.

SPOTLIGHT: As a writer, what qualities did you think T'Challa would bring to the roster of Earth's Mightiest Heroes?

ROY: Besides racial diversity, he was a foreigner, and would have a different outlook, as well as being a good action character, who also had lots of gimmicks that could augment those provided by Tony Stark.

SPOTLIGHT: In his first four *Avengers* appearances, T'Challa sports an unfamiliar half-mask, revealing the color of his skin. Whose idea was that? What prompted the return to the classic full-face mask so soon?

ROY: Stan insisted on that. I was against it. His first *Avengers* appearance had already been drawn by John Buscema with a full face-mask, and we had to change that. It was just around long enough to ruin a few issues of Avengers as far as I was concerned. The Panther looked so much nicer with that serious face-mask. I suppose Stan's thought was that if he stands around in his mask all the time you'd never see he was African. Stan never really liked the idea of full face masks because you don't see a hero's expression that way. This always seemed an odd viewpoint coming from the co-creator of Spider-Man. I think that Jack designed

STILL, PANTHER, MAYBE WE CAN FIGURE OUT THE REASON FOR THE ATTACK!
ANY IDEA OF WHY THE SERPENTS SHOULD SINGLE YOU OUT, MISS...?
THE NAME IS MONICA LYNNE!
AND MY SKIN IS REASON ENOUGH... FOR VERMIN LIKE THAT!
WHAT I WANT TO KNOW IS, WHERE WERE THE POLICE UNTIL THE DANGER WAS OVER?
DIDN'T YOU WANT TO DIRTY YOUR HANDS...TO RESCUE A BLACK GIRL?
WE DO OUR BEST, LADY... BUT WE CAN'T BE EVERY-WHERE AT ONCE!
YOU'VE GOT TO UNDERSTAND...!
PERHAPS I DO UNDERSTAND... BETTER THAN YOU WANT ME TO!
EXCUSE ME, PLEASE! I HAVE TO CALL A MAN... ABOUT A CAUSE...!

MONICA LYNNE: The Panther's first featured lady love was introduced in the Avengers. (Art from *Avengers #73* by Frank Giacoia.)

Black Panther that way so Stan let it go at first as an exception. But as a general rule we tried to avoid too much of that.

Another oft-asked question is why his name was changed to Black Leopard for a little while; another one of Stan's ideas that I didn't agree with, but I understood his reasoning. The thing was that the Black Panther group that had started earlier just was getting famous at the same time that Black Panther appeared in FF and as a result it became a little harder to publicize the character without looking like it was related politically. But after a few issues we just gave up and went back to the Black Panther because the Black Leopard just didn't make it. It was pretty much as good a name, but Panther just had more resonance. Black Panther probably would have been a solo-star at that time if not for the political thing.

SPOTLIGHT: During Panther's stay with the team, you collaborated with comic legends including Gene Colan, Barry Windsor-Smith, and both John and Sal Buscema. Do any pages or sequences featuring the Panther stand out for you?

ROY: They were all fun, but I enjoyed especially doing an almost solo Panther issue with Frank Giacoia [*see Avengers #73 – Ed.*] Frank, one of the best inkers in the business, always longed to become more of a penciler, but he was too slow and meticulous ever to pencil stories on a regular basis. Here he did a fine job; particularly noteworthy is one montage of Black Panther in which an actual dark leopard 'comes on little cat feet' at the top of the page. But it took Frank too long to draw and it was clear to both him and to us that he wouldn't be able to do two issues in a row.

SPOTLIGHT: During your run, you established the dichotomy in T'Challa's life that has influenced many writers since; depicting him as being torn between his homeland Wakanda and sense of responsibility as its ruler on the one hand, and his desire to serve the Earth as a hero and an Avenger and work as an inner city school teacher on the other. Do you think T'Challa could ever truly be happy with only one of these lives?

ROY: I suspect he's a Wakandan at heart. I was mostly interested in the angle of him being the African chieftain of a technological nation. Stan wanted the teacher bit. I wasn't so much interested in the idea of him being an inner city school teacher, though I guess it made a lot of sense. It just wasn't something that appealed to me personally. I liked that he was from a foreign land, as alien to us as Doctor Doom, but on the other side.

SPOTLIGHT: In recent years, during Christopher Priest's run on *Black Panther*, it was 'revealed' that the Panther joined the Avengers in order to spy on the American super team for his home nation of Wakanda. How well does that sit with your interpretation of the character?

ROY: Ridiculous. Some people can't leave well enough alone; I suppose you could make anything justified. I could come around and write a story how he was actually a double agent, he wasn't really spying. Anybody can do anything. Some ideas are better off resisted.

SPOTLIGHT: The Man-Ape, who you introduced as a rival to T'Challa's throne in *Avengers #62*, has been a thorn in his side for decades. What inspired his creation and design?

ROY: I told John to draw a big burly guy in a white ape outfit that didn't look silly... and of course John Buscema pulled it off magnificently. That story was plotted in five or ten minutes over the phone. We also used Klaw, and I remember Jack Kirby's statement at one time about Klaw being a kind of Ahab character. I remember him saying in his stories that the Black Panther was the white whale. He saw the Black Panther as being Moby Dick I guess and he drew this guy Klaw to look like Ahab the hunter.

SPOTLIGHT: Did you have to do a lot of research to put yourself in the head of an African chieftain?

ROY: I'd always had a little interest in Africa, but that was from reading *Tarzan* I think. I didn't do a lot of research. Had I been writing a regular book about Black Panther maybe, but remember most of our stories were either set in America or other worlds. I didn't really do much set in Africa. It was a continent I always wanted to visit though, and we did finally in 1994. We spent two or three weeks in Kenya on safari. That was a lot of fun, but we didn't run into any highly technological hidden civilizations. We saw leopards, cheetahs and lions, plenty of those, but no black panthers.

Thanks for chatting with us about Black Panther, Roy! It's been a blast to relive those great Avengers stories in Marvel Masterworks and Essentials volumes! ●

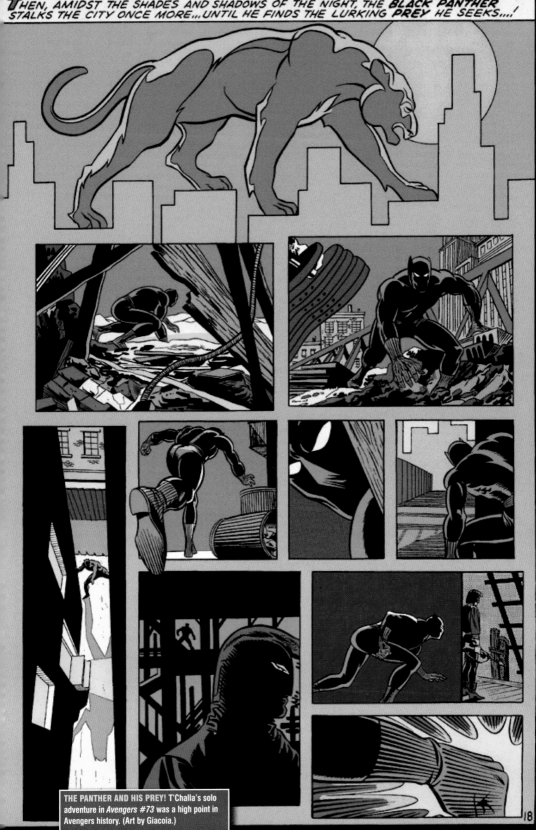

THEN, AMIDST THE SHADES AND SHADOWS OF THE NIGHT, THE **BLACK PANTHER** STALKS THE CITY ONCE MORE...UNTIL HE FINDS THE LURKING **PREY** HE SEEKS....!

THE PANTHER AND HIS PREY! T'Challa's solo adventure in *Avengers #73* was a high point in Avengers history. (Art by Giacoia.)

18

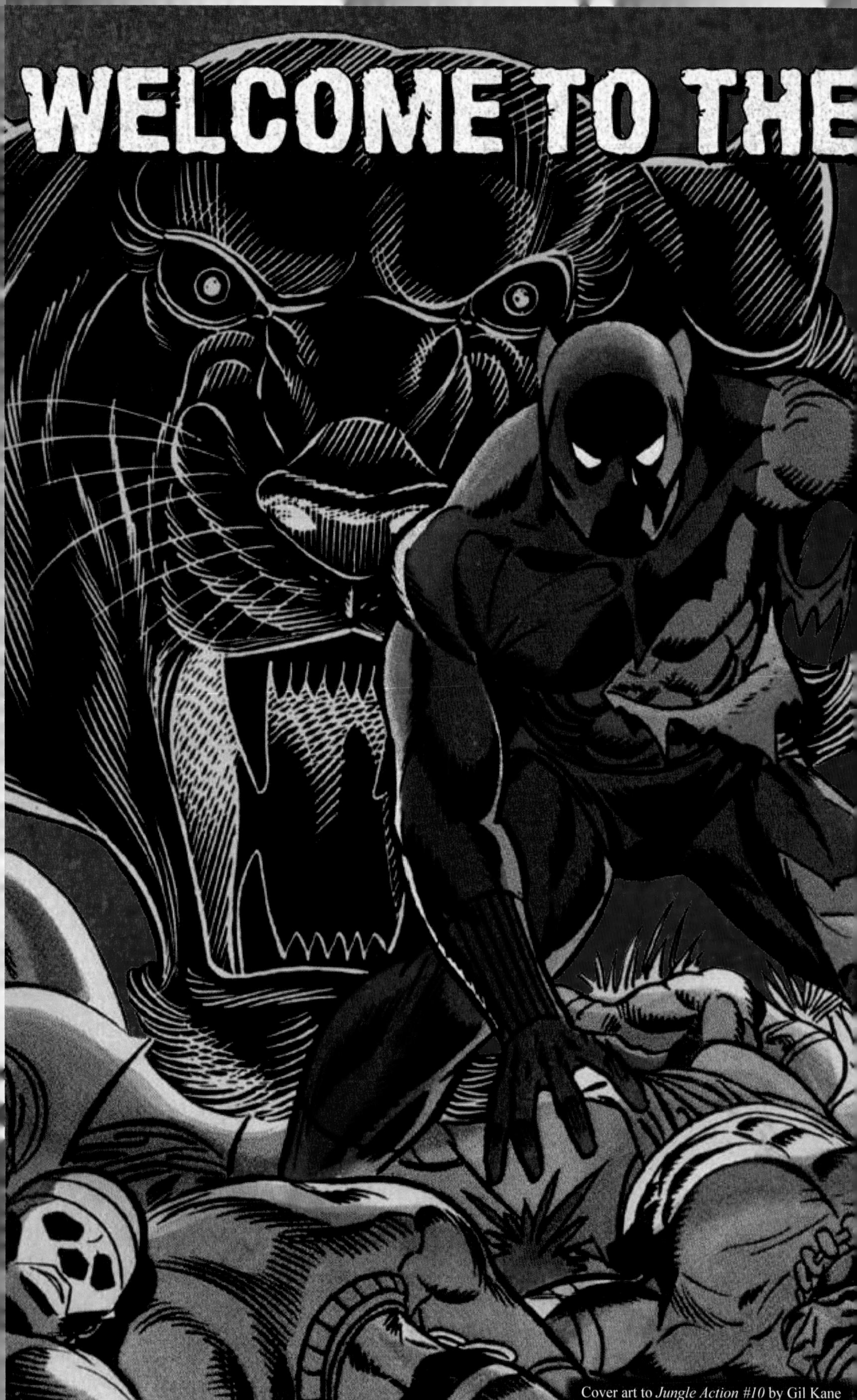
WELCOME TO THE

Cover art to *Jungle Action #10* by Gil Kane

JUNGLE

Don McGregor's Early '70s *Jungle Action* Served As The Panther's First Solo Series

By George Khoury

IN 1972, Marvel Comics relaunched *Jungle Action* as a bi-monthly series reprinting the vintage 1950's Atlas Comics title of the same name; the anthology featured the adventures of scantily dressed, B-level thrillseekers in the wilderness. As the naïve Atlas stories proved to be dated, the Marvel brass felt the time was right to finally have the Panther be a headliner and bestowed the series to the black super hero with issue #5, a reprint of the character's appearance in 1969's *Avengers* #62. With the sixth issue of *Jungle Action* (cover date September 1973,) there began a new age of Marvel Comics storytelling with a young writer and then-Marvel assistant editor named Don McGregor. With his first storyline "Panther's Rage," McGregor penned a strong, complex multi-issue drama that he fully wrote and envisioned as a single epic tale and thus Marvel's first true graphic novel.

Aided by the art of the late Billy Graham, Rich Buckler and others, Don McGregor helped evolve the Marvel method of writing by adding a higher degree of dramatic weight and sophisticated maturity. His Panther stories appealed to a readership looking for a comic that would enrapture them with an epic flair. Since *Jungle Action* was a low editorial priority and a meager seller, it allowed the author and the book's artists enough room to experiment and earn a devoted fan base as it broke new ground in mainstream comics. The Black Panther's stories were tales that portrayed T'Challa as more than a mere cutout super hero, but as a man of great virtue and a leader facing many realistic hurdles trying to lead the people of Wakanda, his nation.

In the thirteen part "Panther's Rage" (*Jungle Action #6-18*), T'Challa faced off with the unrelenting Erik Killmonger, a Wakanda native who wanted the crown for himself. Erik even convinces some of his fellow countrymen that he is the better choice to reign over them since T'Challa is always away from his people and apparently more interested in the ways of the "white colonialist" than their own culture. Throughout each issue of the comic novella, Panther battles an array of Killmonger's soldiers while confronting the problems his citizens and nation must confront together. "Panther vs. Klan," the subsequent saga (*Black Panther #19-24*) dealt head on with the controversial issues of race and the Ku Klux Klan. (With Jack Kirby's return to Marvel in 1976, *Jungle Action* ended midway into the Klan storyline with issue #24 and a farewell letter from the ambitious writer as the title wrapped up to make way for the release of Kirby's 1977 *Black Panther* #1.)

Years later, McGregor would return to script T'Challa in two new sagas: "Panther's Quest" (serialized in the original *Marvel Comics Presents* series) and "Panther's Prey" (a prestige limited series). The *Jungle Action* stories captivated legions of fan, including future creators like Dwayne McDuffie and Christopher Priest. Also evident is the powerful inspiration the book provided to the successful 2005's *Black Panther* series initiated by writer Reginald Hudlin and artist John Romita Jr. In this long and winding road, the pioneering *Jungle Action* title not only made the character socially relevant, but also demonstrated that the Black Panther was a king deserving of his regal title with a bright future amongst the mightiest heroes of the Marvel Universe. ●

PANTHER BY PRIEST

WEDDING HEROIC INTRIGUE WITH SLY, MODERN HUMOR, CHRISTOPHER PRIEST AND BLACK PANTHER WERE A MARVEL KNIGHTS MARRIAGE MADE IN HEAVEN BY JESS HARROLD

"THE *WEST WING* IN A KITTY SUIT." THAT'S HOW WRITER CHRISTOPHER Priest has described his 62-issue stretch on *Black Panther,* the character's longest running series to date. And it became the kind of book that fans of the television drama set at the White House would be at home with – a super-hero book unlike any other. Packed with political intrigue, densely written dialogue, intricately woven plot threads, and non-linear storytelling that kept you guessing until each big reveal, Priest's *Black Panther* was an intelligent book that richly rewarded the attentive reader. Yet at the same time, the title shamelessly brought the funny right from the first page, which introduced Panther's everyman government attaché, Everett K. Ross, and the saga of his stolen pants. Ushered in as one of the inaugural books of the Marvel Knights line, it was presided over by editors Joe Quesada and Jimmy Palmiotti and stood alongside books including Kevin Smith's *Daredevil* and Paul Jenkins' *Inhumans.* Over the next five years, Priest's *Black Panther* would transform T'Challa's role in the Marvel Universe and, in particular, in the Avengers. *Spotlight* asked Priest to dust off the kitty suit, and take a look back at his time on *Black Panther.*

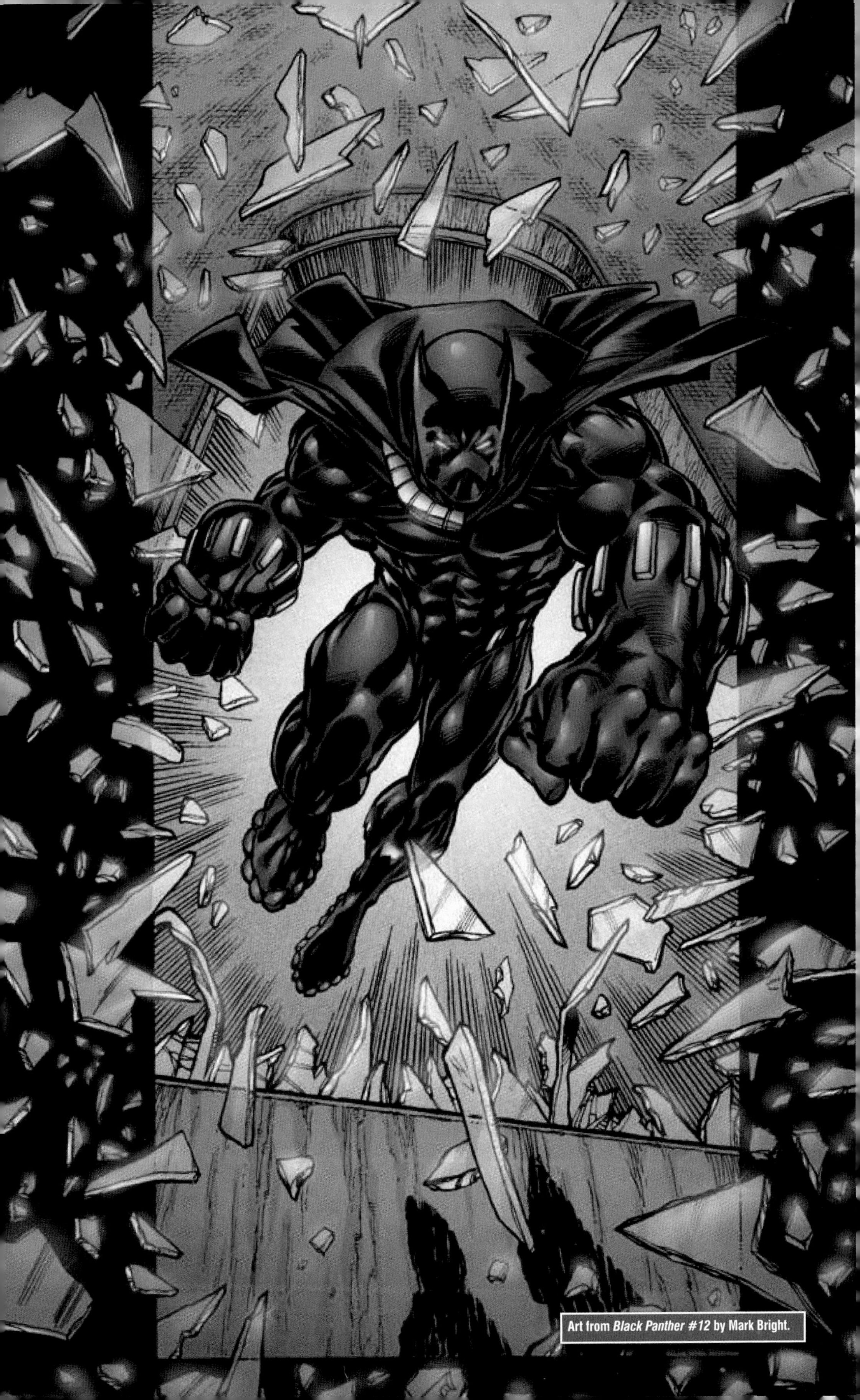

Art from *Black Panther #12* by Mark Bright.

SPOTLIGHT: What was your take on Black Panther as a character when you first launched your run?

PRIEST: I thought he was boring. When I got the call from Joe Quesada, I foolishly assumed he was calling to offer me *Daredevil*. When he said *'Black Panther,'* my heart sank. Joe and Jimmy Palmiotti tag-teamed me with their concept – a riff on the Eddie Murphy film, *Coming To America*. I never liked Panther because he made no sense to me: This powerful king of an advanced nation, a guy with, essentially, below-Captain America strength, who out-witted and beat up the Fantastic Four. Over the years, it seemed like Panther was always an also-ran, standing in the back row of the Avengers – I couldn't imagine why Roy Thomas even put him in the group. Then, over in his own book, Panther got beat up by kids – kids! – lynched and dragged and so forth. I didn't want to write *that* guy.

I got the comedic aspects Joe and Jimmy were pitching, but I was still reluctant. If I was gonna do Panther, I'd have to do him my way. He'd have to stop being the punk of the Marvel Universe. We'd have to go back to the source material, *Fantastic Four #52*. I'd write *that* guy, the guy who *beat* the FF. My take on Panther was simple: He was the most shrewd guy in the Marvel Universe. Additionally, it was important to write him as an African. Over the

years, it seemed to me writers had imbued Panther with American sensitivities, which seemed real wrong to me. I am good friends with a family of Nigerians. I'm sure they love me, but I also get the sense I am more or less tolerated. Their sensibilities are not American, and a lot of what we Americans do frankly disgust them.

Lastly, I've been writing comics for thirty years, and for thirty years I've been passed over to write Batman. I decided to make Panther my own Batman. Only he was a lot more ruthless than Batman, and maybe a tad smarter. Once Mark Texeira and Joe Quesada (who provided layouts on the early issues) began to bring Panther to life, I began to see possibilities with the character. We darkened Panther up quite a bit, which delighted the Marvel Knights crew, making him a kind of evil creature of the night. We played against type and against the expectations that Panther would get beat up every month. I think I only allowed Panther to get beat up once in the entire run (and that was because he was trying not to harm the psycho Dora Milaje, who became the villain Malice).

SPOTLIGHT: To that end, you and artist Mark Texeira introduced a Black Panther with a slightly bolder wardrobe, and a few more tricks up his sleeve. What inspired those changes?

PRIEST: Y'know, I got more grief over the handful of little upgrades we gave Panther... Panther 'purists' whined intensely about the bullet proof costume and the Kimoyo card and the claws. Honestly, so far as I was concerned, I didn't consider any of that to be upgrades to any arsenal. It all seemed like reasonable and com-

A BAD DUDE: Black Panther, that is. Priest wrote him as a cat totally able to take on heavyweights like Mephisto. (Art from *BP #4* by Mark Texeira.)

DORA MILAJE: Priest added the sleek, sexy personal guard to the Panther lexicon. Sample dialogue: "We did not kill them, my lord. There were, however, many injuries." (Art from *BP #2* by Texeira.)

"My take on Panther was simple: He was the most shrewd guy in the Marvel Universe." – PRIEST

mon sense gear, real basic stuff, like an iPhone. I had no idea I'd touch off this storm of protest, to which I replied, "Well, where were you guys when Marvel was cancelling this book?" How dare this genius scientist carry an iPhone? He should stick to the tribal ways! Which was ridiculous - Stan wrote him as a gadget guy. He's always been a gadget guy. I mean, isn't this the guy who designed Falcon's wings? But he should be stumbling around the jungle with a bone through his nose? Enough with that nonsense already.

SPOTLIGHT: Your *Panther* run is very densely written, adding layers of political and economic intrigue not often seen in mainstream superhero comics, as well as addressing racial themes in an honest way. Characters such as Queen Divine Justice are very different from the way African-Americans are often depicted in comics. Do you think *Black Panther* is uniquely suited to that kind of story? Did launching the title under the Marvel Knights banner give you greater freedom to do something readers hadn't seen before?

PRIEST: Undoubtedly. Joe and Jimmy were interested in finding new ground for all of their titles. My thinking was, if this guy is a king, he should be dealing with political issues. Moreover, he needed to confound the expectations of friend and foe alike. It was more than a

race thing – white people being uncomfortable around blacks – it was a cultural difference, Panther understanding American culture much better than the Avengers understood African culture.

Queenie was just me goofing around. I have this little niece that I adore and I tend to write her into everything. She was Queen Divine Justice in *Panther*.

SPOTLIGHT: You also used, particularly in the beginning, a non-linear form of storytelling, with story threads coming together gradually, sometimes over several issues. Looking back, how well do you think this worked, both artistically, and commercially?

PRIEST: Mark Bright and I started doing that over at Acclaim Comics on *Quantum & Woody*, and Joe Q loved it. We actually lampooned *Panther* in Quantum & Woody during our *Dark Kitty* arc, wherein Woody wants to sue Marvel for copyright infringement. We had Jimmy and Joe show up in a cameo, and *Panther* editor Ruben Diaz actually, literally, joined the cast for a few issues. I turned in the first issue script for *Panther*, and Joe and Jimmy rejected it. I felt like I'd crashed and burned. They got on a conference call and said, 'No, do that *Quantum & Woody* riff with

WIND RIDER IN WAKANDA: T'Challa's future bride made a stirring guest appearance in Priest's *BP #25-27*. (Art by Sal Velluto and Bob Almond.)

the out-of-sequence storytelling!' Their problem with the original *Black Panther* #1 was that it was too straight – too much of what the audience would expect from a *Black Panther* #1.

I think sometimes (this device) worked, sometimes it didn't. As with anyone doing a long run, sometimes we hit it out of the park, sometimes we choked. What I will say is, between Joe and Jimmy, then Ruben Diaz, Tom Brevoort and Mike Marts, I was always encouraged to try new things. Sometimes we fell on our face, but we were out there swinging. The main problem with it wasn't the density or the out of sequence storytelling, it was the drips and drabs of story released every four weeks. As a trade, in one sitting, you can read three or four of these and it's a lot less confusing.

SPOTLIGHT: A key character you introduced was Everett K Ross, T'Challa's government attaché. Did you think it was vital to bring in a 'point of view' character for the average comic book guy, whose life experiences almost certainly differ greatly from the warrior monarch of a technologically advanced African nation?

PRIEST: I thought it was in our best interest to deal with fan reluctance and audience expectation head-on, and told Jimmy and Joe that in our first conversations. I didn't have Ross yet, but I knew there had to be a point of view character. I think I was watching *Spin City* and the thought of a Michael J. Fox-type character just made sense to me; of course the State Department would assign someone to T'Challa. I just made the State Department guy the voice of the average fan skeptic who'd assume the book would suck and Panther would get beat up every month The reason those early issues were funny was precisely those reader expectations; that Ross gave voice to them, and

Panther exploded every one of them – like just walking through the door and decking Mephisto.

SPOTLIGHT: As well as Mephisto, your Panther went toe-to-toe with heavyweights including Namor, Doom, Iron-Man and Magneto. Do you think T'Challa should be a major player in the Marvel Universe?

PRIEST: I'm not sure why nobody ever did that before. They always wrote Panther as this passive guy who'd hang back and point, saying, 'Look! A big scaly monster!' and then Thor would go beat up the monster. My Panther wouldn't say a word. He'd just vanish from the room and next thing you know, he's standing over the defeated monster. Several times I had Ross on his cell phone, trying to call the Avengers, while Panther just brushes past him, saying, 'Why?' It was interesting having his super-hero buddies criticize his decisions, which was really arrogant on their part: The Avengers seeing Panther as their buddy while forgetting he is the ruler of a sovereign land and doesn't owe anybody any explanations. Panther is a bad dude. He don't need no stinkin' Avengers. Nothing I did was new or original: I was writing the same guy Stan wrote in *FF #4*. The exact same guy. [*The audacious Namor, the Sub-Mariner, natch! – Ed.*] The fan reaction: "How dare he not get beat up! Priest sucks!" One thing I enjoyed was Panther stealing Stark Enterprises with a phone call, and my favorite line was Henry Peter Gyrich asking Iron Man - who'd just been defeated by, essentially, a non-powered punk - "Excuse me, aren't you supposed to be the *Invincible* Iron Man...?

SPOTLIGHT: There were heavy political overtones to your Panther stories. What was your thinking in that regard?

PRIEST: My thinking was, if this guy is a king, he should be dealing with political issues. I'd edited and later wrote *Conan the King* for Marvel, where we took the barbarian Cimmerian and domesticated him, kind of a homicidal Fred Flintstone. The conflicts revolved around the fact Conan thought it'd be a hoot to be king, but didn't realize all the paperwork involved. Panther intrinsically understood his role as king and embraced it, but the conflicts around him needed to be political. Moreover, he needed to confound the expectations of friend and foe alike.

SPOTLIGHT: Your Panther is also the "man with the plan": charismatic, calculating and downright cool. Is there a real-life T'Challa walking around somewhere that you drew inspiration from?

PRIEST: Denys Cowan and Dwayne McDuffie. The cool edge of Cowan, the scary smarts of McDuffie. Panther's speech pattern and general demeanor were borrowed from my dear father, the late Abi Afonja, a brilliantly wise Nigerian college professor and close friend. The problem with T'Challa being "the man with the plan" was it used to infuriate me when, every time, the audience would assume I'd somehow lost my mind having Panther do these odd things. I mean, every time, you'd have two or three issues of T'Challa being devious, or things apparently not going his way, and then you'd see the final issue and all the mousetraps would snap shut, revealing how Panther had been two steps ahead of the game all along. I mean, I did it so many times it should have been cliché. But, nooooo, every story arc I'd get hate mail

SPOTLIGHT: Your Wakanda was a more fully-realized society than has often been the case in *Panther* stories. Was it important for you to make the culture as believable as possible?

PRIEST: Oh, sure, but I need to stress my Wakanda was Don McGregor's Wakanda. Period. I don't think I changed a thing. I used his map, and I tried to be faithful to his brilliant work. Of course, every artist will realize the place differently, but Don did the heavy lifting so far as Wakanda is concerned. Don also established the internal conflicts in Wakanda. Joe and Jimmy wanted T'Challa's bodyguards to be Tyra Banks and Naomi Campbell. I wanted to give him the female bodyguards in a way that made sense while also building internal conflict. McGregor's wonderful work provided great opportunities for that.

I also kept most if not all of Don's supporting cast, and kept most if not all of their continuity and backstory intact – these are the same guys. They recall events from Don's stories, and those events have shaped who they were in my stories.

SPOTLIGHT: You combined the "real-world" elements and mature storytelling with a great respect for Panther continuity, even including fantastical elements such as King Solomon's time-bending frogs. Which earlier treatments of the character were most influential on your run?

EARTH'S MIGHTIEST: Priest deftly exploited natural tensions between the Avengers and the Wakandan monarch. (Art from *BP #7* by Joe Jusko.)

"**The Avengers (saw) Panther as their buddy while forgetting he is the ruler of a sovereign land and doesn't owe anybody any explanations. Panther is a bad dude. He don't need no stinkin' Avengers.**"

– PRIEST, SIZING UP T'CHALLA'S ROYAL STATURE

PRIEST: I have enormous respect for Don, who carried the water for Panther for a very long time. He was likely the only writer who was truly invested in the character for years and years.

Don's work, so far as I was concerned, was canon. To me, half the fun of writing super heroes is dealing with the continuity. I enjoy all the toys in the box. I enjoy working the puzzle, dealing with the history. It's true the weight of that history can become cumbersome, though. I was determined to find a way to explain

the odd Kirby run (which introduced the frogs). I think, no, I'm sure, our *Enemy of the State II* arc was one of our best and one of our worst. Best because Sal Velluto and Bob Almond just killed on it. I mean, they bled on those pages. *Enemy II* was also our worst in that, if you weren't a fan of the book, you'd have no freaking clue what was going on. Why there were two Panthers, why one was wacky and, *gasp*, dancing. It'd be as if Adam West showed up in the Christian Bale movie in costume, dancing the Batusi.

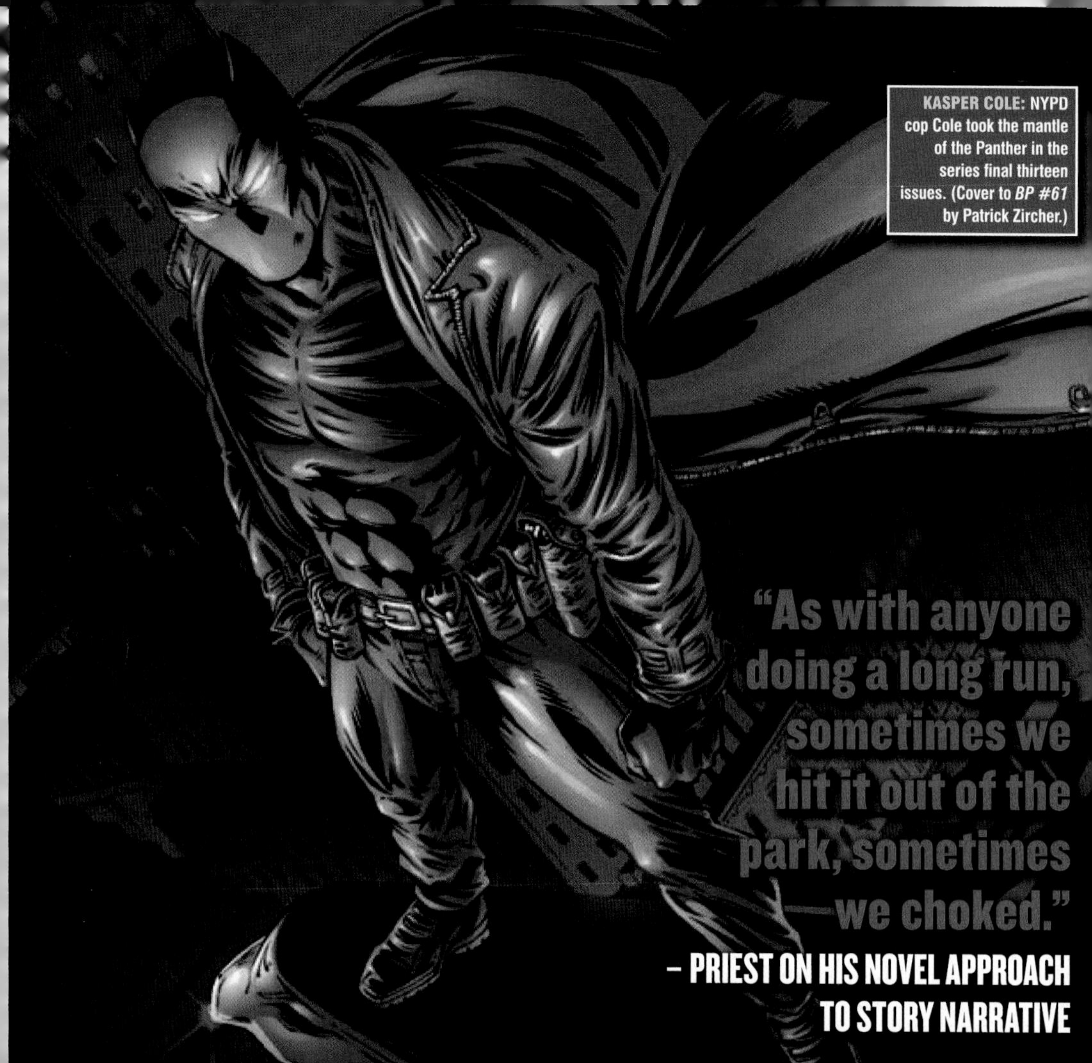

KASPER COLE: NYPD cop Cole took the mantle of the Panther in the series final thirteen issues. (Cover to *BP #61* by Patrick Zircher.)

"As with anyone doing a long run, sometimes we hit it out of the park, sometimes we choked."

– PRIEST ON HIS NOVEL APPROACH TO STORY NARRATIVE

SPOTLIGHT: One key event in Black Panther's life that you put a controversial spin on was his decision to join the Avengers. You revealed this had been part of a spying mission for his native Wakanda, a story that drove a wedge between T'Challa and his former allies. Did it always strike you as odd that he would leave his homeland for life as an American super hero?

PRIEST: It made absolutely no sense. Neither did his stint as a school teacher. I was just trying not to say Roy Thomas' *Avengers* didn't happen. Roy is a national treasure, and I have enormous respect for his talents. His *Avengers* absolutely did happen, and I needed to deal with it in a way that reconciled the history without violating the character. I was unprepared for the uproar, though – that kind of took me by surprise. But, there they were – hundreds of fans who don't buy the book complaining about it.

SPOTLIGHT: Lastly, if you had the time again, is there anything you'd do differently in your approach to the book?

PRIEST: I'd make the stories simpler. I was always asking the reader to invest a little in the story – to think. My major complaint about comic fans was they'd come home from the store with a stack of comics and start ripping through them. Well, you can't rip through *Panther*. I mean, you can, but you'll miss half of what's there. You really needed to work at it a little. I came along during the nine-panel grid days of Jim Shooter, where we gave the reader more bang for the buck. The pictures now are glorious, but either the reader attention span has seriously waned, or somehow we've convinced ourselves we can't cover much ground in 22 pages. As a reader, I liked the density of Frank Miller's seminal work. I am no Frank Miller (much to my horror), but I liked that *Daredevil* and *Dark Knight Returns* and so forth were seriously dense reads, such that, when you finally got to the big double-splash, Frank had earned it: There was real story construction, real depth there. I think we could keep the whole '*The West Wing* with spandex' idea and still make it more accessible. I actually hadn't seen the *The West Wing* until we were done with our series. As complex as the show is, they strive to encapsulate things so new arrivals can get in. In retrospect, I think our series became way too inbred – fun for those who were along for the ride, but perplexing for new arrivals.

The first 12 issues of Priest's Panther saga are available in two trade paperbacks: BLACK PANTHER: THE CLIENT TPB and BLACK PANTHER: ENEMY OF THE STATE TPB. Featuring art by Mark Texeira, Mike Manley and Joe Jusko, they represent some of the most cutting edge comics of the Marvel Knights revival! ●

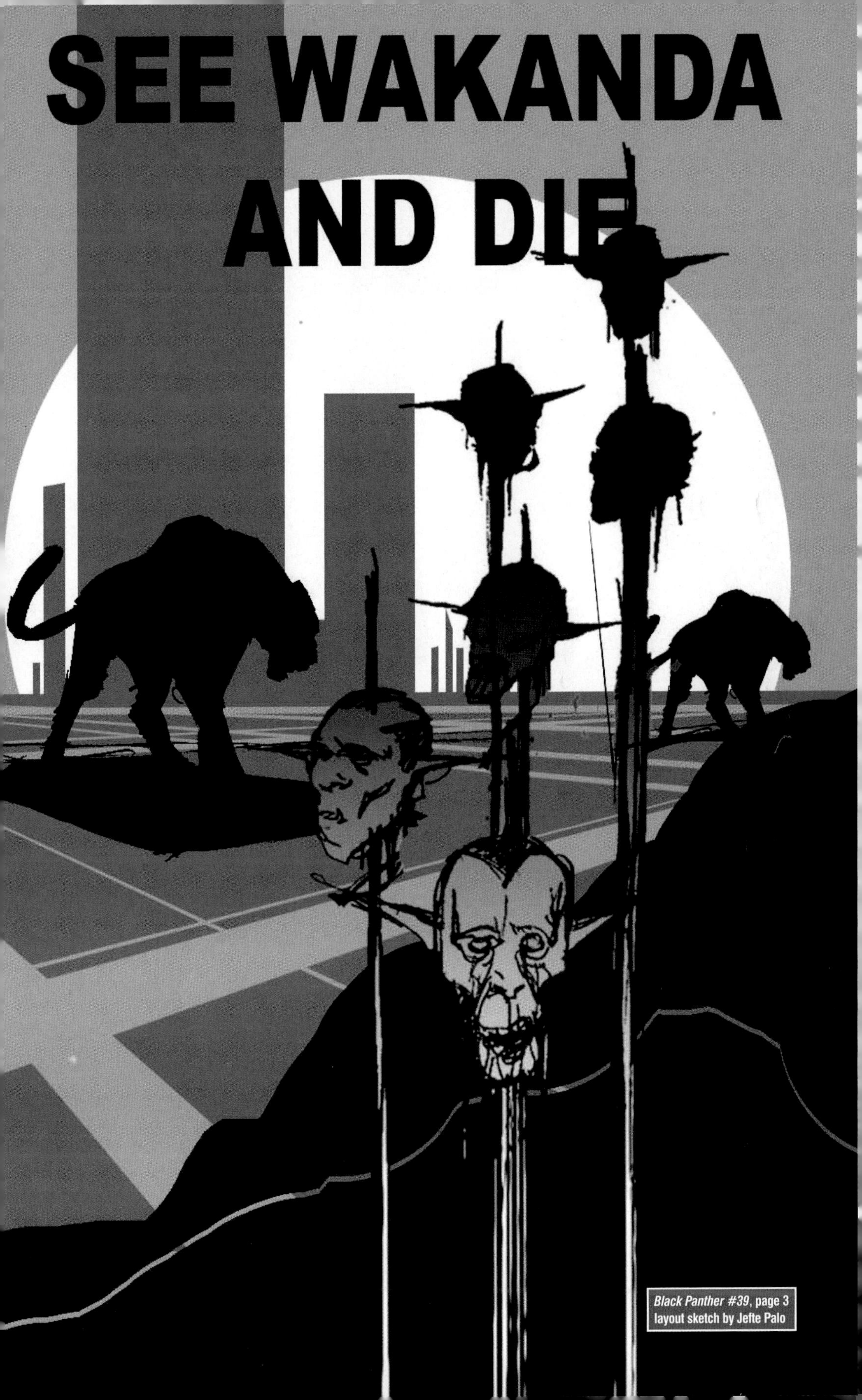
SEE WAKANDA
AND DIE

Black Panther #39, page 3
layout sketch by Jefte Palo

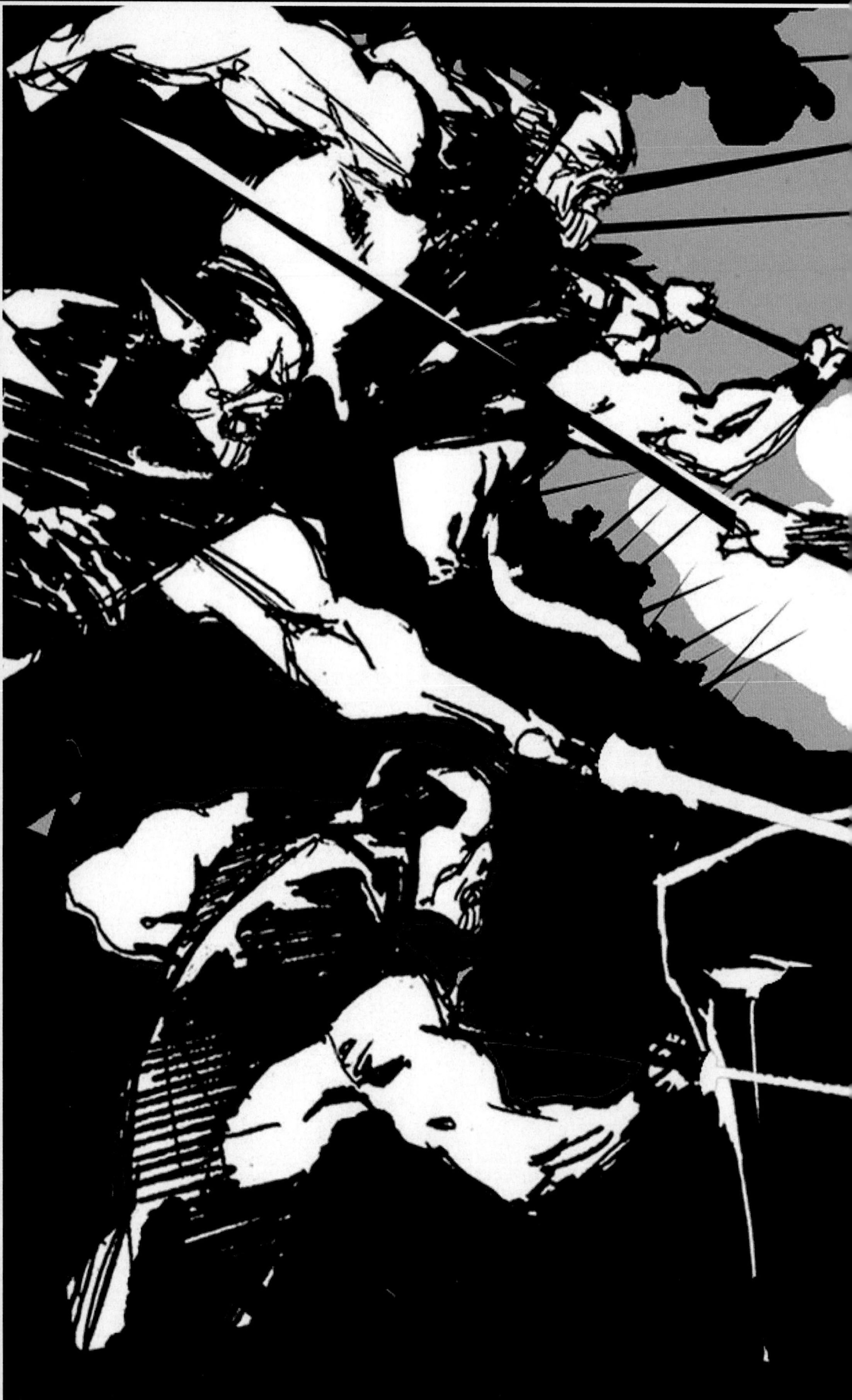

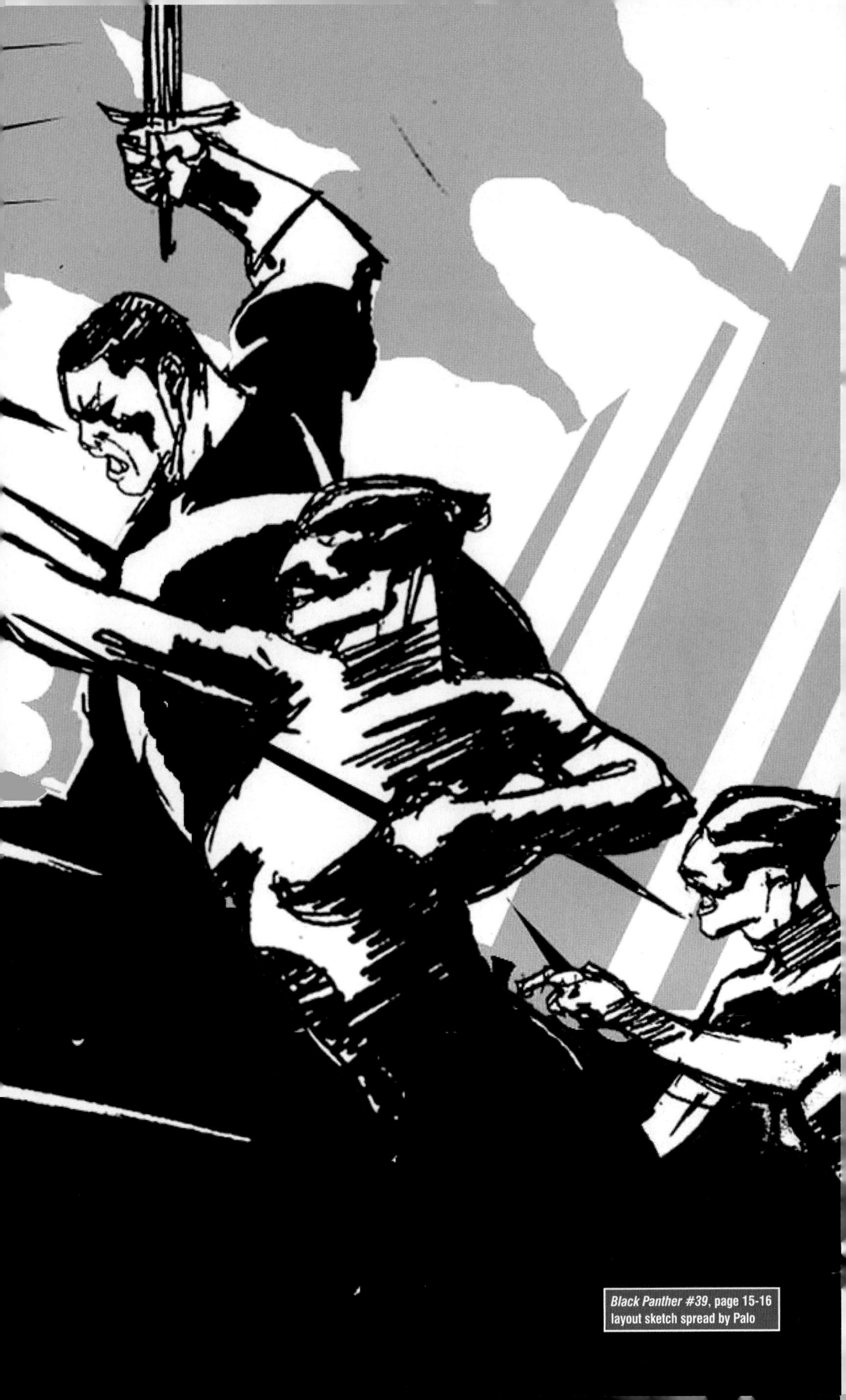

Black Panther #39, page 15-16 layout sketch spread by Palo

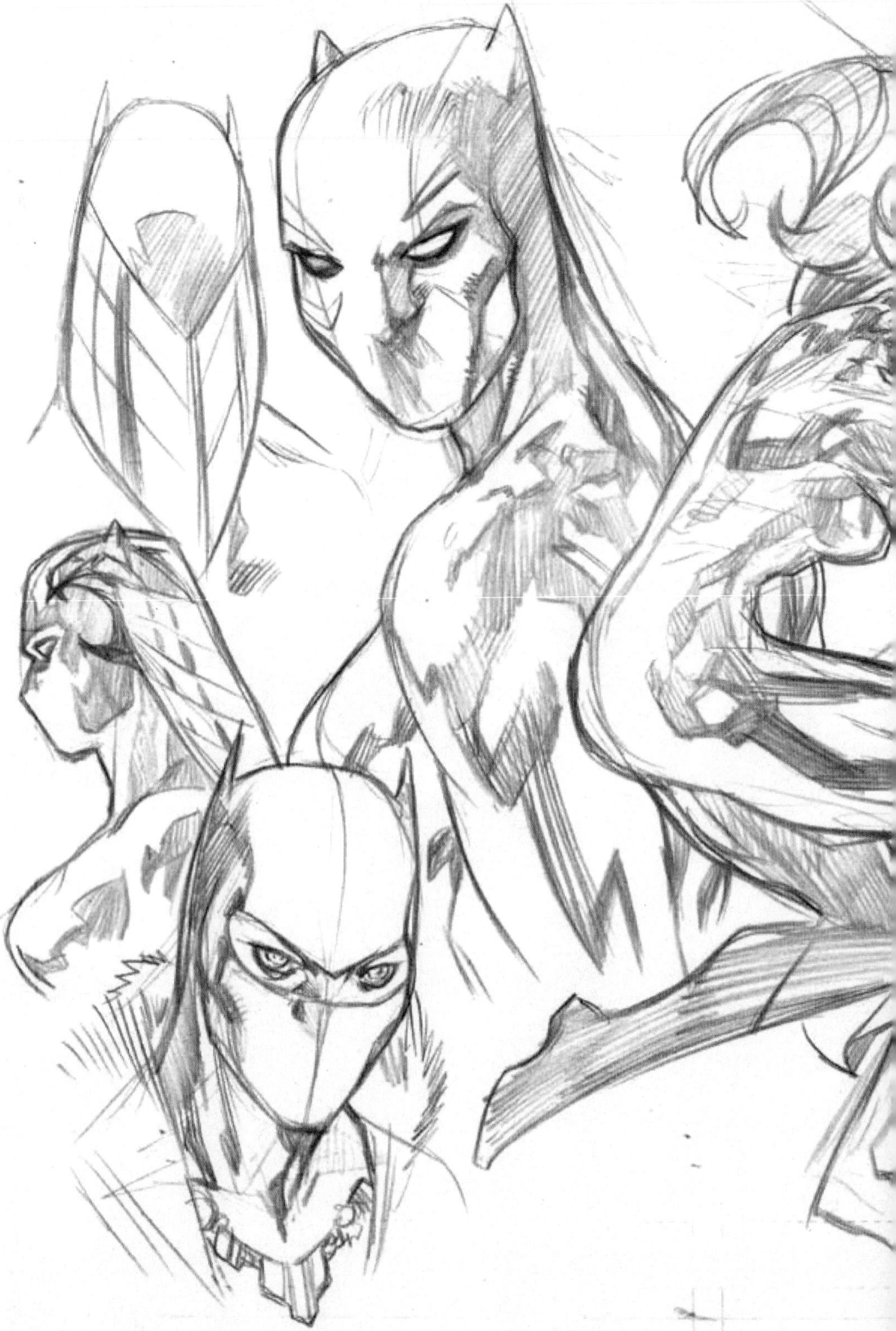

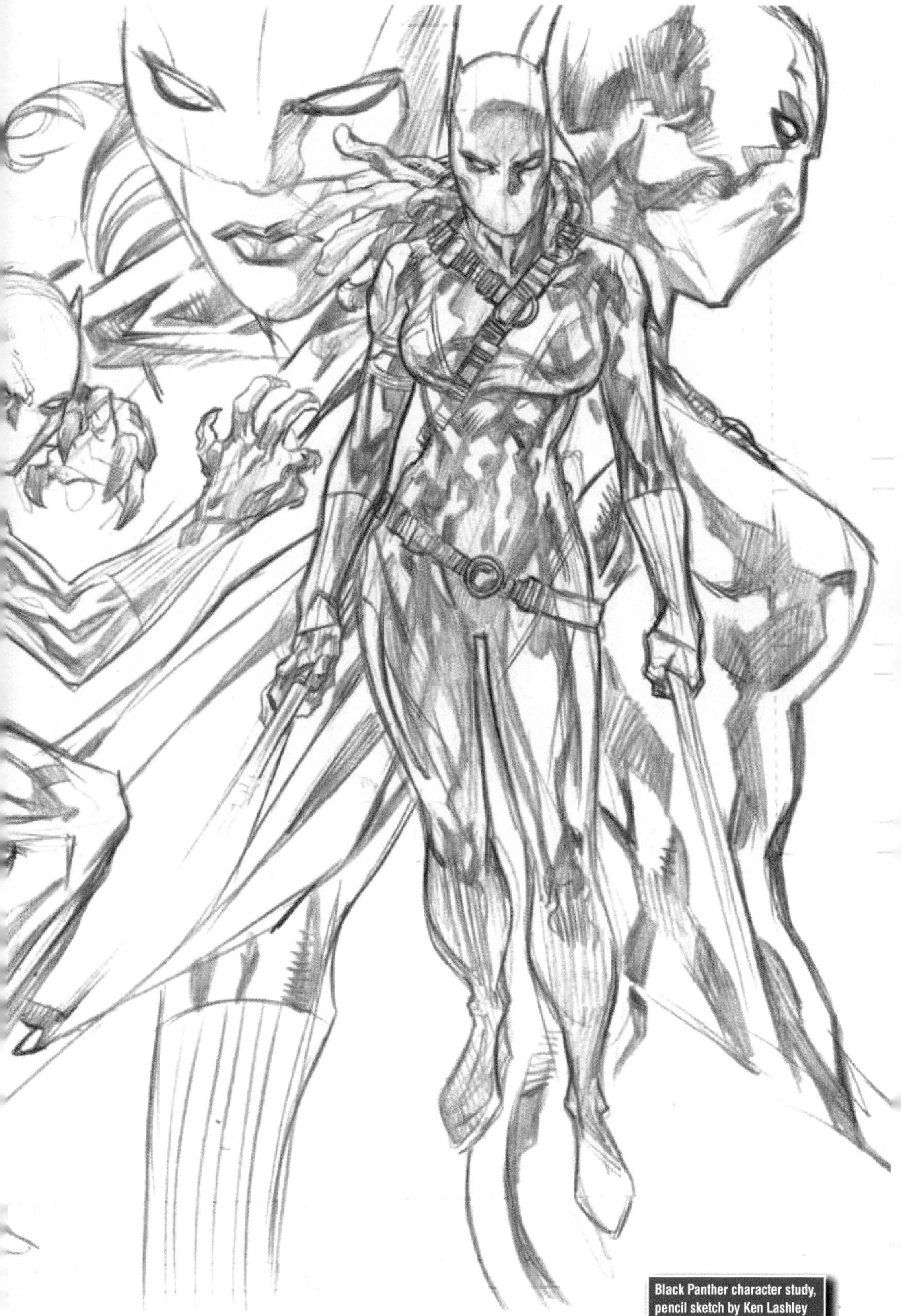

Black Panther character study, pencil sketch by Ken Lashley

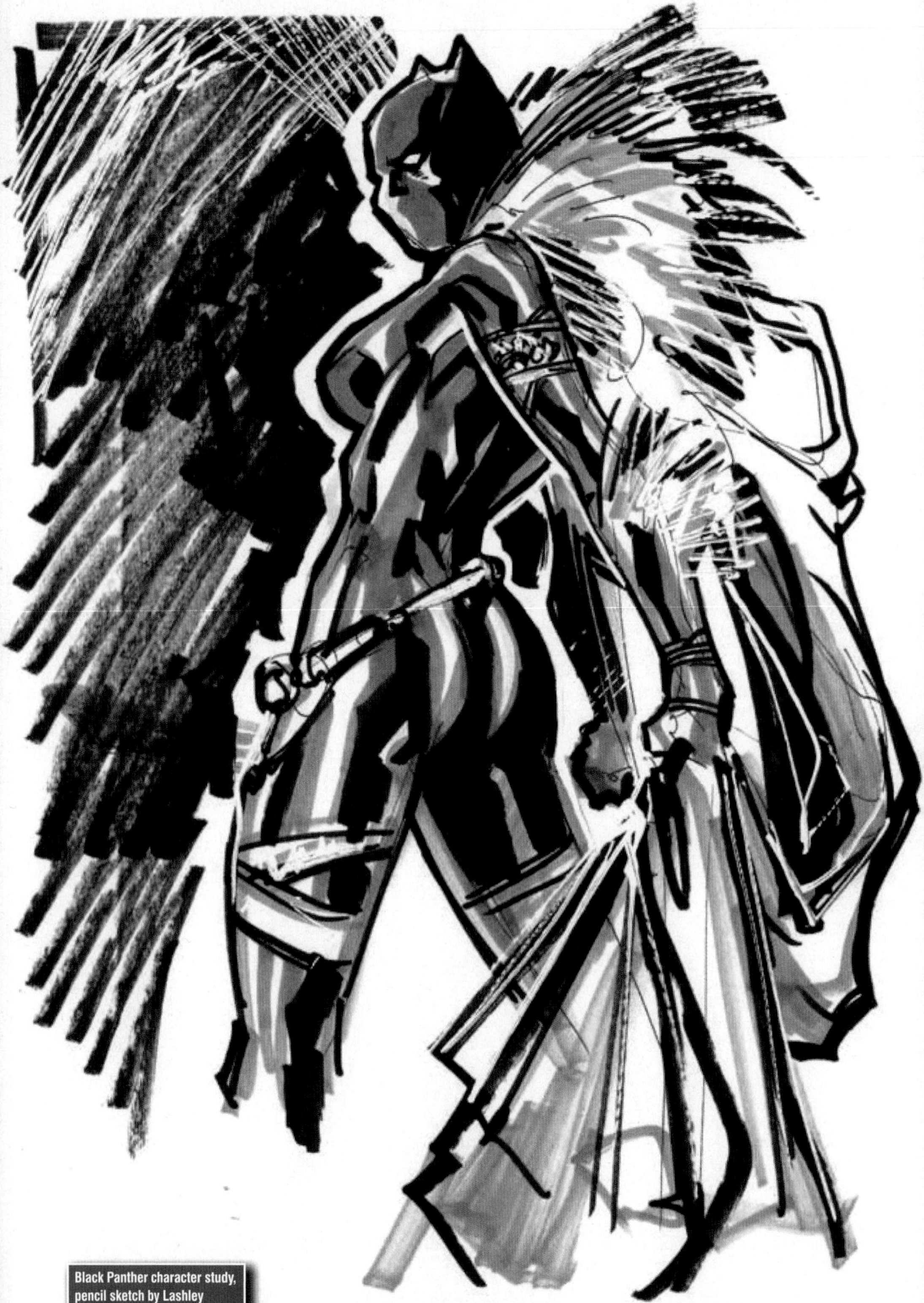

Black Panther character study,
pencil sketch by Lashley

PROMOTIONAL IMAGES FOR THE 2009 *BLACK PANTHER* RELAUNCH. ART BY KEN LASHLEY, PAUL NEARY & PAUL MOUNTS, AND J. SCOTT CAMPBELL & EDGAR DELGADO

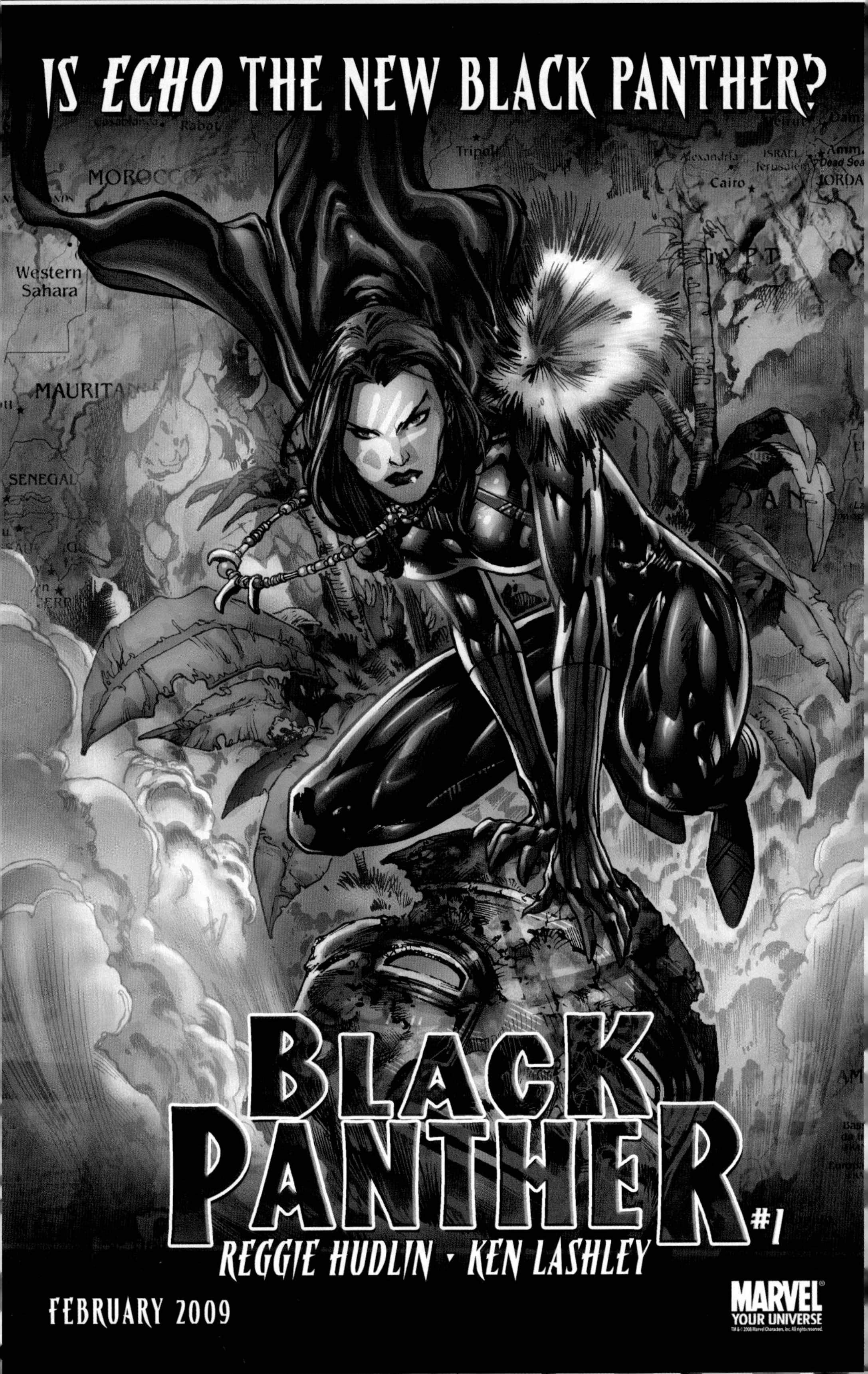

IS *ECHO* THE NEW BLACK PANTHER?
MOROCCO
Western Sahara
Tripoli
Alexandria
Cairo
BLACK PANTHER #1
REGGIE HUDLIN · KEN LASHLEY
FEBRUARY 2009
MARVEL YOUR UNIVERSE

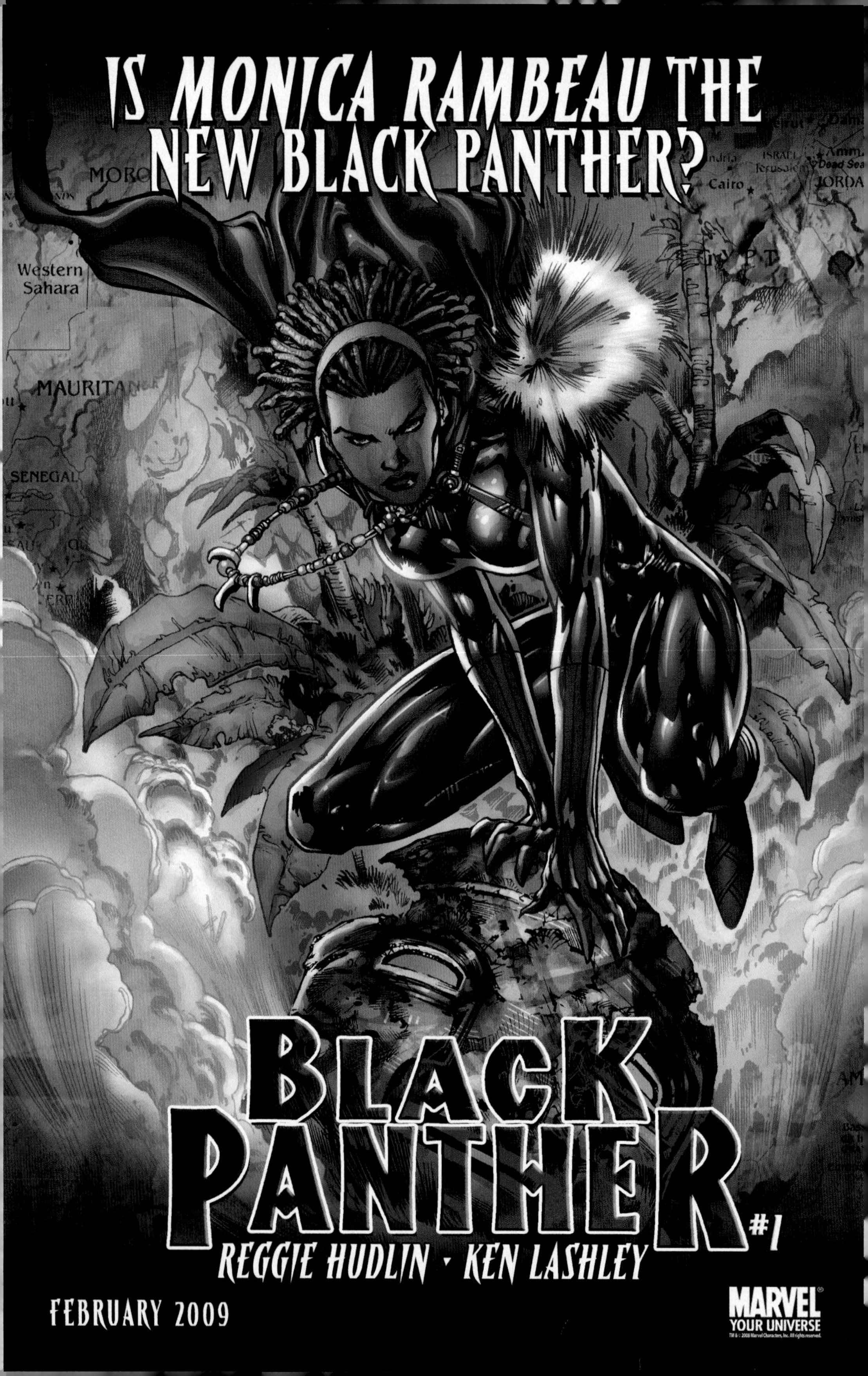
IS MONICA RAMBEAU THE NEW BLACK PANTHER?
Western Sahara
MAURITA
SENEGAL
Cairo
BLACK PANTHER #1
REGGIE HUDLIN · KEN LASHLEY
FEBRUARY 2009
MARVEL YOUR UNIVERSE
TM & © 2008 Marvel Characters, Inc. All rights reserved.

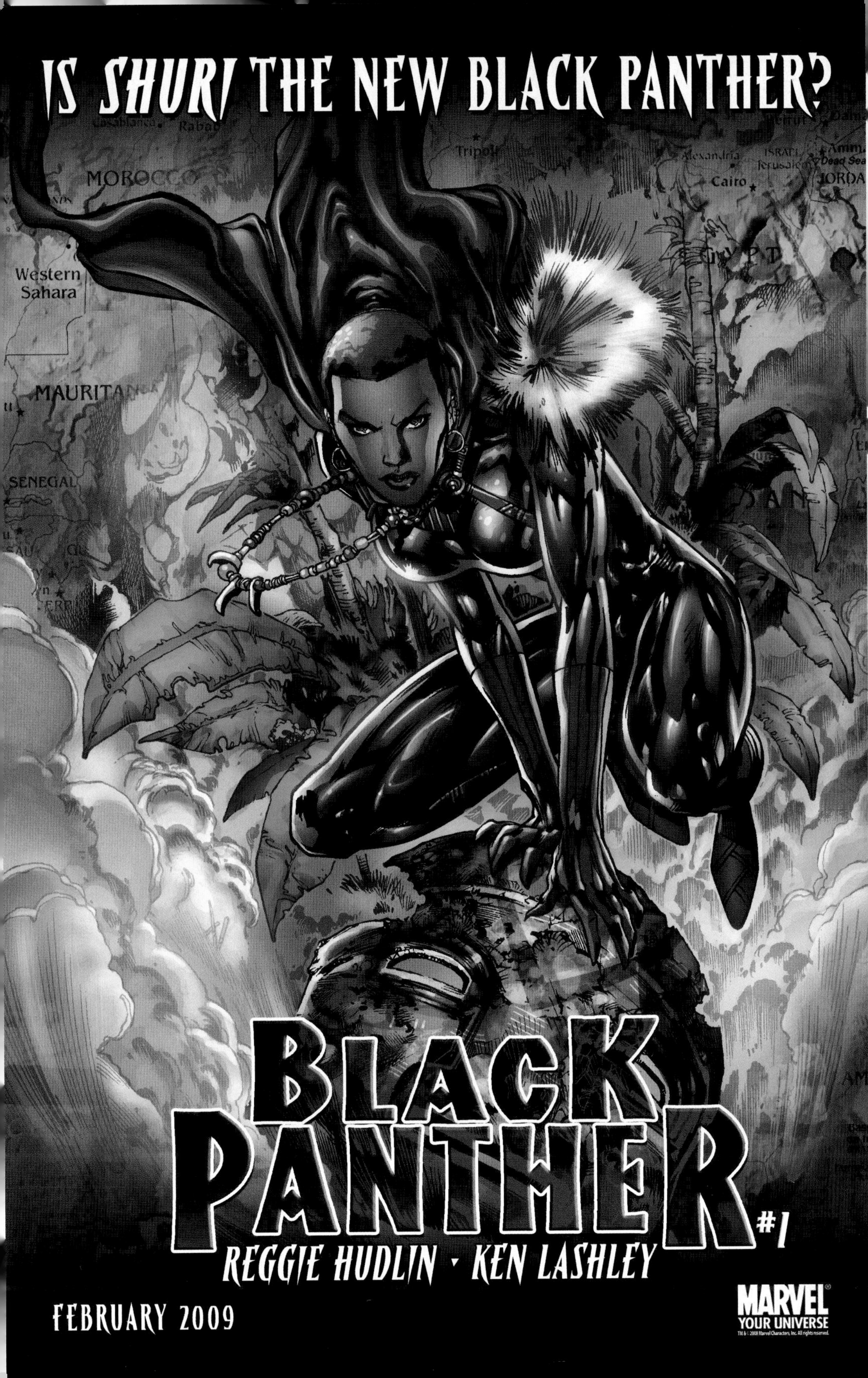
IS SHURI THE NEW BLACK PANTHER?
MOROCCO
Western Sahara
SENEGAL
Tripoli
Alexandria
Cairo
Dead Sea
BLACK PANTHER #1
REGGIE HUDLIN · KEN LASHLEY
FEBRUARY 2009
MARVEL
YOUR UNIVERSE
TM & © 2008 Marvel Characters, Inc. All rights reserved.

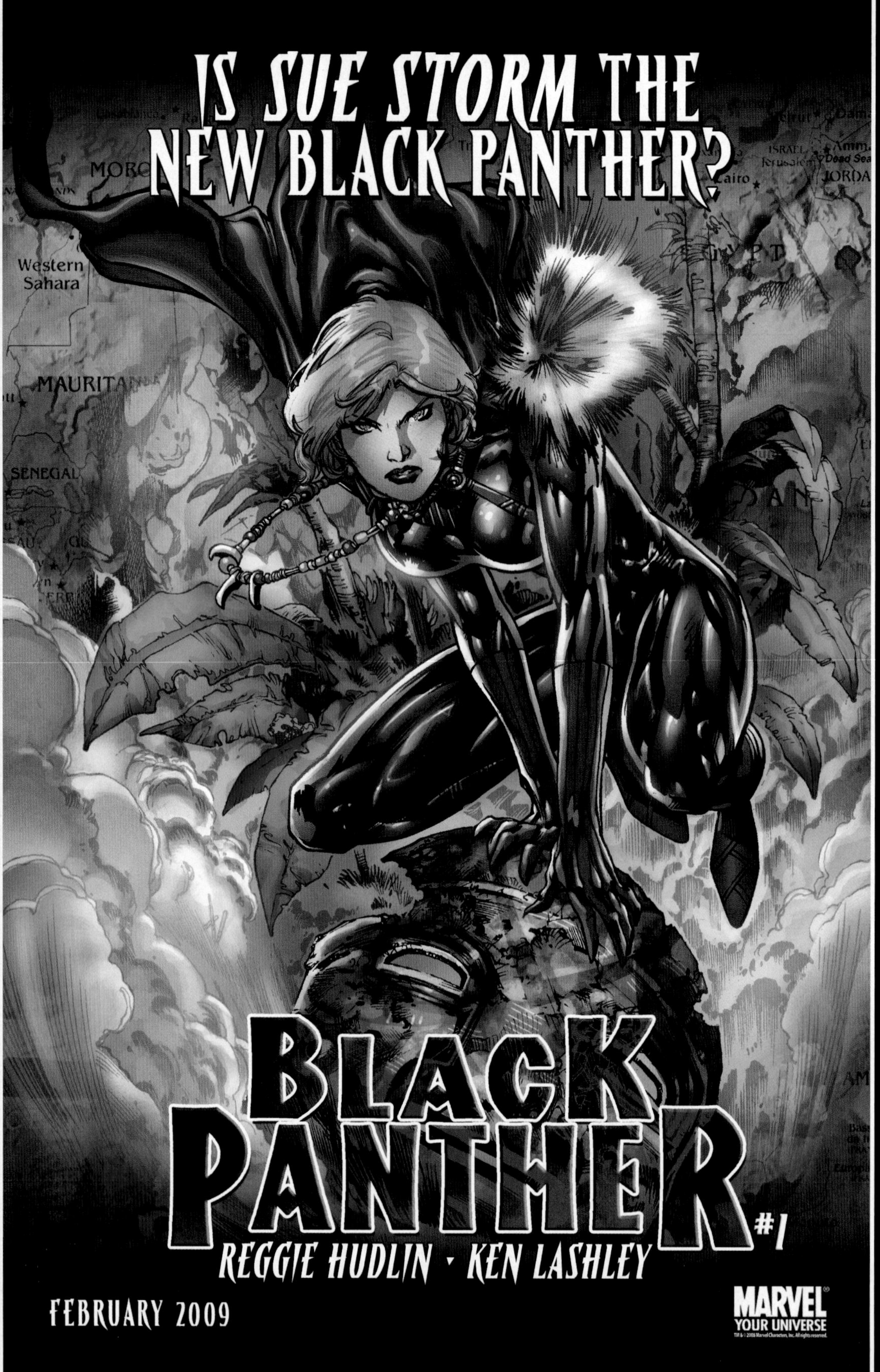
IS SUE STORM THE
NEW BLACK PANTHER?
Western Sahara
SENEGAL
BLACK
PANTHER
#1
REGGIE HUDLIN · KEN LASHLEY
FEBRUARY 2009
MARVEL
YOUR UNIVERSE

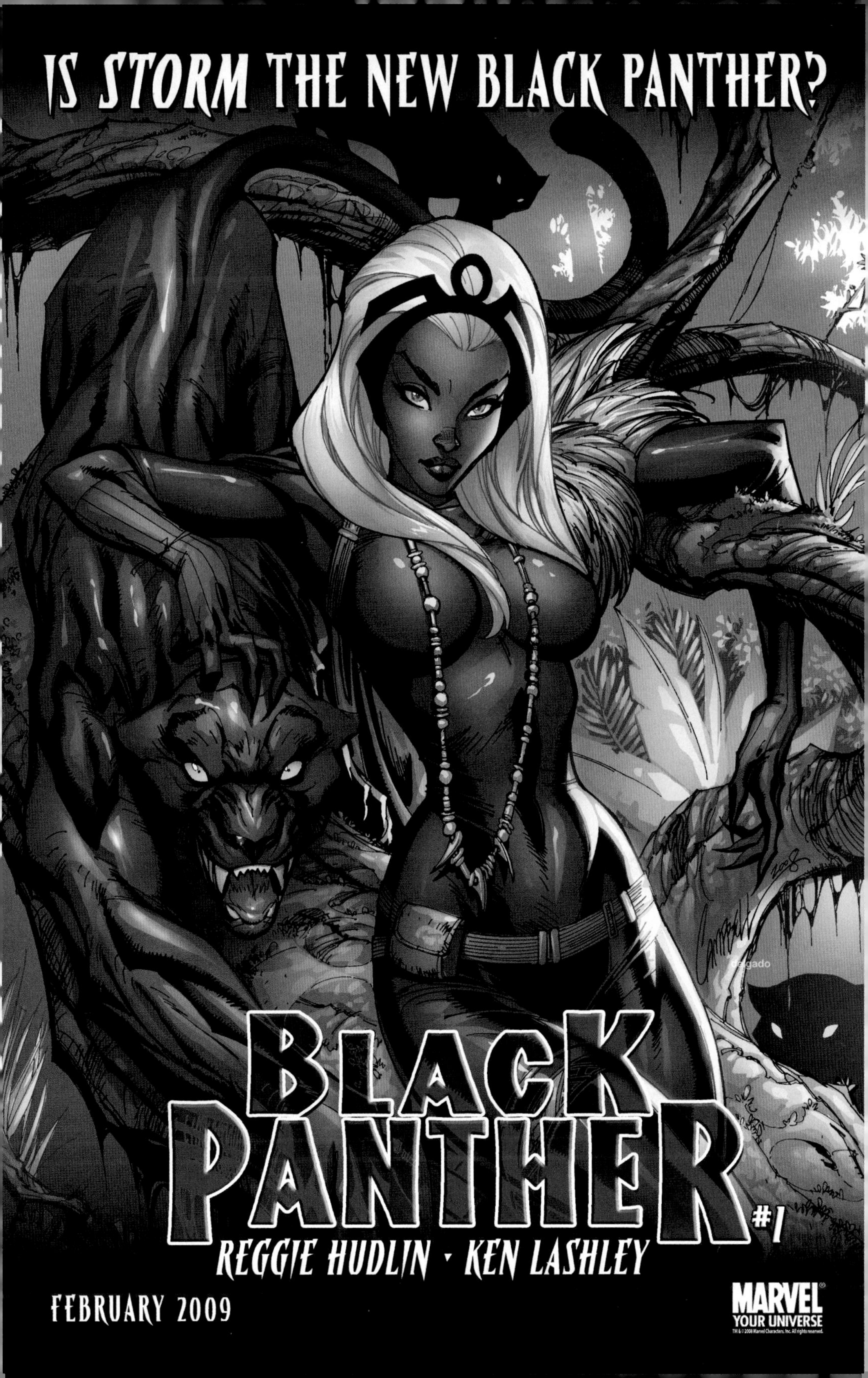
IS STORM THE NEW BLACK PANTHER?
BLACK PANTHER #1
REGGIE HUDLIN · KEN LASHLEY
FEBRUARY 2009
MARVEL
YOUR UNIVERSE
TM & © 2008 Marvel Characters, Inc. All rights reserved.

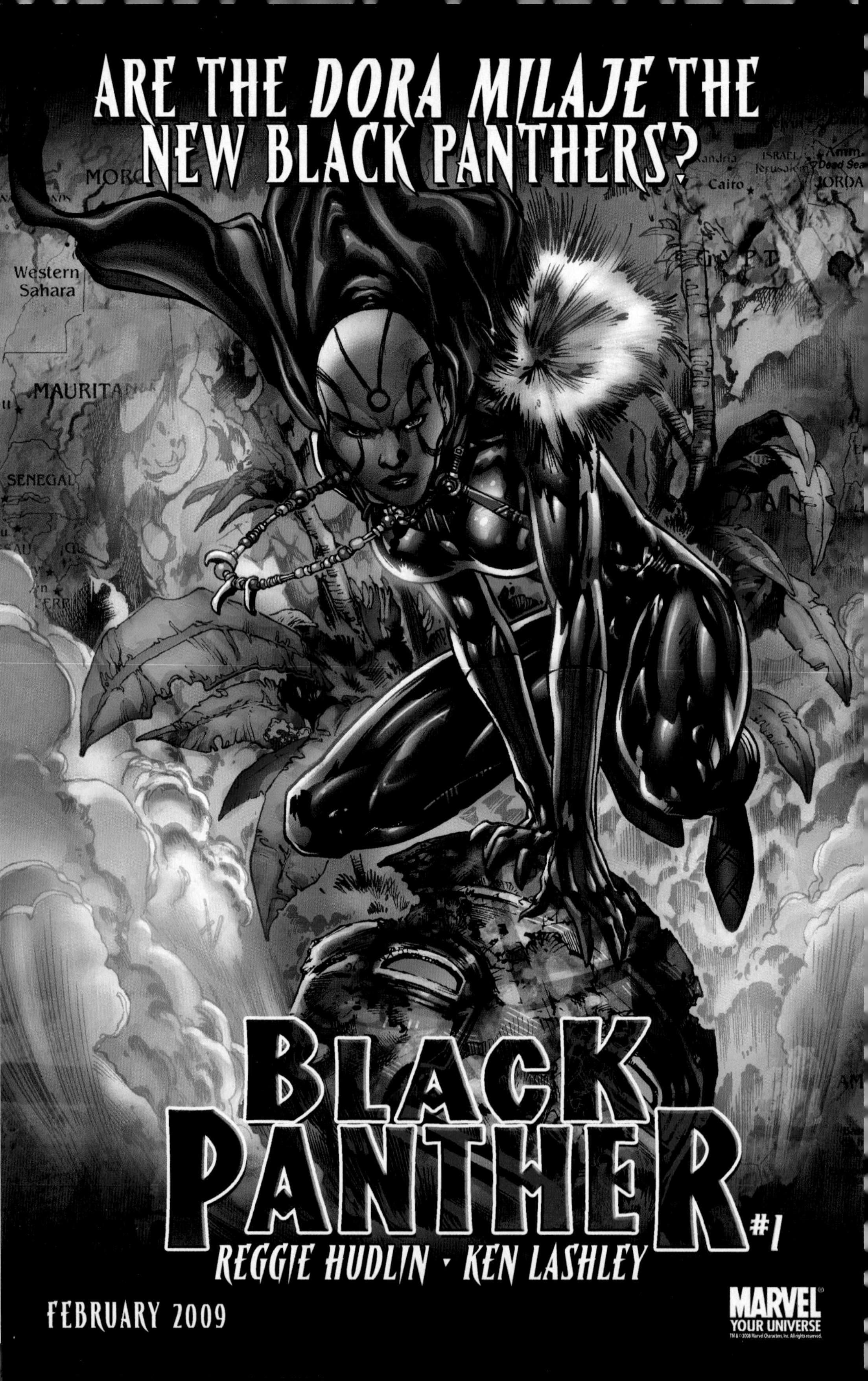
ARE THE DORA MILAJE THE NEW BLACK PANTHERS?
BLACK PANTHER #1
REGGIE HUDLIN · KEN LASHLEY
FEBRUARY 2009
MARVEL YOUR UNIVERSE

BLACK PANTHER (2005) *#37* COVER SKETCHES & PENCILS
BY **ALAN DAVIS**, WITH INKS BY **MARK FARMER**

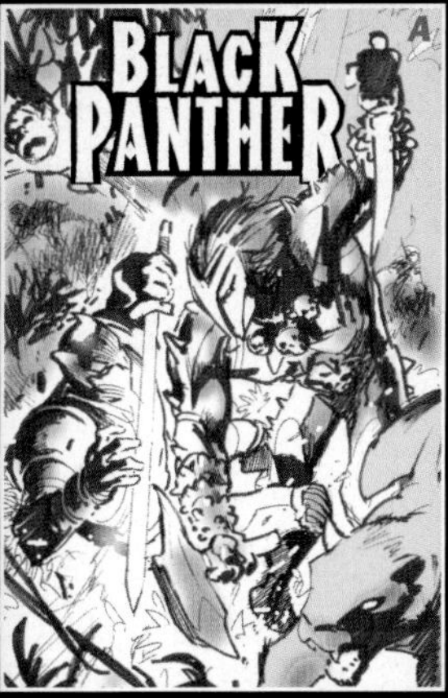
A
BLACK PANTHER

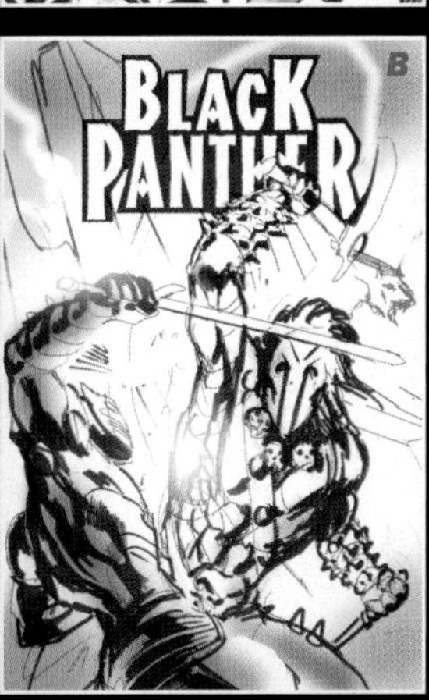
B
BLACK

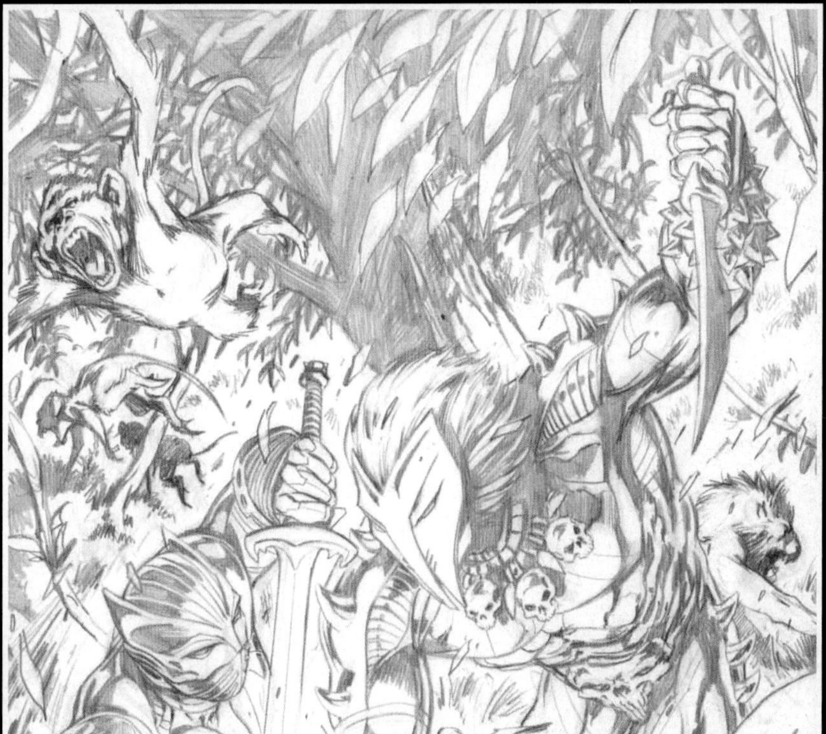

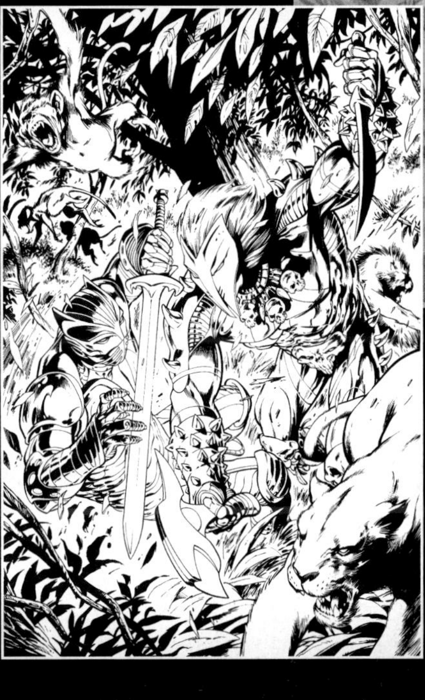

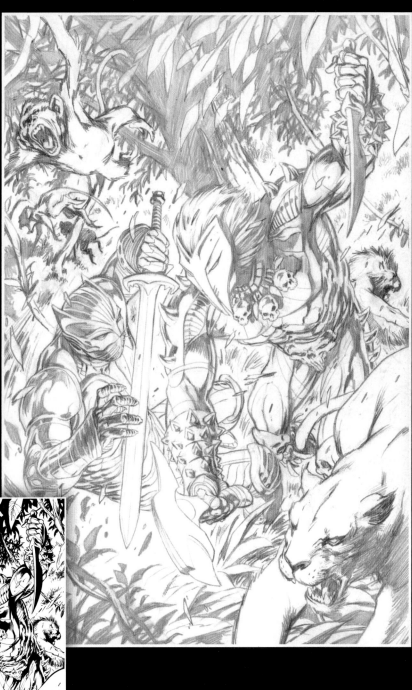

BLACK PANTHER (2005) *#38* COVER SKETCH & PENCILS
BY **ALAN DAVIS**, WITH INKS BY **MARK FARMER**

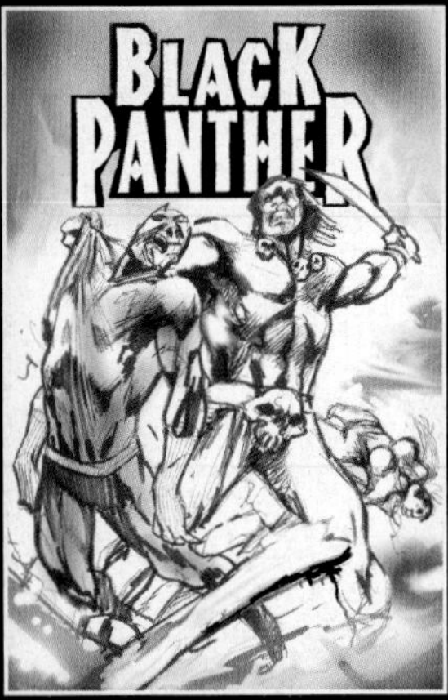
BLACK PANTHER

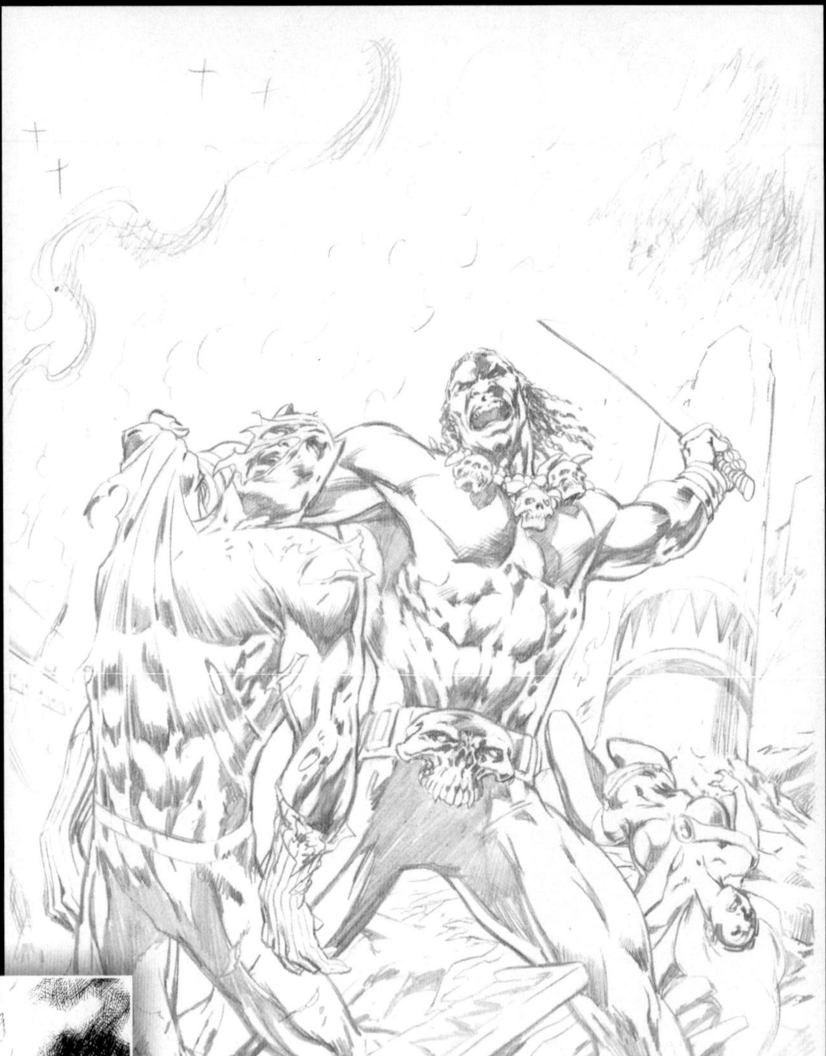

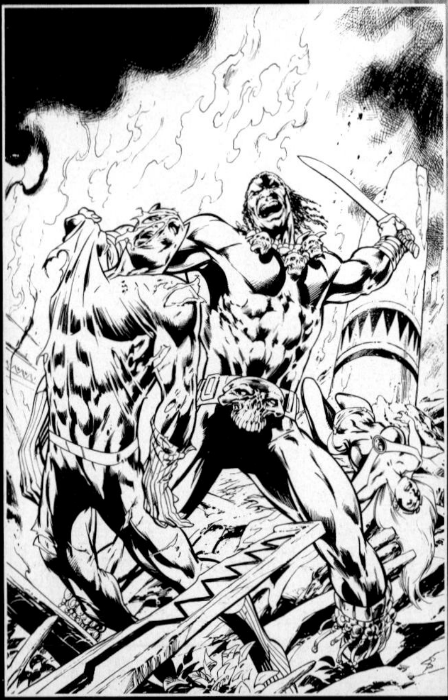

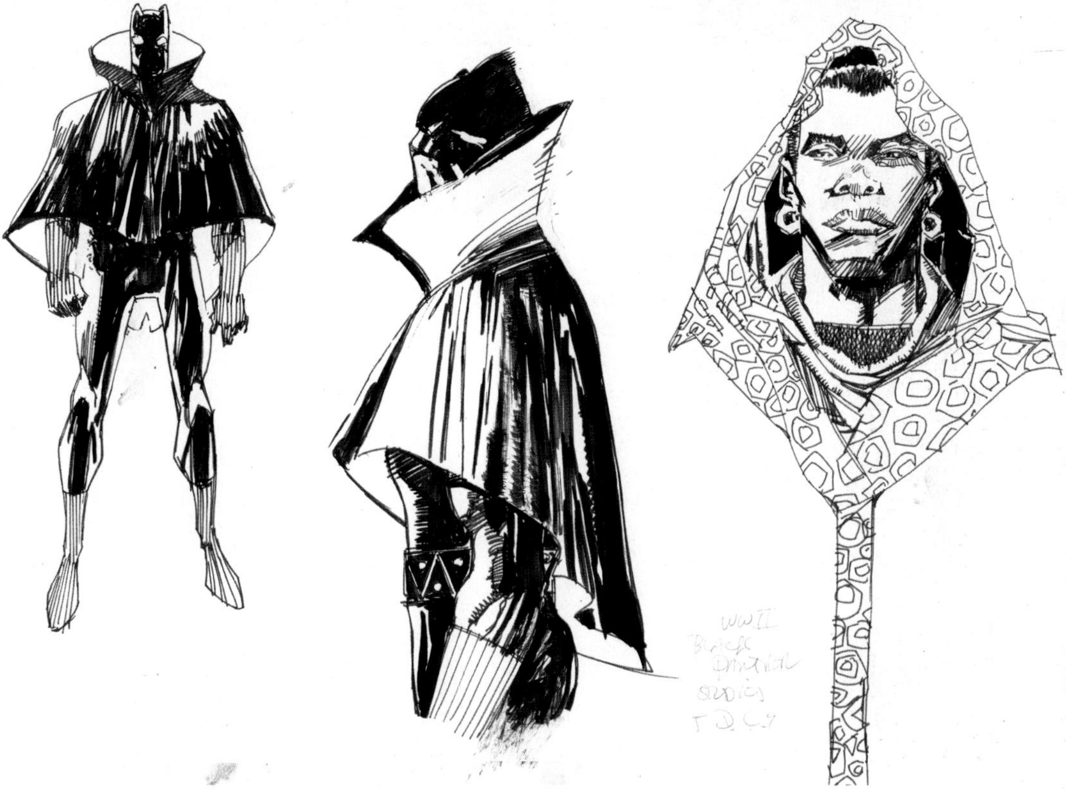
WWII

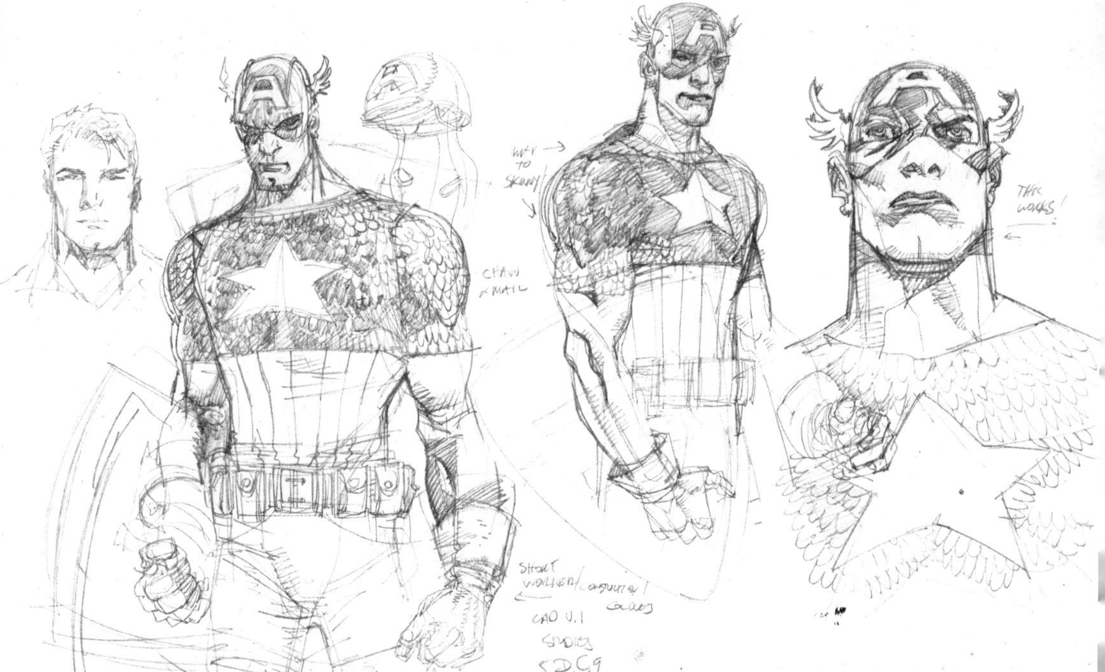
WAY TO SKINNY
CHAIN MAIL
THIS WORKS!

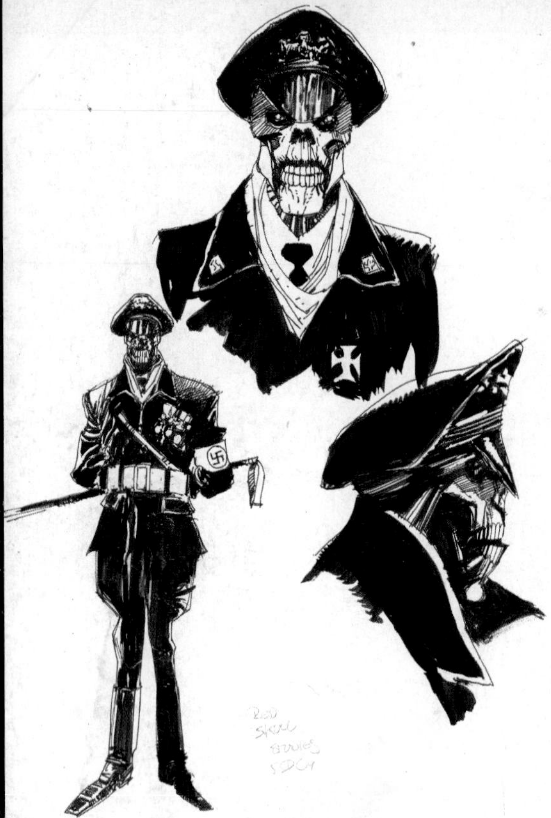

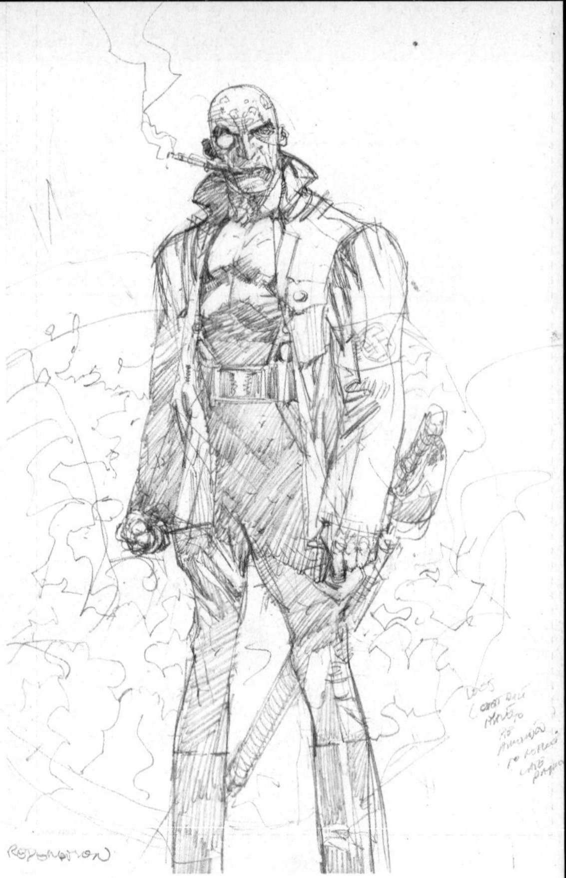

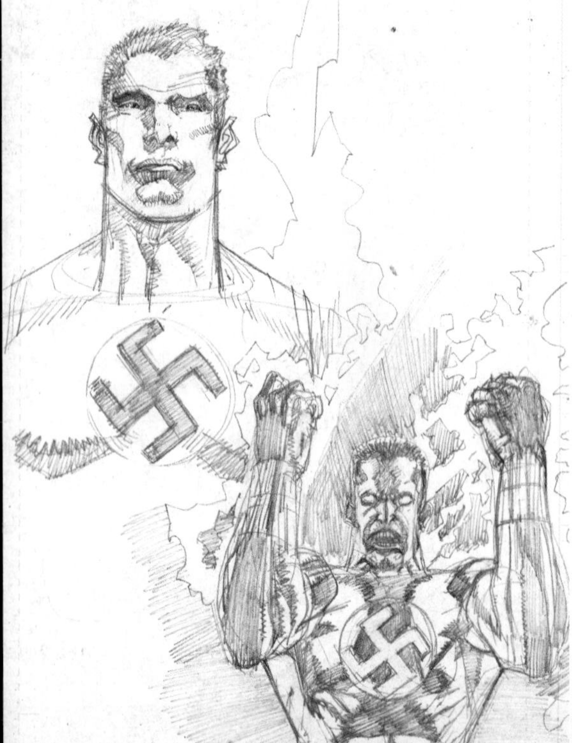

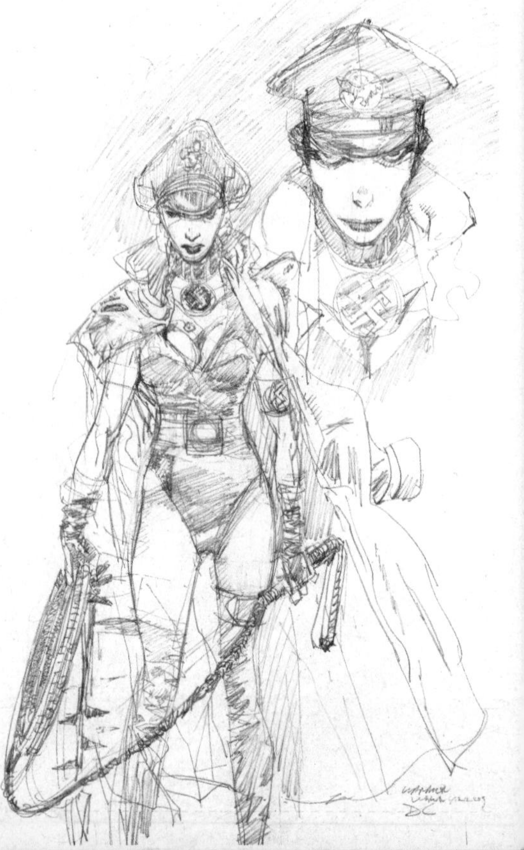